**66th Art
Directors
Annual
and the
First Annual
International
Exhibition**

CREDITS 66TH ART DIRECTORS ANNUAL

ADC Publications, Inc.
Board of Directors
Paul Scher, President
Kurt Haiman
Walter Kaprielian
B. Martin Pedersen
Lou Silverstein
Andrew Kner, Advisory Board

ADC Executive Director
Diane Moore

Editor
Paula Radding

Design Consultant
Sheila McCaffery

Art Director
Dorothy Wachtenheim

Committee
Alice Fernandes Brown
Dianne DePasque
Gerda Anna Deus
Jeff Kushnick
Ryuichi Minakawa
Richard Oriolo
Vittoria Semproni
Elizabeth Slott
Pandora Spelios
Lisa Speroni
Suzanne S. Talbot
Paula Thomson
Penny Wallace

Hall of Fame and Year End Review copy
Dan Forté

Book Packaging
Frank DeLuca
Supermart Graphics, Inc.
PO Box 900
Murray Hill Station
New York, NY 10156

Typography

Fisher Composition
118 East 25th Street
New York, NY 10010

Printing

Toppan Printing Company
Tokyo, Japan

Distribution
United States:

Robert Silver Associates
307 East 37th Street
New York, NY 10016

Canada:

General Publishing Co. Ltd.
30 Lesmill Road
Don Mills, Ontario M3B 2T6
Canada

International:

RotoVision
10 rue de l'Arquebuse
Case postale 434
CH-1211 Geneva
Switzerland

Published by ADC Publications
Copyright © 1987 by The Art
Directors Club, Inc.
ISBN 0-937-414-07-7

TABLE OF CONTENTS

66TH ANNUAL EXHIBITION

FIRST ANNUAL INTERNATIONAL EXHIBITION

HALL OF FAME

The Art Directors Club Hall of Fame was founded essentially to reward exceptional talent.

Yet, this lofty award which chronicles the careers of innovative visual communicators, represents much more than that important quality.

There exists in this award the implicit recognition of tenacity, resiliency, conviction and grit.

Because talent alone is not enough to withstand the repeated client rejections of an individual's work which come inevitably over the course of a lifetime, more is required.

And it is this ability to bounce back; to persist and to help clients understand and eventually support your special view of the world, which matters equally.

To change the way things are doesn't come easily, or without its consequences.

Therefore, this too, is what the Hall of Fame celebrates.

For me, it has been a privilege to serve as Chairman of the Selection Committee which honors this year's inductees to the Hall of Fame. These deserving individuals are: Willy Fleckhaus, Shigeo Fukuda, Steve Horn and Tony Palladino.

And, for only the second time in the history of the Art Directors Club, a Special Award has been given to Leon Friend, an educator who has inspired generations of art directors, designers and photographers.

Amil Gargano
Chairman 1987 Selection Committee

Committee for the Hall of Fame '87

Selection

Amil Gargano, Chairman
Ed Brodsky
Cipe Pineles Burtin
Seymour Chwast
Lou Dorfsman
Gene Federico
Andrew Kner
George Lois
Paul Rand
Paula Scher
Len Sirowitz
Jack Tauss

Patron, Chairman
Sam Scali

Presentation
Andrew Kner

Managing and Planning
William H. Buckley, Chairman
Jack G. Tauss, Co-Chairman

SPECIAL AWARD TO LEON FRIEND (1902–1969)

Born in Warsaw, Poland in 1902, Leon Friend came to the United States at the age of three. He received both his Bachelor and Master degrees from New York's Columbia University.

In 1930, he began his teaching career at Brooklyn's Abraham Lincoln High School. There he became the school's first art department chairman. It was during his almost forty years of inspiring work as an educator that Leon Friend roused the creative juices to flow from his students. He always invited other artists to guest lecture and encouraged everyone to participate in art and design competitions. Friend also founded The Art Squad, an elite group of his students, who created posters and decorated the school's bare walls at a moment's notice.

The partial list of famous pupils who passed through Leon's skillful tutelage possess a fabulously eclectic assortment of talent—George Ancona, Herb Bleiweiss, Seymour Chwast, Tom Courtos, Gene Federico, Jay Maisel, Irving Penn, Alex Steinweiss and Bill Taubin.

Through the years, Leon Friend garnered numerous awards and praise from peers and former students. The Architectural League of New York honored him with an exhibition in 1969 entitled "The Impact of One Art Teacher" and in 1972, The Brooklyn Museum began an advertising and printmaking scholarship in his name that was sponsored by The Art Squad, Inc., an organization of successful art directors, artists, designers and photographers who had studied with him. Friend was also co-author with Joseph Hefter of *Graphic Design,* published by McGraw-Hill in 1936.

Although Leon Friend passed away in 1969 at the age of sixty-seven, his infectious motivational and creative spirit is still with us. Leon's former students see to that! Their work is a direct descendant of his.

The Art Director's Club, recognizing his immense contribution to our profession, posthumously presents this Special Award to Leon Friend. Were it not for his unique prescience in nurturing the abundant talent of the kids from Brooklyn, the design world as we know it, would be a vastly different and lackluster place . . .

1972
M.F. Agha
Lester Beall
Alexey Brodovitch
A. M. Cassandre
René Clarke
Robert Gage
William Golden
Paul Rand

1973
Charles Coiner
Paul Smith
Jack Tinker

1974
Will Burtin
Leo Lionni

1975
Gordon Aymar
Herbert Bayer
Cipe Pineles Burtin
Heyworth Campbell
Alexander Liberman
L. Moholy-Nagy

1976
E. McKnight Kauffer
Herbert Matter

1977
Saul Bass
Herb Lubalin
Bradbury Thompson

1978
Thomas M. Cleland
Lou Dorfsman
Allen Hurlburt
George Lois

1979
W.A. Dwiggins
George Giusti
Milton Glaser
Helmut Krone
Willem Sandberg
Ladislav Sutnar
Jan Tschichold

1980
Gene Federico
Otto Storch
Henry Wolf

1981
Lucian Bernhard
Ivan Chermayeff
Gyorgy Kepes
George Krikorian
William Taubin

1982
Richard Avedon
Amil Gargano
Jerome Snyder
Massimo Vignelli

1983
Aaron Burns
Seymour Chwast
Steve Frankfurt

1984
Charles Eames
Wallace Elton
Sam Scali
Louis Silverstein

1985
Art Kane
Len Sirowitz
Charles Tudor

1986
Walt Disney
Roy Grace
Alvin Lustig
Arthur Paul

1987
Willy Fleckhaus
Shigeo Fukuda
Steve Horn
Tony Palladino

WILLY FLECKHAUS

Calle Hesslefors

When Willy Fleckhaus died suddenly of a heart attack in September of 1983, the design world lost one of its most innovative and stimulating citizens.

Born in Velbert, Germany in 1925, Willy Fleckhaus began his career as a trained journalist and editor. During the 1950's, he wrote for and edited many publications specializing in various subjects; from religion and politics to national labor issues.

Nineteen fifty-nine was a very good year for Willy Fleckhaus. It marked his association with the birth of one of the most intellectually compelling and graphically exciting magazines the world would see: *Twen*.

Twen, short for twenty, catered to the first generation of young German adults who came of age after the end of World War II. It was published from 1959–1970 when deepening political and intellectual thought, combined with increasing sexual awareness, captured the attention of its spirited audience. *Twen* was unmatched in its avant-garde visuals, layouts, typography and fine, literary content.

The late fifties and early sixties were considered renaissance periods for redesigning magazines. Fleckhaus and *Twen* were indeed at the forefront of such a renaissance. What Otto Storch was to *McCall's,* Allen Hurlbert was to *Look* and Henry Wolf was to *Show,* Willy Fleckhaus was to *Twen*.

Fleckhaus, though not a designer by trade, was acutely aware of how *Twen* should look. The format and content obviously reflected the vitality of its readers. He developed a unique design theme based on gut feelings and the trendy subject matter of the magazine.

Published monthly, *Twen's* covers consisted of eye-catching photos or feature copy on black backgrounds. Fleckhaus enjoyed using one typeface in contrasting colors to highlight specific articles. *Twen's* table-of-contents page was different each and every month. They were a marvelous pastiche of layouts adorned with stunning visuals; specifically tailored to each issue's topics. In essence, they were perfect segués to what awaited its readers on succeeding pages.

Twen was unsurpassed when it came to overall design, exhilarating photography and illustration. Fleckhaus always managed to startle, challenge and eventually persuade the reader's eye and mind into the opinionated world of *Twen*. His uncanny ability in selecting visuals by some of the world's finest—Art Kane, Pete Turner, Will McBride, Irving Penn, Richard Avedon, Tomi Ungerer and Hans Hillmann, made *Twen's* impact even more captivating.

Fleckhaus was, in effect, a master of visual montage. He was to magazine design what Sergei Eisenstein was to film. Each, through selective cropping, framing, reducing and enlarging, were able to elicit specific editorial and emotional responses from readers and viewers alike. Power of this magnitude was indeed a stroke of genius!

Such power led to many internal problems at *Twen*. The actual editor became, for all intents and purposes, a ceremonial position. The job was reduced to a revolving door of resignations and damaged egos.

As its readership matured and specific social issues died or shifted, so did the appeal of *Twen*. In 1970, the last of many publishers forced Fleckhaus to resign and *Twen* folded soon after, thus ending an era of magazine brilliance.

Like most successful designers, Fleckhaus pursued other interests. From 1960, he designed countless book covers for *Suhrkamp* and *Insel Verlags* in Frankfurt. His highly sophisticated, yet simplistic designs along with a penchant for selecting or creating the right typefaces, shattered the old adage: You can't judge a book by its cover! If Fleckhaus designed a book jacket, chances are it became a best seller.

Fleckhaus's book jackets mirrored his covers for *Twen* in that they both lured readers into the exciting literary world that awaited them between the covers. His designs, no doubt, put him in high esteem with both publishers and authors alike. All profited financially and grew in popularity from his jacket designs. During a Stuttgart Typographer's Seminar in 1980, Fleckhaus claimed to create a cover a day!

In 1976, *Suhrkamp* publisher, Siegfried Unseld wrote a book chronicling Fleckhaus's immense contribution to book design. It was entitled: *Der Marienbader Korb.* The book, privately published, remains a visual feast and historical retrospective into yet another dimension of the creative mind of Willy Fleckhaus.

In 1974, Fleckhaus became Professor of Graphic Design at Essen University and held the same position from 1981 at Wuppertal University. It was only natural that eager design students wanted to learn from the master. Fleckhaus taught and nurtured only the best and most promising. Bauhaus influences, coupled with the inspirational teachings of Alexey Brodovitch and close friend Max Bill, gave students a working education they couldn't get anywhere else.

There are many Willy Fleckhaus protégés sprinkled throughout the world today. One of the most heralded is Hans-Georg Pospischil, art director of *Frankfurter Allgemeine Zeitung Magazin;* a position he has held since Fleckhaus's death in 1983.

Hans-Georg Pospischil took Professor Fleckhaus's design course for two reasons: curiosity and the satisfaction of a university requirement. After three weeks, Fleckhaus unearthed Pospischil's potential and immediately got him a job as an art director for a magazine in Hamburg. Pospischil recalls: "Fleckhaus never criticized a student's work. You found your design mistakes and corrected them yourself. He taught you to think like a professional; not a student."

Six months later, Fleckhaus called Pospischil back from Hamburg and asked him if he wanted to become his assistant on a new publication venture; one that was to again change the way people look at magazines . . . The date was Friday, March 7, 1980. Another milestone in the life of Willy Fleckhaus. The very conservative daily tabloid, *Frankfurter Allgemeine Zeitung* decided to publish a weekly magazine supplement. Fleckhaus, remembering how much he enjoyed working in *Twen's* stimulating environment, readily accepted the job as art director.

Through his innovative design principles, *F.A.Z. Magazine* achieved the reputation of being the most beautiful and widely read publication in the world! Though editorially the antithesis of *Twen, F.A.Z. Magazine* developed a style reminiscent of its predecessor; only better and more sophisticated.

Fleckhaus's covers for the magazine exuded style. From the elegant Gothic typeface to the compelling, almost sfumato-like visuals, they were common threads for all editorial and graphic inside matter. As an example, one cover features a realistic illustration of a can of red paint. We turn to the table-of-contents page. It centers around a photograph of a tube of spurting blue paint. Subsequently, an article on the power of the color red appears. The eye-popping double-bleed layout is awash with color. Peter Krämer's vivid illustration of a brown, wood paint brush, dripping and streaking across the spread with red paint is absolutely marvelous!

Week after week, page after page, Fleckhaus tempted his readers with such visual artistry. His revolutionary magazine designs were, in sum, achieved through structured, carefully planned chaos. The timely nature of a weekly supplement made for interesting subjects on which to report. Fleckhaus, at times, flexed his journalistic muscles and also contributed editorially to the magazine's success.

Even in his private life, aside from his devotion to family, fine food and wines, Fleckhaus's work was his pleasure. In the third glorious year of his reign at *Frankfurter Allgemeine Zeitung Magazin,* Willy Fleckhaus died at his home in Tuscany. There will never be another Willy Fleckhaus. Yet, the vast legacy of work and list of immensely talented disciples he left us, proves the Genius of Magazine Design is still very much alive.

1

Twen cover, 1960

2

Twen cover, 1970

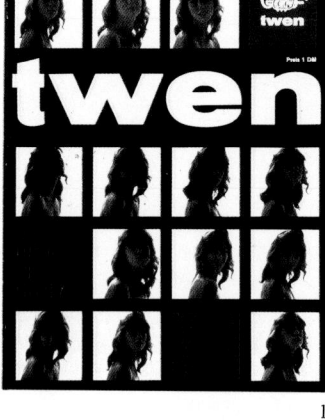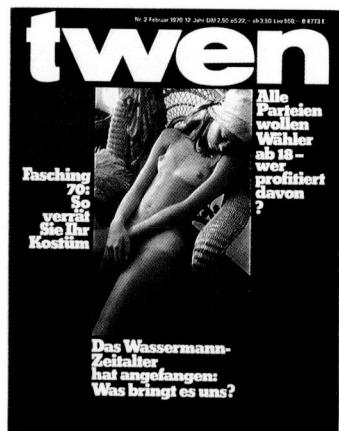

1   2

3

3

Twen table-of-contents page, 1959;
Siegfried Reidie, artist

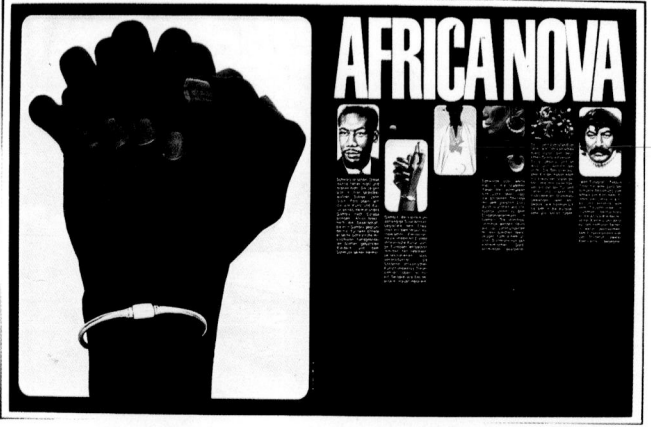

4

4

''Africa Nova'', *Twen;* Horst Munzig,
photographer

5

''Please Steal A Swimming Pool For
Me'', *Twen;* Heinz Edelman, artist

5

6

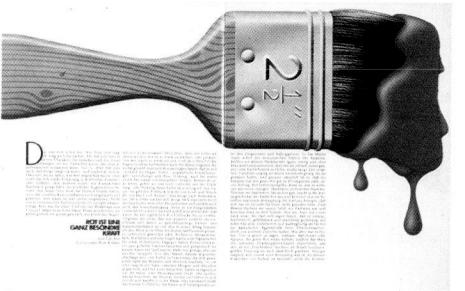

10

11

12

6

Book jacket for Suhrkamp
Publishing, 1967

7

Book jacket for Suhrkamp
Publishing, 1975

8

Frankfurter Allgemeine Magazin
cover, 1980; Andrej Reiser,
photographer

9, 10, 11

Frankfurter Allgemeine Magazin
cover & double-page spread on the
special power of the color red, 1982;
Peter Krämer, artist

12

Frankfurter Allgemeine Magazin
cover, 1982

SHIGEO
FUKUDA

Yasukouchi

Hollywood cinematographer, James Wong Howe once said, "Never state what can be implied." This certainly holds true for modern Japanese communication and design. The Japanese, being culturally homogenous, need not articulate everything in order to be understood. They believe in more indirect and abstract forms of expression.

Shigeo Fukuda is Japan's consummate visual communicator. His induction into the Art Directors Hall of Fame marks the first time for a Japanese designer. Born fifty-five years ago in Tokyo, Fukuda received his design education at that city's National University of Fine Arts & Music. In 1966, his work first gained prominence at a Czechoslovakian graphic design competition. One year later, Fukuda's work graced many posters specially commissioned for Montreal's Expo '67.

It wasn't until later in that year however, that Fukuda's career began to snowball. Fellow Hall of Famer Paul Rand, initially caught sight of his work in an issue of *Japanese Graphic Design Magazine*. Realizing Fukuda's great potential as a world-class designer, Rand helped arrange his first United States exhibition at New York City's IBM Gallery. This, incidentally, also coincided with Fukuda's honeymoon

and his first trip to New York! The exhibit featured his extraordinary, puzzle-like wooden sculptures originally created as playthings for his young daughter. His successful gallery exhibit brought Fukuda even more widespread recognition resulting in Rand's interview with him on Public Television.

Shigeo Fukuda's work is deeply influenced by Takashi Kohno; a pioneer in modern Japanese graphic design. Kohno was purported to be Japan's first designer possessing a distinct objective along with a creative personality. His posters heralded a new era of visual expressionism. Kohno's work was always controversial, yet visually inspiring. His posters were an exhilarating prelude to Fukuda's own imprint on communication design.

During the 1960's, Shigeo Fukuda became interested in illusionism. He illustrated a column on visual magic for the daily *Ashai Newspaper* called: "Ryu Mita Ka?" ("Have You Seen the Dragon?") and presently presides over *Idea Magazine's* "Visual Circus"; an entertaining, bi-monthly feature injected with boyish wit and enthusiasm.

When it comes to illusionism, Fukuda practices what he preaches. The countless awards he continues to win worldwide is living testament to his power of graphic legerdemain. Fukuda's brand of magic and illusion never ceases to amaze and enchant. In an *Idea Magazine* interview, he explains the motivation behind his technique:

"I believe that in design, 30% dignity, 20% beauty and 50% absurdity are necessary. Rather than catering to the design sensitivity of the general public, there is advancement in design, if people are left to feel satisfied with their own superiority; by entrapping them with visual illusion."

Contrary to Western styles of expression, Japanese communication is more emotional than rational. Such emotion is profoundly linked to art. Fukuda dramatically shatters all cultural and linguistic barriers with his universally recognizable style.

Shigeo Fukuda's sense of high moral responsibility as a graphic designer is undertaken with firm conviction. His work effectively mirrors and embraces the worldly causes he believes in. Coupled with his fine flair for color and layout along with advanced Japanese reproduction techniques, Fukuda always manages to get his points across . . . His 1982 *Happy Earthday* posters are prime examples. One is a drawing of an upside-down axe; the tool of destruction spoiling the earth's wilderness. The wooden handle, ironically, sprouts a branch of its own! The second in the series, is an illustration of the earth in the shape of an opening seed awash in a pristine sea-blue background. Fukuda's pro-environmental concepts are indeed abstract, yet globally familiar.

Fukuda's most famous poster, entitled *Victory 1945,* is a bitingly satirical commentary on the senselessness of war. It's an illustration of a cannon barrel with its shell pointing downward; back towards the opening, sealing it forever. In a world where war is big business, Fukuda's chilling, simplistic concept of peace and the containment of nuclear proliferation is absolutely brilliant. It won him a grand prize at the 1975 Warsaw Poster Contest. All proceeds from the competition went to the Peace Fund Movement. As always, Fukuda goes far beyond the bounds of plain function to express a universal plea for peace.

In 1980, Fukuda did another marvelous illusionist poster for Amnesty International. It features a drawing of a clenched fist interwoven with barbed wire. That's not all! The copy at the top simply reads "Amnesty" with the character 's' shaped like a linked shackle. It's work like this that makes Shigeo Fukuda an impeccable communicator.

One of Fukuda's personal favorites is a 1982 poster announcing a ten-man international poster exhibition. He beautifully proclaims the event by showing ten different pairs of colorful hands embraced in friendship. Fukuda's notion of an international forum of design through brotherhood and fraternity is quite a visual feat.

Shigeo Fukuda's abundance of talent goes far beyond his fabulous poster designs. In 1976, Tokyo's *Seibu Department Store* commissioned him to re-design areas of its selling floors. Fukuda rose to the occasion with flying colors. He created shopping rest areas disguised as huge leather briefcases. He linked the store's main wings with gigantic, intricate floor mosaics of Lincoln and Beethoven. The pièce de résistance was, however, a rooftop beer garden complete with eighty model sheep grazing to the piped-in strains of Country & Western music.

Fukuda took his keen sense of design even further with his remarkably futuristic UCC Coffee Pavilion in Tokyo. The entire theme is coffee. From floor to ceiling, the UCC Coffee Pavilion is a swirling marvel of synergistic design. Whether it's the simplicity of the logo, the mixed-media sculpture of Mt. Fuji made of hundreds of coffee cans, the multi-colored, expressionless mannequins holding steaming cups of coffee or the countless burlap sacks containing the mythical bean, Fukuda has created one of the most spirited design wonders the world will see. One can, just by looking at it, smell the delicious aroma of fresh, roasting coffee beans.

Such inventiveness also 'spills' over into Fukuda's home as well. His lawn, shaded by a plastic, fried egg, is adorned with deceptively-realistic bulldog sculptures. Inside, he lives in a Rube Goldberg world of gadgetry no doubt helping him express his peerless individuality.

Shigeo Fukuda is also very involved with education. Aside from attending seminars and being on numerous design committees, he is a Visiting Professor of Design at Yale University. Fukuda is a staunch supporter of teaching art and design in an enjoyable, relaxed manner. He believes that a compulsory, regimented curriculum deters students from developing a personal sense of aesthetics that should otherwise flow freely from within.

Traditionally, Japanese designers looked to the West for innovative solutions. This is no longer the case. The winds are shifting toward an easterly direction. Shigeo Fukuda, Japan's Houdini of Design, is a welcome part of the shifting breeze. His visual originality and deep dedication to worthwhile causes, help keep the sun shining brightly over our ever changing, complex world.

1

Bird Tree sculpture from IBM
Gallery Exhibit, New York City, 1967

2

Victory poster, Grand Prize, Warsaw
Poster Contest, 1975

3

California exhibition poster, 1971

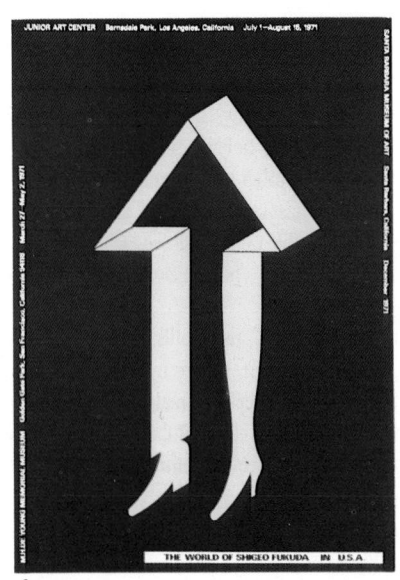

4

Keio Department Store Gallery
Exhibit poster, Tokyo, 1975

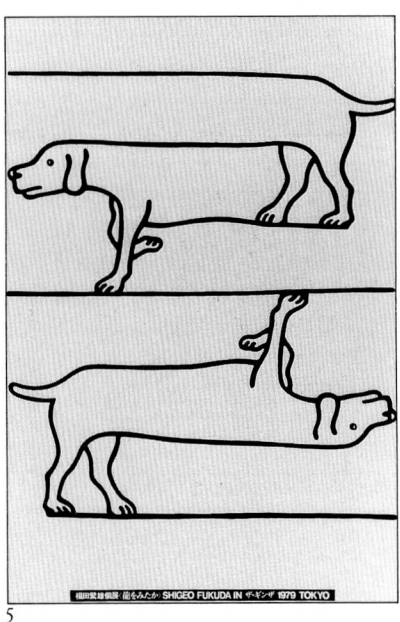

5

Illusion poster, 1979

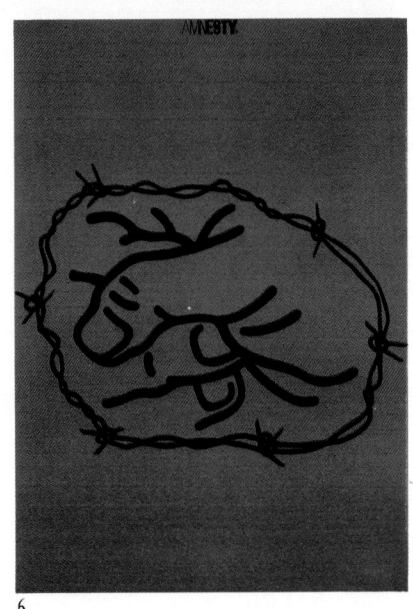

6

Amnesty poster, 1980

7

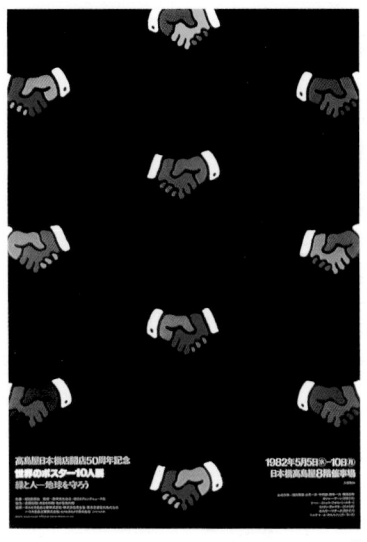

8

7

UCC Coffee Pavilion poster/logo, 1984

8

Ten International Artists poster, 1982

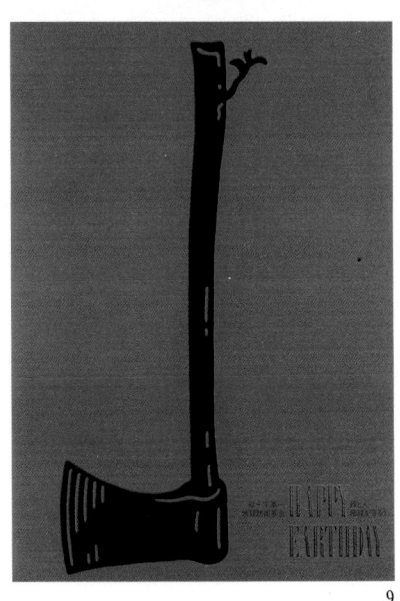

9

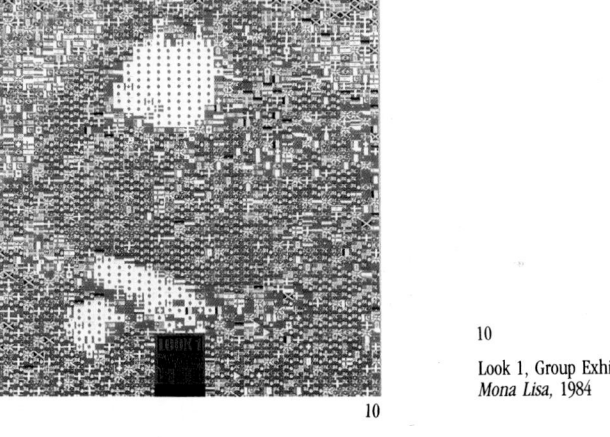

10

9

Happy Earthday poster, 1982

10

Look 1, Group Exhibition Poster: *Mona Lisa,* 1984

11

12

11

Seibu Department Store, customer seating area

12

Seibu Department Store, Beethoven floor mosaic

STEVE HORN

Linda Horn

In 1984, Pratt Institute bestowed its prestigious Alumni Achievement Award upon three people. Two were successful business and engineering executives. The third has sold more soft drinks, automobiles, beer, lipstick, luggage, computers, telephones, gasoline, insurance, airline tickets, motor scooters and sneakers than anyone in the history of television advertising: Steve Horn!

When one walks up the steep staircase leading into Horn's command center, he is greeted by a constant barrage of activity. Aides armed with reels and storyboards move like whirling dervishes, as if part of a well-choreographed ballet. In the middle of all the excitement stands Steve Horn; the Great Communicator; whose consistently high production values are matched only by the fashionable clothes he wears.

Born in Brooklyn in 1932, Steve Horn attended Manhattan's High School of Music & Art. After graduating, the Brooklyn Dodgers offered him a pitching contract. Steve's father, a pharmacist, refused to let him sign. As a result, he went to Pratt Institute on an art scholarship, majoring in advertising. In 1953, Horn went to Columbia University to further his education. He subsequently received a B.A. in Fine Arts and an M.A. in 13th and 14th Century Italian Painting.

Armed with his degrees, Steve Horn landed his first job as an assistant art director with the Reba Sochis Studio. He then went on to take Hal Davis's place at Robert Brandau's Studio. While there, he began dabbling in photography.

In 1957, freelance designer John Berg, invited Steve Horn and another graphic designer, Norm Griner, to his engagement party. A friendship was struck and two years later, they formed Horn/Griner; a partnership that lasted fifteen years.

In the beginning, Horn/Griner was strictly a graphic design firm; shooting an occasional photo for a client's ad or record jacket. John Berg, just beginning his long association with Columbia Records, supplied them with most of their design assignments.

It wasn't until 1961, that Steve Horn's rather uneventful design career changed instantly with the click of a Hasselblad. Steve shot a double-page spread for I. Miller ladies shoes. The moment it hit the newsstands in *Vogue,* Steve Horn began his career as a professional photographer. The ad propelled him into the glamorous world of high-fashion photography. Consisting of a trompe l'oeil painting along with 'live' props, the I. Miller ad was a perfect springboard for Horn's growing expertise as a photographer.

The late fifties and early sixties erupted with slick, chic photography. Besides Horn, some of its major contributors were Richard Avedon and Irving Penn. Both still remain Horn's heroes. Steve began refining a tasteful, technically-sound style of his own; which spills over into his television work of today.

During this time, Steve Horn developed the Hasselblad camera with the Polaroid back. Its discovery came out of his search for total technical control over a photo session. This innovation, now basic equipment in virtually every studio, enables the photographer to immediately check lighting, prop placement and shot composition; avoiding second-guessing and costly re-shoots.

From 1962 to 1964, Steve made several extended trips to Europe on assignment for *Elle* and various other high-fashion magazines. While there, Horn noticed an increasing number of photographers using a wide-angle twenty millimeter lens. Realizing its great visual potential in haute-couture photography, Steve became the first still cameraman to bring this trend to the United States. His work subsequently received rave reviews.

Throughout this period, Horn/Griner became the most sought-after tandem in the business. Their distinct styles and personalities did, however, present some problems. Steve relates a humorous story:

"It was during a Yuban Coffee shoot . . . Norm and I, without regard for each other, would switch props and change lights while the other looked through the camera's viewfinder. From that moment on, we knew we couldn't work together on the same projects."

In 1967, Steve Horn began another segment of his career that would eventually blossom into the most prolific in the business. The late, television art director, Georg Olden, recognized Horn's talent and potential as a commercial director. Consequently, Horn made his directorial debut on an Encyclopedia Brittanica spot. Steve remembers being awed by the sudden shift from Hasselblad to hand-held Arriflex. His proficiency in still work, no doubt, made for a smooth and natural transition.

In addition to directing, Steve Horn also takes great pride in being his own cameraman and lighting director. Very few directors (if any), can effectively do the work of two key crew members. Steve, however, consistently rises to the task. His uncompromising dedication to high production values keep him in constant demand over 200 days a year. Steve's list of satisfied agencies and clients read like a who's who in advertising. Horn's versatility in shooting all types of challenging spots, starring sports figures, celebrities, fashion models and ordinary people is unequaled in the business.

Whether he's shooting the Joffrey Ballet for IBM, staging an Eddie Rabbitt concert with a cast of thousands for Miller Lite or taking over an entire town in Texas for a Bi-Centennial Coke spot, Steve has become *the* most dynamic force in television commercials. He usually shoots very early in the morning or late in the afternoon (the "Golden Hour") in order to produce his distinct, soft and diffused chiaroscuro lighting.

One of Steve's greatest technical triumphs is the "Through-The-Lens-VTR System"; allowing clients to view the action exactly as the director sees it. It works by means of a complex network of ground-glass mirrors. In addition, the images captured on film are also recorded on tape permitting simultaneous playback of questionable scenes. Today, this unique system is standard throughout the film and medical professions.

The late sixties saw Horn/Griner prosper enormously. Beginning in 1967, they produced self-promotional calendars that were distributed industry-wide. Numerous art directors, writers, producers and clients posed for Steve and Norm's twelve abstract, sepia-toned photo vignettes. Today, they remain prized possessions of the fortunate few who still have them.

In 1974, Horn and Griner went their separate ways. Norm collaborated with director Mike Cuesta and

Steve embarked on a partnership with his second wife Linda; forming Steve Horn, Inc.

Steve's flexibility in adapting to and starting new trends keep him at the forefront of an ever-changing profession. It can never be said that Steve Horn is a typecast director. His style doesn't permit directorial pigeon-holing. Steve successfully crosses all genres. His work has earned him innumerable Clios, Gold Lions and Art Directors Cubes. Horn has the distinction of shooting more spots than any other commercial director; at last count, somewhere over 2,000! In 1985, *Advertising Age* named him "Television Commercial Director of the Year." Steve's incredible knack for adding his own dash of visual creativity to a client's board, always enhances the finished product. Each spot inherently becomes a miniature thirty or sixty second work of art.

Over the years, Steve Horn has been an inspiration to many agency art directors and producers—most notably, Bob Giraldi, Rick Levine and Michael Ulick. They all made the switch to commercial directing, undoubtedly catching some of Steve's contagious brand of enthusiasm.

From his timeless Barney's spot to his latest, most daring commercial for Diet Pepsi, Steve Horn always has the power to elicit a positive and memorable response from the usually skeptical consumer. His tireless quest for perfection is the only way he knows how to work. It's no wonder agencies keep calling him . . .

Every year, Steve sets aside time to shoot public service spots. Not just a firm believer in the causes he chooses to represent, Horn also finds them wonderful outlets to create and experiment with. His 1972 hand-held spot for the *Mayor's Narcotics Control Commission* featuring a gritty, cinema-verité style, is a classic. Other stellar examples include work for the *Urban Coalition* and the *Kidney Foundation*.

Today, Steve Horn, Inc., is a thriving, full-service production company. In addition to her duties as executive producer, Steve's wife Linda, also runs a prosperous antique business. Steve still does an occasional print ad. He's been photographing Benson & Hedges and Virginia Slims ads from the beginning. His "Top Gun" spot for Diet Pepsi, has the honor of being the first commercial ever used in all home videocassette copies of the movie bearing the same name. The little leisure time he has is spent playing tennis or restoring houses with his wife.

To list all the spots Steve Horn has shot in his legendary career is indeed an exercise in futility. Through his work, Steve always manages to entertain and delight millions of people. What's Steve Horn doing right now? Chances are he's adjusting lights, creating a new piece of equipment, getting coffee and danish for his appreciative crew or preparing for his next shoot. Whatever spot he's working on, we can't wait to see it . . . Stay tuned!

1

Ad for I. Miller, 1961

2

Horn/Griner calendar, February,
1966

1

2

3

Ad for Volkswagen, 1967

Volkswagen's unique construction keeps dampness out.

4

"Landlord", Urban Coalition, 1968

3

4

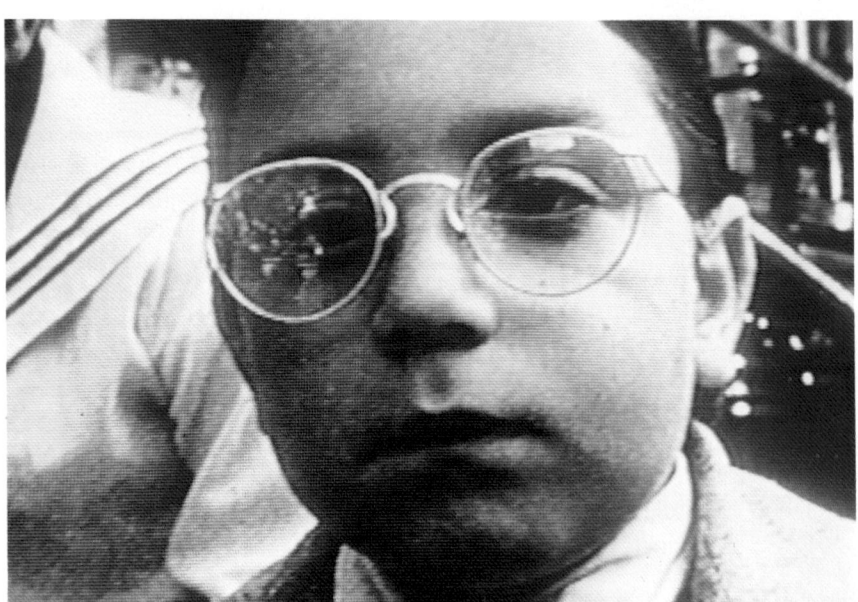

5

"Men of Distinction", Barney's,
1970

5

6

6

Ad for Benson & Hedges, 1973

7

"Thru the Years", Fiat, 1974

8

8

"Dizzy Dean", Exxon, 1976

9

9

"Lou Reed", Honda, 1985

10

10

"Top Gun", Pepsi, 1986

TONY PALLADINO

Carole Cutner

Whatever Tony Palladino creates, it exudes style, beauty and a personal statement. Whether it's a poster, a painting, a book jacket, a sculpture, a print ad or a television spot, the uniquely ubiquitous Palladino Touch is always present and accounted for.

Tony Palladino was born in Manhattan in 1930. His parents were Italian immigrants seeking a new lease on life in America. Times were tough and work was scarce yet Tobio Palladino always managed to put meals on the family dinner table. Growing up amidst the Depression naturally made Tony hard-as-nails. He was street smart and rumor has it, still has a nasty left hook! Behind his stern, compact exterior, however, lurked an artist of immense sensitivity.

In 1938, Tony sneaked into East Harlem's Triboro Burlesque. This proved to be his first memorable visual experience. Such fascination with the stark visual realities of the big city eventually motivated Tony to feature them in his work.

Believing the pen was mightier than the sword, Tony Palladino enrolled in the High School of Music & Art. The year was 1946. During a design class, he met two other brash kids and formed friendships that lasted personally and professionally over the next forty years. Those classmates turned out to be George Lois and Bob Gill. This triumvarite became part of a new breed of maverick graphic designers; a group of highly-motivated movers and shakers that helped reshape modern-day visual ideology. Their vitality on and off the streets of New York gave them the perfect education necessary to take the design world by storm. All rules were effectively broken. When it comes to breaking rules, nobody does it better than Tony Palladino.

He gives new meaning to chewing gum, street signs, hub caps and crushed packs of cigarettes. Each become central themes, resonating and reflecting Tony's inner self. His work is a product of his environment.

At Music & Art, Palladino began his formal training; immersing himself in the art forms that stimulated him. He eventually transformed them into a style that was unmistakably his own.

George Lois expressed it best when he said:

"Tony was light-years ahead of the world. Not the world of art students, but the world of artists! He adored DADA (before MOMA) and drew like a Fra Angelico. He digested Man Ray, Mondrian, Malevich, Magritte and Matisse and it came out pure Palladino."

In 1949, Palladino studied with the founding fathers of Abstract Expressionism, Mark Rothko and Robert Motherwell. The free-flowing, linear and amorphous works of that movement were perfect outlets for Tony's creativity.

The Army put Palladino's creative endeavors on hold in 1950. When he returned in 1953, Palladino began a series of New York street drawings that had their roots in the Triboro Burlesque and other subsequent personal experiences.

The mid-fifties brought Tony Palladino into the mainstream of the creative world. His three, very provocative visual puns promoting his proficiency as a book jacket designer, demonstrate a highly mature, yet playful style. During this period, Palladino designed numerous covers and promotional pieces. His superb selection of typefaces coupled with new graphic concepts exploded everywhere. One of his personal favorites is a promotional piece he did for package designer Irving Werbin. It's a brown paper bag with Werbin's name visually incorporated with the word 'packaging'. Tony created a design that's truly timeless and inspiring.

It was work like this that led Bob Gill to introduce him to Silas Rhodes, the founder of New York's School of Visual Arts. As a result, Palladino began a love affair with teaching and the School that's still going strong.

Aside from his design, illustration and portfolio courses, Tony created a stunning array of posters for S.V.A. They no doubt, captured the enthusiasm and imagination of countless students. His *Flower Pot by Numbers, Pencil* and *Tunnel* posters voice some highly-charged visual and educational statements.

In 1956, Tony designed the book jacket for Robert Bloch's novel *Psycho*. Three years later Alfred Hitchcock bought the movie rights and J. Walter Thompson, Universal's advertising agency, bought

Tony's original collage design. His logo appeared in all the film's advertising. More notably, it inspired Saul Bass to create his visually disturbing animated title sequence. Subliminal as it may be, Palladino's initial design helped make *Psycho* a motion picture classic.

The early and mid-sixties brought sweeping socio-political changes to the world. JFK's assassination and the war in Vietnam became backdrops for "Palladino's Palate." While studying with Ivan Chermayeff and Robert Brownjohn of the Yale School, Tony began experimenting with various forms of mixed-media sculpture. One of his most compelling was done in response to radio censorship. Entitled *Radio Is Dead,* it consists of an old, cathedral-style radio, fitted with copper nailed over the entire wooden shell. What a way to hammer home a point! Again, a potent, almost iconographic message that only Tony Palladino could convey.

Tony's love of architecture resulted in the design of some truly memorable covers for *Architecture & Engineering News.* The covers, brimming with marvelous visual ideas, really didn't need the accompanying feature copy. Tony's designs did all the talking. *AIA In Miami* and *Plastics In Architecture* are particularly wonderful examples.

In 1964, Tony Palladino began another chapter in his illustrious career. His old friend, George Lois, then a principal at Papert, Koenig, Lois Advertising, hired Tony as an art director. Advertising would never be the same! Together, Palladino and Lois blazed new trails blending perfectly with the 1960's impetuous approach to advertising. From sketch pad to finished product, Palladino and Lois breathed new life, wit and panache into an old, somewhat stagnant profession.

Take an ad P.K.L. did for Evan-Picone, selling the merits of resilient, women's sportswear. Art director Sam Scali and copywriter Renée Guion pulled it off by satirizing the popular television series *The Untouchables.* The headline read *The Uncrushables* and featured two women wearing Evan-Picone skirts and blouses surrounded by some ominous-looking 1920's gangsters. One was Lois, the other was Edward G. Palladino. That's the kind of advertising P.K.L. was famous for. Not only did they create great ads, they appeared in them.

Nineteen sixty-five marked another milestone year in the life of Tony Palladino. His cane-shaped lamp design, made of polished aluminum, was accepted into the permanent collection of New York's Museum of Modern Art.

As the turbulent sixties drew to a close, Palladino turned his attention to more artistic endeavors. He worked in various media, from Craypas to plastic milk jugs; each heavily imbued with a basic idea or concept, a vehicle with which to express himself.

Tony Palladino literally has the power to create life in inanimate objects! His 1976 homage to the Triboro Burlesque is a perfect example. At first glance, it's just a strange, colorful medley of pressed pieces of chewing gum. Not to Tony. For him, it's a harsh, visual reminder of what the Triboro was like inside; under the seats and in the seedy dressing rooms. When one looks at such a dazzling visual of Tony's, you can't help hearing the echoes of frantic whistling from its satisfied clientele while a honky-tonk piano trio plays *Night Train.*

The 1970's were wonderfully productive years for Tony Palladino. His abstract sculptures perfectly complemented his soft, Matisse-like paintings and drawings. His posters continued to grace New York's subways; adding a touch of artistic class to an otherwise barren, underground world.

Palladino has always enjoyed the challenge of creating logos and corporate identity programs. His wide range of delighted clients include Conrail, New York's Trattoria Restaurant, Bellevue Hospital and Melsky Zander Films. Whatever the client, Tony's uncanny knack for designing a logo typifying their specific personna is incredible.

Presently, Palladino is as active as ever. His work is still talked about and exhibited throughout the world. He continues to paint, teach and consult with advertising agencies on a variety of interesting assignments.

Palladino's biggest thrill came in 1985, when the School of Visual Arts honored him with a one-man retrospective gallery exhibit. Richard Wilde, S.V.A.'s Co-Chairman of Media Arts, recalls an amusing anecdote leading up to Palladino's opening:

"Tony thought it would be a nice touch to add fresh-cut flowers to the gala opening night reception. Hours before, Tony was walking down Third Avenue and rescued an old, rickety, wooden chair destined for the garbage truck. Palladino, chair in hand, burst into S.V.A., ran upstairs to one of the studios and began painting his own flowers—right on the chair! He then proceeded to hang it on the wall next to the gallery entrance . . ."

Spontaneous? Yes! Impulsive? Yes! Brilliant? Yes!
Borrowing the copy from two of Tony's highly acclaimed School of Visual Arts posters:

"Having talent isn't worth much unless you know what to do with it . . . It isn't the light at the end of the tunnel, it's the light from within."

Tony Palladino has an immeasurable wealth of talent. The joy he's brought to all who have experienced it, is proof he knows what to do with it. His very own special light from within continues to illuminate and enlighten the design world.

1

Book jackets, 1952

1

2

Packaging design, 1954

2

3

Psycho, paper collage used for novel
and movie advertising, 1956 &
1960.

3

4

School of Visual Arts poster, 1959

4

5

Radio Is Dead, 1960

5

6

Ad for Evan-Picone; Papert, Koenig,
Lois Advertising, 1962

6

7

Architecture & Engineering News,
cover, 1963

8

Architecture & Engineering News,
cover, 1963

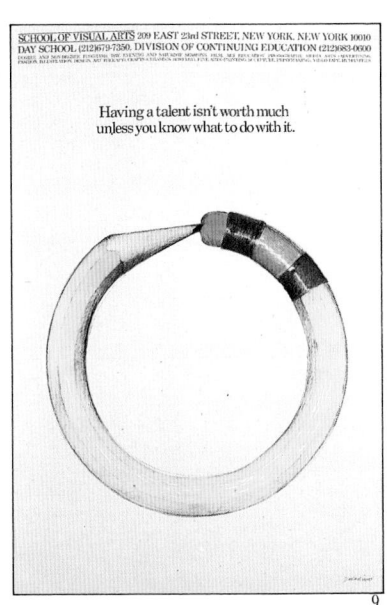

9

School of Visual Arts Poster, 1975

10

Triboro Burlesque, 1976

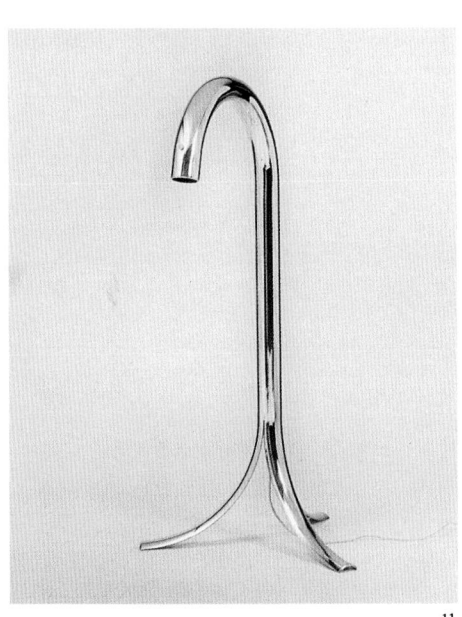

11

Free-standing lamp, Permanent
Collection, Museum of Modern Art,
1965

12

School of Visual Arts poster, 1983

"Call for Phil-ip Mor-ris"

Johnny, the Philip Morris bellhop, began as a drawing on cigarette packages in 1919 and came to life in the person of Johnny Roventini in 1933. Philip Morris decided it wanted a radio voice for the package symbol and Milton Biow set out on a bellhop hunt that led him into most of the hotel lobbies of New York until he discovered the four-foot-two Roventini in uniform at the New Yorker hotel. Johnny's perfect B-flat call was just what Biow was after and a star was born. Johnny stepped "out of store windows and counters all over America" to many top radio shows, including "This Is Your Life", "The Rudy Vallee Show" and "Break The Bank".

66TH ANNUAL EXHIBITION
Gold, Silver and Distinctive Merit Award Winners:

Newspaper Advertising
Magazine Advertising
Newspaper Editorial
Magazine Editorial
Promotion & Graphic Design
Books & Jackets
Posters
Illustration
Photography
Television

1
GOLD AWARD

ART DIRECTOR
Houman Pirdavari
PHOTOGRAPHER
Rick Dublin, Eric Saulitis and
photos courtesy of Isaac Stern,
Zubin Mehta & Ed Koch
WRITER
Bill Miller
CLIENT
Bloomingdale's
AGENCY
Fallon McElligott, Minneapolis, MN

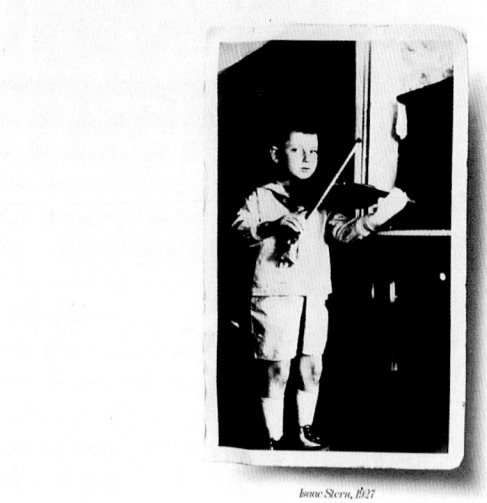

Isaac Stern, 1927

Mom — do you really think
That if I practice very hard
I can really get to Carnegie Hall?

For one hundred years, Bloomingdale's has seen the shadows of great men lengthen along with their pants.

bloomingdale's
It wouldn't be the same without you.

1

Zubin Mehta, 1940

1940 — The world's turmoil is far from
this vacation in Bangalore, India —
So are the dreams that later became the
Philharmonics of New York & Israel!
1986 — Bangalore seems so far away!

For one hundred years, Bloomingdale's has witnessed the dreams of extraordinary people
in an extraordinary city. And they have all been music to our ears.

bloomingdale's
It wouldn't be the same without you.

Ed Koch, 1940

When I was 17, I wanted to look
like a preppy, even though I wasn't
attending a preppy school. And, I also
had hair when I was 17. Today, I
still like to dress informally, although
my hairline has changed.

Ed Koch

For one hundred years, Bloomingdale's sportswear has been pulled over many a changing hairline.

bloomingdale's
It wouldn't be the same without you.

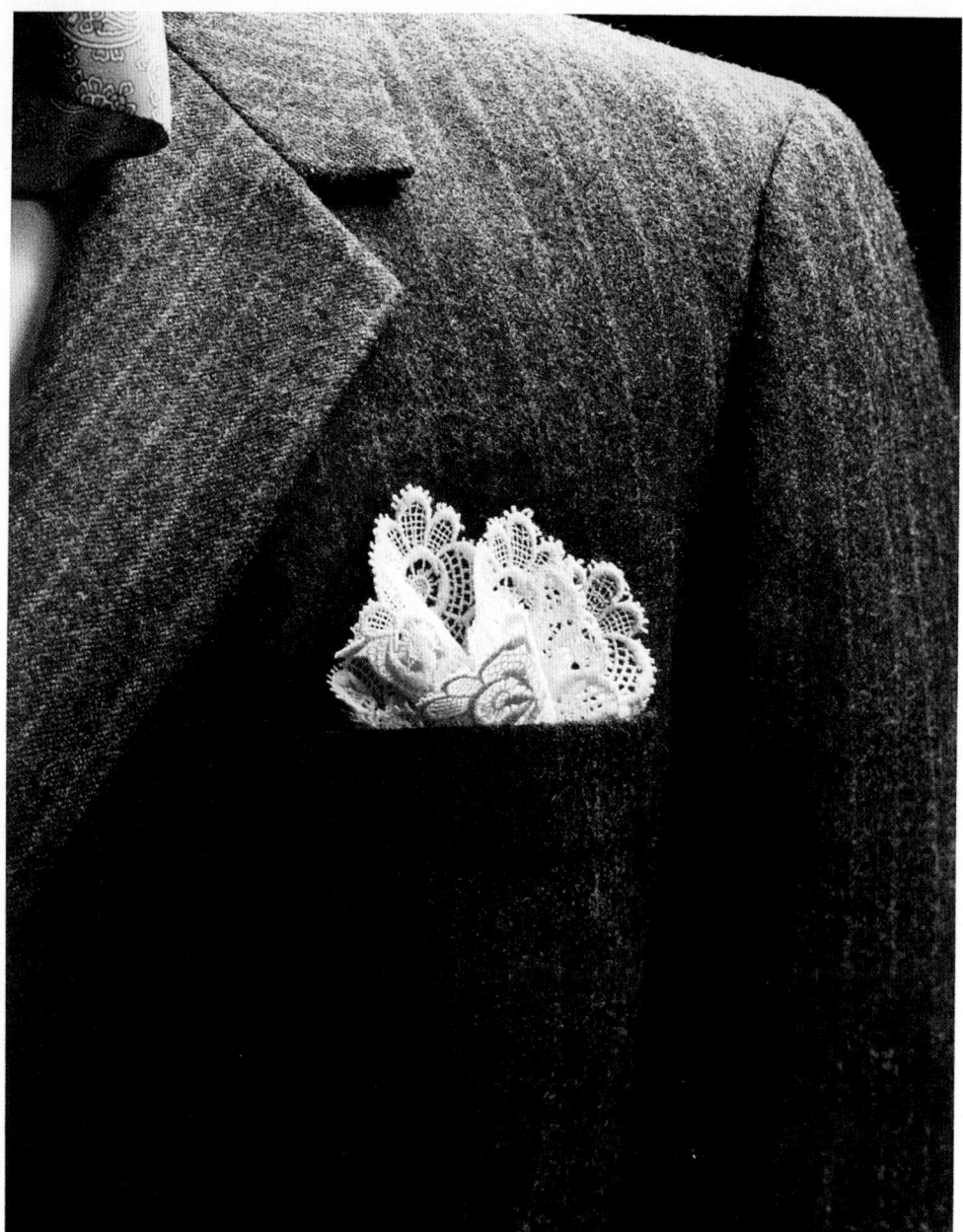

2
SILVER AWARD

ART DIRECTOR
Tom Lichtenheld
PHOTOGRAPHER
Tom Bach/Marvy
WRITER
Jamie Barrett
CLIENT
The Wall St. Journal
AGENCY
Fallon McElligott, Minneapolis, MN

The fabric of American business is changing.

It used to be that wearing a business suit meant being a businessman.

But in recent years, millions of women have entered the workplace. And their arrival has signaled a profound change. Not only in corporate dress, but in the very way of corporate life.

On March 24th, The Wall Street Journal will publish a special report on the increasingly important role of women in business.

Entitled "The Corporate Woman," the section will consider the nature of the new workforce, and the impact of the growing female presence.

It will look at women's problems. Their progress. Their prospects for the future.

And it will measure their influence on some of the basic principles and assumptions of corporate America.

"The Corporate Woman" will be included free of charge in your subscription or newsstand copy of The Wall Street Journal on Monday, March 24th. Be sure to read it.

Whether you're woman enough to or not.

The Wall Street Journal.
The daily diary of the American dream.

3
SILVER AWARD

ART DIRECTOR
John Vitro
DESIGNER
Ron Van Buskirk
PHOTOGRAPHER
Marshall Harrington
WRITER
Mitchell Wein
AGENCY
VW Advertising, San Diego, CA

3

4
SILVER AWARD

ART DIRECTOR
John Vitro
DESIGNER
Ron Van Buskirk
PHOTOGRAPHER
Marshall Harrington
WRITER
John Robertson
CLIENT
United Way/Chad
AGENCY
Phillips-Ramsey Advertising, San
Diego, CA

4

Will it take six strong men to bring you back into the church?

The Episcopal Church welcomes you no matter what condition you're in, but we'd really prefer to see you breathing. Come join us in the love, worship and fellowship of Jesus Christ this Sunday.

The Episcopal Church

5

5
DISTINCTIVE MERIT

ART DIRECTOR
Dean Hanson
PHOTOGRAPHER
Rick Dublin
WRITER
Tom McElligott
CLIENT
Episcopal Ad Project
AGENCY
Fallon McElligott, Minneapolis, MN

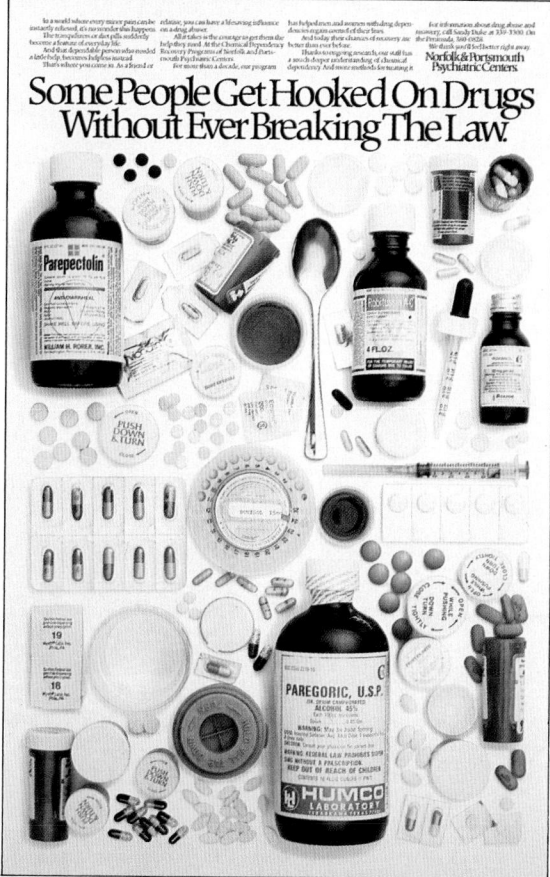

Some People Get Hooked On Drugs Without Ever Breaking The Law.

6

6
DISTINCTIVE MERIT

ART DIRECTOR
Cabell Harris
PHOTOGRAPHER
Pat Edwards
WRITER
Ken Hines
CLIENT
First Hospital
AGENCY
Lawler Ballard Advertising,
Richmond, VA

7
DISTINCTIVE MERIT

ART DIRECTOR
Cabell Harris
PHOTOGRAPHER
John Whitehead
WRITER
Ken Hines
CLIENT
Norfolk General Hospital
AGENCY
Lawler Ballard Advertising,
Richmond, VA

While You're Relaxing With The Sunday Paper, We'd Like To Thank A Few People Who Aren't.

7

8
DISTINCTIVE MERIT

ART DIRECTOR
Mike Murray
DESIGNER
Mike Murray
PHOTOGRAPHER
Eric Saulitis
ILLUSTRATOR/ARTIST
Ron Finger
WRITER
John Francis
CLIENT
Como Park Conservatory
AGENCY
Bozell, Jacobs, Kenyon & Eckhardt,
Minneapolis, MN
PUBLICATION
St. Paul Pioneer Press

Of All The Green Things At The Como Conservatory, This One Is The Rarest.

Help Save The Conservatory At Como Park.

9
DISTINCTIVE MERIT

ART DIRECTOR
Bill Murphy
PHOTOGRAPHER
Michael Pierce
WRITER
Margaret Wilcox
CLIENT
The Boston Globe
AGENCY
Hill, Holliday, Boston, MA
PUBLICATION
The Boston Globe

Last year 26 kids didn't make it to the next grade because of marks like these.

8   9

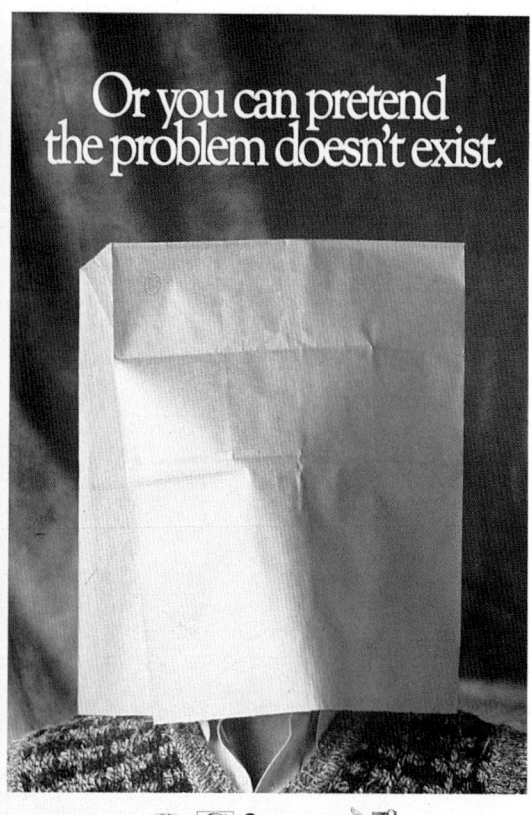

10
DISTINCTIVE MERIT

ART DIRECTOR
Jim Mochnsky
PHOTOGRAPHER
Michael Pohuski
WRITER
Arthur Mitchell
CLIENT
The Baltimore Sun
AGENCY
W. B. Doner Advertising, Baltimore, MD

10

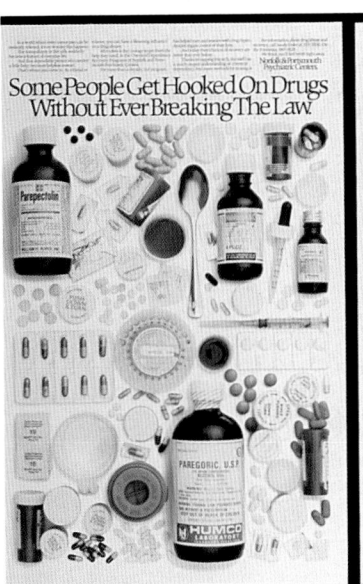

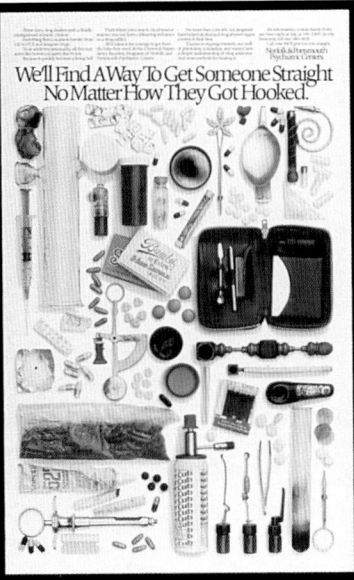

11
DISTINCTIVE MERIT

ART DIRECTOR
Cabell Harris
PHOTOGRAPHER
Pat Edwards
WRITER
Ken Hines
CLIENT
First Hospital
AGENCY
Lawler Ballard Advertising, Richmond, VA

11

12
DISTINCTIVE MERIT

ART DIRECTOR
Marten Tonnis
PHOTOGRAPHER
Bo Hylen
ILLUSTRATOR/ARTIST
Cynthia Shern
WRITER
Penny Kapousouz
CLIENT
Apple Computer, Inc.
AGENCY
Chiat/Day Advertising, Los Angeles, CA
PUBLICATION
USA Today

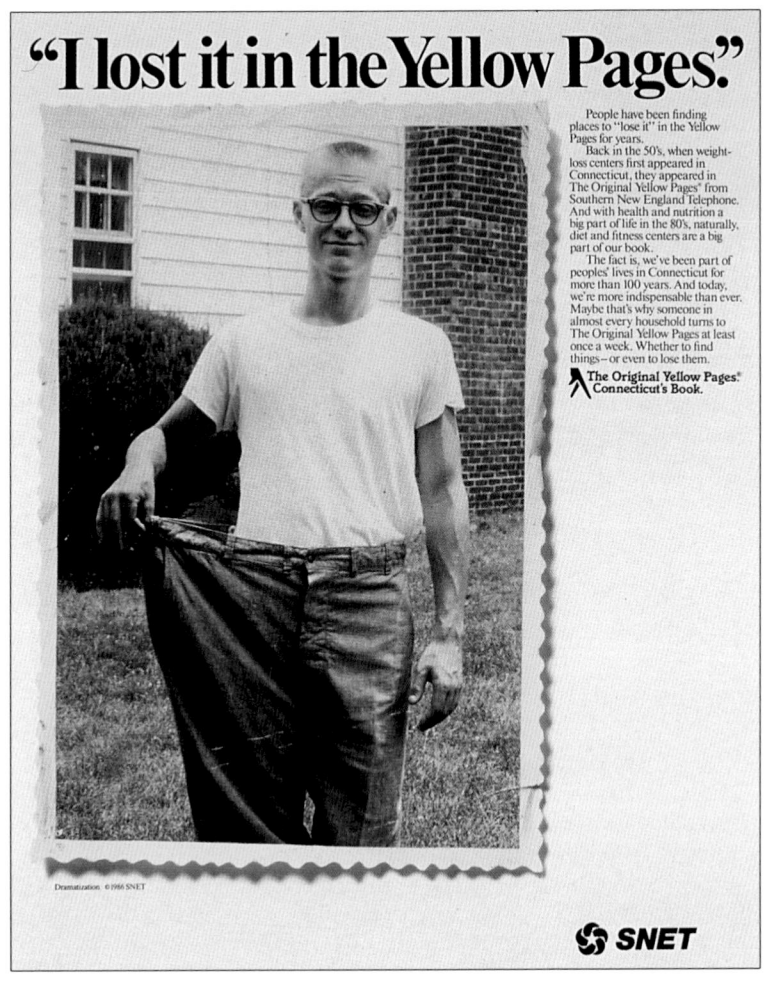

13
DISTINCTIVE MERIT

ART DIRECTOR
Bob Green
PHOTOGRAPHER
Howard Berman
WRITER
Cathy Cole
CLIENT
Southern New England Telephone
DIRECTOR
Arnie Arlow, Peter Lubalin
AGENCY
TBWA, New York, NY

13

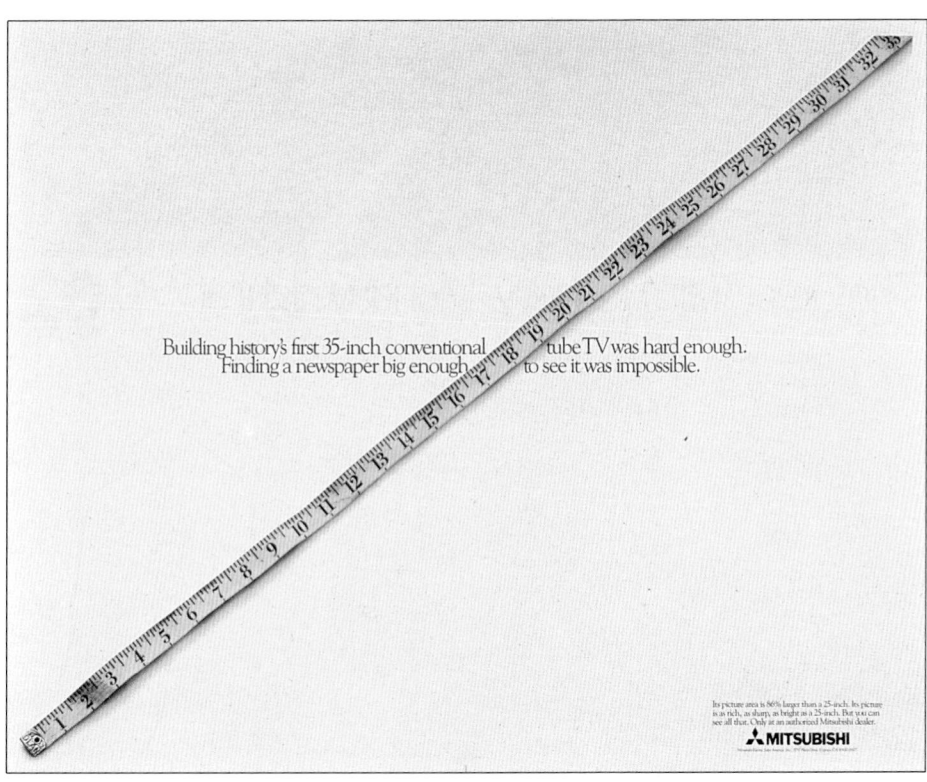

14
DISTINCTIVE MERIT

ART DIRECTOR
Rick Boyko, Andy Dijak
PHOTOGRAPHER
Dennis Manarchy
WRITER
Bill Hamilton
CLIENT
Mitsubishi Electric Sales America
AGENCY
Chiat/Day Advertising, Los Angeles, CA
PUBLICATION
USA Today

14

15
GOLD AWARD

ART DIRECTOR
Houman Pirdavari
ILLUSTRATOR/ARTIST
Dan Craig
WRITER
Mike Lescarbeau
CLIENT
WFLD-TV
AGENCY
Fallon McElligott, Minneapolis, MN

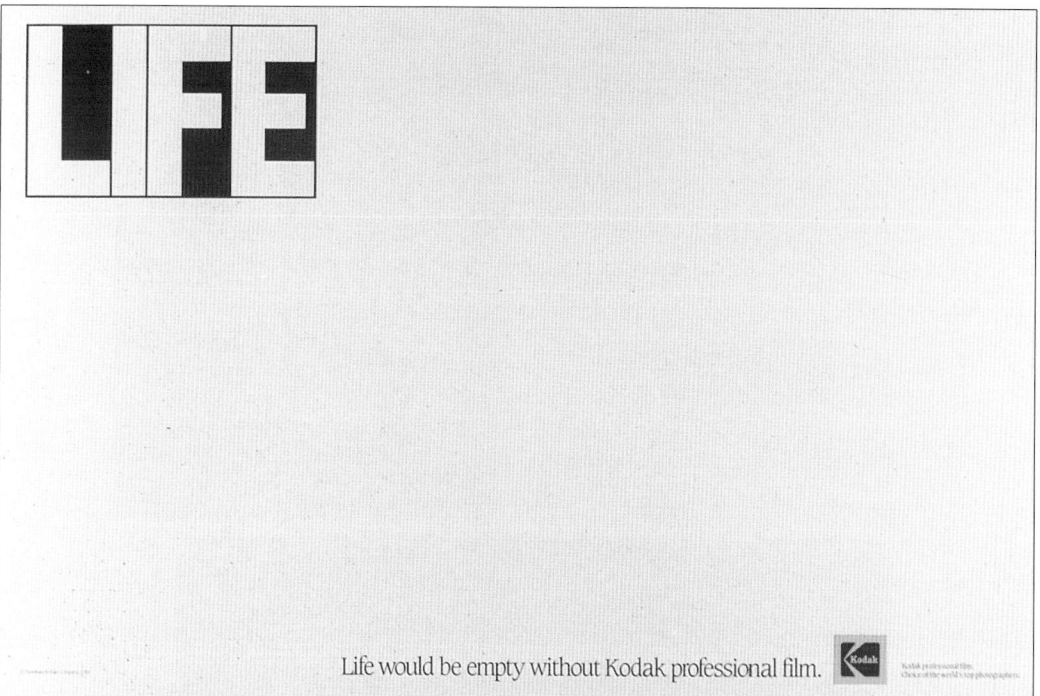

16
SILVER AWARD

ART DIRECTOR
Steve Hall
WRITER
Kenn Jacobs
CLIENT
Eastman Kodak Company
AGENCY
Rumrill-Hoyt, Rochester, NY
PUBLICATION
LIFE Magazine, 50th Anniversary
Issue
PRODUCTION TECHNICIAN
Lou Ann Chatell

17
SILVER AWARD

ART DIRECTOR
Paul Boley
PHOTOGRAPHER
Dewitt Jones, Studio Associates
WRITER
Richard Rand
CLIENT
Schenley/Dewars
AGENCY
Leo Burnett Co., Inc., Chicago, IL
CREATIVE DIRECTOR
John Eding

18
SILVER AWARD

ART DIRECTOR
John C. Jay
DESIGNER
John C. Jay
PHOTOGRAPHER
Ken Matsubara
WRITER
Brian Leitch
CLIENT
Robert Allen Fabrics
AGENCY
John Jay Design, New York, and J.S.
Naren Marketing
DESIGN FIRM
John Jay Design
PUBLICATION
House & Garden, Architectural
Digest and Interior Design

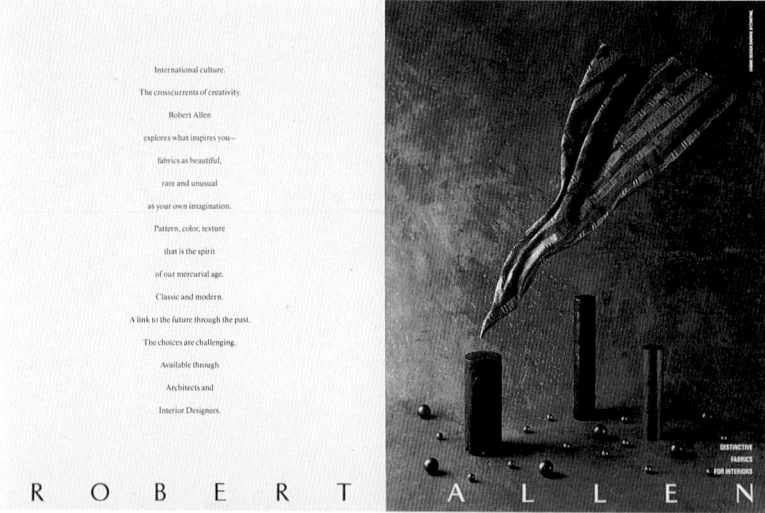

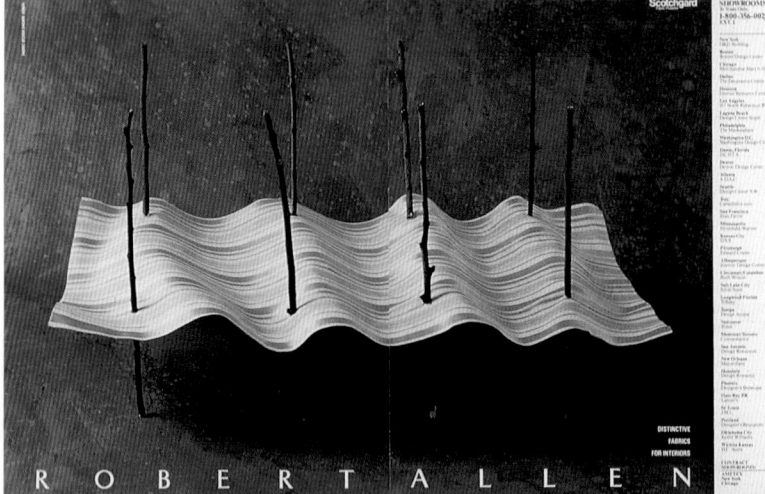

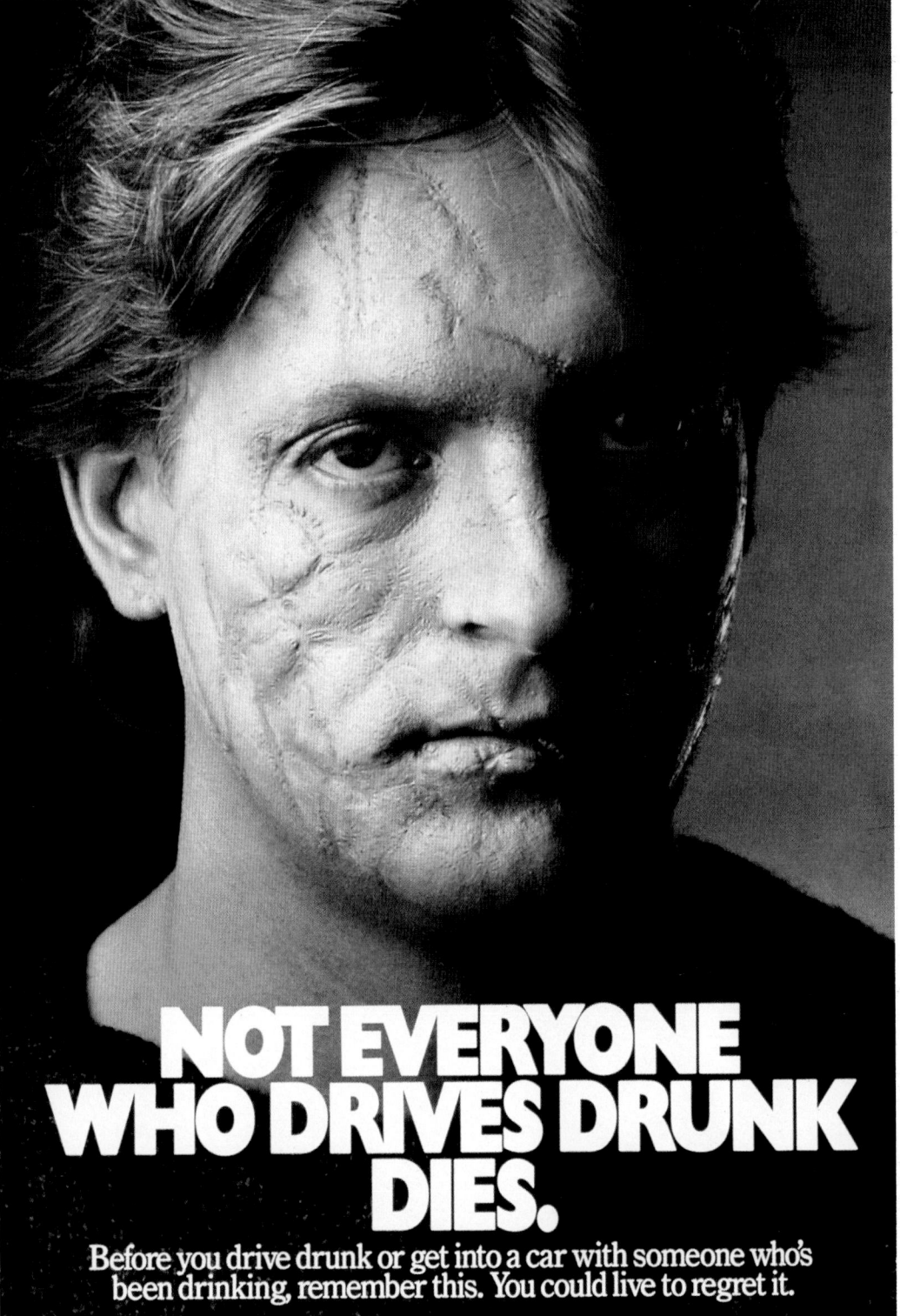

NOT EVERYONE WHO DRIVES DRUNK DIES.

Before you drive drunk or get into a car with someone who's been drinking, remember this. You could live to regret it.

19
SILVER AWARD

ART DIRECTOR
Sal DeVito, Jamie Seltzer
DESIGNER
Sal DeVito
PHOTOGRAPHER
Cailor/Resnick
WRITER
Jamie Seltzer, Sal DeVito
CLIENT
Reader's Digest
AGENCY
Chiat/Day Inc., New York, NY

19

20
SILVER AWARD

ART DIRECTOR
Gary Goldsmith
DESIGNER
Gary Goldsmith
WRITER
Neal Gomberg
CLIENT
Citizens Against Cocaine Abuse
AGENCY
Goldsmith/Jeffrey, New York, NY
PUBLICATION
Format Magazine
ACCOUNT EXECUTIVE
Bob Jeffrey

21
SILVER AWARD

ART DIRECTOR
Miles Turpin
PHOTOGRAPHER
Dana Gluckstein
WRITER
Elizabeth Hayes
CLIENT
Apple Computer, Inc.
AGENCY
Chiat/Day Advertising, Los Angeles,
CA
PUBLICATION
Exceptional Parent

22
SILVER AWARD

ART DIRECTOR
Tom Lichtenheld
PHOTOGRAPHER
Stock
ILLUSTRATOR/ARTIST
Bob Lambert
WRITER
Mike Lescarbeau
CLIENT
Bob Lambert Retouching
AGENCY
Fallon McElligott, Minneapolis, MN

BOB LAMBERT · RETOUCHING · 835-2166

23
SILVER AWARD

ART DIRECTOR
Houman Pirdavari
PHOTOGRAPHER
Rick Dublin
WRITER
Bill Miller
CLIENT
Rolling Stone
AGENCY
Fallon McElligott, Minneapolis, MN
FRAGRANCES
Patchouli, Paco Rabanne

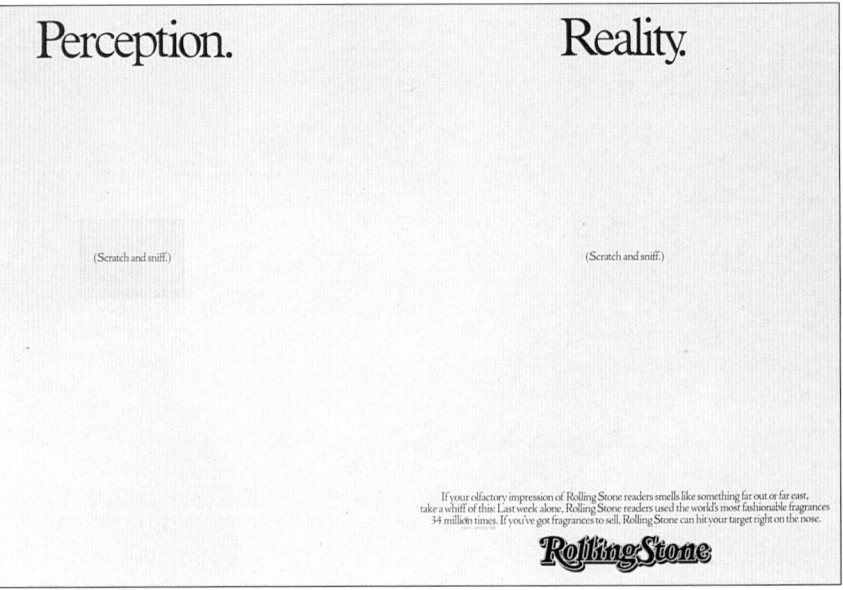

24
SILVER AWARD

ART DIRECTOR
Rick Boyko
PHOTOGRAPHER
Dennis Manarchy
WRITER
Bill Hamilton
CLIENT
Mitsubishi Electric Sales America
AGENCY
Chiat/Day Advertising, Los Angeles, CA
PUBLICATION
Video Review

24

25
DISTINCTIVE MERIT

ART DIRECTOR
Shony Rivnay
DESIGNER
Shony Rivnay
PHOTOGRAPHER
Art Beck
WRITER
Richard Middendorf
CLIENT
Ore-Ida Foods, Inc.
AGENCY
DDB Needham Worldwide, Inc., New York, NY
PUBLICATION
Star, Consumer Mag.

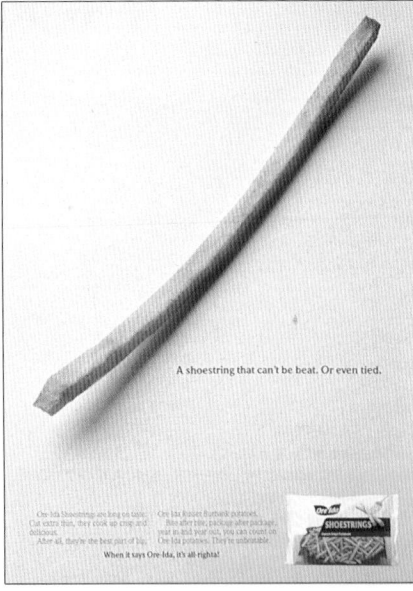

A shoestring that can't be beat. Or even tied.

26
DISTINCTIVE MERIT

ART DIRECTOR
Houman Pirdavari
PHOTOGRAPHER
Rick Dublin
WRITER
Bill Miller
CLIENT
Rolling Stone
AGENCY
Fallon McElligott, Minneapolis, MN

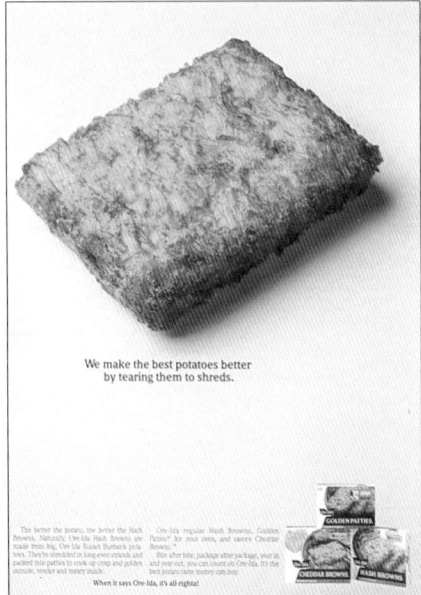

We make the best potatoes better by tearing them to shreds.

27
DISTINCTIVE MERIT

ART DIRECTOR
Dean Hanson
PHOTOGRAPHER
Rick Dublin
WRITER
Tom McElligott
CLIENT
Children's Defense Fund
AGENCY
Fallon McElligott, Minneapolis, MN

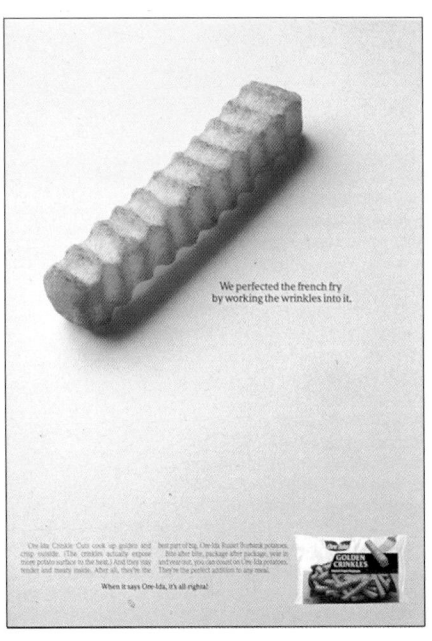

We perfected the french fry by working the wrinkles into it.

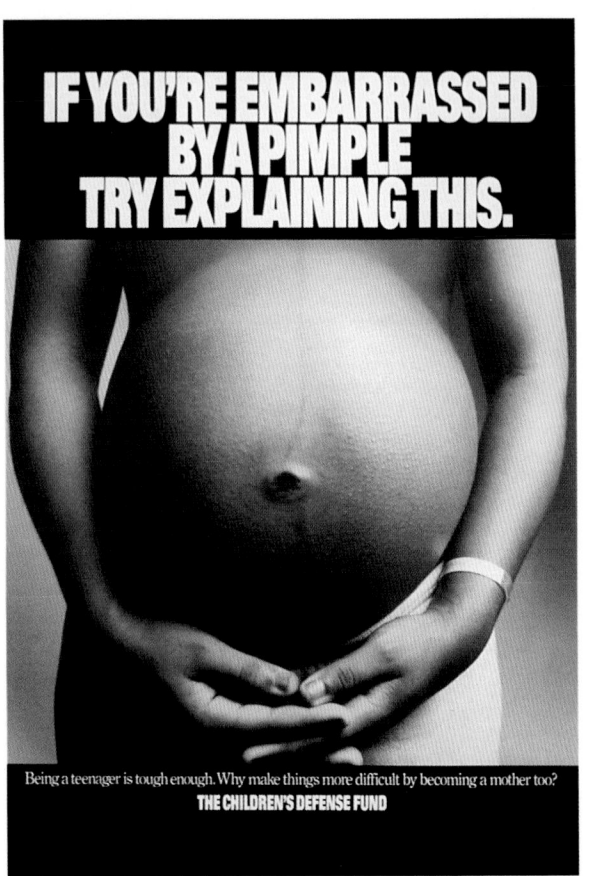

25

27

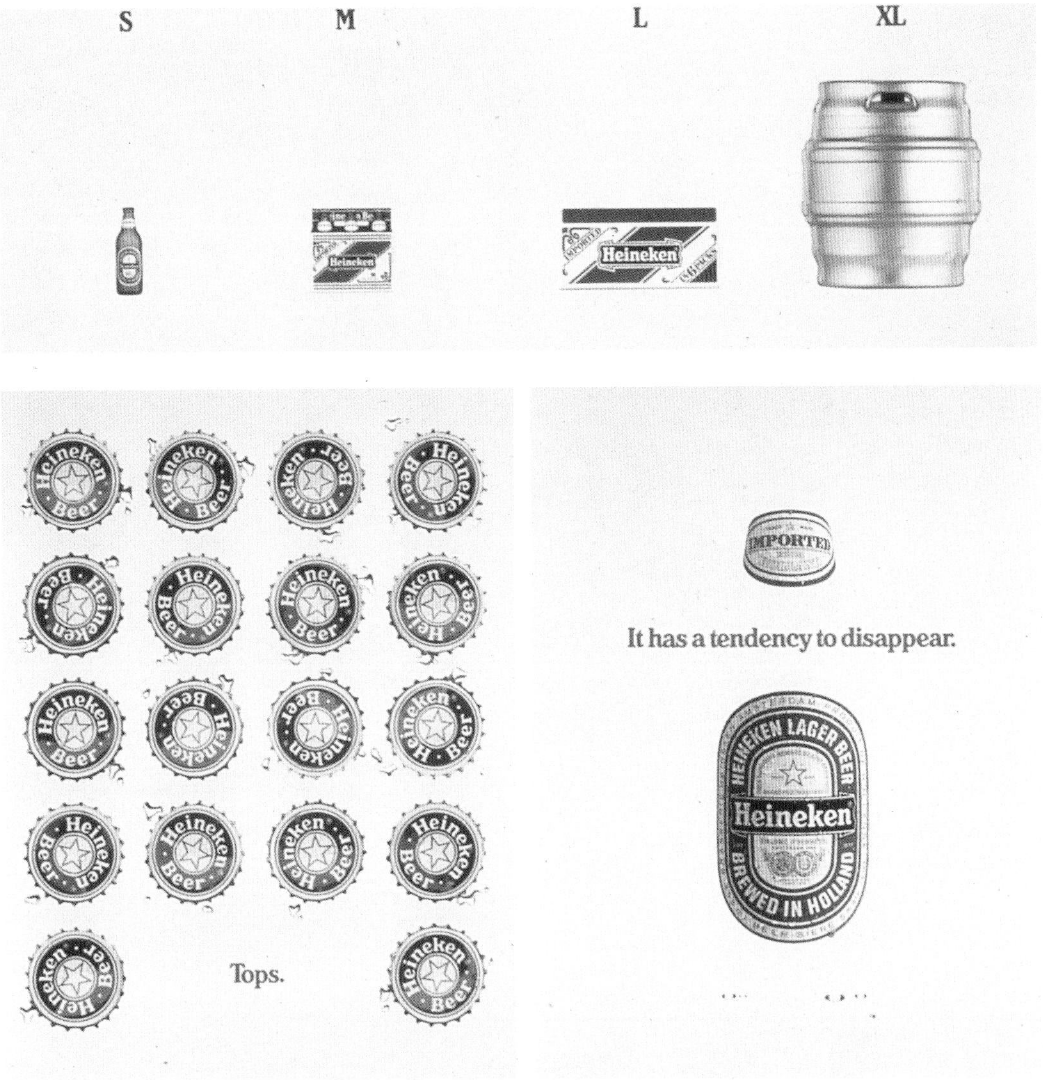

S   M   L   XL

Tops.

IMPORTED

It has a tendency to disappear.

Heineken LAGER BEER
Heineken
BREWED IN HOLLAND

28
DISTINCTIVE MERIT

ART DIRECTOR
Steve Thursby
PHOTOGRAPHER
Ian Campbell
WRITER
Allan Kazmer, Steve Thursby
CLIENT
Heineken Marketing, Canada
AGENCY
DDB Needham Worldwide, Toronto,
Canada
PUBLICATION
Time Magazine
PRODUCTION MANAGER
John Stevenson
TYPE
Typesettra Ltd.

28

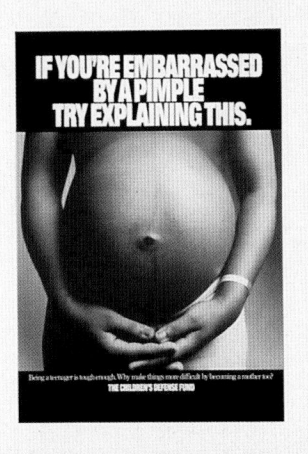

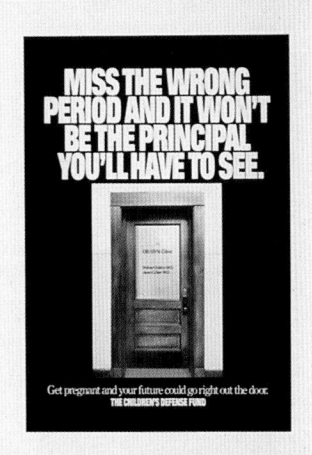

29
DISTINCTIVE MERIT

ART DIRECTOR
Dean Hanson
PHOTOGRAPHER
Marc Hauser, Rick Dublin
WRITER
Tom McElligott
CLIENT
Children's Defense Fund
AGENCY
Fallon McElligott, Minneapolis, MN

29

30
DISTINCTIVE MERIT

ART DIRECTOR
Sharon Roberts
DESIGNER
Clif Bosler
PHOTOGRAPHER
David Leeson
DIRECTOR OF PHOTOGRAPHY
John Davidson
PUBLICATION
The Dallas Morning News, Dallas,
TX

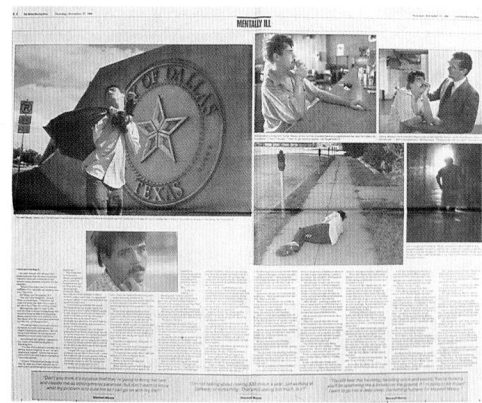

30

31
DISTINCTIVE MERIT

ART DIRECTOR
Nancy Sterngold
DESIGNER
Nancy Sterngold
PHOTOGRAPHER
Thom O'Connor, Dith Pran
ILLUSTRATOR/ARTIST
Keith Bendis
CLIENT
The New York Times Living Section
EDITOR
Margot Slade
PUBLISHER
The New York Times, New York, NY
PUBLICATION
The New York Times

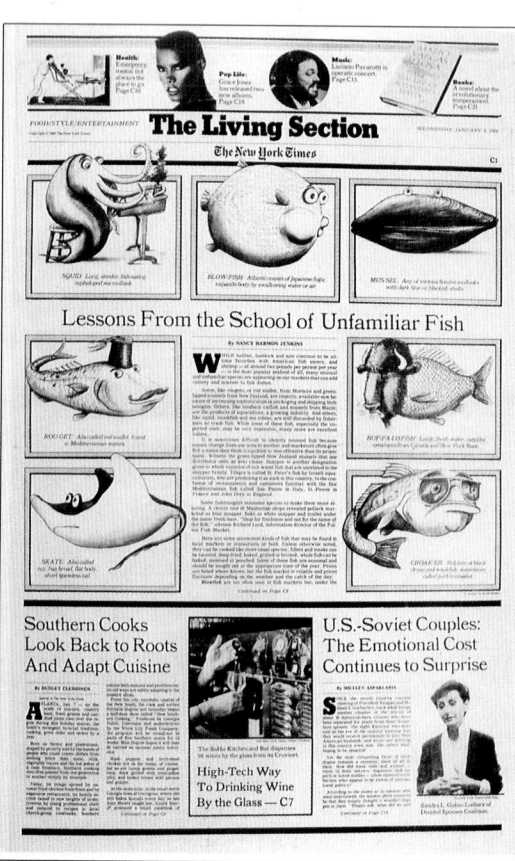

31

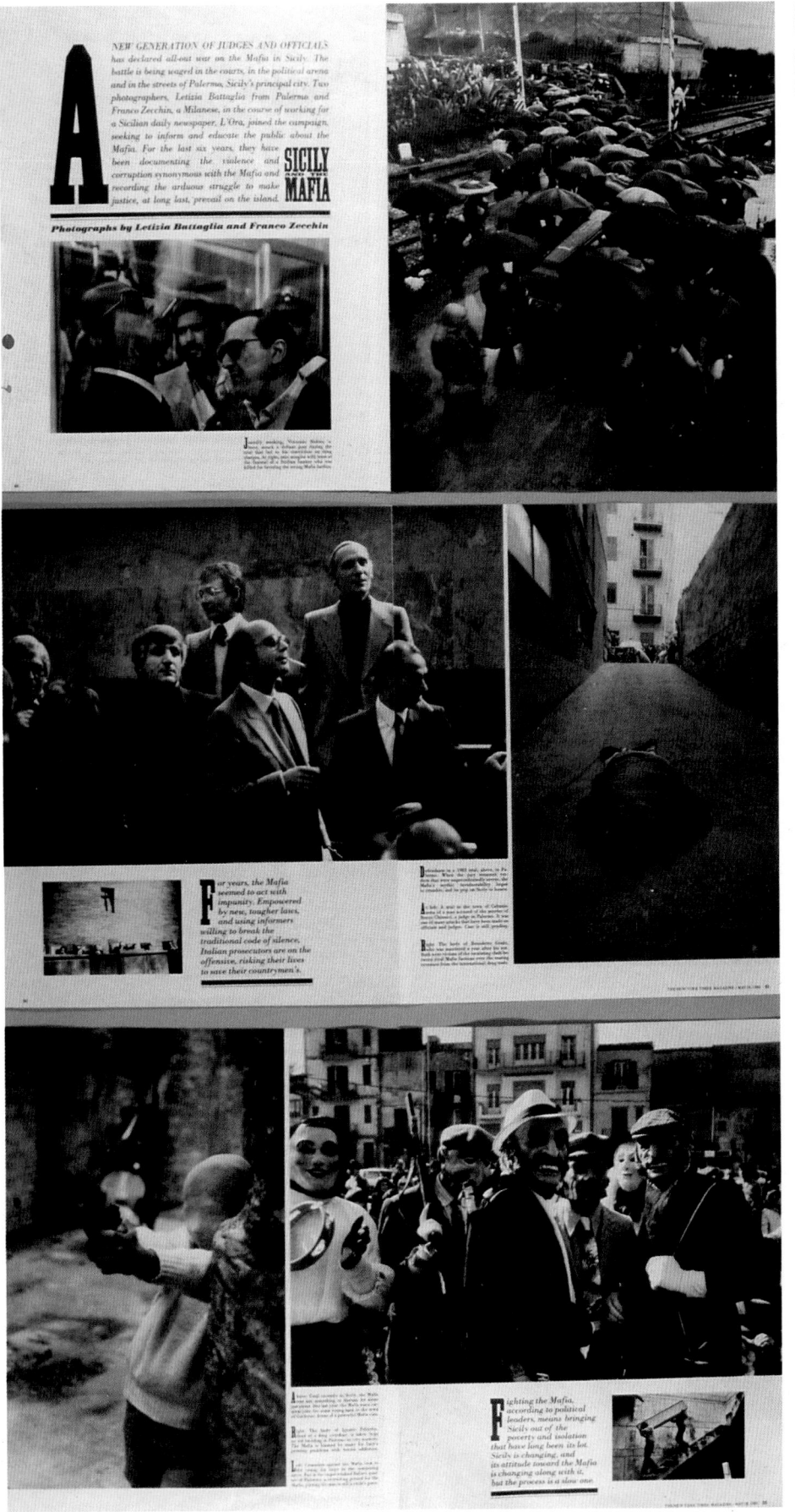

32
GOLD AWARD

ART DIRECTOR
Ken Kendrick
DESIGNER
Ken Kendrick
PHOTOGRAPHER
Letizia Battaglia, Franco Zecchin
CLIENT
The New York Times Magazine
EDITOR
Ed Klein
PHOTO EDITOR
Peter Howe
PUBLISHER
The New York Times, New York, NY
PUBLICATION
The New York Times

33
GOLD AWARD

ART DIRECTOR
Christopher Lione
PHOTOGRAPHER
Lizzie Himmel
WRITER
Patrick Pacheco
EDITOR
Jeffrey Schaire
PUBLISHER
Wick Allison
PUBLICATION
Art & Antiques , New York, NY
PHOTO EDITOR
Denise Dorrance

NEW MEXICO STYLE

How a folk art of dignity, honesty, and proportion arose from a harsh and beautiful land.

Both my mother and father were raised on ranches near the small town of Las Vegas, New Mexico, where, when I was a child, I was often taken to visit *la tias*, "the aunts." They lived in an adobe house, which had been covered with plywood in a nod to modernity, on a rutted sidestreet of the old Spanish section. An overgrown garden of wildflowers encroached on porches leading to a huge door decorated with pendants, which would creak open on rusty hinges.

Inside, the house smelled of rosewater and sanctity; *santos* —

Patrick Pacheco is a writer who lives in New York. He is currently at work on Familia, a history of his ancestors in San Miguel County, New Mexico.

By Patrick Pacheco
Photographs by Lizzie Himmel

New Mexican styles, left to right: a nineteenth-century Hepplewhite "bow-tie" chair, a Spanish chip-carved chair, a pure New Mexican Revival chair, and a nineteenth-century chair from Michoacán in Mexico.

images of the saints—peered from every corner in the gloomy rooms. The high windows let in little light and old lamps banished every trace of the twentieth century. Margarita, the elder of my grandmother's sisters, was forbidding, but her sister Nicolasa favored me with hugs and the occasional conspiratorial sweet. Shortly after we arrived, Nica, as she was called, would announce she was going to get *panela*, tobacco. This was a cue for me to follow her rustling black skirts into her bedroom where, from underneath a high bed piled with dolls in ruffled hoop petticoats, she would draw out what she called her *"cajón de las donas,"* her dowry chest.

In my greedy little mind, the word "chest" was invariably tied to the allure and the romance with which she handled the girl-carved, if worn, box seemed to confirm this. From her pocket she'd withdraw a large ring of keys and open the chest to reveal small compartments, from which she took a bag full of Bull Durham tobacco, rolling papers, and two pieces of buttersweet chocolate.

While I perched on a simple, crudely constructed stool—a *taburete* with the name "Tris" etched into it—she sat at a small table, painstakingly rolling cigarettes. Puffing away, she'd recall her youth in this town of the distant, when New Mexico was still a territory, telling tales of Indians and bandits, of buffalo hunters and land grabbers, and of the coming of the railroad and the Easterners who flocked to the resorts for tubercular patients where she worked as a girl.

As she spoke, I'd gaze the chocolate and mindlessly trace the outline of the rosettes, pomegranates, and fans gouged into the pine wood of the chest, like a blind boy hoping to divine the shape of the life she described in such vivid colors. I didn't know it then, but the furniture in that house—as resistant to the twentieth century as its owners—were the keys to this world. As I grew older, *depressions* these "ranch style" furniture became the symbol of my family's assimilation. We considered the authentic pieces that filled our relatives' ranches and houses in New Mexico little more than junk. Not surprisingly, this "junk," with its simple straight lines and good honest proportions, has become increasingly appreciated as folk art, reflecting the life and times of a people settling a harsh and beautiful land.

"New Mexican" furniture is a term filled with ambiguity, partly because there was little documentation in times that were also subject to the vicissitudes of weather, fire, and hostility. Its temporal parameters stretch between the Spanish Reconquest in 1690, when what Coronado had claimed as "New Spain" a century and a half earlier was wrested back from the Indians, to the 1920s when a confluence of artists, intellectuals, and monied Easterners began to appreciate what my family so cavalierly relegated to the barn and fireplace. In between there are milestones: Mexico's independence in 1821, which ended the Spanish colonial period; the opening of the Santa Fe Trail in 1822; the ceding of the territory to the U.S. by Mexico in 1848; the same year the first period opened in Santa Fe; and 1882, when the Atchison, Topeka, and Santa Fe Railway first reached Las Vegas.

Aunt Nica's *cajón*, made by her father-in-law in the late nineteenth century, was among the most common objects in a culture known for the sparseness of its furnishings. The *cajónes* ranged from *tapetes* in barnacle-massive chests in which those and grain were stored through the winter—to the smaller, more ornate *donas*. Though they were simple and crude, they were well put together

From under a high bed piled with dolls in hoop skirts she would draw out what she called a cajón de las donas *—a dower chest.*

In my greedy little mind, the word "chest" was invariably tied to "treasure."

The dark (previous page) was a ranch version; and while standing, the blue cabinet is made of packing crates. The trasteros on the left here has had its broken linear spindle replaced with panels from a door; on the bottom shelf of the other are indentations for pottery water jugs.

71

The Hanimals, Humands and Humages of Mario Mariotti

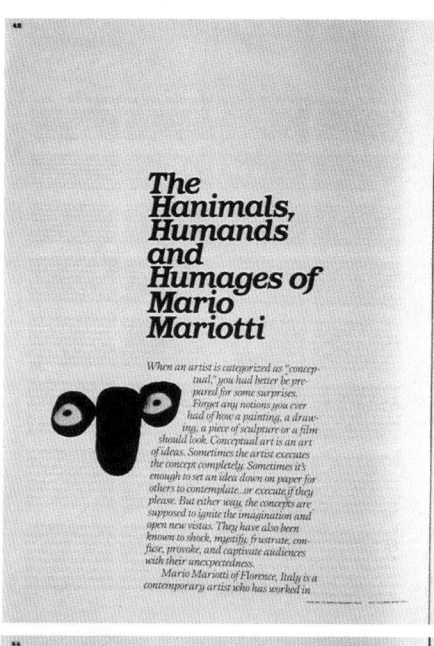

When an artist is categorized as "conceptual," you had better be prepared for some surprises. Forget any notions you ever had of how a painting, a drawing, a piece of sculpture or a film should look. Conceptual art is an art of ideas. Sometimes the artist executes the concept completely. Sometimes it's enough to set an idea down on paper for others to contemplate...or execute if they please. But either way, the concepts are supposed to ignite the imagination and open new vistas. They have also been known to shock, mystify, frustrate, confuse, provoke, and captivate audiences with their unexpectedness.

Mario Mariotti of Florence, Italy is a contemporary artist who has worked in

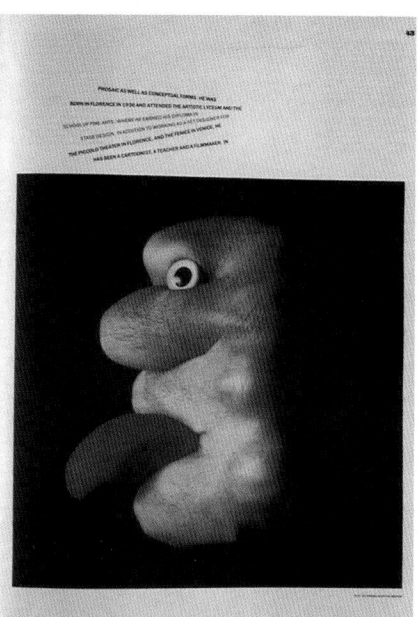

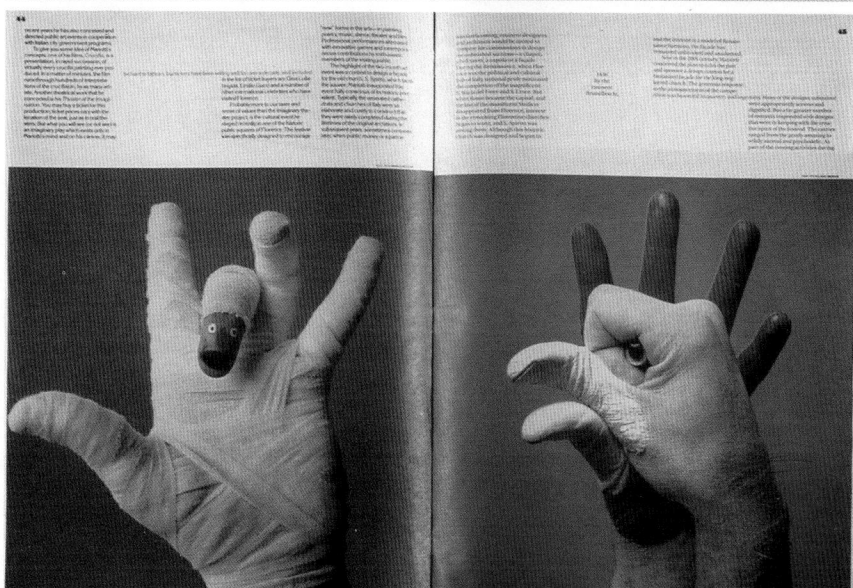

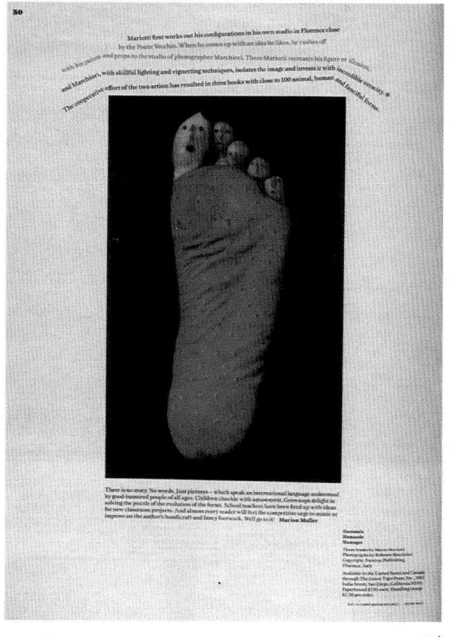

34
GOLD AWARD

ART DIRECTOR
Bob Farber
PHOTOGRAPHER
Roberto Marchiori
ILLUSTRATOR/ARTIST
Mario Mariotti
WRITER
Marion Muller
CLIENT
U & lc (Upper and Lowercase)
EDITOR
Edward Gottschall
PUBLISHER
International Typeface Corporation
DESIGN FIRM
International Typeface Corporation,
New York, NY
PUBLICATION
U & lc (Upper and Lowercase)
ASSISTANT ART DIRECTOR
Ilene Strizver

35
SILVER AWARD

ART DIRECTOR
Carla Barr
DESIGNER
Carla Barr
PHOTOGRAPHER
Sandi Fellman
WRITER
Charles Bricker
PUBLISHER
Hearst Corp.
PUBLICATION
Connoisseur Magazine, New York, NY

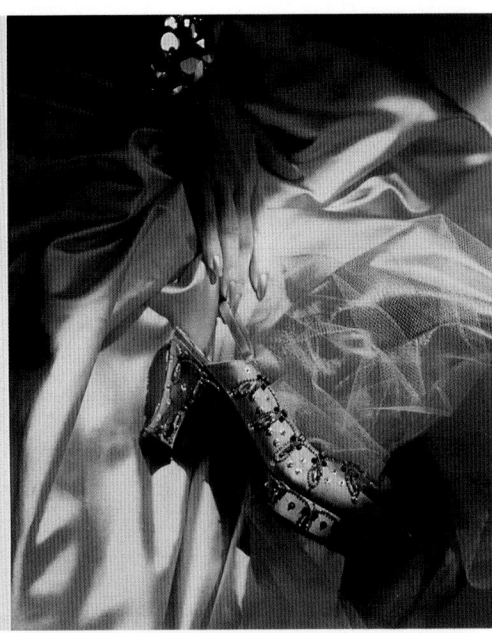

FASHION
AFOOT

ROGER VIVIER, THE SUPREME SHOEMAKER, COMES TO NEW YORK
◆

BY CHARLES BRICKER · PHOTOGRAPHS BY SANDI FELLMAN

Above: Roger Vivier in his Madison Avenue shop. Opposite: "Volga," a shoe designed in 1968, with Romanoff heel and platform sole.

THEY TREAD THE FINE LINE BETWEEN CLASSE AND TARTE.
◆

From last summer's collection, a sandal of gossamer wire gauze, loomed by Geneviève Dupeux. Vivier likens the gauzy stuff to "a puff of smoke" and fastens a cloudlike bow at the instep.

"I NEVER LOOK FOR NEW SHAPES OR IDEAS. THEY SIMPLY MATERIALIZE."
◆

Opposite, left: "Maxim's," a 1954 evening pump of pink satin with beveled heel, embroidered with rhinestones and a large crystal. Right: "Titan," a shoe created in 1954 for Christian Dior, of silver gauze over satin, embroidered with silver thread and topaz rhinestones. It has the Vivier arched heel. Above: From the fall '86 collection, a white satin pump with half-cut counter heel mounted on a rhinestone ball.

DECEMBER 1986

35

36
SILVER AWARD
ART DIRECTOR
Ron Albrecht
PHOTOGRAPHER
Various
EDITOR
Karen Anderegg
PUBLISHER
Marybeth Russell
PUBLICATION
ELLE Magazine, New York, NY
PUBLICATION DIRECTOR
Regis Pagniez

ELLE

BARDOT
DENEUVE
FONDA:
VADIM TALKS

SEAN PENN
FOR REAL

SECRETS
TO FRESH
FRENCH
BEAUTY

COLOR ATTACK
WITTY
MIXINGS,
SUMMER SPARKS,
NEW
IDEAS

MAY 1986
USA $2.50 CANADA $2.95

AUSTRALIA $A4.95 FRANCE FF50 GERMANY DM12
GREECE DR600 ITALY L5200 NETHERLANDS FL13
NEW ZEALAND NZ $9.00 SWITZERLAND FS10

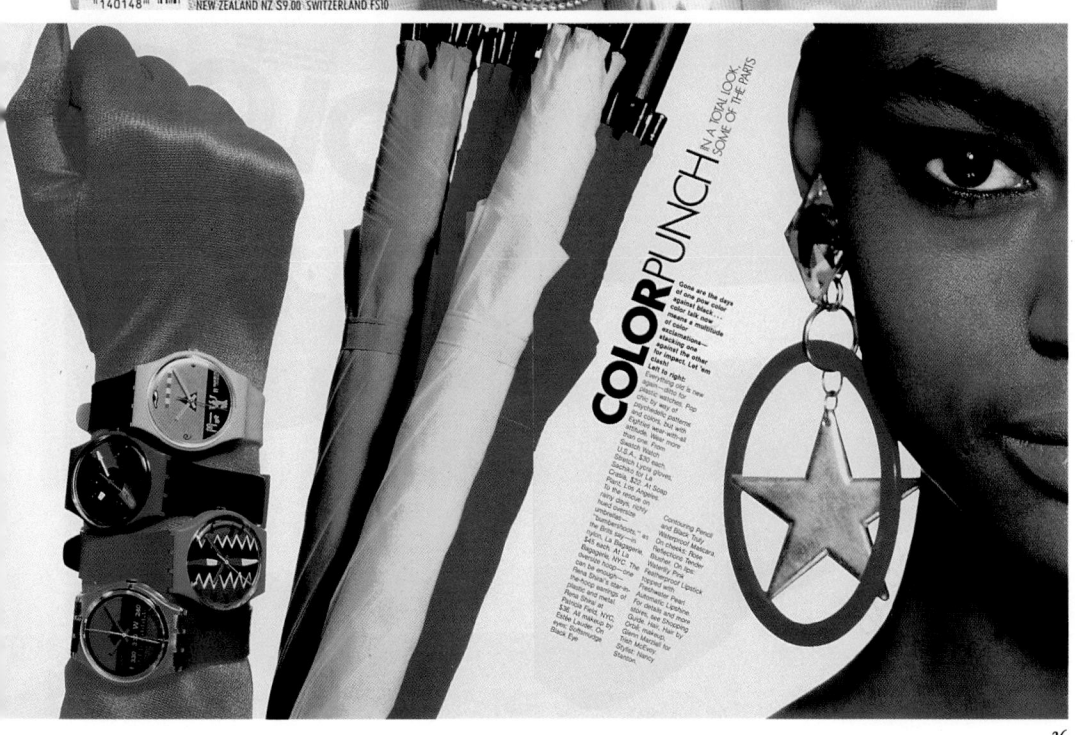

COLORPUNCH IN A TOTAL LOOK, SOME OF THE PARTS

37
DISTINCTIVE MERIT

ART DIRECTOR
Ron Albrecht
PHOTOGRAPHER
Toscani
EDITOR
Karen Anderegg
PUBLISHER
Marybeth Russell
PUBLICATION
Elle Magazine, New York, NY
PUBLICATION DIRECTOR
Regis Pagniez

38
DISTINCTIVE MERIT

ART DIRECTOR
Diana LaGuardia
DESIGNER
Diana LaGuardia
PHOTOGRAPHER
Michael O'Neill
CLIENT
The New York Times Magazine
EDITOR
Ed Klein
PUBLISHER
The New York Times, New York, NY
PUBLICATION
The New York Times

37

38

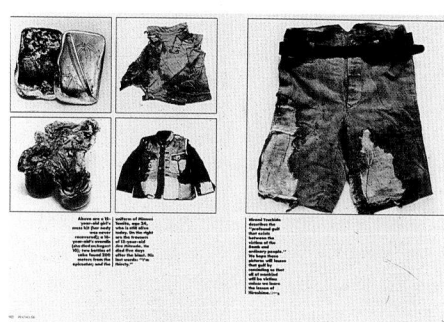

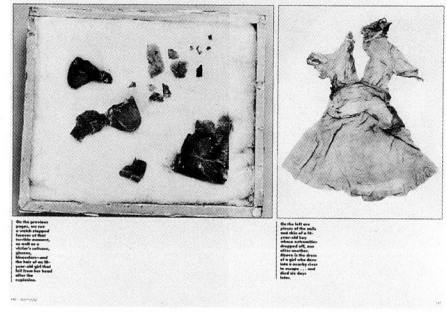

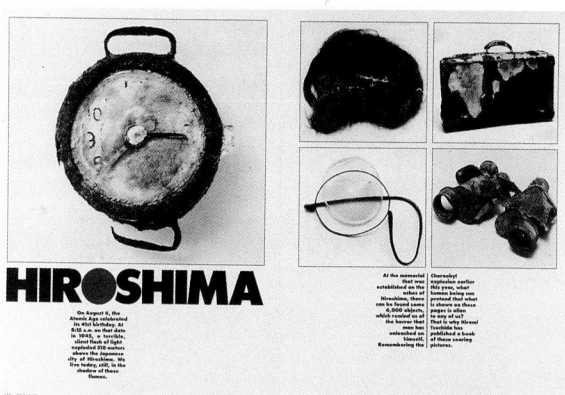

HIROSHIMA

On August 6, the Atomic Age celebrated its 41st birthday. At 8:15 a.m. on that date in 1945, a terrible, silent flash of light exploded 210 meters above the Japanese city of Hiroshima. We live today, still, in the shadow of those flames.

39
DISTINCTIVE MERIT

ART DIRECTOR
Richard Bleiweiss
DESIGNER
Richard Bleiweiss
PHOTOGRAPHER
Hiromi Tsuchida
PUBLISHER
Bob Guccione
PUBLICATION
Penthouse International, New York, NY
GRAPHICS DIRECTOR
Frank Devino

39

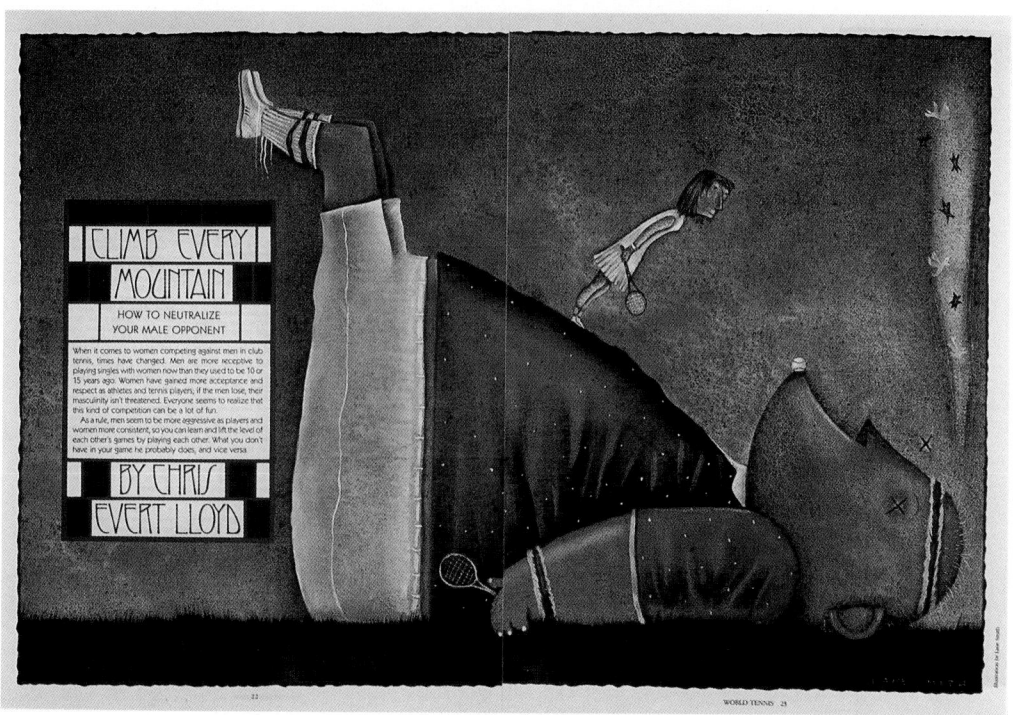

CLIMB EVERY MOUNTAIN

HOW TO NEUTRALIZE YOUR MALE OPPONENT

When it comes to women competing against men in club tennis, times have changed. Men are more receptive to playing singles with women now than they used to be 10 or 15 years ago. Women have gained more acceptance and respect as athletes and tennis players; if the men lose, their masculinity isn't threatened. Everyone seems to realize that this kind of competition can be a lot of fun.

As a rule, men seem to be more aggressive as players and women more consistent, so you can learn and lift the level of each other's games by playing each other. What you don't have in your game he probably does, and vice versa

BY CHRIS EVERT LLOYD

WORLD TENNIS 23

40
DISTINCTIVE MERIT

ART DIRECTOR
Wendy Talve Reingold
DESIGNER
Miriam Campiz
ILLUSTRATOR/ARTIST
Lane Smith
PUBLICATION
World Tennis Magazine, New York, NY

40

41

DISTINCTIVE MERIT

ART DIRECTOR
Scott Menchin

DESIGNER
Scott Menchin

PHOTOGRAPHER
James Dillon

WRITER
Eric Marcus

PUBLISHER
Howard Cadel, RC Publications,
New York, NY

PUBLICATION
How Magazine

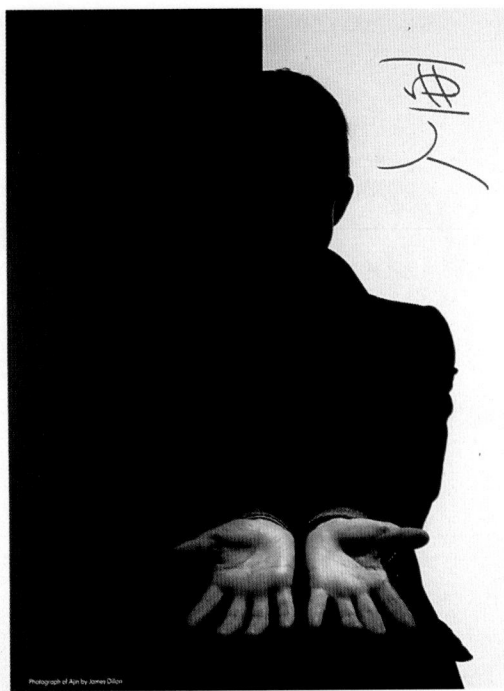

ILLUSTRATION

The Paper Sculptor

With meticulous detail, Ajin
creates paper sculptures
and caricatures using simple
paper and glue. The result is sharp,
insightful work photographed for
magazine illustration.

By Eric Marcus

Photograph of Ajin by James Dillon

22 HOW

41

42

DISTINCTIVE MERIT

ART DIRECTOR
Christopher Lione

PHOTOGRAPHER
Lynn Sugarman

WRITER
Barry Clifford

EDITOR
Margot Guralnick

PUBLISHER
Wick Allison

PUBLICATION
Art & Antiques, New York, NY

PHOTO EDITOR
Denise Dorrance

AN UNDER-
WATER
ODYSSEY

A Cape Cod
dreamer turns a legend
into a reality.

By Barry Clifford
Photographs by Lynn Sugarman

*The Whydah had
been carrying silver coins
and rubies "as big as hen's eggs."*

42

● AMERICAN LANDSCAPE

A TRAIL OF COLOR
AUTUMN HIKES DOWN THE APPALACHIANS

For a half century rugged Americans have taken to the Appalachian Trail, the footpath linking a mountain in Georgia to one in Maine. Blazed by foresters and maintained by volunteers, it rambles through 14 states, cutting deeply into some of the country's wildest lands and skirting some of the most densely settled. A year-round beauty, the trail becomes our shimmering national kaleidoscope when autumn begins its southbound trek.

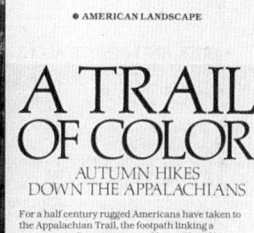

Ambitious through-hikers give five to six months of their lives to go the whole 2,145 miles, from Mt. Springer in Georgia to Maine's Mt. Katahdin. By early October 100 or so will reach Baxter State Park in Maine (above) and earn their reward—scenes of silvery beauty and arcs of dizzying color in the great North Woods.

Shield ferns and fiery maple seedlings cushion a clearing of white birches near the Maine-New Hampshire border. Woods are dense and spooky in these parts, and the Appalachian Trail Guide warns that "the traveller should not proceed more than a sixth of a mile without noticing some Trail indication.... In case of doubt as to the route, stop do not go forward. Retrace the route deliberately...."

Photography: Michael Melford
Reporting: Doris G. Kinney
Text: Vance Muse 59

43

A FOOTPATH WORTH A FIGHT

IN DAVY CROCKETT COUNTRY

43
DISTINCTIVE MERIT
ART DIRECTOR
Bob Ciano
DESIGNER
Robin E. Brown
PHOTOGRAPHER
Michael Melford
WRITER
Vance Muse, Doris Kinney
CLIENT
Life Magazine
EDITOR
Judith Daniels, Mary Simons
PUBLICATION
Life Magazine, New York, NY

44
DISTINCTIVE MERIT
ART DIRECTOR
Paul Davis
DESIGNER
Paul Davis, Jose Conde, Jeanine Esposito
PHOTOGRAPHER
Dominique Nabokov, Richard Corman, Adam Bartos, Robert Mapplethorpe
ARTIST
Weaver, Naggar, Smith, Coale, Johns, Scolari
CLIENT
Normal Inc.
EDITOR
Gini Alhadeff
PUBLISHER
Normal Inc.
PRODUCTION DIRECTOR
Jack Doenias
DESIGN FIRM
Paul Davis Studio, New York, NY
LITERARY EDITOR
Andrew Harvey
MANAGING EDITOR
Myrna Davis

45
DISTINCTIVE MERIT

ART DIRECTOR
Diana LaGuardia
DESIGNER
Kevin McPhee
PHOTOGRAPHER
Sebastiao Salgado
CLIENT
The New York Times Magazine
EDITOR
Ed Klein
PUBLISHER
The New York Times, New York, NY
PUBLICATION
The New York Times

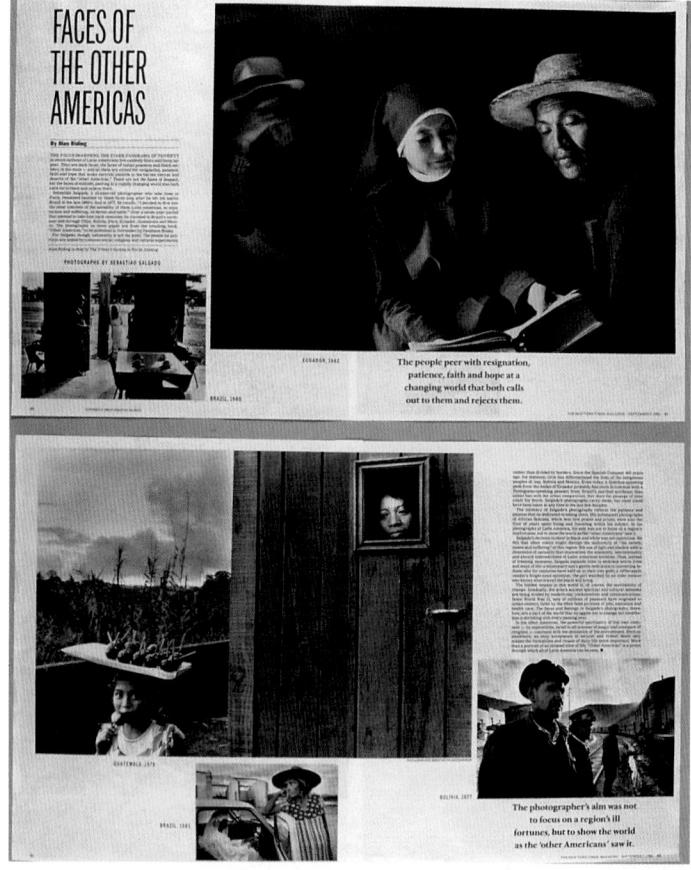

45

46
DISTINCTIVE MERIT

ART DIRECTOR
Richelle J. Huff
DESIGNER
Samuel G. Shelton
PHOTOGRAPHER
Lluis Casals
WRITER
Peter Buchanan
EDITOR
Susan Doubilet, Thomas Fisher
PUBLISHER
Penton Publishing
PUBLICATION
Progressive Architecture, Stamford, CT

46

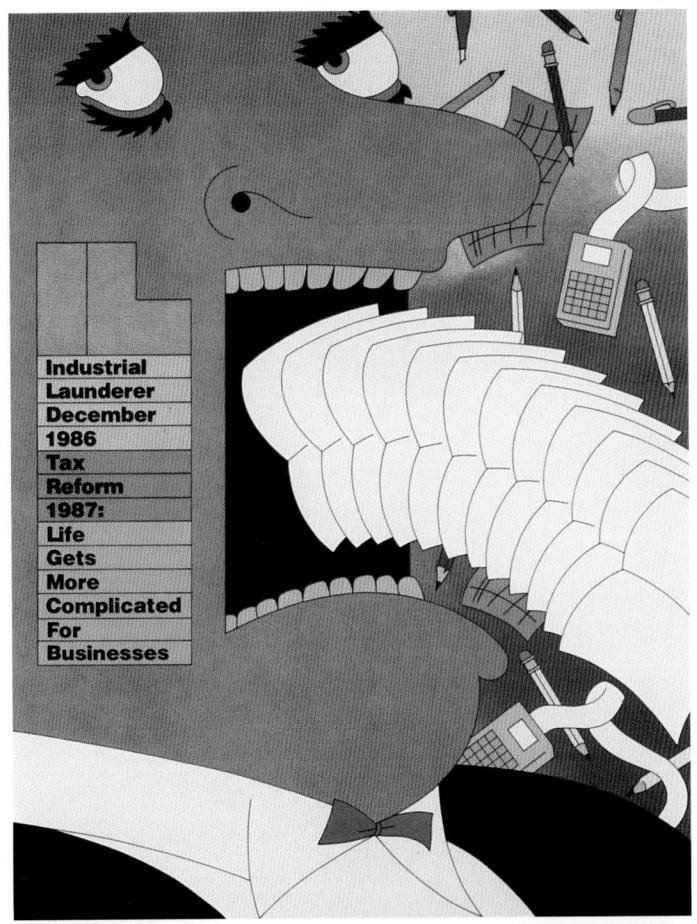

47

47
DISTINCTIVE MERIT
ART DIRECTOR
Jack Lefkowitz
DESIGNER
Jack Lefkowitz
ILLUSTRATOR/ARTIST
Timothy Flatt
WRITER
David Ritchey
CLIENT
Industrial Launderer
EDITOR
David Ritchey
PUBLISHER
Institute of Industrial Launderers
AGENCY
Jack Lefkowitz, Inc., Leesburg, VA
PUBLICATION
Industrial Launderer

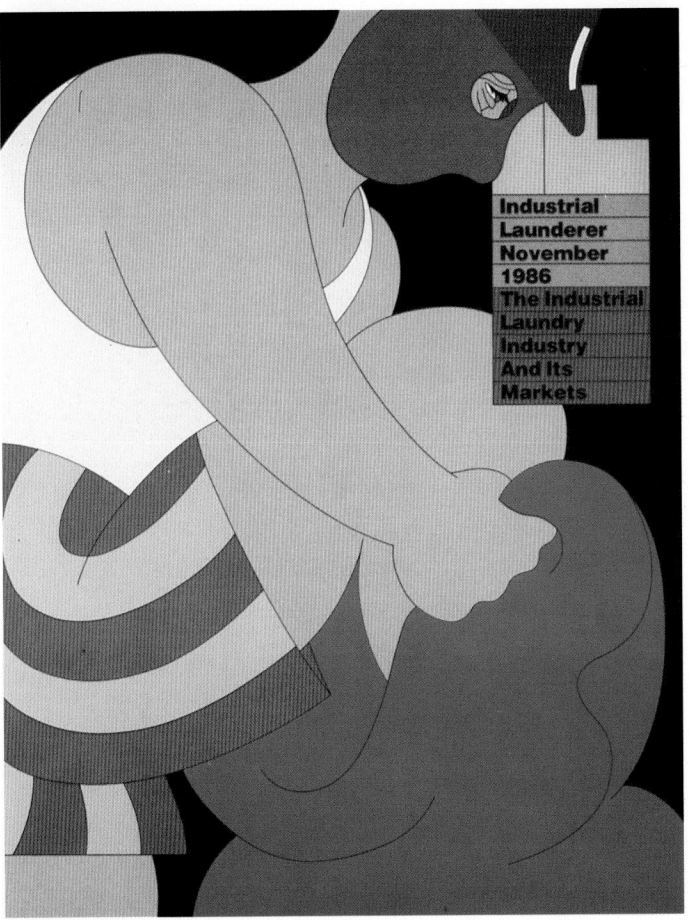

48
DISTINCTIVE MERIT
ART DIRECTOR
Jack Lefkowitz
DESIGNER
Jack Lefkowitz
ILLUSTRATOR/ARTIST
Virginia Strnad
WRITER
David Ritchey
CLIENT
Industrial Launderer
EDITOR
David Ritchey
PUBLISHER
Institute of Industrial Launderers
AGENCY
Jack Lefkowitz, Inc., Leesburg, VA
PUBLICATION
Industrial Launderer

49
DISTINCTIVE MERIT

ART DIRECTOR
Robert Best
DESIGNER
Josh Gosfield, David Walters,
Rhonda Rubinstein
ILLUSTRATOR/ARTIST
Andy Warhol
EDITOR
Edward Kosner
DIRECTOR OF PHOTOGRAPHY
Jordan Schaps, Mike Samson (asst.)
PUBLISHER
Murdoch Magazines
PUBLICATION
New York Magazine, New York, NY

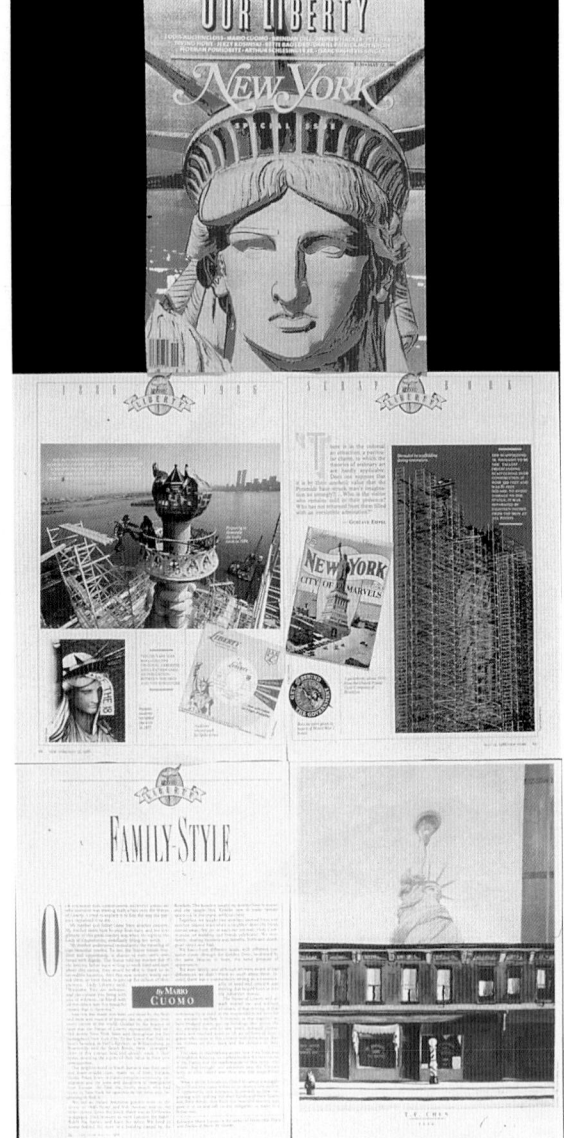

49

50
DISTINCTIVE MERIT

ART DIRECTOR
Helene Silverman
PUBLICATION
Metropolis Magazine, New York, NY

50

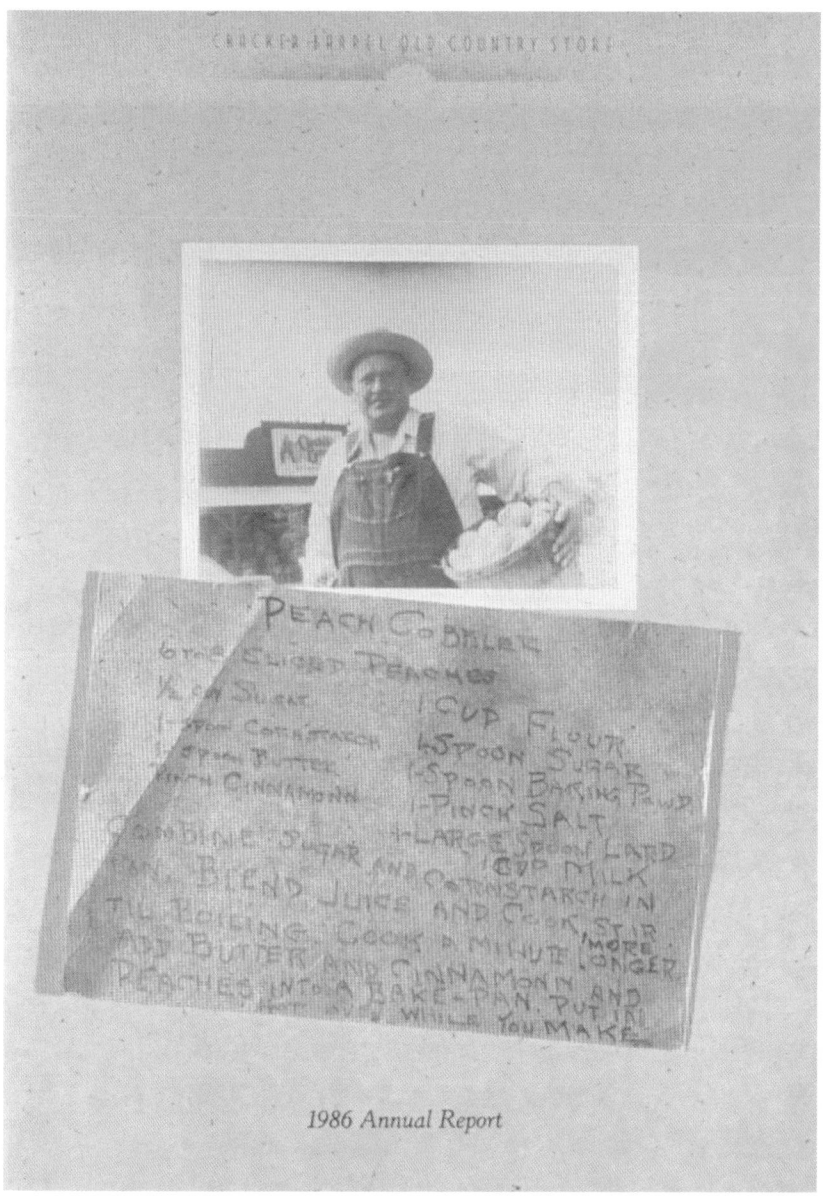

1986 Annual Report

51
GOLD AWARD

ART DIRECTOR
Thomas Ryan
DESIGNER
Thomas Ryan
PHOTOGRAPHER
McGuire
WRITER
John Baeder
CLIENT
Cracker Barrel Old Country Store
EDITOR
Matt Hamilton
AGENCY
Corporate Communications Inc.
DESIGN FIRM
Thomas Ryan Design, Nashville, TN
ENGRAVER
Graphic Process Inc.
PRINTER
Color Graphics, Inc.

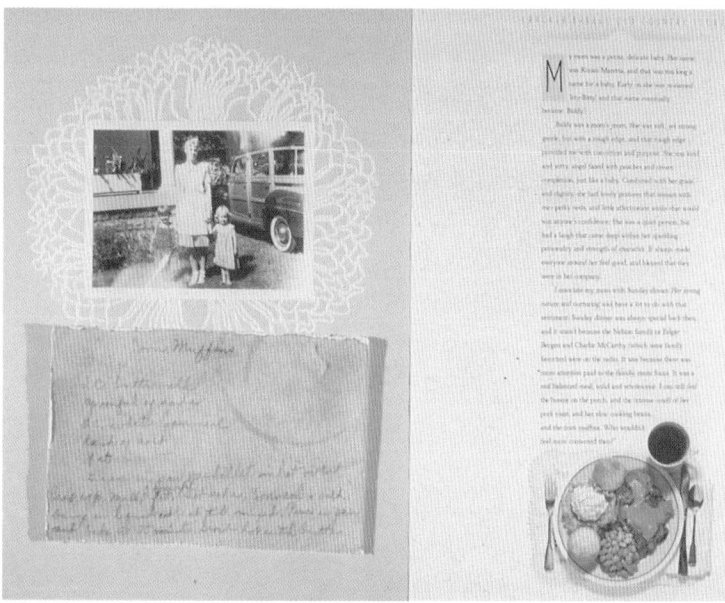

52
GOLD AWARD

ART DIRECTOR
Robert Hyland
DESIGNER
Jon Vopni, Robert Hyland
PHOTOGRAPHER
Peter Christopher
ILLUSTRATOR/ARTIST
Jon Vopni, Larry Bloss, Frank
Bonigut, George Kay
WRITER
David Parry, James Hynes
CLIENT
M.C. Charters & Co. Ltd.
DESIGN FIRM
Robert Hyland Design & Associates,
Toronto, Canada

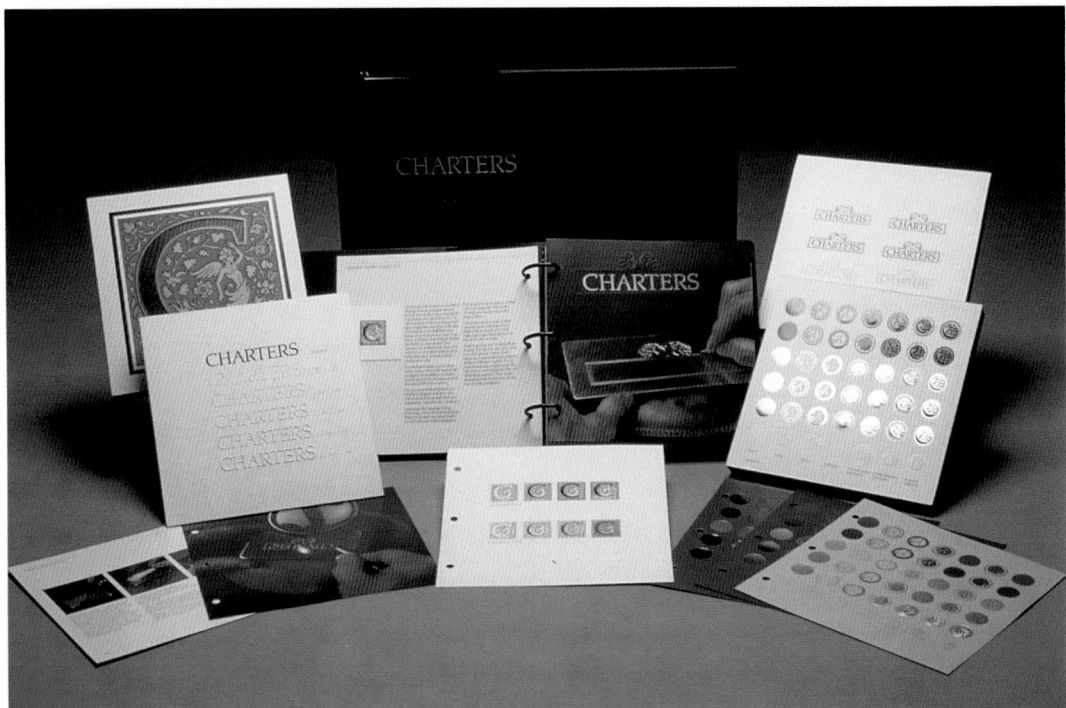

52

53
GOLD AWARD

ART DIRECTOR
Ron Sullivan
DESIGNER
Diana McKnight
PHOTOGRAPHER
Tom Ryan
WRITER
Max Wright
CLIENT
Designers' Chili Cookoff
DESIGN FIRM
Sullivan Perkins, Dallas, TX

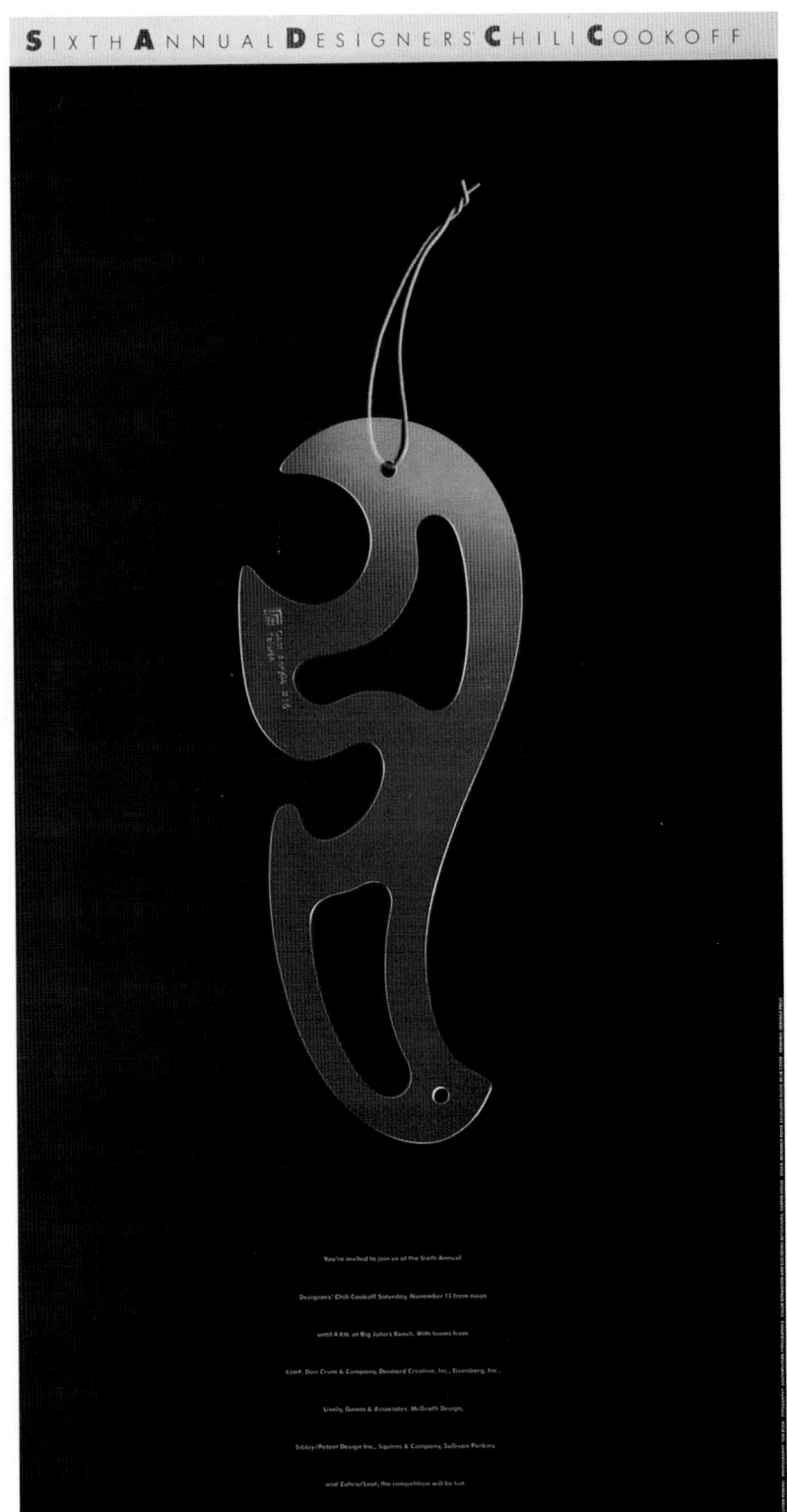

54
GOLD AWARD

ART DIRECTOR
Frank Schulwolf
PHOTOGRAPHER
George Schiavone
ILLUSTRATOR/ARTIST
Paul Salmon, Ted Lodigensky, John Mattos
WRITER
Arthur Low
CLIENT
Aviation Sales Company, Inc.
AGENCY
Susan Gilbert & Company, Coral Gables, FL
PRINTERS
Colour Group, Southwestern Printing

54

55
GOLD AWARD

ART DIRECTOR
David Au, John C. Jay
ILLUSTRATOR/ARTIST
Mark Kostabi, Anthony Russo
CLIENT
Bloomingdale's
AGENCY
Bloomingdale's Special Projects,
New York, NY
CREATIVE DIRECTOR
John C. Jay

56
SILVER AWARD

ART DIRECTOR
Bennett Robinson
DESIGNER
Bennett Robinson, Meera Singh
ILLUSTRATOR/ARTIST
John Berkey, Kinuko Craft, Malcolm
T. Liepke, Julian Allen, Eraldo
Carugati, Max Ginsberg, James
McMullen and others
CLIENT
H J. Heinz Company
DESIGN FIRM
Corporate Graphics Inc., New York,
NY

H.J. HEINZ COMPANY 1986 ANNUAL REPORT IN 1886 THE FOUNDER SAILED FOR ENGLAND...

56

57
SILVER AWARD

ART DIRECTOR
Seymour Chwast
DESIGNER
Seymour Chwast
ILLUSTRATOR/ARTIST
Cover-Seymour Chwast Interior-
Various
WRITER
Steve Heller
CLIENT
Mohawk Paper
EDITOR
Steve Heller
DESIGN FIRM
The Pushpin Group, New York, NY

58
SILVER AWARD

ART DIRECTOR
Michael Mabry
DESIGNER
Michael Mabry, Noreen Fukumori
ILLUSTRATOR/ARTIST
Michael Mabry
CLIENT
SEH Importers, Ltd.
DESIGN FIRM
Michael Mabry Design, San
Francisco, CA

59
SILVER AWARD

ART DIRECTOR
Yvonne Smith, Marc Deschenes
PHOTOGRAPHER
Lamb & Hall
WRITER
Marc Deschenes, Yvonne Smith
CLIENT
Noritsu America Corp.
AGENCY
(213) 827-9695 and Associates,
Venice, CA
AD MANAGER
Brad Moore
PRODUCTION MANAGER
The Production Company

CAN WE ENLARGE SOMETHING FOR YOU?
We'd be more than happy to make 5x7, 8x10 or 11x14 enlargements of your favorite prints.

60
SILVER AWARD

ART DIRECTOR
James A. Sebastian

DESIGNER
James A. Sebastian, Rose Biondi

PHOTOGRAPHER
Bruce Wolf

CLIENT
Martex/West Point Pepperell

DESIGN FIRM
Designframe Incorporated, New York, NY

INTERIOR DESIGNER
William Walter

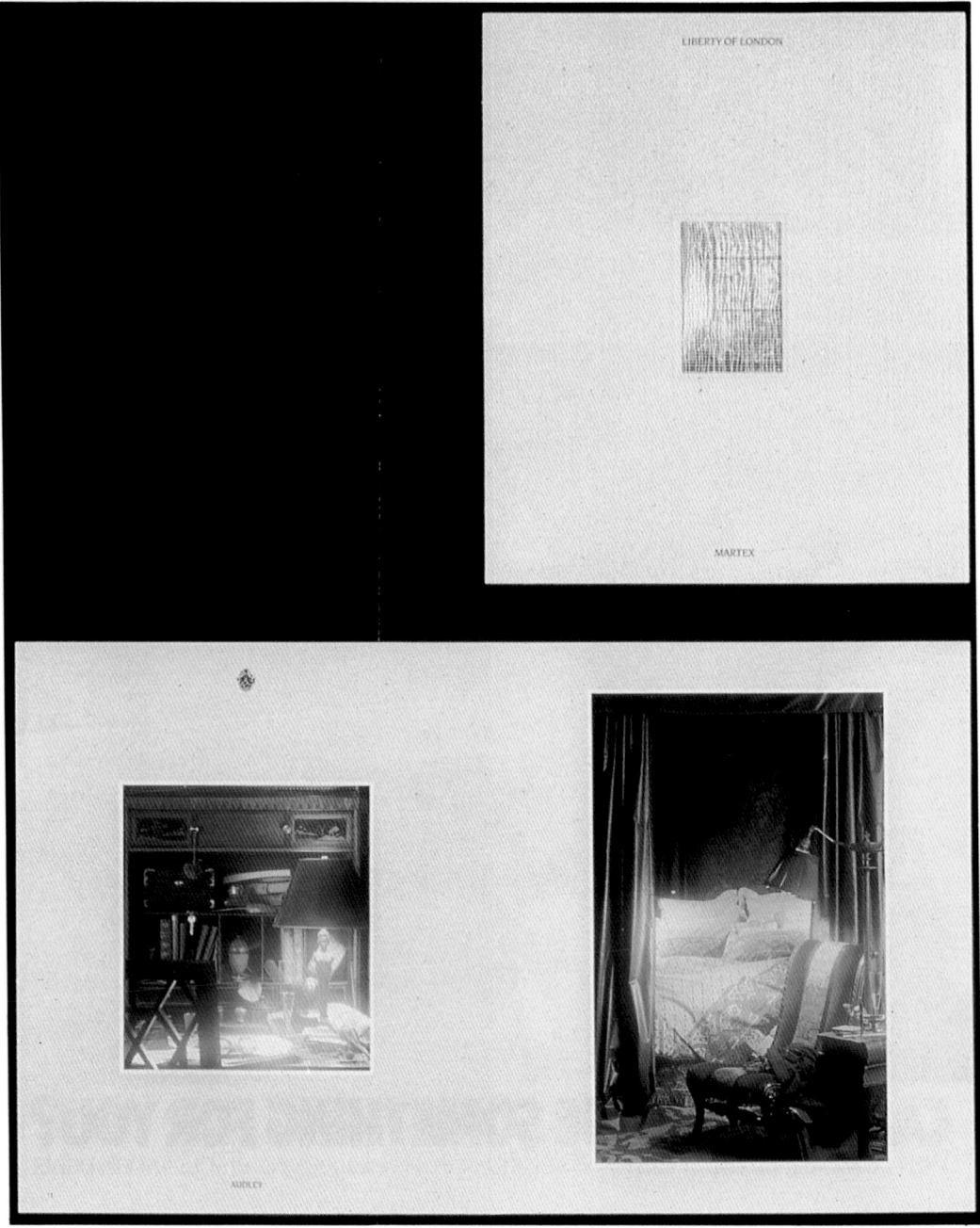

61

61
SILVER AWARD

ART DIRECTOR
Charles Spencer Anderson, Joe Duffy
DESIGNER
Charles Spencer Anderson, Joe Duffy
WRITER
Chuck Carlson
CLIENT
French Paper Company
DESIGN FIRM
Duffy Design Group, Minneapolis, MN

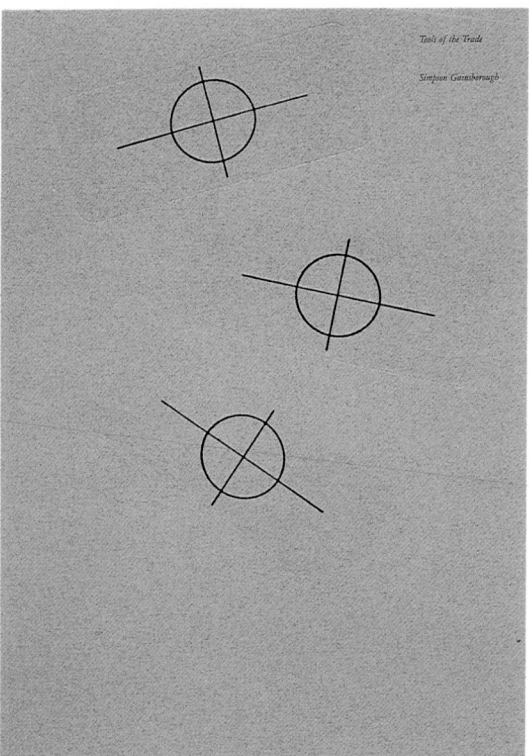

62

62
SILVER AWARD

ART DIRECTOR
James Cross, Michael Skjei
DESIGNER
Michael Skjei
PHOTOGRAPHER
Douglas Manchee
CLIENT
Simpson Paper Company
DESIGN FIRM
Cross Associates, San Francisco, CA
TYPOGRAPHER
McKenzie Harris
PRINTER
Anderson Printing

63
DISTINCTIVE MERIT

ART DIRECTOR
Kit Hinrichs
DESIGNER
Kit Hinrichs, Karen Berndt
PHOTOGRAPHER
Eric Meyer, Terry Heffernan, MGM
Archives
ILLUSTRATOR/ARTIST
Doug Johnson, Dave Stevenson
WRITER
Burson Marsteller
CLIENT
MGM/UA Communications
Corporation
EDITOR
Peter Graves
DESIGN FIRM
Pentagram Design, San Francisco,
CA

By the late 1930s, the movies are an essential part of the audience's lifestyle—a social event as well as entertainment. Unprecedented numbers of people attend movies each week.

Bigger and better are the production watchwords of the day. "Hollywood" comes to mean films of grand proportion and epic spectacles. MGM films— The Good Earth, for example—represent the biggest and the best of the genre.

United Artists continues to build its partnership with the great producers and directors of the day, Samuel Goldwyn, John Ford and others join United Artists. Goldwyn produces 21 films for United Artists release between 1935 and 1940, including such classics as Wuthering Heights, Dodsworth and Dead End.

But the movie event of the decade is MGM's. In 1939, Gone With the Wind pairs Clark Gable with Vivien Leigh, who makes her debut after a highly publicized nationwide search for the ideal Scarlett O'Hara. The film captures the imagination and hearts of the first of several generations of filmgoers, and is an immediate success.

Even today, nearly 50 years after its initial release, Gone With the Wind is still a favorite with theatrical, television and home video audiences all over the world.

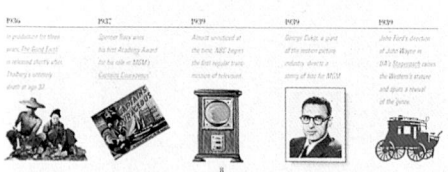

Gone with the Wind, 1939

64
DISTINCTIVE MERIT

ART DIRECTOR
Charles Spencer Anderson
DESIGNER
Sara Ledgard
CLIENT
Typeshooters
DESIGN FIRM
Duffy Design Group, Minneapolis,
MN

63   64

65

65
DISTINCTIVE MERIT

ART DIRECTOR
Larry Phillips
DESIGNER
Larry Phillips
ILLUSTRATOR/ARTIST
Gary Crane
WRITER
Larry Phillips
CLIENT
Goodman Segar Hogan, Inc.
AGENCY
Davis & Phillips, Norfolk, VA
PRODUCER
Tracey Alexander

66
DISTINCTIVE MERIT

ART DIRECTOR
Craig Frazier
DESIGNER
Craig Frazier, Grant Peterson
ILLUSTRATOR/ARTIST
Craig Frazier, Suzanne Frazier
CLIENT
Merlion Winery
DESIGN FIRM
Frazier Design, San Francisco, CA

67
DISTINCTIVE MERIT

ART DIRECTOR
Bennett Robinson
DESIGNER
Bennett Robinson, Adam Shanosky
ILLUSTRATOR/ARTIST
Various
CLIENT
Simpson Paper Company
DESIGN FIRM
Corporate Graphics Inc., New York,
NY

66   67

68
DISTINCTIVE MERIT

ART DIRECTOR
Kit Hinrichs
DESIGNER
Kit Hinrichs, Gwyn Smith
PHOTOGRAPHER
Terry Heffernan
WRITER
Peterson & Dodge
CLIENT
American President Lines
EDITOR
Pamela Peterson
DESIGN FIRM
Pentagram Design, San Francisco,
CA

69
DISTINCTIVE MERIT

ART DIRECTOR
Bradford C. Ghormley
DESIGNER
Bradford C. Ghormley
ILLUSTRATOR/ARTIST
Bradford C. Ghormley
CLIENT
H. Lukens Construction
DESIGN FIRM
Smit Ghormley Sanft, Phoenix, AZ

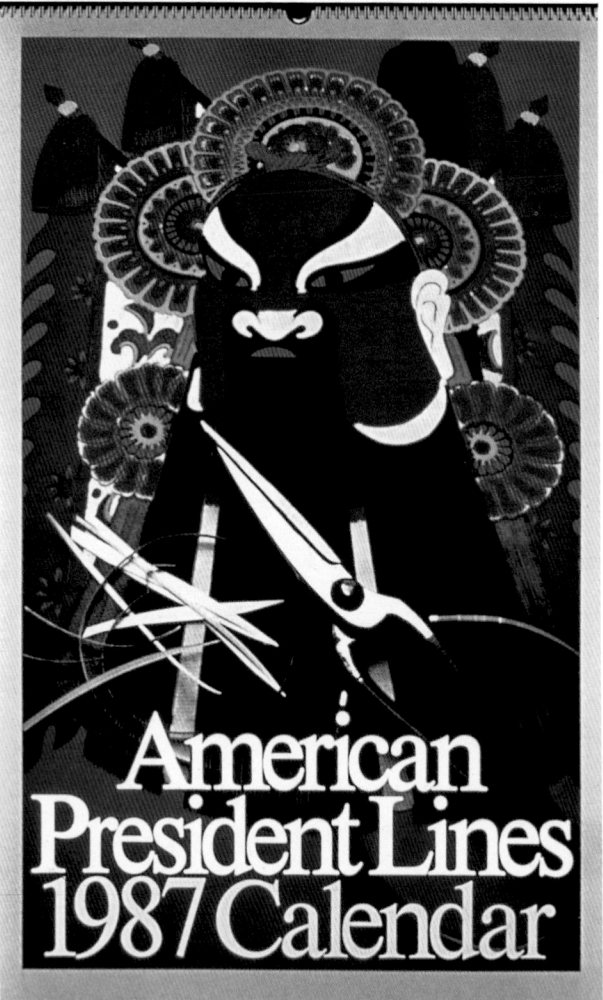

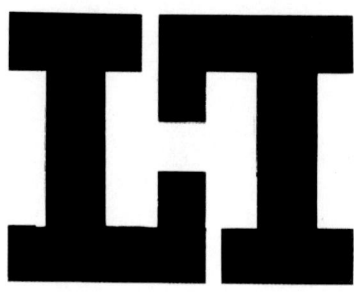

69

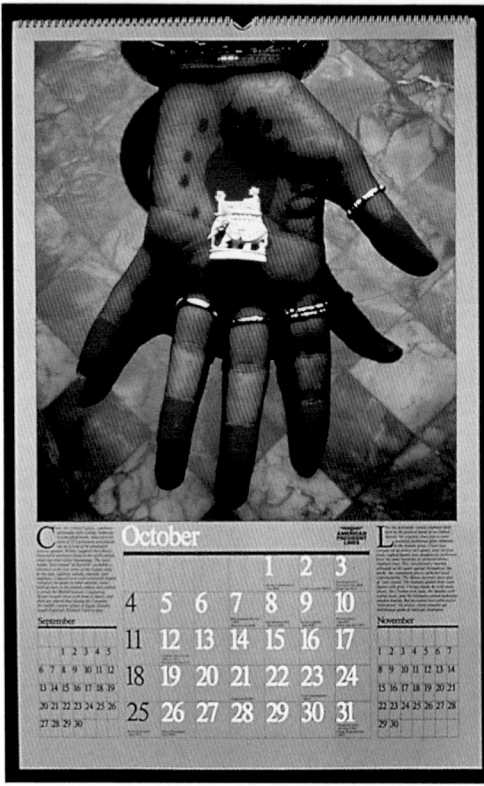

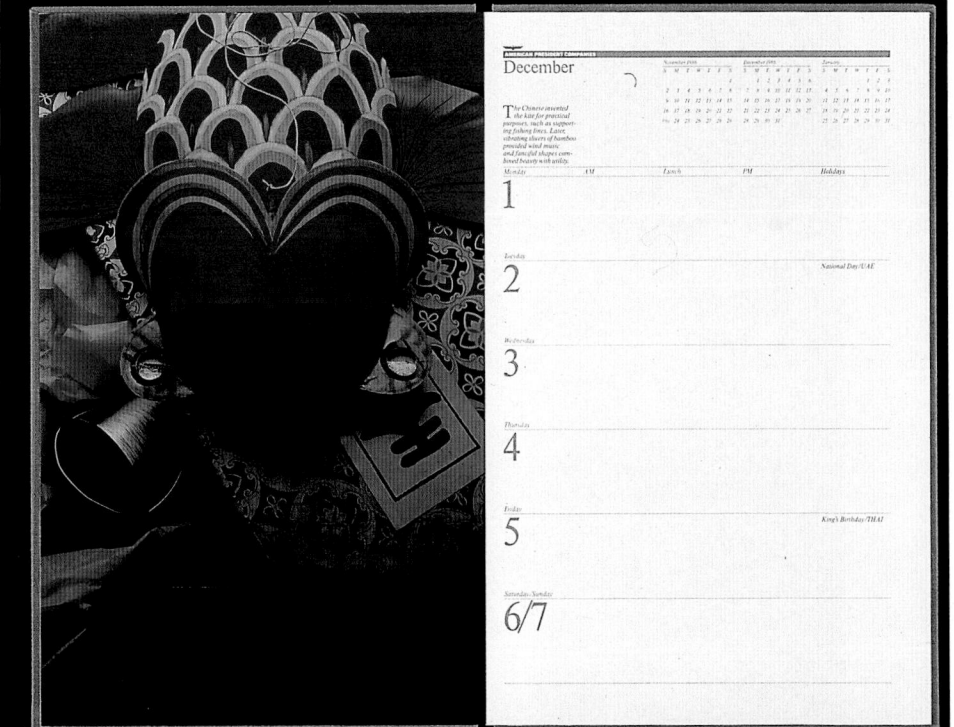

70
DISTINCTIVE MERIT

ART DIRECTOR
Kit Hinrichs
DESIGNER
Kit Hinrichs, Gwyn Smith
PHOTOGRAPHER
Terry Heffernan
WRITER
Peterson & Dodge
CLIENT
American President Lines
EDITOR
Pamela Peterson
DESIGN FIRM
Pentagram Design, San Francisco,
CA

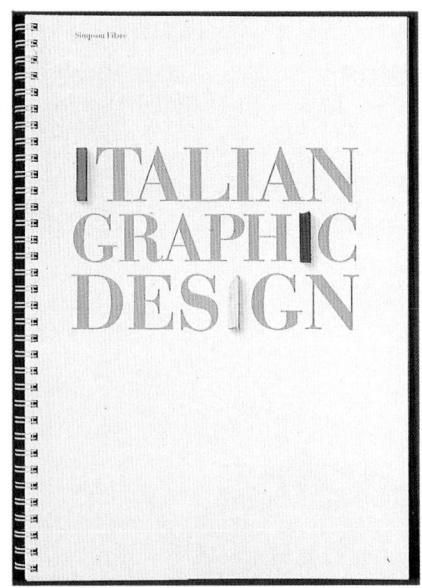

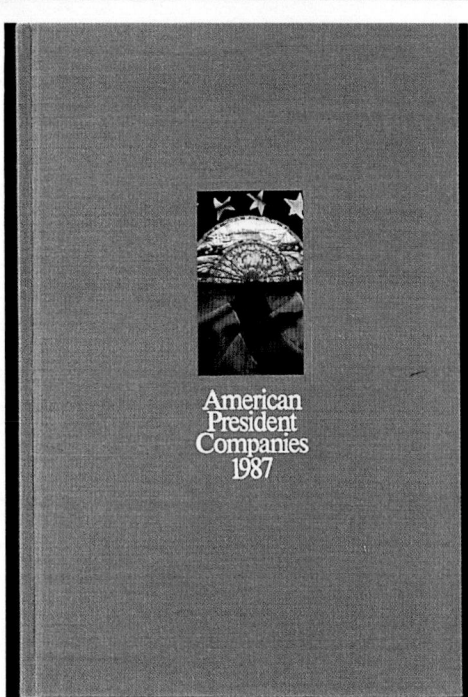

71
DISTINCTIVE MERIT

ART DIRECTOR
James Cross, Michael Mescall
DESIGNER
Michael Mescall
ILLUSTRATOR/ARTIST
14 Italian Graphic Designers
WRITER
John Adams, Cole & Weber
CLIENT
Simpson Paper Company
DESIGN FIRM
Cross Associates, Los Angeles, CA
PRINTER
George Rice & Sons
TYPOGRAPHERS
Andresen Typographers & CCI
Typographers

71   70

72
DISTINCTIVE MERIT

ART DIRECTOR
Steven Michaelson
DESIGNER
Steven Michaelson
ILLUSTRATOR/ARTIST
Charley Brown
WRITER
Robert Sutton
CLIENT
Private Music
AGENCY
Michaelson Sutton Assoc. Inc., New
York, NY

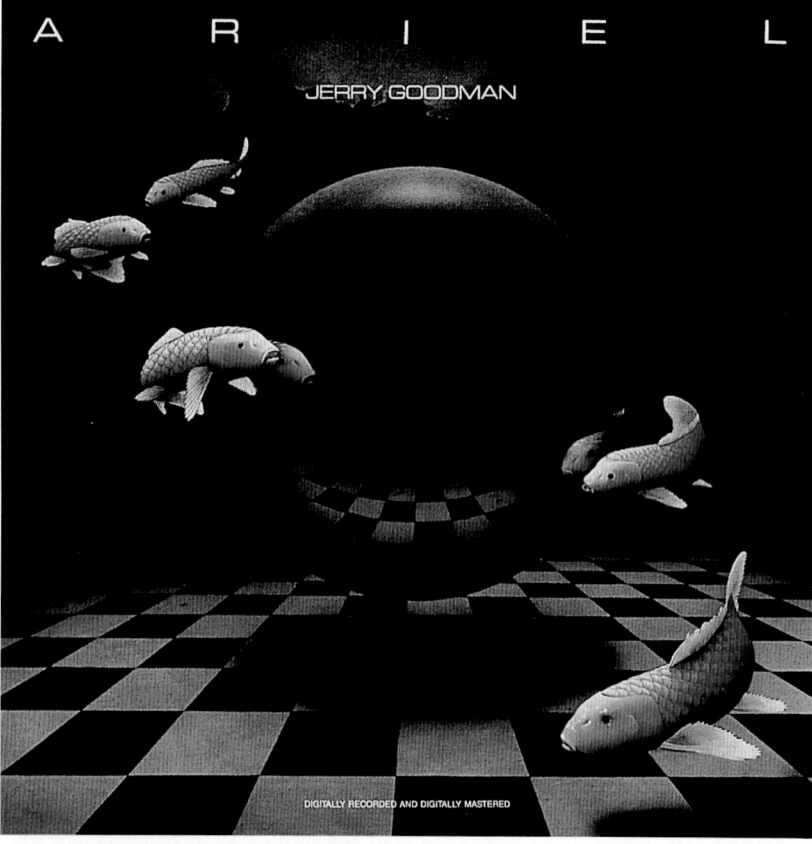

72

73
DISTINCTIVE MERIT

ART DIRECTOR
Bob Defrin
DESIGNER
Javier Romero
ILLUSTRATOR/ARTIST
Javier Romero
CLIENT
Atlantic Records, New York, NY

73

74

74
DISTINCTIVE MERIT

ART DIRECTOR
Nicolas Sidjakov, Jerry Berman
DESIGNER
Barbara Vick, Courtney Reeser
ILLUSTRATOR/ARTIST
Will Nelson
CLIENT
Berkley and Company
DESIGN FIRM
Sidjakov Berman Gomez &
Partners, San Francisco, CA

75

75
DISTINCTIVE MERIT

ART DIRECTOR
Charles Spencer Anderson
DESIGNER
Charles Spencer Anderson
ILLUSTRATOR/ARTIST
Charles Spencer Anderson, Lynn
Schulte
CLIENT
Prince Foods
DESIGN FIRM
Duffy Design Group, Minneapolis,
MN

76
DISTINCTIVE MERIT

ART DIRECTOR
Rex Peteet
DESIGNER
Rex Peteet
ILLUSTRATOR/ARTIST
Rex Peteet, Judy Dolim
WRITER
Rex Peteet
CLIENT
Sibley/Peteet Design
DESIGN FIRM
Sibley/Peteet Design, Dallas, TX

76

77
DISTINCTIVE MERIT

ART DIRECTOR
Jon Reeder
CLIENT
Tom King, Manhattan
Confectioners, Inc.
AGENCY
Thomas Binnion, Los Angeles, CA
CREATIVE DIRECTOR
Tom Binnion

77

78
DISTINCTIVE MERIT

ART DIRECTOR
Jac Coverdale
ILLUSTRATOR/ARTIST
Dan Picasso, Jac Coverdale
CLIENT
Cheetah Pizza
AGENCY
Clarity Coverdale Rueff Advertising,
Minneapolis, MN

78

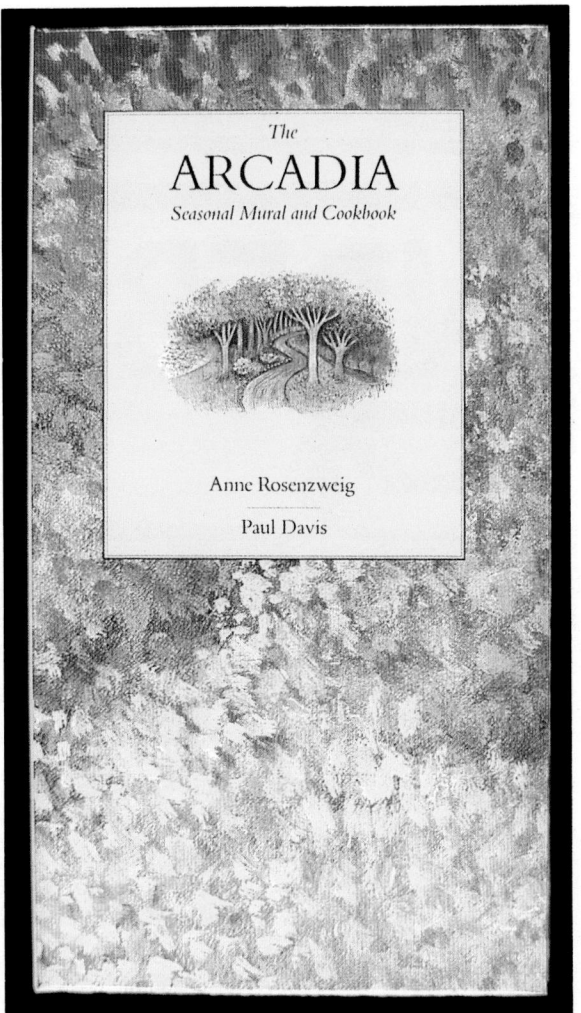

79
SILVER AWARD

ART DIRECTOR
Paul Davis, Sam Antupit
DESIGNER
Jose Conde
ILLUSTRATOR/ARTIST
Paul Davis
WRITER
Anne Rosenzweig
CLIENT
Harry N. Abrams Inc.
EDITOR
Ruth A. Peltason
PUBLISHER
Harry N. Abrams Inc.
DESIGN FIRM
Paul Davis Studio, New York, NY
PROJECT DIRECTOR
Myrna Davis

80
SILVER AWARD

ART DIRECTOR
Massimo Vignelli
DESIGNER
Massimo Vignelli
PHOTOGRAPHER
Margaret Courtney-Clarke
WRITER
Margaret Courtney-Clarke
EDITOR
Lauren Shakely
PUBLISHER
Rizzoli International Publications,
Inc., New York, NY

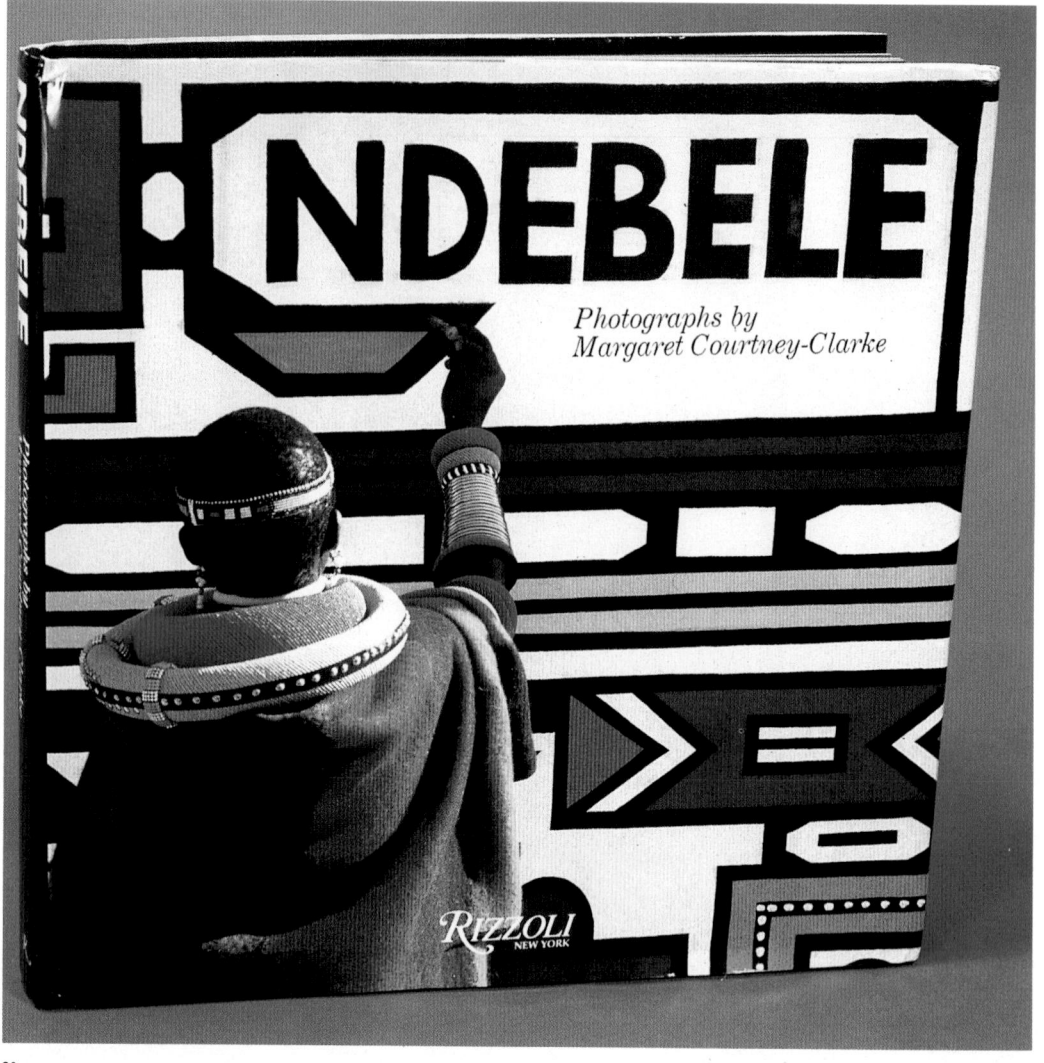

80

81
SILVER AWARD

ART DIRECTOR
Tommy Steele
DESIGNER
Tommy Steele
WRITER
H. Thomas Steele
EDITOR
Walton H. Rawls
DIRECTOR
Robert E. Abrams
PUBLISHER
Abbeville Press, New York, NY

82
SILVER AWARD

ART DIRECTOR
Saul Bass
DESIGNER
Saul Bass, Art Goodman
PHOTOGRAPHER
George Arakaki
EDITOR
Leslie Carr
PUBLISHER
Harper & Row, Publishers, Inc.,
New York, NY
AGENCY
Bass/Yaeger & Associates
PUBLICATION
Psychology by C. Wade & C. Tavris
PRINTER
The Lehigh Press, Inc.
COVER DESIGN COORDINATOR
Mary Archondes

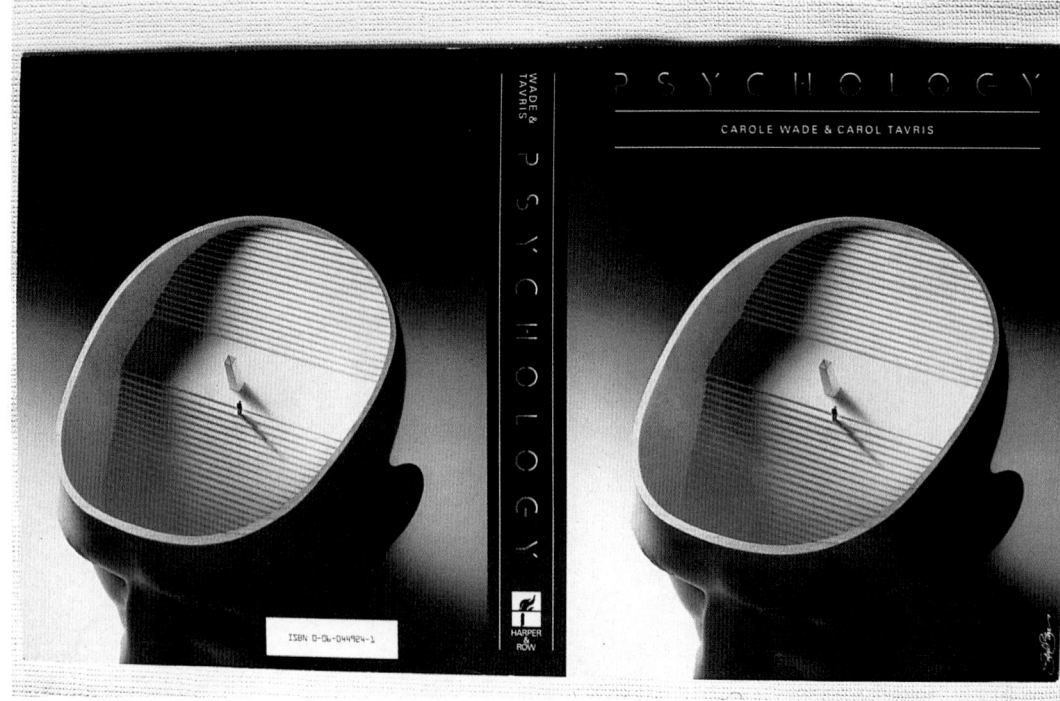

82

83
SILVER AWARD

ART DIRECTOR
James Wageman
DESIGNER
Renée Khatami
WRITER
Kenneth Nebenzahl
EDITOR
Alan Axelrod
DIRECTOR
Robert E. Abrams
PUBLISHER
Abbeville Press, New York, NY

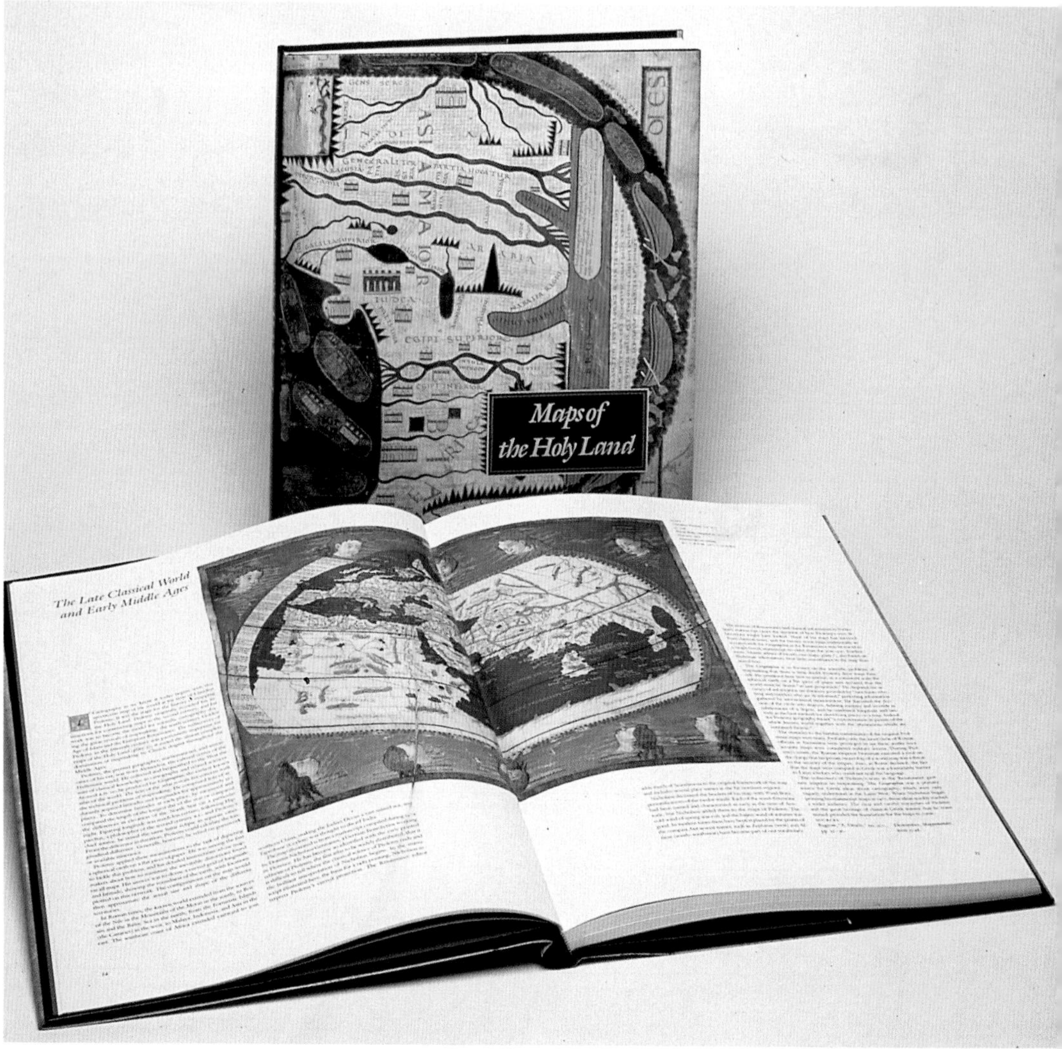

83

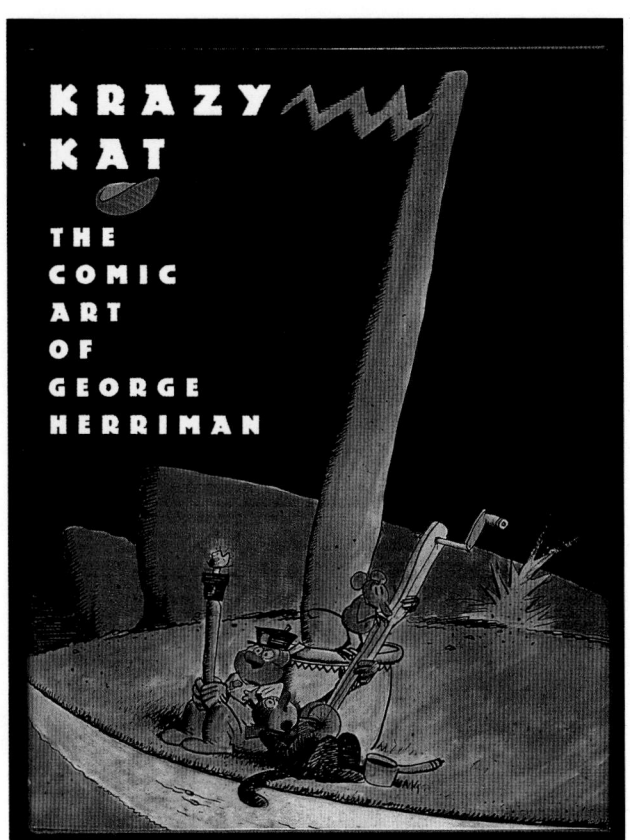

84

84
DISTINCTIVE MERIT

ART DIRECTOR
Samuel N. Antupit
DESIGNER
Samuel N. Antupit
DIRECTOR
Darlene Geis
PUBLISHER
Harry N. Abrams, Inc., New York,
NY

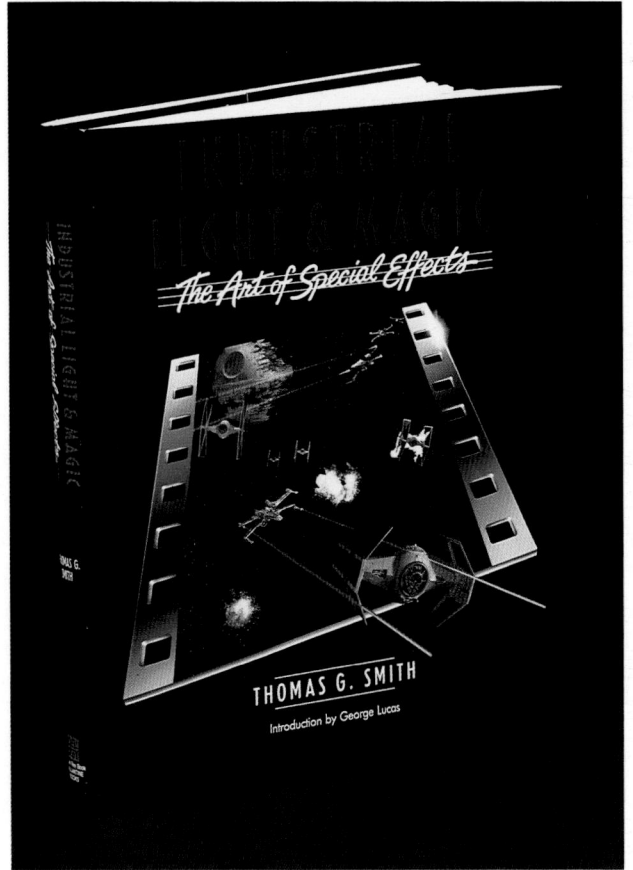

85

85
DISTINCTIVE MERIT

ART DIRECTOR
Sylvain Michaelis
DESIGNER
Sylvain Michaelis
PHOTOGRAPHER
Industrial Light & Magic
ILLUSTRATOR/ARTIST
Ronald Chironna, Richard Kriegler,
Ray Barber
WRITER
Thomas Smith
EDITOR
Anita Gross, Risa Kessler
PUBLISHER
Ballantine Books
DESIGN FIRM
Michaelis & Carpelis Design
Associates, New York, NY
DIRECTOR OF PRODUCTION
Fred Dodnick

86
DISTINCTIVE MERIT

ART DIRECTOR
Myland McRevey
DESIGNER
Myland McRevey
ILLUSTRATOR/ARTIST
Renee Graef, Nancy Niles, Chris
Payne
PUBLISHER
Pleasant Company, Madison, WI
CREATIVE DIRECTOR
Pleasant T. Rowland

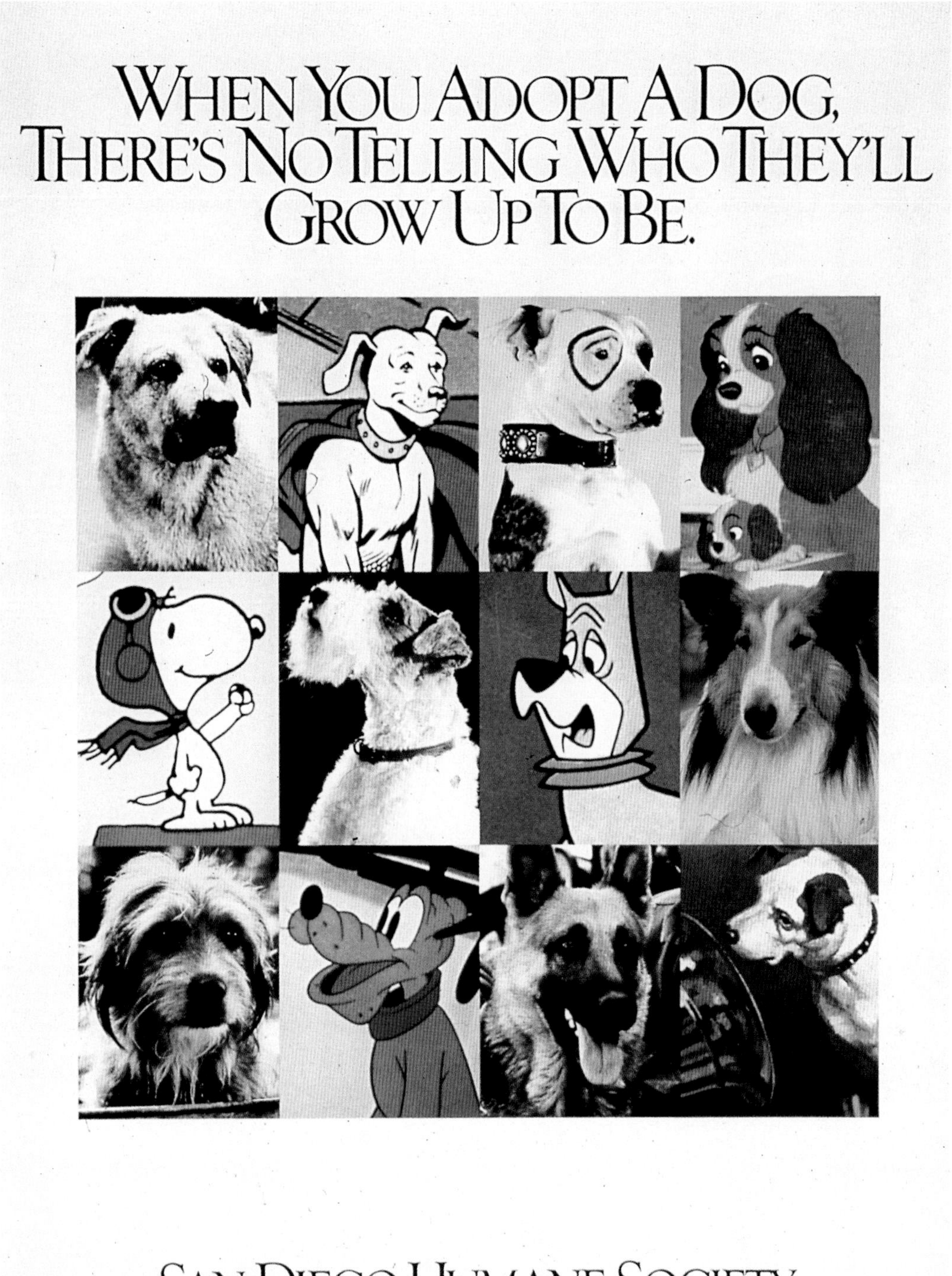

WHEN YOU ADOPT A DOG, THERE'S NO TELLING WHO THEY'LL GROW UP TO BE.

SAN DIEGO HUMANE SOCIETY

Our special thanks to Old Yeller, Krypto, Petey, Lady, Snoopy, Asta, Astro, Lassie, Benji, Pluto, Rin Tin Tin, and Nipper.

87
SILVER AWARD

ART DIRECTOR
John Vitro
DESIGNER
Ron Van Buskirk
PHOTOGRAPHER
Marshall Harrington
WRITER
Mitchell Wein
AGENCY
VW Advertising, San Diego, CA

88
SILVER AWARD

ART DIRECTOR
Gary Greenberg
DESIGNER
Gary Greenberg
PHOTOGRAPHER
Stock
ILLUSTRATOR/ARTIST
Lou Brooks
WRITER
Peter Seronick
CLIENT
Talkabout
AGENCY
Rossin Greenberg Seronick & Hill,
Boston, MA
DESIGN FIRM
Rossin Greenberg Seronick & Hill

88

Contrary to conventional wisdom, stress is not a 20th century phenomenon.

The Episcopal Church

89
SILVER AWARD

ART DIRECTOR
Dean Hanson
PHOTOGRAPHER
Rick Dublin
ARTIST
Rubens, Josse Van Ghent
WRITER
Tom McElligott
CLIENT
Episcopal Ad Project
AGENCY
Fallon McElligott, Minneapolis, MN

Will it take six strong men to bring you back into the church?

The Episcopal Church

For fast, fast, fast relief take two tablets.

The Episcopal Church

Two thousand years later, Christianity's biggest competition is still the Lions.

The Episcopal Church

90
SILVER AWARD

ART DIRECTOR
Charles Spencer Anderson
DESIGNER
Charles Spencer Anderson
ILLUSTRATOR/ARTIST
Charles Spencer Anderson, Lynn
Schulte
DESIGN FIRM
Duffy Design Group, Minneapolis,
MN

91

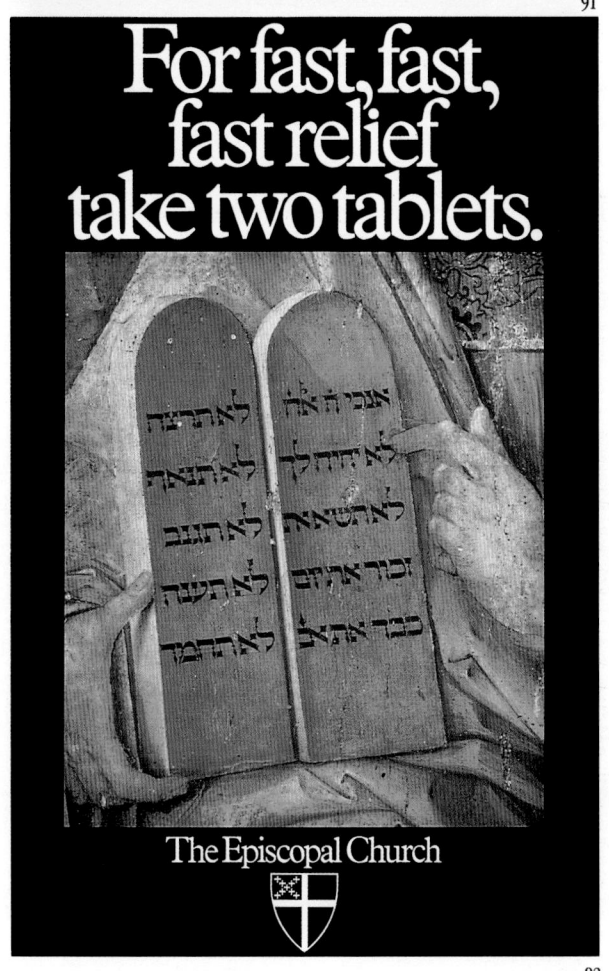

92

91
DISTINCTIVE MERIT

ART DIRECTOR
Milton Glaser
DESIGNER
Milton Glaser
ILLUSTRATOR/ARTIST
Milton Glaser
CLIENT
Catskill Association for Tourism
Services
DESIGN FIRM
Milton Glaser, Inc., New York, NY

92
DISTINCTIVE MERIT

ART DIRECTOR
Dean Hanson
ILLUSTRATOR/ARTIST
Josse Van Ghent
WRITER
Tom McElligott
CLIENT
Episcopal Ad Project
AGENCY
Fallon McElligott, Minneapolis, MN

93
DISTINCTIVE MERIT

ART DIRECTOR
Mike Schroeder
DESIGNER
Mike Schroeder
PHOTOGRAPHER
Robbie McClaran
ILLUSTRATOR/ARTIST
Mike Schroeder
CLIENT
Robbie McClaran
AGENCY
Pirtle Design
DESIGN FIRM
Schroeder Design, Dallas, TX

94
DISTINCTIVE MERIT

ART DIRECTOR
Bob Barrie
WRITER
George Gier
CLIENT
The Adler Planetarium
AGENCY
Fallon McElligott, Minneapolis, MN

95
DISTINCTIVE MERIT

ART DIRECTOR
Bill Oberlander
PHOTOGRAPHER
Dennis Chalkin
WRITER
Nat Russo
CLIENT
Sony
AGENCY
McCann-Erickson, New York, NY
PROPS
Deano Dorgias

93

94

95

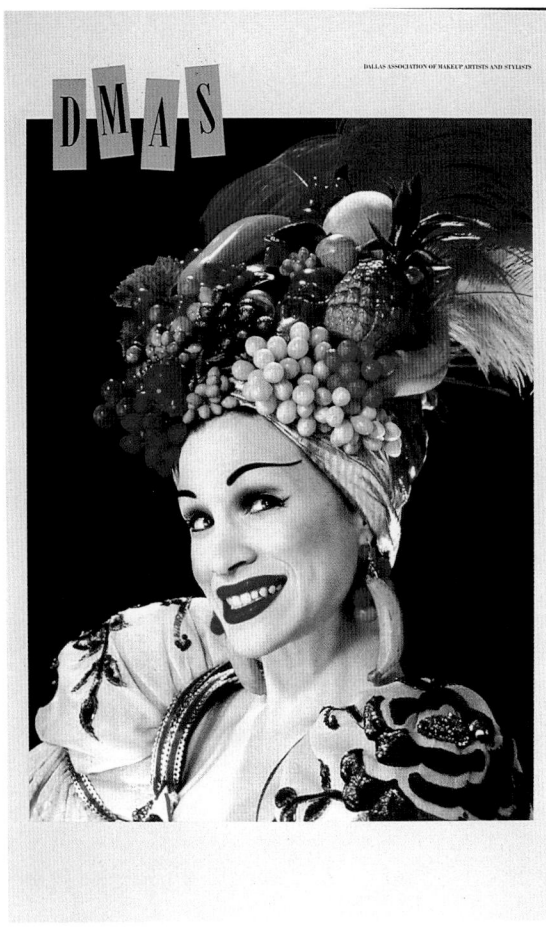

96

96
DISTINCTIVE MERIT

ART DIRECTOR
Mike Schroeder
DESIGNER
Mike Schroeder
PHOTOGRAPHER
Geof Kern
ILLUSTRATOR/ARTIST
Susan Posnick, Lynne Moon
CLIENT
Dallas Association of Make-Up
Artists and Stylists
AGENCY
Pirtle Design
DESIGN FIRM
Schroeder Design, Dallas, TX

97

97
DISTINCTIVE MERIT

ART DIRECTOR
Bob Barrie
PHOTOGRAPHER
Bobby Holland
WRITER
Mike Lescarbeau
CLIENT
Reader's Digest
AGENCY
Fallon McElligott, Minneapolis, MN

98
GOLD AWARD

ART DIRECTOR
Ricardo Van Steen, Ucho Carvalho,
Nancy Rice
ILLUSTRATOR/ARTIST
Braldt Bralds
CLIENT
Pirelli-Brazil, Ad Club of
Minneapolis
EDITOR
Mario Cohen
PUBLISHER
Pirelli-Brazil
AGENCY
Rice & Rice, Minneapolis, MN
DESIGN FIRM
CVS Communications

98

99
SILVER AWARD

ART DIRECTOR
Robert J. Post
DESIGNER
Cynthia Hoffman
ILLUSTRATOR/ARTIST
Eugene Mihaesco
WRITER
Stanley Elkin
CLIENT
Chicago
PUBLISHER
WFMT, Inc.
PUBLICATION
Chicago Magazine, Chicago, IL

100
DISTINCTIVE MERIT
ART DIRECTOR
Anthony Russell
DESIGNER
Anthony Russell
ILLUSTRATOR/ARTIST
David Lesh
CLIENT
Peat Marwick
AGENCY
Anthony Russell Inc., New York, NY
PUBLICATION
World Magazine

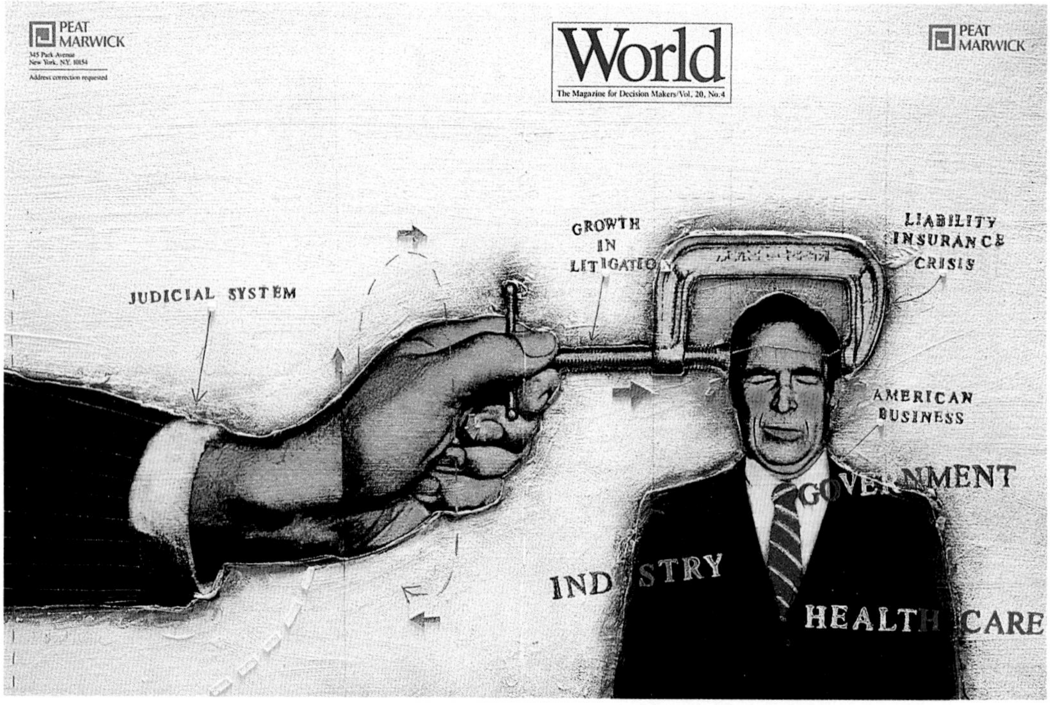

100

101
DISTINCTIVE MERIT
ART DIRECTOR
Jerelle Kraus
DESIGNER
Jerelle Kraus
ILLUSTRATOR/ARTIST
Brad Holland
CLIENT
The New York Times Op-Ed Page
EDITOR
Bob Semple
PUBLISHER
The New York Times, New York, NY
PUBLICATION
The New York Times

101

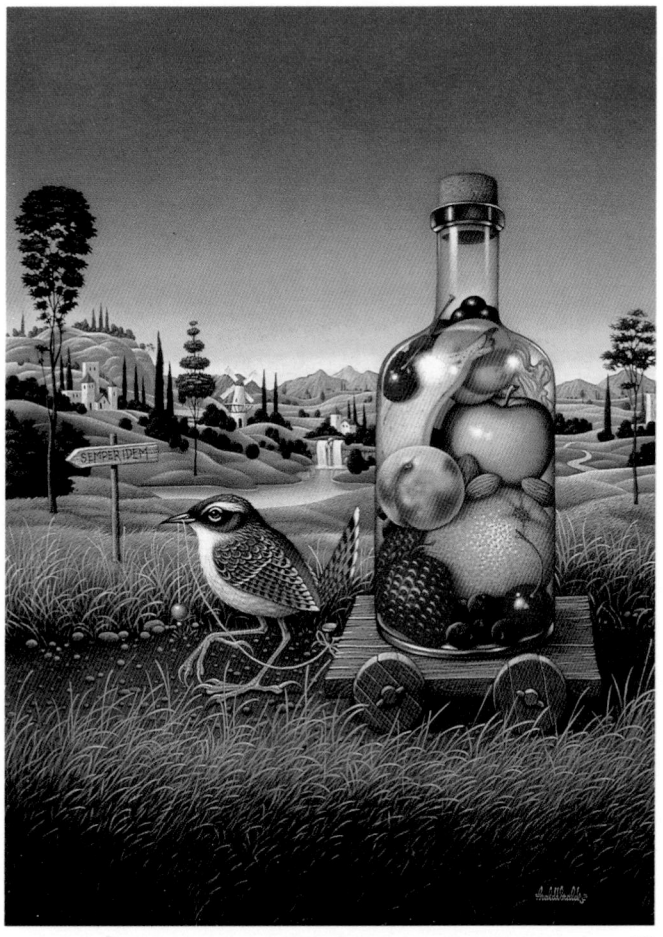

102

102
DISTINCTIVE MERIT

ART DIRECTOR
Braldt Bralds, Victor Vorderstrasse
ILLUSTRATOR/ARTIST
Braldt Bralds
WRITER
Braldt Bralds, Tom Birkenmeier
CLIENT
Bols Liqueurs U.S.A.
AGENCY
BFV & L Advertising, St. Louis, MO

103

103
DISTINCTIVE MERIT
DESIGNER
Alain Filiz, James Fulmer, Roberta
Chiarella, Karen Greenberg
ILLUSTRATOR/ARTIST
Karen Barbour
CLIENT
Polo Ralph Lauren-Cosmair
Designer Fragrance Division
DESIGN FIRM
Cosmair–in house, New York, NY
CREATIVE DIRECTOR
Alain Filiz

104
DISTINCTIVE MERIT

ART DIRECTOR
Bob Paige
DESIGNER
John Alcorn
ILLUSTRATOR/ARTIST
John Alcorn
CLIENT
Mohawk Paper Mills
DIRECTOR
Donald S. Povie
DESIGN FIRM
Jonson Pirtle Pedersen Alcorn
Metzdorf & Hess, New York, NY

104

105
DISTINCTIVE MERIT

ART DIRECTOR
Robert Appleton
DESIGNER
Robert Appleton
ILLUSTRATOR/ARTIST
Diana Minisci Appleton
WRITER
Edwin Simon
CLIENT
Advest Inc.
DESIGN FIRM
Appleton Design Inc., Hartford, CT

106
DISTINCTIVE MERIT

ART DIRECTOR
Bob Defrin
DESIGNER
Bob Defrin
ILLUSTRATOR/ARTIST
Michael Paraskevas
CLIENT
Atlantic Records, New York, NY

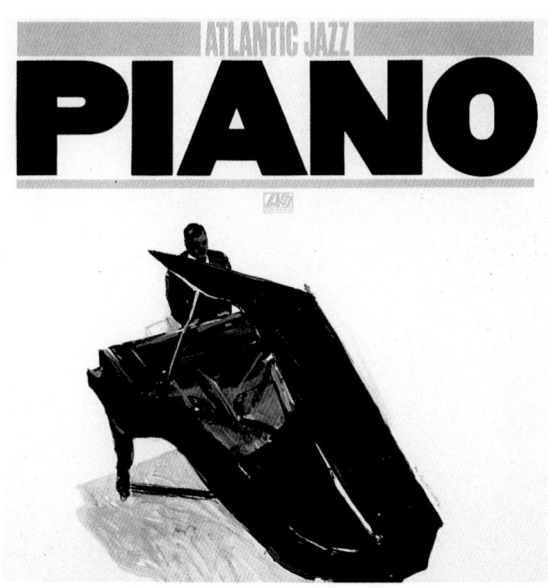

107
GOLD AWARD
ART DIRECTOR
Mark Johnson
PHOTOGRAPHER
Leon Kuzmanoff
WRITER
Sam Avery
CLIENT
Fallon McElligott
AGENCY
Fallon McElligott, Minneapolis, MN

107

108
GOLD AWARD

ART DIRECTOR
Greg Fisher, Mike Campbell
PHOTOGRAPHER
Jay Maisel
CLIENT
Phoenix Society of Communicating
Arts, ASMP , Arizona
AGENCY
Campbell Fisher Design, Phoenix,
AZ

108

109
SILVER AWARD

ART DIRECTOR
Jim Marshall
PHOTOGRAPHER
Jim Marshall, Carefree, AZ
CLIENT
Communication Arts

109

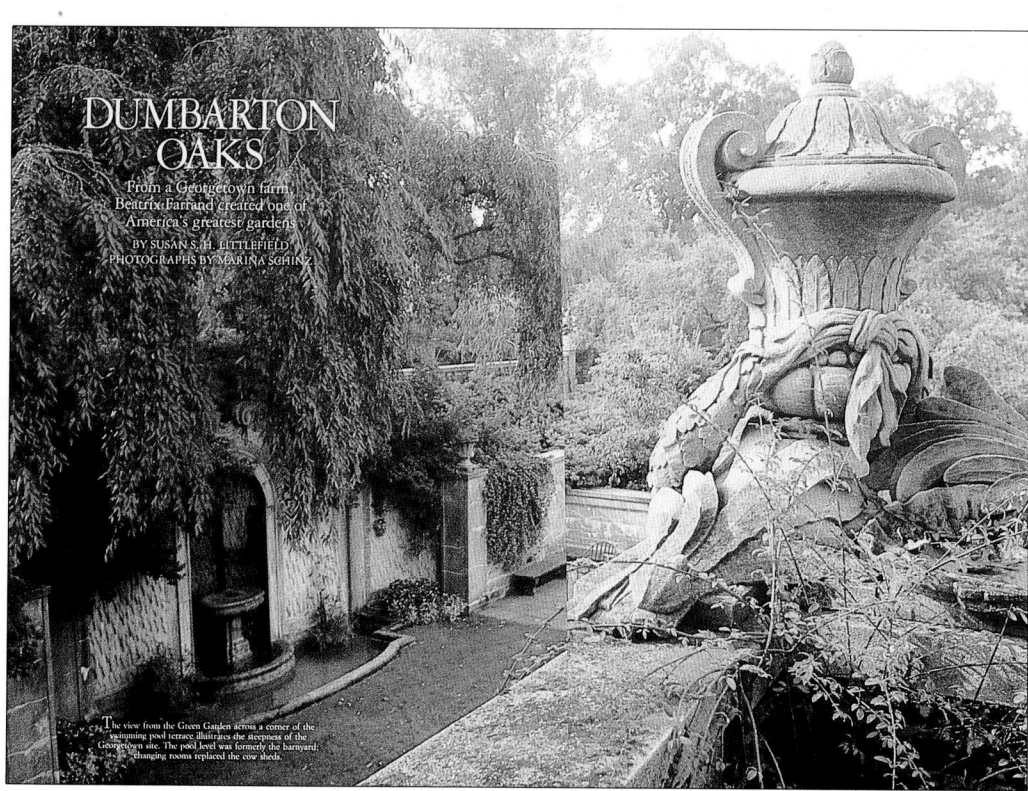

DUMBARTON OAKS

From a Georgetown farm,
Beatrix Farrand created one of
America's greatest gardens

BY SUSAN S. H. LITTLEFIELD
PHOTOGRAPHS BY MARINA SCHINZ

The view from the Green Garden across a corner of the
swimming pool terrace illustrates the steepness of the
Georgetown site. The pool level was formerly the barnyard;
changing rooms replaced the cow sheds.

110
SILVER AWARD

ART DIRECTOR
Lloyd Ziff
DESIGNER
Karen Lee Grant
PHOTOGRAPHER
Marina Schinz
WRITER
Susan H. Littlefield
EDITOR
Louis Oliver Gropp
PUBLISHER
William F. Bondlow, The Conde
Nast Publications Inc., New York,
NY
PUBLICATION
House & Garden

111
SILVER AWARD

PHOTOGRAPHER
Ron Wu
CLIENT
Ron Wu Studios, Rochester, NY

111

112
SILVER AWARD

ART DIRECTOR
Paul Boley
PHOTOGRAPHER
Dewitt Jones, Studio Associates
WRITER
Richard Rand
CLIENT
Schenley/Dewars
AGENCY
Leo Burnett Co., Inc., Chicago, IL
CREATIVE DIRECTOR
John Eding

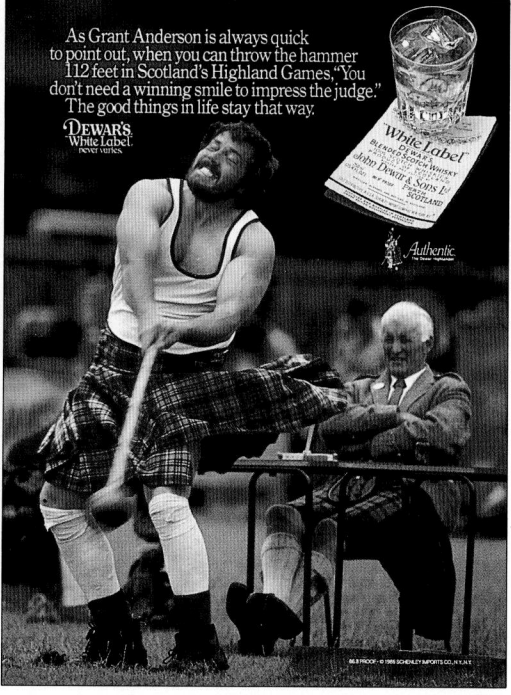

113
SILVER AWARD

ART DIRECTOR
Ken Kendrick
DESIGNER
Ken Kendrick
PHOTOGRAPHER
Peter Lindbergh
CLIENT
The New York Times Magazine
EDITOR
Ed Klein
PUBLISHER
The New York Times, New York, NY
PUBLICATION
The New York Times

1987 CALENDAR

USWEST

114
SILVER AWARD

ART DIRECTOR
Pat Burnham
DESIGNER
Pat Burnham
PHOTOGRAPHER
Kurt Markus
WRITER
Bill Miller
CLIENT
US West
AGENCY
Fallon McElligott, Minneapolis, MN

115
SILVER AWARD

ART DIRECTOR
J. C. Larimore, Arthur Meyerson
DESIGNER
J. C. Larimore
PHOTOGRAPHER
Arthur Meyerson
WRITER
J. C. Larimore
CLIENT
Larimore Creative, Inc.
DESIGN FIRM
Larimore Creative, Inc.,
Albuquerque, NM

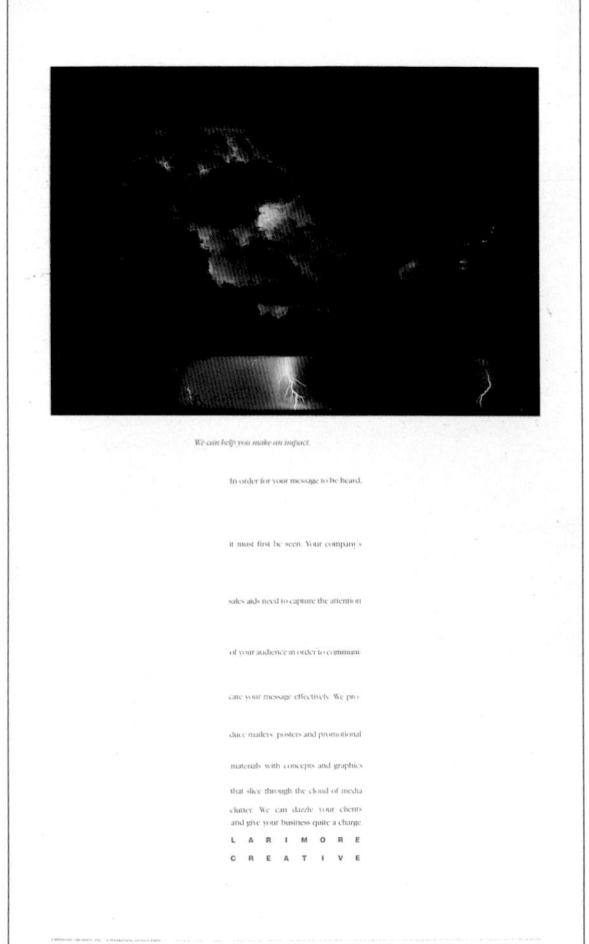

115

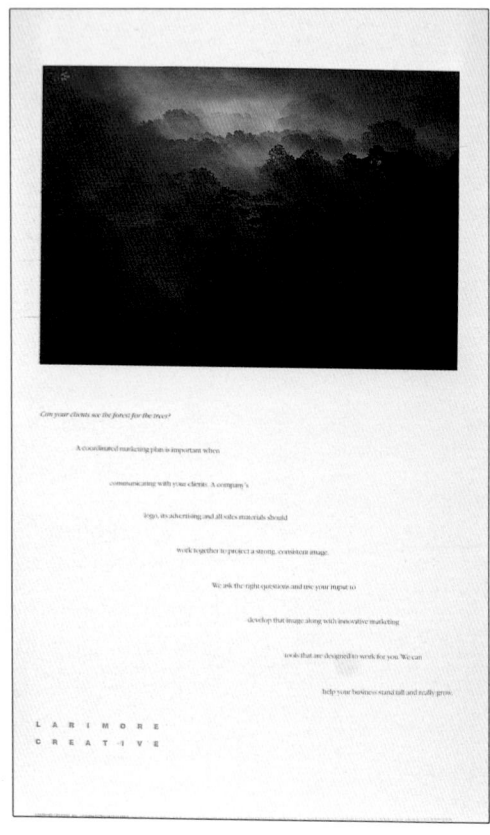

116
DISTINCTIVE MERIT

ART DIRECTOR
Doug Crozier
PHOTOGRAPHER
Ed Zak
WRITER
Paula Rasor
CLIENT
W.R. Grace & Co.
AGENCY
Howard, Merrell & Partners, Inc.,
Raleigh, NC
PUBLICATION
"Grass & Grains"

116

117
DISTINCTIVE MERIT

ART DIRECTOR
Curt Chuvalas
DESIGNER
Curt Chuvalas
PHOTOGRAPHER
Dick Spahr
WRITER
Carole Williams
CLIENT
Indiana Department of Commerce-
Indiana Film Commission
AGENCY
Bloomhorst Story O'Hara Inc.,
Indianapolis, IN
PUBLICATION
Hollywood Reporter, Millimeter,
Variety, Emmy, Ad Week

117

118
DISTINCTIVE MERIT

ART DIRECTOR
Lloyd Ziff
DESIGNER
Karen Lee Grant
PHOTOGRAPHER
Timothy Hursley
WRITER
Lois Wagner Green
EDITOR
Louis Oliver Gropp
PUBLISHER
William F. Bondlow, The Conde Nast Publications Inc.
PUBLICATION
House & Garden, New York, NY

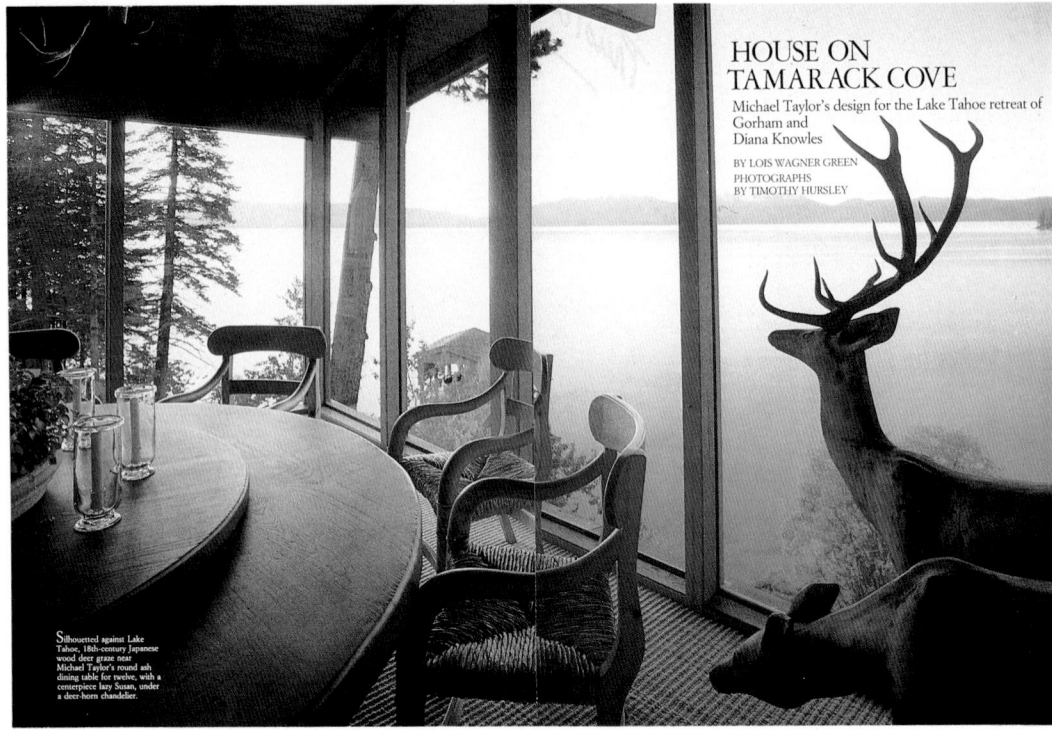

HOUSE ON TAMARACK COVE

Michael Taylor's design for the Lake Tahoe retreat of Gorham and Diana Knowles

BY LOIS WAGNER GREEN
PHOTOGRAPHS
BY TIMOTHY HURSLEY

Silhouetted against Lake Tahoe, 18th-century Japanese wood deer graze near Michael Taylor's round ash dining table for twelve, with a centerpiece lazy Susan, under a deer-horn chandelier.

118

119
DISTINCTIVE MERIT

ART DIRECTOR
Joseph Sachs
PHOTOGRAPHER
Joseph Sachs
CLIENT
Joseph Sachs Photography, New York, NY

JOSEPH SACHS

119

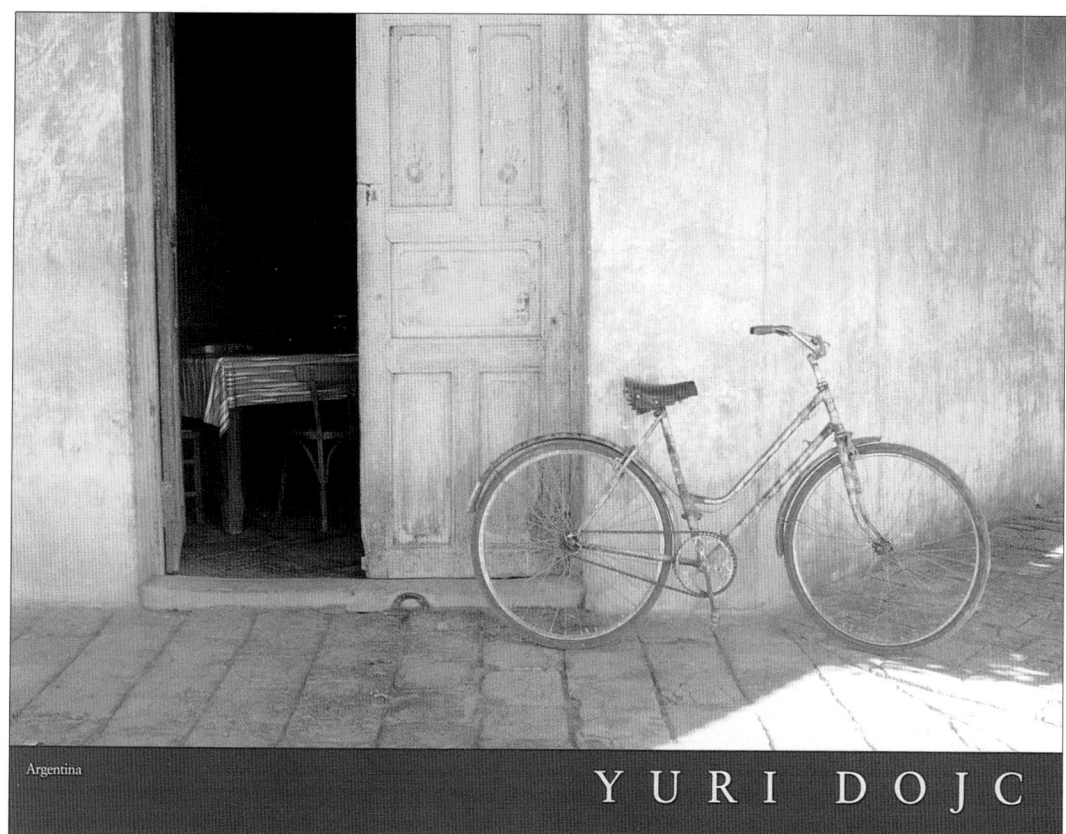

Argentina

YURI DOJC

120

120
DISTINCTIVE MERIT

DESIGNER
Les Hollaway
PHOTOGRAPHER
Yuri Dojc, Toronto, Canada
CLIENT
Yuri Dojc
PUBLISHER
Yuri Dojc Inc.
DESIGN FIRM
Design Source

121

121
DISTINCTIVE MERIT

ART DIRECTOR
Robin Hood
DESIGNER
Tim Kovick
PHOTOGRAPHER
Robin Hood, Franklin, TN

122
DISTINCTIVE MERIT

DESIGNER
John Van Dyke
PHOTOGRAPHER
Terry Heffernan, San Francisco, CA
CLIENT
Mead Paper
DESIGN FIRM
Van Dyke Design, Seattle, WA

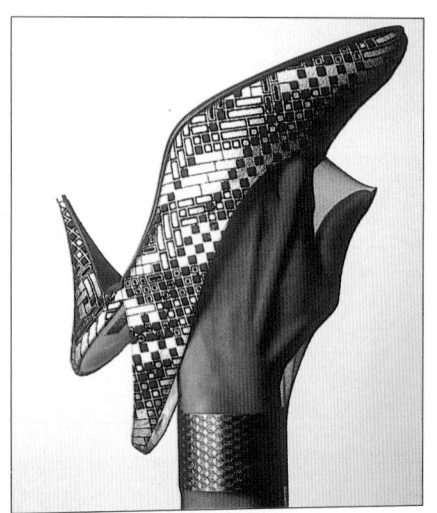

122

123
SILVER AWARD

ART DIRECTOR
Diana La Guardia
DESIGNER
Audrone Razgaitis
PHOTOGRAPHER
Neil Slavin
WRITER
John Russell
CLIENT
New York Times Magazine
EDITOR
Edward Klein
PUBLICATION
New York Times Magazine, New
York, NY
PHOTO EDITOR
Peter Howe

123

124
DISTINCTIVE MERIT

DESIGNER
Kimberlee Keswich, Gretchen Goldie
PHOTOGRAPHER
Terry Heffernan, San Francisco, CA
CLIENT
Wolfer Printing

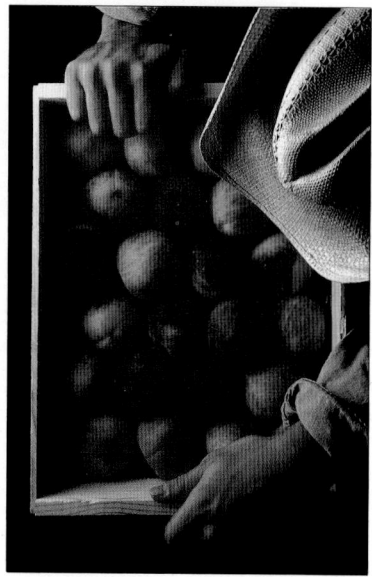

125
GOLD AWARD

ART DIRECTOR
Len McCarron
WRITER
Rick Meyer, Ted Sann
CLIENT
DuPont
EDITOR
Chris Horn, Horn Eisenberg
DIRECTOR
Tom Higgins
PRODUCER/AGENCY
Bob Emerson, BBDO, New York, NY
PRODUCTION COMPANY
BFCS Inc

126
GOLD AWARD

ART DIRECTOR
Mark Haumersen
WRITER
John Jarvis
CLIENT
Marigold Foods
EDITOR
Steve Shepard
DIRECTOR
Steve Griak
DIRECTOR OF PHOTOGRAPHY
John Harvey
PRODUCER/AGENCY
RoseMary Januschka,
Martin/Williams, Minneapolis, MN
PRODUCER/PROD. CO.
Lyle McIntyre, Wilson-Griak

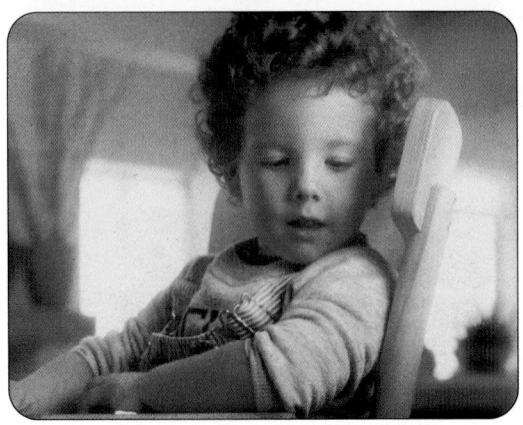 

125

LANDING
30-second
CONTROL TOWER: Flight 124 fly runway heading to 3,000. Right turn to two-seven-zero. You are cleared for take-off.
AVO: Introducing DuPont
certified Stainmaster carpet.
Stainmaster gives you
a revolutionary new level of protection
against stains and spills
that's better than any other carpet you
can buy today.
Because you never know . . .
STARTER: Gentlemen, start your engines.
AVO: New Stainmaster.
AVO: From DuPont Carpet Fibers.

126

GRAFFITI COWS
30-second
Since our last commercial for Kemps Ice Cream, a lot of you have been asking where we get our chocolate cows.. The ones that give Kemps Chocolate Ice Cream its fresh, delicious flavor. I can't tell you that. However one woman wrote wanting to know the difference between Kemps Vanilla Ice Cream and our New York Vanilla flavor. I can answer that. You see, Kemps Vanilla Ice Cream comes from a vanilla cow.
And Kemps New York Vanilla Ice Cream comes from a New York vanilla cow.
ANNCR: Kemps Ice Cream. It's the cows.

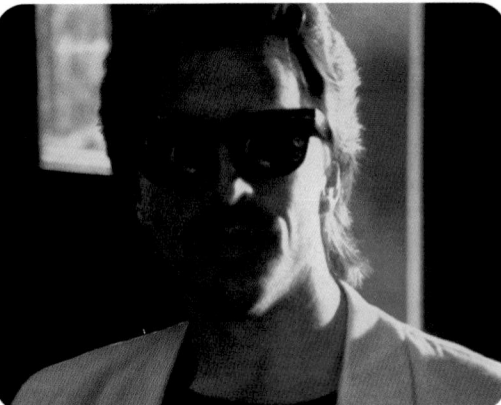

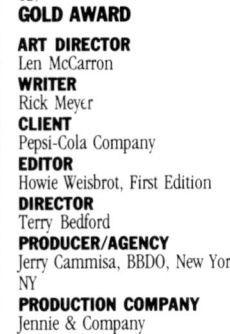

127
GOLD AWARD

ART DIRECTOR
Len McCarron
WRITER
Rick Meyer
CLIENT
Pepsi-Cola Company
EDITOR
Howie Weisbrot, First Edition
DIRECTOR
Terry Bedford
PRODUCER/AGENCY
Jerry Cammisa, BBDO, New York, NY
PRODUCTION COMPANY
Jennie & Company

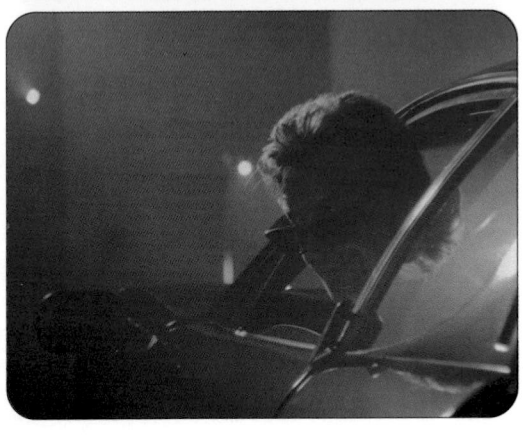

128
GOLD AWARD

ART DIRECTOR
Harvey Hoffenberg
WRITER
Phil Dusenberry, Ted Sann, Susan Procter
CLIENT
Pepsi-Cola Company
EDITOR
Dennis Hayes
DIRECTOR
Ridley Scott
PRODUCER/AGENCY
Gene Lofaro, BBDO, New York, NY
PRODUCTION COMPANY
Fairbanks Films

127

TIME MACHINE
60-second
SFX: ELECTRICAL BUZZING. MUSIC.
SMITH: O.K. Jonathan . . .
SMITH: We're ready to send you back in time.
DOC: Now remember, you're going back before television, before radio,, even before soft drinks.
SMITH: But you're only there to observe. Don't say a word.
DOC: The slightest thing you do or say could change the entire course of history.
JONATHAN: Don't worry, Doc. Mum's the word.
DOC: O.K. Activate time travel mode retrograde to the year 1885.
SFX: MECHANICAL WHIRRING NOISE.
SMITH: He's there.
DOC: We did it! Hey, where's my Pepsi?
SMITH: It's, oh, no. He took it. This could be catastrophic.
SMITH: It could change history.
DOC: Relax, Smith. You don't really think that one can of Pepsi could alter 100 years of history, do you?
SFX: VANISHING SOUND.
SMITH: Nah, I guess not.
SFX: VANISHING SOUND.
DOC: After all, what could twelve little ounces of Pepsi do?
SFX: VANISHING SOUND.
SMITH: Yeah, you're probably right. What could happen?
DOC: What could happen?

128

DON JOHNSON
2-minute
MUSIC: YOU BELONG TO THE CITY
FREY: Go, go left . . . no, no, no, right, right, right.
SFX: TRUCK HORN BLARES.
JOHNSON: Now you've done it.
SFX: MOTOR GRINDING.
FREY: It's your car pal. You fix it.
JOHNSON: Do we have to listen to this?
SFX: MUSIC IN BACKGROUND
FREY: That's my song.
JOHNSON: (MOCKING) That's my song.
FREY: Let's go. Hey, I'm everywhere pal.
SFX:MUSIC, HANDS CLAPPING.
SFX: CAN FALLING ON TURNTABLE.
CROWD: Screams.
JOHNSON: Is there a mechanic in the house?
CROWD: Me!
MUSIC: PEPSI IS THE U.S.A.
SFX: MOTOR TURNING OVER.
GIRL: That's it.
FREY: Thanks alot.
JOHNSON: Yeah, thanks!
GIRL: You drive 'em, we fix em. Bye.
FREY: Cool!
SUPER: Pepsi. The choice of a new geeration.

129
GOLD AWARD

ART DIRECTOR
Bob Meagher
DESIGNER
Bob Meagher
WRITER
Bob Meagher
CLIENT
Lincoln Park Zoological Society
EDITOR
Bob Meagher
PRODUCER/AGENCY
Bob Meagher, Cramer-Krasselt,
Chicago, IL
CREATIVE DIRECTOR
Maureen Moore

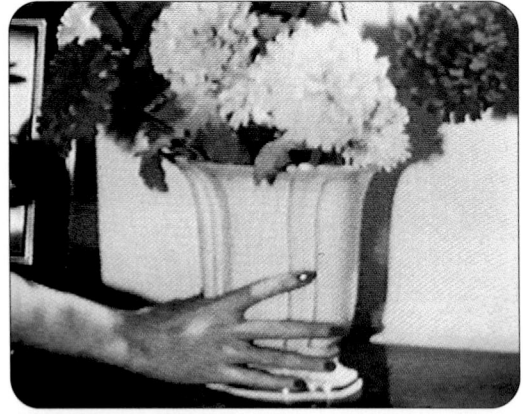

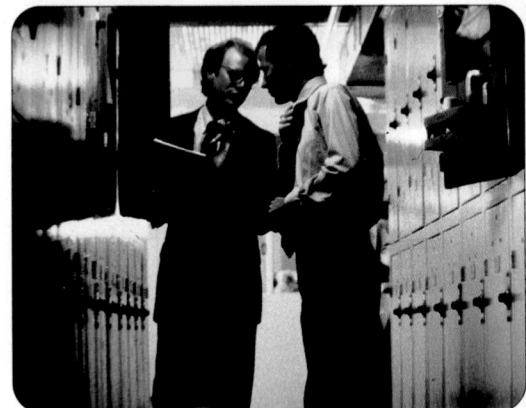

130
GOLD AWARD

ART DIRECTOR
Mike Campbell, Rick Strand
WRITER
Gary Graf, Cynthia Franco, Steve
Diamant
CLIENT
Apple Computer, Inc.
EDITOR
Dennis Hayes
DIRECTOR
Joe Pytka
PRODUCER/AGENCY
Gene Lofaro, BBDO, New York, and
San Francisco
PRODUCTION COMPANY
Pytka

129
THE INCREDIBLE ELEPHANT OFFER
60-second
(FAST TALKING TONGUE-IN-CHEEK DIRECT RESPONSE ANNOUNCER.)
ANNCR: This Valentine's Day you could give your sweetheart flowers but they won't last long . . . and candy's so fattening.
Or you could say "I Love You" in a big way with an Elephant.
Adopt an Elephant at the Lincoln Park Zoo.
This Elephant comes with his very own trunk . . .
. . . and a matching set of precious ivory tusks.
How much would you pay for an Elephant like this? Wait, there's more.
You get a bumper sticker . . . a certificate . . .
. . . and some unknown premium.
Now, how much would you pay? Don't answer—there's more.
You get an elephant fact sheet. An invitation to the Adopt Party.
And your sweetheart gets a card that says he or she has become the proud parent of an Elephant. Imagine their surprise!
How much would you expect to pay for all this? $1,600? $32,000?
You get the Elephant, bumper sticker, certificate,
Unknown premium, Elephant fact sheet, party invitation.
and Valentine Card . . . for only $19.95!
It's the most incredible Elephant offer ever . . . not available in any store.
To order this unforgettable Valentine's gift, call Lincoln Park Zoo at—that's . Major credit cards accepted. Call now! Operators are standing by
(SFX: ELEPHANT TRUMPETS) . . . with your elephant.
To order this unforgettable Valentine's gift call Lincoln Park Zoo at 1-800-977-9600, that's 1-800-977-9600. Visa and MasterCard accepted. Call now. Operators are standing by . . .
(SFX: ELEPHANT TRUMPETS) . . .
with your elephant.

130
THE RIVALRY/THE RED EYE/REPORT
60-second
1ST MAN: Come on admit it, it was a great shot.
2ND MAN: For a beginner.
1ST MAN: Beginner? Two out of three pal two out of three.
2ND MAN: I think you're still trying to get even because I had the higher grade point average.
1ST MAN: Yet as I recall, the lowest starting salary.
2ND MAN: Yea, but at the hottest shop in town.
1ST MAN: Yea, as an assistant to an assistant.
2ND MAN: Oh O.K., O.K. so who was first to the Vice President?
1ST MAN: And last with the corner office. . . .
2ND MAN: But if I can land the North Bay project . . .
1ST MAN: Yea . . .
2ND MAN: I'm talking senior partnership.
1ST MAN: Really?
2ND MAN: How does it look?
1ST MAN: You tell me.
2ND MAN: (WHISTLES) What a production. You guys must have had outside help on this one.
1ST MAN: No way, we put the whole thing together ourselves.
2ND MAN: Come on.
1ST MAN: No really, we did everything on our computer.
2ND MAN: Revenue projections, impact studies?
1ST MAN: Everything.
2ND MAN: So ah what kind of computer?
1ST MAN: Oh, I'm running late.
2ND MAN: Come on, what kind of computer??????

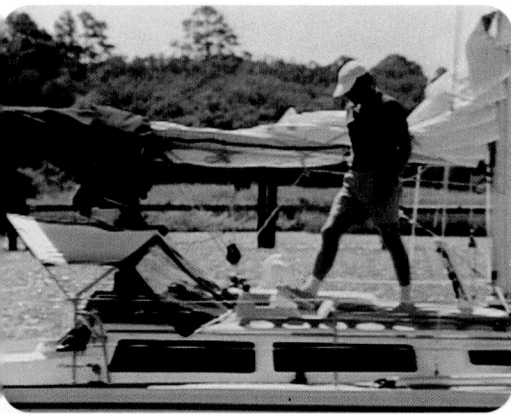

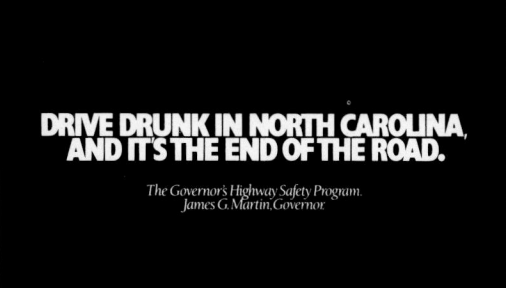

131
SILVER AWARD

ART DIRECTOR
Steve Pharr
WRITER
Sarah Bowman
CLIENT
Georgia Department of Industry & Trade
EDITOR
Wade Watkins
DIRECTOR
John Davis
DIRECTOR OF PHOTOGRAPHY
John Davis
PRODUCER/AGENCY
Steve Pharr, Pringle Dixon Pringle, Atlanta, GA
PRODUCER
Sheryl Myers
PRODUCTION MANAGER
Steve Colby

132
GOLD AWARD

ART DIRECTOR
Michael Winslow
WRITER
Steve Bassett
CLIENT
N.C. Governor's Highway Safety Program
DIRECTOR
Chuck Clemmons
PRODUCER/AGENCY
John Pace, McKinney & Silver, Raleigh, NC
PRODUCTION COMPANY
Michael Moir Productions

131

GEORGIA
30-second
SONG: Georgia, Georgia
the whole day through,
just an old sweet song
keeps Georgia on my mind.
just an old sweet song
keeps Georgia on my mind.
VO: There's a free Georgia vacation planner waiting for you if you call our
toll free number. So why don't you do it now, while it's on your mind?
RAY CHARLES: Yeah!!

132

COOLER
30-second
ANNCR VO: Recently, California introduced America to a new drink called
the wine cooler. But if you drink any kind of alcohol, and then drive . . .
(CUT TO JAIL CELL. DOOR SLAMS SHUT). . . you could get a taste of a
North Carolina cooler. (FADE TO BLACK, FADE UP THEME LINE) Drive
drunk in North Carolina, and it's the end of the road.

133
SILVER AWARD

ART DIRECTOR
Paula Grief
CLIENT
Gene Pressman, Barneys New York,
NY
DIRECTOR OF PHOTOGRAPHY
Peter Kagen
DIRECTOR
Paula Grief, Peter Kagen
CREATIVE DIRECTOR
Neil Kraft, Paula Grief

134
SILVER AWARD

ART DIRECTOR
Saskia Mossel
WRITER
Steve Baer
CLIENT
General Foods Shake 'n Bake
DIRECTOR
David Ashwell
PRODUCER/AGENCY
Al Gay, Ogilvy & Mather, New York
NY
PRODUCER
Danny Boyle
CREATIVE DIRECTOR
Malcolm End

 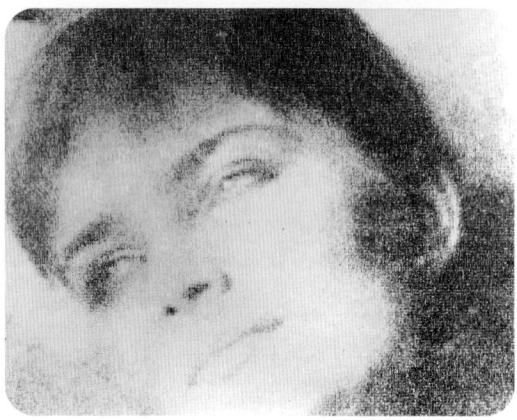 

133
WOMEN'S STORE
30-second
AVO: Whatever you want. All you need. The best of everything. Down to earth. *Out of this world.* A new way to shop. The Women's Store. Barney's New York.

134
SHAKE 'N BAKE "FISH"
30-second
MOM: Shake 'n Bake has this recipe for fish. It makes the fish crunchy on the outside—moist inside.
I serve fish about once a week—because this family loves it.
VO: Shake 'n Bake Coating Mix for Fish.
MOM: And it's good brain food.

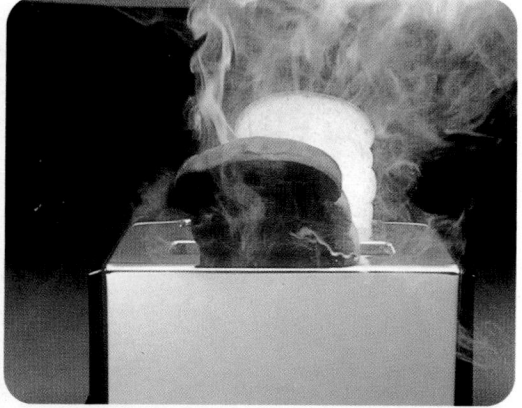

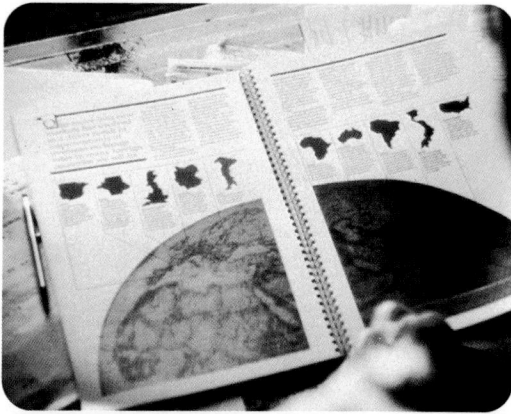

135
SILVER AWARD

ART DIRECTOR
Grant Parrish
WRITER
Tom Rost
CLIENT
American Express
EDITOR
Dennis Hayes Editorial
DIRECTOR
Michael Schrom
DIRECTOR OF PHOTOGRAPHY
Michael Schrom
PRODUCER/AGENCY
Barry Wisotsky, Ogilvy & Mather,
New York, NY
PRODUCER
Carol Brackenridge

136
SILVER AWARD

ART DIRECTOR
Rick Strand
WRITER
Cynthia Franco
CLIENT
Apple Computer, Inc.
EDITOR
Dennis Hayes
DIRECTOR
Joe Pytka
PRODUCER/AGENCY
Gene Lofaro, BBDO, New York, NY
PRODUCTION COMPANY
Pytka

135

BREAKING VERSION 3
30-second
ANNCR: If only things lasted longer.
If only their warranties lasted longer.
If only you had bought them with the American Express Card.
Because from now until December 31, we will extend the free repair period
of the manufacturer's warranty.
In fact, we'll double it, up to an extra year.
American Express introduces "Buyer's Assurance."
Now if something breaks, it won't break you.
But only if you use the American Express Card.
Apply now.

136

THE REPORT
60-second
1ST MAN: Yes, I know but . . . I understand but I still want our attorneys
to handle it. Fine.
2ND MAN: Isn't that thing settled yet?
1ST MAN: Looks like it's gonna drag on forever. What do you think of
Jensons report?
2ND MAN: Looks O.K.
1ST MAN: O.K.?
2ND MAN: Alright it looks terrific. What do you want me to say? This is
great work.
1ST MAN: I thought so too.
2ND MAN: It's nice to see our computer system is finally earning its keep.
1ST MAN: I wish that were true.
2ND MAN: What do you mean?
1ST MAN: Marketing isn't using our system anymore.
2ND MAN: They're not? Then how did they do this?
1ST MAN: They did it on their own system. The one they got a month
ago.
2ND MAN: They put this together in a month?
1ST MAN: Well not quite Frank, they did it in a week.

137
SILVER AWARD

ART DIRECTOR
Bruce Dundore
WRITER
Barry Udoff
CLIENT
Pepsi-Cola Company
EDITOR
Bob DeRise/A Cut Above
DIRECTOR
Joe Pytka
PRODUCER/AGENCY
Gene Lofaro, BBDO, New York, NY
PRODUCTION COMPANY
Pytka

138
SILVER AWARD

ART DIRECTOR
Tom Cordner, Jean Robaire, Doug
Patterson
WRITER
Brent Bouchez, John Stein, Steve
Kessler, Garry Shandling, Tom
Poston, Roseanne Barr
CLIENT
Pizza Hut, Inc.
EDITOR
Rob Watzke
DIRECTOR
David Steinberg
PRODUCER/AGENCY
Elaine Hinton, Vicki Blucher,
Chiat/Day, Los Angeles, CA
PRODUCTION COMPANY
Larkin Prod.

137

COPIER
60-second
SFX: FOOTSTEPS CROSSING LIBRARY FLOOR.
SFX: M.J. FOX DROPS BOOK ON TABLE.
M.J. FOX: Hmmmm.
SFX: BOOK DROPS LOUDLY ON COPIER MACHINE.
M.J. FOX: Somebody have any . . .
STUDENT: Ssssh!
M.J. FOX: . . . change?
SFX: SNAPS FINGERS. CLAPS HANDS. COPIER MACHINE MAKES
PHOTOCOPY OF PEPSI CAN.
SFX: PICKS UP PHOTOCOPY.
SFX: CAN OPENING SOUND. SFX: FIZZING SOUND.
SFX: SQUEAK OF MOISTURE ON CAN. SOUND OF PHOTOCOPY BEING
ROLLED INTO A CAN.
M.J. FOX: Whistles.
SFX: DRINKING SOUNDS.
M.J. FOX: Ahhh.
STUDENT: Ssssh!
SFX: CAN CRUSHING. CAN BANGING IN METAL GARBAGE CAN.
M.J. FOX: Ssssh!
VO AND SUPER: Pepsi. The choice of a new generation.

138

SALAD BAR/DRIVING/MOTHER'S DAY
30-second
(MUSIC UNDER THROUGHOUT)
BARR: So my husband says to me, "Roseanne you've been workin' real
hard. How 'bout if we take the kids out for pan pizza and you can eat at
the salad bar?" So I said, "Well what a great idea honey. While you and
the kids are eatin' a hot, steamy, cheesy pizza, I can be off in the corner
grazing on a delightful array of sprouts and garbanzo beans.
Get real.

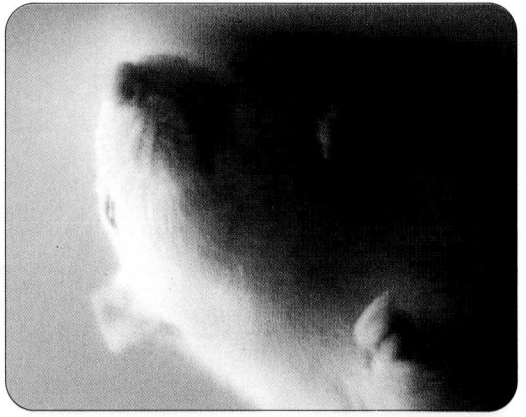

139
SILVER AWARD

ART DIRECTOR
Marisa Acocella
WRITER
Michael Scardino, Leslie Mechanic
CLIENT
Ken Banks, Eckerd Drugs
EDITOR
Mel Cohen
DIRECTOR
David Ashwell
PRODUCER/AGENCY
Tricia Caruso, JWT, New York, NY
PRODUCER
David Ashwell
CREATIVE DIRECTOR
Charles Genneralli

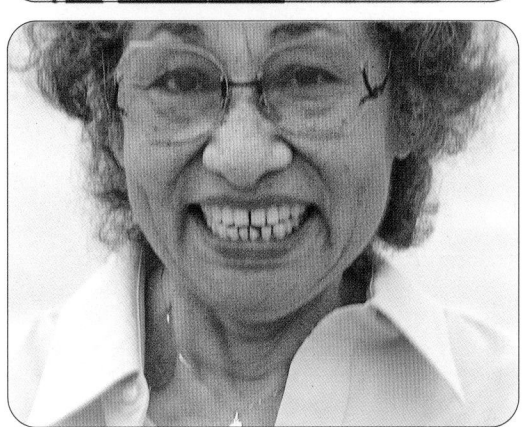

140
SILVER AWARD

ART DIRECTOR
Rick Boyko, Miles Turpin
WRITER
Elizabeth Hayes, Bill Hamilton,
Dustin Jensen, Carmen Cortez, Judy
Kleinmeyer
CLIENT
Home Savings of America
EDITOR
Gayle Grant
DIRECTOR
Leslie Dektor
PRODUCER/AGENCY
Richard O'Neill, David Prince,
Chiat/Day, Los Angeles, CA
PRODUCTION COMPANY
Petermann/Dektor

139
LESSON/POISON/VACCINE
30-second
SUPER: Based on a true story.
VO: In a high school gymnasium, a pharmacist from Eckerd Drugs took the time and trouble to teach an invaluable lesson, and showed 200 teenaged kids what it's really like to get high on drugs.
To an Eckerd pharmacist, nothing's more important than your health.

140
THE CORTEZES/THE KLEINMEYERS/DUSTIN JENSON
60-second
MUSIC: UNDER THROUGHOUT.
CARMEN: Well, I've been saving my money because at our age my husband and I ya know he's still working and one of these days he's gonna retire, and we would like to travel a little bit.
ANNCR: Carmen Cortez. Home Savings of America customer.
CARMEN: I was a widow the first time. With two children. It wasn't easy, I never went anyplace. Because I didn't have the money to do anything or because everything was for the kids you know and pay my bills and make my house payment. And then when I met Mr. Cortez things were a little easier; for me. And he wants to take me to Mexico City and he wants to take me to Cancun and he wants to take me here and there.
But, I want to go to New York.
ANNCR: Home Savings takes very good care of Carmen's money and about a million other people's as well.
CARMEN: Most of all I would like to see Ms. Liberty. And get up way up on her crown and uh get up way up to the top and look from there. This is my country.

141
SILVER AWARD

ART DIRECTOR
Nick Ives
DESIGNER
George Booth
ANIMATOR
Frank Terry
DIRECTOR
Frank Terry
EXECUTIVE PRODUCER
Bonnie Jekel
PRODUCER/AGENCY
Ann O'Keefe, Lord Geller Federico
Einstein
PRODUCER/PROD. CO.
Cheryl Abood, FilmFair, Los Angeles,
CA
CREATIVE DIRECTOR
Chuck Griffith
STYLIST
Carlene Brady

142
DISTINCTIVE MERIT

ART DIRECTOR
Nick Gisonde
WRITER
Charlie Breen
CLIENT
Hyundai Motor America
PRODUCER/AGENCY
Eric Steinhauser, Backer &
Spielvogel, New York, NY

141

WOOF
30-second
DOG (FX): CHEWS LAST BIT, THEN BEGINS TO GIGGLE A LITTLE.
CAT (FX): MEOW AND GIGGLE, AS
DOG (FX): CONTINUES TO GIGGLE.
DOG & CAT (FX): GIGGLES, THEN LAUGHTER GROWS.
DOG & CAT (FX): HYSTERICAL LAUGHTER.
CAT (FX): CONTINUE LAUGHTER.
DOG (FX): BARK!
CAT (FX): SCREAM!
DOG (FX): GROWL!
ANNOUNCER (VO): From the drawings of George Booth, from the pages of
the New Yorker. Yes, the New Yorker.

142

800 NUMBER
15-second
ANNCR VO: With a Mercedes you get an 800 # so you can phone for
assistance day or night.
(HYUNDAI THEME MUSIC THROUGHOUT)
With a Hyundai you get the same thing but you save about $30,000 on
the call.
Hyundai.
Cars that make sense.

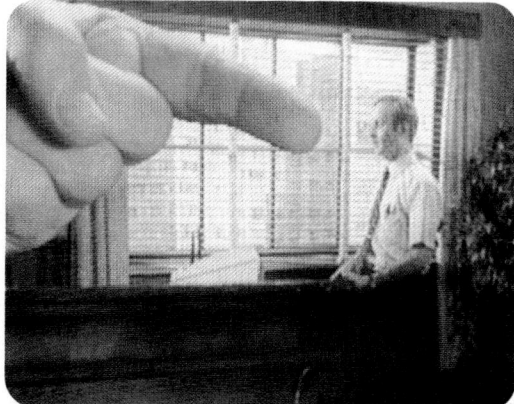

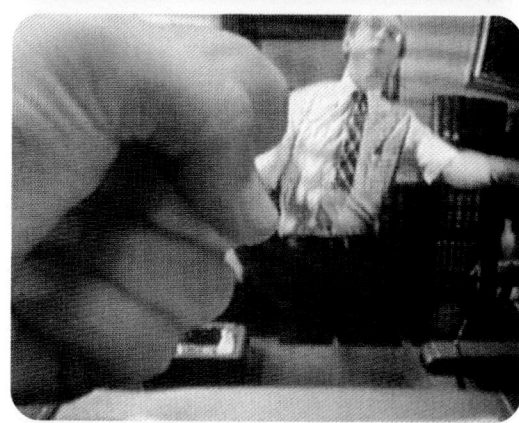

143
DISTINCTIVE MERIT
ART DIRECTOR
Jill McClabb
WRITER
Bruce Richter
CLIENT
WNBC-TV
EDITOR
Ken Coleman
DIRECTOR
Tony Cookson
PRODUCER/AGENCY
Ann O'Keefe, LGFE, New York, NY
PRODUCTION COMPANY
THT Productions

144
DISTINCTIVE MERIT
ART DIRECTOR
Gary Wolfson
WRITER
John De Cerchio
CLIENT
Michigan Lottery
EDITOR
Image Express
DIRECTOR
Bill Dear
PRODUCER/AGENCY
Sheldon Cohn, WB Doner, Southfield, MI
PRODUCTION COMPANY
Magic Lantern

143
MISS HANSTEIN
10-second
HANSTEIN: Now that Donahue's on at 4, I'm never late for work anymore. But I do have to leave early.

144
BILNER
30-second
BOSS: Send in Bilner.
VO: For most of us, there's one person who seems bigger than life.
BILNER: Yes, Boss?
BOSS: Bilner, I'm the boss get that through your head. When I say jump, you jump. Just remember who pays your salary, Bilner. Now, get outta here.
VO: But if you play Super Lotto this Saturday, you could win enough money to do something you've always dreamed of.
BOSS: Bilner, can't you see I'm busy, get back to work right now.
SFX: BITE.
VO: Bit the hand that feeds you.

145
DISTINCTIVE MERIT

ART DIRECTOR
Steve Ohman
WRITER
Harold Karp
CLIENT
W.R. Grace & Co.
EDITOR
Vito DeSario, Pam Powers
DIRECTOR
Ridley Scott
PRODUCER/AGENCY
Mindy Gerber, Lowe Marschalk,
Inc., New York, NY
PRODUCER/PROD. CO.
Richard Goldberg, Fairbanks Films
and RSA Films, London

146
DISTINCTIVE MERIT

ART DIRECTOR
Roger Mosconi, Don Schneider
WRITER
Michael Patti
CLIENT
Chrysler Dodge Corporation
EDITOR
Rye Dolman, Rye Films
DIRECTOR
Jack Churchill
PRODUCER/AGENCY
Jerry Cammisa, BBDO, New York,
NY
PRODUCTION COMPANY
Bean-Kahn with Dreamquest

145

THE DEFICIT TRIALS
60-second
OLD MAN: I've already told you, it was all going to work out somehow.
There was even talk of an amendment. But no one was willing to make
the sacrifices.
I'm afraid you're much too young to understand.
BOY: Maybe so but I'm afraid the numbers speak for themselves. By 1986,
for example, the national debt had reached 2 trillion dollars.
Didn't that frighten you?
VO: No one really knows what another generation of unchecked federal
deficits will bring.
OLD MAN: This frightens me.
BOY: No more questions.
OLD MAN: I have a question. Are you ever going to forgive us?
VO: But we know this much. You *can* change the future. You have to. At
W.R. Grace, we want all of us to stay one step ahead of a changing world.

146

JUNK YARD DOG
60-second
VO: And there came a moment when all the elements came together
Design, engineering, and technology.
Unleashing a new breed of compact car.
The Dodge Shadow. A superbly equipped two door or four door
performance sedan.
With a 5/50 protection plan.
An affordable price.
And an insatiable appetite for the sheer thrill
of driving.
The new Dodge Shadow
is going to cast a giant shadow
across America.

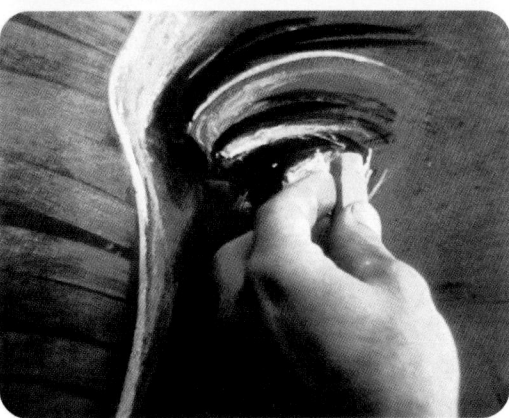

147
DISTINCTIVE MERIT
ART DIRECTOR
Gene Mandarino, Bob Watson
WRITER
Cheryl Berman, Gene Mandarino,
Joe DeVivo
CLIENT
McDonald's
DIRECTOR
Joe Pytka
AGENCY
Leo Burnett, Chicago, IL
PRODUCER
Stuart Kramer, Dave Musial, Mike
Diednich, Bob Koslow
CREATIVE DIRECTOR
Bud Watts, Cheryl Berman, Jack
Smith

148
DISTINCTIVE MERIT
ART DIRECTOR
Tony LaMonte, Len McCarron
WRITER
Phil Dusenberry, Ted Sann, Charlie
Miesmer, Michael Shevack
CLIENT
Apple Computer, Inc.
EDITOR
David Dee, Steve Schreiber
DIRECTOR
Steve Horn, Fred Petermann
AGENCY
BBDO, New York, NY
PRODUCER
Barbara Mullins, Karl Fischer, Vicki
Halliday, Katy O'Brien, Andy
Chinich
PRODUCTION COMPANY
Petermann-Dektor/Steve Horn, New
York & Los Angeles

147

SILENT PERSUASION/RECITAL/GOLDEN TIME
60-second
(MUSIC)
GUY: Surf's up, Lisa.
(MUSIC)
GAL: C'mon you know it's exam time.
GUY: Can't you just smell the sea air?
GAL: Cut it out.
GUY: We could stop on the way for a
Big Mac,
fries,
and an icy Coke.
GAL: I'll get my bike.
SING: It's a good time
For the great taste
Of McDonald's
GAL: Tommy, you really have a way with words.

148

LEFT BRAIN, RIGHT BRAIN/PUT MAC IN/POWER IMAGE
60-second
(SFX)
Imagine a brain who's left side is as brilliant as its right.
A brain as artistic as it is logical. That can calculate and create. Such a
brain exists in the remarkable new Apple II GS.
Brilliant graphics.
Brilliant color.
Brilliant sound.
(SFX)
To help you use both sides of the most personal computer of all.
Your mind.

149
DISTINCTIVE MERIT

DESIGNER
Gary Gutierrez
WRITER
Steven Wright
CLIENT
Warner Brothers Records, Inc.
EDITOR
Susan Crutcher
DIRECTOR
Gary Gutierrez
DIRECTOR OF PHOTOGRAPHY
Rick Fichter
PRODUCTION COMPANY
Colossal Pictures, San Francisco, CA
PRODUCER
Whitney Green, Chris Whitney

150
DISTINCTIVE MERIT

DESIGNER
Eric Jacobson
WRITER
John Miller, Bob Bibb, Eric
Jacobson, Joseph Shields
CLIENT
National Broadcasting Company
EDITOR
Stowell Werden
DIRECTOR
Michel Lichtenstein
DIRECTOR OF PHOTOGRAPHY
Rolf Kesterman
PRODUCER/AGENCY
Eric Jacobson, National
Broadcasting Company, Burbank,
CA
PRODUCTION COMPANY
Bongiovanni/Anlauf Productions
CREATIVE DIRECTOR
John Miller
MUSIC
HEA Productions

149

I HAVE A PONY
4:21-minute
FLASHCUBE VIGNETTE:
SFX ONLY
MUSEUM VIGNETTE:
VENDOR: Can I help you?
MAN (WRIGHT): Yeah, do you have anything I would like?
VENDOR: How do I know what you like?
WRIGHT: You started it.
CROWD: Hey, there he is.
VENDOR: Here, hey!
WRIGHT: Thanks.
VENDOR: That's two dollars.
CROWD: Hey, wait a minute (etc. etc.).
VENDOR: He just stole my hot dog (etc.).
CROWD: Wait a minute (etc.).
BBQ VIGNETTE:
WRIGHT: Last time I went to the movies, I was thrown out for
bringing my own food in. My argument was that
concession stand prices were outrageous.
QUICKSAND VIGNETTE:
WRIGHT: It was always sunny where I grew up, as you can see
in these pictures. When I was little, in our
backyard we had a quicksand box. I was an only
child eventually.
SUSPICIOUS VIGNETTE:
COP: What the hell are you doing around here?

150

COME HOME TO NBC
3-minute
(MUSIC AND THEME PIECE SONG)
PIANO INTRO
Mm-Mm
Had a day of it
Come on home
There's a place
Where your friends are always
Waitin' for you
Make a night of it
Come on home
Take a load off and
Make yourself at
Home is where you
love to be
Home with friends and
family
We've got all you want to see
Home on NBC
Come on home
Come on home . . .
America
From sea to
shining sea
Come on home
Come on home

151
DISTINCTIVE MERIT

DESIGNER
Bob Bibb
ANIMATOR
Pittman Films
WRITER
Bob Bibb
CLIENT
National Broadcasting Company
EDITOR
Tony Lopez
DIRECTOR
Bob Bibb
PRODUCTION COMPANY
NBC Network Advertising &
Promotion, Burbank, CA
MUSIC
Christopher Stone

152
DISTINCTIVE MERIT

ART DIRECTOR
Becky Shaeffer
DESIGNER
George Booth
ANIMATOR
George Booth
WRITER
Ann Olson
CLIENT
George A. Hormel & Co.
EDITOR
Dan Rounds
PRODUCER/AGENCY
Jim Lacey, BBDO, Minneapolis, MN
PRODUCTION COMPANY
Reelworks
CREATIVE DIRECTOR
George Hermelink

151

THE NBC STORY
8-minute, 15-second
(MUSIC IS ALWAYS PLAYING)
MUSIC
(VARIOUS IDENTIFIABLE NBC PERFORMERS)
VO: (SARNOFF) I have in mind a plan which would make radio a
household utility in the same sense as a piano or a phonograph. The idea
is to bring music into the house by wireless. The sale of these radio/music
boxes could yield a handsome profit.
VO: (SARNOFF) Let us create a separate and distinct company known as
the National Radio Broadcasting Company.
Today the National Broadcasting Company will begin the first television
program service in the history of our country.

152

MONSTER
30-second
SFX: CROWD MUMBLING.
VO: Ah excuse me, did you know that Light & Lean ham not only tastes
great, it's low in calories.
CARTOON CHARACTERS (ALL AT ONCE): What?! No way. Com' on! Forget
it. Oh com' on! You gotta be kidding! I don't believe it, no way. Ah . . .

Buster Brown and his dog Tige were famous
cartoon characters in their day. R. F. Outcault,
the creator of the first newspaper comic, the
Yellow Kid, launched Buster Brown in 1902
in the New York Herald. Outcault really went to
town merchandising his character. He set up a
booth at the 1904 St. Louis World's Fair and
sold rights to Buster to anyone willing to pay
the fee. The next few years saw Buster Brown
soap, socks, coffee, flour, harmonicas, apples
and shoes—more than fifty different Buster
Brown products.

The Brown Shoe Company of St. Louis was a
natural. The company promoted its shoes with
touring midget-Busters, who put on shows in
shoe stores, theaters and department stores
between 1904 and 1930. Smilin' Ed
McConnell brought the character and the
shoes to radio in 1943 and to television in
1951.

Buster Brown shoes are still widely advertised
and sold.

NEWSPAPER ADVERTISING:

B&W: half page or less
more than half,
up to including full page
more than full page
campaign
Color: full page or less
more than full page
campaign
Public service: single
campaign
Section, insert, supplement: b&w or color

153

ART DIRECTOR
Woody Kay
DESIGNER
Woody Kay, Doreen Velmer
PHOTOGRAPHER
Ira Garber
WRITER
Ernie Schenck
CLIENT
Blue Cross of Rhode Island
PUBLISHER
Providence Journal
AGENCY
Leonard Monahan Saabye, Providence, RI
PRINTER
Rand

154

ART DIRECTOR
Young & Laramore
DESIGNER
Rob Day
WRITER
Kevin Sutton
CLIENT
Johnson County Memorial Hospital
AGENCY
Young & Laramore, Indianapolis, IN
PUBLICATION
Daily Journal, Franklin, Indiana

155

ART DIRECTOR
Jac Coverdale
PHOTOGRAPHER
Jim Arndt
WRITER
Jerry Fury
CLIENT
YMCA - Metro
AGENCY
Clarity Coverdale Rueff Advertising,
Minneapolis, MN

156

ART DIRECTOR
Gary Greenberg
DESIGNER
Gary Greenberg
PHOTOGRAPHER
Carol Kaplan
WRITER
Tom O'Connor
CLIENT
Pilgrim Health Care
AGENCY
Rossin, Greenberg, Seronick & Hill
DESIGN FIRM
Rossin, Greenberg, Seronick & Hill, Boston,
MA
PUBLICATION
Quincy Patriot Ledger

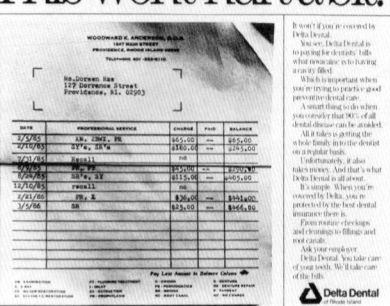

153

155

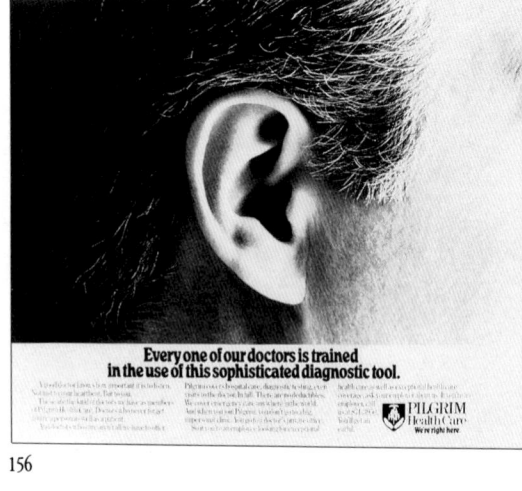

156

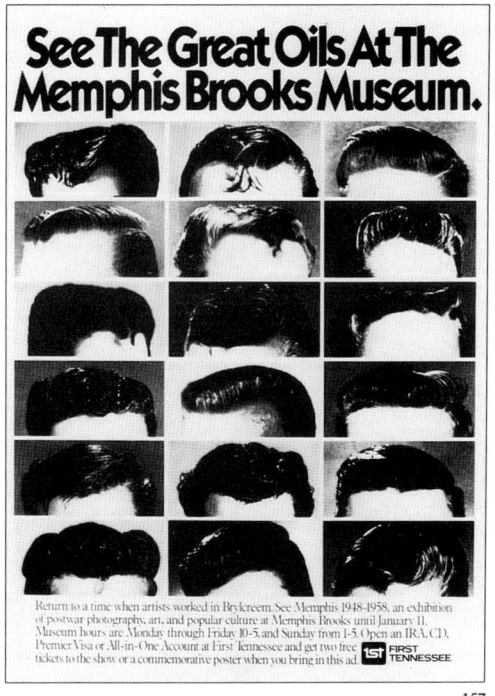

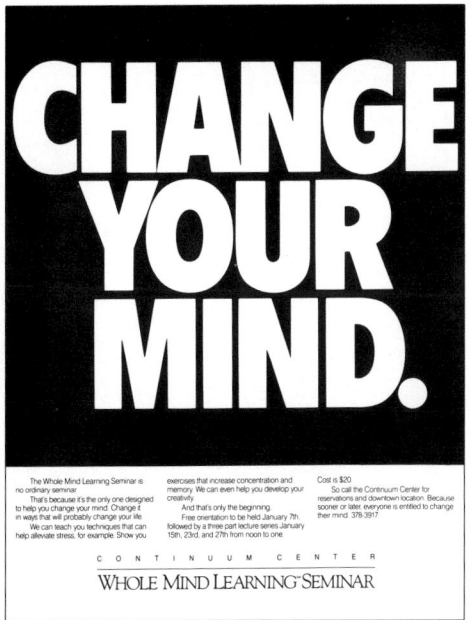

157

ART DIRECTOR
Dean Hanson
WRITER
Jarl Olsen
CLIENT
First Tennessee
AGENCY
Fallon McElligott, Minneapolis, MN

158

ART DIRECTOR
David Peterson
DESIGNER
David Peterson
WRITER
Virg Viner
CLIENT
University of Minnesota Continuum Center
AGENCY
Campbell-Mithun, Inc., Minneapolis, MN

158

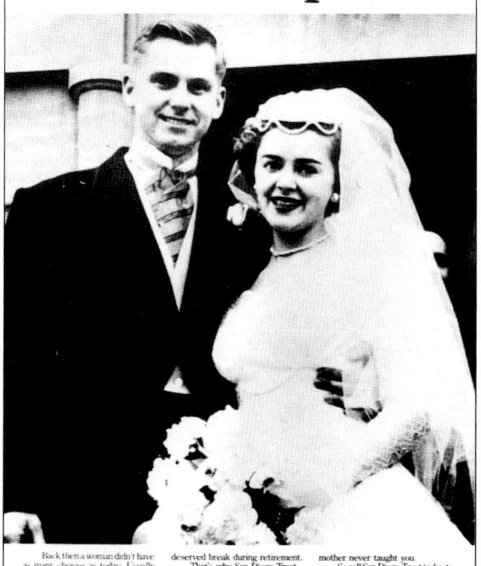

159

ART DIRECTOR
Corey Stolberg
DESIGNER
Corey Stolberg
PHOTOGRAPHER
Bettmann Archive
WRITER
Jill Easton
CLIENT
San Diego Trust & Savings
AGENCY
Phillips-Ramsey, San Diego, CA
PRODUCER
Ron Van Buskirk
PUBLICATION
San Diego Union Tribune

160

159

160

ART DIRECTOR
John Lionti
DESIGNER
John Lionti
WRITER
Laura Owen
CLIENT
AmeriTrust
AGENCY
Liggett-Stashower, Cleveland, OH

161
ART DIRECTOR
Rod Smith
DESIGNER
Rod Smith
PHOTOGRAPHER
Linc Cornell
WRITER
Fred Bertino
CLIENT
James Brown Paint
AGENCY
Smith/Bertino, Boston, MA

162
ART DIRECTOR
Joseph Stryker
DESIGNER
Joseph Stryker
ILLUSTRATOR/ARTIST
John Maggard
WRITER
Marc Harty
CLIENT
Fifth Third Bank
AGENCY
Northlich, Stolley, Inc., Cincinnati, OH

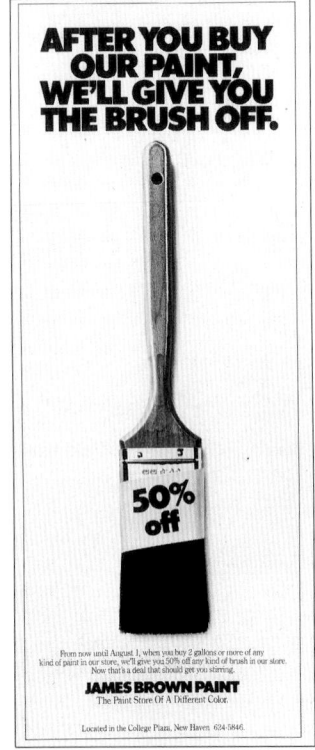

161

162

163
ART DIRECTOR
Pam Conboy
DESIGNER
Pam Conboy
ILLUSTRATOR/ARTIST
Leland Klanderman
WRITER
Lyle Wedemeyer
CLIENT
Skipper's Restaurants
AGENCY
Martin/Williams, Minneapolis, MN

163

164

164
ART DIRECTOR
Rob Dalton
ILLUSTRATOR/ARTIST
Rob Dalton
WRITER
Jamie Barrett
CLIENT
Murray's
AGENCY
Fallon McElligott, Minneapolis, MN

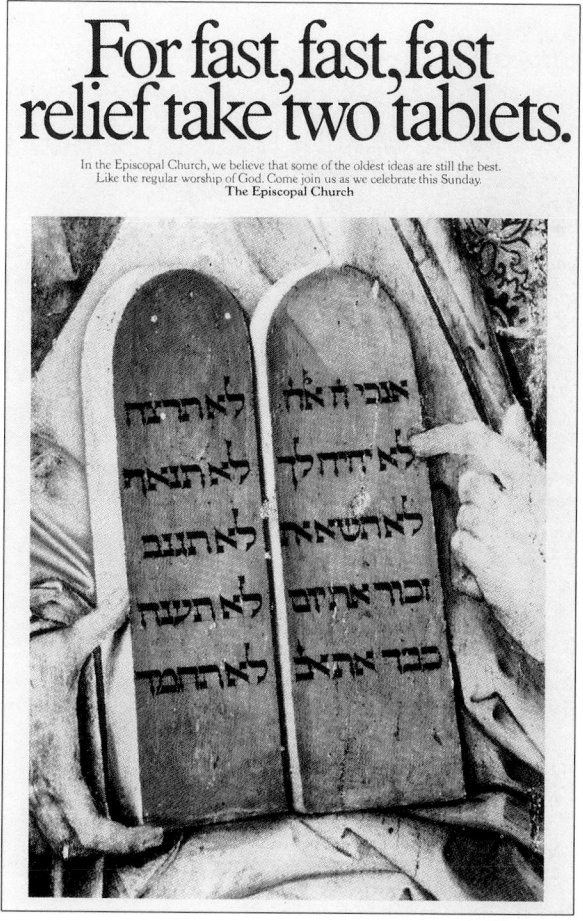

For fast, fast, fast relief take two tablets.

In the Episcopal Church, we believe that some of the oldest ideas are still the best.
Like the regular worship of God. Come join us as we celebrate this Sunday.
The Episcopal Church

165

Are your kids learning about the power of the cross on the late, late show?

With all due regard to Hollywood, there's more to Christianity than stopping vampires. Come with your children
to the Episcopal Church this Sunday as we celebrate the resurrection of Jesus Christ in love and fellowship.
The Episcopal Church

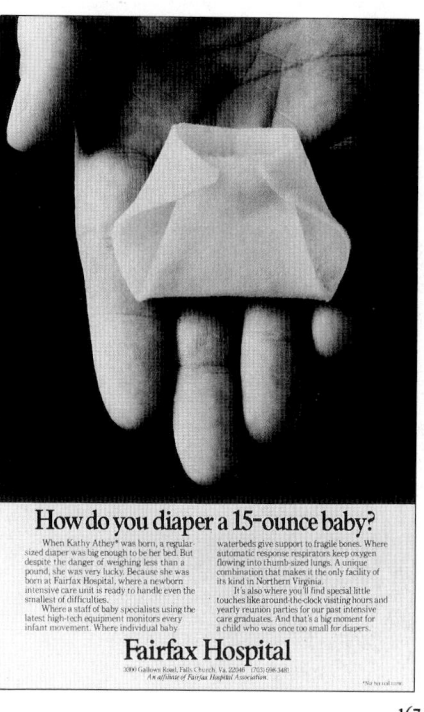

How do you diaper a 15-ounce baby?

When Kathy Athey* was born, a regular-sized diaper was big enough to be her bed. But despite the danger of weighing less than a pound, she was very lucky. Because she was born at Fairfax Hospital, where a newborn intensive care unit is ready to handle even the smallest of difficulties.

Where a staff of baby specialists using the latest high-tech equipment monitors every infant movement. Where individual baby waterbeds give support to fragile bones. Where automatic response respirators keep oxygen flowing into thumb-sized lungs. A unique combination that makes it the only facility of its kind in Northern Virginia.

It's also where you'll find special little touches like around-the-clock visiting hours and yearly reunion parties for our past intensive care graduates. And that's a big moment for a child who was once too small for diapers.

Fairfax Hospital

3300 Gallows Road, Falls Church, Va. 22046   (703) 698-3400
An affiliate of Fairfax Hospital Association.

*Not her real name.

166

167

165
ART DIRECTOR
Dean Hanson
ILLUSTRATOR/ARTIST
Josse Van Ghent
WRITER
Tom McElligott
CLIENT
Episcopal Ad Project
AGENCY
Fallon McElligott, Minneapolis, MN

166
ART DIRECTOR
Dean Hanson
PHOTOGRAPHER
Collection of Dr. Thomas G. Aylesworth
WRITER
Tom McElligott
CLIENT
Episcopal Ad Project
AGENCY
Fallon McElligott, Minneapolis, MN

167
ART DIRECTOR
Jim Spruell
PHOTOGRAPHER
David Sharpe
WRITER
John Sullivan, Terry Coveny
CLIENT
Fairfax Hospital
AGENCY
Abramson Associates, Inc., Washington, DC
PUBLICATION
Washington Post
CREATIVE DIRECTOR
Terry Coveny

168
ART DIRECTOR
Rob Dalton
PHOTOGRAPHER
Eric Saulitis
WRITER
Rod Kilpatrick
CLIENT
The Wall St. Journal
AGENCY
Fallon McElligott, Minneapolis, MN

169
ART DIRECTOR
Tom Lichtenheld
PHOTOGRAPHER
Tom Bach/Marvy
WRITER
Rod Kilpatrick
CLIENT
The Wall St. Journal
AGENCY
Fallon McElligott, Minneapolis, MN

170
ART DIRECTOR
Tom Lichtenheld
PHOTOGRAPHER
Lars Hansen
ILLUSTRATOR/ARTIST
Oasis, Eric Hanson, Jack Malloy
WRITER
Rod Kilpatrick
CLIENT
The Wall St. Journal
AGENCY
Fallon McElligott, Minneapolis, MN

171
ART DIRECTOR
Bob Barrie
ILLUSTRATOR/ARTIST
Bob Barrie
WRITER
Phil Hanft
CLIENT
Minnesota Zoo
AGENCY
Fallon McElligott, Minneapolis, MN

168

169

170

171

172

ART DIRECTOR
Bill Murphy
WRITER
Margaret Wilcox
CLIENT
The Boston Globe
AGENCY
Hill, Holliday, Boston, MA
PUBLICATION
The Boston Globe

173

ART DIRECTOR
Bob Barrie
ILLUSTRATOR/ARTIST
Bob Blewett
WRITER
Phil Hanft
CLIENT
Minnesota Zoo
AGENCY
Fallon McElligott, Minneapolis, MN

173

172

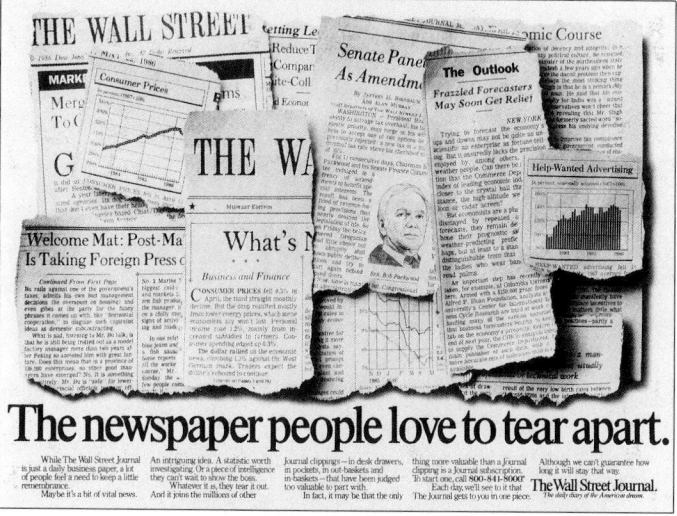

174

ART DIRECTOR
Tom Lichtenheld
PHOTOGRAPHER
Tom Bach/Marvy
WRITER
Rod Kilpatrick
CLIENT
The Wall Street Journal
AGENCY
Fallon McElligott, Minneapolis, MN

175

ART DIRECTOR
Tom Lichtenheld
PHOTOGRAPHER
Tom Bach/Marvy
WRITER
Rod Kilpatrick
AGENCY
Fallon McElligott, Minneapolis, MN

176

175

176

ART DIRECTOR
Bob Barrie
WRITER
Mike Lescarbeau
CLIENT
Mountain Chiropractic
AGENCY
Fallon McElligott, Minneapolis, MN

177
ART DIRECTOR
Martin Schaus, Jeff Abbott
PHOTOGRAPHER
Charles J. Vendetti
WRITER
Jeff Abbott, Martin Schaus
CLIENT
Ted's Giant Grinders
AGENCY
Glory Hounds, Ltd., Birmingham, MI

178
ART DIRECTOR
Martin Schaus, Jeff Abbott
PHOTOGRAPHER
Charles J. Vendetti
WRITER
Martin Schaus, Jeff Abbott
CLIENT
Ted's Giant Grinders
AGENCY
Glory Hounds, Ltd., Birmingham, MI

179
ART DIRECTOR
Jeff Abbott, Martin Schaus
PHOTOGRAPHER
Charles J. Vendetti
WRITER
Jeff Abbott, Martin Schaus
CLIENT
Ted's Giant Grinders
AGENCY
Glory Hounds, Ltd., Birmingham, MI

180
ART DIRECTOR
Lars Anderson
DESIGNER
Lars Anderson
PHOTOGRAPHER
Larry C. Morris
WRITER
Earl Carter
CLIENT
Nikon Corporation
AGENCY
Scali, McCabe, Sloves, New York, NY

181
ART DIRECTOR
Warren Johnson
ILLUSTRATOR/ARTIST
Alex Boies
WRITER
Phil Calvit, Nancy Wellinger
CLIENT
Hotel Sofitel Miami
AGENCY
Carmichael-Lynch, Minneapolis, MN
CREATIVE DIRECTOR
Harry Beckwith

177

178

179

180

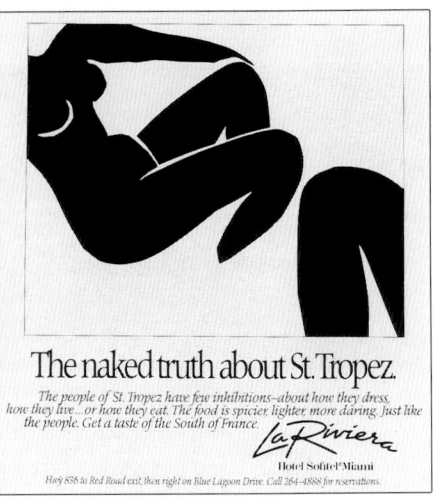

181

How long has it been since you really understood telecommunications?

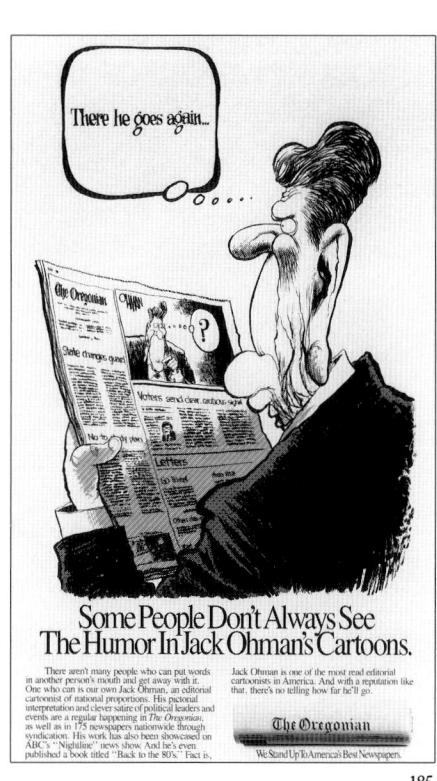

Like many businesspeople, you may have fallen a bit behind in your efforts to keep pace with communications technology.

But on Monday, February 24th, you'll have a rare opportunity to catch up. "Telecommunications," a Wall Street Journal special report.

This extraordinarily useful report not only examines the latest developments in technology. It also investigates how those developments are changing the way business does business.

If your job has anything at all to do with phones, don't miss

"Telecommunications." It will be included free of charge in your subscription or newsstand copy of The Wall Street Journal on Monday, February 24th.

Once you've read it, telecommunications will be child's play. Again.

The Wall Street Journal.
The daily diary of the American dream.

182

ART DIRECTOR
Kathy Sjogren
PHOTOGRAPHER
Christopher Makos
WRITER
Bob Gerke
CLIENT
California Plaza
AGENCY
DJMC, Inc., Los Angeles, CA
CREATIVE DIRECTOR
Peter Coutroulis

183

ART DIRECTOR
Rob Dalton
PHOTOGRAPHER
Kent Severson
WRITER
Rod Kilpatrick
CLIENT
The Wall St. Journal
AGENCY
Fallon McElligott, Minneapolis, MN

183

We Employ More Bozos, Buffoons, Jokesters And Weirdos Than Most Other Newspapers.

Comics are a serious business at *The Oregonian.* Every weekday we devote two full pages to today's best comic strips. You get a much broader selection than most other newspapers offer. And that's nothing to laugh at. Especially if you take comics as seriously as we do.

The Oregonian
We Stand Up To America's Best Newspapers.

182

Some People Don't Always See The Humor In Jack Ohman's Cartoons.

There aren't many people who can put words in another person's mouth and get away with it. One who can is our own Jack Ohman, an editorial cartoonist of national proportions. His pictorial interpretation and clever satire of political leaders and events are a regular happening in *The Oregonian,* as well as in 175 newspapers nationwide through syndication. His work has also been showcased on ABC's "Nightline" news show. And he's even published a book titled "Back to the 80's." Fact is,

Jack Ohman is one of the most read editorial cartoonists in America. And with a reputation like that, there's no telling how far he'll go.

The Oregonian
We Stand Up To America's Best Newspapers.

184

ART DIRECTOR
Ted Gornick
ILLUSTRATOR/ARTIST
Various
DESIGNER
Becky Garvey
WRITER
Steve Lachman
CLIENT
The Oregonian
AGENCY
Morton/Cole & Weber, Portland, OR
CREATIVE DIRECTOR
Bill Casale

185

ART DIRECTOR
Becky Garvey
DESIGNER
Becky Garvey
ILLUSTRATOR/ARTIST
Jack Ohman
WRITER
Steve Lachman
CLIENT
The Oregonian
PUBLISHER
The Oregonian
AGENCY
Morton/Cole & Weber, Portland, OR
CREATIVE DIRECTOR
Bill Casale

184   185

186

ART DIRECTOR
Don Harbor
DESIGNER
Don Harbor
PHOTOGRAPHER
Steve Bronstein/Big City Productions
WRITER
Rebecca Flora
CLIENT
Norfolk General Hospital
AGENCY
Lawler Ballard Advertising, Norfolk, VA

187

ART DIRECTOR
Jerry Gentile
PHOTOGRAPHER
Chuck Kuhn
WRITER
Barbara DeSantis
CLIENT
Cigna Healthplan
AGENCY
DDB Needham Worldwide Inc., Los Angeles,
CA
PRODUCER
Paul Newman
PUBLICATION
Shreveport Times
CREATIVE DIRECTOR
Bob Kuperman

188

ART DIRECTOR
Irv Klein
DESIGNER
Irv Klein
WRITER
Stephanie Arnold
CLIENT
New York Air
AGENCY
Levine, Huntley, Schmidt & Beaver, New
York, NY

186

187

188

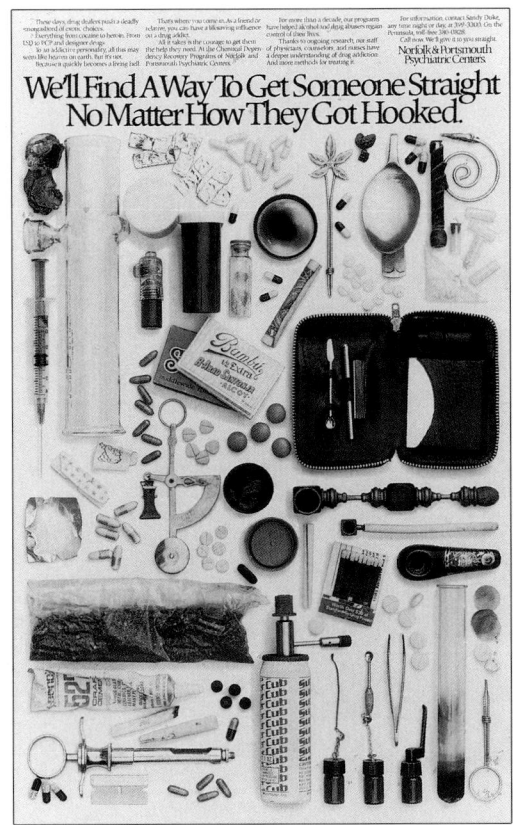

189

189
ART DIRECTOR
Cabell Harris
PHOTOGRAPHER
Pat Edwards
WRITER
Ken Hines
CLIENT
First Hospital
AGENCY
Lawler Ballard Advertising, Richmond, VA

190
ART DIRECTOR
Michael Fazende
PHOTOGRAPHER
David Langley
WRITER
John Stingley
CLIENT
Marine Midland Automotive Financial
AGENCY
Fallon McElligott, Minneapolis, MN

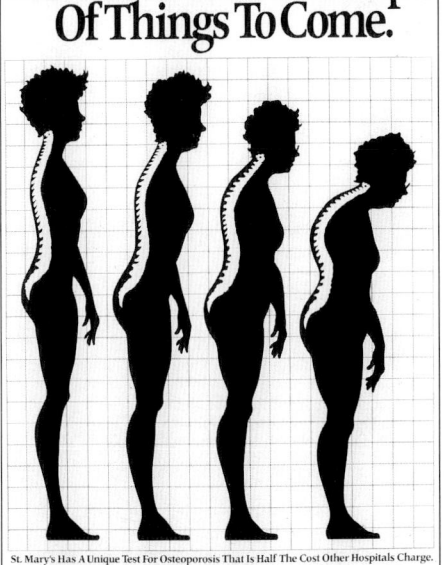

191

190

191
ART DIRECTOR
George Fugate, Kelly O'Keefe
DESIGNER
George Fugate
ILLUSTRATOR/ARTIST
Scott Wright
WRITER
George Fugate
CLIENT
St. Mary's Hospital
AGENCY
Redmond Fugate Amundson Rice & Ross,
Richmond, VA
PRODUCER
Joy Gibrall

192

ART DIRECTOR
Terry Schneider
PHOTOGRAPHER
C.B. Harding
WRITER
Greg Eiden
CLIENT
Zell Bros
AGENCY
Borders, Perrin & Norrander, Inc., Portland,
OR
CREATIVE DIRECTOR
Bill Borders

192

193

ART DIRECTOR
Tom Lichtenheld
PHOTOGRAPHER
Peter B. Kaplan
WRITER
Bruce Bildsten
CLIENT
The Wall St. Journal
AGENCY
Fallon McElligott, Minneapolis, MN

193

  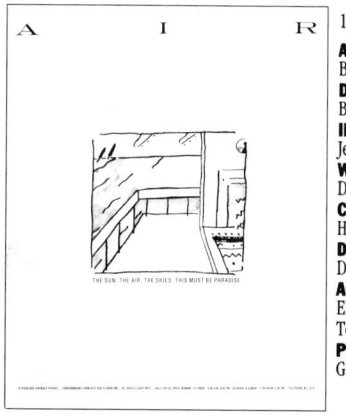

194

ART DIRECTOR
Baiba Black
DESIGNER
Baiba Black
ILLUSTRATOR/ARTIST
Jeff Jackson
WRITER
David Mills
CLIENT
Harbour Terrace
DIRECTOR
David Mills
AGENCY
Elias Marketing & Communications,
Toronto, Canada
PUBLICATION
Globe & Mail

194

195

ART DIRECTOR
Dion Hitchings
DESIGNER
Dion Hitchings
PHOTOGRAPHER
Just Loomis
ILLUSTRATOR/ARTIST
Tim Girvin - (Logotype)
WRITER
Eileen Newman
CLIENT
Bloomingdale's
AGENCY
Bloomingdale's Advertising, New York, NY
PUBLICATION
New York Times
CREATIVE DIRECTOR
John C. Jay

195

196

ART DIRECTOR
Harvey Baron, Ron Louie
DESIGNER
Harvey Baron, Ron Louie
ILLUSTRATOR/ARTIST
Charles Addams, Charles Saxon, Gahan
Wilson
WRITER
John Noble, Patty Volk Blitzer
CLIENT
Audi
AGENCY
DDB Needham Worldwide, Inc, New York, NY
PUBLICATION
Wall Street Journal

196

197

ART DIRECTOR
Scott Eggers
DESIGNER
Curtis Asplund
ILLUSTRATOR/ARTIST
Curtis Asplund
WRITER
Owen Page
CLIENT
Plate & Platter
AGENCY
197 Knape & Knape, Dallas, TX

198

ART DIRECTOR
Chris Conerly
ILLUSTRATOR/ARTIST
David McKelvey
WRITER
Leslie Westlake
CLIENT
Sawgrass Beach Resort
AGENCY
Austin Kelley Advertising, Atlanta, GA

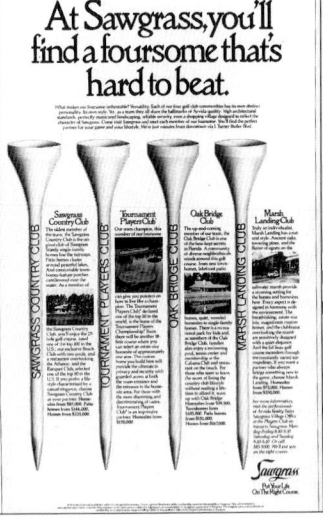

198

199

ART DIRECTOR
Bob Barrie
WRITER
Mike Lescarbeau
CLIENT
American Medcenters
AGENCY
Fallon McElligott, Minneapolis, MN

200

ART DIRECTOR
Sally Oelschlager
PHOTOGRAPHER
Mark LaFavor
WRITER
Jack Supple
CLIENT
Minnesota Office of Tourism
AGENCY
Carmichael-Lynch, Minneapolis, MN
CREATIVE DIRECTOR
Jack Supple

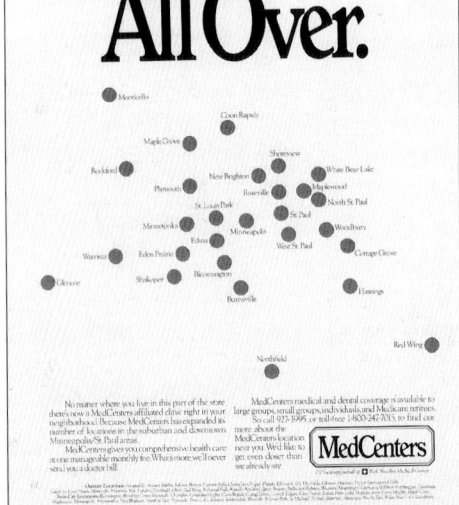

199

200

201

ART DIRECTOR
Paul Jervis
PHOTOGRAPHER
Harry DeZitter
WRITER
Roger Feuerman
CLIENT
Paddington Corp. - Baileys Irish Cream
AGENCY
Backer & Spielvogel, New York, NY

201

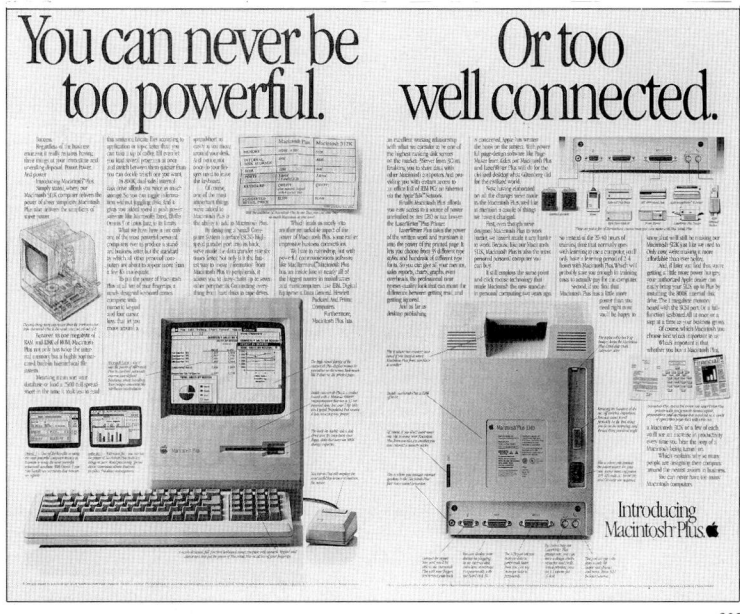

202

202
ART DIRECTOR
John Morrison, Marten Tonnis
PHOTOGRAPHER
Bo Hylen
ILLUSTRATOR/ARTIST
Kathy O'Brien, Jonathan Wright
WRITER
Penny Kapousouz, Steve Rabosky
CLIENT
Apple Computer, Inc.
AGENCY
Chiat/Day Advertising, Los Angeles, CA
PUBLICATION
USA Today

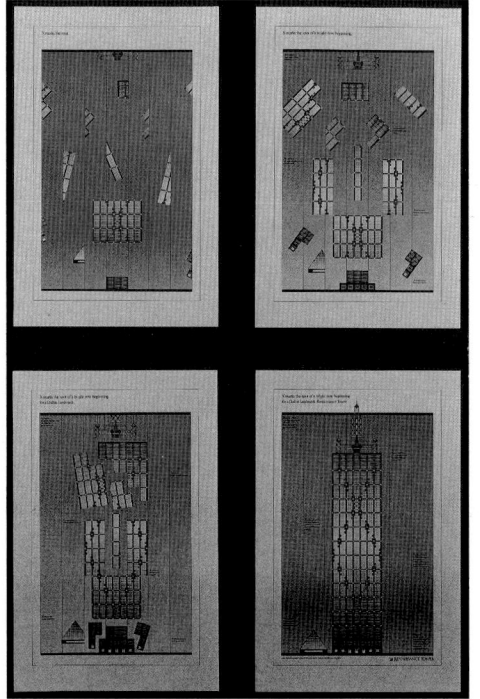

203

204

203
ART DIRECTOR
Rex Peteet
DESIGNER
Rex Peteet
ILLUSTRATOR/ARTIST
Rex Peteet, Penelope Rowland
WRITER
Rex Peteet
CLIENT
LaSalle Partners/Renaissance Tower
DESIGN FIRM
Sibley/Peteet Design, Dallas, TX

204
ART DIRECTOR
Rex Peteet
DESIGNER
Rex Peteet
ILLUSTRATOR/ARTIST
Rex Peteet, Penelope Rowland, Don Roy
WRITER
Rex Peteet
CLIENT
Herring Marathon Group
DESIGN FIRM
Sibley/Peteet Design, Dallas, TX

205

ART DIRECTOR
Warren Eakins
DESIGNER
Warren Eakins
ILLUSTRATOR/ARTIST
George Cheney
WRITER
Bill Borders, Gary Cox
CLIENT
Burgerville USA
AGENCY
Borders, Perrin & Norrander, Inc., Portland.
OR
CREATIVE DIRECTOR
Bill Borders
SPECIAL EFFECTS
True Vistas

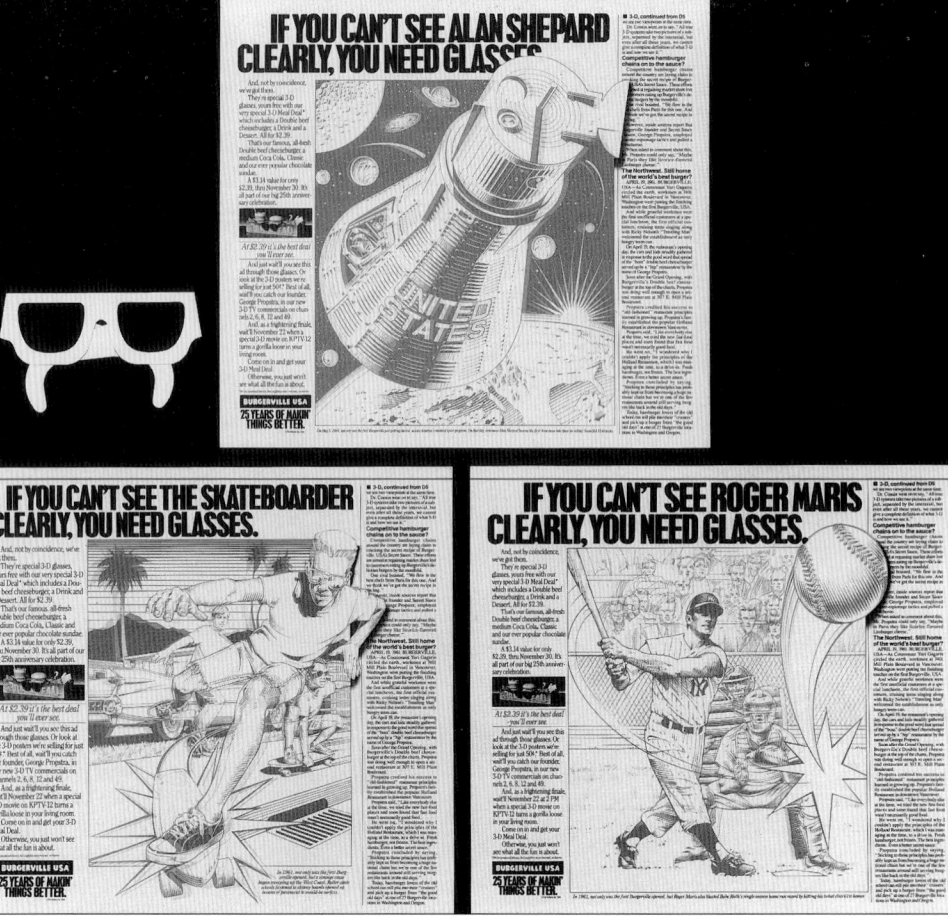

205

206

ART DIRECTOR
Scott Mayeda
DESIGNER
Scott Mayeda
ILLUSTRATOR/ARTIST
Randy Verougstraete
WRITER
David Santiago
CLIENT
Pinery Tree Farms
AGENCY
Wise Communications, San Diego, CA
PUBLICATION
Union-Tribune
ACCOUNT MANAGER
Caren Goldman

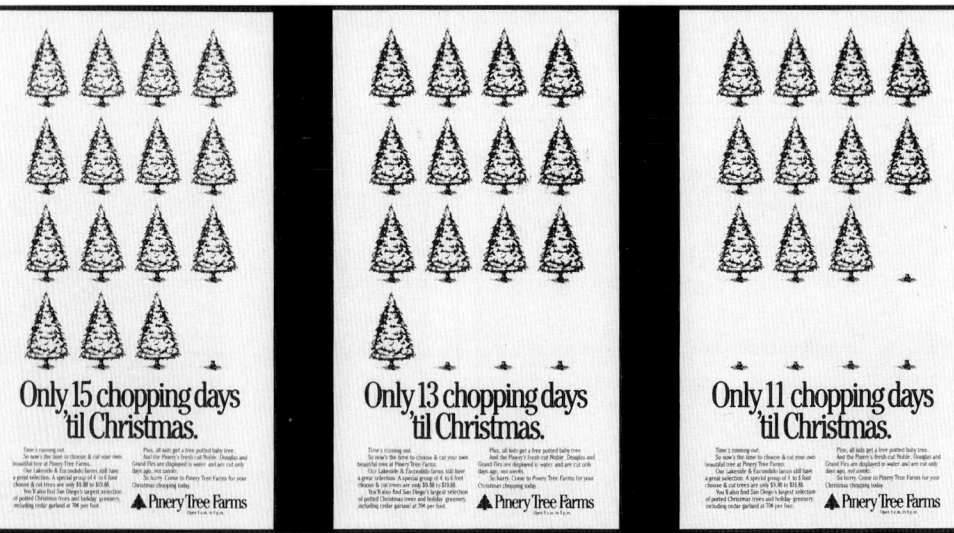

206

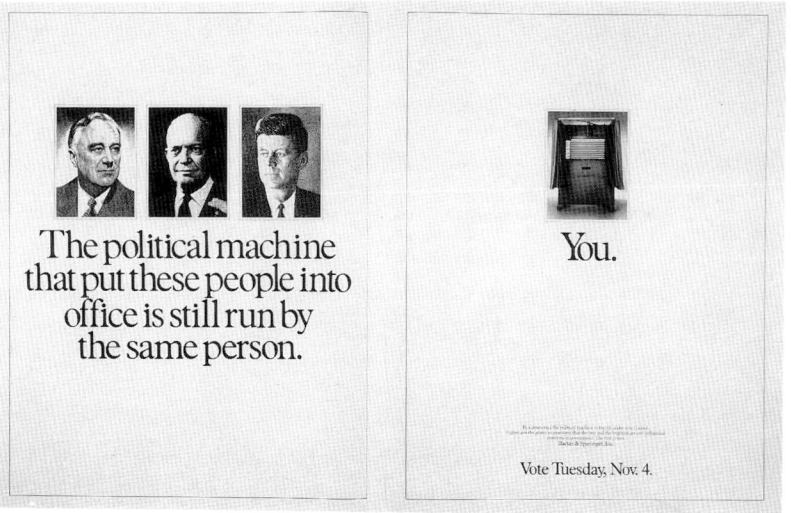

207

207
ART DIRECTOR
Paul Jervis
PHOTOGRAPHER
Gary Perweiler
WRITER
Roger Feuerman
AGENCY
Backer & Spielvogel, New York, NY

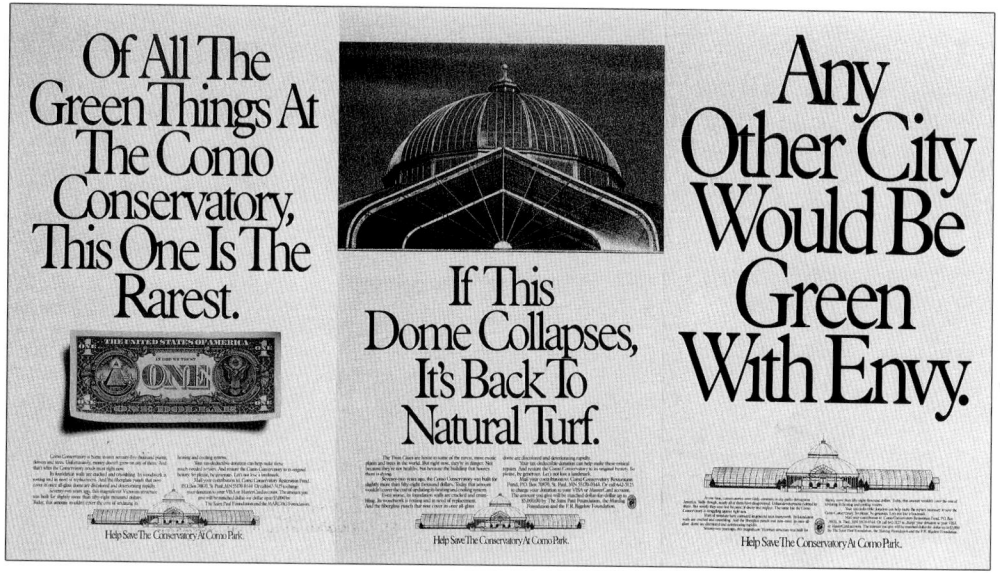

208

208
ART DIRECTOR
Mike Murray
DESIGNER
Mike Murray
PHOTOGRAPHER
Eric Saulitis, "Rarest"
ILLUSTRATOR/ARTIST
Ron Finger
WRITER
John Francis
CLIENT
Como Park Conservatory
AGENCY
Bozell, Jacobs, Kenyon & Eckhardt,
Minneapolis, MN
PUBLICATION
St. Paul Pioneer Press

209

209
ART DIRECTOR
John C. Jay
DESIGNER
John C. Jay
PHOTOGRAPHER
Herb Ritts
ILLUSTRATOR/ARTIST
Tim Girvin - (Logotype)
WRITER
Chris Rockmore, Cynthia Rittenhouse
CLIENT
Bloomingdale's
AGENCY
Bloomingdale's Advertising, New York, NY

According to two surveys in recent years, more people recognize Mr. Clean than the Vice President of the United States. Created in 1959, this unlikely hero has fought valiantly in the battle against dirt. As a mad, "grimefighting" policeman he arrested the dirt problem. As the "New Mean Mr. Clean," he turned into a two-fisted dirt buster who knocked out grime. He has grown whiskers for brute strength, had black eyes to show floor "shiners" and testified in court against dirt. Today, he is still going strong on the bottle whose broad top and tapered base bear a strong resemblance to Mr. Clean's own physique. And he doesn't have a single gray hair.

MAGAZINE ADVERTISING:

Consumer: full page, b&w
spread, b&w
campaign, b&w
full page, color
spread, color
campaign, color
Public service: single
campaign
Business or trade: full page or less, b&w
campaign, b&w
full page or less, color
spread, color
Section, insert, supplement: b&w or color

210
ART DIRECTOR
John Follis, New York, NY
WRITER
Richard Kirshenbaum
CLIENT
Kenneth Cole
ACCOUNT EXEC.
Jon Bond

211
ART DIRECTOR
Mark Oliver
DESIGNER
Mark Oliver
ILLUSTRATOR/ARTIST
Mark Oliver
WRITER
Mark Oliver
CLIENT
Mark Oliver, Inc., Santa Barbara, CA

210

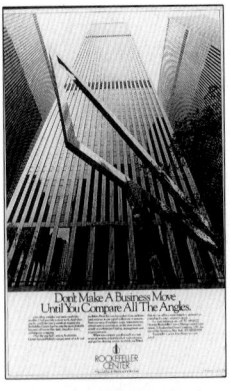

211

212
ART DIRECTOR
Tom Lichtenheld
PHOTOGRAPHER
Steve Umland
WRITER
Greg Beaupré
CLIENT
Murray's Restaurant
AGENCY
Fallon McElligott, Minneapolis, MN

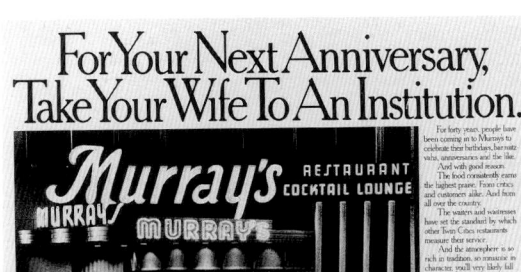

212

213
ART DIRECTOR
Jay Shields
PHOTOGRAPHER
Philip Vullo, Judy Lawne
WRITER
Jim Paddock
CLIENT
Rockefeller Center
AGENCY
Austin Kelley Advertising, Atlanta, GA

214
ART DIRECTOR
Susan Hoffman
PHOTOGRAPHER
Pete Stone
WRITER
Dan Wieden
CLIENT
Nike
AGENCY
Wieden & Kennedy, Portland, OR
PREP
Oregon Printing Plate

213

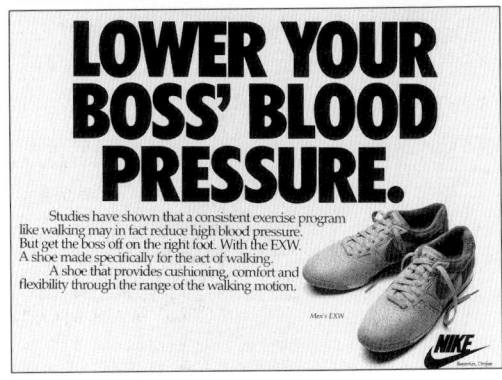

214

215

217

218

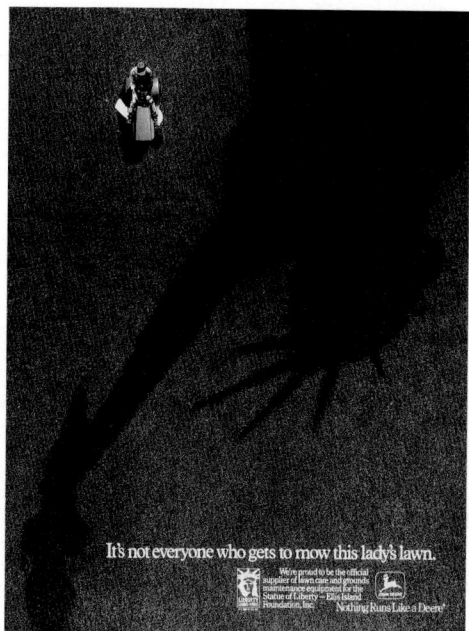

219

216

215

ART DIRECTOR
Paul Boley
PHOTOGRAPHER
Dewitt Jones-Studio Associates
WRITER
Richard Rand
CLIENT
Schenley/Dewars
AGENCY
Leo Burnett Co., Inc., Chicago, IL
CREATIVE DIRECTOR
John Eding

216

ART DIRECTOR
Joel Levinson
PHOTOGRAPHER
Andrew Unangst
WRITER
John Hurst
CLIENT
Hershey Foods Corp./Kisses
AGENCY
Ogilvy & Mather, New York, NY
PUBLICATION
People, Redbook, Reader's Digest, Women's
Day
CREATIVE DIRECTOR
Roy Tuck

217

ART DIRECTOR
James Caporimo
ILLUSTRATOR/ARTIST
R.O. Blechman
WRITER
James Caporimo, Francesca Blumenthal
CLIENT
Perrier Group of America
AGENCY
Waring & LaRosa Inc., New York, NY
PUBLICATION
Food & Wine
CREATIVE DIRECTOR
Joe LaRosa

218

ART DIRECTOR
Marty Weiss
PHOTOGRAPHER
Charles Purvis
WRITER
Ken Sandbank
CLIENT
Braun, Inc.
AGENCY
Lowe Marschalk, Inc., New York, NY

219

ART DIRECTOR
Ernie Cox
DESIGNER
Ernie Cox
PHOTOGRAPHER
Tim Bieber
WRITER
Jerry Craven
CLIENT
John Deere
AGENCY
N W Ayer, Inc., Chicago, IL
PUBLICATION
Time

220

ART DIRECTOR
Ron Louie
DESIGNER
Ron Louie
PHOTOGRAPHER
Neil Barr
WRITER
Dan Brooks
CLIENT
Gold Information Center
AGENCY
DDB Needham Worldwide, Inc., New York, NY

221

ART DIRECTOR
Rick Boyko
PHOTOGRAPHER
Gary McGuire
WRITER
Bill Hamilton
CLIENT
Nike, Inc.
AGENCY
Chiat/Day Advertising, Los Angeles, CA
PUBLICATION
World Tennis

222

ART DIRECTOR
Howard Rieger
WRITER
Lynn McGrath
CLIENT
Club Med
AGENCY
N W Ayer Inc., New York, NY

223

ART DIRECTOR
Tod Seisser
DESIGNER
Tod Seisser
PHOTOGRAPHER
Jerry Friedman
WRITER
Jay Taub
CLIENT
Seagram, Chateau and Estates, Perrier Jouet
AGENCY
Levine, Huntley, Schmidt & Beaver, New York, NY

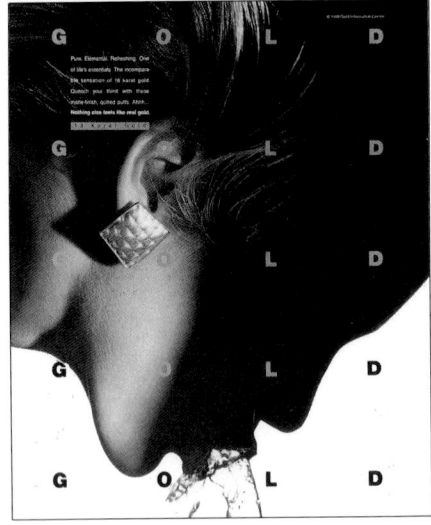

220

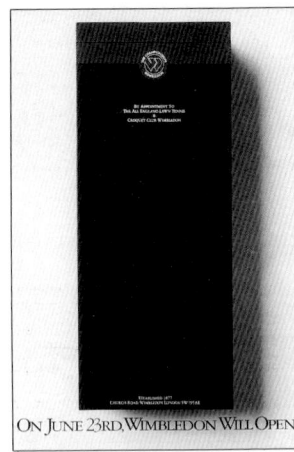

221

222

223

224

ART DIRECTOR
Geoff Hayes
PHOTOGRAPHER
Steve Bronstein
WRITER
Evert Cilliers
CLIENT
Carillon Importers Ltd.
DIRECTOR
Arnold Arlow, Peter Lubalin
AGENCY
TBWA, New York, NY

224

225

ART DIRECTOR
Susan Hoffman
PHOTOGRAPHER
Hank Benson
WRITER
Dan Wieden
CLIENT
Nike
AGENCY
Wieden & Kennedy, Portland, OR

225

226

ART DIRECTOR
Michael Winslow, Mark Oakley
PHOTOGRAPHER
Harry DeZitter
WRITER
Jan Karon
CLIENT
North Carolina Travel & Tourism
AGENCY
McKinney & Silver, Raleigh, NC

226

227

ART DIRECTOR
Mark Nussbaum
PHOTOGRAPHER
Michael Pateman
WRITER
Susan McFeatters
CLIENT
U S Army
AGENCY
N W Ayer Inc., New York, NY
CREATIVE DIRECTOR
Phil Peppis

227

228

ART DIRECTOR
Bruce Arendash
PHOTOGRAPHER
Hiro
WRITER
Michael Jordan
CLIENT
Larry Grunstein, Citizen Noblia Watch
AGENCY
SSC&B Inc., New York, NY
PUBLICATION
People
CREATIVE DIRECTOR
Lynn Giordano
ART SUPERVISOR
Phil Weiner
MAKE-UP ARTIST
Michael Thomas

228

229

ART DIRECTOR
Jud Smith
PHOTOGRAPHER
Marvy! Advertising Photography
WRITER
Jack Supple
CLIENT
3M Scientific Anglers
AGENCY
Carmichael-Lynch, Minneapolis, MN
CREATIVE DIRECTOR
Ron Sackett

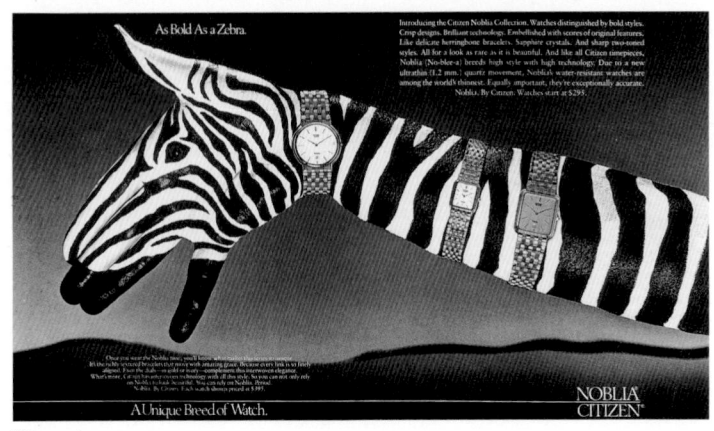

229

230

ART DIRECTOR
Bruce Arendash
PHOTOGRAPHER
Hiro
WRITER
Michael Jordan
CLIENT
Larry Grunstein, Citizen Noblia Watch
AGENCY
SSC&B Inc, New York, NY
PUBLICATION
People
CREATIVE DIRECTOR
Lynn Giordano
ART SUPERVISOR
Phil Weiner
MAKE-UP ARTIST
Michael Jordan

230

231

231
ART DIRECTOR
Joe Genova
DESIGNER
Joe Genova
PHOTOGRAPHER
Hal Davis
WRITER
Tony Chapman
CLIENT
Beiersdorf Inc.
AGENCY
Posey Quest Genova, Inc., Greenwich, CT

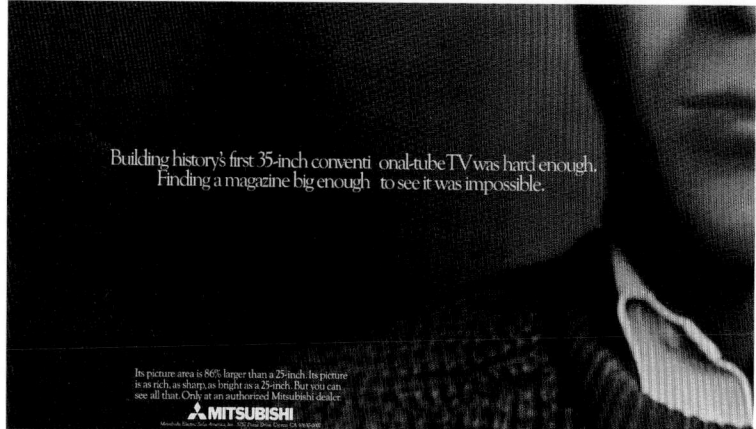

232

232
ART DIRECTOR
Rick Boyko
PHOTOGRAPHER
Dennis Manarchy
WRITER
Bill Hamilton
CLIENT
Mitsubishi Electric Sales America
AGENCY
Chiat/Day Advertising, Los Angeles, CA
PUBLICATION
Life

233

233
ART DIRECTOR
Tom Simons
PHOTOGRAPHER
Jay Maisel
WRITER
Rick Cohn
CLIENT
New England Life
AGENCY
Rizzo Simons Cohn, Boston, MA

234

234
ART DIRECTOR
David Kennedy
PHOTOGRAPHER
Harry DeZitter
WRITER
Dan Wieden
CLIENT
Nike
AGENCY
Wieden & Kennedy, Portland, OR

235

ART DIRECTOR
Tracy Wong
PHOTOGRAPHER
Chuck LaMonica
WRITER
Michael LaMonica
CLIENT
Swanson
AGENCY
Ogilvy & Mather, New York, NY
CREATIVE DIRECTOR
John Doig

236

ART DIRECTOR
Marten Tonnis
PHOTOGRAPHER
Bo Hylen
WRITER
Steve Rabosky
CLIENT
Mitsubishi Electric Sales America
AGENCY
Chiat/Day Advertising, Los Angeles, CA
PUBLICATION
Stereo Review

237

ART DIRECTOR
Raffael Altmann
PHOTOGRAPHER
Beth Galton
WRITER
Stanley Schulman, Eric Jensen
CLIENT
John Thorbeck, Timberland Shoes
AGENCY
SSC&B Inc., New York, NY
PUBLICATION
Field & Stream
CREATIVE DIRECTOR
Don Gill

238

ART DIRECTOR
Raffael Altmann
PHOTOGRAPHER
Beth Galton
WRITER
Eric Jensen
CLIENT
John Thorbeck, Timberland Boots
AGENCY
SSC&B Inc., New York, NY
PUBLICATION
Field & Stream
CREATIVE DIRECTOR
Don Gill

239

ART DIRECTOR
Lois Bender, Jeff Propper
PHOTOGRAPHER
Jim Galate
WRITER
Jane Adamo
CLIENT
Godiva Chocolatier, Inc.
DIRECTOR
John Margeotes, John Weiss
AGENCY
Margeotes Fertitta & Weiss, Inc., New York, NY

235

236

237

238

239

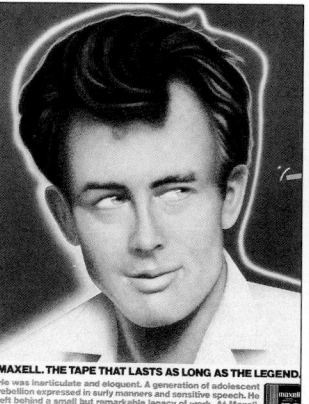

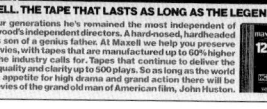

240

240
ART DIRECTOR
Bob Needleman
DESIGNER
Bob Needleman
ILLUSTRATOR/ARTIST
Guy Ferry
WRITER
Gary Gusick
CLIENT
Maxell Corporation
AGENCY
Scali, McCabe, Sloves, New York, NY

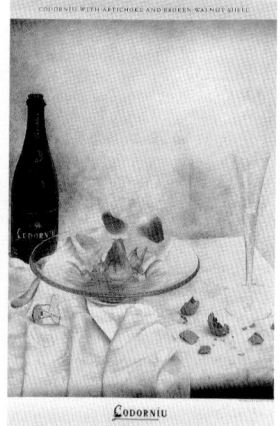

241

241
ART DIRECTOR
Jean Jacques Marc, Janet Trompeter
PHOTOGRAPHER
Francois Gillet
ILLUSTRATOR/ARTIST
Francois Gillet
WRITER
Lynn Dangel
CLIENT
Cordorniu
DIRECTOR
Gordon Bowen
AGENCY
Ogilvy & Mather, New York, NY
PUBLICATION
New York Magazine

242

242
ART DIRECTOR
Roy Carruthers
DESIGNER
Roy Carruthers
PHOTOGRAPHER
Barney Edwards/London
WRITER
Steve Jeffery
CLIENT
Seagram's Glenlivet
AGENCY
Ogilvy & Mather, New York, NY

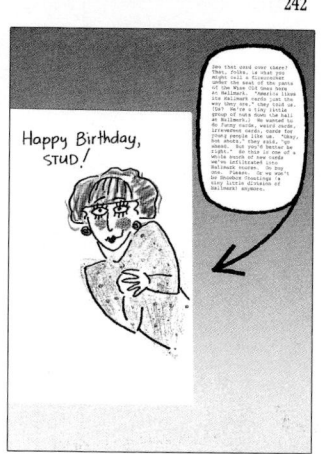

243

243
ART DIRECTOR
Alan Sprules
ILLUSTRATOR/ARTIST
Steve Finkin, Kevin Ahern, Renee Duvall
WRITER
Roger Proulx
CLIENT
Hallmark Cards, Inc.
DIRECTOR
Jay Jasper
AGENCY
Ogilvy & Mather, New York, NY
PRODUCER
Tom Raikakos
PUBLICATION
Cosmopolitan, Glamour,
Rolling Stone, People
ACCOUNT SPVSR
Linda Cornelius

244

ART DIRECTOR
Dick Henderson
DESIGNER
Dick Henderson
PHOTOGRAPHER
Eric Henderson, Jeffrey L. Rotman, Stock
WRITER
Jim Cole
CLIENT
Masland Carpets
AGENCY
Cole Henderson Drake, Atlanta, GA

245

ART DIRECTOR
Bill Shirk, Richard Mantia
DESIGNER
Sue Shirk, Buz Biscay, Chris Flagg, Harold Wetzel
ILLUSTRATOR/ARTIST
Dugald Stermer
WRITER
Allan Godshall, Walt Harrell, Tim Gibson
CLIENT
The Iams Company
AGENCY
Stockton.West.Burkhart, Cincinnati, OH

246

ART DIRECTOR
Clifford Goodenough
PHOTOGRAPHER
Terry Heffernan, Chuck Kuhn
WRITER
Steve Sandoz
CLIENT
Alaska Airlines
AGENCY
Livingston & Company, Seattle, WA
PUBLICATION
Alaska Airlines Magazine
ENGRAVER
Rainier Color

247

ART DIRECTOR
Michael Winslow, Mark Oakley
PHOTOGRAPHER
Harry DeZitter
WRITER
Jan Karon
CLIENT
North Carolina Travel & Tourism
AGENCY
McKinney & Silver, Raleigh, NC

244

245

246

247

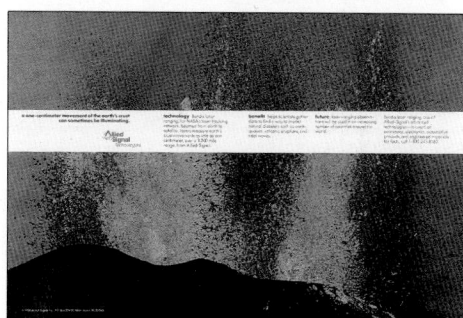

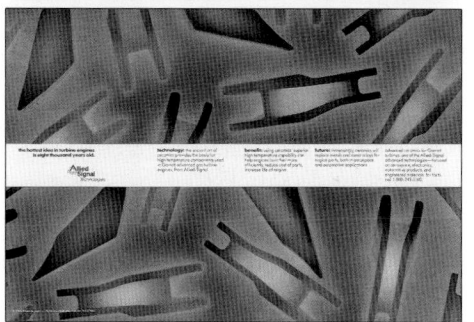

248

ART DIRECTOR
Bruce Arendash
PHOTOGRAPHER
Hiro
WRITER
Michael Jordan
CLIENT
Citizen Noblia - Larry Grunstein
AGENCY
SSC&B Inc., New York, NY
PUBLICATION
People
CREATIVE DIRECTOR
Lynn Giordano
ART SUPERVISOR
Phil Weiner
MAKE-UP ARTIST
Michael Thomas

249

ART DIRECTOR
Mylene Turek
DESIGNER
Mylene Turek
PHOTOGRAPHER
Eric Meola, Gregory Heisler, Joanna
McCarthy
WRITER
Guy Durham
CLIENT
Allied Signal Inc., Mark Whitley
AGENCY
Homer & Durham Advertising, New York, NY

248

249

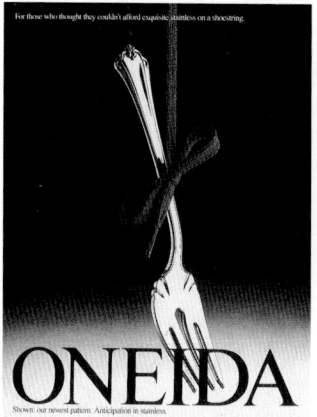

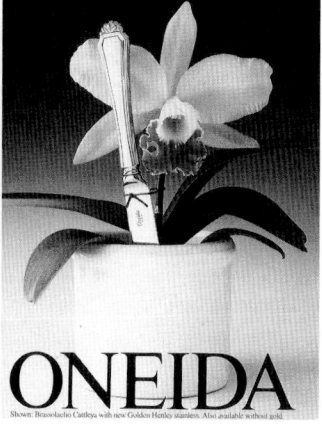

250

ART DIRECTOR
David Deutsch, Rocco Campanelli
PHOTOGRAPHER
Chris Collins
WRITER
Karen Booney
CLIENT
Oneida Tableware
AGENCY
David Deutsch Associates, New York, NY
PUBLICATION
House Beautiful

250

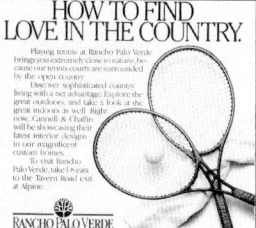

251

ART DIRECTOR
Bill Maddox, Barbie Thompson
PHOTOGRAPHER
Art Fox, Michael Denny
WRITER
Rick Lester
CLIENT
Rancho Palo Verde
AGENCY
Phillips-Ramsey, San Diego, CA
PRODUCER
Barry Whitfield, Ron Van Buskirk
PUBLICATION
San Diego Magazine

251

252
ART DIRECTOR
Tyler Smith
DESIGNER
Tyler Smith
PHOTOGRAPHER
John Goodman
WRITER
Craig Walker
CLIENT
Louis, Boston
DESIGN FIRM
Tyler Smith, Providence, RI

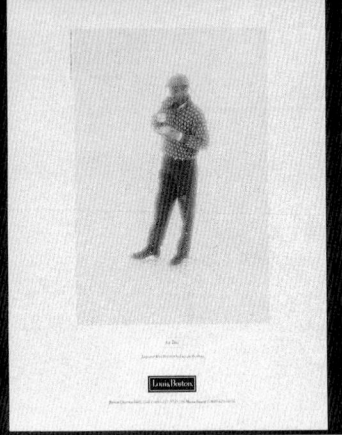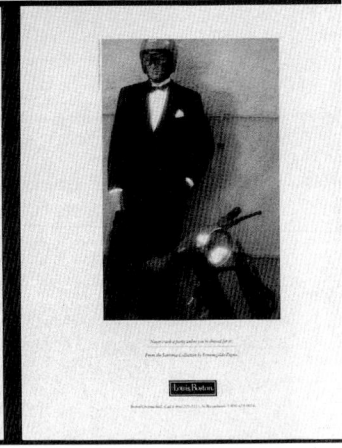

252

253
ART DIRECTOR
Geoff Hayes
PHOTOGRAPHER
Steve Bronstein, Keith Haring
WRITER
Evert Cilliers
CLIENT
Carillon Importers Ltd.
DIRECTOR
Arnold Arlow, Peter Lubalin
AGENCY
TBWA, New York, NY

253

254
ART DIRECTOR
Rick Boyko
PHOTOGRAPHER
Dennis Manarchy
WRITER
Bill Hamilton
CLIENT
Nike, Inc.
AGENCY
Chiat/Day Advertising, Los Angeles, CA
PUBLICATION
Elle

255
ART DIRECTOR
Jud Smith
PHOTOGRAPHER
Dennis Manarchy
WRITER
Ron Sackett
CLIENT
Harley-Davidson
AGENCY
Carmichael-Lynch, Minneapolis, MN

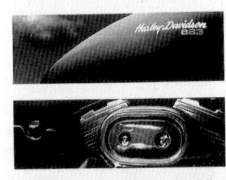

254

255

SHE CAN'T HANDLE HEAVY DRINKING LIKE SHE USED TO.

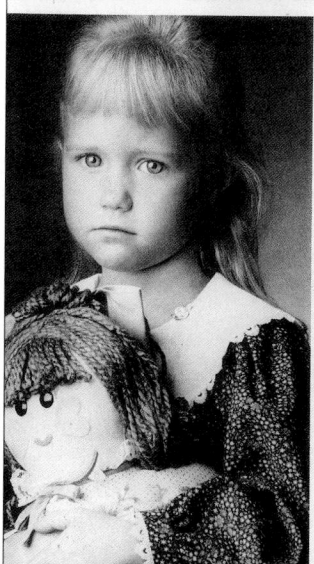

Kate comes home from school every day to the same nightmare. Her mother is an alcoholic. Kate is just one of 7 million children of alcoholics who desperately need help.

Besides problems at home, she's having trouble at school. She feels guilty. (She actually believes it's all her fault.) She also feels very scared and lonely.

Chances are, very soon, things will get worse.

And she will probably start drinking herself.

The evidence suggests that children of alcoholics are four times more likely than other kids to become alcoholics themselves.

It's a cycle that could easily go on forever.

At the Children of Alcoholics Foundation, we know there's no simple answer.

But we do know ways to reduce the suffering of children like Kate. We have educational programs and we promote research.

We can also put sufferers in touch with programs offering guidance to children and parents.

We're trying to break the cycle, but we can't do it alone.

If you'd like to help, send just $10, or more if you can afford it.

In return, we'll send you reports and information about this complex and alarmingly widespread problem.

It's one face of alcoholism that's remained anonymous long enough.

CHILDREN OF ALCOHOLICS FOUNDATION, INC.
P.O. Box 4185, Grand Central Station
New York, NY 10163

256

SHE SUFFERS FROM A SERIOUS DRINKING PROBLEM.

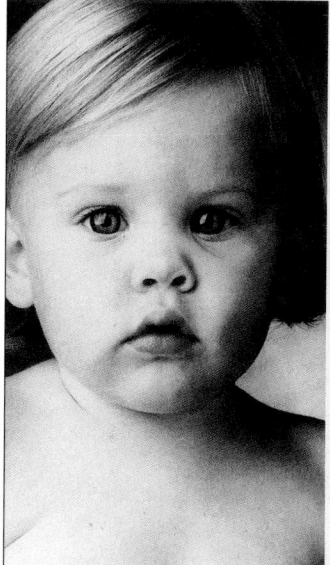

She doesn't know it yet, but Melissa's problem is her Mom. Her mother is an alcoholic.

Melissa is just one of the 7 million children of alcoholics in desperate need of help.

As she grows up, if she conforms to the usual pattern, here's what will happen.

She won't do well in school. She won't have many friends. She'll start feeling guilty. (She'll actually believe it's all her fault.)

She'll also feel very scared.

Later, in her teens, she'll probably start drinking herself.

The evidence suggests that children of alcoholics are four times more likely than other kids to become alcoholics themselves.

It's a cycle that could easily go on forever.

At the Children of Alcoholics Foundation, we know there's no simple answer.

But we do know ways to reduce the suffering of children like Melissa. We have educational programs and we promote research.

We can also put sufferers in touch with programs offering guidance to children and parents.

We're trying to break the cycle, but we can't do it alone.

If you'd like to help, send just $10, or more if you can afford it.

In return, we'll send you reports and information about this complex and alarmingly widespread problem.

It's one face of alcoholism that's remained anonymous long enough.

CHILDREN OF ALCOHOLICS FOUNDATION, INC.
P.O. Box 4185, Grand Central Station
New York, NY 10163

257

Will your child learn to multiply before she learns to subtract?

Adolescent pregnancy isn't just a problem in America, it's a crisis. To learn more about a social issue that concerns all of us, write: *Children's Defense Fund, 122 C Street, N.W., Washington, D.C. 20001.*

The Children's Defense Fund.

258

The one on the left will finish high school before the one on the right.

Adolescent pregnancy isn't just a problem in America, it's a crisis. To learn more about a social issue that concerns all of us, write: *Children's Defense Fund, 122 C Street, N.W., Washington, D.C. 20001.*

The Children's Defense Fund.

259

256
ART DIRECTOR
Joe Genova
DESIGNER
Joe Genova
PHOTOGRAPHER
Bob Brody
WRITER
Tony Chapman
CLIENT
Children of Alcoholics Foundation, Inc.
AGENCY
Posey Quest Genova, Inc., Greenwich, CT

257
ART DIRECTOR
Joe Genova
DESIGNER
Joe Genova
PHOTOGRAPHER
Bob Brody
WRITER
Tony Chapman
CLIENT
Children of Alcoholics Foundation, Inc.
AGENCY
Posey Quest Genova, Inc., Greenwich, CT

258
ART DIRECTOR
Dean Hanson
PHOTOGRAPHER
Jim Arndt
WRITER
Tom McElligott
CLIENT
Children's Defense Fund
AGENCY
Fallon McElligott, Minneapolis, MN

259
ART DIRECTOR
Dean Hanson
PHOTOGRAPHER
Marc Hauser
WRITER
Tom McElligott
CLIENT
Children's Defense Fund
AGENCY
Fallon McElligott, Minneapolis, MN

260
ART DIRECTOR
Dean Hanson
PHOTOGRAPHER
Jim Arndt
WRITER
Tom McElligott
CLIENT
Reader's Digest
AGENCY
Fallon McElligott, Minneapolis, MN

261
ART DIRECTOR
John Muller
DESIGNER
John Muller, Patt Williams
WRITER
Rob Price, John Muller
CLIENT
Kansas City Jazz Commission
DESIGN FIRM
Muller & Company, Kansas City, MO

262
ART DIRECTOR
John Vitro, San Diego, CA
PHOTOGRAPHER
David Kramer
ILLUSTRATOR/ARTIST
Ray Lewis
WRITER
Martha Shaw
CLIENT
Martha Shaw

263
ART DIRECTOR
Nancy Rice, Nick Rice
DESIGNER
Nancy Rice, Nick Rice
PHOTOGRAPHER
Marvy! Advertising Photography
WRITER
Jim Newcombe
CLIENT
The Andersons
AGENCY
Rice & Rice Advertising Inc., Minneapolis, MN
PUBLICATION
Lawn & Garden Marketing

264
ART DIRECTOR
Dave Martin
DESIGNER
Dave Martin
ILLUSTRATOR/ARTIST
U.S. Treasury Department
WRITER
Jeff Linder
CLIENT
Columbia University
AGENCY
DDB Needham Worldwide, Inc., New York, NY
PUBLICATION
Columbia Magazine

260

262

261

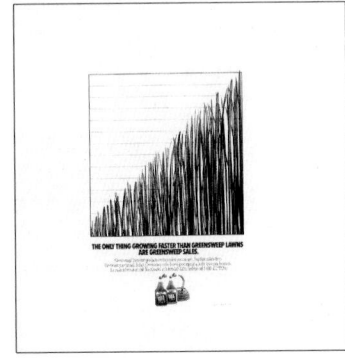

263

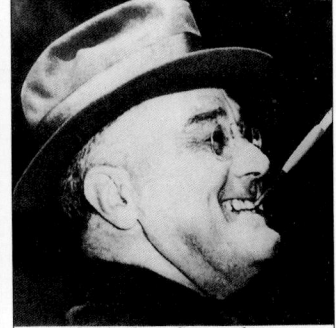

264

265

ART DIRECTOR
Jack Mariucci

DESIGNER
Jack Mariucci

PHOTOGRAPHER
Henry Sandbank

WRITER
Mike Rogers

CLIENT
Michelin

AGENCY
DDB Needham Worldwide, Inc., New York, NY

PUBLICATION
Modern Tire Dealer

265

266

ART DIRECTOR
Miles Turpin

PHOTOGRAPHER
Dana Gluckstein

WRITER
Elizabeth Hayes

CLIENT
Apple computer, Inc.

AGENCY
Chiat/Day Advertising, Los Angeles, CA

PUBLICATION
Exceptional Parent

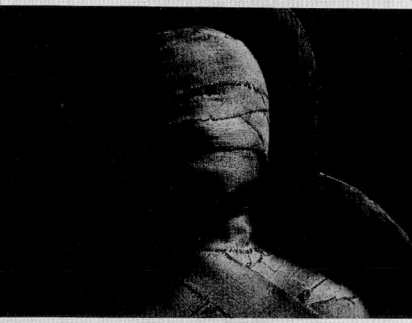

267

ART DIRECTOR
Pat Cornwall

PHOTOGRAPHER
Charles Vendetti

WRITER
Mel Maffei, Rich Swietek

CLIENT
Stanley Hardware

AGENCY
Keiler Advertising, Farmington, CT

267

266

268

ART DIRECTOR
Kevin Kearns

DESIGNER
Nancy Malacaria, Kevin Kearns

PHOTOGRAPHER
Fred Collins

ILLUSTRATOR/ARTIST
John Burgoine

WRITER
Thomas Monahan

CLIENT
Reliance Products

AGENCY
Leonard Monahan Saabye, Providence, RI

PUBLICATION
American Baby

PRINTER
Rand

269

ART DIRECTOR
Jeff Terwilliger

DESIGNER
Jeff Terwilliger

PHOTOGRAPHER
Rick Dublin

WRITER
Pete Pohl

CLIENT
Henkel

AGENCY
Bozell, Jacobs, Kenyon & Eckhardt, Minneapolis, MN

PUBLICATION
Food Technology

269

268

270

ART DIRECTOR
Don Trousdell
DESIGNER
Don Trousdell
PHOTOGRAPHER
Pelosi & Chambers
ILLUSTRATOR/ARTIST
Tom Allen
WRITER
Rich Maender
CLIENT
Customweave Carpets
AGENCY
Fitzgerald & Company
DESIGN FIRM
Don Trousdell Design, Atlanta, GA

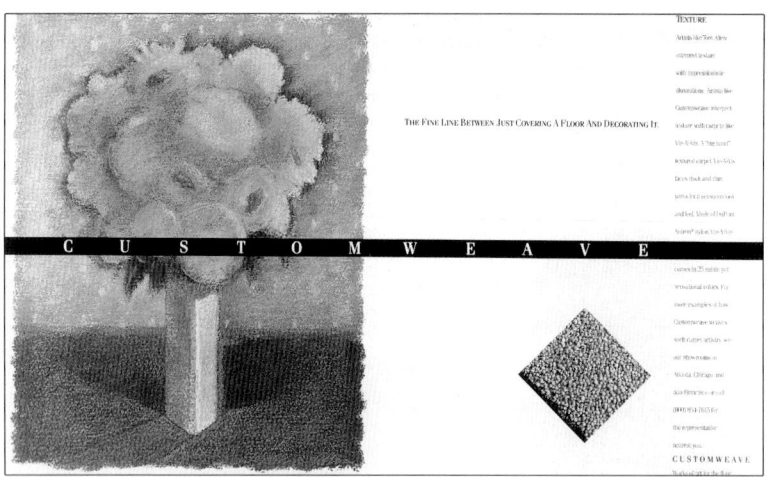

270

271

ART DIRECTOR
Michael McLaughlin
DESIGNER
Michael McLaughlin
PHOTOGRAPHER
Various stock
WRITER
Stephen Creet
CLIENT
Shell Canada Ltd.
AGENCY
Carder Gray Advertising Inc., Toronto,
Canada

271

272

ART DIRECTOR
Greg Nygard
DESIGNER
Greg Nygard
ILLUSTRATOR/ARTIST
Leonard Morgan
WRITER
Mark Fenske
CLIENT
Hollister, Inc.
AGENCY
Zechman & Associates Advertising, Inc.,
Chicago, IL
CREATIVE DIRECTOR
Jan Zechman

272

273

ART DIRECTOR
Vern Scharf
PHOTOGRAPHER
Dennis Gray
WRITER
Mike Hreha
CLIENT
Schlage Lock
AGENCY
Winkler McManus, Santa Clara, CA

273

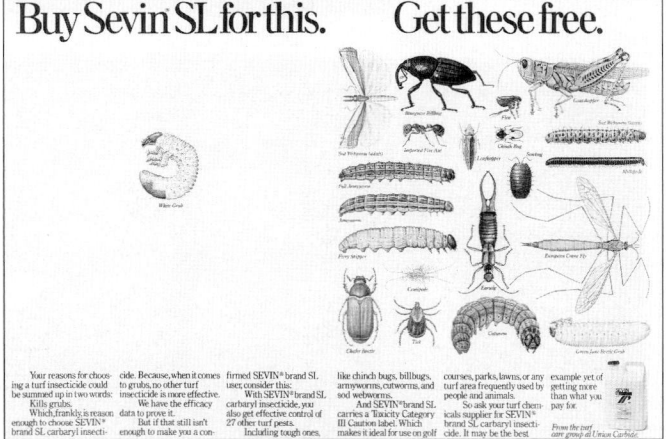

274

ART DIRECTOR
Sharon Brady
PHOTOGRAPHER
Frozen Images
ILLUSTRATOR/ARTIST
Jack Jones
WRITER
Bill Campbell
CLIENT
Royster, Inc.
AGENCY
Barker Campbell & Farley Advertising,
Virginia Beach, VA
MECHANICAL ARTIST
Mary Fritz

274

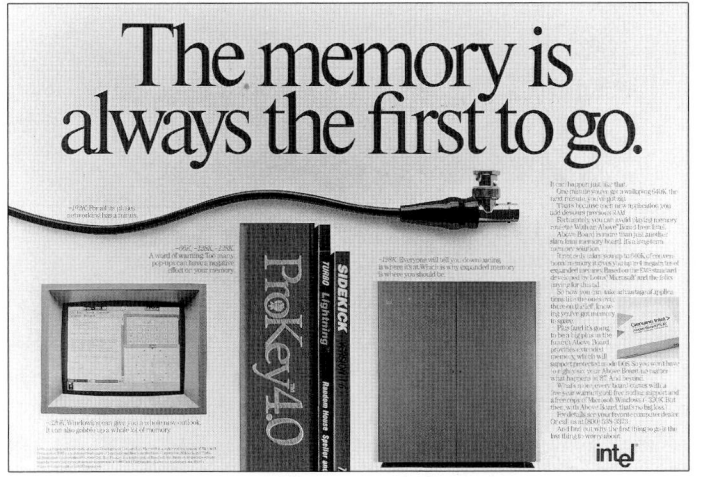

275

ART DIRECTOR
Joe Ivey
ILLUSTRATOR/ARTIST
Biruta Hansen
WRITER
Scott Crawford
CLIENT
Union Carbide Specialty Products
AGENCY
Howard, Merrell & Partners, Inc., Raleigh,
NC
PUBLICATION
Weeds, Trees & Turf, American Lawn
Applicator

275

276

ART DIRECTOR
Andrew Vucinich
PHOTOGRAPHER
Robert Mizono
WRITER
David O'Hare
CLIENT
Intel Corporation
AGENCY
Chiat/Day Advertising, San Francisco, CA
PUBLICATION
PC Week

276

277

ART DIRECTOR
Cap Pannell
DESIGNER
Cap Pannell
PHOTOGRAPHER
Gary Goodwin
ILLUSTRATOR/ARTIST
Cap Pannell
WRITER
Carol St. George
CLIENT
Learning Technologies, Inc.
AGENCY
Alan Weinkrantz & Company
DESIGN FIRM
Pannell/St. George, Dallas, TX
PUBLICATION
Scholastic Magazine, Inc.

277

278

ART DIRECTOR
Chris Poisson
PHOTOGRAPHER
Jerry Sieve
ILLUSTRATOR/ARTIST
Stan Tang
WRITER
Chris Poisson
CLIENT
Woods Lithographics
AGENCY
DuVal Advertising, Phoenix, AZ
PUBLICATION
Arizona Prisma Awards Annual

278

279

ART DIRECTOR
Warren Johnson
ILLUSTRATOR/ARTIST
Andrezej Dudzinski
WRITER
Nancy Wellinger
CLIENT
Network Systems
AGENCY
Carmichael-Lynch, Minneapolis, MN

279

280

ART DIRECTOR
Bill Harris
DESIGNER
Bill Harris, Joe Budne
PHOTOGRAPHER
Boulevard Photographic, Michael Molkenthin
WRITER
Jeff Wolf
CLIENT
Saatchi & Saatchi, Compton Inc., New York, NY
PUBLICATION
Advertising Age

280

281

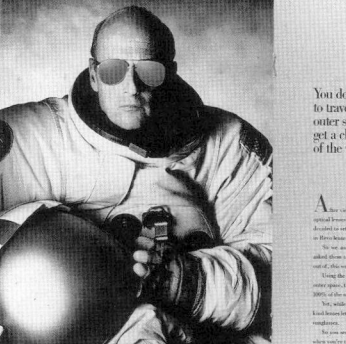

You don't have
to travel to
outer space to
get a clear view
of the world.

281

ART DIRECTOR
Deborah Nichols
DESIGNER
David Pace
PHOTOGRAPHER
Timothy Hursley
WRITER
Alice McGuckin
CLIENT
House & Garden
PUBLISHER
Condé Nast Publications, Inc.
AGENCY
Sacks & Rosen
DESIGN FIRM
House & Garden Promotion, New York, NY
CREATIVE DIRECTOR
Sonda Miller

Now a company with
the reputation for
copying other people's
work, being graphically
explicit by phone,
and snapping at the
slightest provocation,
wants to show you what
it can do for your
computer business.

Eight of the ten reasons why you'll
want to become a Ricoh dealer.

1

Going downhill
at 40 mph is
no time to dim
your lights.

Don't try to
hide behind
these sunglasses.

282

ART DIRECTOR
Antoinette Portis
PHOTOGRAPHER
Matthew Rolston
WRITER
Jaci Sisson, David Bishop
CLIENT
CooperVision/Revo
AGENCY
Della Femina, Travisano & Partners, Los
Angeles, CA
TYPOGRAPHER
John Burton
CREATIVE DIRECTOR
Jim Weller, John Armistead

282

Nine&Ten

283

283

ART DIRECTOR
Dave Nathanson
DESIGNER
Dave Nathanson
ILLUSTRATOR/ARTIST
Dave Nathanson
WRITER
Penny Kapousouz
CLIENT
Ricoh
AGENCY
Chiat/Day Inc., New York, NY
PUBLICATION
Comdex Show Daily

Tetrachloroethylene, Diisobutyl
Ketone 80%, Hydrochloric Acid
(37%), Nitrobenzene, EthylEther,
1, 2 Dichloroethane, Morpholine,
Toluene, Butyl Acetate, Furfural,
Acetaldeh   tyltoluene,
Dioxane, Di   ene, Vinyl
Chloride, D methy   mamide,
1,1,1 Trichlor   hane, Acetonitrile,
Acetone, Sulfuric Acid (3 Molar),
Nitropropane, n-Hexane, Aniline,
Chloroform, Nitric Acid (3 Molar),
Benzene, Carbon Tetrachloride,
Dibutylphthalate, Cyclohexanol,
Ethyl Acetate, Trichloroethylene,

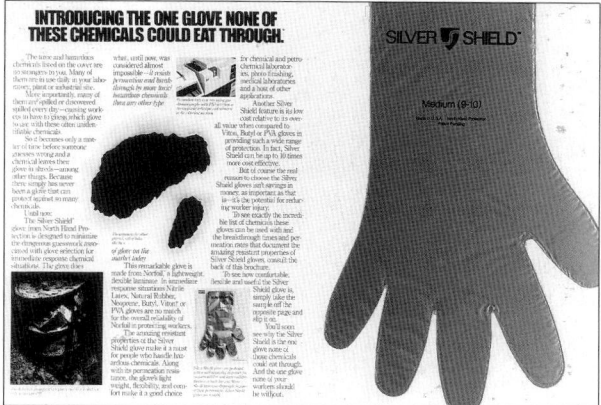

INTRODUCING THE ONE GLOVE NONE OF
THESE CHEMICALS COULD EAT THROUGH.

SILVER SHIELD

284

ART DIRECTOR
Robert Saabye
DESIGNER
Sharon Collins
PHOTOGRAPHER
Myron, Clint Clemens, Gene Dwiggins
WRITER
Jay Williams
CLIENT
Siebe North Inc.
AGENCY
Leonard Monahan Saabye, Providence, RI
PRINTER
United Printing

284

Credit: THE BETTMAN ARCHIVE

"I WANT YOU."

Of all the renditions of Uncle Sam, the most widely-seen has probably been the one painted by James Montgomery Flagg in 1917 for a World War I recruiting poster.

Flagg's Uncle Sam is so strong, so immediate, so powerfully direct that the Army has called him back into service time and time again.

NEWSPAPER EDITORIAL:

Less than full page: b&w or color
Full page: b&w
color
Multi-page section: b&w or color

MAGAZINE EDITORIAL:

Sunday magazine or supplement: full issue
Consumer: multiple pages, single story, b&w
full page, color
spread, color
multiple pages, single story, color
cover
Business trade or house organ: spread, b&w
spread, color
multiple pages, single story, color
cover
Consumer or business magazine: full issue
House organ: full issue

285

ART DIRECTOR
Brad Zucroff
DESIGNER
Kelly Doe
ILLUSTRATOR/ARTIST
Kelly Doe
EDITOR
Elissa Vanaver
PUBLICATION
San Jose Mercury News, San Jose, CA

286

ART DIRECTOR
Michael Keegan
DESIGNER
Carol Porter, Michael Keegan
ILLUSTRATOR/ARTIST
Randall Enos, Becky Heavner, Christopher
Bing, Javier Romero, Guy Billout, Brad
Hamann
CLIENT
The Washington Post - Sunday Show
EDITOR
Ellen Edwards, Jeff Frank
PUBLISHER
The Washington Post
PUBLICATION
The Washington Post, Washington, DC

287

ART DIRECTOR
Terry Redknapp
DESIGNER
Terry Redknapp
PHOTOGRAPHER
Henri Soumireu-Lartigue
EDITOR
Irv Letofsky
PUBLISHER
Los Angeles Times
PUBLICATION
Los Angeles Times Calendar, Los Angeles, CA

288

ART DIRECTOR
Terry Redknapp
DESIGNER
Donald Burgess
PHOTOGRAPHER
Ivy Ney
WRITER
Mary Rourke
EDITOR
Bettijane Levine
PUBLISHER
Los Angeles Times
PUBLICATION
Los Angeles Times, Los Angeles, CA

289

ART DIRECTOR
Terry Redknapp
DESIGNER
Donald Burgess
PHOTOGRAPHER
Stephen Shadley
WRITER
Bettijane Levine
EDITOR
Bettijane Levine
PUBLISHER
Los Angeles Times
PUBLICATION
Los Angeles Times, Los Angeles, CA

285

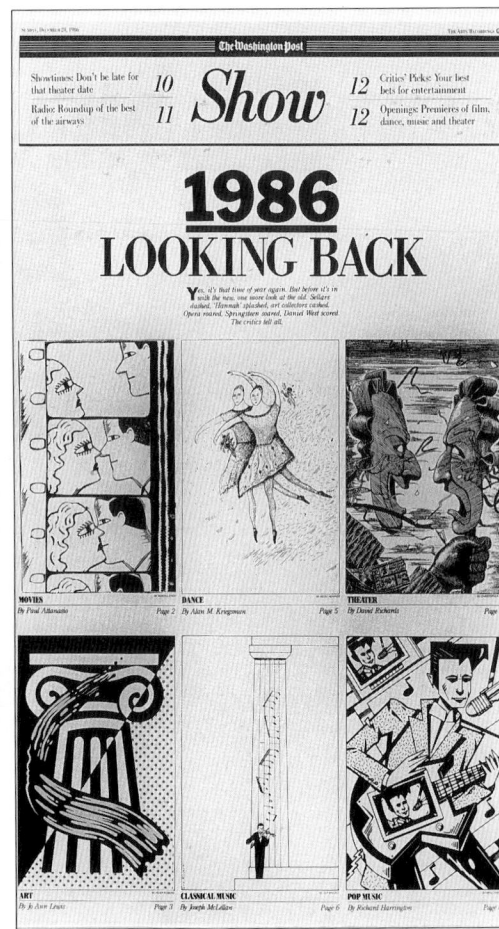

286

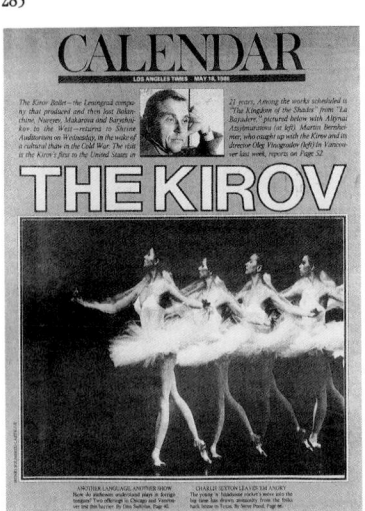

287

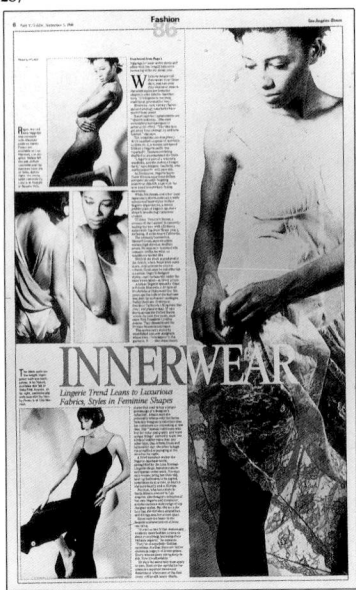

288

289

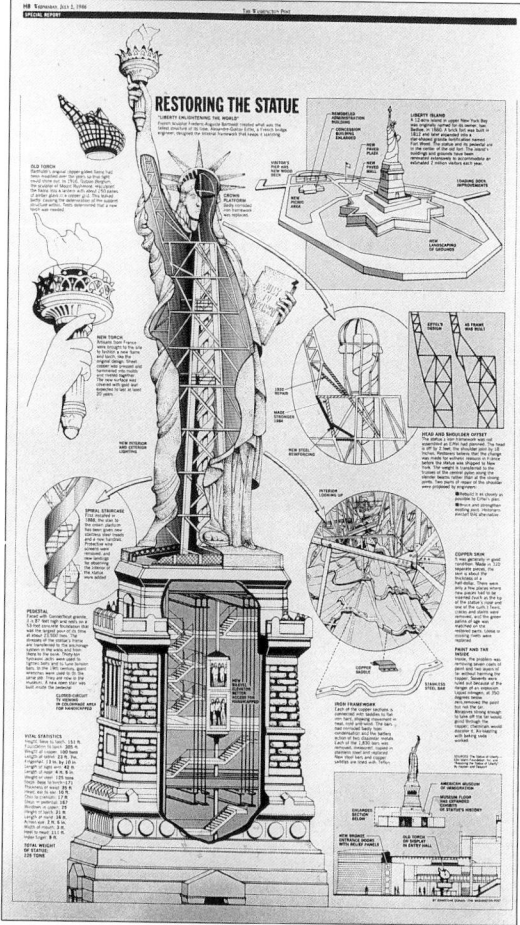

290

291

292

293

294

295

290

ART DIRECTOR
Michael Keegan
DESIGNER
Johnstone Quinan
ILLUSTRATOR/ARTIST
Johnstone Quinan
WRITER
Johnstone Quinan
PUBLISHER
The Washington Post
PUBLICATION
The Washington Post, Washington, DC

291

ART DIRECTOR
Richard Baker
DESIGNER
Richard Baker
PHOTOGRAPHER
Richard Carpenter
PUBLISHER
The Boston Globe, Boston, MA
PUBLICATION
Living Section: Television Man

292

ART DIRECTOR
Aldona Charlton
DESIGNER
Aldona Charlton
PHOTOGRAPHER
Various
WRITER
Diane Nottle
CLIENT
Boston Globe
EDITOR
Gail Ravgiala
PUBLISHER
Boston Globe, Boston, MA
PUBLICATION
Boston Globe

293

ART DIRECTOR
Nicki Kalish
DESIGNER
Nicki Kalish
ILLUSTRATOR/ARTIST
Edward Gorey, Michael Hostovich
CLIENT
The New York Times Living Section
PUBLISHER
The New York Times, New York, NY

294

ART DIRECTOR
Nicki Kalish
DESIGNER
Nicki Kalish
PHOTOGRAPHER
Terrance McCarthy
ILLUSTRATOR/ARTIST
Elwood H. Smith
CLIENT
The New York Times Living Section
EDITOR
Margot Slade
PUBLICATION
The New York Times

295

ART DIRECTOR
Nicki Kalish
DESIGNER
Nicki Kalish
PHOTOGRAPHER
Fred R. Conrad
ILLUSTRATOR/ARTIST
Tom Bloom
CLIENT
The New York Times Living Section
EDITOR
Margot Slade
PUBLISHER
The New York Times, New York, NY

296

ART DIRECTOR
Linda Brewer
DESIGNER
Linda Brewer
ILLUSTRATOR/ARTIST
Shunkin Takahashi
CLIENT
The New York Times Travel Section
EDITOR
Nora Kerr
PUBLISHER
The New York Times, New York, NY
PUBLICATION
The New York Times

297

ART DIRECTOR
Linda Brewer
DESIGNER
Linda Brewer
PHOTOGRAPHER
Jonathan Player, Jonathan Arkin, Nancy Holt
ILLUSTRATOR/ARTIST
Michael Bartalos
CLIENT
The New York Times Travel Section
EDITOR
Nora Kerr
PUBLISHER
The New York Times, New York, NY
PUBLICATION
The New York Times

298

ART DIRECTOR
Linda Brewer
DESIGNER
Linda Brewer
PHOTOGRAPHER
Kit Kittle
ILLUSTRATOR/ARTIST
Perico Pastor
CLIENT
The New York Times Travel Section
EDITOR
Michael Leahy
PUBLISHER
The New York Times, New York, NY
PUBLICATION
The New York Times

299

ART DIRECTOR
Richard Aloisio
DESIGNER
Richard Aloisio
ILLUSTRATOR/ARTIST
Meredith Nemirov
CLIENT
The New York Times Weekend Section
EDITOR
Annette Grant
PUBLISHER
The New York Times, New York, NY
PUBLICATION
The New York Times

300

ART DIRECTOR
Richard Aloisio
DESIGNER
Richard Aloisio
ILLUSTRATOR/ARTIST
Gary Zamchick, Javier Romero
CLIENT
The New York Times Living Section
EDITOR
Margot Slade
PUBLISHER
The New York Times, New York, NY
PUBLICATION
The New York Times

296

297

298

299

300

301

302

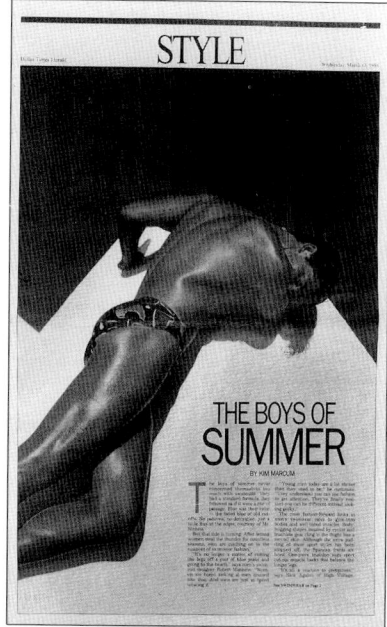

303

305

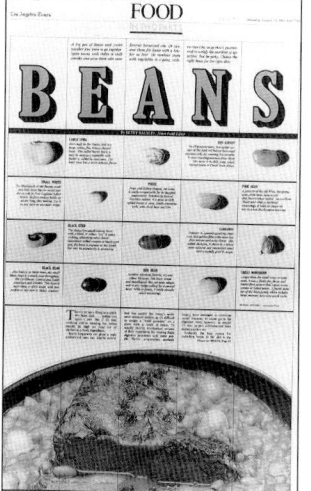

306

304

301

ART DIRECTOR
Margaret O'Connor
DESIGNER
Margaret O'Connor
PHOTOGRAPHER
Barton Silverman, Chester Higgins Jr.
ILLUSTRATOR/ARTIST
Brad Hamann
CLIENT
The New York Times
EDITOR
Steve Rago
PUBLISHER
The New York Times, New York, NY
PUBLICATION
The New York Times

302

ART DIRECTOR
Judy Sell
ILLUSTRATOR/ARTIST
Lee Christiansen
EDITOR
Jean Peterson
PUBLISHER
Minneapolis Star and Tribune, Minneapolis,
MN

303

ART DIRECTOR
Stan Hulen
DESIGNER
Janis Bryza
PHOTOGRAPHER
Michael Wirtz
EDITOR
Kim Marcum
PUBLICATION
Dallas Times Herald, Dallas, TX

304

ART DIRECTOR
Katharine Garraty
DESIGNER
Katharine Garraty
PHOTOGRAPHER
Hal Stoelzle
CLIENT
Orange County Register
PUBLICATION
The Orange County Register, Santa Ana, CA
FOOD STYLIST
Tillie Clements

305

ART DIRECTOR
Keith Branscombe
DESIGNER
Therese Schechter
PHOTOGRAPHER
George Whiteside
WRITER
Greg Quill
CLIENT
What's On
EDITOR
Patrick McCormick
PUBLISHER
The Toronto Star
PUBLICATION
The Toronto Star, Toronto, Canada

306

ART DIRECTOR
Terry Redknapp
DESIGNER
Terry Redknapp
PHOTOGRAPHER
Michael Edwards
WRITER
Betsy Balsley
EDITOR
Betsy Balsley
PUBLISHER
Los Angeles Times
PUBLICATION
Los Angeles Times, Los Angeles, CA

307
ART DIRECTOR
Stan Hulen
DESIGNER
Deborah Withey-Culp
ILLUSTRATOR/ARTIST
Deborah Withey-Culp
WRITER
Maxine Levy
EDITOR
Candy Sagon
PUBLICATION
Dallas Times Herald, Dallas,
TX

308
ART DIRECTOR
Sharon Roberts
DESIGNER
Clif Bosler
PUBLICATION
The Dallas Morning News, Dallas, TX

309
ART DIRECTOR
Margaret O'Connor, Ron Couture
PHOTOGRAPHER
Various
ILLUSTRATOR/ARTIST
Map Dept/N.Y.T.
CLIENT
The New York Times
EDITOR
Steve Rago
PUBLISHER
The New York Times, New York, NY
PUBLICATION
The New York Times
GRAPHIC EDITORS
Nancy Lee, Anne Cronin

310
ART DIRECTOR
Sharon Roberts
DESIGNER
Kathleen Vincent
PHOTOGRAPHER
David Leeson, Lon Cooper
DIRECTOR OF PHOTOGRAPHY
John Davidson
PUBLICATION
The Dallas Morning News, Dallas, TX

307

308

309

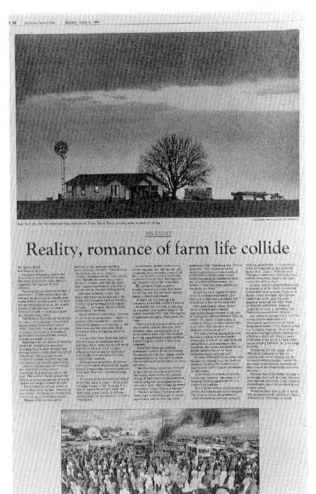

310

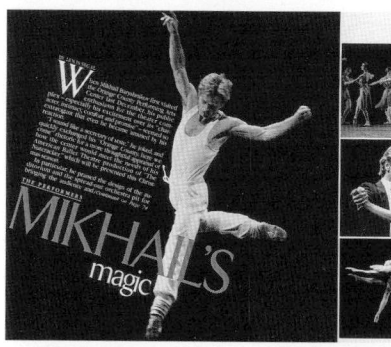

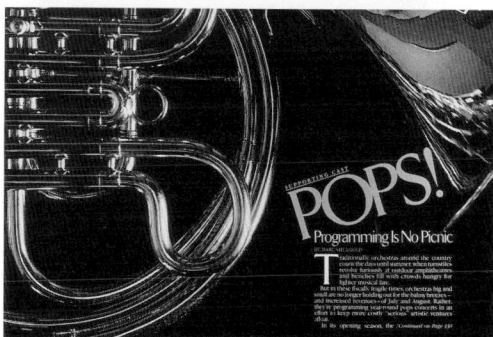

314

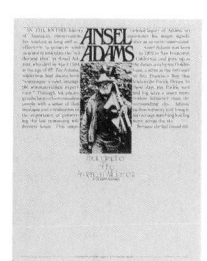

311

311

ART DIRECTOR
Terry Redknapp
DESIGNER
Donald Burgess, Terry Redknapp
PHOTOGRAPHER
Mark Boster
EDITOR
Greta Beigel
PUBLISHER
Los Angeles Times
PUBLICATION
Los Angeles Times, Los Angeles, CA

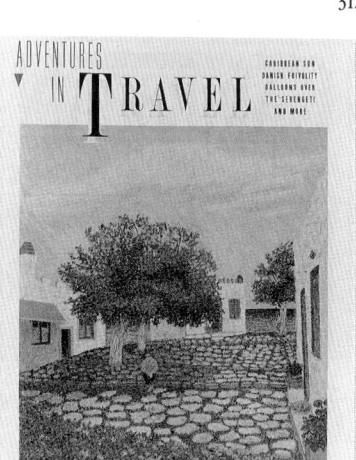

312

312

ART DIRECTOR
Thaddeus A. Miksinski, Jr.
DESIGNER
Thaddeus A. Miksinski, Jr.
PHOTOGRAPHER
Ansel Adams
WRITER
Robert Turnage
CLIENT
TOPIC Magazine
EDITOR
Peter Laine
PICTURE EDITOR
Rosalie Targonski
PUBLISHER
U.S. Information Agency
DESIGN FIRM
U.S. Information Agency, Washington, DC
PUBLICATION
TOPIC Magazine

313

ART DIRECTOR
Ronn Campisi
DESIGNER
Ronn Campisi
EDITOR
Allison Arnett
PUBLISHER
The Boston Globe, Boston, MA

313

314

ART DIRECTOR
Deb Hardison, Bett McLean
DESIGNER
Bett McLean
PHOTOGRAPHER
James Wojcik, Don Dudenbostel
WRITER
Robert Sharoff
CLIENT
Whittle Communications
EDITOR
George Spencer, Thomas G. Lombardo
PUBLISHER
Whittle Communications, Knoxville, TN
PUBLICATION
Connecticut's Finest

315

ART DIRECTOR
John Johanek
PHOTOGRAPHER
Brian Kosoff
WRITER
Joseph Truini
DESIGN DIRECTOR
Bryan Canniff
PUBLICATION
Popular Mechanics, New York, NY

316

ART DIRECTOR
John Johanek
PHOTOGRAPHER
Brian Kosoff
WRITER
Joseph Truini
DESIGN DIRECTOR
Bryan Canniff
PUBLICATION
Popular Mechanics, New York, NY

317

ART DIRECTOR
John Johanek
PHOTOGRAPHER
Brian Kosoff
WRITER
Joseph Truini
DESIGN DIRECTOR
Bryan Canniff
PUBLICATION
Popular Mechanics, New York, NY

318

ART DIRECTOR
John Johanek
PHOTOGRAPHER
Brian Kosoff
WRITER
Joseph Truini
DESIGN DIRECTOR
Bryan Canniff
PUBLICATION
Popular Mechanics, New York, NY

319

ART DIRECTOR
John Johanek
PHOTOGRAPHER
Brian Kosoff
WRITER
Joseph Truini
DESIGN DIRECTOR
Bryan Canniff
PUBLICATION
Popular Mechanics, New York, NY

320

ART DIRECTOR
Nora Sheehan, Mary K. Baumann
DESIGNER
Nora Sheehan, Mary K. Baumann
PHOTOGRAPHER
Peter Zeray
WRITER
Eric Levin
EDITOR
Landon Y. Jones
PUBLISHER
William M. Kelly
PUBLICATION
Quality Magazine, New York, NY

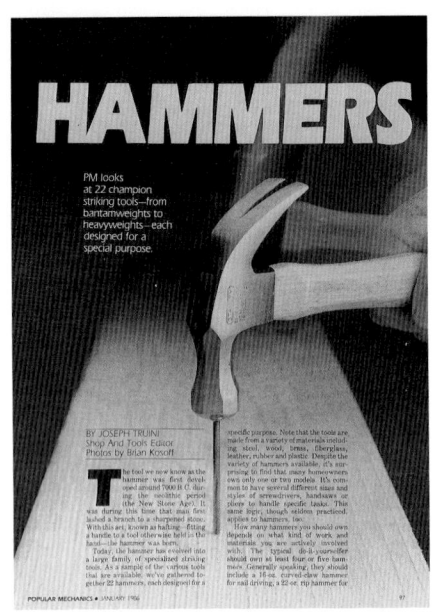

315

316

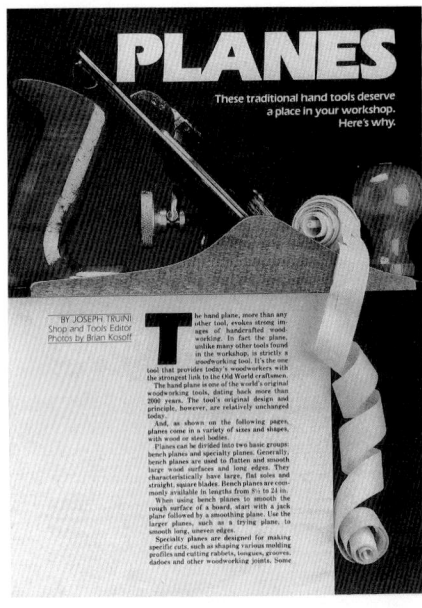

317

318

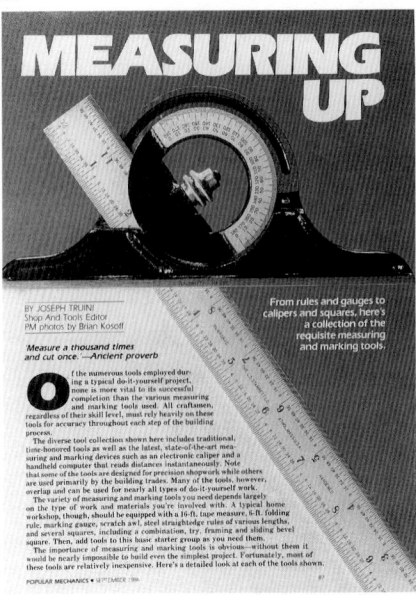

319

320

321

ART DIRECTOR
Jean Griffin, Edward Leida
DESIGNER
Edward Leida
DESIGN DIRECTOR
Owen Hartley
PUBLISHER
Fairchild Publications, New York, NY
PUBLICATION
W Magazine

322

ART DIRECTOR
Melissa Tardiff
DESIGNER
Richard Turtletaub
ILLUSTRATOR/ARTIST
Robert Goldstrom
PUBLISHER
The Hearst Corporation
PUBLICATION
Town & Country, New York, NY

321

322

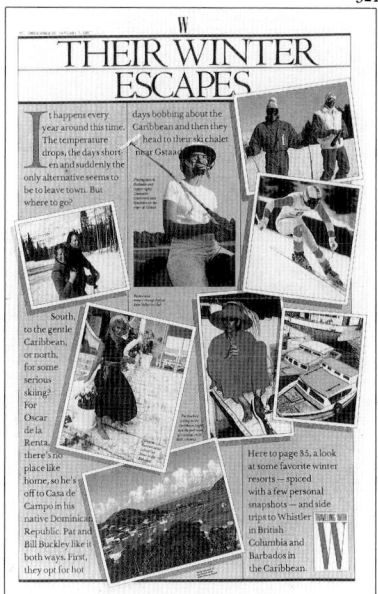

323

ART DIRECTOR
Jean Griffin, Edward Leida
DESIGNER
Edward Leida
DESIGN DIRECTOR
Owen Hartley
PUBLISHER
Fairchild Publications, New York, NY
PUBLICATION
W Magazine

324

ART DIRECTOR
Joseph Yacinski
DESIGNER
Joseph Yacinski
ILLUSTRATOR/ARTIST
Nicholas Gaetano
PUBLISHER
Kiplinger Washington Editors, Washington,
DC
PUBLICATION
Changing Times Magazine

323

324

325

ART DIRECTOR
Owen Hartley
DESIGNER
Owen Hartley
DESIGN DIRECTOR
Owen Hartley
PUBLISHER
Fairchild Publications, New York, NY
PUBLICATION
W Magazine

326

ART DIRECTOR
Shari Spier
DESIGNER
Shari Spier
ILLUSTRATOR/ARTIST
Jamie Bennett
WRITER
John Robertson
CLIENT
Controlled Media Communication
PUBLISHER
Controlled Media Communications, Charlie
Cipolla
DESIGN FIRM
Reactor Art & Design, Toronto, Canada
PUBLICATION
Toronto Blue Jays Scorebook Magazine

325

326

327

ART DIRECTOR
Gary Koepke
DESIGNER
Gary Koepke
ILLUSTRATOR/ARTIST
Gary Mele
EDITOR
Jock Baird
PUBLISHER
Gordon Baird
PUBLICATION
Musician Magazine, Gloucester, MA

328

ART DIRECTOR
Danielle Roy
DESIGNER
Danielle Roy
PHOTOGRAPHER
Tilt Inc.
DESIGN FIRM
Danielle Roy Design et Communication,
Montréal, Canada
PRINTER
Prolith
TYPOGRAPHER
Précicomp

329   330

ART DIRECTOR
Gary Koepke
DESIGNER
Gary Koepke
PHOTOGRAPHER
Davies & Starr
EDITOR
Jock Baird
PUBLISHER
Gordon Baird
PUBLICATION
Musician Magazine, Gloucester, MA

331

ART DIRECTOR
Gary Koepke
DESIGNER
Gary Koepke, Lisa Laarman
PHOTOGRAPHER
Warner Brothers

332

ART DIRECTOR
Adriane Stark
DESIGNER
Adriane Stark
PHOTOGRAPHER
Fred Bauenbam
EDITOR
Michael Robbins
DESIGN FIRM
Stark Design, New York, NY
PUBLICATION
Oceans Magazine

333

ART DIRECTOR
Gary Koepke
DESIGNER
Gary Koepke
PHOTOGRAPHER
Waring Abbott
EDITOR
Jock Baird
PUBLISHER
Gordon Baird
PUBLICATION
Musician Magazine, Gloucester, MA

334

ART DIRECTOR
Bryan Canniff
PHOTOGRAPHER
Becker/Bishop Studios
WRITER
Norman Mayersohn
PUBLICATION
Popular Mechanics, New York, NY

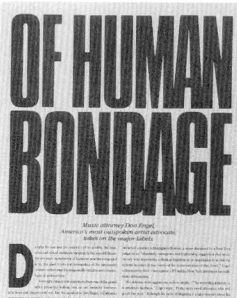
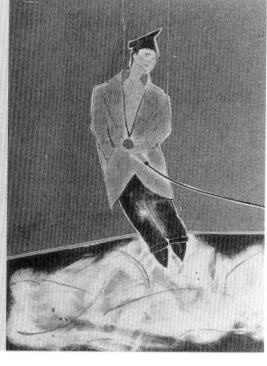

327

328

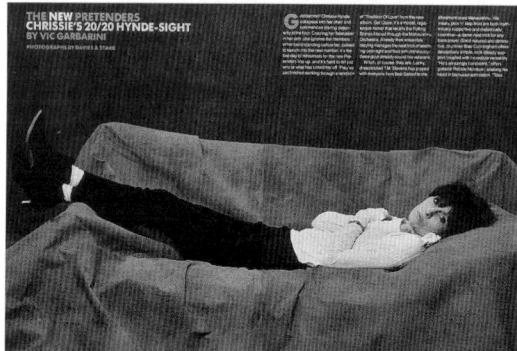

329

330

331

332

333

334

335

336

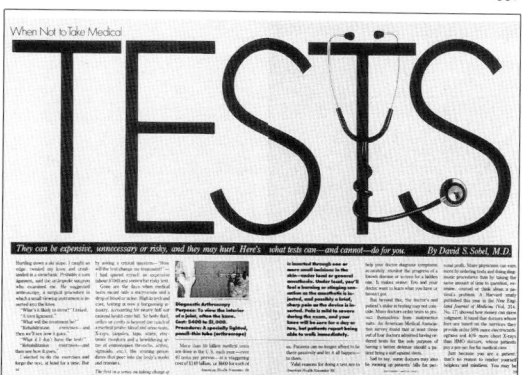

337

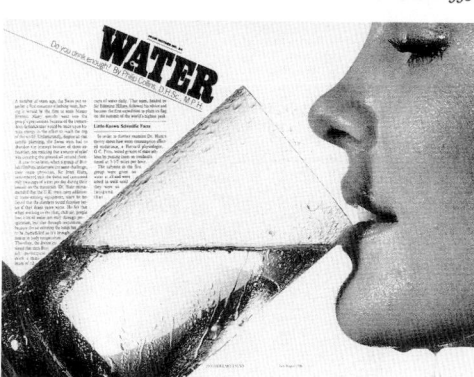

338

339

340

341　342

ART DIRECTOR
Richard Bleiweiss
DESIGNER
Richard Bleiweiss
PHOTOGRAPHER
David Kennedy
GRAPHICS DIRECTOR
Frank Devino
PUBLISHER
Bob Guccione
DESIGNER
Pablo Rodriguez
ILLUSTRATOR/ARTIST
Kunio Hagio
PUBLICATION
Penthouse Int'l, New York, NY

341

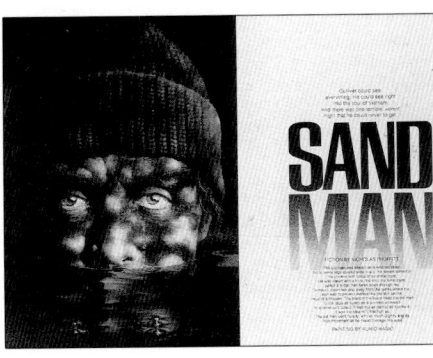

342

343　344

ART DIRECTOR
Nina Ovryn, Morristown, NJ
DESIGNER
Nina Ovryn
PHOTOGRAPHER
Alison Shaw
WRITER
Frank Lowenstein
CLIENT
Eastern Airlines
EDITOR
John Atwood
PUBLISHER
Fred Smith
ILLUSTRATOR/ARTIST
John Craig
WRITER
David Osborne
CLIENT
Eastern Airlines
PUBLICATION
Review Magazine

343

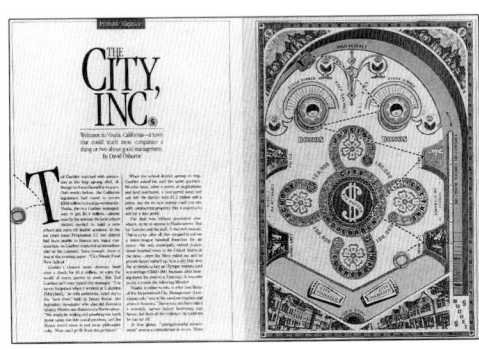

344

345

ART DIRECTOR
Richard M. Baron
DESIGNER
Richard M. Baron
PHOTOGRAPHER
Jeffrey R. Zwart
WRITER
Thos L. Bryant
CLIENT
Road & Track Specials
EDITOR
Thos L. Bryant
PUBLISHER
CBS Magazines
DESIGN FIRM
Road & Track Specials, Newport Beach, CA
PUBLICATION
Road & Track Presents Exotic Cars:4

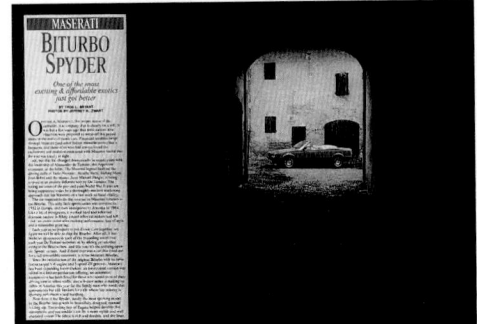

345

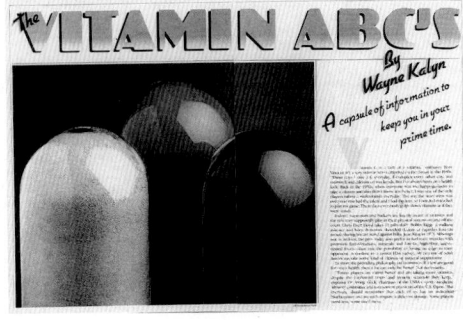

346

346

ART DIRECTOR
Wendy Talve Reingold
DESIGNER
Miriam Campiz
PHOTOGRAPHER
Jeff Smith/Image Bank
PUBLICATION
World Tennis Magazine, New York, NY

347

ART DIRECTOR
Will Hopkins, Ira Friedlander
DESIGNER
Will Hopkins, Ira Friedlander
ILLUSTRATOR/ARTIST
R.J. Kaufman
EDITOR
T. George Harris
PUBLISHER
Owen Lipstein
DESIGN FIRM
Will Hopkins Group, New York, NY
PUBLICATION
American Health

347

It Came from Chicago

348

Ich Bin Ein Artist

350

POWER LUNCH

351

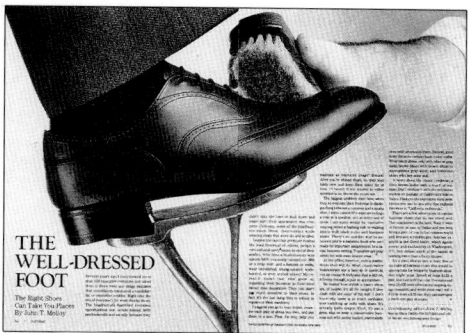

THE WELL-DRESSED FOOT

The Right Shoes
Can Take You Places
By John T. Molloy

352

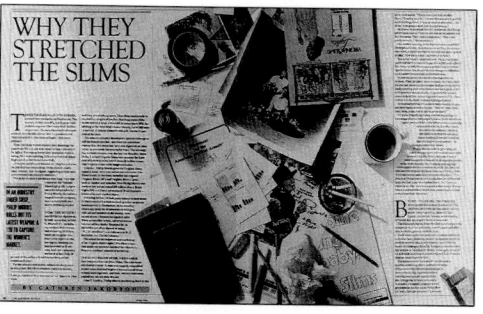

WHY THEY
STRETCHED
THE SLIMS

353

A Yankee
Learns
To Bow

354

348

ART DIRECTOR
Stephen Doyle
DESIGNER
Rosemarie Sohmer
WRITER
Bill Zehme
EDITOR
Susan Morrison
AGENCY
Drenttel Doyle Partners, New York, NY
PUBLICATION
Spy Magazine
SUBJECT
Oprah Winfrey

349

ART DIRECTOR
Stephen Doyle
DESIGNER
Rosemarie Sohmer
PHOTOGRAPHER
George Hein
WRITER
Ann C. Mathers
EDITOR
E. Graydon Carter
PUBLICATION
Spy Magazine

350

ART DIRECTOR
Stephen Doyle
DESIGNER
Rosemarie Sohmer
PHOTOGRAPHER
Enzo Entzel
WRITER
Guy Martin
EDITOR
Kurt Anderson
AGENCY
Drenttel Doyle Partners, New York, NY

351

ART DIRECTOR
Louis F. Cruz
DESIGNER
Louis F. Cruz
PHOTOGRAPHER
Paccione
WRITER
Michael Korda
CLIENT
Success Magazine
EDITOR
Scott DeGarmo
PUBLISHER
Charles S. Bullock
AGENCY
Louis Cruz Creative Group, Inc.

352

ART DIRECTOR
Louis F. Cruz
DESIGNER
Louis F. Cruz
PHOTOGRAPHER
Paccione
WRITER
John T. Malloy
PUBLISHER
Charles S. Bullock
PUBLICATION
Success Magazine

353   354

ART DIRECTOR
Tom Bodkin
DESIGNER
Tom Bodkin
PHOTOGRAPHER
Bruce Wolf
CLIENT
The New York Times Business World
Magazine
EDITOR
Marylin Bender
PUBLISHER
The New York Times, New York, NY
PUBLICATION
The New York Times

355
ART DIRECTOR
David W. Bird II
DESIGNER
David W. Bird II
PHOTOGRAPHER
Roy D. Query
ILLUSTRATOR/ARTIST
David W. Bird
WRITER
Julie M. Fenster
EDITOR
Lowell C. Paddock
PUBLISHER
Richard A. Bartkus, CBS Magazines
PUBLICATION
Automobile Quarterly Magazine, Newport Beach, CA

356
ART DIRECTOR
David W. Bird II
DESIGNER
David W. Bird II
PHOTOGRAPHER
Bill Sumner
CALLIGRAPHER
Lisa L. Tysko
WRITER
Julie M. Fenster
EDITOR
Lowell C. Paddock
PUBLISHER
Richard A. Bartkus, CBS Magazines
PUBLICATION
Automobile Quarterly Magazine, Newport Beach, CA

357
ART DIRECTOR
Wendy Talve Reingold
DESIGNER
Miriam Campiz
ILLUSTRATOR/ARTIST
Robert Risco
PUBLICATION
World Tennis Magazine, New York, NY

358
ART DIRECTOR
Melissa Tardiff
DESIGNER
Maria Cirillo
ILLUSTRATOR/ARTIST
John Glashan
PUBLISHER
The Hearst Corporation
PUBLICATION
Town & Country, New York, NY

355

356

357

358

ANTONIO MARTINO

PAINTING A SMALL WORLD IN A BIG WAY

359

ART DIRECTOR
Clare Cunningham
DESIGNER
Clare Cunningham
PHOTOGRAPHER
Alex Rostocki
ILLUSTRATOR/ARTIST
Antonio Martino
WRITER
Rebecca Smith
CLIENT
Nautical Quarterly
EDITOR
Joseph Gribbins
PUBLISHER
C.S. Lovelace
PUBLICATION
Nautical Quarterly, Essex, CT

359

GONDOLA

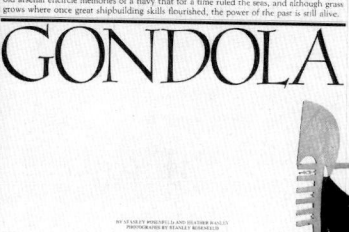

360

ART DIRECTOR
Clare Cunningham
DESIGNER
Clare Cunningham
PHOTOGRAPHER
Stanley Rosenfeld
WRITER
Stanley Rosenfeld, Heather Hanley
CLIENT
Nautical Quarterly
EDITOR
Joseph Gribbins
PUBLISHER
C.S. Lovelace
PUBLICATION
Nautical Quarterly, Essex, CT

360

SHIPS

361

ART DIRECTOR
Clare Cunningham
DESIGNER
Clare Cunningham
PHOTOGRAPHER
Gary Felton
ILLUSTRATOR/ARTIST
Melbourne Smith
WRITER
Stan Grayson
CLIENT
Nautical Quarterly
EDITOR
Joseph Gribbins
PUBLISHER
C.S. Lovelace
PUBLICATION
Nautical Quarterly, Essex, CT

361

OF MICE AND WOMEN

A feminist foible

BY EVELYN RENOLD

continued on page 26

362

ART DIRECTOR
Janet Froelich
DESIGNER
JoDee Stringham
PUBLICATION
NY Daily News, New York, NY

362

363

ART DIRECTOR
David W. Bird II
DESIGNER
David W. Bird II
PHOTOGRAPHER
Leslie L. Bird
WRITER
Jerry Sloniger
EDITOR
Lowell C. Paddock
PUBLISHER
L. Scott Bailey, CBS Magazines
PUBLICATION
Automobile Quarterly Magazine, Newport
Beach, CA

363

364

ART DIRECTOR
Al Foti
DESIGNER
Al Foti
PHOTOGRAPHER
Douglas Kirkland/Sygma, Gareth Hopson
WRITER
Robert Katz
PUBLISHER
MD Publications Inc., New York, NY
PUBLICATION
American Film

364

365

ART DIRECTOR
Karin Burklein Arnold
DESIGNER
Karin Burklein Arnold
PHOTOGRAPHER
Bob Krist
CALLIGRAPHER
Karin Burklein Arnold
WRITER
Peterson & Dodge
CLIENT
Audi of America, Inc.
PRODUCER
Roger Barger
DESIGN FIRM
SHR Communications Planning & Design,
Scottsdale, AZ
PUBLICATION
Spirit of Audi

365

366

ART DIRECTOR
Phyllis Schefer
PHOTOGRAPHER
Various
EDITOR
Karen Anderegg
PUBLICATION DIRECTOR
Regis Pagniez
PUBLISHER
Marybeth Russell
PUBLICATION
Elle Magazine, New York, NY

366

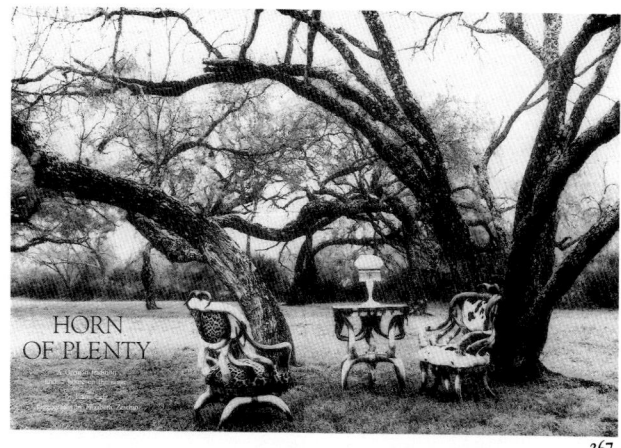

367

ART DIRECTOR
Christopher Lione
PHOTOGRAPHER
Elizabeth Zeschin
WRITER
Franz Lidz
EDITOR
Jeffrey Schaire
PHOTO EDITOR
Denise Dorrance
PUBLISHER
Wick Allison
PUBLICATION
Art & Antiques, New York, NY

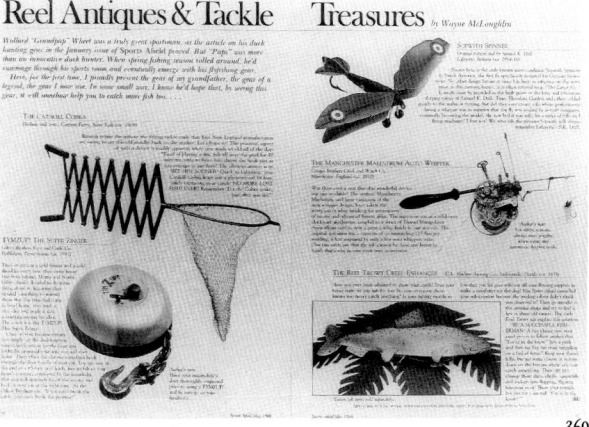

368

ART DIRECTOR
Christopher Lione
PHOTOGRAPHER
Bruce Wolf
WRITER
Catherine Barnett
EDITOR
Catherine Barnett
PHOTO EDITOR
Denise Dorrance
PUBLISHER
Wick Allison
PUBLICATION
Art & Antiques, New York, NY

369

ART DIRECTOR
Gary Gretter
DESIGNER
Carol Rheuban
PHOTOGRAPHER
Amos Chan
ILLUSTRATOR/ARTIST
Wayne McLoughlin
WRITER
Wayne McLoughlin
EDITOR
Tom Paugh
PUBLISHER
Tom Braun
PUBLICATION
Sports Afield Magazine, New York, NY

370

ART DIRECTOR
Richard M. Baron
DESIGNER
Richard M. Baron
PHOTOGRAPHER
Ron Perry
WRITER
Ellida Maki
CLIENT
Road & Track Specials
EDITOR
Thos L. Bryant
PUBLISHER
CBS Magazines
DESIGN FIRM
Road & Track Specials, Newport Beach, CA
PUBLICATION
Road & Track Sports & GT Cars 1987

371

ART DIRECTOR
Will Hopkins, Ira Friedlander
DESIGNER
Will Hopkins, Ira Friedlander
PHOTOGRAPHER
Philippe-Louis Houzé
EDITOR
Bruce Woods
PUBLISHER
Owen Lipstein
DESIGN FIRM
Will Hopkins Group, New York, NY
PUBLICATION
Mother Earth News

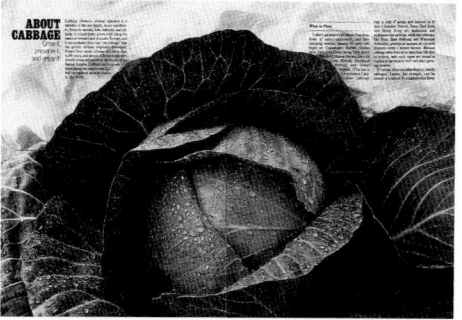

367

368

369

370

371

372

ART DIRECTOR
Lynn Staley
DESIGNER
Lynn Staley
ILLUSTRATOR/ARTIST
Jose Cruz
EDITOR
Ande Zellman
PUBLISHER
The Boston Globe, Boston, MA

372

373

ART DIRECTOR
Danielle Gallo
DESIGNER
Laura Woods
WRITER
A.D. Coleman
EDITOR
Don Myrus
PUBLISHER
Bob Guccione
PUBLICATION
Penthouse Letters, New York, NY

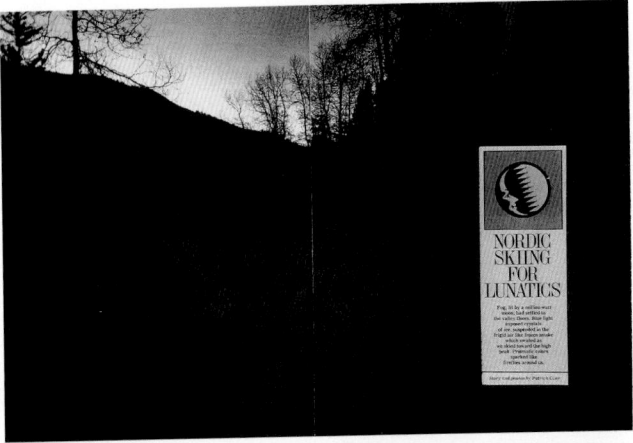

373

374

ART DIRECTOR
Don Weller
DESIGNER
Don Weller
PHOTOGRAPHER
Patrick Cone
ILLUSTRATOR/ARTIST
Don Weller
CLIENT
Lodestar Magazine
PUBLISHER
Jan v. T. Wilking Jr.
DESIGN FIRM
The Weller Institute for the Cure of Design,
Inc., Park City, UT
PUBLICATION
Lodestar Magazine

374

375

ART DIRECTOR
Nora Sheehan, Mary K. Baumann
DESIGNER
Nora Sheehan
PHOTOGRAPHER
Philippe-Louis Houze/Studio Azzuro
WRITER
Leslie N. Vreeland
EDITOR
Landon Y. Jones
PUBLISHER
William M. Kelly
PUBLICATION
Quality Magazine, New York, NY

375

376

ART DIRECTOR
Santiago Cohen
DESIGNER
Carl Barile
PHOTOGRAPHER
Ken Nahoum
WRITER
Alfred Edmond, Jr.
EDITOR
George C. Pryce
PUBLISHER
George C. Pryce
PUBLICATION
MBM Modern Black Men Magazine, New York, NY

376

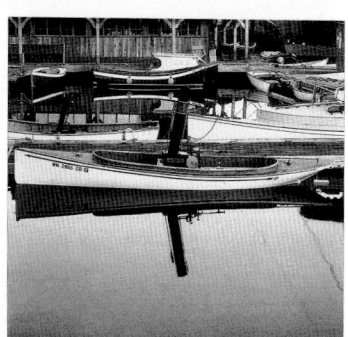

377

ART DIRECTOR
Clare Cunningham
DESIGNER
Clare Cunningham
PHOTOGRAPHER
Marty Loken
WRITER
Bill Durham
CLIENT
Nautical Quarterly
EDITOR
Joseph Gribbins
PUBLISHER
C.S. Lovelace
PUBLICATION
Nautical Quarterly, Essex, CT

377

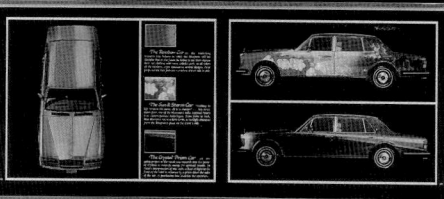

378

ART DIRECTOR
David W. Bird II
DESIGNER
David W. Bird II
PHOTOGRAPHER
Bill Sumner
CALLIGRAPHER
Lisa L. Tysko
WRITER
Julie M. Fenster
EDITOR
Lowell C. Paddock
PUBLISHER
Richard A. Bartkus, CBS Magazines
PUBLICATION
Automobile Quarterly Magazine, Newport Beach, CA

378

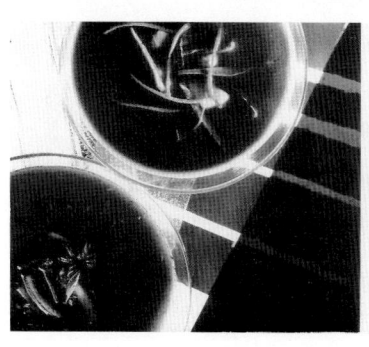

379

ART DIRECTOR
Elizabeth Woodson
DESIGNER
Betty Alfenito
PHOTOGRAPHER
Peter Bosch
CLIENT
American Express Publishing Corp.
EDITOR
Ila Stanger
PUBLICATION
Food & Wine, New York, NY

379

380
ART DIRECTOR
Elizabeth Woodson
DESIGNER
Elizabeth Woodson
PHOTOGRAPHER
Marc David Cohen
CLIENT
American Express Publishing Corp.
EDITOR
Ila Stanger
PUBLICATION
Food & Wine, New York, NY

381
ART DIRECTOR
Elizabeth Woodson
DESIGNER
Elizabeth Woodson
PHOTOGRAPHER
Corinne Colen
CLIENT
American Express Publishing Corp.
EDITOR
Ila Stanger
PUBLICATION
Food & Wine, New York, NY

382
ART DIRECTOR
Christopher Lione
PHOTOGRAPHER
Ianthe Ruthven
WRITER
Alison Beckett
EDITOR
Isolde Motley
PHOTO EDITOR
Denise Dorrance
PUBLISHER
Wick Allison
PUBLICATION
Art & Antiques, New York, NY

383
ART DIRECTOR
Christopher Lione
PHOTOGRAPHER
Kevin Logan
WRITER
Hoagy B. Carmichael
EDITOR
Margot Guralnick
PHOTO EDITOR
Denise Dorrance
PUBLISHER
Wick Allison
PUBLICATION
Art & Antiques, New York, NY

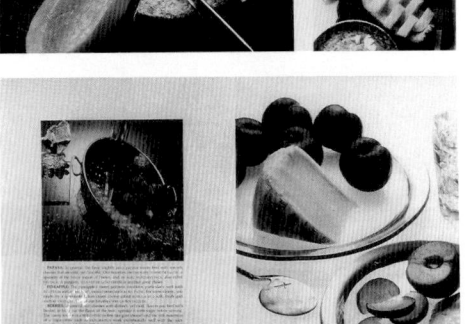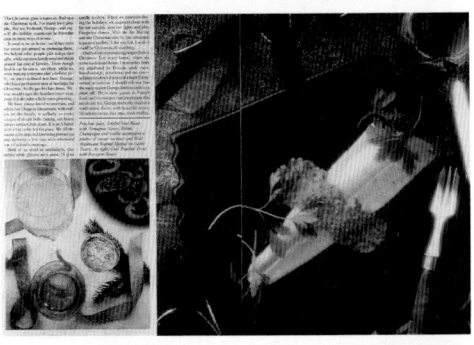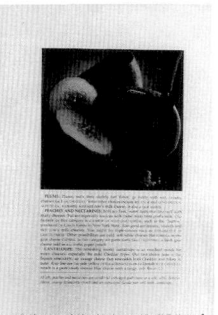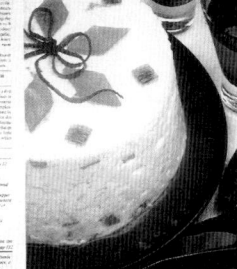

380

381

382

383

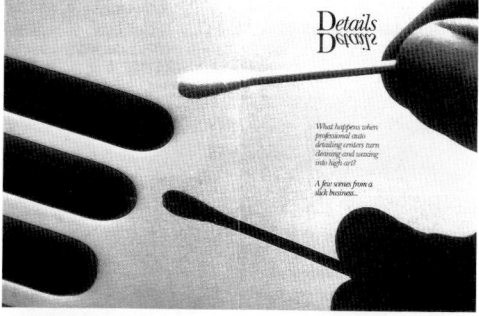

384

ART DIRECTOR
Bridget Desocio, New York, NY
DESIGNER
Diana Kobar
PHOTOGRAPHER
Mark Lyon
CLIENT
Almanac Magazine
EDITOR
Samuel Young
PUBLISHER
Barbara Cady

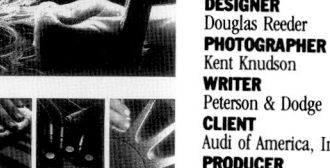

385

ART DIRECTOR
Steve Ditko, Douglas Reeder
DESIGNER
Douglas Reeder
PHOTOGRAPHER
Kent Knudson
WRITER
Peterson & Dodge
CLIENT
Audi of America, Inc.
PRODUCER
Roger Barger
DESIGN FIRM
SHR Communications Planning & Design,
Scottsdale, AZ
PUBLICATION
Spirit of Audi

384

THE INDELIBLE IMAGES OF

Charles Reich

386

ART DIRECTOR
Deb Hardison, Bett McLean
DESIGNER
Deb Hardison
PHOTOGRAPHER
Charles Reich
WRITER
Charles Monagan
CLIENT
Whittle Communications
EDITOR
George Spencer, Thomas G. Lombardo
PUBLISHER
Whittle Communications, Knoxville, TN
PUBLICATION
Connecticut's Finest

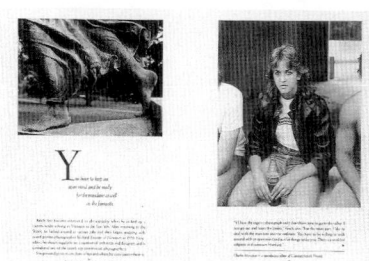

386

387

387

ART DIRECTOR
Joseph Baumer
DESIGNER
Joseph Baumer
PHOTOGRAPHER
Susan Cook, Jack and Linda Vartoogian,
Johan Elbers, Jack Mitchell
WRITER
Joseph H. Mazo
CLIENT
Topic Magazine
EDITOR
Peter Laine
PICTURE EDITOR
Rosalie Targonski
PUBLISHER
U.S. Information Agency
DESIGN FIRM
U.S. Information Agency, Washington DC
PUBLICATION
Topic Magazine

388

ART DIRECTOR
Lloyd Ziff
DESIGNER
Karen Lee Grant
PHOTOGRAPHER
Grant Mudford
WRITER
Martin Filler
EDITOR
Louis Oliver Gropp
PUBLISHER
Conde Nast Publications, Inc., William F.
Bondlow
PUBLICATION
House & Garden, New York, NY

389

ART DIRECTOR
Phyllis Richmond Cox
DESIGNER
Betty B. Saronson
PHOTOGRAPHER
Vanni Burkhart
WRITER
Susan Kuziak
PUBLISHER
Condé Nast Publications, Inc., New York, NY
PUBLICATION
Bride's Magazine
CREATIVE DIRECTOR
Alecia Beldegreen

390

ART DIRECTOR
Bridget Desocio, New York, NY
DESIGNER
Bridget Desocio
PHOTOGRAPHER
Mark Lyon
CLIENT
Almanac Magazine
EDITOR
Samuel Young
PUBLISHER
Barbara Cady

391

ART DIRECTOR
Elizabeth Woodson
DESIGNER
Betty Alfenito
PHOTOGRAPHER
Steven Mark Needham
CLIENT
American Express Publishing Corp.
EDITOR
Ila Stanger
PUBLICATION
Food & Wine, New York, NY

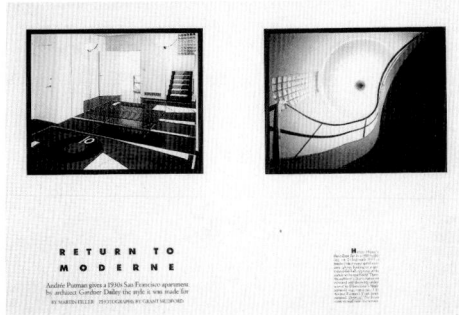

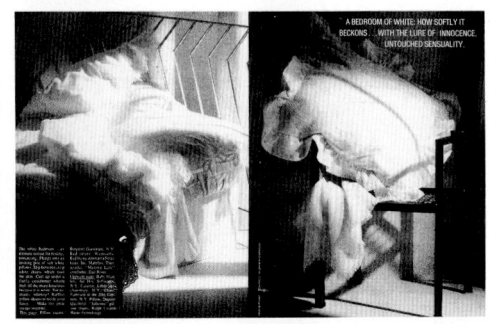
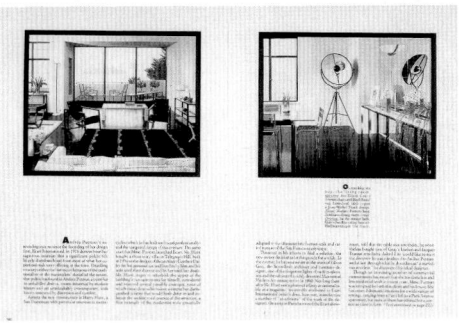

388

389

390

391

392
ART DIRECTOR
Elizabeth Woodson
DESIGNER
Loretta Sala
PHOTOGRAPHER
Michael Skott
CLIENT
American Express Publishing Corp.
EDITOR
Ila Stanger
PUBLICATION
Food & Wine, New York, NY

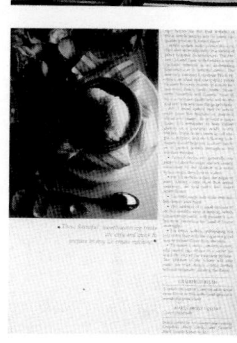
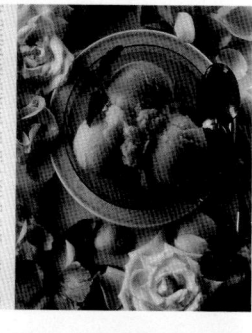

393
ART DIRECTOR
Elizabeth Woodson
DESIGNER
Loretta Sala
PHOTOGRAPHER
Michael Skott
CLIENT
American Express Publishing Corp.
EDITOR
Ila Stanger
PUBLICATION
Food & Wine, New York, NY

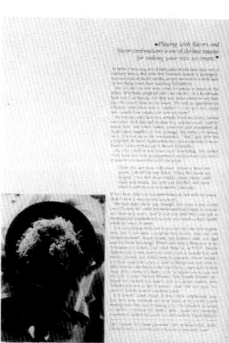

392

393

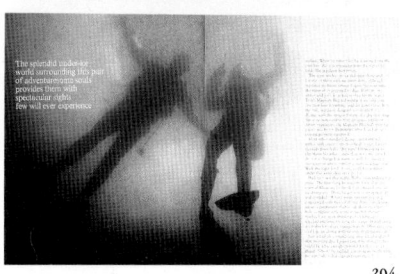

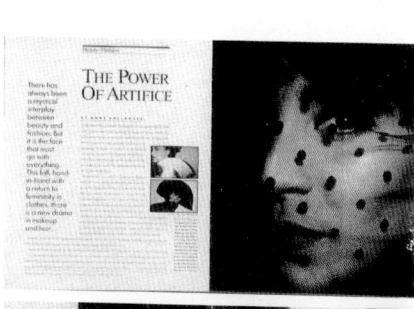

394
ART DIRECTOR
Bill Pope, Gijsbert van Frankenhuyzen
PHOTOGRAPHER
Robert McQuilkin, Glen Ellyn, IL
EDITOR
Geri Nixon, Norris McDowell
PUBLISHER
Nancy Mead
PUBLICATION
Wisconsin Trails Magazine; Michigan Natural
Resources Magazine

395
ART DIRECTOR
Diana LaGuardia
DESIGNER
Kevin McPhee
PHOTOGRAPHER
Various
CLIENT
The New York Times Magazine
EDITOR
Ed Klein
PUBLISHER
The New York Times, New York, NY
PUBLICATION
The New York Times

394

395

396

ART DIRECTOR
Bob Ciano
DESIGNER
Bob Ciano
PHOTOGRAPHER
Mark Sennet, Al Freni
WRITER
David Craig
CLIENT
Life Magazine
EDITOR
Judith Daniels, Jim Watters
PUBLICATION
Life Magazine, New York, NY

396

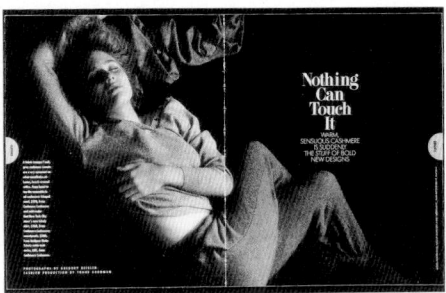

397

ART DIRECTOR
Melissa Tardiff
DESIGNER
Melissa Tardiff
PHOTOGRAPHER
Victor Skrebneski
PUBLISHER
The Hearst Corporation
PUBLICATION
Town & Country, New York, NY

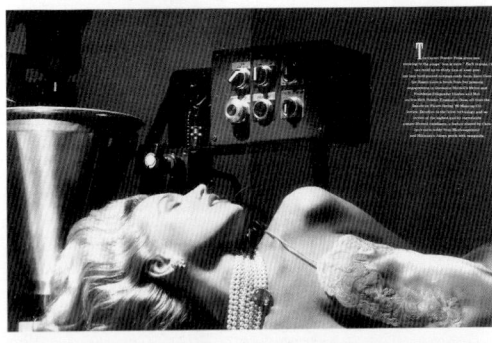

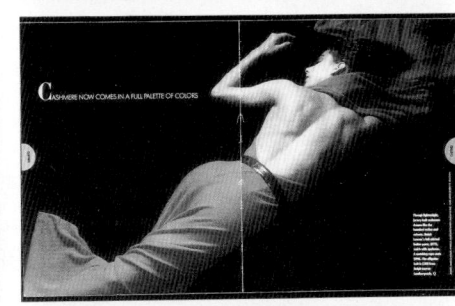

398

ART DIRECTOR
Nora Sheehan, Mary K. Baumann
DESIGNER
Nora Sheehan, Mary K. Baumann
PHOTOGRAPHER
Gregory Heisler
WRITER
Robert Vance
EDITOR
Landon Y. Jones
PUBLISHER
William M. Kelly
PUBLICATION
Quality Magazine, New York, NY

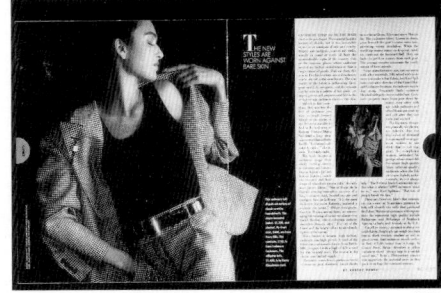

398

397

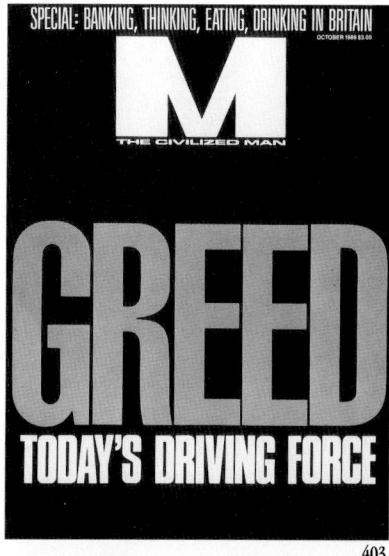

'We Mourn Seven Heroes'

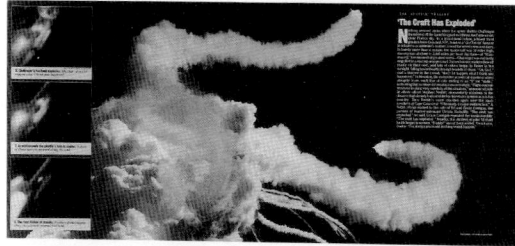

399

BEATING BURNOUT

399

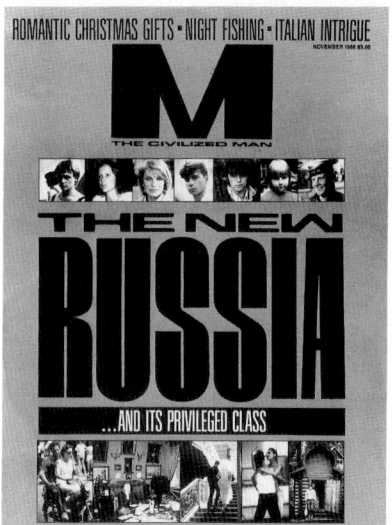

402

SPIDER WEBS &...

...SPHAGNUM BOGS

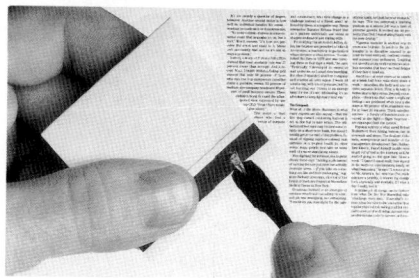

401

400

399

ART DIRECTOR
Roger Black, Ron Meyerson (cover)
PUBLICATION
Newsweek Magazine, New York, NY

400

ART DIRECTOR
Louis F. Cruz
DESIGNER
Louis F. Cruz
PHOTOGRAPHER
Paccione
WRITER
Katy Koontz
CLIENT
Success Magazine
EDITOR
Scott DeGarmo
PUBLISHER
Charles S. Bullock
AGENCY
Louis Cruz Creative Group, Inc.
DESIGN FIRM
Louis Cruz Creative Group, Inc., New York, NY
PUBLICATION
Success Magazine

401

ART DIRECTOR
Louis F. Cruz
DESIGNER
Louis F. Cruz, Pilar Cruz
PHOTOGRAPHER
Sam Prentiss
WRITER
Kathleen Thomas, Sam Prentiss
CLIENT
Adirondack Life Magazine
EDITOR
Jeffrey G. Kelly
PUBLISHER
Arthur Kornhaber
AGENCY
Louis Cruz Creative Group, Inc.
DESIGN FIRM
Louis Cruz Creative Group, Inc., New York, NY

402

ART DIRECTOR
Owen Hartley
DESIGNER
Owen Hartley, Dennis Freedman
PHOTOGRAPHER
Tim Jenkins
CLIENT
M Magazine
EDITOR
Kevin Doyle
PUBLISHER
Fairchild Publications, New York, NY
PUBLICATION
M Magazine

403

ART DIRECTOR
Owen Hartley
DESIGNER
Owen Hartley, John Fairchild, Michael Coady
CLIENT
M Magazine
EDITOR
Kevin Doyle
PUBLISHER
Fairchild Publications, New York, NY
PUBLICATION
M Magazine

404

ART DIRECTOR
Carla Barr
DESIGNER
Carla Barr
PHOTOGRAPHER
Kenro Izu
PUBLISHER
Hearst Corp.
PUBLICATION
Connoisseur Magazine, New York, NY

405

ART DIRECTOR
Carla Barr
DESIGNER
Carla Barr
PHOTOGRAPHER
Brian Hagiwara
PUBLISHER
Hearst Corp.
PUBLICATION
Connoisseur Magazine, New York, NY

406

ART DIRECTOR
Carla Barr
DESIGNER
Carla Barr
PHOTOGRAPHER
Sandi Fellman
PUBLISHER
Hearst Corp.
PUBLICATION
Connoisseur Magazine, New York, NY

407

ART DIRECTOR
Carla Barr
DESIGNER
Carla Barr
PHOTOGRAPHER
Maggie Steber
PUBLISHER
Hearst Corp.
PUBLICATION
Connoisseur Magazine, New York, NY

408

ART DIRECTOR
Carla Barr
DESIGNER
Carla Barr
PHOTOGRAPHER
Sandi Fellman
PUBLISHER
Hearst Corp.
PUBLICATION
Connoisseur Magazine, New York, NY

409

ART DIRECTOR
Vance Jonson, Sara Barbaris
DESIGNER
Vance Jonson, Kim Capone
PHOTOGRAPHER
Richard Felber
WRITER
Judith Hill
EDITOR
Christopher Kimball
DESIGN FIRM
Jonson Pirtle Pedersen Alcorn Metzdorf &
Hess, Rowayton, CT

404

405

407

408

409

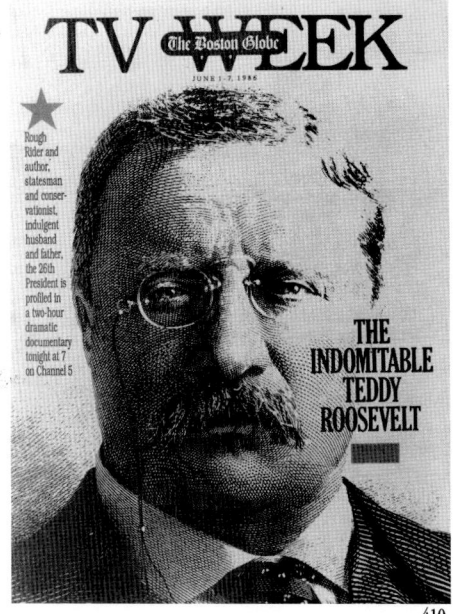

410

411

414

413

415

410
ART DIRECTOR
Lucy Bartholomay
DESIGNER
Lucy Bartholomay
ILLUSTRATOR/ARTIST
Archive
PUBLISHER
The Boston Globe, Boston, MA
PUBLICATION
The Boston Globe TV Week

411
ART DIRECTOR
Lucy Bartholomay
DESIGNER
Lucy Bartholomay
ILLUSTRATOR/ARTIST
Unknown
PUBLISHER
The Boston Globe, Boston, MA
PUBLICATION
The Boston Globe TV Week

412
ART DIRECTOR
Lucy Bartholomay
DESIGNER
Lucy Bartholomay
ILLUSTRATOR/ARTIST
Patrick Blackwell
PUBLISHER
The Boston Globe, Boston, MA
PUBLICATION
The Boston Globe TV Week

413
ART DIRECTOR
Lucy Bartholomay
DESIGNER
Lucy Bartholomay
ILLUSTRATOR/ARTIST
Patrick Blackwell
PUBLISHER
The Boston Globe, Boston, MA
PUBLICATION
The Boston Globe TV Week

414
ART DIRECTOR
Miriam Smith
ILLUSTRATOR/ARTIST
Heino Orro
WRITER
Adrian Peracchio
EDITOR
John Montorio
PUBLISHER
Newsday
PUBLICATION
The Newsday Magazine, Melville, NY

415
ART DIRECTOR
Miriam Smith
ILLUSTRATOR/ARTIST
Mitchell Confer
WRITER
Ann Jones
EDITOR
John Montorio
PUBLISHER
Newsday
PUBLICATION
The Newsday Magazine, Melville, NY

412

416

ART DIRECTOR
Lynn Staley
DESIGNER
Lynn Staley
ILLUSTRATOR/ARTIST
Type
EDITOR
Ande Zellman
PUBLISHER
The Boston Globe, Boston, MA

417

ART DIRECTOR
Lynn Staley
DESIGNER
Lynn Staley
ILLUSTRATOR/ARTIST
Matt Mahurin
EDITOR
Ande Zellman
PUBLISHER
The Boston Globe, Boston, MA

418

ART DIRECTOR
Lynn Staley
DESIGNER
Lynn Staley
ILLUSTRATOR/ARTIST
Marshall Arisman
EDITOR
Ande Zellman
PUBLISHER
The Boston Globe, Boston, MA

419

ART DIRECTOR
Lynn Staley
DESIGNER
Lynn Staley
ILLUSTRATOR/ARTIST
Gene Greif
EDITOR
Ande Zellman
PUBLISHER
The Boston Globe, Boston, MA

420

ART DIRECTOR
Lynn Staley
DESIGNER
Lynn Staley
ILLUSTRATOR/ARTIST
Doug Smith
EDITOR
Ande Zellman
PUBLISHER
The Boston Globe, Boston, MA

421

ART DIRECTOR
Lynn Staley
DESIGNER
Lynn Staley
ILLUSTRATOR/ARTIST
Elmwood Smith
EDITOR
Ande Zellman
PUBLISHER
The Boston Globe, Boston, MA

422

ART DIRECTOR
Melissa Tardiff
DESIGNER
Richard Turtletaub
ILLUSTRATOR/ARTIST
John Rombola
PUBLISHER
The Hearst Corporation
PUBLICATION
Town & Country, New York, NY

416

417

418

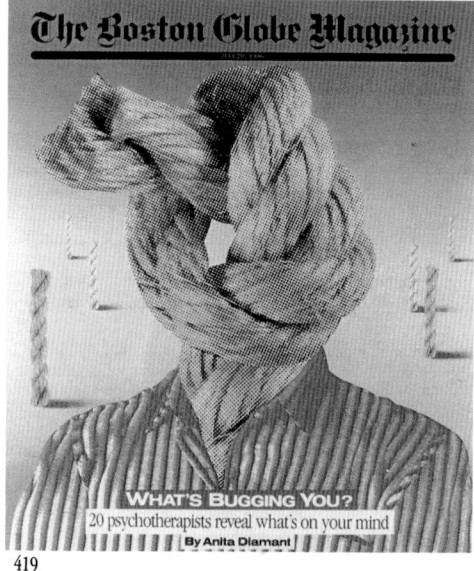

419

420

421

422

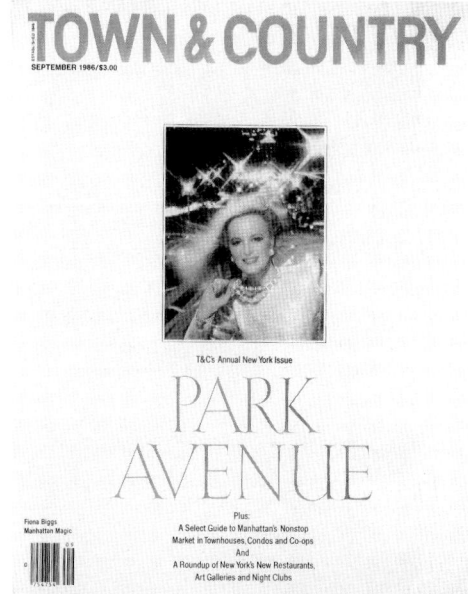

423

423

ART DIRECTOR
Melissa Tardiff
DESIGNER
Richard Turtletaub
PHOTOGRAPHER
Norman Parkinson
PUBLISHER
The Hearst Corporation
PUBLICATION
Town & Country, New York, NY

424

ART DIRECTOR
Phyllis Schefer
PHOTOGRAPHER
Gilles Bensimon
EDITOR
Karen Anderegg
PUBLICATION DIRECTOR
Regis Pagniez
PUBLISHER
Marybeth Russell
PUBLICATION
Elle Magazine, New York, NY

424

425

425

ART DIRECTOR
Ron Albrecht
PHOTOGRAPHER
Gilles Bensimon
EDITOR
Karen Anderegg
PUBLICATION DIRECTOR
Regis Pagniez
PUBLISHER
Marybeth Russell
PUBLICATION
Elle Magazine, New York, NY

426

ART DIRECTOR
Joseph Baumer
DESIGNER
Joseph Baumer
PHOTOGRAPHER
Richard Saunders
WRITER
Andrew M. Bardagjy
PICTURE EDITOR
Rosalie Targonski
PUBLISHER
U.S. Information Agency
CLIENT
Topic Magazine
EDITOR
Peter Laine
PUBLICATION
Topic Magazine

426

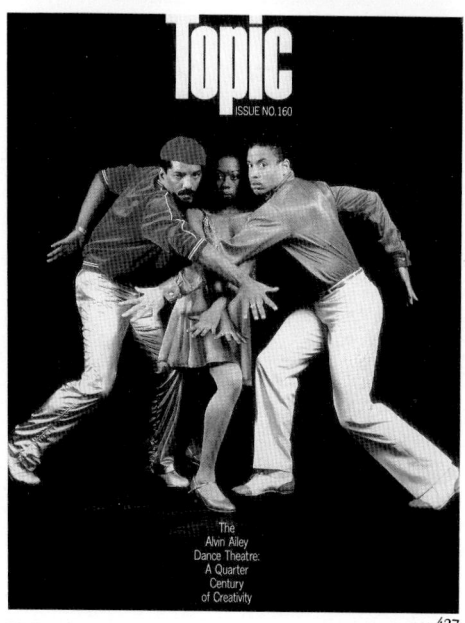

427

427

ART DIRECTOR
Joseph Baumer
DESIGNER
Joseph Baumer
PHOTOGRAPHER
Kenn Duncan
WRITER
Gabrielle Walters
CLIENT
Topic Magazine
EDITOR
Peter Laine
PICTURE EDITOR
Rosalie Targonski
PUBLISHER
U.S. Information Agency
DESIGN FIRM
U.S. Information Agency, Washington, DC
PUBLICATION
Topic Magazine

428

ART DIRECTOR
Helene Silverman
PUBLICATION
Metropolis Magazine, New York, NY

429

ART DIRECTOR
Helene Silverman
PUBLICATION
Metropolis Magazine, New York, NY

430

ART DIRECTOR
Helene Silverman
PUBLICATION
Metropolis Magazine, New York, NY

431

ART DIRECTOR
Helene Silverman
PUBLICATION
Metropolis Magazine, New York, NY

432

ART DIRECTOR
Roger Gorman
DESIGNER
Frances Reinfeld
ILLUSTRATOR/ARTIST
Alexander Calder
CLIENT
Artforum Magazine
EDITOR
Ingrid Sischy
PUBLISHER
Anthony Korner
DESIGN FIRM
Reiner Design Consultants, Inc., New York,
NY
PUBLICATION
Artforum Magazine

433

ART DIRECTOR
Roger Gorman
DESIGNER
Frances Reinfeld
ILLUSTRATOR/ARTIST
Gino De Dominicis
CLIENT
Artforum Magazine
EDITOR
Ingrid Sischy
PUBLISHER
Anthony Korner
DESIGN FIRM
Reiner Design Consultants, Inc., New York,
NY
PUBLICATION
Artforum Magazine

434

ART DIRECTOR
Nancy Kent
DESIGNER
Nancy Kent
ILLUSTRATOR/ARTIST
Milton Glaser
CLIENT
The New York Times Magazine
EDITOR
Alex Ward
PUBLISHER
The New York Times, New York, NY
PUBLICATION
The New York Times

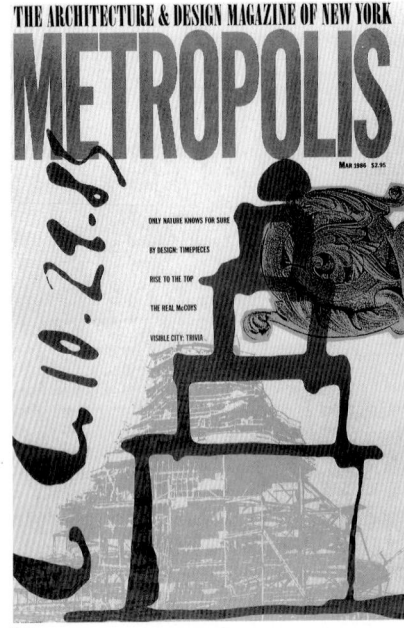

428

429

430

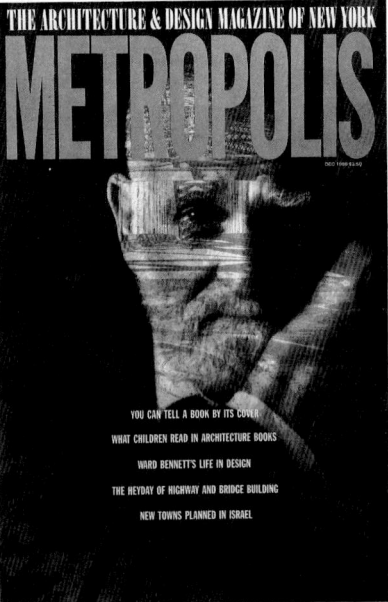

431

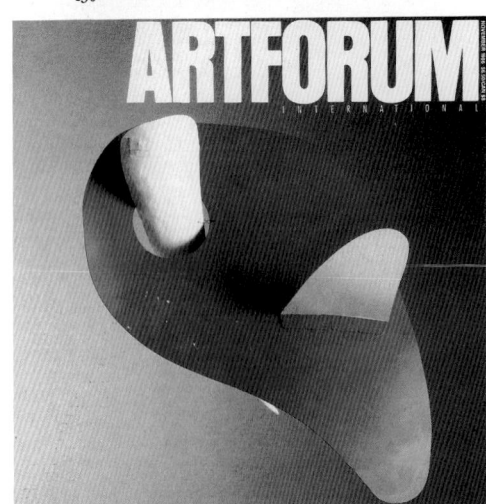

432

433

434

435

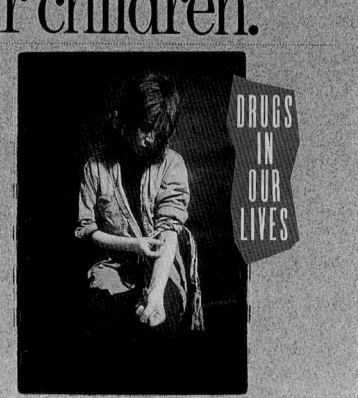

436

437

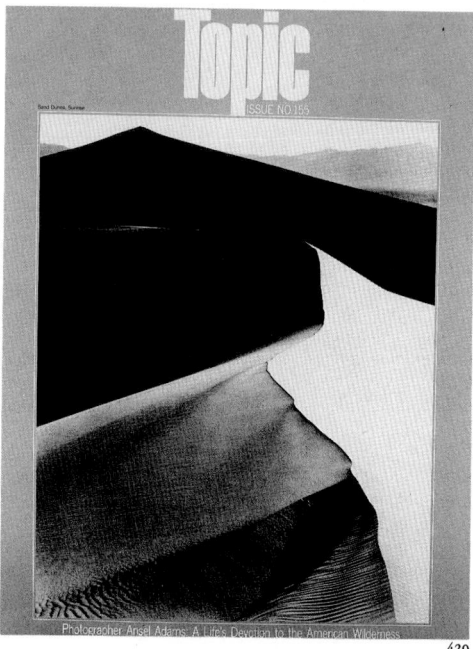

438

439

435
ART DIRECTOR
Ken Kendrick, Diana LaGuardia
DESIGNER
Diana LaGuardia
CLIENT
The New York Times Magazine
EDITOR
Ed Klein
PUBLISHER
The New York Times, New York, NY
PUBLICATION
The New York Times

436
ART DIRECTOR
Lucy Bartholomay
DESIGNER
Lucy Bartholomay
PHOTOGRAPHER
Michael Weisbrot
PUBLISHER
The Boston Globe, Boston, MA
PUBLICATION
Drugs in Our Lives

437
ART DIRECTOR
Richard Baker
DESIGNER
Richard Baker
ILLUSTRATOR/ARTIST
Paula Munck
EDITOR
David E. Young
PUBLISHER
The Boston Globe, Boston, MA
PUBLICATION
Gift Guide

438
ART DIRECTOR
Louis F. Cruz
DESIGNER
Louis F. Cruz, Pilar Cruz
PHOTOGRAPHER
Clyde H. Smith
CLIENT
Adirondack Life Magazine
EDITOR
Jeffrey E. Kelly
PUBLISHER
Howard Fish
AGENCY
Louis Cruz Creative Group, Inc.
DESIGN FIRM
Louis Cruz Creative Group, Inc., New York,
NY
PUBLICATION
Adirondack Life Magazine

439
ART DIRECTOR
Joseph Baumer
DESIGNER
Joseph Baumer
PHOTOGRAPHER
Ansel Adams
WRITER
Gabrielle Walters
CLIENT
Topic Magazine
EDITOR
Peter Laine
PICTURE EDITOR
Rosalie Targonski
PUBLISHER
U.S. Information Agency
DESIGN FIRM
U.S. Information Agency, Washington, DC
PUBLICATION
Topic Magazine

440
ART DIRECTOR
Dwayne Flinchum
PHOTOGRAPHER
Michael Radencich
GRAPHICS DIRECTOR
Frank Devino
PUBLISHER
Bob Guccione
PUBLICATION
Omni Publications International Ltd., New
York, NY

441
ART DIRECTOR
Nigel Holmes
ILLUSTRATOR/ARTIST
James Marsh
CLIENT
Time Magazine, Art Director Rudy Hoglund
PUBLISHER
Time Incorporated, New York, NY
PUBLICATION
Time Magazine

442
ART DIRECTOR
Paul N. Williams
PHOTOGRAPHER
Chuck Place, Santa Barbara, CA
CLIENT
The Yacht Magazine
EDITOR
Roger Vaughan
MANAGING EDITOR
Dan Segal
PUBLICATION
The Yacht

443
ART DIRECTOR
Roxanne Stacheler
DESIGNER
William Wondriska
ASST. ART DIRECTOR
David Kendrick
PHOTOGRAPHER
Jim Meehan
ILLUSTRATOR/ARTIST
William Wondriska
CLIENT
Northeast Magazine, The Hartford Courant
EDITOR
Lary Bloom
PUBLISHER
The Hartford Courant
DESIGN FIRM
Wondriska Associates, Farmington, CT
PUBLICATION
Northeast Magazine

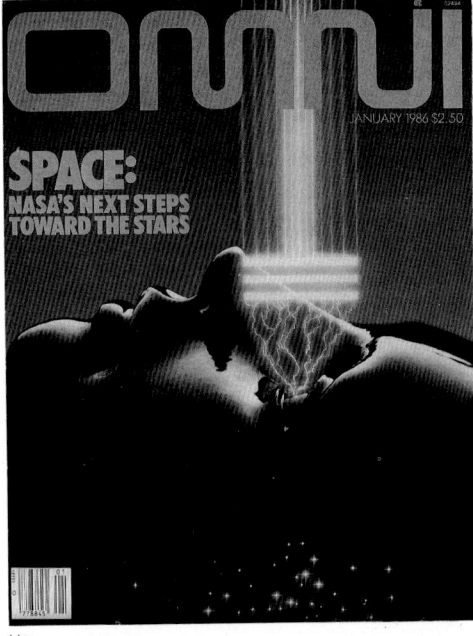

440

441

442

443

444

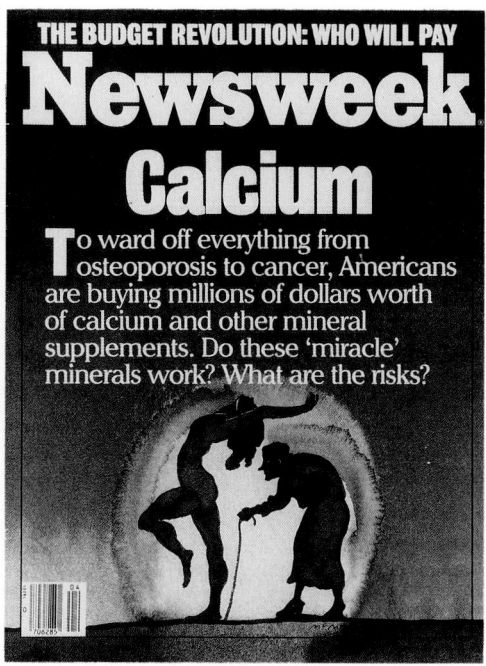

445

444

ART DIRECTOR
Robert Best
ILLUSTRATOR/ARTIST
Michael Witte
EDITOR
Edward Kosner
PUBLISHER
Murdock Magazines, Edward Kosner
PUBLICATION
New York Magazine, New York, NY

445

ART DIRECTOR
Roger Black, Ron Meyerson (cover)
ILLUSTRATOR/ARTIST
James MacMullan
PUBLICATION
Newsweek Magazine, New York, NY

446

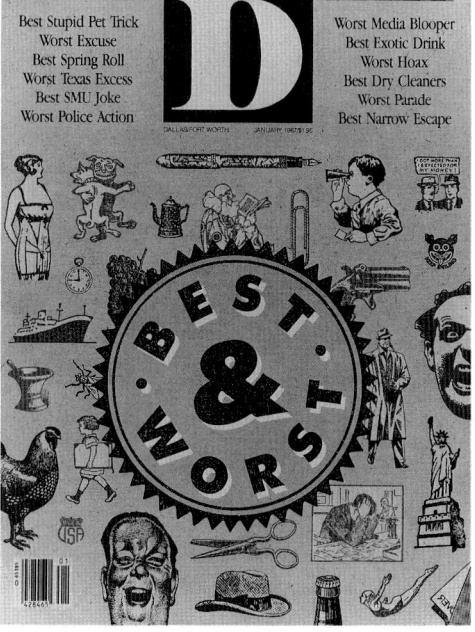

447

446

ART DIRECTOR
Miriam Smith
DESIGNER
Miriam Smith
PHOTOGRAPHER
Ken Spencer
WRITER
A.J. Carter
EDITOR
John Montorio
PUBLISHER
Newsday
PUBLICATION
The Newsday Magazine, Melvilie, NY

447

ART DIRECTOR
Douglas May, Matthew Drace
DESIGNER
Douglas May
ILLUSTRATOR/ARTIST
Bill Nelson
CLIENT
D Magazine
EDITOR
Ruth Miller Fitzgibbons
PUBLISHER
Terry Murphy
DESIGN FIRM
Douglas May Design, Dallas, TX
PUBLICATION
D Magazine

448
DESIGNER
Daniel J. McClain
PHOTOGRAPHER
Gary Braasch, Portland, OR
EDITOR
Martha Hill
PUBLISHER
National Audubon Society
PUBLICATION
Audubon Magazine

448

449
ART DIRECTOR
Claude Skelton
DESIGNER
Claude Skelton
ILLUSTRATOR/ARTIST
Anthony Russo
WRITER
Randel Barnett
EDITOR
Eric Garland
PUBLISHER
The Daily Record/Warfield's
PUBLICATION
Warfield's Magazine, Baltimore, MD

449

450
ART DIRECTOR
Claude Skelton
DESIGNER
Claude Skelton
PHOTOGRAPHER
Tom Wolff
WRITER
Michael Yockel
EDITOR
Eric Garland
PUBLISHER
The Daily Record/Warfield's
PUBLICATION
Warfield's Magazine, Baltimore, MD

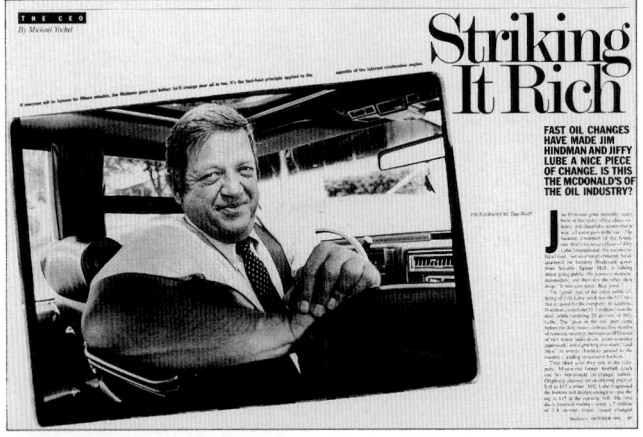

450

451
ART DIRECTOR
Claude Skelton
DESIGNER
Claude Skelton
ILLUSTRATOR/ARTIST
Alan E. Cober
WRITER
Diane Booth
EDITOR
Eric Garland
PUBLISHER
The Daily Record/Warfield's
PUBLICATION
Warfield's Magazine, Baltimore, MD

451

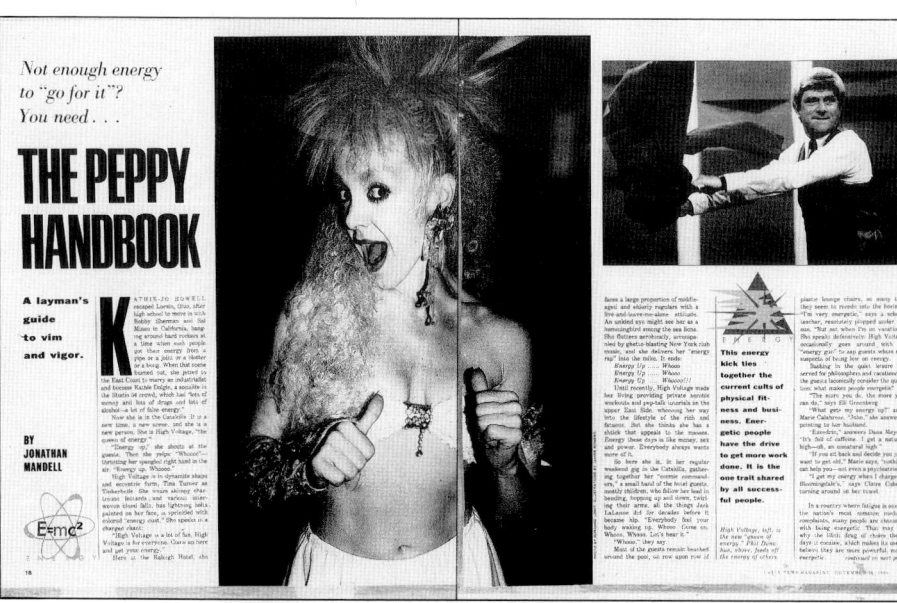

452

ART DIRECTOR
Janet Froelich
DESIGNER
Janet Froelich
ILLUSTRATOR/ARTIST
Javier Romero
PUBLICATION
NY Daily News, New York, NY

452

453

453

ART DIRECTOR
Judy Whitt
ILLUSTRATOR/ARTIST
Judy Whitt
WRITER
James R. Russo
PUBLISHER
Cahners Publishing Co., Des Plaines, IL
PUBLICATION
Packaging

454

454

ART DIRECTOR
Bill Cadge
DESIGNER
Bill Cadge
PHOTOGRAPHER
Randy Duchaine
WRITER
Geoffrey D. Austrian
EDITOR
Chet Hansen
PUBLISHER
IBM
PUBLICATION
Think Magazine, White Plains, NY

455

455

ART DIRECTOR
Owen Hartley
DESIGNER
Owen Hartley
ILLUSTRATOR/ARTIST
Jenny Adams
CLIENT
Philip Morris Magazine
EDITOR
Frank Gannon
PUBLISHER
Eaton Court Publications
DESIGN FIRM
Owen Hartley Design, New York, NY
PUBLICATION
Philip Morris Magazine

456

ART DIRECTOR
Scott Menchin
DESIGNER
Scott Menchin
ILLUSTRATOR/ARTIST
Paul Davis
WRITER
Margaret Richardson
PUBLISHER
RC Publications, Howard Cadel
PUBLICATION
How Magazine, New York, NY

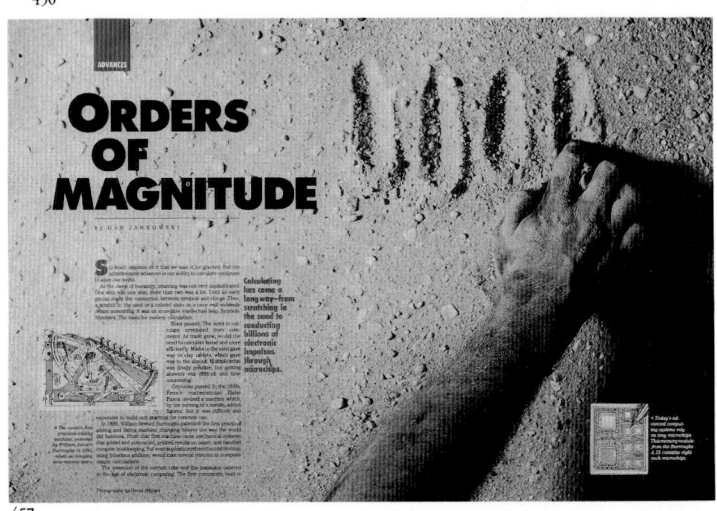

456

457

ART DIRECTOR
Kathy Kelley
DESIGNER
Eric Keller
PHOTOGRAPHER
David Baditoi
WRITER
Dan Jankowski
CLIENT
Unisys Corporation
EDITOR
Dan Jankowski
DIRECTOR
Kirk Cheyfitz
DESIGN FIRM
The Publications Company, Detroit, MI
PUBLICATION
Solutions Magazine

457

458

ART DIRECTOR
John Tom Cohoe
DESIGNER
John Tom Cohoe
PHOTOGRAPHER
Brad Miller
WRITER
William Jeanes
CLIENT
Mercedes-Benz of North America
EDITOR
Tom Parrett
PUBLISHER
Mercedes-Benz of North America
AGENCY
McCaffrey & McCall, New York, NY
PUBLICATION
Mercedes Magazine

458

459

ART DIRECTOR
Wendy Pressley-Jacobs
DESIGNER
Wendy Pressley-Jacobs
PHOTOGRAPHER
James Imbrogno/Imbrogno Photography
ILLUSTRATOR/ARTIST
Amy McCarter
WRITER
K. Wayne Rice, Kent Blair, Robert Poole
CLIENT
Real Estate Today® Magazine
EDITOR
Karin L. Nelson
PUBLISHER
National Association of Realtors®
DESIGN FIRM
Pressley Jacobs Design, Inc., Chicago, IL
PUBLICATION
Real Estate Today®

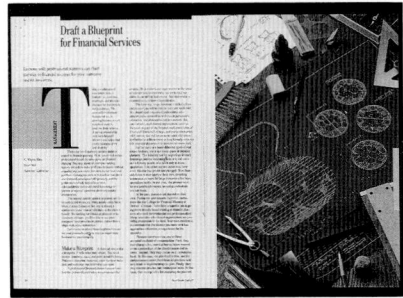

459

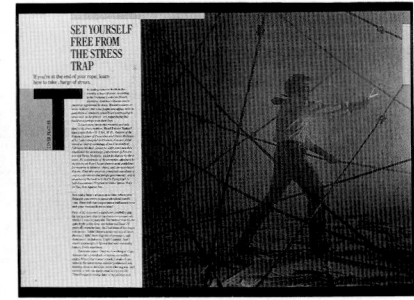

460

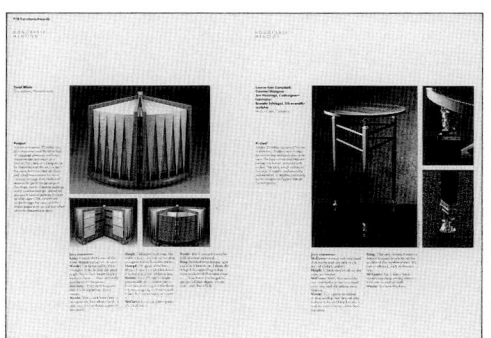

460
ART DIRECTOR
Wendy Pressley-Jacobs
DESIGNER
Wendy Pressley-Jacobs
PHOTOGRAPHER
James Imbrogno/Imbrogno Photography
WRITER
Lynn Koslowsky (staff)
CLIENT
Real Estate Today® Magazine
EDITOR
Karin L. Nelson
PUBLISHER
National Association of Realtors®
DESIGN FIRM
Pressley Jacobs Design, Inc., Chicago, IL
PUBLICATION
Real Estate Today®

461

461
ART DIRECTOR
Richelle J. Huff
DESIGNER
Richelle J. Huff
PHOTOGRAPHER
Keri Pickett, Laurie Ann Campbell
WRITER
Pilar Viladas
EDITOR
Pilar Viladas
PUBLISHER
Penton Publishing
PUBLICATION
Progressive Architecture, Stamford, CT

462

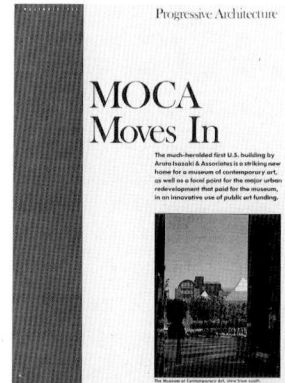

462
ART DIRECTOR
Faye H. Eng, Anthony T. Yee
DESIGNER
Faye H. Eng, Anthony T. Yee
PHOTOGRAPHER
Joseph McDonald, Davis Mather
WRITER
Elizabeth Wecter
CLIENT
The Clarion
EDITOR
Didi Barrett
PUBLISHER
Museum of American Folk Art
DESIGN FIRM
Eng and Yee Designs, Inc., New York, NY

463
ART DIRECTOR
Richelle J. Huff
DESIGNER
Samuel G. Shelton
PHOTOGRAPHER
Richard Bryant
WRITER
Pilar Viladas
EDITOR
Pilar Viladas
PUBLISHER
Penton Publishing
PUBLICATION
Progressive Architecture, Stamford, CT

464
ART DIRECTOR
Richelle J. Huff
DESIGNER
Richelle J. Huff
PHOTOGRAPHER
Tom Crane, Jack Alterman
WRITER
Daralice D. Boles
EDITOR
Daralice D. Boles
PUBLISHER
Penton Publishing
PUBLICATION
Progressive Architecture, Stamford, CT

465
ART DIRECTOR
Eddie Medrano
DESIGNER
Eddie Medrano
PHOTOGRAPHER
Steve Pitkin
WRITER
William H. Skip Boyer
EDITOR
Wendy Black
PUBLISHER
Best Western International
AGENCY
B/W Advertising, Phoenix, AZ
PUBLICATION
Quarterly

466   467
ART DIRECTOR
Jack Lefkowitz
DESIGNER
Jack Lefkowitz
ILLUSTRATOR/ARTIST
Virginia Strnad
WRITER
David Ritchey
CLIENT
Industrial Launderer
EDITOR
David Ritchey
PUBLISHER
Institute of Industrial Launderers
AGENCY
Jack Lefkowitz, Inc., Leesburg, VA
PUBLICATION
Industrial Launderer

468
ART DIRECTOR
Jack Lefkowitz
DESIGNER
Jack Lefkowitz
PHOTOGRAPHER
David Ritchey
ILLUSTRATOR/ARTIST
Virginia Strnad
WRITER
David Ritchey
CLIENT
Industrial Launderer
EDITOR
David Ritchey
PUBLISHER
Institute of Industrial Launderers
AGENCY
Jack Lefkowitz, Leesburg, VA
PUBLICATION
Industrial Launderer

469
ART DIRECTOR
Andrew P. Kner
DESIGNER
Jack Anderson, John Hornall
PHOTOGRAPHER
Mark Burnside
ILLUSTRATOR/ARTIST
Jack Anderson
CLIENT
Print Magazine
EDITOR
Martin Fox
PUBLISHER
Howard Cadel
DESIGN FIRM
Hornall Anderson Design Works, Seattle, WA

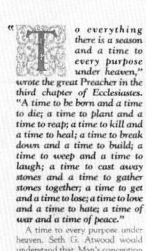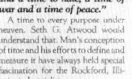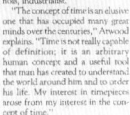
465

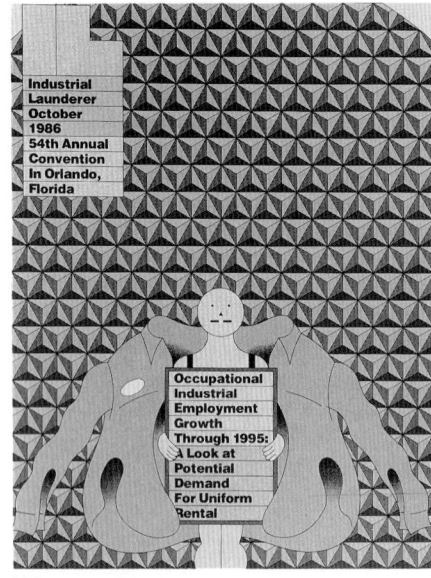
466

467

468

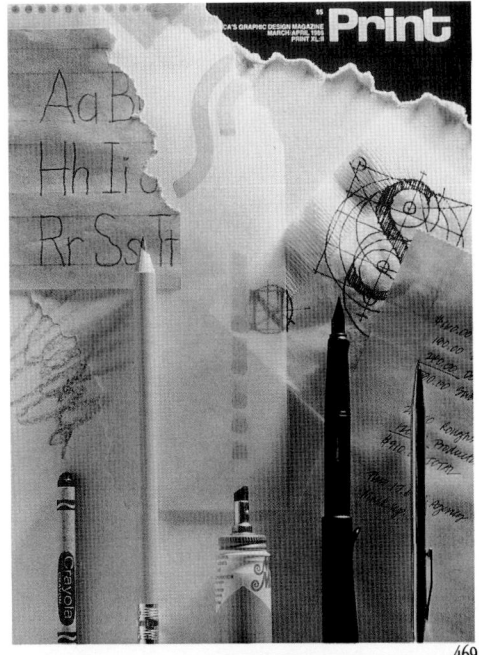

469

470

470

ART DIRECTOR
Scott Menchin
DESIGNER
Paul Davis Studio
ILLUSTRATOR/ARTIST
Paul Davis, Jose Conde, Jeanine Esposito
PUBLISHER
RC Publications, Howard Cadel
PUBLICATION
How Magazine, New York, NY

471

ART DIRECTOR
Fabrizio La Rocca
DESIGNER
Fabrizio La Rocca
PHOTOGRAPHER
Peter Marlow/Magnum
EDITOR
Lee Baier
PUBLICATION
Junior Scholastic, New York, NY
CREATIVE DIRECTOR
Dale Moyer

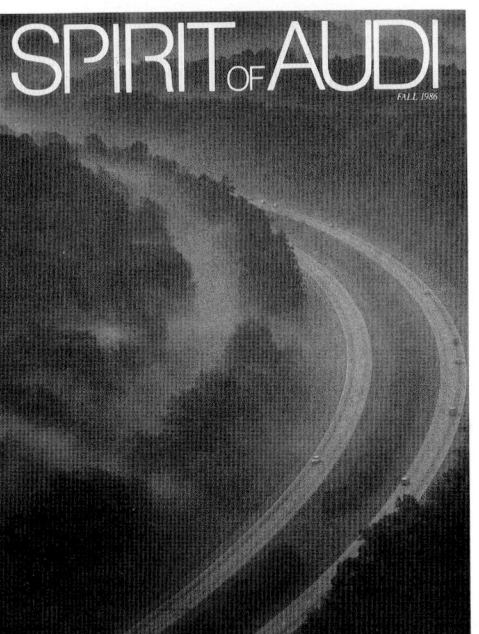

471

472

472

ART DIRECTOR
Steve Ditko
DESIGNER
Steve Ditko
PHOTOGRAPHER
Scott Barrow/Photo Unique
PRODUCER
Roger Barger
DESIGN FIRM
SHR Communications Planning & Design,
Scottsdale, AZ
PUBLICATION
Spirit of Audi

473

ART DIRECTOR
Craig Bernhardt, Janice Fudyma
DESIGNER
Iris Brown, Janice Fudyma
PHOTOGRAPHER
Michael Geiger
CLIENT
W.R. Grace & Co.
EDITOR
Joyce Cole
DESIGN FIRM
Bernhardt Fudyma Design Group, New York,
NY

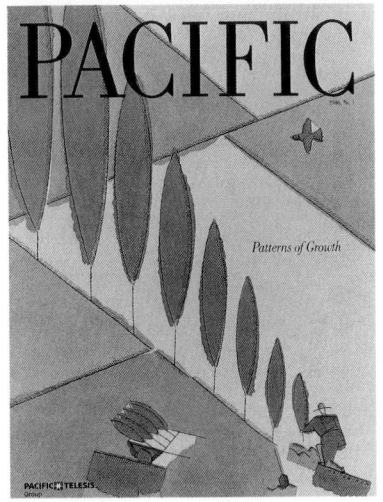

473

474

474

ART DIRECTOR
Michael Mabry
DESIGNER
Michael Mabry
ILLUSTRATOR/ARTIST
Phillipe Weisbecker
CLIENT
Pacific Telesis
EDITOR
Marjorie Wilkens
DESIGN FIRM
Michael Mabry Design, San Francisco, CA
PUBLICATION
Pacific

475

ART DIRECTOR
Lyle Metzdorf
DESIGNER
Lyle Metzdorf
ILLUSTRATOR/ARTIST
R.O. Blechman
WRITER
Lyle Metzdorf
CLIENT
Fidelity Investments
EDITOR
Darla W. Mendales
DESIGN FIRM
Jonson Pirtle Pedersen Alcorn Metzdorf &
Hess, New York, NY
PUBLICATION
Fidelity Investment Vision

476

ART DIRECTOR
Steve Ditko
DESIGNER
Steve Ditko
ILLUSTRATOR/ARTIST
John Kleber
CLIENT
Formal Fashions, Inc.
DESIGN FIRM
SHR Communications Planning & Design,
Scottsdale, AZ

477

ART DIRECTOR
Robert Best
DESIGNER
Josh Gosfield, Betsy Welsh
PHOTOGRAPHER
David Kelley, Larry Bercow, Tohru
Nakamura, Brian Hagiwara
ILLUSTRATOR/ARTIST
Kinuko Y. Craft
PHOTO EDITOR
Jordan Schaps
EDITOR
Edward Kosner
PUBLISHER
Murdoch Magazines, Edward Kosner
PUBLICATION
New York Magazine, New York, NY

478

ART DIRECTOR
Robert Best
DESIGNER
Josh Gosfield, Betsy Welsh
ILLUSTRATOR/ARTIST
Fred Swanson
PHOTO EDITOR
Jordan Schaps, Susan Vermazen
EDITOR
Edward Kosner
PUBLISHER
Murdoch Magazines, Edward Kosner
PUBLICATION
New York Magazine, New York, NY

475

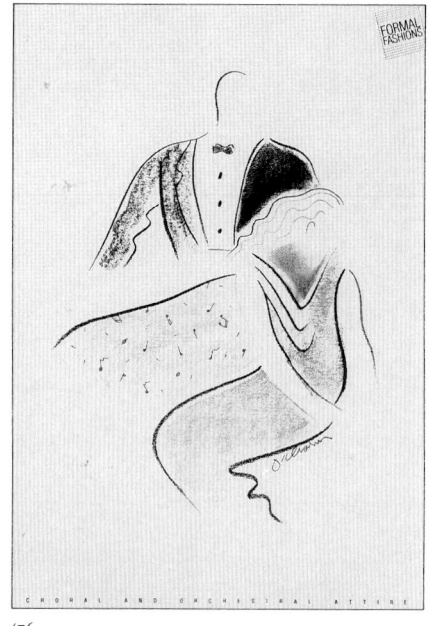

476

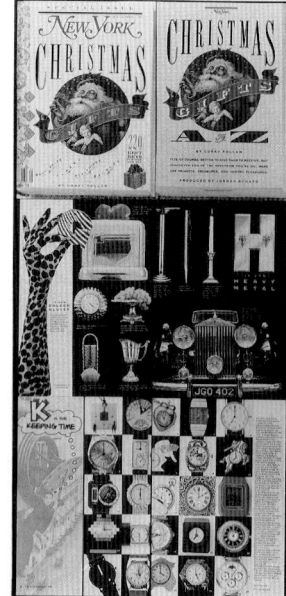

477

478

479

480

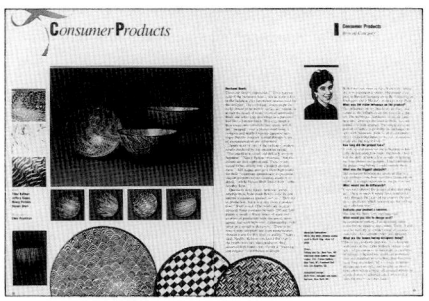

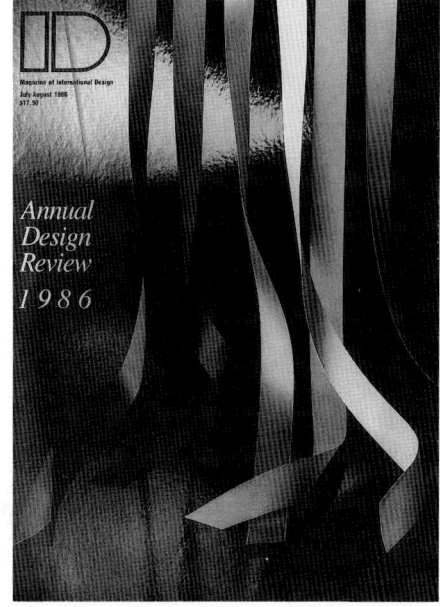

479
ART DIRECTOR
Carla Barr
DESIGNER
Carla Barr, Stephanie Phelan, Albert Chiang,
Bill Naegels
PUBLISHER
Hearst Corp.
PUBLICATION
Connoisseur Magazine, New York, NY

480
ART DIRECTOR
Robert Best
DESIGNER
Josh Gosfield, Betsy Welsh
ILLUSTRATOR/ARTIST
Paul Degan
PHOTO EDITOR
Jordan Schaps, Susan Vermazen
EDITOR
Edward Kosner
PUBLISHER
Murdoch Magazines, Edward Kosner
PUBLICATION
481 New York Magazine, New York, NY

481
ART DIRECTOR
Clive Jacobson
DESIGNER
Clive Jacobson
PHOTOGRAPHER
Richard Levy
CLIENT
Design Publications Inc.
EDITOR
Annetta Hanna
ASSOC. EDITOR
Chee Pearlman
DIRECTOR
Ann Lee Polus
PUBLISHER
Randolph McAusland
DESIGN FIRM
Fulton & Partners Inc., New York, NY
PUBLICATION
482 ID Magazine

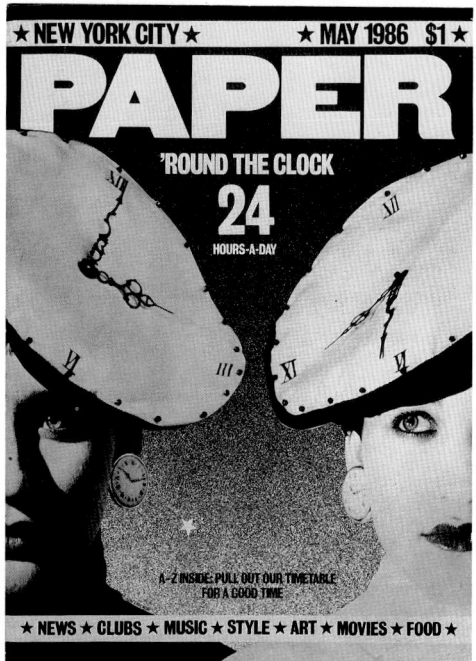

482
ART DIRECTOR
Clare Cunningham
DESIGNER
Clare Cunningham
CLIENT
Nautical Quarterly
EDITOR
Joseph Gribbins
PUBLISHER
C.S. Lovelace
PUBLICATION
Nautical Quarterly, Essex, CT

483
ART DIRECTOR
Richard Pandiscio, Kim Hastreiter
DESIGNER
Richard Pandiscio, John Boyer
PHOTOGRAPHER
Janette Beckman, Jon Ericson, Henny
Garfunkel, Richard Pandiscio, Valerie Shaff
EDITOR
David Hershkovitz, Kim Hastreiter
PUBLISHER
Paper Publishing Co., New York, NY

483

484

ART DIRECTOR
Carole J. Palmer
DESIGNER
Carole J. Palmer
PHOTOGRAPHER
Pavel Stecha
WRITER
Peter Lizon, AIA
CLIENT
The American Institute of Architects
EDITOR
Donald Canty, Hon. AIA
PUBLISHER
Bob G. Kliesch
PUBLICATION
Architecture Magazine, Washington, DC

485

ART DIRECTOR
Richard Pandiscio, Kim Hastreiter
DESIGNER
Richard Pandiscio
PHOTOGRAPHER
Janette Beckman, Jon Ericson, Henny
Garfunkel, Richard Pandiscio, Valerie Shaff
ILLUSTRATOR/ARTIST
Laurie Rosenwald
EDITOR
David Hershkovitz, Kim Hastreiter
PUBLISHER
Paper Publishing Co., New York, NY

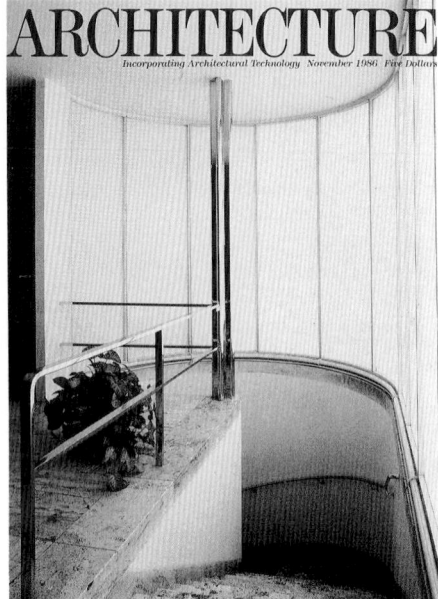

484

485

486

ART DIRECTOR
Richard Pandiscio, Kim Hastreiter
DESIGNER
Richard Pandiscio, John Boyer, Billy Cole
PHOTOGRAPHER
Janette Beckman, Richard Pandiscio, Valerie
Shaff
ILLUSTRATOR/ARTIST
Anne D. Bernstein
EDITOR
David Hershkovitz, Kim Hastreiter
PUBLISHER
Paper Publishing Co., New York, NY

487

ART DIRECTOR
Claude Skelton
DESIGNER
Claude Skelton
PHOTOGRAPHER
Jeremy Green (cover)
EDITOR
Eric Garland
PUBLISHER
The Daily Record/Warfield's
PUBLICATION
Warfield's Magazine, Baltimore, MD

486

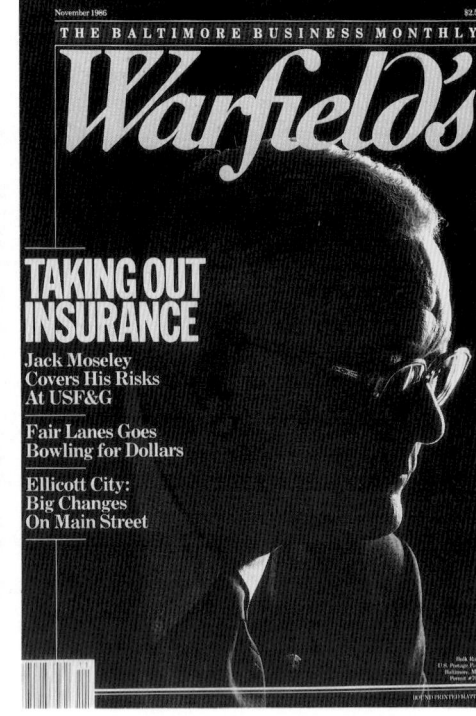

487

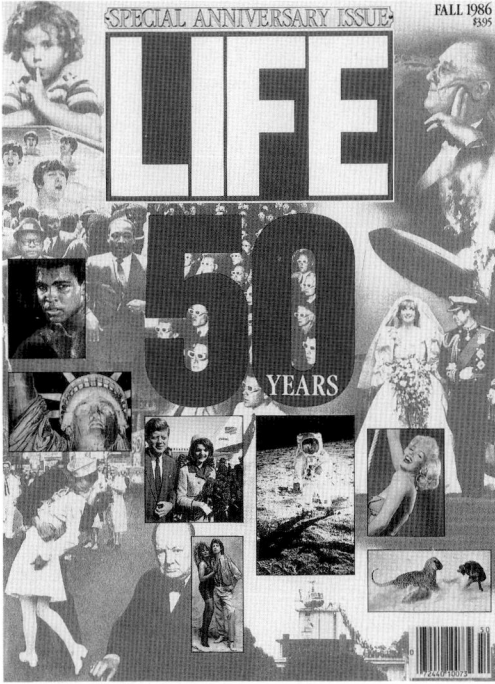

488

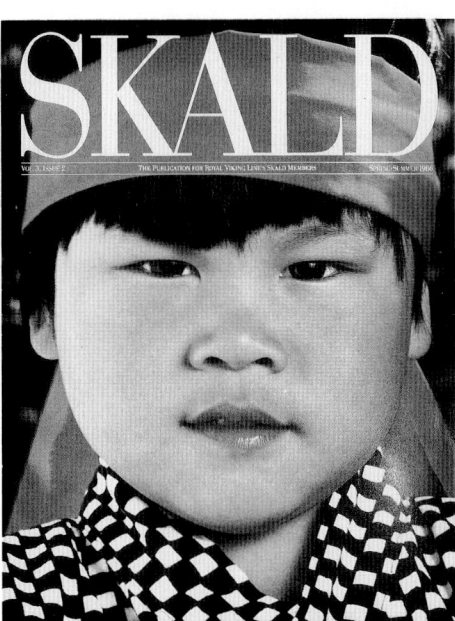

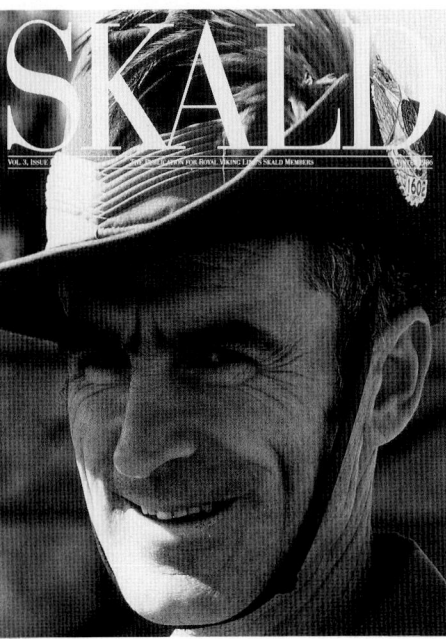

490

491

488

ART DIRECTOR
Jurek Wajdowicz
DESIGNER
Jurek Wajdowicz
CLIENT
The East-West Round Table
EDITOR
Joan Frawley
PUBLISHER
The East-West Round Table
DESIGN FIRM
Emerson, Wajdowicz Studios, Inc., New York, NY
PUBLICATION
The East-West Papers

489

ART DIRECTOR
Charles W. Pates
DESIGNER
Jean Foos, Keith Davis
PHOTOGRAPHER
Various
WRITER
Joe Poindexter, John Neary
CLIENT
Life Magazine
EDITOR
Mary Youatt Steinbauer
PUBLICATION
Life Magazine, New York, NY

490

ART DIRECTOR
Kit Hinrichs
DESIGNER
Kit Hinrichs, Karen Berndt
PHOTOGRAPHER
David Stahl (cover), Henrik Kam, Pete Turner, Allen Miller
ILLUSTRATOR/ARTIST
Ed Lindlof
WRITER
Peterson & Dodge
CLIENT
Royal Viking Lines
EDITOR
George Cruys
DESIGN FIRM
Pentagram Design, San Francisco, CA

491

ART DIRECTOR
Kit Hinrichs
DESIGNER
Kit Hinrichs, Karen Berndt
PHOTOGRAPHER
Michele Clement (cover), Terry Heffernan, Dave Bartruff
ILLUSTRATOR/ARTIST
Jerry Gersten
WRITER
Peterson & Dodge
CLIENT
Royal Viking Lines
EDITOR
George Cruys
DESIGN FIRM
Pentagram Design, San Francisco, CA

His Master's Voice

Credit: THE BETTMAN ARCHIVE

Although Nipper, the RCA dog, spent time in the kennel during the abstract-logo years of the sixties and seventies, a change in company management brought him back in time for his one-hundredth birthday in 1984. A lowly mutt in Bristol, England, the original Nipper was adopted by Francis Barraud, a landscape painter, and delighted his new master by his intent listening to an early phonograph. Sometime in the 1890's Barraud made a painting of Nipper and the phonograph titled "His Master's Voice" and sold it to the Gramophone Company in England.

Nipper came to the United States in 1901 as the trademark of the Victor Talking Machine Company and moved on to the Radio Corporation of America when it purchased Victor. Although Nipper died in 1895, he has lived on as one of the best-loved commercial symbols in the world.

PROMOTION & GRAPHIC DESIGN:

Single Entries: annual report

booklet, folder, brochure

sales kit

direct mail piece, catalog

record album

packaging

calendar

menu, card, announcement

letterhead, envelope & business card

trademark or logo

point-of-purchase design or display

Campaign Entries: booklet, folder, brochure series

sales kit series

direct mail campaign

packaging series

card, menu or announcement series

point-of-purchase design series

corporate identity program

492
ART DIRECTOR
Peter Harrison, Suzanne Morin
DESIGNER
Peter Harrison, Suzanne Morin
PHOTOGRAPHER
Neal Slavin
CLIENT
Hasbro Inc./Robert Hubbell
DESIGN FIRM
Pentagram Design, New York, NY

493
ART DIRECTOR
Wes Massey
DESIGNER
Patti Malone
PHOTOGRAPHER
Pelosi and Chambers
ILLUSTRATOR/ARTIST
Danny Smythe
WRITER
Susan Dodson
CLIENT
John H. Harland Co.
DESIGN FIRM
John H. Harland Co. Idea Market, Atlanta, GA

494
ART DIRECTOR
Chuck Creasy
DESIGNER
Chuck Creasy
PHOTOGRAPHER
Mike Rutherford
CLIENT
Middle Tennessee Council Boy Scouts of America
AGENCY
Brumfield-Gallagher, Inc., Nashville, TN
PRINTER
Lithographics, Inc.
ENGRAVER
Graphic Process, Inc.

495
ART DIRECTOR
Danielle Roy
DESIGNER
Martin Le Sauteur
PHOTOGRAPHER
Jean Tremblay Mia et Klaus
ILLUSTRATOR/ARTIST
Vittorio Fiorucci; Centre Creatif de Mtl. (computer illus.)
CALLIGRAPHER
Gérard Mariscalchi
CLIENT
La Fiducie du Québec
DESIGN FIRM
Danielle Roy Design et Communication, Montréal, Canada
PRINTER
Pierre DesMarais Inc.
TYPOGRAPHER
Avant-Garde

492

493

494

495

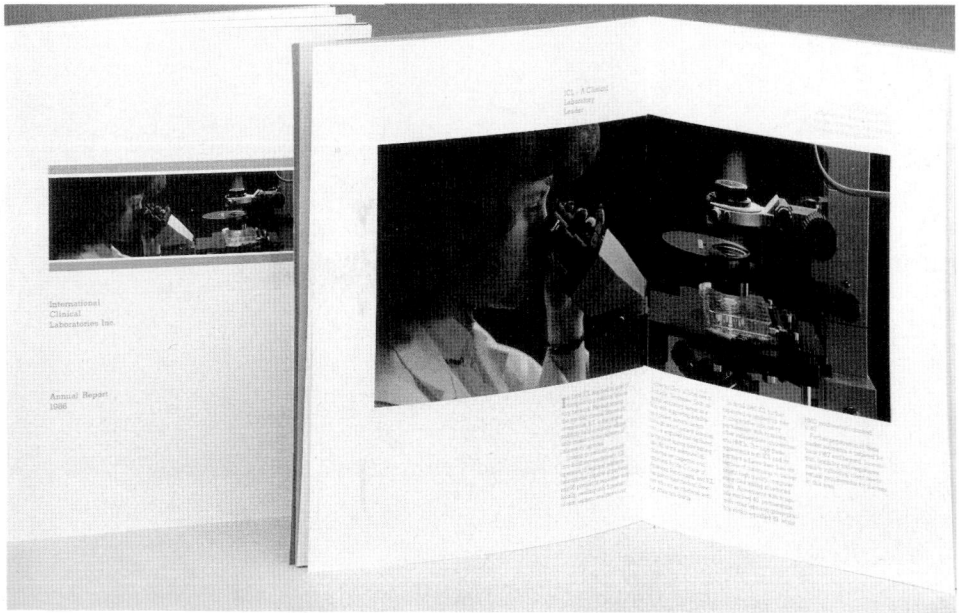

496

ART DIRECTOR
Walter J. Ender
DESIGNER
Walter J. Ender
PHOTOGRAPHER
Michael Morris
WRITER
Walter Barrett, Bill O'Neil
CLIENT
International Clinical Labs
AGENCY
Ender Associates Inc., Dallas, TX

497

ART DIRECTOR
Michael Benes
DESIGNER
Michael Benes
ILLUSTRATOR/ARTIST
Dave Hannum, Nick Fasciano
WRITER
Sam Yanes, Gordon Lewis, Peter Schwartz
CLIENT
Polaroid Corporation
EDITOR
Sam Yanes
PUBLISHER
Polaroid Corporation
AGENCY
Polaroid In-house, Cambridge, MA
DESIGN FIRM
Polaroid In-house
PUBLICATION
Annual Report
DIRECTOR
Michael Benes

496

497

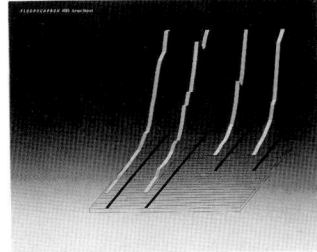

498

ART DIRECTOR
Peter Harrison
DESIGNER
Susan Hochbaum
ILLUSTRATOR/ARTIST
Sue Huntley, Donna Muir
WRITER
David Bither
CLIENT
Warner Communications Inc./David Bither
DESIGN FIRM
Pentagram Design, New York, NY

498

499

ART DIRECTOR
Ron Jefferies
DESIGNER
Susan Garland
PHOTOGRAPHER
Russ Widstrand
WRITER
Ron Bissell, Peter Churm
CLIENT
The Fluorocarbon Company/Ron Bissell
DESIGN FIRM
The Jefferies Association, Los Angeles, CA
PRINTER
George Rice & Sons
TYPOGRAPHER
Typographic Service

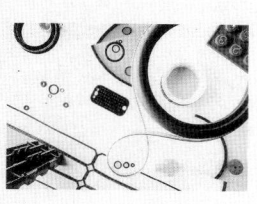

499

500

ART DIRECTOR
Paul Huber
DESIGNER
Paul Huber
PHOTOGRAPHER
Steve Marsel
WRITER
Jennifer French
CLIENT
American Red Cross of Massachusetts Bay
EDITOR
Helen Huber
DESIGN FIRM
Huber & Huber, Watertown, MA

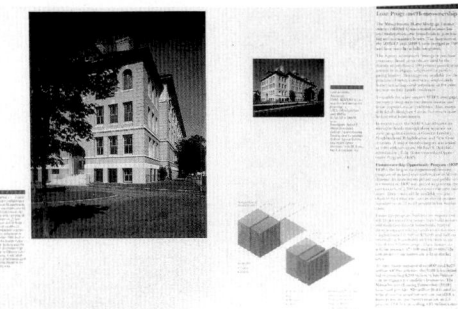

500

501

ART DIRECTOR
Jeffery Dawson
DESIGNER
Jeffery Dawson, Valerie Besser
PHOTOGRAPHER
David Smith and others
WRITER
Therese Pepin, Martha Vaananen
CLIENT
Massachusetts Housing Finance Agency
DESIGN FIRM
Jeffery Dawson Associates, Boston, MA

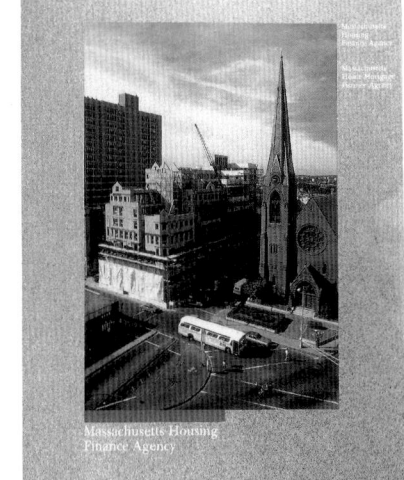

501

502

ART DIRECTOR
Paul Huber
DESIGNER
Paul Huber, Greg Graalfs
PHOTOGRAPHER
Various
WRITER
Marcia Schiff
CLIENT
Polaroid Foundation
DESIGN FIRM
Polaroid Corporation Graphics, Cambridge, MA

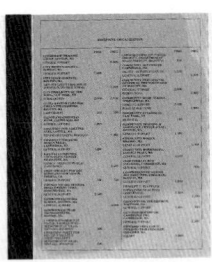

502

503

ART DIRECTOR
Peter Harrison
DESIGNER
Suzanne Morin
PHOTOGRAPHER
Mario Carrieri, Carol Friedman, John Madere
WRITER
Ervin S. Duggan, Ervin S. Duggan Associates
CLIENT
Knoll International Inc., Stuart Silver
DESIGN FIRM
Pentagram Design, New York, NY

503

504

505

504
ART DIRECTOR
John Van Dyke
DESIGNER
John Van Dyke
PHOTOGRAPHER
Ed Giffard, Gordon Fisher, Steve Welsh
WRITER
Stu Clugston
CLIENT
British Columbia Forest Products
AGENCY
Van Dyke Company, Seattle, WA
DESIGN FIRM
Van Dyke Company

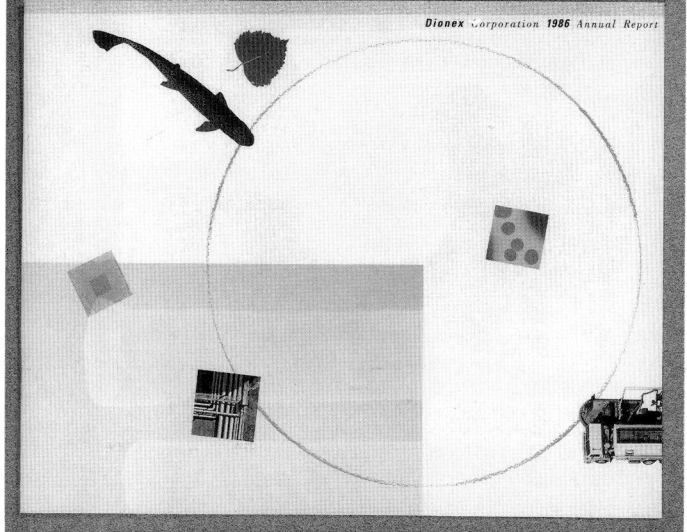

505
ART DIRECTOR
John Van Dyke
DESIGNER
John Van Dyke
PHOTOGRAPHER
Terry Heffernan
WRITER
Elaine Kraft
CLIENT
Weyerhaeuser Paper Company
AGENCY
Van Dyke Company, Seattle, WA
DESIGN FIRM
Van Dyke Company
PRINTER
Graphicolor

506

506
ART DIRECTOR
Terry Eden
DESIGNER
Terry Eden
PHOTOGRAPHER
David Monley
WRITER
Emily Harris
CLIENT
Dionex Corporation
AGENCY
Harris INK, Palo Alto, CA
MARKETING MANAGER
Nancy Zellhoefer, Dionex Corp.

507

507
ART DIRECTOR
Roslyn Eskind
DESIGNER
Christopher Campbell
PHOTOGRAPHER
John James Wood
ILLUSTRATOR/ARTIST
Wendy Wortsman, San Murata, Jamie Bennett, Jean-Christian Knaff
WRITER
Hilton Tudhope
CLIENT
YMCA of Metropolitan Toronto
DESIGN FIRM
Eskind Waddell, Toronto, Canada

508

ART DIRECTOR
Wayne C. Roth
DESIGNER
Wayne C. Roth
PHOTOGRAPHER
Ed Eckstein
WRITER
Gerald Reimel
CLIENT
Alco Standard Corporation
DESIGN FIRM
Roth + Associates, Boonton, NJ

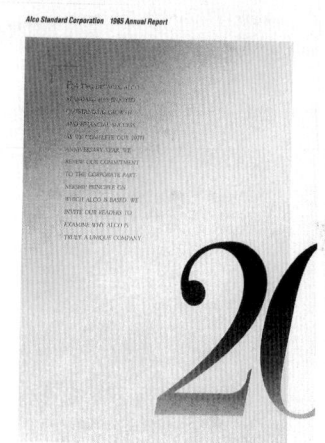
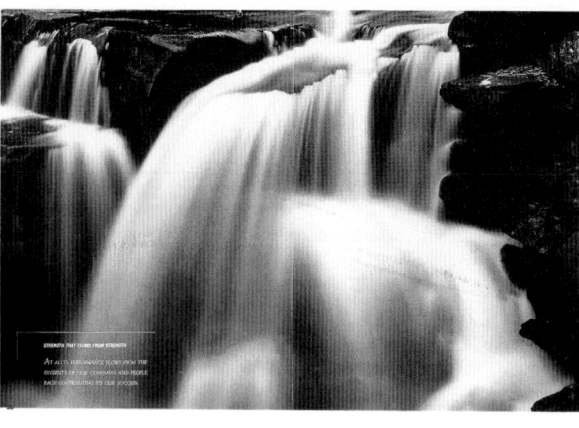

508

509

ART DIRECTOR
Ron Sullivan
DESIGNER
Ron Sullivan, Willie Baronet
PHOTOGRAPHER
Gerry Kano
ILLUSTRATOR/ARTIST
Linda Helton
WRITER
Mark Perkins
CLIENT
Sunbelt Nurseries Group
DESIGN FIRM
Sullivan Perkins, Dallas, TX

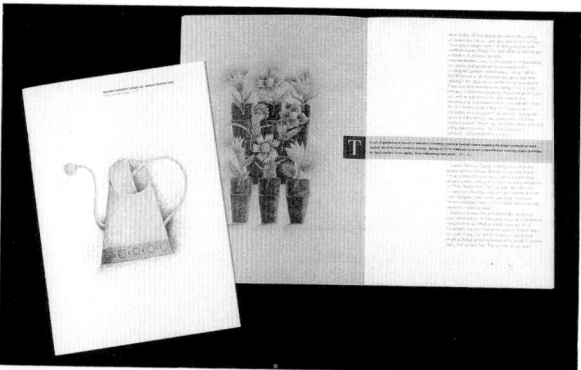

509

510

ART DIRECTOR
Dick Mitchell, Greg Booth
DESIGNER
Dick Mitchell
PHOTOGRAPHER
Greg Booth
WRITER
Mark Perkins
CLIENT
Lomas & Nettleton Financial Corporation
AGENCY
The Richards Group
DESIGN FIRM
Richards Brock Miller Mitchell & Assoc.,
Dallas, TX

510

511

ART DIRECTOR
John Hornall
DESIGNER
Luann Bice, Bruce Hale
ILLUSTRATOR/ARTIST
Bruce Hale
WRITER
Jerry Baglien
CLIENT
Tree Top, Inc.
DESIGN FIRM
Hornall Anderson Design Works, Seattle, WA

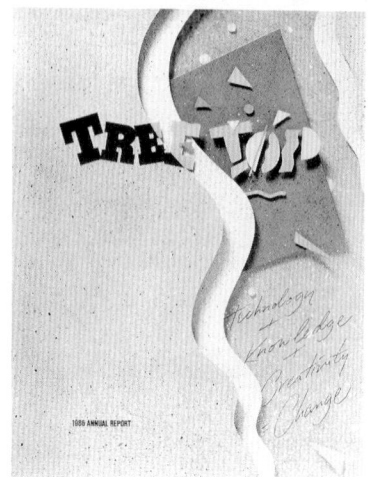

511

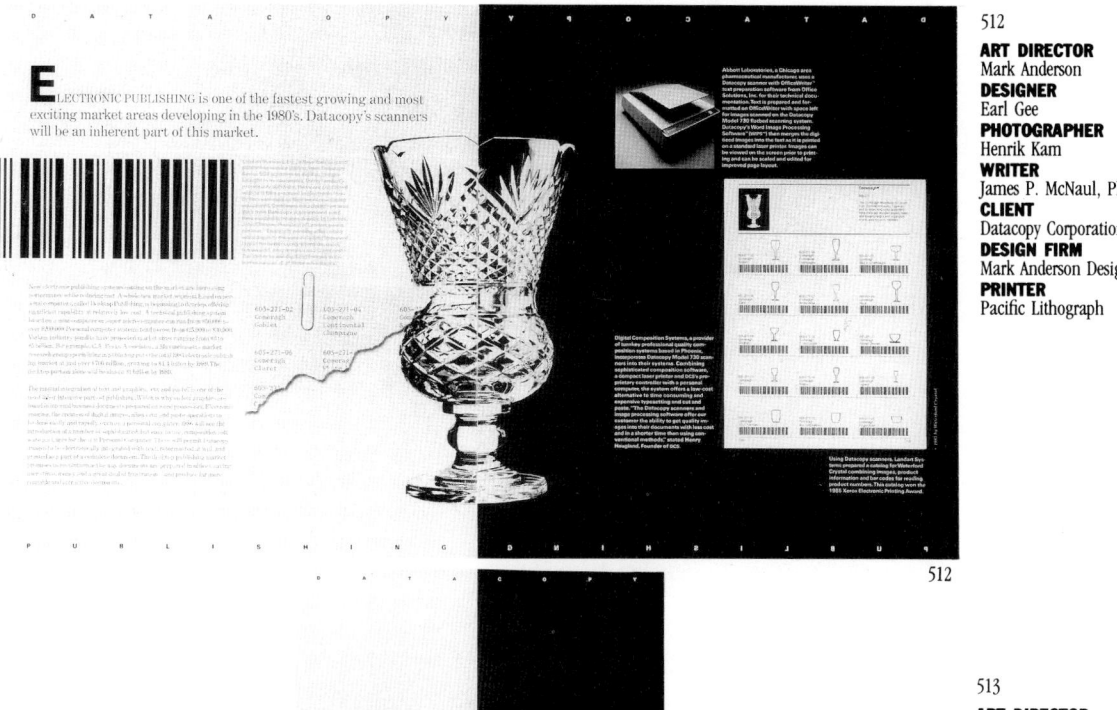

512

513

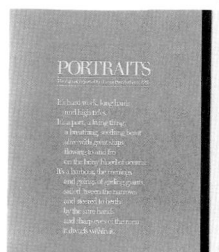

514

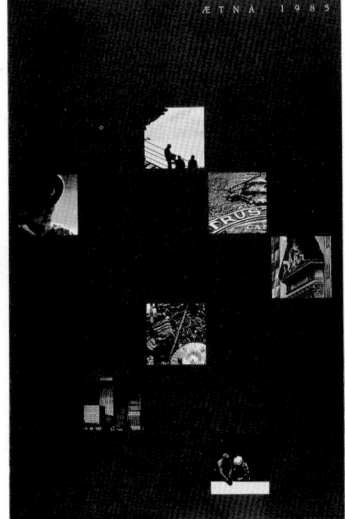

512

ART DIRECTOR
Mark Anderson
DESIGNER
Earl Gee
PHOTOGRAPHER
Henrik Kam
WRITER
James P. McNaul, Phd.
CLIENT
Datacopy Corporation
DESIGN FIRM
Mark Anderson Design, Palo Alto, CA
PRINTER
Pacific Lithograph

513

ART DIRECTOR
David Broom
DESIGNER
David Broom, Michele Wetherbee
PHOTOGRAPHER
Ed Kashi
WRITER
Carol Piasente
CLIENT
The San Francisco Foundation
DESIGN FIRM
Broom & Broom, Inc., San Francisco, CA

514

ART DIRECTOR
Ray Dillman
DESIGNER
Ray Dillman
PHOTOGRAPHER
Dick Dickinson
WRITER
Cameron Dilley
CLIENT
Tampa Port Authority
AGENCY
Benito Advertising, Inc., Tampa, FL

515

ART DIRECTOR
Ken Ko, Lance Matusek
DESIGNER
Ken Ko, Lance Matusek
PHOTOGRAPHER
Jay Maisel
WRITER
Jonathan Powell
CLIENT
Aetna
DESIGN FIRM
Aetna, Hartford, CT

515

516
ART DIRECTOR
Jim Berte
DESIGNER
Jim Berte
PHOTOGRAPHER
Deborah Meyers
CLIENT
Caremark, Inc.
DESIGN FIRM
Robert Miles Runyan & Associates, Playa del
Rey, CA

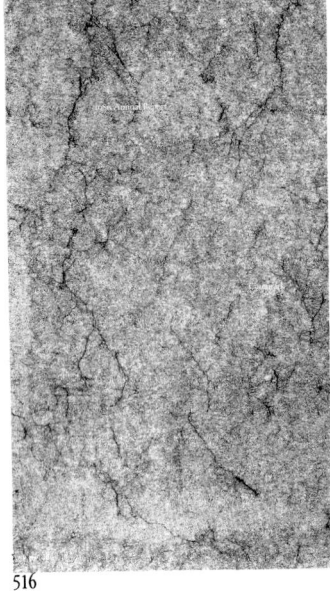
516

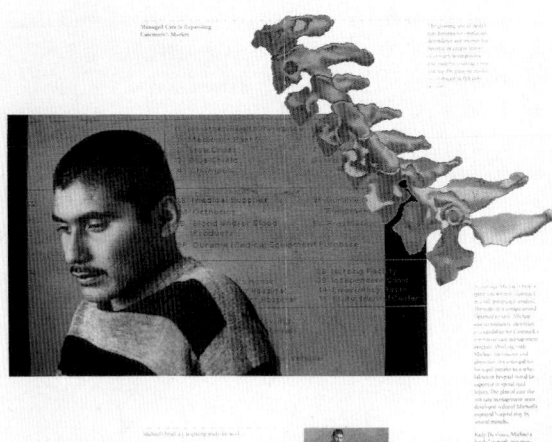

517
ART DIRECTOR
Kit Hinrichs
DESIGNER
Kit Hinrichs, Lenore Bartz
PHOTOGRAPHER
Tom Tracy and others
ILLUSTRATOR/ARTIST
Will Nelson, Lawrence Duke, John Mattos,
Masami Miyamoto
WRITER
Holly Hutchins
CLIENT
Potlatch Corporation
EDITOR
Holly Hutchins
DESIGN FIRM
Pentagram Design, San Francisco, CA

517

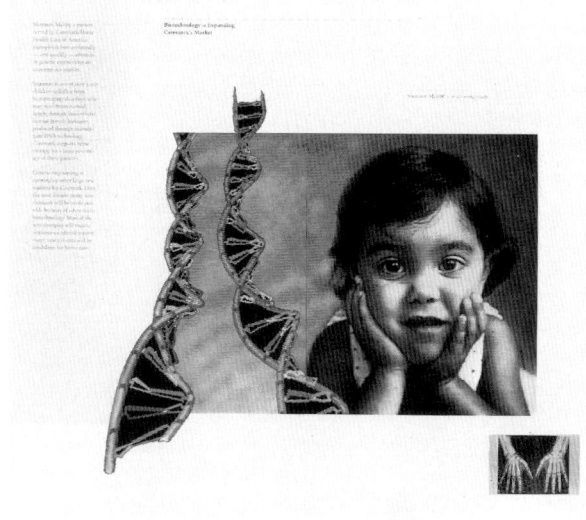

518
ART DIRECTOR
Jamie Feldman
DESIGNER
Jamie Feldman
PHOTOGRAPHER
Roman Sapecki
ILLUSTRATOR/ARTIST
David Lesh
CLIENT
Federal Reserve Bank of Cleveland
DESIGN FIRM
Federal Reserve Bank of Cleveland,
Cleveland, OH
TYPOGRAPHER
Liz Hanna

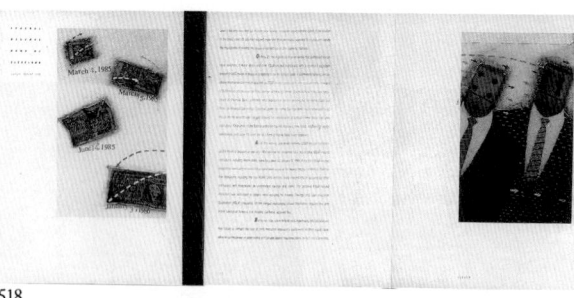
518

519
ART DIRECTOR
Eric Madsen
DESIGNER
Eric Madsen
PHOTOGRAPHER
Stock
WRITER
Dick Russack
CLIENT
Molecular Genetics, Inc.
DESIGN FIRM
Madsen and Kuester, Inc., Minneapolis, MN

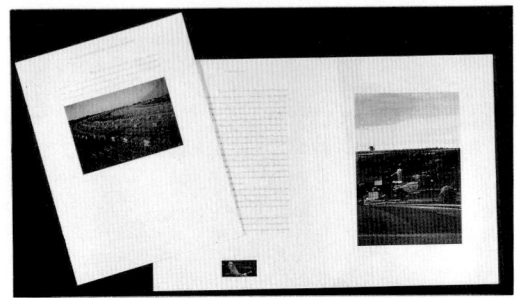
519

520

ART DIRECTOR
Stephen Miller
DESIGNER
Stephen Miller
PHOTOGRAPHER
Greg Booth
WRITER
Mark Perkins, Jess Hay
CLIENT
Lomas & Nettleton Mortgage Investors
AGENCY
The Richards Group
DESIGN FIRM
Richards Brock Miller Mitchell & Assoc.,
Dallas, TX

520

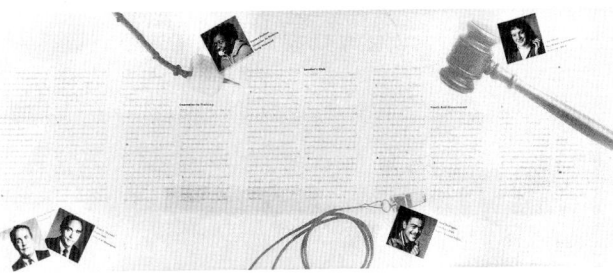

521

ART DIRECTOR
Pat Samata
DESIGNER
Pat Samata
PHOTOGRAPHER
Jean Moss, Dennis Dooley
ILLUSTRATOR/ARTIST
Ann Teson
WRITER
Patrice Boyer
CLIENT
YMCA of Metropolitan Chicago
DESIGN FIRM
Samata Associates, Dundee, IL

522

ART DIRECTOR
Karen Madsen
DESIGNER
Karen Madsen
PHOTOGRAPHER
Doug Evans Photography
WRITER
Mark Phillips, Phillips & Associates
CLIENT
Edmark Corporation
DESIGN FIRM
Karen Madsen Graphic Design, Seattle, WA

521

522

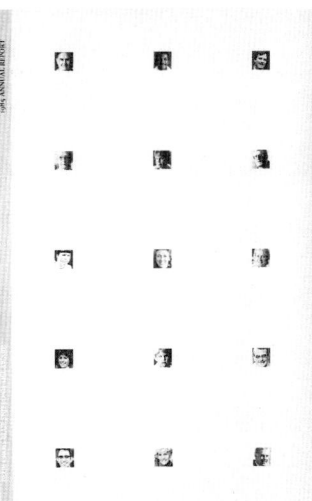

523

ART DIRECTOR
Michael Gunselman
DESIGNER
Michael Gunselman
PHOTOGRAPHER
Ed Eckstein
ILLUSTRATOR/ARTIST
Ralph B. Billings, Jr.
WRITER
Francie Todd
CLIENT
Blue Cross Blue Shield of Delaware, Linda C.
Drake
DESIGN FIRM
Michael Gunselman Inc., Wilmington, DE
PRINTER
Rapoport Printing Inc.

523

524
ART DIRECTOR
Lawrence Bender
DESIGNER
Margaret Hellmann Cheu
PHOTOGRAPHER
Tom Tracy
WRITER
Ann Fenimore
CLIENT
BaronData Systems
DESIGN FIRM
Lawrence Bender & Associates, Palo Alto, CA
PRINTER
Anderson Lithograph

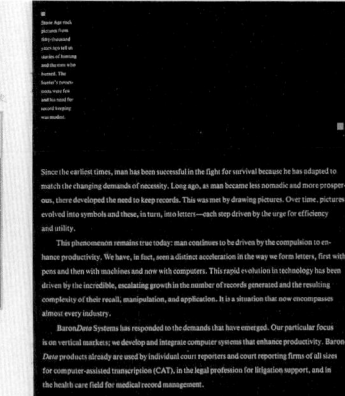

524

525
ART DIRECTOR
Brian Boyd
DESIGNER
Brian Boyd
PHOTOGRAPHER
Robert Latorre
WRITER
David Fowler
CLIENT
Chili's Inc.
PUBLISHER
Heritage Press
AGENCY
The Richards Group
DESIGN FIRM
Richards Brock Miller Mitchell & Assoc.,
Dallas, TX

525

526
ART DIRECTOR
Jerry Demoney
DESIGNER
Jerry Demoney
ILLUSTRATOR/ARTIST
Oren Sherman
CLIENT
Mobil Corporation
EDITOR
Jim Dulicai
PUBLISHER
Mobil Corporation, New York, NY

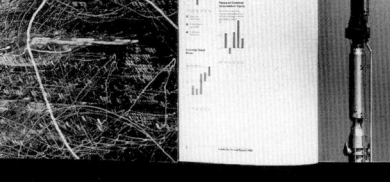

527

526

527
ART DIRECTOR
Robert Appleton
DESIGNER
Robert Appleton
PHOTOGRAPHER
Richard Frank, Arthur Meyerson, Michael
Melford, Al Satterwhite, Pete Turner, Camille
Vickers
WRITER
Carole F. Butenas
CLIENT
Lydall, Inc.
DESIGN FIRM
Appleton Design Inc., Hartford, CT

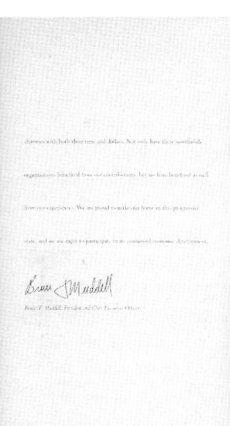

528

ART DIRECTOR
Michael Gunselman
DESIGNER
Michael Gunselman
PHOTOGRAPHER
Kevin Flemming
ILLUSTRATOR/ARTIST
Ralph B. Billings, Jr.
WRITER
Anne S. Bradley
CLIENT
Chemical Bank (Delaware)
DESIGN FIRM
Michael Gunselman Inc., Wilmington, DE
PRINTER
Great Atlantic Graphics

528

529

ART DIRECTOR
Richard Danne
DESIGNER
Eric Atherton, Richard Danne
PHOTOGRAPHER
Cynthia Stern, Bill Farrell
WRITER
Robert Kasmire
CLIENT
The Seagram Company Ltd.
DESIGN FIRM
Richard Danne & Associates, New York, NY

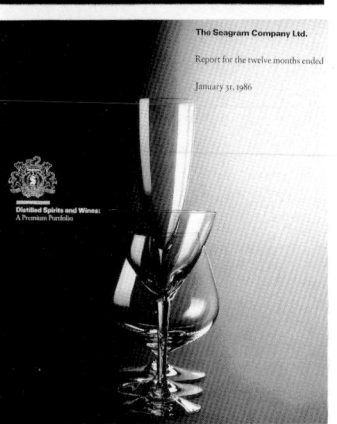

530

530

ART DIRECTOR
John Kirtz
DESIGNER
John Kirtz
PHOTOGRAPHER
Doug Van De Zande (B/W); NC Travel &
Tourism stock (Color)
WRITER
Debbie Lee
CLIENT
Carolina Permanente Medical Group, P.A.
EDITOR
Linda McCrudden
DESIGN FIRM
Sally Johns Design, Raleigh, NC
CREATIVE DIRECTOR
Sally Bruner Johns

529

531
ART DIRECTOR
Laura Nisi
DESIGNER
Laura Nisi
PHOTOGRAPHER
Dennis Iannarelli
WRITER
Lynn Prijatel
CLIENT
The Bibb Company
AGENCY
Liggett-Stashower, Cleveland, OH

532
ART DIRECTOR
Domenica Genovese
DESIGNER
Domenica Genovese
PHOTOGRAPHER
William Denison
ILLUSTRATOR/ARTIST
Richard Waldrep
WRITER
Susann Studz
CLIENT
Franklin & Marshall College
DESIGN FIRM
The North Charles Street Design
Organization, Baltimore, MD

533
ART DIRECTOR
Neil R. Probala
DESIGNER
Neil R. Probala
PHOTOGRAPHER
Carl Fowler, Lad Trepal
ILLUSTRATOR/ARTIST
Rasic Art
WRITER
John Pierce
CLIENT
Industrial Powder Coatings, Inc.
AGENCY
Liggett-Stashower, Cleveland, OH

534
ART DIRECTOR
Brian Harrod
DESIGNER
Brian Harrod
ILLUSTRATOR/ARTIST
Roger Hill
WRITER
Ian Mirlin
CLIENT
The Partners Film Company
AGENCY
Miller Myers Bruce DallaCosta, Toronto,
Canada
PRODUCER
Sam Muffoletto

535
ART DIRECTOR
Kimberlee Keswick, Gretchen Goldie
DESIGNER
Kimberlee Keswick, Gretchen Goldie
PHOTOGRAPHER
Terry Heffernan
WRITER
Debbie Schwartz
CLIENT
Wolfer Printing Company
DESIGN FIRM
Keswick/Goldie & Associates, Los Angeles, CA

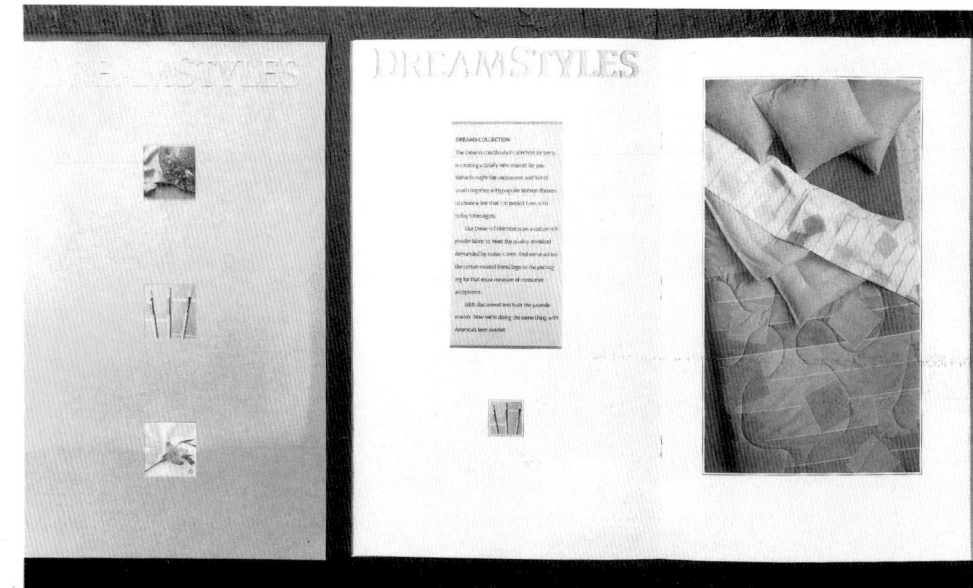

531

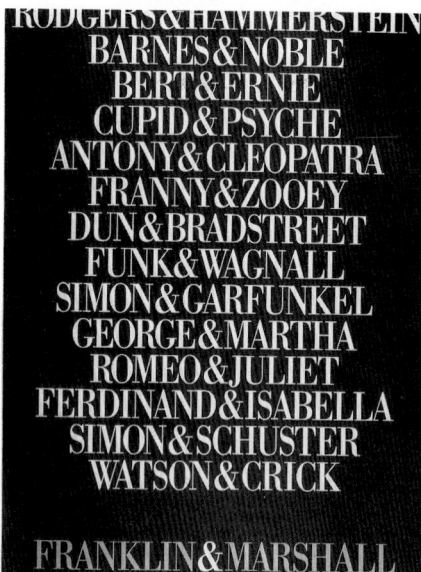

532

533

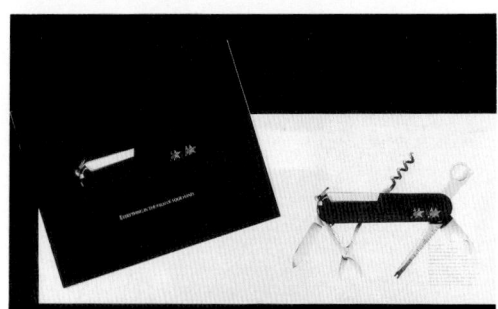

534

535

536

ART DIRECTOR
Cathy Yates
DESIGNER
Cathy Yates
PHOTOGRAPHER
Susie Fitzhugh
WRITER
Tracey Henson Ford, Michele Valle Kogler
CLIENT
Notre Dame Preparatory School
DESIGN FIRM
Shub, Dirksen, Yates & McAllister, Baltimore,
MD
PRINTER
E. John Schmitz & Sons, Inc.

537

ART DIRECTOR
Bradford C. Ghormley
DESIGNER
Steven R. Smit
PHOTOGRAPHER
Craig Wells
WRITER
Sara Harrell
CLIENT
Noel Plastering & Stucco
DESIGN FIRM
Smit Ghormley Sanft, Phoenix, AZ
PRINTER
Woods Lithographics

536

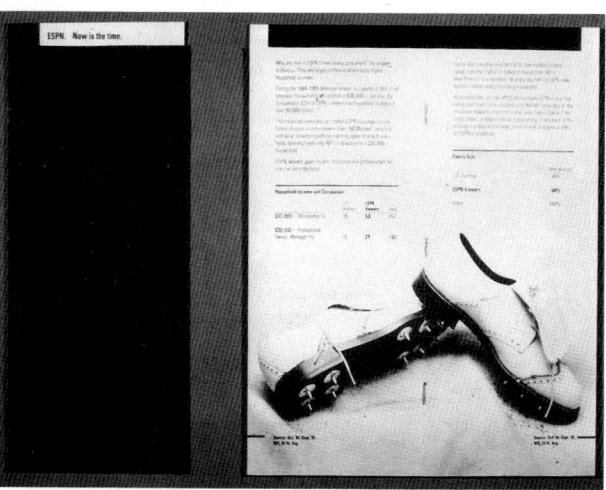

538

ART DIRECTOR
Mark Handler
DESIGNER
Gail Rigelhaupt
PHOTOGRAPHER
Mary McCulley
WRITER
Mark Handler, Howard Flashenburg
CLIENT
ESPN, Inc., Howard Flashenburg
DESIGN FIRM
Handler Group, Inc., New York, NY
PRINTER
Craftsmen Litho

537

538

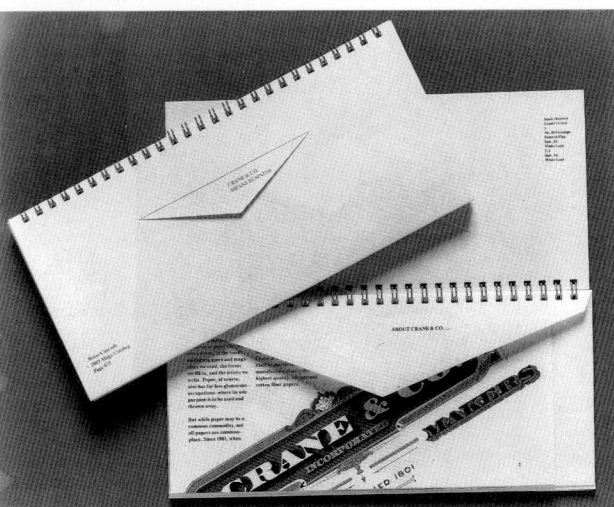

539

ART DIRECTOR
Steff Geissbuhler
DESIGNER
Bill Anton
WRITER
Rose DeNeve
CLIENT
Crane & Co., Richard Kerans
AGENCY
Chermayeff & Geismar Associates, New York,
NY
PRINTER
Andrew Wilson, Tanagraphics

539

540

ART DIRECTOR
Tom Carnase
DESIGNER
Eric Kohler
WRITER
Edward Gottschall
CLIENT
Type Directors Club - N.Y.
PUBLISHER
Type Directors Club - N.Y.
DESIGN FIRM
Carnase, Inc., New York, NY
PRINTER
Flower City Printing
TYPOGRAPHER
Carnase Typography/PDR, Inc.

541

ART DIRECTOR
Tom Zaferes
ILLUSTRATOR/ARTIST
Sal Marese
WRITER
Tina Richter
CLIENT
Hartz Associates
CREATIVE DIRECTOR
Lorraine Borden
AGENCY
Great Scott Advertising, New York, NY
ACCOUNT SUPERVISOR
Lorraine Borden
ACCOUNT EXEC.
Mona Kreaden

542

ART DIRECTOR
Kunio Hayashi
DESIGNER
Kunio Hayashi
PHOTOGRAPHER
Dana Edmunds and others
ILLUSTRATOR/ARTIST
Donna E. Yuen, AIA, Dennis S. Osato, AIA
WRITER
James Conti
CLIENT
Media Five Limited
EDITOR
Peggy E. Kusano
DIRECTOR
Michael J. Leineweber, AIA, Paul Ma, AIA
PUBLISHER
Media Five Limited
DESIGN FIRM
Media Five Limited, Honolulu, HI

543

ART DIRECTOR
Mark Geer, Richard Kilmer
DESIGNER
Mark Geer, Richard Kilmer
PHOTOGRAPHER
Stephanie Radisi
CLIENT
Hermann Hospital
EDITOR
Joyce C. Pyndus
DESIGN FIRM
Kilmer/Geer Design, Inc., Houston, TX
CREATIVE DIRECTOR
Rose Marie Fuller

540

541

542

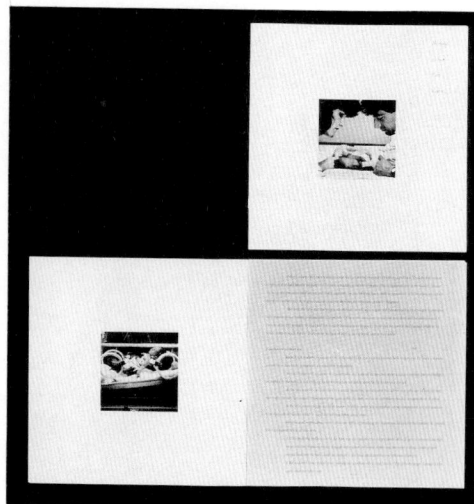

543

544

ART DIRECTOR
Thomas Ryan
DESIGNER
Thomas Ryan
PHOTOGRAPHER
Robert Tolchin (Exteriors), McGuire (Portraits)
WRITER
Mimi Tucker
CLIENT
Aladdin Resources, Inc.
EDITOR
Kelly Hassall
DESIGN FIRM
Thomas Ryan Design, Nashville, TN
ENGRAVER
Graphic Process Inc.
PRINTER
Color Graphics

545

ART DIRECTOR
Eric Rathje
DESIGNER
Eric Rathje
ILLUSTRATOR/ARTIST
Danny Smythe
WRITER
Fran Dyller
CLIENT
Dugan/Farley Communications
AGENCY
Dugan/Farley Communications, Upper Saddle River, NJ

544

Welcome to the creative world of Dugan/Farley

Dugan/Farley
Communications
Associates, Inc.
600 East Crescent Avenue
Upper Saddle River
New Jersey 07458

Here we have only one product to sell. Creativity.

But it comes in many shapes and forms. In many sizes. And with many flavors.

It can be served up piping hot as a small tidbit...

Or we can provide an endlessly replenished groaning board of creative offerings...

A cornucopia of the fruits of our knowledge, skill, and talents.

545

546

ART DIRECTOR
John Dzmil
DESIGNER
John Dzmil
PHOTOGRAPHER
Leslie Deeb, various archives
WRITER
Lee Rosemond
CLIENT
NJ Division of Travel and Tourism
AGENCY
Bozell, Jacobs, Kenyon & Eckhardt, Inc., Union, NJ

547

ART DIRECTOR
Michael Standlee
DESIGNER
Michael Standlee
PHOTOGRAPHER
G. Robert Nease
ILLUSTRATOR/ARTIST
Steven Mitchell
WRITER
Jack Marble
CLIENT
EPSCO
DESIGN FIRM
Michael Standlee Design, Inc., Newport Beach, CA
PRINTER
The Dot Printer
TYPOGRAPHER
Andresen Typographics

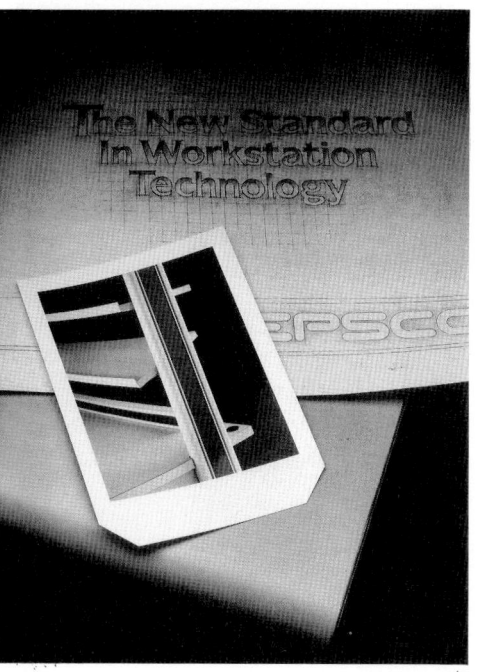

546

547

548
ART DIRECTOR
Kimberly Baer
DESIGNER
Barbara Cooper
PHOTOGRAPHER
Jeff Corwin, George Monserrat
CLIENT
Alex Brands, Inc.
AGENCY
Fleishman & Hillard
DESIGN FIRM
Kimberly Baer Design, Venice, CA

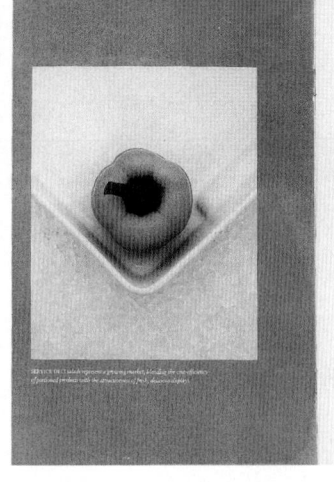

548

549
ART DIRECTOR
Kit Hinrichs
DESIGNER
Kit Hinrichs
PHOTOGRAPHER
Barry Robinson
WRITER
Delphine Hirasuna
CLIENT
Pentagram Design
DESIGN FIRM
Pentagram Design, San Francisco, CA

550
ART DIRECTOR
Milt Simpson
DESIGNER
Jeff Kibler
ILLUSTRATOR/ARTIST
Jeff Kibler
WRITER
Terry Kroloff
CLIENT
Newsletter Ink
DESIGN FIRM
Johnson & Simpson Graphic Designers,
Newark, NJ

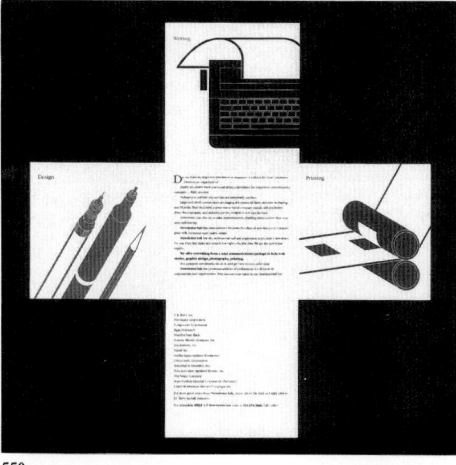

550

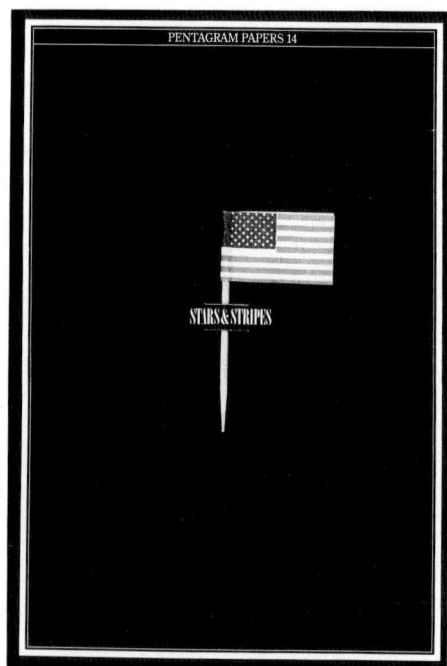

549

551
ART DIRECTOR
David Edelstein, Nancy Edelstein, Lanny
French
DESIGNER
David Edelstein, Nancy Edelstein, Lanny
French, Carol Davidson
PHOTOGRAPHER
Jim Cummins, Glen Erler
WRITER
Nancy Edelstein
CLIENT
Generra Sportswear
AGENCY
Edelstein Associates Advertising, Seattle, WA
DESIGN FIRM
Edelstein Associates Advertising

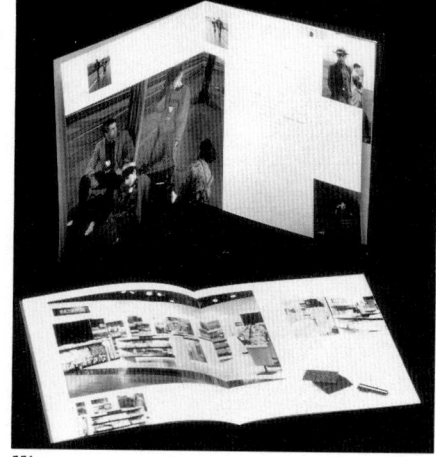

551

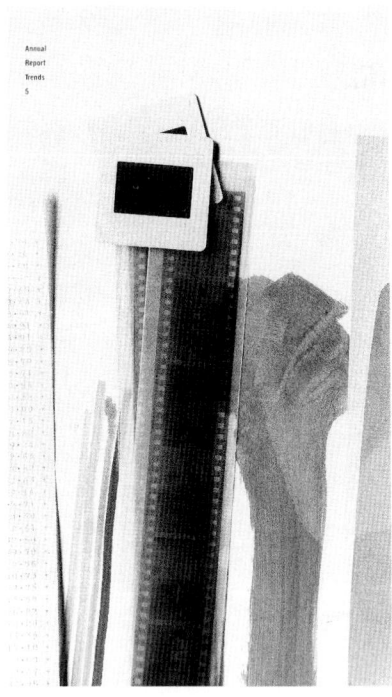

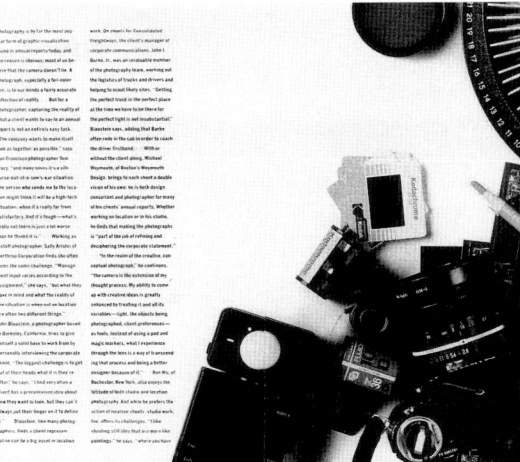

552

ART DIRECTOR
John T. Cleveland
DESIGNER
John T. Cleveland
PHOTOGRAPHER
Peter Darley Miller and various
ILLUSTRATOR/ARTIST
Various
WRITER
Rose DeNeve
CLIENT
S.D. Warren Company
DESIGN FIRM
John Cleveland, Inc., Los Angeles, CA

553

ART DIRECTOR
Lance Matusek
DESIGNER
Lance Matusek
PHOTOGRAPHER
Don Belliveau
ILLUSTRATOR/ARTIST
Lance Matusek
WRITER
Joann Duchesneau
CLIENT
Aetna
DESIGN FIRM
Aetna, Hartford, CT

552

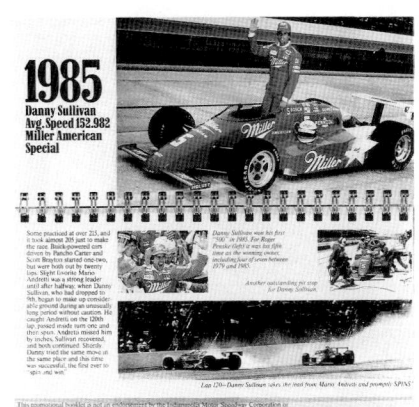

554

ART DIRECTOR
The Marlboro Creative Group
CLIENT
Philip Morris/Marlboro
AGENCY
Leo Burnett Co., Inc., Chicago, IL
CREATIVE DIRECTOR
Ken Krom

554

553

555

ART DIRECTOR
Woody Pirtle
DESIGNER
Woody Pirtle
PHOTOGRAPHER
Gary McCoy
ILLUSTRATOR/ARTIST
Woody Pirtle
WRITER
Woody Pirtle
CLIENT
Pirtle Design
DESIGN FIRM
Pirtle Design, Dallas, TX
PRINTER
Heritage Press

555

556
ART DIRECTOR
Victor Liebert, Liebert Studio
DESIGNER
Ann Galbraith
WRITER
Leslie Teitlebaum
CLIENT
Trevira
AGENCY
Trevira In House, Ina Kahn, New York, NY

556

557
ART DIRECTOR
Wendy Hebborn
DESIGNER
Wendy Hebborn
ILLUSTRATOR/ARTIST
Wendy Hebborn, Carol Burke, Ray Sturdivant
WRITER
Leigh Sander
CLIENT
Lone Star Masters Swim Club
AGENCY
Cox Pippin Communications, Dallas, TX

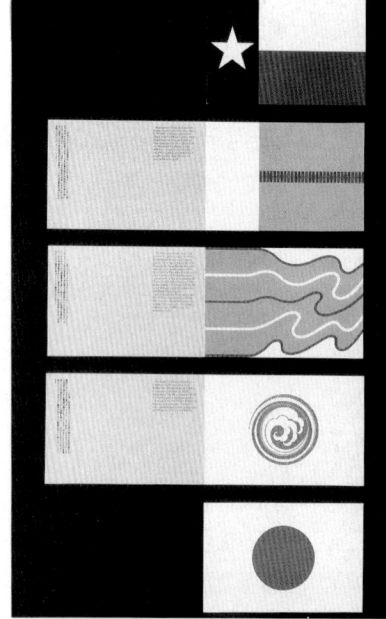

558

558
ART DIRECTOR
Woody Pirtle
DESIGNER
Alan Colvin
PHOTOGRAPHER
Ron Scott
WRITER
Lee Herrick
CLIENT
Olmsted-Kirk Paper Company
DESIGN FIRM
Pirtle Design, Dallas, TX
PRINTER
Williamson Printing Corp.

557

559
ART DIRECTOR
Woody Pirtle
DESIGNER
Jeff Weithman
PHOTOGRAPHER
Jim Olvera
WRITER
Woody Pirtle
CLIENT
Pirtle Design
DESIGN FIRM
Pirtle Design, Dallas, TX
PRINTER
Williamson Printing Corp.

559

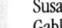

560

ART DIRECTOR
Frank Schulwolf
PHOTOGRAPHER
Mark Weithorn
ILLUSTRATOR/ARTIST
Ted Lodigensky
WRITER
Arthur Low
CLIENT
Aviation Sales Company, Inc.
AGENCY
Susan Gilbert & Company, Inc., Coral Gables, FL
PRINTER
Southeastern Printing

561

ART DIRECTOR
Woody Pirtle
DESIGNER
Alan Colvin
PHOTOGRAPHER
Various
WRITER
Lee Herrick
CLIENT
Pacific Realty
AGENCY
Kagan & Associates
DESIGN FIRM
Pirtle Design, Dallas, TX
PRINTER
Heritage Press

560

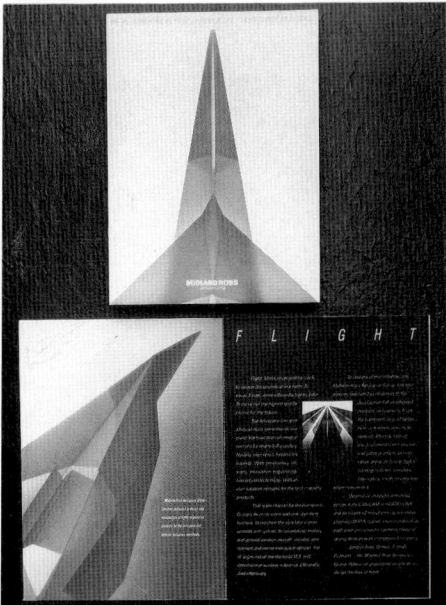

561

562

ART DIRECTOR
Neil R. Probala
DESIGNER
Neil R. Probala, The Wozniaks
PHOTOGRAPHER
Greg Sereta
WRITER
Staff
CLIENT
Midland Ross Aerospace
AGENCY
Liggett-Stashower, Cleveland, OH
CREATIVE DIRECTOR
Ted Kolozsdary

562

563

ART DIRECTOR
Woody Pirtle
DESIGNER
Jeff Weithman
PHOTOGRAPHER
Gary McCoy
WRITER
Gary McCoy, Jeff Weithman
CLIENT
Gary McCoy
DESIGN FIRM
Pirtle Design, Dallas, TX
PRINTER
Williamson Printing Corp.

563

564
ART DIRECTOR
Alan Christie
DESIGNER
Dale Coykendall
PHOTOGRAPHER
Alan Orling
WRITER
Tina Winfield
DESIGN FIRM
SchneiderGraphics, New York, NY

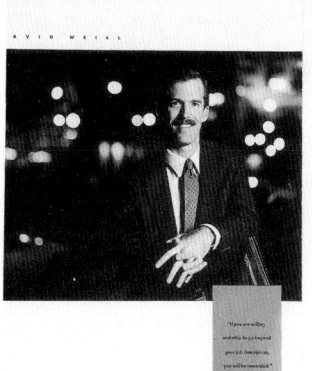

564

565
ART DIRECTOR
Kenneth D. Love
DESIGNER
Robin Andrews, Christopher Johnson,
Constance Birdsall
CLIENT
Unisys Corporation - David Wright, Jeannette
P. Lerman
EDITOR
David Wright
DESIGN FIRM
Anspach Grossman Portugal Inc., New York,
NY

566
ART DIRECTOR
Frank Schulwolf
PHOTOGRAPHER
Mark Weithorn
ILLUSTRATOR/ARTIST
Ted Lodigensky
WRITER
Arthur Low
CLIENT
Aviation Sales Company, Inc.
AGENCY
Susan Gilbert & Company, Inc., Coral
Gables, FL
PRINTER
Southeastern Printing

565

567
ART DIRECTOR
Stephanie Coustenis
DESIGNER
Stephanie Coustenis
PHOTOGRAPHER
Bill Denison
WRITER
Susann Studz
CLIENT
Vassar College
DESIGN FIRM
The North Charles Street Design
Organization, Baltimore, MD

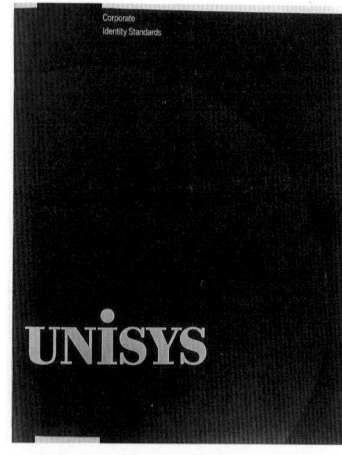

566

567

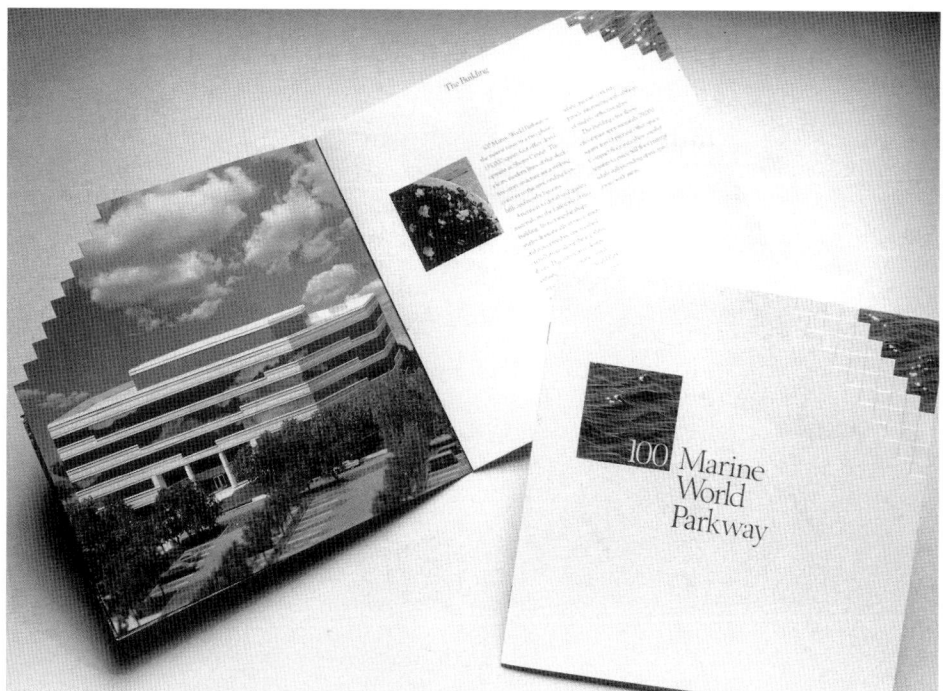

568

ART DIRECTOR
Janet Mumford, Diane Levin
DESIGNER
Janet Mumford, Diane Levin
PHOTOGRAPHER
Henrik Kam
WRITER
Deborah Gallin
CLIENT
William Wilson & Associates
DESIGN FIRM
Design Resource, San Anselmo, CA
PRINTER
Paragraphics

569

DESIGN DIRECTOR
Ivan Chermayeff, Steff Geissbuhler
DESIGNER
Steff Geissbuhler, Danielle Dimston
PHOTOGRAPHER
François Robert
WRITER
Paul Rosenthal
CLIENT
NBC
AGENCY
Chermayeff & Geismar Associates, New York, NY

568

569

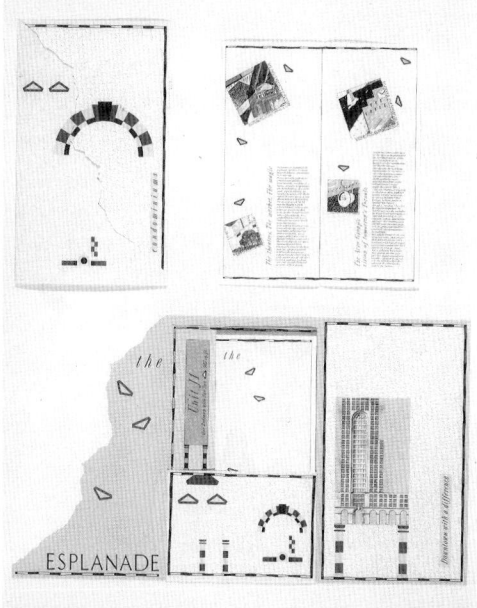

570

ART DIRECTOR
Baiba Black
DESIGNER
Baiba Black, Edda Castellan
ILLUSTRATOR/ARTIST
Jeff Jackson, Fenwick Bonnell
WRITER
David Mills
CLIENT
The Avro Group/The Esplanade
DIRECTOR
David Mills
AGENCY
Elias Marketing & Communications Inc., Toronto, Canada
PRINTER
Bradbury, Tamblyn & Boorne

570

571

ART DIRECTOR
Josh Freeman
DESIGNER
Vickie Sawyer
ILLUSTRATOR/ARTIST
Karen Mercedes McDonald
WRITER
Diana Janus
CLIENT
The Christiana Companies, Inc.
DESIGN FIRM
Josh Freeman/Associates, Los Angeles, CA

571

572
ART DIRECTOR
Frank Schulwolf
PHOTOGRAPHER
George Schiavone
ILLUSTRATOR/ARTIST
Ted Lodigensky, I. Hasegawa, R.G. Smith,
Paul Salmon, Watanabi, William Reynolds
WRITER
Arthur Low
CLIENT
Aviation Sales Company, Inc.
AGENCY
Susan Gilbert & Company, Inc., Coral
Gables, FL
PRINTER
Colour Group

573
ART DIRECTOR
Blake Miller, Wayne Ford
DESIGNER
Blake Miller
PHOTOGRAPHER
Jim Sims, Jim Rantala, Bob Werre
ILLUSTRATOR/ARTIST
Mark Moore, Jack Slattery, Lee Brazeal, Larry
McEntire
WRITER
Jim Sanders
CLIENT
Clampitt Paper Company
DESIGN FIRM
Miller Judson and Ford, Inc., Houston, TX

572

574
ART DIRECTOR
The Brownstone Group, Inc.
DESIGNER
The Brownstone Group, Inc.
WRITER
The Brownstone Group, Inc.
CLIENT
The Brownstone Group, Inc.
DESIGN FIRM
The Brownstone Group, Inc., Brookline, MA
TYPOGRAPHER
Type By Design

573

575
ART DIRECTOR
Colin Forbes
DESIGNER
Michael Gericke
ILLUSTRATOR/ARTIST
Mel Calman
WRITER
Kathy Schleyer
CLIENT
Steelcase, Inc.
DESIGN FIRM
Pentagram Design, New York, NY

575

574

576

576

ART DIRECTOR
Joseph Caroff
DESIGNER
Joseph Caroff
ILLUSTRATOR/ARTIST
Joseph Caroff
WRITER
Gil Liberman
CLIENT
Refco Group Ltd
SENIOR EDITOR
Rick Kaplan
EDITOR
Richard Fran
PUBLISHER
Refco Group Ltd
DESIGN FIRM
J. Caroff Associates, New York, NY

577

ART DIRECTOR
Seymour Chwast
DESIGNER
Seymour Chwast
ILLUSTRATOR/ARTIST
Seymour Chwast (Cover)
WRITER
Steve Heller
CLIENT
Mohawk Paper Mills, Inc.
EDITOR
Steve Heller
DESIGN FIRM
The Pushpin Group, New York, NY
TYPOGRAPHER
Cardinal Type Service, Inc.

577

578

ART DIRECTOR
Jamie Mambro
DESIGNER
Nancy Malacaria
PHOTOGRAPHER
Philip Porcella
WRITER
Thomas Monahan
CLIENT
Lotus Development Corporation
AGENCY
Leonard Monahan Saabye, Providence, RI
PUBLICATION
Scientific American
PRINTER
Rand

578

579

ART DIRECTOR
Colin Forbes, Alan Fletcher
DESIGNER
Colin Forbes, Alan Fletcher
PHOTOGRAPHER
Jean Robert
CLIENT
IBM
EDITOR
Joann Sullivan, IBM
PUBLISHER
S. D. Scott
DESIGN FIRM
Pentagram Design, New York, NY

580
ART DIRECTOR
Paul Huber
DESIGNER
Paul Huber
PHOTOGRAPHER
Steve Brady
WRITER
Dan Altman
CLIENT
Seattle Silicon
AGENCY
Altman & Manley, Boston, MA
DESIGN FIRM
Altman & Manley Design
CREATIVE DIRECTOR
Robert Manley

580

581
ART DIRECTOR
Don Povie
DESIGNER
Seymour Chwast
ILLUSTRATOR/ARTIST
Seymour Chwast
CLIENT
Mohawk Paper
DESIGN FIRM
The Pushpin Group, New York, NY

581

582
ART DIRECTOR
Bob Paganucci
DESIGNER
Bob Paganucci
ILLUSTRATOR/ARTIST
Alex Tiani
WRITER
Bill Littlefield
CLIENT
IBM
AGENCY
Salpeter Paganucci, Inc., New York, NY
DESIGN FIRM
Salpeter Paganucci, Inc.

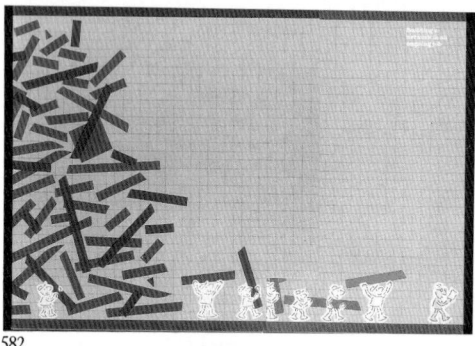

582

583
ART DIRECTOR
Holly Russell
DESIGNER
Holly Russell
ILLUSTRATOR/ARTIST
Phillipe Weisbecker
WRITER
Craig Walker
CLIENT
ABC International
AGENCY
Altman & Manley, Boston, MA
DESIGN FIRM
Altman & Manley Design
CREATIVE DIRECTOR
Robert Manley

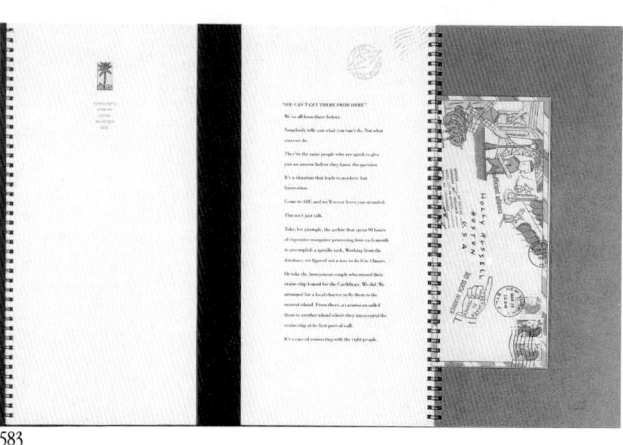

583

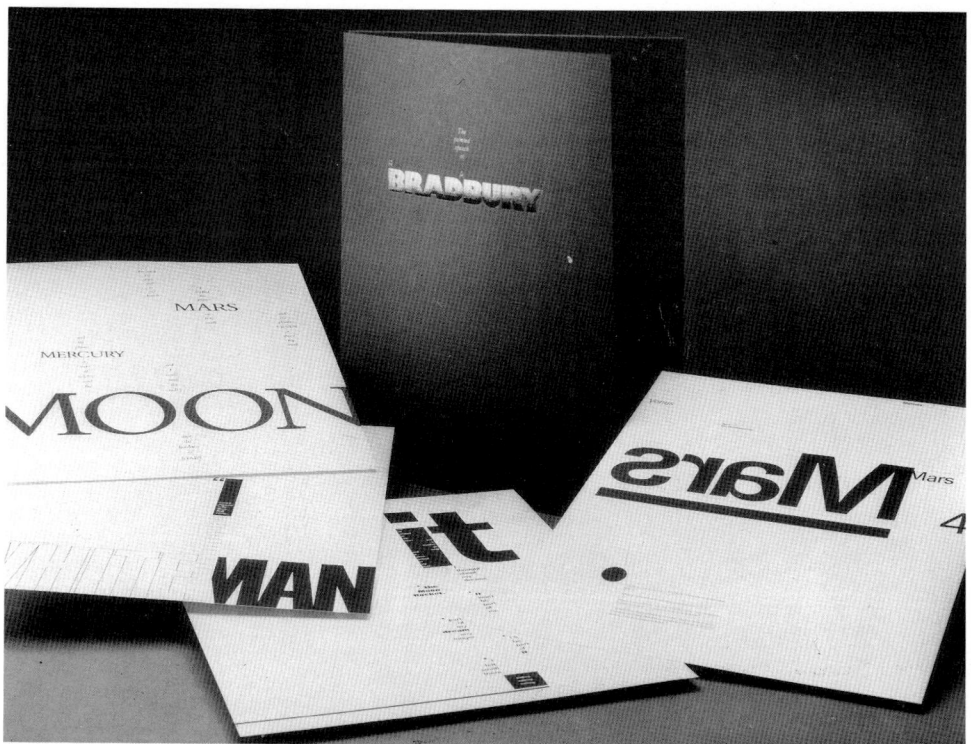

584

ART DIRECTOR
Vance Studley
DESIGNER
Vance Studley
ILLUSTRATOR/ARTIST
Vance Studley
WRITER
Ray Bradbury
CLIENT
Art Center College of Design
DIRECTOR
Vance Studley
PUBLISHER
Art Center College of Design
DESIGN FIRM
Art Center College of Design, Pasadena, CA

585

ART DIRECTOR
Frank Schulwolf
ILLUSTRATOR/ARTIST
John Mattos, Ted Lodigensky, Paul Salmon
WRITER
Arthur Low
CLIENT
Aviation Sales Company, Inc.
AGENCY
Susan Gilbert & Company, Inc., Coral
Gables, FL
PRINTER
Colour Group

584

585

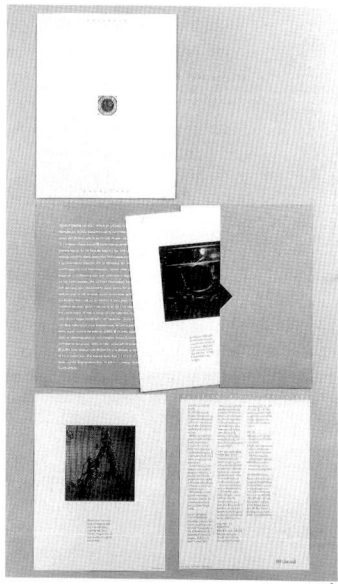

586

ART DIRECTOR
Marie McGinley
DESIGNER
Marie McGinley
WRITER
Brian Flood
CLIENT
Polaroid Holographic Group
PUBLISHER
United Lithograph
DESIGN FIRM
Polaroid In-House, Cambridge, MA
PROJECT MANAGER
Rick Colson
HOLOGRAMS
Polaroid Holographic Group

586

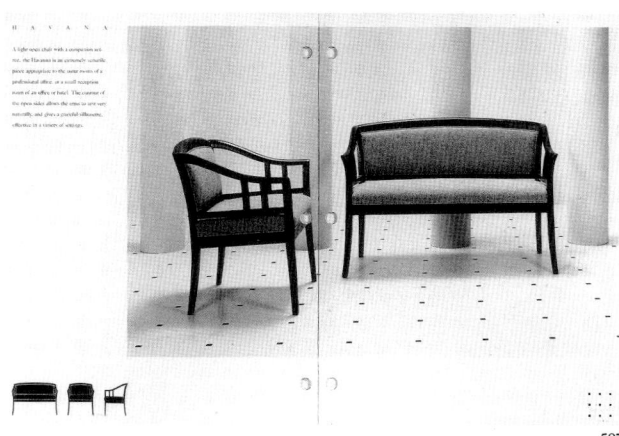

587

ART DIRECTOR
Michael Vanderbyl
DESIGNER
Michael Vanderbyl
PHOTOGRAPHER
Stone and Steccati
CLIENT
Hickory Business Furniture
DESIGN FIRM
Vanderbyl Design, San Francisco, CA
FURNITURE DESIGN
Orlando Diaz-Azcuy

587

588
ART DIRECTOR
Ronald Peterson
DESIGNER
Sharon Gresh
PHOTOGRAPHER
Hing/Norton Studio
ILLUSTRATOR/ARTIST
Elwood Smith, Jose Cruz, Steven Guarnaccia
WRITER
John Salvati, Valerie Stuart
CLIENT
Peterson & Blyth Associates, Inc.
EDITOR
Valerie A. Stuart
DESIGN FIRM
Peterson & Blyth Associates, Inc., New York, NY

589
ART DIRECTOR
Judy Dolim, Rex Peteet
DESIGNER
Judy Dolim, Rex Peteet
PHOTOGRAPHER
Gary McCoy
WRITER
Doris Baron
CLIENT
Herring Marathon Group
DESIGN FIRM
Sibley/Peteet Design, Dallas, TX

590
ART DIRECTOR
Jack Summerford
DESIGNER
Jack Summerford
PHOTOGRAPHER
Arthur Meyerson
WRITER
Linda Bradford, Bob Downs
CLIENT
Heritage Press
DESIGN FIRM
Summerford Design, Inc., Dallas, TX

591
ART DIRECTOR
Jack Summerford
DESIGNER
Jack Summerford
ILLUSTRATOR/ARTIST
Jack Summerford
WRITER
Diane Bullard
CLIENT
Goodwill
DESIGN FIRM
Summerford Design, Inc., Dallas, TX

588

589

590

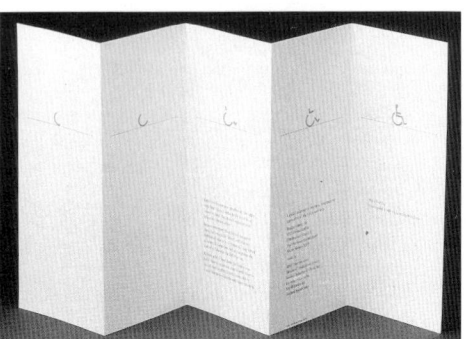

591

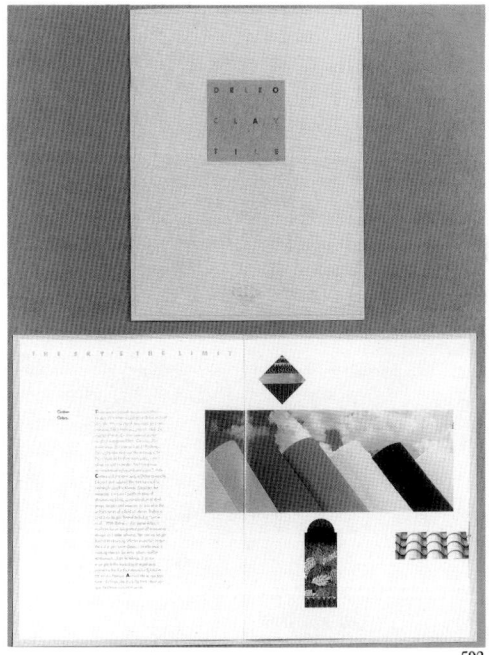

592

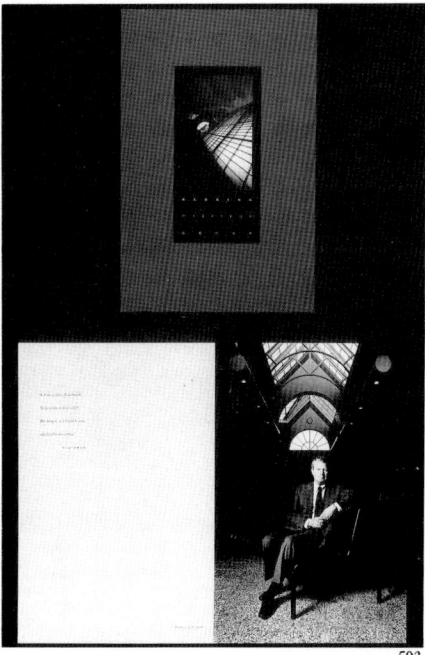

593

592
ART DIRECTOR
Scott Mires
DESIGNER
John Ball
PHOTOGRAPHER
Stephen Simpson
ILLUSTRATOR/ARTIST
John DeMarco
WRITER
Richard Norman Shopplery
CLIENT
Deleo Clay Tile
AGENCY
Hunington Public Relations
DESIGN FIRM
Mires Design, San Diego, CA

593
ART DIRECTOR
Don Sibley
DESIGNER
Don Sibley
PHOTOGRAPHER
Steve Brady
WRITER
Doris Baron
CLIENT
Herring Marathon Group
DESIGN FIRM
Sibley/Peteet Design, Inc., Dallas

594
ART DIRECTOR
Dick Sheaff
DESIGNER
Dick Sheaff, Uldis Purins, Laurie Bohn
WRITER
Charlie Hogg
CLIENT
S.D. Warren Paper Company
EDITOR
Fred Dempsey
DESIGN FIRM
Sheaff Design, Inc., Needham Hts, MA

594

595
ART DIRECTOR
John Muller
DESIGNER
John Muller, Jim Northcraft
PHOTOGRAPHER
Rick Nible
WRITER
Rob Price
CLIENT
North Kansas City Hospital
DESIGN FIRM
Muller + Company, Kansas City, MO

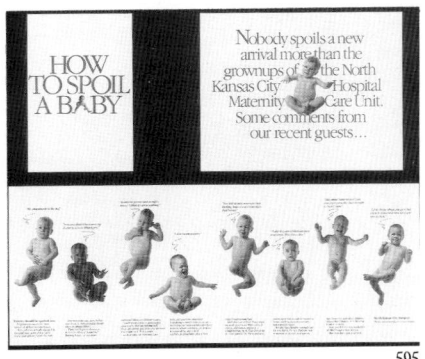

595

597
ART DIRECTOR
Mark Sackett, John Muller
DESIGNER
Mark Sackett, Mark Anderson
PHOTOGRAPHER
David Biegelson, various
ILLUSTRATOR/ARTIST
Hallmark artists
CLIENT
Hallmark Cards Inc.
DESIGN FIRM
Muller + Company, Kansas City, MO

597

598
ART DIRECTOR
Jim Vincent, Henk De Jong
DESIGNER
Jim Vincent, Henk De Jong
PHOTOGRAPHER
Jerry Davidson
WRITER
Martha Pell Stanville, Glen Fitzgerald, Dan
Weiss, Maureen Dolan-Dobson
CLIENT
NBC
EDITOR
Martha Pell Stanville
PUBLISHER
NBC Affiliate Advertising & Promotion
Services
DESIGN FIRM
NBC Print Advertising, Burbank, CA

598

599
PHOTOGRAPHER
Harry Peterson, Washnik Studios
ILLUSTRATOR/ARTIST
Whitman Studios
CLIENT
Gemini Industries
DESIGN FIRM
Ronald Emmerling Design Inc., Montclair,
NJ

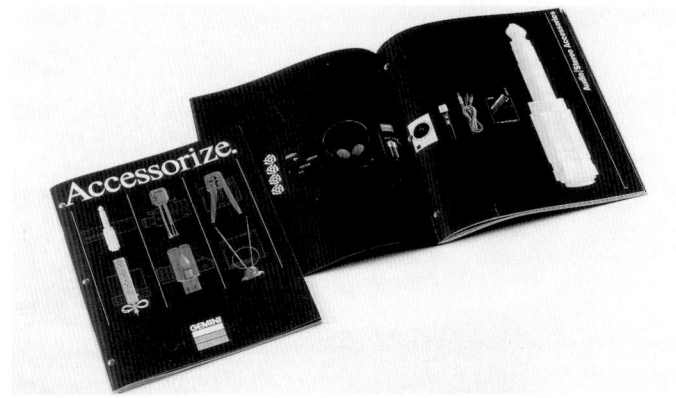

599

600
ART DIRECTOR
Cinda K. Debbink
DESIGNER
Ken Maginnis
PHOTOGRAPHER
Various
WRITER
Mike Heeley
CLIENT
Healthcare International, Inc.
DESIGN FIRM
Creel Morrell Inc., Austin, TX
PRINTER
Communications Specialists Inc.

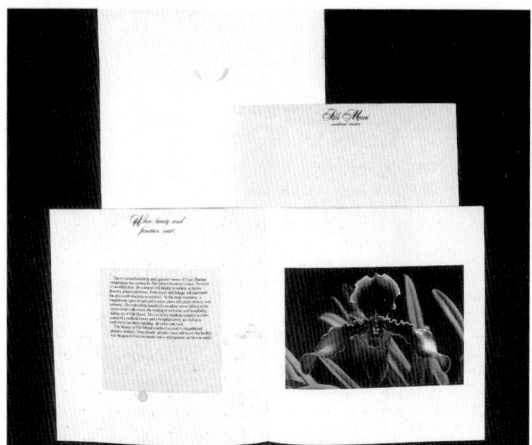

600

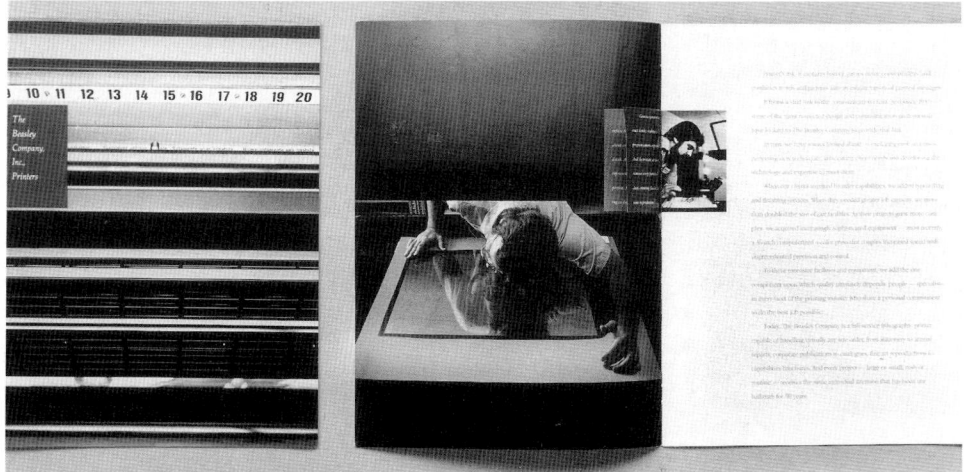

601

ART DIRECTOR
Julia Pepper Thackrey
DESIGNER
Julia Pepper Thackrey
PHOTOGRAPHER
Steve Brady
WRITER
Lee Herrick
CLIENT
The Beasley Company, Inc.
DESIGN FIRM
Savage Design Group, Inc., Houston, TX

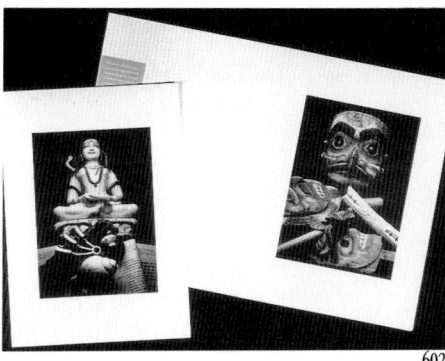

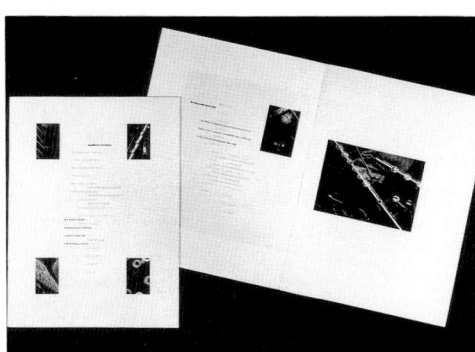

602

ART DIRECTOR
Kevin B. Kuester
DESIGNER
Kevin B. Kuester
PHOTOGRAPHER
Terry Heffernan
WRITER
Dick Cinquina
CLIENT
Potlatch Corporation, Northwest Paper
Division
DESIGN FIRM
Madsen and Kuester, Inc., Minneapolis, MN

602

603

603

ART DIRECTOR
Kevin B. Kuester
DESIGNER
Kevin B. Kuester
PHOTOGRAPHER
Arthur Meyerson
WRITER
Bill Wells
CLIENT
Potlatch Corporation, Northwest Paper
Division
DESIGN FIRM
Madsen and Kuester, Inc., Minneapolis, MN

604

ART DIRECTOR
John Walker
DESIGNER
John Walker
PHOTOGRAPHER
Alan Calhoun
ILLUSTRATOR/ARTIST
Tim Anderson
WRITER
Barbara Goho
CLIENT
North Carolina Zoological Society
PUBLISHER
Hunter Publishing
AGENCY
RJR Nabisco, Inc., Graphic Communications,
Winston-Salem, NC
TYPOGRAPHER
Typography Studio

604

605
ART DIRECTOR
Mark Handler
DESIGNER
Gail Rigelhaupt
PHOTOGRAPHER
Arthur Krasinsky, KPI, Inc.
ILLUSTRATOR/ARTIST
Gail Rigelhaupt
WRITER
Howard Flashenburg, ESPN, Inc.
CLIENT
ESPN, Inc.
PRODUCER
Nancy Bestwick
DESIGN FIRM
Handler Group, Inc., New York, NY
PRINTER
Craftsmen Litho

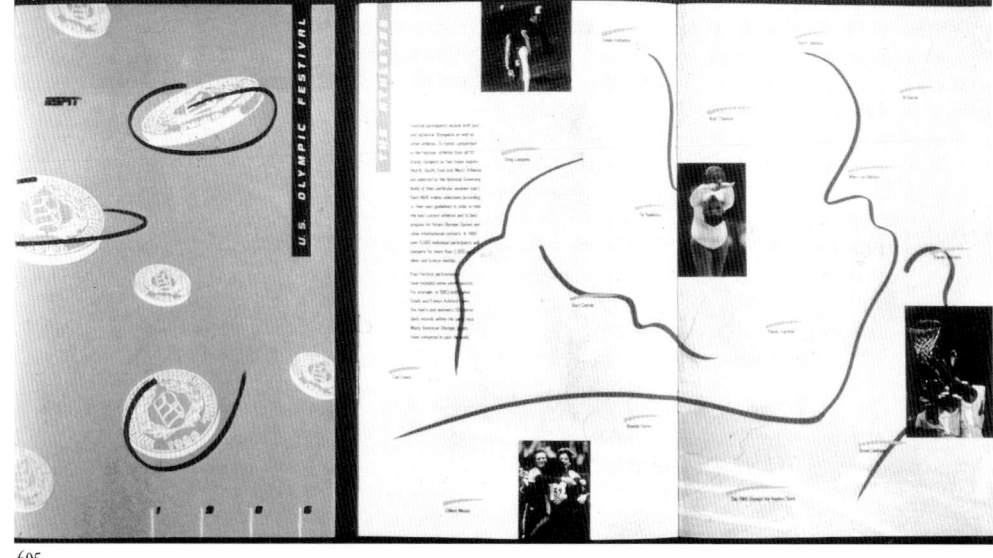

605

606
ART DIRECTOR
Charles Spencer Anderson
DESIGNER
Charles Spencer Anderson
ILLUSTRATOR/ARTIST
Charles Spencer Anderson
CLIENT
Fresh Force Youth Volunteer Group
DESIGN FIRM
Duffy Design Group, Minneapolis, MN

607
ART DIRECTOR
Colin Forbes
DESIGNER
MaryAnn Levesque
PHOTOGRAPHER
Bill Whitehurst (cover)
CLIENT
Interiors Magazine, Beverly Russell
DESIGN FIRM
Pentagram Design, New York, NY

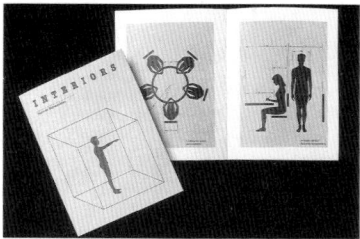

606

607

608
ART DIRECTOR
John Brown, Joan Rutledge
DESIGNER
Joan Rutledge
PHOTOGRAPHER
Alan Calhoun
WRITER
Kay Young
CLIENT
R. J. Reynolds Tobacco USA
EDITOR
Betsy Annese
PUBLISHER
Hunter Publishing
AGENCY
RJR Nabisco, Inc., Graphic Communications,
Winston-Salem, NC
TYPOGRAPHER
Typography Studio
RESEARCH
Barry Miller

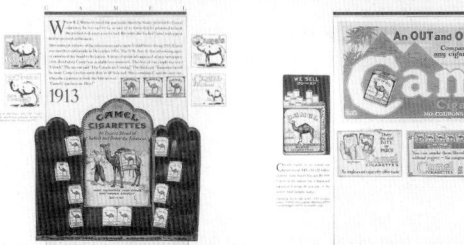

608

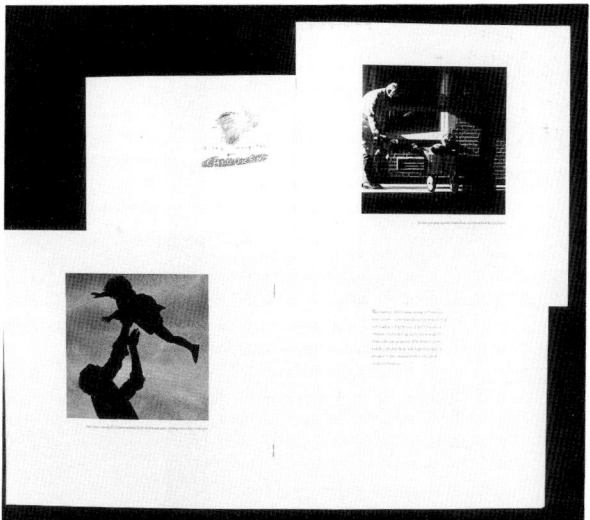

609

ART DIRECTOR
David Lesh, Ellen J. Sickle
DESIGNER
Ellen J. Sickle
PHOTOGRAPHER
Tom Casalini
ILLUSTRATOR/ARTIST
Alan E. Cober
WRITER
Jim Keenan
CLIENT
Riley Hospital for Children
PRODUCER
Emily Gilroy
DESIGN FIRM
Design Solutions, Indianapolis, IN
PRINTER
Metropolitan Printing

609

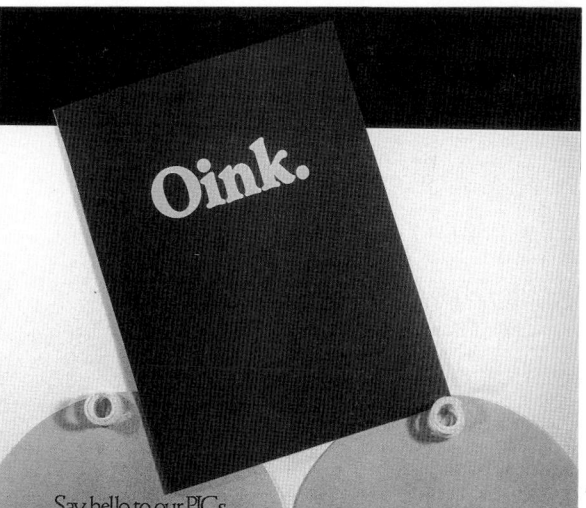

610

ART DIRECTOR
Tom Kaminsky
DESIGNER
Tom Kaminsky
WRITER
Michael Sheehan
CLIENT
New Pig Corp.
AGENCY
ClarkeGowardFitts, Boston, MA
DESIGN FIRM
ClarkeGowardFitts Design

611

ART DIRECTOR
David Wesko
DESIGNER
David Wesko
PHOTOGRAPHER
Robb Debenport
ILLUSTRATOR/ARTIST
David Wesko
WRITER
Nancy Caffoe, David Wesko
CLIENT
Arthur Andersen & Co.; Voluntary Hospitals
of America, Southwest
DESIGN FIRM
Point Design, Dallas, TX

610

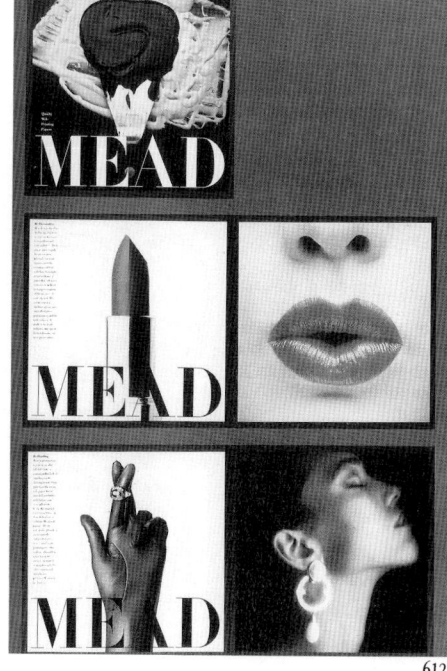

612

ART DIRECTOR
John Van Dyke
DESIGNER
John Van Dyke
PHOTOGRAPHER
Terry Heffernan
WRITER
Peter Maloney
CLIENT
Mead Paper Company
AGENCY
Van Dyke Company, Seattle, WA
DESIGN FIRM
Van Dyke Company

611

612

613
ART DIRECTOR
Don Sibley, Penelope Rowland
DESIGNER
Don Sibley, Penelope Rowland
PHOTOGRAPHER
Steve Brady, Joe Aker
ILLUSTRATOR/ARTIST
Jack Unruh
WRITER
Doris Baron
CLIENT
LaSalle Partners/Renaissance Tower
DESIGN FIRM
Sibley/Peteet Design, Inc., Dallas, TX

614
ART DIRECTOR
Sharon Werner
DESIGNER
Sharon Werner
PHOTOGRAPHER
Terry Heffernan
WRITER
Chuck Carlson (Captions)
DESIGN FIRM
Duffy Design Group, Minneapolis, MN

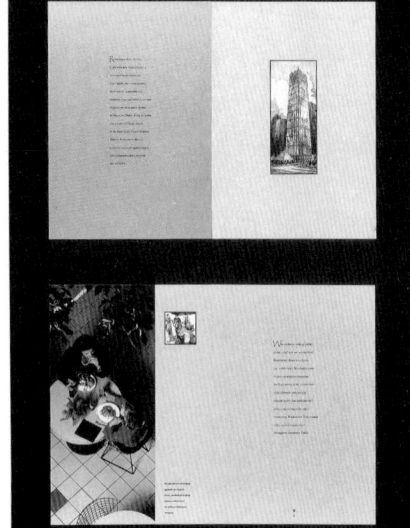

613

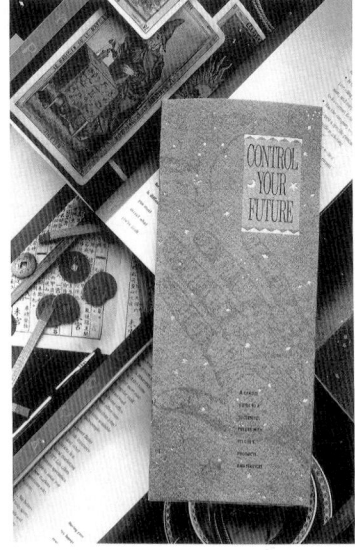

614

615
ART DIRECTOR
Steven Wedeen, Rick Vaughn
DESIGNER
Steven Wedeen
PHOTOGRAPHER
Stephen Marks, Valerie Santagto
ILLUSTRATOR/ARTIST
Kevin Tolman, Mark Chamberlain, Rick Vaughn
WRITER
Mary Langridge
CLIENT
Starline Printing
DESIGN FIRM
Vaughn/Wedeen Creative, Inc., Albuquerque, NM

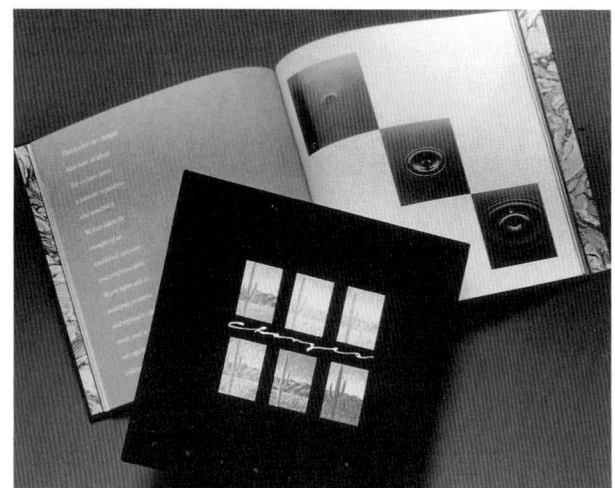

615

616
ART DIRECTOR
Charles Spencer Anderson
DESIGNER
Charles Spencer Anderson
WRITER
Chuck Carlson
CLIENT
Aura
DESIGN FIRM
Duffy Design Group, Minneapolis, MN

616

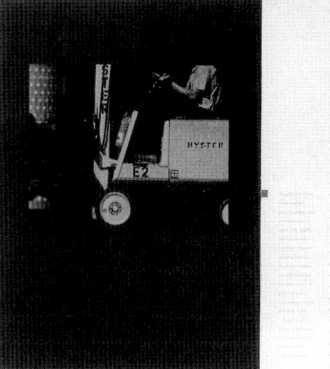

617

618

619

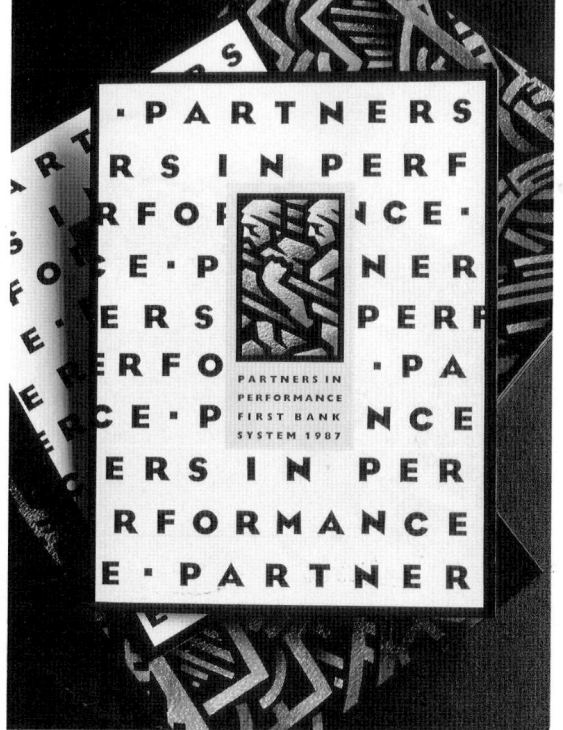

620

617
ART DIRECTOR
Charles Spencer Anderson
DESIGNER
Charles Spencer Anderson
ILLUSTRATOR/ARTIST
Charles Spencer Anderson
WRITER
Chuck Carlson
CLIENT
Morison Asset Management
DESIGN FIRM
Duffy Design Group, Minneapolis, MN

618
ART DIRECTOR
Steven Wedeen
DESIGNER
Steven Wedeen
PHOTOGRAPHER
Michael Barley
WRITER
Penelope Holme, Richard Kuhn
CLIENT
Corporate Security & Investigations
DESIGN FIRM
Vaughn/Wedeen Creative, Inc., Albuquerque, NM

619
ART DIRECTOR
Charles Spencer Anderson
DESIGNER
Charles Spencer Anderson
ILLUSTRATOR/ARTIST
Charles Spencer Anderson, Joe Duffy, Sharon Werner
WRITER
Chuck Carlson
CLIENT
First Bank Minneapolis
DESIGN FIRM
Duffy Design Group, Minneapolis, MN

620
ART DIRECTOR
Charles Spencer Anderson
DESIGNER
Charles Spencer Anderson, Sara Ledgard
ILLUSTRATOR/ARTIST
Charles Spencer Anderson
DESIGN FIRM
Duffy Design Group, Minneapolis, MN

621
ART DIRECTOR
Ron Sullivan
DESIGNER
Diana McKnight
PHOTOGRAPHER
Robert Llewellen
ILLUSTRATOR/ARTIST
Diana McKnight
WRITER
Mark Perkins
CLIENT
Lincoln Property Company
DESIGN FIRM
Sullivan Perkins, Dallas, TX

622
ART DIRECTOR
Joe Duffy
DESIGNER
Joe Duffy, Sharon Werner, Charles Spencer
Anderson
PHOTOGRAPHER
West Light Photography, Craig Aurness
CLIENT
US West
DESIGN FIRM
Duffy Design Group, Minneapolis, MN

623
ART DIRECTOR
Charles Spencer Anderson
DESIGNER
Charles Spencer Anderson
ILLUSTRATOR/ARTIST
Charles Spencer Anderson
WRITER
Chuck Carlson
CLIENT
First Bank of Minneapolis
DESIGN FIRM
Duffy Design Group, Minneapolis, MN

624
ART DIRECTOR
Charles Spencer Anderson
DESIGNER
Charles Spencer Anderson
ILLUSTRATOR/ARTIST
Joe Duffy, Lynn Schulte
WRITER
Chuck Carlson
CLIENT
Shade Information Systems
DESIGN FIRM
Duffy Design Group, Minneapolis, MN

622

623

624

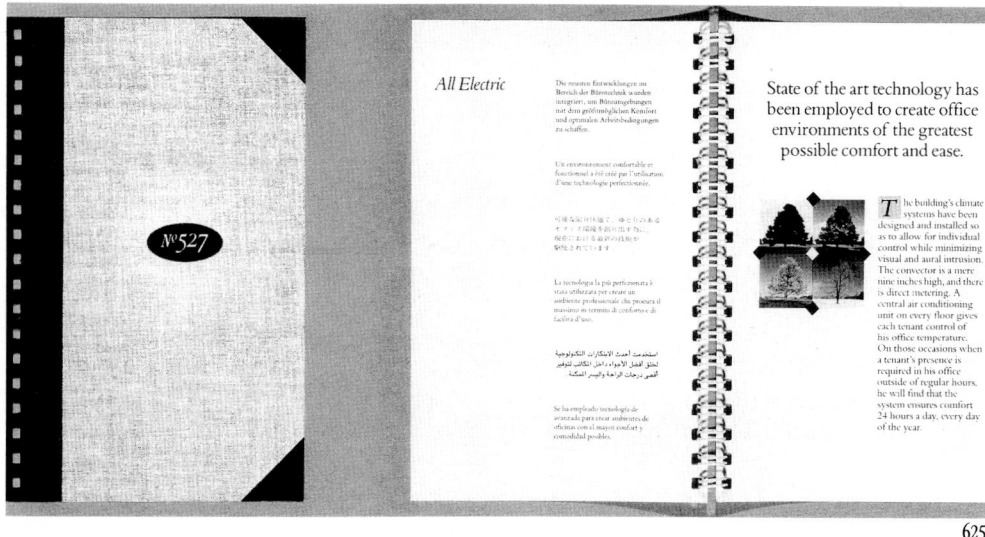

625

ART DIRECTOR
Tibor Kalman
DESIGNER
Alexander Brebner
WRITER
Danny Abelson
CLIENT
Louis Drefus Property Group
DESIGN FIRM
M&Co., New York, NY

625

626

ART DIRECTOR
Richard A. DeOlivera
DESIGNER
Richard A. DeOlivera
WRITER
Marcia Ragonetti ,
CLIENT
Telluride Prospects, LTD
DESIGN FIRM
DeOlivera Creative, Inc., Denver, CO

627

ART DIRECTOR
Rex Peteet
DESIGNER
Rex Peteet
PHOTOGRAPHER
Joe Aker
ILLUSTRATOR/ARTIST
Rex Peteet
WRITER
Rex Peteet, Marguerite Steed
CLIENT
Trammell Crow Company
DESIGN FIRM
Sibley/Peteet Design, Dallas, TX

626

628

ART DIRECTOR
Rex Peteet
DESIGNER
Rex Peteet
PHOTOGRAPHER
Steve Brady
ILLUSTRATOR/ARTIST
Rex Peteet
WRITER
Lee Herrick
CLIENT
The Lehndorff Group
AGENCY
Sibley/Peteet Design, Dallas, TX

627

628

629
ART DIRECTOR
Julia Chong Tam
DESIGNER
Julia Chong Tam
ILLUSTRATOR/ARTIST
Julia Chong Tam
WRITER
Jordan Sollitto
CLIENT
Julia Tam Design
DESIGN FIRM
Julia Tam Design, Palos Verdes, CA
PRINTER
Crown/Sojourn

629

630
ART DIRECTOR
Leslie Smolan
DESIGNER
Eric A. Pike
PHOTOGRAPHER
Barbara Bordnick, E.J. Camp, Bill Hayward,
Steve Krongard, Neil Selkirk
WRITER
Deirdre Peterson
CLIENT
Janet Coombs, Susan Thomas
DESIGN FIRM
Carbone Smolan Associates, New York, NY

630

631
ART DIRECTOR
Edward McDonald, Barry Seifer
DESIGNER
Edward McDonald
PHOTOGRAPHER
Edward McDonald
WRITER
Barry Seifer
CLIENT
Signa Design Group
DESIGN FIRM
Signa Design Group, Ann Arbor, MI
PRINTER
Mossberg & Co.

631

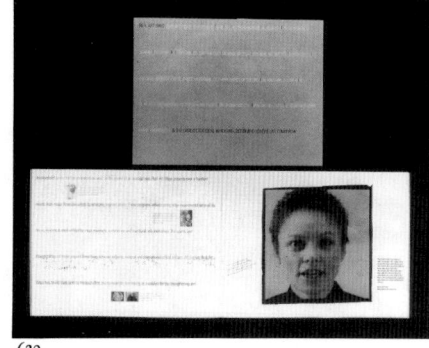

632

632
ART DIRECTOR
Robert Appleton
DESIGNER
Robert Appleton
WRITER
Ellie MacDougall
CLIENT
Real Art Ways
DESIGN FIRM
Appleton Design Inc., Hartford, CT

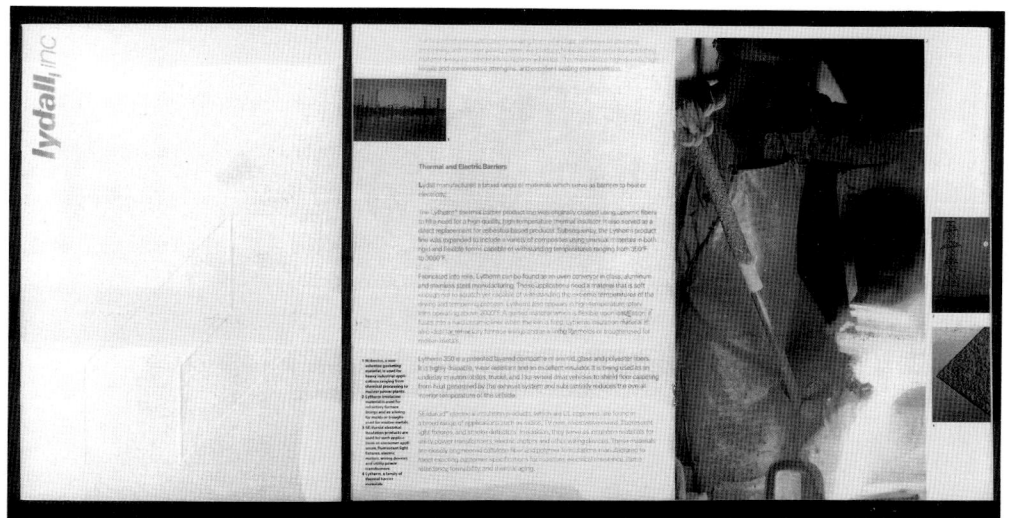

633

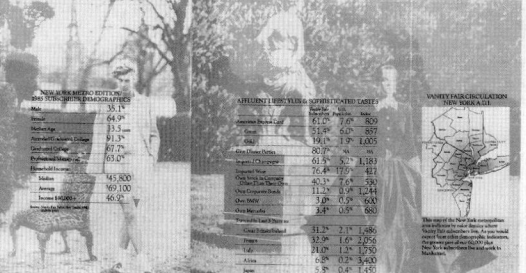

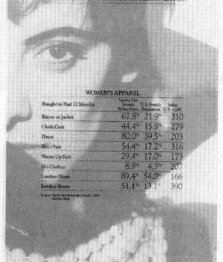

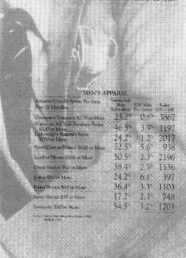

634

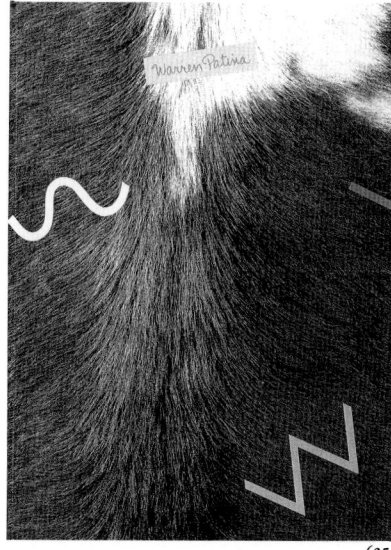

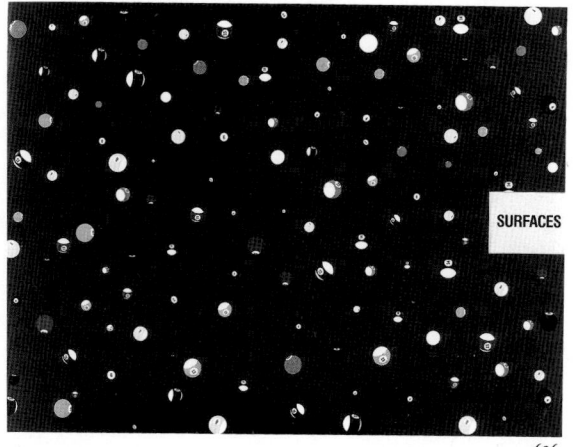

635

636

633

ART DIRECTOR
Robert Appleton
DESIGNER
Robert Appleton
PHOTOGRAPHER
John Earle, Tim Nighswander
ILLUSTRATOR/ARTIST
Natalie Vasa
WRITER
Carole F. Butenas
CLIENT
Lydall, Inc.
DESIGN FIRM
Appleton Design Inc., Hartford, CT

634

ART DIRECTOR
Younghee Choi
DESIGNER
Alice Kenny
WRITER
David Smith
CLIENT
Vanity Fair, New York Metropolitan Edition
DIRECTOR
Jean Karlson
PUBLISHER
G. Douglas Johnston
PRODUCER
Tom Heffernon
PUBLICATION
Vanity Fair Magazine, New York, NY
PRINTER
Master Craft
PROJECT MANAGER
Dierdre Oakley

635

ART DIRECTOR
Cheryl Heller
DESIGNER
Cheryl Heller
PHOTOGRAPHER
Geoffrey Clifford, Myron, William Albert
Allard, Kurt Markus
WRITER
Peter Caroline
CLIENT
S.D. Warren
AGENCY
HBM/Creamer, Inc.
DESIGN FIRM
HBM/Creamer Design Group, Boston, MA

636

ART DIRECTOR
Cheryl Heller
DESIGNER
Cheryl Heller
PHOTOGRAPHER
Clint Clemens
ILLUSTRATOR/ARTIST
Michael Orzech
WRITER
Peter Caroline
CLIENT
S.D. Warren
AGENCY
HBM/Creamer Inc.
DESIGN FIRM
HBM/Creamer Design Group, Boston, MA

637
ART DIRECTOR
Tibor Kalman
DESIGNER
Alexander Isley
WRITER
Danny Abelson
CLIENT
Aaron Green Companies
DESIGN FIRM
M&Co., New York, NY
PUBLICATION
Casa Vogue

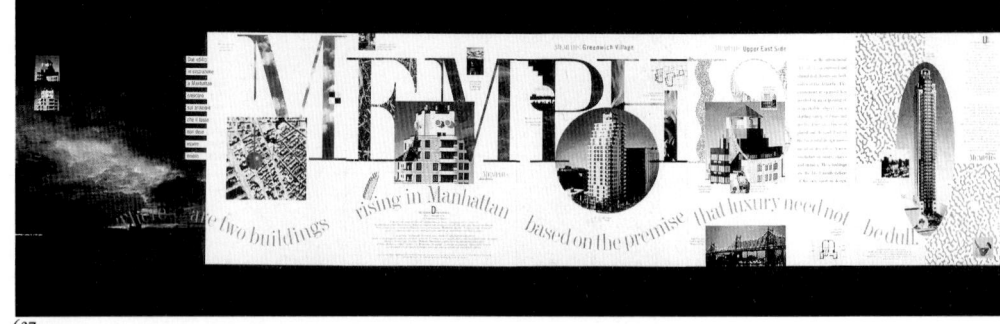

637

638
ART DIRECTOR
Kenneth R. Cooke
DESIGNER
Ken Higgins
PHOTOGRAPHER
Eddie Adams
WRITER
David Breskin, Martin Mayer
CLIENT
SB Lewis & Co.
EDITOR
Wyndham Robertson
PUBLISHER
SB Lewis & Co.
DESIGN FIRM
Identica, Inc., New York, NY

638

639
ART DIRECTOR
Kate Bergquist
DESIGNER
Kate Bergquist
WRITER
Joan Lee Weadock
CLIENT
Drew University
AGENCY
Rutka Weadock Design, Baltimore, MD

639

640
ART DIRECTOR
Curt Chuvalas
DESIGNER
Curt Chuvalas
PHOTOGRAPHER
Dick Spahr
WRITER
Carole Williams
CLIENT
Indiana Department of Commerce, Indiana
Film Commission
AGENCY
Bloomhorst Story O'Hara Inc., Indianapolis,
IN

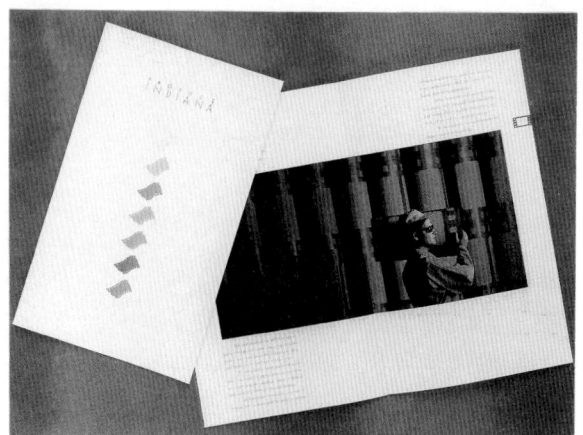

640

641

642

643

644

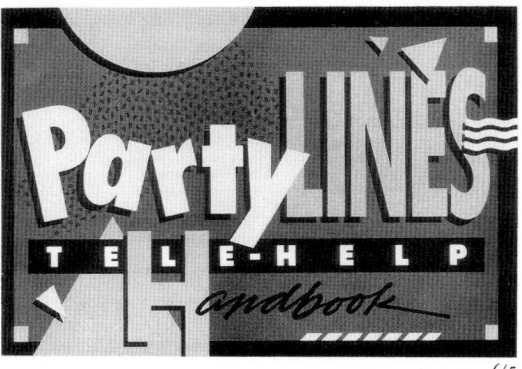

645

641

ART DIRECTOR
Warren A. Kass
DESIGNER
Warren A. Kass
ILLUSTRATOR/ARTIST
Daniel Pelavin
CLIENT
Radio City Music Hall Productions, Tigger
Moscow and Michael Walker
DESIGN FIRM
Kass Communications, New York, NY

642

ART DIRECTOR
Anthony Rutka, Kate Bergquist
DESIGNER
Kate Bergquist
PHOTOGRAPHER
Bill Denison
ILLUSTRATOR/ARTIST
Kimberely Parr
WRITER
Joan Lee Weadock
CLIENT
Washington College
AGENCY
Rutka Weadock Design, Baltimore, MD

643

ART DIRECTOR
Leo Mullen, Helene Patterson
DESIGNER
Leo Mullen, Andres Tremols
WRITER
Peter Muller
CLIENT
Invisions, Ltd.
DESIGN FIRM
Invisions, Ltd., Washington, DC
PRINTER
Stephenson, Inc.

644

ART DIRECTOR
Anthony Rutka, Kate Bergquist
DESIGNER
Kate Bergquist
PHOTOGRAPHER
Bill Denison, Doug Barber
WRITER
Joan Lee Weadock
CLIENT
Trinity College
AGENCY
Rutka Weadock Design, Baltimore, MD

645

ART DIRECTOR
Buck Smith
DESIGNER
Buck Smith
ILLUSTRATOR/ARTIST
Terry Speer, Don Vanderbeek, Buddy
Hickerson, Sean Earley, Steve Sheldon, Jim
Jacobs
CLIENT
Southwestern Bell
AGENCY
Bartels & Carstens, Inc., St. Louis, MO

646
ART DIRECTOR
Kenneth Carbone, Leslie Smolan
DESIGNER
Eric A. Pike,, Thomas Walker
PHOTOGRAPHER
Terry Ferrante
WRITER
Rita D. Jacobs, Rose DeNeve
CLIENT
Carbone Smolan Associates
DESIGN FIRM
Carbone Smolan Associates, New York, NY

646

647
ART DIRECTOR
Dick Bugdal
DESIGNER
Dick Bugdal
PHOTOGRAPHER
Mark Surloff
ILLUSTRATOR/ARTIST
Barbara Neijna
WRITER
Karen Valdés
CLIENT
Museum of Art, Barbara Neijna
DESIGN FIRM
Bugdal Group, Coral Gables, FL

647

648
ART DIRECTOR
Dave Jones
WRITER
Bruce O'Such
CLIENT
Herlin Press
DESIGN FIRM
Dave Jones Design, Middletown, CT

648

649
ART DIRECTOR
Mark Sackett, John Muller
DESIGNER
Mark Sackett, Mark Anderson
PHOTOGRAPHER
David Biegeleson
ILLUSTRATOR/ARTIST
Hallmark artists
CLIENT
Hallmark Cards Inc.
DESIGN FIRM
Muller + Company, Kansas City, MO

649

650

651

652

653

654

650

ART DIRECTOR
Rebecca Dickinson
DESIGNER
Rebecca Dickinson, Connie Formby
PHOTOGRAPHER
Mark Gooch, Lewis Arnold, Ted Tucker
WRITER
Karyn Zweifel, Thomas E. Corts
CLIENT
Samford University
PRODUCER
Richard Urban
DESIGN FIRM
Cruce & Associates/Creative Services,
Birmingham, AL
CREATIVE DIRECTOR
Lu Cruce

651

ART DIRECTOR
Lorraine Louie
DESIGNER
Lorraine Louie
ILLUSTRATOR/ARTIST
Lorraine Louie
CLIENT
Vintage Contemporaries, Random House
DESIGN FIRM
Lorraine Louie Design, New York, NY

652

ART DIRECTOR
Tom Zaferes
PHOTOGRAPHER
Claude Furones, Henry Wolfe, Don
Hammerman, Ruth Orkin, Norm Schneider
ILLUSTRATOR/ARTIST
Rene Caldas
WRITER
George Soter
CLIENT
Trump Corporation
AGENCY
Great Scott Advertising, New York, NY
ACCOUNT SUPERVISOR
Lorraine Borden
ACCOUNT EXEC.
Bob Baldwin

653

ART DIRECTOR
Frank Roehr
DESIGNER
Frank Roehr
PHOTOGRAPHER
Ed Dull
ILLUSTRATOR/ARTIST
Martin Rupert
WRITER
Brian Mount
CLIENT
Freightliner Corp.
AGENCY
Young & Roehr, Portland, OR

654

ART DIRECTOR
Myland McRevey, Katie Brown
DESIGNER
Myland McRevey
ILLUSTRATOR/ARTIST
Renee Graef, Nancy Niles, Chris Payne
WRITER
Jennifer Ellsworth, Pleasant T. Rowland
PUBLISHER
Pleasant Company, Madison, WI
CREATIVE DIRECTOR
Pleasant T. Rowland

655

ART DIRECTOR
Elizabeth C. Ball
DESIGNER
Elizabeth C. Ball, Kathryn Davidian
PHOTOGRAPHER
Jack Pottle
CLIENT
Phoenix Mutual Life Insurance Company
and Shearson Lehman Brothers with Capital
Vectors, Inc.
DESIGN FIRM
Pellegrini and Associates., New York, NY
PRINTER
Daniels Printing Company

655

656

ART DIRECTOR
John Avery
DESIGNER
John Avery
PHOTOGRAPHER
John Goodman, Kurt Stier
ILLUSTRATOR/ARTIST
Andrew Berry
WRITER
Neill Ray
CLIENT
NYNEX Business Centers
AGENCY
Hill, Holliday, Boston, MA
DESIGN FIRM
Hill, Holliday

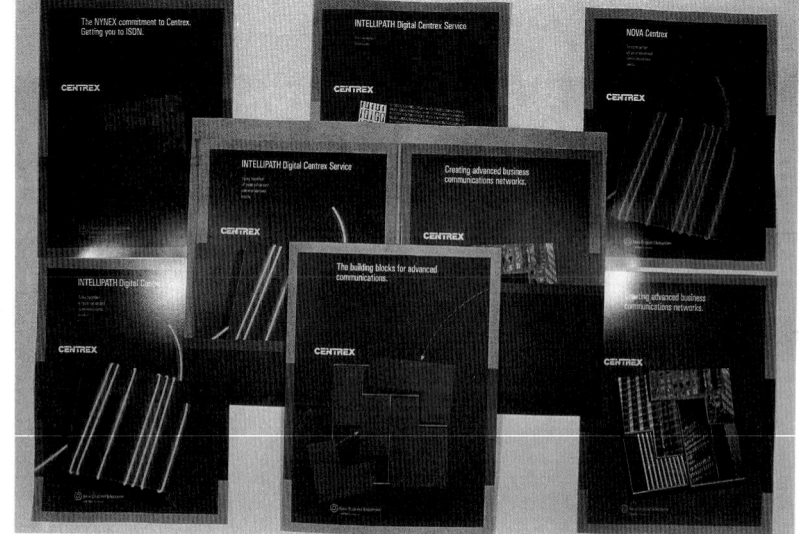
656

657

ART DIRECTOR
Bob Pellegrini, Elizabeth C. Ball
DESIGNER
Elizabeth C. Ball, Robin Williams
PHOTOGRAPHER
Richard Frank (Portraits)
ILLUSTRATOR/ARTIST
Bob Shein
CLIENT
Prime Cable and Shearson Lehman Brothers
with Capital Vectors, Inc.
DESIGN FIRM
Pellegrini and Associates Inc., New York, NY
PRINTER
Daniels Printing Company

657

658

ART DIRECTOR
Jesse Joseph Zellner
DESIGNER
Dan Auman, Draw The Line Studios
WRITER
John McAnulty
CLIENT
The Design Exchange
EDITOR
Jesse Joseph Zellner
AGENCY
Corporate Communications Group, Inc.,
Overland Park, KS
DESIGN FIRM
Draw The Line Studios

658

659

659
ART DIRECTOR
Joyce Schnaufer
DESIGNER
Joyce Schnaufer
ILLUSTRATOR/ARTIST
Nina Manger
WRITER
David Schmida, Jane Schenck
CLIENT
Pellon Company
EDITOR
Ray Pantalone
DESIGN FIRM
Joyce Schnaufer Design, New York, NY
PRINTER
Barton Press

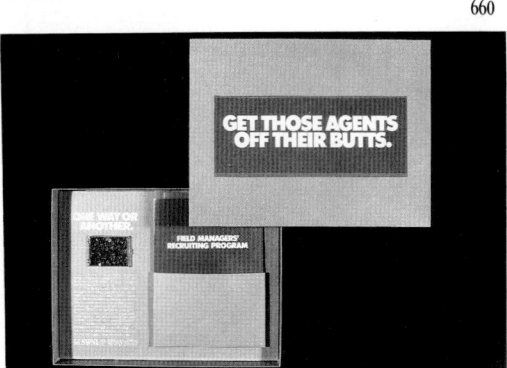

660

660
ART DIRECTOR
Don Trousdell
DESIGNER
Mark Sandlin, Tamila Grogan
PHOTOGRAPHER
Steve Pelosi, Don Chambers
ILLUSTRATOR/ARTIST
Theo Rednak
WRITER
Rich Maender
CLIENT
Kimberly-Clark
DESIGN FIRM
Don Trousdell Design, Atlanta, GA

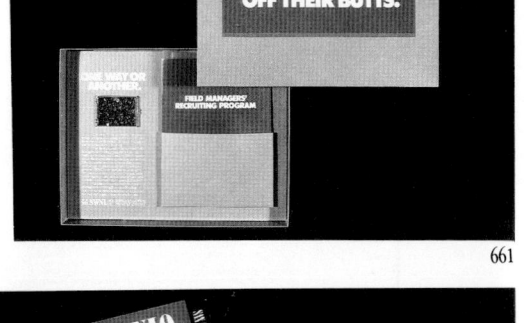

661

661
ART DIRECTOR
Terri Jeszewski
PHOTOGRAPHER
Steve Umland
WRITER
Lee Schmidt
CLIENT
Nick Motu
AGENCY
Martin/Williams, Minneapolis, MN
CREATIVE DIRECTOR
Tom Weyl
ACCOUNT EXEC.
Kay Olson

662

662
DESIGNER
Cheri Groom
ILLUSTRATOR/ARTIST
Dan Soder
WRITER
Tom Norman
CLIENT
San Antonio Convention & Visitors Bureau
AGENCY
Atkins & Associates, San Antonio, TX
PRODUCER
Caryl Berman, Jana Abell
PRINTER
American Printers, Clark Printing, Colad
Corp.
CREATIVE DIRECTOR
David Parker
TYPOGRAPHER
Edie Thompson

663

ART DIRECTOR
Lauren Smith McCombs
DESIGNER
Michael Granberry
CLIENT
Coca-Cola/N.B.D.
AGENCY
Selling Solutions, Inc., Atlanta, GA
PRINTER
Williams Printing
CREATIVE DIRECTOR
William L. Paullin, III

663

664

ART DIRECTOR
Arnold Wechsler
DESIGNER
Stephen J. Visconti
PHOTOGRAPHER
Dick Frank
CLIENT
Shearson Lehman Brothers
DESIGN FIRM
Wechsler & Partners, New York, NY

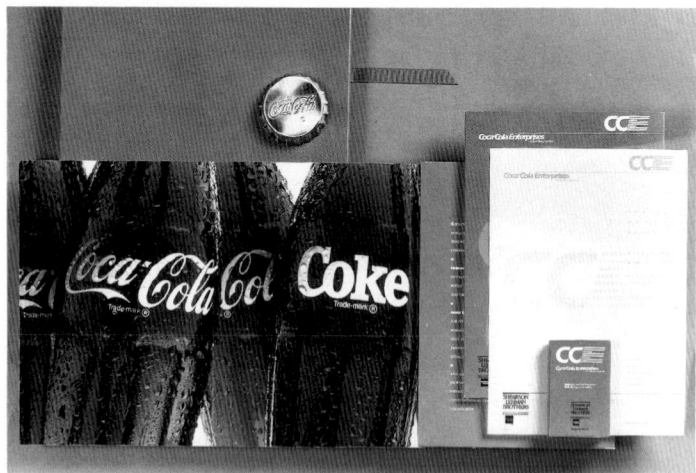

664

665

ART DIRECTOR
Jerry Tokugawa
DESIGNER
Jerry Tokugawa
ILLUSTRATOR/ARTIST
Jerry Tokugawa
WRITER
Jane Morrison
CLIENT
PacTel Publishing
DESIGN FIRM
Way Out West Design Communications, San
Francisco, CA

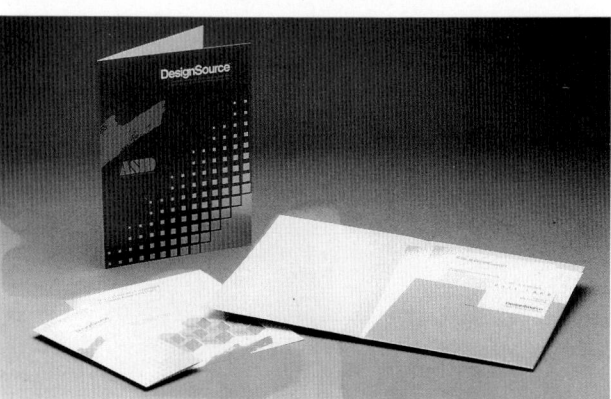

665

666

ART DIRECTOR
Patrick Fultz
DESIGNER
Patrick Fultz
ILLUSTRATOR/ARTIST
Tim Parker
WRITER
Karen Gedney
CLIENT
Oxford Health Plans
AGENCY
Millennium, New York, NY

666

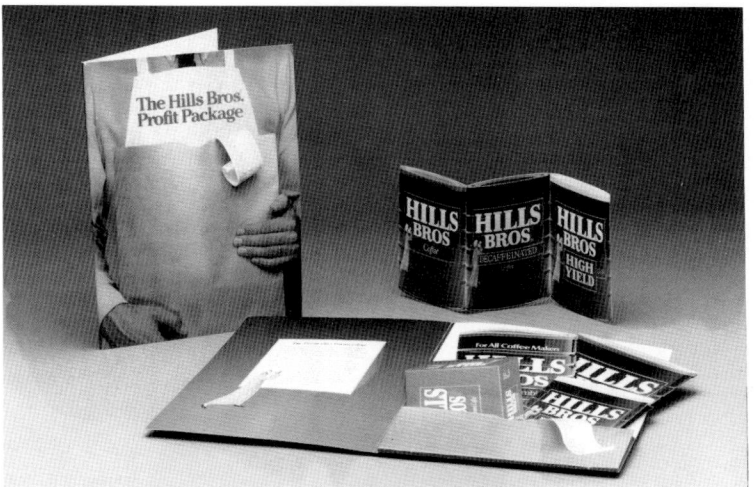

667

ART DIRECTOR
Jerry Tokugawa
DESIGNER
Teri Nishikawa
PHOTOGRAPHER
Bob Montesclaros
ILLUSTRATOR/ARTIST
Jerry Browell, Teri Nishikawa
WRITER
Lon Clark
CLIENT
Mike Shannon, Hills Bros. Coffee
DESIGN FIRM
Way Out West Design Communications, San
Francisco, CA

668

ART DIRECTOR
David Edelstein, Nancy Edelstein, Lanny
French
DESIGNER
David Edelstein, Nancy Edelstein, Lanny
French, Carol Davidson
ILLUSTRATOR/ARTIST
Carol Davidson
WRITER
David Edelstein, Lanny French, Norman
Durkee
CLIENT
Code Bleu
EDITOR
Norman Durkee
AGENCY
Edelstein Associates Advertising, Seattle, WA
DESIGN FIRM
Edelstein Associates Advertising

668

669

ART DIRECTOR
Bruce Dell
DESIGNER
Allen Stoddard, Anne Shecut
WRITER
Stephen Parris
CLIENT
Lockwood Greene
DESIGN FIRM
Lockwood Greene, Spartanburg, SC
PRINTER
Band & White
MARKETING COORDINATOR
Jo Ayers

669

670

ART DIRECTOR
David Stahl
CLIENT
Como Plastics Corporation
AGENCY
Quinlan Advertising, Indianapolis, IN
PRINTER
Metropolitan/D. E. Baugh

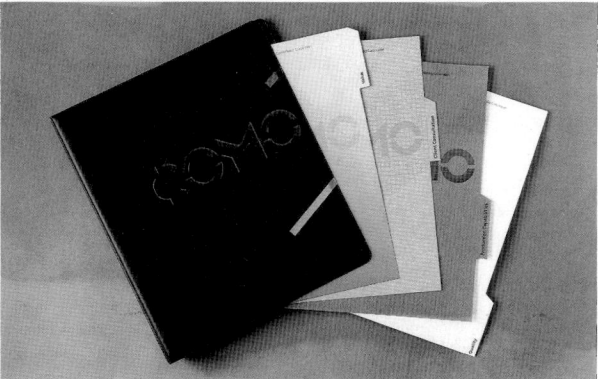

670

671
ART DIRECTOR
Larry A. Profancik
DESIGNER
Larry A. Profancik
PHOTOGRAPHER
Doug Decker
WRITER
Charles K. Cowdery
CLIENT
Brown-Forman Beverage Company
BRAND DIRECTOR
William E. Juckett
AGENCY
PriceWeber Marketing Communications, Inc.,
Louisville, KY

672
ART DIRECTOR
Michael Ostro
DESIGNER
Michael Ostro
ILLUSTRATOR/ARTIST
Michael Ostro
WRITER
Christopher Gregor
CLIENT
Constitution Health Network
AGENCY
The Douglas Group, Inc., Avon, CT

673
ART DIRECTOR
Randi Harper
DESIGNER
Randi Harper, Tim Young
PHOTOGRAPHER
Jim Fagiolo
WRITER
Ginny Willis
CLIENT
ESCA
DIRECTOR OF PHOTOGRAPHY
Pat Hickey
DESIGN FIRM
Harper & Associates, Inc., Bellevue, WA

674
ART DIRECTOR
James Good, Van Hayes
DESIGNER
Van Hayes
ILLUSTRATOR/ARTIST
Van Hayes
WRITER
Linda Bryza
CLIENT
American Airlines Freight
DESIGN FIRM
Good Design, Dallas, TX

675
ART DIRECTOR
Joseph Coleman
DESIGNER
Joseph Coleman
ILLUSTRATOR/ARTIST
Steve Karchin
WRITER
Arlene D. London
CLIENT
Equicor
DESIGN FIRM
Halliday/Herrmann Inc., New York, NY
PRINTER
DePalma Printing Co.

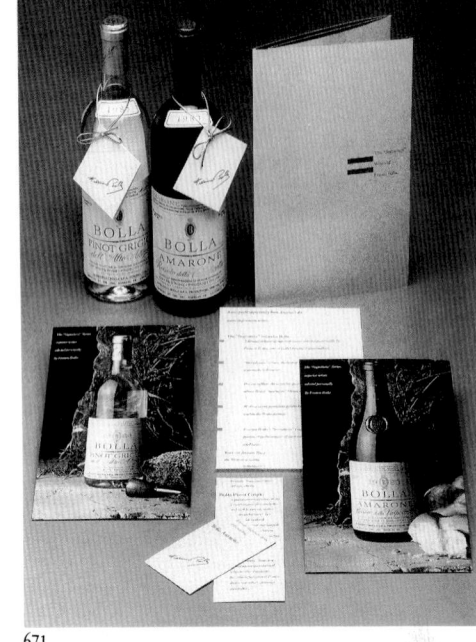

671

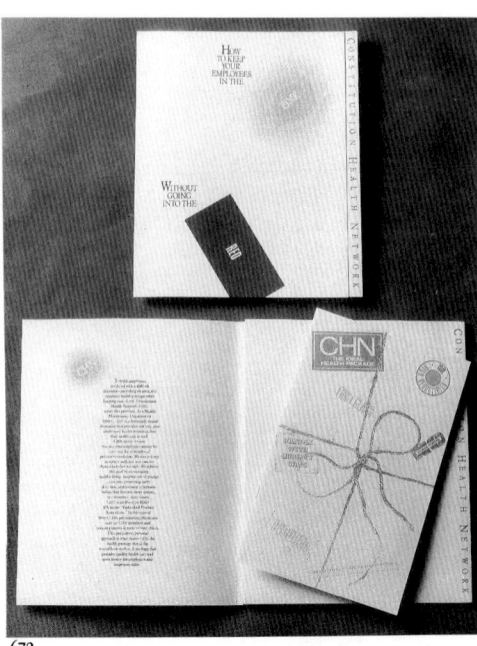

672

673

674

675

676

678

679

676

ART DIRECTOR
Rob Dalton
DESIGNER
Rob Dalton
PHOTOGRAPHER
Kent Severson
WRITER
Mike Lescarbeau
CLIENT
WFLD-TV
AGENCY
Fallon McElligott, Minneapolis, MN

677

ART DIRECTOR
Roger Core
DESIGNER
Roger Core
ILLUSTRATOR/ARTIST
Susan Lawson
WRITER
Roger Core, Linda Trucksis, Susan Lawson
CLIENT
March of Dimes
ADV. DIRECTOR
Virginia Bigenwald
AGENCY
Roger Core Advertising Inc., Weston, CT
ADV. COORDINATOR
Linda Santelli, Peggy White
PRINTER
Thames Printing Company

678

ART DIRECTOR
Gordon Hochhalter
DESIGNER
Bob Meyer
WRITER
Gordon Hochhalter
CLIENT
R. R. Donnelley & Sons Company, Chicago, IL
PRODUCER
Maryann Novak
ACCOUNT SUPERVISOR
Joe Cosgrove

679

ART DIRECTOR
Victor Liebert, Liebert Studio
DESIGNER
Beverly Friedman
WRITER
Larry Miller
CLIENT
Trevira
AGENCY
Trevira In-House, Ina Kahn, New York, NY

680
ART DIRECTOR
Mark Foster
DESIGNER
Mark Foster
PHOTOGRAPHER
Joe Boone, Doug Decker
WRITER
Jim Mabry
CLIENT
Sonn Products, Inc.
AGENCY
PriceWeber Marketing Communications, Inc.,
Louisville, KY
CREATIVE DIRECTOR
Larry A. Profancik

681
ART DIRECTOR
Don Johnson
DESIGNER
Bonnie Berish
PHOTOGRAPHER
Bob Krist, Steve MacNicoll
WRITER
Ann Lewis
CLIENT
Dolan/Wohlers Co.
DESIGN FIRM
Johnson & Simpson Graphic Design, Newark,
NJ

682
ART DIRECTOR
Patricia Robinson
DESIGNER
Patricia Robinson
PHOTOGRAPHER
John Van Schalkwyk, Martin Paul
WRITER
Brian Flood
CLIENT
Polaroid Presentation Products
AGENCY
Cipriani Advertising Inc., Boston, MA
ACCOUNT SUPERVISOR
Stephen A. Swets

683
ART DIRECTOR
Craig Bernhardt, Janice Fudyma
DESIGNER
Janice Fudyma
PHOTOGRAPHER
Bill Haywardt
CLIENT
Bond Investors Guaranty
DESIGN FIRM
Bernhardt Fudyma Design Group, New York,
NY

680

681

682

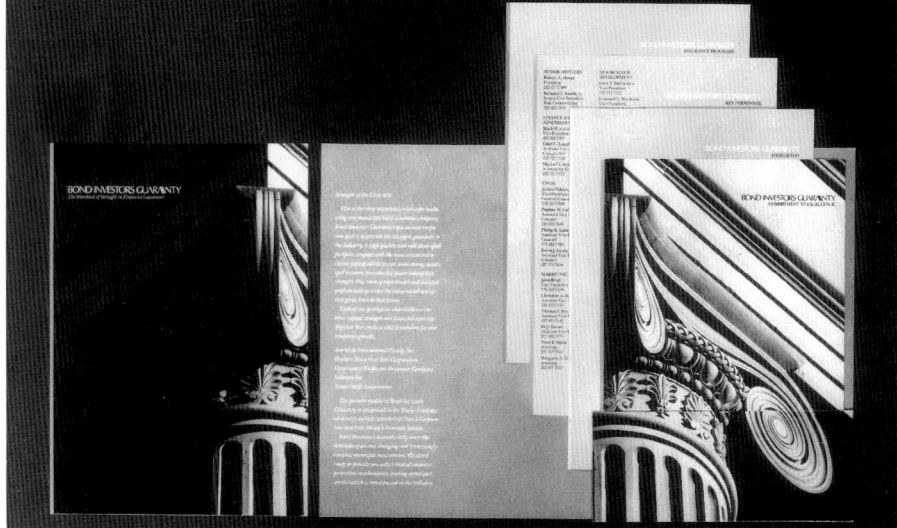

683

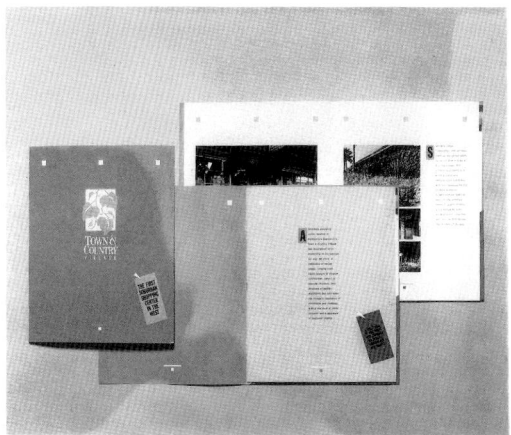

684

684
ART DIRECTOR
Michael Dunlavey
DESIGNER
Michael Dunlavey
PHOTOGRAPHER
Steve Simmons, Keith Jensen
WRITER
Lynda Gianforte Mansfield
CLIENT
Town & Country Village
DESIGN FIRM
The Dunlavey Studio, Inc., Sacramento, CA
PRINTER
Fong & Fong, Printers and Lithographers

685
ART DIRECTOR
Dale Chan
DESIGNER
Dale Chan
ILLUSTRATOR/ARTIST
Susan Blubaugh
WRITER
Gene Schaffer
CLIENT
The New York Times
PUBLISHER
The New York Times, New York, NY

685

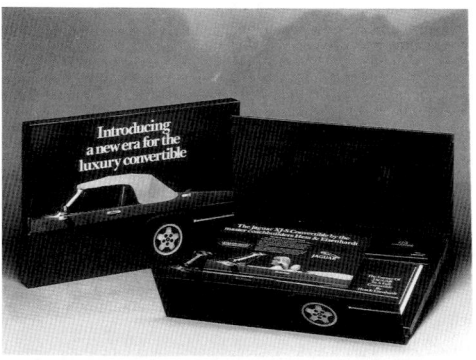

686

686
ART DIRECTOR
Lee Einhorn
DESIGNER
Lee Einhorn, Ron Morgan
PHOTOGRAPHER
Greg Jarem
WRITER
Stu Nickerson
CLIENT
Jaguar Cars Inc.
AGENCY
RMI, Inc., Emerson, NJ
DESIGN FIRM
RMI, Inc.

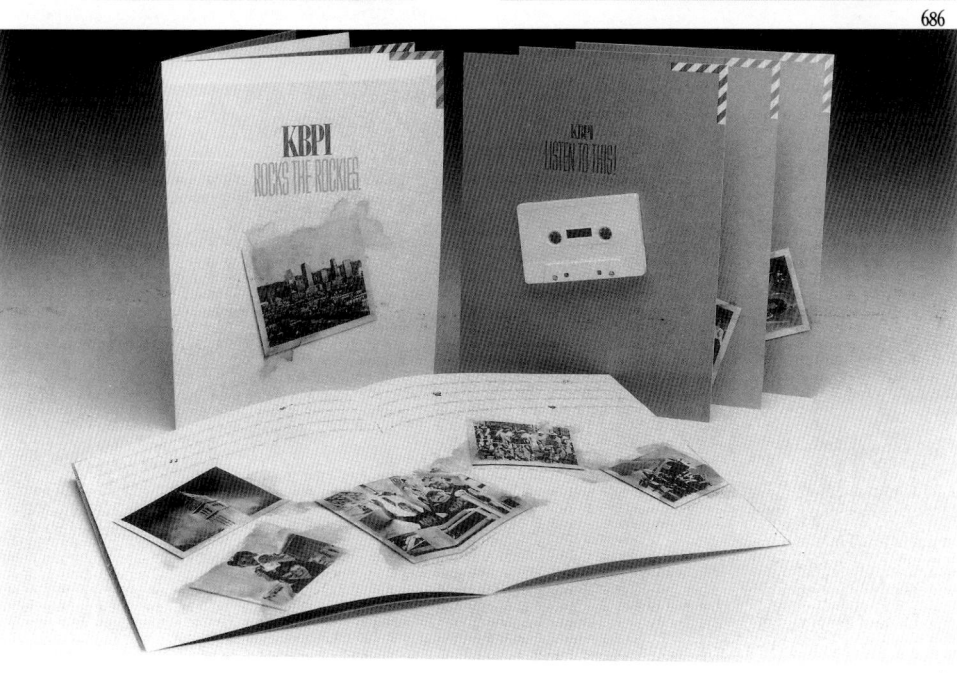

687
ART DIRECTOR
Richard A. DeOlivera
DESIGNER
John Rassman
ILLUSTRATOR/ARTIST
John Rassman
WRITER
Richard Graglia
CLIENT
KBPI Radio
DESIGN FIRM
DeOlivera Creative, Inc., Denver, CO

687

688
ART DIRECTOR
Cheryl Lewin, Gwenne Wilcox
DESIGNER
Gwenne Wilcox
ILLUSTRATOR/ARTIST
Mitchell Confer
CLIENT
Corry Jamestown
DESIGN FIRM
Lewin Design Associates, New York, NY

689
ART DIRECTOR
Cabell Harris
WRITER
Ken Hines
CLIENT
Lawler Ballard Advertising
AGENCY
Lawler Ballard Advertising, Richmond, VA

690
ART DIRECTOR
Joe Paumi
DESIGNER
Joe Paumi
PHOTOGRAPHER
Irv Bahrt
WRITER
Susan Blackwell
CLIENT
Stuart Pharmaceuticals
AGENCY
Sudler & Hennessey, New York, NY
DESIGN FIRM
Sudler & Hennessey

691
ART DIRECTOR
Woody Kay
WRITER
Ernie Schenck
CLIENT
Pagano Shenck & Kay
AGENCY
Pagano Schenck & Kay, Providence, RI

688

689

690

691

FIND OUT IF THE CUTEST CHICK IN HIGH SCHOOL MARRIED A REAL TURKEY.

THE BEREA HIGH SCHOOL CLASS OF '77 REUNION.

692

692

ART DIRECTOR
Jim Proimos
DESIGNER
Janet Stucklak
WRITER
Tom Amico
CLIENT
Berea High School Class Reunion Committee
AGENCY
Meldrum and Fewsmith, Cleveland, OH
TYPESETTER
Camelot Typesetting

693

ART DIRECTOR
John Muller
DESIGNER
John Muller , Patt Williams
PHOTOGRAPHER
Unkown, Archival
WRITER
Rob Price , John Muller
CLIENT
Kansas City Jazz Commission
DESIGN FIRM
Muller + Company, Kansas City, MO

693

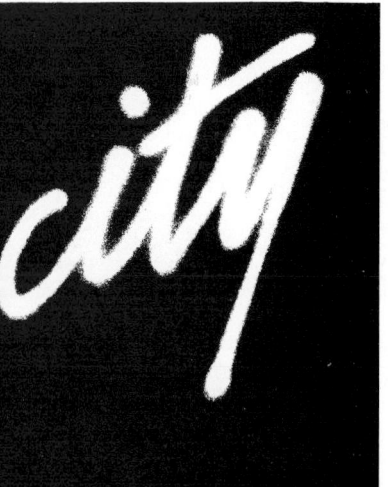

CATALOGUE 1986

694

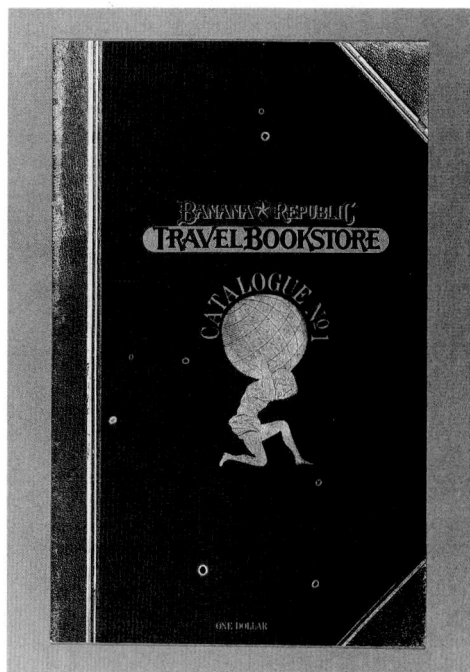

694

DESIGNER
Robert Petrick
PHOTOGRAPHER
Tom Vack , Corinne Pfister
CLIENT
City
DESIGN FIRM
Petrick Design, Chicago, IL

695

ART DIRECTOR
Neil Shakery
DESIGNER
Neil Shakery , Sandra McHenry
ILLUSTRATOR/ARTIST
Ward Schumaker
WRITER
Banana Republic staff
CLIENT
Banana Republic
EDITOR
Bonnie Dahan
DESIGN FIRM
Pentagram Design, San Francisco, CA
HAND TINTING
Sara Anderson

695

696

ART DIRECTOR
Jim Van Noy
DESIGNER
Mutsumi Gregg , Lauren Switz
PHOTOGRAPHER
Dutch Meyers , Christopher Springmann
WRITER
Steve Pressfield , Ann Van Noy
CLIENT
The Van Noy Design Group
DESIGN FIRM
The Van Noy Design Group, Inc., Los
Angeles, CA
PRINTER
Dai Nippon, Tokyo, Japan
TYPOGRAPHER
Alpha Graphix

696

697

ART DIRECTOR
John Amicangelo
DESIGNER
John Amicangelo
PHOTOGRAPHER
Bob Chadbourne
WRITER
John Amicangelo
CLIENT
John Amicangelo
AGENCY
John Amicangelo, Brighton, MA

697

698

ART DIRECTOR
Caron H. Malecki
DESIGNER
Caron H. Malecki
PHOTOGRAPHER
George Kleiman
CLIENT
WestPoint Pepperell
AGENCY
WestPoint Pepperell, New York, NY
STYLIST
Chuck S. Riley

698

699

ART DIRECTOR
Cheryl Meininger
DESIGNER
Cheryl Meininger
ILLUSTRATOR/ARTIST
Jim Lindsay
WRITER
Bruce Carlson
CLIENT
South-Western Publishing
AGENCY
Sive Associates, Cincinnati, OH
CREATIVE DIRECTOR
Mike Kitei
ASSOC. CREATIVE DIR.
Peter Lloyd

699

700

ART DIRECTOR
Warren Johnson
ILLUSTRATOR/ARTIST
Alex Boies
WRITER
Phil Calvit
CLIENT
Hotel Sofitel Miami
AGENCY
Carmichael-Lynch, Minneapolis, MN
CREATIVE DIRECTOR
Harry Beckwith

701

ART DIRECTOR
Doug Fisher
DESIGNER
Doug Fisher
PHOTOGRAPHER
Hickson & Associates
ILLUSTRATOR/ARTIST
Illustrated Alaskan Moose
WRITER
Ron Etter
CLIENT
Nevamar Corporation
AGENCY
Lord, Sullivan & Yoder, Inc., Columbus, OH
DESIGN FIRM
Lord, Sullivan & Yoder, Inc.

702

ART DIRECTOR
Greg Sullentrup
ILLUSTRATOR/ARTIST
Chris Hopkins
WRITER
Steve McCabe
CLIENT
Anheuser-Busch, Inc./Budweiser
AGENCY
D'Arcy Masius Benton & Bowles, St. Louis, MO
CREATIVE DIRECTOR
Dick Zempel

703

ART DIRECTOR
Frank Schulwolf
ILLUSTRATOR/ARTIST
John Mattos , Ted Lodigensky , Paul Salmon
WRITER
Arthur Low
CLIENT
Aviation Sales Company, Inc.
AGENCY
Susan Gilbert & Company, Inc., Coral Gables, FL
PRINTER
Colour Group

704

ART DIRECTOR
Charles Spencer Anderson, Joe Duffy
DESIGNER
Charles Spencer Anderson, Joe Duffy
ILLUSTRATOR/ARTIST
Charles Spencer Anderson, Joe Duffy
WRITER
Chuck Carlson
CLIENT
Speckletone Paper Company
DESIGN FIRM
Duffy Design Group, Minneapolis, MN

705

ART DIRECTOR
Charles Spencer Anderson
DESIGNER
Charles Spencer Anderson
ILLUSTRATOR/ARTIST
Charles Spencer Anderson
CLIENT
Wenger Corp.
DESIGN FIRM
Duffy Design Group, Minneapolis, MN

706

ART DIRECTOR
Logan Broussard
PHOTOGRAPHER
John Katz
CLIENT
Disney On Ice/LLH
AGENCY
Levenson Levenson & Hill, Inc., Irving, TX
PROP
John Sickles
PRINTER
Heritage Press
EXEC. CREATIVE DIRECTOR
William L. Hill

707

ART DIRECTOR
Leo Mullen
DESIGNER
Jeremiah Austin
PHOTOGRAPHER
USIA
WRITER
Robert Anders
CLIENT
Robert Anders, USIA
DESIGN FIRM
Invisions, Ltd., Washington, DC

704

705

706

707

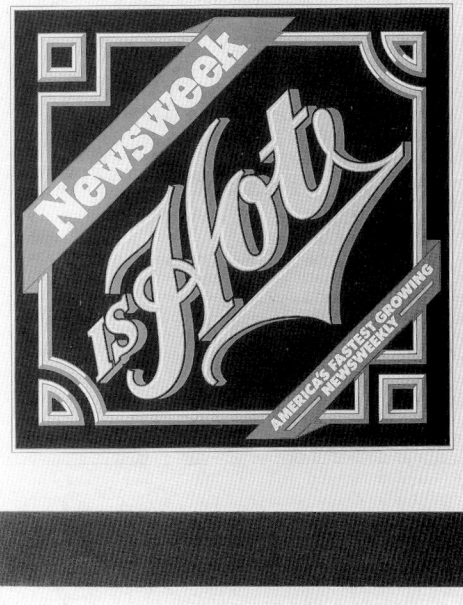

708

ART DIRECTOR
Peter Harrison
DESIGNER
Susan Hochbaum
ILLUSTRATOR/ARTIST
Steven Guarnaccia
CLIENT
Chase Manhattan Bank, Naomi Weiss and
Phil Giaguinto
DESIGN FIRM
Pentagram Design, New York, NY

709

ART DIRECTOR
Nancy Hoefig
DESIGNER
Nancy Hoefig, Ethan Goller
ILLUSTRATOR/ARTIST
Gerard Huerta
WRITER
Melinda Marcus
CLIENT
Newsweek, Bill Bergman
DESIGN FIRM
Nancy Hoefig Design, New York, NY

708

709

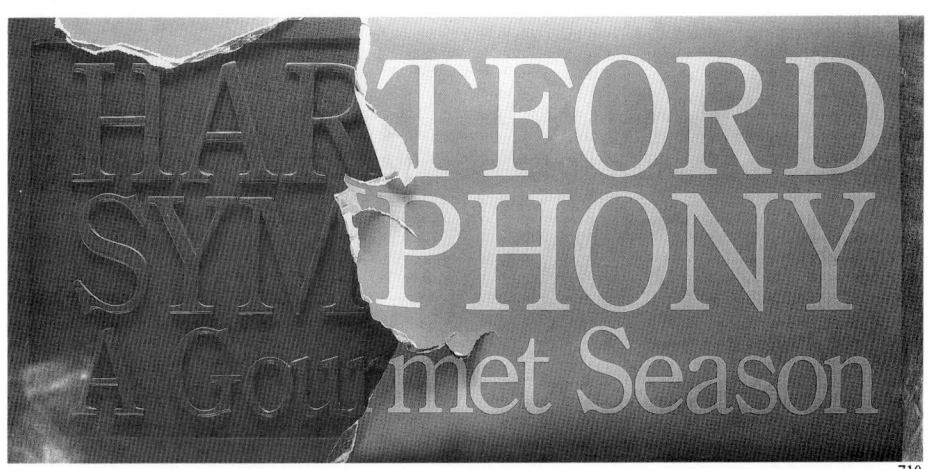

710

ART DIRECTOR
Peter Good
DESIGNER
Peter Good
PHOTOGRAPHER
Christina Howe
ILLUSTRATOR/ARTIST
Peter Good
WRITER
David Snead
CLIENT
Hartford Symphony Orchestra
DESIGN FIRM
Peter Good Graphic Design, Chester, CT

710

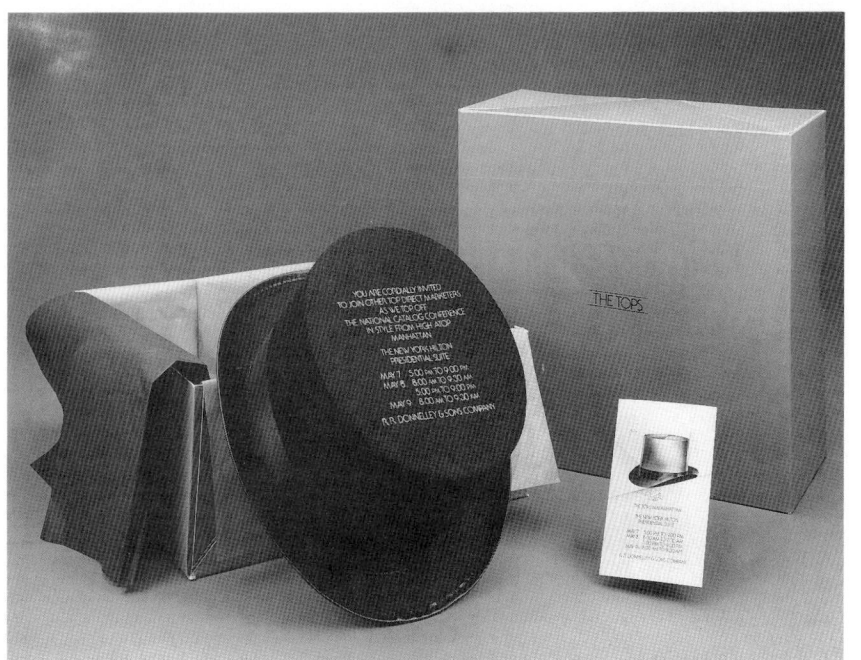

711

ART DIRECTOR
Gordon Hochhalter
DESIGNER
Bob Meyer
WRITER
Gordon Hochhalter
CLIENT
R. R. Donnelley & Sons Company, Chicago,
IL
PRODUCER
Maryann Novak
ACCOUNT SUPERVISOR
Joe Cosgrove

711

712
ART DIRECTOR
Irwin Goldberg
DESIGNER
Irwin Goldberg
PHOTOGRAPHER
Charlie Gold
WRITER
Irwin Goldberg , Nat Russo
CLIENT
Archive Magazine
PUBLISHER
American Showcase
AGENCY
I. Goldberg & Partners Inc., New York, NY

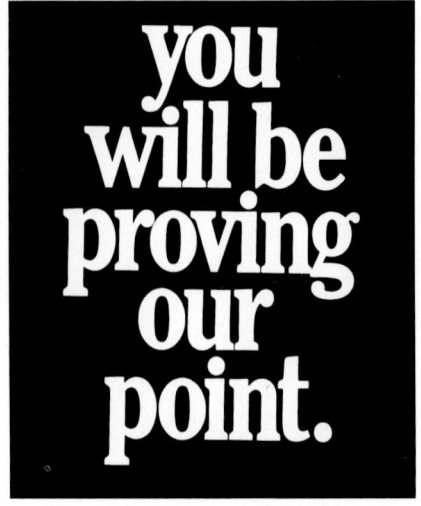

712

713
ART DIRECTOR
John Rieben, Morton Goldsholl
DESIGNER
Jeff Callender
PHOTOGRAPHER
Nick Kolias
WRITER
Morton Goldsholl
DESIGN FIRM
Goldsholl: Design and Film, Northfield, IL
CALLIGRAPHER
John Weber

713

714
ART DIRECTOR
Doug Fisher
DESIGNER
Doug Fisher
ILLUSTRATOR/ARTIST
Rasic Art
WRITER
Ron Etter
CLIENT
Nevamar Corporation
AGENCY
Lord, Sullivan & Yoder, Inc., Columbus, OH
DESIGN FIRM
Lord, Sullivan & Yoder, Inc.

714

715
ART DIRECTOR
Scott Sorokin
WRITER
Leonard Sorcher
CLIENT
Data Switch
AGENCY
Holland Advertising, Inc., New York, NY

715

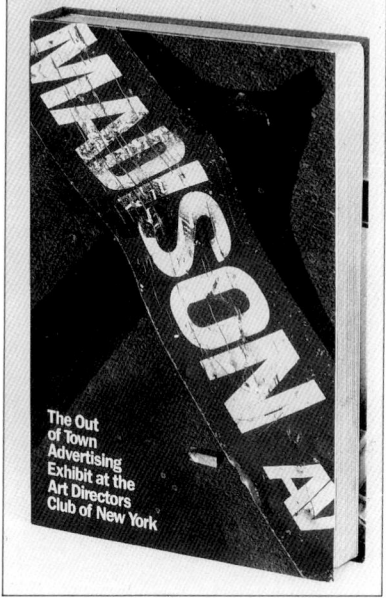

716

717

716
ART DIRECTOR
Joe Duffy
DESIGNER
Joe Duffy
ILLUSTRATOR/ARTIST
Joe Duffy, Lynn Schulte
CLIENT
Memphis Chicks
DESIGN FIRM
Duffy Design Group, Minneapolis, MN

717
ART DIRECTOR
Jamie Mambro
DESIGNER
Nancy Malacaria
PHOTOGRAPHER
Philip Porcella
WRITER
Thomas Monahan
CLIENT
Out of Towners Adverrtising Exhibit
AGENCY
Leonard Monahan Saabye, Providence, RI
PRINTER
National Bickford Foremost

718
DESIGNER
Bridget DeSocio, New York, NY
CLIENT
David Byrne
TYPOGRAPHER
Scarlet Letters

718

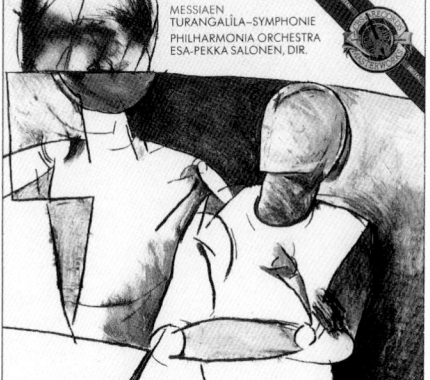

719

719
ART DIRECTOR
Stacy Drummond
DESIGNER
Stacy Drummond
ILLUSTRATOR/ARTIST
Stephen Byram
CLIENT
CBS Records, New York, NY

720
ART DIRECTOR
Christopher Austopchuk
DESIGNER
Christopher Austopchuk
PHOTOGRAPHER
Marc Tauss
DESIGN FIRM
CBS Records, New York, NY

721
ART DIRECTOR
Christopher Austopchuk
DESIGNER
Christopher Austopchuk
ILLUSTRATOR/ARTIST
Roger Huyssen
DESIGN FIRM
CBS Records, New York, NY

722
ART DIRECTOR
Bob Defrin
DESIGNER
Bob Defrin
ILLUSTRATOR/ARTIST
Braldt Bralds
CLIENT
Atlantic Records, New York, NY

723
ART DIRECTOR
Bob Defrin
DESIGNER
Bob Defrin
PHOTOGRAPHER
David Michael Kennedy
CLIENT
Atlantic Records, New York, NY

724
ART DIRECTOR
Allen Weinberg
DESIGNER
Allen Weinberg , Georgina Lehner
CLIENT
CBS Records, New York, NY

725
ART DIRECTOR
Allen Weinberg
DESIGNER
Allen Weinberg
ILLUSTRATOR/ARTIST
Robert Van Nutt
CLIENT
CBS Records, New York, NY

720

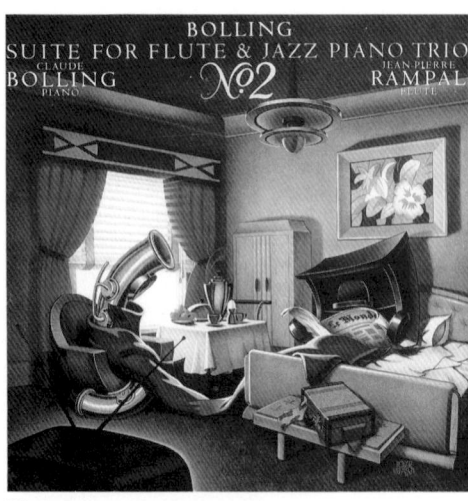
721

722

723

724

725

726

727

728

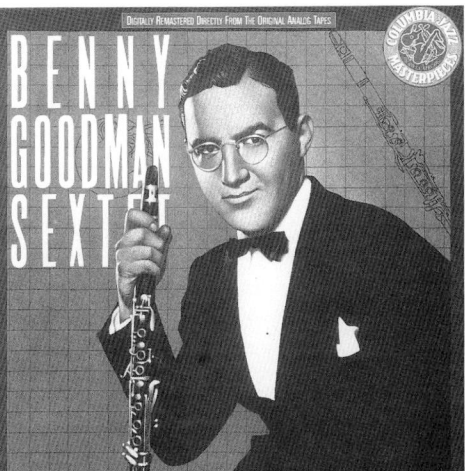

730

731

726
ART DIRECTOR
Neal Pozner
DESIGNER
Neal Pozner
CLIENT
RCA Records
DESIGN FIRM
RCA Records, New York, NY

727
ART DIRECTOR
Neal Pozner
DESIGNER
Neal Pozner
PHOTOGRAPHER
Nick Sangiamo
ILLUSTRATOR/ARTIST
Kinuko Y. Craft
CLIENT
RCA Red Seal
PUBLICATION
RCA Records, New York, NY

728
DESIGN DIRECTOR
Ivan Chermayeff
DESIGNER
Ivan Chermayeff
PHOTOGRAPHER
Alan Shortall
ILLUSTRATOR/ARTIST
Ivan Chermayeff
CLIENT
Gramavision
AGENCY
Chermayeff & Geismar Associates, New York,
NY

729
DESIGN DIRECTOR
Ivan Chermayeff
DESIGNER
Michael Cervantes
PHOTOGRAPHER
Gamma One Conversions
ILLUSTRATOR/ARTIST
Ivan Chermayeff
CLIENT
Gramavision
AGENCY
Chermayeff & Geismar Associates, New York,
NY

730
ART DIRECTOR
Allen Weinberg
DESIGNER
Allen Weinberg
ILLUSTRATOR/ARTIST
Bill Nelson
CLIENT
CBS Records, New York, NY

731
ART DIRECTOR
Allen Weinberg
DESIGNER
Allen Weinberg
ILLUSTRATOR/ARTIST
Brad Holland
CLIENT
CBS Records, New York, NY

732

ART DIRECTOR
Andy Baltimore
DESIGNER
Andy Baltimore
ILLUSTRATOR/ARTIST
Danny Serrano
CLIENT
GRP Records, New York, NY

733

ART DIRECTOR
Josephine DiDonato
DESIGNER
Josephine DiDonato
CLIENT
Columbia Records CBS, New York, NY

734

ART DIRECTOR
Jodi Rovin
ILLUSTRATOR/ARTIST
Javier Romero
CLIENT
Atlantic Records, New York, NY

735

ART DIRECTOR
Norman Moore
DESIGNER
Norman Moore
CLIENT
Jeff Gold, A + M Records
DIRECTOR
Mark Spector
DESIGN FIRM
Design/Art, Inc., Los Angeles, CA
PRINTER
Ed Dwyer, AGI

732

733

734

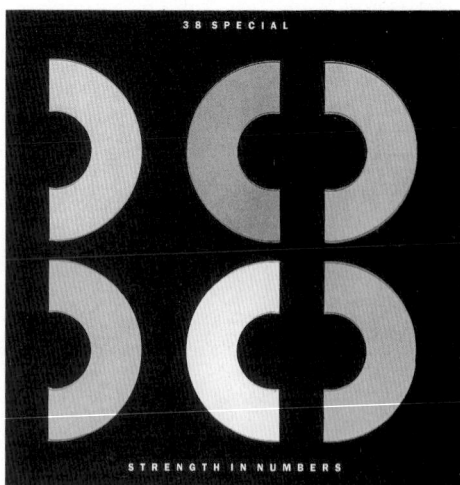

735

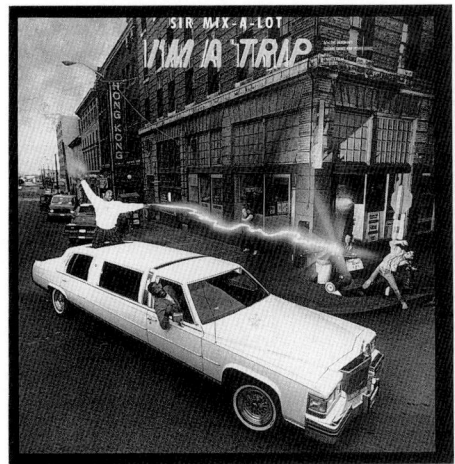
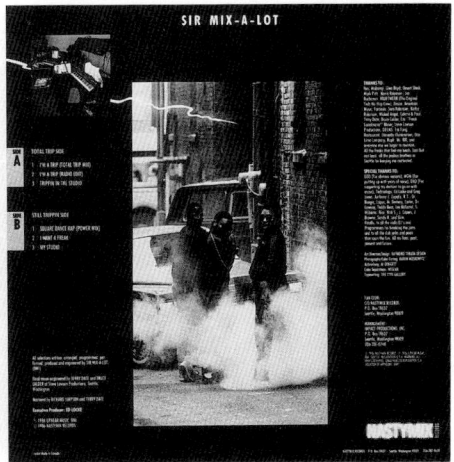

736

ART DIRECTOR
Raymond Terada
DESIGNER
Raymond Terada
PHOTOGRAPHER
Karen Moskowitz
ILLUSTRATOR/ARTIST
Karen Moskowitz (Color Tinting) , Al Doggett (Airbrushing)
CLIENT
Sir Mix-A-Lot, Nastymix Records
DESIGN FIRM
Terada Design, Seattle, WA
PRINTER
Ross Ellis Limited

737

ART DIRECTOR
Joe Vax , Zand Gee
DESIGNER
Joe Vax
PHOTOGRAPHER
John Jensen
WRITER
Pete Barbutti, Herb Wong , Mike Vax
CLIENT
Blackhawk Records
DESIGN FIRM
Crow-Quill Studios, San Francisco, CA

738

ART DIRECTOR
Steven Shmerler
DESIGNER
Maude Gilman
PHOTOGRAPHER
John Pinderhughes
ILLUSTRATOR/ARTIST
Andy Warhol
CLIENT
Aretha Franklin
AGENCY
Arista Records, Inc., New York, NY
DESIGN FIRM
Arista Records

739
ART DIRECTOR
Hal Riney, Jerry Andalin
DESIGNER
Primo Angeli, Ray Honda
ILLUSTRATOR/ARTIST
Mark Jones
CLIENT
'lal Riney & Partners for Blitz Weinhard
Brewing Co.
DESIGN FIRM
Primo Angeli Inc., San Francisco, CA

740
ART DIRECTOR
Primo Angeli
DESIGNER
Primo Angeli
CLIENT
Primo Angeli Inc.
DESIGN FIRM
Primo Angeli Inc., San Francisco, CA

739

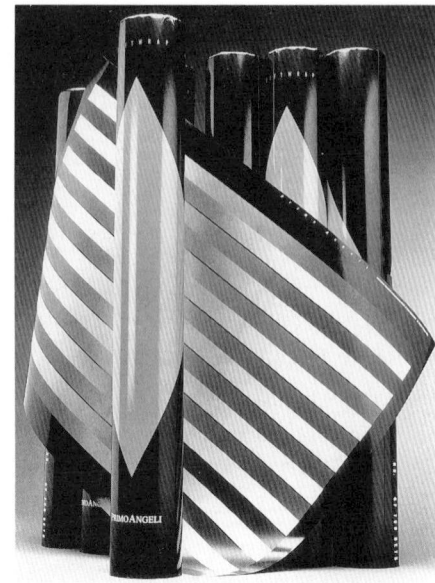

740

741
ART DIRECTOR
Tamotsu Yagi
DESIGNER
Tamotsu Yagi
DESIGN FIRM
Esprit Graphic Design Studio, San Francisco,
CA

742
ART DIRECTOR
Mark Galarneau
DESIGNER
Mark Galarneau
ILLUSTRATOR/ARTIST
Curtis Wong
WRITER
Lisa Layne
CLIENT
Accolade
AGENCY
Darien & Morra
DESIGN FIRM
Galarneau & Sinn, Ltd., Palo Alto, CA

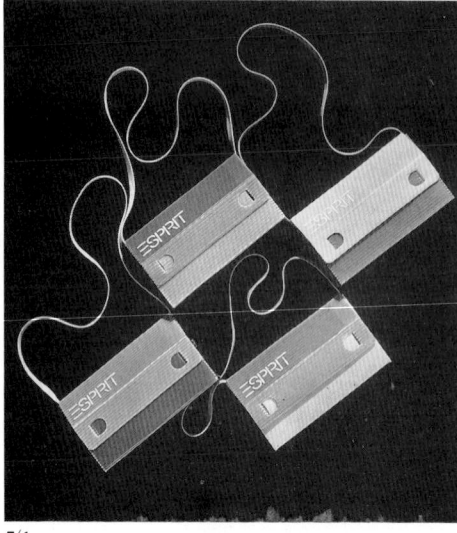

741

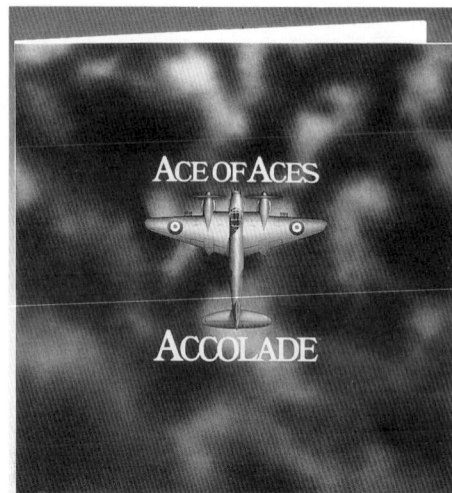

742

743

744

743
ART DIRECTOR
Michael Dunlavey
DESIGNER
Lindy Dunlavey
ILLUSTRATOR/ARTIST
Lindy Dunlavey
CLIENT
Java City
DESIGN FIRM
The Dunlavey Studio, Inc, Sacramento, CA
PRINTER
Graphic Center

744
ART DIRECTOR
Glenn Groglio
DESIGNER
Donald Moruzzi
ILLUSTRATOR/ARTIST
Donald Moruzzi
CLIENT
Dansk International Designs Ltd.
DESIGN FIRM
Dansk International in-house graphics dept.,
Mt. Kisco, NY

745

746

745
ART DIRECTOR
Michael Benes
DESIGNER
Vartus Artinian, Sue Merfeld
PHOTOGRAPHER
Russ Schleipman
ILLUSTRATOR/ARTIST
Margaret Sewell
CLIENT
Polaroid Corporation
DESIGN FIRM
Polaroid Corporation Graphics, Cambridge,
MA

746
ART DIRECTOR
Michael Benes
DESIGNER
Vartus Artinian, Sue Merfeld
PHOTOGRAPHER
Wayne Eastep
ILLUSTRATOR/ARTIST
Margaret Sewell
CLIENT
Polaroid Corporation
DESIGN FIRM
Polaroid Corporate Graphics, Cambridge, MA

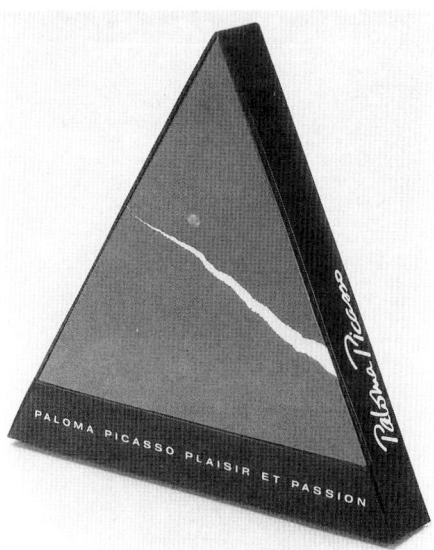

748

748
DESIGNER
Alain Filiz, James Fulmer
CLIENT
Cosmair/Designer Fragrance Division
DESIGN FIRM
Cosmair in-house, New York, NY
CREATIVE DIRECTOR
Alain Filiz

749
ART DIRECTOR
Seth Jaben
DESIGNER
Seth Jaben
PHOTOGRAPHER
Seth Jaben
ILLUSTRATOR/ARTIST
Seth Jaben
WRITER
Seth Jaben
CLIENT
E.G. Smith Color Sock Co. Inc.
EDITOR
Eric Smith
DIRECTOR
Seth Jaben
PUBLISHER
Eric Smith
AGENCY
Seth Jaben Studio, New York, NY

750
ART DIRECTOR
Carol Burke
DESIGNER
Carol Burke
ILLUSTRATOR/ARTIST
Greg King
WRITER
Leigh Sander
CLIENT
H-E-B Food Stores
AGENCY
Cox Pippin Communications, Dallas, TX

751
ART DIRECTOR
Josh Freeman
DESIGNER
Vickie Sawyer
ILLUSTRATOR/ARTIST
Karen Mercedes McDonald
CLIENT
The Christiana Companies, Inc.
DESIGN FIRM
Josh Freeman/Associates, Los Angeles, CA

752
ART DIRECTOR
Jerry Balchunas
DESIGNER
Jerry Balchunas, Cathrine Van Lancker
WRITER
John Elkhay
CLIENT
New England Truffles Inc.
DESIGN FIRM
Adkins/Balchunas Design, Providence, RI

749

750

751

752

753

754

753

ART DIRECTOR
Jack Anderson
DESIGNER
Jack Anderson, Julie Tanagi
ILLUSTRATOR/ARTIST
Hornall Anderson Design Works
CLIENT
Tradewell Group
DESIGN FIRM
Hornall Anderson Design Works, Seattle, WA

754

ART DIRECTOR
William Homan, Minneapolis, MN
DESIGNER
William Homan
CLIENT
Surdyk's

755

ART DIRECTOR
Rick Becker
DESIGNER
Rick Becker
ILLUSTRATOR/ARTIST
Cheri Ryan
WRITER
Mark Eppley
CLIENT
Mark Eppley
DESIGN FIRM
Becker Design Associates, Seattle, WA

755

756

ART DIRECTOR
Michael Mabry
DESIGNER
Michael Mabry, Margie Chu
CLIENT
Thanksgiving Coffee Company
DESIGN FIRM
Michael Mabry Design, San Francisco, CA

756

757
ART DIRECTOR
Syd Hammerquist, Cheryl Fujii
DESIGNER
Anton Kimball
ILLUSTRATOR/ARTIST
Anton Kimball
CLIENT
Nordstrom Advertising
AGENCY
Nordstrom Advertising
DESIGN FIRM
Anton Kimball Design, Portland, OR
LETTERING
Bruce Hale

758
ART DIRECTOR
Jaren Dahlstrom
DESIGNER
Joe Vax, Jaren Dahlstrom
ILLUSTRATOR/ARTIST
Karl Buell
CLIENT
Landmark Vineyards
DESIGN FIRM
Crow-Quill Studios, San Francisco, CA

759
ART DIRECTOR
Tamila Grogan
DESIGNER
Tamila Grogan
ILLUSTRATOR/ARTIST
B.B. Sams
CLIENT
Burger King
AGENCY
Selling Solutions
DESIGN FIRM
Don Trousdell Design, Atlanta, GA

760
ART DIRECTOR
James L. Selak
DESIGNER
James L. Selak
CLIENT
ICE Communications, Inc.
DIRECTOR
Bob MaHarry
AGENCY
ICE Communications, Inc., Rochester, NY

757

758

759

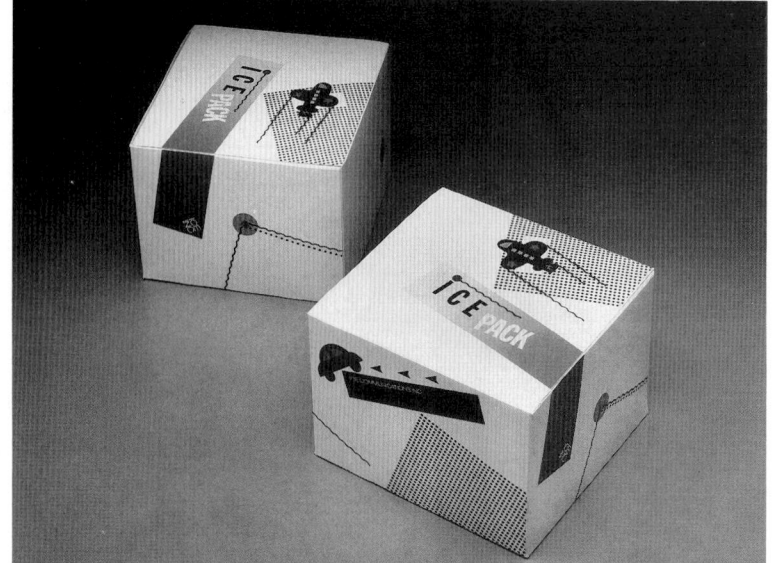

760

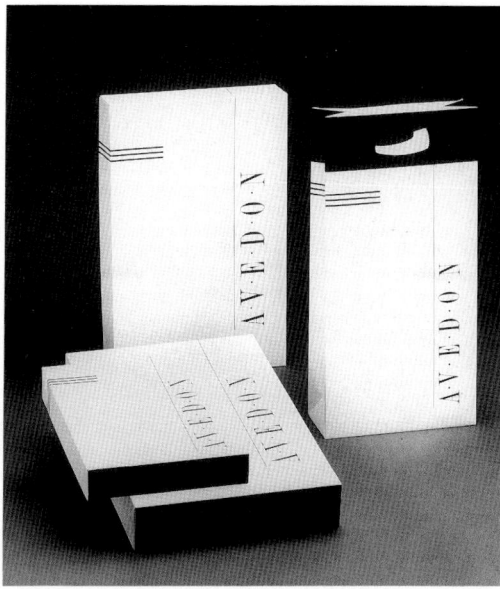

761

762

761

ART DIRECTOR
Tom Hughes
DESIGNER
Tom Hughes, Nancy Noel
PHOTOGRAPHER
Bruno Joachim Studio
ILLUSTRATOR/ARTIST
Katherine Mahoney
CLIENT
Lotus Development Corp.
DESIGN FIRM
Lotus Creative Development, Cambridge, MA

762

ART DIRECTOR
Hal Frazier
DESIGNER
Hal Frazier
ILLUSTRATOR/ARTIST
John Vince
CLIENT
Avedon Retail Clothing Store
DESIGN FIRM
Frazier Design Consultancy, Los Angeles, CA

763

763

ART DIRECTOR
Warren Eakins
DESIGNER
Dan Mandish
ILLUSTRATOR/ARTIST
George Cheney
WRITER
Bill Borders
CLIENT
Burgerville USA
AGENCY
Borders, Perrin & Norrander, Inc., Portland, OR
CREATIVE DIRECTOR
Bill Borders
SPECIAL EFFECTS
True Vistas

764

764

ART DIRECTOR
William Manns, John F. Emery
DESIGNER
John F. Emery
PHOTOGRAPHER
Gordon Smith
CLIENT
Dansk International Designs Ltd.
DESIGN FIRM
Vie Design Studios, Inc., Yellow Springs, OH

765

ART DIRECTOR
Brad Copeland
DESIGNER
Brad Copeland
CLIENT
Contract Design Resources
DESIGN FIRM
Cooper/Copeland, Inc., Atlanta, GA

766

ART DIRECTOR
Sharon Werner
DESIGNER
Sharon Werner
ILLUSTRATOR/ARTIST
Sharon Werner
WRITER
Chuck Carlson
CLIENT
Sonnys Ice Cream
DESIGN FIRM
Duffy Design Group, Minneapolis, MN

767

ART DIRECTOR
Randall Hensley
DESIGNER
Barbara Tanis, Rick Tesoro, Randall Hensley
PHOTOGRAPHER
David Arky
CLIENT
IBM Entry Systems Division, Lee Green
AGENCY
Muir Cornelius Moore, Inc., New York, NY

768

ART DIRECTOR
Ferris Crane
DESIGNER
Ferris Crane
PHOTOGRAPHER
Rick Bolen
DESIGN FIRM
Ferris Crane Graphic Design, San Francisco, CA

765

766

767

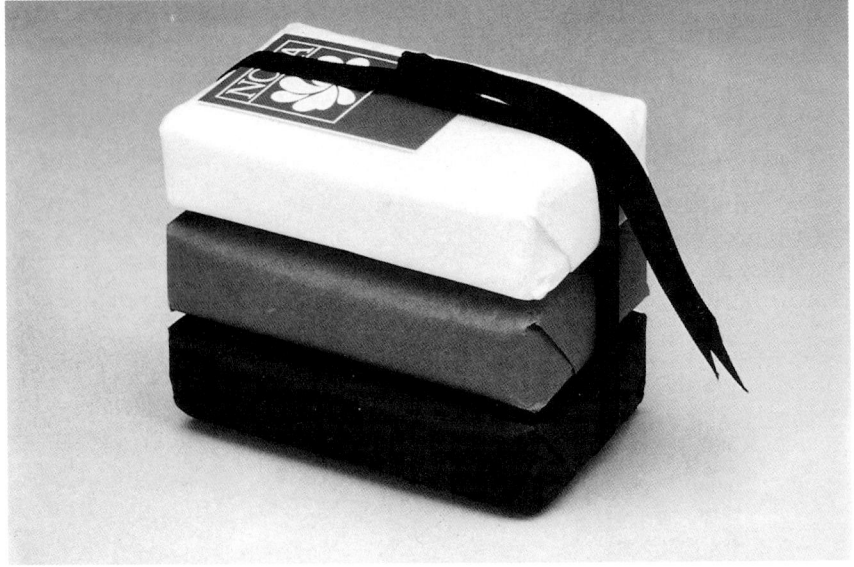

768

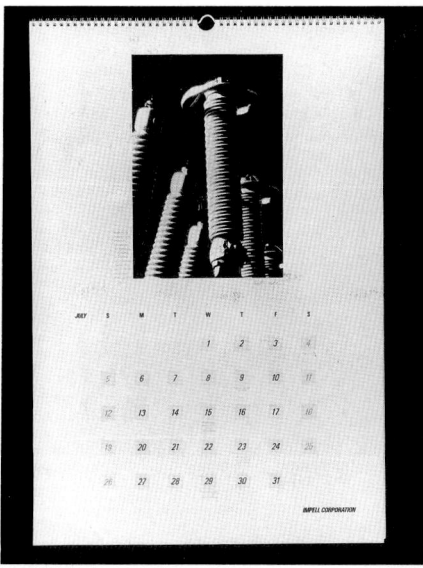

769

770

771

769
ART DIRECTOR
Charles Spencer Anderson
DESIGNER
Charles Spencer Anderson
ILLUSTRATOR/ARTIST
Charles Spencer Anderson, Lynn Schulte
CLIENT
Avant Hair Salon
DESIGN FIRM
Duffy Design Group, Minneapolis, MN

770
ART DIRECTOR
Neil Shakery
DESIGNER
Neil Shakery, Alisa Rudloff
PHOTOGRAPHER
Burton Pritzker
WRITER
Delphine Hirasuna
CLIENT
Impell Corporation
DESIGN FIRM
Pentagram Design, San Francisco, CA

771
ART DIRECTOR
Vance Jonson, Kim Capone
DESIGNER
Vance Jonson
PHOTOGRAPHER
Ross Elmi
WRITER
Vance Jonson
CLIENT
Jonson Pirtle Pedersen Alcorn Metzdorf & Hess
DESIGN FIRM
Jonson Pirtle Pedersen Alcorn Metzdorf & Hess, Rowayton, CT
PRINTER
Baronet Litho

772

772
ART DIRECTOR
Steven Wedeen, Rick Vaughn
DESIGNER
Steven Wedeen
ILLUSTRATOR/ARTIST
Steven Wedeen, Mark Chamberlain
WRITER
Richard Kuhn, Steven Wedeen
CLIENT
Starline Printing
DESIGN FIRM
Vaughn/Wedeen Creative, Inc., Albuquerque, NM

773
ART DIRECTOR
Kurt Tausche
DESIGNER
Kurt Tausche
WRITER
Kerry Casey
CLIENT
Dr. Casey & Dr. O'Kane
AGENCY
Bozell, Jacobs, Kenyon & Eckhardt,
Minneapolis, MN

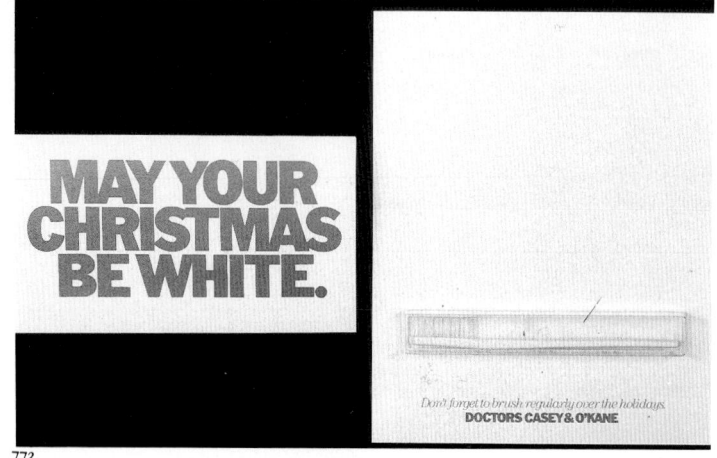

773

774
ART DIRECTOR
Cabell Harris
PHOTOGRAPHER
Pat Edwards
WRITER
Ken Hines
CLIENT
Richmond Renaissance
AGENCY
Lawler Ballard Advertising, Richmond, VA

774

775
ART DIRECTOR
Leila McGrath
DESIGNER
Leila McGrath
PHOTOGRAPHER
Pat Swifka
WRITER
Joel Mitchell
CLIENT
Surdyk's
AGENCY
Bozell, Jacobs, Kenyon & Eckhardt ,
Minneapolis, MN

775

776
ART DIRECTOR
Kirk Souder
DESIGNER
Kirk Souder
WRITER
Kirk Souder
CLIENT
O. Tannenbaum
AGENCY
Homer & Durham Advertising, New York, NY

776

777

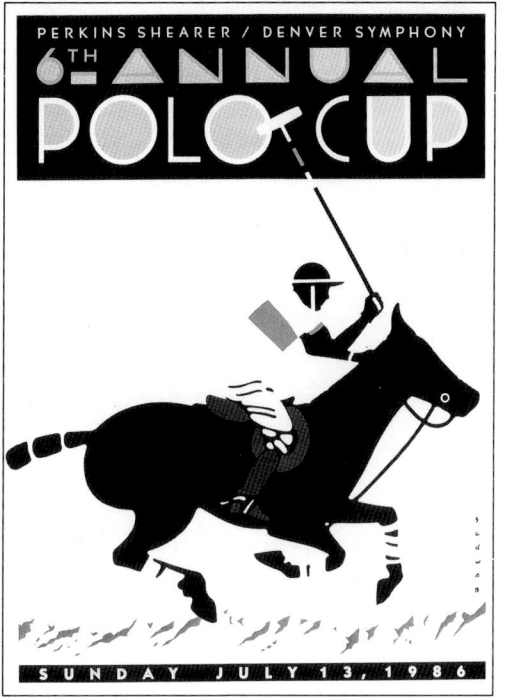

778

777

ART DIRECTOR
Lanny Sommese
DESIGNER
Lanny Sommese
ILLUSTRATOR/ARTIST
Lanny Sommese
CLIENT
The Central Pennsylvania Festival of the Arts
DESIGN FIRM
Lanny Sommese Design, State College, PA
PRINTER
Nittany Valley Offset

778

ART DIRECTOR
Bill Merriken
DESIGNER
Michael Schwab
ILLUSTRATOR/ARTIST
Michael Schwab
CLIENT
Perkins Shearer/Denver Symphony
DESIGN FIRM
Michael Schwab Design, San Francisco, CA

779

ART DIRECTOR
Brad Copeland
DESIGNER
Maxey Andress
PHOTOGRAPHER
Joel Gilmore
ILLUSTRATOR/ARTIST
Maxey Andress, Kathi Roberts, Kevin Irby,
Brad Copeland
WRITER
Staff
CLIENT
Cooper/Copeland, Inc.
DESIGN FIRM
Cooper/Copeland, Inc., Atlanta, GA

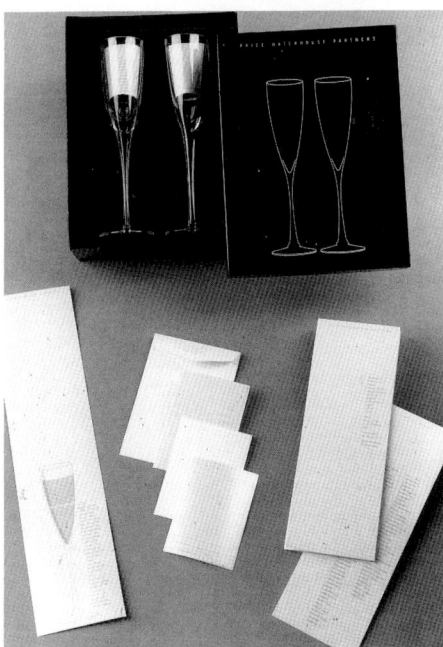

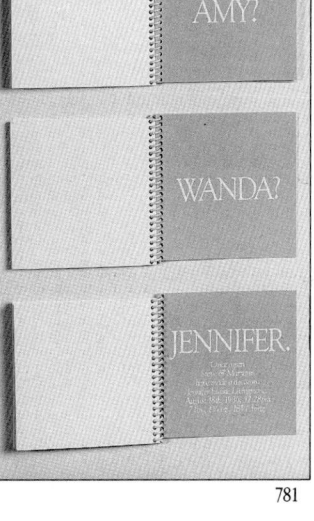

779

780

781

780

ART DIRECTOR
Douglas Reeder
DESIGNER
Douglas Reeder
ILLUSTRATOR/ARTIST
Douglas Reeder
DESIGN FIRM
SHR Communications Planning & Design,
Scottsdale, AZ

781

ART DIRECTOR
Forrest & Valerie Richardson
DESIGNER
Forrest & Valerie Richardson
WRITER
Forrest & Valerie Richardson
CLIENT
Jennifer Livingstone
DESIGN FIRM
Richardson or Richardson, Phoenix, AZ

782

ART DIRECTOR
Tom Kaminsky
DESIGNER
Michele Torok
ILLUSTRATOR/ARTIST
Mike Orzak
WRITER
Michael Sheehan
CLIENT
Price Waterhouse, Clarke & Co.
AGENCY
ClarkeGowardFitts, Boston, MA
DESIGN FIRM
ClarkeGowardFitts Design

782

783
ART DIRECTOR
Lawrence Zempel
DESIGNER
Lawrence Zempel
ILLUSTRATOR/ARTIST
Laura Kootsillas
WRITER
Lawrence Zempel
CLIENT
Zempel Group, Inc.
DESIGN FIRM
Zempel Group, Inc., Los Angeles, CA

783

784
ART DIRECTOR
Lynne Ginsberg
DESIGNER
Lynne Ginsberg
ILLUSTRATOR/ARTIST
Nick Gaetano, John Burgoyne
WRITER
Sara Slater, Dave Idema
CLIENT
Casa Lupita Mexican Restaurant
AGENCY
Geer, DuBois, New York, NY

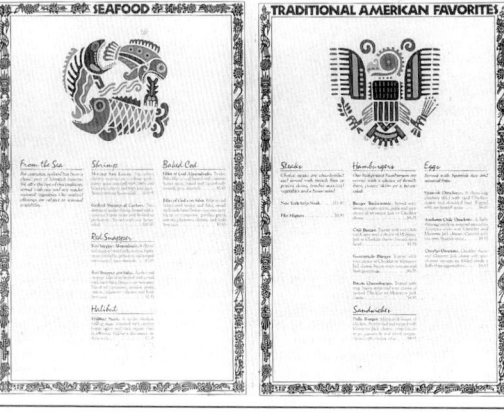

784

785
ART DIRECTOR
Kim Allen
DESIGNER
Kimberly Allen
ILLUSTRATOR/ARTIST
Kimberly Allen
WRITER
Betsy England
CLIENT
American Theatre Company
AGENCY
Brown Bloyed & Associates, Tulsa, OK

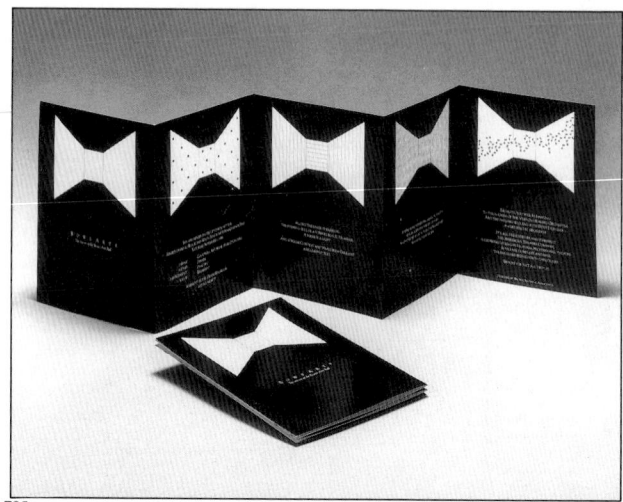

785

786
ART DIRECTOR
Thomas Kluepfel, Stephen Doyle
DESIGNER
Stephen Doyle, Thomas Kluepfel
WRITER
William Drenttel
CLIENT
Drenttel Doyle Partners
AGENCY
Drenttel Doyle Partners, New York, NY

786

787

789

ART DIRECTOR
Charles Spencer Anderson
DESIGNER
Charles Spencer Anderson
CLIENT
Duffy Design Group
DESIGN FIRM
Duffy Design Group, Minneapolis, MN

788

788

ART DIRECTOR
Charles Spencer Anderson
DESIGNER
Sharon Werner
ILLUSTRATOR/ARTIST
Sharon Werner
CLIENT
Nancy Bundt Photography
DESIGN FIRM
Duffy Design Group, Minneapolis, MN

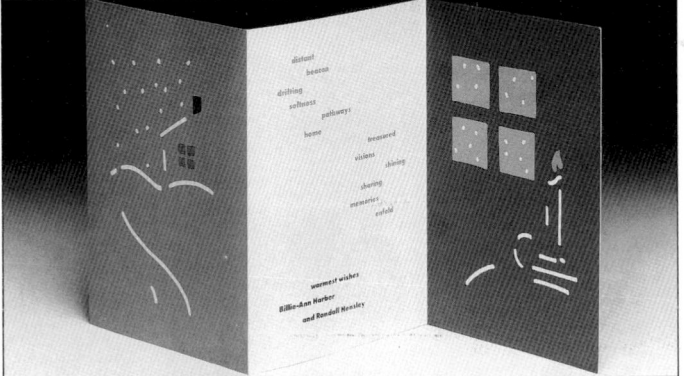

789

789

ART DIRECTOR
Randall Hensley
DESIGNER
Randall Hensley, Billie-Ann Harber
ILLUSTRATOR/ARTIST
Randall Hensley
WRITER
Billie-Ann Harber
CLIENT
Billie-Ann Harber, Randall Hensley
DESIGN FIRM
Articulation, New York, NY
CREATIVE DIRECTOR
Billie-Ann Harber

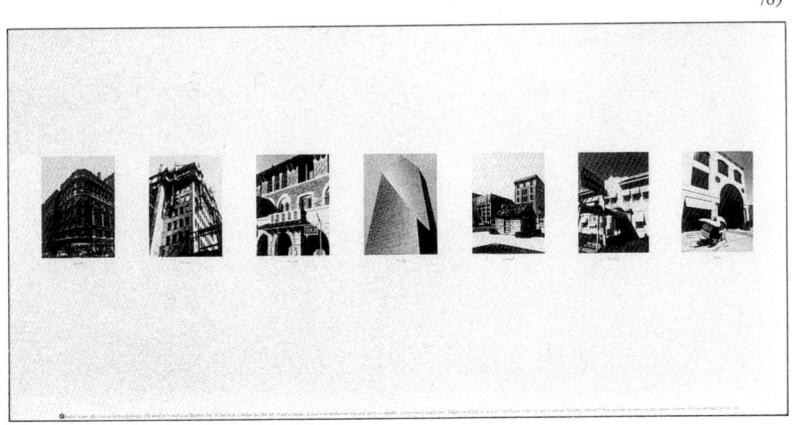

790

790

ART DIRECTOR
Arthur Eisenberg, Don Arday
DESIGNER
Mark Drury
PHOTOGRAPHER
Don Arday
WRITER
Linda Eissler
CLIENT
Eisenberg Inc.
DESIGN FIRM
Eisenberg Inc., Dallas, TX

791
ART DIRECTOR
Paul J. Bussmann
DESIGNER
Paul J. Bussmann
PHOTOGRAPHER
Dan Sindelar
ILLUSTRATOR/ARTIST
R. O. Blechman
WRITER
Carter L. Dunkin
CLIENT
Monsanto Company
EDITOR
Harold Jackson
AGENCY
Fleishman-Hillard, Inc., St. Louis, MO

792
ART DIRECTOR
Tom Kaminsky
DESIGNER
Tom Kaminsky
ILLUSTRATOR/ARTIST
Joyce Culkin
WRITER
Michael Sheehan
CLIENT
New England Home for Little Wanderers
AGENCY
ClarkeGowardFitts, Boston, MA
DESIGN FIRM
ClarkeGowardFitts Design

793
ART DIRECTOR
Andrea Freund Mauro, Charles L. Mauro
DESIGNER
Andrea Freund Mauro
WRITER
Charles L. Mauro
CLIENT
Howe Furniture Corporation, Eric Smith
DESIGN FIRM
Mauro/Mauro/Design, New York, NY

794
ART DIRECTOR
Rex Peteet
DESIGNER
Rex Peteet
ILLUSTRATOR/ARTIST
Rex Peteet, Judy Dolim
WRITER
Rex Peteet
CLIENT
International Paper Company, Kathy Zann
AGENCY
Sibley Peteet Design, Dallas, TX
DESIGN FIRM
Sibley Peteet Design

791

792

793

794

795

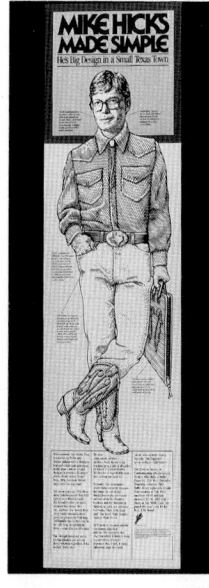

796

795

ART DIRECTOR
Scott Eggers
DESIGNER
Scott Eggers
ILLUSTRATOR/ARTIST
Scott Eggers
WRITER
Scott Eggers
CLIENT
Scott Eggers
AGENCY
Knape & Knape, Dallas, TX

796

ART DIRECTOR
Paul Caldera, Dave Kottler
DESIGNER
Paul Caldera, Dave Kottler
ILLUSTRATOR/ARTIST
Ken Jacobsen
WRITER
Sara Harrell
CLIENT
Phoenix Society of Communicating Arts, Inc.
DESIGN FIRM
The Kottler Caldera Group, Phoenix, AZ
TYPOGRAPHER
Headquarters, Inc.

797

ART DIRECTOR
Richard A. DeOlivera
DESIGNER
Jay Moore
ILLUSTRATOR/ARTIST
Jay Moore
WRITER
Leslie Howard
CLIENT
Green Valley Ranch
DESIGN FIRM
DeOlivera Creative, Inc., Denver, CO

797

798

ART DIRECTOR
John Noone
DESIGNER
John Noone
ILLUSTRATOR/ARTIST
Wangdon Lee
WRITER
John Noone
CLIENT
WBSB Radio
AGENCY
W. B. Doner Advertising, Baltimore, MD

798

799
ART DIRECTOR
Martin Solomon
DESIGNER
Martin Solomon
CLIENT
Lisa & Lawrence Pollack
DESIGN FIRM
Martin Solomon Co., New York, NY

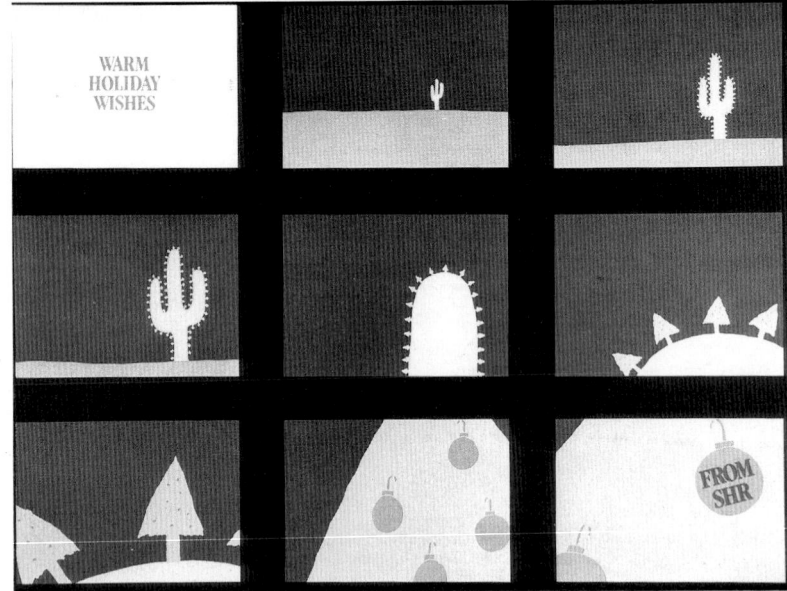

799

800
ART DIRECTOR
Douglas Reeder
DESIGNER
Douglas Reeder
ILLUSTRATOR/ARTIST
Douglas Reeder
DESIGN FIRM
SHR Communications Planning & Design,
Scottsdale, AZ

800

801
ART DIRECTOR
Michael Mabry
DESIGNER
Michael Mabry, Peter Soe Jr.
ILLUSTRATOR/ARTIST
Michael Mabry
WRITER
AIGA New York
CLIENT
AIGA
DESIGN FIRM
Michael Mabry Design, San Francisco, CA

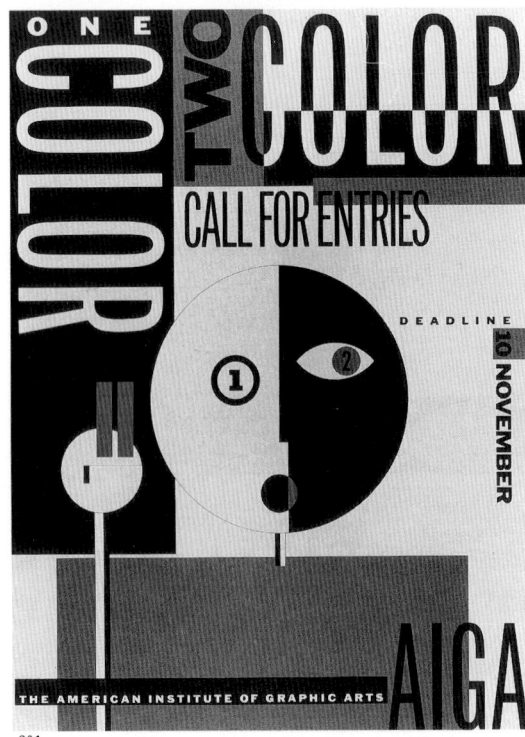

801

802
ART DIRECTOR
Charles Spencer Anderson
DESIGNER
Charles Spencer Anderson
ILLUSTRATOR/ARTIST
Charles Spencer Anderson, Lynn Schulte
CLIENT
Very Light Opera Company
DESIGN FIRM
Duffy Design, Minneapolis, MN

802

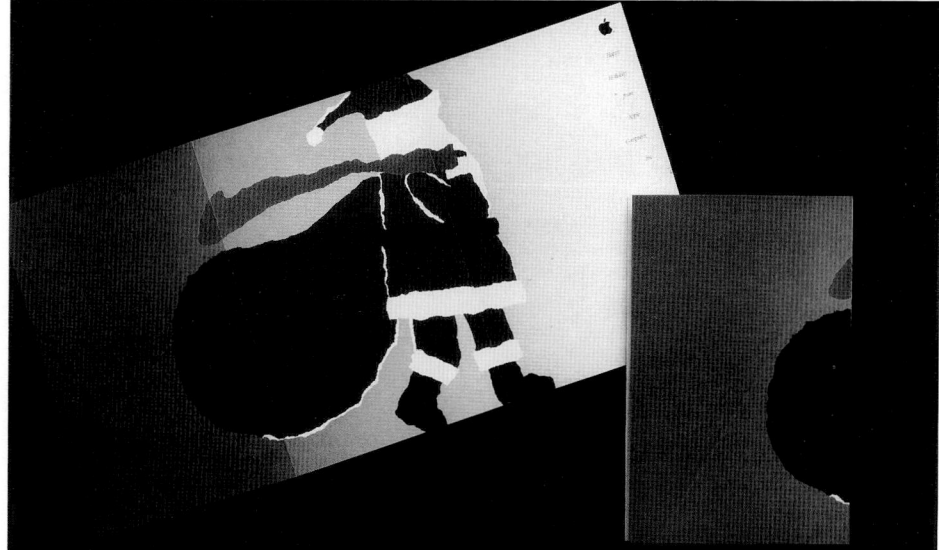

803

ART DIRECTOR
Ellen Romano
DESIGNER
Ellen Romano
ILLUSTRATOR/ARTIST
Ellen Romano
WRITER
Lynda Heideman
CLIENT
Apple Manufacturing
PUBLISHER
Apple Computer, Inc.
DESIGN FIRM
Apple Computer Creative Services, Cupertino, CA

803

804

ART DIRECTOR
Jean McCartney
DESIGNER
Jean McCartney
CLIENT
West Point Pepperell, Martex
AGENCY
West Point Pepperell, New York, NY

804

805

ART DIRECTOR
Paul Huber, Helen Huber
DESIGNER
Paul Huber, Helen Huber
PHOTOGRAPHER
Steve Marsel
WRITER
Paul Huber, Helen Huber
CLIENT
Jesse Bradford Huber
DESIGN FIRM
Huber & Huber, Watertown, MA

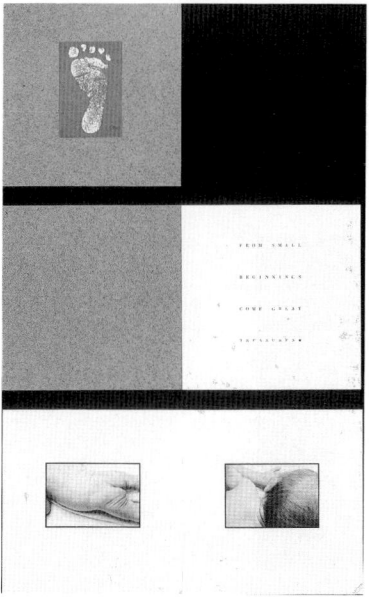

806

ART DIRECTOR
Chris Hill
DESIGNER
Chris Hill, Jeffrey Mckay
PHOTOGRAPHER
Craig Wells
WRITER
Mary Langridge
CLIENT
Craig Wells Photography
DESIGN FIRM
Hill / A Marketing Design Group, Houston, TX

805

806

807
ART DIRECTOR
Charles Spencer Anderson
DESIGNER
Charles Spencer Anderson
ILLUSTRATOR/ARTIST
Joe Duffy, Charles Spencer Anderson, Lynn
Schulte
WRITER
Chuck Carlson
CLIENT
First Bank of Minneapolis
DESIGN FIRM
Duffy Design Group, Minneapolis, MN

808
ART DIRECTOR
Joe Duffy
DESIGNER
Joe Duffy
ILLUSTRATOR/ARTIST
Joe Duffy, Lynn Schulte
CLIENT
Fallon McElligott
DESIGN FIRM
Duffy Design Group, Minneapolis, MN

807

808

809
ART DIRECTOR
Tom Hughes
DESIGNER
Tom Hughes
PHOTOGRAPHER
Bill Gallery
CLIENT
Bill Gallery
AGENCY
Lotus Creative Development, Cambridge, MA

810
ART DIRECTOR
Charles Spencer Anderson
DESIGNER
Sharon Werner, Charles S. Anderson
ILLUSTRATOR/ARTIST
Charles Spencer Anderson
CLIENT
Marine Midland
DESIGN FIRM
Duffy Design Group, Minneapolis, MN

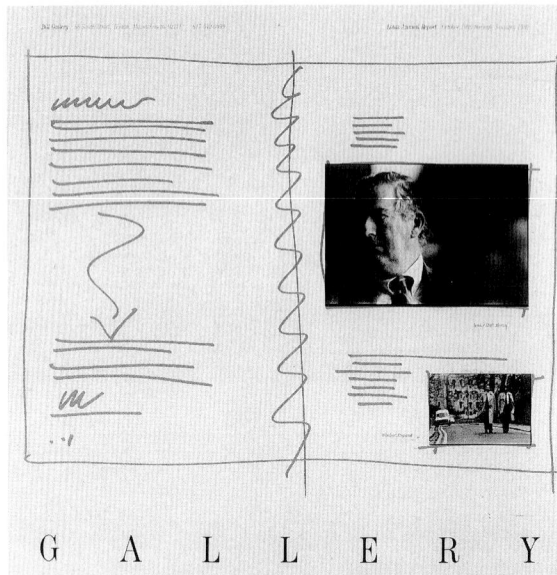

809

810

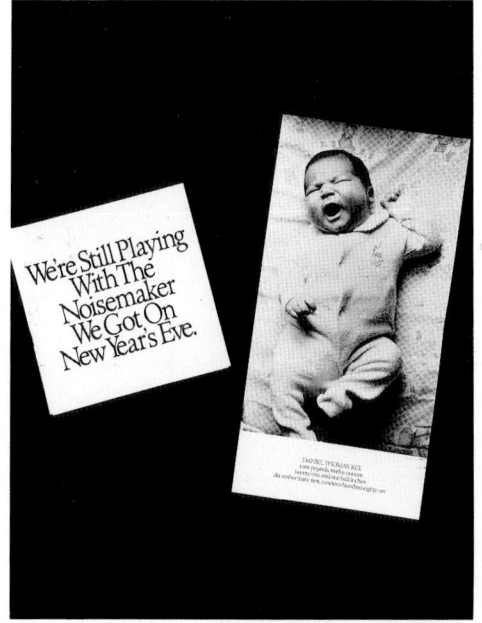

811

812

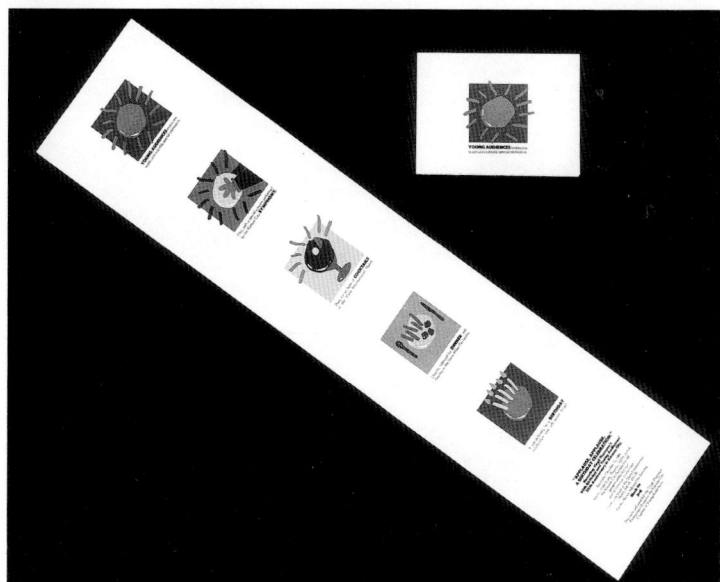

813

814

811
ART DIRECTOR
Jim Proimos
DESIGNER
Jack East, Jr.
PHOTOGRAPHER
Jim Proimos
WRITER
Tom Amico
CLIENT
Mr. and Mrs. Thomas Key
AGENCY
Meldrum and Fewsmith, Cleveland, OH
TYPOGRAPHER
Camelot Typesetting

812
ART DIRECTOR
Danny Boone
DESIGNER
Danny Boone
WRITER
Mike Hughes
CLIENT
Richmond Ad Club
AGENCY
The Martin Agency, Richmond, VA

813
ART DIRECTOR
Michelle Knauss
DESIGNER
Michelle Knauss
ILLUSTRATOR/ARTIST
Michelle Knauss
WRITER
Gail Pasternek
CLIENT
Young Audiences, Kansas City Chapter
PRODUCER
Anita Boyett
DESIGN FIRM
Ann Willoughby & Associates, Kansas City, MO

814
ART DIRECTOR
Ingrid Hansen-Lynch, Martha Carothers
DESIGNER
Ingrid Hansen-Lynch, Martha Carothers
WRITER
Ingrid Hansen-Lynch, Martha Carothers
CLIENT
Jim & Ingrid Lynch
DESIGN FIRM
The Post Press, Newark, DE

815
ART DIRECTOR
Dean Hanson
WRITER
Bill Miller
CLIENT
Next
AGENCY
Fallon McElligott, Minneapolis, MN

Ten years ago, if you wanted to see the future of computers for education, you would have needed the key to Steve Jobs' garage.

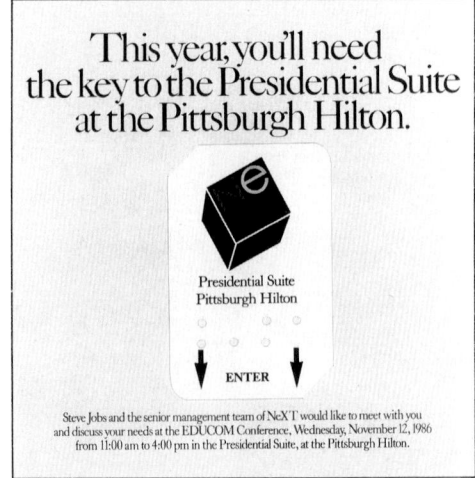

815

816
ART DIRECTOR
Kathy Stanton
DESIGNER
Kathy Stanton
WRITER
Laurel Hamalainen
CLIENT
Herman Miller, Inc.
PRODUCER
Sue Bakker

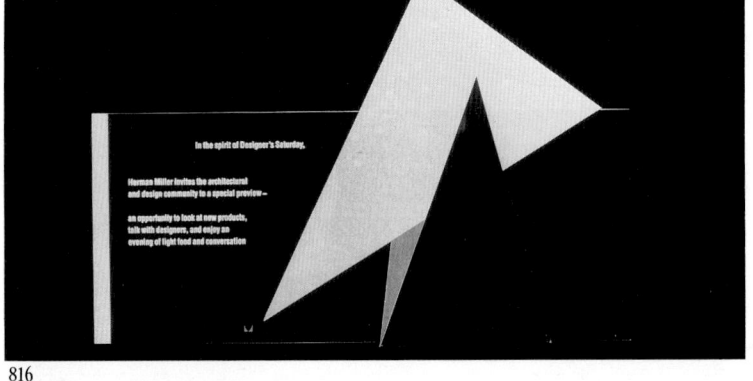

816

817
ART DIRECTOR
Wendy Edwards Lowitz
DESIGNER
Wendy Edwards Lowitz
ILLUSTRATOR/ARTIST
Dan Lampert
CLIENT
Abbott Laboratories
DIRECTOR
Sheryl Bealhen
DESIGN FIRM
Moira & Company, Chicago, IL
TYPESETTER
Compho Graphics
PRINTER
Northwestern Printing House
ACCOUNT EXEC.
Marla Rubin

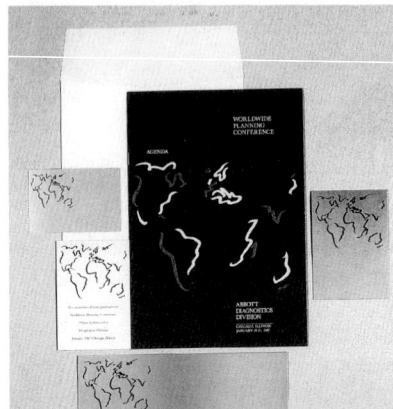

817

818
ART DIRECTOR
Marshall Harmon
DESIGNER
Nancy Laurence
PHOTOGRAPHER
James Wojik
WRITER
Bruce McKenzie
CLIENT
International Paper Company
AGENCY
Harmon Kemp Inc.
DESIGN FIRM
EYE Design, New York, NY

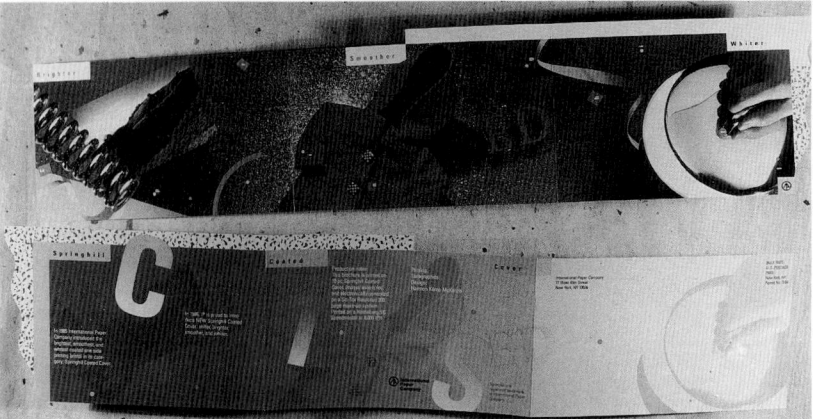

818

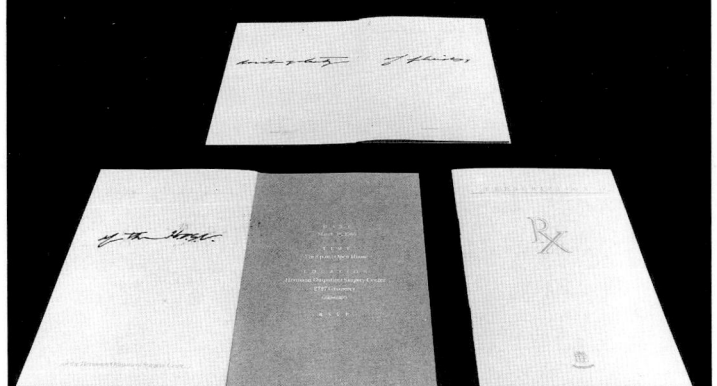

819

ART DIRECTOR
Richard Kilmer, Mark Geer
DESIGNER
Richard Kilmer, Mark Geer
WRITER
Richard Kilmer, Mark Geer
CLIENT
Hermann Hospital
DESIGN FIRM
Kilmer/Geer Design, Inc., Houston, TX

819

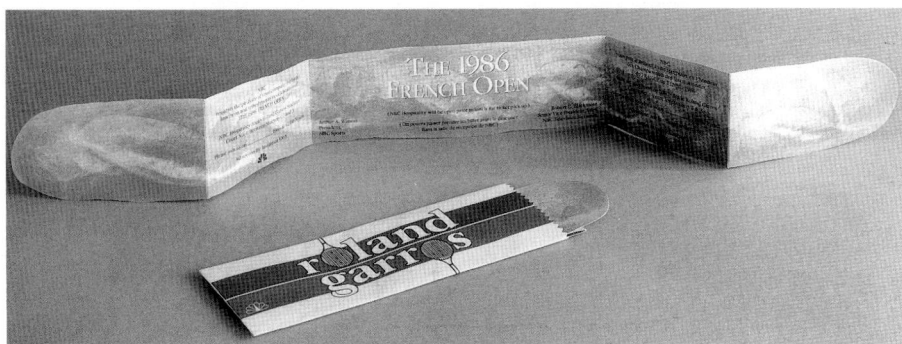

820

ART DIRECTOR
Elaine Zeitsoff
DESIGNER
Marleen Adlerblum
CLIENT
NBC Sports Client Relations
AGENCY
NBC Corporate Advertising & Promotion, New
York, NY
CREATIVE DIRECTOR
Arthur Hecht

820

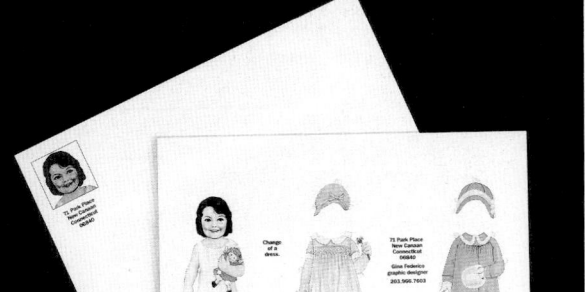

821

ART DIRECTOR
Gina Federico
DESIGNER
Gina Federico
CLIENT
Gina Federico
DESIGN FIRM
Gina Federico Graphic
Design, New Canaan, CT

821

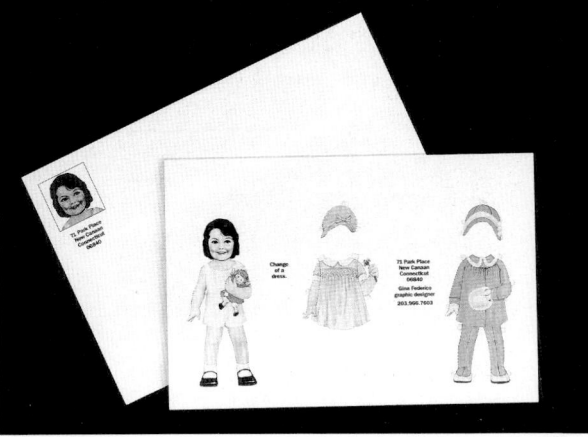

822

ART DIRECTOR
Graphic Design Services/St. Luke's Episcopal
Hospital
DESIGNER
Philip Pinto
ILLUSTRATOR/ARTIST
Dennis Walker
WRITER
Graphic Design Services, St. Luke's Episcopal
Hospital
CLIENT
Graphic Design Services/St. Luke's Episcopal
Hospital
EDITOR
Chris Alexander
DIRECTOR
Phyllis Love
AGENCY
Graphic Design Services/St. Luke's Episcopal
Hospital, Houston, TX
PRINTER
Chas.P.Young Houston

822

823
ART DIRECTOR
Scott A. Mednick
DESIGNER
Scott A. Mednick
PHOTOGRAPHER
Aaron Rapaport
ILLUSTRATOR/ARTIST
Scott Mednick & Associates
DESIGN FIRM
Scott Mednick & Associates, Los Angeles, CA

823

824
ART DIRECTOR
Tamotsu Yagi
DESIGNER
Tamotsu Yagi
DESIGN FIRM
Esprit Graphic Design Studio, San Francisco, CA

824

825
ART DIRECTOR
Kevin B. Kuester
DESIGNER
Kevin B. Kuester
WRITER
Kevin B. Kuester
CLIENT
Madsen and Kuester, Inc.
PRODUCER
Tresa Jahn
DESIGN FIRM
Madsen and Kuester, Inc., Minneapolis, MN

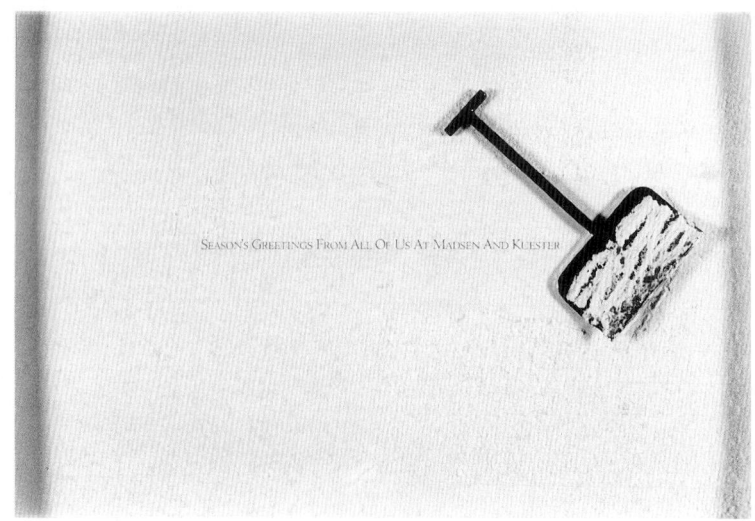

825

826

827

826

ART DIRECTOR
Stephen Miller
DESIGNER
Stephen Miller
ILLUSTRATOR/ARTIST
Robert Forsbach
WRITER
David Fowler
CLIENT
Vecta Contract
AGENCY
The Richards Group
DESIGN FIRM
Richards Brock Miller Mitchell & Assoc.,
Dallas, TX

827

ART DIRECTOR
Effie Meyer
DESIGNER
John McCarthy
ILLUSTRATOR/ARTIST
Lisa Nelson
WRITER
Effie Meyer, Beth Eggert
CLIENT
R.L. Meyer Advertising
AGENCY
R.L. Meyer Advertising, Milwaukee, WI
PRODUCER
Diane Germanotta
DESIGN FIRM
McDill, Ltd.
PRINTER
HM Graphics
TYPESETTER
Peter A. Altenhofen Typographers, Inc.

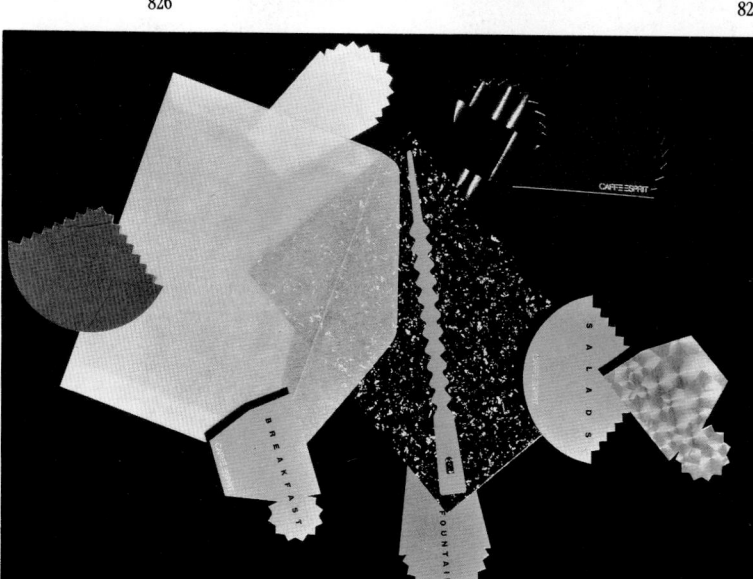

828

828

ART DIRECTOR
Tamotsu Yagi
DESIGNER
Tamotsu Yagi
DESIGN FIRM
Esprit Graphic Design Studio, San Francisco,
CA

829

829

ART DIRECTOR
Robin Ayres, Luis Acevedo
DESIGNER
Robin Ayres
ILLUSTRATOR/ARTIST
Charles McGough
WRITER
Dave Fowler T.G.I. Friday's
CLIENT
T.G.I. Friday's, Inc.
AGENCY
The Richards Group
DESIGN FIRM
Richards Brock Miller Mitchell & Assoc.,
Dallas, TX

830

ART DIRECTOR
Pat Samata
DESIGNER
Pat Samata
PHOTOGRAPHER
Jean Moss
ILLUSTRATOR/ARTIST
Ann Teson, Susan Mechnig, K.C. Yoon, Norm
Lee
WRITER
Nancy Bishop
CLIENT
Samata Associates
DESIGN FIRM
Samata Associates, Dundee, IL
HAND COLORING
George Sawa

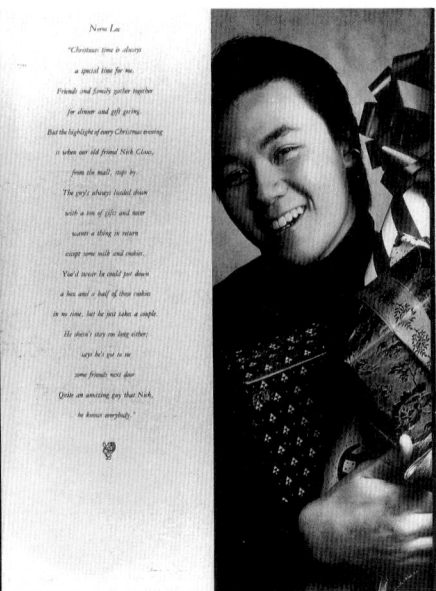

830

831

ART DIRECTOR
Rex Peteet
DESIGNER
Rex Peteet
ILLUSTRATOR/ARTIST
Rex Peteet, Paul Black
WRITER
Rex Peteet
CLIENT
Herring Marathon Group/Alexandria Mall
DESIGN FIRM
Sibley/Peteet Design, Dallas, TX

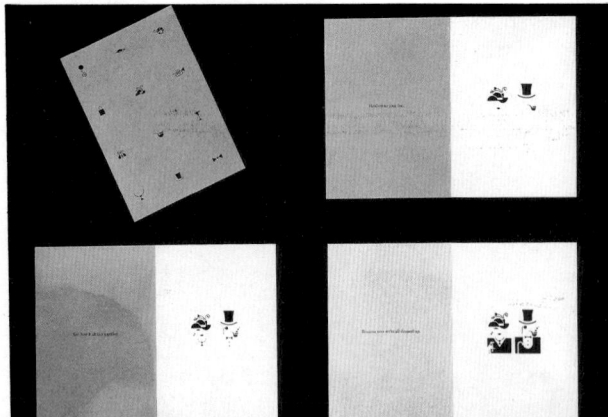

831

832

ART DIRECTOR
Steven Sessions
DESIGNER
Steven Sessions
ILLUSTRATOR/ARTIST
Steven Sessions
WRITER
Steven Sessions
CLIENT
Siori/Ciao, Milan Italy
AGENCY
Steven Sessions, Inc., Houston, TX
DESIGN FIRM
Steven Sessions, Inc.

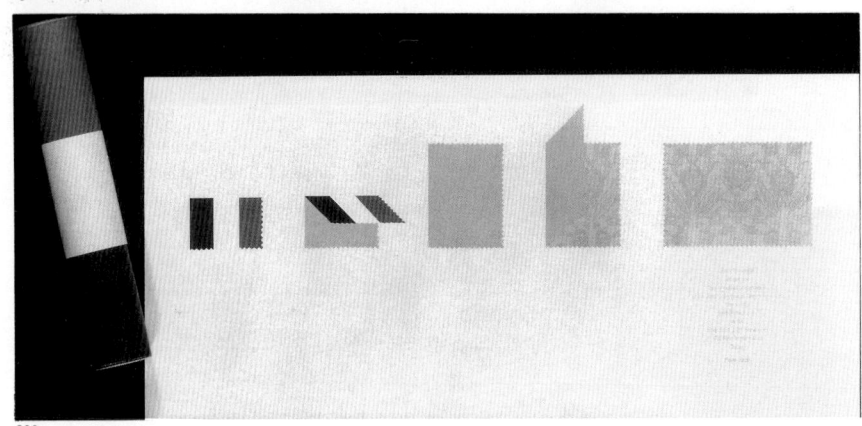

832

833

ART DIRECTOR
Julian Naranjo
DESIGNER
Julian Naranjo
ILLUSTRATOR/ARTIST
Julian Naranjo
WRITER
Jeff Elkind
CLIENT
K-JOY Radio
AGENCY
Wise Communications, San Diego, CA

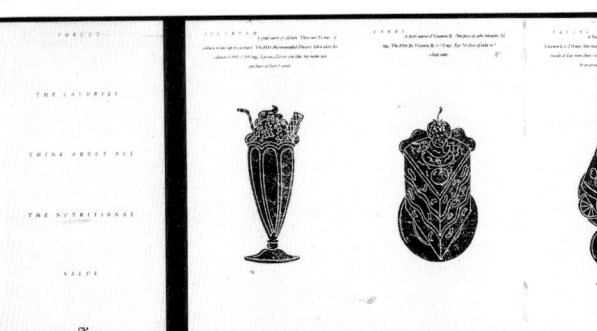

833

834

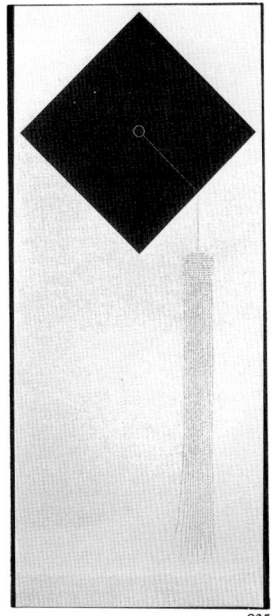

835

834
ART DIRECTOR
Robin Ayres
DESIGNER
Robin Ayres
PHOTOGRAPHER
John Wong, Greg Booth and Associates
WRITER
Linda Bradford, Robin Ayres
CLIENT
Dallas Society of Visual Communications
AGENCY
The Richards Group
DESIGN FIRM
Richards Brock Miller Mitchell & Assoc.,
Dallas, TX

835
ART DIRECTOR
D.C. Stipp
DESIGNER
D.C. Stipp
ILLUSTRATOR/ARTIST
D.C. Stipp
WRITER
David Fowler
CLIENT
Castleberry High School Class of '76
PUBLISHER
Heritage Press
AGENCY
The Richards Group
DESIGN FIRM
Richards Brock Miller Mitchell & Assoc.,
Dallas, TX

836

836
ART DIRECTOR
Tamotsu Yagi
DESIGNER
Tamotsu Yagi
DESIGN FIRM
Esprit Graphic Design Studio, San Francisco,
CA

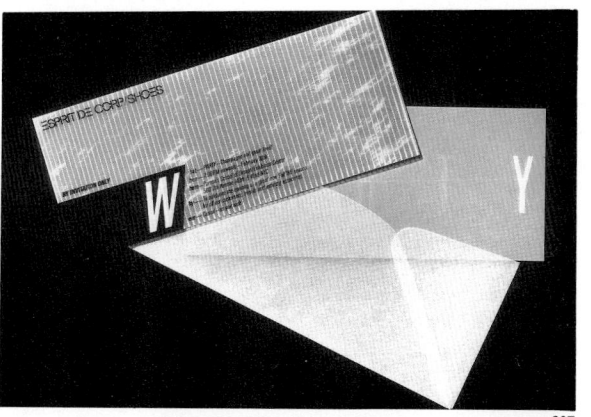

837

837
ART DIRECTOR
Tamotsu Yagi
DESIGNER
Tamotsu Yagi
DESIGN FIRM
Esprit Graphic Design Studio, San Francisco,
CA

838

838
ART DIRECTOR
John Evans, Laurie Malan Evans
DESIGNER
John Evans
ILLUSTRATOR/ARTIST
John Evans
WRITER
John Evans, Laurie Malan Evans
CLIENT
John and Laurie Evans
DESIGN FIRM
Sibley/Peteet Design, Inc., Dallas, TX

839
ART DIRECTOR
Kurt Tausche
DESIGNER
Kurt Tausche
WRITER
Kerry Casey
CLIENT
Joyce's
AGENCY
Bozell, Jacobs, Kenyon & Eckhardt,
Minneapolis, MN

840
ART DIRECTOR
Kurt Tausche
DESIGNER
Kurt Tausche
WRITER
Kerry Casey
CLIENT
Joyce's
AGENCY
Bozell, Jacobs, Kenyon & Eckhardt,
Minneapolis, MN

841
ART DIRECTOR
Kurt Tausche
DESIGNER
Kurt Tausche
WRITER
Kerry Casey
CLIENT
Joyce's
AGENCY
Bozell, Jacobs, Kenyon & Eckhardt,
Minneapolis, MN

842
ART DIRECTOR
Charles Spencer Anderson
DESIGNER
Charles Spencer Anderson, Sara Ledgard
WRITER
Chuck Carlson
CLIENT
First Bank of Minneapolis
DESIGN FIRM
Duffy Design Group, Minneapolis, MN

843
ART DIRECTOR
Mark Geer, Richard Kilmer
DESIGNER
Mark Geer, Richard Kilmer
ILLUSTRATOR/ARTIST
Mark Geer, Richard Kilmer
WRITER
Richard Kilmer, Mark Geer
CLIENT
Decorative Center Houston
AGENCY
Boswell Byers
DESIGN FIRM
Kilmer/Geer Design, Inc., Houston, TX

844
ART DIRECTOR
Robert Anders, Leo Mullen
DESIGNER
Jeremiah Austin
WRITER
Robert Anders
CLIENT
U.S. Information Agency
DESIGN FIRM
Invisions Ltd., Washington, DC

839

840

841

842

843

844

845

ART DIRECTOR
Lisa Halperin, Hasbrouck Heights, NJ
DESIGNER
Lisa Halperin
ILLUSTRATOR/ARTIST
Ed Benguiat
CLIENT
Lisa Halperin

846

ART DIRECTOR
Michael Dunlavey
DESIGNER
Sheree Lum Orsi
CLIENT
Flash Entertainment Corporation
DESIGN FIRM
The Dunlavey Studio, Inc., Sacramento, CA
PRINTER
Fong & Fong, Printers and Lithographers

845

847

ART DIRECTOR
Michael Dunlavey
DESIGNER
Lindy Dunlavey
ILLUSTRATOR/ARTIST
Lindy Dunlavey
CLIENT
Java City
DESIGN FIRM
The Dunlavey Studio, Inc., Sacramento, CA
PRINTER
Graphic Center

846   847

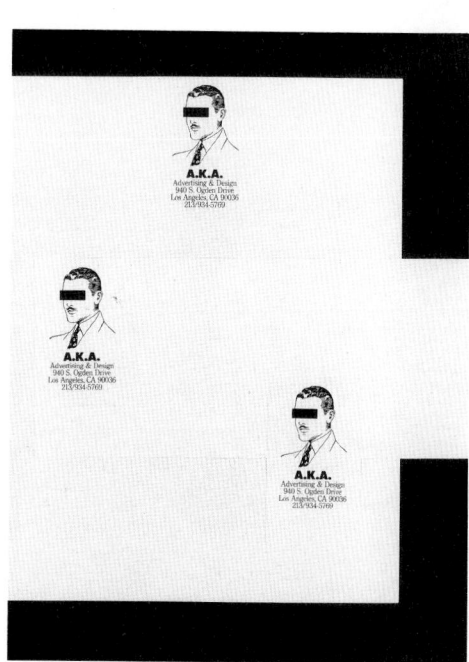

848

ART DIRECTOR
Jeff Denning
DESIGNER
Jeff Denning
CLIENT
Self Images Beauty Salon
DESIGN FIRM
Denning Design, Houston, TX

849

ART DIRECTOR
Gary Johns
DESIGNER
Gary Johns
ILLUSTRATOR/ARTIST
Gary Johns
CLIENT
A.K.A.
DESIGN FIRM
A.K.A., Los Angeles, CA

848   849

850
ART DIRECTOR
Jeff Laramore
DESIGNER
Lisa Thomas
CLIENT
Pages
AGENCY
Young & Laramore, Indianapolis, IN

851
ART DIRECTOR
James Wageman
DESIGNER
James Wageman
CLIENT
Abbeville Press, New York, NY
DIRECTOR
Robert E. Abrams

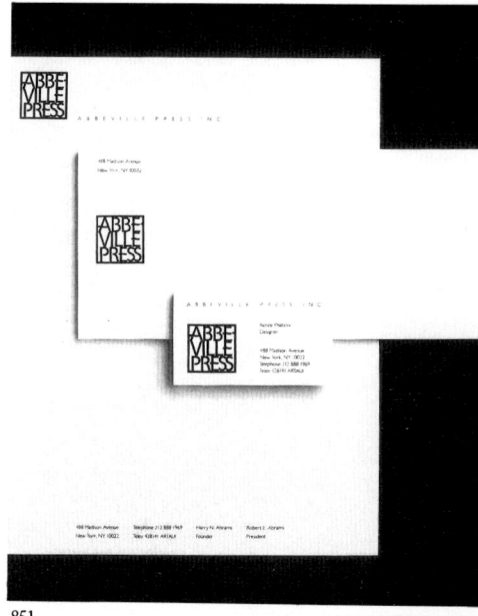

850

851

852
ART DIRECTOR
Don Sibley
DESIGNER
Don Sibley, John Evans
ILLUSTRATOR/ARTIST
Don Sibley
CLIENT
Brophy Bros. Restaurant
DESIGN FIRM
Sibley/Peteet Design, Inc., Dallas, TX

853
ART DIRECTOR
Don Sibley, John Evans
DESIGNER
John Evans
ILLUSTRATOR/ARTIST
John Evans
CLIENT
Mickey Newbury, Songwriter/Composer
DESIGN FIRM
Sibley/Peteet Design, Inc., Dallas, TX

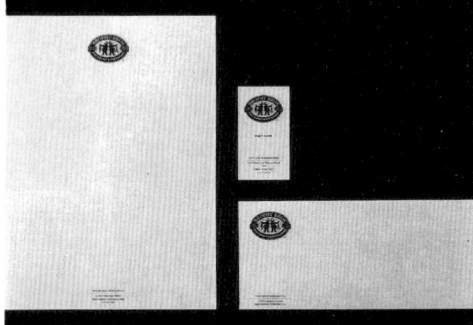

852

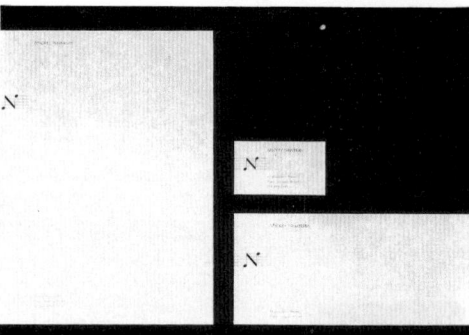

853

854
ART DIRECTOR
Cynthia Friedman, New York, NY
PHOTOGRAPHER
Cynthia Friedman
ILLUSTRATOR/ARTIST
Theodora Skipitares (Sculptor)
CLIENT
Skysaver Productions

855
ART DIRECTOR
Josh Freeman
DESIGNER
Vickie Sawyer
CLIENT
Jennings/Des Anges
DESIGN FIRM
Josh Freeman/Associates, Los Angeles, CA

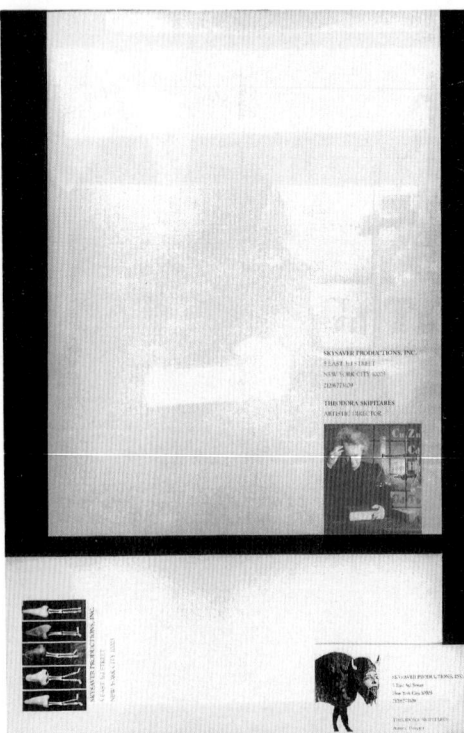

855

854

856

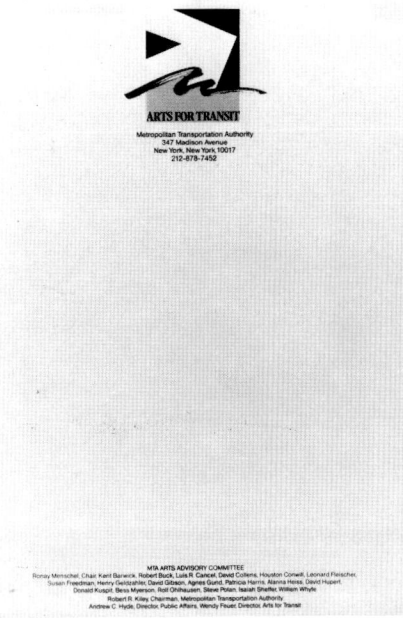

857

858

859

856
ART DIRECTOR
Carol Burke
DESIGNER
Carol Burke
WRITER
Melinda Marcus
AGENCY
Cox Pippin Communications, Dallas, TX

857
ART DIRECTOR
Dean McChesney
DESIGNER
Dean McChesney
CLIENT
Arts for Transit, Metropolitan Transportation
Authority
AGENCY
Metropolitan Transportation Authority, New
York, NY
DESIGN FIRM
Marketing and Graphic Services

858
ART DIRECTOR
Lawrence E. Green
DESIGNER
Lawrence E. Green
CLIENT
G.G. Green
DESIGN FIRM
The Green Co., San Francisco, CA
PRINTER
Technigraphics

859
DESIGNER
Richard Thomas
ILLUSTRATOR/ARTIST
Josie Yee
CLIENT
Conference Call Service
DESIGN FIRM
Richard Thomas, Westport, CT

860
ART DIRECTOR
Charles Spencer Anderson
DESIGNER
Sara Ledgard
CLIENT
Typeshooters
DESIGN FIRM
Duffy Design Group, Minneapolis, MN

861
ART DIRECTOR
Jamie Mambro
DESIGNER
Jamie Mambro, Nancy Malacaria
WRITER
Thomas Monahan
CLIENT
Out of Towners Advertising Exhibit
AGENCY
Leonard Monahan Saabye, Providence, RI
PRINTER
Meridian Printing

860

861

862
ART DIRECTOR
Mike Schroeder
DESIGNER
Mike Schroeder
PHOTOGRAPHER
Robbie McClaran
ILLUSTRATOR/ARTIST
Mike Schroeder
CLIENT
Robbie McClaran
AGENCY
Pirtle Design
DESIGN FIRM
Schroeder Design, Dallas, TX

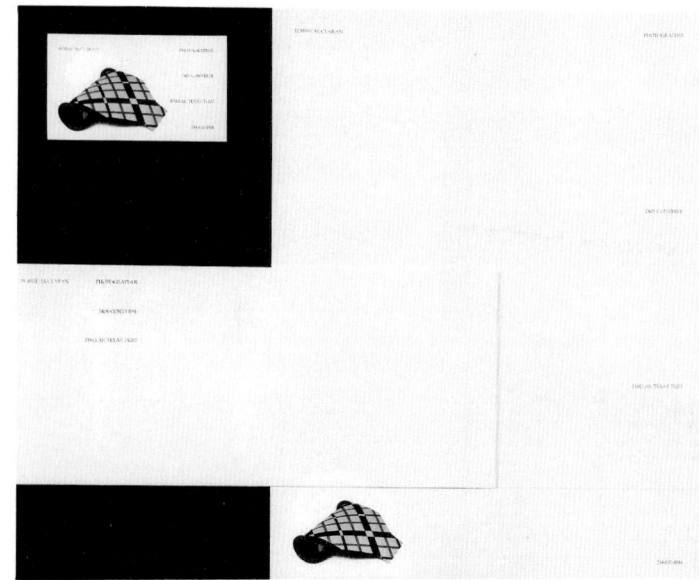

862

863
ART DIRECTOR
John Sposato, New York, NY
ILLUSTRATOR/ARTIST
John Sposato
CLIENT
John Sposato

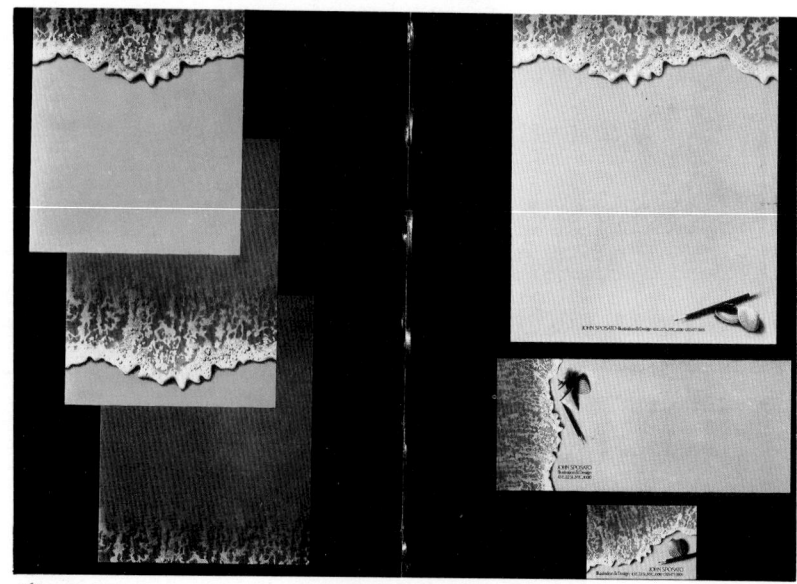

863

864

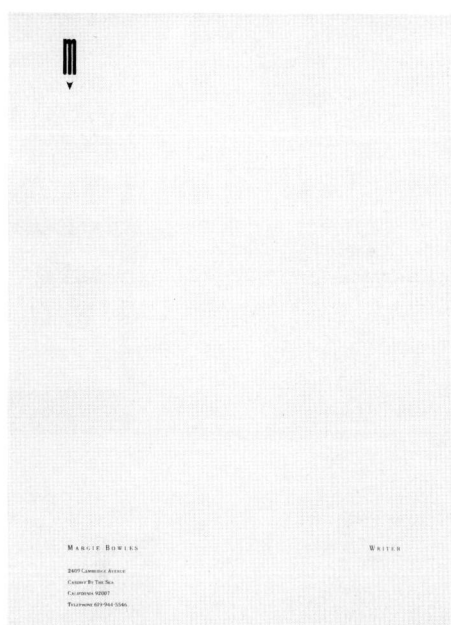

865

864
ART DIRECTOR
John Swieter
DESIGNER
John Swieter
ILLUSTRATOR/ARTIST
John Swieter
CLIENT
Watters & Watters
AGENCY
Swieter Design, Dallas, TX
DESIGN FIRM
Swieter Design

865
ART DIRECTOR
John Benelli
DESIGNER
John Benelli
WRITER
Margie Bowles
CLIENT
Margie Bowles
DESIGN FIRM
Benelli Design, San Diego, CA
PRINTER
Rush Press
TYPE
Central Graphics

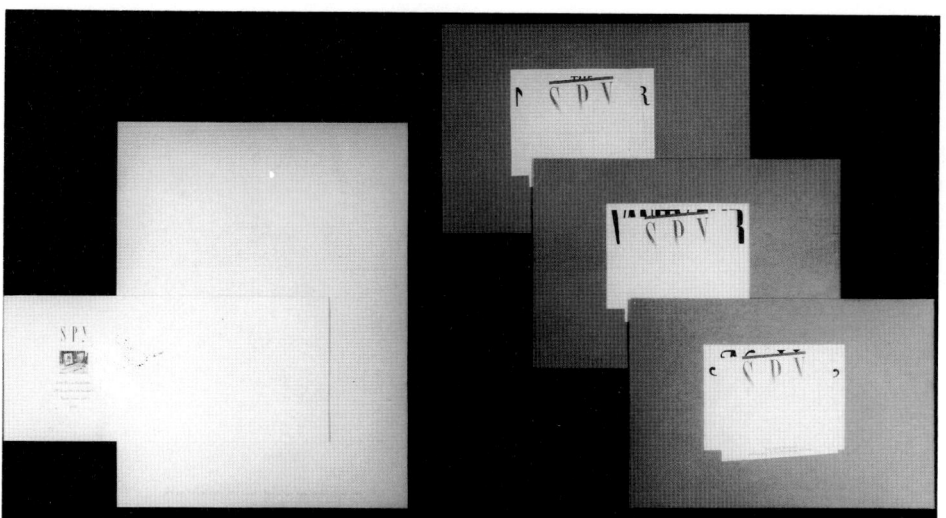

866

866
ART DIRECTOR
Stephen Doyle, Thomas Kluepfel
DESIGNER
Rosemarie Sohmer
CLIENT
Spy Publishing Partners
AGENCY
Drenttel Doyle Partners, New York, NY

867
ART DIRECTOR
Anthony Taibi
DESIGNER
Constance Kovar
CLIENT
Constance Kovar & Company
DESIGN FIRM
Constance Kovar & Company, Woodbury, NY

867

868
ART DIRECTOR
Forrest & Valerie Richardson
DESIGNER
Forrest & Valerie Richardson, Rosemary
Connelley
CLIENT
J.W. Tumbles Childrens Gym
DESIGN FIRM
Richardson or Richardson, Phoenix, AZ

868

869
ART DIRECTOR
Jeff Larson
DESIGNER
Scott Johnson
CLIENT
Stephen Pitkin
DESIGN FIRM
Jeff Larson Design Associates, Rockford, IL

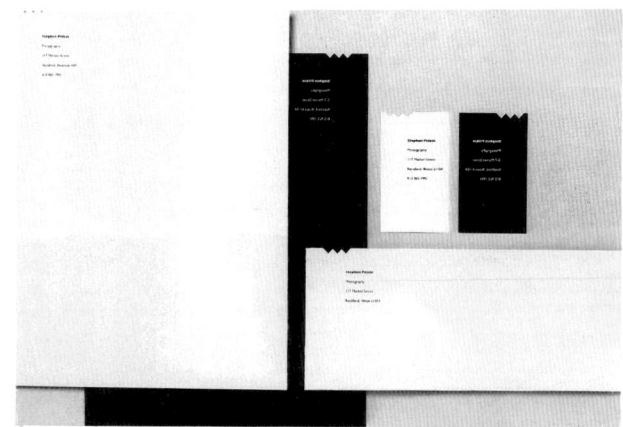

869

870
ART DIRECTOR
Neville Smith
DESIGNER
Neville Smith
ILLUSTRATOR/ARTIST
Neville Smith
CLIENT
Pianocraft
DESIGN FIRM
Neville Smith, Graphic Design, Skyridge,
Québec, Canada
PRINTER
Viki Ball, Screen Printing

870

871
ART DIRECTOR
John Swieter
DESIGNER
John Swieter
ILLUSTRATOR/ARTIST
John Swieter
CLIENT
Winger Muscle Therapy
AGENCY
Swieter Design, Dallas, TX
DESIGN FIRM
Swieter Design

871

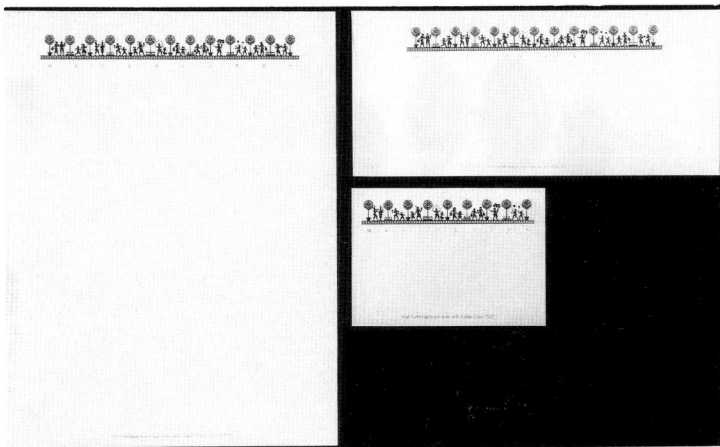

872

ART DIRECTOR
Bob Dennard
DESIGNER
Bob Dennard, Ken Koester
ILLUSTRATOR/ARTIST
Ken Koester
CLIENT
Mallscapes
DESIGN FIRM
Dennard Creative, Dallas, TX

872

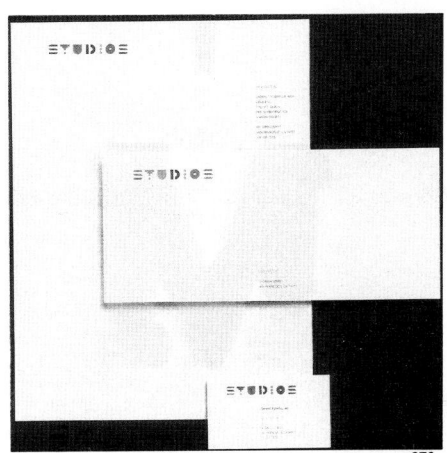

873

ART DIRECTOR
Woody Pirtle
DESIGNER
Woody Pirtle
ILLUSTRATOR/ARTIST
Woody Pirtle
CLIENT
Studios
DESIGN FIRM
Pirtle Design, Dallas, TX
PRINTER
Heritage Press

874

ART DIRECTOR
Tom Binnion, Jon Reeder
CLIENT
Richard C. Hibner D.D.S.
AGENCY
Thomas Binnion, Los Angeles, CA

873

874

875

ART DIRECTOR
Kevin B. Kuester
DESIGNER
Bob Goebel, Kevin B. Kuester
ILLUSTRATOR/ARTIST
Bob Goebel
CLIENT
Parasole Restaurant Holdings
DESIGN FIRM
Madsen and Kuester, Inc., Minneapolis, MN

875

876

ART DIRECTOR
Luis D. Acevedo
DESIGNER
Luis D. Acevedo
ILLUSTRATOR/ARTIST
Luis D. Acevedo
CLIENT
Lewisville Humane Society
AGENCY
The Richards Group
DESIGN FIRM
Richards Brock Miller Mitchell & Assoc.,
Dallas, TX

877

ART DIRECTOR
Dick Mitchell
DESIGNER
Dick Mitchell
ILLUSTRATOR/ARTIST
Dick Mitchell
CLIENT
SellTrack Inc.
AGENCY
The Richards Group
DESIGN FIRM
Richards Brock Miller Mitchell & Assoc.,
Dallas, TX

878

ART DIRECTOR
Craig Frazier
DESIGNER
Craig Frazier
CLIENT
Legname/Bermann Films
DESIGN FIRM
Frazier Design, San Francisco, CA

879

ART DIRECTOR
Bradford C. Ghormley
DESIGNER
Bradford C. Ghormley
ILLUSTRATOR/ARTIST
Bradford C. Ghormley
CLIENT
The Masonry Company
DESIGN FIRM
Smit Ghormley Sanft, Phoenix, AZ

880

ART DIRECTOR
Terry Taylor
DESIGNER
Terry Taylor
CLIENT
Fort Worth Linotyping Co., Inc.
AGENCY
Dally Advertising, Inc., Fort Worth, TX
PRINTER
Higgins Printing
TYPOGRAPHER
Fort Worth Linotyping Co., Inc.

881

ART DIRECTOR
George D'Amato
PHOTOGRAPHER
Irving Penn
WRITER
Herbert Green
CLIENT
Cosmair/L'Oreal
AGENCY
McCann-Erickson, New York, NY

876

878

877

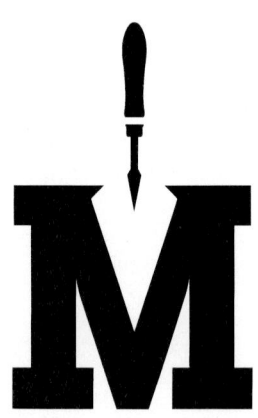

879

880

881

882

883

885

884

882
ART DIRECTOR
Cabell Harris
ILLUSTRATOR/ARTIST
Bill Mayer
WRITER
Ken Hines
CLIENT
Clyde's Restaurant
AGENCY
Lawler Ballard Advertising, Richmond, VA

883
ART DIRECTOR
Joe Duffy
DESIGNER
Joe Duffy
ILLUSTRATOR/ARTIST
Joe Duffy, Lynn Schulte
CLIENT
Donaldson's
DESIGN FIRM
Duffy Design Group, Minneapolis, MN

884
ART DIRECTOR
Anne Baylor Oakley
PHOTOGRAPHER
Greg Slater
WRITER
Mabon Childs
CLIENT
Piedmont Aviation
AGENCY
McKinney & Silver, Raleigh, NC

885
ART DIRECTOR
Denny Gerdeman, Beth Dorsey
DESIGNER
Chris Davis Prater, Scott Stropkay
PHOTOGRAPHER
Sandy Bogart
CLIENT
Hanes Hosiery Manufacturing
DESIGN FIRM
RichardsonSmith, Worthington, OH

886
ART DIRECTOR
Steve Gibbs
DESIGNER
Steve Gibbs
WRITER
Linda Bradford, Carol St. George
CLIENT
VMS Realty
DESIGN FIRM
Gibbs Design, Dallas, TX
PRINTER
Williamson Printing; Classic Color

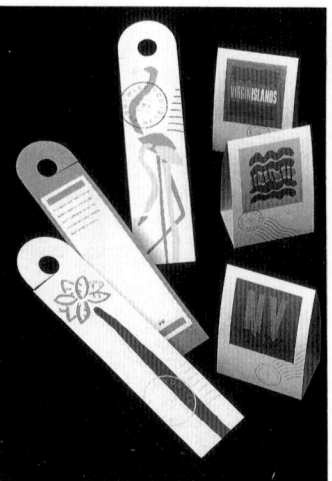
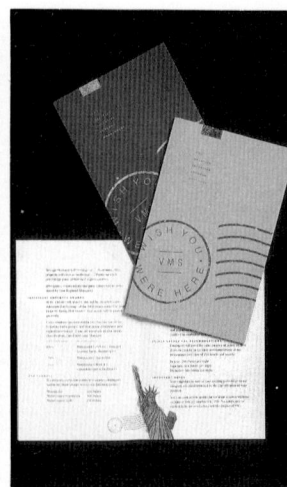

886

887
ART DIRECTOR
Bob Paganucci
DESIGNER
Bob Paganucci, Diana Vasquez, Margaret
Whitchurch
PHOTOGRAPHER
Larry Stein
ILLUSTRATOR/ARTIST
Jean Evans (Calligraphy)
WRITER
Lorraine Pirro
CLIENT
NYNEX
AGENCY
Salpeter Paganucci, Inc., New York, NY
DESIGN FIRM
Salpeter Paganucci, Inc.

887

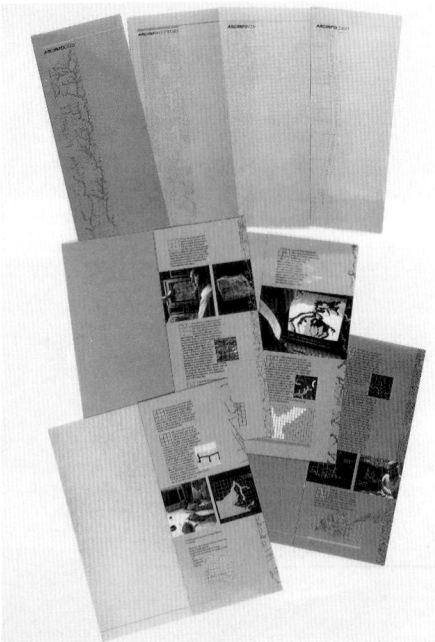

888

888
ART DIRECTOR
Jann Church
DESIGNER
Jann Church
PHOTOGRAPHER
Tibor
ILLUSTRATOR/ARTIST
Shelly Beck
WRITER
Karen Hurlbut
CLIENT
Environmental Systems Research Institute
EDITOR
Jack Dangermond
DIRECTOR
Jann Church
AGENCY
Jann Church Partners Marketing & Graphic
Design, Inc., Newport Beach, CA
DESIGN FIRM
Jann Church Partners Marketing & Graphic
Design, Inc.

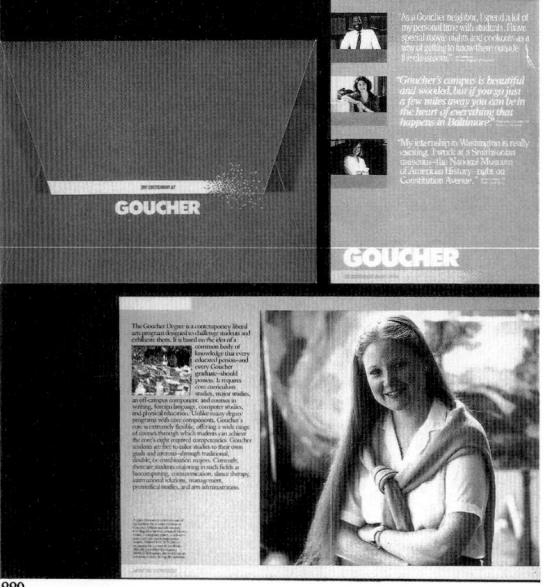

889
ART DIRECTOR
Domenica Genovese
DESIGNER
Domenica Genovese
PHOTOGRAPHER
Kevin Weber, William Denison, Steven
Spartana
WRITER
J. Elizabeth Turner
CLIENT
Goucher College
AGENCY
The North Charles Street Design
Organization, Baltimore, MD

889

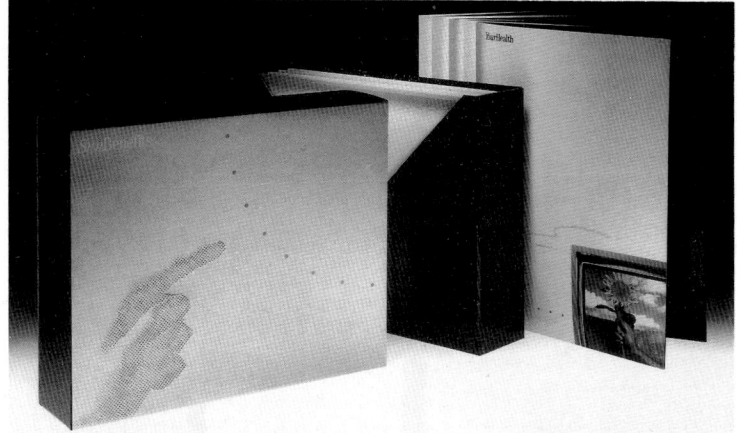

890

ART DIRECTOR
Craig Frazier
DESIGNER
Craig Frazier, Scott Brown
ILLUSTRATOR/ARTIST
Max Seabaugh
CLIENT
Sun Microsystems
DESIGN FIRM
Frazier Design, San Francisco, CA

890

891

ART DIRECTOR
Mark Lichtenstein
DESIGNER
Josanne Nowak
ILLUSTRATOR/ARTIST
Ester Kurti
CLIENT
Automobile Club of Rochester (AAA)
PRODUCER
Michael Tutino
DESIGN FIRM
Lichtenstein Marketing Communications,
Rochester, NY

891

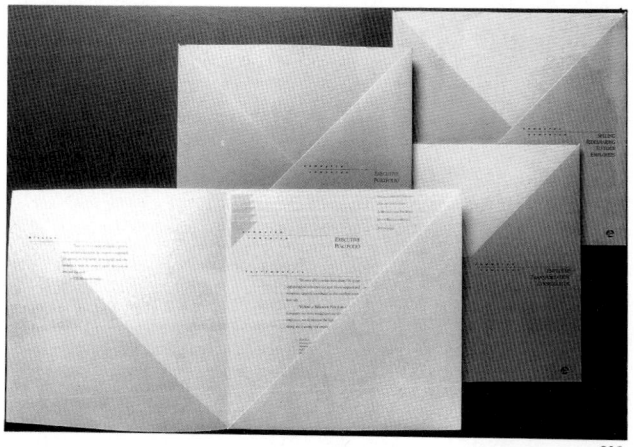

892

ART DIRECTOR
Ken White, Lisa Levin
DESIGNER
Petrula Vrontikis
WRITER
Vicki Thomas
CLIENT
Commuter Computer
DESIGN FIRM
White + Associates, Los Angeles, CA

892

893

ART DIRECTOR
Michael Chikamura
DESIGNER
Michael Chikamura
PHOTOGRAPHER
Don Fogg
WRITER
John Barry, Mark Hall, Mark Jordan, Barbara
Kerns
CLIENT
Sun Microsystems, Inc.
DESIGN FIRM
Michael Chikamura Design, Palo Alto, CA
SET
Scene 2

893

894
DESIGNER
Elaine Shiramizu
ILLUSTRATOR/ARTIST
Bonnie Timmons (Covers), Carol Dufficy
(Medical)
CLIENT
Swedish Medical Center
DESIGN FIRM
Shiramizu Design, Denver, CO

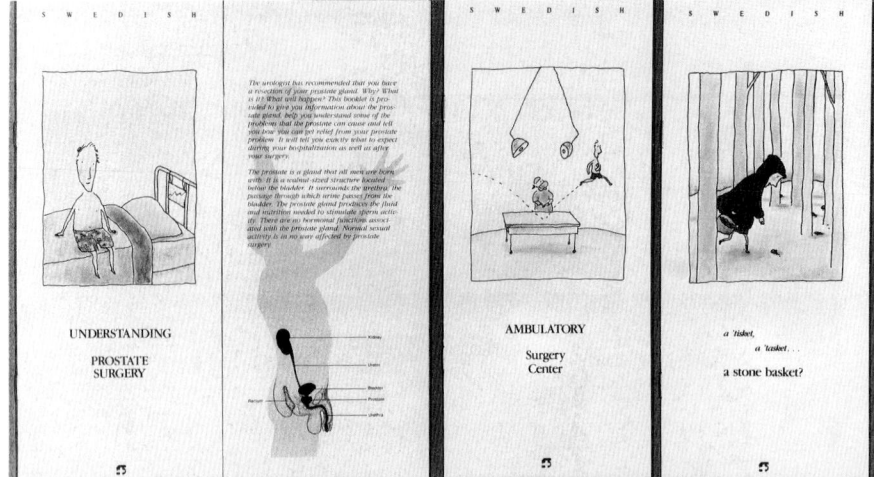

894

895
ART DIRECTOR
Deborah Nichols
DESIGNER
David Pace, Deborah Nichols
PHOTOGRAPHER
House & Garden photographers
WRITER
Alice McGuckin
CLIENT
House & Garden
PUBLISHER
Condé Nast Publications, Inc.
DESIGN FIRM
House & Garden Promotion, New York, NY
CREATIVE DIRECTOR
Sonda Miller

895

896
ART DIRECTOR
Wendy Pressley-Jacobs
DESIGNER
Amy Warner McCarter
PHOTOGRAPHER
Michael Weinstein
WRITER
Hewitt Associates
CLIENT
Baxter Travenol Laboratories Inc.
AGENCY
Hewitt Associates
DESIGN FIRM
Pressley Jacobs Design Inc., Chicago, IL

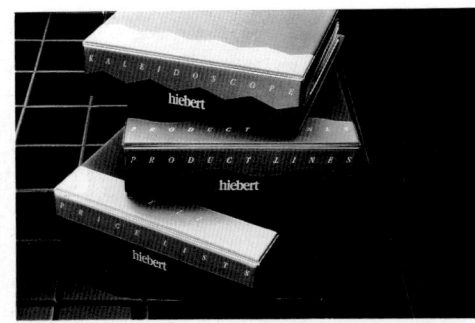

897
ART DIRECTOR
Jeff Fear, Ken White
DESIGNER
Vernon Hahn
WRITER
Jeff Fear
CLIENT
Hiebert, Inc.
DESIGN DIRECTOR
Lisa Levin
DESIGN FIRM
White + Associates, Los Angeles, CA

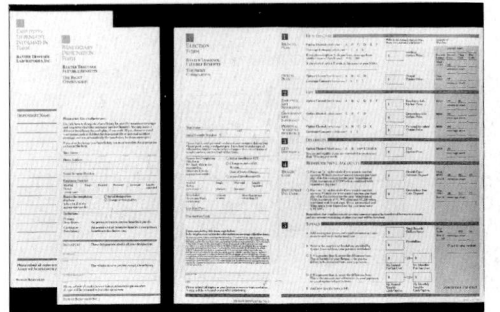

896

897

898

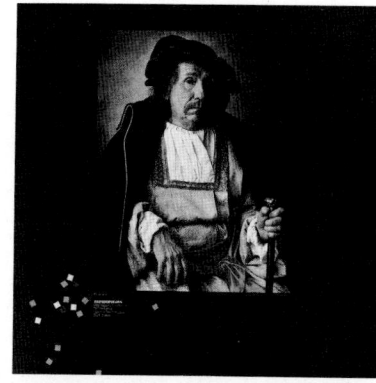

898
DESIGNER
Gary W. Priester
WRITER
Mary E. Carter
CLIENT
Singer Printing, Inc.
AGENCY
The Black Point Group, Novato, CA

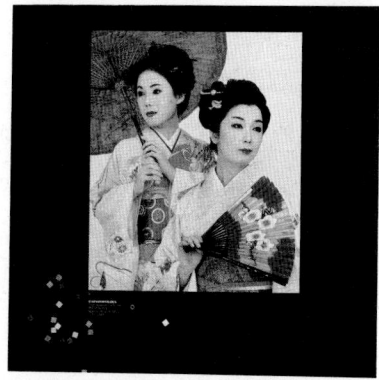

899
ART DIRECTOR
Ken Sausville
DESIGNER
Ken Sausville
PHOTOGRAPHER
Peter Papadopolous
CLIENT
Peter Papadopolous, Inc., New York, NY

900

899

900
ART DIRECTOR
Peter Harrison, Susan Hochbaum
DESIGNER
Susan Hochbaum
ILLUSTRATOR/ARTIST
Jean Tuttle, Susan Hochbaum
CLIENT
Chase Manhattan Bank, Naomi Weiss and
Phil Giaquinto
DESIGN FIRM
Pentagram Design, New York, NY

901

901
ART DIRECTOR
James A. Sebastian
DESIGNER
James A. Sebastian, Michael McGinn,
Francois Asselin
PHOTOGRAPHER
Stock
WRITER
David Konigsberg
CLIENT
Champion International
DESIGN FIRM
Designframe Incorporated, New York, NY

902

ART DIRECTOR
Jack Anderson
DESIGNER
Jack Anderson, Julie Tanagi
ILLUSTRATOR/ARTIST
Hornall Anderson Design Works
WRITER
Hal Hilts
CLIENT
Tradewell Group
DESIGN FIRM
Hornall Anderson Design Works, Seattle, WA

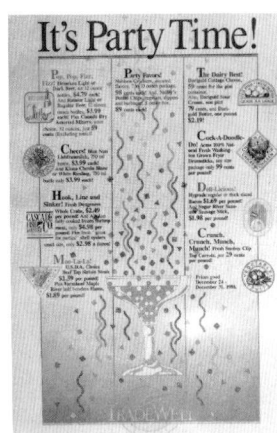

902

903

ART DIRECTOR
Scott Eggers
DESIGNER
Scott Eggers
ILLUSTRATOR/ARTIST
Curtis Asplund
WRITER
Melinda Marcus
CLIENT
Ellis, Inc.
AGENCY
Knape & Knape, Dallas, TX

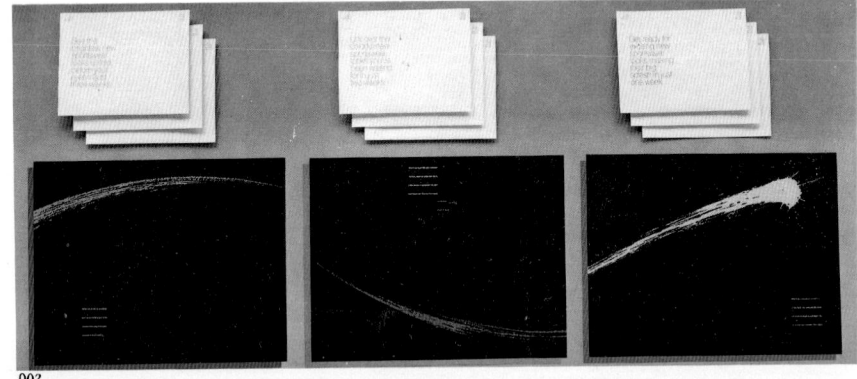

903

904

ART DIRECTOR
Julianna Kovach
DESIGNER
Jim McWilliams
WRITER
Michael G. Zimmerman
CLIENT
MEDNET
AGENCY
Watt, Roop & Co., Cleveland, OH

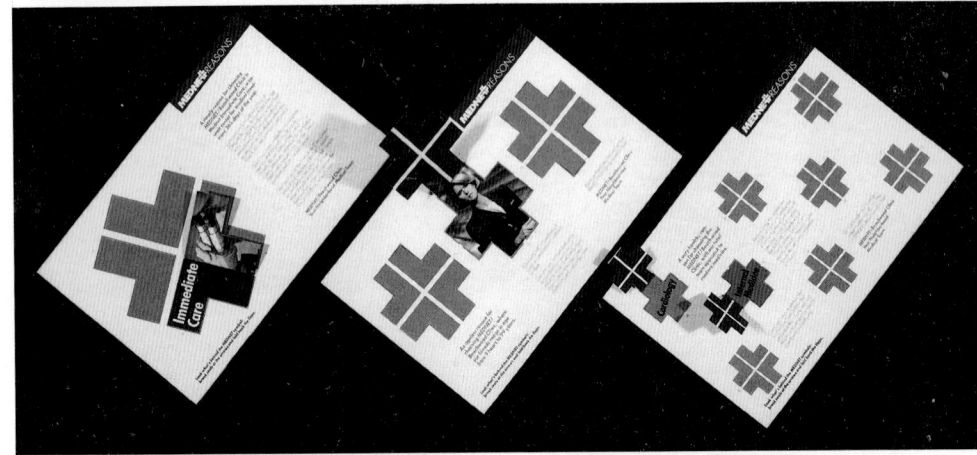

904

905

ART DIRECTOR
Kevin B. Kuester
DESIGNER
Kevin B. Kuester
PHOTOGRAPHER
Arthur Meyerson, Greg Edwards
ILLUSTRATOR/ARTIST
Elwood Smith, Mischa Richter, Henry Martin
WRITER
Bill Wells
CLIENT
Federal Express Corporation
EDITOR
Joan McPeak
DESIGN FIRM
Madsen and Kuester, Inc., Minneapolis, MN

905

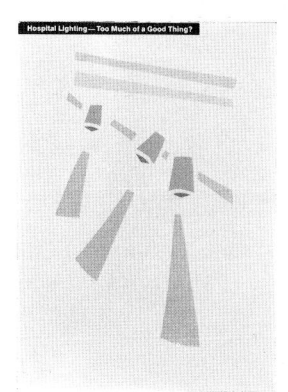

906

ART DIRECTOR
Doug Akagi
DESIGNER
Doug Akagi, Sharrie Brooks
ILLUSTRATOR/ARTIST
Sharrie Brooks, Gwen Terpstra
CLIENT
Stone, Marraccini and Patterson
DESIGN FIRM
Akagi Design, San Francisco, CA

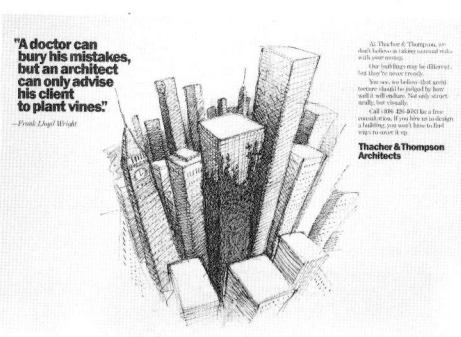
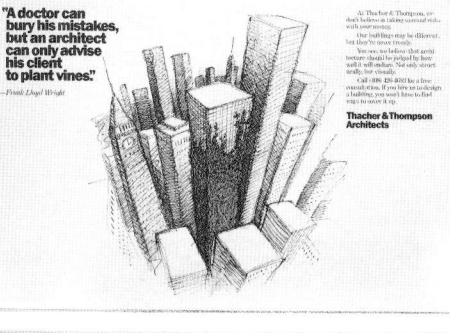
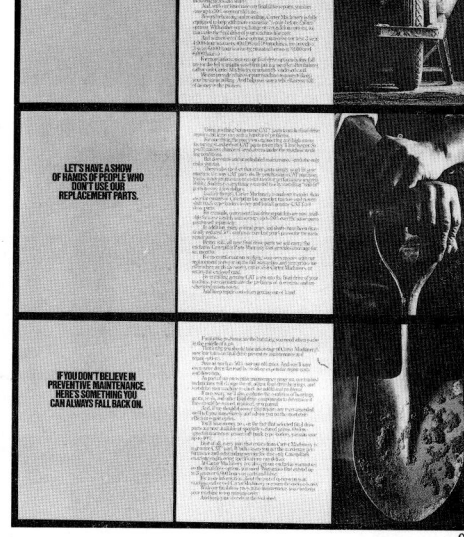

908

907

907

ART DIRECTOR
Sue Crolick
DESIGNER
Sue Crolick
ILLUSTRATOR/ARTIST
Stan Olson, Mike Reed
WRITER
Gary LaMaster
CLIENT
Thacher & Thompson, Architects
AGENCY
Sue Crolick Advertising & Design,
Minneapolis, MN
KEYLINER
Nancy Johnson

908

ART DIRECTOR
Cabell Harris
PHOTOGRAPHER
I.B.I.D.
WRITER
Joel Jamison
CLIENT
Carter Machinery Company
AGENCY
Lawler Ballard Advertising, Richmond, VA

909

909

ART DIRECTOR
Art Lofgreen
DESIGNER
Art Lofgreen
PHOTOGRAPHER
Rick Rusing
WRITER
Leslie Johnson
CLIENT
Rusing Photography
DESIGN FIRM
Parker, Johnson, Lofgreen, Mesa, AZ

910
ART DIRECTOR
David Hadley
DESIGNER
David Hadley
ILLUSTRATOR/ARTIST
Seymour Chwast
WRITER
Mary Beaudoin
CLIENT
Minneapolis Star and Tribune, Minneapolis,
MN

911
ART DIRECTOR
Nancy Rice, Nick Rice
DESIGNER
Nancy Rice, Nick Rice
WRITER
Jim Newcombe
CLIENT
Lamination Concepts
AGENCY
Rice & Rice Advertising Inc., Minneapolis,
MN

910

911

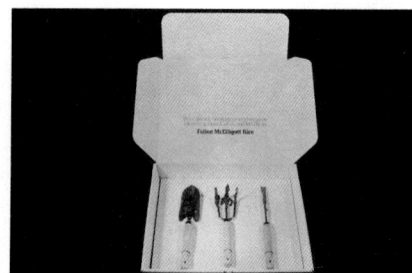

912
ART DIRECTOR
Michael Fazende
WRITER
John Stingley
CLIENT
Fallon McElligott
AGENCY
Fallon McElligott, Minneapolis, MN

912

913
ART DIRECTOR
Frank Schulwolf
PHOTOGRAPHER
George Schiavone
ILLUSTRATOR/ARTIST
Paul Salmon, Ted Lodigensky, John Mattos,
Frank Wooton, Robert Taylor
WRITER
Arthur Low
CLIENT
Aviation Sales Company, Inc.
AGENCY
Susan Gilbert & Company, Inc., Coral
Gables, FL
PRINTER
Colour Group, Southeastern Printing

913

914

915

914

914
ART DIRECTOR
Craig Frazier, Scott Brown
DESIGNER
Craig Frazier, Scott Brown
WRITER
Craig Frazier, Scott Brown
CLIENT
Frazier Design
DESIGN FIRM
Frazier Design, San Francisco, CA

915
CLIENT
Keystone Camera Corporation
DESIGN FIRM
Ronald Emmerling Design Inc., Montclair,
NJ

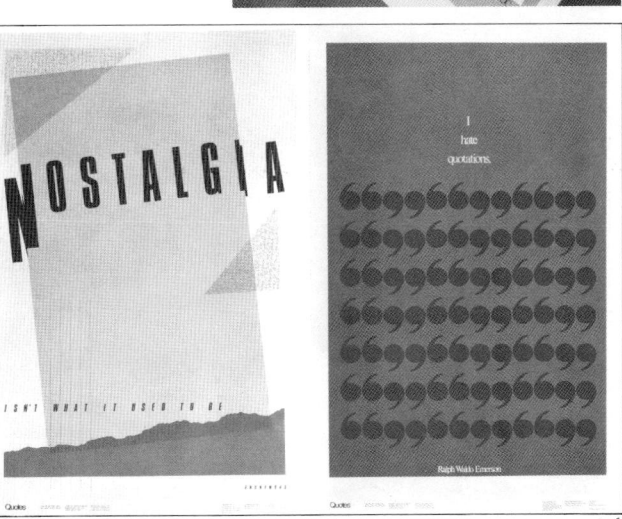

916

917

916
ART DIRECTOR
Dan Stewart, Karen Abney
DESIGNER
Karen Abney, Dan Stewart
ILLUSTRATOR/ARTIST
Garry Kaulitz, Silkscreen Artist
CLIENT
Stewart Winner, Inc.
DESIGN FIRM
Stewart Winner, Inc., Louisville, KY

917
ART DIRECTOR
Michael Fazende
PHOTOGRAPHER
Dave Jordano
WRITER
Mike Lescarbeau
CLIENT
Vander Zanden, Inc.
AGENCY
Fallon McElligott, Minneapolis, MN

918

ART DIRECTOR
Bob Defrin
DESIGNER
Bob Defrin
ILLUSTRATOR/ARTIST
Michael Paraskevas
CLIENT
Atlantic Records, New York, NY

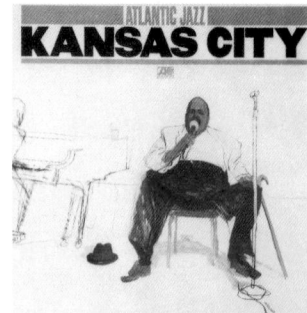

918

919

ART DIRECTOR
Tamotsu Yagi
DESIGNER
Tamotsu Yagi
DESIGN FIRM
Esprit Graphic Design Studio, San Francisco,
CA

920

ART DIRECTOR
Tamotsu Yagi
DESIGNER
Tamotsu Yagi
DESIGN FIRM
Esprit Graphic Design Studio, San Francisco,
CA

919

920

921

ART DIRECTOR
Dorris Kennedy, Michael Landon
DESIGNER
Michael Landon, John Norman
PHOTOGRAPHER
Tomio Hashimoto
ILLUSTRATOR/ARTIST
John Norman
CLIENT
Southland Corporation
DESIGN FIRM
Landon Design, Inc., Dallas, TX

921

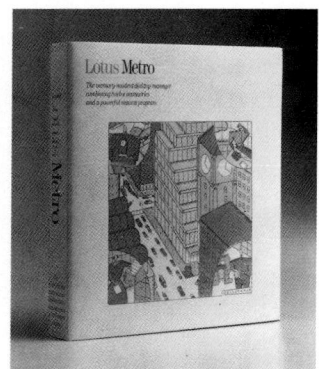

922

ART DIRECTOR
Tom Hughes, George Martin
DESIGNER
Tom Hughes, Celia Miller, Carolina Sterling,
Gary Gibson, Nancy Noel, George Martin
ILLUSTRATOR/ARTIST
Lonni Sue Johnson, Phillipe Weisbecker,
Katherine Mahoney
CLIENT
Lotus Development Corp.
DESIGN FIRM
Lotus Creative Development, Cambridge, MA

923

ART DIRECTOR
Doug Crozier
ILLUSTRATOR/ARTIST
Doug Crozier
WRITER
Bob McQueen
CLIENT
Farr Better Feeds (Div. of W.R. Grace & Co.)
AGENCY
Howard, Merrell & Partners, Inc., Raleigh,
NC

924

ART DIRECTOR
Charles Spencer Anderson
DESIGNER
Charles Spencer Anderson
ILLUSTRATOR/ARTIST
Charles Spencer Anderson, Lynn Schulte
CLIENT
Avant Hair Products
DESIGN FIRM
Duffy Design Group, Minneapolis, MN

923

924

925

ART DIRECTOR
Primo Angeli
DESIGNER
Lew Karchin
ILLUSTRATOR/ARTIST
Mark Jones
CLIENT
National Oats Co., Inc.
DESIGN FIRM
Primo Angeli Inc., San Francisco, CA

925

926

ART DIRECTOR
Nicolas Sidjakov, Jerry Berman
DESIGNER
Jackie Foshaug, Courtney Reeser
PHOTOGRAPHER
Michael LaMotte, Henrik Kam
CLIENT
Berkley and Company
DESIGN FIRM
Sidjakov Berman Gomez & Partners, San
Francisco, CA

926

927

ART DIRECTOR
Lauren Smith McCombs
ILLUSTRATOR/ARTIST
Jeffery Mangiat
CLIENT
Burger King Corporation
AGENCY
Selling Solutions, Inc., Atlanta, GA
PRINTER
Waldorf Corporation
CREATIVE DIRECTOR
William L. Paullin, III

928

ART DIRECTOR
Tamila Grogan
ILLUSTRATOR/ARTIST
B.B. Sams
CLIENT
Burger King Corporation
AGENCY
One Up Studio, Atlanta, GA
PRINTER
Waldorf Corporation
CREATIVE DIRECTOR
William L. Paullin, III

927

928

929

DESIGN DIRECTOR
Jacqueline Ghosin
DESIGNER
Jacqueline Ghosin
PHOTOGRAPHER
Sven-Olof Linblad
CLIENT
Integon Corporation, Arthur E. Hall
DESIGN FIRM
S&O Consultants Inc., San Francisco, CA
PRINTER
Graphic Arts of Marin
TYPE
Eurotype
CREATIVE DIRECTOR
David Canaan

929

930

ART DIRECTOR
Robert Patrick DeVito
DESIGNER
Eric Jon Read
CLIENT
Memtek Products
DESIGN FIRM
Axion Design Inc., San Anselmo, CA

930

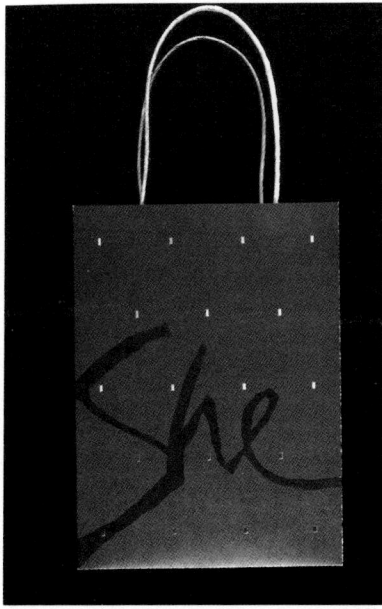

931

ART DIRECTOR
Dan Stewart
DESIGNER
Karen Abney
CLIENT
SHE, Pat Burkhart Schilling
DESIGN FIRM
Stewart Winner, Inc., Louisville, KY

931

932

ART DIRECTOR
Douglas May, Lynn Bernick
DESIGNER
Douglas May, Lynn Bernick
ILLUSTRATOR/ARTIST
Laura Smith
WRITER
Bill Pierce
CLIENT
Imagination Incorporated
DESIGN FIRM
Douglas May Design, Dallas, TX

933

ART DIRECTOR
Ann Clementino
DESIGNER
Ann Clementino
PHOTOGRAPHER
Kasia Gruda, Astoria, NY
WRITER
Ellie MacDougall
CLIENT
Kasia Gruda

932

933

934

ART DIRECTOR
Martin Solomon
DESIGNER
Martin Solomon, Alexa Nosal
ILLUSTRATOR/ARTIST
Martin Solomon, Alexa Nosal
WRITER
Martin Solomon
CLIENT
Royal Composing Room
DESIGN FIRM
Royal Composing Room, New York, NY

934

935

ART DIRECTOR
Charles Spencer Anderson
DESIGNER
Charles Spencer Anderson, Sara Ledgard
ILLUSTRATOR/ARTIST
Charles Spencer Anderson, Joe Duffy, Lynn Schulte
WRITER
Chuck Carlson
CLIENT
First Bank of Minneapolis
DESIGN FIRM
Duffy Design Group, Minneapolis, MN

935

936

ART DIRECTOR
Charles Spencer Anderson
DESIGNER
Charles Spencer Anderson
ILLUSTRATOR/ARTIST
Charles Spencer Anderson
CLIENT
Fresh Force Youth Volunteer Group
DESIGN FIRM
Duffy Design Group, Minneapolis, MN

937

ART DIRECTOR
Charles Spencer Anderson
DESIGNER
Charles Spencer Anderson
ILLUSTRATOR/ARTIST
Charles Spencer Anderson, Lynn Schulte
CLIENT
Avant Hair Products
DESIGN FIRM
Duffy Design Group, Minneapolis, MN

 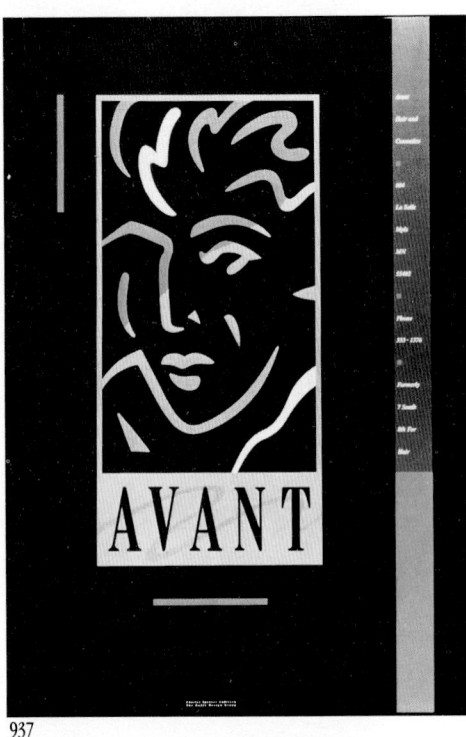

936   937

938

ART DIRECTOR
Stan Gellman
DESIGNER
Stan Gellman
ILLUSTRATOR/ARTIST
Professor Shozo Sato
WRITER
Jim Gobberdiel
CLIENT
University of Illinois Foundation
EDITOR
Jim Gobberdiel
PUBLISHER
University of Illinois Foundation
AGENCY
Stan Gellman Graphic Design, Inc., St. Louis, MO
DESIGN FIRM
Stan Gellman Graphic Design, Inc.

938

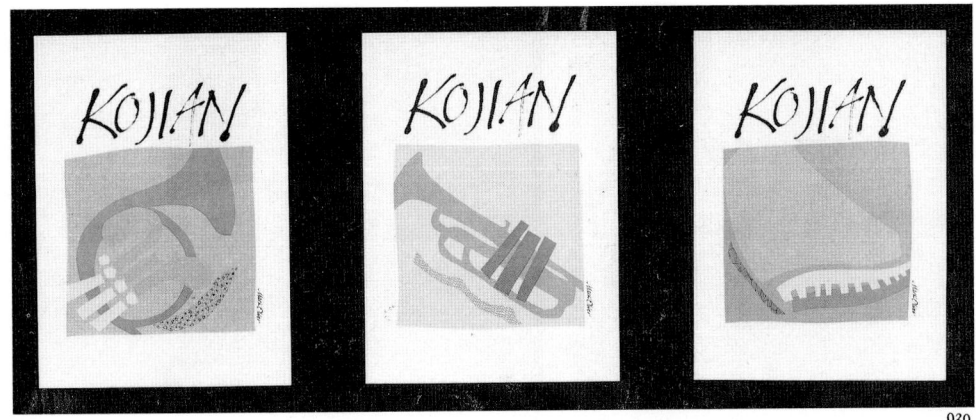

939

ART DIRECTOR
Mark Oliver
DESIGNER
Mark Oliver
ILLUSTRATOR/ARTIST
Mark Oliver
WRITER
Mark Oliver
CLIENT
Santa Barbara Symphony
AGENCY
Mark Oliver, Inc., Santa Barbara, CA

939

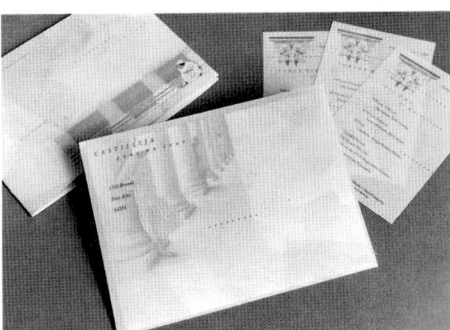

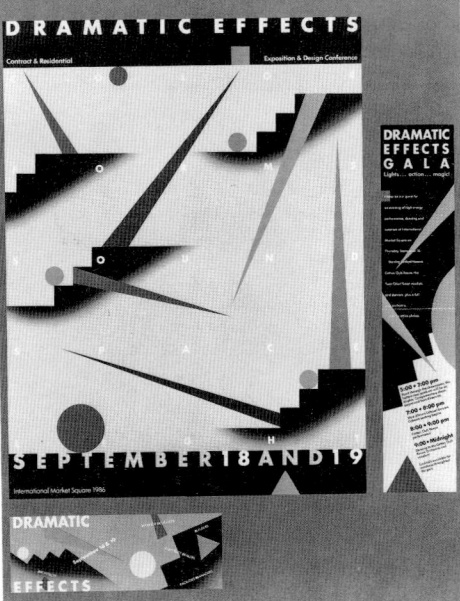

940

DESIGNER
Tracy Evan Moon
PHOTOGRAPHER
Jennifer Abbe
ILLUSTRATOR/ARTIST
Tracy Evan Moon
CLIENT
Castilleja School
DIRECTOR
Susan Collins, Janna Shennan
DESIGN FIRM
S&O Consultants Inc., San Francisco, CA
PRINTER
Cannon Press
TYPE
ReproType
CREATIVE DIRECTOR
David Canaan

941

ART DIRECTOR
Jim Cordaro
DESIGNER
William Homan
CLIENT
International Market Square
DESIGN FIRM
Rubin Cordaro Design, Minneapolis, MN
PRINTER
Bolger Publications
TYPOGRAPHER
P&H Photo Composition

940

941

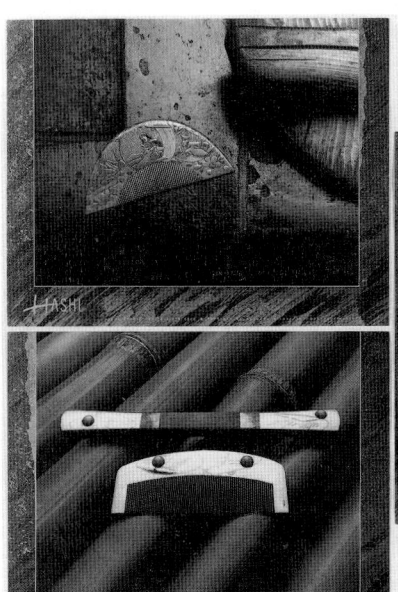

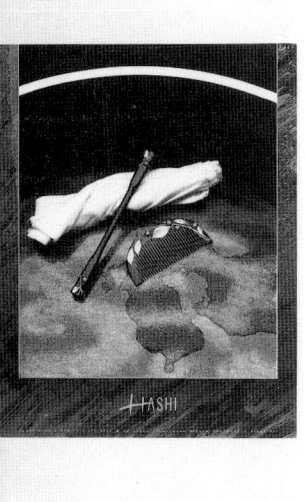

942

ART DIRECTOR
Hashi
DESIGNER
Coco Masuda, Hashi
PHOTOGRAPHER
Hashi
CLIENT
Hashi Studio, Inc.
DESIGN FIRM
Studio Cygnus, New York, NY

942

943
ART DIRECTOR
Richard Poulin
DESIGNER
Richard Poulin
CLIENT
United Nations Plaza Hotel
DESIGN FIRM
Rudolph de Harak & Associates, Inc., New York, NY

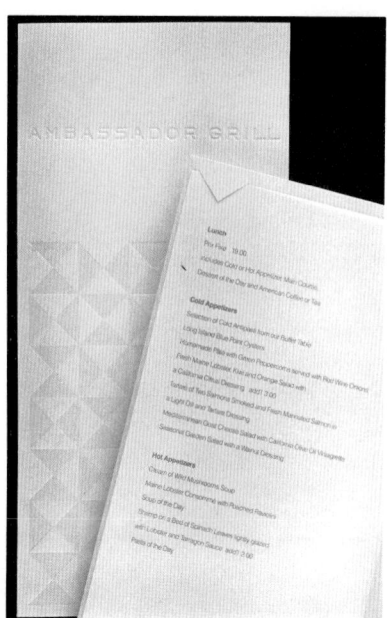

943

944
ART DIRECTOR
Louis Charpentier, Claude A. Garneau
ILLUSTRATOR/ARTIST
Louis Charpentier, Claude A. Garneau
CLIENT
Sorena
DESIGN FIRM
Charpentier/Garneau, Montreal, Canada

944

945
ART DIRECTOR
Forrest & Valerie Richardson
DESIGNER
Forrest & Valerie Richardson, Rosemary Connelly
WRITER
Forrest & Valerie Richardson
CLIENT
DigiType Typographers
DESIGN FIRM
Richardson or Richardson, Phoenix, AZ

946
ART DIRECTOR
Paul Haslip
DESIGNER
Paul Haslip
PHOTOGRAPHER
Steven Evans
ILLUSTRATOR/ARTIST
Rene Zamic
WRITER
David Mills
CLIENT
Daniels Equities/The Dakota
DIRECTOR
David Mills
AGENCY
Elias Marketing & Communications, Toronto, Canada

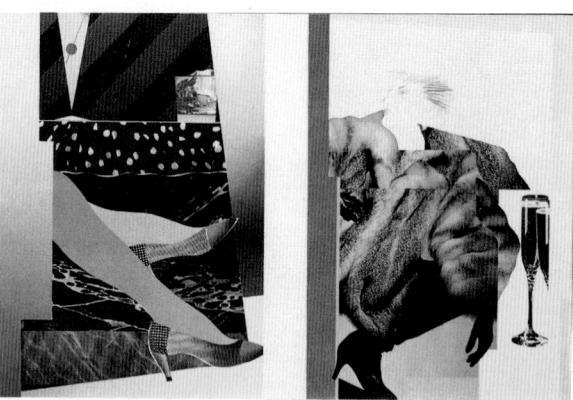

945   946

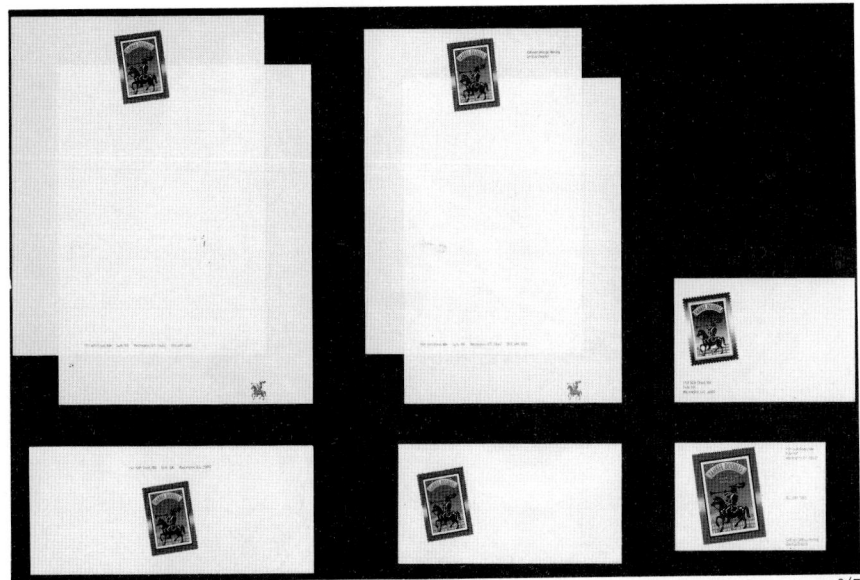

947

ART DIRECTOR
Kathleen Wilmes Herring
DESIGNER
Kathleen Wilmes Herring
ILLUSTRATOR/ARTIST
Barry Zaid
WRITER
Thomas S. Simmons
CLIENT
Yankee Doodles
PRODUCER
Mark H. Lakefish
DESIGN FIRM
Yankee Doodles, Washington, DC
PRINTER
Westland Printers, Inc.

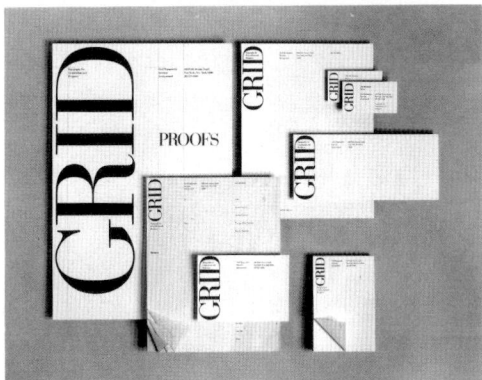

948

DESIGNER
Kenichi Nishiwaki
ILLUSTRATOR/ARTIST
Kenichi Nishiwaki, Mitsukoshi Corporate Art Department
CLIENT
Mitsukoshi Department Stores
DESIGN DIRECTOR
Jacqueline Ghosin
PROJECT DIRECTOR
James Shennan
DESIGN FIRM
S&O Consultants Inc., San Francisco, CA
CREATIVE DIRECTOR
David Canaan
ACCOUNT MANAGER
Hisao Ishiwata

949

ART DIRECTOR
Richard Rogers
DESIGNER
Richard Rogers, David Scott
ILLUSTRATOR/ARTIST
Robert Rosenberg
CLIENT
Grid Typographic Services Incorporated
DESIGN FIRM
Richard Rogers Inc., New York, NY

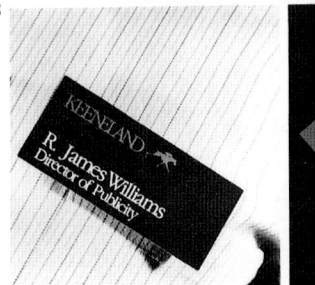

950

ART DIRECTOR
Dan Stewart
DESIGNER
Dan Stewart, Steve Hutchison
ILLUSTRATOR/ARTIST
Steve Hutchison
CLIENT
Keeneland Association
DIR. OF PUBLICITY
Jim Williams
DESIGN FIRM
Stewart Winner, Inc., Louisville, KY

BOOKS & JACKETS:

Book: general trade
special trade
juvenile
text or reference
series
Jacket: single
series

*"Buy me some peanuts and Cracker Jack
I don't care if I never come back."*

*In 1893, F. W. Rueckheim, a young German
immigrant, sold a new popcorn, peanut and
molasses candy at Chicago's World
Columbian Exposition visited by twenty-one
million people from around the world. It was
the forerunner of what would become Cracker
Jack. Three years later Rueckheim combined a
new manufacturing process and two words
just entering popular usage and launched
Cracker Jack nationwide. In 1908 it earned
the candy hall-of-fame status in "Take Me Out
To The Ballgame" and in 1912 a key
feature—the prize in every box—was added.*

*Sailor Jack and his dog stepped onto the box
in 1919. The little boy was modeled on
Rueckheim's grandson Robert, who died of
pneumonia soon after the new box appeared.
He is buried in St. Henry's cemetery, near
Chicago, under a headstone carving of him in
his sailor suit.*

951
ART DIRECTOR
Susan Mitchell
DESIGNER
Susan Mitchell
WRITER
Inea Bushnaq
EDITOR
Wendy Wolf
PUBLISHER
Pantheon Books, New York, NY

952
ART DIRECTOR
Susan Mitchell
DESIGNER
Susan Mitchell
PHOTOGRAPHER
Stephen Deutch, Archie Lieberman, Marc Pokempner, Arthur Shay, Richard Younker
WRITER
Studs Terkel
EDITOR
André Schiffrin
PUBLISHER
Pantheon Books, New York, NY

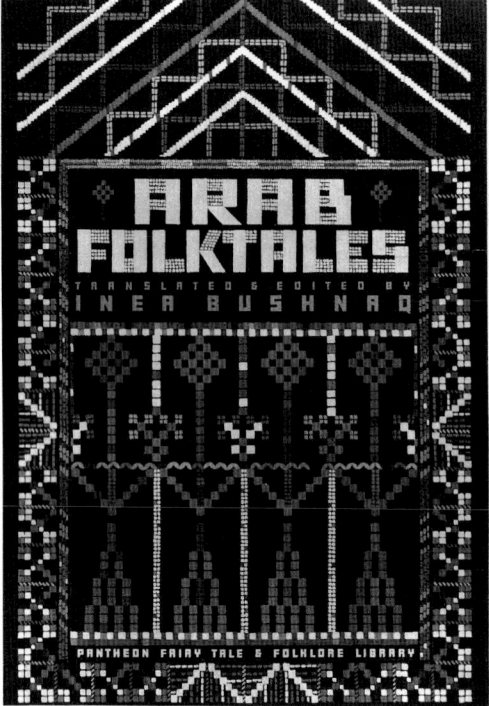

951

952

953
ART DIRECTOR
Susan Mitchell
DESIGNER
Susan Mitchell
WRITER
Elena Poniatowska
EDITOR
Tom Engelhardt
PUBLISHER
Pantheon Books, New York, NY

953

954

954
DESIGNER
Karen M. Bloom
CLIENT
Westvaco Corporation, New York, NY
PRODUCER
Anagraphics, Inc.
PRINTER
Meriden-Stinehour Press
TYPOGRAPHER
Finn Typographic
BINDER
Zahrndt, Inc.

955

ART DIRECTOR
Pat Samata
DESIGNER
Pat Samata
PHOTOGRAPHER
Jean Moss
ILLUSTRATOR/ARTIST
Susan Mechnig
WRITER
Nancy Bishop
CLIENT
A.T. Kearney Management Consultants
DESIGN FIRM
Samata Associates, Dundee, IL

955

956

DESIGNER
Tyler Smith
PHOTOGRAPHER
Clint Clemens
WRITER
Juan Jose Arreola (foreword)
CLIENT
Sergio Bustamante
DESIGN FIRM
Tyler Smith Art Direction, Inc., Providence,
RI

956

957

ART DIRECTOR
Ken Sansone
DESIGNER
George Corsillo
WRITER
Stephen C. Wagner, Michael Closen
EDITOR
Brandt Aymar
PUBLISHER
Crown Publishers, Inc., New York, NY

957

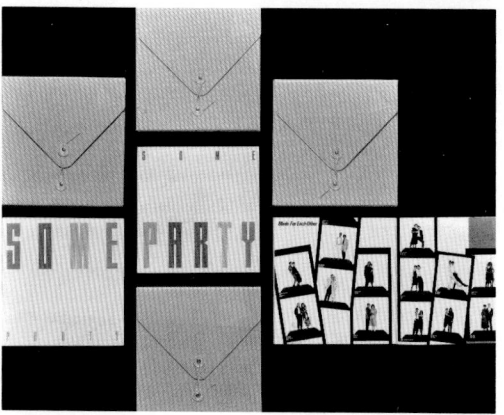

958

ART DIRECTOR
Tamotsu Yagi
DESIGNER
Hiroshi Serizawa
PHOTOGRAPHER
Roberto Carra
WRITER
Beth LaDove
DESIGN FIRM
Esprit Graphic Design Studio, San Francisco,
CA

958

959
ART DIRECTOR
Patrick Dooley
DESIGNER
Patrick Dooley
PHOTOGRAPHER
Julia Margaret Cameron
WRITER
Mike Weaver
CLIENT
The J. Paul Getty Museum
EDITOR
Andrea Belloli
PUBLISHER
The J. Paul Getty Museum
PRODUCER
Karen Schmidt
DESIGN FIRM
The J. Paul Getty Museum Design
Department, Malibu, CA
PUBLICATION
Whisper of the Muse: The Overstone Album
and Other Photographs by Julia Margaret
Cameron

960
ART DIRECTOR
Louise Fili
DESIGNER
Art Speigelman, Louise Fili
ILLUSTRATOR/ARTIST
Art Speigelman
WRITER
Art Speigelman
PUBLISHER
Pantheon Books, New York, NY

961
ART DIRECTOR
Gael Towey
DESIGNER
Gael Towey
PHOTOGRAPHER
Michael Skott
WRITER
Lois Dwan
CLIENT
Los Angeles County Museum
EDITOR
Carolyn Hart
DIRECTOR
Carol Southern
PUBLISHER
Clarkson N. Potter, Inc.Crown Publishers,
Inc.
DESIGN FIRM
Clarkson N. Potter in-house, New York, NY

962
ART DIRECTOR
Samuel N. Antupit
DESIGNER
Judith Michael
PHOTOGRAPHER
Andreas Feininger
WRITER
Andreas Feininger
EDITOR
Eric Himmel
DIRECTOR
Robert Morton
PUBLISHER
Harry N. Abrams, Inc., New York, NY

963
ART DIRECTOR
Charles Spencer Anderson, Joe Duffy
DESIGNER
Charles Spencer Anderson, Joe Duffy
WRITER
Chuck Carlson
CLIENT
French Paper Company
DESIGN FIRM
Duffy Design Group, Minneapolis, MN

959

960

961

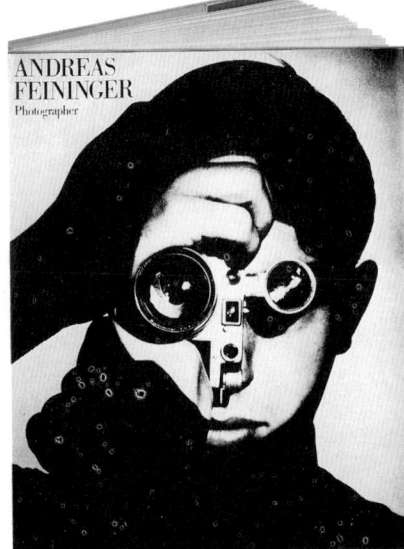

962

963

964

965

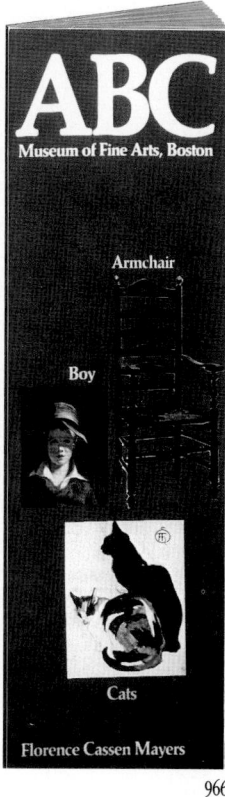

966

964
ART DIRECTOR
Charles Spencer Anderson
DESIGNER
Charles Spencer Anderson
ILLUSTRATOR/ARTIST
Charles Spencer Anderson
CLIENT
Fresh Force Youth Volunteer Group
DESIGN FIRM
Duffy Design Group, Minneapolis, MN

965
ART DIRECTOR
Florence Cassen Mayers
DESIGNER
Florence Cassen Mayers
EDITOR
Sheila Franklin
PUBLISHER
Harry N. Abrams, Inc., New York, NY

966
ART DIRECTOR
Florence Cassen Mayers
DESIGNER
Florence Cassen Mayers
EDITOR
Sheila Franklin
PUBLISHER
Harry N. Abrams, Inc., New York, NY

967
ART DIRECTOR
Paula Meyers
DESIGNER
Keith J. McPherson
PHOTOGRAPHER
George Kamper
CLIENT
Business Publications, Inc.
PUBLISHER
Richard D. Irwin, Inc., Homewood, IL

967

968

ART DIRECTOR
Charles Spencer Anderson
DESIGNER
Charles Spencer Anderson
WRITER
Pamela Espeland
CLIENT
Wenger Corporation
DESIGN FIRM
Duffy Design Group, Minneapolis, MN

969

ART DIRECTOR
Barbara Schneider
DESIGNER
Kathleen Cunningham
ILLUSTRATOR/ARTIST
Candace Haught
WRITER
Robert A. Divine, T.H. Breen, George M.
Fredrickson, R. Hal Williams
EDITOR
Barbara Muller, Louise Howe, Ann-Marie
Buesing
PUBLISHER
Scott, Foresman and Company, Glenview, IL

968

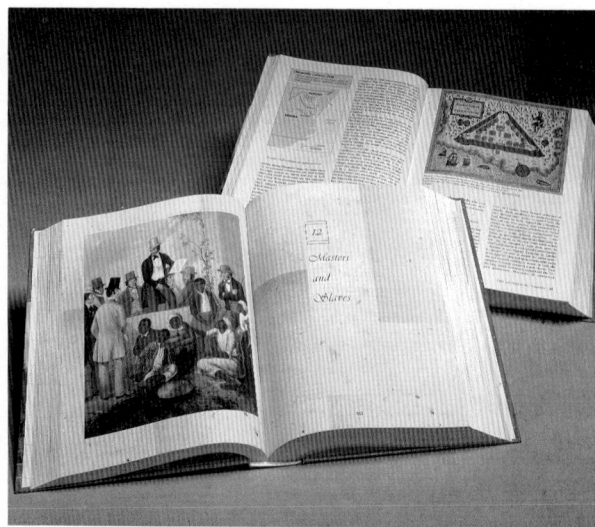

969

970

ART DIRECTOR
Barbara S. Olejniczak, Chip MacCormack
DESIGNER
Barbara S. Olejniczak, Chip MacCormack
PHOTOGRAPHER
Tom Warren, Ed Parinello,
Noel Allum
CLIENT
Sotheby's
DESIGN FIRM
Sotheby's In-house Creative Department, New
York, NY

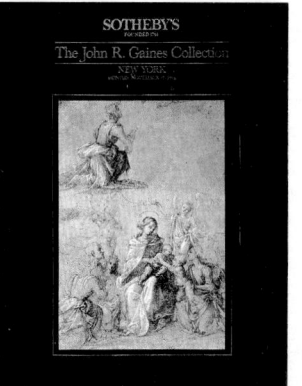

970

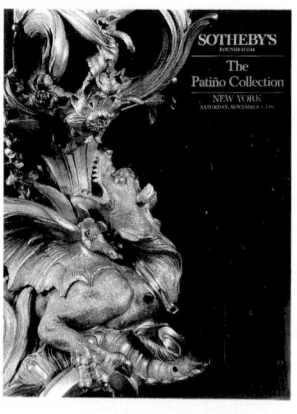

971

ART DIRECTOR
Katie Brown
DESIGNER
Myland McRevey
ILLUSTRATOR/ARTIST
Renee Graef, Nancy Niles, Chris Payne, Rob
Grace
EDITOR
Jeanne Thieme
PUBLISHER
Pleasant Company, Madison, WI
CREATIVE DIRECTOR
Pleasant T. Rowland

971

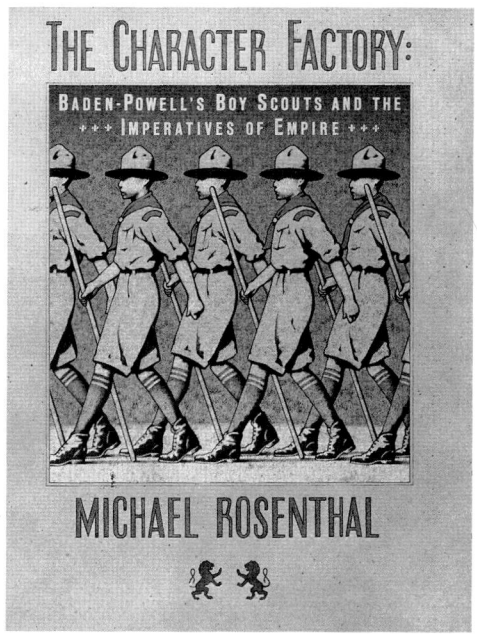

972

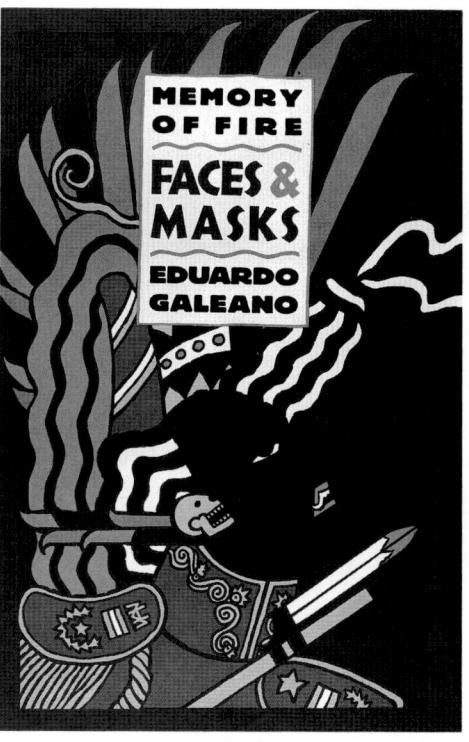

972

ART DIRECTOR
Joseph Montebello
DESIGNER
Carin Goldberg
PUBLISHER
Harper & Row, New York, NY

973

ART DIRECTOR
Louise Fili
DESIGNER
Phil Huling
973 **ILLUSTRATOR/ARTIST**
Phil Huling
WRITER
Michael Rosenthal
EDITOR
Wendy Wolf
PUBLISHER
Pantheon Books, New York, NY

974

ART DIRECTOR
Joseph Montebello
DESIGNER
Lynn Dreese Breslin
CLIENT
Harper & Row, New York, NY

975

ART DIRECTOR
Louise Fili
DESIGNER
Louise Fili
ILLUSTRATOR/ARTIST
John Martinez
WRITER
Eduardo Galeano
EDITOR
Tom Engelhardt
PUBLISHER
Pantheon Books, New York, NY

974

975

976
ART DIRECTOR
Louise Fili
DESIGNER
John Craig
ILLUSTRATOR/ARTIST
John Craig
EDITOR
Wendy Wolf
PUBLISHER
Pantheon Books, New York, NY

977
ART DIRECTOR
Sara Eisenman
DESIGNER
Fred Marcellino
ILLUSTRATOR/ARTIST
Fred Marcellino
WRITER
David Leavitt
EDITOR
Bobbie Bristol
PUBLISHER
Alfred A. Knopf, New York, NY

978
ART DIRECTOR
Carin Goldberg
DESIGNER
Carin Goldberg
ILLUSTRATOR/ARTIST
Barbara Nessim
CLIENT
Simon & Schuster
PUBLISHER
Simon & Schuster
DESIGN FIRM
Nessim & Associates, New York, NY

979
ART DIRECTOR
Sara Eisenman
DESIGNER
Sara Eisenman
ILLUSTRATOR/ARTIST
Douglas Fraser
WRITER
Gabriel Garcia Marquez
EDITOR
Ashbel Green
PUBLISHER
Alfred A. Knopf, New York, NY

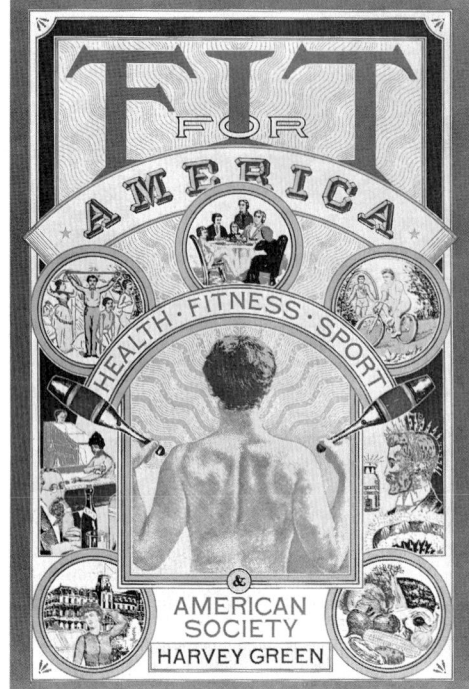

976

977

978

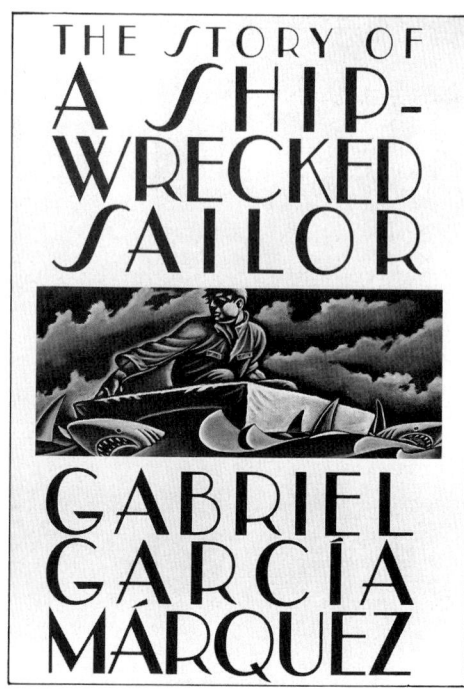

979

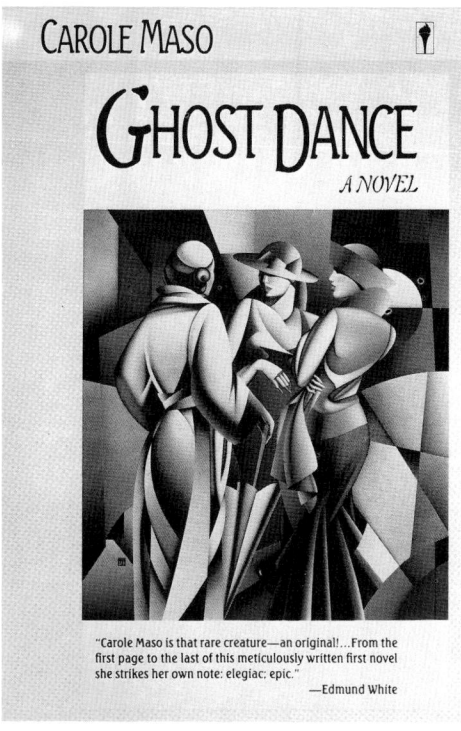

980

981

982

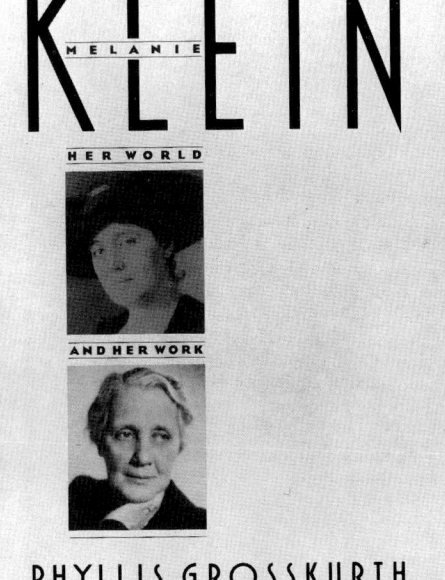

983

980

ART DIRECTOR
Joseph Montebello
DESIGNER
Gloria Adelson
ILLUSTRATOR/ARTIST
John Jinks
PUBLISHER
Harper & Row, New York, NY

981

ART DIRECTOR
Judith Loeser
DESIGNER
Lorraine Louie
ILLUSTRATOR/ARTIST
Lorraine Louie
EDITOR
Gordon Lish
PUBLISHER
Vintage Books
DESIGN FIRM
Lorraine Louie Design, New York, NY

982

ART DIRECTOR
Joseph Montebello
DESIGNER
Gloria Adelson
ILLUSTRATOR/ARTIST
Dan Reed
PUBLISHER
Harper & Row, New York, NY

983

ART DIRECTOR
Sara Eisenman
DESIGNER
Carin Goldberg
WRITER
Phyllis Grosskurth
EDITOR
Lee Goerner
PUBLISHER
Alfred A. Knopf, New York, NY

984
ART DIRECTOR
Carin Goldberg
DESIGNER
Carin Goldberg
ILLUSTRATOR/ARTIST
Barbara Nessim
CLIENT
Harper & Row
PUBLISHER
Harper & Row
DESIGN FIRM
Nessim & Associates, New York, NY

985
ART DIRECTOR
Judith Loeser
DESIGNER
Daniel Pelavin
ILLUSTRATOR/ARTIST
Daniel Pelavin, New York, NY
PUBLISHER
Vintage Books

986
ART DIRECTOR
Louise Fili
DESIGNER
Louise Fili
WRITER
Elena Poniatowska
EDITOR
Tom Engelhardt
PUBLISHER
Pantheon Books, New York, NY

987
ART DIRECTOR
Louise Fili
DESIGNER
Nancy Brescia
ILLUSTRATOR/ARTIST
David Johnson
PUBLISHER
Pantheon Books, New York, NY

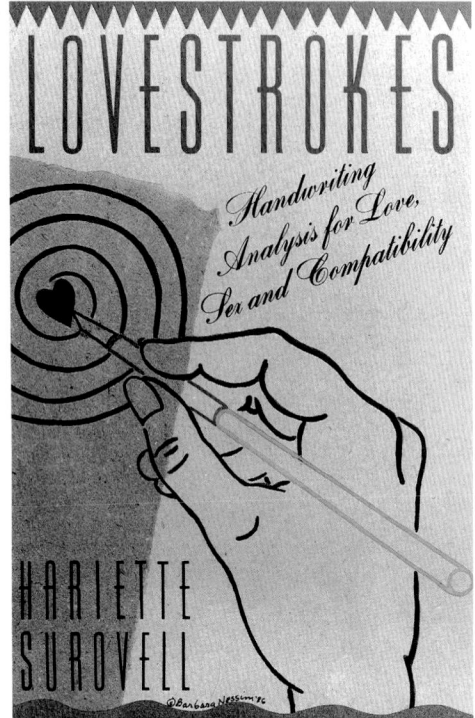

984

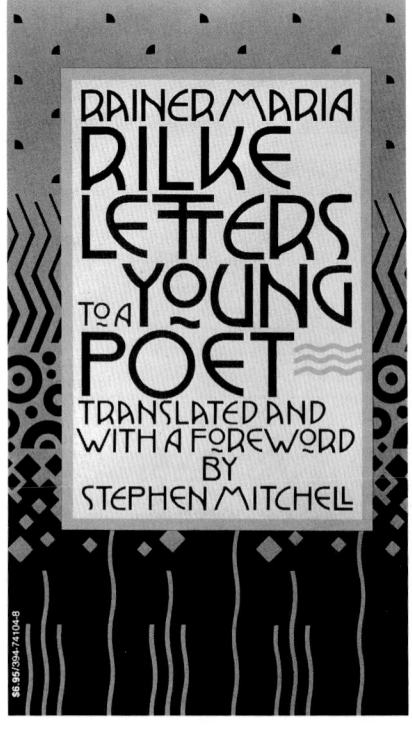

985

986

987

988

989

990

991

988
ART DIRECTOR
Judith Loeser
DESIGNER
Carin Goldberg
CLIENT
Vintage
EDITOR
Anne Freedgood
PUBLISHER
Random House, New York, NY

989
ART DIRECTOR
Victoria Wong
DESIGNER
Daniel Pelavin
ILLUSTRATOR/ARTIST
Daniel Pelavin, New York, NY
PUBLISHER
Oxford University Press

990
ART DIRECTOR
Judith Loeser
DESIGNER
Carin Goldberg
CLIENT
Vintage
EDITOR
Anne Freedgood
PUBLISHER
Random House, New York, NY

991
ART DIRECTOR
Neal Stuart
DESIGNER
William Sloan
ILLUSTRATOR/ARTIST
William Sloan
PUBLISHER
Viking Penguin
DESIGN FIRM
Three, New York, NY

992
ART DIRECTOR
Jackie Merri Meyer
DESIGNER
David Tamura
ILLUSTRATOR/ARTIST
David Tamura
PUBLISHER
Warner Books, New York, NY

993
ART DIRECTOR
Jackie Merri Meyer
DESIGNER
Carol Bokuniewicz
ILLUSTRATOR/ARTIST
Darryl Zudeck
PUBLISHER
Mysterious Press, New York, NY

992

993

994
ART DIRECTOR
Frank Metz
DESIGNER
Louise Fili, New York, NY
PHOTOGRAPHER
Jack Mitchell
ILLUSTRATOR/ARTIST
Louise Fili
WRITER
Yehudi Menuhin
CLIENT
Simon & Schuster
PUBLISHER
Simon & Schuster

995
ART DIRECTOR
Frank Metz
DESIGNER
Louise Fili
PHOTOGRAPHER
Francisco Hidalgo
WRITER
André Brink
CLIENT
Simon & Schuster
PUBLISHER
Simon & Schuster
DESIGN FIRM
Louise Fili Design, New York, NY

994

995

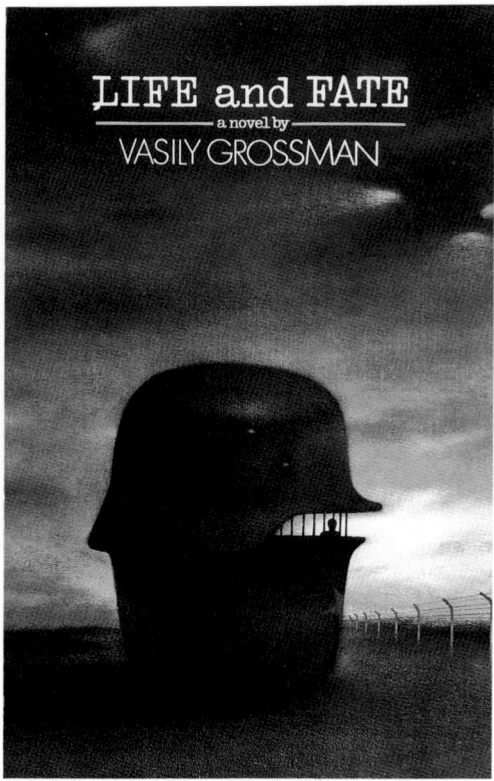

996

997

996
ART DIRECTOR
Jackie Merri Meyer
ILLUSTRATOR/ARTIST
Brian Davis
PUBLISHER
Warner Books, New York, NY

997
ART DIRECTOR
Joseph Montebello
DESIGNER
James Victore
ILLUSTRATOR/ARTIST
Christopher M. Zacharow
PUBLISHER
Harper & Row, New York, NY

998
ART DIRECTOR
Jackie Merri Meyer
DESIGNER
Stanislaw Fernandez
ILLUSTRATOR/ARTIST
Stanislaw Fernandez
PUBLISHER
Warner Books, New York, NY

999
ART DIRECTOR
Joseph Montebello
DESIGNER
Gloria Adelson
ILLUSTRATOR/ARTIST
Dan Reed
PUBLISHER
Harper & Row, New York, NY

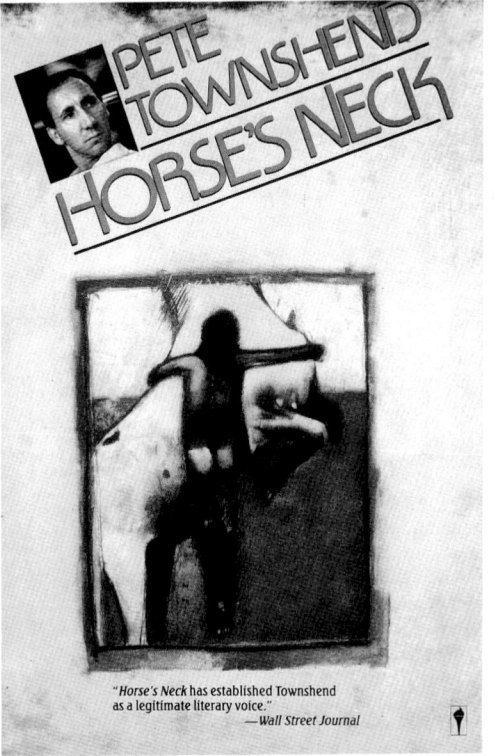

998

999

1000

COVER DESIGN COORDINATOR
Mary Archondes
DESIGNER
Joan Greenfield
PHOTOGRAPHER
Photo courtesy Louis K. Meisel Gallery, New York
ILLUSTRATOR/ARTIST
Michael Gallagher from the collection of Louis K. and Susan Pear Meisel.
WRITER
J.W. Coleman, D.R. Cressey
EDITOR
Alan McClare
PUBLISHER
Harper & Row, Publishers, Inc., New York, NY
PUBLICATION
Social Problems, Third Edition
PRINTER
The Lehigh Press, Inc.

1001

COVER DESIGN COORDINATOR
Mary Archondes
DESIGNER
Robin Hessel
WRITER
P. Chirlian
EDITOR
Peter Richardson
PUBLISHER
Harper & Row, Publishers, Inc., New York, NY
DESIGN FIRM
Brand X Studios
PUBLICATION
Analysis and Design of Integrated Electronic Circuits, Second Edition
PRINTER
New England Book Components

1002

COVER DESIGN COORDINATOR
Mary Archondes
DESIGNER
Edward A. Butler
WRITER
S. Moriarity, C.P. Allen
EDITOR
Peter Coveney
PUBLISHER
Harper & Row, Publishers, Inc., New York, NY
PUBLICATION
Cost Accounting, Second Edition
PRINTER
The Lehigh Press, Inc.

1003

COVER DESIGN COORDINATOR
Mary Archondes
DESIGNER
Tomoko Miho
WRITER
R.G. Lipsey, P.O. Steiner, D.D. Purvis
EDITOR
John Greenman
PUBLISHER
Harper & Row, Publishers, Inc., New York, NY
PUBLICATION
Economics, Eighth Edition
PRINTER
The Lehigh Press, Inc.

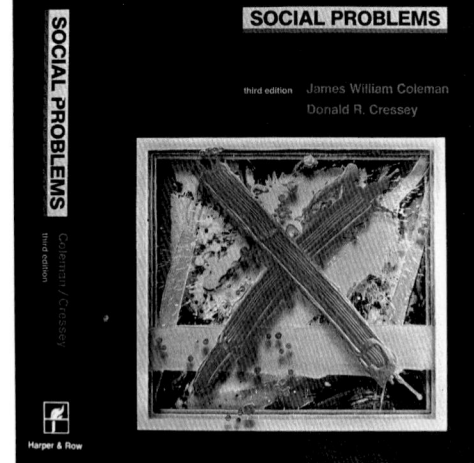
1000

1001

1002

1003

1004

1005

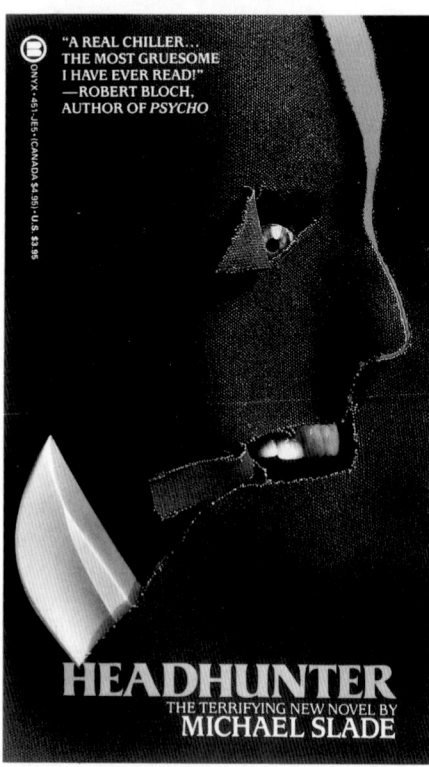
1006

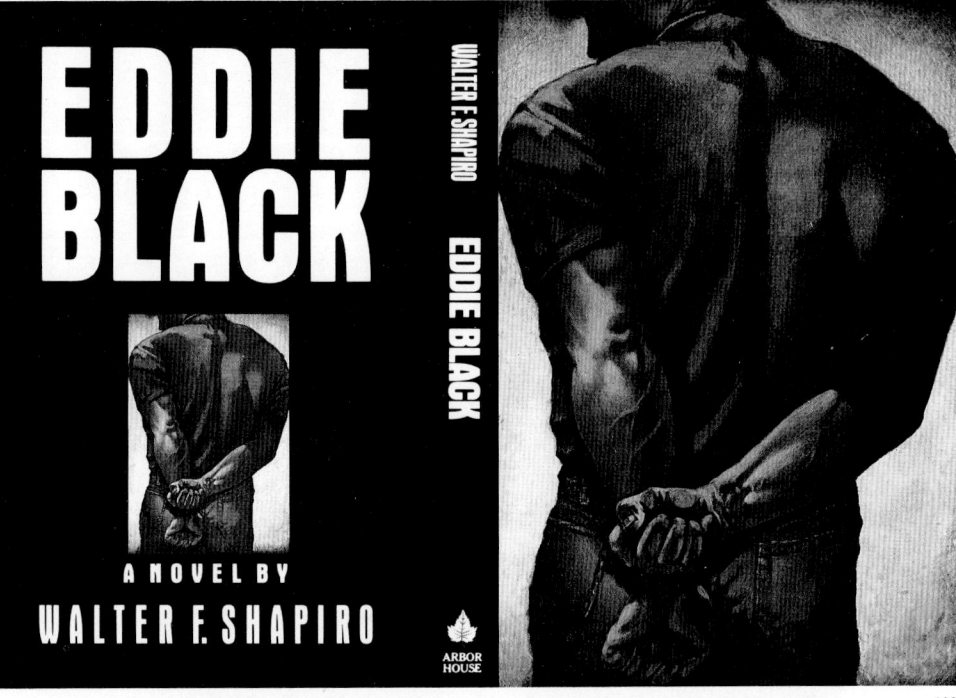

1004
ART DIRECTOR
Samuel N. Antupit
DESIGNER
Robert McKee
EDITOR
Robert Morton
PUBLISHER
Harry N. Abrams, Inc., New York, NY

1005
ART DIRECTOR
Dorothy Wachtenheim
DESIGNER
Carin Goldberg
PUBLISHER
Arbor House, New York, NY

1006
ART DIRECTOR
George Cornell
DESIGNER
E. Rouya
PHOTOGRAPHER
Victorio Sartor
PUBLISHER
New American Library (Onyx Books), New
York, NY

1007
ART DIRECTOR
Dorothy Wachtenheim
DESIGNER
Dorothy Wachtenheim
ILLUSTRATOR/ARTIST
Winslow Pinney Pels
PUBLISHER
Arbor House, New York, NY

1008
ART DIRECTOR
B. Martin Pedersen
DESIGNER
B. Martin Pedersen
PHOTOGRAPHER
Richard Levy
CLIENT
Society of Publication Designers
PUBLISHER
Madison Square Press
DESIGN FIRM
Jonson Pirtle Pedersen Alcorn Metzdorf &
Hess, New York, NY

1009
ART DIRECTOR
Joseph Montebello
ILLUSTRATOR/ARTIST
Robert Crawford
PUBLISHER
Harper & Row, New York, NY

1010
ART DIRECTOR
Robert Scudellari
DESIGNER
Robert Scudellari
WRITER
John Lecarré
EDITOR
Robert Gottlieb
PUBLISHER
Alfred A. Knopf, New York, NY

1011
ART DIRECTOR
Alex Gotfryd
DESIGNER
Craig DeCamp
EDITOR
Sally Arteseras
PUBLISHER
Doubleday & Company, New York, NY

1012
ART DIRECTOR
Judie Mills
DESIGNER
Lynn Dreese Breslin
PHOTOGRAPHER
UPI, Bettmann Newsphotos
CLIENT
Franklin Watts
EDITOR
Edward F. Breslin
DESIGN FIRM
Lynn Dreese Breslin Design, New York, NY

1013
ART DIRECTOR
Art Chantry
WRITER
Leif Davidsen
PUBLISHER
Steve Murray, Fjord Press
DESIGN FIRM
Art Chantry Design, Seattle, WA
TRANSLATOR
Tiina Nunnally, Fjord Press

1010

1011

1012

1013

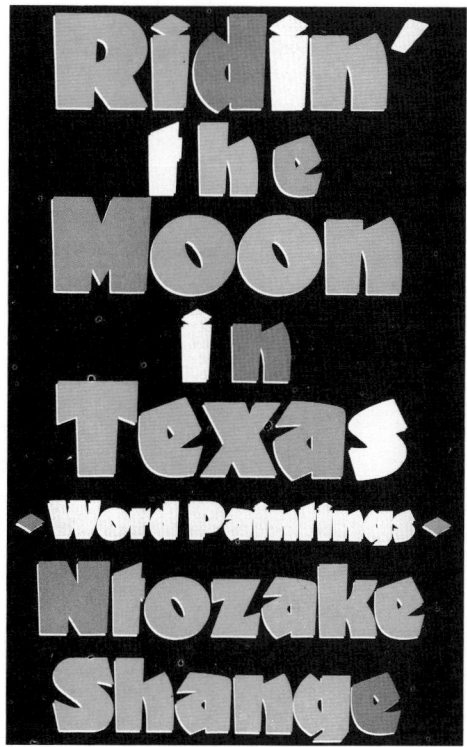

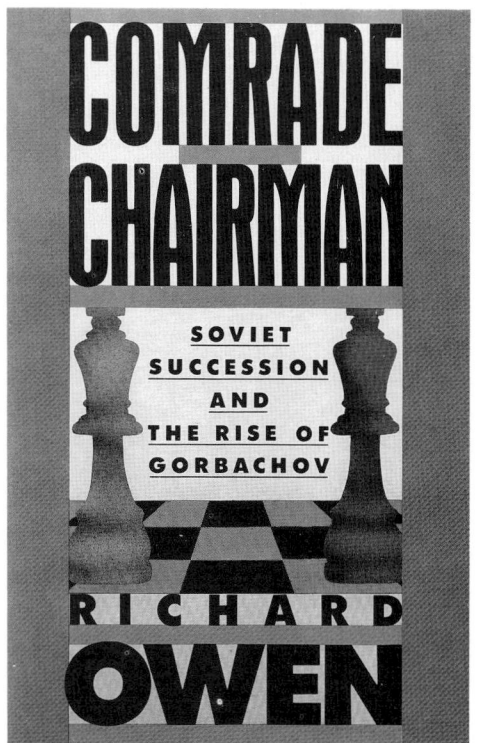

1014

1015

1014

ART DIRECTOR
Andy Carpenter
DESIGNER
Andy Carpenter
WRITER
Ntozake Shange
EDITOR
Michael Denneny
PUBLISHER
St. Martin's Press, New York, NY

1015

ART DIRECTOR
Dorothy Wachtenheim
DESIGNER
Karen Katz
PUBLISHER
Arbor House, New York, NY

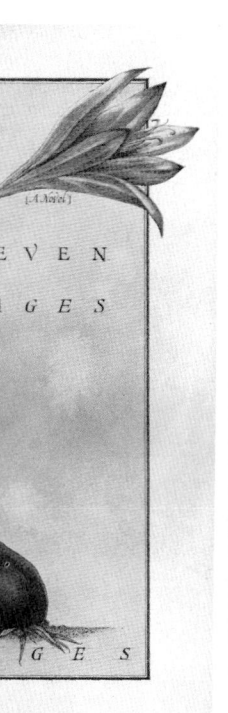

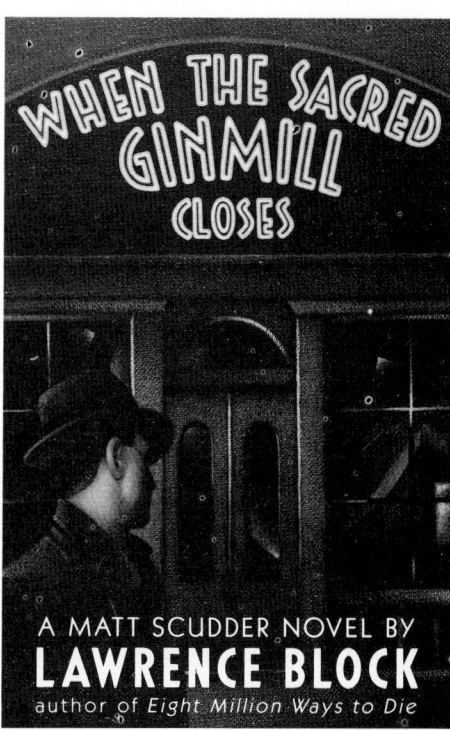

1016

1017

1016

ART DIRECTOR
Louise Fili
DESIGNER
Dugald Stermer
ILLUSTRATOR/ARTIST
Dugald Stermer
WRITER
Eva Figes
EDITOR
Tom Engelhardt
PUBLISHER
Pantheon Books, New York, NY

1017

ART DIRECTOR
Dorothy Wachtenheim
DESIGNER
Dorothy Wachtenheim
ILLUSTRATOR/ARTIST
M. Christopher Zacharow
PUBLISHER
Arbor House, New York, NY

1018
ART DIRECTOR
Louise Fili
DESIGNER
Louise Fili
WRITER
Marguerite Duras
EDITOR
André Schiffrin
PUBLISHER
Pantheon Books, New York, NY

1019
ART DIRECTOR
Louise Fili
DESIGNER
Louise Fili
ILLUSTRATOR/ARTIST
Robert Goldstrum
WRITER
James McClure
PUBLISHER
Pantheon Books, New York, NY

1020
ART DIRECTOR
Andy Carpenter
DESIGNER
Doris Borowsky
WRITER
Margaret George
EDITOR
Hope Dellon
PUBLISHER
St. Martin's Press, New York, NY

1021
ART DIRECTOR
Sara Eisenman
DESIGNER
Sara Eisenman
ILLUSTRATOR/ARTIST
Philippe Weisbecker
WRITER
Ann Arensberg
EDITOR
Alice Quinn
PUBLISHER
Alfred A. Knopf, New York, NY

1022
ART DIRECTOR
Char Lappan
DESIGNER
Louise Fili, New York, NY
CLIENT
Atlantic Monthly Press
PUBLISHER
Atlantic Monthly Press

1023
ART DIRECTOR
Louise Fili
DESIGNER
Louise Fili
ILLUSTRATOR/ARTIST
John Martinez
WRITER
Dan Kavanagh
EDITOR
André Schiffrin
PUBLISHER
Pantheon Books, New York, NY

1018

1019

1020

1021

1022

1023

1024

1024
ART DIRECTOR
Barbara Schneider
DESIGNER
Candace Haught, Ellen Pettengell
EDITOR
Louise Howe, Barbara Muller
PUBLISHER
Scott, Foresman and Company, Glenview, IL

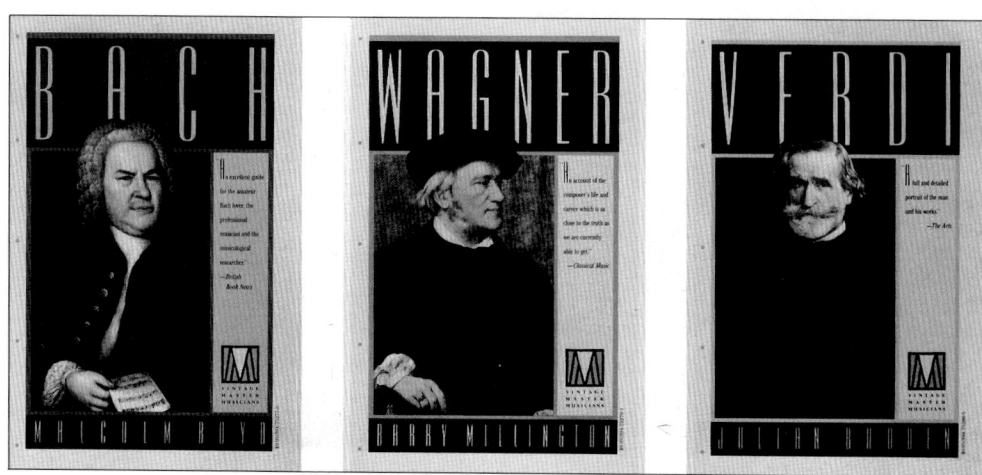

1025

1025
ART DIRECTOR
Judith Loeser
DESIGNER
Carin Goldberg
CLIENT
Vintage
EDITOR
Anne Freedgood
PUBLISHER
Random House, New York, NY

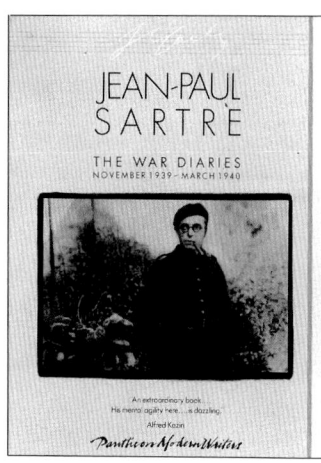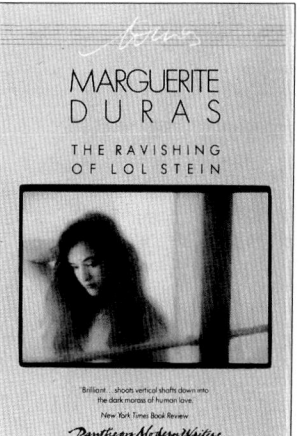

1026

1026
ART DIRECTOR
Louise Fili
DESIGNER
Louise Fili
PHOTOGRAPHER
Christine Rodin
WRITER
Jean-Paul Sartre, Harry Mulisch, Marguerite
Duras
PUBLISHER
Pantheon Books, New York, NY

Until the turn of the century peanuts were used primarily as a low cost nutritional food for animals. With the advent of new machinery and the compelling salesmanship of Amedeo Obici, "the peanut specialist", peanuts became a major product of the Planters Nut and Chocolate Company. In 1916 a national advertising campaign introduced "Mr. Peanut", a spritely figure that soon became familiar to people everywhere. Mr. Peanut actually was the creation of a thirteen-year old schoolchild, Antonio Gentile, who won $5 for the idea in a contest. Mr. Obici's energy and leadership eventually made Suffolk, Virginia, the peanut center of the world.

POSTERS:

Single Entries: outdoor billboard

transit

public service or political

in-store, promotional

Campaign Entries: outdoor billboard

public service or political

in-store, promotional

1027
ART DIRECTOR
Bob Jensen
PHOTOGRAPHER
David Ludwigs
WRITER
David Marks
CLIENT
Blue Cross and Blue Shield
AGENCY
Valentine-Radford, Kansas City, MO
PUBLICATION
Gannett Outdoor Co. of Kansas City
CREATIVE DIRECTOR
Bob Jensen

1027

1028
ART DIRECTOR
Tom Bleakly
PHOTOGRAPHER
Steve Umland
WRITER
Tom Bleakly
CLIENT
Bethesda Lutheran Medical Center
AGENCY
Blaisdell & Westlie Advertising, St. Paul, MN

1028

1029
ART DIRECTOR
Bob Akers
WRITER
Richard Rand
CLIENT
Schenley/Dewars
AGENCY
Leo Burnett Co., Inc., Chicago, IL
CREATIVE DIRECTOR
John Eding

1029

1030
ART DIRECTOR
Phill Cooper
PHOTOGRAPHER
Ralph Cole
WRITER
Jimmy Bloyed
CLIENT
Tulsa World Newspaper
AGENCY
Brown Bloyed & Associates, Tulsa, OK

1030

1031

1032

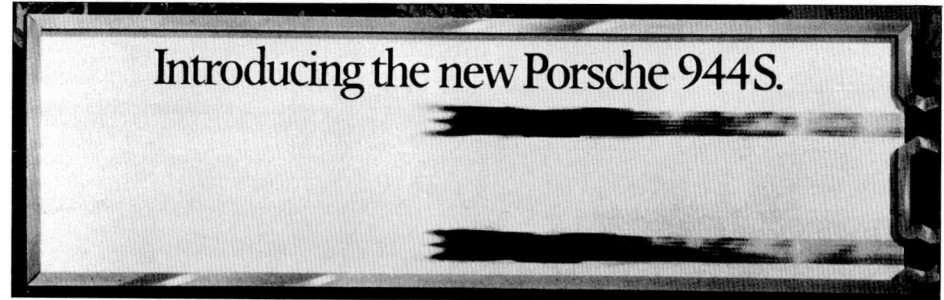

1033

1034

1031
ART DIRECTOR
Craig Thompson
DESIGNER
Craig Thompson
PHOTOGRAPHER
Phillip Parker
WRITER
Kathy Pfeifle, John Malmo
CLIENT
Regency Travel
AGENCY
John Malmo Advertising, Inc., Memphis, TN
CONSTRUCTION
Cummings Sign Co., Naegele Outdoor
Advertising

1032
ART DIRECTOR
Paul Cournoyer
ILLUSTRATOR/ARTIST
Rick Patterson
WRITER
Michele McKenna
CLIENT
Metro Transit
AGENCY
Cole & Weber/Seattle, Seattle, WA

1033
ART DIRECTOR
Peter Day
ILLUSTRATOR/ARTIST
Francoise Shartier
WRITER
Viv Tate
CLIENT
Volkswagen Canada Inc.
AGENCY
DDB Needham Worldwide, Toronto, Canada
PRODUCER
John Stevenson
TYPE
Typsettra Ltd.

1034
ART DIRECTOR
Michael Fazende
PHOTOGRAPHER
Graham Brown
WRITER
Bruce Bildsten
CLIENT
Minnesota Orchestra
AGENCY
Fallon McElligott, Minneapolis, MN

1035
ART DIRECTOR
Bob Kuperman, David Breznau
ILLUSTRATOR/ARTIST
Roger Bergendorf
WRITER
Bob Kuperman, Buddy Weiss
CLIENT
Sea World Orlando
AGENCY
DDB Needham Worldwide Inc., Los Angeles, CA
PRODUCER
Barry Brooks
CREATIVE DIRECTOR
Bob Kuperman

1035

1036
ART DIRECTOR
Paul J. Collins
DESIGNER
Paul J. Collins
PHOTOGRAPHER
Clint Clemens
WRITER
Paul J. Collins
CLIENT
Readers Digest
AGENCY
Collins&Reilly, Inc., Boston, MA

1036

1037
ART DIRECTOR
Jane Rubini
PHOTOGRAPHER
Richard Noble
WRITER
Cathy Cole
CLIENT
Evian Waters of France, Inc.
DIRECTOR
Arnold Arlow, Peter Lubalin
AGENCY
TBWA, New York, NY

1037

1038
ART DIRECTOR
Bob Taylor
WRITER
Bob Taylor
CLIENT
McDonald's
AGENCY
Leo Burnett Co., Inc., Chicago, IL
CREATIVE DIRECTOR
Bob Taylor

1038

1039

1040

1041

1042

1039
ART DIRECTOR
Mas Yamashita
WRITER
Karen Winters
CLIENT
Sea World San Diego
AGENCY
DDB Needham Worldwide Inc., Los Angeles, CA
PRODUCER
Barry Brooks
CREATIVE DIRECTOR
Bob Kuperman

1040
ART DIRECTOR
David Garcia
DESIGNER
David Garcia
PHOTOGRAPHER
Derek Gardner
ILLUSTRATOR/ARTIST
R/V Studios
WRITER
Ken Shuldman
CLIENT
Volkswagen USA
AGENCY
Doyle Dane Bernbach, New York, NY

1041
ART DIRECTOR
Greg Clancey
ILLUSTRATOR/ARTIST
Doug Fraser
WRITER
Dann Wilkens
CLIENT
Levi Strauss and Co.
AGENCY
Foote, Cone and Belding, San Francisco, CA

1042
ART DIRECTOR
Ron Louie
DESIGNER
Ron Louie
PHOTOGRAPHER
George Holz
WRITER
David Warren
CLIENT
Cruise Line International
AGENCY
DDB Needham Worldwide, Inc., New York, NY

1043

ART DIRECTOR
Rich Silverstein
PHOTOGRAPHER
Hank Benson
WRITER
Andy Berlin
CLIENT
San Francisco Examiner
AGENCY
Goodby, Berlin & Silverstein, San Francisco, CA

1043

1044

ART DIRECTOR
Mark Haumersen
DESIGNER
Mark Haumersen
ILLUSTRATOR/ARTIST
Leland Klanderman
WRITER
John Jarvis
CLIENT
Marigold Foods
AGENCY
Martin/Williams, Minneapolis, MN

1044

1045

ART DIRECTOR
Brian D. Fox
DESIGNER
Georgia Young
ILLUSTRATOR/ARTIST
Mike Bryan
WRITER
Marshall Drazen
CLIENT
New World Pictures, Steve Werndorf
AGENCY
B.D. Fox & Friends, Inc., Santa Monica, CA
DESIGN FIRM
B.D. Fox & Friends, Inc.

1046

ART DIRECTOR
Meg Moorhead
DESIGNER
Meg Moorhead
ILLUSTRATOR/ARTIST
Meg Moorhead
WRITER
Susan Brophy
CLIENT
Long Island Rail Road
AGENCY
Metropolitan Transportation Authority, New York, NY
DESIGN FIRM
Marketing and Graphic Services

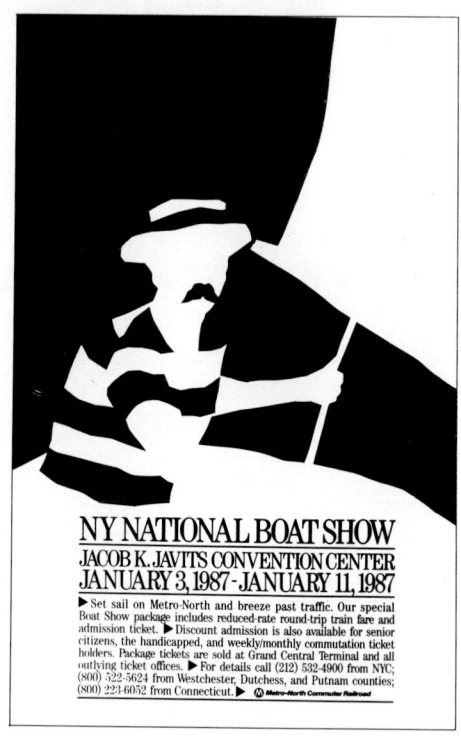

1045

1046

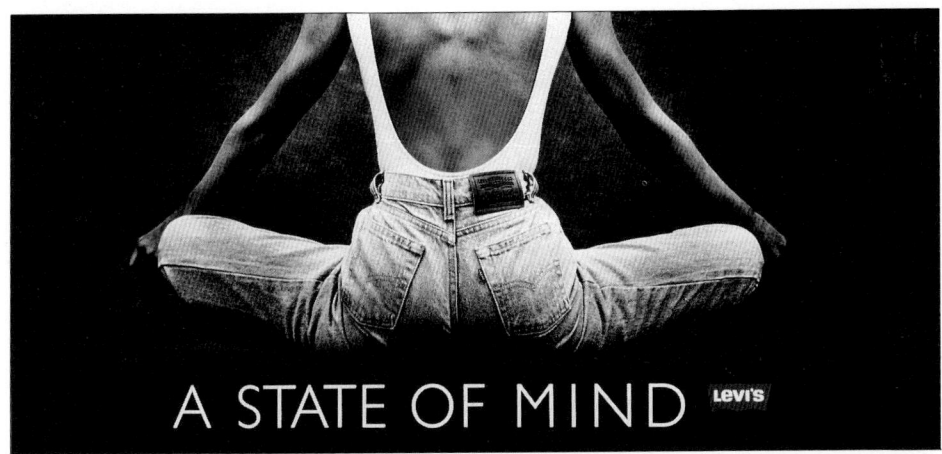

A STATE OF MIND Levi's

1047

Last year 125,000 junior high students flunked this simple test.

HOME PREGNANCY TEST

The Children's Defense Fund.

1048

New York nonstop to Munich daily.
Lufthansa

1049

NEW YORK BEGINS AT THE DECK
AT THE WORLD TRADE CENTER

1050

1047
ART DIRECTOR
Peter Day
PHOTOGRAPHER
Shin Sugino
WRITER
Viv Tate
CLIENT
Levi Strauss Canada
AGENCY
DDB Needham Worldwide, Toronto, Canada
PRODUCER
John Stevenson
TYPE
Typsettra Ltd.

1048
ART DIRECTOR
Dean Hanson
PHOTOGRAPHER
Kerry Peterson
WRITER
Tom McElligott
CLIENT
Children's Defense Fund
AGENCY
Fallon McElligott, Minneapolis, MN

1049
ART DIRECTOR
Bill Oberlander
PHOTOGRAPHER
Steve Bronstein, Big City Productions
WRITER
Steve Jaffe
CLIENT
Lufthansa
AGENCY
McCann-Erickson, New York, NY

1050
ART DIRECTOR
John Bloch
DESIGNER
John Bloch, Paul Shaw
ILLUSTRATOR/ARTIST
Paul Shaw (Calligraphy)
WRITER
Karen Cure
CLIENT
Port Authority of New York and New Jersey /
World Trade Center
AGENCY
McCaffery & Ratner, Inc.
DESIGN FIRM
Paul Shaw / Letter Design, New York, NY

1051

ART DIRECTOR
Pam Conboy
DESIGNER
Pam Conboy
PHOTOGRAPHER
Rick Dublin
WRITER
Kerry Casey
CLIENT
Minneapolis Star and Tribune
AGENCY
Bozell, Jacobs, Kenyon & Eckhardt,
Minneapolis, MN

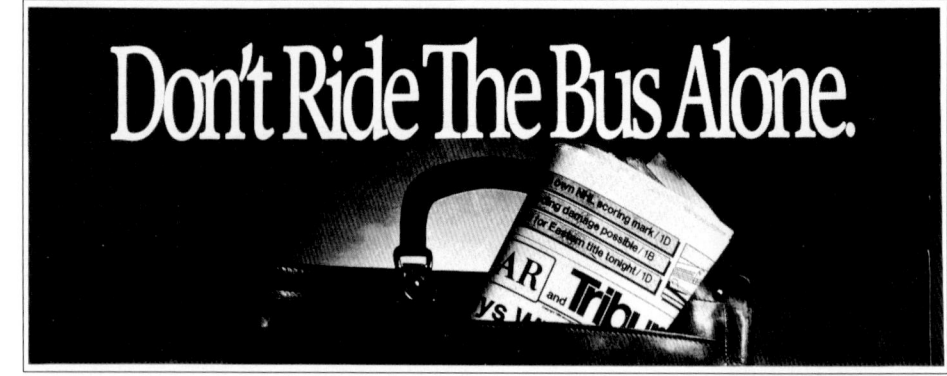

1051

1052

ART DIRECTOR
Bob Barrie
PHOTOGRAPHER
Rick Dublin
WRITER
Mike Lescarbeau
CLIENT
Continental Illinois
AGENCY
Fallon McElligott, Minneapolis, MN

1052

1053

ART DIRECTOR
Meg Moorhead
DESIGNER
Meg Moorhead
ILLUSTRATOR/ARTIST
Meg Moorhead
WRITER
Susan Brophy
CLIENT
Metro-North Commuter Railroad
AGENCY
Metropolitan Transportation Authority, New
York, NY
DESIGN FIRM
Marketing and Graphic Services

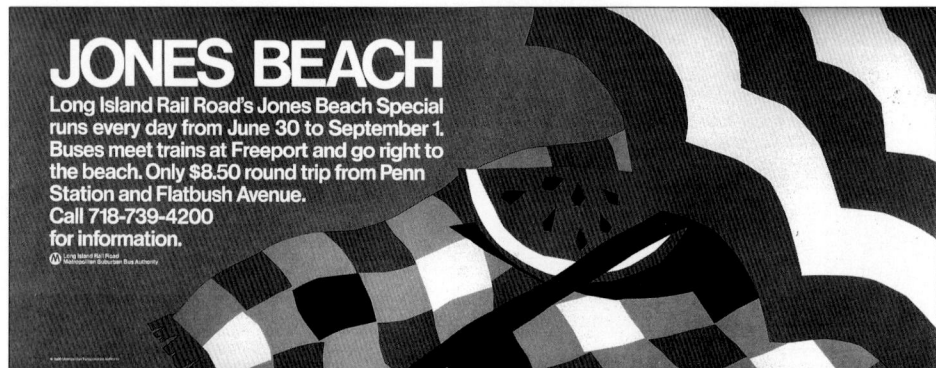

1053

1054

ART DIRECTOR
Steve Thursby
ILLUSTRATOR/ARTIST
Desmond Montague
WRITER
Allan Kazmer, Steve Thursby
CLIENT
Levi Strauss Canada
AGENCY
DDB Needham Worldwide, Toronto, Canada
PRODUCER
John Stevenson
TYPE
Typsettra Ltd.

1054

1055

1056

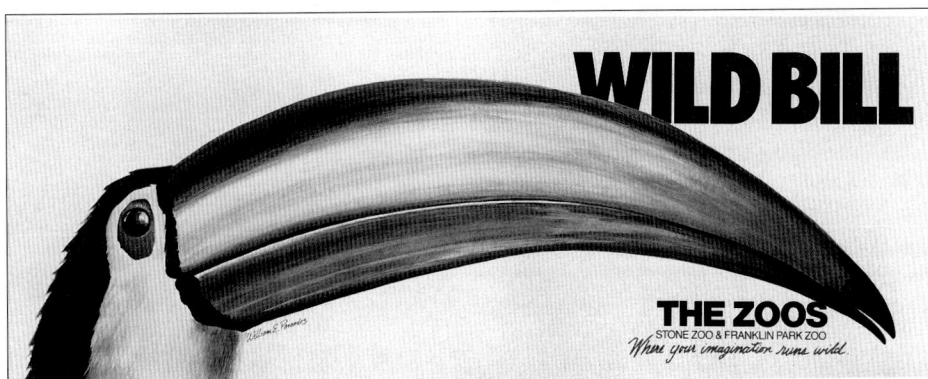

1057

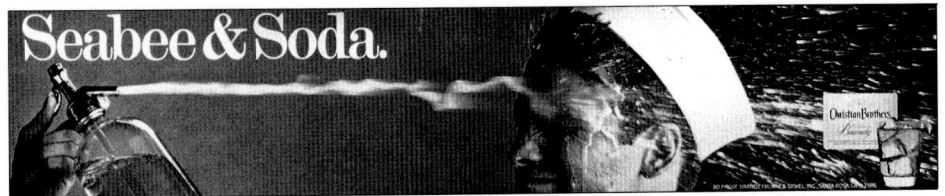

1058

1055
ART DIRECTOR
Pam Conboy
DESIGNER
Pam Conboy
PHOTOGRAPHER
Rick Dublin
WRITER
Kerry Casey
CLIENT
Minneapolis Star and Tribune
AGENCY
Bozell, Jacobs, Kenyon & Eckhardt,
Minneapolis, MN

1056
ART DIRECTOR
Pam Conboy
DESIGNER
Pam Conboy
PHOTOGRAPHER
Rick Dublin
WRITER
Kerry Casey
CLIENT
Minneapolis Star and Tribune
AGENCY
Bozell, Jacobs, Kenyon & Eckhardt,
Minneapolis, MN

1057
ART DIRECTOR
Stavros Cosmopulos, Richard Hydren
DESIGNER
Richard Hydren
ILLUSTRATOR/ARTIST
William Parandes
WRITER
Stavros Cosmopulos
CLIENT
Metropolitan Boston Zoos
AGENCY
Cosmopulos, Crowley & Daly, Inc., Boston,
MA
DESIGN FIRM
Cosmopulos, Crowley & Daly, Inc.

1058
ART DIRECTOR
John Morrison
DESIGNER
Dennis Manarchy
WRITER
Jarl Olsen, Jeff Goodby
CLIENT
Christian Brothers Winery
AGENCY
Goodby, Berlin & Silverstein, San Francisco,
CA

1059
ART DIRECTOR
Terri Small
WRITER
Margy Tylczak
CLIENT
Seattle Post-Intelligencer
AGENCY
Elgin Syferd, Seattle, WA

1059

1060
ART DIRECTOR
Rick James
PHOTOGRAPHER
Bruno
WRITER
John Berners
AGENCY
Young & Rubicam, New York, NY
ASSOC. CREATIVE DIRECTOR
Vince Daddiego

1061
ART DIRECTOR
Dean Hanson
PHOTOGRAPHER
Rick Dublin
WRITER
Tom McElligott
CLIENT
Children's Defense Fund
AGENCY
Fallon McElligott, Minneapolis, MN

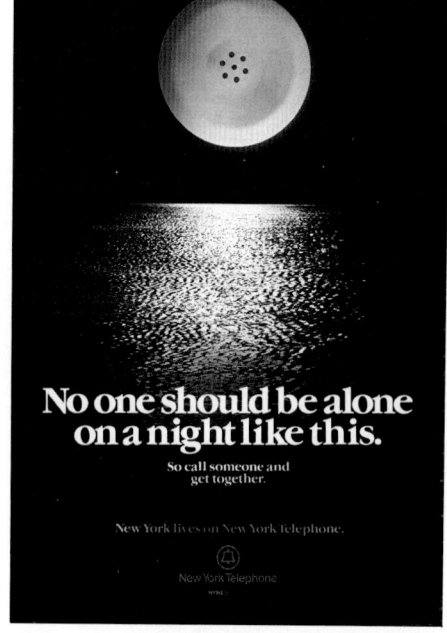

1060

1061

1062
ART DIRECTOR
Brian Aldrich
ILLUSTRATOR/ARTIST
Mark Steele
WRITER
Jon Goward
CLIENT
Prudential Center
AGENCY
ClarkeGowardFitts, Boston, MA

1062

1063

1064

1065

1066

1063
ART DIRECTOR
Pam Conboy
DESIGNER
Pam Conboy
PHOTOGRAPHER
Rick Dublin
WRITER
Kerry Casey
CLIENT
Minneapolis Star and Tribune
AGENCY
Bozell, Jacobs, Kenyon & Eckhardt,
Minneapolis, MN

1064
ART DIRECTOR
Bob Barrie
PHOTOGRAPHER
Bob Barrie
WRITER
Mike Lescarbeau
CLIENT
Hennepin County Newborn Care Unit
AGENCY
Fallon McElligott, Minneapolis, MN

1065
ART DIRECTOR
Ben Hillman
DESIGNER
Ben Hillman
PHOTOGRAPHER
Raymond Buckner
WRITER
Ben Hillman, Jack Huttner, Nora Bredes
CLIENT
Meenan Oil Co.
AGENCY
Huttner & Hillman, Inc., New York, NY

1066
ART DIRECTOR
Dean Hanson
PHOTOGRAPHER
Marc Hauser
WRITER
Tom McElligott
CLIENT
Children's Defense Fund
AGENCY
Fallon McElligott, Minneapolis, MN

1067

ART DIRECTOR
Steve Thursby
ILLUSTRATOR/ARTIST
Desmond Montague
WRITER
Allan Kazmer, Steve Thursby
CLIENT
Levi Strauss Canada
AGENCY
DDB Needham Worldwide, Toronto, Canada
PRODUCER
John Stevenson
TYPE
Typsettra Ltd.

1068

ART DIRECTOR
Bill Freeland
DESIGNER
Bill Freeland
PHOTOGRAPHER
Matthew Klein
ILLUSTRATOR/ARTIST
Jordan Steckel
WRITER
Bill Freeland
CLIENT
LaGuardia Community College
AGENCY
LaGuardia Communications, New York, NY

1069

ART DIRECTOR
Clifford Goodenough
PHOTOGRAPHER
Gerry Ellis
WRITER
Steve Sandoz
CLIENT
Woodland Park Zoo
AGENCY
Livingston & Company, Seattle, WA

1070

ART DIRECTOR
Bruce Blackburn
DESIGNER
Bruce Blackburn
ILLUSTRATOR/ARTIST
Bruce Blackburn
CLIENT
Napoli 99 Foundation
DESIGN FIRM
Blackburn & Associates, Inc., New York, NY

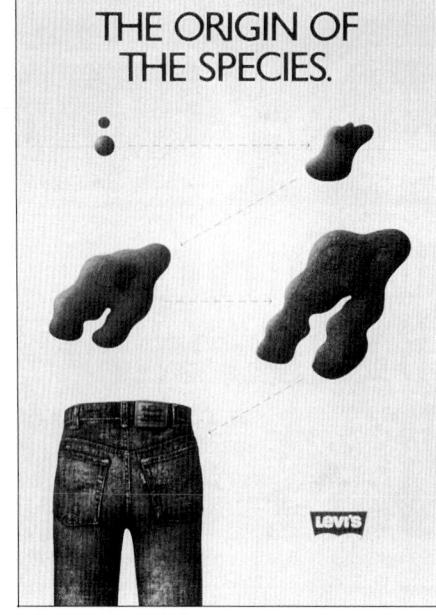

1067

1068

1069

1070

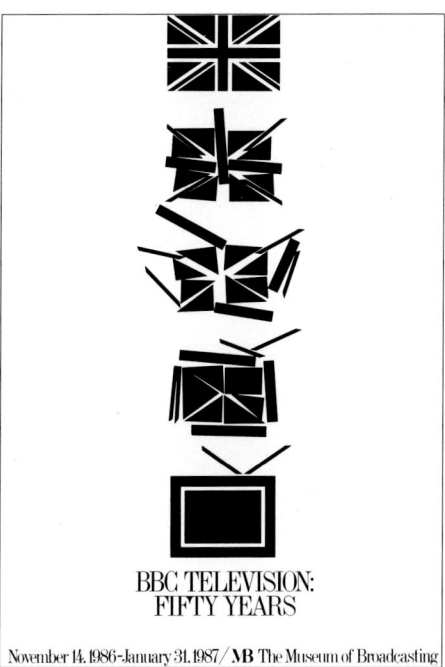

BBC TELEVISION:
FIFTY YEARS

November 14, 1986–January 31, 1987 / **MB** The Museum of Broadcasting

1071

1072

1071
ART DIRECTOR
Charles Spencer Anderson
DESIGNER
Charles Spencer Anderson
ILLUSTRATOR/ARTIST
Charles Spencer Anderson, Lynn Schulte
DESIGN FIRM
Duffy Design Group, Minneapolis, MN

1072
ART DIRECTOR
Paula Reedy, The Museum of Broadcasting
DESIGNER
David Suh
ILLUSTRATOR/ARTIST
David Suh
EDITOR
Paula Reedy
PUBLISHER
The Museum of Broadcasting, New York, NY

"NO" "NO" "NO" "NO" "YES"

IT
ONLY
TAKES
ONCE.

For more information
or help call: 379-6363
CHILDREN'S DEFENSE FUND

1073

1073
ART DIRECTOR
Dean Hanson
PHOTOGRAPHER
Rick Dublin
WRITER
Tom McElligott
CLIENT
Children's Defense Fund
AGENCY
Fallon McElligott, Minneapolis, MN

If You Liked Vietnam, You'll Love Nicaragua.

Don't Let It Happen Again. Call Women Against Military Madness, 827-5364.

1074

1074
ART DIRECTOR
Len Mitsch
DESIGNER
Len Mitsch
PHOTOGRAPHER
Eddie Adams
WRITER
Pete Smith
CLIENT
Women Against Military Madness
AGENCY
Martin/Williams Advtsg, Minneapolis, MN

1075
ART DIRECTOR
Marc English
DESIGNER
Marc English
ILLUSTRATOR/ARTIST
Marc English
CLIENT
Massachusetts College of Art
DESIGN FIRM
Design Research Unit, Boston, MA

1076
ART DIRECTOR
Kurt Tausche
DESIGNER
Kurt Tausche
WRITER
Pete Smith
CLIENT
Yellow Cab
AGENCY
Bozell, Jacobs, Kenyon & Eckhardt,
Minneapolis, MN

1075

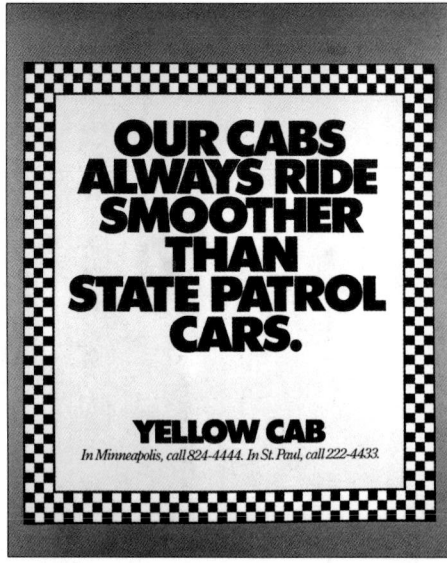

1076

1077

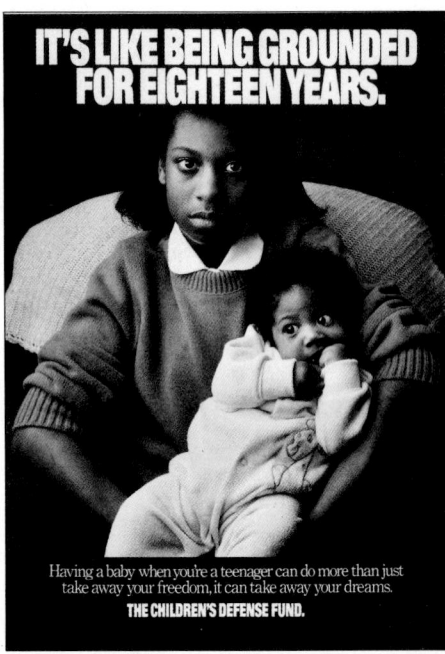

1078

1077
ART DIRECTOR
Bryan L. Peterson
DESIGNER
Bryan L. Peterson
ILLUSTRATOR/ARTIST
Bryan L. Peterson
WRITER
Norman A. Darais
CLIENT
Zale Corporation
DESIGN FIRM
Peterson & Company, Dallas, TX

1078
ART DIRECTOR
Dean Hanson
PHOTOGRAPHER
Marc Hauser
WRITER
Tom McElligott
CLIENT
Children's Defense Fund
AGENCY
Fallon McElligott, Minneapolis, MN

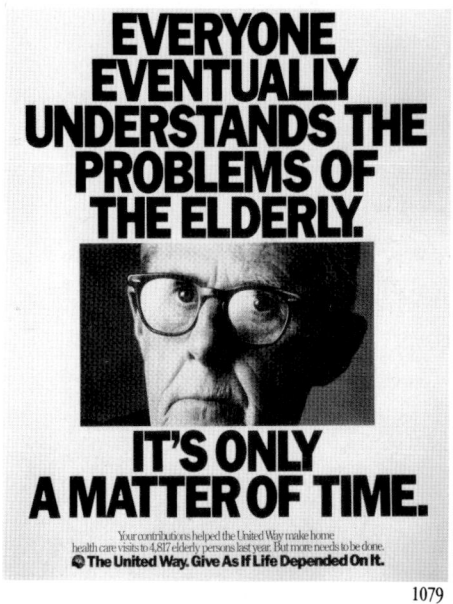

EVERYONE EVENTUALLY UNDERSTANDS THE PROBLEMS OF THE ELDERLY.

IT'S ONLY A MATTER OF TIME.

Your contributions helped the United Way make home health care visits to 4,817 elderly persons last year. But more needs to be done.
The United Way. Give As If Life Depended On It.

1079

Where Would The Beaver Be Without A Big Brother?

Become A Big Brother Or Big Sister. 871·3939.
Play a big role in the life of a child.

1080

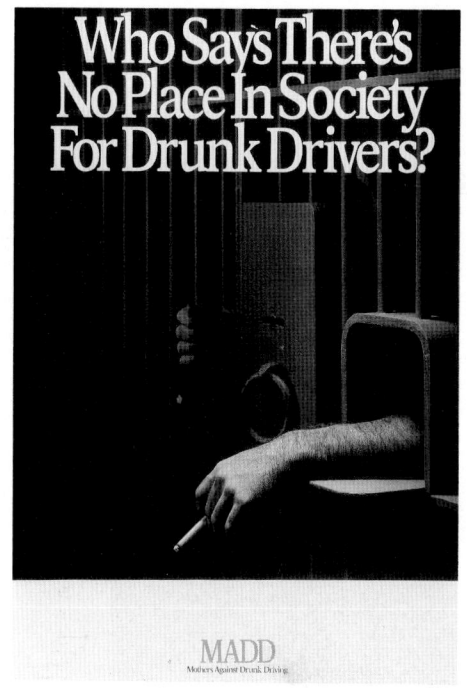

Who Says There's No Place In Society For Drunk Drivers?

MADD
Mothers Against Drunk Driving

1081

FIDM

1082

1079
ART DIRECTOR
Ron Sandilands
PHOTOGRAPHER
Ibid
WRITER
Bernie Hafeli
CLIENT
United Way of King County
AGENCY
Livingston & Company, Seattle, WA

1080
ART DIRECTOR
Bill Zabowski
DESIGNER
Bill Zabowski
PHOTOGRAPHER
Jim Arndt
WRITER
John Jarvis
CLIENT
Big Brothers/Big Sisters of Minneapolis
AGENCY
Martin/Williams, Minneapolis, MN

1081
ART DIRECTOR
Ken Butts
DESIGNER
Ken Butts
PHOTOGRAPHER
Dick Baker
WRITER
Kirk Ruhnke
CLIENT
Mothers Against Drunk Driving
AGENCY
Frankenberry, Laughlin & Constable,
Milwaukee, WI
PRODUCER
Paula Rothe

1082
ART DIRECTOR
Tom Antista
DESIGNER
Tom Antista
CLIENT
Fashion Institute of Design and
Merchandising
DESIGN FIRM
Antista Design, Santa Monica, CA

1083

ART DIRECTOR
Herbert Rogalski
DESIGNER
Herbert Rogalski, Patrick King
ILLUSTRATOR/ARTIST
Herbert Rogalski, Rick Rizzotto
WRITER
Herbert Rogalski
CLIENT
Saengerchor Boston
DESIGN FIRM
Rogalski Associates, Inc., Boston, MA

1084

ART DIRECTOR
Bob Dennard
DESIGNER
Chuck Johnson
ILLUSTRATOR/ARTIST
Glyn Powell, Chuck Johnson
CLIENT
Susan G. Komen Foundation
DESIGN FIRM
Dennard Creative, Dallas, TX

1085

ART DIRECTOR
Mike Zender
DESIGNER
Mike Zender, David Steinbrunner, Nancy
McIntosh, Darla Haven, Priscilla Fisher
CLIENT
WGUC FM/90.9 Fine Arts Public Radio, Kathy
Panoff, Development Director
DESIGN FIRM
Zender + Associates, Inc., Cincinnati, OH
PRINTER
The Hennegan Company

1086

ART DIRECTOR
Bryan L. Peterson
DESIGNER
Bryan L. Peterson
ILLUSTRATOR/ARTIST
Bryan L. Peterson
WRITER
Al Younts
CLIENT
Council for the Advancement and Support of
Education
DESIGN FIRM
Peterson & Company, Dallas, TX

1087

ART DIRECTOR
Scott Ray
DESIGNER
Scott Ray
ILLUSTRATOR/ARTIST
Scott Ray
CLIENT
Southern Methodist University
DESIGN FIRM
Peterson & Company, Dallas, TX

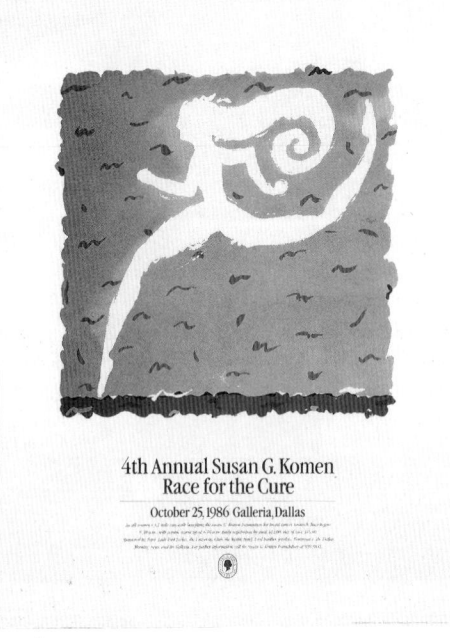

1083

1084

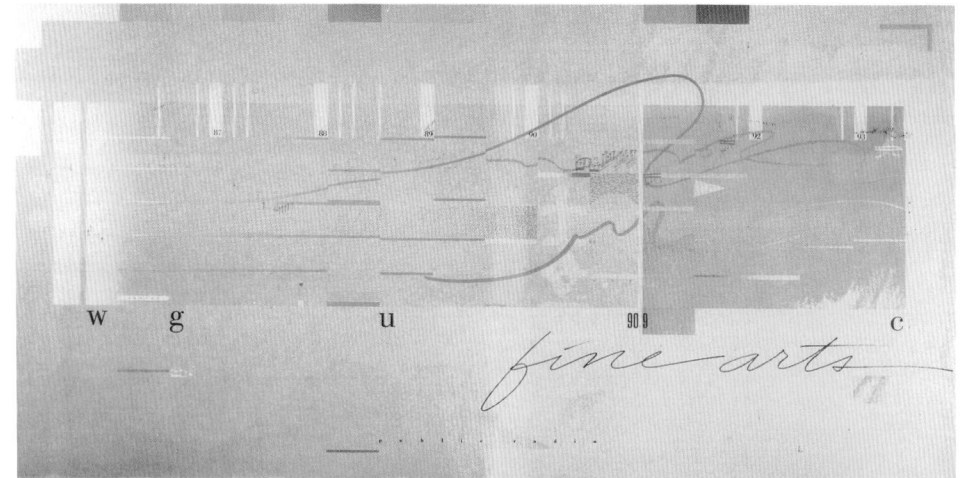

1085

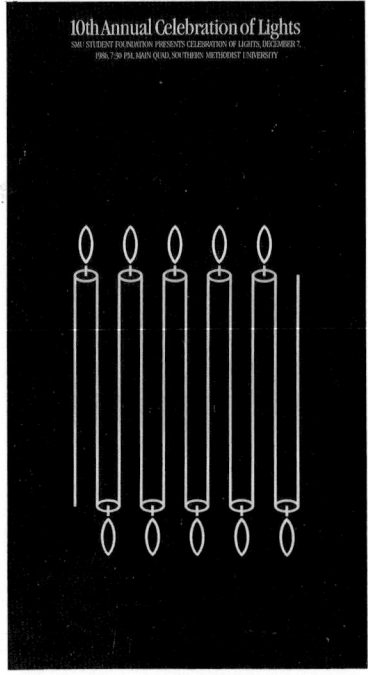

1086

1087

1088

1089

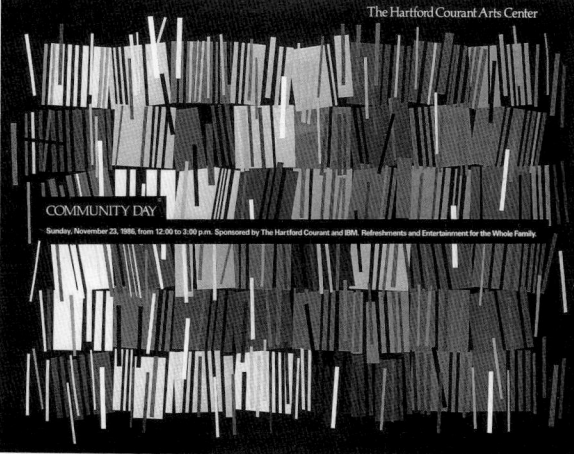

1090

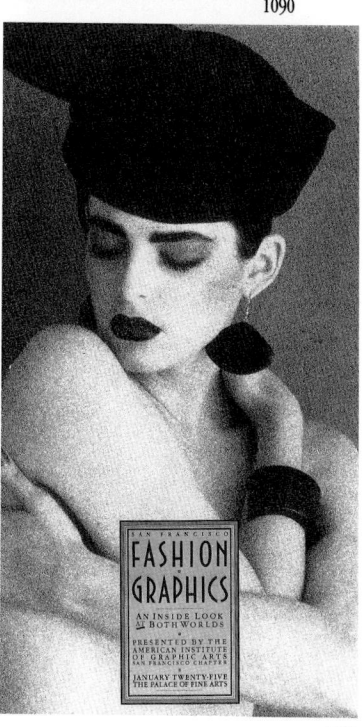

1091

1092

1088
ART DIRECTOR
Mary Mentzer, Larry Jarvis
PHOTOGRAPHER
Ferderbar Studios
WRITER
Mary Mentzer, Larry Jarvis
CLIENT
Advocates for Retarded Citizens
AGENCY
Frankenberry, Laughlin & Constable,
Milwaukee, WI

1089
ART DIRECTOR
Peter Good, Gordon Bowman
DESIGNER
Peter Good
ILLUSTRATOR/ARTIST
Janet Cummings Good
WRITER
Gordon Bowman
CLIENT
Canton Creative Arts Council / United
Technologies Corporation
PUBLISHER
United Technologies Corporation
DESIGN FIRM
Peter Good Graphic Design, Chester, CT

1090
ART DIRECTOR
William Wondriska
DESIGNER
Gilberto Pocaterra
ILLUSTRATOR/ARTIST
Gilberto Pocaterra
WRITER
Sylvia Levy
CLIENT
The Hartford Courant
EDITOR
Sylvia Levy
DIRECTOR
Michael Davies
PUBLISHER
The Hartford Courant
DESIGN FIRM
Wondriska Associates, Farmington, CT
PRINTER
Allied Printing Services

1091
ART DIRECTOR
Nancy Davis
DESIGNER
Nancy Davis
PHOTOGRAPHER
Gary Nolton
ILLUSTRATOR/ARTIST
David Davis
CLIENT
Oregon Special Olympics
PUBLISHER
Errolgraphics, Inc.
AGENCY
Nancy Davis, Design and Illustration,
Portland, OR
COORDINATOR
Errol M. Beard
FOOD STYLIST
Carolyn Schirmacher

1092
ART DIRECTOR
Jennifer Morla
DESIGNER
Jennifer Morla
PHOTOGRAPHER
Michele Clement
WRITER
Marianne Smith
CLIENT
American Institute of Graphic Arts (AIGA)
DESIGN FIRM
Morla Design, Inc., San Francisco, CA

1093

ART DIRECTOR
Barry Slavin
DESIGNER
John Siebert
ILLUSTRATOR/ARTIST
Ken Goldammer
DESIGN FIRM
Slavin Asssociates, Inc., Chicago, IL

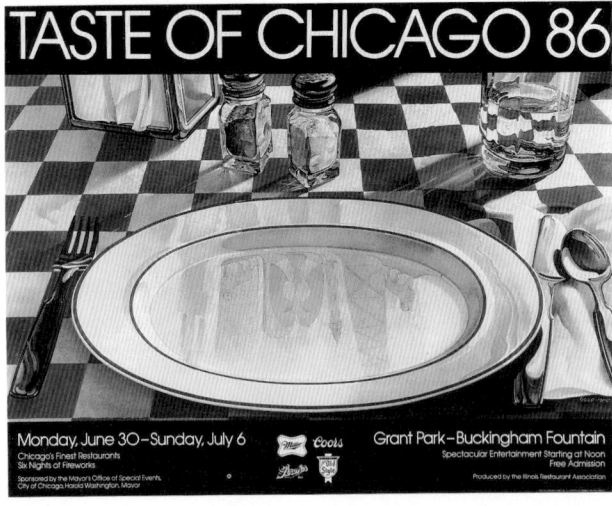

1093

1094

ART DIRECTOR
Mike Quon
DESIGNER
Mike Quon
ILLUSTRATOR/ARTIST
Mike Quon
CLIENT
The Shoshin Society
DESIGN FIRM
Mike Quon Design Office, Inc., New York, NY

1095

ART DIRECTOR
Lanny Sommese
DESIGNER
Lanny Sommese
ILLUSTRATOR/ARTIST
Lanny Sommese
CLIENT
Penn State Amnesty International Chapter
DESIGN FIRM
Lanny Sommese Design, State College, PA

1094

1095

1096

ART DIRECTOR
Seymour Chwast
DESIGNER
Seymour Chwast
ILLUSTRATOR/ARTIST
Seymour Chwasst
CLIENT
Shoshin Society
DIRECTOR
Charles Michael Helmken
PUBLISHER
Shoshin Society
DESIGN FIRM
The Pushpin Group, New York, NY

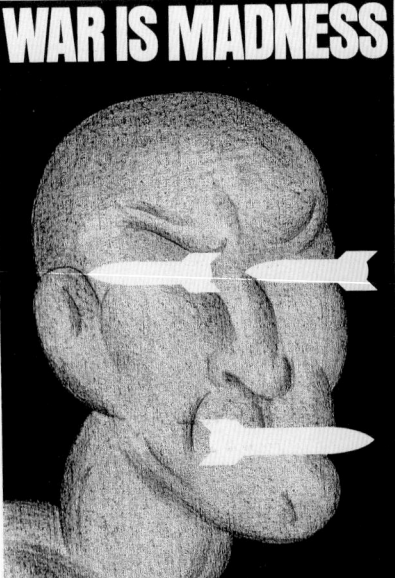

1096

1097

1098

1099

1100

1097
ART DIRECTOR
Peter Good, Gordon Bowman
DESIGNER
Peter Good
PHOTOGRAPHER
Jean-Luc Bureau
WRITER
Lis Ingoldsby
CLIENT
Wadsworth Atheneum / United Technologies Corporation
PUBLISHER
United Technologies Corporation
DESIGN FIRM
Peter Good Graphic Design, Chester, CT

1098
ART DIRECTOR
Liz Kathman Grubow
DESIGNER
Liz Kathman Grubow
PHOTOGRAPHER
Alan Brown / Photo Design
ILLUSTRATOR/ARTIST
Liz Kathman Grubow, Alan Brown
CLIENT
Cincinnati Symphony Orchestra
DESIGN FIRM
Libby Perszyk Kathman, Cincinnati, OH

1099
ART DIRECTOR
Peter Good
DESIGNER
Peter Good
PHOTOGRAPHER
Wes Garrison
ILLUSTRATOR/ARTIST
Peter Good
WRITER
Steve Campo
CLIENT
TheaterWorks
PUBLISHER
TheaterWorks
DESIGN FIRM
Peter Good Graphic Design, Chester, CT

1100
ART DIRECTOR
Liz Kathman Grubow
DESIGNER
Liz Kathman Grubow
PHOTOGRAPHER
Alan Brown, PhotoDesign
ILLUSTRATOR/ARTIST
Liz Kathman Grubow
CLIENT
Downtown Council of Cincinnati
DESIGN FIRM
Libby Perszyk Kathman, Cincinnati, OH

POSTERS

1101
ART DIRECTOR
Sarah Lavicka
DESIGNER
Sarah Lavicka
ILLUSTRATOR/ARTIST
Ernst Ludwig Kirchner
CLIENT
Virginia Museum of Fine Arts, Richmond
EDITOR
Anne Barriault
PUBLISHER
Virginia Museum of Fine Arts, Richmond
DESIGN FIRM
Virginia Museum of Fine Arts, Publications
Dept., Richmond, VA
PRINTER
Teagle & Little Inc.

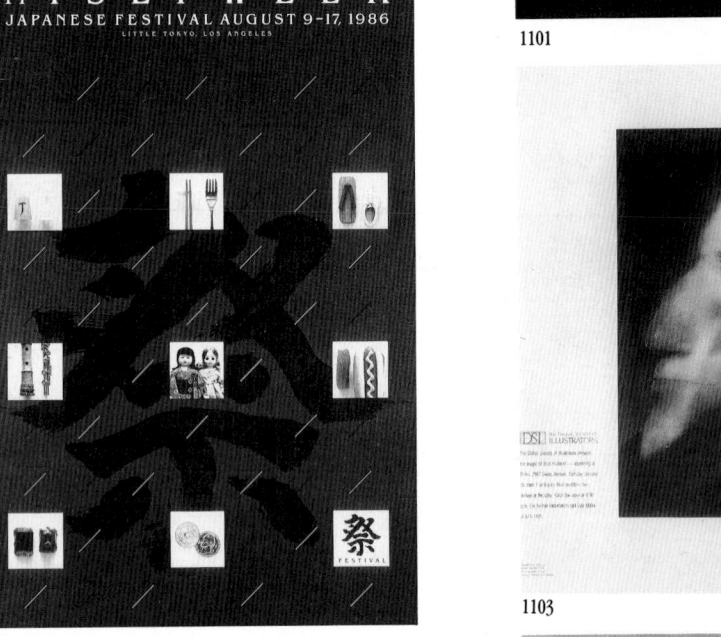
1101

1102
ART DIRECTOR
Tets Yamashita
DESIGNER
Tets Yamashita
PHOTOGRAPHER
Roger Marshutz
ILLUSTRATOR/ARTIST
Hiroko Ikuta
CLIENT
Kats Kunitsugu, Nisei Week Festival
Committee
DIRECTOR
Art Mochizuki
PUBLISHER
James Ludan, Labelcraft Lithographics
DESIGN FIRM
Harte Yamashita & Forest, Los Angeles, CA

1102

1103
DESIGNER
Lyle Miller
ILLUSTRATOR/ARTIST
Brad Holland, New York, NY
CLIENT
Dallas Society of Illustrators
DESIGN FIRM
Flying Colors Studio, Dallas, TX

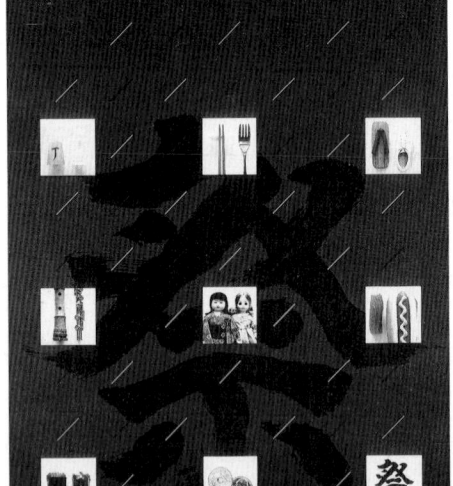
1103

1104
ART DIRECTOR
Milton Glaser
DESIGNER
Milton Glaser
ILLUSTRATOR/ARTIST
Milton Glaser
CLIENT
Charvoz Carsen Corporation
DESIGN FIRM
Milton Glaser, Inc., New York, NY

1104

1105

1106

1108

1107

1105
ART DIRECTOR
Milton Glaser
DESIGNER
Milton Glaser
ILLUSTRATOR/ARTIST
Milton Glaser
WRITER
Milton Glaser
CLIENT
The Brooklyn Museum
DESIGN FIRM
Milton Glaser, Inc., New York, NY

1106
ART DIRECTOR
Brad Holland
ILLUSTRATOR/ARTIST
Brad Holland, New York, NY
CLIENT
Tulsa Art Directors Club

1107
ART DIRECTOR
Steve Sieler
ILLUSTRATOR/ARTIST
Brad Holland, New York, NY
CLIENT
Apple Computers

1108
ART DIRECTOR
Milton Glaser
DESIGNER
Milton Glaser
ILLUSTRATOR/ARTIST
Milton Glaser
CLIENT
The James Beard Foundation, and American Express
DESIGN FIRM
Milton Glaser, Inc., New York, NY

1109
ART DIRECTOR
Alan Lidji
DESIGNER
Alan Lidji
ILLUSTRATOR/ARTIST
Alan Lidji
CLIENT
NHAB-McSam
AGENCY
Rosenberg & Company, Dallas, TX

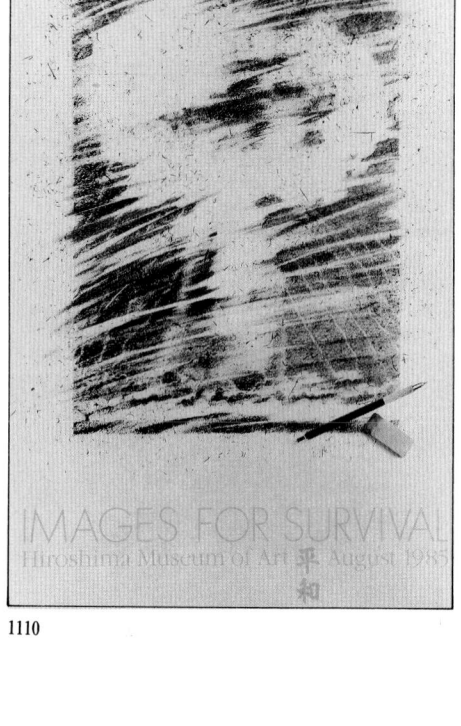

The 1986 McSam Awards

1109

IMAGES FOR SURVIVAL
Hiroshima Museum of Art ・ August 1985

1110

1110
ART DIRECTOR
Alan Lidji
DESIGNER
Alan Lidji
PHOTOGRAPHER
Charlie Freeman
ILLUSTRATOR/ARTIST
Alan Lidji
CLIENT
The Shoshin Society
AGENCY
Rosenberg & Company, Dallas, TX

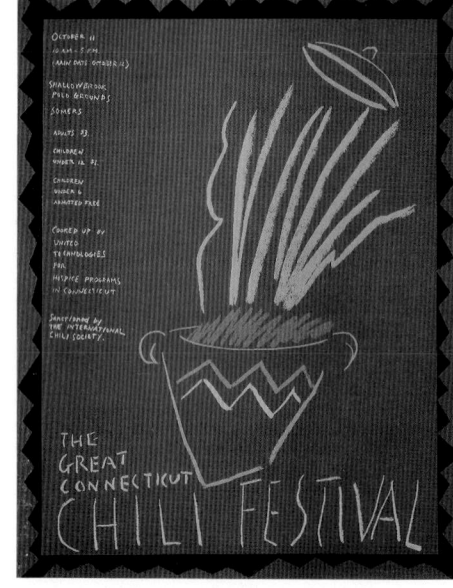

1111

1111
ART DIRECTOR
Gordon Bowman
DESIGNER
Merle Nacht
ILLUSTRATOR/ARTIST
Merle Nacht, Wethersfield, CT
CLIENT
United Technologies
PRODUCER
Lis Ingoldsby

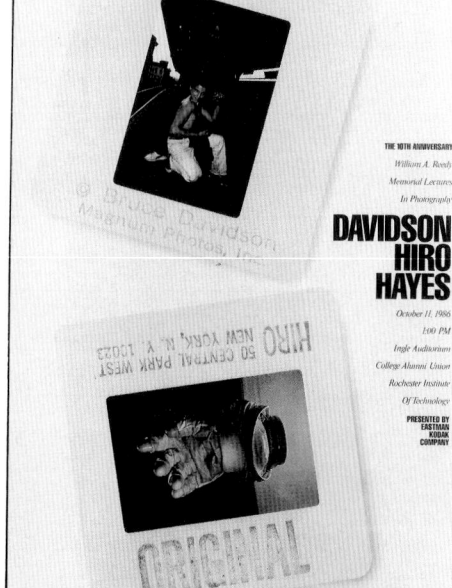

1112

1112
ART DIRECTOR
Ronald Peterson
DESIGNER
Sharon Gresh
PHOTOGRAPHER
Bruce Davidson, Hiro
CLIENT
William A. Reedy Memorial Lectures in
Photography
DESIGN FIRM
Peterson & Blyth Associates, Inc., New York,
NY

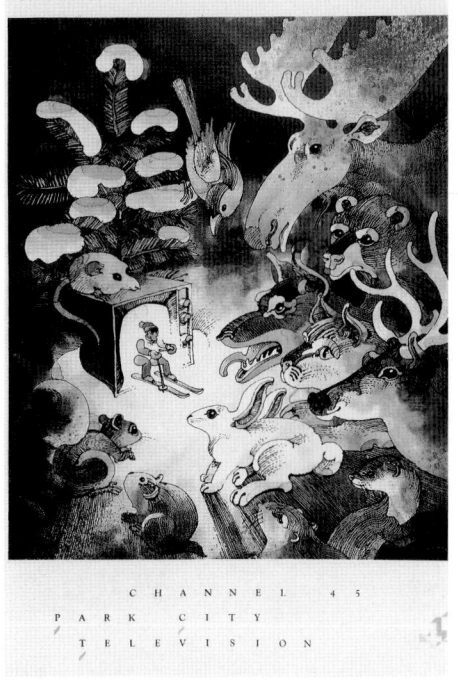

1113

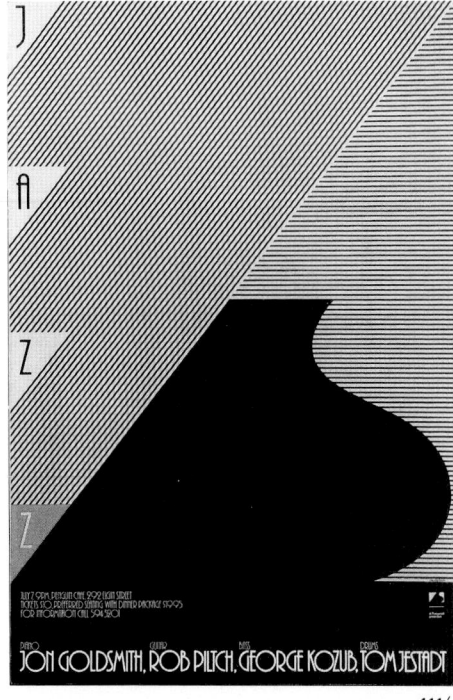

1114

1113
ART DIRECTOR
Don Weller
DESIGNER
Don Weller
ILLUSTRATOR/ARTIST
Don Weller
CLIENT
Channel 45 Park City Television
PUBLISHER
Channel 45 Park City Television
AGENCY
The Weller Institute for the Cure of Design, Inc., Park City, UT
DESIGN FIRM
The Weller Institute for the Cure of Design, Inc.

1114
ART DIRECTOR
Neville Smith
DESIGNER
Neville Smith
ILLUSTRATOR/ARTIST
Neville Smith
CLIENT
Pianocraft
DESIGN FIRM
Neville Smith, Graphic Design, Skyridge, Quebec, Canada
PRINTER
Malmberg Printers

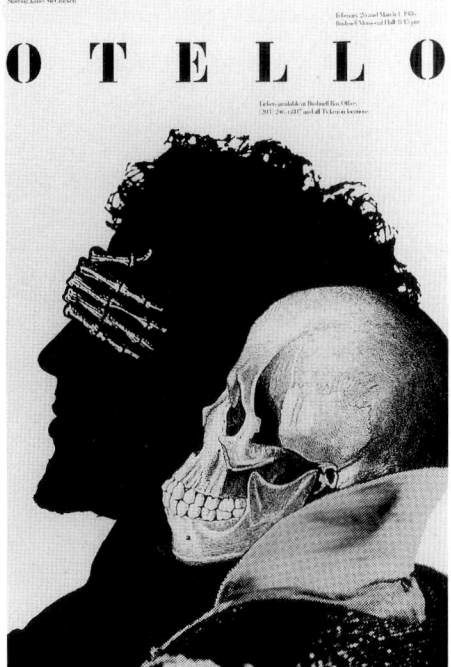

1115

1115
ART DIRECTOR
Robert Appleton
DESIGNER
Robert Appleton
ILLUSTRATOR/ARTIST
Robert Appleton
CLIENT
The Connecticut Opera
DESIGN FIRM
Appleton Design Inc., Hartford, CT

1116

1116
ART DIRECTOR
Charles Spencer Anderson
DESIGNER
Charles Spencer Anderson
ILLUSTRATOR/ARTIST
Charles Spencer Anderson
CLIENT
Washburn Child Guidance Center
DESIGN FIRM
Duffy Design Group, Minneapolis, MN

1117
ART DIRECTOR
David Fox
PHOTOGRAPHER
Rick Dublin
WRITER
Jerry Fury
CLIENT
First Federal of La Crosse
AGENCY
Clarity Coverdale Rueff Advertising,
Minneapolis, MN

1117

1118
ART DIRECTOR
Mark Johnson
DESIGNER
Dennis Manarchy
WRITER
Phil Hanft
CLIENT
ITT Corp.
AGENCY
Fallon McElligott, Minneapolis, MN

1119
ART DIRECTOR
Houman Pirdavari
PHOTOGRAPHER
Jim Arndt
WRITER
Jarl Olsen
CLIENT
Brief Encounter
AGENCY
Fallon McElligott, Minneapolis, MN

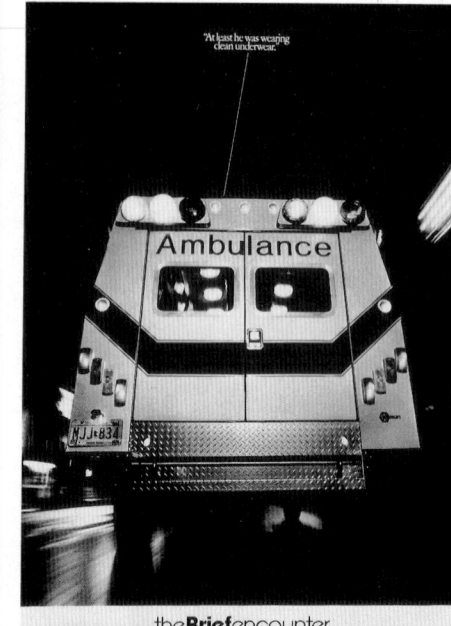

1118

1119

1120
ART DIRECTOR
John Malinowski
PHOTOGRAPHER
Jim Barber
WRITER
Craig Demeter
CLIENT
Procter & Gamble
AGENCY
D'Arcy Masius Benton & Bowles, New York,
NY
CREATIVE DIRECTOR
Ken Charof

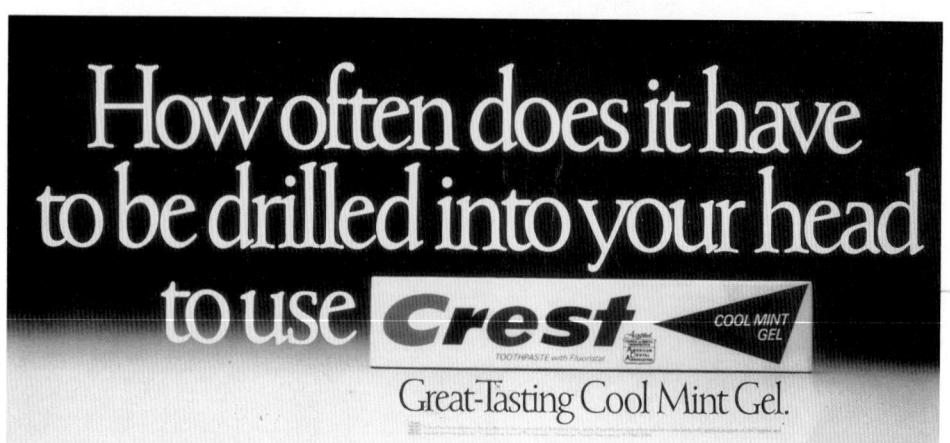

1120

1121

1121
ART DIRECTOR
Marty Neumeier
DESIGNER
Marty Neumeier
PHOTOGRAPHER
Chuck Place, Thomas Upton
CLIENT
Santa Barbara Metropolitan Transit District
DESIGN FIRM
Neumeier Design Team, Atherton, CA
PRINTER
Gore Graphics

1122

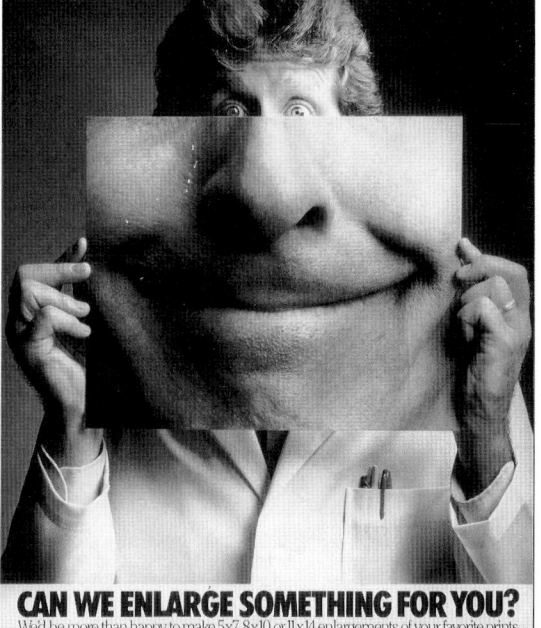

1123

1122
ART DIRECTOR
Robert Appleton
DESIGNER
Robert Appleton
ILLUSTRATOR/ARTIST
Robert Appleton
CLIENT
The Connecticut Opera
DESIGN FIRM
Appleton Design Inc., Hartford, CT

1123
ART DIRECTOR
Yvonne Smith, Marc Deschenes
PHOTOGRAPHER
Lamb & Hall
WRITER
Marc Deschenes, Yvonne Smith
CLIENT
Noritsu America Corp.
AGENCY
(213) 827-9695 And Associates, Venice, CA
PRODUCER
The Production Company
AD MANAGER
Brad Moore

1124

1124
ART DIRECTOR
Susan Hoffman, Dan Wieden
PHOTOGRAPHER
Pete Stone
CLIENT
Nike
AGENCY
Wieden & Kennedy, Portland, OR

1125
ART DIRECTOR
Dean Hanson
DESIGNER
Kerry Peterson
WRITER
Bruce Bildsten
CLIENT
First Tennessee
AGENCY
Fallon McElligott, Minneapolis, MN

1126
ART DIRECTOR
Marilyn Hoffner
DESIGNER
Seymour Chwast
ILLUSTRATOR/ARTIST
Seymour Chwast
PUBLISHER
Cooper Union
DESIGN FIRM
The Pushpin Group, New York, NY

1127
ART DIRECTOR
Jack Mariucci
DESIGNER
Jack Mariucci
PHOTOGRAPHER
Bob Stern
WRITER
Mike Rogers
CLIENT
Michelin
DIRECTOR
Jack Mariucci
AGENCY
DDB Needham Worldwide, Inc., New York,
NY
PUBLICATION
Motor Trend, Car & Driver

1128
ART DIRECTOR
Randall Hensley
DESIGNER
Tom Bazzel, Diana DeLucia
ILLUSTRATOR/ARTIST
Soren Arutunyan, Carol Ferrante
WRITER
Robert S. Byer
CLIENT
IBM Entry Systems Division, Lee Green and
Patricia Armstrong
AGENCY
Muir Cornelius Moore, Inc., New York, NY
ACCOUNT MANAGER
Robert S. Byer; Lisa Nagursky

1125

1126

1127

1128

1129

1130

1129

ART DIRECTOR
Ira Barkoff
DESIGNER
Kathy Kunkel
PHOTOGRAPHER
Barry Blackman
WRITER
Judy Olstein
CLIENT
Sony Tape
AGENCY
Burkhardt & Christy/NY, New York, NY
CREATIVE DIRECTOR
Ron Burkhardt

1130

ART DIRECTOR
James Cross, John Clark
DESIGNER
James Cross
PHOTOGRAPHER
James Cross
CLIENT
University of California at Los Angeles
(Extension)
DESIGN FIRM
Cross Associates, Los Angeles, CA

1131

1131

ART DIRECTOR
Jeffrey Schneider
DESIGNER
Jeffrey Schneider
ILLUSTRATOR/ARTIST
Eric Dinyer
CLIENT
Anheuser-Busch
AGENCY
AdWorks, Inc., St. Louis, MO

1132

1132

ART DIRECTOR
Tyler Smith
DESIGNER
Tyler Smith
ILLUSTRATOR/ARTIST
Anthony Russo
CLIENT
Trinity Rep.
DESIGN FIRM
Tyler Smith, Providence, RI

1133
ART DIRECTOR
Linda Sullivan
DESIGNER
Linda Sullivan
ILLUSTRATOR/ARTIST
Linda Sullivan
WRITER
Norman A. Darais
CLIENT
BYU Graphics
DESIGN FIRM
BYU Graphics, Provo, UT
PRINTER
Rob Carawan
TYPOGRAPHER
Jonathan Skousen

1134
ART DIRECTOR
I.L. Fraiman
DESIGNER
I.L. Fraiman
PHOTOGRAPHER
George Simboni
DESIGN FIRM
Fraiman Design Inc., Toronto, Canada
PRINTER
Proving Specialties Ltd.
COLOR SEPARATOR
Formart Graphics

1135
ART DIRECTOR
Chris Hill
DESIGNER
Chris Hill, Margaret Kim
PHOTOGRAPHER
Mike Schneps
CLIENT
Art Directors Club of Houston
DESIGN FIRM
Hill/A Marketing Design Group, Houston, TX

1136
ART DIRECTOR
Chris Hill
DESIGNER
Chris Hill
PHOTOGRAPHER
Bancroft Library University of California,
Berkeley, Dan Coolidge Collection
CLIENT
Southwest Texas State University
DESIGN FIRM
Hill/A Marketing Design Group, Houston, TX

1133

1134

1135

1136

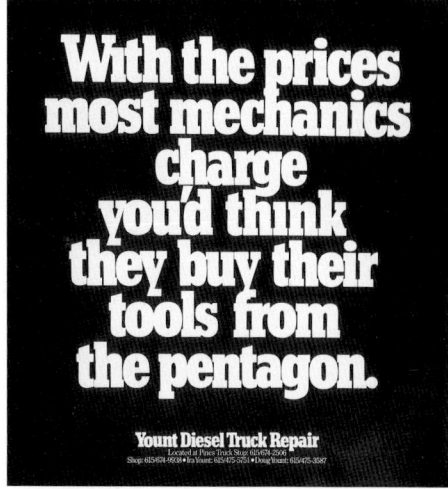

1137

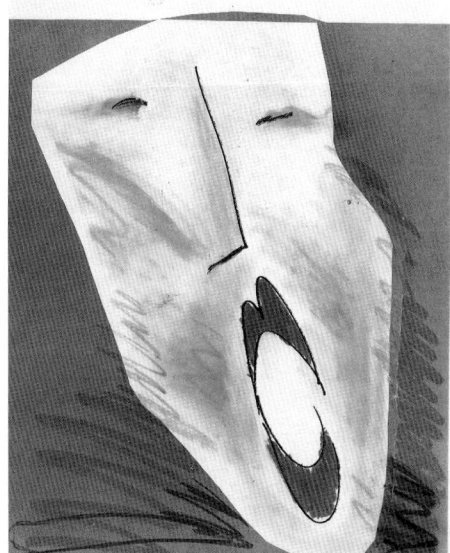

1139

1138

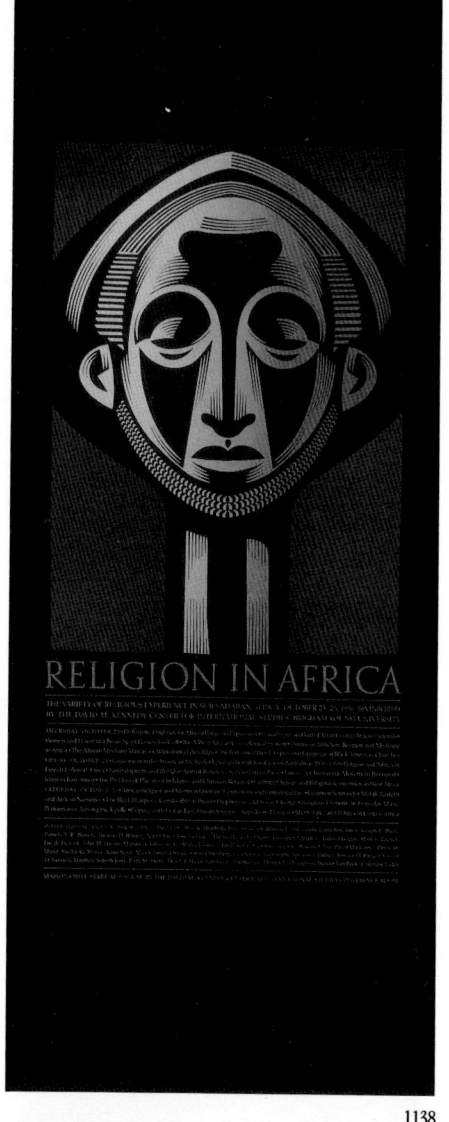

1140

1137
ART DIRECTOR
Larry Jarvis
DESIGNER
Larry Jarvis
WRITER
Larry Jarvis
CLIENT
Yount Diesel Truck Repair
AGENCY
Bozell, Jacobs, Kenyon & Eckhardt,
Minneapolis, MN

1138
ART DIRECTOR
McRay Magleby
DESIGNER
McRay Magleby
ILLUSTRATOR/ARTIST
McRay Magleby
WRITER
Thomas D. Blakely, Pamela A. R. Blakely
CLIENT
David M. Kennedy Center for International
Studies, BYU
DESIGN FIRM
BYU Graphics, Provo, UT
PRINTER
Nathan Richards
TYPOGRAPHER
Jonathan Skousen

1139
ART DIRECTOR
William Wondriska
DESIGNER
Dennis Russo
ILLUSTRATOR/ARTIST
Dennis Russo
CLIENT
Simsbury Light Opera Company / The
Hartford Insurance Company
PUBLISHER
Simsbury Light Opera Company
DIRECTOR
William K. Erhart, Music Director, Ron
Luchsinger, Artistic Director
DESIGN FIRM
Wondriska Associates, Farmington, CT

1140
ART DIRECTOR
Louis Fishauf
DESIGNER
Louis Fishauf
ILLUSTRATOR/ARTIST
Jean Tuttle
CLIENT
Bata Industries Ltd.
DESIGN FIRM
Reactor Art & Design, Toronto, Canada
ACCOUNT MANAGER
Robert Young

1141

DESIGN DIRECTOR
Rolando Rosler
DESIGNER
Anthony Paul Hyun
ILLUSTRATOR/ARTIST
Anthony Paul Hyun
CLIENT
Ensemble Studio Theatre
DIRECTOR
Margaret H. Widelock
DESIGN FIRM
S&O Consultants Inc., San Francisco, CA
CREATIVE DIRECTOR
David Canaan

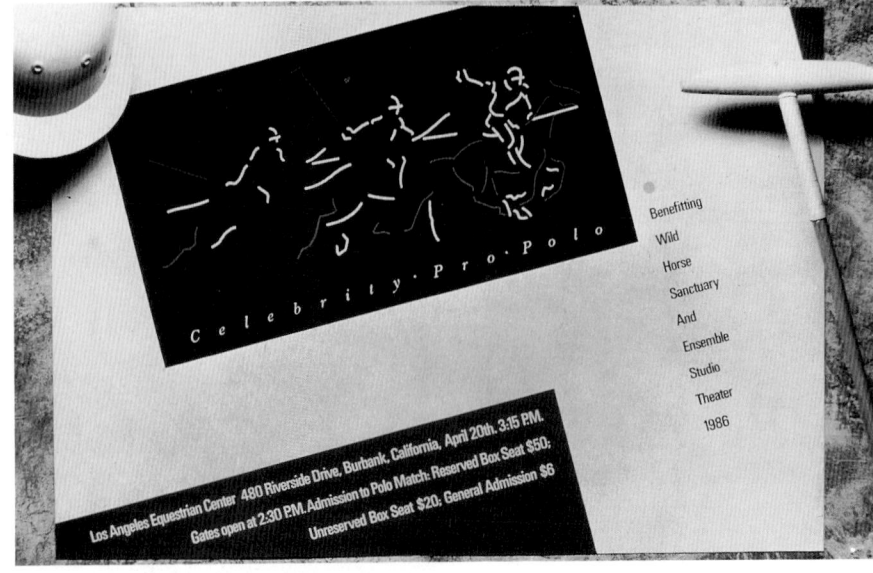

1141

1142

ART DIRECTOR
Stephen Frykholm
DESIGNER
Stephen Frykholm
ILLUSTRATOR/ARTIST
Stephen Frykholm
CLIENT
Herman Miller, Inc
PRINTER
Continental Identification
TYPOGRAPHER
Type House Inc.

1142

1143

ART DIRECTOR
Stephen Kashtan
DESIGNER
Stephen Kashtan
PHOTOGRAPHER
Gabe Palmer
CLIENT
Shearson Lehman Brothers
AGENCY
Madris, Nelson & Colleagues, New York, NY

1143

1144

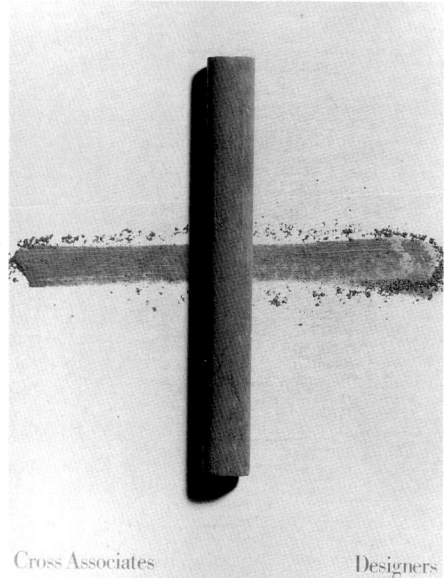

Cross Associates   Designers

1145

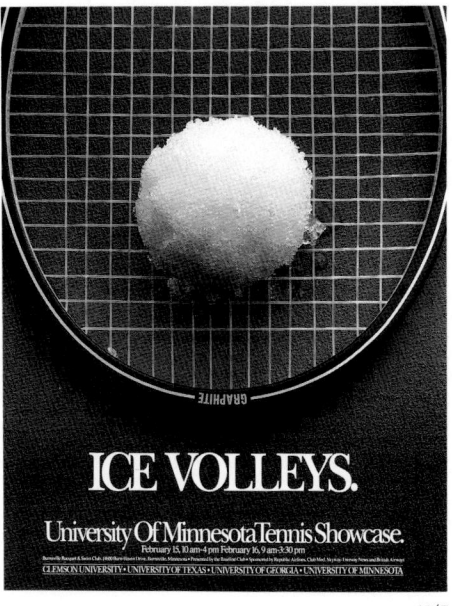

1147

1146

1144
ART DIRECTOR
Saul Bass, Art Goodman
DESIGNER
Saul Bass
PHOTOGRAPHER
Energy Productions
CLIENT
Directors Guild of America
DESIGN FIRM
Bass/Yager & Assoc., Los Angeles, CA

1145
ART DIRECTOR
James Cross, John Clark
DESIGNER
John Clark
PHOTOGRAPHER
David Randle
CLIENT
Cross Associates
DESIGN FIRM
Cross Associates, Los Angeles, CA
PRINTER
Anderson Printing

1146
ART DIRECTOR
Ken Parkhurst
DESIGNER
Ken Parkhurst, Denis Parkhurst
ILLUSTRATOR/ARTIST
Denis Parkhurst
WRITER
Ken Parkhurst
CLIENT
Scott & Scott Lithography
PUBLISHER
Scott & Scott Lithography
DESIGN FIRM
Ken Parkhurst & Associates, Inc., Los
Angeles, CA

1147
ART DIRECTOR
Mark Haumersen
DESIGNER
Mark Haumersen
PHOTOGRAPHER
Crofoot Photography
WRITER
Lyle Wedemeyer
CLIENT
University of Minnesota Athletics
AGENCY
Martin/Williams, Minneapolis, MN

1148
ART DIRECTOR
Karen Brown
PHOTOGRAPHER
Peggy Sirota
WRITER
Cathy Berg
CLIENT
Dayton Hudson Department Stores
DESIGN FIRM
Dayton Hudson Dept. Store in-house,
Minneapolis, MN

1149
ART DIRECTOR
Craig Frazier, Jeff Hurn
DESIGNER
Craig Frazier
WRITER
Jeff Hurn
CLIENT
Artificial Intelligence
DESIGN FIRM
Frazier Design, San Francisco, CA

1150
ART DIRECTOR
Thomas G. Hair
DESIGNER
Thomas G. Hair
PHOTOGRAPHER
Pete Lacker
ILLUSTRATOR/ARTIST
Thomas G. Hair
WRITER
Thomas G. Hair
CLIENT
Clampitt Paper Company
DIRECTOR
Thomas G. Hair
PUBLISHER
Harp Press
AGENCY
Rosenberg & Company, Dallas, TX
PRODUCTION ARTIST
Cyndi Brock

1151
ART DIRECTOR
Richard Console, Linda Canale
DESIGNER
Mike Quon
ILLUSTRATOR/ARTIST
Mike Quon
CLIENT
PaineWebber
DESIGN FIRM
Mike Quon Design Office, Inc., New York, NY

1148

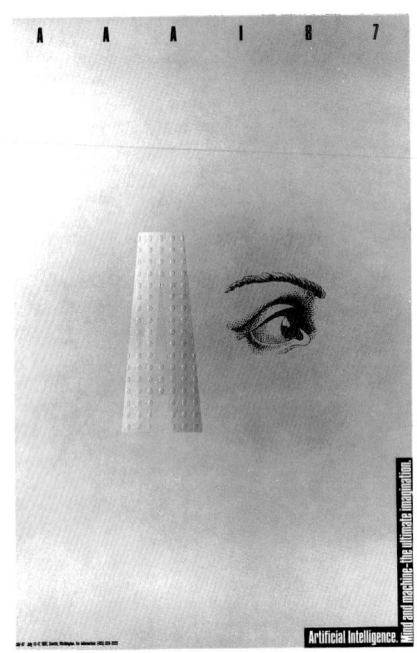

1149

1150

1151

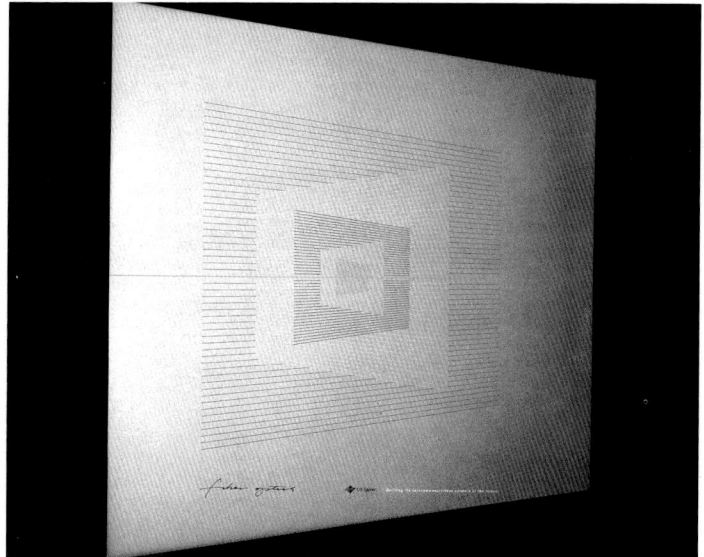

1152

1153

1154

1155

1152
ART DIRECTOR
Mark Anderson, Antony Milner
DESIGNER
Earl Gee
ILLUSTRATOR/ARTIST
Earl Gee
CLIENT
US Sprint Communications Corporation
DESIGN FIRM
Mark Anderson Design, Palo Alto, CA
PRINTER
Overland Printers, Inc.

1153
ART DIRECTOR
Linda Tom
DESIGNER
Michael Orr, Peggy Personious
CLIENT
IBM Endicott Communications
AGENCY
IBM Endicott Design Center, Endicott, NY
DESIGN FIRM
Michael Orr & Associates, Inc.

1154
DESIGNER
Charles Spencer Anderson
ILLUSTRATOR/ARTIST
Joe Duffy, Lynn Schulte
DESIGN FIRM
Duffy Design Group, Minneapolis, MN

1155
ART DIRECTOR
Thomas Lehman
DESIGNER
Thomas Lehman Design
ILLUSTRATOR/ARTIST
Gary Jacobsen
CLIENT
Pacific Northwest Ballet
DESIGN FIRM
Thomas Lehman Design, Seattle, WA

1156

ART DIRECTOR
Craig Frazier
DESIGNER
Craig Frazier
ILLUSTRATOR/ARTIST
Craig Frazier
CLIENT
AIGA - San Francisco
DESIGN FIRM
Frazier Design, San Francisco, CA

1157

ART DIRECTOR
Diana Howard
ILLUSTRATOR/ARTIST
Rodger Duncan
WRITER
Jayne Ingram
EDITOR
Jayne Ingram
AGENCY
Vogue Promotion, New York, NY
PUBLICATION
Vogue
CREATIVE DIRECTOR
Robin Sweet

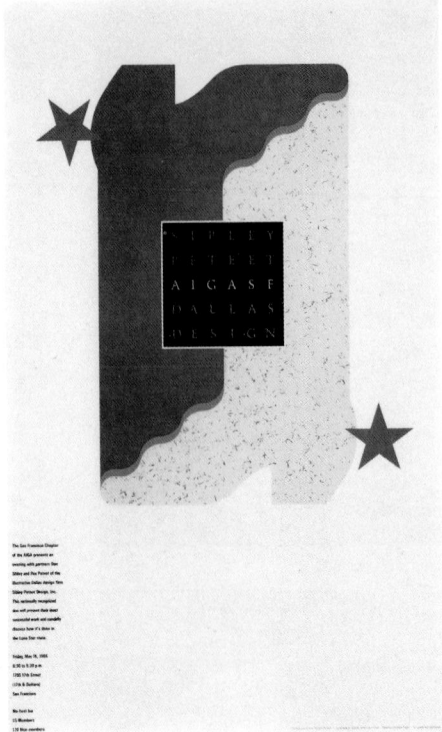

1156

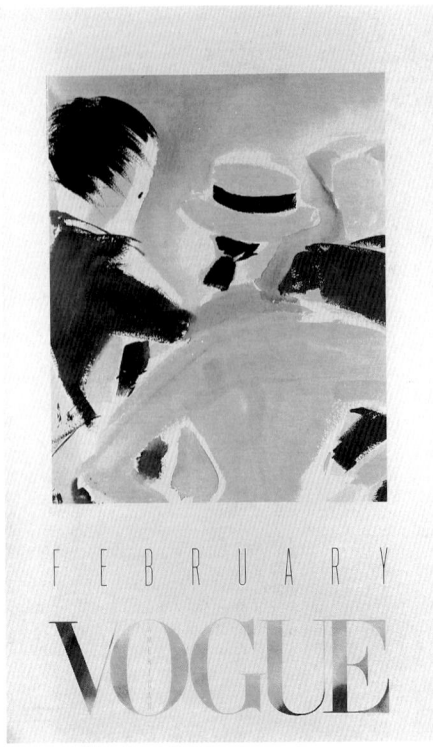

1157

1158

ART DIRECTOR
Steven Sessions
DESIGNER
Steven Sessions
ILLUSTRATOR/ARTIST
Jesus Felix, Steven Sessions
WRITER
Don Gordon, Steven Sessions
CLIENT
Houston Advertising Federation
AGENCY
Steven Sessions, Inc., Houston, TX
DESIGN FIRM
Steven Sessions, Inc.

1158

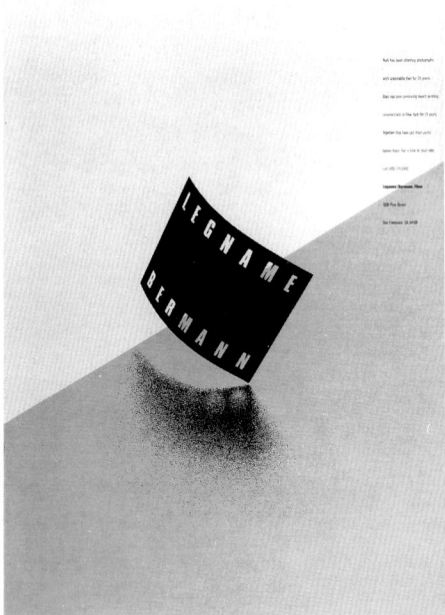

1159

1159

ART DIRECTOR
Craig Frazier
DESIGNER
Craig Frazier
CLIENT
Legname/Bermann Films
DESIGN FIRM
Frazier Design, San Francisco, CA

1160

1161

1162

1163

1160
ART DIRECTOR
Diana Howard
ILLUSTRATOR/ARTIST
Rodger Duncan
WRITER
Jayne Ingram
EDITOR
Jayne Ingram
AGENCY
Vogue Promotion, New York, NY
PUBLICATION
Vogue
CREATIVE DIRECTOR
Robin Sweet

1161
ART DIRECTOR
William Wondriska
DESIGNER
William Wondriska
ILLUSTRATOR/ARTIST
William Wondriska
CLIENT
Boston Symphony Orchestra at Tanglewood
EDITOR
Vera Gold
DIRECTOR
Seiji Ozawa, Music Director
PUBLISHER
Tanglewood Music Center
DESIGN FIRM
Wondriska Associates, Farmington, CT
PRINTER
Allied Printing Services

1162
ART DIRECTOR
William Wondriska
DESIGNER
William Wondriska, Laura Smith
ILLUSTRATOR/ARTIST
Laura Smith
CLIENT
Boston Symphony Orchestra
EDITOR
Vera Gold
DIRECTOR
Seiji Ozawa, Music Director
PUBLISHER
Boston Symphony Orchestra
DESIGN FIRM
Wondriska Associates, Farmington, CT
PRINTER
Finlay Brothers

1163
ART DIRECTOR
Ken Harris
DESIGNER
Ken Harris
PHOTOGRAPHER
Eric Roth
ILLUSTRATOR/ARTIST
Jack Crompton
CLIENT
Great Woods Educational Foundation
DESIGN FIRM
Grand Design/Boston, Marblehead, MA

1164
ART DIRECTOR
Dean Hanson
PHOTOGRAPHER
Rick Dublin
WRITER
Tom McElligott
CLIENT
Episcopal Ad Project
AGENCY
Fallon McElligott, Minneapolis, MN

1165
ART DIRECTOR
George Tscherny
DESIGNER
George Tscherny
ILLUSTRATOR/ARTIST
George Tscherny
CLIENT
Samuel C. Florman
AGENCY
George Tscherny, Inc., New York, NY
DESIGN FIRM
George Tscherny, Inc.

1166
ART DIRECTOR
Jeff Terwilliger
DESIGNER
Jeff Terwilliger
PHOTOGRAPHER
Steve Umland
WRITER
Kerry Casey
CLIENT
Surdyk's
AGENCY
Bozell, Jacobs, Kenyon & Eckhardt,
Minneapolis, MN

1167
ART DIRECTOR
Michael Vanderbyl
DESIGNER
Michael Vanderbyl
ILLUSTRATOR/ARTIST
Michael Bull
CLIENT
Hickory Business Furniture
DESIGN FIRM
Vanderbyl Design, San Francisco, CA

1164

1165

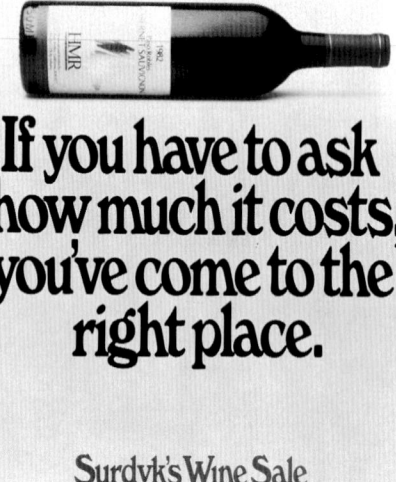

1166

1167

1168

ART DIRECTOR
Marcia Stone
PHOTOGRAPHER
Rick Dublin
WRITER
Joe Milla
CLIENT
McDonald's (Upper Midwest)
AGENCY
Carmichael-Lynch, Minneapolis, MN
CREATIVE DIRECTOR
Dan Krumwiede

1168

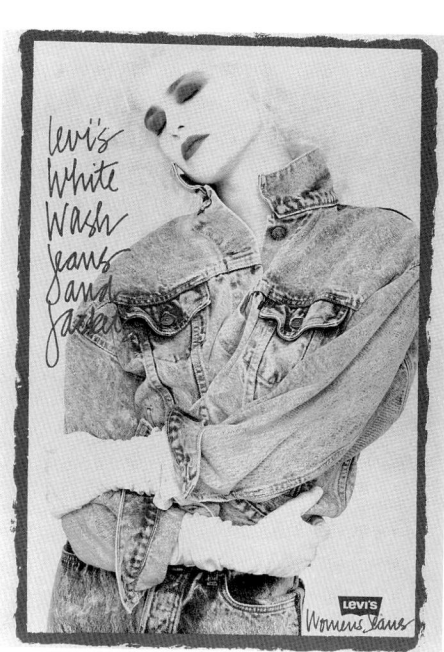

1169

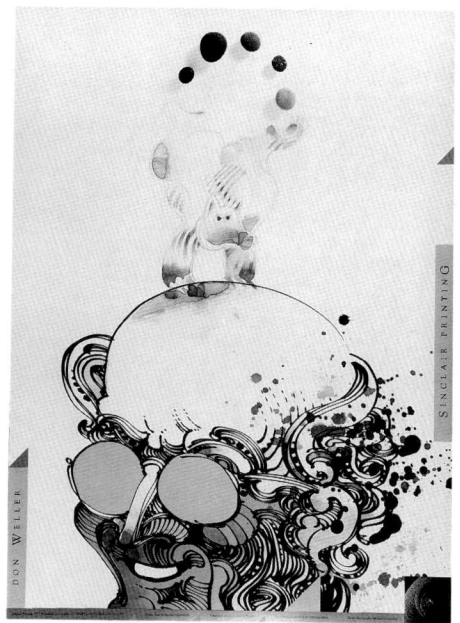

1170

1169

ART DIRECTOR
Jennifer Morla
DESIGNER
Jennifer Morla
PHOTOGRAPHER
Matthew Rolston
CLIENT
Levi Strauss & Co.
DESIGN FIRM
Morla Design, Inc., San Francisco, CA

1170

ART DIRECTOR
Don Weller with Harold Burch
DESIGNER
Don Weller
PHOTOGRAPHER
Michael Schoenfeld
ILLUSTRATOR/ARTIST
Don Weller
CLIENT
Sinclair Printing
PUBLISHER
Sinclair Publishing
DESIGN FIRM
The Weller Institute for the Cure of Design,
Inc., Park City, UT

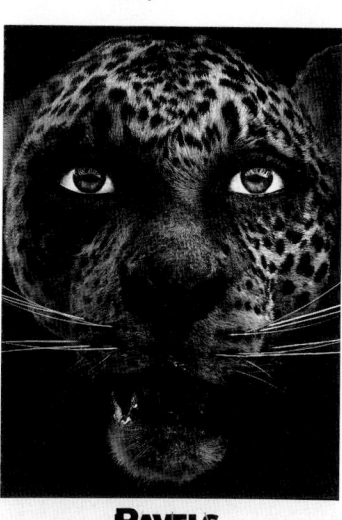

1171

1171

ART DIRECTOR
Alan Lidji
DESIGNER
Alan Lidji
PHOTOGRAPHER
Robert Latorre
WRITER
Mike Kirby
CLIENT
The Registry Hotel
AGENCY
Rosenberg & Company, Dallas, TX

1172

ART DIRECTOR
Jerry Requa
DESIGNER
Kelly Smith
ILLUSTRATOR/ARTIST
Kurt Holloman, Stephen Peringer, Leslie
Hale, Vickie Wordworth, Renae DeMartin,
Kurt Reifschneider
WRITER
Kathe Fraga
CLIENT
Washington State Tourism
AGENCY
Cole & Weber/Seattle, Seattle, WA

1172

1173

1174

1173

ART DIRECTOR
Wes Massey
DESIGNER
Wes Massey
ILLUSTRATOR/ARTIST
Bill Mayer
WRITER
Carla Herrin
CLIENT
John H. Harland Co.
DIRECTOR
Greg Resler
DESIGN FIRM
John H. Harland Co. Idea Market, Atlanta,
GA

1174

ART DIRECTOR
Joe Duffy
DESIGNER
Joe Duffy
ILLUSTRATOR/ARTIST
Joe Duffy, Lynn Schulte
DESIGN FIRM
Duffy Design Group, Minneapolis, MN

1175

ART DIRECTOR
Greg Sullentrup, Jim White
PHOTOGRAPHER
Bill Debold, Bob Ebel, Chuck Kuhn
CLIENT
Anheuser-Busch, Inc.—Budweiser
AGENCY
D'Arcy Masius Benton & Bowles, St. Louis,
MO
CREATIVE DIRECTOR
Gerry Mandel

1175

1176

Celebrate the San Diego Zoo's 70th birthday.

1177

1176

ART DIRECTOR
Charles Spencer Anderson
DESIGNER
Charles Spencer Anderson
ILLUSTRATOR/ARTIST
Charles Spencer Anderson, Lynn Schulte
CLIENT
Wenger Corporation
DESIGN FIRM
Duffy Design Group, Minneapolis, MN

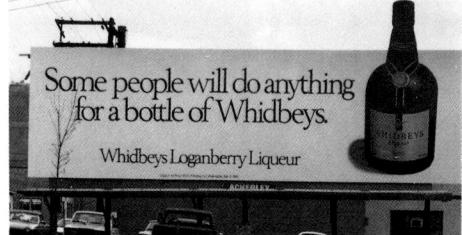

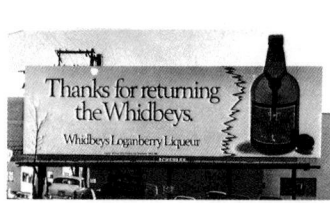

1178

1177

ART DIRECTOR
Bob Kwait
DESIGNER
Bob Kwait
ILLUSTRATOR/ARTIST
Darrel Millsap
WRITER
Rich Badami
CLIENT
San Diego Zoo
AGENCY
Phillips-Ramsey, San Diego, CA
PRODUCER
Ron Van Buskirk

1178

ART DIRECTOR
Angela Bogdanovich
PHOTOGRAPHER
Fred Milkie, Gary Benson
WRITER
Kathe Fraga
CLIENT
Chateau Ste. Michelle
AGENCY
Cole & Weber/Seattle, Seattle, WA

1179

1179

ART DIRECTOR
Paul Nye
WRITER
Bob Conlon
CLIENT
Joanna Robinson, Diner's Club International
AGENCY
SSC&B Inc., New York, NY
CREATIVE DIRECTOR
Michael Shalette

1180

ART DIRECTOR
Dean Hanson
PHOTOGRAPHER
Jim Arndt, Kerry Peterson, Marc Hauser
WRITER
Tom McElligott
CLIENT
Children's Defense Fund
AGENCY
Fallon McElligott, Minneapolis, MN

1180

1181

ART DIRECTOR
Dean Hanson
PHOTOGRAPHER
Marc Hauser, Rick Dublin
WRITER
Tom McElligott, George Gier
CLIENT
Children's Defense Fund
AGENCY
Fallon McElligott, Minneapolis, MN

  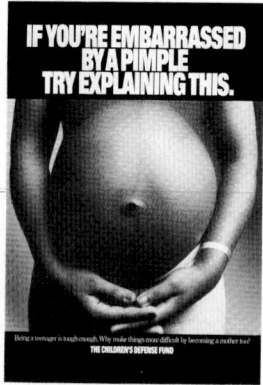

1181

 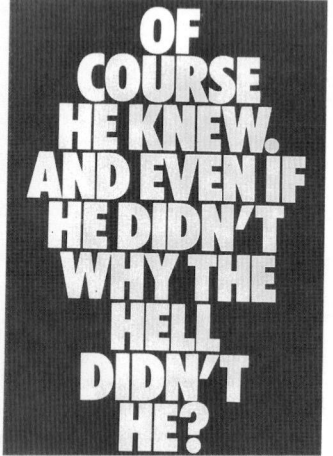

1182

ART DIRECTOR
Bill Caldwell
DESIGNER
Bill Caldwell
PHOTOGRAPHER
Bill Caldwell
ILLUSTRATOR/ARTIST
Bill Caldwell
WRITER
Bill Caldwell
CLIENT
Just Imagine Communications
EDITOR
Bill Caldwell, Marcia Schmitz
PUBLISHER
Just Imagine Communications
DESIGN FIRM
Just Imagine Communications, Arlington, VA
PRINTER
Cardany Printing

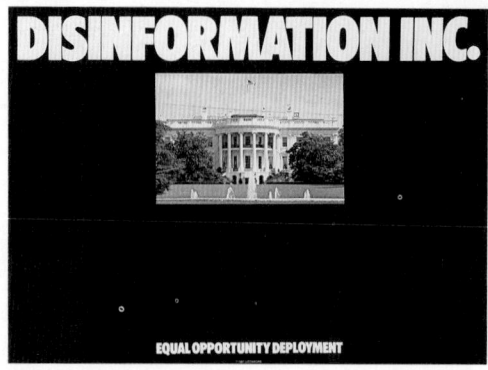

1182

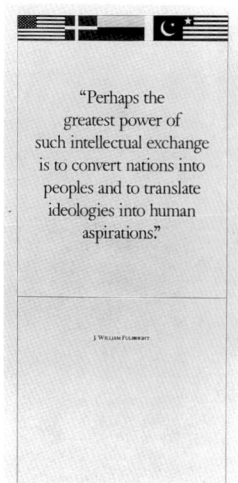

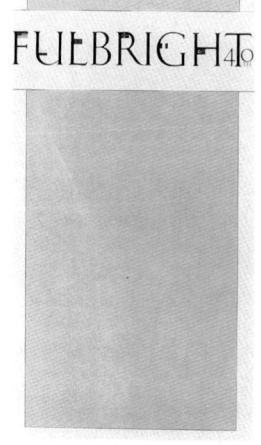

1183

1183
ART DIRECTOR
Alan Nurmi
DESIGNER
Nan Dearborn
CLIENT
U.S. Information Agency
EDITOR
Martha Williams
DIRECTOR
Karen Starkey

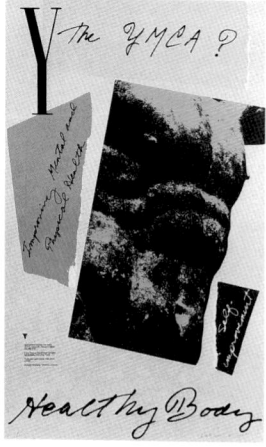

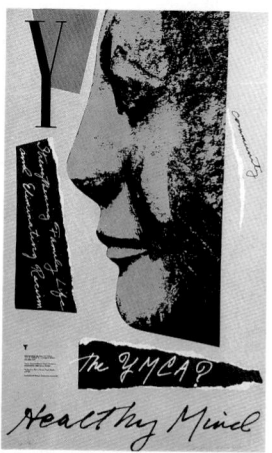

1184

1184
ART DIRECTOR
Katherine Lorenzetti
DESIGNER
Katherine Lorenzetti
ILLUSTRATOR/ARTIST
Katherine Lorenzetti
WRITER
Katherine Lorenzetti
CLIENT
New City YMCA
PRODUCER
Gary Grube, Proto-Grafix Limited
DESIGN FIRM
Katherine Lorenzetti, Chicago, IL

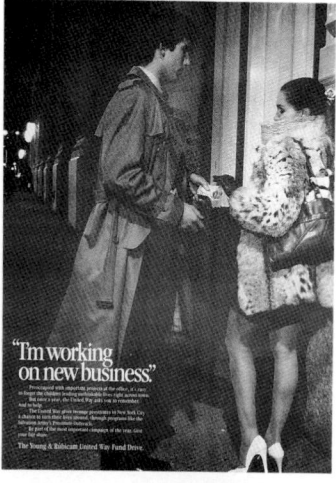

1185

1185
ART DIRECTOR
John Polachek
PHOTOGRAPHER
Chris Pizzolorusso
WRITER
Howard Gould
AGENCY
Young & Rubicam, New York, NY
CREATIVE DIRECTOR
Lou DiJoseph

1186
ART DIRECTOR
Ron Anderson
DESIGNER
Ron Anderson, Leila McGrath
WRITER
Dick Thomas
CLIENT
Presbyterian Church
AGENCY
Bozell, Jacobs, Kenyon & Eckhardt,
Minneapolis, MN

1187
ART DIRECTOR
Alan Nurmi
DESIGNER
Caesar Jackson
ILLUSTRATOR/ARTIST
Dagmar Frinta, Brian Leister, John Collier,
Becky Heavner
CLIENT
U.S. Information Agency
EDITOR
Martha Williams
DIRECTOR
Karen Starkey

1188
ART DIRECTOR
Kurt Tausche
DESIGNER
Kurt Tausche
WRITER
Pete Smith
CLIENT
Yellow Cab
AGENCY
Bozell, Jacobs, Kenyon & Eckhardt,
Minneapolis, MN

1186

1187

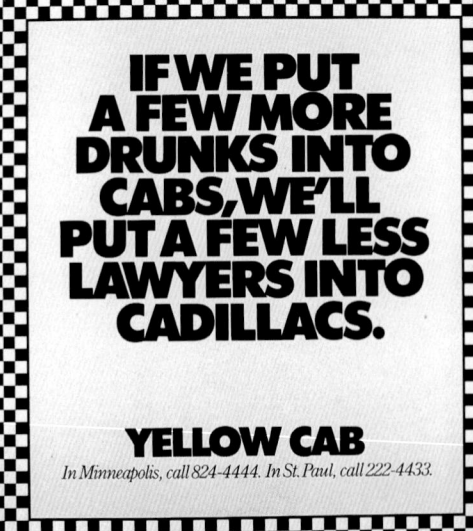
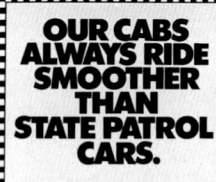
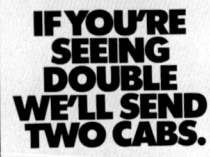

1188

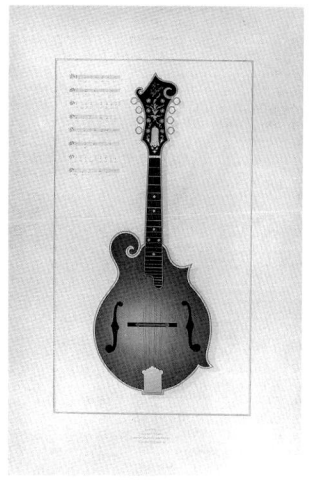
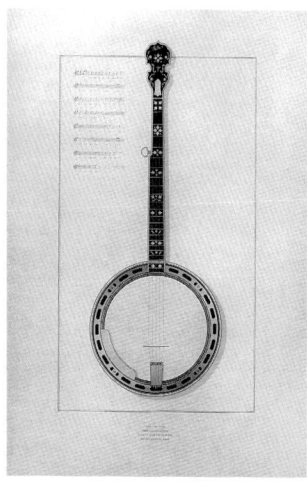

1189

ART DIRECTOR
McRay Magleby
DESIGNER
McRay Magleby
ILLUSTRATOR/ARTIST
Shari Hall, McRay Magleby, Joleen Roos
WRITER
Norman A. Darais
CLIENT
Brigham Young University Registration
DESIGN FIRM
BYU Graphics, Provo, UT
PRINTER
Nathan Richards
TYPOGRAPHER
Jonathan Skousen

1189

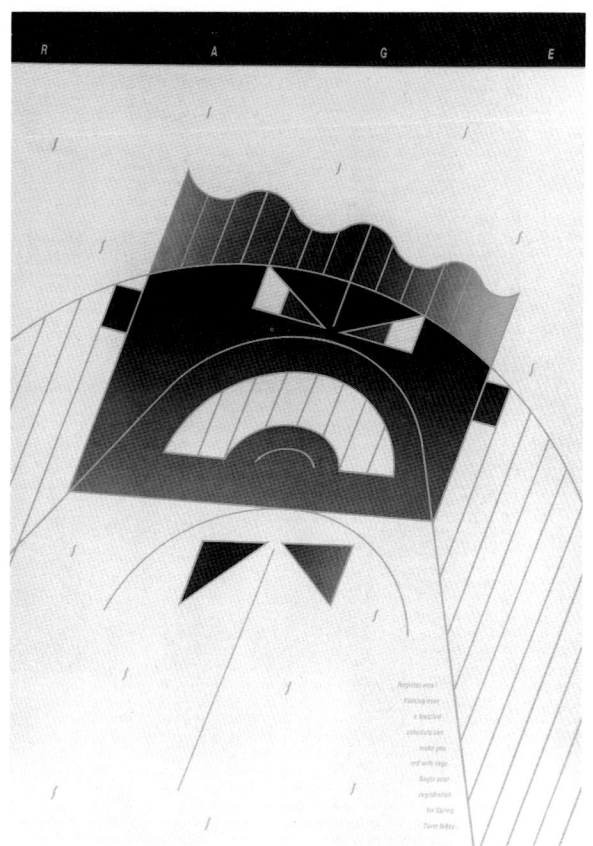

1190

ART DIRECTOR
McRay Magleby
DESIGNER
McRay Magleby
ILLUSTRATOR/ARTIST
Shari Hall, McRay Magleby
CLIENT
Brigham Young University Registration
DESIGN FIRM
BYU Graphics, Provo, UT
PRINTER
Nathan Richards

1190

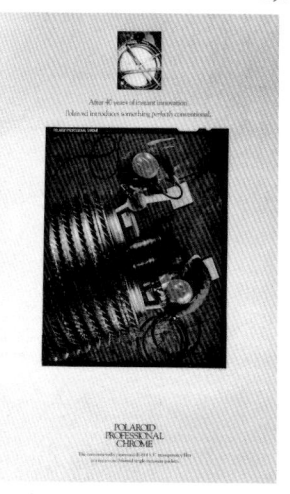

1191

ART DIRECTOR
Marie McGinley
DESIGNER
Marie McGinley
PHOTOGRAPHER
Mark Green, Richard Payne, Douglas Hopkins
WRITER
Rick Colson, Cameron Foote
CLIENT
Polaroid
PUBLISHER
Daniels Printing
DESIGN FIRM
Polaroid in-house, Cambridge, MA

1191

1192
ART DIRECTOR
Ellen Romano
DESIGNER
Ellen Romano, Richard Vaughn
PHOTOGRAPHER
Stuart Schwartz
WRITER
Lynda Heideman, Eric Stouffer
CLIENT
Apple Business Marketing
PUBLISHER
Apple Computer, Inc.
DESIGN FIRM
Apple Computer Creative Services, Cupertino,
CA

  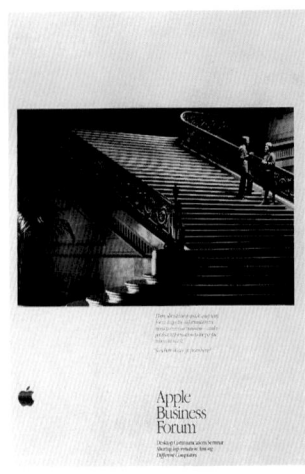

1192

1193
ART DIRECTOR
McRay Magleby
DESIGNER
McRay Magleby
ILLUSTRATOR/ARTIST
McRay Magleby, Gail Watne, Shari Hall
WRITER
Norman A. Darais
CLIENT
Brigham Young University Registration
DESIGN FIRM
BYU Graphics, Provo, UT
PRINTER
Jed Porter
TYPOGRAPHER
Jonathan Skousen

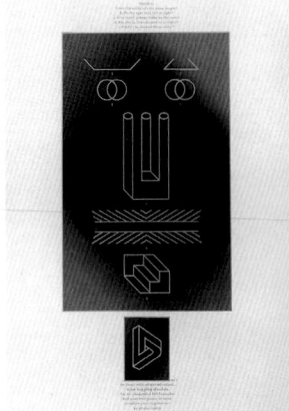

1194
ART DIRECTOR
Scott A. Mednick
DESIGNER
Scott A. Mednick, Daniel J. Simon
PHOTOGRAPHER
Ken Merfeld
WRITER
Scott A. Mednick, Lori Precious, Daniel J.
Simon, Cathy Linstrom
CLIENT
Pogo Pizza
DESIGN FIRM
Scott Mednick & Associates, Los Angeles, CA

1193

1195
ART DIRECTOR
Steven Noxon
DESIGNER
John Dudek, Steven Noxon
ILLUSTRATOR/ARTIST
Leo Skidmore, Leonard Bertin, Bob Andrews
WRITER
James Turnbull III, Susan Logar
CLIENT
Hill's Pet Products, Inc.
AGENCY
(Y&R) Wunderman, Ricotta & Kline, Inc.,
Detroit, MI
DESIGN FIRM
Skidmore Sahratian, Inc.
TYPOGRAPHER
Willens/Michigan

1194

1195

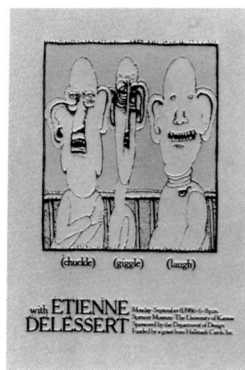 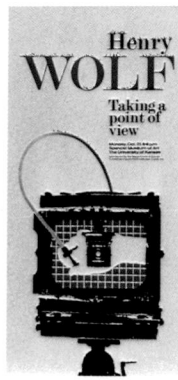 

1196

 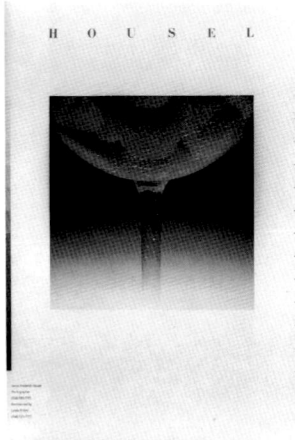 

1197

1198

1199

1196
ART DIRECTOR
Richard Varney, Keith Jones
DESIGNER
Richard Varney, Keith Jones, Kathy O'Meara
CLIENT
Hallmark Symposium Lecture Series
AGENCY
University of Kansas Department of Design,
Lawrence, KS

1197
ART DIRECTOR
Jack Anderson
DESIGNER
Jack Anderson, Heidi Hatlestad
PHOTOGRAPHER
James Frederick Housel
CLIENT
James Frederick Housel
DESIGN FIRM
Hornall Anderson Design Works, Seattle, WA

1198
ART DIRECTOR
George Delany
DESIGNER
Catherine McGuinness, George Delany
ILLUSTRATOR/ARTIST
Catherine McGuinness (Calligraphy)
CLIENT
Delany Design Group, Inc.
DESIGN FIRM
Delany Design Group, Inc., Providence, RI
PRINTER
Graphic Images Screen Printing

1199
ART DIRECTOR
Rick Vaughan, Steve Wedeen
DESIGNER
Kevin Tolman (Smell), Steven Wedeen
(Taste), Rick Vaughn (Hearing)
ILLUSTRATOR/ARTIST
Kevin Tolman, Mark Chamberlain, Rick
Vaughn
WRITER
Kevin Tolman, Steven Wedeen
CLIENT
Academy Printers
DESIGN FIRM
Vaughn/Wedeen Creative, Inc., Albuquerque,
NM

ILLUSTRATION:

"Ho Ho Ho"

In 1925, the Minnesota Valley Canning Company wanted to introduce a new type of pea as "Green Giant". But the company's trademark attorney warned that the name alone would not afford brand name protection and suggested that a picture of a giant be added to the label. That way it could be argued that the name referred to the giant and not the peas.

The first giant, a wild-haired creature with a fur wrap, muscled his way past the trademark examiners. In 1935, a young Chicago ad man named Leo Burnett gave the giant a total renovation—adding a green skin, leaf cloak and a smile.

1200
ART DIRECTOR
Steve Scholem
DESIGNER
Mike Quon, Sam Gunn
ILLUSTRATOR/ARTIST
Mike Quon
WRITER
Norah Delaney
CLIENT
Hennessey
AGENCY
Lord, Geller, Federico, Einstein Inc.
DESIGN FIRM
Mike Quon Design Office, Inc., New York, NY

1200

1201
ART DIRECTOR
Bob Eisner
DESIGNER
Jack Sherman, Gary Viskupic
ILLUSTRATOR/ARTIST
Gary Viskupic
WRITER
Richard Rosecrance
CLIENT
Newsday
EDITOR
Ilene Barth
PUBLISHER
Newsday Inc.
DESIGN FIRM
Newsday Editorial Art Dept., Melville, NY
PUBLICATION
Newsday 'Ideas' section

1201

1202
ART DIRECTOR
Brad Zucroff
DESIGNER
Doug Griswold
ILLUSTRATOR/ARTIST
Doug Griswold
EDITOR
Sheila Himmel
PUBLICATION
San Jose Mercury News, San Jose, CA

1202

1203
ART DIRECTOR
Bob Barthelmes
ILLUSTRATOR/ARTIST
John Rombola
WRITER
Buddy Radisch
CLIENT
Zeckendorf Company
AGENCY
Great Scott Advertising, New York, NY
CREATIVE DIRECTOR
Lorraine Borden
SR. ACCOUNT SPVSR
Lorraine Borden
ACCOUNT SPVSR
Gene Messinger

1203

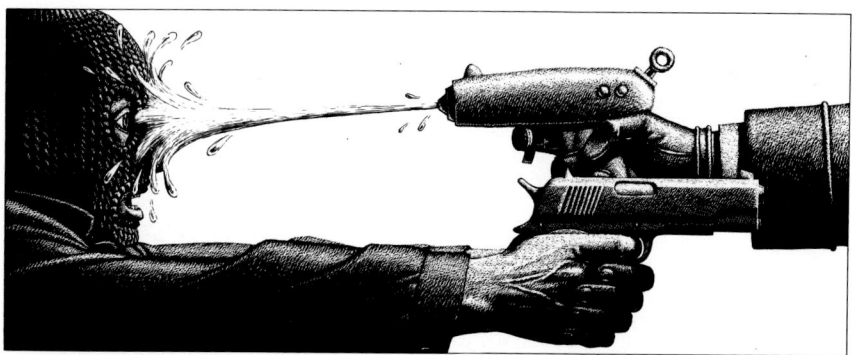

1204

ART DIRECTOR
Tom Trapnell
ILLUSTRATOR/ARTIST
Mirko Ilic
PUBLISHER
LA Times, Los Angeles, CA
PUBLICATION
LA Times

LIVING WITH DEATH

ESSAY

A walk through a cemetery can teach us something about ourselves. It can tell us less about death than about the way we live and the way we deal with our past — and our inevitable future.

BY ADRIAN PERACCHIO

1205

ART DIRECTOR
Miriam Smith
DESIGNER
Lee Hill
ILLUSTRATOR/ARTIST
Gary Viskupic
WRITER
Adrian Peracchio
CLIENT
Newsday Magazine
DESIGN FIRM
Newsday Editorial Art Dept., Melville, NY
PUBLICATION
Newsday Magazine

Out Of Control

BEHAVIOR

"You can't control me," the daughter gloated. And, for a while she was right — inexplicably turning into a raging, foul-mouthed stranger, defiant both at home and at school. The reason eventually became painfully clear; the remedy, painfully uncertain.

BY JESSICA SHANNON

1206

ART DIRECTOR
Miriam Smith
DESIGNER
George Ramos
ILLUSTRATOR/ARTIST
Gary Viskupic
WRITER
Jessica Shannon
CLIENT
Newsday Magazine
EDITOR
John Montorio
PUBLISHER
Newsday Inc.
DESIGN FIRM
Newsday Editorial Art Dept., Melville, NY
PUBLICATION
Newsday Magazine

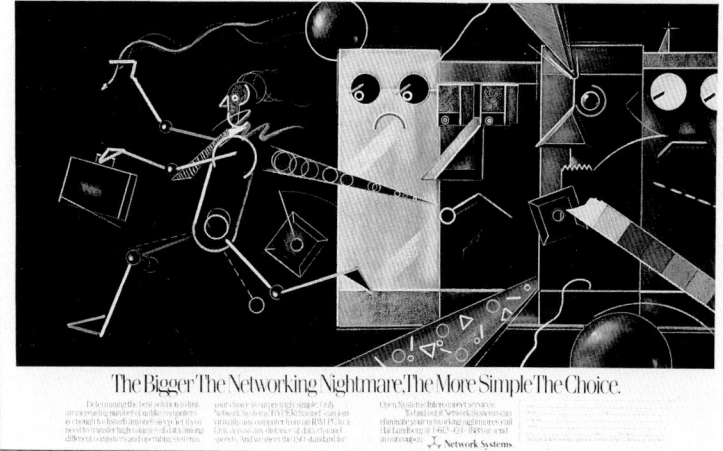

The Bigger The Networking Nightmare, The More Simple The Choice.

1207

ART DIRECTOR
Warren Johnson
ILLUSTRATOR/ARTIST
Andrezej Dudzinski
WRITER
Nancy Wellinger
CLIENT
Network Systems
AGENCY
Carmichael-Lynch, Minneapolis, MN

1208
ART DIRECTOR
Gordon Hochhalter
ILLUSTRATOR/ARTIST
Vivienne Flesher
WRITER
Gordon Hochhalter
CLIENT
R.R. Donnelly & Sons Company
PRODUCER
Maryann Novak
ACCOUNT SUPERVISOR
Joe Cosgrove

1209
ART DIRECTOR
Victor Liebert
ILLUSTRATOR/ARTIST
Thea Kliros
CLIENT
Trevira
AGENCY
Trevira in-house, Ina Kahn, New York, NY
DESIGN FIRM
Liebert Studio

1208

1209

1210
ART DIRECTOR
Tom Clemente
DESIGNER
John Sullivan
ILLUSTRATOR/ARTIST
Mark English
WRITER
Hank Simons
CLIENT
Newspapers of U.S. and Canada
DESIGN FIRM
Newspaper Advertising Bureau, New York, NY
PUBLICATION
Creative Newspaper II

1211
ART DIRECTOR
Nancy Walker
ILLUSTRATOR/ARTIST
Bill Mayer, Decator, GA
CLIENT
Coors Town Point Jazz Festival

1210

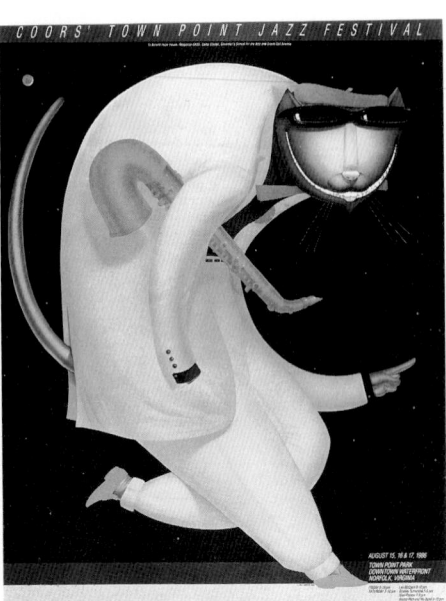
1211

1212

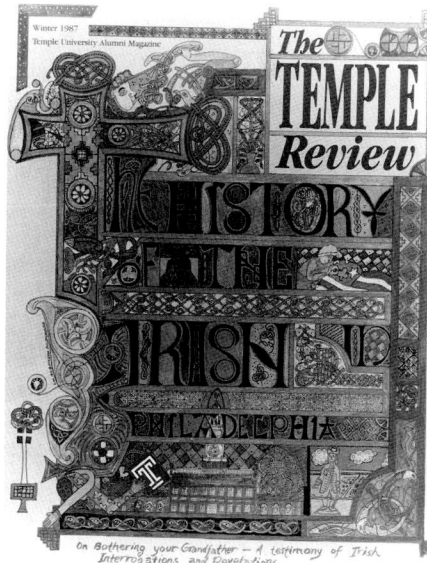

1213

1214

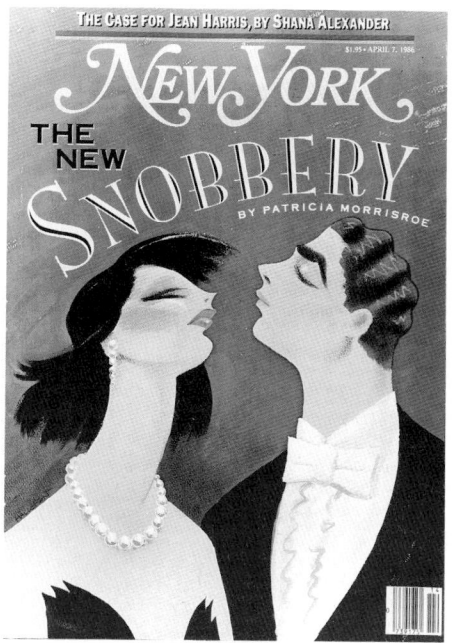

1215

1212
ART DIRECTOR
Sara Eisenman
DESIGNER
Sara Eisenman
ILLUSTRATOR/ARTIST
Walton Ford
WRITER
Dalene Mathee
EDITOR
Robert Gottlieb
PUBLISHER
Alfred A. Knopf, New York, NY

1213
DESIGNER
Laura M. Robinson Pritchard
ILLUSTRATOR/ARTIST
Laura M. Robinson Pritchard
WRITER
Dennis Clark
CLIENT
The Temple Review
EDITOR
Bonnie Squires
ASSOC. EDITOR
Ruth Schultz
PUBLISHER
Temple University
DESIGN FIRM
Laura M. Robinson Pritchard, Philadelphia,
PA
PUBLICATION
The Temple Review

1214
ART DIRECTOR
Diana LaGuardia
DESIGNER
Audrey Razgaitis
ILLUSTRATOR/ARTIST
Larry Rivers
CLIENT
The New York Times Magazine
EDITOR
Ed Klein
PUBLISHER
The New York Times, New York, NY
PUBLICATION
The New York Times

1215
ART DIRECTOR
Robert Best
DESIGNER
Josh Gosfield
ILLUSTRATOR/ARTIST
Gary Hallgren
EDITOR
Edward Kosner
PUBLISHER
Edward Kosner, Murdoch Magazines
PUBLICATION
New York Magazine, New York, NY

1216

ART DIRECTOR
Dwayne Flinchum
DESIGNER
Dwayne Flinchum
ILLUSTRATOR/ARTIST
Don Eddy
GRAPHICS DIRECTOR
Frank Devino
PUBLISHER
Bob Guccione
PUBLICATION
Omni Publications International Ltd., New
York, NY

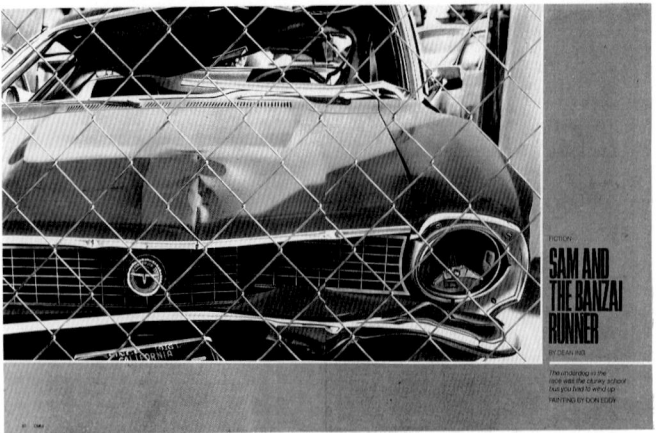

1216

1217

ART DIRECTOR
Lois Erlacher
DESIGNER
Marlene Goldman
ILLUSTRATOR/ARTIST
Peter DeSéve
WRITER
Alan Fitch
EDITOR
Douglas W.E. Wagner
PUBLICATION
Emergency Medicine Magazine, New York,
NY

1217

1218

ART DIRECTOR
Lois Erlacher
DESIGNER
Lois Erlacher
ILLUSTRATOR/ARTIST
Bradley Clark
WRITER
Hilda Regier
EDITOR
Douglas W.E. Wagner
PUBLICATION
Emergency Medicine Magazine, New York,
NY

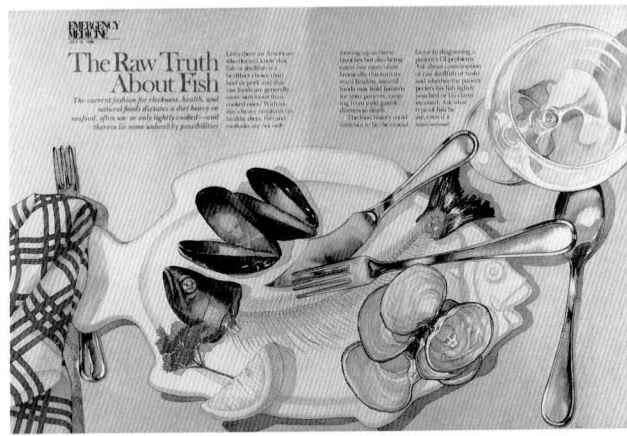

1218

1219

ART DIRECTOR
Lois Erlacher
DESIGNER
Marlene Goldman
ILLUSTRATOR/ARTIST
Sherilyn Van Valkenburgh
WRITER
Edward D. Harris Jr., M.D., Adele Zinberg
EDITOR
Douglas W.E. Wagner
PUBLICATION
Emergency Medicine Magazine, New York,
NY

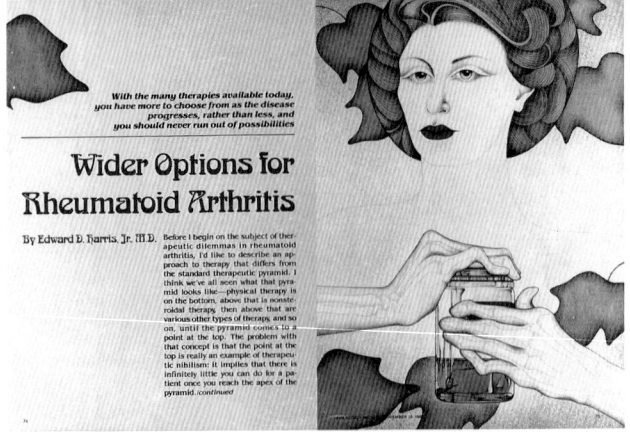

1219

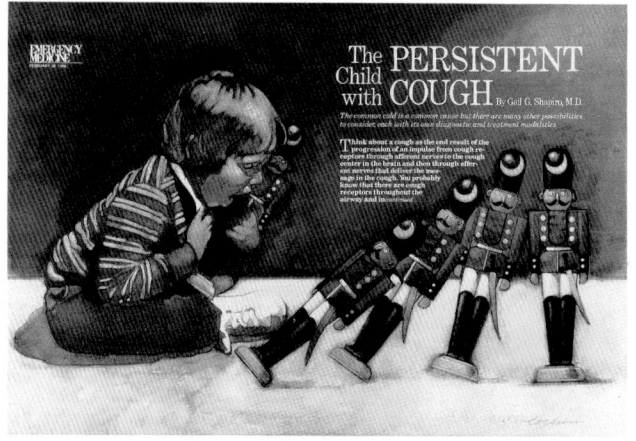

1220

1220

ART DIRECTOR
Lois Erlacher
DESIGNER
Marlene Goldman
ILLUSTRATOR/ARTIST
Rick McCollum
WRITER
Gail Shapiro
EDITOR
Douglas W.E. Wagner
PUBLICATION
Emergency Medicine Magazine, New York,
NY

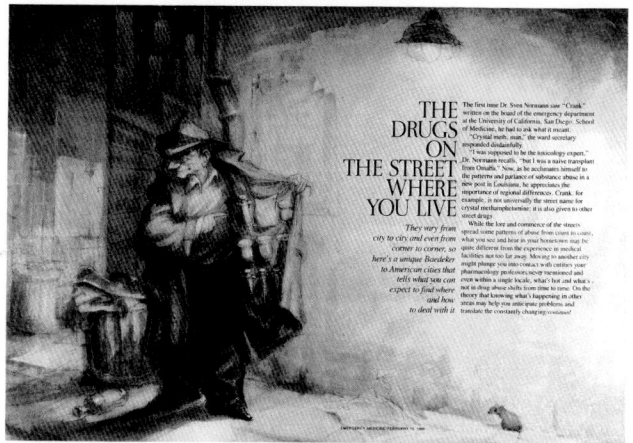

1221

1221

ART DIRECTOR
Lois Erlacher
DESIGNER
Lois Erlacher
ILLUSTRATOR/ARTIST
Peter DeSéve
WRITER
Hilder Regier
EDITOR
Douglas W.E. Wagner
PUBLICATION
Emergency Medicine Magazine, New York,
NY

1222

1222

ART DIRECTOR
Lois Erlacher
DESIGNER
Marlene Goldman
ILLUSTRATOR/ARTIST
Bonnie Hofkin
EDITOR
Douglas W.E. Wagner
PUBLICATION
Emergency Medicine Magazine, New York,
NY

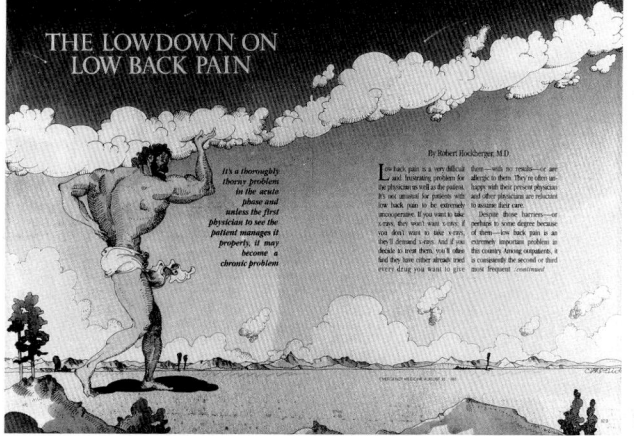

1223

1223

ART DIRECTOR
Lois Erlacher
ILLUSTRATOR/ARTIST
Joseph Ciardiello
WRITER
Robert Hockberger, M.D., Alan Fitch
EDITOR
Douglas W.E. Wagner
PUBLICATION
Emergency Medicine Magazine, New York,
NY

1224
ART DIRECTOR
Harold A. Perry
DESIGNER
Harold A. Perry
ILLUSTRATOR/ARTIST
Steve Dininno
CLIENT
Hearst Business Publications
EDITOR
Kenneth Zino
PUBLICATION
Motor Magazine, New York, NY

1224

1225
ART DIRECTOR
Allen Carroll
ILLUSTRATOR/ARTIST
Davis Meltzer
CLIENT
National Geographic Magazine
EDITOR
W.E. Garrett
PUBLISHER
National Geographic Society
PUBLICATION
National Geographic Magazine, Washington,
DC

1225

1226
ART DIRECTOR
Thomas Darnsteadt
DESIGN DIRECTOR
John Newcomb
ILLUSTRATOR/ARTIST
Brian Ahjar
CLIENT
Medical Economics Co., Inc.
EDITOR
Valentine Cardinale
PUBLISHER
William J. Reynolds
PUBLICATION
Drug Topics Magazine

1227
ART DIRECTOR
William J. Kuhn
DESIGN DIRECTOR
John Newcomb
PHOTOGRAPHER
Stephen E. Munz
ILLUSTRATOR/ARTIST
Gordon Swenarton
WRITER
Mark Crane
CLIENT
Medical Economics Co., Inc.
EDITOR
Joel Goldberg
PUBLISHER
Jim Jenkins
PUBLICATION
Medical Economics for Surgeons, Oradell, NJ

1226

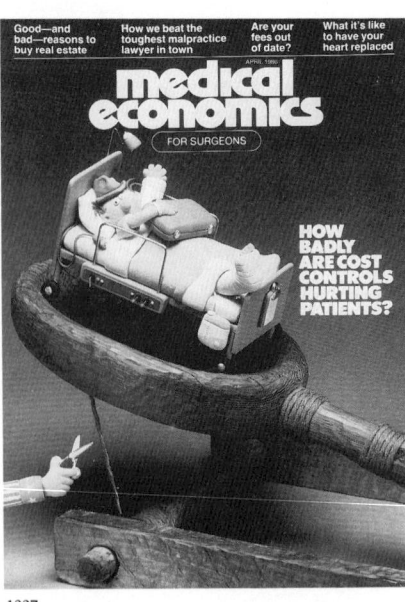

1227

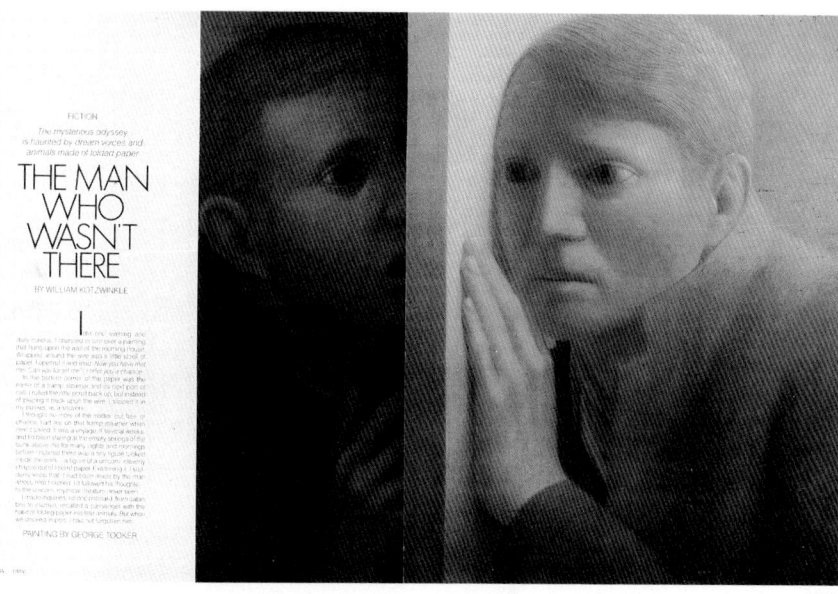

1228

ART DIRECTOR
Dwayne Flinchum
DESIGNER
Dwayne Flinchum
ILLUSTRATOR/ARTIST
George Tooker
GRAPHICS DIRECTOR
Frank Devino
PUBLISHER
Bob Guccione
PUBLICATION
Omni Publications International Ltd., New York, NY

1228

1229

ART DIRECTOR
Diana LaGuardia
DESIGNER
Audrey Razgaitis
ILLUSTRATOR/ARTIST
Matt Mahurin
CLIENT
The New York Times Magazine
EDITOR
Ed Klein
PUBLISHER
The New York Times, New York, NY
PUBLICATION
The New York Times

1229

1230

ART DIRECTOR
Bill Cadge
DESIGNER
Bill Cadge
ILLUSTRATOR/ARTIST
Bernie Fuchs
WRITER
Peter Hillyer
EDITOR
Woody Klein
PUBLISHER
IBM
PUBLICATION
Think Magazine, White Plains, NY

1231

ART DIRECTOR
Richard Bleiweiss
DESIGNER
Daryl Phillips
ILLUSTRATOR/ARTIST
Ori Hofmekeler
GRAPHICS DIRECTOR
Frank Devino
PUBLISHER
Bob Guccione
PUBLICATION
Penthouse International, New York, NY

1230   1231

1232
ART DIRECTOR
Victor J. Closi
DESIGNER
Victor J. Closi
ILLUSTRATOR/ARTIST
Shannon Stirnweis
WRITER
Jim Merritt
CLIENT
Field & Stream Magazine
EDITOR
Duncan Barnes
PUBLISHER
Gene Bay
DESIGN FIRM
CBS Magaziness/Field & Stream, New York,
NY
PUBLICATION
Field & Stream

1232

1233
ART DIRECTOR
Robert Best
ILLUSTRATOR/ARTIST
Alan Reingold
EDITOR
Edward Kosner
PUBLISHER
Edward Kosner, Murdoch Magazines
PUBLICATION
New York Magazine, New York, NY

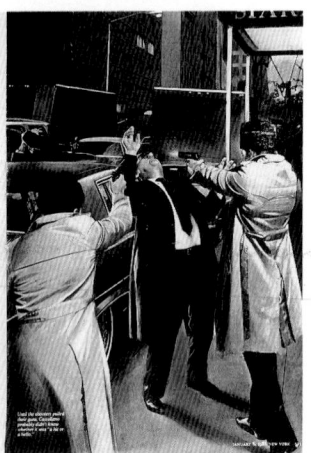

1233

1234
ART DIRECTOR
Su Pogany
DESIGNER
Su Pogany
ILLUSTRATOR/ARTIST
Andrzej Dudzinski
WRITER
Jim Auchmutey
CLIENT
Whittle Communications
EDITOR
Cynthia Lollar
PUBLICATION
Campus Voice Magazine, Knoxville, TN

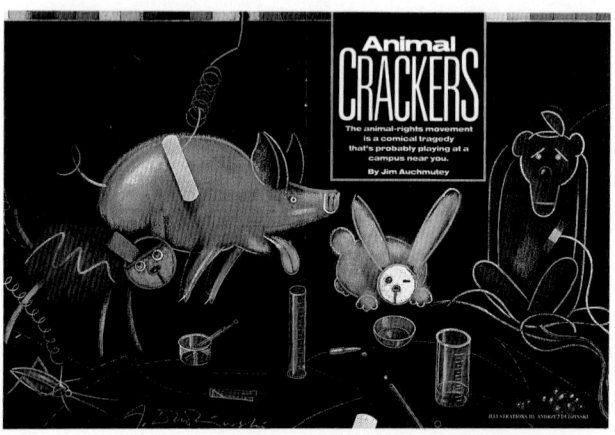

1234

1235
ART DIRECTOR
Wendy Talve Reingold
DESIGNER
Miriam Campiz
ILLUSTRATOR/ARTIST
Lane Smith
PUBLICATION
World Tennis Magazine, New York, NY

1235

DAMN! I'M GOING TO DIE ON THIS FISHING TRIP

Life couldn't get better. This doctor had just landed a big one in a fishing tournament. Then sport became a life-and-death contest.

By John A. Ward, D.O.

1236

1237

HOW DOES THE GARDEN GROW?

1238

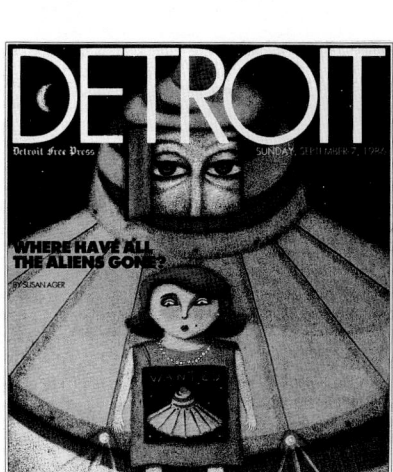

1239

1236

ART DIRECTOR
Roger Dowd
DESIGNER
Michelle Gerdes
ILLUSTRATOR/ARTIST
Jerry Pinkney
WRITER
John A. Ward, D.O.
CLIENT
Medical Economics Co., Inc.
EDITOR
Don L. Berg
DESIGN DIRECTOR
John Newcomb
PUBLISHER
Jim Jenkins
PUBLICATION
Medical Economics Magazine, Oradell, NJ

1237

ART DIRECTOR
Howard E. Paine
ILLUSTRATOR/ARTIST
Karel Havlicek
EDITOR
W. E. Garrett
PUBLICATION
National Geographic, Washington, DC

1238

ART DIRECTOR
Will Hopkins, Ira Friedlander
DESIGNER
Will Hopkins, Ira Friedlander
ILLUSTRATOR/ARTIST
Joan Landis
EDITOR
Bruce Woods
PUBLISHER
Owen Lipstein
DESIGN FIRM
Will Hopkins Group, New York, NY
PUBLICATION
Mother Earth News

1239

ART DIRECTOR
Sheila Young Tomkowiak
DESIGNER
Lona O'Connor
ILLUSTRATOR/ARTIST
Bob Zuba, Plains, PA
CLIENT
Detroit Free Press
PUBLICATION
Detroit Magazine

1240

ART DIRECTOR
Richard Bleiweiss
DESIGNER
Pablo Rodriguez
ILLUSTRATOR/ARTIST
Michael Parkes
GRAPHICS DIRECTOR
Frank Devino
PUBLISHER
Bob Guccione
PUBLICATION
Penthouse International, New York, NY

1240

1241

ART DIRECTOR
Dwayne Flinchum
DESIGNER
Eric Bacon
ILLUSTRATOR/ARTIST
Fernando Botero
GRAPHICS DIRECTOR
Frank Devino
PUBLISHER
Bob Guccione
PUBLICATION
Omni Publications International Ltd., New
York, NY

1241

1242

ART DIRECTOR
Dwayne Flinchum
DESIGNER
Eric Bacon
ILLUSTRATOR/ARTIST
Claudio Bravo
ART EDITOR
Hilde Kron
GRAPHICS DIRECTOR
Frank Devino
PUBLISHER
Bob Guccione
PUBLICATION
Omni Publications International Ltd, New
York, NY

1242

1243

ART DIRECTOR
Richard Bleiweiss
DESIGNER
Daryl Phillips
ILLUSTRATOR/ARTIST
Daniel Riberzani
GRAPHICS DIRECTOR
Frank Devino
PUBLISHER
Bob Guccione
PUBLICATION
Penthouse International, New York, NY

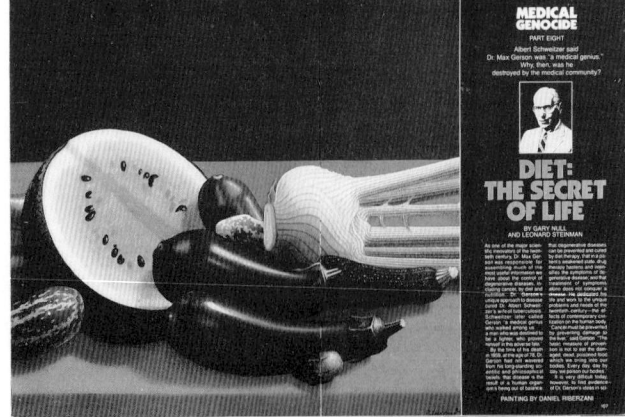

1243

1244

1245

1246

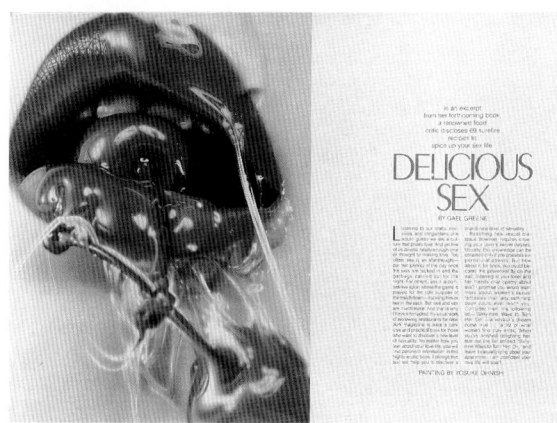

1247

1244
ART DIRECTOR
Richard Bleiweiss
DESIGNER
Pablo Rodriguez
ILLUSTRATOR/ARTIST
Alan Reingold
GRAPHICS DIRECTOR
Frank Devino
PUBLISHER
Bob Guccione
PUBLICATION
Penthouse International, New York, NY

1245
ART DIRECTOR
Dwyane Flinchum
DESIGNER
Dwayne Flinchum
ILLUSTRATOR/ARTIST
Paul Wunderlich
GRAPHICS DIRECTOR
Frank Devino
PUBLISHER
Bob Guccione
PUBLICATION
Omni Publications International Ltd., New York, NY

1246
ART DIRECTOR
Sara Eisenman
DESIGNER
Sara Eisenman
ILLUSTRATOR/ARTIST
Rafal Olbinski
WRITER
Joseph Kastner
EDITOR
Charles Elliot
PUBLISHER
Alfred A. Knopf, New York, NY

1247
ART DIRECTOR
Richard Bleiweiss
DESIGNER
Kay Cardwell
ILLUSTRATOR/ARTIST
Yosuke Ohnishi
GRAPHICS DIRECTOR
Frank Devino
PUBLISHER
Bob Guccione
PUBLICATION
Penthouse International., New York, NY

1248

ART DIRECTOR
George Hartman
DESIGNER
Kenneth Nadel
ILLUSTRATOR/ARTIST
Joe Ciardiello
PUBLICATION
Glamour Magazine, New York, NY

1248

1249

ART DIRECTOR
Wm. A. Motta
DESIGNER
Richard M. Baron
ILLUSTRATOR/ARTIST
Jorge Garcia
WRITER
Ronald Hansen
EDITOR
John Dinkel
PUBLISHER
Richard A. Bartkus
PUBLICATION
Road & Track Magazine, Newport Beach, CA

1249

1250

ART DIRECTOR
Richard Bleiweiss
DESIGNER
Joann Agress
ILLUSTRATOR/ARTIST
Ajin
GRAPHICS DIRECTOR
Frank Devino
PUBLISHER
Bob Guccione
PUBLICATION
Penthouse International, New York, NY

1250

1251

ART DIRECTOR
Rosslyn A. Frick
DESIGNER
Rosslyn A. Frick
ILLUSTRATOR/ARTIST
Doug Smith
EDITOR
Dennis Brisson
PUBLISHER
Stephen Twombly
PUBLICATION
Run Magazine, CW Communications,
Peterborough, NH

1251

1252

1252
ART DIRECTOR
Jan Adkins
ILLUSTRATOR/ARTIST
Pierre Mion
CLIENT
National Geographic Magazine
EDITOR
W. E. Garrett
PUBLISHER
National Geographic Magazine
PUBLICATION
National Geographic Magazine, Washington, DC

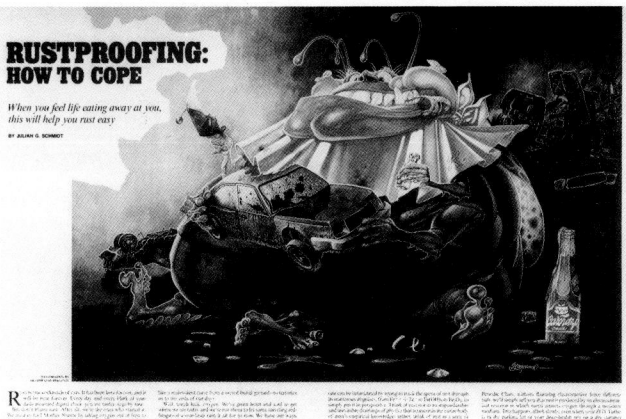

RUSTPROOFING: HOW TO COPE

When you feel life eating away at you, this will help you rust easy

BY JULIAN G. SCHMIDT

1253

1253
ART DIRECTOR
Wm. A. Motta
DESIGNER
Henry Thomas
ILLUSTRATOR/ARTIST
Héctor Luis Bergandi
WRITER
Julian G. Schmidt
EDITOR
John Dinkel
PUBLISHER
Richard A. Bartkus
PUBLICATION
Road & Track Magazine, Newport Beach, CA

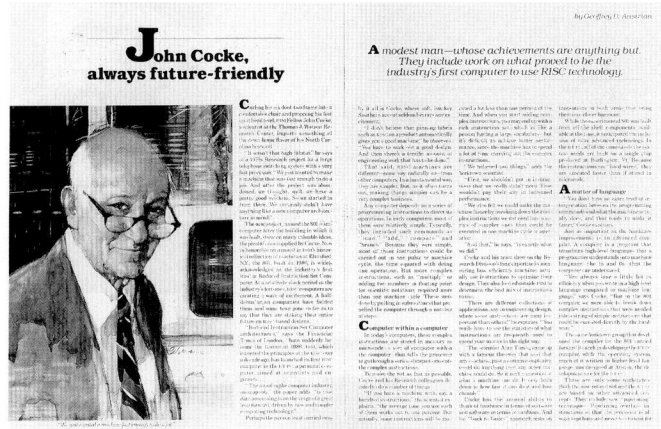

By Geoffrey D. Austrian

John Cocke, always future-friendly

A modest man—whose achievements are anything but. They include work on what proved to be the industry's first computer to use RISC technology.

1254

1254
ART DIRECTOR
Bill Cadge
DESIGNER
Bill Cadge
ILLUSTRATOR/ARTIST
Burt Silverman
WRITER
Geoffrey D. Austrian
EDITOR
Woody Klein
PUBLISHER
IBM
PUBLICATION
Think Magazine, White Plains, NY

FICTION
The challenge: to master the raw flames that burned deep within

FIRE CATCHER

BY RICHARD KADREY

PAINTING BY
MICHAEL PARKES

1255

1255
ART DIRECTOR
Amy Seissler
DESIGNER
Amy Seissler
ILLUSTRATOR/ARTIST
Michael Parkes
GRAPHICS DIRECTOR
Frank Devino
PUBLISHER
Bob Guccione
PUBLICATION
Omni Publications International Ltd., New York, NY

1256
ART DIRECTOR
Dwayne Flinchum
DESIGNER
Eric Bacon
ILLUSTRATOR/ARTIST
Armodio
GRAPHICS DIRECTOR
Frank Devino
PUBLISHER
Bob Guccione
PUBLICATION
Omni Publications International Ltd., New
York, NY

1256

1257
ART DIRECTOR
Rosslyn A. Frick
ILLUSTRATOR/ARTIST
Paul Mock
EDITOR
Dennis Brisson
PUBLISHER
Stephen Twombly
PUBLICATION
Run Magazine, CW Communications,
Peterborough, NH

1258
ART DIRECTOR
Walter Bernard, Milton Glaser
DESIGNER
Colleen McCudden
ILLUSTRATOR/ARTIST
Guy Billout
CLIENT
Insurance Review
EDITOR
Colleen Katz
PUBLISHER
Insurance Informtion Institute
DESIGN FIRM
WBMG, Inc., New York, NY
PUBLICATION
Insurance Review

1257   1258

1259
ART DIRECTOR
Hulon Noe
DESIGNER
Hulon Noe
ILLUSTRATOR/ARTIST
Geoffrey Moss
PUBLISHER
Kiplinger Washington Editors, Washington,
DC
PUBLICATION
Changing Times Magazine

1259

1260

1261

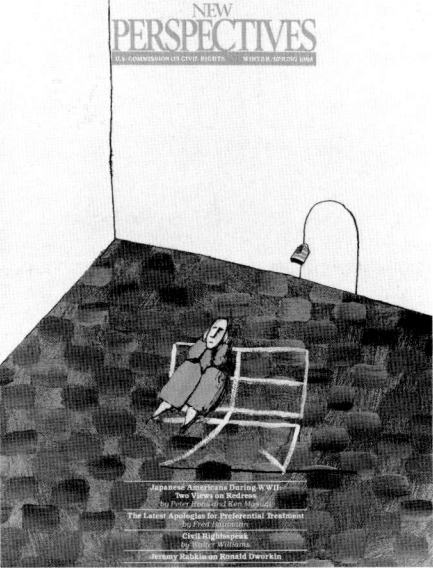

1262

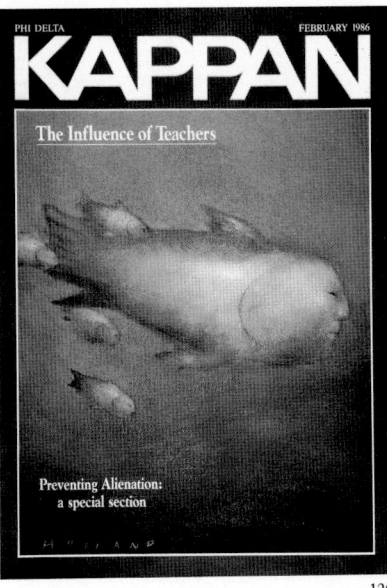

1263

1260
ART DIRECTOR
Kerig Pope
ILLUSTRATOR/ARTIST
Braldt Bralds, New York, NY
WRITER
Francisco Goldman
CLIENT
Playboy Magazine
PUBLISHER
Playboy Enterprises

1261
ART DIRECTOR
Seymour Chwast
DESIGNER
Seymour Chwast
ILLUSTRATOR/ARTIST
Seymour Chwast
WRITER
Dan Weaver, Charles Dickens
EDITOR
Deborah Brodie
PUBLISHER
Viking Penguin
DESIGN FIRM
The Pushpin Group, New York, NY

1262
ART DIRECTOR
Joe Swanson
DESIGNER
Design Network, Inc.
ILLUSTRATOR/ARTIST
James Yang, Greenbelt, Md.
CLIENT
U.S. Commission on Civil Rights
PUBLICATION
New Perspectives, Washington, DC

1263
ART DIRECTOR
Kristin Herzog
DESIGNER
Kristin Herzog
ILLUSTRATOR/ARTIST
Brad Holland
WRITER
Robert W. Cole, Jr.
CLIENT
Phi Delta Kappan
PUBLICATION
Phi Delta Kappan, Bloomington, IN

1264
ART DIRECTOR
Peggy Robertson
DESIGNER
Peggy Robertson
ILLUSTRATOR/ARTIST
Richard Downs
WRITER
Gina Kolata
PUBLISHER
The Washington Post
PUBLICATION
The Washington Post, Washington, DC

1265
ART DIRECTOR
Miriam Smith
ILLUSTRATOR/ARTIST
R. Newman
EDITOR
John Montorio
PUBLICATION
The Newsday Magazine, Melville, NY

1266
ART DIRECTOR
Danielle Gallo
DESIGNER
Laura Woods
ILLUSTRATOR/ARTIST
Alan Daniels
EDITOR
Don Myrus
PUBLISHER
Bob Guccione
PUBLICATION
Penthouse Letters, New York, NY

1267
ART DIRECTOR
Joe Swanson
DESIGNER
Design Network, Inc.
ILLUSTRATOR/ARTIST
James Yang, Greenbelt, MD
CLIENT
U.S. Commission on Civil Rights
PUBLICATION
New Perspectives Magazine, Washington, DC

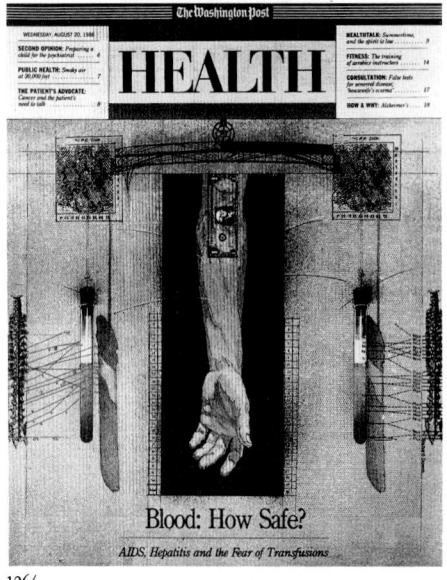
1264

1265

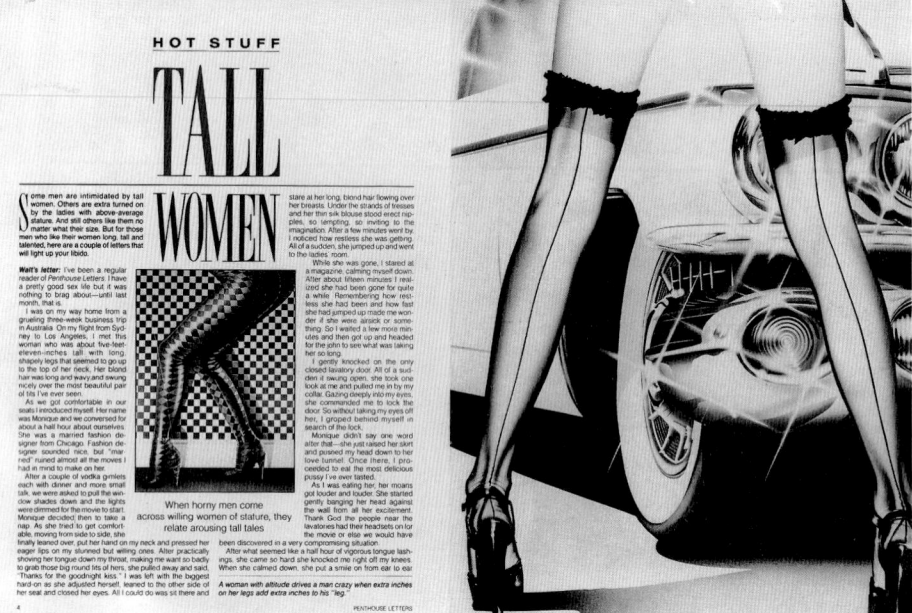
1266

1267

1268

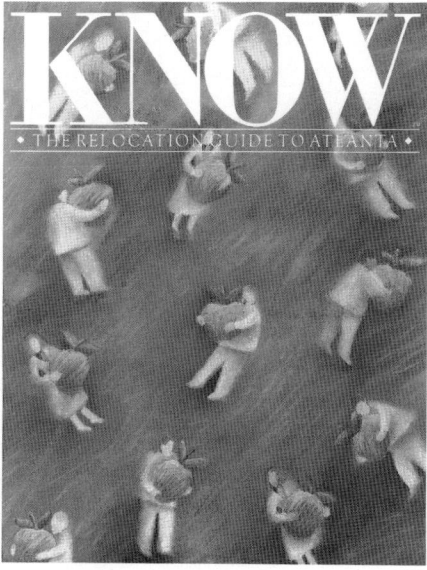

1269

1268
ART DIRECTOR
Robert J. Post
DESIGNER
Cynthia Hoffman
ILLUSTRATOR/ARTIST
Mark Penberthy
WRITER
Gene Mustain, Rick Soll
CLIENT
Chicago
PUBLISHER
WFMT
PUBLICATION
Chicago Magazine, Chicago, IL

1269
ART DIRECTOR
Mark Sandlin
DESIGNER
Mark Sandlin
ILLUSTRATOR/ARTIST
Mark Sandlin
CLIENT
Bryant Litho
DESIGN FIRM
Don Trousdell Design, Atlanta, GA

Hungry for Apple Pie

*H*ow long will it be before a foreign or domestic terrorist group initiates substantial activity in the US? Between 1968 and 1985, terrorists were responsible for 557 attacks against US bases and personnel overseas, including the fatal bombings at Rhein-Main Air Force Base in West Germany in August 1985 and the assassination of four Marines on embassy duty in El Salvador in summer 1985. Future terrorist activity within the continental United States seems certain.

BY LEE RONSO JR.

> Imagine the shock effect if a key military officer were assassinated in the US.

1270

1270
ART DIRECTOR
Cecily Roberts
DESIGNER
Cecily Roberts
ILLUSTRATOR/ARTIST
James Yang, Greenbelt, Md.
DESIGN FIRM
Security Management Magazine

'Crack'
Early report on a new drug epidemic

Arnold M. Washton, PhD   Mark S. Gold, MD   A. Carter Pottash, MD

Preview
The popularity of smoking freebase cocaine, or "crack," has risen precipitously in recent years because of widespread availability and cheap prices. In this report on a random sample of hotline callers, Drs Washton, Gold, and Pottash suggest a basic treatment plan for abusers of this exceptionally addictive drug and warn the healthcare community to prepare for an unprecedented influx of patients as the problem becomes even more prevalent.

During the past three years, a growing epidemic of cocaine use in the United States has resulted in widespread physical, psychiatric, and social problems that have alarmed medical experts, parents, and law enforcement officials. Although the most common method of use has been nasal inhalation, or "snorting," of cocaine hydrochloride powder, recent observations point to a sudden and dramatic rise in the popularity of freebase smoking. This is apparently linked to a shift in cocaine distribution patterns, as dealers in many areas switch from selling cocaine powder to selling freebase cocaine to tiny chunks or rocks known on the street as "crack."

Crack is extracted from cocaine powder in a procedure using sodium bicarbonate, heat, and water. The process is simple and relatively safe compared with the more volatile method of processing cocaine powder, which uses ether. Unlike cocaine powder, which has a high vaporization point and decomposes with

heating, the basic cocaine alkaloid, or freebase, can be readily volatilized into smoke at moderate temperatures using a regular match or lighter.

When smoked as freebase, cocaine is rapidly absorbed into the pulmonary circulation and is transmitted to the brain in less than ten seconds. The drug's euphoric effects are intensified and compressed into three to five minutes of intoxication, followed by an equally acute dysphoria and intense cravings that may promote a rapidly escalating pattern of compulsive use.

Dealers prefer to sell crack rather than cocaine powder because of crack's high addiction potential, low unit cost, and ease of handling. A self-marketing product, crack assures the dealer a reliable clientele and a high profit margin. It is typically dispensed on the illegal market in small plastic vials (figure 1) containing one, two, or three rocks. Each rock weighs approximately 100 mg and sells for $5 to $10 on the street.

This article presents survey data on the demographics, patterns, and consequences of crack use in a random sample of callers to our national drug abuse hotline 800-COCAINE.

Survey methods
The survey included 458 primary cocaine abusers who called the hotline during the first two weeks of May 1986 and voluntarily consented to a 20- to 30-minute anonymous telephone interview during which a structured questionnaire on crack use was administered. Only adult users, at least 20 years old, were included in the sample. Adolescent users participated in a separate survey, not reported here.

Results
Among the 458 adults, 144 (31%) reported that crack was their primary drug of abuse. All results of this survey are based on information from these 144 users (table I). The calls came from 13 states, spanning a wide geographic area of the United States. Most callers noted that crack was "very easy" to obtain in their locale and that cocaine powder was becoming less available.

Most subjects (81%) said they had been snorting cocaine powder before switching to crack, but only 32% of these subjects had considered themselves addicted to the powder form. Of the sample, 54% said they had "fallen continued"

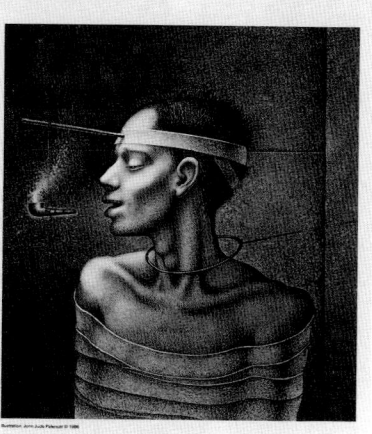

1271

1271
ART DIRECTOR
Tina Adamek
ILLUSTRATOR/ARTIST
John Jude Palencar
CLIENT
Postgraduate Medicine
PUBLISHER
McGraw-Hill Publishing, Minneapolis, MN
PUBLICATION
Postgraduate Medicine

1272

ART DIRECTOR
Alyce Mathias
ILLUSTRATOR/ARTIST
Theo Rudnak
PUBLISHER
Gulfshore Publishing Co., Naples FL
PUBLICATION
Gulfshore Life Magazine

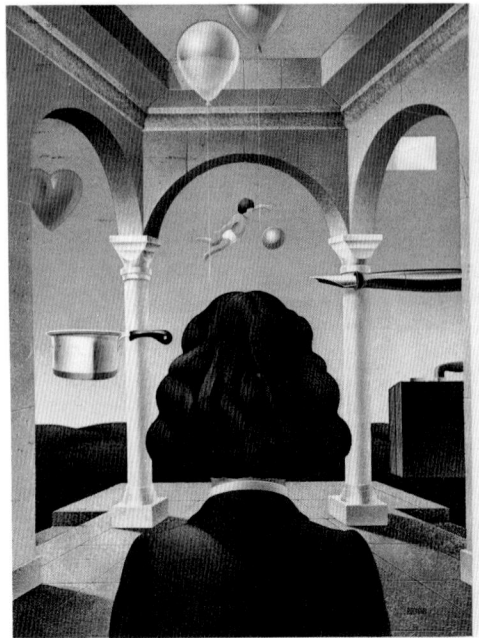

1272

1273

ART DIRECTOR
Robert J. Post
DESIGNER
Cynthia Hoffman
ILLUSTRATOR/ARTIST
Richard A. Goldberg
CLIENT
Chicago
PUBLISHER
WFMT Inc.
PUBLICATION
Chicago Magazine, Chicago, IL

1274

ART DIRECTOR
Robert J. Post
DESIGNER
Cynthia Hoffman
ILLUSTRATOR/ARTIST
John Kleber
WRITER
Eugene Wildman
PUBLICATION
Chicago Magazine, Chicago, IL

1273

1274

1275

ART DIRECTOR
Tina Adamek
ILLUSTRATOR/ARTIST
Mary Grandpré
CLIENT
The Physician and Sportsmedicine Magazine
PUBLISHER
McGraw-Hill Publishing, Minneapolis, MN
PUBLICATION
The Physician and Sportsmedicine

1275

First of three
symposium articles
in this issue

John W. Malo, MD
Barbara J. Bezdicek, MD

Secondary amenorrhea

A protocol for pinpointing the underlying cause

Preview questions

Of which disease is amenorrhea often the first clinically apparent symptom?

What physiologic and pharmacologic factors must be considered during evaluation of amenorrheic patients with hyperprolactinemia?

How can ovarian unresponsiveness be differentiated from inadequate gonadotropin stimulation?

■ Secondary amenorrhea is classically defined as the absence of menses for six months or for the equivalent of three previous cycle intervals, whichever is longer. Because the normal menstrual cycle is dependent on the intricate interplay within the hypothalamic-pituitary-ovarian-uterine axis, a change in the cycle, such as secondary amenorrhea, is often the first clinical sign of significant physical, psychological, or nutritional stress.

When to initiate evaluation
The clinician must use common sense in deciding when to initiate an evaluation of secondary amenorrhea. In most clinical situations, a thorough history and physical examination, including a pelvic examination, should be performed 90 days after the patient's last menstrual period. Amenorrheic patients at high risk of having a serious underlying disorder, such as those who also have galactorrhea, should be evaluated before 90 days have passed. Patients at lower risk, such as those who have voluntarily lost weight, are experiencing considerable psychological stress, or have a history of irregular menstrual cycles, can usually wait for the classic interval of six months before undergoing comprehensive evaluation.

At the Twin City Fertility Center, St Paul, we initiate a careful history and physical examination as soon as the patient perceives that she has a problem. Usually, the problem is a change in the menstrual pattern that she accepts as "normal" for her. The history and results of the physical examination are then used to guide the timing and extent of further laboratory evaluation.

Compartmentalization of cycle dysfunction
Although some disorders underlying secondary amenorrhea tend to occur more often in one age group than another, the distinction is too slight to
continued

1276

1276

ART DIRECTOR
Tina Adamek
ILLUSTRATOR/ARTIST
Susi Kilgore
CLIENT
Postgraduate Medicine
PUBLISHER
McGraw-Hill Publishing, Minneapolis, MN
PUBLICATION
Postgraduate Medicine

1277

1277

ART DIRECTOR
Jurek Wajdowicz
DESIGNER
Jurek Wajdowicz
ILLUSTRATOR/ARTIST
Andrzej Dudzinski
CLIENT
Dalton Communications
EDITOR
Don S. Johnson
PUBLISHER
Peter Betuel
DESIGN FIRM
Emerson, Wajdowicz Studios, Inc., New York, NY
PUBLICATION
Administrative Management

1278

1278

ART DIRECTOR
Robert J. Post
DESIGNER
Robert J. Post
ILLUSTRATOR/ARTIST
Robert J. Post
WRITER
Celestine C. Ware
CLIENT
Chicago
PUBLISHER
WFMT, Inc.
PUBLICATION
Chicago Magazine, Chicago, IL

First of four
symposium articles
in this issue

David K. Sarver, MD

Hepatitis in clinical practice

1. Hepatitis A and B

Preview questions

How effective is hepatitis A prophylaxis with immune globulin?

What are the possible vehicles for transmission of hepatitis B virus (HBV)?

Why does AIDS transmission via HBV vaccine not appear to be a possibility?

■ Many new findings and issues have recently come to light regarding the classification, epidemiology, pathogenesis, pathology, clinical manifestations, laboratory diagnosis, treatment, prophylaxis, and prevention of hepatitis A and B infections. Part 1 of this two-part article focuses on these most interesting aspects and provides a general review of the two diseases.

Hepatitis A
Hepatitis A (HA) has been recognized for many years. It was originally called infectious hepatitis.

ETIOLOGY—Hepatitis A virus (HAV) is a 27-nanometer (nm) single-stranded RNA virus without an envelope. It is classified as an enterovirus, type 72. Only one serotype has been identified.

EPIDEMIOLOGY—Hepatitis A occurs worldwide. Infection is not persistent, nor is viremia continuous. HAV is present in the feces of all persons with acute illness. Parenteral transmission by blood or blood products is rare. Posttransfusion hepatitis A has been reported.

Fecal-oral spread via water or food is the most common means of transmission. Spread by serum, bile, sputum, saliva, or urine is not of major significance. Humans seem to be the only natural hosts since there is no nonhuman reservoir or persistent infection; human disease must be maintained by serial spread from persons with acute illness to susceptible hosts. The incidence appears to be highest in the fall and winter. HAV antibody is more prevalent in older than
continued

1279

1279

ART DIRECTOR
Tina Adamek
DESIGNER
Cary Henrie
CLIENT
Postgraduate Medicine Magazine
PUBLISHER
McGraw-Hill Publishing, Minneapolis, MN
PUBLICATION
Postgraduate Medicine Magazine

1280

ART DIRECTOR
Tina Adamek
ILLUSTRATOR/ARTIST
Enid Hatton
CLIENT
Postgraduate Medicine
PUBLISHER
McGraw-Hill Publishing, Minneapolis, MN
PUBLICATION
Postgraduate Medicine

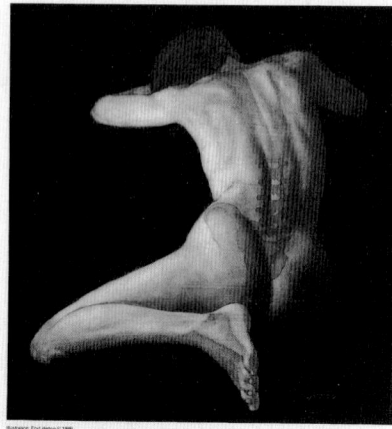

1280

1281

ART DIRECTOR
Craig Bernhardt, Janice Fudyma
ILLUSTRATOR/ARTIST
Brian Ajhar
CLIENT
Maxwell House
EDITOR
Nan Haley Redmond
DESIGN FIRM
Bernhardt Fudyma Design Group, New York, NY

1281

1282

ART DIRECTOR
Dwayne Flinchum
DESIGNER
Eric Bacon
ILLUSTRATOR/ARTIST
George Tooker
GRAPHICS DIRECTOR
Frank Devino
PUBLISHER
Bob Guccione
PUBLICATION
Omni Publications International Ltd., New York, NY

1282

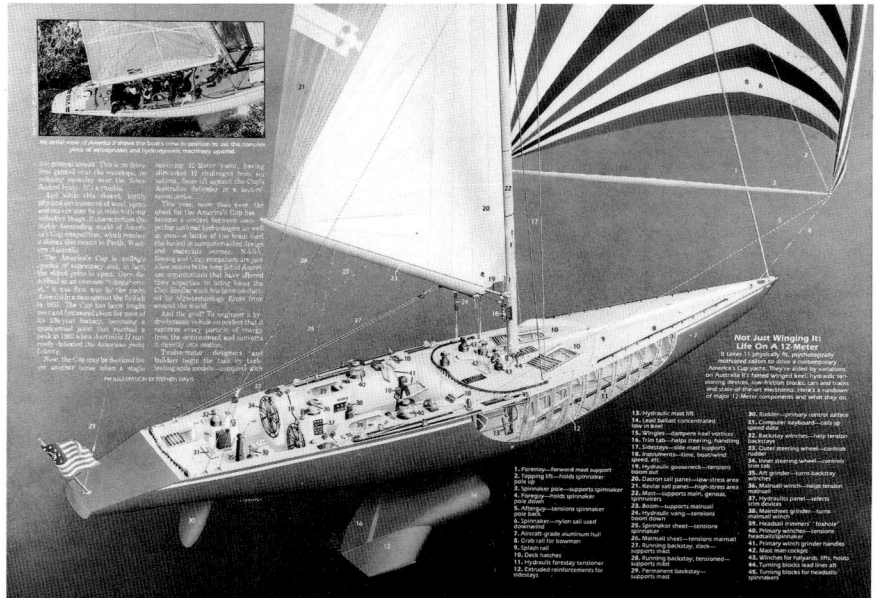

1283

ART DIRECTOR
Ann Bennett
ILLUSTRATOR/ARTIST
Stephen Davis
WRITER
Tim Cole
DESIGN DIRECTOR
Bryan Canniff
PUBLICATION
Popular Mechanics, New York, NY

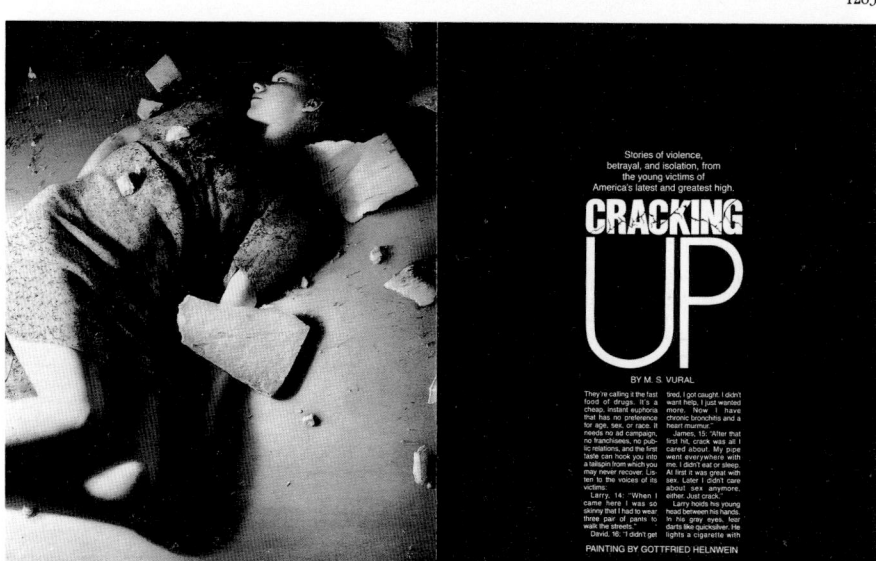

1284

ART DIRECTOR
Richard Bleiweiss
DESIGNER
Daryl Phillips
ILLUSTRATOR/ARTIST
Gottfried Helnwein
GRAPHICS DIRECTOR
Frank Devino
PUBLISHER
Bob Guccione
PUBLICATION
Penthouse International, New York, NY

1285

ART DIRECTOR
Janet Froelich
DESIGNER
Randy Dunbar
ILLUSTRATOR/ARTIST
Dave Shannon
PUBLICATION
NY Daily News, New York, NY

1286

ART DIRECTOR
Bob Conge
DESIGNER
Bob Conge
ILLUSTRATOR/ARTIST
Bob Conge
WRITER
Steve Roberts & Co.
CLIENT
Rochester Society of Communicating Arts
DESIGN FIRM
Conge Design, Rochester, NY
PRINTER
G.M. DuBois Corp.

1287

ART DIRECTOR
Jodi Rovin
ILLUSTRATOR/ARTIST
Javier Romero
CLIENT
Atlantic Records, New York, NY

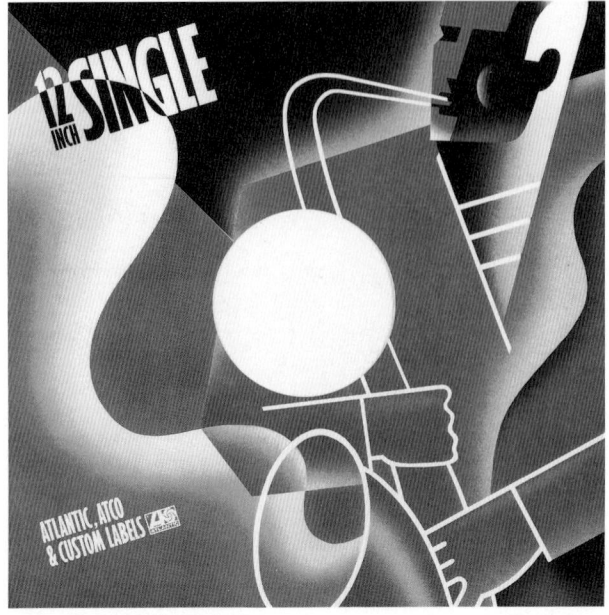

1287

1288

ART DIRECTOR
Bob Conge, Bill McElveney
DESIGNER
Joe LaMay
ILLUSTRATOR/ARTIST
Bob Conge
CLIENT
Rochester Club of Printing House Craftsmen
DESIGN FIRM
Conge Design, Rochester, NY
PRINTER
Flower City Printing Inc.

1288

1289

ART DIRECTOR
Bob Conge
DESIGNER
Bob Conge
ILLUSTRATOR/ARTIST
Bob Conge
CLIENT
Park Avenue Merchants Association
DESIGN FIRM
Conge Design, Rochester, NY
PRINTER
G.M. DuBois Corp.

1289

1290

1290
ART DIRECTOR
Shinichiro Tora
DESIGNER
Chris Hill
ILLUSTRATOR/ARTIST
Leo Dillon, Diane Dillon
CLIENT
Hotel Barmen's Association
AGENCY
DNP America Inc., New York, NY
DESIGN FIRM
Hill/A Graphic Design Group

1291

1291
ART DIRECTOR
Kathleen C. Howell
ILLUSTRATOR/ARTIST
Linda Montgomery, Toronto, Canada
CLIENT
Harry Hoffman & Sons Printing
PUBLICATION
Air Canada enRoute Magazine, Airmedia

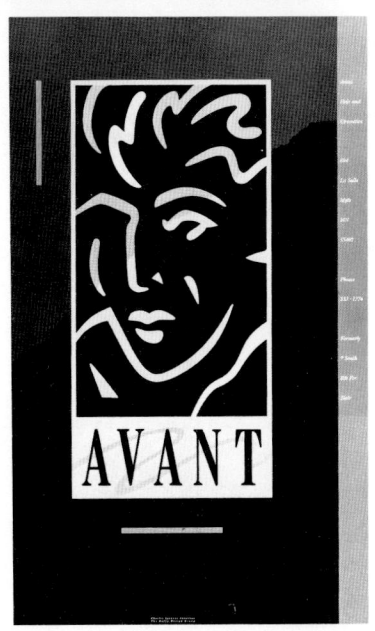

1292

1292
ART DIRECTOR
Charles Spencer Anderson
DESIGNER
Charles Spencer Anderson
ILLUSTRATOR/ARTIST
Charles Spencer Anderson, Lynn Schulte
DESIGN FIRM
Duffy Design Group, Minneapolis, MN

1293

ART DIRECTOR
Christopher Mayes
DESIGNER
Christopher Mayes
ILLUSTRATOR/ARTIST
Val Tillery, Hungry Dog Studio
CLIENT
American Institute of Graphic Arts, Texas
Chapter
EDITOR
Don Gordon
PUBLISHER
American Institute of Graphic Arts, Texas
Chapter
DESIGN FIRM
Christopher Mayes Design, Houston, TX
PUBLICATION
AIGA/TEXAS JOURNAL

1293

1294

ART DIRECTOR
Deborah Lawrence
ILLUSTRATOR/ARTIST
Braldt Bralds
WRITER
Leslie Lawton, Frances Frazer
CLIENT
Chevron
AGENCY
J. Walter Thompson USA, San Francisco, CA

1294

1295

ART DIRECTOR
Stavros Cosmopulos, Tom Demeter
DESIGNER
Tom Demeter
ILLUSTRATOR/ARTIST
John Thompson
WRITER
Stavros Cosmopulos, Sam Bregande, Steve
Lynch
CLIENT
Allendale Insurance
AGENCY
Cosmopulos, Crowley & Daly, Inc., Boston,
MA
DESIGN FIRM
Cosmopulos, Crowley & Daly, Inc.

1295

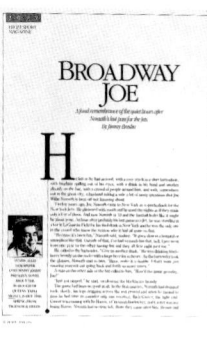

1296

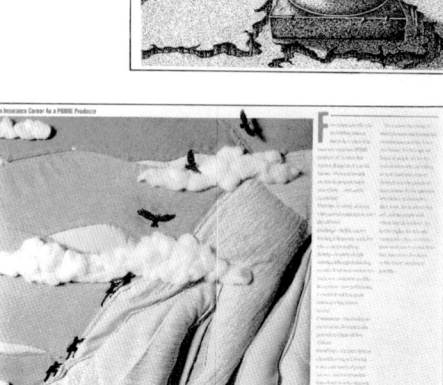

1297

1296

ART DIRECTOR
Nina Ovryn
DESIGNER
Nina Ovryn, Woodbridge, NJ
ILLUSTRATOR/ARTIST
Greg Spalenka, Jeffrey Smith, James Endicott
WRITER
Jimmy Breslin, Tennessee Williams, Woody Allen
CLIENT
Eastern Airlines
EDITOR
John Atwood
PUBLISHER
Fred Smith
PUBLICATION
Review Magazine

1297

ART DIRECTOR
Lance Matusek
DESIGNER
Lance Matusek
PHOTOGRAPHER
Don Belliveau
ILLUSTRATOR/ARTIST
Ken Ko, Lance Matusek, Karen Ouimet, Bob Gallagher, Rex Ruden, Bob Hunt, Bob Faucher
WRITER
Joann Duchesneau
CLIENT
Aetna
DESIGN FIRM
Aetna, Hartford, CT

1298
ART DIRECTOR
Harry Kerker
ILLUSTRATOR/ARTIST
Jim Dietz
WRITER
Murray Kalis
CLIENT
Flying Tigers
AGENCY
HCM, Los Angeles, CA

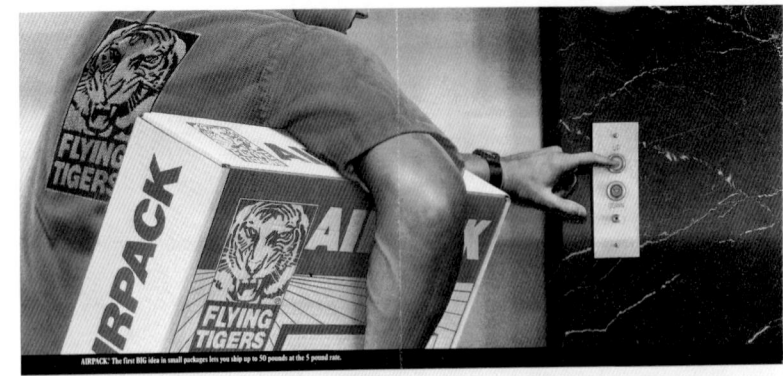

Today, you can count on this AIRPACK.

1298

1299
ART DIRECTOR
Jamie Feldman
DESIGNER
Jamie Feldman
ILLUSTRATOR/ARTIST
David Lesh, Indianapolis, IN
CLIENT
Federal Reserve Bank of Cleveland
PUBLICATION
Federal Reserve Bank of Cleveland Annual
Report

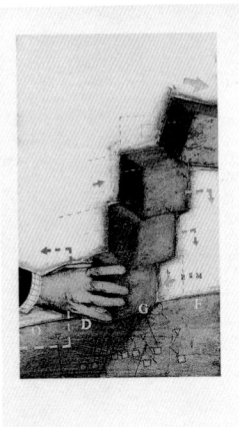

1299

1300

1300

ART DIRECTOR
Bennett Robinson
DESIGNER
Bennett Robinson, Meera Singh
ILLUSTRATOR/ARTIST
Julian Allen (Venezuela), Eraldo Carugati
(Italy), James McMullan (Zimbabwe)
WRITER/RESEARCH
Oscar Shefler, John Aspery, Emily Dibb,
James Milton, Andrew Mulligan, Bennett
Robinson
CLIENT
H J Heinz Company
DESIGN FIRM
Corporate Graphics Inc., New York, NY

1301

1301

ART DIRECTOR
Bennett Robinson
DESIGNER
Bennett Robinson, Meera Singh
ILLUSTRATOR/ARTIST
Malcolm T Liepke (Canada), Max Ginsberg
(Australia), John Berkey (Holland)
WRITER/RESEARCH
Oscar Shefler, John Aspery, Emily Dibb,
James Milton, Andrew Mulligan, Bennett
Robinson
CLIENT
H J Heinz Company
DESIGN FIRM
Corporate Graphics Inc., New York, NY

1302

1302

ART DIRECTOR
Charles Spencer Anderson
DESIGNER
Charles Spencer Anderson
ILLUSTRATOR/ARTIST
Charles Spencer Anderson, Lynn Schulte
DESIGN FIRM
Duffy Design Group, Minneapolis, MN

1914    1921    1933

1941    1956    1968

PHOTOGRAPHY:

Single Entries: advertising, b&w
editorial, b&w
advertising, color
editorial, color
promotion, color

Campaign Entries: promotion, b&w
editorial, color
promotion, color

*In 1911, the Morton Salt Company engaged
N. W. Ayer to develop a campaign of twelve ads
to promote its new free-running salt in* Good
Housekeeping. *Ayer also submitted an
alternate—a picture of a little girl under an
umbrella, with a container of salt pouring
out behind her, captioned "Even in rainy
weather it flows freely". Morton loved the
concept, "the whole story in a picture", but
decided that the line needed work. In one of
the earliest brainstorming sessions ever
recorded, the client-agency group settled on
"when it rains it pours". Three years later they
adopted the girl and the line for the package
and, updated through the years, they survive
today.*

1303
ART DIRECTOR
Daniel Cooper-Bey
DESIGNER
Annie Leibovitz
CLIENT
Kenneth Cole Productions
AGENCY
Grace Kent Sage Inc., New York, NY
PUBLICATION
US, New York Talk, Rolling Stone, Details,
Interview, Vogue
CREATIVE DIRECTOR
Grace Sage

1303

1304
ART DIRECTOR
John Morrison
PHOTOGRAPHER
Dennis Manarchy
WRITER
Jarl Olsen, Jeff Goodby
CLIENT
Christian Brothers Winery
AGENCY
Goodby, Berlin & Silverstein, San Francisco,
CA

1304

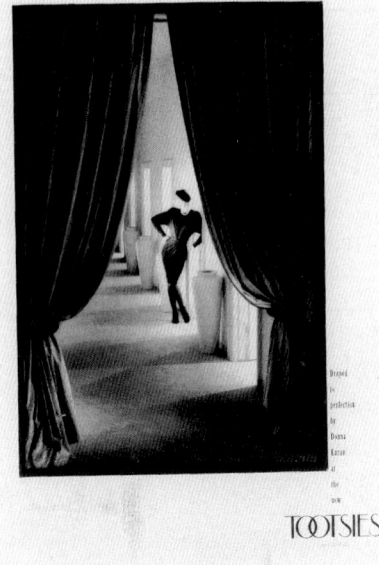

1305
ART DIRECTOR
Steven Sessions
DESIGNER
Steven Sessions
PHOTOGRAPHER
Jim Sims Sims/Boynton Photography,
Houston, TX
CLIENT
Tootsie's
AGENCY
Steven Sessions Design
DESIGN FIRM
Steven Sessions Design
PUBLICATION
''W'' Magazine

1305

1306
ART DIRECTOR
John Muller
DESIGNER
John Muller
PHOTOGRAPHER
Rick Nible
WRITER
Grant Pace
CLIENT
Rick Nible
DESIGN FIRM
Muller & Company, Kansas City, MO

1306

1307

1309

1308

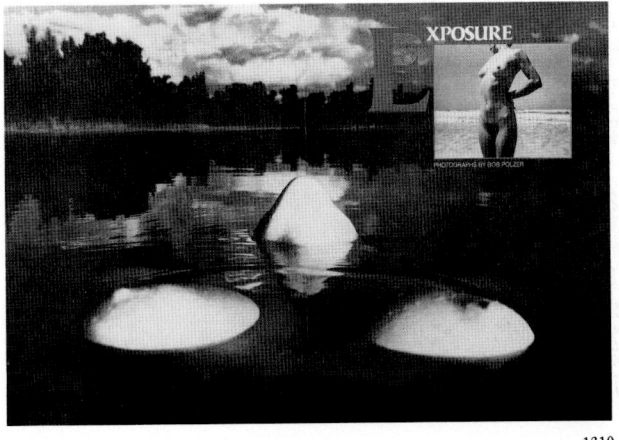

1310

1307
ART DIRECTOR
Walter Kaprielian
DESIGNER
Walter Kaprielian
PHOTOGRAPHER
Skrebneski
CLIENT
Natori
AGENCY
Kaprielian O'Leary, New York, NY

1308
ART DIRECTOR
Robert J. Post
DESIGNER
Robert J. Post
PHOTOGRAPHER
Dennis Manarchy
WRITER
Marcia Froelke Coburn
CLIENT
Chicago
PUBLISHER
WFMT
PUBLICATION
Chicago Magazine, Chicago, IL

1309
ART DIRECTOR
Marc Balet
PHOTOGRAPHER
Charles Purvis, New York, NY
PUBLICATION
Interview

1310
ART DIRECTOR
Danielle Gallo
DESIGNER
Danielle Gallo
PHOTOGRAPHER
Bob Polzer
EDITOR
Don Myrus
PUBLISHER
Bob Guccione
PUBLICATION
Penthouse Letters, New York, NY

1311

ART DIRECTOR
Jim Frazier
PHOTOGRAPHER
Herman Kokojan, Black Star
WRITER
Bob Power
CLIENT
Phillips 66 Co.
AGENCY
Tracy-Locke, Dallas, TX

1312

ART DIRECTOR
Ron Louie
PHOTOGRAPHER
Neal Barr
WRITER
Dan Brooks
CLIENT
Gold Information Center
AGENCY
DDB/Needham, New York, NY

1311

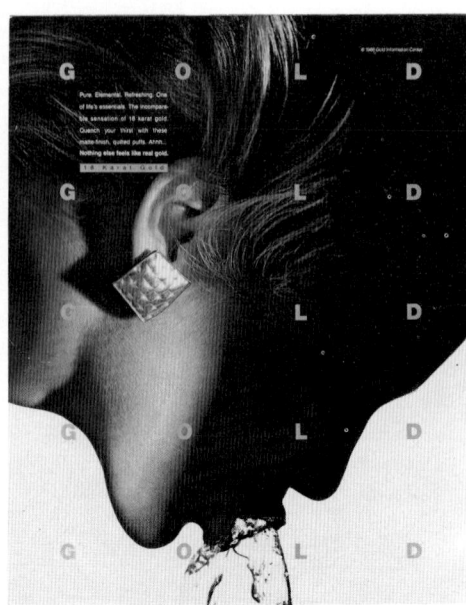

1312

1313

ART DIRECTOR
Tom Simons
PHOTOGRAPHER
Jay Maisel
WRITER
Rick Cohn
CLIENT
New England Life
AGENCY
Rizzo Simons Cohn, Boston, MA

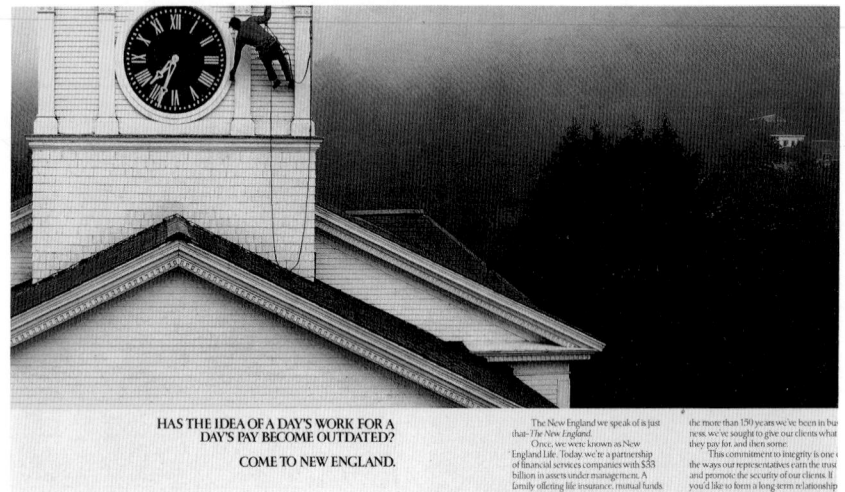

1313

1314

ART DIRECTOR
Gary Custer
PHOTOGRAPHER
Glen Wans
WRITER
Scott McCormick
CLIENT
Mobay Corporation, Agricultural Chemicals
Division
AGENCY
Valentine-Radford, Kansas City, MO
PUBLICATION
Farm Futures
CREATIVE DIRECTOR
Bob Jensen

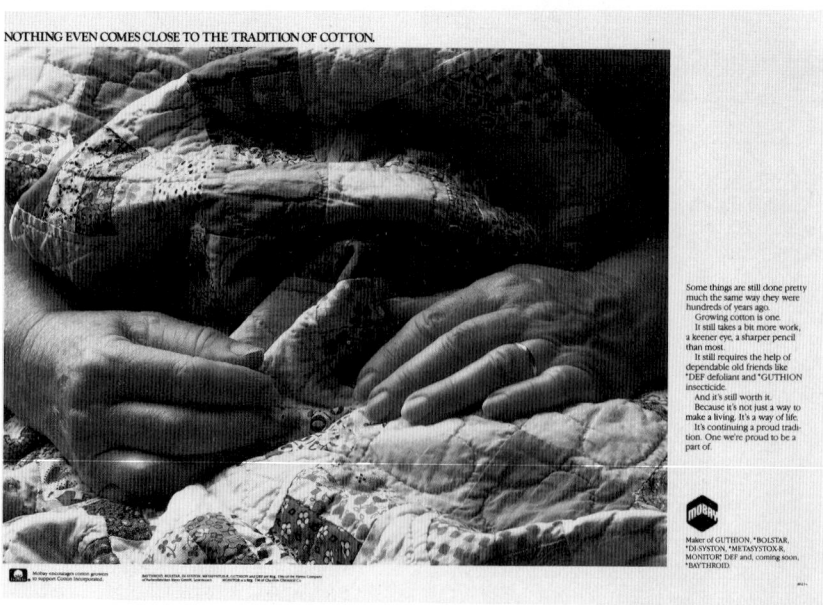

1314

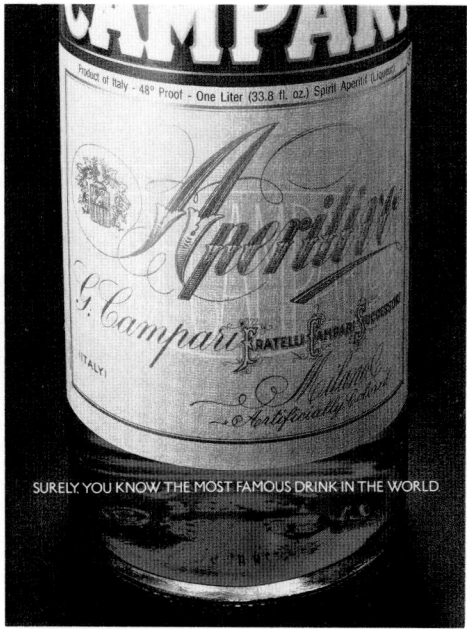

1315

1316

1315
ART DIRECTOR
Stavros Cosmopulos
DESIGNER
Stavros Cosmopulos
PHOTOGRAPHER
Onofrio Paccione
WRITER
Stavros Cosmopulos
CLIENT
Dorfman Jewelers
AGENCY
Cosmopulos, Crowley & Daly, Inc., Boston, MA
DESIGN FIRM
Cosmopulos, Crowley & Daly, Inc.

1317

1316
ART DIRECTOR
Robert Reitzfeld
DESIGNER
Robert Reitzfeld
PHOTOGRAPHER
Hashi
WRITER
David Altschiller
CLIENT
Campari USA Inc.
AGENCY
Altschiller Reitzfeld, New York, NY

1317
ART DIRECTOR
Steven Sandstrom
PHOTOGRAPHER
Stephen Wilkes, New York, NY
CLIENT
Pictorial Offset

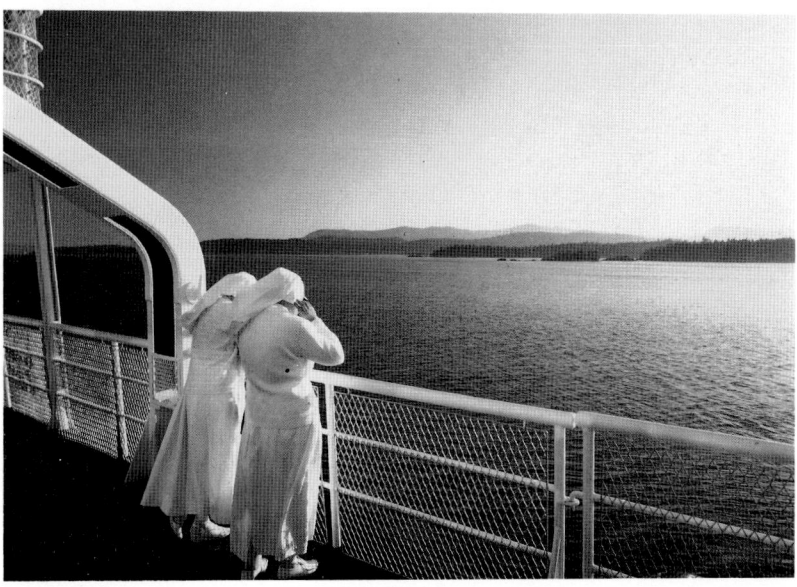

1318

1318
ART DIRECTOR
Barbara Hodgson
DESIGNER
Barbara Hodgson
PHOTOGRAPHER
Andras Dancs
CLIENT
Government of British Columbia
EDITOR
Saeko Usukawa
PUBLISHER
Douglas & McIntyre Ltd.
DESIGN FIRM
North Light, Vancouver, Canada
PUBLICATION
British Columbia—Time of Our Lives
PHOTO RESEARCHER
Kate Poole

1319

ART DIRECTOR
Bernard Rotondo
PHOTOGRAPHER
Rudi Legname
WRITER
Ken Hom
CLIENT
Bon Appetit Magazine
EDITOR
William Garry
PUBLISHER
Knapp Communications, Los Angeles, CA

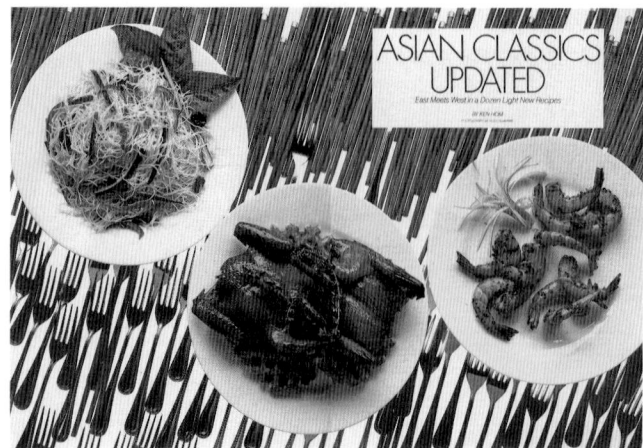

1319

1320

ART DIRECTOR
Ira Friedlander, Will Hopkins
PHOTOGRAPHER
Carl Fischer
CLIENT
American Health
EDITOR
T. George Harris
PUBLISHER
Owen J. Lipstein
DESIGN FIRM
The Will Hopkins Group, New York, NY
PUBLICATION
American Health

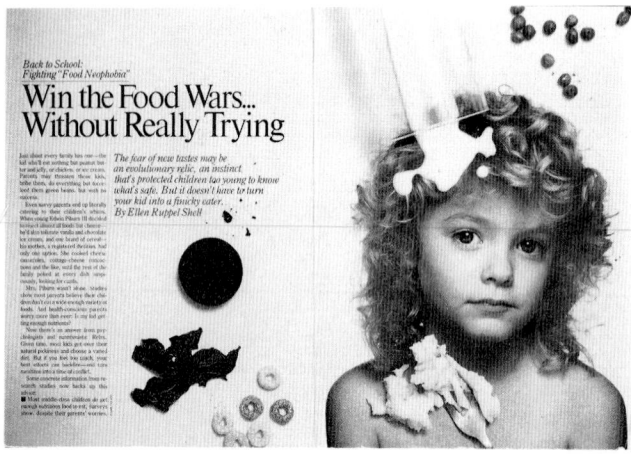

1320

1321

ART DIRECTOR
Lindsay Beaudry
DESIGNER
Maggie Finnegan
PHOTOGRAPHER
Yuri Dojc, Toronto, Canada
WRITER
Harriet Eisenkraft
CLIENT
Toronto Life Magazine
EDITOR
Marq de Villiers
PUBLISHER
Peter Herrndorf
PUBLICATION
Toronto Life Magazine

1321

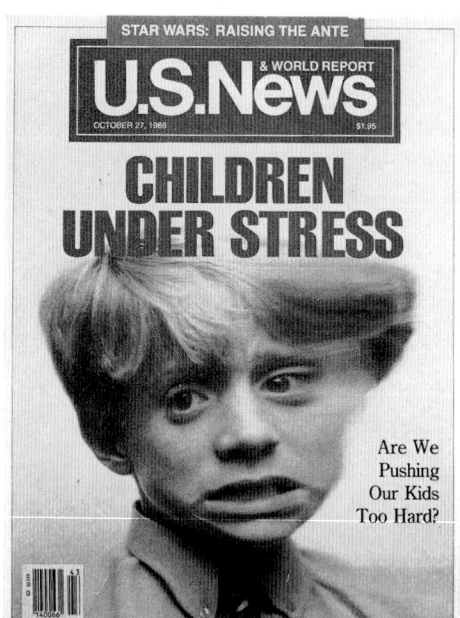

1322

ART DIRECTOR
Walter Bernard, Milton Glaser
PHOTOGRAPHER
Carl Fischer
CLIENT
U.S. News & World Report
EDITOR
David R. Gergen
DESIGN FIRM
W.B.M.G., Inc., New York, NY
PUBLICATION
U.S. News & World Report

1322

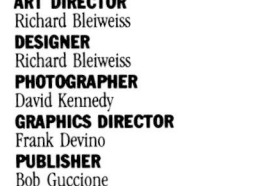

1323

1323
ART DIRECTOR
Richard Bleiweiss
DESIGNER
Richard Bleiweiss
PHOTOGRAPHER
David Kennedy
GRAPHICS DIRECTOR
Frank Devino
PUBLISHER
Bob Guccione
PUBLICATION
Penthouse International, New York, NY

1324

1324
ART DIRECTOR
Amy Seissler
DESIGNER
Amy Seissler
PHOTOGRAPHER
Mike Mitchell
GRAPHICS DIRECTOR
Frank Devino
PUBLISHER
Bob Guccione
PUBLICATION
Omni Publications International Ltd., New
York, NY

1325

1325
ART DIRECTOR
Rod Della Vedova
DESIGNER
Rod Della Vedova
PHOTOGRAPHER
Skip Dean, Toronto, Canada
CLIENT
Comac Communications Inc. / City Woman
Magazine
EDITOR
Karen Hanley
PUBLISHER
Comac Communications Inc.
PUBLICATION
City Woman Magazine
FOOD STYLIST
Olga Truchan

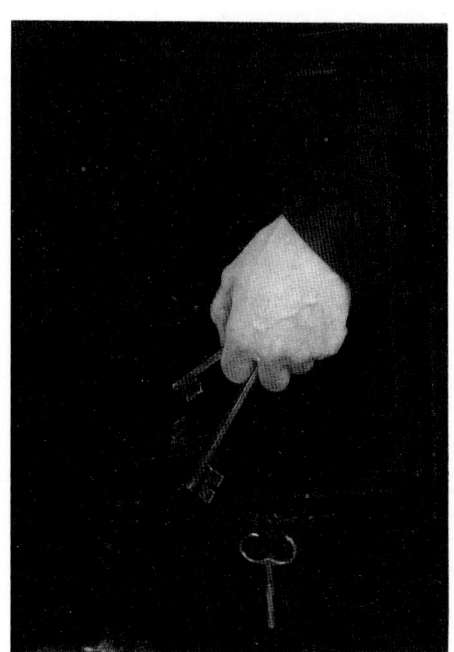

1326

1326
ART DIRECTOR
Wayne Hulse
PHOTOGRAPHER
Robert McQuilkin, Glen Ellyn, IL
CLIENT
Lens Magazine
EDITOR
Barry Tanenbaum
PUBLISHER
Hearst Business Communications
PUBLICATION
Lens Magazine

1327
ART DIRECTOR
Dwayne Flinchum
DESIGNER
Dwayne Flinchum
ILLUSTRATOR/ARTIST
H.R. Giger
ART EDITOR
Hilde Kron
GRAPHICS DIRECTOR
Frank Devino
PUBLISHER
Bob Guccione
PUBLICATION
Omni Publications International Ltd., New
York, NY

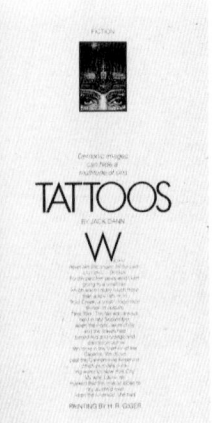

1327

1328
ART DIRECTOR
Clare Cunningham
DESIGNER
Clare Cunningham
PHOTOGRAPHER
Benjamin Mendlowitz
WRITER
Joseph Gribbins
CLIENT
Nautical Quarterly
EDITOR
Joseph Gribbins
PUBLISHER
C.S. Lovelace
PUBLICATION
Nautical Quarterly, Essex, CT

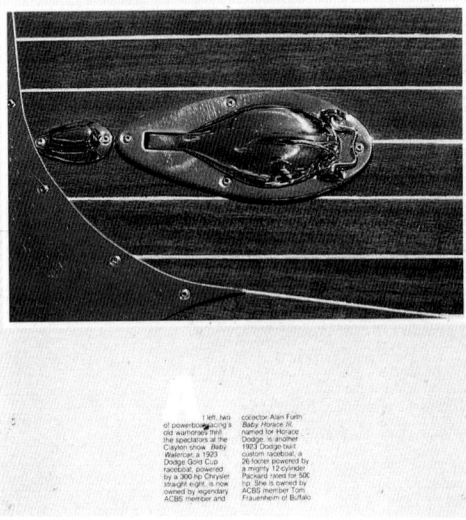

1328

1329
ART DIRECTOR
Gary Bennett
DESIGNER
Jim Marshall, Carefree, AZ
CLIENT
Arizona Highways
PICTURE EDITOR
Pete Ensenberger

1329

1330
ART DIRECTOR
Steve Brady
PHOTOGRAPHER
Steve Brady, Houston, TX
CLIENT
Palm Press
PUBLISHER
Palm Press

1330

1331

1331
ART DIRECTOR
John Goodman
DESIGNER
Ken Silvia
PHOTOGRAPHER
John Goodman, Boston, MA
PUBLISHER
Boston Business Magazine

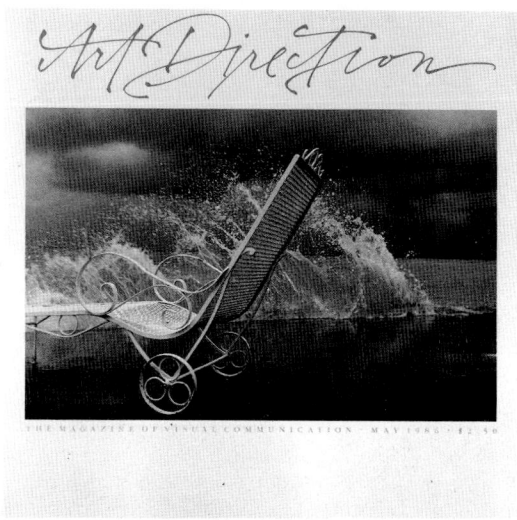

1332

1332
ART DIRECTOR
Carla Block
DESIGNER
Carla Block
PHOTOGRAPHER
Yuri Dojc, Toronto, Canada
CLIENT
Art Direction Magazine
EDITOR
Hedi Levine
PUBLISHER
Dan Barron
PUBLICATION
Art Direction Magazine

1333

1333
ART DIRECTOR
David Kramer
DESIGNER
Noreen Bonkers
PHOTOGRAPHER
David Kramer, San Diego, CA
CLIENT
Champion Products, John Connell
PUBLISHER
Champion Products

1334

1334
ART DIRECTOR
Osamu Iijima
PHOTOGRAPHER
Michael S. Yamashita, Mendham, NJ
CLIENT
Nikon, Tadashi Watarai

1335
ART DIRECTOR
Christopher Mayes, Bryan Kuntz
DESIGNER
Christopher Mayes
PHOTOGRAPHER
Bryan Kuntz
WRITER
Kay Hairgrove
CLIENT
Printing Industries of the Gulf Coast
DESIGN FIRM
Christopher Mayes Design, Houston, TX
PRINTER
Wetmore & Company

1335   1336

1336
ART DIRECTOR
Ervin Advertising and Design, Inc.
CLIENT
Fukuhara, Inc. Photography, Orange, CA
PRINTER
Colour Image, Direct Color
CREATIVE DIRECTOR
Richard Y. Fukuhara
TYPE
Photo-Graphix

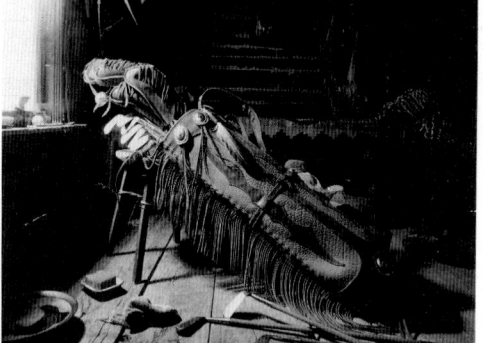

1337

1337
ART DIRECTOR
Pat Burnham
PHOTOGRAPHER
Dennis Manarchy
WRITER
Bill Miller
CLIENT
US West
AGENCY
Fallon McElligott, Minneapolis, MN

1338
DESIGNER
Rob MacIntosh
PHOTOGRAPHER
Kurt Stier
CLIENT
Monadnock Paper Mills
DESIGN FIRM
Rob MacIntosh Communications, Boston, MA

1338

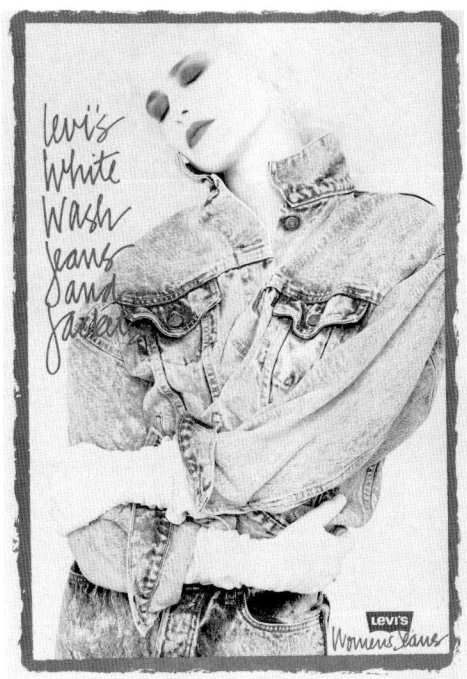

1339

1340

1342

1339
ART DIRECTOR
Jennifer Morla
DESIGNER
Jennifer Morla
PHOTOGRAPHER
Matthew Rolston
CLIENT
Levi Strauss & Co., Inc.
DESIGN FIRM
Morla Design, Inc., San Francisco, CA

1340
ART DIRECTOR
Carlos Caicedo
PHOTOGRAPHER
Frank White
CLIENT
Texas Opera Theater
AGENCY
Ogilvy & Mather, Houston, TX

1341
ART DIRECTOR
Steve Ditko
PHOTOGRAPHER
Rick Rusing
CLIENT
Valley National Bank
DESIGN FIRM
SHR Communcations, Scottsdale, AZ

1342
ART DIRECTOR
Woody Pirtle, Mike Schroeder, Arthur
Meyerson
DESIGNER
Woody Pirtle, Mike Schroeder
PHOTOGRAPHER
Arthur Meyerson
WRITER
Woody Pirtle, Mike Schroeder
CLIENT
The Image Bank—Texas
DESIGN FIRM
Pirtle Design, Dallas, TX

1343
ART DIRECTOR
Pat Burnham
PHOTOGRAPHER
Jim Arndt
WRITER
Bill Miller
CLIENT
US West
AGENCY
Fallon McElligott, Minneapolis, MN

1343

1344
ART DIRECTOR
Woody Pirtle
DESIGNER
Jeff Weithman
PHOTOGRAPHER
Gary McCoy
CLIENT
Gary McCoy
DESIGN FIRM
Pirtle Design, Dallas, TX
PRINTER
Williamson Printing Corp.

1344

1345

1345
ART DIRECTOR
Doug Fisher, Bob Bender
DESIGNER
Doug Fisher, Bob Bender
PHOTOGRAPHER
Hickson & Associates
WRITER
Ron Etter
CLIENT
Nevamar Corporation
AGENCY
Lord, Sullivan & Yoder, Inc., Columbus, OH
DESIGN FIRM
Lord, Sullivan & Yoder, Inc.
PUBLICATION
Progressive Architecture

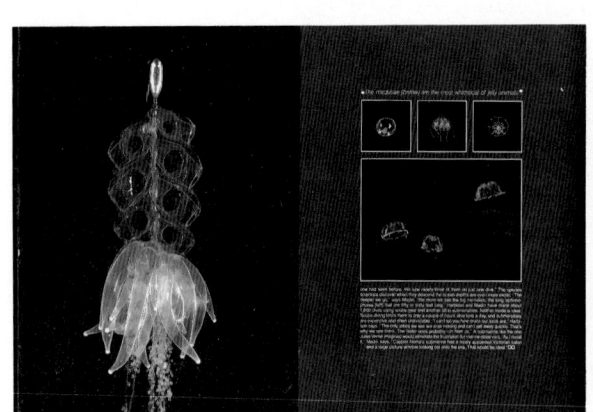

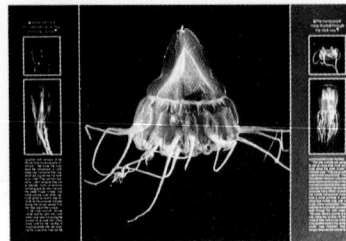

1346
ART DIRECTOR
Dwayne Flinchum
DESIGNER
Dwayne Flinchum
ART EDITOR
Hilde Kron
GRAPHICS DIRECTOR
Frank Devino
PUBLISHER
Bob Guccione
PUBLICATION
Omni Publications International Ltd., New York, NY

1346

1347

1347

ART DIRECTOR
Joe Baraban
DESIGNER
John Weaver
PHOTOGRAPHER
Joe Baraban
ILLUSTRATOR/ARTIST
Ric Borum
CLIENT
Joe Baraban Photography, Inc.
PUBLISHER
Superb Litho
DESIGN FIRM
Gluth/Weaver, Houston, TX

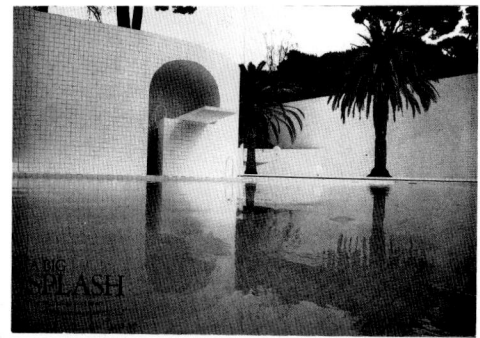

1348

1348

ART DIRECTOR
Lloyd Ziff
DESIGNER
Karen Lee Grant
PHOTOGRAPHER
Francois Halard
EDITOR
Louis Oliver Gropp
PUBLISHER
William F. Bondlow, The Conde Nast
Publications Inc., New York, NY
PUBLICATION
House & Garden

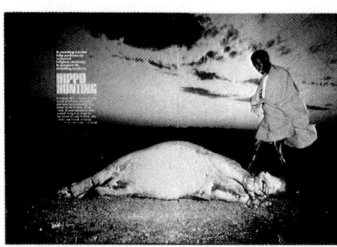

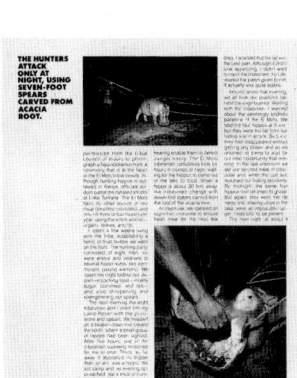

1349

ART DIRECTOR
Richard Bleiweiss
DESIGNER
Richard Bleiweiss
PHOTOGRAPHER
Jeff Rotman
GRAPHICS DIRECTOR
Frank Devino
1349 **PUBLISHER**
Bob Guccione
PUBLICATION
Penthouse International, New York, NY

1350
ART DIRECTOR
Joel Laroche, Arthur Meyerson
DESIGNER
Joel Laroche
PHOTOGRAPHER
Arthur Meyerson, Houston, TX
CLIENT
Zoom, The Image Bank
EDITOR
Joel Laroche
PUBLISHER
Joel Laroche
PUBLICATION
Zoom

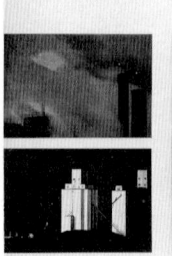

1350

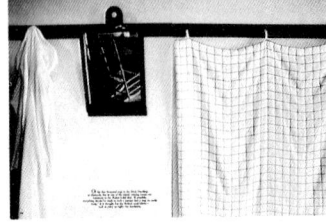

1351
ART DIRECTOR
Lloyd Ziff
DESIGNER
Karen Lee Grant
PHOTOGRAPHER
Jacques Dirand
WRITER
Guy Davenport
EDITOR
Louis Oliver Gropp
PUBLISHER
William F. Bondlow, The Conde Nast
Publications Inc., New York, NY
PUBLICATION
House & Garden

1351

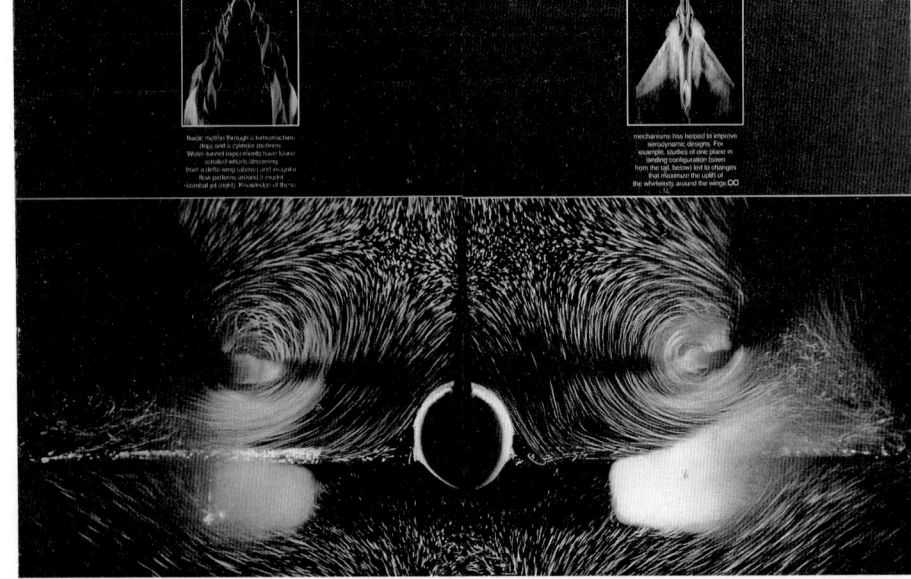

1352
ART DIRECTOR
Dwayne Flinchum
DESIGNER
Dwayne Flinchum
PHOTOGRAPHER
Henri Werlé
ART EDITOR
Hilde Kron
GRAPHICS DIRECTOR
Frank Devino
PUBLISHER
Bob Guccione
PUBLICATION
Omni Publications International Ltd., New
York, NY

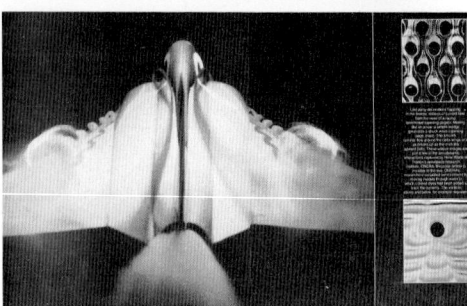

1352

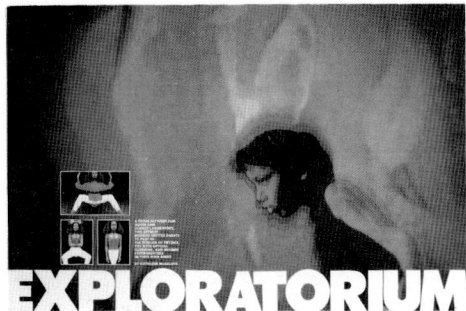

EXPLORATORIUM

1353

ART DIRECTOR
Amy Seissler
DESIGNER
Amy Seissler
PHOTOGRAPHER
Alan Levenson
GRAPHICS DIRECTOR
Frank Devino
PUBLISHER
Bob Guccione
PUBLICATION
Omni Publications International Ltd., New York, NY

1353

1354

1354

ART DIRECTOR
Tom Bentkowski
PHOTOGRAPHER
Eric Meola, Dennis Brack/Black Star, Ted Thai, Neil Leifer
CLIENT
Time Magazine, Rudy Hoglund
PUBLISHER
Time Incorporated, New York, NY
PUBLICATION
Time Magazine

BACK-ROOM BESTIARY

A photographic safari of hidden animal exotica

BY STEPHEN JAY GOULD

 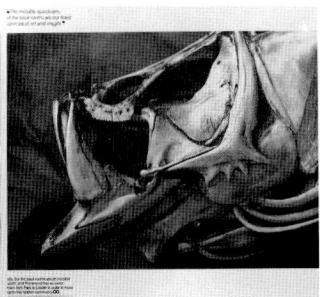 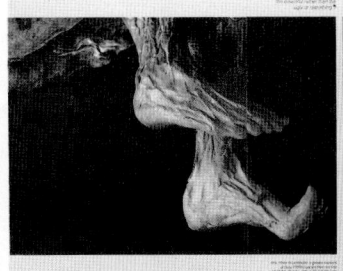 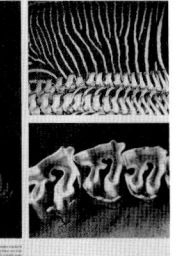

1355

ART DIRECTOR
Dwayne Flinchum
DESIGNER
Dwayne Flinchum
PHOTOGRAPHER
Rosmond Wolff Purcell
GRAPHICS DIRECTOR
Frank Devino
PUBLISHER
Bob Guccione
PUBLICATION
Omni Publications International Ltd., New York, NY

1355

1356

ART DIRECTOR
Richard Bleiweiss
DESIGNER
Richard Bleiweiss
PHOTOGRAPHER
Howard Hall
GRAPHICS DIRECTOR
Frank Devino
PUBLISHER
Bob Guccione
PUBLICATION
Penthouse International, New York, NY

1356

1357

ART DIRECTOR
Robert Appleton
DESIGNER
Robert Appleton
PHOTOGRAPHER
Pete Turner, Arthur Meyerson, Camille Vickers
WRITER
Carol F. Butenas
CLIENT
Lydall, Inc.
DESIGN FIRM
Appleton Design, Inc., Hartford, CT

1357

1358

ART DIRECTOR
James B. Patrick
DESIGNER
Donald G. Paulhus
PHOTOGRAPHER
Robert Llewellyn, Charlottesville, VA
PUBLISHER
Foremost Publishers, Inc., an affiliate of Yankee Publishing, Inc.

1358

1359
ART DIRECTOR
Kevin Kuester, Arthur Meyerson
DESIGNER
Kevin Kuester
PHOTOGRAPHER
Arthur Meyerson
WRITER
Wells & Company
CLIENT
Potlatch Corporation
DESIGN FIRM
Madsen & Kuester, Inc., Minneapolis, MN

1359

1360
ART DIRECTOR
Lisa Jenks (cards), Tibor Kalman (package)
DESIGNER
Tim Horn
PHOTOGRAPHER
Chris Callis
CLIENT
Chris Callis
DESIGN FIRM
M & Company, New York, NY

1360

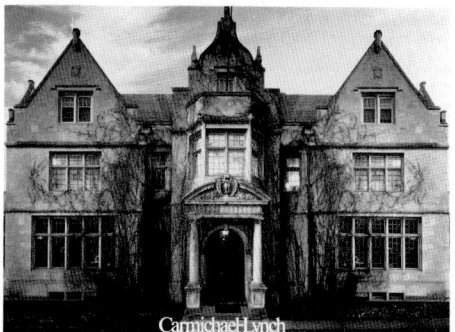

1361

1361
ART DIRECTOR
Marcia Stone
PHOTOGRAPHER
Rick Dublin
WRITER
Cathy Madison, Joe Milla
CLIENT
Carmichael-Lynch
AGENCY
Carmichael-Lynch,
Minneapolis, MN

Though most Americans in 1956 were still watching TV on their old black and white sets, NBC's new emblem, the peacock, suggested that the industry was entering the world of color. This vibrant symbol, sporting a tail of bright hues, established NBC as a live color network. A year later, the NBC peacock became animated. Dropped in 1959 for another symbol, the peacock returned to NBC twenty-one years later, this time, coupled with the big "N." In May, 1986, NBC resurrected the solitary peacock, now festooned with a tail of six feathers instead of the original eleven.

TELEVISION:

Commercial: 10 or 15 seconds
30 seconds
45 or 60 seconds
campaign, 10 or 15 seconds each spot
campaign, 30 seconds each spot
campaign, 45 or 60 seconds each spot
Public service: single
campaign
Political
Film titles, logos, signatures, cable breaks
Industrial, educational or promotional film
Film promos: 10, 30 or 60 seconds
Animation

1362

ART DIRECTOR
William J. Ludwig
WRITER
William J. Ludwig
CLIENT
Chevrolet Motor Division
EDITOR
Stewart Shevin
DIRECTOR
Dennis Grippentrog
BROADCAST DIRECTOR
Dennis H. Plansker
AGENCY
Campbell-Ewald Company, Warren, MI
PRODUCER
David A. Dreschel
PRODUCTION COMPANY
Sundog Productions
CREATIVE DIRECTOR
Dennis H. Plansker

1363

ART DIRECTOR
Joe Staluppi, Stuart Pittman
WRITER
Richard Levy
CLIENT
Black & Decker
EDITOR
Alan Eisenberg, Horn-Eisenberg
DIRECTOR
Mark Story
AGENCY
McCann-Erickson, New York, NY
PRODUCER
Joanne Murino, Linda Kramer
PRODUCTION COMPANY
Cami Taylor, Story Piccolo Guliner

1362

CAVALIER THIRTY FOUR SECONDS
15-second
SFX: CLOCK TICKING MIXED WITH HEARTBEAT.
ANNCR: Every thirty-four seconds, somebody buys a new Chevy Cavalier.
In fact, before this day is through . . .
. . . over 1,000 people will drive away in new Cavaliers.
There goes another one.
MUSIC: THE HEARTBEAT OF AMERICA. THAT'S TODAY'S CHEVROLET.

1363

A CUTTING IDEA
15-second
ANNCR VO: What's a quicker easier way to chop, slice and shred?
The compact Black & Decker Shortcut food processor.
It does everyday jobs without a big mess.
The Shortcut food processor.
Black & Decker. Ideas at work.

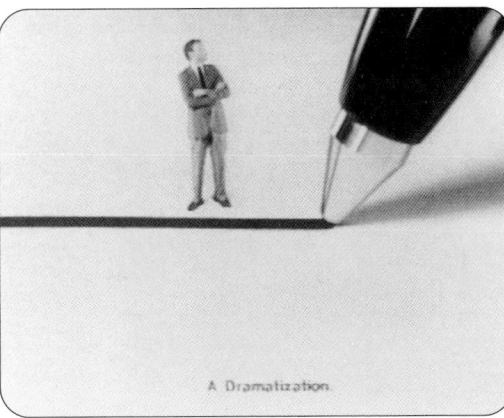

A Dramatization.

PAPER☺MATE
METAL ROLLER

One Neat Pen.

©The Gillette Company, 1986

1364

ART DIRECTOR
Mike Moser, Lee Clow
WRITER
David O'Hare, David Woodside
CLIENT
California Cooler
EDITOR
Steve Wystrach
DIRECTOR
Mark Coppos
DIRECTOR OF PHOTOGRAPHY
Peter Brown
AGENCY
Francesca Cohn, Chiat/Day, San
Francisco, CA
PRODUCTION COMPANY
Mike Appell, Coppos Films

1365

ART DIRECTOR
Bob Jeffers, Bill Oberlander
WRITER
Philip Davidson
CLIENT
Gillette/Papermate
DIRECTOR
Jerry Collamer, Phil Kellison
AGENCY
Tony Silano, McCann-Erickson, New
York, NY
PRODUCTION COMPANY
Tom Mitchell, Ron Seawright,
Hogarth Films, Coast Productions

64

TTI FRUTTI
-second
NCR (VO): The FDA requires that we inform you of the ingredients in
ery California Cooler. Okay.
JSIC UP: "TUTTI FRUTTI" THROUGHOUT

1365

MACRO
15-second
OCP (TIM DOYLE)
1. The new Paper Mate Metal Roller pen dries fast . . .
OCP
2. so it doesn't smudge or smear
OCP
3. like . . . the leading roller ball pen.
AVO The new Paper Mate Metal Roller. One neat pen.
SUPER: ONE NEAT PEN.

1366
ART DIRECTOR
Sally Wagner
WRITER
John Jarvis
CLIENT
Abbott Northwestern Hospital
DIRECTOR
John Harvey
AGENCY
Rosemary Januschka, Martin/
Williams, Minneapolis, MN
PRODUCTION COMPANY
Mark Setterholm, Setterholm Prod.

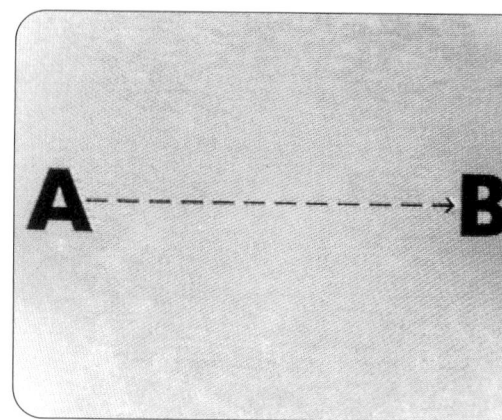

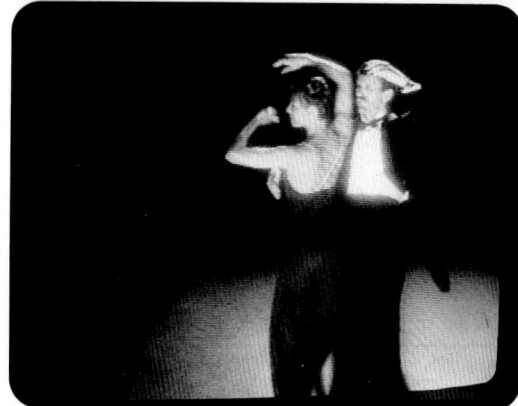
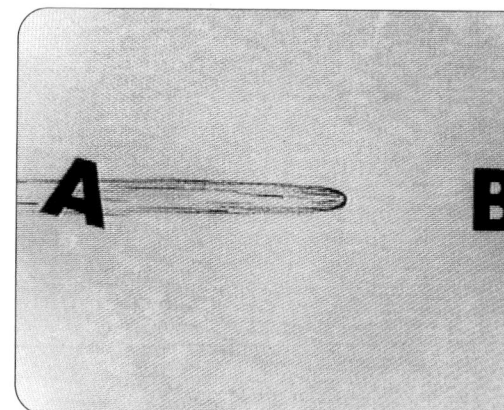

1367
ART DIRECTOR
Steve Thursby
ANIMATOR/ARTIST
Michael Mills
WRITER
Allan Kazmer
CLIENT
Volkswagen Canada Inc.
DIRECTOR
Michael Mills
AGENCY
Louis Blouin, DDB Needham
Worldwide, Toronto, Canada
PRODUCTION COMPANY
Michael Mills, Michael Mills
Production
AUDIO
David Fleury
V.O.
Graeme Campell

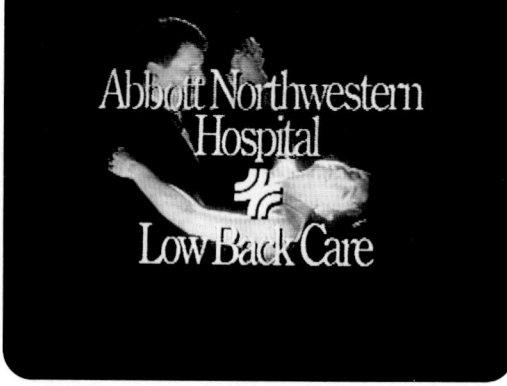

1366

DANCERS
10-second
VO ANNCR: Now you can . . .
get immediate help for . . .
low back pain.
From the low back specialists . . .
(SFX: LOUD "SPRONG" AS SHE BENDS BACK.)
At Abbott Northwestern Hospital.

1367

A TO B
15-second
VO: The most dependable distance . . .
SFX: "BLIP, BLIP, BLIP"
. . . from A to B is . . .
. . . VW . . .
VO: The shortest distance . . .
SFX: WHOOSH!
. . . from A to B is . . .
. . . GTI.

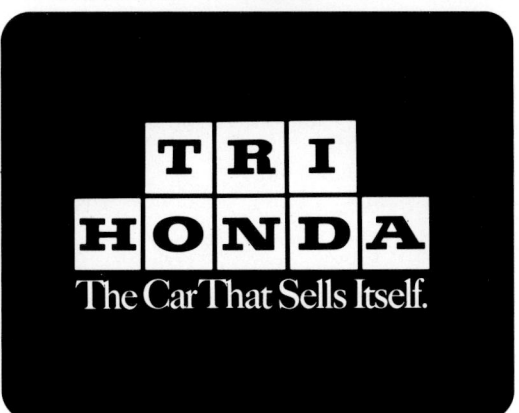

1368
ART DIRECTOR
Stuart Pittman, Joe Staluppi
WRITER
Sal Finazzo, Debbie Kasher
CLIENT
Black & Decker
EDITOR
Alan Eisenberg, Horn-Eisenberg
DIRECTOR
Mark Story
AGENCY
Linda Kramer, McCann-Erickson,
New York, NY
PRODUCTION COMPANY
Cami Taylor, Story Piccolo Guliner

1369
ART DIRECTOR
Allen Kay
WRITER
Lois Korey
CLIENT
Tri-Honda Auto Dealers Association
AGENCY
Korey, Kay & Partners, New York,
NY
PRODUCER
Milda Misevicius

68

UNBEATABLE IDEA
second
ITRESS VO: Western omelette, blueberry pancakes.
NCR VO: Making everyday kitchen chores
smoothly is no short order. But with the
ndymixer cordless beater from Black & Decker
u can beat, mix,
and blend quickly
d easily,
d be
e that everything will come out
FX: CRASH)
fectly.

1369

FIRST/REV. 3
10-second
ANNCR: In the latest customer satisfaction survey, this car came in first.
For about $30,000 more, you can have the car that came in second.

1370

ART DIRECTOR
Gary Ennis
WRITER
Richard Kaufman
CLIENT
Gillette Co., Personal Care Division
EDITOR
Frankie Cioffredi
AGENCY
Lowe Marschalk, Inc., New York, NY
PRODUCER
Cynthia Woodward
PRODUCTION COMPANY
Lowe Marschalk, Inc.

 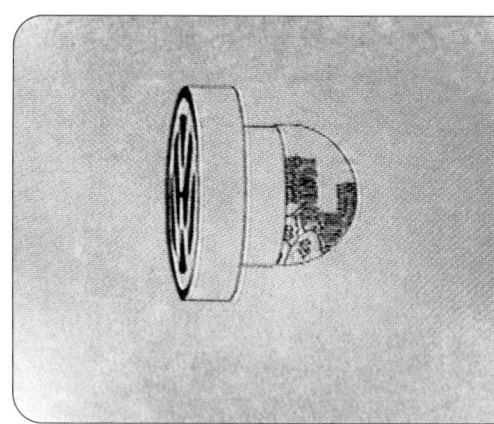

 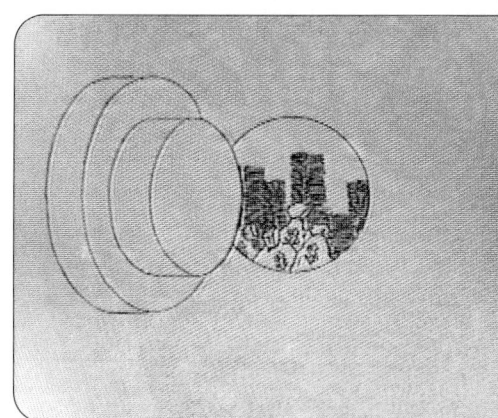

1371

ART DIRECTOR
Steve Thursby
ANIMATOR/ARTIST
Michael Mills
WRITER
Allan Kazmer
CLIENT
Volkswagen Canada Inc.
DIRECTOR
Michael Mills
AGENCY
Louise Blouin, DDB Needham
Worldwide, Toronto, Canada
PRODUCTION COMPANY
Michael Mills, Michael Mills
Production
AUDIO
David Fleury
V.O.
Graeme Campbell

1370

ABBOTT & COSTELLO (NEW)
15-second
LAUGH TRACK (UNDER)
VO: No one really knows how your skin got sensitive.
But if it is, try the shave cream with more advanced lubricants than any other.
New Gillette Foamy for Sensitive Skin.

1371

VAULT
15-second
VO: Now you can own a German-engineered road sedan . . .
. . . and laugh all the way to the bank.
SFX: CLANG!
. . . The Volkswagen Jetta. The affordable German-engineered road seda

1372
ART DIRECTOR
Ernie Cox
DESIGNER
Ernie Cox
WRITER
Jim Doherty
CLIENT
John Deere
AGENCY
N W Ayer, Inc., Chicago, IL
PRODUCER
Ellen Israel
PRODUCTION COMPANY
Kurtz & Friends

1373
ART DIRECTOR
Betsy Nathane, Robert Chandler
WRITER
Betsy Nathane, Robert Chandler
CLIENT
Jerseymaid
DIRECTOR
Gary Johns, Jeff Gorman
DIRECTOR OF PHOTOGRAPHY
Amir Hamed
AGENCY
Harvey Greenberg, keye/donna/
pearlstein
PRODUCTION COMPANY
Sam Shapiro, Lilly Weingarten,
Johns&Gorman Films, Los Angeles,
CA

1372

DEERE SEASON
10-second
SFX: BIRDS CHIRPING
AVO: Looks like Deere Season again.
SFX: LAWN MOWER SOUND
AVO: Nothing runs like a Deere.

1373

BOARD OF DIRECTORS
10-second
ANNCR: Our distinguished board of directors. Nothing important happens
here without their full participation.
SUPER: Jerseymaid

1374

ART DIRECTOR
Walter Molano
WRITER
Noel Nauber
CLIENT
Pontiac Motor Division, Charlene
Curry
EDITOR
Bill Riss
DIRECTOR
Jack Churchill
AGENCY
DMB&B, Bloomfield Hills, MI
PRODUCER
Jere Chamberlin
MUSIC
Steve Karmen

1375

ART DIRECTOR
Gary Ennis
WRITER
Richard Kaufman
CLIENT
Gillette Co., Personal Care Division
EDITOR
Frankie Cioffredi
AGENCY
Lowe Marschalk, Inc., New York, NY
PRODUCER
Cynthia Woodward
PRODUCTION COMPANY
Lowe Marschalk, Inc.

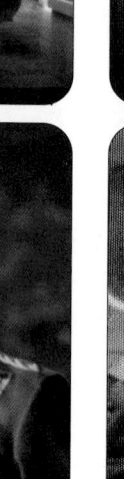

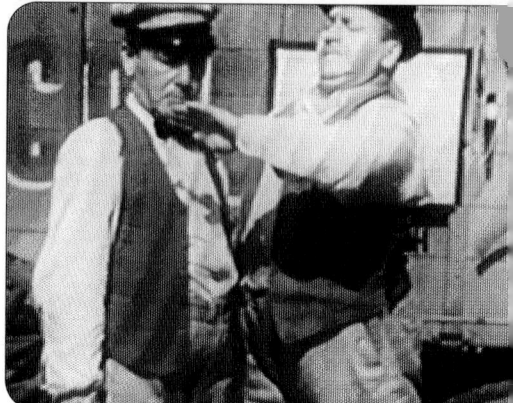

1374

CASINO
15-second
SINGER: PONTIAC!
SFX: NATURAL . . . INCLUDING ENGINE START.
MR. X: The red job over there, Pierre.
PIERRE (VO): Italian, Monsieur, eh!?
MR. X (VO): Picked it up in America, actually.
PIERRE: The Americans, they make such a car?
MR. X: Yes, extraordinary outfit called Pontiac . . . their new Fiero
GT . . .
Mid-engine, fuel-injected V-6 and all that.
PIERRE: . . . ahhh, it looks like a billion francs!
MR. X: A bientôt, Pierre.
PIERRE: Give my regards to the princess.
VALET: Isn't that . . . uh. . . ?
PIERRE: But of course . . . the new Pontiac Fiero GT!
SINGERS: We build excitement . . . Pontiac!

1375

STOOGES
15-second
VO: No one really knows how your skin got sensitive.
But if it is, try the shave cream with more advanced lubricants than any
other.
New Gillette Foamy for Sensitive Skin.

1376
ART DIRECTOR
William J. Ludwig, Barry Lund
WRITER
Jon M. Cashen
CLIENT
Chevrolet Motor Division
EDITOR
Stewart Shevin
DIRECTOR
Dennis Grippentrog
BROADCAST DIRECTOR
Dennis H. Plansker
AGENCY
Campbell-Ewald Company, Warren, MI
PRODUCER
David A. Dreschel
PRODUCTION COMPANY
Sundog Productions
CREATIVE DIRECTOR
Sean Kevin Fitzpatrick

1377
ART DIRECTOR
Gary Ennis
WRITER
Richard Kaufman
CLIENT
Gillette Co., Personal Care Division
EDITOR
Frankie Cioffredi
AGENCY
Lowe Marschalk, Inc., New York, NY
PRODUCER
Cynthia Woodward
PRODUCTION COMPANY
Lowe Marschalk, Inc.

1376

NOVA—KITCHEN SINK
15-second
MUSIC: HEARTBEAT THEME.
ANNCR: Instead of showing you all of the things you can get with new Chevy Nova . . .
. . . we thought we'd show you one of the things you can't get.
SFX: METALLIC CLUNK.
MUSIC: HEARTBEAT INSTRUMENTAL CLOSE.

1377

COWBOYS NON-NEW REV
15-second
COWBOY MUSIC UNDER
SFX: SLAP!
SFX: SLAP!
SFX: SLAP!
VO: No one really knows how your skin got sensitive . . .
SFX: SLAP!
VO: But if it is . . .
SFX: SLAP! SLAP!
VO: . . . try the shave cream with more advanced lubricants than any other.
VO: Gillette Foamy for Sensitive Skin.

1378

ART DIRECTOR
Betsy Nathane, Robert Chandler
WRITER
Betsy Nathane, Robert Chandler
CLIENT
Jerseymaid
DIRECTOR
Gary Johns, Jeff Gorman
DIRECTOR OF PHOTOGRAPHY
Amir Hamed
AGENCY
Harvey Greenberg, keye/donna/
pearlstein
PRODUCTION COMPANY
Sam Shapiro, Lilly Weingarten,
Johns&Gorman Films, Los Angeles,
CA

1379

ART DIRECTOR
Bob Meagher
WRITER
Bob Meagher, Dave Ullman
CLIENT
Skil Corporation
EDITOR
Chris Claeys
DIRECTOR
Steve Griak
AGENCY
Bob Meagher, Dave Ullman,
Cramer-Krasselt, Chicago, IL
PRODUCTION COMPANY
Mike Monten, Wilson-Griak
CREATIVE DIRECTOR
Maureen Moore

1378

DAY CARE CENTER
10-second
ANNCR: At the dairies of Jerseymaid we maintain a model day care center;
for the benefit of all our working moms.
SUPER: Jerseymaid

1379

DUELING SCREWS
15-second
(SFX: SQUEAKING OF A SCREW BEING DRIVEN IN WITH MANUAL
SCREWDRIVER.)
(SFX: WHIRR OF THE SKIL TWIST CORDLESS POWER SCREWDRIVER.
IT DRIVES THE SCREW ON THE RIGHT IN QUICKLY.)
(SFX: OUT)
ANNCR VO: The Skil Twist cordless power screwdriver.
ANNCR VO: It's a new twist on an old idea.

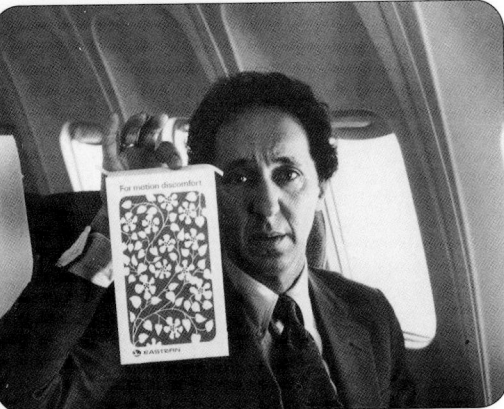

1380
ART DIRECTOR
Tod Seisser
WRITER
Jay Taub
CLIENT
New York Air
DIRECTOR
Henry Sandbank, Sandbank Films, Inc.
AGENCY
LHS&B, New York, NY
PRODUCER
Rachel Novak

1381
ART DIRECTOR
Donna Tedesco
DESIGNER
Tony Meininger
WRITER
Yoni Mozeson
CLIENT
Duracell
EDITOR
Mike Charles Editorial
DIRECTOR
Dick Miller
AGENCY
Mootsy Elliot, Ogilvy & Mather, New York, NY
PRODUCTION COMPANY
Carol Herrick, Director's Chair
CREATIVE DIRECTOR
Mike Pitts

1380
OUR BAG
15-second
ANNCR: Fly New York Air's Super Shuttle and get a bagel and cream cheese or an apple; all in this handy little bag. Or fly the Eastern Shuttle and get this handy little bag.
SILENT SUPER: New York Air Shuttle Service.

1381
55 CHEVY
15-second
SFX: MUSIC UP AND UNDER.
ANNCR VO: Today's Duracell Battery.
SFX: TIRES SCREECH.
ANNCR VO: It lasts up to 30% longer than the ones we made just last year. Duracell . . .
SFX: TONES. SLAM-AROUND.
ANNCR VO: The best a battery can be.

1382

ART DIRECTOR
John Colquhoun
WRITER
Arthur Bijur
CLIENT
North American Philips Lighting
Company
DIRECTOR
Mark Story, Piccolo Story Guliner
AGENCY
DFS Dorland, New York, NY
PRODUCER
Steven Friedman

1383

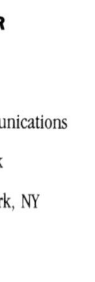

ART DIRECTOR
Michael Vitiello
WRITER
Lee Garfinkel
CLIENT
Tel Plus Communications
DIRECTOR
Henry Sandbank
AGENCY
LHS&B, New York, NY
PRODUCER
Rachel Novak

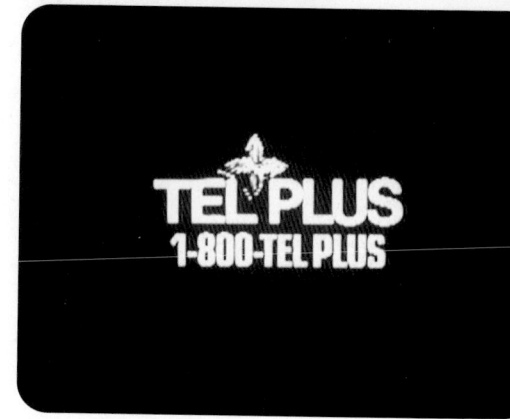

1382

VACUUM
10-second
SFX: VACUUM SOUND.
SEE WOMAN VACUUMING AROUND HER CAT.
SFX: LIGHT BULB BLOWS OUT (BLACK OUT)
SFX: CAT SCREECHING.
WOMAN VACUUMS UP HER CAT IN THE DARKNESS.
ANNCR: It's time to change your light bulb. Philips longer life square
bulbs last 33% longer than ordinary round bulbs.

1383

ROTARY INSPECTOR
15-second
ANNCR: For 100 years Bell specialized in Western Electric business phones.
But now they're selling phones they have little experience with.
And while it's possible to change phones overnight, can they change their
people overnight?
For the business phone experts, call Tel Plus.
SUPER: TEL PLUS 1-800-TEL-PLUS.

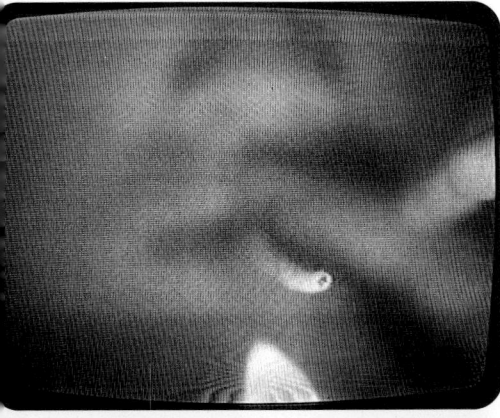

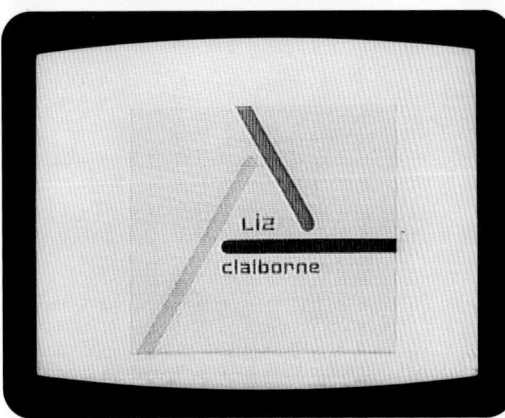

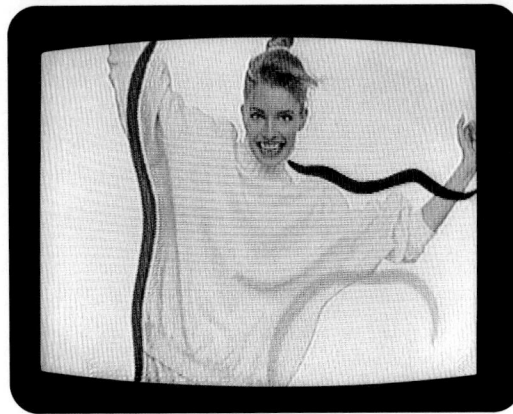

1384
ART DIRECTOR
Bill Murphy
WRITER
Margaret Wilcox
CLIENT
The Boston Globe
DIRECTOR
Bob Brown
AGENCY
Hill Holliday, Boston, MA
PRODUCER
Amy Wilcox
PRODUCTION COMPANY
Viz Whiz

1385
ART DIRECTOR
Joanne Pateman
ANIMATOR/ARTIST
Charlex
WRITER
Phyllis Robinson
CLIENT
Liz Claiborne Cosmetics
EDITOR
Morty's
DIRECTOR
Barrie Lategan
AGENCY
DDB Needham, New York, NY
PRODUCER
Carolyn Roughsedge
PRODUCTION COMPANY
Fairbanks

84

RUGS
-second
): The drug problem in this country gets smaller every year. Find out
out drugs in America, this Sunday in The Boston Globe.

1385

A GREAT MOOD TO BE IN
10-second
MUSIC UP
ANNOUNCER VO: Liz Claiborne Fragrance.
A great mood to be in.

1386

ART DIRECTOR
Betsy Nathane, Robert Chandler
WRITER
Betsy Nathane, Robert Chandler
CLIENT
Jerseymaid
DIRECTOR
Gary Johns, Jeff Gorman
DIRECTOR OF PHOTOGRAPHY
Amir Hamed
AGENCY
Harvey Greenberg, keye/donna/
pearlstein
PRODUCTION COMPANY
Sam Shapiro, Lilly Weingarten,
Johns & Gorman Films, Los
Angeles, CA

1387

ART DIRECTOR
John Staffen
WRITER
Ken Shuldman
CLIENT
Volkswagen
DIRECTOR
Dick James
DIRECTOR OF PHOTOGRAPHY
Dick James
AGENCY
DDB Needham, New York, NY
PRODUCER
Jim DeBarros

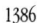

1386

PHYLLIS
10-second
ANNCR: From Phyllis to your 'fridge in 24 hours.
SUPER: Jerseymaid
ANNCR: Jerseymaid. Behind every great dairy is a great bunch of cows.

1387

YAHOO
15-second
ANNCR: Ei Deutschland, ein Wort
fur das Gefuhl
einen Volkswagen Golf GT
zu fahren,
Yahoo!

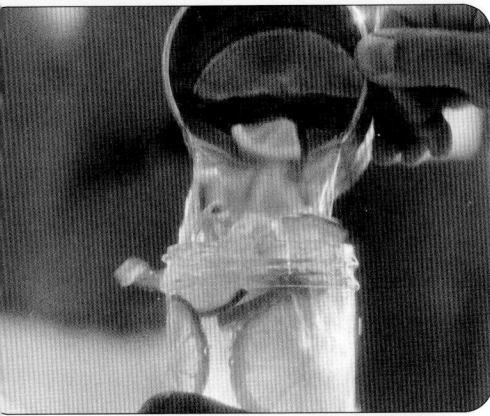

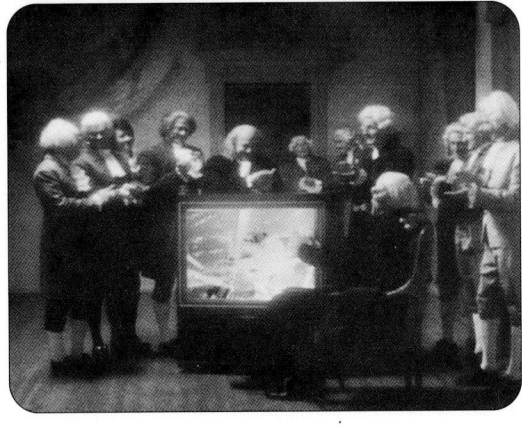

1388
ART DIRECTOR
Mike Moser, Lee Clow
WRITER
Dave O'Hare, Dave Woodside
CLIENT
California Cooler
EDITOR
Steve Wystrach
DIRECTOR
Mark Coppos
DIRECTOR OF PHOTOGRAPHY
Peter Brown
AGENCY
Francesca Cohn, Chiat/Day, San
Francisco, CA
PRODUCTION COMPANY
Mike Appell, Coppos Films

1389
ART DIRECTOR
Eric Gardner
DESIGNER
Eric Gardner
WRITER
Dudley Fitzpatrick
CLIENT
Pioneer Electronics (USA) Inc.
EDITOR
Jacques Dury
DIRECTOR
James B. Wood
DIRECTOR OF PHOTOGRAPHY
James B. Wood
AGENCY
Ed Chapman, DFS Dorland
Worldwide, Torrance, CA
PRODUCTION COMPANY
Dan Lindquist, James B. Wood
Production
CREATIVE DIRECTOR
John Mead
ASSOC. CREATIVE DIR.
Larry Rosenberg

8

TE NIGHTS
second
SIC UP: "LOUIE LOUIE"
NCR (VO): Thousands of people worked
nights,
kends,
holidays
fecting the original wine coolers.
ifornia Cooler.
real stuff.

1389

INDEPENDENCE
15-second
DRAMATIC MUSICAL CORD.
ANNCR (VO: Unprecedented brilliance.
Inspired innovation.
The best and the brightest on earth.
Pioneer's 40" projection monitor.
Not evolutionary,
revolutionary. (SFX: FOUNDING FATHERS START TO APPLAUD).
SFX: FULL ROUSING APPLAUSE.

1390

ART DIRECTOR
Nick Gisonde
WRITER
Charlie Breen
CLIENT
Hyundai Motor America
AGENCY
Backer & Spielvogel, New York, NY
PRODUCER
Eric Steinhauser

1391

ART DIRECTOR
Jeff Roll, Andy Dijak
WRITER
David Butler, Phillip Lanier
CLIENT
Porsche Cars North America
EDITOR
Rob Watzke
DIRECTOR
Mark Coppos
AGENCY
Chiat/Day, Los Angeles, CA
PRODUCER
Susan Ashmore
PRODUCTION COMPANY
Coppos Films

1390

REAR DEFROSTER
30-second
(MUSIC UP AND THROUGHOUT)
ANNCR VO: A rear window defroster comes standard
on the new Hyundai Excel.
Because it always pays
to know
what's behind you.
Hyundai. Cars that make sense.

1391

ZERO TO ZERO
15-second
MUSIC: SUBTLE, RHYTHMIC THROUGHOUT.
SFX: SOUNDS OF 928S 4 VERY FAR AWAY.
SFX: 928S 4 SOUNDS GET LOUDER.
SFX: AND LOUDER
SFX: AND LOUDER
ANNCR VO: In under 10 seconds, the new Porsche 928S 4 can go from
zero to sixty . . .
SFX: APPROPRIATE.
ANNCR VO: . . . and back to zero.

SIMPLE INSTRUCTIONS FOR CHANGING YOUR SPARE TIRE.

1392
ART DIRECTOR
Steve Fong
WRITER
David Woodside
CLIENT
California Cooler
EDITOR
Steve Wystrach
DIRECTOR
Mark Coppos
DIRECTOR OF PHOTOGRAPHY
Peter Brown
AGENCY
Peter Valentine, Chiat/Day, San Francisco, CA
PRODUCTION COMPANY
Mike Appell, Coppos Films

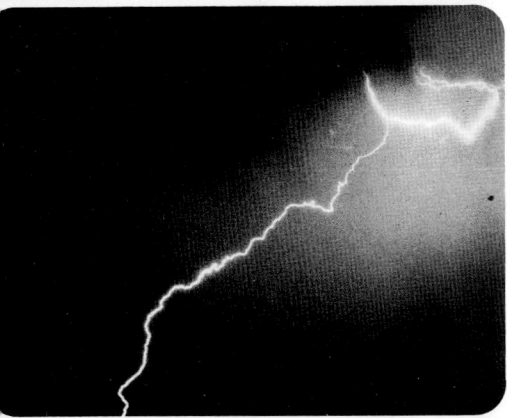

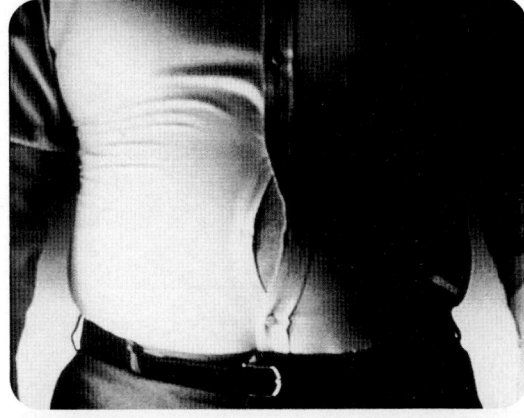

JOIN THE YMCA

1393
ART DIRECTOR
Jac Coverdale
WRITER
Jerry Fury
CLIENT
YMCA–Metro
AGENCY
Clarity Coverdale Rueff, Minneapolis, MN
PRODUCER
Ruby Polnau

1392

OUGH
5-second
MUSIC: "LOUIE LOUIE" UP)
NNCR (VO): California Cooler reminds you . . . when the going gets
ough . . .
. . the tough go indoors.
alifornia Cooler. Official drink of the indoor party season.

1393

SPARE TIRE
10-second
SCRIPT: And now, some simple instructions for changing your spare tire.
Join the YMCA.

1394

ART DIRECTOR
Eric Steinhauser
WRITER
Charlie Breen
CLIENT
Miller Brewing Company — Lite
Beer
AGENCY
Backer & Spielvogel, New York, NY
PRODUCER
Andy Cornelius

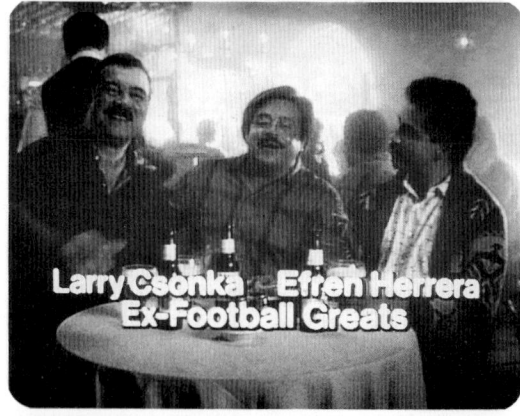

1395

ART DIRECTOR
Jim Cox, Boyd Jacobsen
WRITER
Tony Durket
CLIENT
General Dynamics
DIRECTOR
Gary Johns, Jeff Gorman
DIRECTOR OF PHOTOGRAPHY
Amir Hamed
PRODUCER
Jim Cox
PRODUCTION COMPANY
Sam Schapiro, Lilly Weingarten,
Johns&Gorman Films, Los Angeles,
CA

1394

HERRERA & CSONKA
30-second
EFREN: My amigo Juan just came up from Mexico so I'm introducing
him to my American friend Larry and our favorite beer Miller Lite.
LARRY (BUTCHERING SPANISH): Efren, por fador. Mi Miller Lite gusto
porque. It tastes mui bieno.
EFREN: Larry . . .
LARRY: Lite has mimosa calorios and no gusto filli uppo.
LARRY: El comprende?
JUAN (SARCASTICALLY): No, not really.
CROWD: LAUGHS.
AVO: For mucho great taste . . .
MUSIC IN.
. . . there's only one Lite Beer.
Miller Lite.
JUAN (TO EFREN): Does your friend speak
any English?
CROWD: LAUGHS.
MUSIC OUT.

1395

FARMHOUSE
30-second
SFX: RADIO PLAYING.
SFX: DOG WHINES.
VO: The security of our country is something most people don't think
about every day. We do our part to make sure they don't have to.

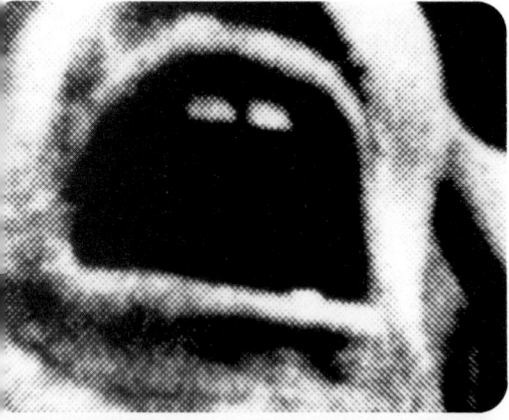

1396
ART DIRECTOR
Milt Marcus
WRITER
George Adels
DIRECTOR
Richard Greenberg
AGENCY
Peter Barg, McCann-Erickson, New
York, NY
PRODUCTION COMPANY
Chris Woods, Richard Greenberg

1397
ART DIRECTOR
Janet Guillet
WRITER
Jane Talcott
CLIENT
Miles Lab, Marty Redlin
EDITOR
Howie Lazarus
DIRECTOR
Paul Guliner
DIRECTOR OF PHOTOGRAPHY
John Crawford
AGENCY
Ellyn Epstein, DDB Needham, New
York, NY
PRODUCTION COMPANY
Steve Eshelman, Story Piccolo
Guliner

1396

INSTANT COVERAGE
30-second
SUPER: AT&T IS IN INSTANT COVERAGE
(SFX: RIOT SCENE—CROWD NOISES)
VO: This is a cover story taking shape for TIME Magazine. But late
breaking news stops the presses.
(SSFX: CROWD'S NOISE CEASES)
VO: TIME puts AT&T SKYNET Digital Service into action.
(SFX: ELECTRONIC TRANSMISSION OF COVER BEGINS)
VO: Via satellite, a new cover story is transmitted instantly, accurately,
and rolls off the presses in under 24 hours.
(ELECTRONIC TRANSMISSION OF COVER ENDS; COVER APPEARS)
(DISSOLVE TO MNEMONIC)
VO: Let us show you how AT&T Digital services can help your business.
SUPER: AT&T. The right choice.
(SIMULATED TIME® COVER. USED WITH PERMISSION.)

1397

BANGING HEADS REV. 5
30-second
(MUSIC THROUGHOUT)
VO: S.O.S. introduces a glass cleaner that really works . . .
. . . Glass Works.
Glass Works, made with vinegar instead of ammonia, cleans better than
Windex.
New Glass Works with vinegar cuts through the toughest, greasy smudges
faster and easier, so there's *less* work for you.
And everything you clean . . . is shiny and streak-free.
New Glass Works . . .
. . . made with vinegar.
Cleans with less work.
Maybe it works too well.

1398
ART DIRECTOR
Alan Chalfin
WRITER
David Tessler
CLIENT
Chiquita
DIRECTOR
Len Fulford
AGENCY
Ammirati & Puris Inc., New York,
NY
PRODUCER
Susan Shipman

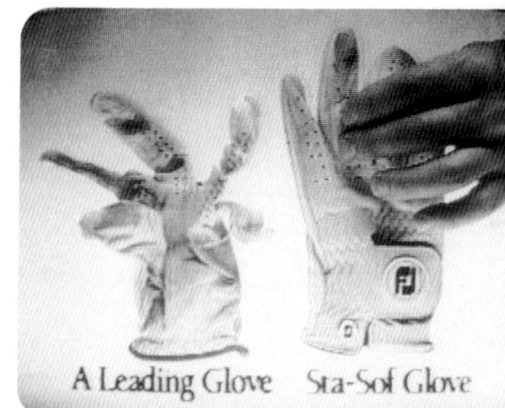

1399
ART DIRECTOR
Bill Boch
WRITER
Ron Lawner
CLIENT
Foot-Joy
DIRECTOR OF PHOTOGRAPHY
Clint Clemens
DIRECTOR
Clint Clemens
AGENCY
HBM/Creamer, Boston, MA
PRODUCER
Bob Shriber

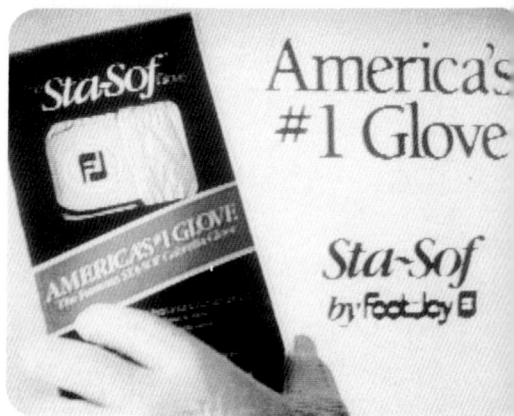

1398

DRACULA VERSION
30-second
VO: Over the years, the banana has inspired a lot of laughs . . .
The banana peel, the banana cream pie, going bananas, and of course,
"Yes, we have no bananas"
Orange juice, however, rarely even got a smile until Chiquita introduced
Orange Banana Juice. A smooth refreshing blend of pure orange juice with
just the right touch of Chiquita banana.
So orange juice has finally gone bananas.

1399

CHOICE ISN'T HARD
30-second
MUSIC: BEETHOVEN'S 5TH SYMPHONY
VO: You're about to see the difference between a leading golf glove and the
Sta-Sof glove by Foot-Joy after 5 rounds of golf.
As you can see the competition is stiff.
The Sta-Sof glove isn't.
With WR200 leather, created exclusively for Foot-Joy by Pittard's of
England, Sta-Sof gloves dry soft, and Sta-Soft.
Sta-Sof. Once you feel the difference the choice isn't hard.
America's number one glove. Sta-Sof by Foot-Joy.

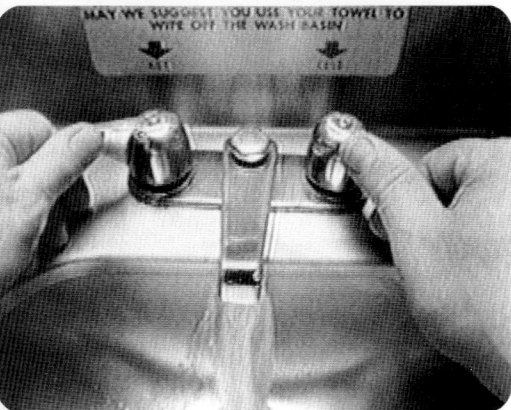

He's Lying.

House Not Included.

You have my word on it.

1400

ART DIRECTOR
Ron Anderson
WRITER
Bert Gardner
CLIENT
Minnetonka, Inc.
DIRECTOR
Joe Sedelmaier
AGENCY
Bozell, Jacobs, Minneapolis, MN
PRODUCER
Judy Wittenberg
PRODUCTION COMPANY
Sedelmaier

1401

ART DIRECTOR
Jeanne Marie Obeji, John Armistead
WRITER
Matt Bogen, Rick Carpenter
CLIENT
American Isuzu Motors, Inc.
EDITOR
Stuart Waks
DIRECTOR
Graham Baker
DIRECTOR OF PHOTOGRAPHY
John Jensen
AGENCY
Frank Tammariello, Della Femina, Travisano, Los Angeles, CA
PRODUCTION COMPANY
Steven Monkarsh, Elite Films
CREATIVE DIRECTOR
Jim Weller, John Armistead

1400

AIRPLANE/REV.
30-second
(MUSIC UNDER & THROUGHOUT)
SFX OF ICE IN DRINK GLASSES.
SFX: BRUSHING.
SFX: FAUCETS SHUTTING OFF AND WATER GURGLING DOWN DRAIN.
SFX: WATER GURGLING DOWN DRAIN.
VO: It's becoming harder and harder . . .
. . . to brush after eating.
SFX: WATER RUNNING AND FAUCET SHUTTING OFF.
SFX: SEAT BELT SIGNAL.
SFX: PLANE SWERVING.
VO: Introducing Check•Up plaque fighting gum.
It's clinically tested to help remove plaque . . . gracefully.
Check•Up Gum. When you can't brush, chew.

1401

THE LIAR
30-second
LIAR: The amazing Isuzu I-Mark. Rated one of the best of the best by *Car and Driver* Magazine.
It gets 94 miles per gallon, city, 112, highway.
SUPER: HE'S LYING. 34 mpg CITY 40 HIGHWAY
Its top speed is three hundred miles per hour.
SUPER: DOWNHILL IN A HURRICANE.
And Isuzu dealers have millions in stock, so they're selling them for nine dollars.
SUPER: CLOSE. WE HAVE HUNDREDS.
SUPER: WRONG. PRICES START AT $6999.
And if you come in tomorrow, you'll get a free . . . house.
SUPER: HOUSE NOT INCLUDED.
You have my word on it.

1402

ART DIRECTOR
Andrew O'Connor
WRITER
Neil Ira Needleman
CLIENT
Nestle Foods Corporation
EDITOR
Alan Eisenberg
DIRECTOR
Ian Leech
AGENCY
McCann-Erickson, New York, NY
PRODUCER
Elaine Mixson

1403

ART DIRECTOR
Tod Seisser
WRITER
Jay Taub
CLIENT
New York Air
EDITOR
Morty's Place
DIRECTOR
Henry Sandbank, Sandbank Films,
Inc.
AGENCY
LHS&B, New York, NY
PRODUCER
Rachel Novak

1402

CRUISIN'
30-second
Camera Voice: Yo. What are you guys doin'?
Character: We're takin' a vacation from carbonation.
VO: Nestle Quik. The great chocolate escape.

1403

WASHINGTON OFFICIALS
30-second
ANNCR: Recently, the United States government purchased flashlights. The price: $170. Each. Nuts: $2,0043. Each. Socket Wrenches $404. Each. And the list goes on.
That's why New York Air offers Washington low fares to Florida.
You see, some people in Washington already know how to spend more. We think it's time they learned how to spend less.
(SFX: PLANE TAKING OFF)

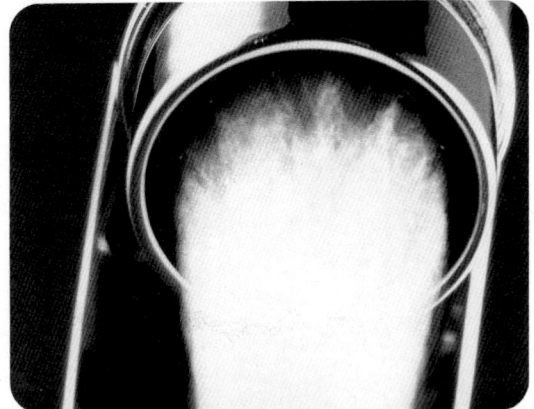

1404
ART DIRECTOR
Dianne Rella, Carol Goldstein
WRITER
Rich Roth
CLIENT
The Hershey Pasta Group, Skinner Pasta
EDITOR
Arthur Williams, Editing Concepts
DIRECTOR
Chris Nolan
AGENCY
Della Femina Travisano, New York, NY
PRODUCER
Debbie Lawrence
PRODUCTION COMPANY
Partners USA
ASSOCIATE CREATIVE DIR.
Karen Larson, Kathy Kiely

1405
ART DIRECTOR
Stephen Parker
DESIGNER
Peter Richardson
WRITER
Jan Egan
CLIENT
Peerless Faucet
EDITOR
Mike Miller, Tony Nardone
DIRECTOR
Peter Richardson
AGENCY
Debbie Dunlap, RS&H, New York, NY
ACCOUNT SPVSR.
Harvey Kipnis
PRODUCTION COMPANY
Carolyn Judd, Paisley Prod.

404

ERFECT FAMILY I—BOX VERSION
)-second
MUSIC UNDER THROUGHOUT)
NNOUNCER (VO): Skinner Spaghetti presents the perfect family.
USBAND: Hi hon. How was your day?
IFE: Perfect. And yours?
USBAND: Perfect. And look who's here for dinner.
IFE: Your mother. Oh, perfect.
IRL: I'll set the table.
OY: I'll shampoo the rug.
IFE: And I'll make the perfect dinner . . . Skinner spaghetti.
ou just cook & stir Skinner for 12 minutes,
dd sauce, and it's . . .
IOTHER: Perfect! I may stay a few weeks.
MILY IN UNISON: That's perfect!
NNOUNCER: Skinner. The perfect spaghetti for the perfect family. And the
st of us.

1405

2001 MULTIFAUCET
30-second
ANNCR VO: To Peerless Faucet, durability means solid brass, resilient copper,
and stainless steel construction.
It also means if you install your Peerless washerless faucet today, it will not only still be working in the year 2001 . . .
it will still be under warranty.
Peerless do-it-yourself faucets
Install in no time. . . .
. . . and last a long time.

1406

ART DIRECTOR
Steve Diamant
WRITER
Pacy Markman
CLIENT
Sea World San Diego
EDITOR
Charlie Chubak
DIRECTOR
Neil Tardio
AGENCY
Beth Hagen, DDB Needham
Worldwide Inc., Los Angeles, CA
PRODUCTION COMPANY
Stacey Kahn, Neil Tardio
Productions
CREATIVE DIRECTOR
Bob Kuperman

1407

ART DIRECTOR
Danny Boone
DESIGNER
Danny Boone
WRITER
Andy Ellis
CLIENT
Virginia Power
DIRECTOR
Jim Lund
AGENCY
The Martin Agency, Richmond, VA
PRODUCER
Craig Bowlus
PRODUCTION COMPANY
James Productions

1406

MISS ROONEY'S CLASS
30-second
ANNCR VO: Last month . . .
. . . Miss Rooney's fourth-grade class went to Sea World.
They played with dolphins.
They saw a seal and otter show.
And four-ton killer whales that were . . . actually cuddly.
But of all the wonderful things Miss Rooney's . . .
. . . fourth-graders saw that day . . .
. . . some cute black and white birds from the Antarctic . . .
. . . made the biggest impression of all.
ANNCR VO: No other day makes you feel this way.

1407

SAFETY
30-second
SPOKESMAN: This is a reminder from Virginia Power . . . that when
trimming limbs, cleaning gutters, using ladders . . . *look* for power lines.
They're there and can be dangerous . . . even deadly. Because electrical
shock is a crush injury. Simply put, it can carry the same impact as being
hit . . . by a truck.
VO ANNOUNCER: Virginia Power periodically includes safety tips in your
bill to bring the facts to light.

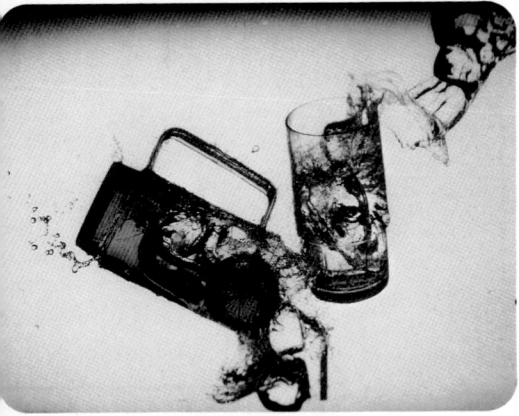

1408

ART DIRECTOR
Tom Shortlidge, Parker Lienhart
WRITER
Mike Faems
CLIENT
Tupperware Home Parties
EDITOR
Jerry Hastings
DIRECTOR
Peter Elliott, Peter Elliot
Productions
AGENCY
Y&R, Chicago, IL
PRODUCER
Pat McNaney

1409

ART DIRECTOR
Neil Leinwohl
WRITER
Kevin McKeon
CLIENT
Tri-Honda Auto Dealers Association
DIRECTOR
Ross Cramer
AGENCY
Milda Misevicius, Korey, Kay &
Partners, New York, NY
PRODUCTION COMPANY
Pete Christy, Power & Light

1408

TUMBLING TUMBLERS
30-second
ANNCR: Tupperware's ® Deluxe Tumblers ® are so elegant
they're perfect for cocktail parties,
dinner parties,
pool parties,
barbeque parties,
little kids' parties,
or any party who's (just)
a little clumsy.
Because, Tupperware® tumblers are
the fine tumblers
that are guaranteed to last a lifetime.
Tupperware®. We're in the White Pages.

1409

MOM
30-second
MOM: My boy Tommy isn't exactly a born salesman. In kindergarten, he
sold lemonade for 3¢. The boy next door sold it for a dime, and ran him
out of business.
When he was a scout, he sold candy door to door.
Even I pretended I wasn't home.
Then he became a Honda salesman. Now my son Tommy is a huge
success!
(CONFIDENTIALLY) Those Honda's must be *very* good cars.
ANNCR: Honda. The Car that sells itself. See the new '87 Hondas at your
New York, New Jersey, Connecticut Tri-Honda dealer.

1410

ART DIRECTOR
Arnold Blum
WRITER
Paul Cappelli
CLIENT
The Coca-Cola Company/USA
Division
DIRECTOR
Chris Hartwill
AGENCY
McCann-Erickson, New York, NY
PRODUCER
Steve Shore
PRODUCTION COMPANY
RSA Film Ltd.

1411

ART DIRECTOR
Frank Byron Tucker
DESIGNER
Steve Walker, Vince Peranio (Props
& sets)
WRITER
Bill Fidel
CLIENT
Minolta Corp. (Business Division)
EDITOR
Lee Bonner
DIRECTOR
Lee Bonner, Bonner Films
AGENCY
Vicki Romine, Eisner & Associates,
Baltimore, MD
PRODUCER
Mary Holland
MUSIC
Jack Heyrman, Clean Cuts

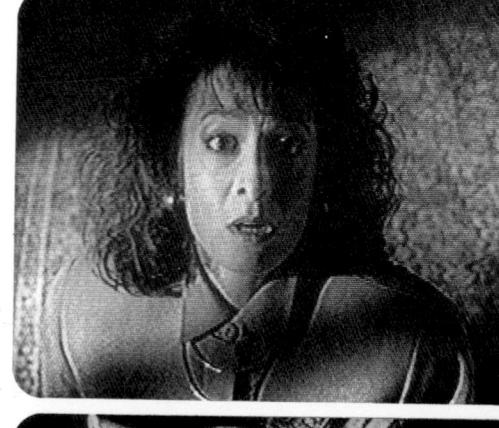

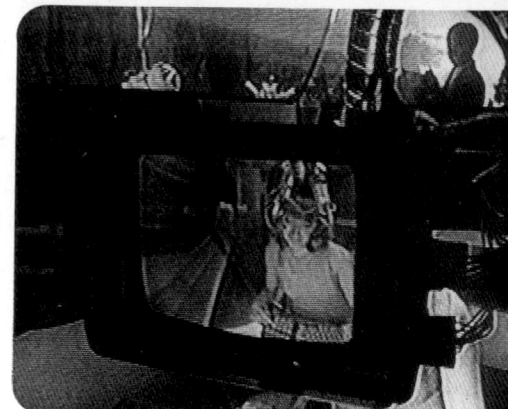

1410

MAX INTEVIEW
30-second
Max Headroom speaks throughout—
Hi, Max Headroom here with . . .
Is this my guest?
I heard you were big time in the old Pop days.
Huh? Huh? Huh?
Well, I'm going to take that as a no comment— So nitty gritty time.
What I'm talking about, and you're not is that more people prefer the
new . . .
refreshing taste of Coke over Pepsi.
Sweating?
It's true, more people are, as we Cokeologists say . . .
Catching the Wave.
Catch it if you can, can . . .
Catch the Wave.
Coke. (MAX SIGHS)

1411

CHAMBER OF HORRORS
30-second
CHAIRMAN OF THE BOARD: It's your turn Eileen.
EILEEN: Oh . . . no!
CHAIRMAN OF THE BOARD: You're going to learn word processing.
EILEEN (BEING DRAGGED AWAY) It's not my turn! It's not my turn!
SFX: ELECTRONIC WHOOSH AND SLAM OF CLOSING DOOR
VO: There is an easy way to learn word processing. With the Minolta Offic
System. It's so simple, you can teach yourself how to use it. Or you could
learn the hard way!
SFX: ZZZ OF ELECTRIC SHOCK
VO: Call today for your free one-week trial. The Minolta Office System.

 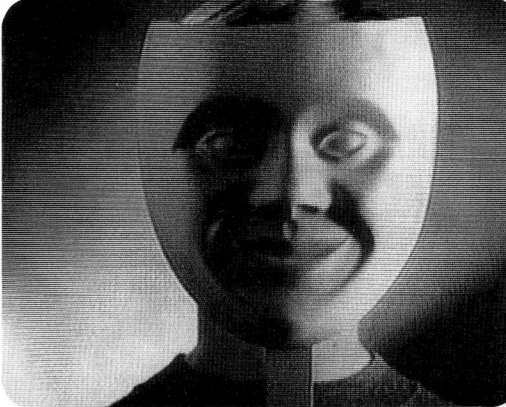

 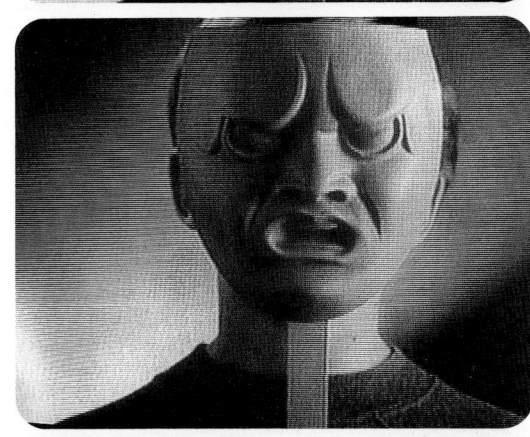

1412
ART DIRECTOR
Neil Leinwohl
WRITER
Kevin McKeon
CLIENT
Tri-Honda Auto Dealers Association
DIRECTOR
Ross Cramer
AGENCY
Milda Misevicius, Korey, Kay &
Partners, New York, NY
PRODUCTION COMPANY
Pete Christy, Power & Light

1413
ART DIRECTOR
Holland Henton
WRITER
Brett Robbs, Dean Tepper
CLIENT
Rivendell of America
EDITOR
Editing Concepts, The Tape House
DIRECTOR
Gary Perweiler
DIRECTOR OF PHOTOGRAPHY
Jamie Jacobson
AGENCY
Cris Hardaway, Walker & Associates,
Memphis, TN
PRODUCTION COMPANY
Exit Films
CREATIVE DIRECTOR
Joe Pizzirusso
MUSIC
Rich Sanders
PROPS
Brooklyn Model Works

VERSAL
-second
ALER: And this is our new Honda Accord LXi.
STOMER: Oh, so this is the new LXi, uh? Very impressive. 2 liter 12
ve engine, fuel injection, variable assist power steering, alloy wheels,
8570-R13 Michelin radials, 4-wheel double wishbone suspension. And
k! A rear stabilizer bar, plus power moonroof, air conditioning, cruise
ntrol, full logic stereo, even power windows and door locks. O.K. you
ked me into it!
NCR: Honda. The car that sells itself. At your New York, New Jersey,
nnecticut Tri-Honda dealer.

MASK
30-second
Some children mask their real feelings. Seeming happy,
when they're not.
And underneath the sadness may lie even stronger feelings,
dark emotions which they hide no matter how you seek them out.
But there are programs to help children show their feelings. So they can
face themselves and the world again.
For help, call your local mental health agency or physician.

1413

1414

ART DIRECTOR
Holland Henton
WRITER
Brett Robbs
CLIENT
HealthMark
EDITOR
Em Com
DIRECTOR
Allen Grey
AGENCY
Cris Hardaway, Walker & Associates,
Memphis, TN
PRODUCTION COMPANY
EmCom
CREATIVE DIRECTOR
Joe Pizzirusso
MUSIC
Songstaff

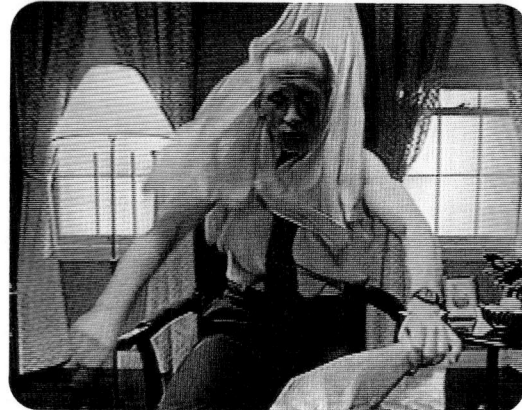

1415

ART DIRECTOR
Jill Stone
WRITER
Mike Smith
CLIENT
Secure Horizons
EDITOR
Jim Edwards
DIRECTOR
Leslie Dektor
DIRECTOR OF PHOTOGRAPHY
Amir Hamed
AGENCY
Helen Erb, Cochrane, Chase,
Livingston, Newport Beach, CA
PRODUCTION COMPANY
Faith Dektor, Petermann/Dektor

1414

FALLING MAN
30-second
ANNCR: Feel good about your health insurance?
With most plans medical bills can take the shirt off your back.
Or cost an arm and a leg.
And when you think you've recovered, know what happens then? They'll pull the rug out from under you.
But the Baptist HealthMark plan relieves painful costs and provides expert care.
So with high cost hanging over you don't wait till the bottom drops out.
Ask your employer about HealthMark.

1415

HARRY'S NEIGHBORHOOD
30-second
HARRY: It's a heart attack. I had a heart attack. It hit me like . . . bam.
Downtown. And boy, that Secure Horizons Health Plan. I mean, they too care of everything.
ANNOUNCER: Secure Horizons is a Zero Premium health plan for peopl on Medicare. Call toll free 1-800-453-8822 for a free information packet
HARRY: This is my neighborhood. I love this neighborhood.

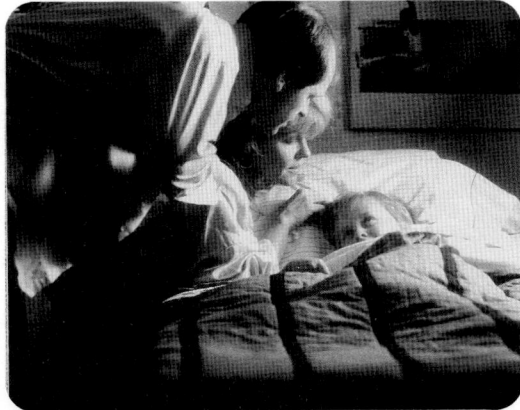

1416
ART DIRECTOR
Kate Corr
WRITER
Sharon Glazer
CLIENT
Continental Baking/Hostess
EDITOR
Billy Williams
DIRECTOR
Santiago Suarez
AGENCY
Sam Pillsbury, Ted Bates, New York, NY
PRODUCER
Joan Vitaliano
MUSIC
Rick Ulfic, Fred Miller

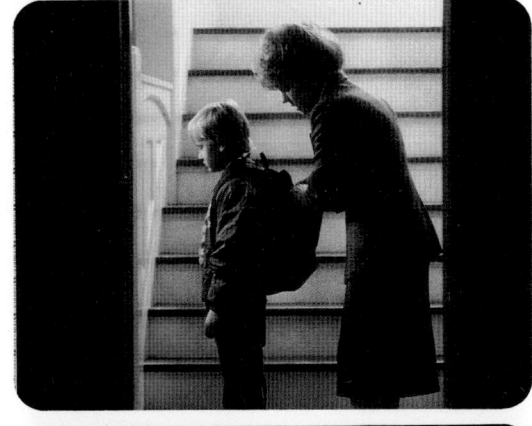

1417
ART DIRECTOR
Jeff Gorman
WRITER
Bill Force, Jeff Gorman
CLIENT
Video Technology
DIRECTOR
Jeff Gorman
DIRECTOR OF PHOTOGRAPHY
Matt Cantrell
AGENCY
Zwiren & Partners
PRODUCER
Kitty Rosenbluth
PRODUCTION COMPANY
Sam Shapiro, Lilly Weingarten, Johns&Gorman Films, Los Angeles, CA

16

VEET SENSATION
-second
NG: Oh what a Sweet Sensation
n Hostess this is gonna be
ch a luscious gooey, flakey
veet Sensation
n Hostess this is ecstasy
s a fruity fuit pie
: Apple
NG: That I'm dreamin of
: Berry
NG: This is Hostess
: Cherry
P SINC: I'm in love!
: And Hostess Twinkies
kes, Cupcakes, too.
NG: Oh Hostess what a
veet Sensation!

1417

MOM & DAD
30-second
MOM: Morning, honey.
DAD: When was the Magna Carta signed?
DAD: Spell meringue.
MOM: What's the symbol for oxygen?
ANNCR: Some parents believe kids have to be forced to learn.
MOM: Next.
DAD: Next.
MOM: True or false? a total eclipse is when Mars. . . .
ANNCR: But with Talking Whiz Kids' computer-like keyboard, spelling, reading, music and math can be fun.
WHIZ KID COMPUTER: Yes, you are right.
TAPE RECORDER: While we're out, name the five major food groups.
ANNCR: Something some parents still haven't learned.
ANNCR: Talking Whiz Kid. From Video Technology.

1418
ART DIRECTOR
Clarice Bonzer
WRITER
Jim Glynn
CLIENT
Mountain Bell
DIRECTOR
Jim Lund
AGENCY
Tracy-Locke, Dallas, TX
PRODUCER
Julie Weyand
PRODUCTION COMPANY
James Productions

1419
ART DIRECTOR
Steve Monchak, John Trzuskowski
WRITER
Bill Hartsough
CLIENT
U.S. Navy
EDITOR
Stuart Waks
DIRECTOR
Michael Werk
AGENCY
Jim Callan, Ted Bates, New York, NY
PRODUCTION COMPANY
Joanne Wood, Rick Levine Productions
MUSIC
Fred Miller

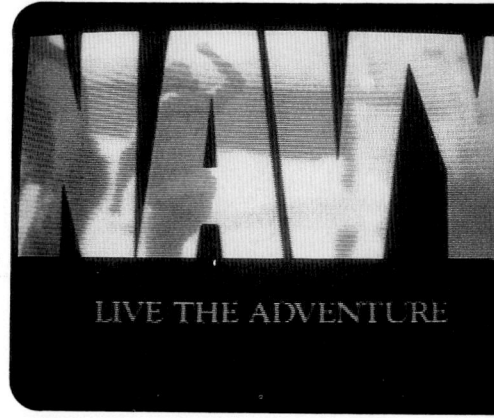

1418

CHEAPEST ISN'T
30-second
ANNCR (VO): There was a reason why you didn't get the cheapest projector.
And there was a reason why you didn't get the cheapest typewriter.
So when you look at
perhaps your most important business tool . . .
your long distance service, there's a reason why you should get the one rated better for quality and dependability. Mountain Bell.
And that reason is simple.
Cheapest isn't always cheapest.
Mountain Bell Business Long Distance.
ALT TAG: Mountain Bell. Answers.

1419

U.S. NAVY
30-second
SONG: Fight fire on the blue horizon
Gonna lay it on the line
Take it to the limit
VO: To reach for something bigger
To master a more challenging world
To feel the confidence and pride
of knowing who you are
What you can do
Show the world your U.S. Navy
Live the adventure
Call 1-800-327-NAVY.

1420
ART DIRECTOR
Dianne Rella, Carol Goldstein
WRITER
Rich Roth
CLIENT
The Hershey Pasta Group/Skinner
Pasta
EDITOR
Jay Gold
DIRECTOR
Stan Dragoti
AGENCY
Della Femina Travisano, New York,
NY
PRODUCER
Richard Burke
PRODUCTION COMPANY
EUE/LA
ASSOC. CREATIVE DIR.
Karen Larson, Kathy Kiely

1421
ART DIRECTOR
Tim Hannell
WRITER
Rob Feakins
CLIENT
Mountain Bell
EDITOR
Ilene Hochman
DIRECTOR
Mike Cuesta
AGENCY
Tracy-Locke, Denver, CO
PRODUCER
Carol Williams
PRODUCTION COMPANY
Griner Cuesta

:0

RFECT FAMILY II—BOX VERSION
second
USIC UNDER THROUGHOUT)
NOUNCER: Skinner brings you the perfect family.
RL: I got all A pluses.
MILY IN UNISON: Perfect.
SBAND: And how did you do Pet?
Y: All A pluses for me.
MILY IN UNISON: Perfect!
FE: Perfect grades deserve a perfect dinner . . . Skinner spaghetti.
u just cook & stir Skinner for twelve minutes,
l sauce, and it's . . .
SBAND & CHILDREN: Perfect, mother.
FE: I guess we're just an A plus family.
NOUNCER: Skinner. The perfect spaghetti for the perfect family. And the
t of us.

1421

ANSWERING MACHINE
30-second
SFX: (BEEP)
ANWERING MACHINE: Hi, this is Chris. Just leave your name and number
and I'll get back to you.
SFX: (BEEP)
ASSISTANT: The Boss is going crazy, where are you? . . .
(LOUD CLICK)
ANNCR (VO): Ever miss an important call?
SFX: (BEEP)
DJ: This is KRICH Radio with our $5000 giveaway but since you're not
home . . . (CLICK)
ANNCR (VO): Then get call forwarding from Mountain Bell. It costs a little
more, but what have those missed calls cost you?
SFX: (BEEP)
SEXY GIRL: Oh Chris, I was going to ask you over, but since you're
out . . .
SFX: (CLICK)

1422

ART DIRECTOR
Bill Halladay
WRITER
Norah Delaney, Chuck Griffith
CLIENT
IBM
DIRECTOR
Henry Sandbank
AGENCY
Ann O'Keefe, LGFE, New York, NY
PRODUCTION COMPANY
Henry Sandbank, Henry Sandbank
Film

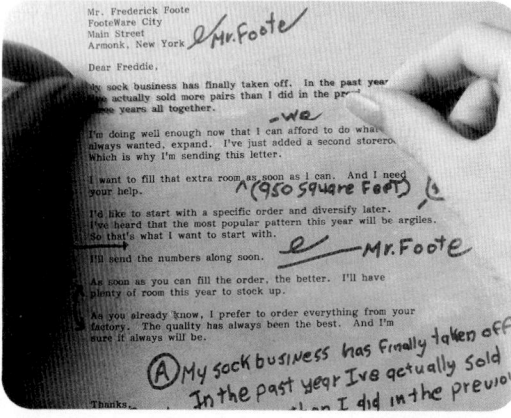
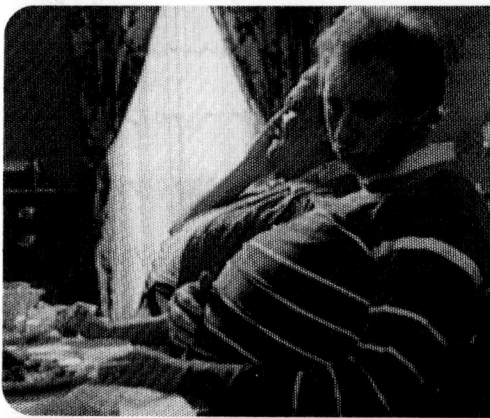

1423

ART DIRECTOR
Barbara Livenstein
WRITER
Debbie Kasher
CLIENT
Miles Laboratories/Alka-Seltzer
DIRECTOR
Mark Story
AGENCY
McCann-Erickson, New York, NY
PRODUCER
Margaret Cancassi
PRODUCTION COMPANY
Story Piccolo Guliner

1422

MAGIC PAPER
30-second
ANNCR: Just when you think everything's . . .
under control . . .
someone else thinks it isn't.
If only you could . . .
rewrite it as easily as the boss did . . .
change words . . .
correct your spelling . . .
make room for new . . .
ideas . . .
and numbers . . .
and best of . . .
all . . .
do it quickly. If only you had a personal computer and . . .
Displaywrite software from IBM.

1423

THE FULLERS
30-second
ANNCR VO: This is the Fuller family. The Fullers have just filled full wi
four fried foods and this is the fullest the Fullers have ever felt, folks.
Alka-Seltzer to the rescue.
Alka-Seltzer fights your acid indigestion and fixes your headache in a
flash.
So when you've finished a few too many forkfulls of your favorite food,
send Alka-Seltzer to the rescue. And feel your finest, *fast.*
CHORUS: Alka-Seltzer to the rescue. Ahh . . .

1424

ART DIRECTOR
Jeanne Marie Obeji, John Armistead
WRITER
Matt Bogen, Jim Weller, Rick Carpenter
CLIENT
American Isuzu Motors, Inc.
EDITOR
Decoupage
DIRECTOR
Gary Johns, Jeff Gorman
AGENCY
Della Femina, Travisano, Los Angeles, CA
PRODUCER
Howard Bailin
CREATIVE DIRECTOR
Jim Weller, John Armistead

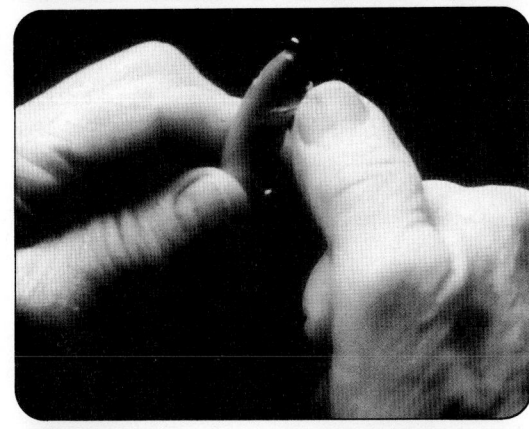

1425

ART DIRECTOR
Frank Haggerty
WRITER
Jack Supple
CLIENT
Normark/Rapala
DIRECTOR
Richard Klug
AGENCY
Cathy Grayson, Carmichael-Lynch, Minneapolis, MN
PRODUCER
Dan Orren
CREATIVE DIRECTOR
Ron Sackett

1424

PINNACLE
30-second
MAR: The amazing Isuzu Trooper II. Its four-wheel drive can take you anywhere.
In fact, I drove it up here myself.
SUPER: HE'S LYING.
It has more seats than the Astrodome.
SUPER: ALMOST. IT SEATS FIVE.
Plus, enough cargo space to carry Texas.
SUPER: 79 CUBIC FEET OF IT.
And Isuzu will accept marbles and sea shells as payment.
SUPER: $10,599. MARBLES AND SHELLS NOT ACCEPTED.
But they're selling fast, so you have to come in in five minutes.
SUPER: GIVE OR TAKE A WEEK.
You have my word on it.

1425

THAT'S ONE
30-second
(GENTLE FINNISH PIANO ARRANGEMENT, UNDER.)
ITALIC: (OLDER FINNISH GENTLEMAN PAINSTAKINGLY HAND TUNES A RAPALA FISHING LURE. EXTREME CLOSE-UPS OF FACE, HANDS AND LURE.)
(HE MUTTERS TO HIMSELF IN FINNISH AS HE TRIES TO PERFECT THE SWIMMING ACTION OF THE LURE. PULLS IT THROUGH A TEST TANK.)
(HE SHAVES IT WITH A KNIFE HERE, TWEAKS IT WITH A PLIERS THERE.)
(THE LURE SWIMS AS IT SHOULD.)
(HE SETS THE LURE DOWN ON HIS WORKBENCH.)
FINLANDER: "yo tambana uuksi"
SUBTITLE: That's one.
SUPER: Individually hand tuned and tank tested.
SUPER: Rapala

1426

ART DIRECTOR
John Sapienza
WRITER
Jim Kochevar
CLIENT
Eureka Vacuums
DIRECTOR
Gary Johns, Jeff Gorman
DIRECTOR OF PHOTOGRAPHY
Matt Cantrell
AGENCY
Jan Collins, Young & Rubicam
PRODUCTION COMPANY
Sam Schapiro, Lilly Weingarten,
Johns&Gorman Films, Los Angeles,
CA

1427

ART DIRECTOR
Tim Hannell
WRITER
Chris Preston
CLIENT
Mountain Bell
EDITOR
Sheila Sweeney
DIRECTOR
Bill Timmer
AGENCY
Tracy-Locke, Denver, CO
PRODUCER
Carol Williams
PRODUCTION COMPANY
Harmony Pictures

1426

ANOTHER ERA
30-second
ANNCR: You have modern appliances all over your home, but when it comes to vacuum cleaners are you living in another era?
SFX: MUSIC
ANNCR: Now, there's the Eureka Express power team, with our powerhead for carpets, and attachments for everything else.
ANNCR: Eureka. Vacuum cleaners for today, not yesterday.

1427

FISHING BUDDIES
30-second
MARY: (KINDLY GRANDMOTHER)
What's the matter with you this morning?
ELMER: (GRUFF GRANDFATHER)
Oh nothing.
MARY: Come on you old mule, call your grandson.
ELMER: Nahh, he doesn't want to spend his Saturday with a fossil like me.
MARY: When has that boy *ever* turned down a day on the lake with his ol' fishin' buddy?
ELMER: Oh all right, make a federal case, I'll call, but he's not coming.
ANNCR: (NATURAL AMBIANCE UNDER)
Everyday, we handle over 42 million phone calls. But none more important than yours.
GRANDSON: I'm glad you called Grampa.
ELMER: Me too Brian.

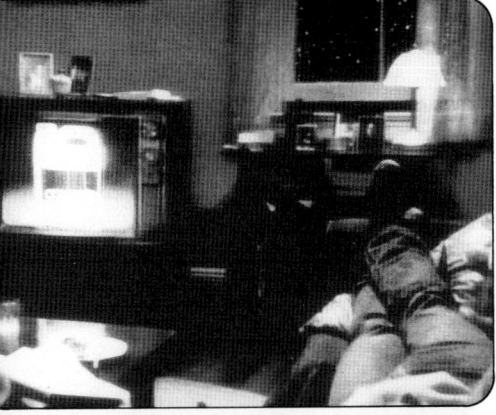 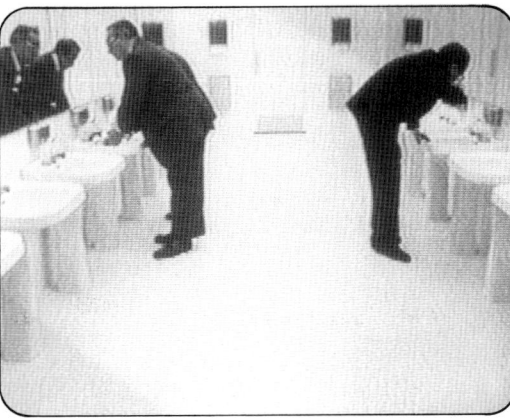

1428
ART DIRECTOR
Diane Cook Tench
DESIGNER
Diane Cook Tench
WRITER
Luke Sullivan
CLIENT
FMC
DIRECTOR
Peter Corbett
AGENCY
The Martin Agency, Richmond, VA
PRODUCER
Craig Bowlus
PRODUCTION COMPANY
Peter Corbett & Associates

1429
ART DIRECTOR
Ron Anderson
WRITER
Bert Gardner
CLIENT
Minnetonka, Inc.
DIRECTOR
Joe Sedelmaier
AGENCY
Bozell Jacobs, Minneapolis, MN
PRODUCER
Judy Wittenberg
PRODUCTION COMPANY
Sedelmaier

28

SET
-second
X: SOME BLAND TV FARE DRONING ON IN BACKGROUND.
roducing Command from FMC. It's everything a soybean farmer's ever
nted to do to a weed . . .
. in one convenient package.
s the only soybean herbicide that kills grasses . . .
. as well as the major broadleaf weeds.
thout damaging the crop.
cause you see, Comma . . . (ABRUPT STOP)
X: HOOTING INDIANS AND COWBOY GUNS.
SSOLVE TO LOGO.
PER: "Command. Read and follow label directions."
IC (R) (LOGO) (c) 1987 FMC Corporation

1429

WASHROOM/REV.
30-second
(MUSIC UNDER & THROUGHOUT)
SFX: WATER RUNNING AND GURGLING DOWN DRAIN, BRUSHING.
MAN: Excellent lunch, Mr. Runstead.
RUNSTEAD: Yes, it was.
SFX: BRUSHING CONTINUES.
RUNSTEAD: Benson, I'm of the understanding that your presentation kicks
off this afternoon's session.
BENSON: Mmmm-hmmmm.
(NODS) Mmmm-hmmmm.
SFX: WATER IN SINK GURGLING DOWN DRAIN.
RUNSTEAD: I needn't stress the importance of that presentation, Benson.
BENSON: Mmmmm-hmmmm.
VO: It's not hard to figure out why people don't always brush after eating
BENSON: UMMMM.
VO: But now, Check•Up toothpaste introduces . . .
VO: . . . Check•Up plaque fighting gum.
It's clinically tested.
VO: . . . to help remove plaque . . . with dignity.
VO: Check•Up Gum. When you can't brush, chew.

1430

ART DIRECTOR
Jim White
WRITER
Jim Welborn
CLIENT
Anheuser-Busch, Inc./Budweiser
DIRECTOR
Ian Leech
AGENCY
D'Arcy Masius Benton & Bowles, St.
Louis, MO
PRODUCER
Michael Windler
CREATIVE DIRECTOR
Dick Zempel

1431

ART DIRECTOR
Dennis H. Plansker
WRITER
Mike McCaffrey
CLIENT
Chevrolet Motor Division
EDITOR
Roger Harrison
DIRECTOR
Peter Heath
BROADCAST DIRECTOR
Dennis H. Plansker
AGENCY
Campbell-Ewald Company, Warren,
MI
PRODUCER
Robert J. Solano
PRODUCTION COMPANY
N. Lee Lacy
CREATIVE DIRECTOR
Sean Kevin Fitzpatrick
MUSIC
Robert J. Solano; Joey Levine,
Crushing Enterprises

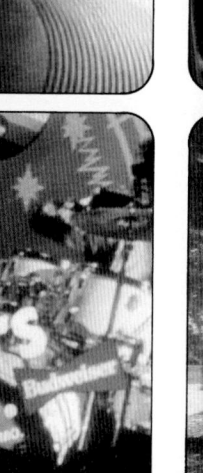

1430

JUKEBOX
30-second
SFX: BAR AMBIENCE
SFX: SOUND OF QUARTER BEING DROPPED IN
MUSIC: INTRO NOTES BEGIN
SINGER: This Bud's for all that you do
BAND: We say Bud. The boys say Bud.
SINGER: Nobody plays 'em like you
You call the tune
And we'll rock the room
You keep the music goin', yeah
You really make it work and
SINGER: This Bud's for . . . (SFX: SKIP)
This Bud's for (SFX: SKIP)
SFX: SLAM/NEEDLE SLIDE/JUKEBOX RUMBLING
SINGER: This Bud's for you.

1431

CAMPUS RIDE
30-second
SFX: HEARTBEAT
MUSIC: PIANO VERSION OF HEARTBEAT.
SINGER: Listen to the heartbeat . . .
. . . of America.
ANNCR: When you're ready for the real world . . .
. . . put yourself in
Today's Chevy Sprint . . .
. . . and listen to your heartbeat.
SINGERS: The Heartbeat of America (Chevrolet)
That's today's Chevrolet.
MUSIC AND HEARTBEAT FADES.

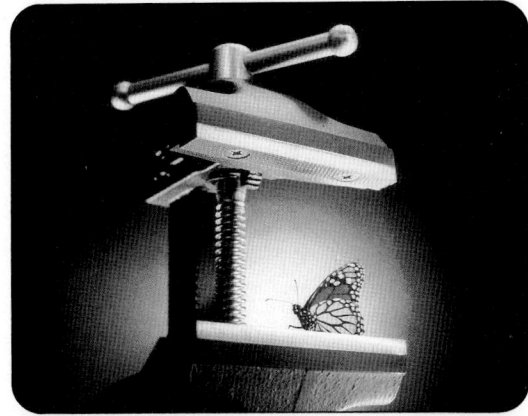

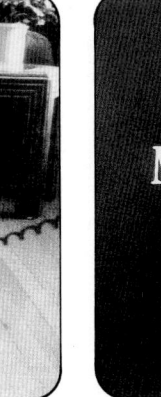

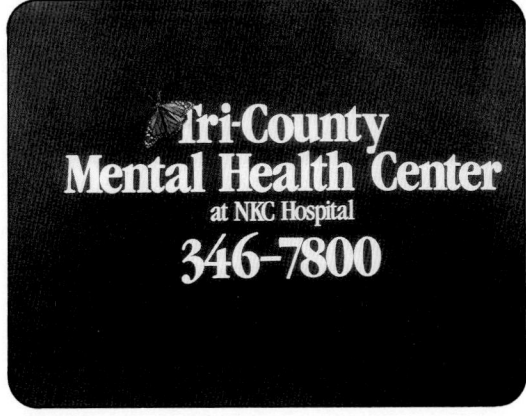

1432

ART DIRECTOR
Tim Hannell
WRITER
Rob Feakins
CLIENT
Mountain Bell
EDITOR
Ilene Hochman
DIRECTOR
Mike Cuesta
AGENCY
Tracy-Locke, Denver, CO
PRODUCER
Carol Williams
PRODUCTION COMPANY
Griner Cuesta

1433

ART DIRECTOR
John Muller
DESIGNER
John Muller
WRITER
Rob Price
CLIENT
North Kansas City Hospital
EDITOR
Northwest Teleproductions
DIRECTOR
Bob Jones
DIRECTOR OF PHOTOGRAPHY
Bob Jones
AGENCY
Rob Price, Muller & Company,
Kansas City, MO
PRODUCTION COMPANY
Bob Jones, Jones Productions

2

LL WAITING
second
N: Max, if they call me for that job, we'll be eating T-bones for a
nth.
: (RING)
N: Hello! Oh, hi, Shirley, no I'm expecting an important call. No, I'm
implying you're not important.
NCR: For everyone who's afraid of tying up their phone . . .
N: I kiss the earth you walk on, my pet . . .
NCR: Mountain Bell presents call waiting.
N: Shirley . . . how do I love you? Well, I (CLICK, BUZZ) Hello? Hello?
NCR: Because you never want to miss an important call.

1433

BUTTERFLY
30-second
ANNCR VO: No matter how tough you try to be on the outside, there's a
part of you that's very fragile indeed. Your job; your marriage; even your
children, can add up to more pressure than you think you can take. If
that's happening to you now, do something about it. Call Tri-County
Mental Health Center at North Kansas City Hospital. It'll take a load off
your mind.

1434

ART DIRECTOR
Stan Jones
WRITER
Alan Proctor
CLIENT
Comprehensive Care Corporation
EDITOR
Charlie Chubak
DIRECTOR
Norman Griner
AGENCY
Elaine Lord, DDB Needham
Worldwide Inc., Los Angeles, CA
PRODUCTION COMPANY
Chris Stefani, Griner Cuesta
Productions
CREATIVE DIRECTOR
Bob Kuperman

1435

ART DIRECTOR
Bob Barrie
WRITER
Phil Hanft
CLIENT
Allnet Communication Services, Inc.
EDITOR
Steve Shepherd, Wilson-Griak
DIRECTOR
Henry Sandbank
AGENCY
Fallon McElligott, Minneapolis, MN
PRODUCER
Judy Brink
PRODUCTION COMPANY
Sandbank Films
V.O.
Michael Kane

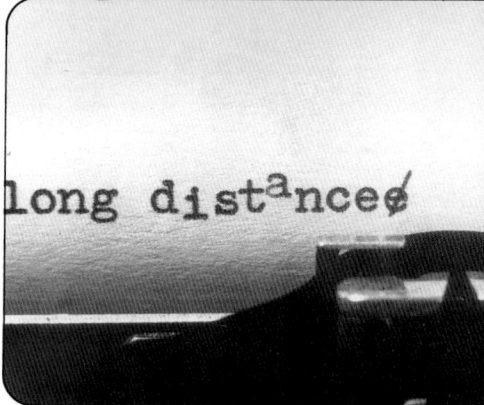

1434

OATH
30-second
ANNCR VO
(WOMAN): (SEDUCTIVE, ALLURING): Will you lie, cheat and steal for me?
BOY: Sure.
ANNCR VO: Will you give up your job?
MAN: Okay.
ANNCR VO: Will you risk prison?
WOMAN: Yes.
ANNCR VO: Will you abandon your family?
(MAN NODS HIS HEAD)
ANNCR VO: Will you die for me, if I ask?
MAN: I'll die.
ANNCR VO: I knew you would.
ANNCR VO
(MALE): If you or someone you love loves cocaine, call CareUnit. We can
help.

1435

BUSINESS LETTER
30-second
ANNCR: Presenting Allnet Business Long Distance. Bargain rates. Not
bargain service.

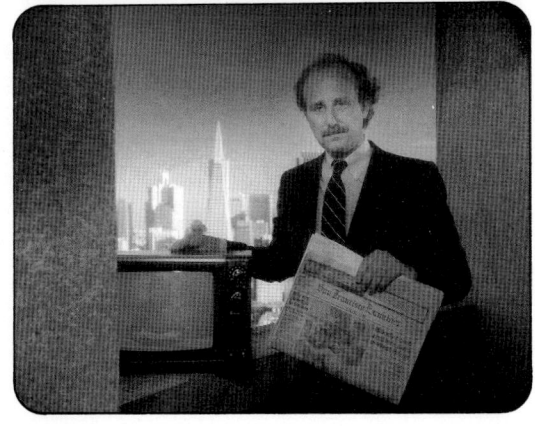

1436

ART DIRECTOR
Neil Leinwohl
WRITER
Kevin McKeon
CLIENT
Tri-Honda Auto Dealers Association
DIRECTOR
Ross Cramer
AGENCY
Milda Misevicius, Korey, Kay &
Partners, New York, NY
PRODUCTION COMPANY
Pete Christy, Power & Light

1437

ART DIRECTOR
Rich Silverstein
WRITER
Jeff Goodby, Andy Berlin
CLIENT
San Francisco Newspaper Agency/
San Francisco Examiner
EDITOR
Jim Heygood, One Pass
DIRECTOR
Jon Francis
DIRECTOR OF PHOTOGRAPHY
Dan Cundey
AGENCY
Debbie King, Goodby, Berlin &
Silverstein, San Francisco, CA
PRODUCTION COMPANY
Sandra Marshall, Jon Francis Films
MUSIC
Independent Sound

36

AIT
-second
EALER: . . . and we'll put the new Accord LX right here.
JSTOMER: I'll take it.
EALER: What?
JSTOMER: That Accord. I'll take it!
EALER: What Accord?
JSTOMER: *That* Accord.
EALER: Where?
JSTOMER: There!
EALER: There?
JSTOMER: There!
EALER: There's no Accord there.
JSTOMER: I'll take it anyway.
EALER: But that Accord won't be there for weeks!
JSTOMER: I'll wait!
NNCR: If you want a new '87 Honda you may have to wait. Sorry. But
e're making them as fast as we can. Honda. The car that sells itself. At
ur New York, New Jersey, Connecticut Tri-Honda dealer.
JSTOMER: Ah, excuse me, this Accord's taken.

1437

GALILEO
30-second
(MUSIC UNDER THROUGHOUT)
WILL (VO): We're re-enacting Galileo's experiment to find out . . .
. . . which is heavier? TV? Or *The Examiner?*
The Examiner has in-depth reporting . . .
. . . that TV usually doesn't have time for.
The Examiner has sections on science, entertainment, business,
neighborhoods, style and . . .
(CRASH) . . . well, more *substance.* And this week, we'll deliver a special
copy to you so you can try this test yourself.
ANNCR: *The San Francisco Examiner.* A better way to spend your time.

1438

ART DIRECTOR
Steve Fong, Mike Moser
WRITER
David O'Hare, David Woodside
CLIENT
California Cooler
EDITOR
Steve Wystrach
DIRECTOR
Mark Coppos
DIRECTOR OF PHOTOGRAPHY
Peter Brown
AGENCY
Peter Valentine, Chiat/Day, San
Francisco, CA
PRODUCTION COMPANY
Mike Appell, Coppos Films

1439

ART DIRECTOR
Alex Fenton
WRITER
Dave Wesolowski
CLIENT
Fisher Price
DIRECTOR
Gary Johns, Jeff Gorman
DIRECTOR OF PHOTOGRAPHY
Laszlo Kovacs
AGENCY
Liz Wedlan, J. Walter Thompson
PRODUCTION COMPANY
Sam Schapiro, Lilly Weingarten,
Johns&Gorman Films, Los Angeles,
CA

1438

INDOOR PARTY SEASON
30-second
(MUSIC UNDER: "NOBODY BUT ME")
ANNCR (VO): California Cooler reminds you. The indoor party season is
now open.
(MUSIC UP)
ANNCR: California Cooler. Official drink of the indoor party season.

1439

CHILD'S PLAY
30-second
ANNCR: The Fisher Price tape recorder.
ANNCR: Built tough enough for child's play.

1440
ART DIRECTOR
Bob Barrie
WRITER
Mike Lescarbeau
CLIENT
Continental Illinois Bank
EDITOR
Jeff Stickles, Wilson-Griak
DIRECTOR
Mark Coppos
AGENCY
Fallon McElligott, Minneapolis, MN
PRODUCER
Char Loving
PRODUCTION COMPANY
Coppos Films
MUSIC
John Trivers
V.O.
Karl Webber

1441
ART DIRECTOR
Joe Minnella
WRITER
John De Cerchio, Dale Silverberg
CLIENT
Sohio
EDITOR
Bill Riss
DIRECTOR
Ron Finley
AGENCY
W.B. Donor, Southfield, MI
PRODUCER
Sheldon Cohn
PRODUCTION COMPANY
Ron Finley Films

1440
SPORTS
30-second
MUSIC THROUGHOUT
(SFX: WHACK—THUNK)
(SFX: WHACK—THUNK)
(SFX: BOWLING BALL RUMBLE)
ANNCR: When you work at Continental Illinois, you have time to be a good banker . . .
(SFX: RUMBLE)
(SFX: GOLF SWING)
. . . and that's about it.
(SFX: PLUNK)
The new Continental Illinois. We work hard. We have to.

1441
FROZEN SOLID
30-second
GUY: (TO HIMSELF) Hmmmmppff. Sure hope it starts.
VO: On typical Ohio winter mornings you'll be glad you filled up at Sohio.
GUY: (TO HIMSELF) Ice is kind of thick today.
VO: Because Sohio Unleaded gasolines and Diesel Supreme with Ice-Gard are guaranteed to prevent fuel line freeze-up.
GUY: (TO HIMSELF) Well, here goes.
(SFX . . . START-UP)
VO: Sohio with Ice-Gard. You go or we pay the tow.
(WAVES TO NEIGHBOR)
NEIGHBOR: Morning, Frank.

1442

ART DIRECTOR
Pat Burnham
WRITER
Bill Miller
CLIENT
KRON-TV (Chronicle Broadcasting)
EDITOR
Tony Fischer, James Productions
DIRECTOR
Mark Story
AGENCY
Fallon McElligott, Minneapolis, MN
PRODUCER
Judy Brink
PRODUCTION COMPANY
Story Piccolo Guliner
V.O.
Eddie Barth

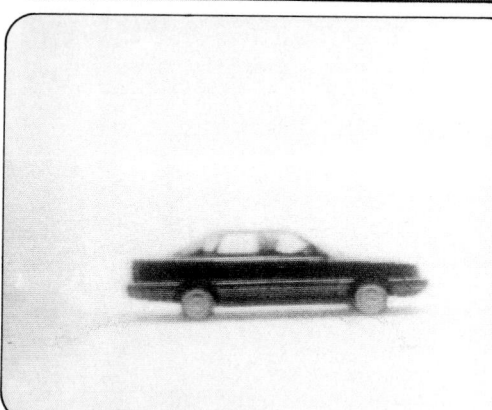

1443

ART DIRECTOR
Terry Iles
WRITER
Rick Davis
CLIENT
Volkswagen Canada Inc.
DIRECTOR
Paul Cade
AGENCY
Louise Blouin, DDB Needham
Worldwide, Toronto, Canada
PRODUCTION COMPANY
Chris Money, Boardwalk Pictures
Limited
MUSIC
David Fleury
CAMERAMAN
Harry Lake

1442

CHEESECAKE
30-second
ANNCR VO: Awhile back, we, here at Newscenter 4, did a little story on
cheesecakes. Then, Channel 5 did a little story on cheesecakes.
We did a story on shooting birds on the golf course. Then, they did a story
on shooting birds on the golf course.
We did a story on peacocks. Then they did a story on peacocks.
You want to know their next story? Take a look at our next story.
You can get the story straight from us or once they get our story straight,
you can get it from them.
Newscenter 4. At 5, 6 and 11.

1443

CHALLENGE
30-second
MUSIC: (UNDERSTATED, ORCHESTRAL)
SFX: (CARS START)
ANNCR: (VO) (CONFIDENT, UNDERSTATED)
Because an Audi with quattro-drive virtually doubles road grip, it's really
for two kinds of drivers.
SFX: (CARS PULLING AWAY)
Those who like to feel the challenge of the road.
And those who don't.

1444

ART DIRECTOR
Michael Fazende
WRITER
John Stingley
CLIENT
O.M. Scott
EDITOR
Steve Shepherd, Wilson-Griak
DIRECTOR
Joe Pytka
AGENCY
Fallon McElligott, Minneapolis, MN
PRODUCER
Judy Brink
PRODUCTION COMPANY
Pytka
V.O.
Michael Stull

1445

ART DIRECTOR
Brad J. Neely
WRITER
Cerves T. McNeill
CLIENT
Chevrolet Motor Division
EDITOR
Roger Harrison
DIRECTOR
Peter Heath
BROADCAST DIRECTOR
Dennis H. Plansker
AGENCY
Campbell-Ewald Company, Warren, MI
PRODUCER
Robert J. Solano
PRODUCTION COMPANY
N. Lee Lacy
CREATIVE DIRECTOR
Sean Kevin Fitzpatrick
MUSIC
Denise Abood Sidlow; Joey Levine, Crushing Enterprises

1444

SOD FIELDS
30-second
ANNCR: In Marysville, Ohio, people spend a lifetime watching the grass grow.
GUY 1: Ustilago striiformis in test plot 4.
GUY 2: Yep.
ANNCR: Because Marysville is the home of Scotts lawn products.
GUY 1: Plot 10 looks good.
GUY 2: Yep.
ANNCR: It has been for *three* generations.
GUY 2: 'Cept for that centella asiatica . . .
ANNCR: That's why Scotts can guarantee you a beautiful lawn.
GUY 1: (SURPRISED) Yep.
ANNCR: After 60 years, we could do it with our eyes closed. When all there is to do is watch the grass grow . . . you really get to know grass.
LOGO: Scott's The Lawn People. See Bag for Guarantee.

1445

NOVA AUDITION
30-second
SFX: HEARTBEAT EFFECT.
MUSIC: CLASSICAL ARRANGEMENT OF HEARTBEAT THEME.
SFX: HEARTBEAT EFFECT.
SINGERS: Listen to the heartbeat
SINGERS: of America
ANNCR: When your standards . . .
. . . are higher than you think you can afford . . .
. . . put yourself in today's Chevy Nova and listen to your heartbeat.
SINGERS: The Heartbeat of America
SINGERS: That's today's
Chevrolet.
MUSIC: CLASSICAL MUSIC.
SFX: HEARTBEAT

1446

ART DIRECTOR
Dianne Rella
WRITER
Rich Roth
CLIENT
A & W Beverage Company
EDITOR
Arthur Williams, Editing Concepts
DIRECTOR
Chris Nolan
AGENCY
Della Femina Travisano, New York, NY
PRODUCER
Debbie Lawrence
PRODUCTION COMPANY
Partners USA
ASSOC. CREATIVE DIR.
Jim Ross, John Peebles

1447

ART DIRECTOR
Tom Lichtenheld
WRITER
Bruce Bildsten
CLIENT
O.M. Scott
EDITOR
Steve Shepherd, Wilson-Griak
DIRECTOR
Mark Story
AGENCY
Fallon McElligott, Minneapolis, MN
PRODUCER
Char Loving
PRODUCTION COMPANY
Story Piccolo Guliner
V.O.
Michael Stull

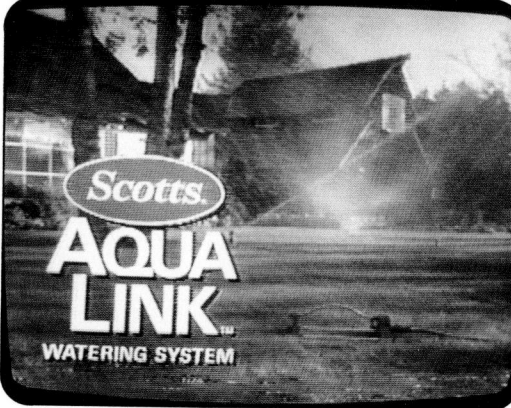

1446

FAN CLUB
30-second
As you can see I have a large and adoring fan club. To show how much . . .
I appreciate their good taste, I'm throwing them an A&W Root Beer Float party.
Now the first thing you do is flip in your ice cream.
FANS: Ooh!
Then you pour in your rich, creamy A&W Root Beer.
Now you kids try it.
Just because they have good taste, don't mean they have good aim.
Pour yourself an A&W Root Beer Float.

1447

CHIMP
25-second
SFX: (CHIMPANZEE NOISES)
SFX: (ESPECIALLY LOUD AND ANGRY CHIMPANZEE NOISES.)
VO: Scotts AquaLink Watering System. The hardest part is turning it on.

1448
ART DIRECTOR
Eugene Turner
WRITER
Tucker Coon
CLIENT
Chevrolet Motor Division
EDITOR
Bill Riss
DIRECTOR
Ian Leech
BROADCAST DIRECTOR
Dennis H. Plansker
AGENCY
Campbell-Ewald Company, Warren, MI
PRODUCER
Albert E. Schacherer
PRODUCTION COMPANY
Ian Leech & Associates
CREATIVE DIRECTOR
Sean Kevin Fitzpatrick
MUSIC
Denise Abood Sidlow; Joey Levine, Crushing Enterprises

1449
ART DIRECTOR
Ernie Cox
WRITER
Jim Doherty
CLIENT
Illinois Bell
DIRECTOR
Stan Schofield
AGENCY
N W Ayer, Inc., Chicago, IL
PRODUCER
Ellen Israel
PRODUCTION COMPANY
Sandbank Films

1448

AMERICAN BLAZER-HEARTBEAT
30-second
FEMALE SINGER: Listen to the heartbeat
(ooh ooh)
of America
MALE SINGER: It's the rhythm of the road
It's the pulse on the street (PULSE ON THE STREET)
A city, town, magic sound (oooh)
ANNCR: If you want the adventure of it all . . .
Put yourself in Today's Chevy S-10 Blazer . . .
. . . and listen to your heartbeat.
FEMALE SINGER: Ooh! The heartbeat of America (Chevrolet)
MALE SINGER: That's today's Chevrolet.
SFX: HEARTBEAT FADES OUT.

1449

SALON
30-second
RECEPTIONIST: And your appointment is with. . . ?
PATRON: Oh, I don't have one.
RECEPTIONIST: Well, it's by appointment only.
PATRON: Oh really? I just need a quick trim.
WOMAN (INTO PHONE): Hi. I'm in the neighborhood and I'd like to get my hair cut right away.
RECEPTIONIST (THROUGH PHONE): How soon can you be here?
WOMAN: How's 5 minutes?
RECEPTIONIST (THROUGH PHONE): Monique will be waiting. Thank you for calling.
RECEPTIONIST: And your appointment is with. . . ?
WOMAN: Monique.
RECEPTIONIST: Miss Francis. Of course!
Shampoooooo!!
CHORUS: Phone First.

1450

ART DIRECTOR
Diane Cook Tench
DESIGNER
Diane Cook Tench
WRITER
Luke Sullivan
CLIENT
FMC
DIRECTOR
Peter Corbett
AGENCY
The Martin Agency, Richmond, VA
PRODUCER
Craig Bowlus
PRODUCTION COMPANY
Peter Corbett & Associates

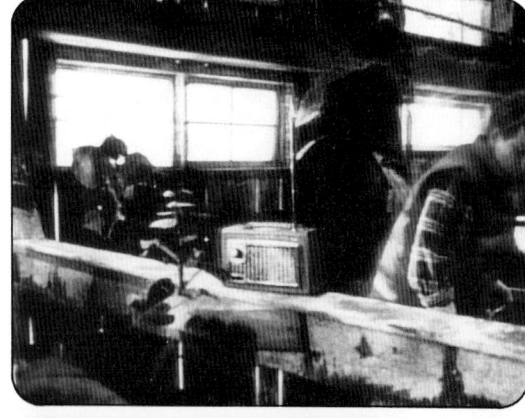

1451

ART DIRECTOR
Candy Greathouse, Roberta Williams
WRITER
John Lyons
CLIENT
Procter & Gamble — Bounce
EDITOR
Howard Weisbrot
DIRECTOR
Ed Bianchi
DIRECTOR OF PHOTOGRAPHY
Andrzej Bartkowiak
AGENCY
Karen Spector, DMB&B, New York, NY
PRODUCTION COMPANY
Ann Friedman, Bianchi Films
MUSIC
Michael Zager

1450

RADIO SET
30-second
SFX: Radio playing country music.
ANNCR: Introducing Command from FMC. It's everything a soybean farmer has ever wanted to do to a weed in one convenient package. The only soybean herbicide that kills grasses as well as the major broadleaf weeds, without damaging the crop.
And it controls weeds all . . .
season long. Because you see, Comma . . .
SFX: PLOP.

1451

SOFT/FP
30-second
SFX: MUSIC THROUGHOUT.
SONG: How soft
Jump.
So soft.
Jump.
Ooh. Very soft.
Jump. Jump. Jump. Jump.
Bounce.
For so soft clothes
you can't wait to jump into.
Jump.
Feels so good.
Jump in
You are the one
so warm and soft around me.
Jump. Jump. Jump. Jump. Jump.
Bounce. For so soft clothes you can't wait to jump into.
Jump.

1452
ART DIRECTOR
Gus Shoukas
WRITER
D. Linder
CLIENT
Eastern Airlines
DIRECTOR
Cosimo
DIRECTOR OF PHOTOGRAPHY
Cosimo
AGENCY
B. Schenkel, Campbell-Ewald, New
York, NY
PRODUCTION COMPANY
Morty Dubin, Iris Films

1453
ART DIRECTOR
Michael Fazende
WRITER
John Stingley
CLIENT
O.M. Scott
EDITOR
Steve Shepherd, Wilson-Griak
DIRECTOR
Joe Pytka
AGENCY
Fallon McElligott, Minneapolis, MN
PRODUCER
Judy Brink
PRODUCTION COMPANY
Pytka
V.O.
Michael Stull

52

OUVENIRS
-second
e souvenirs all you save when you take a trip?
so, Eastern Airlines has an announcement for you.
ght now what's really memorable are Eastern's prices.
w York is only $99
iami is only $79
d almost a hundred other cities are just as affordable
call Eastern and save something besides souvenirs.

1453

PARK BENCH
30-second
ANNCR: In Marysville, Ohio about all there is to do is watch the grass
grow.
GUY #1: Looks good this year.
GUY #3: Yep.
ANNCR: Coincidentally, Marysville is the home of Scotts lawn products.
GUY #1: Must be the trionized carrier molecular bonding process . . .
ANNCR: Which explains Scott's superior technology.
GUY #3: Could be the short chain polymer nitrogen . . . Gordon?
GORDON: Well, we've had a lot of rain.
ANNCR: When all there is to do is watch the grass grow . . . you really get
to know grass.

1454

ART DIRECTOR
Ken Amaral
WRITER
Jim Doherty
CLIENT
John Deere
DIRECTOR
Mike Cuesta
AGENCY
Bob Carney, N W Ayer, Inc.,
Chicago, IL
PRODUCTION COMPANY
Erwin Cramer, Griner Cuesta

1455

ART DIRECTOR
Dennis H. Plansker
WRITER
Sean Kevin Fitzpatrick
CLIENT
Chevrolet Motor Division
EDITOR
Roger Harrison
DIRECTOR
Peter Smillie
BROADCAST DIRECTOR
Dennis H. Plansker
AGENCY
Campbell-Ewald Company, Warren,
MI
PRODUCER
Kenneth J. Domanski
PRODUCTION COMPANY
Berkofsky, Smillie & Barrett
CREATIVE DIRECTOR
Sean Kevin Fitzpatrick
MUSIC
Denise Abood Sidlow; Joey Levine,
Crushing Enterprises

1454

NEIGHBORS
30-second
NEIGHBOR: Hey, Ol' Buddy! My mower broke down. Mind if I borrow yours?
OWNER: Sure . . . Ol' Buddy.
AVO: Why is it that . . .
. . . The grass is always greener wherever there's a John Deere Lawn mower?
NEIGHBOR #2: You weren't around . . . So I helped myself.
AVO: Because you can always depend on a John Deere Lawn Mower to keep running when others don't.
It's got adjustable speed drive, a blade brake clutch and a 2 or 4 cycle engine.
NEIGHBOR #3: Hi
OWNER (ANTICIPATES NEIGHBOR #3): Don't tell me . . . your mower's not working.
NEIGHBOR #3: Nah! I don't even own one.
AVO: Nothing runs like a Deere.

1455

EUROFORCE-TRIATHLON
30-second
SFX: HEARTBEAT
SINGER: Listen to the heartbeat . . .
. . . of America.
Listen to the heartbeat . . .
. . . of America.
ANNCR: When you've got what it takes . . .
Put yourself in Today's Chevrolet Celebrity Eurosport . . .
And listen to your heartbeat
SINGERS: The heartbeat of America (Chevrolet)
That's today's Chevrolet.

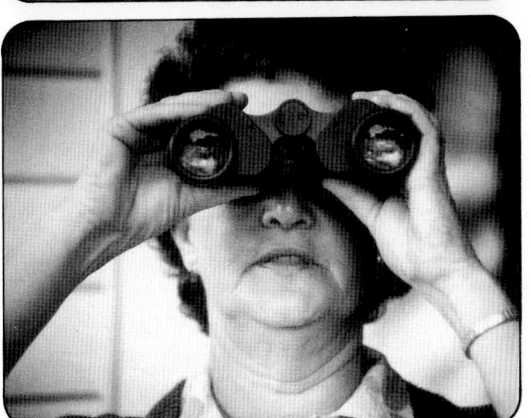

1456

ART DIRECTOR
Hector Robledo
WRITER
Ted Littleford
CLIENT
Data General
DIRECTOR
Lee Lacy
AGENCY
Herb Miller, FCB Leber Katz, New York, NY
PRODUCTION COMPANY
Dick Ashe, N. Lee Lacy & Assoc.

1457

ART DIRECTOR
Michael Fazende
WRITER
John Stingley
CLIENT
O.M. Scott
EDITOR
Steve Shepherd, Wilson-Griak
DIRECTOR
Joe Pytka
AGENCY
Fallon McElligott, Minneapolis, MN
PRODUCER
Judy Brink
PRODUCTION COMPANY
Pytka
V.O.
Michael Stull

1456

SOMEDAY WE'LL BE TOGETHER
30-second
VOCAL: Mmmmm someday we'll be together . . .
yes we will, yes we will . . .
someday . . .
we'll be together.
ANNCR: Why wait for someday to bring all of your different computers together? At Data General, we're leaders in making computers work together today. With the best integrated computer solutions . . .
VOCAL: Someday . . .
ANNCR: Talk to Data General today.
Because you can't wait for someday.

1457

BINOCULARS
30-second
ANNCR: An evening in Marysville, Ohio is different.
MAN: Mother it appears we have prunella vulgaris.
ANNCR: Because Marysville is the home of Scott's lawn products.
WOMAN: We've never had prunella vulgaris.
MAN: Well, we do now.
ANNCR: It's living here that inspired our toll-free number for lawn advice.
WOMAN: That's malva neglecta.
ANNCR: Because our idea of fun . . .
MAN: Oh.
ANNCR: May not be yours.
ANNCR: When all there is to do is watch the grass grow, you really get to know grass.

1458

ART DIRECTOR
Candy Greathouse, Roberta Williams
WRITER
John Lyons
CLIENT
Procter & Gamble — Bounce
EDITOR
Howard Weisbrot
DIRECTOR
Ed Bianchi
DIRECTOR OF PHOTOGRAPHY
Andrzej Bartkowiak
AGENCY
Karen Spector, DMB&B, New York, NY
PRODUCTION COMPANY
Ann Friedman, Bianchi Films
MUSIC
Michael Zager

1459

ART DIRECTOR
Leif Nielsen
WRITER
Steve Conover
CLIENT
Chieftain Products Inc.
DIRECTOR
Paul Cade
AGENCY
Louise Blouin, DDB Needham Worldwide, Toronto, Canada
PRODUCTION COMPANY
Chris Money, Boardwalk Pictures Limited
MUSIC
John Capon
CAMERAMAN
Bill Gimmi

1458

NO CLING/FP
30-second
SFX: MUSIC THROUGHOUT
SONG: No cling nightgowns
Jump.
No cling skirts.
Jump
No cling to most anything
Jump. Jump. Jump. Jump.
Bounce for no cling
things you can't wait to jump into
Jump. Feel the touch.
Jump in
You are the one
so smooth and free around me.
Jump. Jump. Jump. Jump.
Bounce. For no cling things
you can't wait to jump into
Jump.

1459

PABLO
30-second
MUSIC: GUITAR AND FLUTE DUET THROUGHOUT
BOY: (VO) Mama, come see.
MOTHER: (VO) Oh, it's beautiful.
But Pablo, why two noses?
ANNCR: (VO) Etch-A-Sketch.
Lots of fun for budding young Picassos.

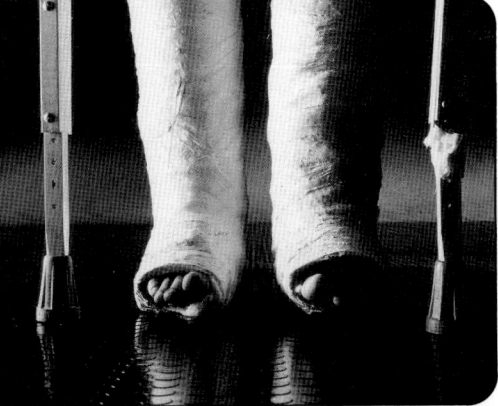

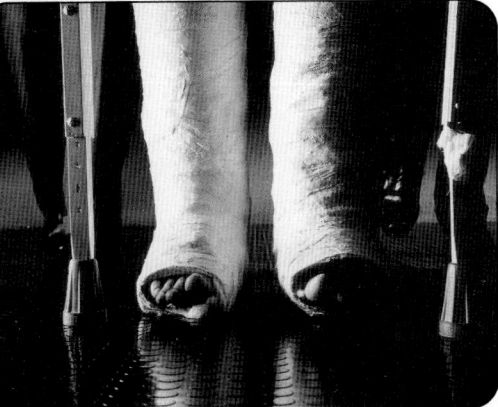

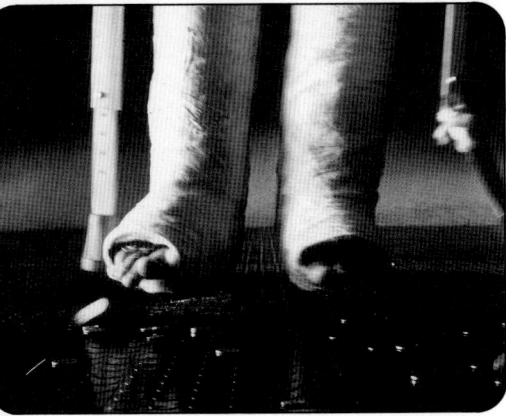

1460

ART DIRECTOR
Tom Lichtenheld
WRITER
Rod Kilpatrick
CLIENT
American Medcenters
EDITOR
Steve Shepherd, Wilson-Griak
DIRECTOR
Mark Story
AGENCY
Fallon McElligott, Minneapolis, MN
PRODUCER
Char Loving
PRODUCTION COMPANY
Story Piccolo Guliner
MUSIC
Tom Lescher, City-Post
V.O.
Fred Gwynne

1461

ART DIRECTOR
Mike Moser, David Bigman, Lee Clow
WRITER
David O'Hare, David Woodside
CLIENT
California Cooler
EDITOR
Steve Wystrach
DIRECTOR
Mark Coppos
DIRECTOR OF PHOTOGRAPHY
Peter Brown
AGENCY
Francesca Cohn, Chiat/Day, San Francisco, CA
PRODUCTION COMPANY
Mike Appell, Coppos Films

460

ASTS
)-second
NNCR VO: When you join MedCenters health plan, MedCenters pays
·actically all your health-care costs from the very first penny.
hile with regular health insurrance, you'll probably have to pay the first
200.
very year.
edCenters. Where everything's taken care of.

1461

MEET THE PEOPLE
30-second
STOCKTON, CALIFORNIA
ANNCR (VO): Meet the people who made the original wine coolers.
MUSIC UP: "Surfin' Bird" THROUGHOUT
California white wine and real fruit.
Blended in a tub.
At a party.
On the beach.
And now that original blend
comes in a bottle.
MUSIC: (GURGLING PART OF SONG)
ANNCR: California Cooler.
The real stuff.

1462

ART DIRECTOR
Jo Ann Meyer
WRITER
Doug Pippin
CLIENT
Popsicle
EDITOR
Ed Friedman, DJM
DIRECTOR
Bob Bierman
AGENCY
Steve Friedman, DFS Dorland, New York, NY
PRODUCTION COMPANY
Bruce Mellon, Elite Films
EXEC. CREATIVE DIR.
Eric Weber
CREATIVE DIRECTOR
Stephen Dolleck

1463

ART DIRECTOR
Dennis H. Plansker
WRITER
Sean Kevin Fitzpatrick
CLIENT
Chevrolet Motor Division
EDITOR
Bill Riss
DIRECTOR
Bruce Dowad
BROADCAST DIRECTOR
Dennis H. Plansker
AGENCY
Campbell-Ewald Company, Warren, MI
PRODUCER
Kenneth J. Domanski
PRODUCTION COMPANY
Jennie & Co.
CREATIVE DIRECTOR
Sean Kevin Fitzpatrick
MUSIC
Denise Abood Sidlow; Joey Levine, Crushing Enterprises

1462

REALLY RICH
30-second
ANNCR: Do you know how rich you'd have to be to be as rich as new Fruitsicle bars?
GIRL 1: Daddy bought Connecticut today.
GIRL 2: Really.
ANNCR: You'd have to be richer than that.
BOY 1: Shall we take the red or the blue yacht this evening?
ANNCR: Much richer than that. Because new Fruitsicle Smooth-n-Fruity bars take real fruit juice and whip it ever so lightly for a most uncommonly smooth and creamy texture. So how rich do you have to be to be as rich as new Fruitsicle bars?
BOY 2: We struck oil. Again.
ANNCR: Richer than that.

1463

HEARTBEAT OF AMERICA/WOMEN'S
30-second
(MUSIC STING)
FEMALE SINGER: Listen to the heartbeat
(ooh, ooh)
of America
Listen to the heartbeat
(heartbeat)
of America
Oh Yeah
(ooh, ooh)
It's the rhythm of the road
It's the pulse on the street
(pulse on the street)
A city, town,
a magic sound
(ooh, ooh)
FEMALE SINGER: Feel the heartbeat of America
CHORUS: Chevrolet
That's today's Chevrolet
(HEARTBEAT EFX UNDER AND OUT)

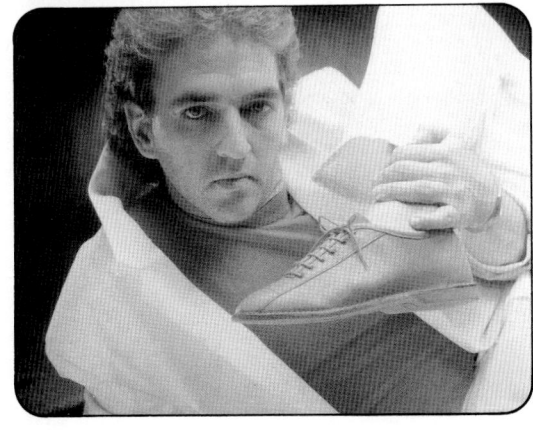

1464
ART DIRECTOR
John Guliner
WRITER
Molly Clevenger
CLIENT
Procter & Gamble — Always
EDITOR
Ed Friedman
DIRECTOR
Richard Chambers
DIRECTOR OF PHOTOGRAPHY
Ralph Young
AGENCY
Alan Clark, DMB&B, New York, NY
PRODUCTION COMPANY
Ken Peat, Chambers & Associates
MUSIC
John Silberman

1465
ART DIRECTOR
Claudia Stroud
WRITER
Kathleen O'Brien
CLIENT
Capezio Shoes for Men
EDITOR
Bill Riss
DIRECTOR
Ron Castorri
DIRECTOR OF PHOTOGRAPHY
Tom Houghton
AGENCY
Jere Chamberlin, DMB&B,
Bloomfield Hills, MI
PRODUCER
Bob Long
V. P. PLANNING
John Greening

1464
UOTES CD III/FP
)-second
FX: MUSIC THROUGHOUT
OMAN: It's different all right. I mean different.
ND WOMAN: Did you see it? The darn thing has wings.
OMAN: Wings?
ND WOMAN: Wings.
VO: New Always Plus. The maxi with panty protectors.
ONG: Wait til you see.
RD WOMAN: Wrap around. What an idea.
TH WOMAN: Terrific idea.
TH WOMAN: It's so logical
ND WOMAN: You gotta see it.
VO: New Always Plus. Better protection than any other maxi.
ONG: Wait til you see
TH WOMAN: It's so simple.
VO: See ordinary maxis can leave the sides of your panties unprotected.
ut new Always Plus has panty protectors.
TH WOMAN: What an idea.
VO: Amazing flaps that wrap around and protect better than any other
naxi.
TH WOMAN: This is a big idea.
VO: And the special dri-weave covering means it's cleaner and drier too.
ONG: See what we've done.
TH WOMAN: A maxi with sides.
TH WOMAN: Did you see it? You didn't see it? Oh you gotta see it.

1465
CONTORTIONIST
24-second
ANNCR (VO): When you wear Capezios for men, it's almost a shame your
feet are so far away. Because Capezio's are great shoes. The colors are
unbelievable.
And the styles are, well, *incredible.*
They *all* look as good comin', as they do goin'.
So, hey, why settle for a shoe that just looks good from a distance? When
you can wear Capezios. Take a closer look at Capezio for men by calling
this toll-free number for a store near you.

1466

ART DIRECTOR
Stan Jones
WRITER
Mark Monteiro
CLIENT
Audi of America
EDITOR
Charlie Chubak
DIRECTOR
Neil Tardio
AGENCY
Beth Hagen, DDB Needham
Worldwide Inc., Los Angeles, CA
PRODUCTION COMPANY
Stacey Kahn, Neil Tardio
Productions
CREATIVE DIRECTOR
Bob Kuperman

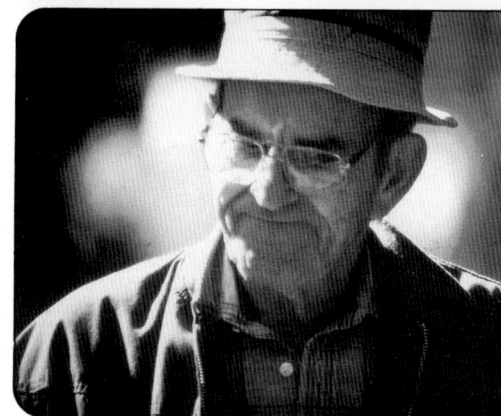

1467

ART DIRECTOR
Michael Fazende
WRITER
John Stingley
CLIENT
O.M. Scott
EDITOR
Steve Shepherd, Wilson-Griak
DIRECTOR
Joe Pytka
AGENCY
Fallon McElligott, Minneapolis, MN
PRODUCER
Judy Brink
PRODUCTION COMPANY
Pytka
V.O.
Michael Stull

1466

STOLEN PARTS
30-second
ANNCR VO: You're looking at the Audi 5000. A lot of our competitors have
also been looking at it.
ANNCR VO: The Japanese were interested in its flush-mounted windows.
ANNCR VO: While certain American firms became very attached to its
body.
ANNCR VO: And certain German companies,
ANNCR VO: . . . are getting excited about all wheel drive.
ANNCR VO: Now you can buy one of their cars . . .
ANNCR VO: . . . but why get just a piece of an Audi . . . when you can
have the whole thing.
ANNCR VO: You're ready for an Audi.

1467

GUARANTEE/ALT VERSION 2
30-second
ANNCR: In Marysville, Ohio, it doesn't take much to draw a crowd.
GUY 1: It just up and died.
ANNCR: That's because Marysville is the home of Scotts lawn products.
GUY 2: Coulda' used some ergosterol bio-synthesis inhibitors.
ANNCR: So people understood how different Scotts products are.
GUY 3: And trionized carrier bonded nitrogen.
ANNCR: So different . . . they're guaranteed. When all there is to do is
watch the grass grow . . .
GUY 1: And the yard was only two years old.
ANNCR: . . . you really get to know grass.

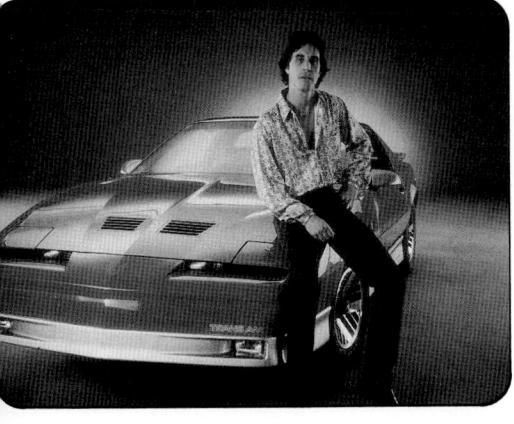

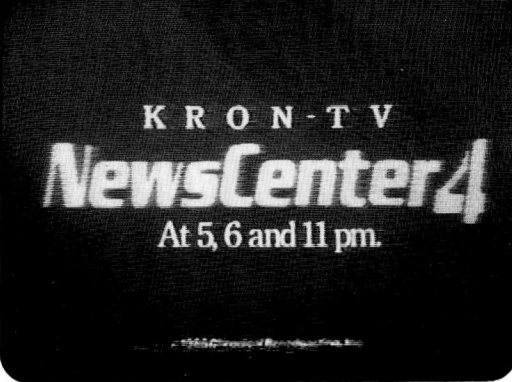

1468
ART DIRECTOR
Amy Mizner
WRITER
Don Deutsch
CLIENT
The Pontiac Dealer Association of
NY/NJ/CT
EDITOR
Jerry Fried
DIRECTOR
John O'Driscoll
DIRECTOR OF PHOTOGRAPHY
John Crawford
AGENCY
Randy Cohen, David Deutsch Assoc.,
New York, NY
PRODUCER
Pete Christy

1469
ART DIRECTOR
Pat Burnham
WRITER
Bill Miller
CLIENT
KRON-TV (Chronicle Broadcasting)
EDITOR
Tony Fischer, James Productions
DIRECTOR
Mark Story
AGENCY
Fallon McElligott, Minneapolis, MN
PRODUCER
Judy Brink
PRODUCTION COMPANY
Story Piccolo Guliner
V.O.
Eddie Barth

468

OU POTENZA
0-second
ye, My name is Lou Potenza and I drive a Trans Am. Now I would never
o a commercial for something I didn't believe in. I mean like if they
sked me I would also do one for that gum that squirts that stuff in your
nouth because I like that also. Now this Trans Am. Heh, You listen to me
: is the machine and I think it's the best. Lou Potenza speaks the truth.
ey, you call me. I'll tell you right to your face.

1469

DAY LATE
30-second
ANNCR VO: Some time ago, we, here at Newscenter 4, were first to report a
story on toxic pollution in the Kesterson reservoir.
Cable News Network rushed over and picked up the story from us.
The next day, KCRA in Sacramento rushed over and picked up the story
from them.
Later, KGO rushed over and picked up the story from KCRA.
And went on their air . . .
SFX: ("CHANNEL 7 NEWS IS LEARNING TONIGHT . . .")
. . . with our story. You can get our story straight from us. Or once they
get our story straight, you can get it from them.
Newscenter 4. At 5, 6 and 11.

1470

ART DIRECTOR
Richard Mahan
WRITER
Phil Guthrie
CLIENT
Miller Brewing Company — Meister Brau
AGENCY
Backer & Spielvogel, New York, NY
PRODUCER
Michael Berkman

1471

ART DIRECTOR
John Colquhoun, Steve Miller
WRITER
Clifford L. Freeman, Arthur Bijur
CLIENT
North American Philips Lighting Company
DIRECTOR
Mark Story, Story Piccolo Guliner
AGENCY
DFS Dorland, New York, NY
PRODUCER
Steven Friedman

1470

SHOW BIZ
30-second
AGENT: Ok, Kiddo, I'm going to give it to you straight.
GIRL: Hi, Max. (GIGGLE)
AGENT: (TO GIRL) Love you babe.
(TO KIDDO) The studios aren't calling any more.
Your bank accounts . . . they've dried up!
The houses, the cars, the boats . . .
Listen to me sweetheart . . . you can kiss them all goodbye.
Frankly, there's only one luxury you can still afford . . .
. . . and you're looking at it. Meister Brau.
ANNCR VO: You don't have to be rich to enjoy a beer as rich and smooth as Meister Brau. It only tastes expensive.
KIDDO: Whoa, Max . . . you really had me worried for a minute pal.
AGENT: (GROAN)

1471

ELEVATOR
30-second
MAN: Hello
HE SHRUGS OFF HER REJECTION. RAISES NEWSPAPER UP IN FRONT OF HIS FACE.
1ST GUY: I guess you know I think you're extremely attractive.
MAN WHO GOT ON ELEVATOR: Gee, Thank you very much.
SFX: (LIGHT CLICKS ON)
ANNCR: It's time you changed your light bulb.
Philips Longer Life square bulbs.
lasts 33% longer than ordinary bulbs.

1472
ART DIRECTOR
Tony DeGregorio
WRITER
Lee Garfinkel
CLIENT
Citizen Watch Company of America
EDITOR
David Dee
DIRECTOR
Steve Horn, Steve Horn, Inc.
AGENCY
LHS&B, New York
PRODUCER
Bob Nelson

1473
ART DIRECTOR
Ron Taylor
WRITER
Pat O'Neil
CLIENT
Pillsbury
EDITOR
Bobby Smalheiser, First Editions
DIRECTOR
Graham Baker
AGENCY
BBDO, New York, NY
PRODUCER
Alice Chevalier
PRODUCTION COMPANY
Elite Films

1472

QUARTER TO NINE
30-second
LYRICS: The stars are gonna' twinkle and shine, how they'll shine
This evening about a quarter to nine
I know I won't be late, cause at half past eight
I'm gonna' hurry there . . . I'll be waiting you on
needles and pins . . . About a quarter to nine.
ANNCR: They say time is what you make it. At Citizen we prefer making it
beautiful . . . Citizen.
SUPER: CITIZEN. NO OTHER WATCH EXPRESSES TIME AS BEAUTIFULLY.

1473

COCKNEY
30-second
ENGLISH BAKER: Me puffin' s stuffin's are date at eight.
But you Yanks have got
new Pillsbury fig and poster puffin' stuffin's.
Puffin' stuffin's from a fig and poster?
Ain't nothing like puffin' stuffin's.
Mmm, bunchy croppings
true merries
heave'n hoist in the cat 'n fiddle.
But taste?
Ey, that's a bit awright!
Stone the crows, strike the light!
AVO: New Pillsbury Toaster Muffins and Toaster Strudel.
DOUGH BOY: You never toasted anything like it!
Hee, Hee!

1474

ART DIRECTOR
Amy Mizner
WRITER
Don Deutsch
CLIENT
The Pontiac Dealer Association of
NY/NJ/CT
EDITOR
Jerry Fried
DIRECTOR
John O'Driscoll
DIRECTOR OF PHOTOGRAPHY
John Crawford
AGENCY
Randy Cohen, David Deutsch Assoc.,
New York, NY
PRODUCER
Pete Christy

1475

ART DIRECTOR
George Halvorson
WRITER
Terry Bremer
CLIENT
The Toro Company
EDITOR
Dale Cooper
DIRECTOR
Denny Harris
DIRECTOR OF PHOTOGRAPHY
Bobby Burns
AGENCY
George Halvorson, Terry Bremer,
Campbell-Mithun, Minneapolis, MN
PRODUCER
Jeff Scruton
CREATIVE DIRECTOR
Ed Des Lauriers

1474

RHONDA WEISSMAN
30-second
I'm Rhonda Weissman from Great Neck and I'm not a princess. I hate
when people call me that. Are you ready? Like this Fiero, the cutest. I went
on my own without my parents and I paid for it— Four thousand dollars.
OK, OK my father did kick in six thousand but I'm not a princess. If I
were a princess I would not have paid for anything.
Does anyone have any gum?

1475

SON OF FATHER AND SON
30-second
KID #1: Come on, let's go.
KID #2: Can't, gotta cut the grass.
KID #1: Hey . . . maybe the mower won't start.
KID #2: It'll start.
Come 'ere, I'll show ya.
KID #1: Oh nooo.
KID #2: Oh yeah.
ANNCR: Toro introduces the two year starting guarantee. Your Toro with
the new GTS engine will start on the first or second pull for two years, or
Toro will fix it free.
DAD: Hey Billy come 'ere.
KID #2: Yeah Dad.
KID #1: Oh no.
KID #2: Oh yeah.
(SFX: STARTS ENGINE) . . . (DEALER TAG)

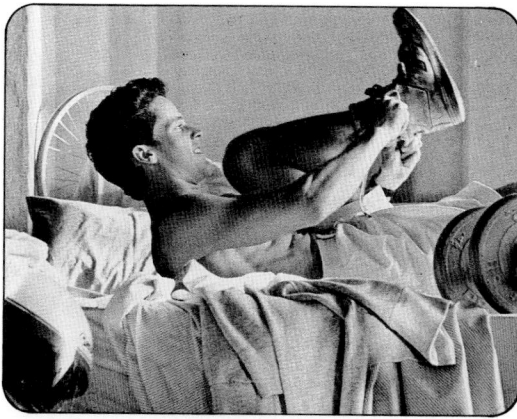
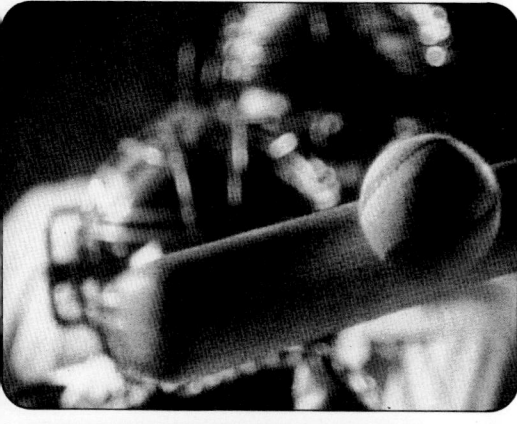
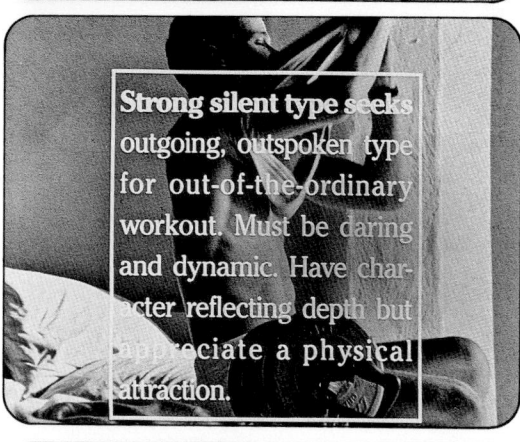
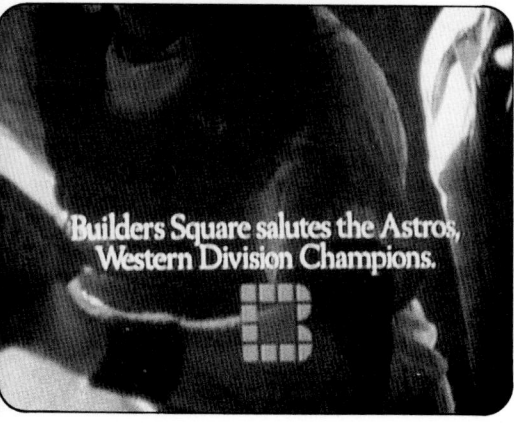

1476
ART DIRECTOR
Roger Christian
WRITER
Ann Ecklund-Phillips
CLIENT
Builders Square
EDITOR
Match Frame
DIRECTOR
Steve Johnson
AGENCY
Roger Christian & Co., Inc., San
Antonio, TX
PRODUCER
Glynda Smith
PRODUCTION COMPANY
Steve Johnson Film Production Inc.
CINEMATOGRAPHER
Karl Gerber

1477
ART DIRECTOR
Maryanne Fisher
WRITER
Chris Laubach
CLIENT
Dr. Pepper Company — Diet
EDITOR
Clay Warnick
DIRECTOR
Patrick Russell
DIRECTOR OF PHOTOGRAPHY
Andy Dittenfass
AGENCY
Young & Rubicam, New York, NY
PRODUCER
Roseanne Horn
PRODUCTION COMPANY
Rick Levine Production
TYPE DIRECTOR
Dick Mullen

1476
ASTROS
30-second
T - minus 20 seconds, to mark, stand by sequence start
T minus 15, 14 . . . 10, 9, we have a go for main engine start, and we
have main engine start, four, three, two, one, ignition, and lift off.
Hot dog! Look at that Jack. Roll program initiated Houston now
controlling.
Voice Over is from actual NASA soundtrack from several different lift-offs.

1477
STRONG SILENT TYPE
30-second
(MUSIC UNDER)
(MUSIC)
MAN (VO): Strong silent type seeks outgoing, outspoken type for out-of-
the-ordinary work-out.
Must be daring and dynamic.
Have character reflecting depth but appreciate a physical attraction.
FEMALE SINGER: Meet the daring, dynamic new taste of
Diet Dr Pepper.
Throw your diet a curve.
Diet Dr Pepper.

1478

ART DIRECTOR
Gerry Pfiffner
WRITER
Gerry Pfiffner
CLIENT
Hyundai Motor Company
AGENCY
Backer & Spielvogel, New York, NY

1479

ART DIRECTOR
Ron Wolin, Eric Gardner
DESIGNER
Ron Wolin, Eric Gardner
WRITER
Dudley Fitzpatrick
CLIENT
Pioneer Electronics (USA) Inc.
EDITOR
Jacques Dury
DIRECTOR
Jean Marie Perier
DIRECTOR OF PHOTOGRAPHY
Jean Marie Perier
AGENCY
Ed Chapman, DFS Dorland
Worldwide, Torrance, CA
PRODUCTION COMPANY
Blair Hayes, Bill Hudson &
Associates
ASSOC. CREATIVE DIRECTOR
Larry Rosenberg
CREATIVE DIRECTOR
John Mead

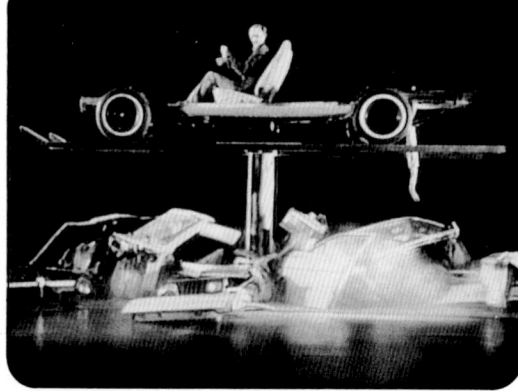

1478

USED CAR/PRICE
30-second
SFX: TICKING.
AVO: Another thirty seconds of common sense.
DUNNE: Should you buy another used car . . . or a new Hyundai Excel.
With used, you never really know how much is left unused.
But right now, for the average price of a used car,
you can get a brand new Hyundai Excel.
Thoroughly equipped. Never used.
Never abused.
And starting at only $4,995.
I suggest you pull yourself together and get down to your Hyundai dealer.
Hurry.
AVO: Local dealer tag copy.

1479

SIX OF A KIND
30-second
ANNCR: One disc . . . interesting. Six discs . . . fantastic.
SONG: It's the spirit in the air, the sound that you hear. It's the spirit that exists in a true Pioneer.
ANNCR: Introducing the only CD Player that plays six discs. It's a Pioneer. (MUSICAL SFX) And with the push of a button (MUSICAL SFX) it'll play your musical fantasies forever, and ever.
MUSIC: CATCH THE SPIRIT OF A TRUE PIONEER.

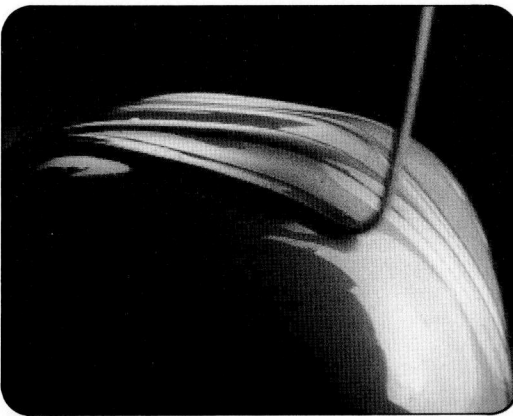

1480

ART DIRECTOR
Teri Walker
WRITER
Susan Dilallo
CLIENT
M.L.Polaner
EDITOR
David Dee
DIRECTOR
Henry Holtzman
DIRECTOR OF PHOTOGRAPHY
Ric Waite
AGENCY
Alice Mintzer, Lowe-Marschalk
PRODUCTION COMPANY
Barbara Gold, Holtzman/Stavros,
New York, NY

1481

ART DIRECTOR
Gene Mandarino
WRITER
Cheryl Berman
CLIENT
Ethel M Chocolates
EDITOR
John Komanich
DIRECTOR
Michael Schrom
AGENCY
Sam Patrino, Leo Burnett, Chicago,
IL
PRODUCTION COMPANY
Dick Hall, Griner Cuesta
CREATIVE DIRECTOR
Cheryl Berman

480

DON'T DARE
30-second
(VIOLIN MUSIC/RESTAURANT AMBIENCE)
LADY DOWAGER: Please pass the All Fruit.
YOUNG MAN: Pass the Polaner All Fruit.
YOUNG WOMAN (VO): Pass the Polaner All Fruit.
TEXAN: Would ya please pass the jelly?
(SFX: CRASH!)
LADY DOWAGER: Ah-h-h.
YOUNG MAN: Ach!!
LITTLE GIRL: Ha, ha!
ANNCR (VO): Polaner All Fruit is real fruit . . . sweetened only with fruit
juice, and no added sugar.
ANNCR (VO): You'll call it delicious . . .
TEXAN: Umm . . . Mmmm!
ANNCR (VO): You'll call it remarkable . . .
But please don't dare call it jelly!
ANNCR (VO): Polaner All Fruit. The spreadable fruit.

1481

LOVE
30-second
ANNCR: Ethel M would like to show you all the things we do for love.
(MUSIC UNDER)
ANNCR: Ethel M.
For the love of chocolate.

1482

ART DIRECTOR
Tony LaMonte
WRITER
Charlie Miesmer, Michael Shevack
CLIENT
Apple Computer, Inc.
EDITOR
David Dee, Eventime
DIRECTOR
Steve Horn
AGENCY
BBDO, New York, NY
PRODUCER
Barbara Mullins, Katy O'Brien, Andy Chinich
PRODUCTION COMPANY
Steve Horn Productions

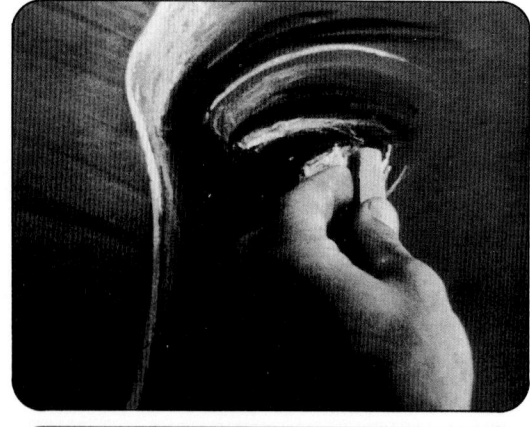

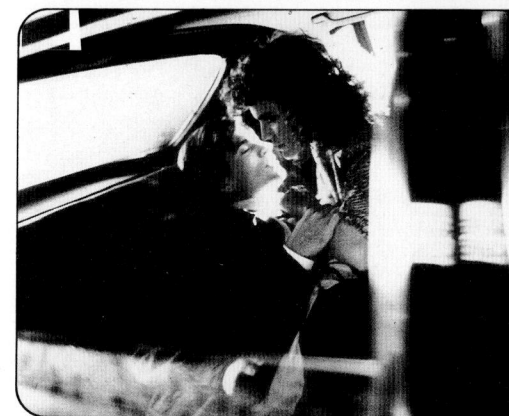

1483

ART DIRECTOR
Vince Taschetti
WRITER
Glenn Miller
CLIENT
Jacqueline Cochran
EDITOR
Bob DeRise, A Cut Above
DIRECTOR
Leslie Dektor
AGENCY
BBDO, New York, NY
PRODUCER
Tony Frere
PRODUCTION COMPANY
Petermann-Dektor

1482

LEFT BRAIN, RIGHT BRAIN
30-second
(SFX)
Imagine a brain who's left side is as brilliant as its right.
A brain as artistic as it is logical. That can calculate and create. Such a brain exists in the remarkable new Apple II GS.
Brilliant graphics.
Brilliant color.
Brilliant sound.
(SFX)
To help you use both sides of the most personal computer of all.
Your mind.

1483

WEAR IT WELL INTO THE NIGHT
30-second
(SOUND EFFECTS-HEARTBEAT)
(SOUND EFFECTS-HEARTBEAT)
(SOUND EFFECTS-HEARTBEAT)
(SOUND EFFECTS-HEARTBEAT)
(SOUND EFFECTS-HEARTBEAT)
(SOUND EFFECTS-HEARTBEAT)
(SOUND EFFECTS-HEARTBEAT)
(SOUND EFFECTS-HEARTBEAT)
(SOUND EFFECTS-HEARTBEAT)
(SOUND EFFECTS-HEARTBEAT)
(SOUND EFFECTS-HEARTBEAT)
AVO: Pierre Cardin Man's Musk.
Wear It Well Into The Night.

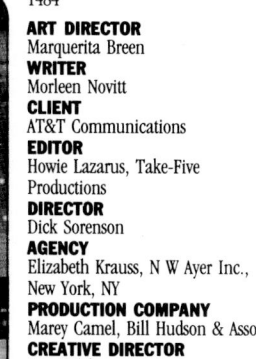

1484

ART DIRECTOR
Marquerita Breen
WRITER
Morleen Novitt
CLIENT
AT&T Communications
EDITOR
Howie Lazarus, Take-Five
Productions
DIRECTOR
Dick Sorenson
AGENCY
Elizabeth Krauss, N W Ayer Inc.,
New York, NY
PRODUCTION COMPANY
Marey Camel, Bill Hudson & Assoc.
CREATIVE DIRECTOR
Ron Salzberg

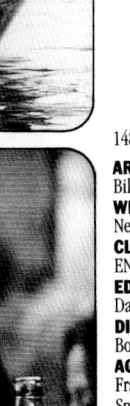

1485

ART DIRECTOR
Bill Puckett
WRITER
Neil Calet
CLIENT
ENIT
EDITOR
David Seeger, Today Video
DIRECTOR
Bob Giraldi
AGENCY
Frank DiSalvo, Calet Hirsch &
Spector, New York, NY
MNG. SUPERVISOR
Susan Goldin
PRODUCER
Patricia Greaney

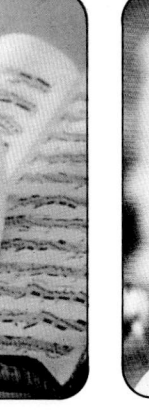

484

'S MOZART
0-second
INGERS: Reach out
IRL: Maestro, What's missing?
MAESTRO: Just let the joy in you come out.
MAESTRO OFF CAMERA: It's Mozart.
MAESTRO: Yes
ist be yourself.
MAESTRO VO: Be yourself.
OBERTSON VO: When you can hear the joy. That's AT&T
INGERS: Reach out and touch someone.

1485

FEAST VERSION 2
30-second
Some people come to Italy for our magnificent art. And our pasta.
Some come for our incomparable music.
And our gelato.
While others wish only to drink in our matchless scenery . . . and our
wine.
No other country gives you so much to see, to hear, to feel . . . and to
eat.
Italy. There's more to it.

1486

ART DIRECTOR
Marty Weiss
WRITER
Ken Sandbank
CLIENT
Braun, Inc.
EDITOR
Take Five
DIRECTOR
Michael Schrom
AGENCY
Lowe Marschalk, Inc., New York, NY
PRODUCER
Peggy Moore
PRODUCTION COMPANY
Griner Questa
MUSIC
Elias Associates

1487

ART DIRECTOR
Mike Moser, Lee Clow
WRITER
David O'Hare, David Woodside
CLIENT
California Cooler
EDITOR
Steve Wystrach
DIRECTOR
Mark Coppos
DIRECTOR OF PHOTOGRAPHY
Peter Brown
AGENCY
Francesca Cohn, Chiat/Day, San Francisco, CA
PRODUCTION COMPANY
Mike Appell, Coppos Films

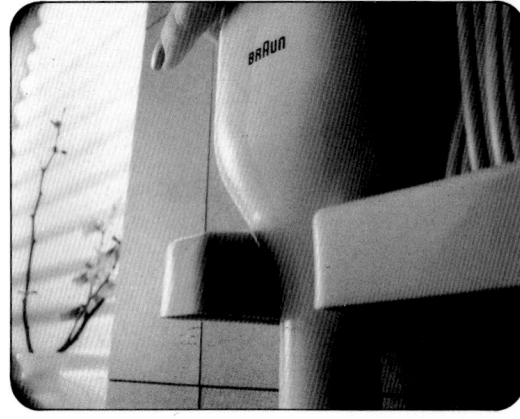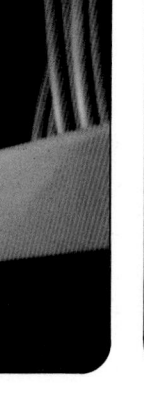 

1486

47 SECONDS
30-second
ANNCR VO: This is the Braun handblender.
With it you can puree tomatoes
for sauce in minutes.
Make salad dressing in seconds.
You can prepare fresh vegetable
soup in almost no time.
And even make
a strawberry parfait in under a
minute.
Who knows? With the Braun handblender
you just may acquire a taste for
fast food.
Braun. Designed to perform better.

1487

GREEN ONIONS
30-second
MUSIC UP: GREEN ONIONS THROUGHOUT
ANNCR (VO): Up and down the coast of California, the locals made a drink they called "cooler." Using white wine and real fruit, they made it on beaches like Rincon, San Onofre, The Ranch.
And now that original blend comes in a
bottle, and you'll find it in
places like
Shreveport, Newark,
Des Moines, Boise . . . (FADE)

1488

ART DIRECTOR
Frank Rizzo
WRITER
Doug Rucker
CLIENT
Hagger Apparel Co.
DIRECTOR
Linton Suttner
AGENCY
Tracy-Locke, Dallas, TX
PRODUCTION COMPANY
Film Fair

1489

ART DIRECTOR
Susan Kruskopf
WRITER
Pat Hanlon
CLIENT
Lamaur, Inc.
EDITOR
Wilson-Griak, Inc.
DIRECTOR
Jimmy Moore
AGENCY
Campbell-Mithun, Minneapolis, MN
PRODUCER
Ray Seide
CREATIVE DIRECTOR
Bob Fugate

1488

ALLERY/SURREAL
0-second
USIC: SYNTHESIZED JAZZ.
'O: Styles in pure wool
ave never been in better shape.
he fit for the fit.
allery by Haggar.

1489

FRENCHIE
30-second
(ANNCR VO): Perma Soft and The Foreign Exchange.
FRENCHIE: La France vous a apporté La mode . . .
Le parfum . . .
Le champagne.
C'est votre tour maintenant avec Perma Soft.
C'est le seul shampooing pour ma permanente.
Il adouci . . .
vous voyez, pas de frisure.
et mes booucles: Oh LA LA! Elles tiennent toutes seules.
Il doit y avoir quelque chose de magique dedans.
Malheuresment, ma copine ne m'en a envoyé qu'une seule bouteille.
(ANNCR VO): Perma Soft. Shampoo, Conditioner, Mousse, Hair Spray, and
now . . .
Extra Body Perm Soft for Fine, Limp Hair.
FRENCHIÉ: S'il vous plait . . .
envoyez-moi du Perma Soft!

1490

ART DIRECTOR
Rich Martel
WRITER
Al Merrin
CLIENT
Pepsi-Cola Company/Diet Pepsi
EDITOR
Steve Bodner, The Editors
DIRECTOR
Patrick Russell
AGENCY
BBDO, New York, NY
PRODUCER
Phyllis Landi
PRODUCTION COMPANY
Rick Levine Productions

1491

ART DIRECTOR
Bud Watts
WRITER
Greg Taubeneck
CLIENT
United Airlines
EDITOR
Bruce Frankel
DIRECTOR
Henry Holtzman
DIRECTOR OF PHOTOGRAPHY
Ric Waite
AGENCY
T. Artman, Leo Burnett
PRODUCTION COMPANY
Barbara Gold, Holtzman Stavros,
New York, NY

1490

BILLY CRYSTAL
30-second
MUSIC THROUGHOUT
BILLY CRYSTAL: You changed the way you look. Can you see that?
Up close it's exciting, and I'll tell you something, dahling, you look
mahvelous!
SINGERS: No other taste attracts
so much attention.
BILLY: Absolutely mahvelous!
SINGERS: Diet Pepsi,
the most refreshingest
invention.
BILLY: And not only do you look mahvelous, my little 12 oz. dahling,
but you taste mahvelous!
SINGERS: No other taste attracts so much attention.
BILLY: Do you come here often? I'm kidding you, I'm a kidder.
SINGERS: Diet Pepsi.
SUPER: THE ONE CALORIE CHOICE OF A NEW GENERATION.

1491

UMPIRE/NETWORK
30-second
UMPIRE: Sa-a-fe!
ANNCR VO: Not everyone got a vacation this summer.
SING: I need a vacation
PLAYER: Whaddya need? Some glasses? How many fingers can ya' see?
SING: Like nobody's business
UMP: Ye-r-r-r- . . .
SING: I need a vacation
ANNCR VO: This fall, you can still get great low fares to more places. On
the biggest bargain airline . . . United.
SING: I got a vacation
UMP: Have a nice shower, Pokorny.,
SING: And I'm not just flyin'
I'm flyin' the friendly skies
UMP: I'm 'outta there.

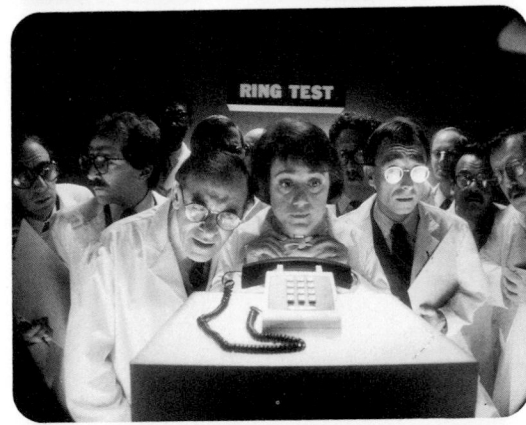

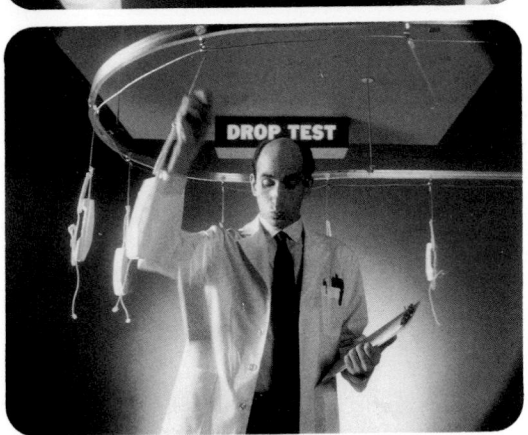

1492
ART DIRECTOR
Gene Mandarino
WRITER
Cheryl Berman, Gene Mandarino
CLIENT
McDonald's
EDITOR
Tony Izzo
DIRECTOR
Joe Pytka
AGENCY
Stuart Kramer, Leo Burnett,
Chicago, IL
PRODUCTION COMPANY
Brenda Haverstock, Pytka Prod.
CREATIVE DIRECTOR
Cheryl Berman

1493
ART DIRECTOR
Leslie Karkus
WRITER
Janet Kraus
CLIENT
AT&T Consumer Products
EDITOR
Michael Shankheim, MS Editorial
DIRECTOR
Mike Cuesta
AGENCY
Sam Cernichiari, N W Ayer Inc.,
New York, NY
PRODUCTION COMPANY
Maddi Carlton, Griner/Cuesta
CREATIVE DIRECTOR
Mickey Tender

1492

GOLDEN TIME
50-second
GENT (VO): I've seen her here many times before.
But I forgot all the right things to say.
LADY (VO): I'm too old to be smitten . . . besides it's not fittin' for me to
be lookin' his way.
BOY: Mr . . . You're up.
CREW GIRL: May I help you please?
GENT: Oh . . . Big Mac, fries and Coke, please.
CREW GIRL: Thank you . . . come again.
SING: It's a good time . . .
GENT (VO): Well, who knows?
SING: For the great taste
GENT (VO): O.K. . . . here goes . . .
GENT: Excuse me . . . is this seat taken?
LADY: No.

1493

TESTING
30-second
ANNCR (VO): The way cheap phones break down, the companies that
make them must do some pretty interesting tests.
MAN 1: I hear you.
WOMAN: Hear me?
MAN 1: I hear you. I heard something.
ANNCR (VO): . . . Real torture tests . . .
SFX: WHISTLE AND THUD.
ANNCR (VO): . . . and ring tests . . .
SFX: WIMPY RING
WOMAN 2: I heard it.
MAN 2: What did you hear?
WOMAN 2: I heard it.
MAN 3: I didn't hear anything . . .
MAN 2: Are you sure you heard it?
WOMAN 2: I heard it.
ANNCR (VO): Well for over 100 years, AT&T's made phones that passed
the real test. You.
SFX: SERIOUS PHONE DROP.
GUY: Nothing. I dropped the phone.
ANNCR: You get what you pay for. AT&T. The right choice.

1494

ART DIRECTOR
Howard Hellams
WRITER
Howard Hellams
CLIENT
Georgia Railroad Bank
EDITOR
Dean Pernaci, Crawford Post
Production
DIRECTOR
Bryan Elsom, Kingfisher
Productions
AGENCY
Howard Hellams, Cook Ruef,
Columbia, SC
PRODUCER
Nan Robinson

1495

ART DIRECTOR
George Halvorson
WRITER
Terry Bremer
CLIENT
The Toro Company
EDITOR
Peter Dalton, Optimus
DIRECTOR
Phil Murray
DIRECTOR OF PHOTOGRAPHY
John Bartley
AGENCY
George Halvorson, Terry Bremer,
Campbell-Mithun, Minneapolis, MN
PRODUCTION COMPANY
Mark Carter, Dalton Fenske
CREATIVE DIRECTOR
Terry Bremer

1494

YUPPIE I.R.A.
30-second
. . . so it turns out—are you ready for this—she's an accountant! And
she's telling me how I oughta' open up this Individual Retirement
Account at The Georgia Railroad Bank, and how I can get one for only a
hundred dollars a month. And I'm thinking, give me a break, right? Then
she tells me I could wind up with a quarter of a million dollars.
I mean, do you have any idea how many Rolex watches you could buy
with a quarter of a million dollars?

1495

#1 RATED 521
30-second
ANNCR VO: This Toro 521 was rated America's #1 standard size
snowthrower . . .
and nothing else comes close.
Well . . . almost nothing.
The Toro throws up to 15 inches . . .
of wet snow effortlessly.
. . . this does too.
The Toro cleans right down to the pavement.
. . . so does this.
The Toro throws snow a long way . . .
in either direction.
HMMM . . .
And finally, the Toro 521 fits nicely in the garage.
(SFX: PLOW)
Haven't you done without a Toro long enough?

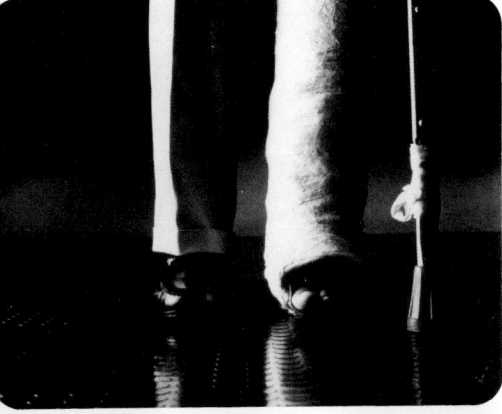

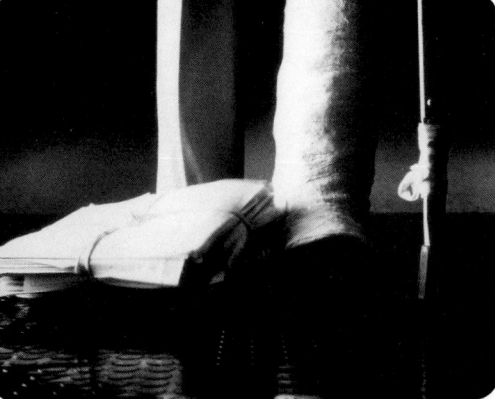

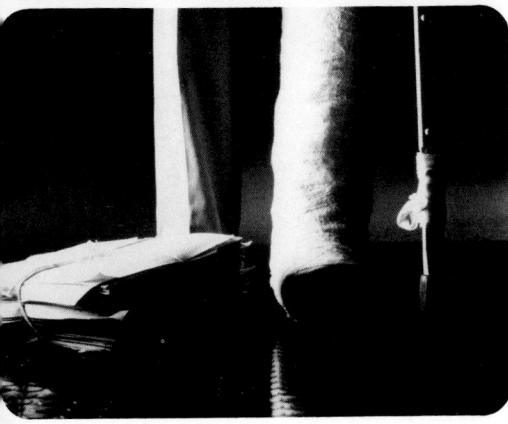

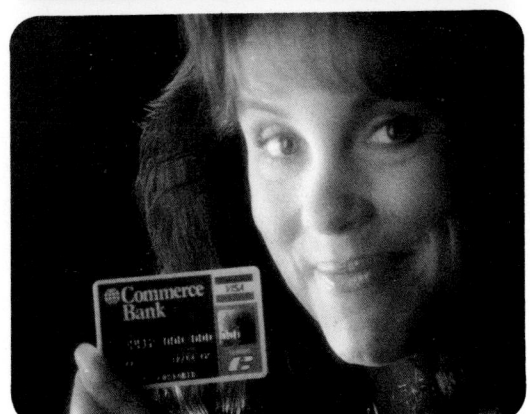

1496
ART DIRECTOR
Tom Lichtenheld
WRITER
Rod Kilpatrick
CLIENT
American Medcenters
EDITOR
Steve Shepherd, Wilson-Griak
DIRECTOR
Mark Story
AGENCY
Fallon McElligott, Minneapolis, MN
PRODUCER
Char Loving
PRODUCTION COMPANY
Story Piccolo Guliner
MUSIC
Tom Lescher, City-Post
V.O.
Fred Gwynne

1497
ART DIRECTOR
Mark Wolf
WRITER
David Marks
CLIENT
Commerce Bank
AGENCY
Valentine-Radford, Kansas City, MO
PRODUCER
David Schutten, Laura Fields
PRODUCTION COMPANY
Bob Jones Film Productions

496

FOOT
30-second
ANNCR VO: When you join MedCenters Health Plan, you won't get hit with
doctor bills, claim forms and other medical paperwork.
SFX: (WHISTLING, AS FALLING BOMB.)
ANNCR VO: While with regular health insurance . . .
. . . you will.
MedCenters. Where everything's taken care of.

1497

LOW
30-second
MUSIC: BLUESY ''DETECTIVE'' MUSIC THROUGHOUT.
WOMAN: I always knew you were low. But this is incredible.
You really are the lowest.
But you know something, the lower you get, the more I want you.
ANNCR: Missouri's lowest bank card rate has just gotten lower. Seventeen-
and-a-half percent. But there's another reason to call and switch to ·
Commerce VISA or MasterCard.
Our annual fee.
WOMAN: You're not only low. You're cheap.

1498
ART DIRECTOR
Hans Kageneck, Bob Hinden
PHOTOGRAPHER
Bob Porche
WRITER
Barbara Siegel
CLIENT
McNeil Consumer Products
Company
EDITOR
David Stone
DIRECTOR
Jeffrey Metzner
AGENCY
Vera Samamma, Lowe Marschalk,
Inc., New York, NY
PRODUCTION COMPANY
Joan Babchak, Metzner Productions
MUSIC
David Horowitz

1499
ART DIRECTOR
Donna Weinheim
WRITER
Clifford L. Freeman
CLIENT
Wendy's International
DIRECTOR
Mark Story, Story Piccolo Guliner
AGENCY
DFS Dorland, New York, NY
PRODUCER
Jill Paperno

1498

ANTHOLOGY/REV/CBS
30-second
ANNCR VO: Introducing Medipren.
When your body hasn't got time for the pain.
SONG: I haven't got time for the pain.
No, I haven't got time for the pain anymore.
ANNCR VO: Medipren has ibuprofen, the prescription ingredient
recommended by doctors 2 to 1 over aspirin for body pain, including
minor arthritis. And it's safer to your stomach than aspirin.
SONG: No, I haven't got time for the pain.
(MUSIC UNDER)
ANNCR VO: When your body hasn't got time for the pain. New Medipren.
From the makers of Tylenol products.

1499

INVENTOR
30-second
INTERVIEWER: Sir, would you choose Hamburger A, a Wendy's
hamburger with fresh toppings or Hamburger B which uses things like
reconstituted onions?
MAN: I'd pick Hamburger B because it's got reconstituted onions. I'm
working on tomatoes myself, got 'em shrunk down to the size of a garden
pea. I got 300 or 400 of 'em right here in my pocket.
(LITTLE TOMATOES SPILL OUT OF POCKET, ONTO TABLE)
ANNCR: Wouldn't you choose the one with fresh toppings? Choose fresh,
Choose Wendy's.

1500

ART DIRECTOR
Ros Van Dusen, John DeBonis
WRITER
Joe Garrett
CLIENT
Worlds of Wonder (Lazer Tag)
EDITOR
Gayle Grant
DIRECTOR
Peter Smillie
DIRECTOR OF PHOTOGRAPHY
Richard Bowen
AGENCY
Richard O'Neill, Chiat/Day, San
Francisco, CA
PRODUCTION COMPANY
Cindy Akins, Robert Abel & Assoc.

1501
WRITER
Linda Waldman
CLIENT
WLS-AM 89
DIRECTOR
Robin Rutledge
AGENCY
Waldman & Associates, Inc.,
Chicago, IL

He sounds even better.
Fred Winston Mornings on

WLS
▶AM 89◀

1500

LAZER TEASE
30-second
MUSIC: MOMENTOUS SCORE THROUGHOUT
METALLIC VOICE: Players to the stadium now. Players to the stadium
now.
CROWD CHEERING IN BACKGROUND: Lazer! Lazer!
ANNCR (VO): Lazer Tag. The games begin in August.

1501

SILENT FILM
30-second
MUSIC UP (NO DIALOGUE)
MUSIC OUT

1502

ART DIRECTOR
Peter Hirsch
WRITER
Ken Majka
CLIENT
Toshiba
EDITOR
Bobby Smalheiser, First Edition
DIRECTOR
Colin Chilvers
AGENCY
Calet Hirsch & Spector, New York,
NY
PRODUCER
Frank DiSalvo
MNG. SUPERVISOR
Sandy Goebel

1503

ART DIRECTOR
Dave Kingman
WRITER
Maryann Renz
CLIENT
AT&T Corp. Arts
EDITOR
Howie Lazarus, Take-Five
Productions
DIRECTOR
Caleb Deschanel
AGENCY
Patti McGuire, N W Ayer Inc., New
York, NY
PRODUCTION COMPANY
Ted Malan, Knightsbridge Prod.
CREATIVE DIRECTOR
Jim Murphy

1502

CHANGE HISTORY
30-second
(MUSIC THROUGHOUT)
ANNCR: You're witnessing one of the
most momentous
events of all time—
The world's
first digital video system. From
Toshiba.
The Toshiba digital VCR
creates unforgettable
special effects.
And the first 525-line
digital tv
is incredible.
Toshiba digital video. It'll
change history.
See Toshiba change history at
booth 700.
0435C

1503

MADAME MONET/NATIONAL
30-second
VO: What happend on this
windswept hill 100
years ago shocked and
outraged Paris.
Now you can see for yourself
what the commotion was all about.
When AT&T brings you
an extraordinary
exhibition . . . .
The New Painting:
Impressionism:
1874–1886 . . .
In Washington, D.C.
and San Francisco.
This celebration of
vision is made
possible by AT&T.

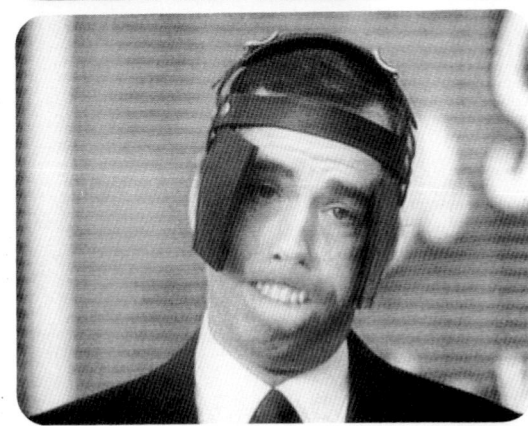

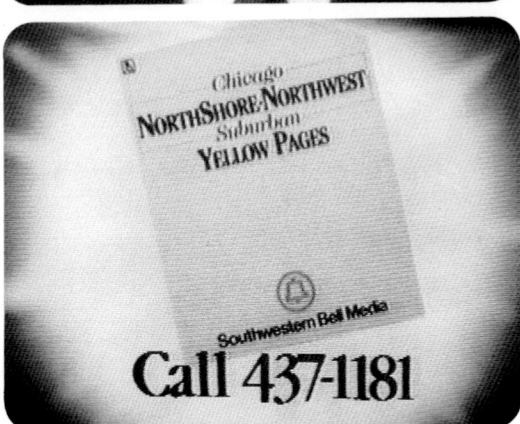

1504

ART DIRECTOR
Joe Perz
WRITER
Larry Laiken
CLIENT
Miller Brewing Company — Lite Beer
AGENCY
Backer & Spielvogel, New York, NY
PRODUCER
Andy Cornelius

1505

ART DIRECTOR
Paul Behnen
WRITER
Tom Townsend, Steve Puckett
CLIENT
Southwestern Bell Media
EDITOR
Chris Taylor
DIRECTOR
Glen Swanson
AGENCY
Gardner Advertising, St. Louis, MO
PRODUCER
Wendy Littlefield
PRODUCTION COMPANY
Film Fair
MUSIC
HLC

1504

CONRAD DOBLER/TROUBLEMAKER
30-second
DOBLER: When I played football, they called me a troublemaker. But really, I'm just a nice guy who likes to watch a game with a Miller Lite. I see you're drinking Lite, too.
MAN ON LEFT: Yeah, it tastes great.
DOBLER: I agree, but he drinks it 'cause it's less filling.
MAN ON LEFT: Tastes great.
DOBLER: Did you hear that?
MAN ON RIGHT: It's less filling.
DOBLER: Pretty strong words.
MAN ON LEFT: It tastes great!
MAN ON RIGHT: Less filling!
CROWD: Tastes great! Less filling!
ANNCR VO: There's no argument. There's only one Lite Beer. Miller Lite.
(CROWD CONTINUES TO ARGUE UNDER ANNOUNCER)
DOBLER: That a Lite Beer you're drinking?
(CROWD IS STILL ARGUING FAINTLY IN BACKGROUND)
MAN ON LEFT: Yeah, it tastes great!
DOBLER: I agree, but that's not what he said!
MAN ON LEFT: Who?!!

1505

BLINDERS
30-second
ANNCR: When you shop Greater Baltimore with your current yellow pages . . .
you might as well have blinders on.
You may never see some of the best businesses in the area . . .
because you only get part of the picture.
But later this year you'll have one convenient yellow pages
for all the best shopping areas around.
Look for the Greater Baltimore Metropolitan Yellow Pages from Southwestern Bell Media.
And see everything . . .
you've been missing.

1506

ART DIRECTOR
Michael Vitiello
WRITER
Lee Garfinkel
CLIENT
Tel Plus Communications
EDITOR
The Editors
DIRECTOR
Henry Sandbank, Sandbank Films, Inc.
AGENCY
LHS&B, New York, NY
PRODUCER
Rachel Novak

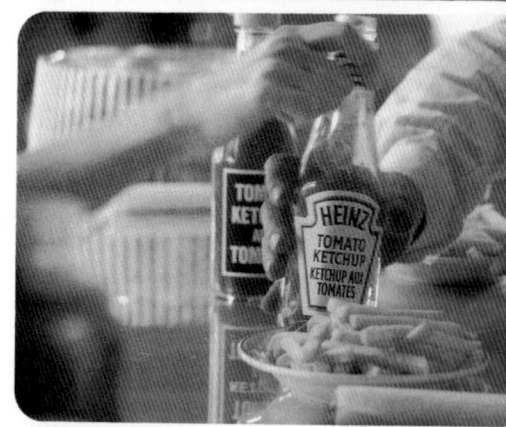

1507

ART DIRECTOR
Michael McLaughlin
WRITER
Stephen Creet
CLIENT
H.J. Heinz Company of Canada Ltd.
EDITOR
Bob Kennedy
DIRECTOR
Eugene Beck
DIRECTOR OF PHOTOGRAPHY
Guy Furner
AGENCY
Doug Lowe, Carder Gray Advertising Inc., Toronto, Canada
PRODUCER
Sue Percival

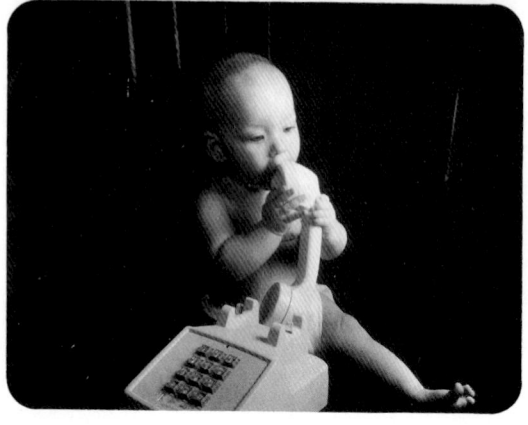

1506

MA BELL
30-secoond
ANNCR: For 100 years, Ma Bell was the voice of experience in the phone business.
But times have changed.
Ma Bell is now selling business phones she has little experience with. Little experience installing. And little experience servicing.
So if you call the voice of experience today, you're really calling a company going through a learning experience.
For the business experts, call Tel Plus. The nation's largest independent business phone company.
SUPER: TEL PLUS 1-800-TEL-PLUS.

1507

GOOD TASTE
30-second
1ST MAN: Didn't we go to school with her?
SECOND MAN LOOKS TO SEE GIRL AS FIRST MAN SWITCHES PLATES.
2ND MAN: I think you made a mistake.
1ST MAN: (TASTES HEINZ) Oh, I don't think so.
ANNCR VO: Once you've tasted Heinz, there are no other kinds.

1508
ART DIRECTOR
Donna Weinheim
WRITER
Clifford L. Freeman
CLIENT
Wendy's International
DIRECTOR
Mark Story, Story Piccolo Guliner
AGENCY
DFS Dorland, New York, NY
PRODUCER
Jill Paperno

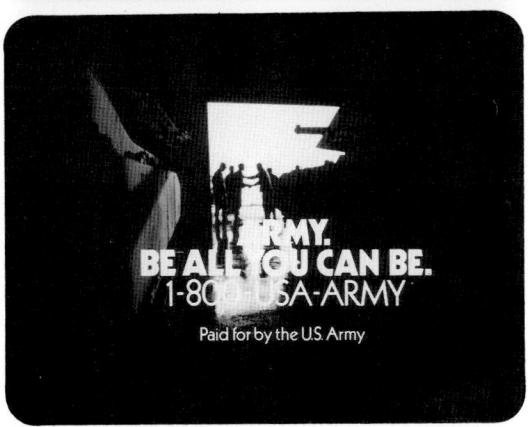

1509
ART DIRECTOR
Kevin Reilly
WRITER
Gordon Hasse
CLIENT
US Army
EDITOR
Rick Mabley, PSI Editorial
DIRECTOR
Neil Tardio
AGENCY
Jim McMenemy, N W Ayer Inc., New York, NY
PRODUCTION COMPANY
Stacy Kahn, Neil Tardio Prod.
CREATIVE DIRECTOR
Phil Peppis

508
OT SIDE/COLD SIDE
)-second
NTERVIEWER: Would you rather have Hamburger A, a Wendy's
amburger served fresh or Hamburger B, where there's a cold side and a
ot side? And the cold side's kept cold by putting it under a heating unit.
ait a minute. There's a cold side (PICKS UP BOX—SWITCHES IT
ROUND). And they put it under a heating unit. (SWITCHES BOX
ROUND AGAIN) Put the heating unit here (POINTS TO COLD SIDE) and
ne cold side stays cold. Okay that much we know.
•LDER MAN: Are you making this up?
NTERVIEWER: See, no, no. Okay. (POINTS TO HAMBURGER A) This is a
amburger.
NNCR: Wouldn't you choose the fresh one? Choose fresh, Choose
/endy's.

1509
THE LETTER
30-second
SERGEANT: Where's Schooler?
SCHOOLER: Here, Sergeant!
SERGEANT: Got a letter here for ya . . .
SCHOOLER: Thank you, Sergeant.
ANNCR (VO): The Army's special Two-Year Enlistment can get you to
college two years wiser—and with The GI Bill and The Army College
Fund—up to $17,000 richer.
SCHOOLER: (READING ALOUD) We are holding a place for you in our
next Freshman class. I'm in! I got it!
ANOTHER SOLDIER: All right!
MUSIC: BE ALL YOU CAN BE. . . .
SERGEANT: Schooler . . .
SCHOOLER: Yes, Sergeant.
SERGEANT: Just one more thing . . .
SCHOOLER: What's that, Sergeant?
SERGEANT: Graduate!
MUSIC: FIND YOUR FUTURE IN THE ARMY.

1510

ART DIRECTOR
Alan Koenke
WRITER
Debbi Smith
CLIENT
Pepsi Bottling Group
EDITOR
Lisa Breitenwischer
DIRECTOR
John Urie
AGENCY
Tracy-Locke, Dallas, TX
PRODUCTION COMPANY
Wright Banks Films
CREATIVE DIRECTOR
Alan Koenke
MUSIC
Cry Wolf Productions

1511

ART DIRECTOR
Marty Weiss
WRITER
Ken Sandbank
CLIENT
Citibank
DIRECTOR
Bill Hudson
AGENCY
Lowe Marschalk, Inc., New York, NY
PRODUCER
Robin Dobson
PRODUCTION COMPANY
Hudson Films
MUSIC
Webster Lewis; David Horowitz
Music Assoc.

1510

MASTERPIECE
30-second
SFX: ORCHESTRA TUNING UP
ANNCR: (SOFT SPOKEN POSSIBLY ENGLISH ACCENT)
The following performance is brought to you *free* from Pepsi-Cola.
SFX: TAPPING OF A BATON ON MUSIC STAND.
MUSIC: BEGIN LIVELY, FUN MOVEMENT FROM NUTCRACKER SUITE, OR SIMILAR FUN CLASSICAL PIECE.
MUSIC: STOPS
SFX: AUDIENCE APPLAUDS.
ANNCR: Bravo.
Create your own masterpiece with Crayola Markers. Free when you buy Pepsi-Cola products at your supermarket display.

1511

REACH OUT ALT.
30-second
SINGERS: Reach out and touch somebody's hand. Make this world a better place, if you can.
VO: On May 25, millions of Americans will join hands to fight hunger and homelessness in their own country.
We at Citibank are proud to help fund this important event, and you can help fund it every time you use the Citibank Visa and Mastercard.
SINGERS: Reach out and touch somebody's hand. Make this world a better place, if you can.

1512

ART DIRECTOR
Kim C. White
DESIGNER
Kim C. White
WRITER
Peter Lloyd
CLIENT
Murray Ohio Manufacturing Co.
DIRECTOR
David Dryer
AGENCY
Sive Associates, Inc., Cincinnati, OH
PRODUCER
Donna Gary
PRODUCTION COMPANY
Dexter-Dryer-Lai
ASSOC. CREATIVE DIRECTOR
Peter Lloyd
CREATIVE DIRECTOR
Mike Kitei
MUSIC
John Henry, Radio Theatre Group

1513

ART DIRECTOR
Mike Schell
WRITER
Joyce King-Thomas
CLIENT
SB Thomas Company — English
Muffins
EDITOR
Barry Stillwell
DIRECTOR
Patrick Russell
DIRECTOR OF PHOTOGRAPHY
Ron Fortunato
AGENCY
Young & Rubicam, New York, NY
PRODUCER
Roseanne Horn
PRODUCTION COMPANY
Rick Levine Production

1512

1040 STREET MACHINE
30-second
FRIEND (ON MONITOR): "I'm beamin' down to the Dunes."
BOY: "I'll race you."
SINGERS: "Street Machine
Murray moves!
Two-speed Street Machine
Easy shiftin' Street Machine
Murray moves!
Drum brake Street Machine
Quick stop Street Machine."
BOY: "What took you so long?"
SINGERS: "Murray moves you faster!"

1513

BUSINESSMAN
30-second
MALE (VO): Soon, this man's morning will take off with all the restraint of a runaway roller coaster. He'll face questions, challenges, dilemmas. Which is why he's having a Thomas English Muffin. Not only do Thomas's taste delicious and wholesome, they're light enough to keep him on his toes. Yet give him just what he needs to make it through the morning. Thomas English Muffins. Every day should start out this good.

1514

ART DIRECTOR
Amy Mizner
WRITER
Don Deutsch
CLIENT
The Pontiac Dealer Association of
NY/NJ/CT
EDITOR
Jerry Fried
DIRECTOR
John O'Driscoll
DIRECTOR OF PHOTOGRAPHY
John Crawford
AGENCY
Randy Cohen, David Deutsch Assoc.,
New York, NY
PRODUCER
Pete Christy

1515

ART DIRECTOR
Michael Fazende
WRITER
Phil Hanft
CLIENT
KTTV-TV (Metromedia)
EDITOR
Beth Dougherty, Wilson-Griak
DIRECTOR
Mark Story
AGENCY
Fallon McElligott, Minneapolis, MN
PRODUCER
Judy Brink
PRODUCTION COMPANY
Story Piccolo Guliner
PERFORMER
Ian Shoales

1514

CAR DEALER
30-second
My name is Jim Morrell. I am one of the Pontiac Dealers. I'm here to tell
you about Lease Excitement. Through December 31 that's right through
December 31 lease a Pontiac for the following—Fiero $169 a month,
6000 $199 a month, Grand Am Sedan—$189 a month, Sunbird Coupe
$169 a month, some other models are available. I was in the service with
an honorary discharge so you know you can take my word.
Did I say December 31.

1515

FEEL GOOD
30-second
IAN SHOALES: Let's say you're on your way home and you're an hour
behind schedule. Well at Channel 11 the news is an hour behind schedule
too. So if you're an hour behind schedule, you're actually right on
schedule. Or looking at it a different way, the news at Channel 11 is right
on schedule if you're an hour behind schedule. Or if you're right on
schedule, the news at Channel 11 is an hour late. So if you're an hour
late . . . as usual . . . and Channel 11 is an hour late . . . like they
always are . . . everybody's on schedule. For the first time in your life
you're actually rewarded for being late. Doesn't that make you feel good?
I'd feel good too, but I don't know how. I gotta go.

1516
ART DIRECTOR
Rick Paynter
WRITER
Leland Rosemond
CLIENT
New Jersey Division of Travel &
Tourism
EDITOR
Scott Hudson
DIRECTOR
Dick Richards
DIRECTOR OF PHOTOGRAPHY
Richard Shore
AGENCY
Dan Kohn, US Advertising, Union,
NJ
PRODUCTION COMPANY
Howard Schaller, Knightsbridge
Prod.

1517
ART DIRECTOR
David Thall
WRITER
Larry Sokolove
CLIENT
Miller Brewing Company — Lite
Beer
AGENCY
Backer & Spielvogel, New York, NY
PRODUCER
Eric Steinhauser

1516

TRENTON
30-second
SFX: DRUM BEATS . . .
ANNOUNCER (VO): The battle of Trenton was an American triumph. One
of many ways New Jersey helped shape America's proud heritage. Share
your pride—come to New Jersey.

1517

PYTHON PISCOPO
30-second
PYTHON: I used to be the roughest, toughest, meanest wrestler in the
world.
MAN IN CROWD: Hey, Python, how ya' doin?
PYTHON: Hey, how are ya? Good to see ya . . . Sorry.
PYTHON: But now I've mellowed out. Excuse me.
MAN IN CHAIR: Whoaaa!
SFX: BREAKING PLASTER.
PYTHON: And there ain't nothing I like better than hanging out with my
friends and sharing some Miller Lites. They love it cause it's less filling.
SFX: SCREAM.
PYTHON: Me, I love it 'cause it tastes great.
SFX: GLASS BEING CHEWED.
ANNCR VO: It's no match, there's only one Lite Beer. Miller Lite.

1518

ART DIRECTOR
Ron Anderson
WRITER
Bert Gardner
CLIENT
Minnetonka, Inc.
DIRECTOR
Joe Sedelmaier
AGENCY
Bozell, Jacobs, Minneapolis, MN
PRODUCER
Judy Wittenberg
PRODUCTION COMPANY
Sedelmaier

 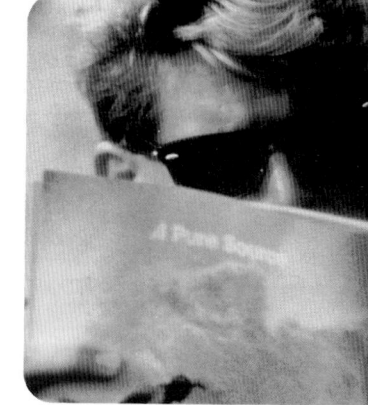

1519

ART DIRECTOR
Mike Moser, Lee Clow
WRITER
David O'Hare, David Woodside
CLIENT
California Cooler
EDITOR
Steve Wystrach
DIRECTOR
Mark Coppos
DIRECTOR OF PHOTOGRAPHY
Peter Brown
AGENCY
Francesca Cohn, Chiat/Day, San
Francisco, CA
PRODUCTION COMPANY
Mike Appell, Coppos Films

 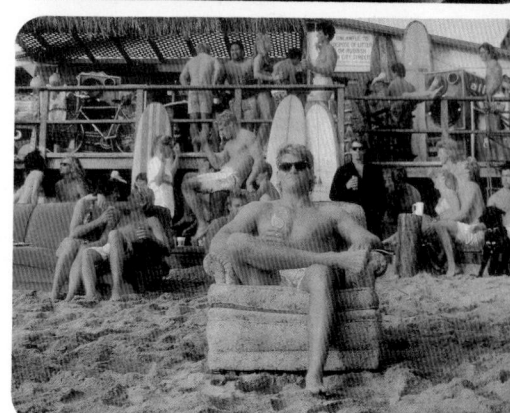

1518

TAXI/REV.
30-second
(MUSIC UNDER & THROUGHOUT)
VO: It's not always . . .
. . . practical . . .
. . . to brush after eating.
VO: Introducing Check•Up plaque fighting gum . . .
. . . from Check•Up Toothpaste.
It's clinically tested to help remove plaque . . .
. . . peacefully.
VO: Check•Up Gum. When you can't brush, chew.

1519

PARTY (TUB)
30-second
MUSIC: "GIMME SOME LOVIN'" THROUGHOUT
ANNCR (VO): For years, it was made by guys with names like Rabbit,
Quasimodo,
The Chairman.
SINGERS: HEY!
ANNCR: Real fruit and white wine. Blended under ideal conditions.
MUSIC: LYRICS UP
ANNCR: California Cooler. The real stuff.

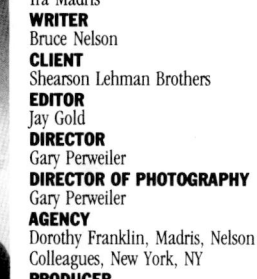

1520
ART DIRECTOR
Ira Madris
WRITER
Bruce Nelson
CLIENT
Shearson Lehman Brothers
EDITOR
Jay Gold
DIRECTOR
Gary Perweiler
DIRECTOR OF PHOTOGRAPHY
Gary Perweiler
AGENCY
Dorothy Franklin, Madris, Nelson &
Colleagues, New York, NY
PRODUCER
Mike Lupino
MUSIC
Charles Gross

1521
ART DIRECTOR
Donna Weinheim
WRITER
Clifford L. Freeman
CLIENT
Diet Rite Cola
AGENCY
DFS Dorland, New York, NY
PRODUCER
Jill Paperno

1520

ROCK AND HARD PLACE
30-second
VO: A rock and a hard place.
Many who find themselves there resign themselves to a no-win situation.
Others are paralyzed into making no decision at all.
We, however, believe that between a rock and a hard place is a solution
searching to be found.
Seeking what others don't see is capitalism at its best.
And why you'll never look at a hard decision quite the same again.
Shearson Lehman Brothers.
Minds Over Money.

1521

YOU'LL DO
30-second
SINGER: Everybody's gotta Diet Rite, it doesn't matter who you are, it's
going to be a tough fight. So give yourself salt-free Diet Rite Cola.
WOMAN: Lee, Ahhh, you look great.
LEE: Not that great.
WOMAN: I think you'll do.
SINGER: Everybody's gotta Diet Rite.
SUPER: The Salt Free One.

1522

ART DIRECTOR
Ken Boyd
ANIMATOR
The Animation House
WRITER
Terry Bell
CLIENT
Cadbury Schweppes Canada Inc.
DIRECTOR
Bob Fortier
AGENCY
Nicole Tardif, Scali, McCabe, Sloves,
Toronto, Canada
PRODUCER
Sam Gardner
TECH. PRODUCER
John Burtcher
V.O.
Alfred Humphreys, Len Carlson

1523

ART DIRECTOR
Richard Mahan
WRITER
Phil Guthrie
CLIENT
Arby's
AGENCY
Backer & Spielvogel, New York, NY
PRODUCER
Michael Berkman

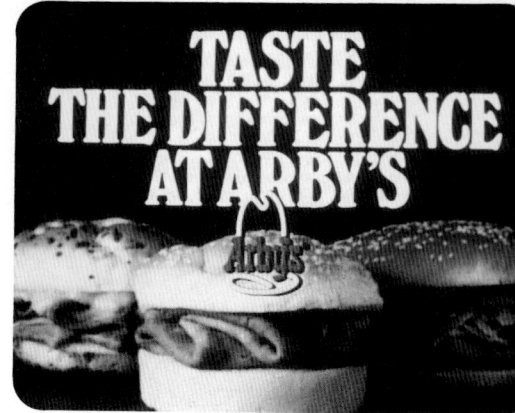

1522

THICKLISH
30-second
VIGNETTE 1
Brush is applying new price to bar.
Bar is squirming in reaction to brush.
Bar is laughing.
Laughter builds in intensity as brush continues to paint.
The brush has completed painting in price. We hear bar give a sigh of relief.
VIGNETTE 2
We see the 55¢ price appear on Einstein's bar. Freud, Shakespeare and Mozart look at the bar above Einstein's head.
55¢ price bubbles rise above the heads of Freud, Shakespeare and Mozart. All bars above all heads now reads 55¢.
VIGNETTE 3
Theme music from Looney Tune Cartoons plays throughout.
Bars dance to music.
Voice of Porky Pig. . . .
"TH-TH-TH-THICKS ALL FOLKS."

1523

NOT ANOTHER HAMBURGER
30-second
#1: Oh, whatta surprise. A hamburger.
#2: Golly, gee, whiz. Another hamburger.
#3: Whoopee.
#4: Yahoo.
ANNCR: Every year people consume over 7 billion hamburgers. That's a lot of hamburgers, a lot of the same old thing. But there is something different. Arby's delicious slow-roasted roast beef. Different sandwiches, lo of different toppings. So before you say . . .
#5: Oh, no, another hamburger.
ANNCR: Say Arby's. And taste the difference.

1524
ART DIRECTOR
David Edelstein, Nancy Edelstein,
Lanny French
DESIGNER
David Edelstein, Nancy Edelstein,
Lanny French
WRITER
Jeremy Wolff, Linda Yellin
CLIENT
Generra Sportswear
EDITOR
Michael Krupnick
DIRECTOR
Peter Heath
DIRECTOR OF PHOTOGRAPHY
Peter Heath
AGENCY
Terry Thompson, Edelstein Assoc.,
Seattle, WA
PRODUCTION COMPANY
Robin Benson, N. Lee Lacy

1525
ART DIRECTOR
Art Mellor
WRITER
H. Robert Greenbaum
CLIENT
Visa
EDITOR
Bob DeRise, A Cut Above
DIRECTOR
Gerard Hameline
AGENCY
BBDO, New York, NY
PRODUCER
Tonie Deon
PRODUCTION COMPANY
Gerard Hameline Productions

1524

PAPER CLIP
30-second
JEFFREY: Life is a paper clip, just waiting to be twisted into funny little
shapes.
JANELLE: He always dressed great. Too bad his personality was part of the
deal.
ROBERT: There was something I wanted to say about my clothes, but I
forgot.
JANELLE: Anyone who has ever put a staple into their own thumb, knows
exactly what my last relationship was like.
JEFFREY: Is Phil Donohue watching? I just want to know if Phil Donohue
is watching?

1525

FRANCE
30-second
AVO: High above the Loire Valley
is a castle that
has enchanted travelers since the
Middle Ages.
But now travelers
of all ages can be
enchanted at the Hotel De La
Bretesche.
So if you go there, remember,
bring your nose for wine and
your Visa card. Because you can't
check out without a glass of Pouilly
Fume, and you can't check in with
American Express.
Visa. It's everywhere you want to be.

1526

ART DIRECTOR
John DeCerchio
WRITER
John DeCerchio
CLIENT
Little Caesars
DIRECTOR
Dan Nichols
AGENCY
Sheldon Cohn, W.B. Donor,
Southfield, MI
PRODUCER
Michael Daniel

1527

ART DIRECTOR
John Armistead
WRITER
Jim Weller, Dick Sittig, Rick
Carpenter
CLIENT
American Isuzu Motors, Inc.
EDITOR
Decoupage
DIRECTOR
Gary Johns, Jeff Gorman
DIRECTOR OF PHOTOGRAPHY
Matt Cantrell
AGENCY
Della Femina, Travisano, Los
Angeles, CA
PRODUCER
Howard Bailin
CREATIVE DIRECTOR
Jim Weller, John Armistead

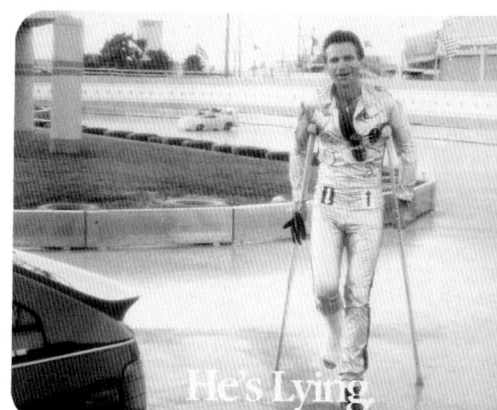

1526

FARM
30-second
FARMER: Whatta we got here Sam?
(READS)
Dear Mason Dairy; We have some good news to pass along. More and
more folks have been telling us lately how much they like Little Caesars
pizza, especially our fresh, all natural cheese. We're very anxious to hear
this praise, since all of you at the dairy played such an important role.
Girls I got some good news.
Sincerely yours, Little Caesars.

1527

RACE TRACK
30-second
LIAR: Ban journo. I'm the world's greatest race car driver.
SUPER: He's lying.
Recently, I had a little problem here at Monte Carlo.
SUPER: He slipped in the bathtub.
So I switched to this $200,000 Formula Isuzu.
SUPER: The Isuzu Impulse: from $12,059
It comes with driving gloves, and a pit crew. All standard.
SUPER: Well, it does have air conditioning, cruise control standard.
It's so fast it will go from Paris to Rome in two minutes.
SUPER: Turbo Impulse 0-60 in 8.3 seconds.
And the bank gave me 5.9% financing.
Just because they like my face.
SUPER: Almost anyone can get 5.9% financing, right now.

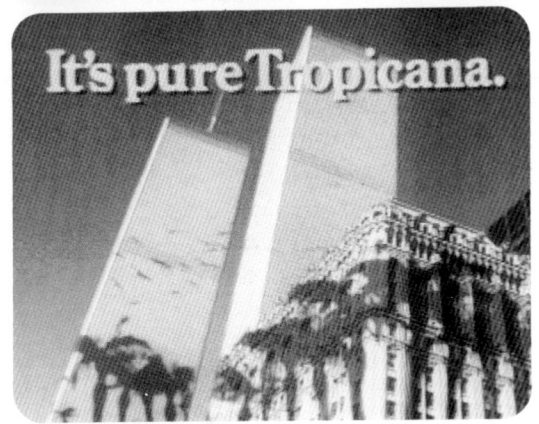

1528

ART DIRECTOR
Ernie Cox
WRITER
Bill Teitelbaum
CLIENT
Bon Ami
DIRECTOR
Peter Cooper
AGENCY
N W Ayer, Inc., Chicago, IL
PRODUCER
Phil Smith
PRODUCTION COMPANY
Cooper & Co.

1529

ART DIRECTOR
Alex Lopez
WRITER
Chris Helbling
CLIENT
Beatrice/Tropicana
EDITOR
Katherine Campbell
DIRECTOR
Stephen Goldblatt
AGENCY
Darr Hawthorne, Leo Burnett, Chicago, IL
PRODUCTION COMPANY
Marlon Staggs, Robert Abel
CREATIVE DIRECTOR
Dave Allemeier

1528

CHEMICAL WARFARE
30-second
Mother was here today; does it show? She says that my house doesn't smell clean. Now you have to understand that my mother does not clean—my mother engages in chemical warfare. Before cleaning day she should be required to file an environmental impact statement. *Her* house smells like a swimming pool. At a hospital. Now *that's* clean. But *my* house doesn't smell clean. (BEAT) It's only clean.
(SILENT.)

1529

CITY
30-second
AVO: Come. Feel the freshness.
SONG: TROPICANA
AVO: Tropicana Pure Premium
shades your morning with a taste so
fresh, so pure, so natural.
SONG: TROPICANA
AVO: Pure Premium,
only Florida oranges,
with nothing added, nothing taken away.
The taste could only be one:
SONG: TROPICANA
AVO: Feel the freshness. It's pure Tropicana.

1530

ART DIRECTOR
Tony Carillo
WRITER
Florence Granello
CLIENT
General Foods — Sanka
EDITOR
Joe Pellicano
DIRECTOR
Ed Bianchi
DIRECTOR OF PHOTOGRAPHY
Andrzej Bartkowiak
AGENCY
Texas East, Young & Rubicam, New
York, NY
PRODUCTION COMPANY
Bianchi Films

1531

ART DIRECTOR
Tom Cordner, Jean Robaire
WRITER
Brent Bouchez, John Stein, Garry
Shandling
CLIENT
Pizza Hut, Inc.
EDITOR
Rob Watzke
DIRECTOR
David Steinberg
AGENCY
Chiat/Day, Los Angeles, CA
PRODUCER
Elaine Hinton
PRODUCTION COMPANY
Larkin Prod.

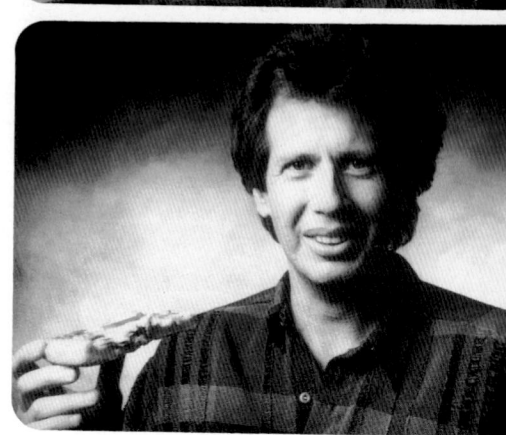

1530

CUPS/HINES NATURAL
30-second
(MUSIC UNDER) SONG: I love coffee. I love me. I love my
Sanka, 'cause it loves me.
Sanka and me; I'm glad I'm caffeine free
A cup, a cup, a cup, a cup, a cup.
ANNCR (VO): Smooth, satisfying Sanka Brand Decaffeinated Coffee. You
can drink it all day long, and feel good about it.
(MUSIC)
(MUSIC)
(MUSIC)
SONG: Sanka and me.
(MUSIC OUT)

1531

MOTHER'S DAY
30-second
MUSIC: UNDER THROUGHOUT.
GARRY SHANDLING: You know, I'm very loyal in a relationship, any
relationship, even when I go out with my Mom, I don't, I don't think,
"Oh, I wonder what that Mom is like. I wonder what her macaroni and
cheese tastes like."
I love my Mom. On Mother's Day I take her out for pizza. Say, "Mom, ge
whatever you want on your half."
She's in heaven.

1532
ART DIRECTOR
William McCaffery
WRITER
Jay Cheek
CLIENT
Bulova Watch Company
EDITOR
Alan Eisenberg, Horn/Eisenberg
DIRECTOR
Melvin Sokolsky, Sunlight Films, Inc.
AGENCY
Russell Hudson, McCaffery & Ratner, Inc., New York, NY
PRODUCER
John Danischewsky
MUSIC
Walter Raim, HEA Music

1533
ART DIRECTOR
Tod Seisser
WRITER
Jay Taub
CLIENT
New York Air
EDITOR
Morty's Place
DIRECTOR
Henry Sandbank, Sandbank Films, Inc.
AGENCY
LHS&B, New York, NY
PRODUCER
Rachel Novak
MUSIC
Michael Small

532

VIETNAM
30-second
ANNCR VO: On October 1, 1961, Roger Maris hit number 61 at precisely . . .
. . 2:46 p.m. Bulova Watch time.
On February 23, 1971, Bert Moss came home . . .
. . 2:01 p.m. Bulova Watch time.
And today Jennifer Barrett took a giant step . . .
at 7:20 a.m. Bulova Watch time.
Bulova measures every minute of our lives, large and small
Bulova. It's America's time.

1533

FEATHERS
30-second
ANNCR: At New York Air, we wondered how does Eastern earn their wings everyday.
Unlike our shuttle, Eastern doesn't offer food or drinks. It doesn't offer you an assigned seat. And the seat you do get is 23% less roomy than ours.
Of course, the Eastern shuttle does have lots of flights. About one third less than we have.
New York Air's Super Shuttle Service. We clip Eastern's wings, everyday.
SILENT SUPER: New York Air Super Shuttle* Service.
*We offer confirmed reservations instead of back up sections.

1534

ART DIRECTOR
Ron Condon
WRITER
Jennie Fields
CLIENT
Heinz Ketchup
EDITOR
Ed Hall
DIRECTOR
J. Wesley Jones
AGENCY
Jim McAward, Leo Burnett, Chicago,
IL
PRODUCTION COMPANY
Alice Carroll, J. Wesley Jones
CREATIVE DIRECTOR
Ron Condon

1535

ART DIRECTOR
Lee Clow, Mike Moser
WRITER
David O'Hare, David Woodside
CLIENT
California Cooler
EDITOR
Steve Wystrach
DIRECTOR
Mark Coppos
DIRECTOR OF PHOTOGRAPHY
Peter Brown
AGENCY
Francesca Cohn, Chiat/Day, San
Francisco, CA
PRODUCTION COMPANY
Mike Appell, Coppos Films

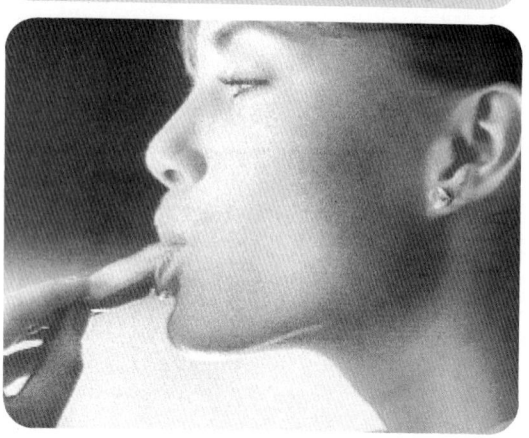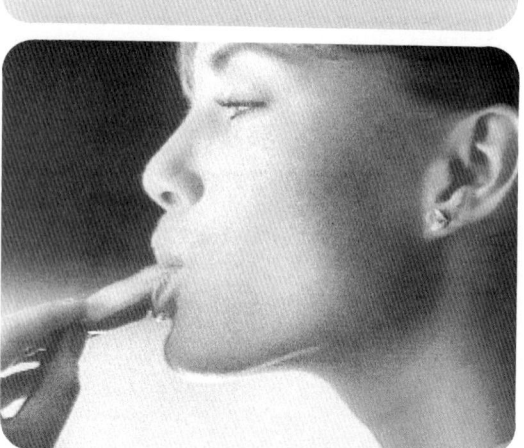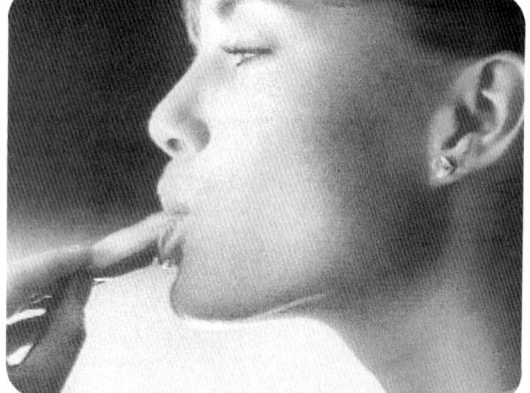

1534

KNIFE REV.
30-second
ANNCR: The point of this knife
is to show you how thick and rich
Heinz Ketchup is.
Ready, set, pour.
Heinz is so thick, so rich, it clings.
Even upside down.
SFX: (SIZZLE)
ANNCR: Still, what counts
when it comes to ketchup
is how it tastes.
And Heinz tastes like no other ketchup
can.
Only Heinz
can say it's
America's thickest, richest, best-
tasting ketchup. Heinz.

1535

20 YRS. OF R&D
30-second
MUSIC UP: LOUIE LOUIE
(CONTINUES THROUGHOUT)
ANNCR (VO): Over 20 years of research and development have gone into
every bottle of California Cooler.
ANNCR: California Cooler. The real stuff.
MUSIC: "LET'S GO!"

1536
ART DIRECTOR
Tod Seisser
WRITER
Jay Taub
CLIENT
New York Air
EDITOR
Morty's Place
DIRECTOR
Henry Sandbank, Sandbank Films, Inc.
AGENCY
LHS&B, New York, NY
PRODUCER
Rachel Novak

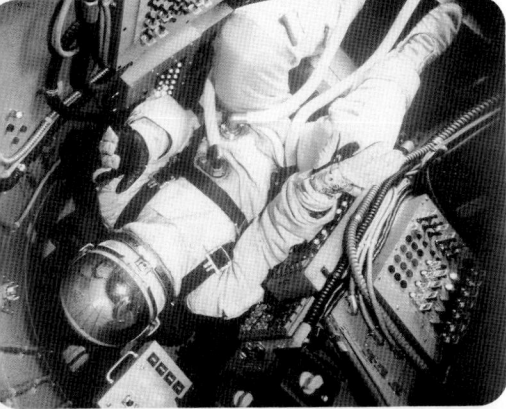

1537
ART DIRECTOR
Tony DeGregorio
WRITER
Lee Garfinkel
CLIENT
Subaru of America
EDITOR
David Dee, Eventime
DIRECTOR
Steve Horn, Steve Horn, Inc.
AGENCY
LHS&B, New York, NY
PRODUCER
Bob Nelson

1536

BORMAN
30-second
ANNCR: Before he became the chairman of Eastern Airlines, Frank Borman was an astronaut. So he flew in some pretty cramped quarters. Maybe that's why the average seat on the Eastern shuttle offers a mere 475 square inches of room.
But on New York Air's Super Shuttle, the average seat is a full 23% roomier.
You see, Frank Borman had to fly like this. But you don't.

1537

JERRY'S NEW CAR
30-second
WOMAN: Here's Jerry with a new car.
MAN: What did you pay for it?
JERRY: About $5,500. (EVERYONE TREATS THE CAR GINGERLY)
COUSIN: Are you kidding?
MAN: Does it run on batteries?
GIRL: What's it made of, crepe paper?
TWIN #1: Does it have a motor?
TWIN #2: Does it have a motor?
COUSIN: Can I kick the tires?
UNCLE: Will the doors come off the hinges?
RELATIVE: Hey, guess what? It's a Subaru.
CROWD: Oh, a Subaru! (EVERYONE BANGS THE DOORS, THE HOOD AND THE TRUNK)
TWIN #1: A Subaru!
TWIN #2: A Subaru!
ANNCR: Only one inexpensive car is built like a Subaru.
Introducing the Subaru Justy.
Inexpensive. And built to stay that way.
WOMAN: Such a smart boy.

1538

ART DIRECTOR
Fred Massin, Eric Glickman, Rex Wilder
WRITER
Fred Massin, Eric Glickman, Rex Wilder
CLIENT
RC Cola Company
DIRECTOR
Dominick Rossetti
AGENCY
DFS Dorland, New York, NY
PRODUCER
Deb Wagner

1539

ART DIRECTOR
Tom Walker
WRITER
Kent Middleton
CLIENT
McDonald's
AGENCY
Leo Burnett, Chicago, IL
PRODUCER
Mike Diedrich
CREATIVE DIRECTOR
Bud Watts

1538

TOO FAR
30-second
ANNCR: A certain American institution allows their people only Coke and Pepsi, which means they're sentenced to a life of Coke and Pepsi.
But there will always be some people who'll go out of their way for the taste of RC Cola. A taste that's unrestrained.
Yes, some people will go out of their way for the taste of RC.
But sometimes they go too far.

1539

WHO'S PLAYING
30-second
BROCK: Who's playing McDonald's NFL Kickoff Payoff?
LINEMEN: I'm playing. He's playing . . . Are you playing?
LINEMEN: We're all playing!
ANNCR: Collect trading cards of your favorite NFL stars.
COACH: I got your card and I got your card I don't have your card yet . . .
ANNCR: Every Kickoff Payoff card is a winner. Win a McDonald's sandwich, fries or Coca-Cola.
REF: Cards must be redeemed during the following week.
LINEMAN: Hey wanna play?
LINEMAN: NFL Kickoff Payoff
LINEMAN: Great idea.
LINEMAN: C'mon let's go!

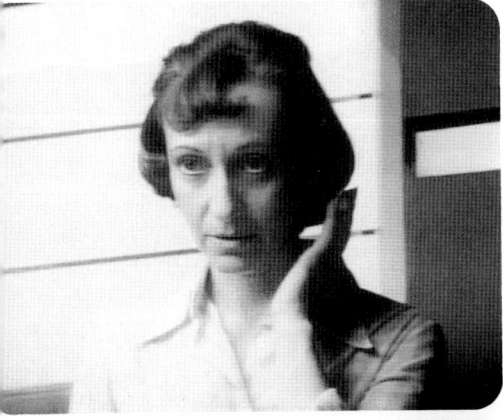

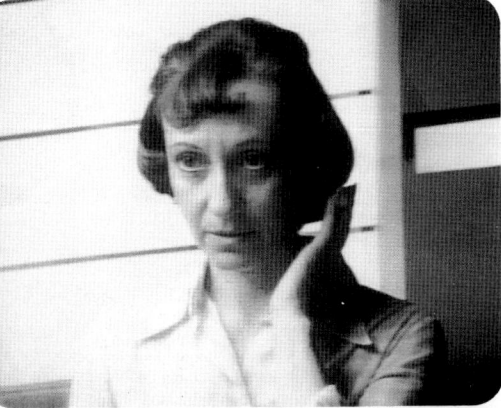

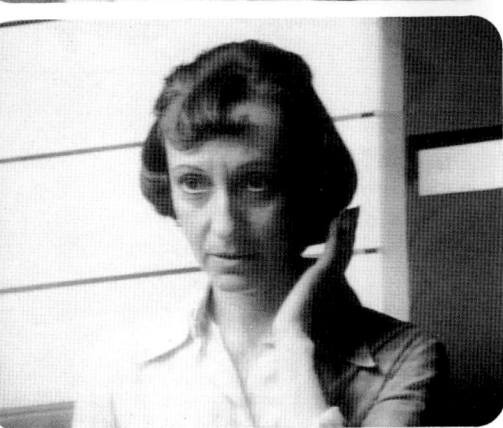

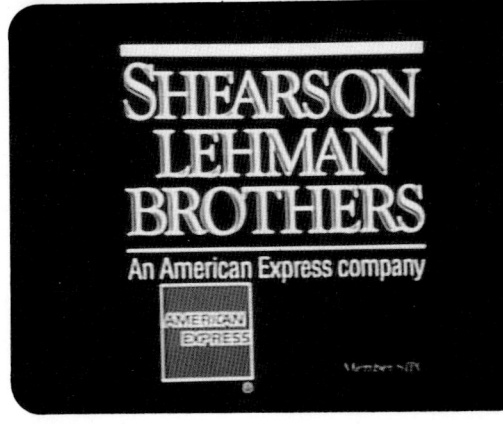

1540
ART DIRECTOR
Donna Weinheim
WRITER
Clifford L. Freeman, Arthur Bijur,
Donna Weinheim
CLIENT
Wendy's International
DIRECTOR
Mark Story, Story Piccolo Guliner
AGENCY
DFS Dorland, New York, NY
PRODUCER
Jill Paperno

1541
ART DIRECTOR
Ira Madris
WRITER
Bruce Nelson
CLIENT
Shearson Lehman Brothers
EDITOR
Howie Lazarus
DIRECTOR
Gary Perweiler
DIRECTOR OF PHOTOGRAPHY
Gary Perweiler
AGENCY
Peter Barg, Madris, Nelson &
Colleagues, New York, NY
PRODUCER
Doug Friedman
MUSIC
Charles Gross

1540

HAIRDO
30-second
INTERVIEWER: Would you choose Hamburger A, a Wendy's hamburger in
which you get the fresh toppings you want or Hamburger B where you
take the toppings they give you?
WOMAN: B. I'm not used to getting what I want. I went to the beauty
parlor and asked for a glamorous hairdo (TOUCHES HAIR). I don't think
I got it. What do you think?
INTERVIEWER: I love it.
ANNCR: Wouldn't you prefer your choice of fresh toppings? Choose fresh,
choose Wendy's.

1541

GLASS
30-second
VO: The pessimist sees the glass as half-empty. The optimist sees the glass
as half-full. We, however, see it as a way to . . . quench a thirst . . . boil
an egg . . . or . . . make something grow.
Seeing the possibilities is capitalism at its best.
And why you'll never look at a glass of water quite the same again.
Shearson Lehman Brothers.
Minds Over Money.

1542

ART DIRECTOR
Darrell Wilks
WRITER
Larry Volpi, Dennis Ferrone
CLIENT
Warner Lambert-Sticklets, Mike
Soriano
EDITOR
Al Derise
DIRECTOR
Martin Bell
AGENCY
Eric Lassoff, JWT, New York, NY
PRODUCTION COMPANY
Don Lumpkin, THT Productions
CREATIVE DIRECTOR
Bernie Owett

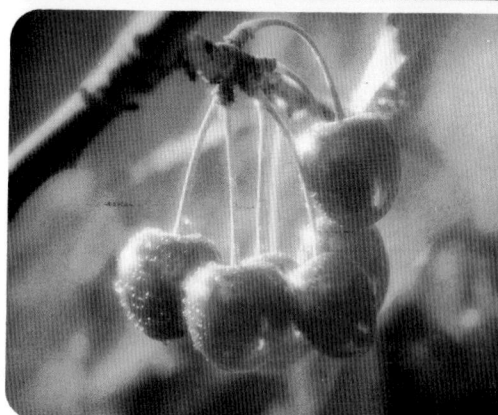

1543

ART DIRECTOR
Richard Voehl
WRITER
Alan Saperstein
CLIENT
The J.M. Smucker Company, John
Carpenter
EDITOR
Stu Zavolinsky
DIRECTOR
Hobby Morrison
AGENCY
Elaine Rehfuss, Wyse Advertising,
New York, NY
PRODUCER
John Marias, Hunt Lowry
MNG. SUPERVISOR
John Lippmann

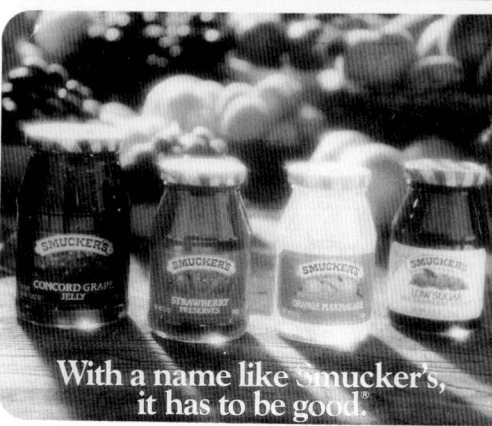

1542

TANGO
30-second
SONG: Skinny Sticklets. Fat with flavor.
Skinny, skinny, that's the shape of,
Skinny Sticklets. Fat with flavor.
See how Skinny. Taste how fat.
ANNCR: Only one gum gives you nine slim sticks instead of seven wide
ones in a regular pack. New Sticklets in natural spearmint or peppermint.
SONG: Skinny Sticklets. Fat with flavor.
See how skinny. Taste how fat.

1543

TASTE TIME REV.1
30-second
If you could taste time,
caring . . .
dedication.
If you could taste the sun . . .
rain . . .
fresh air.
If you could taste tradition . . .
and pride . . .
this is what it would taste like.
Every time.
With a name like Smucker's,
it has to be good.

1544
ART DIRECTOR
Pat Burnham
WRITER
Bill Miller
CLIENT
Don Biehn
EDITOR
Jeff Stickles, Lighthouse
DIRECTOR
Joe Pytka
AGENCY
Fallon McElligott, Minneapolis, MN
PRODUCER
Judy Brink
PRODUCTION COMPANY
Pytka
V.O.
Percy Rodriguez

1545
ART DIRECTOR
Frank Costantini
WRITER
Nina DiSesa
CLIENT
Kentucky Fried Chicken — Coop
EDITOR
Barry Stillwell
DIRECTOR
George M. Cochran
DIRECTOR OF PHOTOGRAPHY
Joe Rivers
AGENCY
Young & Rubicam, New York, NY
PRODUCER
Louise Kirsch
PRODUCTION COMPANY
G. M. Cochran Production

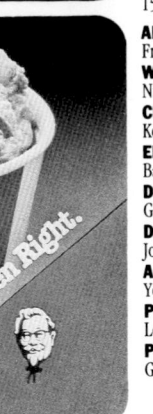

1544

CAMPFIRE
30-second
SFX: LONELY. HARMONICA, CRICKETS, A COYOTE HOWLS IN DISTANCE.
VO: When most people think of beans, they think of the kind of beans you eat around a campfire.
But in Minneapolis, when art directors think of beans, they think of Biehn's Full Service Art Studio, tasteful illustration and graphic design.
SFX: FLATULENCE.
VO: They might sound the same. But they're spelled differently.

1545

FRESH CHICKEN
30-second
(MUSIC UNDER)
EMPLOYEE: At some places, you never know if chicken is fresh or frozen.
(MUSIC)
Or just how long it's been sitting around. At Kentucky Fried Chicken our Extra Crispy and Original Recipe chicken starts fresh and it's cooked fresh all day long. So for great-tasting chicken that's fresh and freshly made you know who to come to, the chicken experts.
Other places may sell you chicken, no matter what shape it's in.
SINGERS: Kentucky Fried Chicken . . . We do chicken right.

1546

ART DIRECTOR
Tod Seisser
WRITER
Jay Taub
CLIENT
New York Air
EDITOR
Morty's Place
DIRECTOR
Henry Sandbank, Sandbank Films,
Inc.
AGENCY
LHS&B, New York, NY
PRODUCER
Rachel Novak

1547

ART DIRECTOR
Mike Moser
WRITER
Brian O'Neill
CLIENT
Worlds of Wonder (Teddy Ruxpin)
EDITOR
Rob Watzke
DIRECTOR
Mike Cuesta
DIRECTOR OF PHOTOGRAPHY
David Castillo
AGENCY
Francesca Cohn, Chiat/Day, San
Francisco, CA
PRODUCTION COMPANY
Erwin Kramer, Griner-Cuesta

1546

CONTORTIONIST
30-second
ANNCR: Every once in a while, you hear people complain about how
small the seats are on the Eastern Shuttle.
Come on, I've been taking the shuttle for years. I even hear New York Air
bragging that their seats are 23% roomier. But, that's not going to make
me switch shuttles. No sir. I mean Eastern's fine. They give me all the
room I need to stretch out.

1547

SCHOOL BUS
30-second
MUSIC: SWEET PIANO MUSIC
KIDS' CHATTER IN BACKGROUND
TEDDY: Hi.
My name is Teddy Ruxpin. Can you and I be friends? I really enjoy . . .
DRIVER: Everybody out!
TEDDY: Then one day, we found an old treasure map.
ANNCR (VO): The world of Teddy Ruxpin.

1548
ART DIRECTOR
Dennis H. Plansker
WRITER
Sean Kevin Fitzpatrick
CLIENT
Chevrolet Motor Division
EDITOR
Roger Harrison
DIRECTOR
Peter Smillie
BROADCAST DIRECTOR
Dennis H. Plansker
AGENCY
Campbell-Ewald Company, Warren, MI
PRODUCER
Kenneth J. Domanski
PRODUCTION COMPANY
Berkofsky, Smillie & Barrett
CREATIVE DIRECTOR
Sean Kevin Fitzpatrick
MUSIC
Dennis H. Plansker, Christopher Firestone

1549
ART DIRECTOR
Paul Walter
WRITER
Charlie Miesmer, Lance Mald
CLIENT
Polaroid
EDITOR
Howie Weisbrot, First Edition/Composite
DIRECTOR
Terry Bedford
AGENCY
BBDO, New York, NY
PRODUCER
Jack Harrower
PRODUCTION COMPANY
Jennie & Co.

548

IROC THUNDER
30-second
(HEARTBEAT MUSICAL EFFECTS UNDER THROUGHOUT)
SINGERS: Listen to the heartbeat
(ooh, ooh)
of America
(ooh, ooh)
ANNCR: When you want to feel the thunder . . .
. . . put yourself in Today's Chevrolet Camaro IROC-Z and listen to your heart beat.
SINGERS: The heartbeat of America
SFX: (LOUD REVERBERATING HEARTBEAT)
SINGERS: That's today's Chevrolet

1549

RED DRESS
30-second
AVO: If you are a dark-haired girl
in a bright red dress
I will steal you away.
If you are an ancient cathedral
I will capture you.
Instantly.
If you are an explosion of brilliant flowers,
I will catch you.
And I will keep you, all of you,
in all the splendor of your glorious colors.
The amazing new
Polaroid Spectra System.
Polaroid. We take your pictures seriously.

1550

ART DIRECTOR
Michael Bays
WRITER
Jim Grodd
CLIENT
Ray-O-Vac Batteries
AGENCY
Tony Macchia, FCB/Leber Katz
Partners, New York, NY
PRODUCTION COMPANY
Chris Woods, R/Greenberg Assoc.

1551

ART DIRECTOR
Nick Gisonde
WRITER
Charlie Breen
CLIENT
Hyundai Motor America
AGENCY
Backer & Spielvogel, New York, NY
PRODUCER
Eric Steinhauser

1550

EARTH
30-second
ANNCR (VO): What's the power that makes the world go round? Well, when things start to run down on this planet, there's simply no better way to start them up again than by reaching for a Rayovac battery. So powerful. So dependable. And Rayovac created the Smart Pack so you'll never run out. The Smart Pack from Rayovac. We give you the power.

1551

MASERATI/COP
30-second
ANNCR VO: The new frontwheel drive Hyundai Excel was designed by the same man who designed this Maserati.
But they are a little different.
The Excel has room for 3 more passengers.
It's more economical,
and it costs about $40,000 less.
It's only $4995.
Of course the Hyundai Excel doesn't go
quite as fast as the Maserati, but
in the long run,
that may save you even more money.
Hyundai.
Cars that make sense.

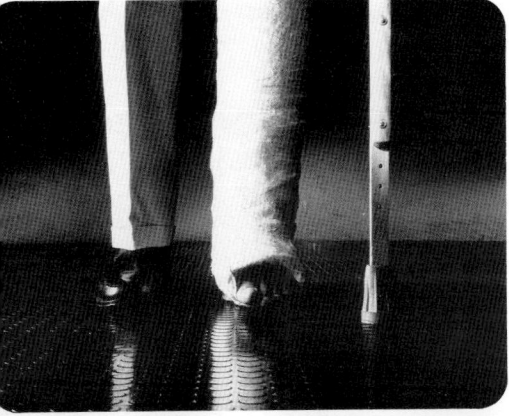

1552
ART DIRECTOR
Tom Lichtenheld
WRITER
Rod Kilpatrick
CLIENT
American Medcenters
EDITOR
Steve Shepherd, Wilson-Griak
DIRECTOR
Mark Story
AGENCY
Fallon McElligott, Minneapolis, MN
PRODUCER
Char Loving
PRODUCTION COMPANY
Story Piccolo Guliner
MUSIC
Tom Lescher, City-Post
V.O.
Fred Gwynne

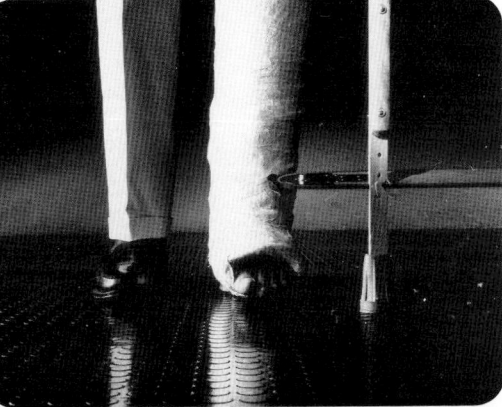

1553
ART DIRECTOR
Larry Sommerville
WRITER
Janine Klayman
CLIENT
McDonald's
DIRECTOR
Don Guy
AGENCY
Leo Burnett, Chicago, IL
PRODUCER
Jerry Chodera
PRODUCTION COMPANY
Dennis, Guy & Hirsch
CREATIVE DIRECTOR
Bob Taylor

1552

CRUTCH
30-second
ANNCR VO: When you join MedCenters Health Plan, practically all your
health-care costs are covered 100%.
While regular health insurance cuts you off at 80%.
(SAW ENTERS, CUTS OFF CRUTCH; MAN TIPS OVER.)
Which plan would you rather lean on?
MedCenters. Where everything's taken care of.

1553

WELCOME HOME CC
30-second
(MUSIC)
ANNCR: When those that are kept
apart . . . finally come together . . .
it's not just good . . . it's fantastic.
McDonald's New McDLT.

1554

ART DIRECTOR
David Edelstein, Nancy Edelstein,
Lanny French
WRITER
Jeremy Wolff
CLIENT
Generra Sportswear
EDITOR
Michael Krupnick
DIRECTOR
Peter Heath
DIRECTOR OF PHOTOGRAPHY
Peter Heath
AGENCY
Terry Thompson, Edelstein Assoc.,
Seattle, WA
PRODUCTION COMPANY
Robin Benson, N. Lee Lacy

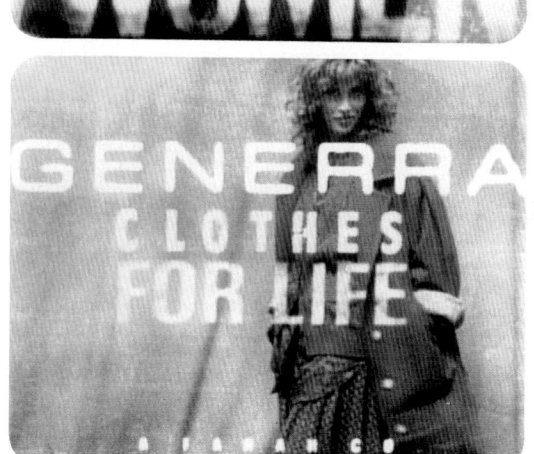

1555

ART DIRECTOR
Rich Martel
WRITER
Al Merrin
CLIENT
Pepsi-Cola Company/Pepsi Free
EDITOR
David Dee, Eventime
DIRECTOR
Steve Horn
AGENCY
BBDO, New York, NY
PRODUCER
Barbara Mullins
PRODUCTION COMPANY
Steve Horn Productions

1554

PRETEND
30-second
KEVIN: Okay, let's just say I'm standing right here, okay?
I turn around, I walk right up, and I confront her.
And she says Yes, a white lie.
She says, A white lie goes better with what I have on.
AMANDA: When he says I do it on purpose, I say I don't.
When he says I do it unconsciously I say, I'm not doing it at all.
I guess I lead him on, but it's not my fault.
I wouldn't do it if he didn't follow.

1555

FISHING
30-second
SFX: FISHING LINE BEING PULLED.
MAN: Honey!
MAN: Honey!
SFX: SPLASH.
SFX: UNDERWATER SOUNDS.
SFX: SPEED BOAT APPROACHING.
MAN: Whaaaa!
MAN: Ah, let go!
VO: To those whose lives are stimulating enough, we offer
the caffeine free choice of a new generation . . .
SFX: SPLASH
Pepsi Free,
made with absolutely no caffeine.
Just great Pepsi taste.
Caffeine free Pepsi Free . . .
SFX: FISHING LINE BEING PULLED.
because life . . .
MAN & WOMAN: Whaaaa!!
VO: is stimulating enough. In regular and diet.
SUPER: The caffeine free choice of a new generation.

1556
ART DIRECTOR
Doug Patterson
WRITER
Steve Kessler, Roseanne Barr
CLIENT
Pizza Hut, Inc.
DIRECTOR
David Steinberg
AGENCY
Chiat/Day, Los Angeles, CA
PRODUCER
Vicki Blucher
PRODUCTION COMPANY
Larkin Prod.

1557
ART DIRECTOR
Jim Doyle
DESIGNER
Jim Doyle
ANIMATOR/ARTIST
Kurtz and Friends
WRITER
Bill Brooke
CLIENT
Toyota Motor Sales, U.S.A., Inc.
EDITOR
Steve McCoy, Sim Sadler
DIRECTOR
Bill Butler
DIRECTOR OF PHOTOGRAPHY
Bill Butler
AGENCY
Sheldon Levy, DFS Dorland S.
Calif., Torrance, CA
PRODUCTION COMPANY
Chris Petersen, Brian Donnelly,
Petersen Communications
CREATIVE DIRECTOR
John Mead, Kevin Begos

1556
SALAD BAR
30-second
(MUSIC UNDER THROUGHOUT)
BARR: So my husband says to me, "Roseanne you've been workin' real hard. How 'bout if we take the kids out for pan pizza and you can eat at the salad bar?" So I said, "Well what a great idea honey. While you and the kids are eatin' a hot, steamy, cheesy pizza, I can be off in the corner grazing on a delightful array of sprouts and garbanzo beans. Get real."

1557
PERFORMANCE
30-second
MUSIC: (EFFECT)
ANNCR: You've shaped it in your mind: total performance. (EFFECT). Now the all-new Toyota Supra brings it alive. (EFFECT). Supra power: created by a three-liter 24-valve, 200-horsepower engine. Supra suspension: racing-type double wishbone fully independent. Supra cockpit: where you perform. (EFFECT). The new Toyota Supra. (EFFECT). Performance without compromise. Now, the Supra Dynasty begins. "Who could ask for anything more!"

1558

ART DIRECTOR
Maryanne Fisher
WRITER
Chris Laubach
CLIENT
Dr Pepper Company — Diet
EDITOR
Clay Warnick
DIRECTOR
Patrick Russell
DIRECTOR OF PHOTOGRAPHY
Andy Dittenfass
AGENCY
Young & Rubicam, New York, NY
PRODUCER
Roseanne Horn
PRODUCTION COMPANY
Rick Levine Production
TYPE DIRECTOR
Dick Mullen

1559

ART DIRECTOR
Gene Mandarino
WRITER
Gene Mandarino
CLIENT
McDonald's
DIRECTOR
Steve Horn
AGENCY
Dave Musial, Leo Burnett, Chicago,
IL
PRODUCTION COMPANY
Linda Horn, Steve Horn Prod.
CREATIVE DIRECTOR
Cheryl Berman

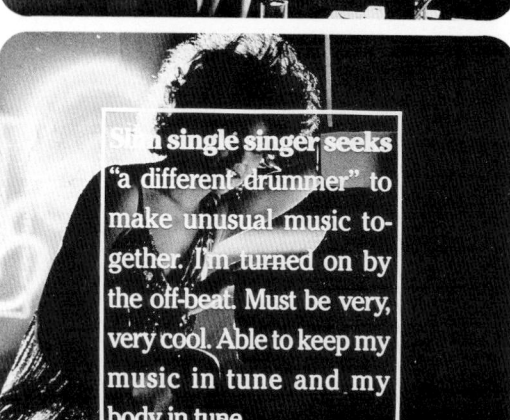

1558

SLIM SINGLE SINGER
30-second
(MUSIC UNDER)
(MUSIC)
WOMAN (VO): Slim single singer seeks "a different drummer" to make
unusual music together. I'm turned on by the off-beat. Must be very, very
cool. Able to keep my music in tune and my body in tune.
MALE SINGER: Meet the off-beat, very cool new taste of Diet Dr Pepper.
Throw your diet a curve. Diet Dr Pepper.

1559

SILENT PERSUASION
30-second
(MUSIC)
GUY: Surf's up, Lisa.
(MUSIC)
GAL: C'mon you know it's exam time.
GUY: Can't you just smell the sea air?
GAL: Cut it out.
GUY: We could stop on the way for a
Big Mac,
fries,
and an icy Coke.
GAL: I'll get my bike.
SING: It's a good time
for the great taste
of McDonald's
GAL: Tommy, you really have a way with words.

1560
ART DIRECTOR
Melinda Mettler
WRITER
Victor Levin
CLIENT
General Foods/Jell-O Instant
Pudding
DIRECTOR
Steve Horn
DIRECTOR OF PHOTOGRAPHY
Steve Horn
AGENCY
Texas East, Young & Rubicam, New
York, NY
PRODUCTION COMPANY
Steve Horn Production

1561
ART DIRECTOR
Rick Boyko, Doug Patterson
WRITER
Bill Hamilton, Ed Cole, Pat Morita
CLIENT
Pizza Hut, Inc.
EDITOR
Gayle Grant
DIRECTOR
Norman Seeff
AGENCY
Chiat/Day, Los Angeles, CA
PRODUCER
Elaine Hinton
PRODUCTION COMPANY
Richard Marlis Prod.

1560

HIGH NOON
30-second
COSBY: Frank Doyle is coming on the noontime train.
I need deputies fast.
Can't offer you much,
Just my thanks, and a tin star.
KID: That ain't gonna do it marshall.
COSBY: Okay. How'about if I throw in some smooth, creamy Jell-O Instant
Pudding.
KID 2: Can you have it ready in five minutes?
(SNAPS FINGERS)
ANNCR: Jell-O Instant Pudding regular and sugar-free. Moms love it cause
it's made with milk.
Kids just love it.
KID: I always wanted to be a lawman.

1561

CHOPSTICKS
30-second
MUSIC: UNDER THROUGHOUT.
PAT MORITA: I'm eating pizza . . .
eh eh . . .
um . . . ah . . . um . . . um . . . ah . . .
This is no good, you can't eat
pizza with chopsticks . . .
Ah-ha . . .

1562

ART DIRECTOR
Richard Mahan
WRITER
Phil Guthrie
CLIENT
Miller Brewing Company — Meister
Brau
AGENCY
Backer & Spielvogel, New York, NY
PRODUCER
Michael Berkman

1563

ART DIRECTOR
Rich Martel
WRITER
Al Merrin
CLIENT
Pepsi-Cola Company/Pepsi Free
EDITOR
David Dee, Eventime
DIRECTOR
Steve Horn
AGENCY
BBDO, New York, NY
PRODUCER
Barbara Mullins
PRODUCTION COMPANY
Steve Horn Productions

1562

BROKERAGE HOUSE
30-second
CHAIRMAN: As some of you may know, this has not been a bad year for
the firm financially. It has been a disaster!
. . . That means no more limos . . . no more wining and dining of
clients . . . no more perks!
. . . In short, the only luxury we can still afford is this . . .
. . . Meister Brau.
ANNCR VO: You don't have to be rich to enjoy a beer as rich and smooth
as Meister Brau. It only tastes expensive.
OFFICER: Oh, don't be a fool Wickham. Come on down from there. Have
a Meister Brau.

1563

PIANO
30-second
SFX: PIANO KEYS BANGING.
MAN: Easy! Easy!
WOMAN: Wooahh!
SFX: PIANO MUSIC THROUGHOUT
SFX: DING, DING, DING.
CAR HORNS.
WOMAN: Aaaahh!!
VO: To those whose lives
are stimulating enough, we offer
SFX: CRASHES.
the caffeine free choice of a new generation . . .
Pepsi Free, made with absolutely no caffeine. Just great Pepsi taste.
Caffeine free Pepsi Free . . .
because life . . .
is stimulating enough. In regular and diet.
SUPER: The caffeine free choice of a new generation.

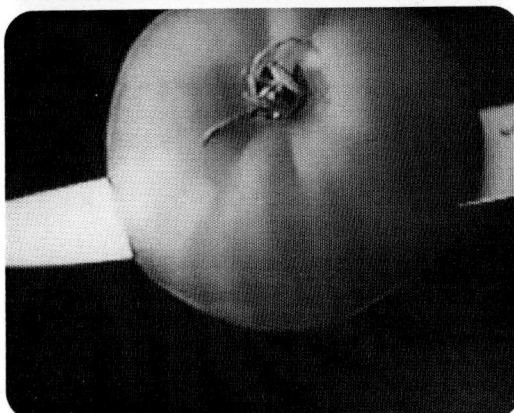

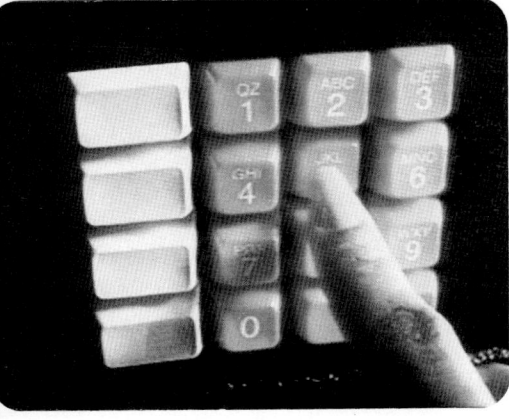

1564
ART DIRECTOR
Shelley Doppelt
WRITER
Susan Dowd
CLIENT
Mellon Bank/CashStream
EDITOR
Morris Albenda
DIRECTOR
Bruce Nadel
AGENCY
Gordon Kolvenbach, Brouillard
Comm., New York, NY
PRODUCTION COMPANY
Bob Ramos, Associates and Nadel
PROPS
H. Aoki Studio

1565
ART DIRECTOR
Hillary Tannenbaum
WRITER
Molly Clevenger
CLIENT
Wiltshire Knives
EDITOR
Jay Gold
DIRECTOR
Bill Marshall
DIRECTOR OF PHOTOGRAPHY
Ian Holmes
AGENCY
Karen Spector, DMB&B, New York,
NY
PRODUCTION COMPANY
David Sussan, Sussan/Santandrea
MUSIC
David Dundas

564

INGERS
0-second
NNCR VO: Fingers everywhere are in training.
imbering up for a race that'll challenge even the nimblest!
ashStream's "Finest Hour" Sweepstakes.
rand prize—one hour at a CashStream machine where you punch out
p to twenty-five thousand dollars!
very deposit or withdrawal's an entry.
nd a chance for *instant* cash.
's one hundred thousand dollars in all.
o *run* for a CashStream card.
nd start training for CashStream's "Finest Hour" Sweepstakes.
he quicker you are, the richer you get.

1565

TOMATO TOO/FP
30-second
SFX: MUSIC THROUGHOUT.
AVO: You're seeing what makes one knife different from any other. The
patented spring loaded tungsten carbide sharpening heads inside the case
of the Wiltshire staysharp knife. Just put it in or take it out and the
Wiltshire stays as sharp as the day you bought it. A very useful tool
to have around the kitchen.
Wiltshire. The sharp knife that stays that way.

1566

ART DIRECTOR
Lauren Deane, Steve Ohler
WRITER
Marvin Waldman
CLIENT
New York Telephone — Residence
Usage
EDITOR
C. Franklin
DIRECTOR
Henry Holtzman
AGENCY
Young & Rubicam, New York, NY
PRODUCER
Brendan O'Malley
PRODUCTION COMPANY
N. Lee Lacy

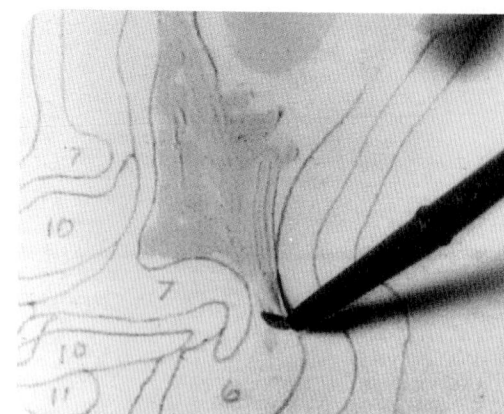
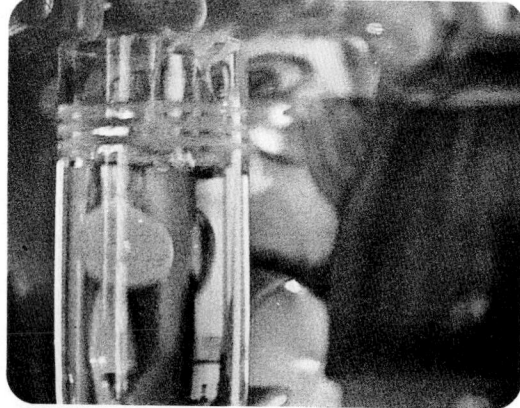

1567

ART DIRECTOR
Bill Foster
WRITER
Bert Kemp
CLIENT
Fred Alger Management
DIRECTOR
Michael Schron
AGENCY
Cynthia Fleury, FCB Leber Katz,
New York, NY
PRODUCTION COMPANY
Carol Breckenridge, Griner Cuesta

1566

THE THANK YOU CALL
30-second
ANNCR VO: New York Telephone presents the thank you call.
WOMAN: Lauren, thanks again for dinner. Nice to know my new
daughter-in-law can cook . . .
ANNCR VO: Return the favor with a call.
WOMAN: Good? It was . . . indescribable!
ANNCR VO: A call that's welcome with New York Telephone's low Regional
Calling Area Rates.
WOMAN: Next week? Again? Could I get back to you on that?
ANNCR VO: So call and say thank you, please.
SINGERS: . . . I can't live without you . . .

1567

MONA LISA
30-second
ANNCR (VO): Investing by the numbers
is a little like painting by the numbers . . .
everybody else's research . . .
produces everybody else's results.
And that's less than inspired . . . that's ordinary!
At Fred Alger, we create our own research . . .
for our own clients.
Ten thousand dollars invested with Fred Alger
in 1965 . . . would be worth nearly six hundred
eighty thousand dollars today.
That's more than inspired . . . that's genius.
A genius for managing money . . . Fred Alger
Management, Inc.

1568
ART DIRECTOR
Larry Sommerville
WRITER
Janine Klayman
CLIENT
McDonald's
DIRECTOR
Don Guy
AGENCY
Leo Burnett, Chicago, IL
PRODUCER
Jerry Chodera
PRODUCTION COMPANY
Dennis, Guy & Hirsch
CREATIVE DIRECTOR
Bob Taylor

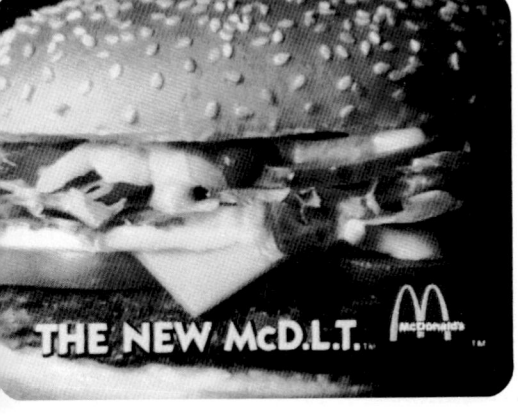

1569
ART DIRECTOR
Jeff France
WRITER
Bruce Mansfield
CLIENT
WLTY/FM
EDITOR
Pat Pranica
DIRECTOR
Bill Randall
AGENCY
Lawler Ballard, Norfolk, VA
PRODUCER
Bruce Mansfield, Jeff France
PRODUCTION COMPANY
AFI

1568

SHALL WE DANCE REV. CC
30-second
(MUSIC)
ANNCR: When those that are kept apart . . . finally come together . . . it's
not just good . . . it's fantastic.
McDonald's New McDLT.

1569

BOSS
30-second
ANNCR: Some radio stations only listen to national sales charts but at Y96
we listen to you.
Y96 does local surveys to find out exactly what you want to hear.
WLTY/FM. We Listen To You.

1570

ART DIRECTOR
Dennis H. Plansker
WRITER
Patrick G. O'Leary
CLIENT
Chevrolet Motor Division
EDITOR
Roger Harrison
DIRECTOR
Peter Smillie
BROADCAST DIRECTOR
Dennis H. Plansker
AGENCY
Campbell-Ewald Company, Warren, MI
PRODUCER
Kenneth J. Domanski
PRODUCTION COMPANY
Berkofsky, Smillie & Barrett
CREATIVE DIRECTOR
Sean Kevin Fitzpatrick
MUSIC
Denise Abood Sidlow; Joey Levine, Crushing Enterprises

1571

ART DIRECTOR
Gary Wolfson
WRITER
John De Cerchio
CLIENT
Sohio
DIRECTOR
Dennis Gelbaum
AGENCY
W.B. Donor, Southfield, MI
PRODUCER
Bob Rashid
PRODUCTION COMPANY
Coast Productions

1570

BOY AND CAR VERSION 2
30-second
AUDIO EFFECTS: HEARTBEAT THROUGHOUT UNDER MUSIC.
SINGERS: Listen to the heartbeat.
SINGERS: Listen to
the heartbeat
ohh, ohh
of America.
ANNCR (VO): If you have a dream . . .
. . . put yourself in Today's Chevrolet Corvette . . .
. . . and listen to *your* heartbeat.
MUSIC/SFX UNDER: LOUD REVERBERATING HEARTBEAT.
SINGERS: The heartbeat of America.
(Chevrolet)
That's today's Chevrolet.
SFX: (HEARTBEAT FADES).

1571

DEMONSTRATION
30-second
MAN: Pretend my finger is your car's fuel-injector. It sprays gas into your cylinder . . .
SFX: HISS
MAN: . . . And with your piston, it creates this explosion.
SFX: 2 LOUD BANGS
MAN: But fuel-injectors can clog, robbing your car's performance.
SFX: 2 WEAK SPUTTERS
MAN: That's why you need New Gulf Super, specially formulated to keep fuel injectors clean . . . for better performance.
SFX: LOUD BANGS CONTINUE UNDER VO.
VO: New Gulf Super. The gasoline for today's cars.
SFX: STEAM ESCAPING
MAN: (SIGH OF RELIEF) Ahhhhh!

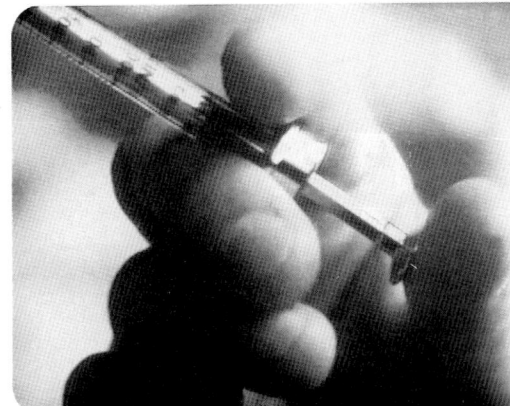

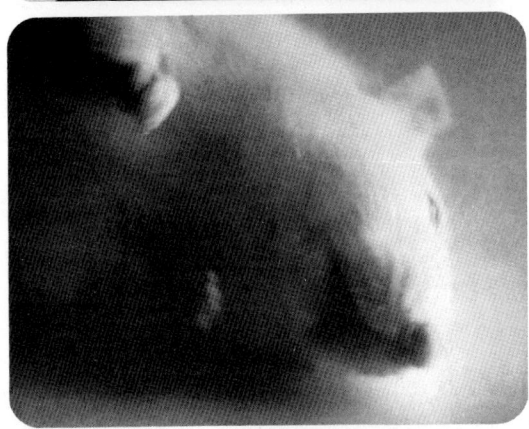

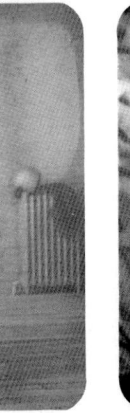

NOTHING'S MORE IMPORTANT THAN YOUR HEALTH

1572
ART DIRECTOR
Susan Hoffman
WRITER
Jim Riswold
CLIENT
Honda Scooters
DIRECTOR
Graham Henman, Michael Karbelnikoff
AGENCY
Wieden & Kennedy, Portland, OR
PRODUCER
Bill Davenport
PRODUCTION COMPANY
HKM Productions

1573
ART DIRECTOR
Marisa Acocella
WRITER
Michael Scardino, Leslie Mechanic
CLIENT
Eckerd Drugs, Ken Banks
EDITOR
Mel Cohen, DJM
DIRECTOR
David Ashwell
AGENCY
Tricia Caruso, JWT, New York, NY
PRODUCTION COMPANY
David Ashwell, David Ashwell
CREATIVE DIRECTOR
Charles Genneralli

1572

MCMAHON
30-second
MCCMAHON: Outrageousness?
MCMAHON: Outrageousness?
MCMAHON: Outrageousness?
(CRAZY MUSIC KICKS IN)
MCMAHON: Outrageousness? It's nothin' more than a way to wake people up. Wake 'em up!
MCMAHON: Especially yourself.
MCMAHON: Wasn't that fun?

1573

LESSON
30-second
SUPER: BASED ON A TRUE STORY.
VO: In a high school gymnasium, a pharmacist from Eckerd Drugs took the time and trouble to teach an invaluable lesson, and showed 200 teenaged kids what it's really like to get high on drugs.
To an Eckerd pharmacist, nothing's more important than your health.

1574

ART DIRECTOR
Chuck Anderson
WRITER
Chuck Anderson, Bob Feinberg,
Harry Ralston
CLIENT
Coleco Industries
EDITOR
Stu Eisenberg
DIRECTOR
Bob Bean
AGENCY
Liza Leeds, Bozell, Jacobs, Kenyon &
Eckhardt, Inc., New York, NY
PRODUCTION COMPANY
Michael Salzer, Bean-Kahn Int'l.

1575

ART DIRECTOR
Chris Lezotte
WRITER
Chris Lezotte, John Richards
CLIENT
Sinai Hospital
AGENCY
W.B. Donor, Southfield, MI
PRODUCER
Kurt Kulas

1574

IT'S AN ALIEN
30-second
ANNCR (VO): It's an alien!
ALF: No kiddin'? Where?
ANNCR (VO): It's living in America.
ALF: I like what they've done with the place.
ANNCR (VO): It loves cats.
ALF: Can't get enough of 'em!
(SFX: CAT MEOWS)
ANNCR (VO): It's ALF!
(MUSIC UNDER)
GIRL #1: He's debonair and yet fuzzy.
GIRL #2: My parents just don't understand our relationship.
BOY: I mean, this whole cat thing's been blown all out of proportion.
(SFX: MEOW)
BOY: ALF!
(MUSIC ENDS)
ANNCR (VO): Alf. Alien life form. New from Coleco.

1575

PLAY BALL
30-second
VO: Although never quite a star, Tom loves to play ball. But for a time he
thought he'd never play again. When he discovered his heart was failing.
Fortunately, Tom's doctor sent him to Sinai Hospital, one of the world's
leading heart centers. Sinai's cardiac team intervened with testing, therapy
and individualized treatment. So Tom can get out there and play ball.
(PLOP)
As well as he always could.
This is Sinai. Using all we know to make you well.

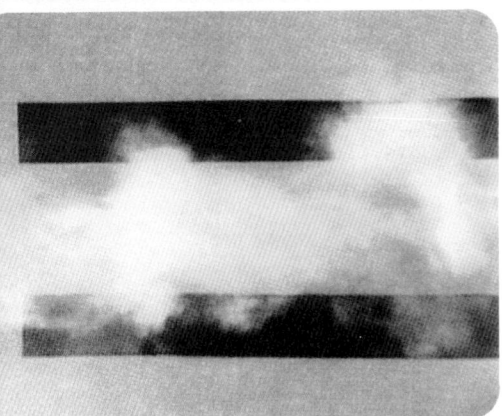

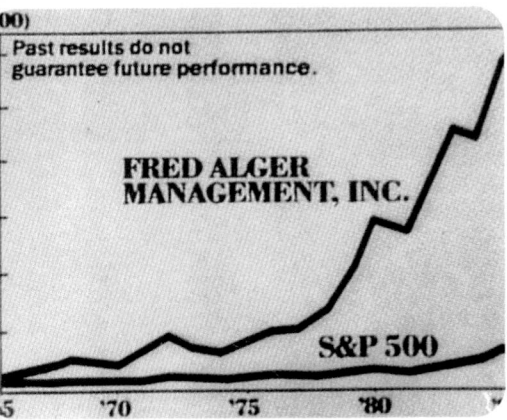

1576
ART DIRECTOR
Bill Foster
WRITER
Ted Littleford
CLIENT
Fred Alger Management
DIRECTOR
Michael Schron
AGENCY
Cynthia Fleury, FCB Leber Katz,
New York, NY
PRODUCTION COMPANY
Carol Breckenridge, Griner-Cuesta

1577
ART DIRECTOR
Brian Gregg
WRITER
John Montgomery
CLIENT
McDonald's
EDITOR
David Szabo
DIRECTOR
Peter Moss
AGENCY
David Geeting, Leo Burnett,
Chicago, IL
PRODUCTION COMPANY
Barbara Schenk, Partners
CREATIVE DIRECTOR
Rob Nolan

576

RAGSTER
-second
FX: MOTOR RUNNING)
FX: MOTOR RUNNING)
FX: MOTOR REVVING)
ILENCE)
NCR (VO): In the high performance world of investing . . .
FX: CAR SCREECHING OFF)
ILENCE)
. what does it take
turn ten thousand dollars
o nearly six hundred eighty thousand
llars in 21 years . . .
d out-perform the Standard & Poor's
0 more than ten to one?
genius for managing money. Fred Alger
anagement, Inc.

1577

DOODLIN'
30-second
(MUSIC: TENSE.)
SFX: TIC . . . TIC . . . TIC . . .
KID VO: Almost twelve . . .
(TEACHER LECTURING: Which is why you'll find Geometry a
fascinating . . .).
KID VO: I'm starved . . .
(MUSIC: LIVELY AS . . .)
(ALSO: Miscellaneous mumbles from character.)
(MUSIC: STOPS OR "COOLS" AS TEACHER TALKS).
TEACHER: Brian . . . Brian . . .
SONG: It's a good time . . .
TEACHER: Brian? Would you care to share with the rest of the class?
SONG: For the great taste of McDonald's.

1578

ART DIRECTOR
Chuck Anderson
WRITER
Bob Feinberg
CLIENT
Coleco Industries
DIRECTOR
Alex Weill
AGENCY
Bozell, Jacobs, Kenyon & Eckhardt,
Inc., New York, NY
PRODUCER
Liza Leeds

1579

ART DIRECTOR
Lisa Scott
WRITER
Shawne Cooper
CLIENT
WNBC-TV
EDITOR
Lenny Friedman
DIRECTOR
Bob Pasqualina
AGENCY
Neal Bergman, LGFE, New York, NY
PRODUCTION COMPANY
Abby Margolis, Myers Films

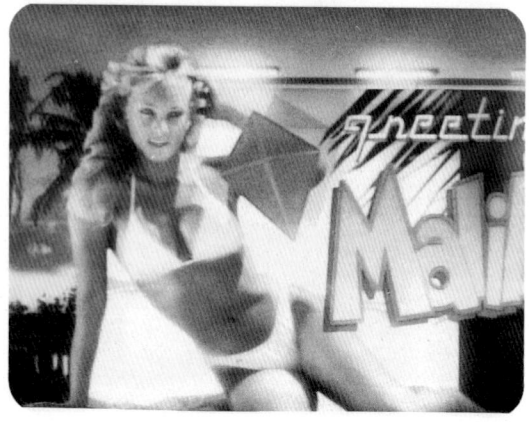

1578

THE WORLD ACCORDING TO UBI
30-second
MUSIC BEGINS (I SPY)
VO: In the game The World According To UBI the object is to win the ruby
UBI. But where on earth will the clue be?
MUSIC CHANGES (HAIL BRITTIANA)
Maybe where Big Ben's bong be?
MUSIC ENDS
SFX: UBI. UBI. DESERT WINDS
VO: Or will the clue be where very few be.
SFX: UBI. MUSIC BEGINS (1812 OVERTURE)
VO: It might be where Waterloo be.
SFX: SACRE BLEU UBI. MUSIC ENDS
VO: Or even where a zoo be.
SFX: UBI, UBI.
VO: Or where the Cambridge racing crew be?
VO: Or will the clue be where Malibu be?
SFX: HI, UBI.
MUSIC BEGINS
VO: Discover the World According To UBI. The addictive new game from
those very weird people who created the Trivial Pursuit game. UBI's ready,
will you be?
MUSIC OUT
SFX: UBI!

1579

DRUG TESTING
30-second
ANNCR: These days to get a job . . .
you have to be bright, . . .
attractive, . . .
educated, articulate, . . .
hard working, ambitious . . .
and, do-you-know-what in a cup.
Will it be your turn next
to take a drug test?
Watch a special report by
David Diaz: The Drug Testing
Dilemma. This week at 5 and 6
on Channel 4.

1580
ART DIRECTOR
Charles McQuilkin
WRITER
Julie Burmeister
CLIENT
Citizens & Southern Banks
EDITOR
Michael Charles
DIRECTOR
Michael Moir
DIRECTOR OF PHOTOGRAPHY
Greg Califano
AGENCY
Julie Burmeister, Ogilvy & Mather,
Atlanta, GA
PRODUCER
Barbara Baumann
MUSIC
Doppler Studios

1581
ART DIRECTOR
Nik Ives
WRITER
Frederick Barthelme, Chuck Griffith
CLIENT
The New Yorker Magazine
EDITOR
Lenny Friedman
DIRECTOR
Bob Giraldi
AGENCY
Ann O'Keefe, LGFE, New York, NY
PRODUCTION COMPANY
Patty Greaney, GASP

80

ONEY, THAT'S WHAT I WANT
-second
USIC; BEATLES "MONEY"
NGER: The best things in life are free
NGER: But you can keep 'em for the birds and bees
NGER: Now give me money . . .
NGER: That's what I want
INGER: That's what I want
NGER: That's what I want
NGER: That's what I want
NGER: That's what I want
NNCR: For whatever you want,
NNCR: We've got the money you need.
NNCR: Find out about a C&S loan today.
INGER: Just give me money, that's whaat I want . . .
NGER: Ahhh!
USIC OUT

1581

DRIVER
30-second
NARRATOR: I sat in the dark and imagined flirting with a pretty Latin girl
in a short, tight, shiny dress: her skin perfect and brown, on a glittering
street on a hot summer night, with the smell of gasoline in the air. And
me, slouched behind the wheel, ready to pop the front end for a smile.
ANNCR VO: From "Driver" by Frederick Barthelme in a recent issue of The
New Yorker, Yes, The New Yorker.

1582

ART DIRECTOR
Brian Harrod
WRITER
Ian Mirlin
CLIENT
Wm. Neilson Ltd.
EDITOR
Jim Munro
DIRECTOR
Graham Hunt
DIRECTOR OF PHOTOGRAPHY
Nick Allen-Woolfe
AGENCY
Angela Carroll, Miller Myers Bruce,
Toronto, Canada
PRODUCER
Laurie Sawlor

1583

ART DIRECTOR
C. Bryant Loftis, Joe Sedelmaier
WRITER
Douglas Hardee, Joe Sedelmaier
CLIENT
James C. Craig, Independent Life
EDITOR
Peggy DeLay
DIRECTOR
Joe Sedelmaier
AGENCY
Douglas Hardee, West & Company,
Jacksonville, FL
PRODUCTION COMPANY
Marsie Wallach, Sedelmaier Film
ACCOUNT SPVSR.
Benjamin B. West

1582

HOT (REVISED)
30-second
MUSIC UNDER THROUGHOUT
VO: You want to know how hot it was?
It was so hot, even the dogs were wearing shoes.
The flowers had moved into the shade.
The birds were wearing hats.
Well, my watch didn't know what time it was.
But man, I was hungry.
Neilson now makes ice cream bars for days like this. Five cold snacks to choose from. So I made my choice.
Cooled my hunger.
And stepped back onto the streets of fire.

1583

DEPARTMENT STORE INSURANCE
30-second
MUSIC
FIRST MAN: Pardon me. I understand you sell life insurance.
CLERK: We certainly do.
SECOND MAN: Where's hardware?
CLERK: On the second floor . . .
ANNCR (VO): These days it seems like everyone's trying to sell life insurance.
CLERK: . . . at the north end of the store. You can take either the escalator or the elevator . . . Fill out the application.
THIRD MAN: Young man, I'm looking for socks.
CLERK: Socks are on fourth . . . Listing any childhood diseases or communicable diseases.
FIRST MAN: Communal diseases?
THIRD MAN: On fourth.
CLERK: Communicable diseases. On fourth.
FOURTH MAN: What?
WOMAN: Communiable diseases on fourth.
FOURTH MAN: Communicable diseases on fourth!
CROWD: Communicable diseases on fourth.
ANNCR (VO): At Independent Life, insurance is all we sell. With personal service from a full-time insurance professional, your Independent Life Agent.

1584
ART DIRECTOR
Nelsena Burt
WRITER
Barry Hoffman
CLIENT
Fuji
EDITOR
Ken Coleman
DIRECTOR
Jim Johnston
AGENCY
LGFE, New York, NY
PRODUCER
Jack Harrower
PRODUCTION COMPANY
Jim Johnston Films
PERFORMER
Maurice La Marche

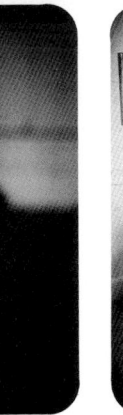

1585
ART DIRECTOR
Sal DeVito
WRITER
Mike Drazen
CLIENT
Peugeot Motors of America, Inc.
EDITOR
Dennis Hayes
DIRECTOR
Henry Sandbank
AGENCY
HCM, New York, NY
PRODUCER
Charlie Curran

1584

BAD GUYS
30-second
ANNCR VO: Fuji video tape presents the 'Bad Guys.'
COMEDIAN: Everyone knows a bad guy on tv they really like.
You come to me on my father's wedding day.
Ah, hee, hee, hee . . .
Riddle me this, Cape Crusader.
You, dirty rat.
Natasha, we must get moose and squirrel.
Rick, don't let them take me, Rick.
Egor, I need you.
It's curtains for you, see . . . nawhhh . . .
Go ahead, make my day.
ANNCR VO: Replay the bad guys on Fuji video tape. And put the good stuff on the good stuff.

1585

BEDROOM WINDOW
30-second
VO: If you think this is where the French perform best,
SFX: SHATTERING GLASS
VO: we suggest you test drive the 6-cylinder Peugeot 505.

1586
ART DIRECTOR
Dan Krippahne
WRITER
Sandy Mairs
CLIENT
IBM PC Convertible
EDITOR
Allen Rozek
DIRECTOR
Stu Hagman
AGENCY
LGFE, New York, NY
PRODUCER
Bob Warner
PRODUCTION COMPANY
HISK Productions
MUSIC
David Horowitz
PERFORMER
Billy Scudder

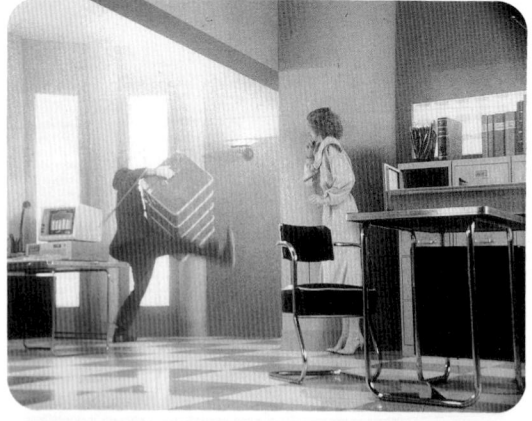

1587
ART DIRECTOR
Dextor Fedor, Greg Clancey
ANIMATOR/ARTIST
Will Vinton
WRITER
Seth Werner
CLIENT
California Raisin Advisory Board
AGENCY
Flo Babbitt, Robert Gondell, FCB,
San Francisco, CA
PRODUCER
Will Vinton
MUSIC
Mark & Jeff's Jingle Company

1586

THE CONVERTIBLE
30-second
VO: Taking your business on the road can be a cumbersome task . . . and
productivity can easily . . . fall off.
Presenting the IBM PC Convertible. A powerful personal computer that
easily converts to a full-function portable . . .
one you can use in a train . . . a plane . . . a car . . . or a meeting. And
be as productive on the road as you are at the office.
The IBM PC Convertible.
One computer . . . for people who really need two.

1587

LATE SHOW
30-second
(MUSIC UP)
(SFX: FINGER SNAPS)
SINGERS: Ooo, Ooo I heard it through the grapevine.
Raised in the California sunshine.
ANNCR VO: California Raisins from the California vineyards.
SINGERS: Don't ya know I heard it through the grapevine.
ANNCR VO: Sounds grape, doesn't it?
(MUSIC OUT)

1588

ART DIRECTOR
Mark Haumersen
WRITER
John Jarvis
CLIENT
Marigold Foods
EDITOR
Steve Shepherd
DIRECTOR
Steve Griak
DIRECTOR OF PHOTOGRAPHY
John Harvey
AGENCY
RoseMary Januschka, Martin/
Williams, Minneapolis, MN
PRODUCTION COMPANY
Lyle McIntyre, Wilson-Griak

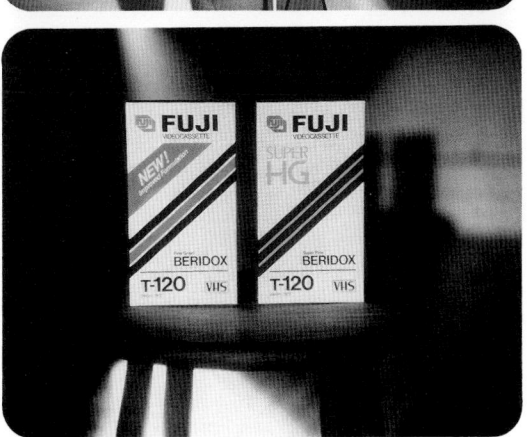

1589

ART DIRECTOR
Nelsena Burt
WRITER
Barry Hoffman
CLIENT
FUJI
EDITOR
Ken Coleman
DIRECTOR
Jim Johnston
AGENCY
LGFE, New York, NY
PRODUCER
Jack Harrower
PRODUCTION COMPANY
Jim Johnston Films
ASSOC. DIRECTOR
Maurice La Marche

1588

GREEN COW
30-second
As you probably know Kemps Ice Cream comes in over 30 delicious
flavors. But did you ever stop to think of where we get 'em all?
Well, Kemps Vanilla Ice Cream comes from one of these—a vanilla cow.
Our Chocolate Ice cream . . . a chocolate cow.
And Kemps Chocolate Chip Ice Cream comes from one of these.
OK! you ask. Where does Kemps Peppermint Bon Bon Ice Cream come
from? Well, uh, where do you think?
ANNCR: Kemps Ice Cream. It's the cows.

1589

TENDER MOMENTS
30-second
ANNCR VO: Fuji video tape presents 'Tender Moments.'
COMEDIAN: Everyone has a favorite love scene on tv.
I will always have Paris.
Ooh, Mindy, ooh wow.
Don't Willie Nell.
I shall protect you.
Oh, Archie.
Gez, Edith, will you stifle there.
Oh, Kermie.
Ah, gee, Piggy, I gotta show to do.
Oh, I'm going to see my sweetie, Olive . . .
Uh guh guh guh guh guh. Wow.
Baby, you're the greatest.
ANNCR VO: Live your favorite love scenes over again on Fuji video tape.
And put the good stuff on the good stuff.

1590

ART DIRECTOR
Wes Hotchkiss
WRITER
Joanne DeMenna
CLIENT
Bell of Pennsylvania
EDITOR
Burke Moody, Seventh Art
DIRECTOR
Norman Griner
DIRECTOR OF PHOTOGRAPHY
Victor Hammer
AGENCY
Lewis Gilman Kynett, Philadelphia, PA
PRODUCER
Peg Finucan
PRODUCTION COMPANY
Griner/Cuesta & Assoc.
CREATIVE DIRECTOR
Jacqueline Lowell

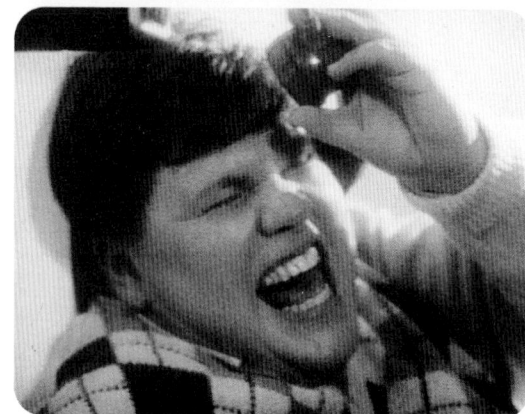

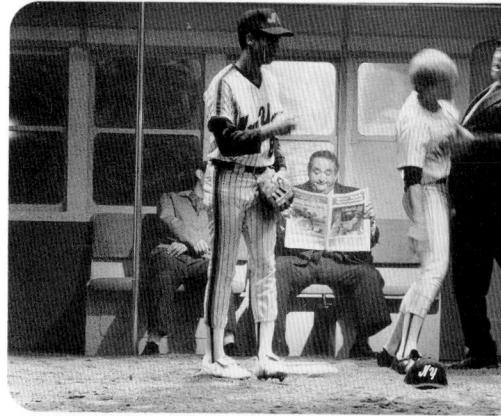

1591

ART DIRECTOR
Cathie Campbell
WRITER
Dana Jones
CLIENT
New York Newsday
EDITOR
Milt Loonan
DIRECTOR
Patrick Pitelli
AGENCY
Hill, Holliday, New York, NY
PRODUCER
Nick Ciarlante
PRODUCTION COMPANY
Pitelli Productions
CREATIVE DIRECTOR
Mal MacDougall

1590

LAUGHTER
30-second
SFX: PEOPLE LAUGHING ON PHONE THROUGHOUT
ANNCR: Whenever you want to share good times, we'll be there.
Bell of Pennsylvania.

1591

SUBWAY/SPORTS NEWS
30-second
ANNCR: New York sports are more colorful in *New York Newsday*.
More colorful baseball, football, horseracing. Plus baseball bonus pages season long.
There's a more colorful New York in *New York Newsday*.

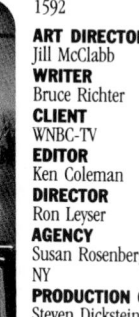

1592
ART DIRECTOR
Jill McClabb
WRITER
Bruce Richter
CLIENT
WNBC-TV
EDITOR
Ken Coleman
DIRECTOR
Ron Leyser
AGENCY
Susan Rosenberg, LGFE, New York, NY
PRODUCTION COMPANY
Steven Dickstein, RHA Productions

1593
ART DIRECTOR
Brian Harrod
WRITER
Ian Mirlin
CLIENT
Canada Packers Inc.
EDITOR
Louise Moritsuga
DIRECTOR
Peter James
DIRECTOR OF PHOTOGRAPHY
Peter James
AGENCY
Angela Carroll, Miller Myers Bruce, Toronto, Canada
PRODUCER
Kate Hunter

1592

MUSIC VIDEOS
30-second
GIRL: (SINGING) Like a virgin, touched for the very first time. Like a vir--ir-gin, when your heart beats next to mine.
ANNCR: Are music videos teaching your kids things you don't want them to know? Watch Chuck Scarborough's special report, "Music Videos: Kids under the Influence." This week at 6 on Channel 4.

1593

BLUES
30-second
SFX: NATURAL SOUNDS OF SHOWER.
SS: Today
doo doo
Hello kitty
What do you say?
Today is going to be uh . . .
be bop a doo dah
Scrubbing all the blues away
Hey- hey
Today is going to be mine
Come rain or come shine
And that's all I've got to say
Okay.
VO: Feel glad all over.
Feel glad all day.
Dial Deodorant Soap.

1594

ART DIRECTOR
George Booth, Nik Ives
ANIMATOR/ARTIST
George Booth
WRITER
Chuck Griffith
CLIENT
The New Yorker Magazine
DIRECTOR
Frank Terry
AGENCY
Ann O'Keefe, LGFE, New York, NY
PRODUCTION COMPANY
Cheryl Abood, Film Fair, Inc.
MUSIC
David Horowitz

1595

ART DIRECTOR
Martine Beudert
WRITER
Anne Conlon
CLIENT
Parfums Stern
EDITOR
Allen Rosek
DIRECTOR
Willie Patterson
AGENCY
LGFE, New York, NY
PRODUCER
Sandy Bachom
PRODUCTION COMPANY
Fairbanks

1594

WOOF
30-second
ANNCR VO: From the drawings of George Booth. From the pages of The New Yorker. Yes, The New Yorker.

1595

RITES OF PASSAGE
30-second
ANNCR (VO): Valentino. Born to reveal the woman you've become. Not just a perfume. A rite of passage.

1596

ART DIRECTOR
Greg Clancey, Claude Jacques
ANIMATOR/ARTIST
Will Vinton
WRITER
Seth Werner, Michael Hutchinson
CLIENT
California Raisin Advisory Board
AGENCY
Flo Babbitt, FCB, San Francisco, CA
PRODUCER
Will Vinton
MUSIC
Mark & Jeff's Jingle Company

1597

ART DIRECTOR
Jill McClabb
WRITER
Bruce Richter
CLIENT
WNBC-TV
EDITOR
Ken Coleman
DIRECTOR
Ron Leyser
AGENCY
Susan Rosenberg, LGFE, New York,
NY
PRODUCTION COMPANY
Steven Dickstein, RHA Productions

1596

LUNCH BOX
30-second
(SFX: LIQUID BEING POURED INTO A CONTAINER).
(MUSIC IN)
(SFX: LUNCH BOX TOP SLAMMING CLOSED.)
(MUSIC OUT)
(SFX: SQUEAKY TOP OF LUNCH BOX OPENING.)
(MUSIC IN)
SOLO RAISIN SINGER: Ooh, ooh, I heard it through the grapevine. . . .
BACK-UP RAISIN SINGERS: Ooh.
SOLO RAISIN SINGER: . . . raised in the California sun . . . shine.
SOLO RAISIN (SPOKEN): California raisins. . . .
. . . from the California vineyards.
SOLO RAISIN SINGER: Don'cha know that I. . . .
ALL RAISIN SINGERS: . . . heard it through the . . .
ALL RAISIN SINGERS VO: . . . grapevine.
THIRD STEELWORKER: Sounds better'n what I got.
(SFX: AUTOMOBILE HORN).

1597

LOVE/HATE
30-second
ANNOUNCER (VO): Watch Love Connection, 4:00 weekdays, where people
get together. Then, at 4:30, watch People's Court, where people get even.
Love Connection and People's Court. Weekdays on Channel 4.

1598

ART DIRECTOR
Michael Vitiello
WRITER
Rich Pels
CLIENT
Subaru of America
EDITOR
David Dee, Eventime
DIRECTOR
Steve Horn, Steve Horn, Inc.
AGENCY
LHS&B, New York, NY
PRODUCER
Bob Nelson

1599

ART DIRECTOR
Tony DeGregorio
WRITER
Rich Pels
CLIENT
Subaru of America
EDITOR
David Dee, Eventime
DIRECTOR
Steve Horn, Steve Horn, Inc.
AGENCY
LHS&B, New York, NY
PRODUCER
Bob Nelson

1598

BANANAS
30-second
ANNCR: A lot of people are disappointed with the traction they're getting from their present car.
Which is why more and more of them are looking into the number one four wheel drive car in America at their Subaru dealer.
SUBARU. INEXPENSIVE. AND BUILT TO STAY THAT WAY.

1599

GETTING THERE
30-second
ANNCR VO: In 1981 the French Ski Team missed an important meet.
The U.S. Team arrived early.
And in '86 the Italians ran into a small problem.
For 10 years, the 4 wheel drive Subaru has helped the U.S. Ski Team get jump on the competition.
Except in '84 when the Swedish women's team broke down.
U.S. SKIER: Howdy, Ma'am.
SUBARU. THE OFFICIAL CAR OF THE U.S. SKI TEAM.

1600
ART DIRECTOR
Ron Sandilands
WRITER
Steve Sandoz
CLIENT
Alaska Airlines
EDITOR
Peggy Delay
DIRECTOR
Joe Sedelmaier
DIRECTOR OF PHOTOGRAPHY
Joe Sedelmaier
AGENCY
Cindy Henderson, Livingston &
Company, Seattle, WA
PRODUCER
Marsie Wallach

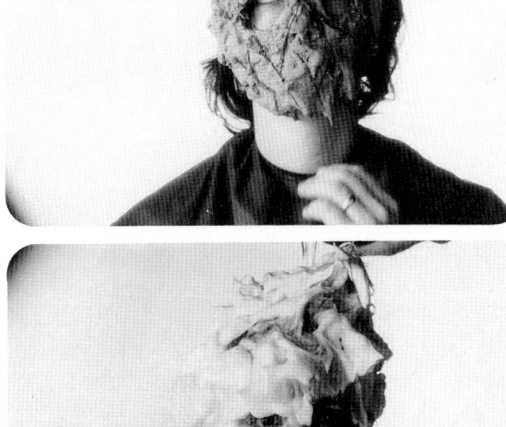

1601
ART DIRECTOR
Bob Tore
WRITER
Eileen Sandler
CLIENT
WNBC-TV
EDITOR
Lenny Friedman
DIRECTOR
Bob Pasqualina
AGENCY
Neal Bergman, LGFE, New York, NY
PRODUCTION COMPANY
Abby Margolis, Myers Films
PERFORMER
Patty Kelly Byer

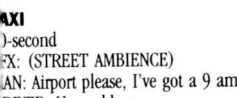

1600

TAXI
30-second
SFX: (STREET AMBIENCE)
MAN: Airport please, I've got a 9 am flight.
DRIVER: No problem.
MAN: Good.
DRIVER: What airline?
MAN: Alaska.
DRIVER: Alaska?
SFX: (TIRE SQUEAL)
DRIVER: First time Alaska?
MAN: Yes it is. But airlines never take off on time.
DRIVER: First time Alaska.
MUSIC: (UP TEMPO MUSIC GOES THROUGHOUT)
VO: When Alaska Airlines says a plane will leave at 9 am, we do our best
to make sure it does. . . .
MAN: I tell you, they never leave on time.
VO: So usually, the only time you'll have to wait for a plane . . .
SFX: (TIRE SCREECH)
VO: . . . Is when you miss one.
MAN: What's the world coming to?

1601

FOUNTAIN OF YOUTH
30-second
(MUSIC) Baby face, you've got the cutest little baby face,
There's not another one to take your place, my little baby face,
My poor heart is jumpin', you sure have started somethin', baby face . . .
ANNCR VO: Last year, we spent over one billion dollars searching for the
fountain of youth.
But, who's getting soaked? Join Betty Furness for her special report,
"The Fountain of Youth", this week at 5 and 6 on Channel 4.

1602

ART DIRECTOR
Clifford Goodenough
WRITER
Steve Sandoz
CLIENT
Skipper's Seafood & Chowder
Houses
DIRECTOR
Norman Seeff
AGENCY
Cindy Henderson, Livingston &
Company, Seattle, WA
PRODUCTION COMPANY
Lynn Pateman, Richard Marlis
Productions

1603

ART DIRECTOR
Donna Weinheim
WRITER
Clifford L. Freeman
CLIENT
Diet Rite Cola
AGENCY
DFS Dorland, New York, NY
PRODUCER
Jill Paperno

1602

GAME WARDEN
30-second
GAME WARDEN: This is a fishing license. It costs around $15.00. With it,
your legal limit is seven fish. If you take more I am obligated to arrest
you. This is a receipt for $4.39 from Skipper's. With it you may take as
much golden fried fish, cole slaw, french fries and chowder as you want.
And there's not a darned thing I can do about it.
ANNCR: The Skipper's all you can eat special. All you can eat any day,
anytime, for just $4.39.
GAME WARDEN: There ought to be a law.

1603

LEE & SON
30-second
SON: Dad, help me get in shape. I feel like I've lost the edge.
LEE: You've lost the edge?
SINGER: Everybody's got to Diet Rite, it doesn't matter who you are, it's
going to be a tough fight. So give yourself the greatest taste, Diet Rite
Cola.
LEE: I bet you didn't know that Diet Rite has no salt.
SON: Technically speaking Dad, it's sodium. I've been avoiding salt myse
for 4 or 5 years now. Furthermore, I like the way Diet Rite tastes . . .
SINGER: Everybody's gotta Diet Rite!

An ordinary hotel room.

A Red Lion Inn room.

1604
ART DIRECTOR
Terry Schneider
WRITER
Greg Eiden
CLIENT
Red Lion Inns
DIRECTOR
Jim Lund
AGENCY
Borders, Perrin & Norrander, Inc.,
Portland, OR
PRODUCTION COMPANY
James Productions
CREATIVE DIRECTOR
Bill Borders

1605
ART DIRECTOR
David Kennedy, Peter Moore
WRITER
Jim Riswold
CLIENT
Nike
AGENCY
Wieden & Kennedy, Portland, OR
PRODUCER
Bill Davenport
PRODUCTION COMPANY
Pytka Productions

1604

SILENCE
30-second
VOICEOVER: Imagine trying to sleep in an ordinary hotel room. Where
you can get to know your neighbors without ever seeing them.
(SFX: TV DRONING ON . . . ADD DOOR OPEN, CLOSE . . . ADD
MUFFLED CONVERSATION . . . ADD CACKLING LAUGHTER.)
Now imagine trying to sleep in a room in a Red Lion Inn.
(SFX: DEAD SILENCE.)
With double-insulated, 10-inch thick walls.
RED LION INNS. You can tell the difference with your eyes closed.
(SFX: GENTLE SNORT SIGH OF SOMEONE FALLING ASLEEP.)

1605

JORDAN ROCKABABY
30-second
(INTRO TYPE MUSIC)
(MUSIC KICKS IN TO UPBEAT NUMBER. ARIA SINGER.)
ANNCR: Air Jordan. It's all in the imagination.

1606

ART DIRECTOR
Lisa Scott
WRITER
Shawne Cooper
CLIENT
WNBC-TV
EDITOR
Lenny Friedman
DIRECTOR
Bob Pasqualina
AGENCY
Neal Bergman, LGFE, New York, NY
PRODUCTION COMPANY
Abby Margolis, Myers Films

 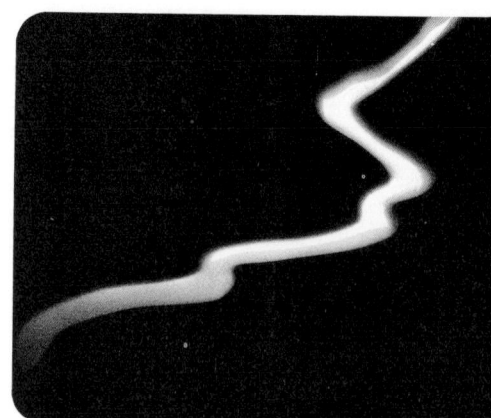

 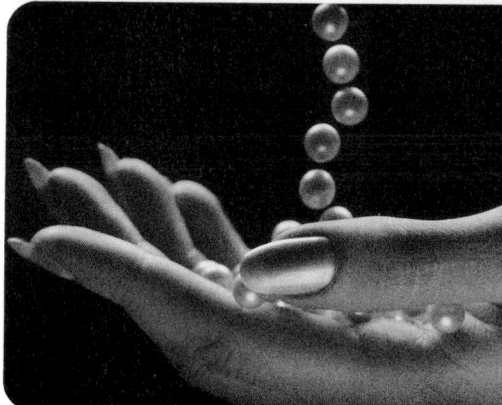

1607

ART DIRECTOR
Jayne Rumolo
WRITER
Jeanne-marie Lonza
CLIENT
Peter Troup, Luminesse Nail Color
EDITOR
Bobby Smalheiser
AGENCY
Carole Gersten, SSC&B Inc., New York, NY
PRODUCTION COMPANY
Ingrid Lacis, Phil Marco Prod.
CREATIVE DIRECTOR
Lynn Giordano

1606

SEXUAL HARASSMENT
30-second
MAN #1: So, you want a promotion? What are you going to do to make it worth my while, Miss Cooper?
SUPER: A SPECIAL REPORT BY CHUCK SCARBOROUGH
MAN #2: I could be good for your career. *Very* good.
SUPER: SEXUAL HARASSMENT ON THE JOB
MAN #3: I'd hate to see you be a secretary all your life, if you know what I mean.
SUPER: THIS WEEK AT 5 AND 6 ON NEWS 4 NEW YORK.
MAN #4: I've had my eye on you for a long time.

1607

RIBBON
30-second
ANNCR (VO): Cover Girl looks at polish in a whole new light. The colors . . . luminous. A finish that catches and reflects light like satin. The shimmer of pearls. The look elegant. The name Luminesse. Luminesse Satin Finish Nailcolor. So new. From Cover Girl.

1608

ART DIRECTOR
Christie Kelly
WRITER
Tom Nelson
CLIENT
General Foods Corporation/Instant
Maxwell House
EDITOR
Billy Williams
DIRECTOR
Patrick Russel
AGENCY
Ogilvy & Mather, New York, NY
PRODUCER
John Massey
CREATIVE DIRECTOR
Roy Tuck

1609

ART DIRECTOR
Rick McQuiston
WRITER
Barrett Rossie
CLIENT
Nike
DIRECTOR
Bill Butler
AGENCY
Wieden & Kennedy, Portland, OR
PRODUCER
Lesley Bloom
PRODUCTION COMPANY
Petersen Comm.

1608

INSTANT RELAXATION/JUSTINE BATEMAN
30-second
JUSTINE: Please. Unbelievable.
Do you believe this?
It says, TV star reveals terrible secret.
And there's a picture of me.
When I get a break, I fix myself a cup of Maxwell House Instant.
You know, something nice, warm.
So I can kick back.
Relax.
Put my feet up.
Must be workin'.
'Cause I'm not even upset to find out I'm the daughter of alien visitors.
(SUPER)
Where do they get this stuff?

1609

BARKLEY AIR FORCE
30-second
CHARLES BARKLEY (THINKING TO HIMSELF WHILE DRIVING TO THE
BASKET): If you don't get out of my way, there's a couple of ways I can
handle this.
I can go around you . . .
I can go through you . . .
or, I can just do . . .
what I do . . .
best.
ANNCR: Basketball by Barkley.
Shoes by Nike.

1610

ART DIRECTOR
Marian Monsen
WRITER
Kathleen Malone
CLIENT
Bill Strauss, Panadol
EDITOR
Frank Herold
AGENCY
Lori Danenberg, SSC&B Inc., New York, NY
PRODUCTION COMPANY
Marjorie Clark, Videoworks
CREATIVE DIRECTOR
Betty Fitterman

1611

ART DIRECTOR
David Kennedy, Peter Moore
WRITER
Jim Riswold, Dan Wieden
CLIENT
Nike
DIRECTOR
Joe Pytka
AGENCY
Wieden & Kennedy, Portland, OR
PRODUCER
Bill Davenport
PRODUCTION COMPANY
Pytka Productions

1610

FACES
30-second
BRITISH WOMAN: I get headaches. But I'm not alone. Every day,
SWISS MAN: people all over the world get headaches. You probably do, too.
AMERICAN INDIAN WOMAN: So discover the strong relief millions depend on
JAMAICAN MAN: in country after country and doctors recommend worldwide.
ORIENTAL WOMAN: Aspirin-free Panadol. Panadol relieves my headache fast,
EAST INDIAN WOMAN: without upsetting my stomach. Nothing you can buy has been proven
AMERICAN WOMAN: more effective. Prove it to yourself. Aspirin-free Panadol.
VOICE-OVER: What the world takes for pain.

1611

ROCKABABY ONE SHOT
30-second
("URBAN BEAT BOX" MUSIC THROUGHOUT)
ANNCR: Air Jordan. It's all in the imagination.

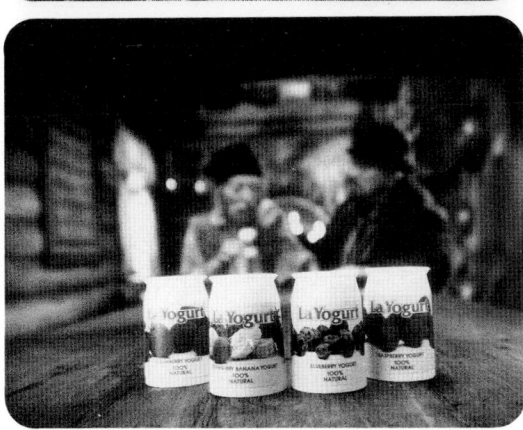

1612

ART DIRECTOR
Rich Park
WRITER
Richard Marchesano, Melissa Ennis
CLIENT
IKEA
EDITOR
John Prescott
DIRECTOR
John Prescott
DIRECTOR OF PHOTOGRAPHY
Peter Reiners
AGENCY
Goldberg/Marchesano, Washington, DC
PRODUCTION COMPANY
John Prescott & Associates

1613

ART DIRECTOR
Tony DeGregorio
WRITER
Lee Garfinkel
CLIENT
La Yogurt/Johanna Farms
EDITOR
Ciro DeNettis, The Editors
DIRECTOR
Michael Cuesta, Griner-Cuesta
AGENCY
LHS&B, New York, NY
PRODUCER
Bob Nelson

12

T OF TOWN
-second
EA Theater presents—They Came From Out of Town!
rill—as you search for extra beds!
ill—the good dishes! (CRASH)
ill—with last-minute linens! (BRR!)
EA to the rescue, (CHEERS) with beds that work undercover!
bles that grow with extra chairs.
d a cast of thousands!
en your in-laws will love IKEA's quality . . .
t (SUSPENSE CHORD) can you afford it?
RUMPET) You bet! IKEA's prices are impossibly low!
e love a happy ending. (SNIFF)

1613

CRYING RUSSIAN
30-second
ANNCR: It is said that Russians who live long lives eat a lot of yogurt. So who better to taste test a yogurt than someone who's eaten it for over a century.
RUSSIAN MAN: (HE HANDS 139 YEAR OLD MAN LA YOGURT)
139 YEAR OLD MAN: (EATS A SPOONFUL OF LA YOGURT AND STARTS TO WEEP)
RUSSIAN MAN: Do you not like it?
139 YEAR OLD MAN: (CONTINUS TO SOB) I *do* like it.
RUSSIAN MAN: Then, Comrade, why do you weep so?
139 YEAR OLD MAN: Because I've been eating that other stuff for over 139 years. (SOBS UNCONTROLLABLY).
ANNCR: Life is too short to miss out on La Yogurt.

1614
ART DIRECTOR
Rosalind Schell
WRITER
Doug Houston
CLIENT
Jordan Marsh
DIRECTOR
Norman Seeff
AGENCY
Maggie Hines, Hill Holliday, Boston, MA
PRODUCER
Richard Marlis

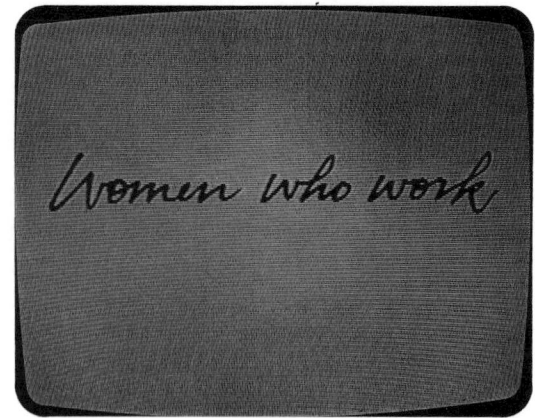

1615
ART DIRECTOR
Susan Hoffman
WRITER
Jim Riswold
CLIENT
Honda Scooters
DIRECTOR
Graham Henman, Michael Karbelnikoff
AGENCY
Wieden & Kennedy, Portland, OR
PRODUCER
Bill Davenport
PRODUCTION COMPANY
HKM Productions

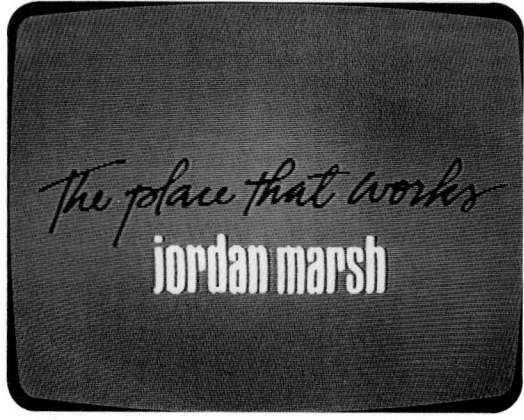

1614

UNGLUED
30-second
VO: A friend of mine had called him and said, "Do you want to meet this writer?".
And I was with him when he made the call, so I knew he didn't tell this person that I, you know, a black person was going to come in.
And it's interesting if you've ever seen anyone sort of fall apart, and immediately glue themselves back together again real fast.
That's kind of what he did. He kind of had one of those internal eruptions where he went, "Omigod, she's black . . . Oh, it's alright." (LAUGH)
You have to deal with that.

1615

MCMAHON-BERNHARD/FOOTBALL
30-second
MCMAHON: Outrageousness?
(CRAZY MUSIC KICKS IN)
MCMAHON: Outrageousness? It's nothin' more than a way to wake people up.
MCMAHON: Especially yourself.
BERNHARD: Okay, so I'm not some macho football hero.
BERNHARD: I'm Sandra Bernhard and I'm a woman.
BERNHARD: And I have a woman's needs.

1616
ART DIRECTOR
Jagdish Prabhu
WRITER
Chuck Hoffman
CLIENT
Larry Bice, Eastman Kodak
EDITOR
Dennis Hayes
DIRECTOR
Thomas Higgins
AGENCY
Bruce Davidson, JWT, New York, NY
PRODUCTION COMPANY
Joan Laxer, BFSC
CREATIVE DIRECTOR
Charles Genneralli

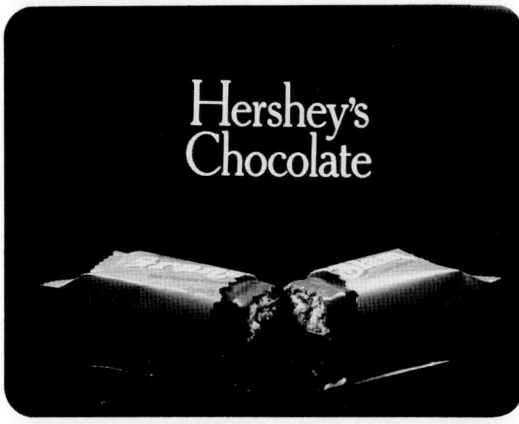

1617
ART DIRECTOR
Mitch Davidson
WRITER
David Apicella
CLIENT
Hershey Foods
EDITOR
Mitchell Hart, Editor's GAS
DIRECTOR
Alan Orpin
AGENCY
Skip Allocco, O&M, New York, NY
PRODUCTION COMPANY
Laurie Kay, Melsky Zander

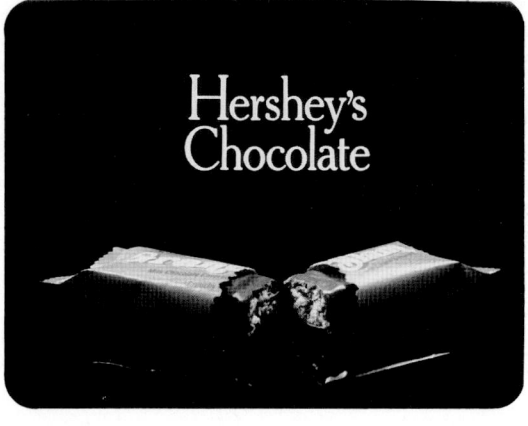

6

GUITAR
second
: Just when you're ready to knock 'em dead
r battery dies.
Kodak created Supralife alkaline batteries,
long lasting battery
h the real gold tip
the best contact.
w, do you settle for the ordinary?
go for the gold.
O
PER: GO FOR THE GOLD.

1617

GRAND SLAM/FOOTBALL
30-second
LEADER: Grand Slam! . . .
. . . How could Hershey's give a great tasting new candy bar a baseball
name?
GUYS: Yeah! . . .
LEADER: They shoulda called it . . .
LINEBACKER: Linebacker!
GUYS: Yeah!
NOSETACKLE: Or Nosetackle . . .
GUYS: Yeah! Right!
TIGHT END: What about Tight End?
GUYS: Yeah!
ALL: or . . . or . . . ah . . . ah . . . how about, uh . . .
. . . pulling guard . . .
yeah, that's good, pulling guard.
SFX: WE HEAR THE CRACK OF A BASEBALL BAT.
ALL: What about . . . what about . . .
KID: I got it . . . Homerun!!
SFX: JEERS, BOOS, HISSES, ETC.

1618

ART DIRECTOR
David Kennedy
WRITER
Jim Riswold
CLIENT
Nike
AGENCY
Bill Davenport, Wieden & Kennedy,
Portland, OR
PRODUCTION COMPANY
David Altschul, Will Vinton Prod.

1619

ART DIRECTOR
Gary Goldsmith
DESIGNER
Gary Goldsmith
WRITER
Robin Ray
CLIENT
NYNEX
DIRECTOR
Henry Sandbank
AGENCY
Chiat/Day, New York, NY
PRODUCER
Carol Lee Keliher
PRODUCTION COMPANY
Sandbank Films

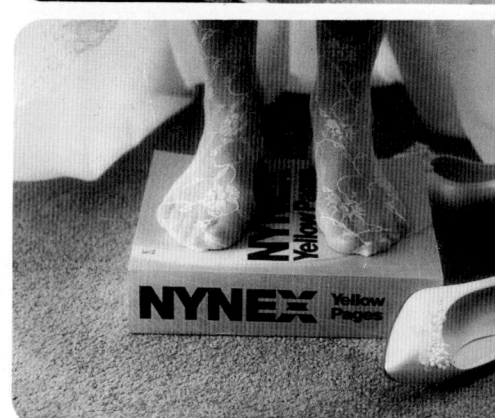

1618

SHOEBOX
30-second
Nike makes shoes for kids.
Running shoes.
Basketball shoes.
Aerobic shoes.
Tennis shoes.
Baseball shoes.
Shoes to cheer about.
Fitness shoes.
Soccer shoes.
Shoes to jump up and down about.
Shoes that will get you pumped.
Wrestling shoes.
Hey, wait a minute.
Whew!
Nike. You can't keep a lid on it.

1619

WEDDING
30-second
SFX: NATURAL SOUNDS OF BRIDE'S QUARTERS; CONVERSATION IS
FAST-PACED. BRIDE REMAINS CALM THROUGHOUT.
DAD: (ENTERS) The limo service is overbooked. We need another limo.
MOM: Check the Yellow Pages.
GNDM: Fix her veil.
DAD: Where is the Yellow Pages?
SIS 1: It was here this morning.
GRDM: Don't touch her hair.
SIS 2: Maybe Auntie has it.
GRDM: Don't touch her hair . . .
VO: One book is in more homes, helping people find more goods and
services . . . the official directory of New York Telephone . . .
DAD: Oh!
(REVEAL) The NYNEX Yellow Pages.
(OVER TITLE) It's always there when you need it . . .

1620
ART DIRECTOR
Ruth Spitzer
WRITER
Jeff Atlas
CLIENT
Duracell
EDITOR
Dennis Hayes Editorial
DIRECTOR
Steve Tobin
AGENCY
Nancy Perez, Ogilvy & Mather, New
York, NY
PRODUCTION COMPANY
Michelle Krause, Steifel & Co.
CREATIVE DIRECTOR
Mike Pitts

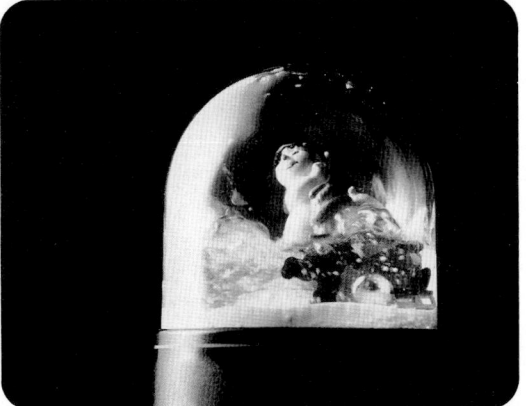

1621
ART DIRECTOR
Grant Parrish
WRITER
Tom Rost
CLIENT
American Express
EDITOR
Dennis Hayes Editorial
DIRECTOR
Michael Schrom
DIRECTOR OF PHOTOGRAPHY
Michael Schrom
AGENCY
Sande Breakstone, Ogilvy & Mather,
New York, NY
PRODUCER
Carol Brackenridge

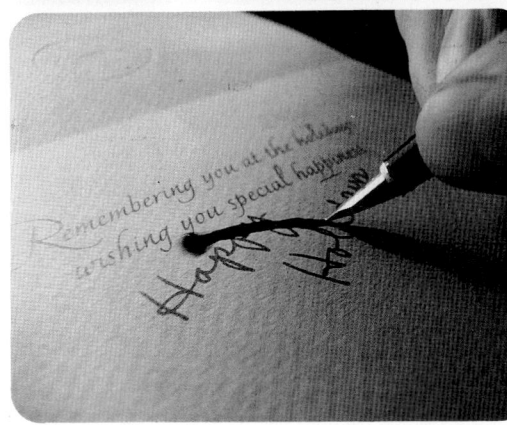

1620

1992
30-second
ANNCR (VO): A Japanese baseball team has won the world's series. You
can cross the Atlantic by plane in 47 minutes. A computer has been
elected mayor of Cupertino, California.
SFX: FLASH
And the revolutionary
SFX: FLASH
Duracell XL Lithium battery
SFX: FLASH
you put in your
SFX: FLASH
auto-focus camera in 1986,
SFX: FLASH
is still
SFX: FLASH
going strong.
SFX: FLASH
Duracell XL . . .
SFX: TONES. SLAM-AROUND.
The long life lithium.

1621

BREAKING/XMAS VERSION
30-second
ANNCR: As the holidays come around, it's nice to know that even if
something breaks, it won't break you, if you shop with the American
Express Card.
Because until December 31st, we will extend the free repair period of the
manufacturer's warranty.
In fact, we'll double it up to an extra year, just in case the things you buy
aren't all that they're cracked up to be.
Be sure to register your purchase with ''Buyer's Assurance'' and use the
American Express Card.

1622

ART DIRECTOR
Susan Hoffman
PHOTOGRAPHER
Pete Stone
WRITER
Dan Wieden
CLIENT
Nike
AGENCY
Wieden & Kennedy, Portland, OR

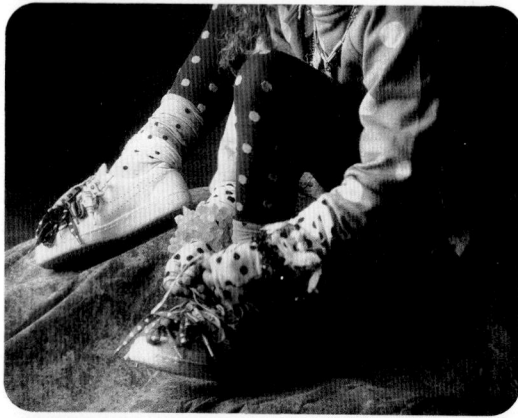

1623

ART DIRECTOR
Christie Kelly
WRITER
Tom Nelson
CLIENT
General Foods Corporation/Instant
Maxwell House
EDITOR
Billy Williams
DIRECTOR
Patrick Russel
AGENCY
Ogilvy & Mather, New York, NY
PRODUCER
John Massey
CREATIVE DIRECTOR
Roy Tuck

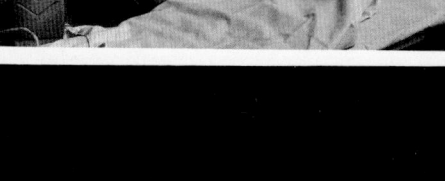

Maxwell House Instant Coffee
Instant Civilization

1622

KID'S SHOELACES
30-second
TALENT: Text
DWAYNE: This is it. This is ours.
ZOE: This is what's prime. Mint.
JOSH: Tie them like this and it gets the girls totally shocked.
HEATHER: You've got to be original. You've got to be primo perfect.
MATT: Like, they're definitly in.
CHAD: So fine, so funky.
CHENNA: They're cool.
KOBIE: What's cool is what I do in them.

1623

INSTANT CIVILIZATION/BRONSON PINCHOT
30-second
BRONSON: You know, when people drop by my apartment they say.
Well, this is the apartment.
You can guess what they say.
They say, don't you have a couch?
Don't you have a dining room set?
(DINING ROOM SET.)
I do, however, have Maxwell House Instant Coffee.
That seems to reassure most folks that I'm a reasonably tasteful guy.
And after 1 or 2 cups.
They forget they're sitting on lawn furniture.
(SUPER)
And when they get up.
The backs of their thighs look like Belgian waffles.

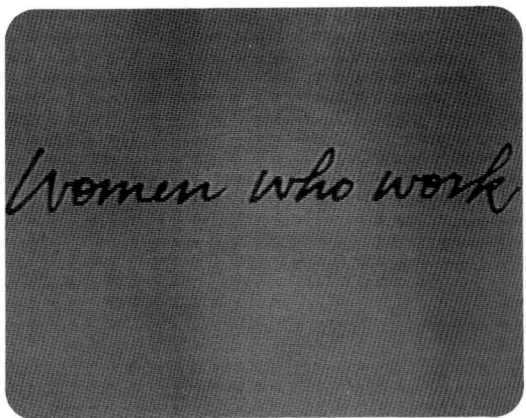

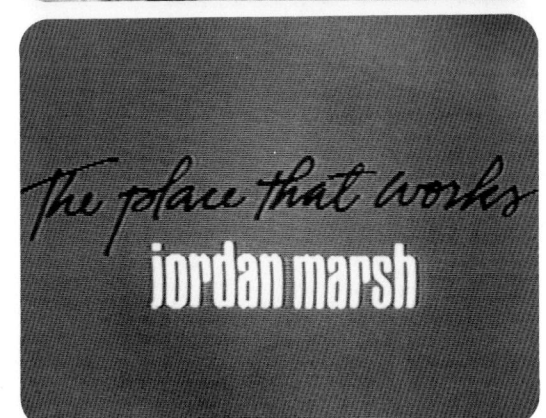

1624
ART DIRECTOR
Gary Shapiro
ANIMATOR/ARTIST
Paul Vester, Lee Dyer, Mark Kausler,
Barry Bruce
WRITER
Laurie Solomon
CLIENT
Hershey
EDITOR
Rick Haber
DIRECTOR
Paul Vester
DIRECTOR OF PHOTOGRAPHY
Paul Vester
AGENCY
Kathy DiToro, Ogilvy & Mather,
New York, NY
PRODUCER
Keri Batten, Linda Stewart

1625
ART DIRECTOR
Rosalind Schell
WRITER
Doug Houston
CLIENT
Jordan Marsh
DIRECTOR
Norman Seeff
AGENCY
Maggie Hines, Hill Holliday, Boston,
MA
PRODUCER
Richard Marlis

624

ALL TIME GREATS—KIDS
30-second
(MUSIC UNDER)
SINGERS: H-h-h-Hershey's One of the all time greats.
MUMMY: Hershey.
SINGERS: H-h-h-h-Hershey's . . .
One-one-one-one of the all time greats.
Pure milk chocolate, delicious and smooth;
Hershey's is a fun one.
H-h-
n-Hershey's
One-one-one-one of the all time greats
(SFX: BEEP, BEEP)

1625

SUCCESS CAN BE VERY SEXY
30-second
VO: I love working hard.
'Cuz I love what I do for a living.
I also like caring alot. I have a family that I care for.
And I enjoy that very much.
I love dressing stylishly; it's fun.
It makes me feel good and if I feel good I work better.
Being a successful businesswoman is being a good businessperson.
But you don't have to hide the fact that you are a woman.
Success is very sexy.

1626

ART DIRECTOR
F. Paul Pracilio
WRITER
Robert Neuman
CLIENT
American Express
DIRECTOR
Bob Eggers, Eggers Films
EDITOR
Steve Schreiber, Editor's Gas
AGENCY
Ann Marcato, Ogilvy & Mather, New
York, NY
PRODUCTION COMPANY
Sterling Ray, Eggers Films
CREATIVE DIRECTOR
Tom Rost

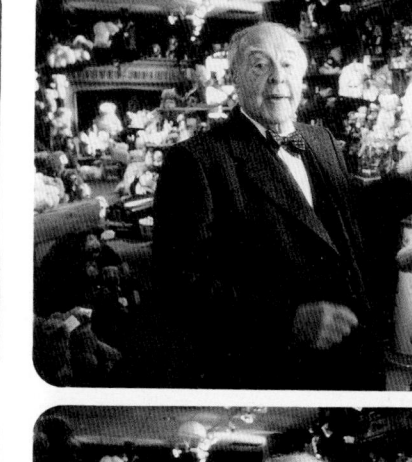

1627

ART DIRECTOR
F. Paul Pracilio
WRITER
Roger Butler
CLIENT
Smith Barney, Harris Upham & Co.,
Robert Connor
EDITOR
Ilene Hochman, Startmark
DIRECTOR
Stan Schofield
AGENCY
Ann Marcato, Ogilvy & Mather, New
York, NY
PRODUCTION COMPANY
Richard Cohen, Sandbank Films
CREATIVE DIRECTOR
Robert Neuman

1626

DO YOU KNOW ME/RON REAGAN, JR.
30-second
RON REAGAN, JR.: Do you know me?
Every time I appear on a talk show, people ask me about my father.
Every time I do an interview, people ask me about my father.
Every time I pull out the American Express Card, people treat me like my
father.
Come to think of it, that's not so bad . . .
ANNCR: To apply for the Card, look for an application. And take one.
RON REAGAN: The American Express Card. Don't leave home without it.
Hello, Dad? Excuse me . . .

1627

TEDDY RUXPIN
30-second
ANNCR: John Houseman, for the investment firm of Smith Barney.
HOUSEMAN: Nurturing today's tots. Some may become tomorrow's
tycoons.
(BEAR TALKS)
Smith Barney nurtures fledgling companies by helping to finance their
growth. Like the company that makes this noisy . . . little . . . bear. It
started small. It's now rather substantial.
Smith Barney. They make money the old-fashioned way. They . . .
(BEAR SAYS: "THEY EARN IT." HE MUFFLES BEAR WITH HAND.)

1628
ART DIRECTOR
Dennis D'Amico
DESIGNER
Dennis D'Amico
WRITER
Robin Raj
CLIENT
NYNEX
DIRECTOR
Mike Cuesta
AGENCY
Chiat/Day, New York, NY
PRODUCER
Paul Gold
PRODUCTION COMPANY
Griner-Cuesta

1629
ART DIRECTOR
Ron Hartley, Don Nevins
WRITER
Ray Hirschman
CLIENT
Al Neilson, Heineken
EDITOR
John Patestrini
AGENCY
Eric Brenner, SSC&B Inc., New
York, NY
PRODUCTION COMPANY
Patricia Phillips Marco, Phil Marco
Productions
CREATIVE DIRECTOR
Bob Conlon

1628

VIOLATION
30-second
SFX: NATURAL SOUNDS
COP: In a hurry, huh? (PAUSE AS HE EXAMINES DOCUMENTS) What's in back?
MAN: Yellow Pages.
COP: (COP ABSORBED IN WRITING. HE DOES DOUBLE-TAKE OF TRUCK; RAISES EYEBROW) The Yellow Pages Yellow Pages?
MAN: (SHRUGS) It's a Yellow Pages.
COP: (STOPS WRITING; TRIES TO UNDERSTAND) If it's not the NYNEX Yellow Pages . . . then what exactly is it?
MAN: (SHRUGS) It's, it's a Yellow Pages.
COP: (FOLDS ARMS, LOOKS AT HIM SQUARELY) Why would anyone need another?
(HOLD ON DRIVER'S FACE AS HE SINKS IN SEAT. COP HANDS HIM TICKET; CUT TO TRUCK LEAVING TOWN. END ON NYNEX BOOK.)
VO: For 75 years, there's always been one book when you've needed it.
(TO BOOK) The NYNEX Yellow Pages. Look out for imitations . . .

1629

DROP
30-second
ANNCR (VO): Climbing. Reaching for the top.
Thirsting for the best in life.
Only one beer can satisfy a thirst like yours.
The world's best beer.
Come to think of it, I'll have a Heineken.
Heineken.
Satisfy your thirst for the best.

1630

ART DIRECTOR
Dave Nathanson
DESIGNER
Dave Nathanson
WRITER
Penny Kapousouz
CLIENT
Ricoh
DIRECTOR
Richard Loncraine
AGENCY
Chiat/Day, New York, NY
PRODUCER
Bertelle Selig
PRODUCTION COMPANY
Garnett & Co.

1631

ART DIRECTOR
Roy Carruthers
WRITER
Steve Jeffery
CLIENT
Seagram's Golden Wine Cooler
EDITOR
David Dee
DIRECTOR
David Ashwell
AGENCY
Nancy Braunstein, Ogilvy & Mather,
New York, NY
PRODUCER
Danny Boyle
CREATIVE DIRECTOR
Malcolm End

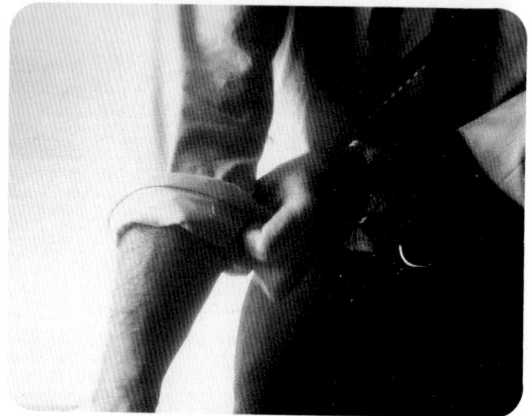

1630

REPAIRMAN
25-second
ANNCR VO: This man is not a company president.
Or a vice president.
While his face is well known to everyone in the office . . . his name
doesn't appear on the company phone list.
Yet he controls the productivity of this office . . . down to the last sheet of
paper.
And that's a serious problem.
Because business should depend on a copier that works . . . not a
repairman.
(REVISED TAG)
Ricoh. Copiers built to work. And work. And work.

1631

JAMMING
30-second
BRUCE: Hit me fellas . . . Look here . . . (SINGS)
Seagram's Golden Wine Cooler
(BOYS JOIN IN)
Seagram's Golden Wine Cooler
BRUCE: It's wet and it's dry.
BOY: Golden Wine Cooler.
BRUCE: My, my, my, my . . .
BOYS: Golden Wine Cooler
BRUCE: Me and the boys . . . love, love, love it all the time.
BOYS: Seagram's Golden Wine Cooler.
BRUCE: It's wet and it's dry.
BOYS: Golden Wine Cooler.

1632
ART DIRECTOR
Losang Gyatso, David Mangan
WRITER
Pete Kellogg, Dan Sheehan
CLIENT
Diet Coke
EDITOR
Jeff Kahn
AGENCY
Eric Brenner, SSC&B Inc., New York, NY
PRODUCER
Paul Wieland
CREATIVE DIRECTOR
Don Gill

1633
ART DIRECTOR
Carolyne Diehl
WRITER
Mimi Emilita
CLIENT
American Red Cross, Christy Phillips
EDITOR
Editors Gas, Steve Schreiber
DIRECTOR
John Korty
AGENCY
JWT, New York, NY
PRODUCER
Beth Stewart Morris
PRODUCTION COMPANY
John Korty Films
CREATIVE DIRECTOR
Jim Patterson

1632

SYMPHONY
30-second
O: Just for the fun of it. The London Symphony Orchestra for diet Coke.
SOPRANO SOLOIST: Just for the light of it.
BASS SOLOIST: The smooth taste of it.
SOPRANO & BASS: diet Coke.
CHORUS: Just for the ah-ah-ah
SOPRANO: ah-ahhhhhh!
CHORAL GROUP: Ahhh! Just for the taste of it.
TENOR: From Coca-Cola.
TUTTI: Diet Coke. Diet Coke. Diet Coke. Diet Coke. Diet Coke.
TYMPANY: Boom, Boom!
SINGERS: Diet Coke!
MAN BLOWS LAST NOTE FROM BOTTLE: Wooh!

1633

FATHER
30-second
FATHER: Ma'am, excuse me, could you help me please?
Sir, could you help me, please; my little girl, she needs blood.
Could you help me?
WOMAN: I'm sorry.
FATHER: Somebody, somebody, please.
My daughter, she needs blood, could you please help?
Somebody, somebody help me.
ANNCR VO: Imagine if you had to ask for blood to save the life of someone you love.
Next time the American Red Cross asks, give blood, please.

1634
ART DIRECTOR
Mitch Davidson
WRITER
David Apicella
CLIENT
Hershey Foods
EDITOR
Mitchell Hart, Editor's GAS
DIRECTOR
Alan Orpin
AGENCY
Skip Allocco, O&M, New York, NY
PRODUCTION COMPANY
Laurie Kay, Melsky-Zander

1635
ART DIRECTOR
Gary Goldsmith
DESIGNER
Gary Goldsmith
WRITER
Robin Raj
CLIENT
NYNEX
AGENCY
Chiat/Day, New York, NY
PRODUCER
Carol Lee Keliher
PRODUCTION COMPANY
Sandbank Films

1634

GRAND SLAM/BASEBALL
30-second
CAPTAIN: Hey guys, you know this new Hershey Grand Slam candy bar?
GUYS: Yeah, it's great . . . love it . . .
CAPTAIN: Well, you know what I heard?
GUYS: What?
CAPTAIN: I heard some football players don't like the name.
GUYS: Oh yeah?
CAPTAIN: And they wanna change it to—you're gonna love this—
LINEBACKER!
GUYS: Get outta here!
SFX: LAUGHTER
CAPTAIN: I'm not kidding . . .
. . . or tight end . . .
SFX: LAUGHTER GETS LOUDER
SFX: WE HEAR THE CRACK OF A BAT.
SFX: LAUGHTER CONTINUES EVEN LOUDER THAN BEFORE.
CAPTAIN: . . . this is the best . . . NOSETACKLE!!!
SFX: UNCONTROLLED HYSTERICAL LAUGHTER

1635

ELEVATOR
30-second
SFX: NATURAL SOUNDS.
VO: One book reaches more homes, helping people throughout the
Northeast find more goods and services . . .
The Nynex Yellow Pages.
(WEDGES BOOK BETWEEN DOORS)
It's always there when you need it . . .
SFX: ELEVATOR BELL.
MAN: (OVER TITLE) Can you press two? . . .

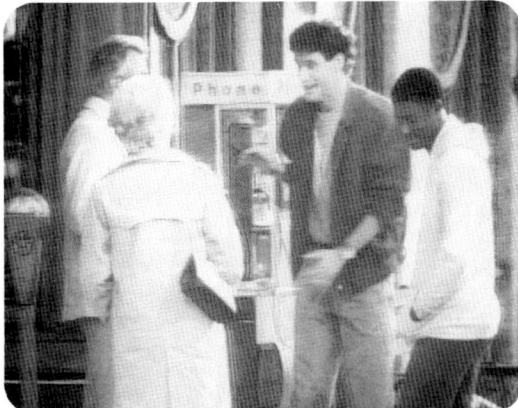

1636

ART DIRECTOR
Nick Vitale
WRITER
Brian Sitts
CLIENT
Burger King, Kendall Crolius
EDITOR
Bob Derise, A Cut Above
DIRECTOR
Joseph Hanwright
AGENCY
JWT, New York, NY
PRODUCER
Ric Wylie, John Maritato, David Schneiderman
PRODUCTION COMPANY
Steven Cohen, KIRA Films
CREATIVE DIRECTOR
Hal Friedman

1637

ART DIRECTOR
Maryann Christopher
WRITER
Michael Delaney, Alan Brunstein
CLIENT
Warner Lambert, EPT Plus, Russ Moran
EDITOR
Michael Charles, Michael Chas
DIRECTOR
Norman Seeff
AGENCY
Randy Hecht, JWT, New York, NY
PRODUCTION COMPANY
Richard Marlis, Marlis Prod.
CREATIVE DIRECTOR
Bernie Owett

36

ACKYARD/BBQ
-second
RIC: My kind of people. My kind of taste. Something special about this ace. Got no reason to stray too far, cause it's all right here in my own ackyard.
): There's no secret to the taste of a Burger King burger. We just watch w you cook over an open flame and do the same thing.
RIC: This is a Burger King town. We know how burgers should be.

1637

PHONE CALL
30-second
MAN: Look, you can't use the phone right now. She's calling right back, and then we'll know if we're, if *she's* pregnant. She said ten minutes. What's ten minutes, huh?
ANNCR: EPT Plus. The fastest home pregnancy test ever. Use EPT Plus on your first late day.
MAN: A simple color change tells her in as soon as ten minutes if she's pregnant. My wife's name is Janice. We met on a blind date. I know, these things never work out, but this one did, obviously. 'T' minus three— Where you folks from, huh?
ANNCR: EPT Plus. On your first late day.
MAN: (RING) It's for me.

1638
ART DIRECTOR
Terry O'Leary
DESIGNER
Tony Meininger
WRITER
Doug Feinstein
CLIENT
Duracell
EDITOR
Mike Charles Editorial
DIRECTOR
Dick Miller
AGENCY
Mootsy Elliot, Ogilvy & Mather, New York, NY
PRODUCTION COMPANY
Carrol Herrick, Director's Chair
CREATIVE DIRECTOR
Mike Pitts

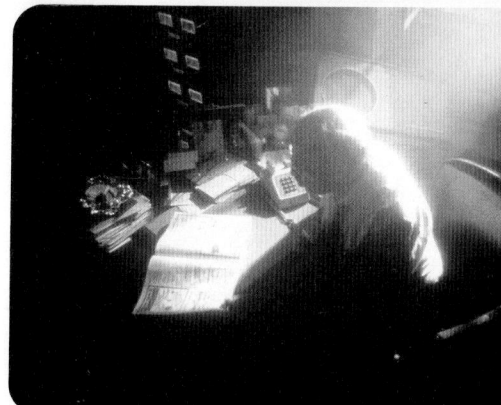

1639
ART DIRECTOR
Gary Goldsmith
DESIGNER
Gary Goldsmith
WRITER
Robin Raj
CLIENT
NYNEX
AGENCY
Chiat/Day, New York, NY
PRODUCER
Carol Lee Keliher
PRODUCTION COMPANY
Sandbank Films

1638

SPIES
30-second
SFX: MUSIC UP AND UNDER.
ANNCR (VO): It's no secret. Today's copper-top battery makes yesterday's look, well, not too swift. In fact it's so completely improved it will last up to 30% longer than the ones we made just two years ago. It'll keep going long after our old battery is . . . dead in the water. Today's Duracell . . .
SFX: TONES. SLAM-AROUND.
ANNCR (VO): No battery lasts longer.

1639

FLY
30-second
SFX: BUZZING OF FLY WEAVES IN & OUT.
GUY: You're open weekends? Good . . . My air-conditioner's not working . . . it's not running at all . . . the filter seems fine . . . (RELIEVED) Today would be great . . . Uh, two two one five . . . I mean, two two fi one North Brennen, turn left, right . . . no left! . . .
VO: One book is in more offices, helping people find more goods and services . . . the official directory of New York Telephone . . .
(SLAMS BOOK SHUT, BUZZING STOPS) The Nynex Business-to-Business Yellow Pages.
(OVER TITLE) It's always there when you need it . . .
SFX: BUZZING OF FLY RESUMES AGAIN BEFORE FADE.

1640
ART DIRECTOR
Tony DeGregorio
WRITER
Lee Garfinkel
CLIENT
La Yogurt/Johanna Farms
EDITOR
Ciro DeNettis, The Editors
DIRECTOR
Michael Cuesta, Griner-Cuesta
AGENCY
LHS&B, New York, NY
PRODUCER
Bob Nelson

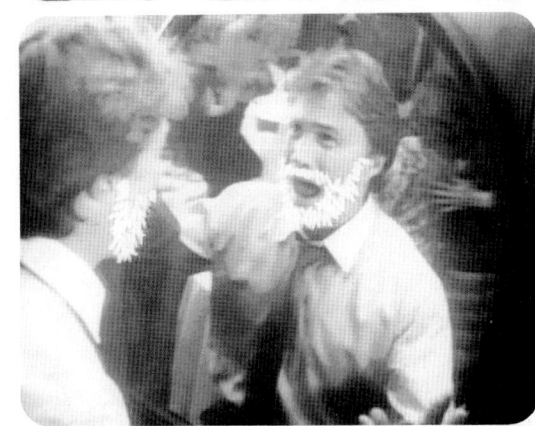

1641
ART DIRECTOR
Len Fink
WRITER
Drake Sparkman
CLIENT
Warner Lambert-Schick, Don Benes,
Vince Termini
EDITOR
Billy Rohn, Editors Gas
DIRECTOR
Rose Cramer
AGENCY
JWT, New York, NY
PRODUCER
Beth Stewart Morris
PRODUCTION COMPANY
Power & Light Picture Co.
CREATIVE DIRECTOR
Charles Genneralli

40

RED RUSSIANS
-second
NCR: Years ago Dannon discovered Russians who lived long lives ate a
of yogurt.
ey didn't tell you *how* they lived. So we gave them La Yogurt. The great
sting yogurt from America. So now they not only can live longer, they
n live better.
(MUSIC BECOMES EXCITING, THEY START DANCING)
NCR: Life is too short to miss out on La Yogurt.

1641

RESTAURANT
30-second
WOMAN: (SCREAMS)
MAN: (SCREAMS)
SONG: The beard is back. Schick Schick Schick.
The beard is back. Schick Schick Schick.
It's back again.
I need to get.
You better get.
Gotta get, gotta get Schick.
New Schick Super II Plus leaves a lubricant behind with each stroke.
Super II Plus. Every stroke's as comfortable as the first.
SONG: I need to get,
You better get,
Gotta get, get Schick.

1642

ART DIRECTOR
Marisa Acocella
WRITER
Michael Scardino, Leslie Mechanic
CLIENT
Eckerd Drugs, Ken Banks
EDITOR
Mel Cohen, DJM
DIRECTOR
David Ashwell
AGENCY
Tricia Caruso, JWT, New York, NY
PRODUCTION COMPANY
David Ashwell, David Ashwell
CREATIVE DIRECTOR
Charles Genneralli

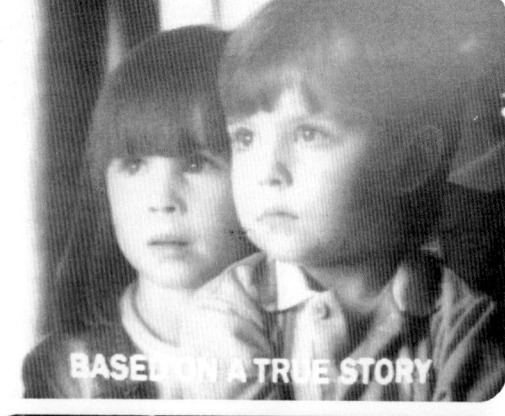

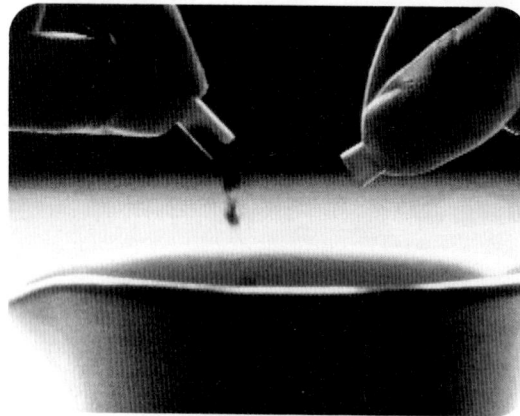

1643

ART DIRECTOR
Saskia Mossel
WRITER
Steve Baer
CLIENT
G.F. Shake 'n Bake
EDITOR
Stuart Waks
DIRECTOR
David Ashwell
AGENCY
Elaine Keeve, Ogilvy & Mather, New York, NY
PRODUCER
Danny Boyle
CREATIVE DIRECTOR
Malcolm End

1642

VACCINE
30-second
SUPER: BASED ON A TRUE STORY.
VO: When 100 nursery school kids were exposed to spinal meningitis, 2 pharmacists from Eckerd Drugs worked overtime, against time itself, mixing enough antibiotic, dose by dose, for each and every child. And through their dedication and concern, they stopped an epidemic before it started.
To an Eckerd pharmacist, nothing's more important than your health.

1643

JUICY
30-second
BOY: What's this for?
GRANDMA: Dinner.
BOY: We're eating napkins?
MOTHER: We're eating crispy chicken.
FATHER: I could eat a horse.
MOTHER: This was easier.
GIRL: It's crispy chicken.
GRANDMA: From Shake 'n Bake.
MOM: Please use your napkins, it's juicy. (TO SON) You're lucky the la says I have to feed you until you're eighteen.
BOY: It is juicy. I could use another leg.
VO: Shake 'n Bake Coating Mix.
TEENAGE GIRL: I think you better look for another brain.
VO: The chicken that's crispy outside, juicy inside.

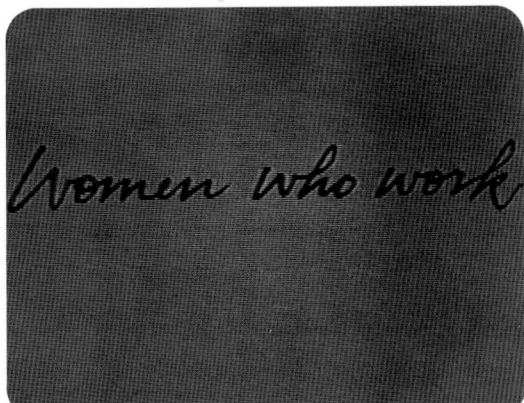

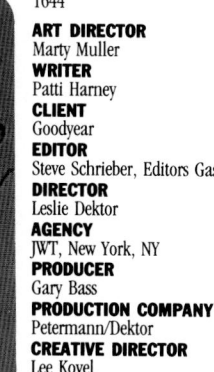

1644
ART DIRECTOR
Marty Muller
WRITER
Patti Harney
CLIENT
Goodyear
EDITOR
Steve Schrieber, Editors Gas
DIRECTOR
Leslie Dektor
AGENCY
JWT, New York, NY
PRODUCER
Gary Bass
PRODUCTION COMPANY
Petermann/Dektor
CREATIVE DIRECTOR
Lee Kovel

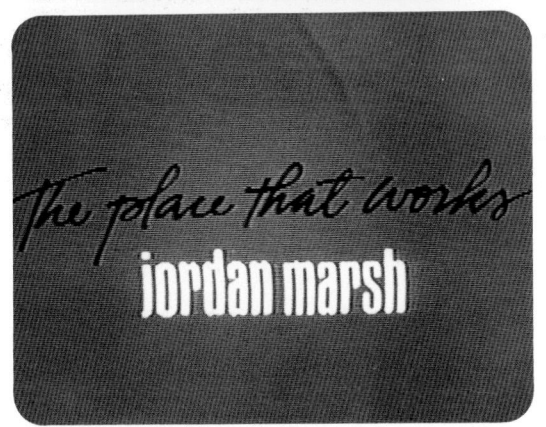

1645
ART DIRECTOR
Rosalind Schell
WRITER
Doug Houston
CLIENT
Jordan Marsh
DIRECTOR
Norman Seeff
AGENCY
Maggie Hines, Hill Holliday, Boston, MA
PRODUCER
Richard Marlis

644

OST PET
0-second
UNG: Take me back where I belong
ake me where it's safe and warm
NNCR: The Goodyear Vector is the all season radial that pumps water
way to keep more tire tread on the road. And for some . . . that's a
omforting thought.
UNG: Take me home, Goodyear
ake me home
lever matters how far I go
oodyear, take me home

1645

BORN TO BE WILD
30-second
VO: I used to be wild.
I had about 10 jobs. Let's see. I moved from Boston to Dallas to LA to
Boston again.
My job's pretty good.
The money's very good.
And I live in this beautiful house with my husband and the best little baby
girl.
I'm not wild anymore.
I'm too tired.

1646

ART DIRECTOR
Frank Parke
WRITER
Clifford L. Freeman, Frank Parke,
Dan O'Neill
CLIENT
Wendy's International
AGENCY
DFS Dorland, New York, NY

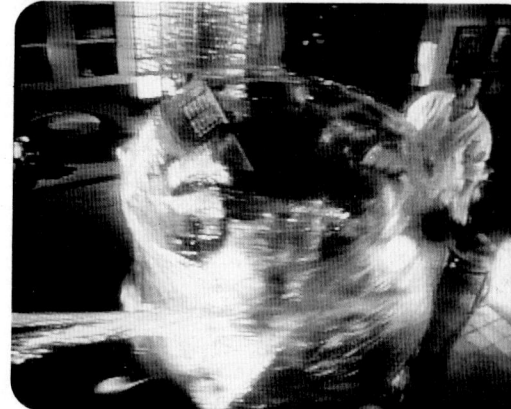

1647

ART DIRECTOR
Len Fink
WRITER
Lori Korchek
CLIENT
Reynolds Plastic Wrap, Doug Mickel
EDITOR
Dennis Hayes, Barry Stillwell
DIRECTOR
Ross Cramer
AGENCY
JWT, New York, NY
PRODUCER
Sid Horn
PRODUCTION COMPANY
Power and Light
CREATIVE DIRECTOR
Lee Kovel

1646

BETTY LOU
30-second
Swimsuit Competition begins soon. And you know how Betty Lou looks in
a bathing suit. Better look into Wendy's Light Menu. Hundreds of lower
calorie salads, fresh fruit and pasta salad. Even lower calorie multi-grain
buns.
Try Wendy's Light Menu.
See you at the beach.

1647

MIND OF ITS OWN
30-second
ANNCR VO: Ever notice how some plastic wraps seem to have a mind of
their own?
How they don't seem to cling where you want them to?
Well, Reynolds Plastic Wrap clings better than any other plastic wrap. And
it clings where it's supposed to cling.
So, get Reynolds Plastic Wrap before yours get out of hand.

1648
ART DIRECTOR
Frank Kirk
WRITER
Jim Weller
CLIENT
Transamerica Corporation
EDITOR
Jacques Dury, Decoupage
DIRECTOR
Gary Johns, Jeff Gorman
DIRECTOR OF PHOTOGRAPHY
Laszlo Kovaks A.S.C.
AGENCY
Della Femina, Travisano, Los
Angeles, CA
PRODUCER
Shannon Silverman
PRODUCTION COMPANY
Johns & Gorman Films
MUSIC
Donall Piestrup, Piece of Cake

1649
ART DIRECTOR
Margot Olshan Clapps
WRITER
J. Gregory Alderisio
CLIENT
Proctor & Gamble/Spic and Span
EDITOR
Patrick Udale, Tony Siggia
DIRECTOR
David Lane
DIRECTOR OF PHOTOGRAPHY
Peter Hanman
AGENCY
Mary Kaplun, Wells, Rich, Greene,
New York, NY
PRODUCTION COMPANY
Robert Cardona, Michelle Fabian-
Jones, Clearwater Films, Inc.
CREATIVE DIRECTOR
Nancy Vaughan

48

KING KONG II
-second
GIRL: I want to talk to you about something that could change your life. Insurance.
SFX: BANG!
GIRL: This is a policy from one of the world's biggest insurance specialists.
SFX: BANG!
GIRL: For almost any kind of insurance . . .
SFX: BANG!
GIRL: Because you never know when you're going to need insurance . . .
SFX: BANG!
GIRL: Excuse me.
SFX: CRACK!
GIRL: Hey, you big ape. Who's going to pay for this mess!!!
ANCR: Transamerica. For insurance and financial services, the power of the pyramid is working for you.

1649

DRAG RACE
30-second
SPORTSCASTER 1: (DON) (AS MOPS PULL TO STARTING LINE) It's the racing showdown we've been waiting for between old Spic and Span . . .
SPORTSCASTER 2: (JIM) . . . and new No Rinse Spic and Span.
DON: (ON GREEN LIGHT) And they're off!
JIM: Heck, Don, I've got to say I'm real impressed with new No Rinse Spic and Span. It's got the same great cleaning power, but doesn't streak like you-know-who.
DON: They're in the home stretch . . .
JIM: . . . and old Spic and Span's in a tailspin! It's going back to rinse!
DON: That makes new Spic and Span our winner! It's faster to the finish because there's no rinsing.
SUPER: FASTER TO THE FINISH

1650

ART DIRECTOR
Hal Tench
DESIGNER
Hal Tench
WRITER
Andy Ellis
CLIENT
Barnett Banks
DIRECTOR
Stu Hagmann
AGENCY
The Martin Agency, Richmond, VA
PRODUCER
Frank Soukup
PRODUCTION COMPANY
HISK Productions

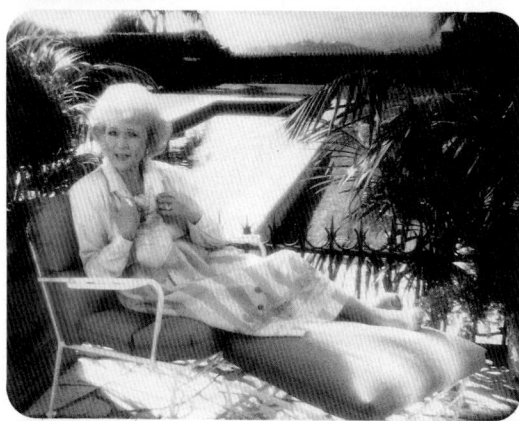

1651

ART DIRECTOR
Herb Jager
WRITER
William Lower
CLIENT
Pan American World Airways/The
Pan Am Shuttle
EDITOR
Jay Gold
DIRECTOR
Bill Hudson
DIRECTOR OF PHOTOGRAPHY
Salvatore Guida
AGENCY
Tony Perrotto, Wells, Rich, Greene,
New York, NY
PRODUCTION COMPANY
Sabrina Palladino, Bill Hudson &
Assoc.
CREATIVE DIRECTOR
Charles Moss
MUSIC
Larry Levenson, Neil Warner,
Warner/Levinson

1650

BETTY WHITE
30-second
BETTY WHITE: My character on TV lives in Florida. *I* live in California.
They're not that different. You have warm weather . . . we have warm
weather. You have palms . . . we have palms. You have Barnett's Senior
Partners . . . (BRIEF PAUSE) . . . we have earthquakes. So, you get free
checking, free checks, itemized statements . . . we get smog, mud slides,
and raw fish. I'm moving to Florida the day I turn 55. I can wait 20
years.

1651

AMERICAN ADVANTAGE/SCHEDULE
30-second
FRENCH MUSIC UNDER AND THROUGHOUT
SPOKESMAN: American Advantage member who fly the new Pan Am
Shuttle can accrue mileage on American's Advantage program and earn
free trip to Europe . . .
Advantage members who fly Eastern won't.
SPOKESMAN: Now you don't have to worry about missing the Eastern
Shuttle because the Pan Am Shuttle leaves on the half hour.
And once you've flown the new Pan Am Shuttle, we don't think you'll
miss the Eastern Shuttle.
ANNCR VO: The Pan Am Shuttle. The first choice in shuttles.

1652
ART DIRECTOR
Monte Hallis
WRITER
David Bishop
CLIENT
Six Flags Magic Mountain
EDITOR
Larry Bridges, Red Car
DIRECTOR
Jordan Cronenweth
DIRECTOR OF PHOTOGRAPHY
Jordan Cronenweth
AGENCY
Frank Tammariello, Della Femina,
Travisano, Los Angeles, CA
PRODUCTION COMPANY
David Dwiggins, Riverrun City Films
CREATIVE DIRECTOR
John Armistead, Jim Weller
MUSIC
Warren Dewey

1653
ART DIRECTOR
Duncan Milner
WRITER
Hal Maynard
CLIENT
San Diego Tribune
DIRECTOR
Gary Johns, Jeff Gorman
DIRECTOR OF PHOTOGRAPHY
Amir Hamed
AGENCY
Judy Stamp, WFC Advertising
PRODUCTION COMPANY
Sam Shapiro, Lilly Weingarten,
Johns&Gorman Films, Los Angeles,
CA

1652

SHOCK WAVE
30-second
SFX: EERIE, FUTURISTIC MUSIC.
ANNCR: Introducing Shock Wave.
Do you think you can take it . . .
. . . stand up.

1653

TRUE STORY
30-second
VO: Not long ago, the Carlsbad City Council was voting on plans to build
new condominiums in an old Eucalyptus grove.
BOY: You know, lots of us play in those trees. Please don't cut them down.
VO: Those trees still stand.
VO: There were bigger stories that day, but none more important.

1654

ART DIRECTOR
Stuart Pittman
WRITER
Sal Finazzo, Debbie Kasher, Fred Siegel
CLIENT
Black & Decker
EDITOR
Bob DeRise, A Cut Above
DIRECTOR
Mark Story
AGENCY
Joanne Murino, McCann-Erickson, New York, NY
PRODUCTION COMPANY
Cami Taylor, Story Piccolo Guliner
LIGHTING
Robert Liiv

1655

ART DIRECTOR
Carlton Taylor
WRITER
John Weil
CLIENT
Granny Goose Chips
DIRECTOR
Jon Francis
DIRECTOR OF PHOTOGRAPHY
Keith Mason
PRODUCER
Carrie Crosby
EXEC. PRODUCER
Sandra Marshall
PRODUCTION COMPANY
Deborah Billig, Jon Francis Films, San Francisco, CA

1654

A TIMELY IDEA
30-second
SFX: INTERCOM BUZZER
VO: (DOORMAN) "Mrs. Philpot on her way up."
VO (ANNCR): "4.3 minutes
from the lobby to the 5th floor.
Just enough time for the Dustbuster Plus.
It gets rid of fern leaves
basil leaves, bonsai leaves,
potato chips, corn chips,
barbecue banana chips.
Cat hairs dog hairs,
long hairs short hairs
dustballs
furfurballs
caraway seeds, sesame seeds,
cookie crumbs, cracker crumbs,
crumb cake crumbs.
In fact it
gets rid of just about
everything, except your
mother-in-law.

1655

HONK
30-second
VO: Recently, in a major city . . . people who know chips gathered to discuss the taste of Granny Goose.
MAN 1: Honk!
WOMAN 1: Honk, honk, honk.
VO: They tried tortilla chips . . .
MAN 2: Honk, honk.
VO: They tried corn chips . . .
WOMAN 2: Honk, honk.
MAN 3: Honk, honk.
MAN 4: Honk, honk.
MAN 5: Honk, honk.
VO: Finally, when all was said and done, . . . they came to one conclusion . . . Words cannot describe the great taste of Granny Goose

1661
ART DIRECTOR
Tony LaMonte
WRITER
Michael Shevack
CLIENT
Apple Computer, Inc.
EDITOR
David Dee, Eventime
DIRECTOR
Steve Horn
AGENCY
BBDO, New York, NY
PRODUCER
Barbara Mullins, Katy O'Brien, Andy
Chinich
PRODUCTION COMPANY
Steve Horn Productions

1662
ART DIRECTOR
Jeff France
WRITER
Bruce Mansfield
CLIENT
Sovran Bank
EDITOR
Tim Golbluff
DIRECTOR
Michael McNamara
AGENCY
Lawler Ballard, Norfolk, VA
PRODUCER
Bruce Mansfield
PRODUCTION COMPANY
Film Fair

661

EACH YOUR CHILDREN
-second
USIC.
ONG: Teach
ur children well
eir skill will tell how life will go by . . .
nd show them their own dreams, the one they'll
ck, is the one they'll know by.
each them how to think, teach them the things
at they can live by
nd show them how to grow because they know
ow much they must try.
O: Nothing's more important than teaching children well.
hat's why more schools teach on Apple than any other computer.
ONG: So just look at them and sigh . . . and know they love you.

1662

A MOVING STORY
60-second
ANNCR: Life in the Washington area is a moving experience. We live,
work, shop in lots of different places. Even different states. And now there's
a financial institution with offices in the District and Maryland and
Virginia, offering far more locations than anyone else. Now what could be
more fitting for such a mobile society than a bank that's so obviously on
the move.
Sovran Bank. We're right for the times.

1663

ART DIRECTOR
Jamie Carlson
WRITER
Frank Merriam
CLIENT
First of America Bank Corporation
EDITOR
Janice Rosenthal, Avenue Edit
DIRECTOR
Joe Murray, Film Fair
AGENCY
Lawler Ballard Advertising,
Kalamazoo, MI
PRODUCER
Joanne Bettman
PRODUCTION COMPANY
FilmFair
CREATIVE DIRECTOR
Frank Merriam

1664

ART DIRECTOR
Rich Kimmel, Ken Amaral
WRITER
Walt Hampton
CLIENT
Citicorp Savings
DIRECTOR
Jack Piccolo
AGENCY
N W Ayer, Inc., Chicago, IL
PRODUCER
Bob Carney
PRODUCTION COMPANY
Story Piccolo Guliner

1663

DECISION MAKING
60-second
VO: Behind every loan we make is a story.
And behind every story, a dream.
At First of America, we've become one of the Midwest's biggest bank
companies. By being, one of its biggest lenders.
All on a local level. In nearly 200 communities.
Around the region.
For a change of scenery . . . a change of pace.
Home improvement . . . self-improvement.
Ways to get around . . . ways to get away.
It's the stuff that, dreams are made of.
First of America. We're community banks, first.
An equal housing lender.
LOGO: First of America®.
We're Community Banks First.
Members FDIC.

1664

CONFERENCE ROOM
60-second
OPERATOR: The marketing plan of the Western Region . . .
MAN (TO ANOTHER): Is it 3:30?
OTHER MAN: Yeah.
FIRST MAN: I got to go.
SFX
MAN: C'mon. C'mon.
SFX
MAN: Excuse me.
MAN: No . . .
MAN: Wait.
(VO) How far do you have to go to do your banking?
(VO) At Citicorp Savings, we think no matter where you live or work, you
should be close to your money.
That's why we've built 46 branches.
. . . So there's always one nearby.
We've also built new Citicard Banking Centers . . .
. . . out of the weather, where you can bank 24 hours a day . . . every
day of the week.
And we've built a CitiPhone Service.
(VO) Now you can move money between accounts and check balances.
Everyday. 7 a.m. to 11 p.m.
MAN: Hello Citicorp . . .
WIFE: They're open?
(VO) Citicorp Savings. The Citi . . . is built for you.

1665

ART DIRECTOR
Kurt Tausche
WRITER
Kerry Casey
CLIENT
University of Minnesota
EDITOR
Tony Fischer
DIRECTOR
Jim Lund
AGENCY
Lisa Jarrard, Bozell, Jacobs,
Minneapolis, MN
PRODUCTION COMPANY
Jim Lund, James Productions

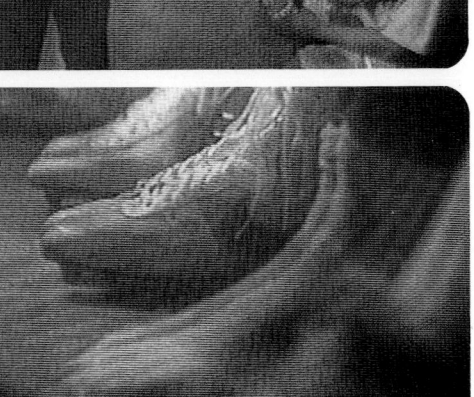

1666

ART DIRECTOR
Harvey Hoffenberg
WRITER
Ted Sann
CLIENT
Pepsi-Cola Company
EDITOR
Bob DeRise, A Cut Above
DIRECTOR
Joe Pytka
AGENCY
BBDO, New York, NY
PRODUCER
Gene Lofaro
PRODUCTION COMPANY
Pytka

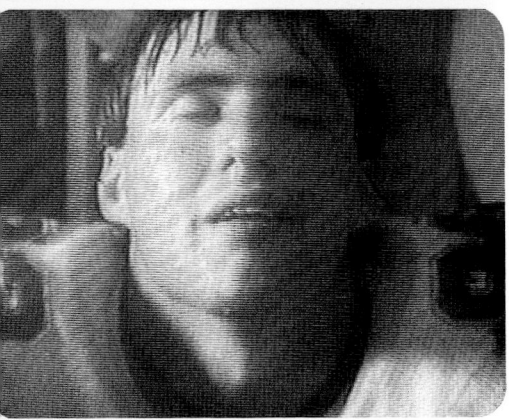

1665

OME
0-second
(MELLOW MUSIC UP AND UNDER THROUGHOUT)
PLAYERS: (CLAPS & CHEERS)
UTE: Alright, listen up! Listen up.
UTE: It's very, *very* hard to win on the road. But you guys did it.
UTE: I know you're beat up . . .
UTE: I know you're tired, but remember . . .
UTE: . . . next week we play at home. And there's no place . . .
MUSIC: (SWITCHES TO LIGHT MUSIC UP AND UNDER THROUGHOUT)
UTE: . . . like home.
PLAYER #1: Home. There's no place like home.
LL PLAYERS: There's no place like home . . .
LL PLAYERS: There's no place like home . . . There's . . .
LL PLAYERS: . . . no place like home.
FX: (VOICES BUILDING, MUSIC BUILDING)
LAYERS: There's no place like home . . . There's no place like
ome . . .
PLAYERS: There's no place like home!!
PLAYERS: There's no place like home.
LAYERS: There's no place like home.
FX: (STADIUM AMBIANCE.)
PLAYERS: Let's go.
TH PLAYER: I have a feeling we're not in Kansas anymore.
FX: (STADIUM UNDER)
MUSIC: (MINNESOTA ROUSER UP AND CONTINUE)
NNCR VO: Thanks to you, . . .
NNCR VO: . . . there's no place like home.
MUSIC FADES.

1666

TELEKINESIS
60-second
SCIENTIST: Experiment Number 128: Telekinesis. Subject will attempt to
move an object using only the power of his mind.
COACH: C'mon, Kravatz. All you gotta do is think refreshment . . . and
you can move that can right into your hand.
SCIENTIST: C'mon, concentrate.
SFX: MUSIC, MONITORING DEVICES.
METER READER: Nothing.
HEADSET OPERATOR: Think harder.
SFX: FAUCET OPENING. DROP OF WATER HITS BOTTOM OF SINK.
COACH: Think big refreshment.
METER READER: Still nothing.
SFX: FIRE HYDRANT SPRAYS
COACH: Think of the biggest refreshment you've ever had.
SFX: RUMBLING OF VENDING MACHINE VIBRATING.
HEADSET OPERATOR: Concentrate, Kravatz. Can't you taste it?
SCIENTIST: It's not happening. Let's take a break.FX: SELECT BUTTON,
CAN OPENING.
SCIENTIST: Kravatz, uh, could you think down . . . slowly?
SUPER & VO: Pepsi. The choice of a new generation.

1667

ART DIRECTOR
Rick Boyko, Miles Turpin
WRITER
Elizabeth Hayes, Bill Hamilton,
Dustin Jensen
CLIENT
Home Savings of America
EDITOR
Gayle Grant
DIRECTOR
Leslie Dektor
AGENCY
Chiat/Day, Los Angeles, CA
PRODUCER
Richard O'Neill, David Prince
PRODUCTION COMPANY
Petermann/Dektor

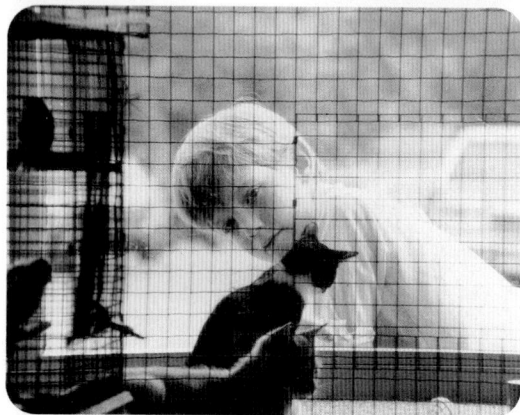

1668

ART DIRECTOR
Walt Taylor
WRITER
Laura Whitacre
CLIENT
Sovran Bank
EDITOR
Tim Golbluff
DIRECTOR
Joe Murray
AGENCY
Lawler Ballard, Norfolk, VA
PRODUCER
Jeff France, Bruce Mansfield
PRODUCTION COMPANY
Film Fair

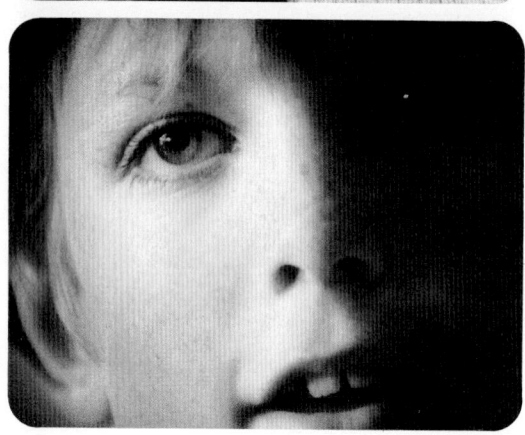

1667

DUSTIN JENSEN
60-second
MUSIC: THROUGHOUT.
DUSTIN: Well usually sometimes if I keep my room clean I will get an
allowance. Which I probably will get an allowance this week.
ANNCR: Dustin Jensen, Home Savings customer.
DUSTIN: Sometimes I'll get money from maybe a birthday or maybe like
my Mom instead of giving me a present put a hundred dollars in the
bank. I'm looking for a paper job that's just the only ways I get money.
I'm saving for mainly college. I was kinda hoping to get a scholarship.
But my grades aren't that hot.
I think I want to be a veterinarian when I grow 'cuz I really like animals.
I have a hamster, a bird . . .
ANNCR: Dustin is one of Home Savings' smartest customers. He's in the
fifth grade.
DUSTIN: I think it's a smart thing to save money because if nobody saved
money then it'd be kinda hard to get around in the world.

1668

SUMMER OF '86
60-second
ANNCR: Summertime.
It's the best time to visit a Sovran Bank.
We're all across Virginia, Maryland and D.C.
For floating a loan.
Getting away from home.
Or a little cold cash on a hot summer night.
Come see us this summer.

1669

ART DIRECTOR
Dennis Kightley
DESIGNER
Dennis Kightley
WRITER
Kevin Begos
CLIENT
Toyota Motor Sales, U.S.A., Inc.
EDITOR
Michael Miller
DIRECTOR
Brent Thomas
DIRECTOR OF PHOTOGRAPHY
Brent Thomas
AGENCY
Susan Hallinan, DFS Dorland
Worldwide, Torrance, CA
PRODUCTION COMPANY
Bill Braikowski, Michael King,
Coppos Films
CREATIVE DIRECTOR
John Mead, Kevin Begos
ASSOC. CREATIVE DIRECTOR
Richard Calvelli

1670

ART DIRECTOR
Nick Gisonde, Howard Smith
WRITER
Charlie Breen, Seth Fried
CLIENT
Miller Brewing Co. — Lite Beer
AGENCY
Backer & Spielvogel, New York, NY
PRODUCER
Eric Steinhauser

1669

GETAWAY
30-second
ANNCR: Whoa. There it goes. And it's getting away. The all-new getaway car from Toyota. Corolla FX16 for 1987.
Tough and agile on sticky tires and 4-wheel disc brakes, it slips through traffic snarls. The snarl is its gutsy, 16-valve, twin cam engine.
Zero to whatever's legal is immediate gratification. And it likes the passing lane. It'll hold highway cruising speeds all day long.
Sports car zoom. Liftback room. You can get away with more in an FX16. Just fold the rear seatbacks down. It hauls.
Looking good. Even as a blur. The all-new Toyota Corolla FX16 is. The getaway car.
Who could ask for anything more! Toyota.

1670

THE CASE OF THE MISSING CASE/SOLUTION
75-second
ANNCR VO: And now the conclusion of "The Case of The Missing Case."
(MUSIC UNDER)
MICKEY: It started out as a party, but turned into . . .
. . . The Case of The Missing Case.
SFX: LIGHTNING NOISE, THUNDER, PARTY NOISES.
BEN: (GRUNT)
DAVE: Incredible feat.
BOB: Thank you.
SFX: ELECTRICAL NOISE UPSET CROWD.
JOHN MADDEN: Hey! Who turned out the lights?!!! (DRAMATIC MUSIC BEGINS)
LEE MEREDITH: Ooh! Mickey.
MICKEY: It's OK Doll.
BEN DAVIDSON: No it's not, there's a case of Miller Lite missing.
RAY NITSCHE: Who took it?
MICKEY: It had to be somebody in this room.
GROUP: Rodney!! (ACCUSINGLY)
RODNEY: Hey guys take it easy, will ya.
BOOG POWELL: Why did you do it Rodney! Because Lite tastes great?
GROUP: Yeah!
L.C.: Or cause Lites' less filling.
GROUP: Yeah!
RODNEY: I tell ya I didn't do it. Well I'm not even Rodney.
(MUSIC CHANGES)

1671

ART DIRECTOR
Rick Boyko, Miles Turpin
WRITER
Elizabeth Hayes, Bill Hamilton, Judy Kleinmeyer
CLIENT
Home Savings of America
EDITOR
Gayle Grant
DIRECTOR
Leslie Dektor
AGENCY
Chiat/Day, Los Angeles, CA
PRODUCER
Richard O'Neill, David Prince
PRODUCTION COMPANY
Petermann/Dektor

1672

ART DIRECTOR
Tony DeGregorio
WRITER
Rich Pels
CLIENT
Subaru of America
EDITOR
David Dee, Eventime
DIRECTOR
Steve Horn, Steve Horn, Inc.
AGENCY
LHS&B, New York, NY
PRODUCER
Bob Nelson

1671

THE KLEINMEYERS
60-second
MUSIC: UNDER THROUGHOUT.
WOMAN: Well . . . it's a long skinny house.
You know the rooms are long and skinny, and I've got my big shade tree. I've got a porch where I can hang a porch swing and sit out on the front porch and watch the traffic go up and down the street.
ANNCR: Judy Kleinmeyer, Home Savings customer.
JUDY: You sit down on the porrch swing with, you know, the lil' old lady next door and visit with her in the evening in the summertime and talk about her dog and her arthritis and her tomato plants in the backyard. And . . . you just feel like you belong there. I'm content with the area. Some people don't think it's the best but like I say my house payment is a lot different than their house payment. I can change the color of the carpet every 2-3 years if I want to.
FENNEMAN: When Judy Kleinmeyer called Home Savings for a home loan she said she found the perfect front porch with a wonderful house attached.
JUDY: I have felt at home in it from the time I moved in . . .
. . . it's just one of those places that I felt at home in immediately.

1672

GETTING THERE
45-second
ANNCR VO: In 1981, the French Ski Team missed an important meet.
The U.S. Team arrived early.
In '82 the Austrians were stranded.
The U.S. Team arrived early.
And in '86 the Italians ran into a small problem.
For 10 years, the 4 wheel drive Subaru has helped the U.S. Ski Team get a jump on the competition.
Except in '84 when the Swedish women's team broke down.
U.S. SKIER: Howdy Ma'am.
Subaru. The official car of the U.S. Ski Team.

1673
ART DIRECTOR
Gary Conway
WRITER
Gary Conway
CLIENT
Seven-Up
EDITOR
Bob Carr
DIRECTOR
Leslie Dektor
AGENCY
Gary Conway, Leo Burnett, Chicago, IL
PRODUCTION COMPANY
Phyllis Koenig, Petermann/Dektor
CREATIVE DIRECTOR
Phil Raskin

1674
ART DIRECTOR
Roy Carruthers
WRITER
Steve Jeffery
CLIENT
Seagram's Golden Wine Cooler
EDITOR
Stuart Waks
DIRECTOR
David Ashwell
AGENCY
Nancy Braunstein, Ogilvy & Mather, New York, NY
PRODUCER
Danny Boyle
CREATIVE DIRECTOR
Malcolm End

1673

SUNNY LANE HOME/MONO/REV.
30-second
SFX: CAN POP, FIZZ
SONG: Feels so good
Comin' down
Feels so good
Comin' down
Seven-Up splashin'
On the fun
Pourin' cool 'n clear
On everyone! Seven-Up
SONG; Feels so good 7Up pure refreshment
Seven-Up

1674

WEDDING
60-second
BUTLER: Bride's party or groom's party.
BRUCE WILLIS: Who's having the best party . . .
Hey Max . . . Hi buddy . . . he remembers me.
(TO WAITER) Thank you Seagram's.
WAITER: My name's not Seagram's sir.
BRUCE WILLIS: If you're watching Mr. Seagram's, I want to thank you for bringing us Seagram's Golden Wine Cooler. It's brand new . . . and you did a great job.
GROOM: Who invited him?
BRIDE: I did.
BRUCE WILLIS: (TO GUESTS) I knew the bride when she liked to Rock n' Roll.
(TO BRIDE) Now what's he got that I haven't got.
BRIDE: He's got me.
BRUCE: I have a toast. Seagram's Golden. It's wet and it's dry.
BRIDE: Is that the toast?
BRUCE: Nah, that's the commercial. To Rock 'n Roll.
BRIDE: Golden days.
VO: Seagram's Golden Wine Cooler. It's wet and it's dry.

1675

ART DIRECTOR
Tony Kremka
WRITER
John LaRock
CLIENT
Eveready Battery Co.
EDITOR
Norman O'Dell, FlashCut
DIRECTOR
Bruce Dowad
DIRECTOR OF PHOTOGRAPHY
Fred Schuller
AGENCY
Natalie Quinn, Avrett, Free &
Ginsberg, New York, NY
PRODUCTION COMPANY
Mindy Goldberg, Jennie & Co.

1676

ART DIRECTOR
David Kennedy, Peter Moore
WRITER
Jim Riswold
CLIENT
Nike
DIRECTOR
Joe Pytka
AGENCY
Wieden & Kennedy, Portland, OR
PRODUCER
Bill Davenport
PRODUCTION COMPANY
Pytka Productions

1675

MORE POWER TO THE USA
60-second
MUSIC & LYRICS: MORE POWER TO LIVE
MORE POWER TO GIVE
MORE POWER TO PLAY
MORE POWER TO DO THE THINGS
WE DO TODAY—
EVEREADY—MORE POWER TO THE USA.
MORE POWER TO FLY
MORE POWER TO SING.
MORE POWER TO PLAY
MORE POWER TO DO THE THINGS
WE DO TODAY—
EVEREADY—MORE POWER TO THE USA.
ANN VO: No one gives you more power than Eveready . . . Eveready leads
the world in portable power and light, with every kind of battery for every
kind of need.
MUSIC & LYRICS: EVEREADY—MORE POWER TO THE USA!

1676

MEN AT WORK
60-second
MUSIC THROUGHOUT)
SFX: PLAYER BANTER.
MOSES (UNDER LOGO): Hey, way to work, man.

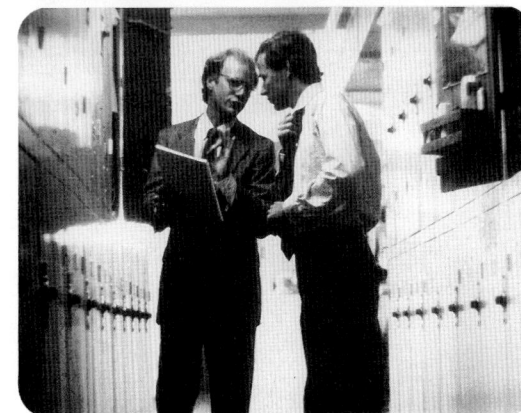

1677

ART DIRECTOR
Ross Sutherland
WRITER
John Doig
CLIENT
Pepsico
DIRECTOR
David Mallet
AGENCY
Ed Kleban, Ogilvy & Mather, New
York, NY
PRODUCTION COMPANY
Jackie Byford, Tara McCarthy,
MGMM London
MUSIC
David Dundas

1678

ART DIRECTOR
Mike Campbell
WRITER
Gary Graf
CLIENT
Apple Computer, Inc.
EDITOR
Dennis Hayes
DIRECTOR
Joe Pytka
AGENCY
BBDO, New York, NY
PRODUCER
Gene Lofaro
PRODUCTION COMPANY
Pytka

1677

TINA
60-second
TINA: We're in the mood for moving,
moving into something new
We got the taste for living . . .
We got the taste for love.
We got the taste for Pepsi
and we just can't get enough.
We got the taste for living,
We got the taste for love,
We got the taste for Pepsi and we
just can't get enough.

1678

THE RIVALRY
60-second
1ST MAN: Come on admit it, it was a great shot.
2ND MAN: For a beginner.
1ST MAN: Beginner? Two out of three pal two out of three.
2ND MAN: I think you're still trying to get even because I had the higher
grade point average.
1ST MAN: Yet as I recall, the lowest starting salary.
2ND MAN: Yea, but at the hottest shop in town.
1ST MAN: Yea, as an assistant to an assistant.
2ND MAN: Oh O.K., O.K. so who was first to the Vice President?
1ST MAN: And last with the corner office. . . .
2ND MAN: But if I can land the North Bay project . . .
1ST MAN: Yea . . .
2ND MAN: I'm talking senior partnership.
1ST MAN: Really?
2ND MAN: How does it look?
1ST MAN: You tell me.
2ND MAN: (WHISTLES) What a production. You guys must have had
outside help on this one.
1ST MAN: No way, we put the whole thing together ourselves.
2ND MAN: Come on.
1ST MAN: No really, we did everything on our computer.
2ND MAN: Revenue projections, impact studies?
1ST MAN: Everything.
2ND MAN: So ah what kind of computer?
1ST MAN: Oh, I'm running late.
2ND MAN: Come on, what kind of computer??????

1679

ART DIRECTOR
Jim Doyle
DESIGNER
Jim Doyle
ANIMATOR/ARTIST
Kurtz and Friends
WRITER
Bill Brooke
CLIENT
Toyota Motor Sales, U.S.A., Inc.
EDITOR
Steve McCoy, Sim Sadler
DIRECTOR
Bill Butler
DIRECTOR OF PHOTOGRAPHY
Bill Butler
AGENCY
Sheldon Levy, DFS Dorland
Worldwide, Torrance, CA
PRODUCTION COMPANY
Chris Petersen, Brian Donnelly,
Petersen Communications
CREATIVE DIRECTOR
John Mead, Kevin Begos

1680

ART DIRECTOR
Paul Rubinstein
DESIGNER
Paul Rubinstein
WRITER
Mike Pitts
CLIENT
Hardee's
EDITOR
Jay Gold Films
DIRECTOR
David Mallet
DIRECTOR OF PHOTOGRAPHY
Nick Knowland
AGENCY
Ed Kleban, Ogilvy & Mather, New
York, NY
PRODUCTION COMPANY
Jackie Byford, MGMM London
CREATIVE DIRECTOR
Mike Pitts

1679

DYNASTY
60-second
MUSIC: (EFFECT)
ANNCR: You've shaped it in your mind: total performance.
MUSIC: (EFFECT)
ANNCR: Now the all-new Toyota Supra brings it alive. (EFFECT) Supra
shape: designed by the wind. (EFFECT) Supra power: created by a three
liter 24-valve 200 horsepower engine that is all heart. Supra suspension:
racing-type double wishbone, fully independent. Supra cockpit: where you
perform.
MUSIC UP: (EFFECT)
ANNCR: The new Toyota Supra. This is performance without compromise.
(EFFECT). Now, the Supra Dynasty begins. "Who could ask for anything
more!"

1680

BURGER WARS
60-second
SFX: MARTIAL DRUMS
CLOWN ADJUTANT: Huh, huh, gener'l, the troops are ready, huh, huh,
CLOWN GENERAL: Okay, huh, huh, let's go!
CLOWNS: Huh, huh, huh . . .
OLD LADY: Here they come, girls! Let's get 'em!
OLD LADIES: Where's the . . .
SFX: THUMP OF RAMP DOOR
ANNCR (VO): They called it the Burger Wars. But now that the smoke's
starting to clear one thing's pretty obvious: The big boys, for all their
noise, didn't really have anything new to say . . . did they?
SFX: BAM!
ANNCR (VO): Well now, someone does. Someone who's taken the burger,
rethought it, made it thicker, succulent, full of natural juices. Taken it off
the battlefield and brought it closer to where it shuld have been all along
Home.
ADJUTANT: Cheer up, Gener'l. *This*'ll really get 'em . . .
SFX: BOINGGG!!!
ANNCR (VO): The new quarter-pound burgers. From Hardee's. A little
closer to home.

1681
ART DIRECTOR
Rick Boyko, Miles Turpin
WRITER
Elizabeth Hayes, Bill Hamilton,
Carmen Cortez
CLIENT
Home Savings of America
EDITOR
Gayle Grant
DIRECTOR
Leslie Dektor
AGENCY
Chiat/Day, Los Angeles, CA
PRODUCER
Richard O'Neill, David Prince
PRODUCTION COMPANY
Petermann/Dektor

1682
ART DIRECTOR
Bob Watson
WRITER
Joe DeVivo
CLIENT
McDonald's
DIRECTOR
Steve Horn
AGENCY
Bob Koslow, Mike Diedrich, Leo
Burnett, Chicago, IL
PRODUCTION COMPANY
Linda Horn, Steve Horn Prod.
CREATIVE DIRECTOR
Bud Watts

1681

THE CORTEZES
60-second
MUSIC: UNDER THROUGHOUT.
CARMEN: Well, I've been saving my money because at our age my
husband and I ya know he's still working and one of these days he's
gonna retire, and we would like to travel a little bit.
ANNCR: Carmen Cortez. Home Savings of America customer.
CARMEN: I was a widow the first time. With two children. It wasn't easy, I
never went anyplace. Because I didn't have the money to do anything or
because everything was for the kids you know and pay my bills and make
my house payment. And then when I met Mr. Cortez things were a little
easier; for me. And he wants to take me to Mexico City and he wants to
take me to Cancun and he wants to take me here and there.
But, I want to go to New York.
ANNCR: Home Savings takes very good care of Carmen's money and about
a million other people's as well.
CARMEN: Most of all I would like to see Ms. Liberty. And get up way up
on her crown and uh get up way up to the top and look from there. This
is my country.

1682

RECITAL
60-second
BECKY: I don't want to do this.
DAD: You'll be great.
BECKY: I'll be scared.
DAD: Just think of how glad you'll be when you're all done and maybe
we'll all go to McDonald's.
BECKY (VO): I'll be glad when I'm done.
I'll be glad when I'm done. I'll be glad . . . (SIGH) . . .
Think McDonald's
BECKY (VO) SONG: Oh I wish I were already there
Instead of here playing this song.
Oh I would have a big
Chocolate shake
A cheeseburger
BECKY (VO) SONG: And also whoops and also fries.
And I would eat all my fries myself
And not give any to my dumb brother
Hands off,
They're mine
All mine
Oh boy my recital is almost done
It wasn't bad,
I'm still alive
And now I can have my chocolate shake
My cheeseburger and also whoops

1683
ART DIRECTOR
Bruce Dundore
WRITER
Ted Sann
CLIENT
Pepsi-Cola Company
EDITOR
Steve Schreiber, Editors Gas
DIRECTOR
Joe Pytka
AGENCY
BBDO, New York, NY
PRODUCER
David Frankel
PRODUCTION COMPANY
Pytka

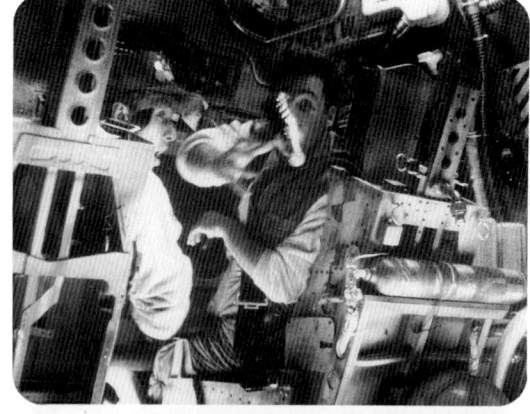 

1684
ART DIRECTOR
Tony LaMonte, Phil Triolo
WRITER
John Greenberger, Jimmy Siegel
CLIENT
Apple Computer, Inc.
EDITOR
David Dee, Eventime
DIRECTOR
Steve Horn
AGENCY
BBDO, New York, NY
PRODUCER
Barbara Mullins, Katy O'Brien, Andy Chinich
PRODUCTION COMPANY
Steve Horn Productions

1683

FLOATS
60-second
COMMAND CONTROL: Good work, Starship. We'll talk to you at O-six-hundred.
PILOT #1: That's a copy.
COMMAND CONTROL: Why don't you guys take a break?
PILOT #2: How 'bout a Pepsi?
SFX: BUTTON PRESSED. LATCH OPENS.
PILOT #1: There's only one left.
SFX: WALTZ MUSIC.
SFX: HATCH OPENING.
SUPER & VO: Pepsi. The choice of a new generation.

1684

NIGHTMARE
60-second
ANDY: Hi girls.
ANDY: Hi Doreen.
GIRLS: Hi Andy ready for the history final?
ANDY: History final? Is that today?
GIRLS: It sure is.
ANDY: Ah man, I forgot all about it. Let me borrow your notes will ya?
GIRLS: Andy, class starts in 5 minutes.
ANDY: What?
GIRLS: See ya Andy.
GIRLS: Hope you have your term paper finished. LAUGHING. . . .
ANDY: Wait, I haven't been to history class in awhile. I've forgotten which room it's in.
GIRLS: It's right here Andy.
SFX.
GIRLS: Mr. Spencer's gonna kill you.
SFX.
GASP.
MUSIC
ANNCR: The reason more kids use Apple than any other personal computer is because it makes keeping up with school a lot easier.
ANNCR: And that makes waking up to school a lot nicer.
MUSIC.

1685
ART DIRECTOR
Peter Lauer
DESIGNER
Peter Lauer
ANIMATOR/ARTIST
Rick Spain, Ann St. Pierre, Howard Post
WRITER
David Felton
CLIENT
MTV, New York, NY
EDITOR
Tim Farrell
PRODUCER
Peter Lauer
AUDIO ENGINEER
Tom Clack

1686
ART DIRECTOR
Arnold Blum, Arthur Vibert
WRITER
Paul Cappelli
CLIENT
Coca-Cola Company/USA Division
EDITOR
Bob Derise
DIRECTOR
Ridley Scott
DIRECTOR OF PHOTOGRAPHY
Huey Johnson
AGENCY
McCann-Erickson, New York, NY
PRODUCER
Maryellen Pirozzoli
PRODUCTION COMPANY
RSA Film Ltd.

1685

RACHEL—NEW FALL SEASON
30-second
STUDIO: As Rachel turned on the TV
she knew her life would never be the same
MTV's new fall season:
Shoot Madonna's next video
Manage David Lee Roth
What the . . .
Work out all week with Janet Jackson
Fly to a private concert with Tina Turner
Spend a weekend in the studio with Don Johnson
Send a week on the road with Van Halen
Rick never told me about this!
Take a vacation with Huey Lewis
Spend a week with Paul McCartney
Catch the Clapton and Friends concert and
the Weird Halloween video special
And don't forget every Friday night is party night!
I feel so strange . . . yet wonderful!
MTV's new fall season . . . get yours now!!

1686

MAX TRUCK
30-second
(SFX)
(SUPER: SOME TIME NEXT WEEK)
(MUSIC BEGINS)
BOY 1: What's that?
BOY 3: Looks like a cross-hatch generator.
(MUSIC FADES OUT)
MAX HEADROOM: (JUMBLED "MAX" JIBBERISH).
MAX HEADROOM: This is Ma ma ma Max Headroom . . .
BOY 2: Max Headroom?
MAX: Ahhhhhh . . .
MAX: Cokeologists.
BOY 3: He sees us.
MAX: Where there's a wave, there's a Coke.
BOY 2: I like him.
MAX: Join the club.
MAX: Ya know . . . more people prefer the new taste of Coke over
Pepsi. . . .
BOY 1: Let's take him home.
MAX: Good idea.
MAX: So you Pepsi drinkers
now's your chance. Become a Cokeologist.
MAX: (SHOUTS IN ECHO)
Catch the Wave. Coke.

1687
ART DIRECTOR
Paul Walter
WRITER
John Greenberger
CLIENT
Polaroid
EDITOR
Larry Bridges, Red Car
DIRECTOR
Tony Richardson
AGENCY
BBDO, New York, NY
PRODUCER
Jeff Felter
PRODUCTION COMPANY
Dreamquest

1688
ART DIRECTOR
Don Easdon
WRITER
Bill Heater
CLIENT
John Hancock Financial Services
DIRECTOR
Joe Pytka
AGENCY
Hill Holliday, Boston, MA
PRODUCER
Mary Ellen Argentieri
PRODUCTION COMPANY
Joseph Pytka Productions

1687

JOURNEY
60-second
ANNCR VO: I'd like you to join me on a journey through the most unique total photographic system ever made.
It's the completely automatic new Spectra System from Polaroid.
Let's go inside.
Simply press the shutter and two separate systems measure me . . . and the background for light.
I'm also automatically measured by sonar for distance,
and in 1/20th of a second an amazing new lens automatically snaps my image into sharp focus.
Now, the flash goes off, and
my precisely measured smiling face hurtles through space . . .
Down onto a brilliant new Polaroid film.
A churning, molecular sea of stunning new colors that will result in a brilliant new
Polaroid picture.
A larger, more beautiful picture. Picture, after picture.
And I'm able to do all this. Simply by doing this.
The new Polaroid Spectra System. We take your pictures seriously.

1688

TRADITIONAL FAMILY
30-second
(SFX) BOYS: (GIGGLES)
MAN: Man, that gas bill last month was a real choker.
WOMAN: You're not kidding.
(SFX) BOYS: (GIGGLES-KITCHEN UTENSILS)
MAN: How's work going?
WOMAN: Real good.
SFX: (CONTINUED)
MAN: Ahem.
You heard any good jokes?
WOMAN: No.
MAN: Too bad, these boys would love to hear them.
SFX: (CONTINUED)
MAN: Hey boys, get smart.
BOYS: (SNICKER)

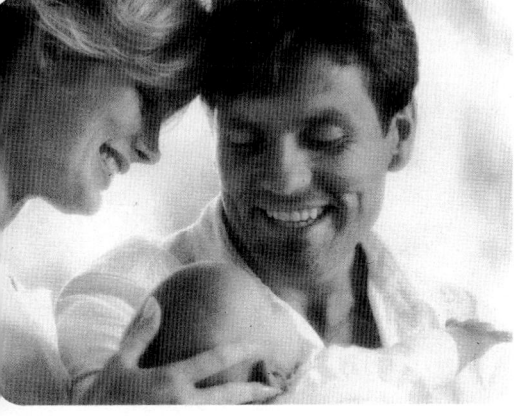

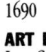

1689
ART DIRECTOR
Susan Barron
WRITER
Susan Barron
CLIENT
Proctor & Gamble
EDITOR
Alan Eisenberg
DIRECTOR
Greg Weinschenker
AGENCY
Pam Buckner, DFS Dorland, New York, NY
PRODUCER
Sharon Starr
CREATIVE DIRECTOR
Jean-Manuel Guyader
EXEC. CREATIVE DIRECTOR
Eric Weber

1690
ART DIRECTOR
Lou Carvell
WRITER
Abbie Simon
CLIENT
Ad Council — Food Stamps
EDITOR
Billy Williams
DIRECTOR
Stan Schofield
AGENCY
Danni Jesudowich, RS&H, New York, NY
PRODUCTION COMPANY
John Kamen, Sandbank Films
ACCOUNT SPVSR.
Harvey Kipnis

1689

IMAGINE
30-second
MUSIC UNDER THROUGHOUT
ANNCR (VO): If you knew absolutely nothing of the ways of the world and couldn't speak and could barely see—can you imagine how important touch would be? That's what it's like to be a baby. In fact, it's only through touch that a new baby discovers the world. So it's vitally important that everything surrounding him be clean enough to trust against his tender skin. As clean as clothes washed in Dreft. Dreft with enriched borax for a clean you can trust.

1690

TOUGH TIMES/MEALTIMES
60-second
MUSIC UP
ANNCR: Here, in this land of plenty, about 10 million people are hungry. Many don't know they're eligible for Food Stamps.
Most are family people going through some temporary troubles. They've lost a job, a farm or a husband.
Food Stamps can help. You don't have to be on public assistance. You can have a job and still qualify.
Now one phone call can get you information to tell you if you qualify for Food Stamps and how to get them.
America has made a place at our table of plenty for you. We want to make sure you get there.
Call for a free brochure. 1-800-453-4000 Food Stamps.
Meal times don't have to be tough times.

1691

ART DIRECTOR
Len McCarron
WRITER
Phil Dusenberry, Ted Sann
CLIENT
Apple Computer, Inc.
EDITOR
Steve Schreiber, Editors Gas
DIRECTOR
Steve Horn
AGENCY
BBDO, New York, NY
PRODUCER
Barbara Mullins
PRODUCTION COMPANY
Steve Horn Productions

1692

ART DIRECTOR
Don Easdon
WRITER
Bill Heater
CLIENT
John Hancock Financial Services
DIRECTOR
Joe Pytka
AGENCY
Hill Holliday, Boston, MA
PRODUCER
Mary Ellen Argentieri
PRODUCTION COMPANY
Joseph Pytka Productions

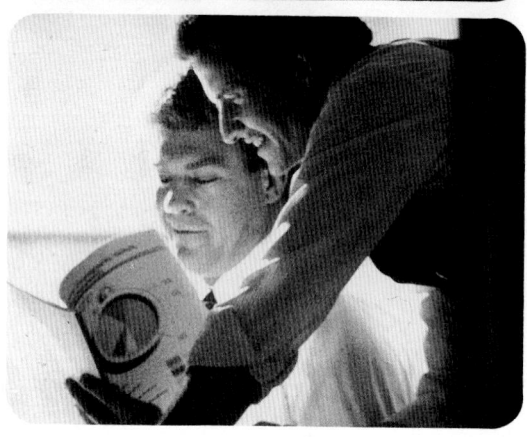

1691

PUT MAC IN
60-second
MUSIC THROUGHOUT . . .
Put MacIntosh in the middle of your company and see remarkable things start to happpen.
Those who shoot from the hip suddenly show signs of organization.
And those who live by the book show glimmers of Creativity.
Ideas surface from people you thought had retired.
Reports that could bore the dead, sparkle with graphic clarity.
Your 8th floor will actually communicate with your 7th.
Presentations begin to border on the flamboyant.
And your most tireless worker will actually have time to take an afternoon off.
And a budding genius will be found, where once a face was seen but not heard.
And one by one each and every person in your company will begin to discover the power of MacIntosh. The Power, To Be Your Best.

1692

SAM OSTROFF
60-second
(SCENE: SAM AND BARBARA EATING IN A RESTAURANT)
B: (OPENS A FORTUNE COOKIE)
Be fruitful and multiply
(BOTH LAUGH)
S: You know apart from the fact that we love each other and we know we can live together . . . it makes sense from a financial point also.
B: Is that how you see it?
S: No. No . . . it's just that along with everything else there's that as well
B: I don't know. You make it sound like . . . a merger or something.
S: All I meant is that we wouldn't need two cars . . . two apartments . . . two of everything. That's all I meant.
S: Let's just forget that. Um. The important thing is . . . is that we love each other . . . and

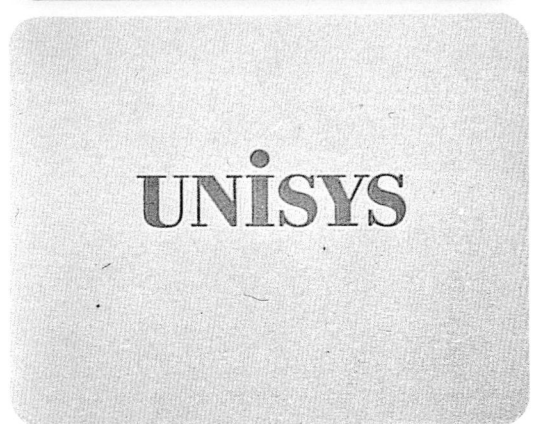

1693
CLIENT
Tourism Canada
EDITOR
Norm Odell
DIRECTOR
Bruce Dowad
DIRECTOR OF PHOTOGRAPHY
Brian Thomson
AGENCY
Derek Ellis, Bob Kirk, Camp
Associates, Ltd., Toronto, Canada
PRODUCER
Candace Conacher
CREATIVE DIRECTOR
John McIntyre, Arnold Wicht

1694
ART DIRECTOR
Matt Basile
WRITER
Marvin Waldman
CLIENT
Unisys
EDITOR
Ashkinos
DIRECTOR
Neil Tardio
AGENCY
Young & Rubicam, New York, NY
PRODUCER
Texas East
PRODUCTION COMPANY
Neil Tardio Production

1693

NEW WORLD REVISED
60-second
Canada
Come widen your horizons
Canada
Come to the world next door
Canada
Come & widen your horizons
Come to the world next door
SUPER: Canada
The World Next Door

1694

CREATION
60-second
VO: Imagine the power of two great computer companies coming together as one.
Resources . . . not just doubled, but raised to the power of two.
Introducing UNISYS.
True competition in the computer industry.
And a single winner will emerge. You.

1695
CLIENT
Tourism Canada
EDITOR
Bob Kennedy
DIRECTOR
Bruce Dowad
DIRECTOR OF PHOTOGRAPHY
Brian Thomson
AGENCY
Derek Ellis, Bob Kirk, Camp
Associates Ltd., Toronto, Canada
PRODUCER
Candace Conacher
CREATIVE DIRECTOR
John McIntyre, Arnold Wicht

1696
ART DIRECTOR
Tom Walker
WRITER
Ted Naron
CLIENT
United Airlines
AGENCY
Leo Burnett, Chicago, IL
PRODUCER
Dave Musial
CREATIVE DIRECTOR
Bud Watts

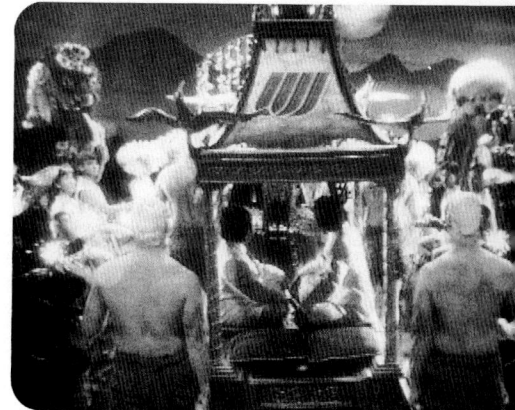

1695

OLD WORLD
60-second
SFX WAVES ON SHORE
MUSIC BEGINS
SFX BELL RINGING
SFX CARRIAGE ON COBBLESTONES
SFX STEAM ENGINE
SFX TRAIN WHISTLE
SFX HOTEL DESK BELL
Come to Canada
And widen your horizons
SFX GUNFIRE
Come to the world next door

1696

KING REV
60-second
NARRATOR VO: (YOUNG ORIENTAL WOMAN) Once upon a time,
far across the great ocean,
there flew a gleaming carriage on the wings of birds. The carriage was
called United, and the people who flew in it were happy, for everywhere
the carriage flew, the skies were friendly.
WOMEN CHANTERS: Friendly skies, friendly skies,
NARRATOR VO: But people were sad too. Why cannot we fly through
friendly skies to other side of great ocean.
Then one day, a new wind blew.
It blew and blew the friendly skies from all fifty states to our land . . . to
Beijing, Shanghai, Osaka, Tokyo, Melbourne, Sydney, Seoul, Manila,
Auckland, Singapore, Taipei, Bangkok, Hong Kong.
Welcome, gleaming carriage of United.
United Royal Pacific Service truly a fresh breeze across the Pacific.
SONG: You're not just flying . . .
You're flying
The friendly skies.

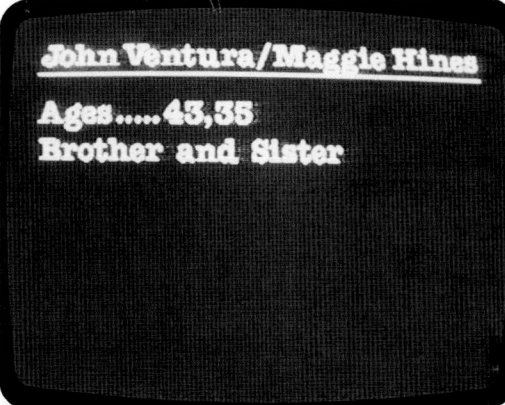

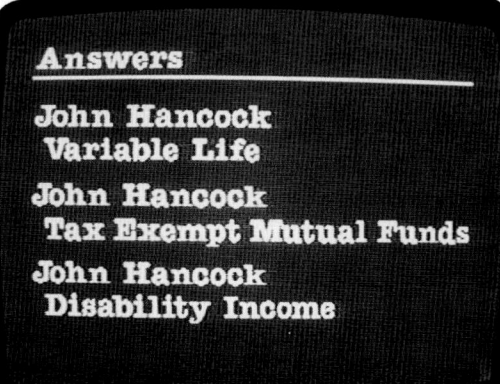

1697

ART DIRECTOR
Don Schneider
WRITER
Jonathan Mandell
CLIENT
Polaroid
EDITOR
Rob Tortoriello, Bert's Place
DIRECTOR
Jim Spencer
AGENCY
BBDO, New York, NY
PRODUCER
Jerry Cammisa
PRODUCTION COMPANY
Dreamquest

1698

ART DIRECTOR
Don Easdon
WRITER
Bill Heater
CLIENT
John Hancock Financial Services
DIRECTOR
Joe Pytka
AGENCY
Hill Holliday, Boston, MA
PRODUCER
Mary Ellen Argentieri
PRODUCTION COMPANY
Joseph Pytka Productions

97

ORLDS
0-second
(MUSIC—SINGERS)
ne world of art.
uid. Inspired.
eled by passion and bound by man's imagination.
(MUSIC—SINGERS)
ne world of science. Logical.
athematical.
he purest distillation of information.
USIC
ut, throughout time, when logic and order have meshed with inspiration
nd imagination,
e results have been some of men's greatest accomplishments.
n May 5th,
olaroid Corporation will introduce the Spectra System
nd the world of science and the world of art
ill become one.

1698

BROTHER & SISTER
60-second
BRO: Ah gee. I don't know.
You remember . . . Maggie . . . I certainly remember. When he could
pick up the both of us in one hand. One hand.
SIS: I know.I remember.
BRO: Oh man. Now . . . it's like it's our turn. You know what I mean?
SIS: I know. I know.
BRO: He can't drive at night anymore. Did you know that? Mom told me
that.

1699

ART DIRECTOR
Randy Akers
DESIGNER
Randy Akers, Nancy Laurence
ANIMATOR/ARTIST
Nancy Laurence
CLIENT
TIME
EDITOR
Randy Akers, Bob Resler
DIRECTOR
Randy Akers
DIRECTOR OF PHOTOGRAPHY
Bob Lyons, Don Canfield, Glen
Claybrook, David Phillips
AGENCY
Amy Wagoner, Hill, Holiday,
Connors, Cosmopulos, New York, NY
PRODUCTION COMPANY
Richard Quan, Broadcast Arts

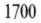

1700

ART DIRECTOR
Jeff Vetter
WRITER
Tim Kidwell
CLIENT
Anheuser-Busch, Inc.—Budweiser
DIRECTOR
Joe Pytka
AGENCY
D'Arcy Masius Benton & Bowles, St.
Louis, MO
PRODUCER
Jeb Schary
CREATIVE DIRECTOR
Gerry Mandel

1699

TIME HAS COME TODAY
2-minute
Time has come today
Young hearts can go their way
Can't put it off another day
I don't care what others say
They say we don't listen anyway
Time has come today
Now the time has come
No place to run
I might get burned up by the sun
But I had my fun
Now the time has come
There are things to realize
Time has come today
Time

1700

A CHANCE
60-second
SFX: ROOM AMBIENCE
STEWARD: OK, let me have your attention, guys . . .
(VO): . . . assignments for the day!
MUSIC: THEME, IN AND UNDER
SINGER: This Bud's . . . for all that you do . . .
AVO: Like many before, you came here asking for just one thing—
—a chance.
STEWARD: . . . and Sid—Sidowski!
HERO: Szydlowski!
STEWARD: Si—wha?
HERO: It's pronounced Shi-*dwo*-ski . . .
MUSIC: BUILDING, TEMPO QUICKENS
SINGER: It's time to
Make your new start
SINGER: You know that
You'll do your part
Whatever the test
You give it your best
You'll show you've
Got the heart
'Cause you—
SINGERS: (You) make
America work—and—
This Bud's for you . . .

1701
WRITER
Phil Dusenberry, Ted Sann
CLIENT
Apple Computer, Inc.
EDITOR
David Dee, Eventime
DIRECTOR
Fred Petermann
AGENCY
BBDO, New York, NY
PRODUCER
Karl Fischer, Vicki Halliday
PRODUCTION COMPANY
Petermann/Dektor

1702
ART DIRECTOR
Vicki Smith
WRITER
Scott Crawford
CLIENT
Costa Del Mar
EDITOR
Kevin Doran
DIRECTOR
Bill Randall
AGENCY
Howard, Merrell & Partners, Inc.,
Raleigh, NC
PRODUCTION COMPANY
AFI

1701

POWER IMAGE
60-second
SFX THROUGHOUT . . .
Think of all the power on this earth.
The power of nature and human endurance.
The power of spirit and speed and determination.
And then realize that of all this power none is more potent than the power
that resides within the minds of us all.
The power to learn,
to communicate.
To imagine, to create.
The Power To Be Your Best.

1702

COOL
60-second
(SFX: GULLS, OCEAN WAVES.)
CORKY CARROLL (OC): People ask, "Corky, how can you be so *way*
cool?" Either you're cool or you're not. Am I right? Or am I right? I'm
right. Take these shades, Costa Del Mars. Sure, they look great. And
they're made in America. That's cool. But you gotta do more than look
cool to be cool, right?
GIRL #1: (OC) Right, Corky.
CORKY: So Costa Del Mar uses the same polarized and polycarbonate
lenses eye docs do. No distortion. No funky colors. Perfect! They block out
more gnarly UV rays than two tons o' sunscreen. And the frames? Almost
too cool. Try this with your cheapo nylon frames. No way, Bud. Only Zyl
frames from Costa twist and turn like this. So even if you've got a head
like a melon, they're gonna fit. Perfect. They're even guaranteed to last a
lifetime. Outrageous.
(SFX: CRASH OF WAVE OVER SET.)
CORKY: (SPITTING OUT WATER) That was cool.

1703

ART DIRECTOR
Clark Frankel
WRITER
Florence Granello
CLIENT
Jamaica Tourist Board
EDITOR
Alan Rozek
DIRECTOR
Ed Bianchi
DIRECTOR OF PHOTOGRAPHY
Andrzej Bartkowiak
AGENCY
Young & Rubicam, New York, NY
PRODUCER
Laurie Kahn
PRODUCTION COMPANY
Bianchi Films

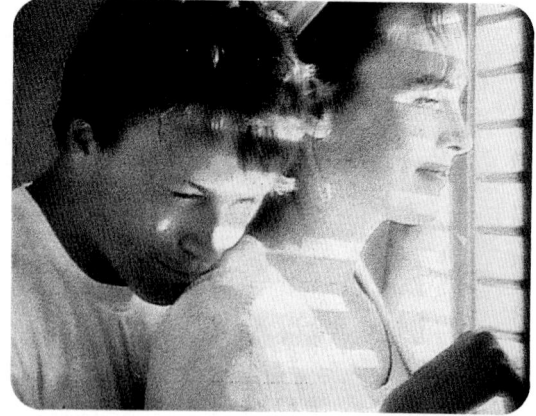
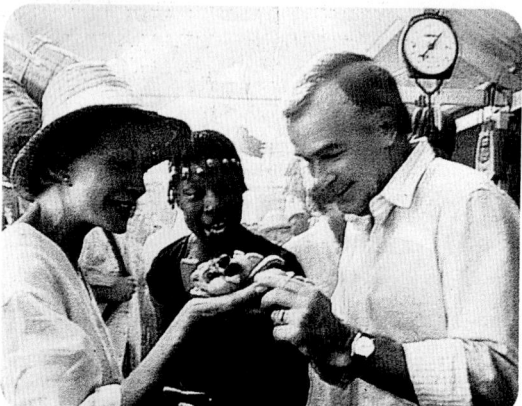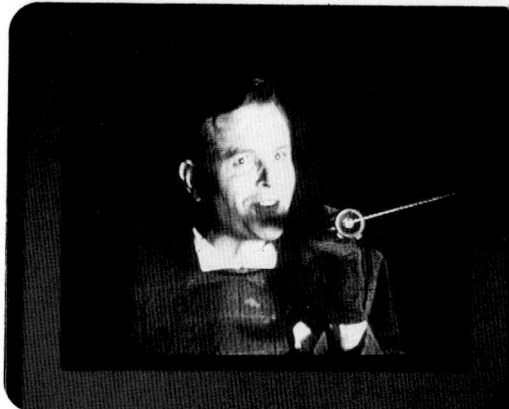

1704

ART DIRECTOR
Gary Johns
WRITER
Jeff Gorman
CLIENT
Chevrolet Nova
DIRECTOR
Gary Johns, Jeff Gorman
DIRECTOR OF PHOTOGRAPHY
Laszlo Kovacs
AGENCY
Bill Donaldson, Vic Olesen &
Partners, Los Angeles, CA
PRODUCTION COMPANY
Sam Schapiro, Lilly Weingarten,
Johns + Gorman Films

1703

COME BACK TO ROMANCE
60-second
(MUSIC: JAMAICA THEME MUSIC THROUGHOUT)
(SFX: LAUGHTER AND WATER SPLASH)
(SFX: OCEAN SURF)
(SFX: SHARP RAPS OF TENNIS GOLF AND TENNIS GAMES)
SOLO SINGER: (VO) Jamaica . . .
(SFX: SPLASHING WATER)
MAN: What is this?
SOLO SINGER: (VO) Oh-uhhhh Jamaica.
MAN: Oh.
(SFX: WATER SPLASHING)
SOLO SINGER: (VO) Jamaica. Come back to romance.
GROUP SINGERS: (VO) Jamaica. Jamaica.

1704

ANTIQUE AUCTION
60-second
AUCTIONEER: The winning bid on the 1996 Raydion microwave is fifteen
hundred. Now ladies and gentlemen, bidding will commence on the 1987
Chevrolet Nova. This mint condition, and original color and finish,
vintage automobile is a highly prized example of Japanese design and
American workmanship from the late 20th century. Bidding will
commence at 120. Now do I hear any advance on . . . Yes, I have a bid
of 130. Do I hear 140?
MAN: 140.
AUCTIONEER: 140. 150, do I hear?
WOMAN: 150.
AUCTIONEER: 150. Now come on ladies and gentlemen, nothing but 150
for one of the best built automobiles of its time?
MAN: 160.
AUCTIONEER: I have 160, thank you. One seve . . . and 170.
WOMAN: 180.
MAN: 190.
AUCTIONEER: 190.
MAN: 200.
AUCTIONEER: Two, yes I have a bid of two, going now for two, any
advance on two? Yours sir for $200,000 . . . the gentleman on screen 17.
VO: Who knows what a Chevy Nova will go for in the future.
But today you can get one for considerably less.

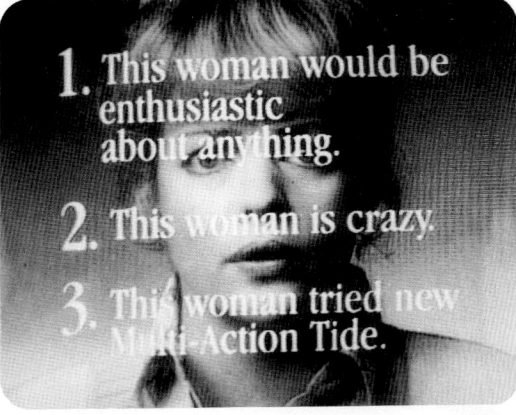

1705
ART DIRECTOR
Arnold Blum, Arthur Vibert
WRITER
Paul Cappelli, Teri Boesvert
CLIENT
Coca-Cola Company/USA Division
DIRECTOR
Howard Guard
AGENCY
McCann-Erickson, New York, NY
PRODUCER
Brad Christian
PRODUCTION COMPANY
Howard Guard Prod.

1706
ART DIRECTOR
Bob Meyerson
WRITER
Jeffery Frey
CLIENT
Proctor & Gamble
DIRECTOR
Norman Seeff
DIRECTOR OF PHOTOGRAPHY
Norman Seeff
AGENCY
Liza Leeds, SS&C, New York, NY
PRODUCER
Richard Marlis

1705

HORIZONTAL POUR
30-second
VO: You are about to
VO: Experience
VO: Something new
VO: A new wave of taste
VO: That will
VO: Stretch your imagination
VO: A taste
VO: So smooth
VO: So refreshing
VO: So
VO: Irresistible
VO: Your only choice
VO: Will be to
VO: Catch it
VO: Catch the wave
VO: Coke

1706

KNOCK YOUR SOCKS OFF
90-second
WOMAN 1: It's like something from Mars. I can't believe it. *You* won't believe it. It's incredible. Unbelievable. I'm repeating myself.
ANNCR: Which statement is true? One, this woman would be enthusiastic about anything. Two, this woman is crazy. Three, this woman tried new Multi-Action Tide. The answer is three!
Introducing new Multi-Action Tide. It'll knock your socks off, and it'll get 'em cleaner!
WOMAN 2: It gets things cleaner than any detergent. I mean, the way it works is just so amazing. I mean, it works. It really works.
ANNCR: One, this woman was a high school cheerleader and never got over it. Two, this woman sees what she wants to see. Three, this woman tried new Multi-Action Tide. This woman tried new Multi-Action Tide. With ingredients so special, so superior, we had to bring them to you in a whole new form. Just one sheet in the washer . . . and the most effective detergent ingredients ever created are released. Then come whiteners more effective than any bleach. Then you keep that same sheet of Multi-Action Tide for your dryer . . . where the fabric softener is activated for unbeatable static control.
WOMAN 3: I could believe cleaner and harder. But cleaner and easier just blows my mind!
ANNCR: One, this woman's mind was blown a long time ago. Two, this woman leads a very dull life. Three, this woman tried . . . You know the answer. For the cleanest, brightest, most static-free wash you've ever had from one product, new Multi-Action Tide. It'll knock your socks off, and

1707

ART DIRECTOR
Larry Larsen, Paul Dabrowski
WRITER
Steve Turner
CLIENT
Miller/Dakota
EDITOR
Tony Izzo, Vince Izzo
DIRECTOR
Graham Henman, Michael Karbalnikoff
AGENCY
Michael Birch, Leo Burnett, Chicago, IL
PRODUCTION COMPANY
Tom Mickel, HKM
CREATIVE DIRECTOR
Bob Welke

1708

ART DIRECTOR
Ross Van Dusen, John DeBonis
WRITER
Joe Garrett
CLIENT
Worlds of Wonder (Lazer Tag)
EDITOR
Gayle Grant
DIRECTOR
Peter Smillie
DIRECTOR OF PHOTOGRAPHY
Richard Bowen
AGENCY
Richard O'Neill, Chiat/Day, San Francisco, CA
PRODUCTION COMPANY
Cindy Akins, Robert Abel & Assoc.

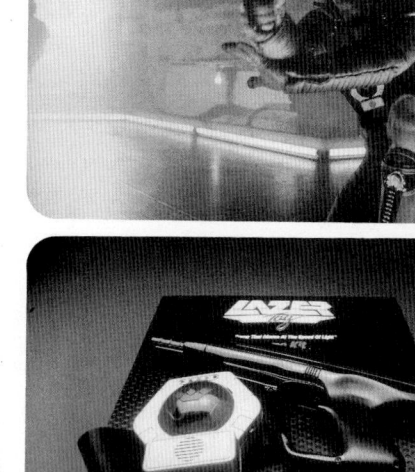

1707

MEN
60-second
MUSIC: (SCRATCHY RECORDING OF MAN SINGING:)
My boy follow me
It's for us to grow wheat
For as long as the land
lets us be
It's a hard life my son
For there's work to be done.
Stand tall
In this family's tree.
MUSIC: (SHIFTS TO HARD ROCK).
MUSIC: (UP CONTINUED).
SFX: (MUSIC UNDER)
ANNCR (VO): Out here, they brew a beer from the pride of the land. A wheat brewed beer. with a taste of the Heartland. Born wild. Raised proud. Miller makes it. And they call it . . . QBIII.
SFX: (POP!)
YNG FARMER: A wheat-brewed beer. You know, my granddaddy would've liked that.
ANNCR (VO): Straight . . . from the Heartland.
QBIII. The wheat-brewed beer.

1708

LAZER TAG
60-second
MUSIC: MOMENTOUS SCORE THROUGHOUT
METALLIC VOICE: Players to stadium now. Players to stadium now.
CROWD CHEERING IN BACKGROUND: Lazer! Lazer!
CROWD CHEERING THROUGHOUT.
REFEREE: On my signal, begin.
Now!
Out! You're out!
Out!
ANNCR (VO): Lazer Tag. The game that moves at the speed of light. From Worlds of Wonder.
Stadium not included.

1709
ART DIRECTOR
Dennis H. Plansker
WRITER
Sean Kevin Fitzpatrick
CLIENT
Chevrolet Motor Division
EDITOR
Bill Riss
DIRECTOR
Bruce Dowad, Jennie & Co.
BROADCAST DIRECTOR
Dennis H. Plansker
AGENCY
Campbell-Ewald Company, Warren, MI
PRODUCER
Kenneth J. Domanski
PRODUCTION COMPANY
Jennie & Co.
CREATIVE DIRECTOR
Sean Kevin Fitzpatrick
MUSIC
Denise Abood Sidlow; Joey Levine, Crushing Enterprises

1710
ART DIRECTOR
Harvey Hoffenberg
WRITER
Phil Dusenberry, Ted Sann, Susan Procter
CLIENT
Pepsi-Cola Company
EDITOR
Dennis Hayes
DIRECTOR
Ridley Scott
AGENCY
BBDO, New York, NY
PRODUCER
Gene Lofaro
PRODUCTION COMPANY
Fairbanks Films

709
HEARTBEAT OF AMERICA
0-second
MALE SINGER: (HEARTBEAT SFX)
Listen to the heartbeat of America
(HEARTBEAT SFX)
Listen to the heartbeat of America
(MUSIC STING)
(HEARTBEAT SFX)
FEMALE SINGER: Listen to the heartbeat
(ooh ooh)
of America
(ooh ooh)
FEMALE SINGER: Listen
to the heartbeat
(HEARTBEAT)
of America
(oh yeah)
MALE SINGER: It's the rhythm on the road
It's the pulse
on the street
(PULSE ON THE STREET)
a city,
town
a magic sound
(oooh)
Feel the heartbeat of America

1710
DON JOHNSON
60-second
MUSIC: YOU BELONG TO THE CITY.
FREY: Go, go left . . . no, no, no, right, right, right.
SFX: TRUCK HORN BLARES.
JOHNSON: Now you've done it.
SFX: MOTOR GRINDING.
FREY: It's your car pal. You fix it.
JOHNSON: Do we have to listen to this?
SFX: MUSIC IN BACKGROUND
FREY: That's my song.
JOHNSON: (MOCKING) That's my song.
FREY: Let's go. Hey, I'm everywhere pal.
SFX: MUSIC, HANDS CLAPPING.
SFX: CAN FALLING ON TURNTABLE.
CROWD: Screams.
JOHNSON: Is there a mechanic in the house?
CROWD: Me!
MUSIC: PEPSI IS THE U.S.A.
SFX: MOTOR TURNING OVER.
GIRL: That's it.
FREY: Thanks alot.
JOHNSON: Yeah, thanks!
GIRL: You drive 'em, we fix em. Bye.
FREY: Cool!
SUPER: Pepsi. The choice of a new generation.

1711

ART DIRECTOR
Rich Silverstein
WRITER
Jeff Goodby, Andy Berlin
CLIENT
San Francisco Newspaper Agency/
San Francisco Examiner
EDITOR
Jacques Dury, Decoupage, LA
DIRECTOR
Jon Francis, Jon Francis Films
DIRECTOR OF PHOTOGRAPHY
Dean Cundey, Keith Mason
AGENCY
Debbie King, Goodby, Berlin &
Silverstein, San Francisco, CA
PRODUCTION COMPANY
Sandra Marshall, Jon Francis Films
MUSIC
Don Piestrup, Piece of Cake

1712

ART DIRECTOR
Ed Martel
WRITER
Joel Shinsky
CLIENT
Anheuser-Busch, Inc.—Budweiser
EDITOR
Terry Richter
DIRECTOR
Joseph Hanright
AGENCY
D'Arcy Masius Benton & Bowles, St.
Louis, MO
PRODUCER
Michael Windler
CREATIVE DIRECTOR
Ed Martel

1711

DREAM
60-second
(MUSIC UNDER THROUGHOUT)
BUM: Mr. Hearst, listen, I got this idea for your newspaper.
WILL: So that's it. I'll be overseeing the deal personally.
RPTRS: Mr. Hearst, Mr. Hearst, Mr. Hearst!
ANCR: A half-price moneyback guarantee . . .
MAN: Good idea.
ANCR: But would they call?
WOMAN: Let's act now!
OPER: Examiner . . . may I help you?
(CONTINUE UNDER)
ANCR: They called. And called. Until . . .
MEN: Chief, chief, we can't print 'em fast enough!
WILL: Then buy more presses.
ANCR: Success . . . Sweet . . . Resounding . . .
A young publisher's pledge captures the hearts of the world
SFX: (THUNDER)
WILL: Nah . . .
ANCR: Now, for a limited time . . .
The Examiner . . . at half price . . . with a moneyback guarantee from
Will Hearst himself. Call 800-543-1200 now. Operators are standing by.

1712

TRAINER/REV
60-second
SINGER: This Bud's for all that you do.
OLDER TRAINER: I'd like to help you . . . I just don't have the time.
OWNER: Bob I need a trainer.
OLDER TRAINER: Talk to Eddie.
OWNE: (SKEPTICAL) He's just a kid.
OLDER TRAINER: So was I.
OWNER: Hey Eddie!
AVO: You've worked long and hard to get there . . .
AVO: . . . when the time comes, you hope you're ready.
OWNER: Son, I'm counting on you.
SINGER: You make America work. This Bud's for you.
ANNCR (VO): Here's to you. Beechwood aged for that distinctively clean,
crisp taste that makes Budweiser the King of Beers.
OLDER TRAINER: You're doin' great.
EDDIE: Thanks.
OLDER TRAINER: Who's talking to you.
SINGER: This Bud's for you.

1713

ART DIRECTOR
Fred Braidman, Rich Johnson
WRITER
Rob Nolan
CLIENT
McDonald's
EDITOR
Chris Claes, Cutters
DIRECTOR
Michael Moir
DIRECTOR OF PHOTOGRAPHY
Greg Califano
AGENCY
Cathy Nelson, Leo Burnett, Chicago, IL
PRODUCTION COMPANY
Steve Morris, Moir Productions
CREATIVE DIRECTOR
Rob Nolan

1714

ART DIRECTOR
Rick Strand
WRITER
Cynthia Franco
CLIENT
Apple Computer, Inc.
EDITOR
Dennis Hayes
DIRECTOR
Joe Pytka
AGENCY
BBDO, New York & San Francisco
PRODUCER
Gene Lofaro
PRODUCTION COMPANY
Pytka

1713

FIRST DAY
30-second
PRINCIPAL: (VO) Welcome freshmen, to Montclair High School.
This year, this class is special.
Because, this year, this class is challenged.
BOY 1 & 2: (OC) Oh, great.
SONG: How come it's so big?
Are you gonna be late?
Why does everyone look older than you?
OLDER GIRL: (OC) Do you have a pass?
BOY 1: (OC) I'm looking for my homeroom.
OLDER GIRL: (OC) I need your pass.
BOY 1: (IMPATIENTLY) (OC) I'm new here.
OLDER GIRL: (OC) I *need* your pass.
SONG: Why can't you go in the right direction?
How come you just don't know what to do?
TEACHER: (VO) Welcome to Agronomy Two.
BOY: (OC) Oops.
SONG: By the end of the day you're findin' your place.
Learnin' the ropes, learnin' the pace
Time to get away to a familiar face.
It's a good time for the great taste.
BOY 1: Fifty pages tonight.
BOY 1 & 2: Oh, great!
SONG: It's a good time for the great taste
BOY 2: Tomorrow'll be better.
BOY 3: You mean we gotta go back?
SONG: Of McDonald's.

1714

GOING TO WORK
60-second
They here yet?
Plenty of time, it's only 7:45.
What's so interesting?
Those two down there.
Oh, that's Wilson and Bennett. Couple of hot shots from finance.
What are they carrying?
Oh those are computers.
Computers? They're taking our computers home at night?
Not exactly. They're bringing their computers in.
You're kidding? What for?
Well for one thing that's how they put together these killer forecasts.
You mean we can't do this on our system?
Nope. Not like this.
O.K., two questions, what kind of computers are they using . . .
And?
And why don't we have them?

1726

ART DIRECTOR
Steve Thursby
ANIMATOR/ARTIST
Michael Mills
WRITER
Allan Kazmer
CLIENT
Volkswagen Canada Inc.
DIRECTOR
Michael Mills
AGENCY
Louise Blouin, DDB Needham
Worldwide, Toronto, Canada
PRODUCTION COMPANY
Michael Mills, Michael Mills
Production
AUDIO
David Fleury
V.O.
Graeme Campbell

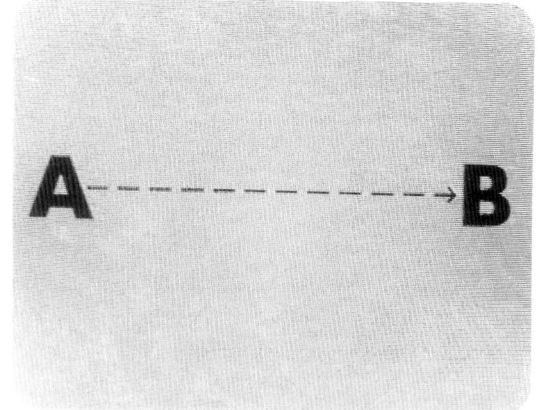

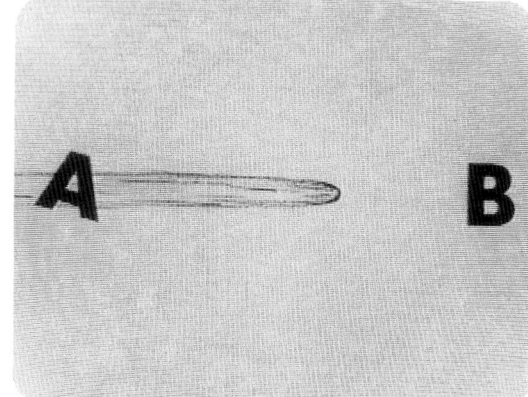

1727

ART DIRECTOR
Joel Machak
WRITER
Jim Ferguson, Bob Taylor
CLIENT
Ad Council/Safety Belts
EDITOR
Chris Claeys
DIRECTOR
William Dear
AGENCY
Darr Hawthorne, Leo Burnett,
Chicago, IL
PRODUCTION COMPANY
Julie Larson, Boardwalk Prod.
CREATIVE DIRECTOR
Bob Taylor

1726

A TO B/VAULT/DOLLAR
15-second
VO: The most dependable distance . . .
SFX: BLIP, BLIP, BLIP
. . . from A to B is . . .
. . . VW . . .
VO: The shortest distance . . .
SFX: WHOOSH!
. . . from A to B is . . .
. . . GTI.

1727

SAFETY BELTS × 3
10-second
VINCE: Do not attempt this at home. We are professional crash dummies
BOTH: Ah!
ANNCR: You could learn a lot from a dummy. Buckle your safety belt.

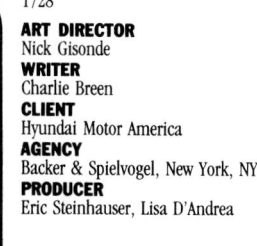

1728
ART DIRECTOR
Nick Gisonde
WRITER
Charlie Breen
CLIENT
Hyundai Motor America
AGENCY
Backer & Spielvogel, New York, NY
PRODUCER
Eric Steinhauser, Lisa D'Andrea

1729
ART DIRECTOR
Ray Groff
WRITER
Jim Lawson
CLIENT
Xerox
EDITOR
Marty's
DIRECTOR
Howard Zieff
AGENCY
Carolyn Roughsedge, DDB
Needham, New York, NY
PRODUCER
Howard Zieff

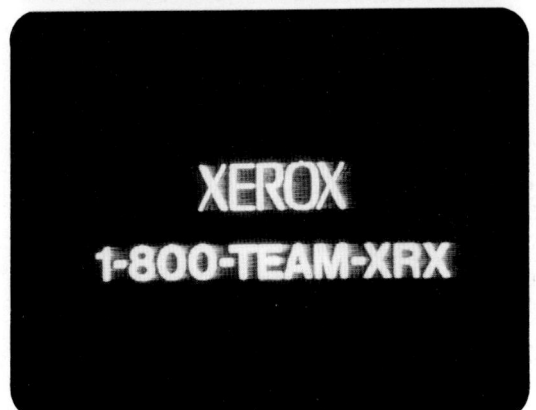

728

AR POOL, REAR DEFROSTER/800 NUMBER/MASERATI
0-second
MUSIC UP AND THROUGHOUT)
NNCR VO: A rear window defroster comes standard
n the new Hyundai Excel.
ecause it always pays
 know
hat's behind you.
yundai. Cars that make sense.

1729

CHARITY/PROMO/APPLY FOR JOB
15-second
MAN: For a copier as dependable as this liitle Xerox Marathon, how much
would you pay?
Really?
Can we take that much?
No, we can't take that much.
Why not?
ANNCR: For Lazer sharp documents, call Team Xerox.

1730

ART DIRECTOR
Tod Seisser
WRITER
Jay Taub
CLIENT
New York Air
EDITOR
Morty's Place
DIRECTOR
Henry Sandbank, Sandbank Films, Inc.
AGENCY
Rachel Novak, LHS&B, New York
PRODUCTION COMPANY
John Kamen, Sandbank Films

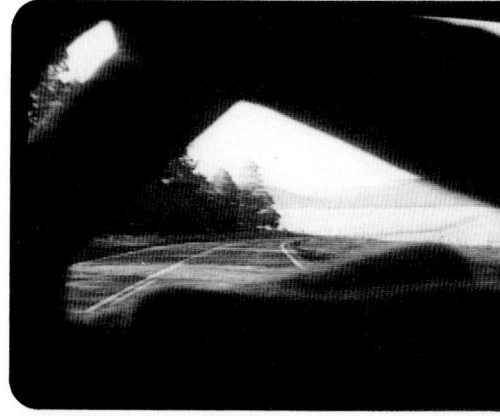

1731

ART DIRECTOR
Mark Hughes, Bill Yamada, Neil Raphan
WRITER
Dean Hacohen, Ed Smith
CLIENT
Volkswagen of America
EDITOR
Ciro DeNettis, Joe Laliker
DIRECTOR
Michael Karbelnikoff, Michael Werk, Owen Roizman
DIRECTOR OF PHOTOGRAPHY
Mike Karbelnikoff, Mike Werk, Owen Roizman
AGENCY
Lorraine Schaffer, Ugo Pergolloti, DDB Needham, New York, NY
PRODUCER
Tom Mickel

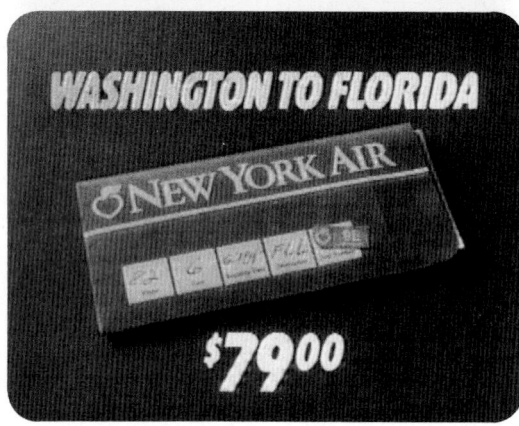

1730

WASHINGTON OFFICIALS/OUR BAG/SEATING
15-second
ANNCR: Recently, the United States government paid some extraordinary prices for some ordinary items. Obviously, some people in Washington already know how to spend more.
We think it's time they learned to spend less.
SUPER: New York Air Super Shuttle Service.

1731

MOTHER, SON/MOTHER/FATHER,DAUGHTER
30-second
SFX: CAR'S REVVING ENGINE (THROUGHOUT).
SON: Ma, take your hands off your eyes.
MOTHER: I can't.
SON: Not even doing 55.
MOTHER: That's a mater of opinion.
What is it you call this . . . this uh . . .
SON: German engineered 16 valve Volkswagen Scirocco.
MOTHER: It should be outlawed.
SON: Ma.
MOTHER: Your father used to own a Volkswagen
It was a nice little car.
This is not a nice little car.
SON: It's not supposed to be. This is the 80's.
SON: Power, control.
MOTHER: Umm.
SON: That's what really counts.
MOTHER: I'm sure it does.
Could you please pull over.
SON: You want to drive?
MOTHER: I want to walk.

1732
ART DIRECTOR
Maryanne Fisher
WRITER
Chris Laubach
CLIENT
Dr Pepper Company — Diet
EDITOR
Clay Warnick
DIRECTOR
Patrick Russell
DIRECTOR OF PHOTOGRAPHY
Andy Dittenfass
AGENCY
Young & Rubicam, New York, NY
PRODUCER
Roseanne Horn
PRODUCTION COMPANY
Rick Levine Production
TYPE DIRECTOR
Dick Mullen

1733
ART DIRECTOR
Candy Greathouse, Roberta Williams
WRITER
John Lyons
CLIENT
Procter & Gamble — Bounce
EDITOR
Howard Weisbrot
DIRECTOR
Ed Bianchi
DIRECTOR OF PHOTOGRAPHY
Andrzej Bartkowiak
AGENCY
Karen Spector, DMB&B, New York,
NY
PRODUCTION COMPANY
Ann Friedman, Bianchi Films
MUSIC
Michael Zager

1732

ORPORATE EXEC/SLIM SINGLE SINGER/STRONG SILENT TYPE
0-second
MUSIC UNDER)
MUSIC)
WOMAN: (VO) Curvaceous corporate executive seeks fellow mover and
haker to shake up my life.
Must have a strong personality to make me weak at the knees and must
neasure up to my measurements.
MALE SINGER: Meet the movin' and shakin' new taste of
iet Dr Pepper
hrow your diet a curve.
iet Dr Pepper.

1733

NO CLING/SOFT/SCENT
30-second
SFX: MUSIC THROUGHOUT.
SONG: No cling nightgowns
Jump.
No cling skirts.
Jump
No cling to most anything
Jump. Jump. Jump. Jump.
Bounce for no cling
things you can't wait to jump into
Jump. Feel the touch.
Jump in
You are the one
so smooth and free around me.
Jump. Jump. Jump. Jump.
Bounce.
for no cling things you can't
wait to jump into
Jump.

1734

ART DIRECTOR
Gavino Sanna
WRITER
Andrea Concato
CLIENT
Barilla G&R F.LLI
EDITOR
Roberto Crescenzi
DIRECTOR
Norman Griner
DIRECTOR OF PHOTOGRAPHY
Norman Griner
PRODUCER
Alessandra Ferrari, Sergio Castellani
PRODUCTION COMPANY
Film Master/Griner Cuesta

1735

ART DIRECTOR
Amy Mizner
WRITER
Don Deutsch
CLIENT
The Pontiac Dealer Association of
NY/NJ/CT
EDITOR
Jerry Fried
DIRECTOR
John O'Driscoll
DIRECTOR OF PHOTOGRAPHY
John Crawford
AGENCY
Randy Cohen, David Deutsch Assoc.,
New York, NY
PRODUCER
Pete Christy

1734

GIRL & KITTEN/DIVORCED FATHER/CADETS
30-second
NO SOUND.

1735

RHONDA WEISMANN/LOU POTENZA/RICHARDS BROTHER
30-second
I'm Rhonda Weissman from Great Neck and I'm not a princess. I hate
when people call me that. Are you ready? Like this Fiero, the cutest. I we
on my own without my parents and I paid for it— Four thousand dolla
OK, OK my father did kick in six thousand but I'm not a princess. If I
were a princess I would not have paid for anything.
Does anyone have any gum?

1736
ART DIRECTOR
Joe Perz, Nick Gisonde, Howard
Smith
WRITER
Larry Laiken, Seth Fried, Charlie
Breen
CLIENT
Miller Brewing Company — Lite
Beer
AGENCY
Backer & Spielvogel, New York, NY
PRODUCER
Eric Steinhauser, Andy Cornelius

1737
ART DIRECTOR
Dennis H. Plansker, Eugene Turner
WRITER
Sean Kevin Fitzpatrick, Tucker Coon
CLIENT
Chevrolet Motor Division
EDITOR
Bill Riss
DIRECTOR
Bruce Dowad, Ian Leech
AGENCY
Campbell-Ewald Co., Warren, MI
PRODUCER
Kenneth J. Domanski, Albert E.
Schacherer
PRODUCTION COMPANY
Jennie & Co./Ian Leech & Associates
CREATIVE DIRECTOR
Sean Kevin Fitzpatrick

1736

HALLEY'S COMET/CONRAD DOBLER/MISSING CASE
30-second
BOB: Nope.
TOMMY: Ueck, you've been here three weeks waiting for Halley's comet?
BOB: Yup, and I already started celebrating with a cold Lite Beer from Miller.
TOMMY: Lite tastes great.
BOB: Lite's less filling too, Tommy. And I can't get filled up, been waiting all my life to spot this baby.
TOMMY: Well how 'bout one for me?
BOB: Sure.
TOMMY: Wow!
TOMMY: Incredible.
BOB: What was?
TOMMY: Uh, nothing Ueck, uh, listen, uh . . . I gotta run.
BOB: Ok. But you're gonna miss it. There. no—oh!
ANNCR: Wherever you look, there's only one Lite Beer.
Miller Lite.

1737

HEARTBEAT OF AMERICA × 3
30-second
FEMALE SINGER: Listen to the heartbeat
(ooh ooh)
of America
Listen to the heartbeat
(HEARTBEAT)
of America
(oh yeah)
MALE SINGER: It's the rhythm
on the road
It's the pulse
on the street
(PULSE ON THE STREET)
a city, town,
a magic sound
(ooh, ooh)
FEMALE SINGER: Feel the heartbeat
of America
CHORUS: Chevrolet
MALE SINGER: That's today's Chevrolet
(HEARTBEAT EFX UNDER AND OUT)

1738

ART DIRECTOR
Barbara Kanowitz
DESIGNER
Ruth Aamon
WRITER
Gilbert Gottfried
CLIENT
MTV, New York, NY
EDITOR
John Tierney, Bob Gleason
DIRECTOR
Barbara Kanowitz
DIRECTOR OF PHOTOGRAPHY
John McNolte, Bob Achs

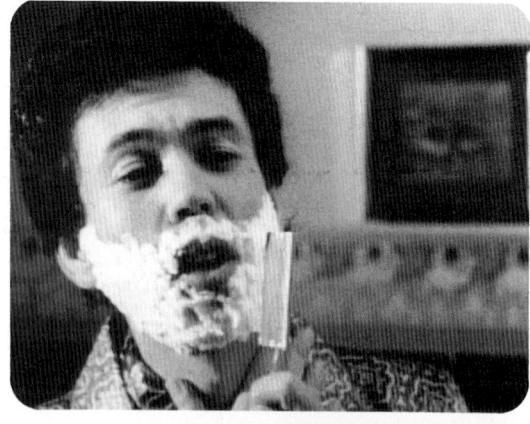

1739

ART DIRECTOR
Mike Ciranni
DESIGNER
Mike Ciranni
WRITER
Jamie Seltzer
CLIENT
NYNEX
DIRECTOR
Henry Sandbank
AGENCY
Chiat/Day, New York, NY
PRODUCER
Bertelle Selig
PRODUCTION COMPANY
Sandbank Films

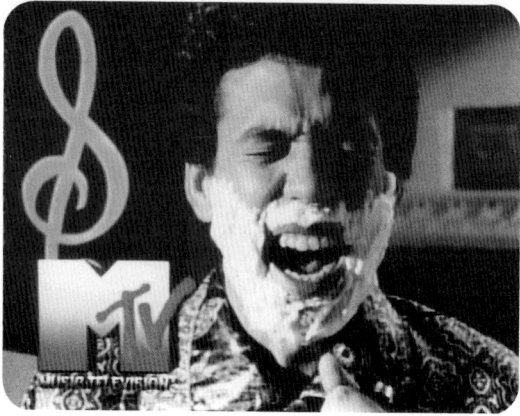

1738

GILBERT GOTTFRIED—BATHROOM/DAVID & DAVID/ON THE WHO
30-second
You know most television executives
can't look at themselves in the mirror
I can, because I'm not embarrassed about what I show
I don't show shows like "Two Girls and A Chimp,"
"Armando the Talking Amoeba" or shows from the green grocer
No!! I'll be showing you more videos in an hour
More videos in a row
More videos by new breaking artists
That's MTV's personal guarantee to you
Excuse me
Ahhhhhhhhhhhhhhhhhhhhhhh!!!!

1739

SEAFOOD RESTAURANT/SELTZER/MIKE PERRELLA
30-second
OWNER: The coat check girl comes running in.
Tells me there's a guy up front talking to the lobsters. Sure enough, he's
up here. Practicing his sales pitch.
Says to them "Hello. I'm from the Southwestern Bell Yellow Pages."
I tell him don't count on their business. They got about 10 more minute
to live.
As for me, I use the NYNEX Yellow Pages. Everyone in town uses it. I
wouldn't think of using any other book.
I told him he's wasting his time, but if he wants to keep rehearsing I ha
some fresh swordfish in the back that are pretty good listeners.
VO: There's only one official Yellow Pages for New York Telephone.
SUPER: The NYNEX Yellow Pages.
There's only one.

He's Lying

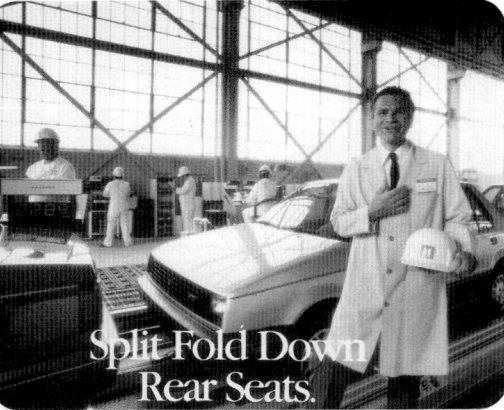

Split Fold Down Rear Seats.

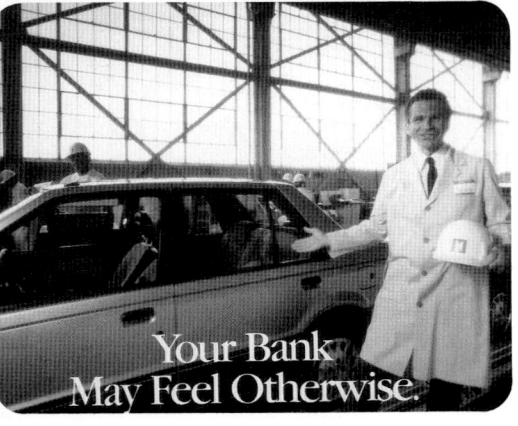

Your Bank May Feel Otherwise.

IT'S A GOOD TIME FOR THE GREAT TASTE

1740
ART DIRECTOR
Jeanne Marie Obeji, John Armistead
WRITER
Matt Bogen, Rick Carpenter, Jim
Weller, Dick Sittig, Laurie
Brandalise
CLIENT
American Isuzu Motors, Inc.
AGENCY
Della Femina Travisano, Los
Angeles, CA
PRODUCER
Frank Tammariello, Howard Bailin,
Nancy Koch
PRODUCTION COMPANY
Elite Films/Johns & Gorman Films

1741
ART DIRECTOR
Brian Gregg, Fred Braidman, Rich
Johnson
WRITER
John Montgomery, Rob Nolan
CLIENT
McDonald's
DIRECTOR
Peter Moss, Michael Moir
AGENCY
Leo Burnett, Chicago, IL
PRODUCER
David Geeting, Cathy Nelson, David
Beller
CREATIVE DIRECTOR
Rob Nolan

1740

FACTORY/THE LIAR/PINNACLE
30-second
LIAR: Hi. I'm Joe Isuzu.
SUPER: He's lying.
Here in my factory I equip these I-Marks with millions of standard
features.
SUPER: Close. It has dozens of standard features.
Like a breakfast nook.
SUPER: Split fold down rear seats.
Twin satellite dishes.
SUPER: Dual electric mirrors.
And for those kids—a frozen yogurt machine.
SUPER: A peppy 1.5 liter engine.
Prices start at $6999. With 5.9% financing.
SUPER: Hurry. He's not lying.
And if you miss 8 or 9 payments, that's okay. I trust you.
SUPER: Your bank may feel otherwise.

1741

FIRST DAY/DOODLIN'/SINGIN'
30-second
PRINCIPAL (VO): Welcome freshmen, to Montclair High School.
This year, this class is special.
Because, this year, this class is challenged.
BOY 1 & 2: (OC) Oh, great.
SONG: How come it's so big?
Are you gonna be late?
Why does everyone look older than you?
OLDER GIRL: (OC) Do you have a pass?
BOY 1: (OC) I'm looking for my homeroom.
OLDER GIRL: (OC) I need your pass.
BOY 1: (IMPATIENTLY) (OC) I'm new here.
OLDER GIRL: (OC) I *need* your pass.
SONG: Why can't you go in the right direction?
How come you just don't know what to do?
TEACHER: (VO) Welcome to Agronomy Two.
BOY: (OC) Oops.
SONG: By the end of the day you're findin' your place.
Learnin' the ropes, learnin' the pace
Time to get away to a familiar face.
It's a good time for the great taste.
BOY 1: Fifty pages tonight.
BOY 1 & 2: Oh, great!
SONG: It's a good time for the great taste
BOY 2: Tomorrow'll be better.

1742

ART DIRECTOR
Ron Anderson
WRITER
Bert Gardner
CLIENT
Minnetonka, Inc.
DIRECTOR
Joe Sedelmaier
AGENCY
Bozell, Jacobs, Minneapolis, MN
PRODUCER
Judy Wittenberg
PRODUCTION COMPANY
Sedelmaier

1743

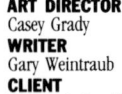

ART DIRECTOR
Casey Grady
WRITER
Gary Weintraub
CLIENT
Proctor & Gamble
EDITOR
Frank Ciofredi
DIRECTOR
Greg Weinschenker
AGENCY
Ann Broderick, DFS Dorland, New York, NY
PRODUCER
Sharon Starr
EXEC. CREATIVE DIR.
Eric Weber
CREATIVE DIRECTOR
Jean-Manuel Guyader
GROUP HEAD
Rita Senders, Beverly Okada

1742

TAXI/AIRPLANE/WASHROOM
30-second
(MUSIC UNDER & THROUGHOUT)
VO: It's not always . . .
. . . practical . . .
. . . to brush after eating.
VO: Introducing Check•Up plaque fighting gum . . .
. . . from Check•Up Toothpaste. It's clinically tested to help remove plaque . . .
. . . peacefully.
VO: Check•Up Gum. When you can't brush, chew.

1743

SOUTHERN BELLE/HATE/MOON
30-second
TESS: Uh, oh, it's Mary Alice.
BESS: Well if she complains about her leaky diaper again, I'll scream!
MARY ALICE: Ooo, girls! My diaper's killin' me! I declare, it springs bigger leaks than the Titanic!
BESS: Should we tell her?
MARY ALICE: Tell me what?
ANNCR/VO: Introducing Luvs Super Baby Pants with leakproof padding.
BESS: My new Luvs diaper. The padding's practically leakproof!
MARY ALICE: And thin, too!
BESS: Just takes the worry out of my day.
MARY ALICE: Leakproof padding! Well, shut my mouth!
TESS: For how long?
ANNCR/VO: New Luvs, it's got babies talking.

1744
ART DIRECTOR
Michael Hart, Nick Vitale, Frank
Perry
WRITER
Brian Sitts
CLIENT
Tom Kettinger, Burger King
EDITOR
Bob Derise, A Cut Above
DIRECTOR
Joseph Hanwright
AGENCY
JWT, New York, NY
PRODUCER
Ric Wylie, John Maritato, David
Schneiderman, Stu Raffell
PRODUCTION COMPANY
Steven Cohen, KIRA Films
CREATIVE DIRECTOR
Hal Friedman, Brian Sitts, Nick
Vitale

1745
ART DIRECTOR
Richard Chasey
WRITER
L. Keith Stentz
CLIENT
Chevrolet Motor Division
EDITOR
Bill Riss
DIRECTOR
Ron Dexter
BROADCAST DIRECTOR
Dennis H. Plansker
AGENCY
Campbell-Ewald Company, Warren,
MI
PRODUCER
Albert E. Schacherer
PRODUCTION COMPANY
The Dextr's
CREATIVE DIRECTOR
Sean Kevin Fitzpatrick
MUSIC
Denise Abood Sidlow, Bill Withers,
Billy Eaton

1744

TOWN ANTHEM/DIRECTIONS/BACKYARD BBQ
30-second
LYRIC: My kind of people, my kind of taste
Somethin' special about this place
Got no reason to stray too far
'Cause it's all right here in my own backyard
This is a Burger King town
It's made just for me
This is a Burger King town
We know how burgers should be
Right up the road, left at the sign
My way, your way, one at a time
Hot off the fire, with anything on it
Don't it feel good when it's just how you
Want it. This is a Burger King town
It's made just for me
This is a Burger King town
We know how burgers should be

1745

LEAN ON ME × 3
30-second
SINGERS: Lean on me
When you're not strong
and I'll be your friend
I'll help you
Carry on
For . . .
It won't be long
Till you're gonna need
SINGERS: Somebody
to lean on
VO: When you need a truck you can lean on, nothing works like a Chevy
Truck.
SINGERS: Lean on me . . .

1746
ART DIRECTOR
Tony DeGregorio, Michael Vitiello
WRITER
Lee Garfinkel, Rich Pels
CLIENT
Subaru of America
EDITOR
David Dee, Eventime
DIRECTOR
Steve Horn, Steve Horn, Inc.
AGENCY
Bob Nelson, LHS&B, New York, NY
PRODUCTION COMPANY
Linda Horn, Steve Horn Inc.

 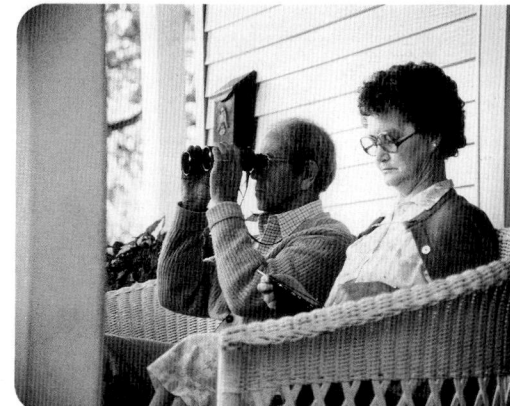

1747
ART DIRECTOR
Michael Fazende
WRITER
John Stingley
CLIENT
O.M. Scott
EDITOR
Steve Shepherd, Wilson-Griak
DIRECTOR
Joe Pytka
AGENCY
Fallon McElligott, Minneapolis, MN
PRODUCER
Judy Brink
PRODUCTION COMPANY
Pytka
V.O.
Michael Stull

 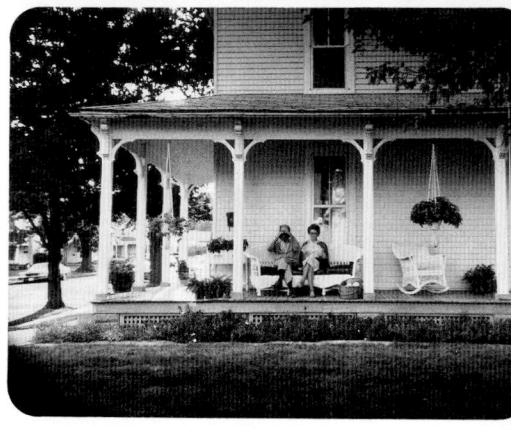

1746

BANANAS/GETTING THERE/JERRY'S NEW CAR
30-second
ANNCR: A lot of people are disappointed with the traction they're getting from their present car.
Which is why more and more of them are looking into the number one 4 wheel drive car in America at their Subaru dealer.
Subaru. Inexpensive. And built to stay that way.

1747

BINOCULARS/PARK BENCH/GUARANTEE
30-second
ANNCR: An evening in Marysville, Ohio is different.
MAN: Mother it appears we have prunella vulgaris.
ANNCR: Because Maryville is the home of Scott's lawn products.
WOMAN: We've never had prunella vulgaris.
MAN: Well, we do now.
ANNCR: It's living here that inspired our toll-free number for lawn advice.
WOMAN: That's malva neglecta.
ANNCR: Because our idea of fun . . .
MAN: Oh.
ANNCR: May not be yours.
ANNCR: When all there is to do is watch the grass grow, you really get to know grass.

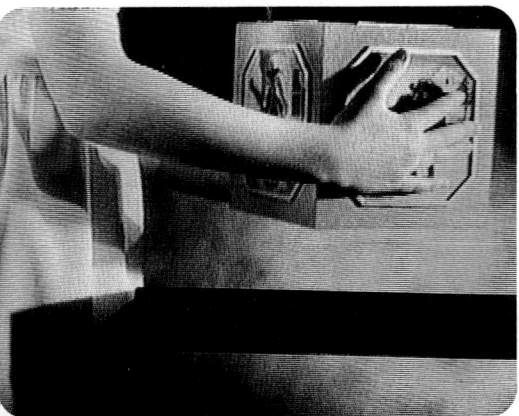

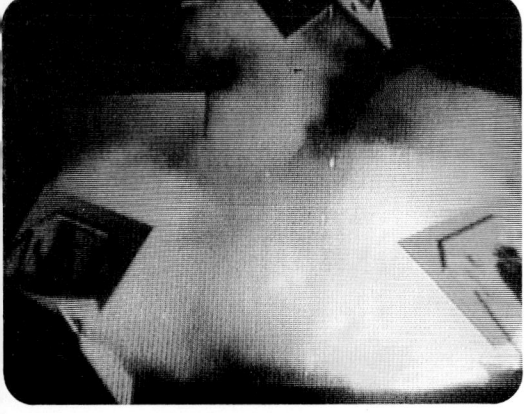

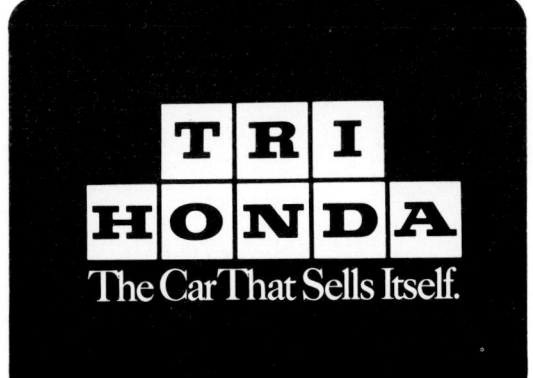

1748

ART DIRECTOR
Holland Henton
ANIMATOR/ARTIST
Doron Ben-Ami
WRITER
Brett Robbs, Dean Tepper
CLIENT
Rivendell of America
EDITOR
Editing Concepts/The Tape House
DIRECTOR
Gary Perweiler
DIRECTOR OF PHOTOGRAPHY
Jamie Jacobson
AGENCY
Walker & Associates, Memphis, TN
PRODUCER
Cris Hardaway
PRODUCTION COMPANY
Exit Films
CREATIVE DIRECTOR
Joe Pizzirusso
MUSIC
Rich Sanders
PROPS
Brooklyn Model Works

1749

ART DIRECTOR
Neil Leinwohl
WRITER
Kevin McKeon
CLIENT
Tri-Honda Auto Dealers Association
DIRECTOR
Ross Cramer
AGENCY
Milda Misevicius, Korey, Kay &
Partners, New York, NY
PRODUCTION COMPANY
Pete Christy, Power & Light

1748

JACK IN THE BOX/MASK/FINGER PRISM
30-second
You try and help your child get a handle on life.
But some children still come to feel like black sheep.
As they get older, they begin to play with fire, living more and more
dangerously.
So it just gets harder for you to keep the lid on.
Before things go to pieces, seek help.
Call your local mental health agency or physician.

1749

MOM/REVERSAL/WAIT
30-second
MOM: My boy Tommy isn't exactly a born salesman. In kindergarten, he
sold lemonade for 3¢. The boy next door sold it for a dime, and ran him
out of business.
When he was a scout, he sold candy door to door. Even I pretended I
wasn't home.
Then he became a Honda salesman. Now my son Tommy is a huge
success!
(CONFIDENTIALLY) Those Honda's must be *very* good cars.
ANNCR: Honda. The Car that sells itself. See the new '87 Hondas at your
New York, New Jersey, Connecticut Tri-Honda dealer.

1750
ART DIRECTOR
Danny Boone
DESIGNER
Danny Boone
WRITER
John Mahoney, Andy Ellis
CLIENT
Theatre Virginia
DIRECTOR
Danny Boone
AGENCY
Danny Boone, The Martin Agency,
Richmond, VA
PRODUCTION COMPANY
John Parks, Mirage

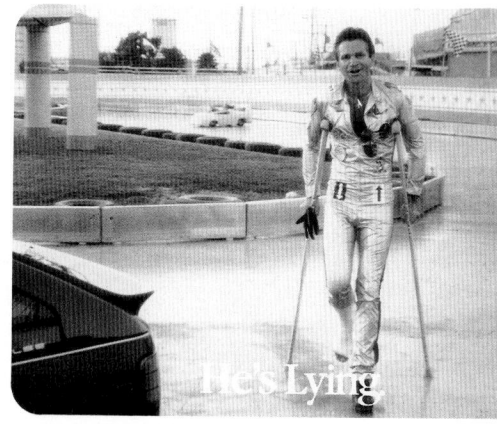

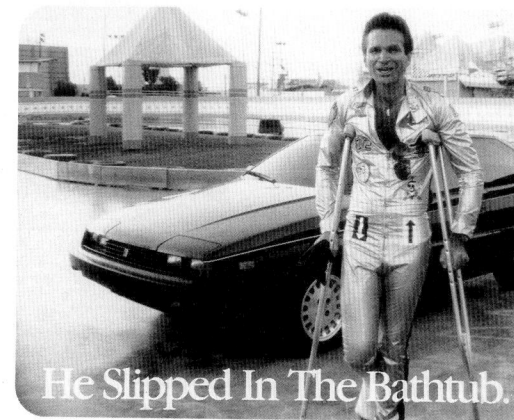

1751
ART DIRECTOR
Rick Carpenter, John Armistead,
Jeanne Marie Obeji
WRITER
Jaci Sisson, Jim Weller, Dick Sittig,
Matt Bogen
CLIENT
American Isuzu Motors, Inc.
DIRECTOR
Gary Johns, Jeff Gorman
AGENCY
Howard Bailin, Della Femina
Travisano
PRODUCTION COMPANY
Sam Schapiro, Lilly Weingarten,
Johns + Gorman Films, Los Angeles,
CA

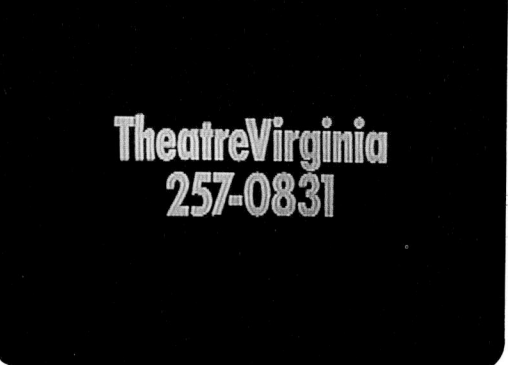

1750

BILLY BISHOP/SCHOOL FOR WIVES/WIRELESS CHRISTMAS
30-second
BILLY BISHOP: So Albert says, "Bishop. I have a vision. Two pilots,
compatriots in glory, like ghosts in the night hurl ourselves against the
whole German aerodrome. The unsuspecting Hun lies asleep in his bed.
There is no defense." Hell of a plan, Albert, I say. But how do we get out?
He looks at me funny and says, "Out?"

1751

RACE TRACK/JUDGE/PINNACLE
30-second
LIAR: Bon Journo. I'm the world's greatest race car driver.
SUPER: He's lying.
LIAR: Recently, I had a little problem here at Monte Carlo.
SUPER: He slipped in the bathtub.
LIAR: So I switched to this $200,000 Formula Isuzu.
SUPER: The Isuzu Impulse: From $12,059 Mfr.'s sugg. retail price excl.
tax license and transp. fee. Price subject to change.
LIAR: It comes with driving gloves, and a pit crew. All standard.
SUPER: Well, it does have air conditioning and cruise control standard.
LIAR: It's so fast it will go from Paris to Rome in two minutes.
SUPER: Turbo impulse 0-60 in 8.3 seconds.
LIAR: And the bank gave me 5.9% financing. Just because they like my
face.
SUPER: Almost anyone can get 5.9% financing right now. Annual
percentage rate for qualified buyers. See your participating dealer for
details.
ANNCR: The Isuzu Impulse. Now, for a limited time with 5.9% financing.

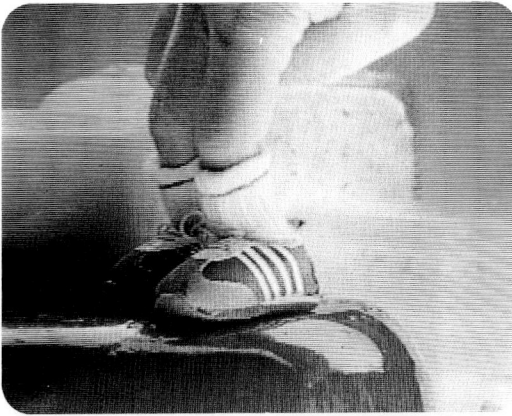

1752
ART DIRECTOR
Mackie Rosen
WRITER
David Uskali
CLIENT
M&M/Mars-Kudos
EDITOR
Morty Ashkinos
DIRECTOR
Jeremiah Chechik
AGENCY
Lynne Lyons, Ted Bates, New York, NY
PRODUCTION COMPANY
Jean-Michel Ravon, Bill Hudson & Assoc.
MUSIC
Sara Lovell, Fred Miller

1753
ART DIRECTOR
Holland Henton, Dan Acree
WRITER
Brett Robbs
CLIENT
Big Apple Foods
EDITOR
Modern Video Productions
DIRECTOR
Jeffrey Berry
DIRECTOR OF PHOTOGRAPHY
Kyle Rudolph
AGENCY
Cris Hardaway, Walker & Associates, Memphis, TN
PRODUCTION COMPANY
Alice Haynsworth, SBK Productions
CREATIVE DIRECTOR
Joe Pizzirusso
MUSIC
Modern Audio Productions

1752

I'M YOURS × 3
30-second
SINGERS: You'll love the first bite
New "KUDOS" Granola Snacks
Outrageously right
Electrifying
Granolafying
"KUDOS I'm yours!"
KIDS: I'm yours!
SONG: Rich and Jazzy
Hot and Snazzy
KUDOS I'm yours
I'm yours, I'm yours, I'm yours
Nutty Fudge,
Chocolate Chip or Peanut Butter
Simply nutritious
Outrageously delicious
"KUDOS I'm yours!"
KIDS: I'm yours!

1753

FINGERS/MEAT/EXPRESS
30-second
Running all over to find all you need.
Can wear you out.
But at the new Big Apple, you'll run across everything you want in one place.
You'll find a variety of imported cheeses,
great tasting deli meats
plus our bakery's fresh-baked bread.
Sail through our seafood department for shrimp, fresh fish and live lobster
even tiptoe through our tulips.
Shopping's a kick with over 25,000 great values to choose from.
At the new Big Apple. The pick of Atlanta.

1754

ART DIRECTOR
Jeff Layton
WRITER
Jim Catlin
CLIENT
General Foods Ltd.
EDITOR
Mick Griffin, Magnetic North
DIRECTOR
Alan Marr
DIRECTOR OF PHOTOGRAPHY
Stan Mestel
AGENCY
Kay Brown, Grey Advertising, Ltd.,
Toronto, Canada
PRODUCTION COMPANY
Nancy Lee, The Partners Film Co.
Ltd.
MUSIC
The Air Company

1755

ART DIRECTOR
Matt Fischer
WRITER
Suellen Gelman
CLIENT
National Institute on Drug Abuse
EDITOR
Steve Bodner
DIRECTOR
John Bonanno
AGENCY
DDB Needham, New York, NY
PRODUCER
Tony Compitello
PRODUCTION COMPANY
Neil Tardio Films

1754

GONE WITH THE KOOL-AID/KOOL-A-BLANCA
30-second
TARA'S THEME UNDER
SCARLETT KID: Oh Rhett! The Yankees stole our Kool-Aid!
RHETT KID: Don't fret Scarlett. I have my pesonal stock.
SCARLETT: Oh fiddle-de-dee! Orange, grape, cherry and mah
favourite . . .
Mountain Berry Punch!
RHETT: At pennies a glass, we'll stay cool
all summer
SCARLETT: We'll need it. Atlanta's burnin' up . . .
and so am I.
RHETT: Frankly, my dear, with Kool-Aid, I don't give a darn.
SCARLETT: Rhett! I swear I'll never be thirsty again!

1755

MIKE SCHMIDT/REGGIE JACKSON/NANCY REAGAN
30-second
SUPER: Mike Schmidt Philadelphia Phillies
MIKE: I don't need drugs.
I believe in me and my ability.
I don't want anything interfering with the way I
play the game.
Cocaine's no way to believe in yourself . . .
It can kill you.
If you're into cocaine, get off it.
You're living a lie.
Get off it while you still have a life.
VO & SUPER: Cocaine the big lie
Call 1-800-662-HELP.

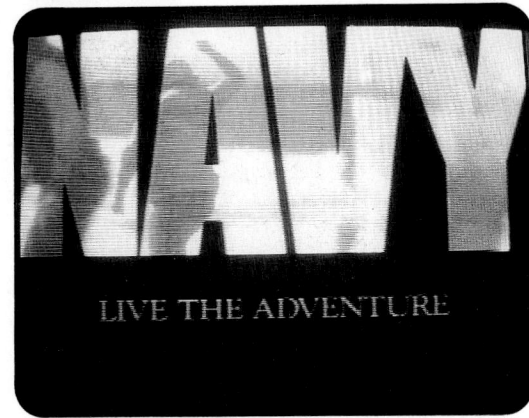

1756
ART DIRECTOR
Hal Tench
DESIGNER
Hal Tench
WRITER
Mike Hughes
CLIENT
Barnett Banks
DIRECTOR
Mike Cuesta
AGENCY
The Martin Agency, Richmond, VA
PRODUCER
Craig Bowlus
PRODUCTION COMPANY
Griner/Cuesta

1757
ART DIRECTOR
Steve Monchak, John Trzuskowski
WRITER
Bill Hartsough
CLIENT
U.S. Navy
EDITOR
Stuart Waks, Pelco
DIRECTOR
Michael Werk
AGENCY
Ted Bates, New York, NY
PRODUCER
Jim Callan

1756

SERVICE/LOCAL DECISIONS/SIMPLICITY
30-second
ANNCR: Some financial institutions have become a little . . . impersonal.
BIG SHOT BANKER: I'll need your driver's license and two forms of identification.
WOMAN: Will this take long, Jerry?
BIG SHOT BANKER: I'm moving as fast as I can, Mom.
ANNCR: Others aren't very business like.
TELLER: Has your rash cleared up, Alvin?
MAN: Yes, Mrs. Tunney, can I cash a check?
TELLER: That was a nasty rash . . .
MAN: Yes, Mrs. Tunney, can I cash a check?
ANNCR: Instead, come to Barnett. We've struck a balance between personal service and professional service. And that's what makes us Florida's bank.

1757

CATAPULT/ANCHOR I/TO RISE
30-second
U.S. NAVY
SONG: Fight fire on the blue horizon
Gonna lay it on the line
Take it to the limit
VO: Reach for something bigger
To master a more challenging world
To feel the confidence and pride
of knowing who you are
What you can do
Show the world your U.S. Navy
Live the adventure
Call 1-800-327-NAVY.

1758

ART DIRECTOR
Rich Silverstein
WRITER
Jeff Goodby, Andy Berlin
CLIENT
The Christian Brothers Winery,
Fromm & Sichel, Inc.
EDITOR
Jacques Dury, Decoupage, LA
DIRECTOR
Norman Seeff
DIRECTOR OF PHOTOGRAPHY
John Fleckenstein, Sean Doyle
AGENCY
Debbie King, Goodby, Berlin &
Silverstein, San Francisco, CA
PRODUCTION COMPANY
Lynne Pateman, Richard Marlis
Productions
MUSIC
Don Piestrup, Piece of Cake, Inc.

1759

ART DIRECTOR
Roy Carruthers
WRITER
Steve Jeffery
CLIENT
Seagram's Golden Wine Cooler
EDITOR
David Dee, Stuart Waks
DIRECTOR
David Ashwell
AGENCY
Nancy Braunstein, Ogilvy & Mather,
New York, NY
PRODUCER
Danny Boyle
CREATIVE DIRECTOR
Malcolm End

1758

BROTHER TIMOTHY/MODERATION/HOLIDAY DINNER
30-second
(MUSIC UNDER THROUGHOUT)
TIMOTHY: It's a beautiful day, and uh, no clouds in the sky . . . the vines
are growing very fast . . . they're growing about one inch per day.
We've gotten by this year without any frost, so we're just delighted with the
way the vine are coming along and the way, the uhm, the prospects for
this year's crop.
Thank you all.

1759

WEDDING/JAMMING/IT'S A START
30-second
BRUCE WILLIS: Thank you Seagram's.
WAITER: My name's not Seagram's sir.
BRUCE WILLIS: If you're watching Mr. Seagram's, I want to thank you fo
bringing us Seagram's Golden Wine Cooler. It's brand new . . . and you
did a great job.
GROOM: Who invited him?
BRIDE: I did.
BRUCE WILLIS: I have a toast. Seagram's Golden. It's wet and it's dry.
BRIDE: Is that the toast?
BRUCE: Nah, that's the commercial.
To rock 'n roll.
BRIDE: Golden days.
VO: Seagram's Golden Wine Cooler. It's wet and it's dry.

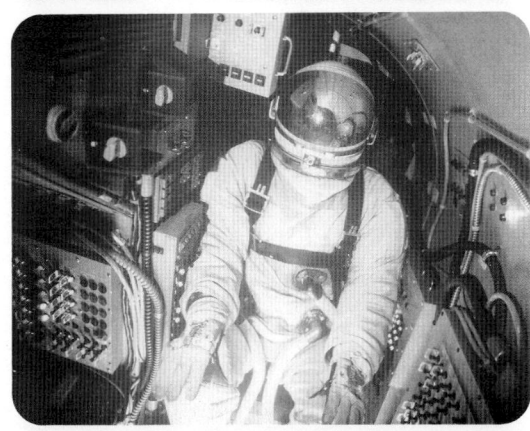

1760
ART DIRECTOR
Gary Goldsmith
DESIGNER
Gary Goldsmith
WRITER
Robin Raj
CLIENT
NYNEX
DIRECTOR
Henry Sandbank
AGENCY
Chiat/Day, New York, NY
PRODUCER
Carol Lee Keliher
PRODUCTION COMPANY
Sandbank Films

1761
ART DIRECTOR
Tod Seisser
WRITER
Jay Taub
CLIENT
New York Air
EDITOR
Morty's Place
DIRECTOR
Henry Sandbank, Sandbank Films
AGENCY
Rachel Novak, LHS&B, New York,
NY
PRODUCTION COMPANY
John Kamen, Sandbank Film

1760

WEDDING/FLY/ELEVATOR II
30-second
SFX: NATURAL SOUNDS OF BRIDE'S QUARTERS; CONVERSATION IS
FAST-PACED. BRIDE REMAINS CALM THROUGHOUT.
DAD: (ENTERS) The limo service is overbooked. We need another limo.
MOM: Check the Yellow Pages.
GNDM: Fix her veil.
DAD: Where is the Yellow Pages?
SIS 1: It was here this morning.
GRDM: Don't touch her hair.
SIS 2: Maybe Auntie has it.
GRDM: Don't touch her hair . . .
VO: One book is in more homes, helping people find more goods and
services . . . the official directory of New York Telephone . . .
DAD: Oh!
(REVEAL) The NYNEX Yellow Pages.
(OVER TITLE) It's always there when you need it . . .

1761

BORMAN/WASHINGTON OFFICIALS/CONTROTIONIST
30-second
ANNCR: Before he became the chairman of Eastern Airlines, Frank
Borman was an astronaut. So he flew in some pretty cramped quarters.
Maybe that's why the average seat on the Eastern shuttle offers a mere 475
square inches of room.
But on New York Air's Super Shuttle, the average seat is full 23% roomier.
You see, Frank Borman had to fly like this.
But you don't.

1762

ART DIRECTOR
John Colquhoun, Steve Miller
WRITER
Clifford L. Freeman, Arthur Bijur
CLIENT
North American Philips Lighting
Company
DIRECTOR
Mark Story, Story Piccolo Guliner
AGENCY
DFS Dorland, New York, NY
PRODUCER
Steven Friedman

1767

ART DIRECTOR
Len McCarron, Bruce Dundore
WRITER
Ted Sann, Rick Meyer, Barry Udoff
CLIENT
Pepsi-Cola Company
EDITOR
Steve Schreiber, Bob DeRise, Howie
Weisbrot
DIRECTOR
Joe Pytka, Terry Bedford
AGENCY
BBDO, New York, NY
PRODUCER
Gene Lofaro, David Frankel, Jerry
Cammisa
PRODUCTION COMPANY
Jennie & Co/Pytka

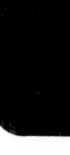

1762

CABIN/ELEVATOR/CAT
30-second
1ST GUY: What was that?
2ND GUY: They said don't worry as long as the lights are on.
1ST GUY: What was that?
2ND GUY: They said don't worry as long as the lights are on.
1ST GUY: What was that?
2ND GUY: They said don't worry as long as the lights are on.
1ST GUY: What did they say to do if the lights go out?
2ND GUY: They didn't say.
ANNCR: It's time you changed your light bulb.
Philips Longer Life square bulbs last 33% longer than ordinary bulbs.

1767

FLOATS/TIME MACHINE/COPIER
60-second
COMMAND CONTROL: Good work, Starship. We'll talk to you at O-six-hundred.
PILOT #1: That's a copy.
COMMAND CONTROL: Why don't you guys take a break?
PILOT #2: How 'bout a Pepsi?
SFX: BUTTON PRESSED. LATCH OPENS.
PILOT #1: There's only one left.
SFX: WALTZ MUSIC
SFX: HATCH OPENING.
SUPER & VO: Pepsi. The choice of a new generation.

1768
ART DIRECTOR
Mary Morant, Dan Krippahne, Bill Halladay
WRITER
Eileen Sandler, Sandy Mairs, Norah Delaney
CLIENT
IBM
DIRECTOR
Dick Loew, Stu Hagman, Henry Sandbank
AGENCY
LGFE, New York, NY
PRODUCER
Bob Schenkel, Bob Warner, Ann O'Keefe
PRODUCTION COMPANY
Gome Loew, HISK Prod., Henry Sandbank Films

1769
ART DIRECTOR
Mark Ryan
WRITER
Elin Jacobson
CLIENT
General Motors Corp.
EDITOR
Michael Shankheim, MS Editorial
DIRECTOR
Rocky Morton, Annabel Jankel
AGENCY
Jim McMenemy, NW Ayer Inc., New York, NY
PRODUCTION COMPANY
Steve Ross, Paula Harwood, Jennie & Co.
EXEC. CREATIVE DIRECTOR
Keith Gould

1768

THE CONVERTIBLE/BUSY BUSINESS/MAGIC PAPER
60-second
VO: When it comes time to take your business on the road . . . some weighty problems can arise.
Information can disappear.
Time can be lost in the shuffle.
And productivity can take a tumble.
Presenting the IBM PC Convertible. A powerful personal computer that easily converts to a full-function portable . . .
an IBM PC you can use on a train . . . a plane . . . at home . . . even in your car.
It runs many of today's most popular business programs . . . and is available with a modem and a snap-on printer to let you print reports on the spot.
All to make you a "big deal" on the road . . . and a big hit back in the office.
The IBM PC Convertible.
One computer . . . for people who really need two.
See your authorized dealer. Or call IBM.

1769

DESIGN/ROBOTICS/COLLISION AVOIDANCE
60-second
(MUSIC UNDER THROUGHOUT)
TEACHER: Kevin . . .
Kevin!
What do you think you're doing young man?
KEVIN: It's a car.
TEACHER: Well I bet everyone would love to see it wouldn't they?
Up front, go on . . .
KEVIN: It's long and low like this,
and the engine is back here and. . . .
TEACHER: And, does it have a name?
KEVIN: Well, I was kind of thinking of . . .
ADULT KEV: . . . Wildcat.
LOUISE: Wildcat?
RUSSELL: That's what it's called.
LOUISE: And you say a computer helped design it?
RUSSELL: By using computers, our design team can get people the kind of GM cars they want much faster
TEACHER: Well Kevin do you have a name for it?
KEVIN: Well, I was kind of thinking of Wildcat?
ANNOUNCER: The GM Odyssey: Science not Fiction

1770

ART DIRECTOR
Don Schneider, Paul Walter
WRITER
Jonathan Mandell, John Greenberger
CLIENT
Polaroid
EDITOR
Rob Tortoriello, Larry Bridges
DIRECTOR
Jim Spencer, Tony Richardson
AGENCY
BBDO, New York, NY
PRODUCER
Jerry Cammisa, Jeff Felter, Jeff Fischgrund
PRODUCTION COMPANY
Dreamquest

1771

CLIENT
Tourism Canada
EDITOR
Norm Odell, Bob Kennedy
DIRECTOR
Bruce Dowad, Ousama Rawi
DIRECTOR OF PHOTOGRAPHY
Brian Thomson, Ousama Rawi
AGENCY
Camp Associates Ltd, Toronto, Canada
PRODUCER
Candace Conacher, Ann Henney
CREATIVE DIRECTOR
John McIntyre, Arnold Wicht

1770

WORLDS/JOURNEY/STOLEN MOMENTS
60-second
(MUSIC—SINGERS)
The world of art.
Fluid. Inspired.
Fueled by passion and bound by man's imagination.
(MUSIC—SINGERS)
Mathematical.
The purest distillation of information.
MUSIC
But, throughout time, when logic and order have meshed with inspiration and imagination,
the results have been some of men's greatest accomplishments.
On May 5th,
Polaroid Corporation will introduce the Spectra System
and the world of science and the world of art
will become one.

1771

WILD WORLD/OLD WORLD/NEW WORLD
60-second
SFX—EARLY MORNING
MUSIC BEGINS
Come to Canada
And widen your horizons
Canada
Come to the world next door
Canada
Come and widen your horizons
Come to the world next door.
SFX—EVENING

1772
ART DIRECTOR
Mike Bade, Bob Steigelman, Howie Cohen, Paul Frahm
WRITER
David Hale, Laurie Birnbaum, Brian Sitts, Frank Nicolo, Brian Mullaney
CLIENT
Miller Brewing Co.
EDITOR
Bob DeRise, Mitchell Hart, Steve Schreiber
DIRECTOR
Tim Newman, Joe Hanwright, Don Guy, Steve Horn, Brian Cummins, Ron Dexter
AGENCY
John Scarola, Michael LaGattuta, JWT, New York, NY
PRODUCTION COMPANY
Randy Stith, Jenkins/Covington and KIRA, Dennis Guy Hirsch, Steve Horn Prod., Fred Levinson Prod.
CREATIVE DIRECTOR
Jim Patterson, Frank Nicolo, David Hale, Bob Steigelman

1773
ART DIRECTOR
Nick Gisonde, Howard Smith
WRITER
Charlie Breen, Seth Fried
CLIENT
Miller Brewing Company — Lite Beer
AGENCY
Backer & Spielvogel, New York, NY
PRODUCER
Eric Steinhauser

1772

ANTHEM III/LONG RYDERS/ANTHEM II
60-second
SONG: Just as proud as the people
Who are making it today . . .
Where I come from folks don't say too much,
But you know where they stand.
A place where doin what you say you will,
Is part of bein' a man.
Where people understand what's right and wrong.
And you know they're sincere.
It's where your word is your word.
A friend's a friend.
And Miller's the beer.
ANNCR: Miller contains no additives or preservatives.
Purity you can see.
Quality you can taste.
SONG: Miller's made the American way.

1773

THE CASE OF THE MISSING CASE SOLUTION × 2/VOTE
75-second
ANNCR VO: And now the conclusion of "The Case of The Missing Case."
(MUSIC UNDER)
MICKEY: It started out as a party, but turned into . . .
. . . The Case of The Missing Case.
SFX: LIGHTENING NOISE, THUNDER, PARTY NOISES.
BEN: (GRUNT)
DAVE: Incredible feat.
BOB: Thank you.
SFX: ELECTRICAL NOISE UPSET CROWD
JOHN MADDEN: Hey! Who turned out the lights?!!! (DRAMATIC MUSIC BEGINS)
LEE MEREDITH: Ooh! Mickey.
MICKEY: It's OK Doll.
BEN DAVIDSON: No it's not, there's a case of Miller Lite missing.
RAY NITSCHE: Who took it?
MICKEY: It had to be somebody in this room.
GROUP: Rodney!! (ACCUSINGLY)
RODNEY: Hey guys take it easy, will ya.
BOOG POWELL: Why did you do it Rodney! Because Lite tastes great?
GROUP: Yeah!
L.C.: Or cause Lites' less filling.
GROUP: Yeah!
RODNEY: I tell ya I didn't do it. Well I'm not even Rodney.
(MUSIC CHANGES)

1774

ART DIRECTOR
Clark Frankel
WRITER
Florence Granello
CLIENT
Jamaica Tourist Board
EDITOR
Alan Rozek
DIRECTOR
Ed Bianchi
DIRECTOR OF PHOTOGRAPHY
Andrzej Bartkowiak
AGENCY
Young & Rubicam, New York, NY
PRODUCER
Laurie Kahn
PRODUCTION COMPANY
Bianchi Films

1775

ART DIRECTOR
Tony LaMonte, Phil Triolo
WRITER
Michael Shevack, John Greenberger,
Jimmy Siegel
CLIENT
Apple Computer, Inc.
EDITOR
David Dee, Eventime
DIRECTOR
Steve Horn
AGENCY
BBDO, New York, NY
PRODUCER
Barbara Mullins, Katy O'Brien, Andy
Chinich
PRODUCTION COMPANY
Steve Horn Productions

1774

COME BACK TO ROMANCE/EXCITEMENT/YOURSELF
60-second
SFX: (TYPEWRITER CLATTER)
ANNCR (VO): This time, this place has done a lot for me.
MUSIC: JAMAICA THEME IN BACKGROUND
SFX: OCEAN SURF
ANNCR (VO): As I write this, on a beach just this side of paradise, I reflect
that life is only as complicated as we choose to make it.
SINGERS (VO): Jamaica
ANNCR (VO): There's a kind of thing that happens when the beauty of a
place overwhelms you. You look at yourself in a whole new way. Think
about things, about people, differently. I think more positively.
SINGERS (VO): Jamaica
ANNCR (VO): I'll be going home in a few days . . . but if there's one
thing I'm certain of
SINGERS (VO): Jamaica
ANNCR (VO): it's that I'll be back.
SINGERS (VO): Come back to yourself.

1775

NIGHTMARE/INFLUENCES/TEACH YOUR CHILDREN
60-second
ANDY: Hi girls.
ANDY: Hi Doreen.
GIRLS: Hi Andy ready for the history final?
ANDY: History final? Is that today?
GIRLS: It sure is.
ANDY: Ah man, I forgot all about it. Let me borrow your notes will ya?
GIRLS: Andy, class starts in 5 minutes.
ANDY: What?
GIRLS: See ya Andy.
GIRLS: Hope you have your term paper finished.
LAUGHING. . . .
ANDY: Wait, I haven't been to history class in awhile. I've forgotten which
room it's in.
GIRLS: It's right here Andy.
SFX.
GIRLS: Mr. Spencer's gonna kill you.
SFX.
GASP.
MUSIC.
ANNCR: The reason more kids use Apple than any other personal
computer is because it makes keeping up with school a lot easier.
ANNCR: And that makes waking up to school a lot nicer.
MUSIC.

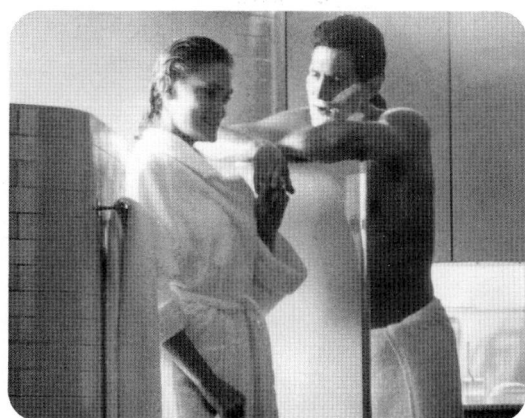

1776

ART DIRECTOR
Bill Oakley
WRITER
Dave Henke, Bill Oakley
CLIENT
Southwestern Bell Telephone
DIRECTOR
John Pytka
AGENCY
D'Arcy Masius Benton & Bowles, St. Louis, MO
PRODUCER
Jane Liepshutz
CREATIVE DIRECTOR
Dave Henke

1777

ART DIRECTOR
Bill Harris
DESIGNER
Bill Harris
WRITER
Jeff Wolf
CLIENT
New York Life
EDITOR
Steve Schreiber, Editor's Gas
DIRECTOR
Jeff Lovinger
DIRECTOR OF PHOTOGRAPHY
John Fleckenstein
AGENCY
Raquel Celenza, Saatchi & Saatchi Compton, New York, NY
PRODUCER
Sheila Mahoney
MUSIC
David Horowitz

1776

MAILBOX/DADDY IT'S ME/BEING HEARD/
60-second
LIGHT MUSIC UP AND UNDER THROUGHOUT
SFX: EARLY MORNING ATMOSPHERE, BIRDS, A CAR DRIVING BY, DOG BARKING IN DISTANCE
AVO: This morning, in communities all over, certain people will find something special in their mailbox.
It's not a new catalog. Or the latest contest. Or a letter from a far-away friend.
MUSIC CONTINUES
AVO: It's a Tele-Help booklet . . . from Southwestern Bell Telephone.
Inside are ways to help senior citizens get a little more out of their phone service . . .
like controlling the cost, special equipment, and long distance services.
Now, while all this may seem very *simple* to *most* of us . . .
AVO: It could turn out to be very *special* for *all* of us.
GIRL: (LAUGHTER) . . . You know Grandma . . . I'm really glad you called.
(CONVERSATION CONTINUES UNDER)
AVO: For your free copy, call 1-800-325-2686.
(TDD Number: 1-800-423-4565)
GRANDMA: (CONTINUES UNDER)
AVO: At Southwestern Bell Telephone. We're here to help.

1777

MIRROR/ARCHITECTS/INSOMNIA/
60-second
BETH: You know Jerry, sometimes I take you for granted. You're a terrific husband, a great golfer . . . and a super salesman.
JERRY: Hey Beth . . . what is this?
BETH: A financial genius you're not.
JERRY: Well I got an idea . . . why don't we get some advice.
VO: You put a lot into life . . . you deserve to get the most out of it. We can help.
AGENT: Mike Stone . . . New York Life.
VO: At New York Life we have the resources to make the most of your resources. We offer a range of financial opportunities . . . including mutual funds, universal life, IRA's, and limited partnerships.
AGENT: Jerry, you're making the right choice . . . Beth . . .
VO: Don't settle for less than you deserve. Get the most out of life with New York Life.

1778

ART DIRECTOR
Roger Mosconi, Don Schneider, Dan Long
WRITER
Michael Patti, Walter Bishop
CLIENT
Chrysler/Dodge Corporation
EDITOR
Rye Dolman, Allen Rozek
DIRECTOR
Jack Churchill, Terry Bedford
AGENCY
BBDO, New York, NY
PRODUCER
Jerry Cammisa, Jack Harrower, Cate Donovan
PRODUCTION COMPANY
Jennie & Co, Bean-Kahn, Dreamquest

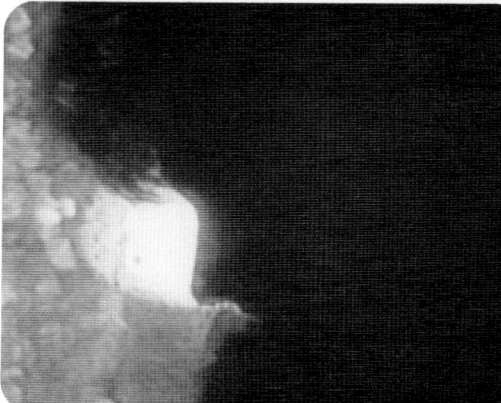

1779

ART DIRECTOR
Don Easdon
WRITER
Bill Heater
CLIENT
John Hancock Financial Services
DIRECTOR
Joe Pytka
AGENCY
Hill Holliday, Boston, MA
PRODUCER
Mary Ellen Argentieri
PRODUCTION COMPANY
Joseph Pytka Productions

1778

JUNK YARD DOG/PRE-LAUNCH/LIGHTNING
60-second
VO: And there came a moment when all the elements came together . . .
Design, engineering, and technology.
Unleashing a new breed of compact car.
The Dodge Shadow. A superbly equipped two door or four door performance sedan.
With a 5/50 protection plan.
An affordable price.
And an insatiable appetite for the sheer thrill of driving.
The new Dodge Shadow is going to cast a giant shadow across America.

1779

DIVORCE/BROTHER & SISTER/WE LOVE EACH OTHER
60-second
How are you.
Yes. Yes I'm fine. Ya, ya.
Well I'm calling because you forgot David's birthday yesterday.
Ya, ya . . . I'm busy, too. I have responsibilities but I manage.
Well enough.
Yes this is new for me you know.
Look. I can't. I can't.
. . . I'm at a pay phone. Ya.
Alright. Call tonight. OK? Bye
Real life, real answers.

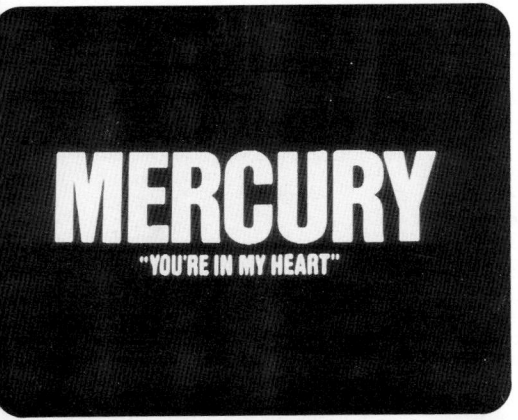
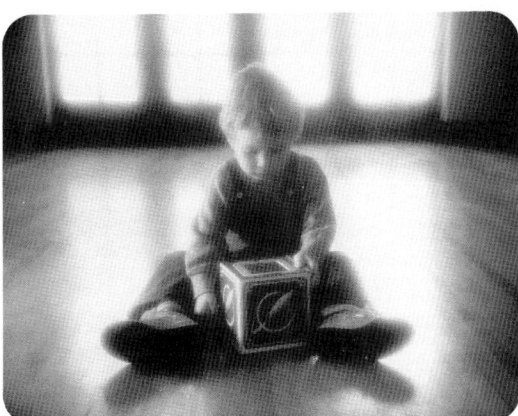

1780
ART DIRECTOR
Joe Puhy
WRITER
Jim Hayman, Brad Justus
CLIENT
Lincoln Mercury — Full Line
EDITOR
Howie Weisbrot
DIRECTOR
Howard Guard
DIRECTOR OF PHOTOGRAPHY
H. Johnson
AGENCY
Young & Rubicam, New York, NY
PRODUCER
Joe Puhy
PRODUCTION COMPANY
Iris Films

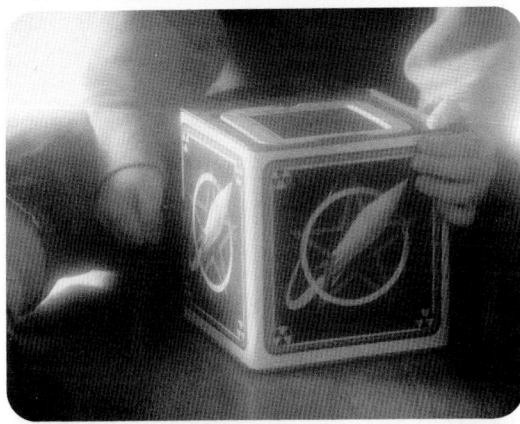

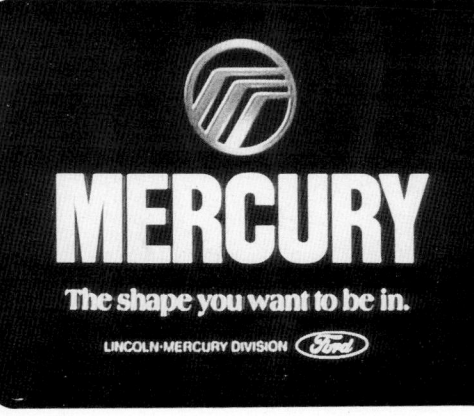
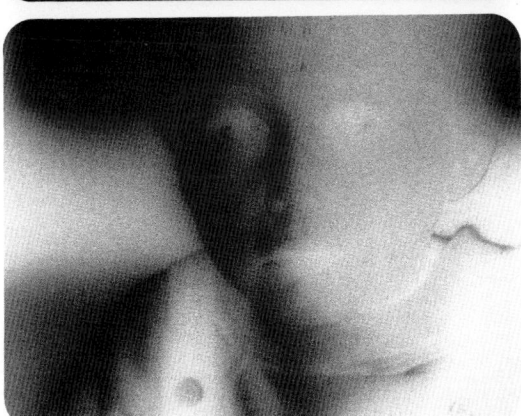

1787
ART DIRECTOR
Young & Laramore
CLIENT
Indianapolis Nuclear Weapons
Freeze
EDITOR
Scofield Editorial
DIRECTOR
Craig Somers
AGENCY
Young & Laramore, Indianapolis,
IN
PRODUCER
Somers & Somers

1780

YOU'RE IN MY HEART/PASSION/TONIGHT'S THE NIGHT
60-second
(MUSIC THROUGHOUT)
(SONG: Rod Stewart's "You're in my Heart")
(MUSIC AND LYRICS)
ANNCR (VO): Mercury for 1987. Shaped to hold the road, and to capture
your heart.
(MUSIC AND LYRICS)
(MUSIC AND LYRICS)
Mercury. The shape you want to be in.

1787

NUCLEAR JACK-IN-THE-BOX
30-second
SFX: DEEP SYNTHESIZED HEARTBEAT THROUGHOUT
(SLOWLY BUILDS IN VOLUME).
SFX: JACK-IN-THE-BOX MUSIC—"ALL AROUND THE COBBLER'S BENCH"
SLOWLY PLAYS AND BECOMES SLIGHTLY DISTORTED.
SFX: (AT THE POINT OF "POP GOES THE WEASEL")
EXPLOSION—FADES TO SILENCE
SCREEN GOES WHITE AND DISSOLVES TO INDIANAPOLIS NUCLEAR
WEAPONS FREEZE LOGOTYPE.

1788
ART DIRECTOR
Stephen A. Pharr
WRITER
Sean Burgett
CLIENT
Governor's Safety Council
DIRECTOR
George Watkins
DIRECTOR OF PHOTOGRAPHY
John Davis
AGENCY
Pringle Dixon Pringle, Atlanta, GA
PRODUCTION COMPANY
Fireside Productions
CREATIVE DIRECTOR
Perry Mitchell
MUSIC
Doppler's Studios

1789
ART DIRECTOR
Rosalind Schell
WRITER
Vashti Brotherhood
CLIENT
Casa Myrna Vasquez
DIRECTOR
Mathew Harris
AGENCY
Hill Holliday, Boston, MA
PRODUCER
Amy Wagoner
PRODUCTION COMPANY
September

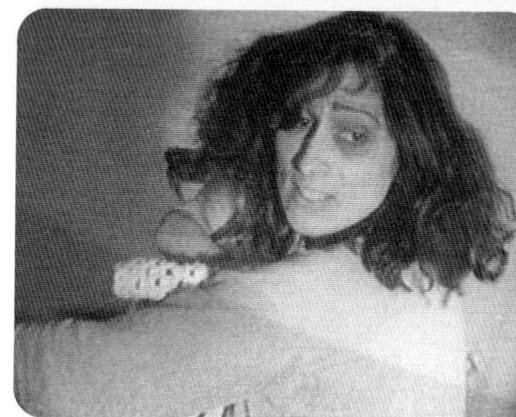

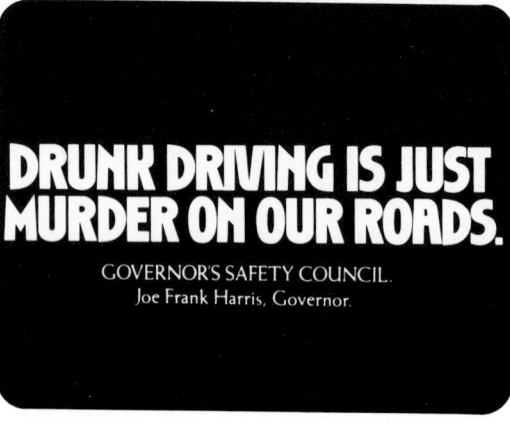

1788

THE FUNERAL
30-second
When anybody talked about Eric, they would always mention things like . . .
he was a model student.
He was captain of the football team.
He used to be such a responsible person.
Everyone, all of his friends looked up to him.
But Eric had one flaw, he drank too much and then got behind the wheel of a car . . .
And killed his best friend. Now he'll have to live with that for the rest of his life.
Drunk driving is just murder on our roads.

1789

FIRE
30-second
SFX: HEAVY, FOOTSTEPS COMING UPSTAIRS POUNDING/ YELLING-(UNDER-GETTING CLOSER)
MOTHER: C'mon-*hurry!* Where's your shirt?
SFX: FOOTSTEPS/POUNDING/YELLING
VO: When you are tired of the beatings and fear
CHILD: Momma?
MOTHER: your shoes . . .
VO: When you have children . . . no job . . . and no money . . .
SFX: FOOTSTEPS/POUNDING AT DOOR
Where do you go?
MOTHER: Hurry—get your coat, go on . . . there's not much time.
SFX: POUNDING-ARE COMING THROUGH DOOR
VO: White, black, hispanic, many battered women and their children lived at a place called Casa Myrna . . . (FIREMAN BREAKS THROUGH DOOR) until it burned down.
Give to Casa Myrna—a home for battered women that's taken a beating of its own.

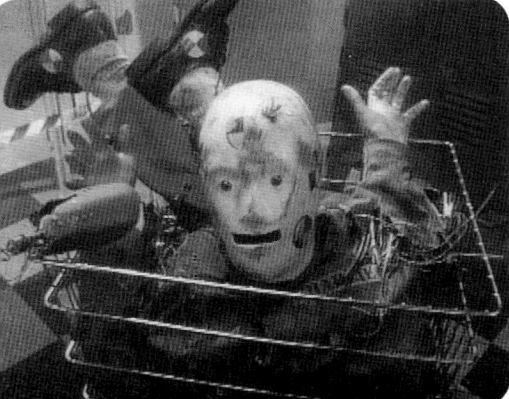

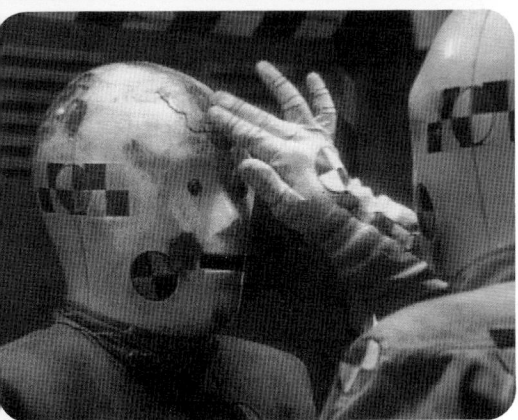

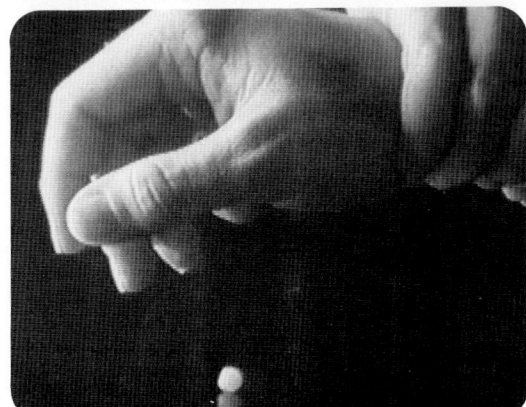

1790

ART DIRECTOR
Joel Machak
WRITER
Jim Ferguson
CLIENT
Ad Council/Safety Belts
EDITOR
Chris Claeys
DIRECTOR
William Dear
AGENCY
Darr Hawthorne, Leo Burnett,
Chicago, IL
PRODUCTION COMPANY
Julie Larson, Boardwalk Prod.
CREATIVE DIRECTOR
Bob Taylor

1791

ART DIRECTOR
Kurt Tausche
WRITER
Kerry Casey
CLIENT
Better Business Bureau
EDITOR
City Post
DIRECTOR
Denny Carlson
AGENCY
Bozell, Jacobs, Minneapolis, MN
PRODUCER
Lisa Jarrard

790

LOCKER ROOM
30-second
LARRY: Hey, Charlie, looks like you could use a shoulder to cry on.
CHARLIE: There's one in here somewhere.
LARRY: Vince, whataya doing?
VINCE: Gettin' out of the crash dummy business. No way I'm ending up like Charlie there.
LARRY: But, Vince, how else can we prove safety belts save lives.
VINCE: We could buckle up.
LARRY: How many times I gotta tell ya? We're dummies. We don't wear safety belts.
TECH: Vince. Larry. Your number's up. Heh. Heh.
LARRY: Could save a life.
VINCE: I'm with ya, pardner.
CHARLIE: Vince. Break a leg.
VINCE: A regular comedian.
ANNCR: You could learn a lot from a dummy. Buckle your safety belt.

1791

SHELL GAME
30-second
MUSIC UP AND UNDER THROUGHOUT
ANNCR VO: In theory, advertising exists to inform you . . .
ANNCR VO: . . . about a product. Unfortunately in practice advertising . . .
ANNCR VO: . . . isn't always . . .
ANNCR VO: . . . that simple.
ANNCR VO: Sometimes it's . . .
ANNCR VO: . . . confusing, misleading or blatantly deceptive.
ANNCR VO: If you've been fooled by an advertiser, call the Advertising Review Committee.
ANNCR VO: We're a program of the Better Business Bureau.
ANNCR VO: And we're here . . .
ANNCR VO: . . . to lend a hand.

1792

ART DIRECTOR
Dean Hanson
WRITER
George Gier
CLIENT
Children's Defense Fund
EDITOR
Beth Dougherty, Wilson-Griak
DIRECTOR
Mark Story
AGENCY
Fallon McElligott, Minneapolis, MN
PRODUCER
Char Loving
PRODUCTION COMPANY
Story Piccolo Guliner
V.O.
Alan Bevis

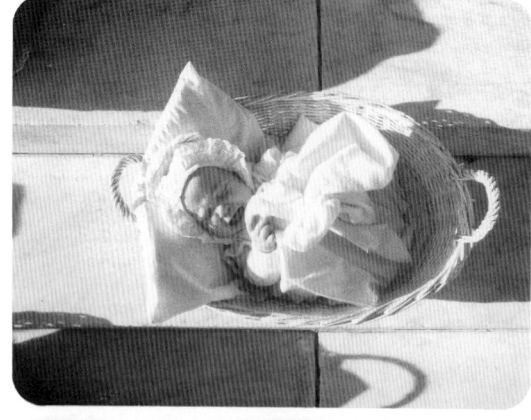

1793

ART DIRECTOR
Nancy Rorabaugh
WRITER
Sarah Bowman
CLIENT
Georgia Council on Child Abuse
DIRECTOR
Rod Paul
DIRECTOR OF PHOTOGRAPHY
Rod Paul
AGENCY
Pringle Dixon Pringle, Atlanta, GA
PRODUCTION COMPANY
Paul Rodman Productions
CREATIVE DIRECTOR
Perry Mitchell

1792

BABIES
30-second
SFX: (BABY CRYING)
VO: There's a growing problem being left on the doorstep of every American.
Last year, nearly half a million babies were born to teenage girls.
The cost to our country was over a billion dollars.
But the human costs are incalculable.
If we don't do something soon,
we'll all have something to cry about.
SFX: (THOUSANDS OF CRYING BABIES)

1793

VICIOUS CYCLE
30-second
CHILD (UNDER): Humming lullaby.
CHILD (UNDER): Stop crying. Mommy wants you to stop crying.
VO: It's a vicious cycle. The victims of child abuse can, and often do, grow up to be abusing parents.
CHILD (UNDER): Mommy takes such good care of you. Why won't you stop crying?
VO: It doesn't have to be. The Georgia Council on Child Abuse provides help to the victims of child abuse and to those who may become child abusers.
CHILD (UNDER): Stop crying! Stoppit! Why are you doing this to me? I'll make you stop crying!
VO: If you need help, call us toll-free, 24 hours a day. Together we can stop the cycle. Before it starts again.

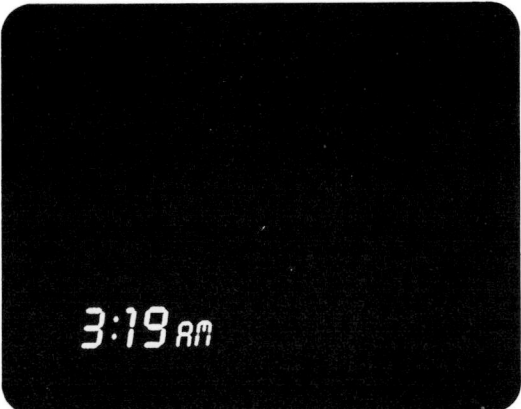

1794
ART DIRECTOR
Joel Machak
WRITER
Jim Ferguson
CLIENT
Ad Council/Safety Belts
EDITOR
Chris Claeys
DIRECTOR
William Dear
AGENCY
Darr Hawthorne, Leo Burnett,
Chicago, IL
PRODUCTION COMPANY
Julie Larson, Boardwalk Prod.
CREATIVE DIRECTOR
Bob Taylor

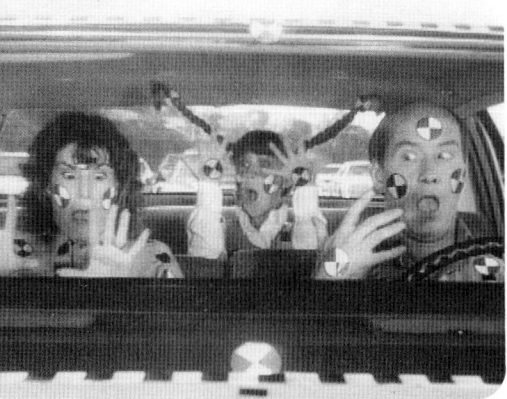

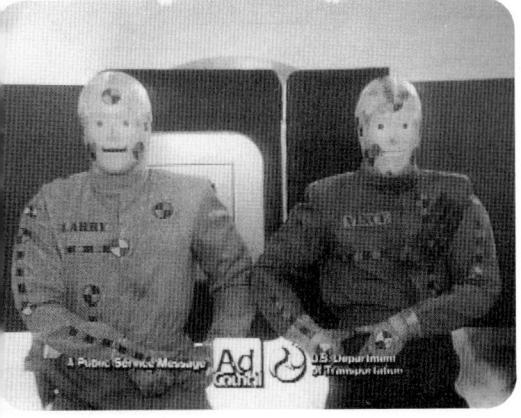

1795
ART DIRECTOR
Peter Norris
WRITER
Winston Albert
CLIENT
L.A. Earthquake Preparedness
Committee
EDITOR
Realtime Video Productions
DIRECTOR
Bill Bayne
DIRECTOR OF PHOTOGRAPHY
Rick Wise
AGENCY
Cheryl Egan, DJMC Advertising, San
Francisco, CA
PRODUCTION COMPANY
Aileen Timmers, Landvoigt-Bayne
CREATIVE DIRECTOR
Brad Ball

1794

THE VINCE AND LARRY SHUFFLE
30-second
MUSIC: (A HEAVY RAP BEAT)
SFX: (LOUD CRASH)
VINCE & LARRY: We are the dummies. The car crashing crew.
Bustin' our heads.
Doin' it for you.
VINCE: My name is Vince. This job makes me sore.
If you'd buckle up,
VINCE: I wouldn't have to do it no more.
LARRY: They call me Larry. I'm a dummy, too.
When you don't buckle up,
Then the dummy's *you.*
NASAL ANNCR: These are professional crash dummies.
Do not attempt this at home.
DUMMIES: Buckle that belt.
Buckle, buckle, buckle that belt.
VINCE & LARRY: We got one thing to say
and we know we're not wrong.
When you go for a ride, put your safety belt on.

1795

THE BIG QUAKE
30-second
SFX: DISTANT DOG BARKING (UP AND OUT)
SFX: CHINA CHATTERING, FURNITURE RATTLING (RISING)
SFX: HOUSEHOLD EFFECTS CRASHING TO FLOOR (RISING)
SFX: WINDOWS BREAKING, CONCRETE AND PLASTER CRUMBLING,
TIMBERS FALLING, GROUND RUMBLING (RISING TO CRESCENDO)
SFX: ALL SFX (OUT)
ANNCR VO: The California Earthquake. It could happen . . . any time.
SUPER: Call (213) PRE-PARE.
SUPER: Furnished by the Los Angeles City and County Earthquake
Preparedness Committee.

1796

ART DIRECTOR
Larry Fredette
WRITER
George Evans
CLIENT
Coalition for Addictive Diseases
EDITOR
Chuck Aikman
DIRECTOR
Paul Hartwick
DIRECTOR OF PHOTOGRAPHY
Paul Hartwick
AGENCY
HBM/Creamer,Inc., Pittsburgh, PA
PRODUCTION COMPANY
Hartwick Przyborski Productions
CREATIVE SUPERVISOR
Bill Gruber

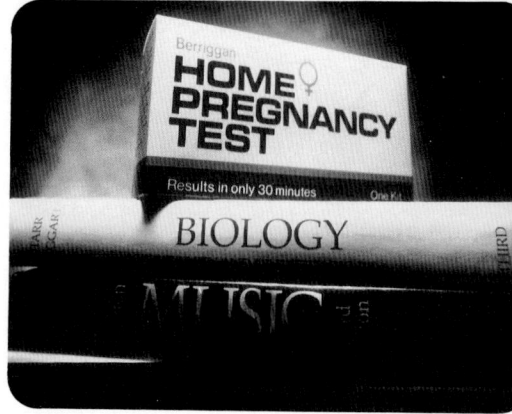

1797

ART DIRECTOR
Dean Hanson
WRITER
George Gier
CLIENT
Children's Defense Fund
EDITOR
Beth Dougherty, Wilson-Griak
DIRECTOR
Eric Young
AGENCY
Fallon McElligott, Minneapolis, MN
PRODUCER
Char Loving
PRODUCTION COMPANY
Wilson-Griak
V.O.
Alan Blevis

1796

KILLING HERSELF
30-second
You're watching someone kill herself.
It might be someone you know. Someone you love.
And you're watching . . . you're letting . . .
her kill herself.
You just refuse to admit it.
You say things like . . .
"How could it be happening to her . . .
or
"I know she has a problem, but
what can *I* do?"
You're watching someone kill herself.
Do something.
Before it's too late.
Drug addiction is treatable. Help someone
you love get help.

1797

BOOKS
15-second
Last year, one hundred twenty five thousand junior . . .
VO: . . . high school students . .
. . . took a very simple test.
And failed.
Let's Prevent Teen Pregnancy.
The Children's Defense Fund
Washington, D.C.

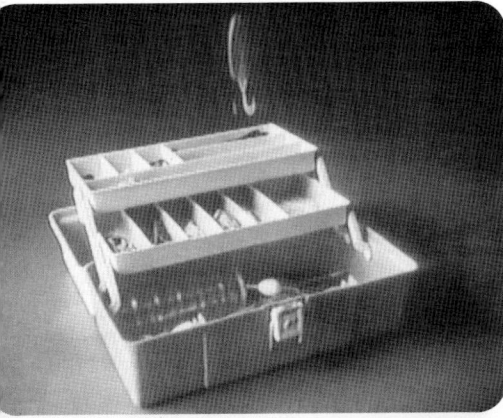

1798
ART DIRECTOR
George Halvorson
WRITER
Tom Evans
CLIENT
Minnesota Institute of Public
Health/Dept. of Natural Resources
EDITOR
Dale Cooper
DIRECTOR
Denny Carlson
AGENCY
Campbell-Mithun, Minneapolis, MN
PRODUCER
George Halvorson, Tom Evans
CREATIVE DIRECTOR
Terry Bremer

1799
ART DIRECTOR
Jeff Roll
WRITER
David Butler
CLIENT
Blind Children's Center
EDITOR
Gayle Grant
DIRECTOR
Mark Coppos
AGENCY
Chiat/Day, Los Angeles, CA
PRODUCER
Francesca Cohn
PRODUCTION COMPANY
Coppos Films

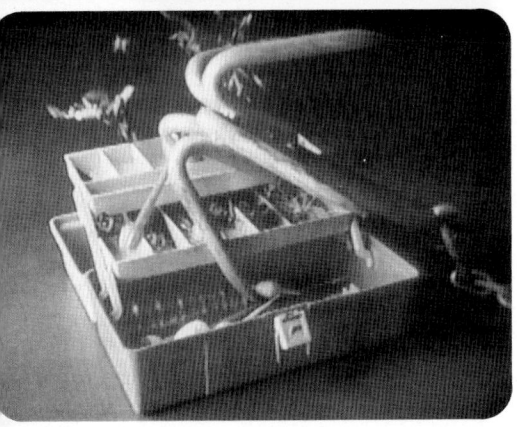

798

IFEJACKET
0-second
OPEN ON A TACKLE BOX)
NNCR (VO): Last year, Minnesotans pulled 6 million walleyes out of
Minnesota lakes . . . using one of these.
CRANKBAIT LURE FALLS INTO TACKLE BOX)
NNCR (VO): They pulled 4 million northerns out . . . using one of these.
SPOON LURE FALLS INTO TACKLE BOX)
NNCR (VO): They pulled 3 million bass out . . . using one of these.
SPINNEBAIT LURE FALLS INTO TACKLE BOX)
NNCR (VO): Unfortunately, Minnesotans also pulled 25 Minnesotans out
f Minnesota lakes . . . using one of these.
GRAPPLING HOOK FALLS INTO TACKLE BOX)
UPER: Wear your life jacket

1799

I CAN SEE CLEARLY NOW
60-second
SINGER: I can see clearly now, the rain is gone. I can see all obstacles in
my way. Gone are the dark clouds that had me blind . . . Gonna be a
bright, bright sunshiney day. Gonna be a bright, bright sunshiney day.
Look all around, there's nothing but blue skies . . . look straight ahead
nothing but blue skies . . .
ANNCR: With the extra love, care and support of the Blind Children's
Center, you'd be amazed at how much a blind child can see.
SINGER: Gonna be a bright, bright sunshiney day.

1800

ART DIRECTOR
Tom Tieche
WRITER
Michael Leonard
CLIENT
United Way of The Bay Area
EDITOR
Michael Leonard
DIRECTOR
Jon Francis
DIRECTOR OF PHOTOGRAPHY
Bob Brown
PRODUCER
Deborah Billig
PRODUCTION COMPANY
Elizabeth O'Toole, Jon Francis
Films, San Francisco, CA
EXECUTIVE PRODUCER
Sandra Marshall

1801

ART DIRECTOR
Cabell Harris
WRITER
Ken Hines
CLIENT
Division of Litter Control
DIRECTOR
Tom Ferrell
AGENCY
Lawler Ballard, Richmond, VA
PRODUCTION COMPANY
Thom II

1800

KHAMPHY
60-second
KHAMPHY: When I first came to San Francisco, I had no money. I had no food. I had no place to live. All I had was memories of my home.
(BLACK AND WHITE WAR FOOTAGE)
KHAMPHY: A home I had to leave, and could never return to.
(BLACK AND WHITE WAR FOOTAGE)
KHAMPHY: So I thank you for the Chinatown Youth Center. You got me work so I can bring my family here.
(BLACK AND WHITE WAR FOOTAGE)
KHAMPHY: We still remember ever day . . . what our old home was like.
(BLACK AND WHITE WAR FOOTAGE)
KHAMPHY: So every day we are grateful for our new home.
(IN LAOTIAN WITH ENGLISH SUBTITLES)
I don't know you, but I love you.
LOGO: United Way for the Bay Area.

1801

RECYCLE
30-second
OC ANNCR: Recycling one glass bottle saves enough energy to burn this lightbulb for four hours. Recycling this can saves enough energy to fix your toast every morning for eight months. What do you save when you recycle this many newspapers? Let me give you a hint.
VO ANNCR: Get the facts on recycling. Call us toll free.
SUPER: Logo
1-800-KEEP ITT

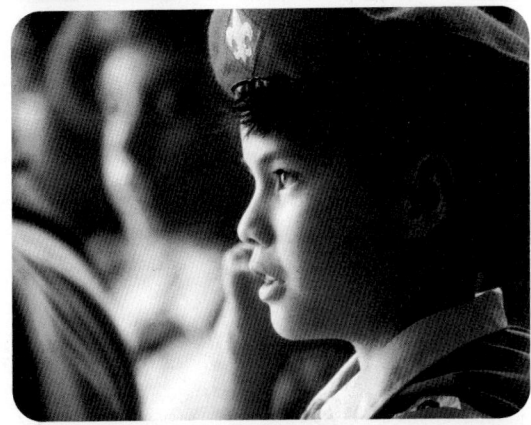

1802
ART DIRECTOR
Larry Fredette
WRITER
George Evans
CLIENT
Coalition for Addictive Diseases
EDITOR
Chuck Aikman
DIRECTOR
Paul Hartwick
DIRECTOR OF PHOTOGRAPHY
Paul Hartwick
AGENCY
HBM/Creamer, Inc., Pittsburgh, PA
PRODUCTION COMPANY
Hartwick Przyborski Productions
CREATIVE SUPERVISOR
Bill Gruber

1803
ART DIRECTOR
Tom Tieche
WRITER
Michael Leonard
CLIENT
United Way of The Bay Area
DIRECTOR
Jon Francis
DIRECTOR OF PHOTOGRAPHY
Bob Brown
PRODUCER
Deborah Billig
PRODUCTION COMPANY
Elizabeth O'Toole, Jon Francis
Films, San Francisco, CA
EXECUTIVE PRODUCER
Sandra Marshall

1802

KILLING HIMSELF
30-second
You're watching someone kill himself.
It might be someone you know. Someone you love.
And you're watching . . . you're letting . . . him kill himself.
You just refuse to admit it.
You say things like . . .
"How could it be happening to him . . ."
or
"I know he has a problem, but what can *I* do?"
You're watching someone kill himself.
Do something.
(SFX—GUN SHOT)
Before it's too late. Alcoholism . . . is treatable. Help someone you love get help.

1803

BOY SCOUTS
60-second
TROOP LEADER: Attention
VO: This is Troop 555
TROOP LEADER: At ease . . . Michael Halloran
VO: Michael Halloran knows first aid as well as many paramedics. Michael is also what is sometimes called retarded.
TROOP LEADER: Migel
VO: Migel Lepe could guide you home if you were lost in the Sierras. Migel is also legally blind.
TROOP LEADER: And John
VO: John Maso has a defect that left his heart outside his chest cavity. He's also an Eagle Scout.
VO: Most of the scouts in Troop 555 are disabled in one way or another, but thanks to your contributions to the United Way, they seldom feel that way or act it.
SCOUTS: . . . to keep myself physically strong, mentally awake, and morally straight.
VO: Troop 555 never asks for favors, but they do appreciate them.
SCOUTS: We don't know you, but we love you.
VO: At ease troop, at ease.
LOGO: United Way for the Bay Area.

1804

ART DIRECTOR
Margaret Noon
DESIGNER
Margaret Noon
WRITER
Robin Silverman
CLIENT
Pharmaceutical Advertising Council,
Food & Drug Administration
DIRECTOR
Daniel Cooperbey
DIRECTOR OF PHOTOGRAPHY
Motion Picture Services
AGENCY
Sudler & Hennessey, New York, NY
PRODUCER
Daniel Cooperbey

1805

ART DIRECTOR
Stan Jones
DESIGNER
Peter Politanoff
WRITER
Alan Proctor
CLIENT
Compcare
EDITOR
Charlie Chubak, Filmcore
DIRECTOR
Norman Griner
DIRECTOR OF PHOTOGRAPHY
Norman Griner
AGENCY
Elaine Lord, DDB
PRODUCTION COMPANY
Chris Stefani, Griner Cuesta, New
York, NY

1804

OPERATION QUACKDOWN
30-second
SFX: SOUNDS OF THE WILD, QUACKING SOUNDS
ANNCR (VO): Quack. Another word for fraud or fake. Thousands of quack
medical products are advertising simple cures for problems ranging from
baldness to cancer . . .
. . . luring you into believing they're the real thing.
All are a waste of money; many endanger your health.
So before buying a questionable cure, ask your doctor or pharmacist first.
Because the next dead duck . . .
SFX: CRUNCHING SOUND OF TWIG BEING STEPPED ON
. . . could be you.
For a free booklet on quackery, write to: Quackery, HFE 55, Rockville,
Maryland 20857.

1805

OATH
30-second
WOMAN'S VO: (SEDUCTIVE, ALLURING): Will you lie, cheat and steal for
me?
YOUNG WHITE KID: I will.
WOMAN'S VO: Will you abandon your family?
PROFESSIONAL MAN: (NODS SILENTLY)
WOMAN'S VO: Will you risk prison?
WORKING WOMAN: Yes.
WOMAN'S VO: Will you give me your health?
YOUNG BLACK KID: O.K.
ANNCR: When you say yes to cocaine, you're saying yes to all these things
WOMAN'S VO: Will you die for me, if I ask?
YOUNG MAN: I'll die.
WOMAN'S VO: I knew you would. (LIGHT, TINKLING LAUGH)
ANNCR: If you or someone you love loves cocaine, call CareUnit before it's
too late.
We can help.

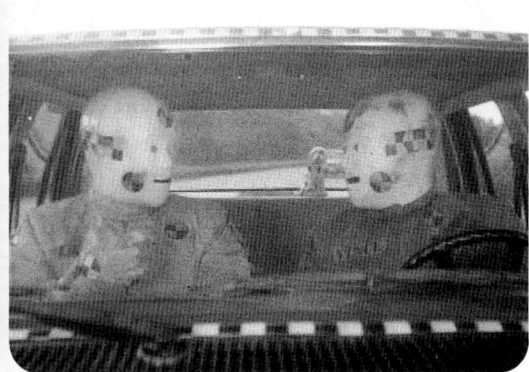

1806

ART DIRECTOR
Joel Machak
WRITER
Jim Ferguson
CLIENT
Ad Council/Safety Belts
EDITOR
Chris Claeys
DIRECTOR
William Dear
AGENCY
Darr Hawthorne, Leo Burnett,
Chicago
PRODUCTION COMPANY
Julie Larson, Boardwalk Prod.
CREATIVE DIRECTOR
Bob Taylor

1807

ART DIRECTOR
Paul Matthaeus
WRITER
Paul Matthaeus, Rick Peterson
CLIENT
Seattle Art Museum
DIRECTOR
David Culp
AGENCY
Cynthia Hartwig, Sharp Hartwig,
Seattle, WA
PRODUCER
Karen Coucher, Kaye Smith
CREATIVE DIRECTOR
Cynthia Hartwig

1806

THE GETAWAY
30-second
SFX: (CAR ZOOMING TOWARD THE TARGET.)
(SCREECH)
LARRY: Whataya doin', Vince?
Have you lost your head?
VINCE: That's what I'm tryin' to avoid, my friend.
LARRY: But, Vince, if we don't belly up to the bullseye how else can we
prove that safety belts save lives?
VINCE: It ain't workin', Larry. Nobody's listening.
LARRY: Sure they are. Look at them. They're buckled up.
Them, too.
VINCE: so maybe eating all these dashboard hors d'oeuvres is worth it.
Let's head back. Wanna drive, pal?
LARRY: Can I, Vince?
VINCE: Sure, take the wheel.
LARRY: Who-o-o-o-a!
ANNCR: You could learn a lot from a dummy. Buckle your safety belt.

1807

OUT OF THE DARK
30-second
MUSIC: CHAMBER
VO: The Seattle Art Museum is home to an extensive collection of
European paintings, sculpture and decorative arts. And to most of Seattle,
they look like this. (DARKNESS)
MUSIC: MANDARIN
VO: We also have one of the finest collections of Asian art on the West
Coast. But to most of Seattle, it looks like this. (DARKNESS)
MUSIC: STOP
SFX: LIGHTBULB CORD
ANNCR: You see, 97 percent of Seattle's art is in the dark, hidden away in
storage. There just isn't room to show it. That's why we're building a
bigger museum downtown. The new Seattle Art Museum downtown.
Please. Help bring Seattle's art out of the dark.

1808

ART DIRECTOR
Rob Rich
WRITER
Michael Sheehan
CLIENT
AIDS Action Committee
DIRECTOR
Mike Mascioli
DIRECTOR OF PHOTOGRAPHY
Rick Ashley
AGENCY
Terri McGroary, ClarkeGowardFitts,
Boston, MA
PRODUCER
Rick Ashley

1809

ART DIRECTOR
Michael Edwards
WRITER
Bruce MacDonald
CLIENT
Ministry of the Attorney General for
Ontario
EDITOR
Mick Griffin
DIRECTOR
Stanley Mestel
DIRECTOR OF PHOTOGRAPHY
Stanley Mestel
AGENCY
Angela Carroll, Miller Myers Bruce,
Toronto, Canada
PRODUCER
Evelyn Arthur

1808

HOME MOVIES
30-second
SFX: HOME MOVIE PROJECTOR.
ANNCR VO: AIDS. It takes all kinds.
For more information, call.

1809

IMPACT
30-second
MUSIC: UP AND UNDER.
SS: You are so beautiful . . .
SFX: CAR HORN, SQUEALING TIRES, SKIDDING SOUNDS.
SS: to me.
SS: You're everything . . .
SFX: Brakes, skid, explosive impact.
SS: I hoped for.
SS: You're everything . . .
SFX: SOUND OF IMPACT, TIRES SQUEALING, BRAKES GRINDING.
SS: I need.
SS: You are so beautiful . . .
SS: to me.

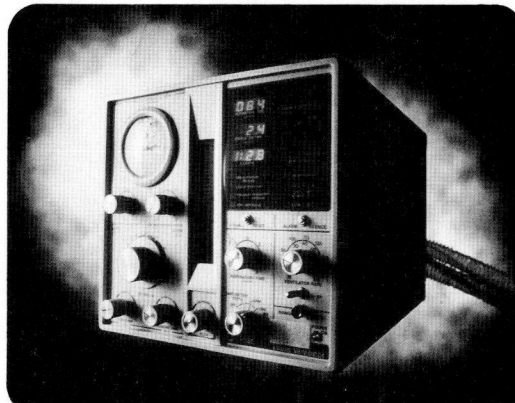

Fight low birthweight.
March of Dimes.

(212) 922-1460

1810
ART DIRECTOR
Gary Greenberg
WRITER
Peter Seronick
CLIENT
Rosie's Place
DIRECTOR
Bill Cuchinello
AGENCY
Rossin Greenberg Seronick & Hill,
Boston, MA
PRODUCTION COMPANY
Viz Wiz

1811
ART DIRECTOR
Kirk Souder
WRITER
Martin Canellakis
CLIENT
March of Dimes
DIRECTOR
Gary Perweiler
DIRECTOR OF PHOTOGRAPHY
Gary Perweiler
AGENCY
Homer & Durham Advertising, New
York, NY
PRODUCTION COMPANY
Exit Films

1810

PLACE TO CALL HOME
30-second
FEMALE: There's an intimate place in Boston that serves good food. And
has lodging for guests. It doesn't accept credit cards. Doesn't have maid
service. Doesn't take reservations. Yet every night the dining room is
packed and the rooms are full. You could stay there or dine there. And it
won't cost you a penny. All you have to do is be a homeless woman with
nowhere else to turn.
Rosie's Place.

1811

LUNGS
30-second
You wouldn't want us to show you 3 day old Janice Thompson.
So instead we're showing you her lungs.
You see, Janice was born with what's known as low birth-weight. She was
only 1½ pounds.
Because Janice's mother didn't know getting pregnant was any reason to
see a doctor.
Janice sees a lot of doctors now.

1812

ART DIRECTOR
Wes Hotchkiss
WRITER
Joanne DeMenna
CLIENT
United Way
EDITOR
Annie Taylor, Seventh Art
DIRECTOR
Sid Myers
DIRECTOR OF PHOTOGRAPHY
Richard Henry
AGENCY
Lewis Gilman & Kynett,
Philadelphia, PA
PRODUCER
Peg Finucan
PRODUCTION COMPANY
Myers Films Inc.
CREATIVE DIRECTOR
Jacqueline Lowell

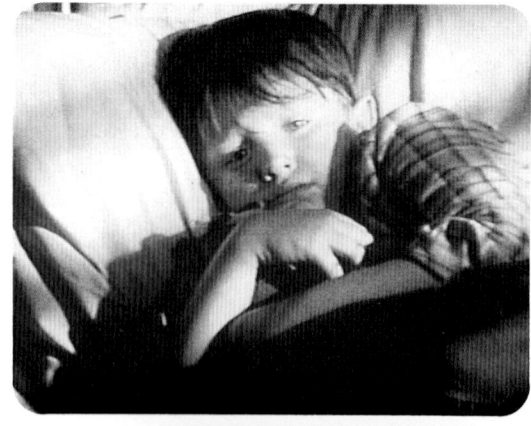

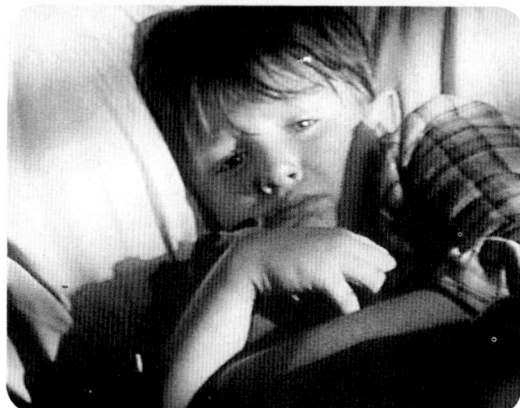

1814

ART DIRECTOR
Michael Winslow
WRITER
Steve Bassett
CLIENT
N.C. Governor's Highway Safety
Program
DIRECTOR
Chuck Clemmons
AGENCY
McKinney & Silver, Raleigh, NC
PRODUCER
John Pace
PRODUCTION COMPANY
Michael Moir Productions

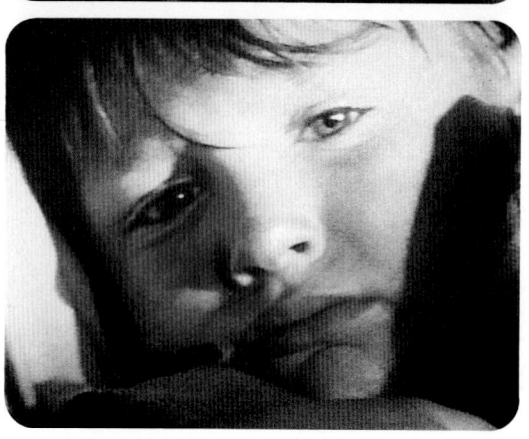

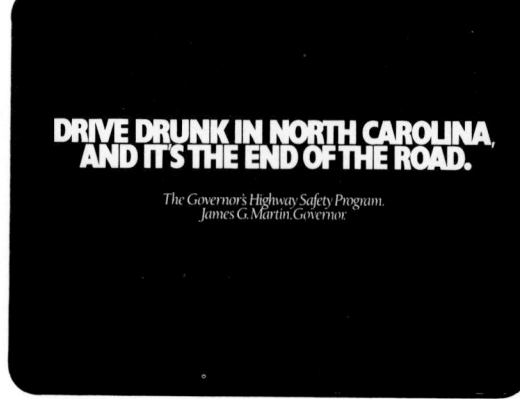

1812

BOY
30-second
SFX: LOUD SCREAMING BETWEEN PARENTS DOWNSTAIRS
Abuse comes in many forms.
ANNCR: When families can't turn to each other, there's got to be a place
to turn.
Don't give up.
Give.
It's the American way.
It's the United Way.

1814

COOLER/CAN/TOUGH LAWS
30-second
ANNCR VO: Recently, California introduced America to a new drink called
the wine cooler. But if you drink any kind of alcohol, and then drive . . .
(CUT TO JAIL CELL. DOOR SLAMS SHUT) . . . you could get a taste of a
North Carolina cooler. (FADE TO BLACK, FADE UP THEME LINE) Drive
drunk in North Carolina, and it's the end of the road.

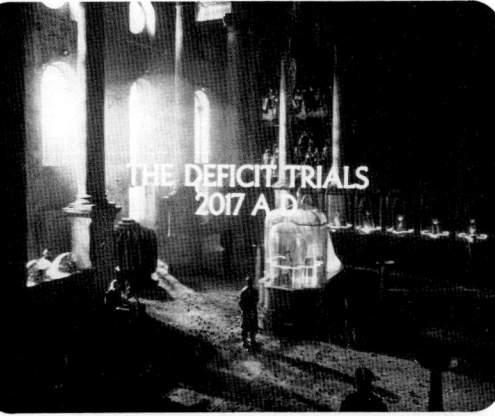

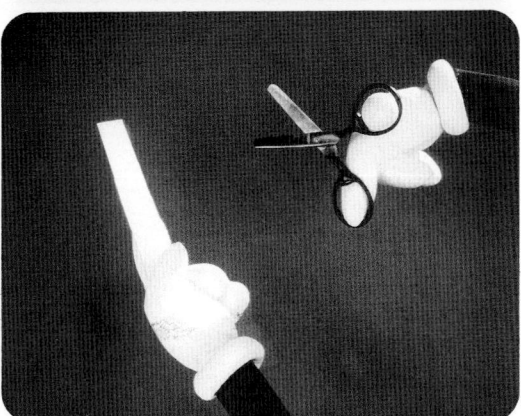

1815
ART DIRECTOR
Steve Ohman
WRITER
Harold Karp
CLIENT
W.R. Grace & Co.
EDITOR
Vito DeSario, Pam Powers
DIRECTOR
Ridley Scott
AGENCY
Mindy Gerber, Lowe Marschalk,
Inc., New York, NY
PRODUCTION COMPANY
Richard Goldberg, Fairbanks Films;
RSA Films

1816
ART DIRECTOR
Carl Willat
DESIGNER
George Evelyn
ANIMATOR/ARTIST
Carl Willat
WRITER
George Evelyn
CLIENT
The Disney Channel
EDITOR
Carol Brzezinski
DIRECTOR
Carl Willat
DIRECTOR OF PHOTOGRAPHY
Carl Willat
PRODUCER
Chris Whitney
PRODUCTION COMPANY
Colossal Pictures, San Francisco, CA
DIRECTOR CREATIVE SERVICES
Mike Nichols, The Disney Channel

1815

HE DEFICIT TRIALS
)-second
LD MAN: I've already told you, it was all going to work out somehow.
here was even talk of an amendment. But no one was willing to make
e sacrifices.
m afraid you're much too young to understand.
OY: Maybe so but I'm afraid the numbers speak for themselves. By 1986,
r example, the national debt had reached 2 trillion dollars.
idn't that frighten you?
): No one really knows what another generation of unchecked federal
eficits will bring.
LD MAN: This frightens me.
OY: No more questions.
LD MAN: I have a question. Are you ever going to forgive us?
): But we know this much. You *can* change the future. You have to. At
".R. Grace, we want all of us to stay one step ahead of a changing world.

1816

MICKEY ORIGAMI
10-second
NO SCRIPT.
MUSIC TRACK ONLY.

1817

ART DIRECTOR
Abby Terkuhle
ANIMATOR/ARTIST
Caesar Video Graphics
CLIENT
MTV, New York, NY
EDITOR
Bob Gleason
AGENCY
Ohlmeyer Communications

1818

ART DIRECTOR
Bob Pook
DESIGNER
Bob Pook
CLIENT
NBC Late Night With David
Letterman
PROJECT DIRECTOR
Bob Pook
DIRECTOR OF PHOTOGRAPHY
Marc Karzen
AGENCY
NBC, New York, NY
PRODUCER
Barry Sand
PROJECT PRODUCER
Edd Hall

1817

**1986 VIDEO MUSIC AWARDS SHOW CHERRY
BOMB/OREO/SPEAKER**
50-second
MUSIC: David Bowie and Mick Jagger/Dancin' in the Streets
Dire Straits/Money for Nothing
Robert Palmer/Addicted to Love
Bruce Springsteen/Glory Days
Sting/If You Love Somebody Set Them Free

1818

LATE NIGHT WITH DAVID LETTERMAN
30-second
MUSIC ONLY.

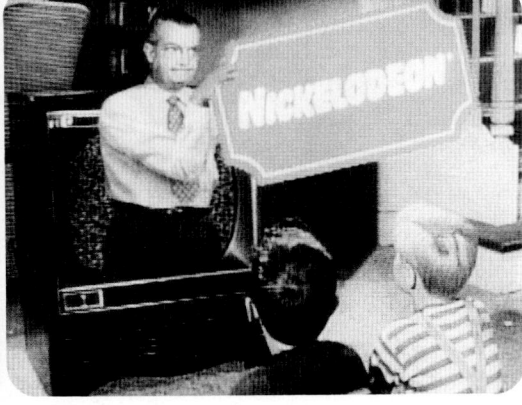

1819
ART DIRECTOR
Alex Weil, Chris Harvey
ANIMATOR/ARTIST
Gordon DeWolf, Page Wood, Henry Baker
WRITER
Scott Webb
CLIENT
Nickelodeon/MTV Networks, New York, NY
EDITOR
David Rothenberg, Jonathan Vesey, David Hyland
DIRECTOR
Betty Cohen
PRODUCER
Scott Webb, Ralph Horan

1820
ART DIRECTOR
George Evelyn
DESIGNER
George Evelyn
ANIMATOR/ARTIST
Catherine Margerin
CLIENT
The Disney Channel
DIRECTOR
George Evelyn
DIRECTOR OF PHOTOGRAPHY
Don Smith
PRODUCER
Chris Whitney
PRODUCTION COMPANY
Colossal Pictures, San Francisco, CA
DIRECTOR CREATIVE SERVICES
Mike Nichols, The Disney Channel

1819

DENNIS THE MENACE BUMPER
5-second
VO: You're watching Nickelodeon
Now back to Dennis the Menace

1820

MICKEY SHADOW
10-second
NO SCRIPT.
MUSIC TRACK ONLY.

1821

ART DIRECTOR
Orest Woronewych
DESIGNER
Tom Gericke, Roger Chouinard,
Jean Perramon
ANIMATOR/ARTIST
Roger Chouinard, Jean Perramon
CLIENT
HBO, New York, NY
DIRECTOR
Tom Gericke
PRODUCER
Tom Gericke
PRODUCTION COMPANY
Campbell & Gericke, Inc.

 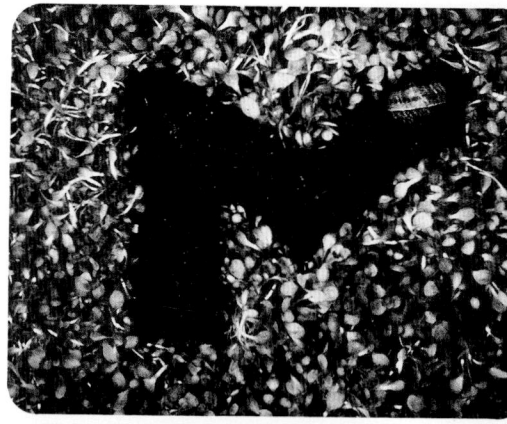

1822

ART DIRECTOR
Carl Willat
DESIGNER
Carl Willat
CLIENT
MTV Networks, Inc., Marcy Brafman
EDITOR
Vickie Lewis, Carol Brzezinski
DIRECTOR OF PHOTOGRAPHY
Carl Willat
PRODUCER
Jane Antee
PRODUCTION COMPANY
Colossal Pictures, San Francisco, CA
MUSIC
Greg Jones

1821

FAMILY SHOWCASE

No dialogue

1822

M-MOLLUSK
10-second
NO SCRIPT.
MUSIC TRACK ONLY.

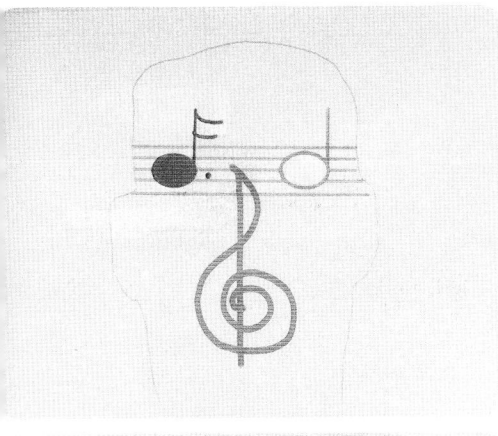

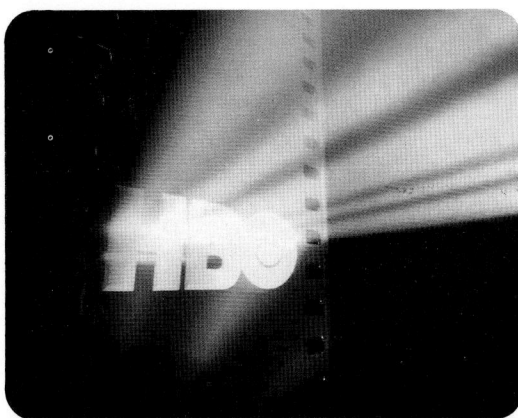

1823

ART DIRECTOR
B.T. Whitehill
DESIGNER
B.T. Whitehill
CLIENT
American Masters
PRODUCER
WNET/Thirteen Design Dept.
PRODUCTION COMPANY
Editel, New York, NY

1824

ART DIRECTOR
Orest Woronewych, HBO and Cheri
Du Sair, California Films
DESIGNER
Wendy Vanguard-Dobrowner,
California Films
ANIMATOR
Adam B. Chin, Pacific Data Images
PRODUCER
Mitchell Dobrowner
PRODUCTION COMPANY
Calif. Films
TECHNICAL DIRECTOR
Terry O'Brien, California Films

823

AMERICAN MASTERS OPENING
0-second
ORIGINAL THEME MUSIC BY JONATHAN TUNICK.

1824

MOVIE OPEN

No dialogue

1825

ART DIRECTOR
Nan Cadorin, John Payson
DESIGNER
Nan Cadorin, John Payson
ANIMATOR/ARTIST
Nan Cadorin, John Payson
WRITER
John Tierney, Dick Seeback, Matty
Powers, Rob Ortiz
CLIENT
MTV, New York, NY
PRODUCER
Linda Corradina, John Payson

1826

ART DIRECTOR
Orest Woronewych
DESIGNER
Michael Busch, Campbell &
Gericke, Inc.
ANIMATOR/ARTIST
Mark Kirkland, Justin Carroll
CLIENT
HBO, New York, NY
DIRECTOR
Tom Gericke, Campbell & Gericke,
Inc.
PRODUCER
Tom Gericke
PRODUCTION COMPANY
Campbell & Gericke, Inc.

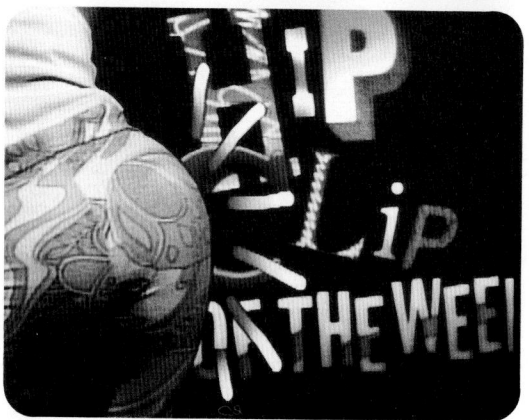

1825

HIP CLIP OF THE WEEK OPEN/MUSIC NEWS/YEAR IN ROCK
4-second
AUDIO: Hip
Clip
of the week.

1826

ON LOCATION

No dialogue

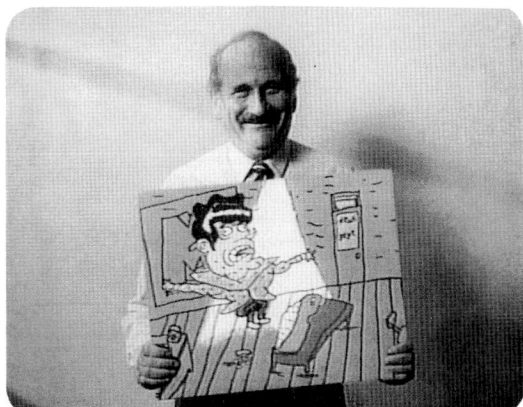

1827
ART DIRECTOR
Richard Greenberg
DESIGNER
Paul Johnson
ANIMATOR/ARTIST
Paul Johnson
WRITER
Tom Wehner
CLIENT
General Motors
PRODUCER
Jim McMenemy
PRODUCTION COMPANY
Robert M. Greenberg, R/Greenberg
Associates, Inc.
CREATIVE DIRECTOR
Keith Gould

1828
ART DIRECTOR
R. O. Blechman
DESIGNER
Mark Marek, R. O. Blechman
ANIMATOR
Tony Eastman, Ed Smith
CLIENT
MTV Networks
EDITOR
Bruce Knapp, The Ink Tank
DIRECTOR
R. O. Blechman, The Ink Tank
PRODUCER
Nina Silvestri, Marcie Brafman
PRODUCTION COMPANY
J. J. Sedelmaier, The Ink Tank, New
York, NY

1827

GM BILLBOARD
30-second
GEORGE WASHINGTON: The forging of a nation . . .
is one of several television specials to be presented by GM in the coming
year . . .
marking the bicentennial of the Constitution of the United States.
This program is a General Motors Mark of Excellence Presentation.

1828

MTV ROCK 'N' ROLL OPEN/ROCK NEWS/MUSIC NEWS
4-second
AUDIO: Hip
Clip
Of the week.

1829
CREATIVE DIRECTOR
John McIntyre, Arnold Wicht
CLIENT
Tourism Canada
EDITOR
Norm Odell
DIRECTOR
Bruce Dowad, Ousama Rawi
DIRECTOR OF PHOTOGRAPHY
Brian Thomson, Ousama Rawi
AGENCY
Derek Ellis, Bob Kirk, Camp
Associates Ltd., Toronto, Canada
PRODUCER
Candace Conacher, Ann Henney

 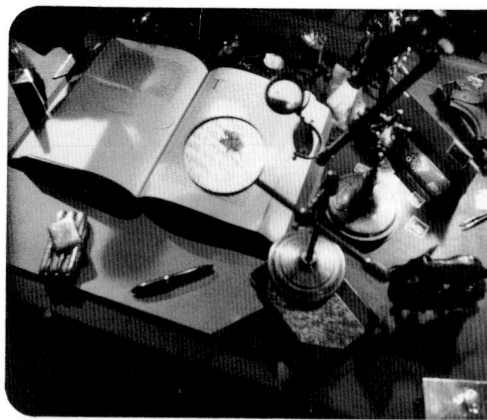

1832
ART DIRECTOR
Rick Boyko
ILLUSTRATOR/ARTIST
Jaime Seltzer
WRITER
Jaime Seltzer
CLIENT
Amblin Entertainment
EDITOR
Rob Watzke
DIRECTOR
Ken Davis
AGENCY
Chiat/Day, Los Angeles, CA
PRODUCER
Richard O'Neill
PRODUCTION COMPANY
RSA

 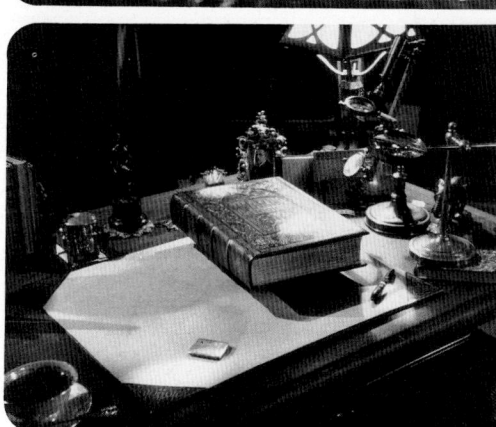

1829

CANADA: THE WORLD NEXT DOOR
8-minute
SCENE LOCATIONS IN:
LOUISBOURG, NOVA SCOTIA;
FORT HENRY GUARD, KINGSTON, ONTARIO;
SOUTH WESTERN ALBERTA;
UPPER CANADA VILLAGE, MORRISBURG, ONTARIO;
ROYAL HUDSON, SQUAMISH, BRITISH COLUMBIA;
MONTREAL;
QUEBEC CITY;
PLACE JACQUES CARTIER, MONTREAL;
OLD MONTREAL;
ST. JOSEPH'S ORATORY, MONTREAL;
CHATEAU FRONTENAC, QUEBEC CITY;
HOLY TRINITY UKRAINIAN CHURCH, LEDUC, ALTA.; ETC.

1832

FLY
10-second
ANNCR VO: Discover the Wonder.
Monday nights on NBC.

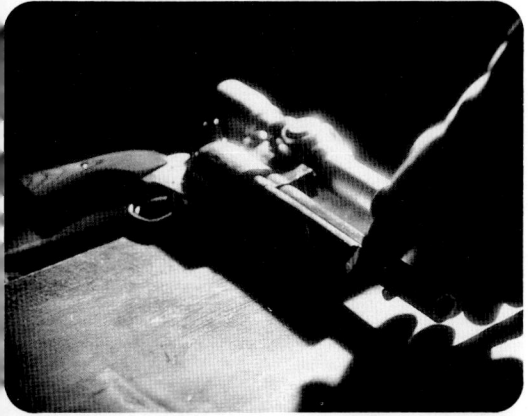

1833
ART DIRECTOR
Paula Silver
WRITER
Kate Cox
CLIENT
Columbia Pictures
EDITOR
Bill Lattanzi
DIRECTOR
Richard Greenberg
DIRECTOR OF PHOTOGRAPHY
Jerry Hartleben
PRODUCER
Ken Stewart
LINE PRODUCER
Brian Williams
PRODUCTION COMPANY
Robert M. Greenberg, R/Greenberg
Associates, Inc., New York, NY

1834
ART DIRECTOR
Rick Boyko
WRITER
Jaime Seltzer
CLIENT
Amblin Entertainment
EDITOR
Rob Watzke
DIRECTOR
Ken Davis
AGENCY
Chiat/Day, Los Angeles, CA
PRODUCER
Richard O'Neill
PRODUCTION COMPANY
RSA

1833

ARMED & DANGEROUS TRAILER
90-second
VO: Defiled and humiliated. Set up and put down. Pushed beyond the
limits of human endurance.
VO: Targeted for destruction.
VO: They're not just going to get even . . .
VO: They're going to get donuts.
CANDY: Give us those curly ones with coconut on it and a couple of
coffees, no sugar.
CANDY TO LEVY: No sugar?
LEVY: No.
CANDY: Yah.
VO: John Candy and Eugene Levy are . . .
VO: Armed & Dangerous.

1834

DOG
20-second
ANNCR VO: Discover the Wonder.
Monday nights on NBC.

1835

ART DIRECTOR
Janet Scabrini
DESIGNER
Janet Scabrini
ANIMATOR/ARTIST
Janet Scabrini
CLIENT
USA Sports
EDITOR
Bill Mahler
DIRECTOR
Gordon Beck, Steve Feder
PRODUCTION COMPANY
Compugraph Designs, New York, NY

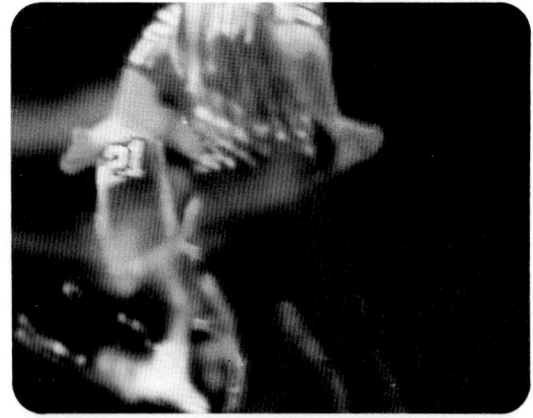 

1836

ART DIRECTOR
Rich Park
WRITER
Richard Marchesano
CLIENT
VF Factory Outlet
AGENCY
Goldberg/Marchesano, Washington, DC
PRODUCTION COMPANY
Spicer Productions

1835

USA SPORTS: COLLEGE BASKETBALL
15-second
NO SCRIPT.
FX ONLY

1836

BACK TO THE SOURCE
30-second
Long ago when you wanted something you went straight to the source and paid a modest price.
(SFX: Bonk!)
As time passed, people were forced to pay more and more.
(SFX: Bonk! Bonk!)
Soon the phrases "paying through the nose" (SFX: Bonk!) (SFX: Ouch!) and "getting clobbered"
(SFX: Bonk!) (SFX: Ahah!) came about.
A million years later, man would finally get relief.
On October 2nd, the VF Factory Outlet opens to save people up to one-half on brand-name goods.
(SFX: Birds)
Now, you don't have to take a beating for the things you want.
Get back to the source at the VF Factory Outlet.
(SFX: Whistle!)

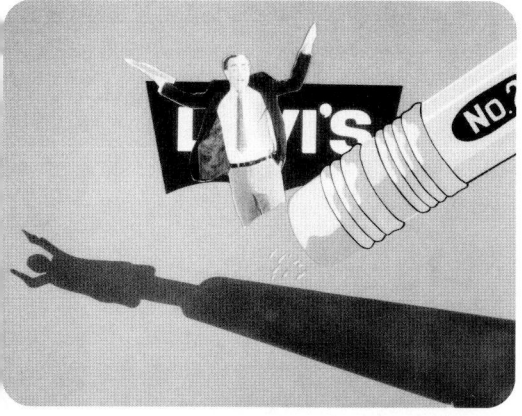

1837
ART DIRECTOR
Michael Brunsfeld, George Evelyn,
Kirk Henderson, Catherine
Margerin; Martha Anne Booth,
Foote Cone & Belding
CLIENT
Levi Strauss Youthwear Division
EDITOR
Richard Childs
AGENCY
Ed Galvezy, Foote Cone & Belding
PRODUCTION COMPANY
Jana Canellos, Colossal Pictures,
San Francisco, CA

1838
ART DIRECTOR
John LeeWong
WRITER
Ken Fitzgerald
CLIENT
Hawaiian Punch
DIRECTOR
Randy Roberts
AGENCY
DYR Inc., Los Angeles, CA
PRODUCER
Susan Hallinan
PRODUCTION COMPANY
Abel & Associates
ASSOC. CREATIVE DIRECTOR
Judy Johnson

1837

LEVI'S COLLAGE '86
30-second
ANNCR: Here are a few words about Levi's jeans and cords . . .
(VOICE FADES AS ANNOUNCER IS ERASED).
BLUES BEAST SONG: I got my two-tone shoes and my 5-0-1 blues. How
. . I love 'em.
LINEMAN: Leeee . . . vi's.

1838

ROBOTS EPIC
60-second
SFX: (WIND, TRAIN, HORN—FADES . . .)
SFX: (POP, SIP, GULP, AHHH. PING!)
BED & CHANT: Ha-wai-ian-Pun-ch
Ha-wai-ian-Pun-ch
VOCAL: Ow!
SFX: (CANS OPENING—CLICK-CLICK)
VOCAL: Hawaiian Punch. It hits you in all the right places.
SFX: (REWIND)
SFX: (RATCHET)
CHANT: Hawaiian Punch.
SFX: (SIP-AHH-SIP-AHH)
GROUP: It hits you in all the right places.
SFX: (POP, SIP, GULP, AHH, OW!)
(FACTORY MUSIC BED)
(MUSIC AND VOCALS UP)
MUSIC & VOCALS: Hawaiian Punch. It hits you in all the right places.
Hawaiian Punch. It hits you in all the right places. Ahhh!

1839

ART DIRECTOR
Marshall Taylor
WRITER
George Watts
CLIENT
Metropolitan Life Insurance
Company
DIRECTOR
Bill Melendez
DIRECTOR OF PHOTOGRAPHY
Bill Melendez
AGENCY
Young & Rubicam, New York, NY
PRODUCER
Ted Storb
PRODUCTION COMPANY
Bill Melendez Production

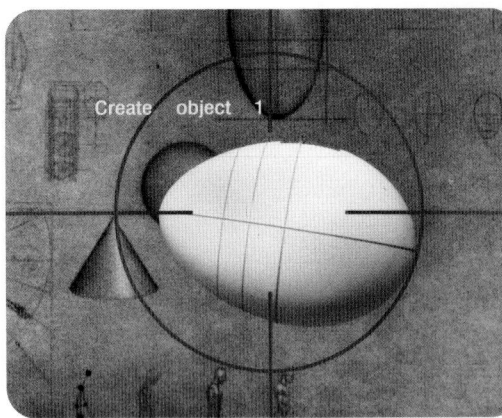

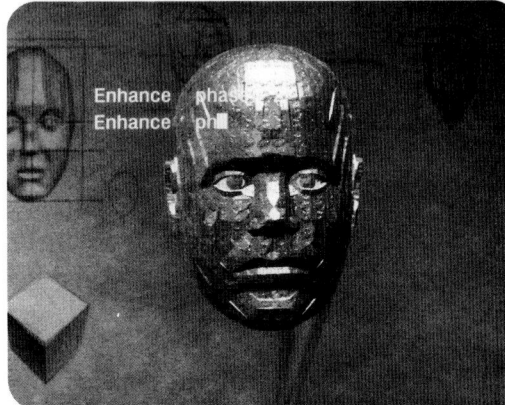

1840

ART DIRECTOR
Tom Smith
DESIGNER
Ken Mirman
ANIMATOR/ARTIST
Dana Duff
WRITER
Chuck Withrow, Mike Dreyfuss
CLIENT
TRW
AGENCY
Roseanne Lowe, WYSE Advertising,
Cleveland, OH
PRODUCTION COMPANY
Robert Abel & Associates
MUSIC
HK Sound

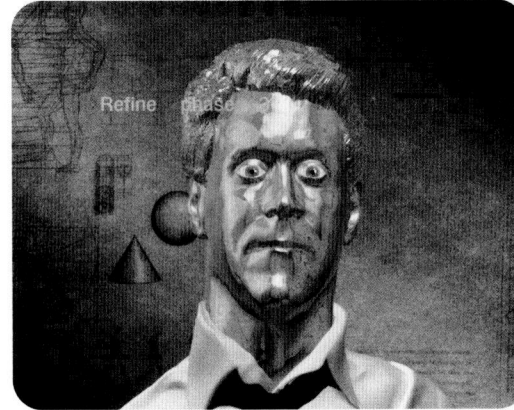

1839

THE BIRDS
30-second
(MUSIC UNDER) (SFX: BIRDS CHIRPING) SALLY: One, two three . . .
(SFX) . . . two hundred two, two hundred eleven . . . The birds! The
Birds!
(SFX: CRASH)
LINUS: What's that all about?
CHARLIE: Snoopy is holding tryouts for another Met Life Prompt Payment
Squadron. See?
Met Life believes it's really important to pay insurance claims promptly, no
matter what the size. That one is for really big checks.
LINUS: Get Met. It pays.
(MUSIC OUT)

1840

RAPID PROTOTYPING
30-second
VO: A simple idea from a company called TRW lets the person who will
use a computer system help design it.
First, TRW engineers make a rough prototype. Then the user tries it,
changes it, until it reflects his needs.
SS: "Okay that's it.
We've got it."
VO: This satisfies the most crucial element in any system. The human
one.
SS: "Perfect"
VO: Tomorrow is taking shape at a company called TRW. (DING)

1841

ART DIRECTOR
Tyler Vogel, Monique Risch
DESIGNER
Bob Kurtz
ANIMATOR/ARTIST
Pam Cooke, Gary Mooney
WRITER
Sharon Goldberg
CLIENT
ComputerLand
EDITOR
Kurtz & Friends
DIRECTOR
Bob Kurtz
AGENCY
Patty Dudgeon, Lewis, Browand &
Associates, Oakland, CA
PRODUCTION COMPANY
Lorraine Roberts, Kurtz & Friends
CREATIVE DIRECTOR
Bob Browand

1841

"I RECOMMEND COMPUTERLAND"
30 second
AUDIO:
Brunswick: As President of Loomis & Brunswick, I recommend that we buy
a computer at ComputerLand.
Loomis: As Chairman, I must consider our frugal fiscal policy.
Brunswick: As Comptroller, I'm sure we'll be very fiscal and save money
too.
Loomis: Well, as Personnel Director, I'd like to know who the heck is
gonna teach us to use it and if it breaks down who'll fix it.
Brunswick: Well, as Research Director, I found the answer to both . . .
Loomis: Yeah?
Brunswick: It's ComputerLand.
Loomis: Ok, let's call ComputerLand. Where's that secretary?
Brunswick: It's your turn.
Loomis: I know that.

1842

ART DIRECTOR
Michael Patterson, Candace
Reckinger
ANIMATOR/ARTIST
Michael Patterson, Candace
Reckinger
WRITER
John Miller, Lewis Goldstein, Bob
Bibb
CLIENT
National Broadcasting Company —
Entertainment
EDITOR
Jerry O'Neill
PRODUCER
Lewis Goldstein, Bob Bibb
PRODUCTION COMPANY
National Broadcasting Company,
Burbank, CA

1842

HILL STREET BLUES—TRIBUTE
30-second
It began as a vision
and became a tradition.
America, you'll never be over the hill.

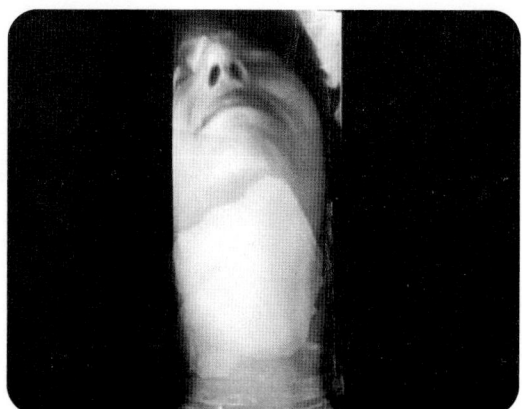

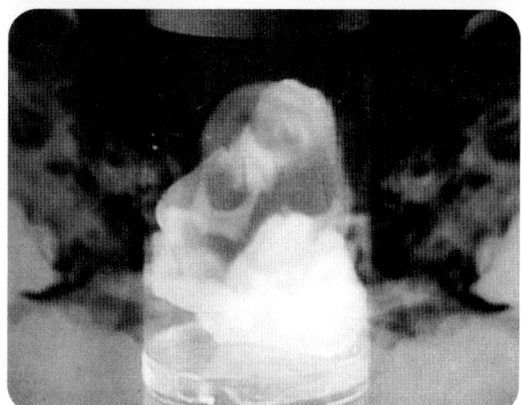

1843
ART DIRECTOR
Ned Steinberg, CBS News
ANIMATOR/ARTIST
Penelope W. Ashman, CBS News
EDITOR
David Seeger, Today Video, Inc.
DIRECTOR
Kyle Good, CBS News, New York, NY

1843

48 HOURS ON CRACK STREET

No dialogue

FIRST ANNUAL INTERNATIONAL EXHIBITION:

Gold, Silver and Distinctive Merit Award Winners
Newspaper Advertising
Magazine Advertising
Magazine Editorial
Promotion
Posters
Books & Jackets
Illustration
Photography
Television

Johnnie Walker opened his first grocery, wine and spirit shop in Kilmarnock in 1820 and introduced his first brand—Walker's Kilmarnock Whisky. By the early 1900's expansion demanded new sales ideas and advertising techniques. Most notable of these was the introduction of the striding man trademark.

The figure was designed in 1908 by Tom Browne, a successful commercial artist. It was Lord Stevenson, later a joint managing director of the firm, who first wrote: "Johnnie Walker: born 1820—still going strong." Both words and design were registered as the company trademark in 1910. Two new brands were also introduced with striking red and black labels set at a slant on square bottles.

These two brands along with a famous trademark have helped make Johnnie Walker's blending and bottling operation the largest in Scotland.

FIRST
INTERNATIONAL
EXHIBITION

Karl Eric Steinbrenner

Before being given the new hat of the presidency to wear, I took on the chairmanship of the First Annual International Show, which proved to be a great pleasure. When you see the winning work, you'll see some of the reasons why it was such a treat.

This year marks the Club's long overdue involvement in the world of international advertising, communications, design and promotion. While the Club made an attempt at doing so several years ago, it may have been an idea too far ahead of its time.

The idea of "Global Advertising" or "Global Communications" isn't a new one. A few well-known people in our business had the foresight to understand the ramifications of international marketing and advertising a couple of generations ago.

People like Ray Rubicam, H.K. McCann, J. Walter Thompson, the Grants of St. Louis and a handful of others said to their key clients, "Wherever you do business, we'll be there, too."

The result was the gradual growth of multi-national advertising and marketing. An additional result was the recruitment of adventurous creative people to go overseas and influence marketing and advertising communications; to improve the creative product and to train local staff in order to better serve their clients.

The vast majority of people in our business were disdainful of "International" unless it meant shooting a commercial in some exotic place. Most of them held the quality of design and advertising over there in low esteem; including some of the people in our home offices. They didn't know and they didn't much care . . .

It wasn't until the Saatchi brothers and lately, the WPP Group focused our attention on "global" advertising through the drama of reverse acquisition (they were now buying *our* communication companies and ad agencies, where ten years ago, *we* were doing the buying). Subsequently, we became painfully aware that the rest of the world was doing our kind of work very well. So well, that John O'Toole, former chairman of FCB, could host a panel discussion of creative leaders to determine where in the world the best work is now being done and why much of it is no longer coming from the traditional centers of marketing and advertising.

Indeed, those of us who were a part of international marketing and communications, who had something to do with its growth and development, are now seeing our efforts bear fruit. We're seeing the pupils outshine the teachers and we're seeing their work taking rightful places in the spotlight of peer recognition. That's what this First International Exhibition represents: a long overdue recognition by the Art Directors Club of the outstanding communications design being done throughout the world.

The permanent jury for this important event is comprised of internationally renowned members of the prestigious ADC Hall of Fame. The jury will be augmented yearly by a select group of their peers from overseas. In addition, an International Communications Design Conference is being planned and will soon be hosted by the Art Directors Club here in New York.

So, while the size of our First Annual International Exhibition is modest, the quality is outstanding. We look forward to greater participation in the coming years and we look forward to sharing with you, some of the best communications design the world has to offer. Cheers!

KARL H. STEINBRENNER,
Chairman,
First Annual
International
Exhibition

Shinichiro Tora

2
INTERNATIONAL JUDGES,
Milton Glaser, Massimo Vignelli,
Gene Federico and Len Sirowitz

1845
SILVER AWARD

ART DIRECTOR
Hermann Gottschalk, Klaus
Heckhoff
PHOTOGRAPHER
Christian Délu
WRITER
Monika Fammler
CLIENT
SOPEXA, François Pommereau
DIRECTOR
Klaus Heckhoff
AGENCY
IdeenService, Meerbusch, West
Germany
PRODUCER
Vera Hufnagel
PUBLICATION
Frankfurter Allgemeine Zeitung

1845

1846
DISTINCTIVE MERIT

ART DIRECTOR
Digby Atkinson
WRITER
Christopher Waite
CLIENT
K.M.G.
AGENCY
Saatchi & Saatchi Compton Ltd.,
London

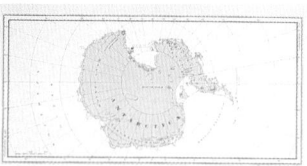

The last tax haven?

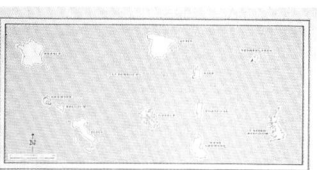

Europe doesn't exist.

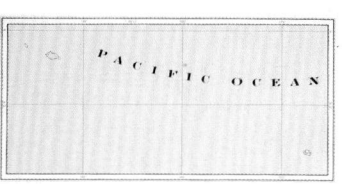

In 10 years will this be the financial centre of the earth?

1846

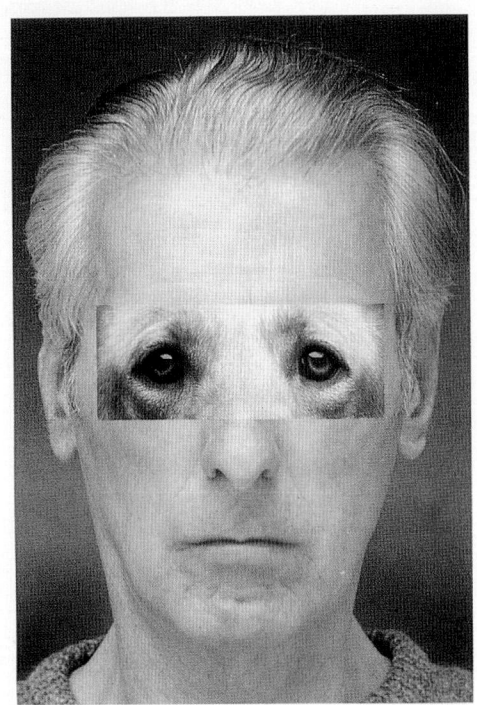

NO SURGEON IN THE WORLD CAN HELP
THIS BLIND MAN SEE. BUT A DOG CAN.

Try going blind.

Walk to the corner of the street with your
eyes closed.

Post a letter with your eyes closed.

Buy a loaf of bread with your eyes closed.

Discover how the simplest tasks become
a nightmare with your eyes closed.

Now walk to the corner of the street and
post a cheque with your eyes wide open.

THE GUIDE DOGS FOR THE BLIND ASSOCIATION
Department 3, 9 Park Street, Windsor, Berkshire SL4 1JR.

1847
GOLD AWARD
ART DIRECTOR
Mike Shafron
PHOTOGRAPHER
Peter Lavery
WRITER
Jeff Stark
CLIENT
Guide Dogs for the Blind Association
AGENCY
Saatchi & Saatchi Compton Ltd.,
London
PUBLICATION
Reader's Digest

1847

1848
GOLD AWARD

ART DIRECTOR
Zelda Malan
PHOTOGRAPHER
Andreas Heumann
ILLUSTRATOR
Dan Tierney (hand colour)
WRITER
Tim Mellors
CLIENT
J.R. Phillips
AGENCY
Saatchi & Saatchi Compton Ltd,
London
PUBLICATION
Tatler

1848

1849

1849
SILVER AWARD
ART DIRECTOR
Gerard v.d. Hart
PHOTOGRAPHER
Will v.d. Vlugt
WRITER
Ron Walvisch
CLIENT
Tom van Oosterhout, John v.d. Zwan
AGENCY
Noordervliet & Winninghoff/Leo Burnett, Amsterdam

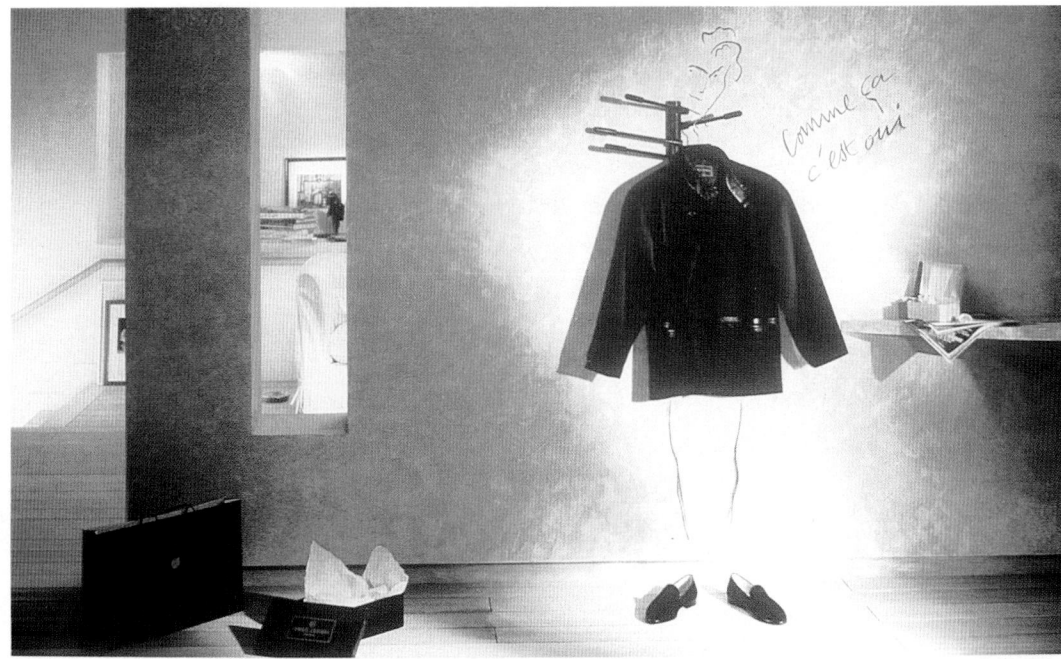

1850

1850
DISTINCTIVE MERIT
ART DIRECTOR
Sylvia Schildge
PHOTOGRAPHER
Martin Fraudreau
WRITER
Gregoire Delacourt
AGENCY
FCB, Neuilly, France
ART BUYER
Christine Pugeaux

1851
GOLD AWARD

ART DIRECTOR
Hans-Georg Pospischil
DESIGNER
Bernadette Gotthardt
PHOTOGRAPHER
Serge Cohen
PUBLISHER
Dr. Bruno Dechamps
PUBLICATION
Frankfurter Allgemeine Magazin,
Frankfurt

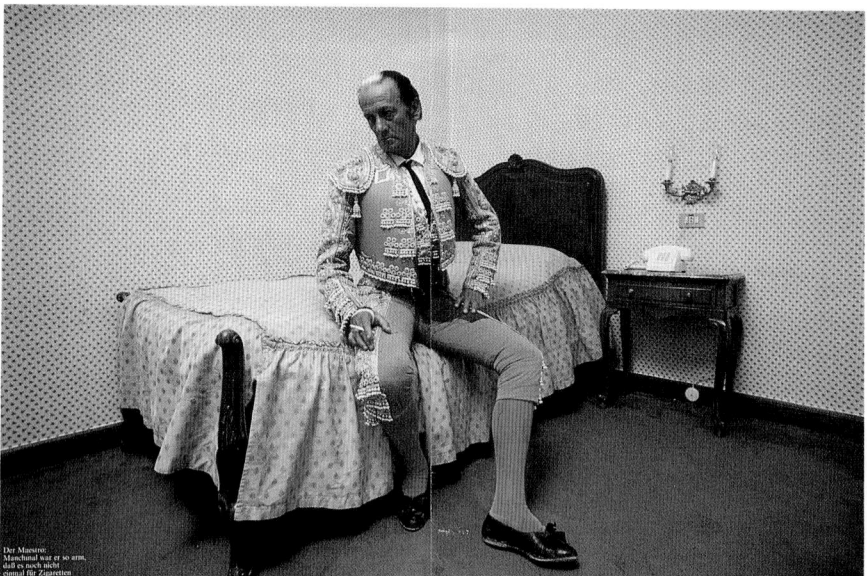

1851

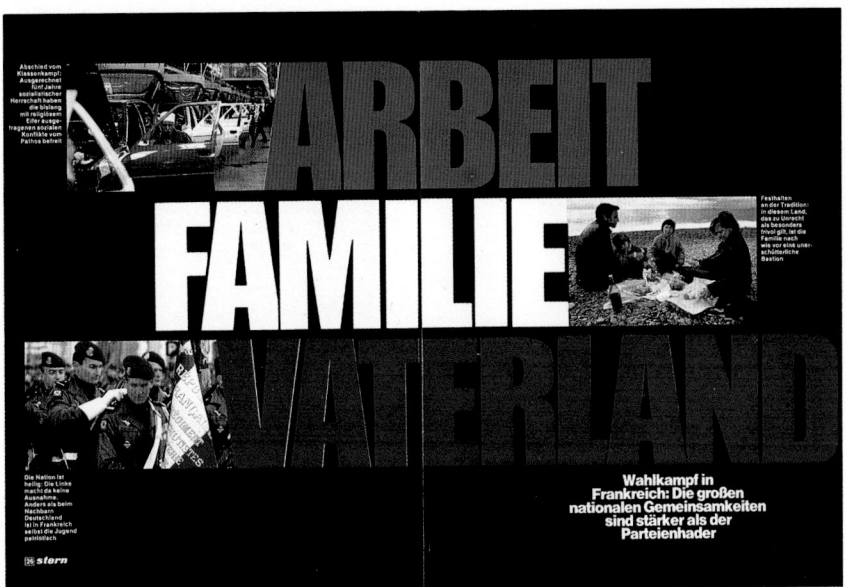

1852
GOLD AWARD
ART DIRECTOR
Wolfgang Behnken
DESIGNER
Herbert Suhr
PHOTOGRAPHER
Bob Lebeck
PUBLICATION
Stern, Hamburg

1853
SILVER AWARD

ART DIRECTOR
Hans-Georg Pospischil
DESIGNER
Bernadette Gotthardt
PHOTOGRAPHER
Burkhard von Harder
PUBLISHER
Dr. Bruno Dechamps
PUBLICATION
Frankfurter Allgemeine Magazin,
Frankfurt

Kein Strom auf Erden läßt sich mit dem Ganges an Heiligkeit messen, an heiligen Tagen in ihm zu baden wäscht die Sünden ab, an seinem Ufer zu sterben und verbrannt zu werden sichert ewigen Frieden, wer weit entfernt lebt, nimmt sein Wasser in einem kupfernen Gefäß nach Hause, um es beim Herannahen des Todes zu trinken, und läßt seine Asche in den Ganges streuen, und weil Almosengeben dem Frommen nützt, säumen Bettler den Weg zum Strom.

Von den heiligen Städten, die um Benares die heilige, eine Stätte des Badens und Brennens, die Betens und Betteins, keine schöne Stadt, eher schrecklich, ein Labyrinth der Frömmigkeit, von Schmutz starrend, vom heiseren

Murmeln der Bettler und Vogi und den kreischenden Rufen der Händler gefüllt. Verwundert sieht der Fremde, wie religiös gestimmte Männer und Frauen, bis zur Brust oder bis zum Kopf im Strom stehend, mit der hohlen Hand das Wasser schöpfen, gurgeln, den Mund reinigen, trinken, ungeachtet daß einige Meter entfernt der Rest einer menschlichen Leiche, ein roter Hund und allerlei Unrat treiben. Längst haben Wissenschaftler die seltsam reinigende Kraft des Ganges, zumal bei Benares, untersucht, wie sie mit der besonderen produzierten Beschaffenheit des Flußbodens erklärt wird.

Kein anderes Volk begibt sich in solcher Zahl, in solchen Massen und deren häufig auf Pilgerfahrt wie die Inder, und immer ist das

Wallfahrten mit Wasser verbunden, vor allem mit Flüssen. Das Sanskrit-Wort für einen Pilgerort heißt "tirtha", in seinem ursprünglichen Sinn ein Badeplatz. Seit alters bis zum heutigen Tag sind die Inder, Männer wie Frauen, zu den größten Anstrengungen und Entbehrungen bereit, um nach Benares zu pilgern.

HEILIGE STADT
AM HEILIGEN STROM

Von Thomas Ross
Fotos Burkhard von Harder

Baden und waschen.
Die heißesten Flüten des Ganges
und wir alten bei ihr
religiöse Hindus die begehrteste
Wallfahrtsziel

Wann und warum der Ganges und andere Flüsse heilig wurden, bleibt im dunkeln, doch wird es im allgemeinen mit der Einwanderung und Ausbreitung der Indoarier in Zusammenhang gebracht. Im Ramayana wird erzählt, daß die Nymphe Ganga, die älteste Tochter von Himan oder Himalaya, durch das Gebet des frommen Bhagirath bewogen wurde, vom Himmel auf die Erde hinabzusteigen; so entstand der Fluß. Einem anderen Mythos zufolge war der Ganges ein himmlischer Fluß, die Göttin Ganga, die auf die Erde gebracht ward, um die Söhne des Sagar wieder zum Leben zu erwecken, die der Zorn eines Weisen zu Asche verbrannt hatte. Als sie auf die Erde fiel, floß sie die Haare Shivas herab. Von den 1450 Tempeln in Benares sind die meisten Shiva geweiht, voran der Goldene Tempel.

Baden, waschen, sich reinigen gehört zum Kern indischer Religiosität, dem eine ganz spezifische Idee der Reinheit innewohnt. Die Unreinheit, schreibt Louis Dumont, entspricht dem organischen Aspekt des Menschen. Und weiter heißt es "Die Religion, in der im allgemeinen im Namen der universellen Ordnung auftritt, setzt, indem sie die

Reinheit verkündet, den religiösen und gesellschaftlichen Menschen in Gegensatz zur Natur".

Reinheit und Unreinheit haben viele Aspekte, so sind sie eine Basis der Kastenordnung, doch jedoch Inder, dem Brahmanen wie dem Paria, ist das Baden, das Waschen, zumindest bei bestimmten Gelegenheiten und Festen, eine religiöse Pflicht. Nun wird nach all der Liebhaber und Bewunderer Indiens schwerlich behaupten, daß es ein reinliches, ein sauberes Land sei, im Gegenteil. Sein Leben lang kämpft der Inder gegen Druck, gegen Verschmutzung, gegen Unreinheit, es ist ein Kampf, den ihm Natur und Klima aufzwingen.

In der Trockenzeit dringt der feine Staub durch Türen und Fenster, ja durch die schmalsten Ritzen und bedeckt alles; in der Regenzeit versinken die Dörfer und die meisten Städte in Schlamm und brackigem Wasser, die extreme Feuchtigkeit läßt in wenigen Tagen Schuhe und Kleidung, Bücher und Speisen schimmeln, die Ziegeln schwitzen, die Lehmwände bröckeln, der Putz schwärzt sich und wird mit Schmutz überzogen, keine Wasser, keine Hauswand widersteht dem Einwirken der tropischen Witterung.

Beten und
beten, Von den heiligen
Städten, die
um Ufer des Ganges liegen, ist
Benares die heiligste

Freilaufende Kühe, ihrer Heiligkeit wegen mit größerer Rücksicht behandelt als viele Menschen, platschen Wege und Straßen voll mit Mist und Urin, der Mangel an hygienischen Einrichtungen, an Toiletten, Latrinen, Abflußröhren, macht aus der menschlichen Dorn- und Harnblasentätigkeit auf dem Dorf und in der Stadt, selbst in Neu-Delhi, ein öffentliches Geschäft mit besonderer Parfümmarke. Leider gibt es in der indischen Mythologie kein Pendant zu Sisyphos, aber es läßt sich unschwer vorstellen: ein Mann oder eine Frau, die unentwegt wäscht und badet, ohne jemals den erstrebten Gipfel der Reinheit zu erreichen, weder der eigenen Physis noch der Umgebung. Mau-

che Soziologen sprechen von einer Waschmanie der Inder, jedenfalls ist sie die gewissermaßen weltliche, materielle, ludische Seite der Dualität Reinheit und Unreinheit. Jedes Mitglied der indischen Gesellschaft ist der Verunreinigung ausgesetzt, und sein sozialer Status, seine Kaste, wird unter anderem davon bestimmt, mit welchen Wirkkräften der Verunreinigung und in welchem Maße er damit in Berührung kommt: Leichen, Aas, Leder, Unrat stehen ganz u vorn. Solche Form der Verunreinigung wurde - und wird weitgehend noch immer - als abscheulich und ehrlich betrachtet. Daneben gibt es Formen der zeitweisen Verunreinigung, die der einzelne mittels ritueller Purifikation über-

Meditieren
und notieren: Jeder Hindu
soll wenigstens
einmal im Leben als Pilger in
Benares gewesen sein

1854
SILVER AWARD

ART DIRECTOR
Urs Schwerzmann
PHOTOGRAPHER
Dietmar Henneka, Stuttgart
WRITER
Claudia Jaekel
CLIENT
PSL Hamburg

1854

1855
DISTINCTIVE MERIT

ART DIRECTOR
Hans-Georg Pospischil
DESIGNER
Bernadette Gotthardt
PHOTOGRAPHER
Susan Lamér
PUBLISHER
Dr. Bruno Dechamps
PUBLICATION
Frankfurter Allgemeine Magazin,
Frankfurt

1855

1856
GOLD AWARD

ART DIRECTOR
Derek Birdsall
DESIGNER
Derek Birdsall
PHOTOGRAPHER
Paul Rocheleau
WRITER
June Sprigg
CLIENT
United Technologies Corp.
DIRECTOR
Tom Armstrong
PUBLISHER
Whitney Museum of American Art
PRODUCER
Omnific Studios, London

1856

1857
GOLD AWARD

ART DIRECTOR
Seiichi Maeda,
Kazuki Maeda, Osaka
DESIGNER
Kazuki Maeda
ILLUSTRATOR/ARTIST
Seiichi Maeda
CLIENT
Souhonke Surugaya

1857

1858
SILVER AWARD

ART DIRECTOR
Pierre Bernard, Jean Paul Bachollet,
Gerard Paris-Clavel, Alex Jordan
DESIGNER
Guy Chagot, Simone Christ, Silvia
Goëtze, Anne Marie Latremoliere,
Pierre Milville, Pierre Laurent
Theve, Vincent Perottet
CLIENT
Etablissement Public de la Villette
PRODUCER
Etablissement Public de la Villette

1858

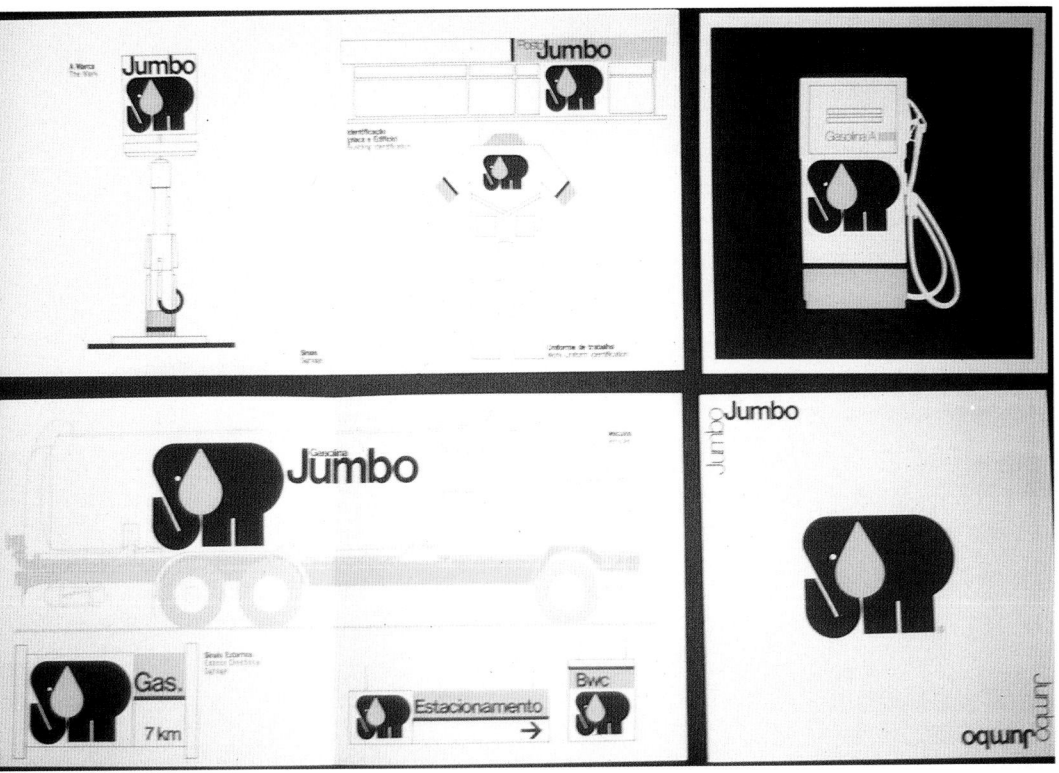

1859

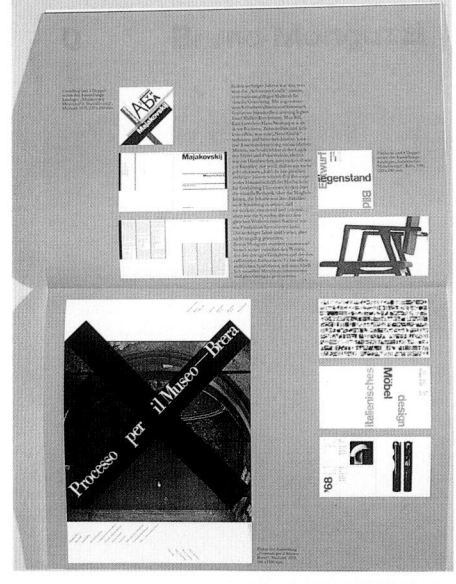

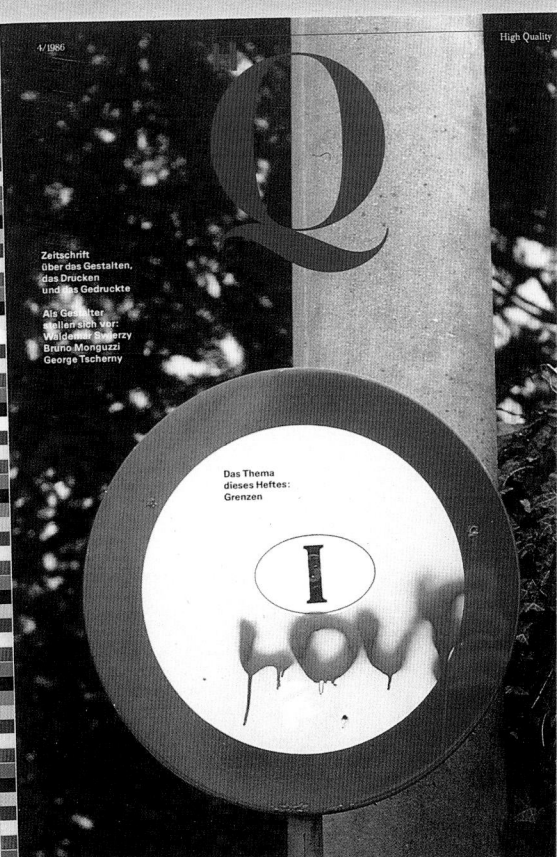

1860

1859
DISTINCTIVE MERIT
ART DIRECTOR
Oswaldo Miranda, Curitiba, Brazil
CLIENT
Jumbo Gas Station

1860
DISTINCTIVE MERIT
ART DIRECTOR
Rolf Müller, München
DESIGNER
Barbara Miedaner, Roman Lorenz
CLIENT
Heidelberger Druckmaschinen AG
EDITOR
Rolf Müller, Günter Braus
PRODUCER
Paul Simon

1861
DISTINCTIVE MERIT

ART DIRECTOR
Toru Ando, Tokyo
DESIGNER
Minako Asano

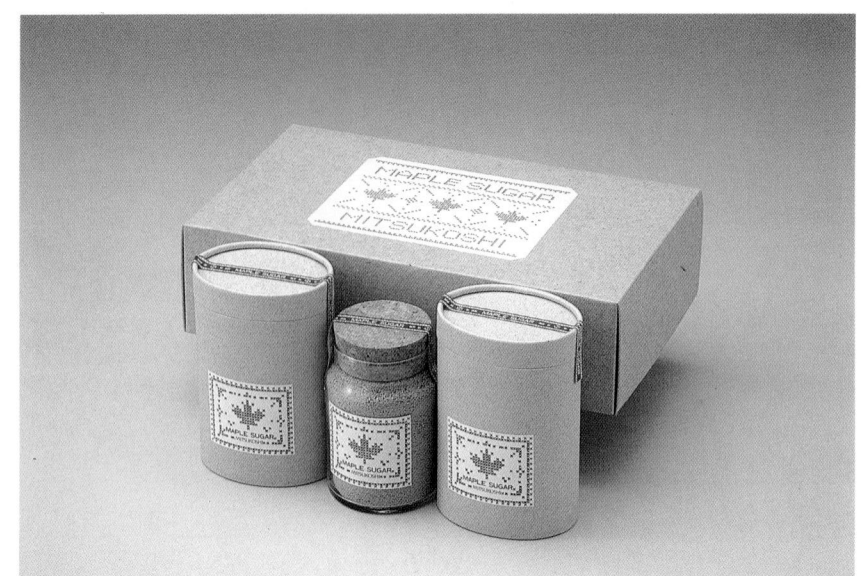

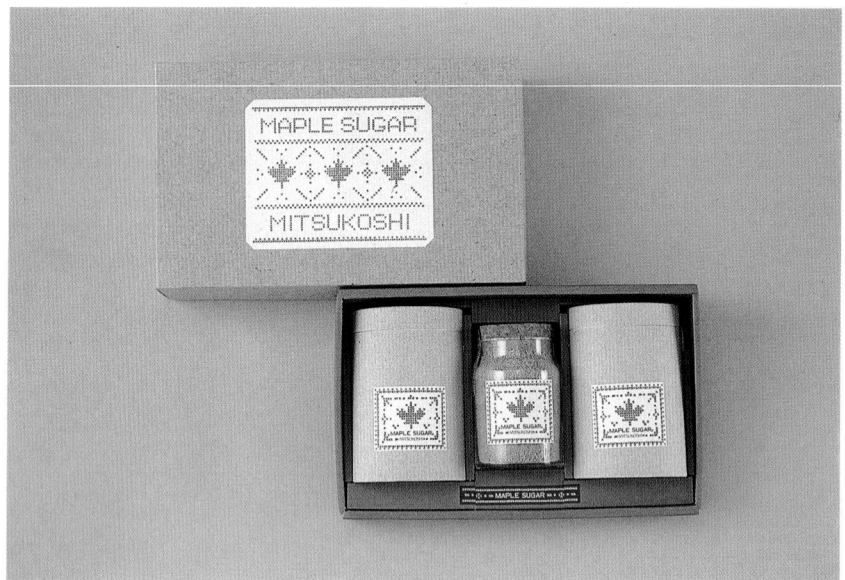

1861

1862
DISTINCTIVE MERIT

ART DIRECTOR
Andy Schmid, Elwood, Australia
DESIGNER
Andy Schmid
PHOTOGRAPHER
Edy Gaber
ILLUSTRATOR/ARTIST
Andy Schmid
CLIENT
The Decor Corporation Pty Ltd

1862

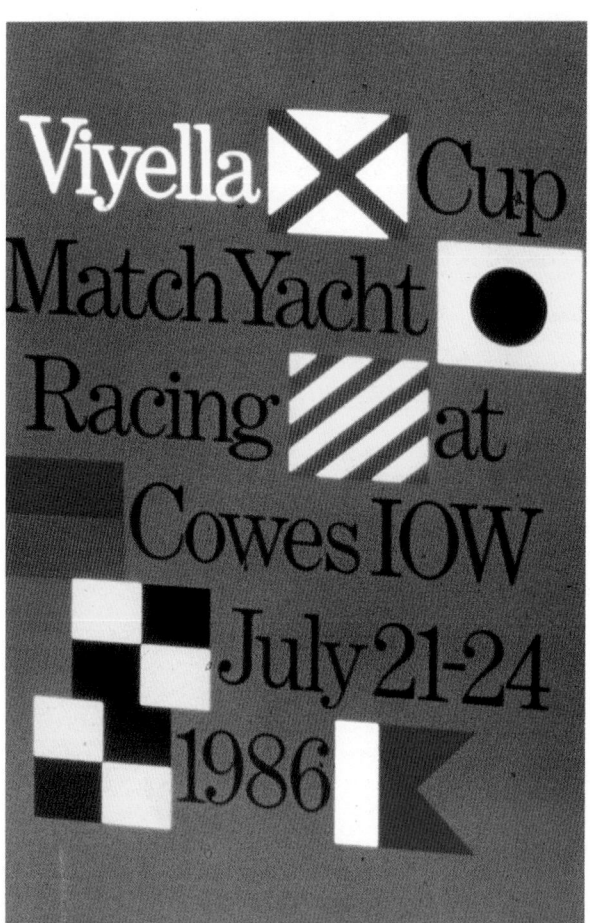

1863
DISTINCTIVE MERIT

ART DIRECTOR
Keith Murgatroyd
DESIGNER
Keith Murgatroyd
PHOTOGRAPHER
Ken Gilliam
CLIENT
Viyella
AGENCY
RMDA Ltd, London

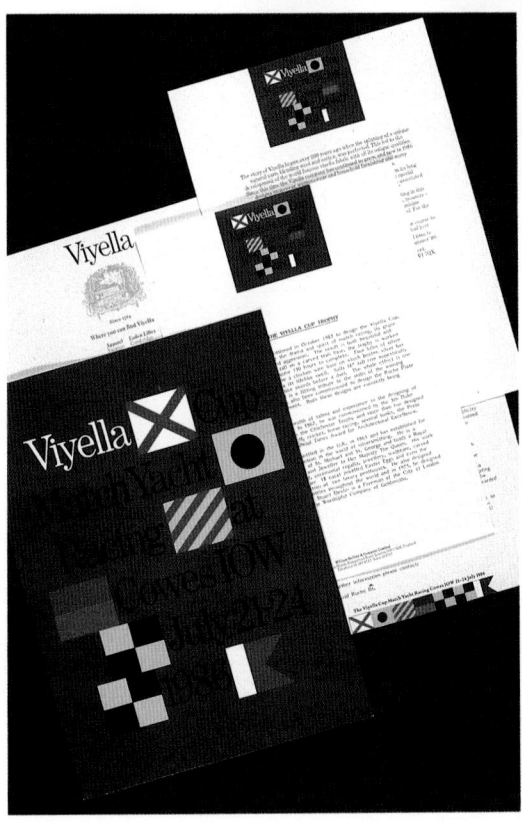

1863

1864
SILVER AWARD

ART DIRECTOR
Otmar Bucher
EDITOR
Angelika Bucher, Otmar Bucher
PUBLISHER
H. H. Coninx,
Tages Anzeiger
PUBLICATION
SPICK, Children's Magazine, Zurich

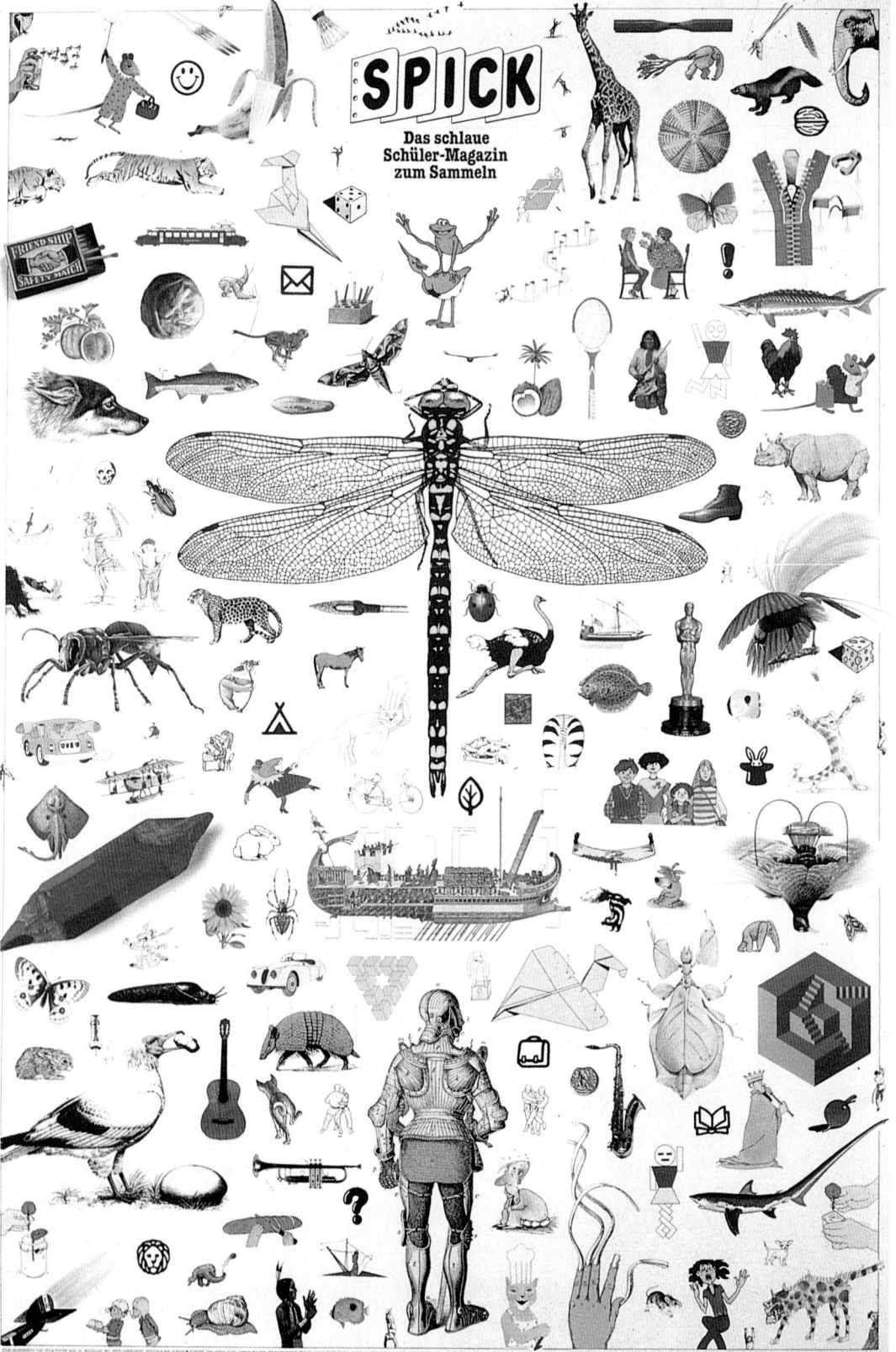

1865
GOLD AWARD

ART DIRECTOR
Wolfgang Behnken
DESIGNER
Franz Epping
PHOTOGRAPHER
Olaf Gollnek
PUBLISHER
Stern, Hamburg

1865

1866
GOLD AWARD

ART DIRECTOR
Makoto-Saito, Tokyo
DESIGNER
Makoto Saito
PHOTOGRAPHER
Tsutomu Wakatsuki
CLIENT
Taiyo Printing Co., Ltd.

1866

1867
GOLD AWARD

ART DIRECTOR
Grapus
CLIENT
A.N.C./Grapus, Montreuil, France

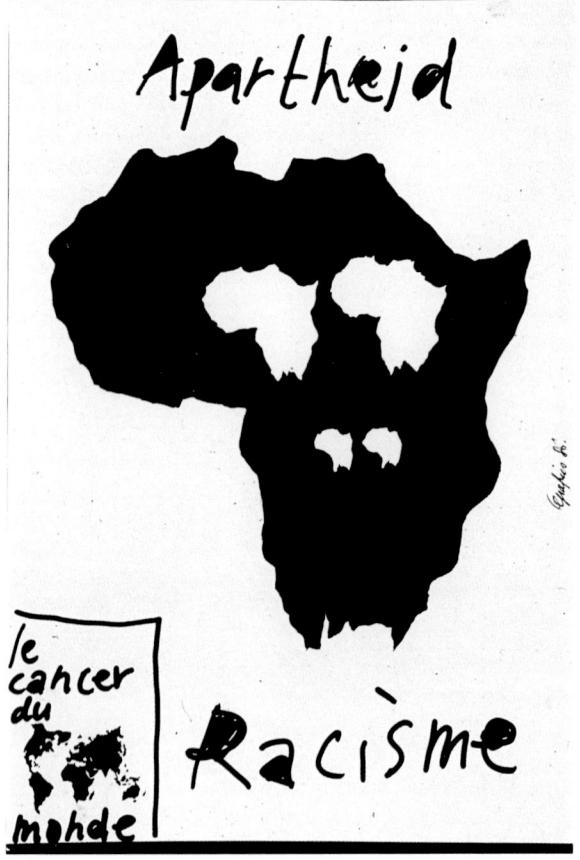

1867

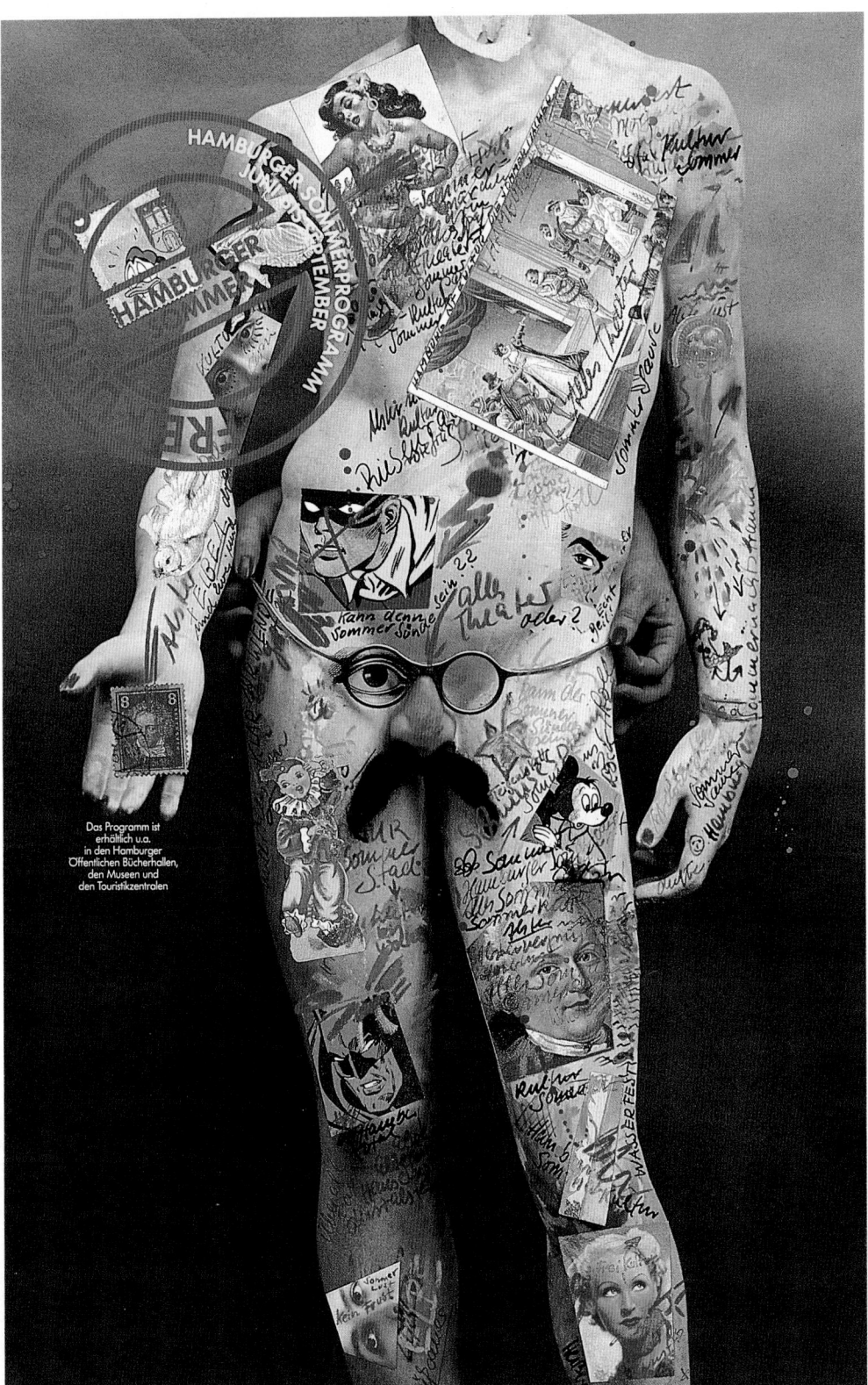

1868
SILVER AWARD

ART DIRECTOR
Holger Matthies
DESIGNER
Holger Matthies
PHOTOGRAPHER
Holger Matthies
ILLUSTRATOR
Gabi & Holger Matthies
CLIENT
Kulturbehörde , Hamburg

1868

1869
SILVER AWARD

ART DIRECTOR
Koji Mizutani, Tokyo
DESIGNER
Hirokazu Kurebayashi, Osamu
Kitazima
PHOTOGRAPHER
Kastuo Hanzama, Kazumi Kurigami

SA.t

SA.t

SA.t

1869

1870
DISTINCTIVE MERIT

ART DIRECTOR
Takeshi Ohtaka, Osaka
DESIGNER
Takeshi Ohtaka
CLIENT
Morisawa & Company Ltd

SMILE OF 37,180 WORDS

1870

1871

1871
DISTINCTIVE MERIT

ART DIRECTOR
Fumihiko Enokido, Shizuoka, Japan
DESIGNER
Fumihiko Enokido
ILLUSTRATOR/ARTIST
Fumihiko Enokido

1872

1872
DISTINCTIVE MERIT

ART DIRECTOR
Kyoji Nakatani, Tokyo
DESIGNER
Kyoji Nakatani
PHOTOGRAPHER
Masatomo Kuriya
ILLUSTRATOR/ARTIST
Kyoji Nakatani
CLIENT
Seibu Department Store

1873
GOLD AWARD

ART DIRECTOR
Urs Schwerzmann
PHOTOGRAPHER
Dietmar Henneka, Stuttgart
CLIENT
Michael Cromer
ADVERTISING MGR
Michela Schmidt

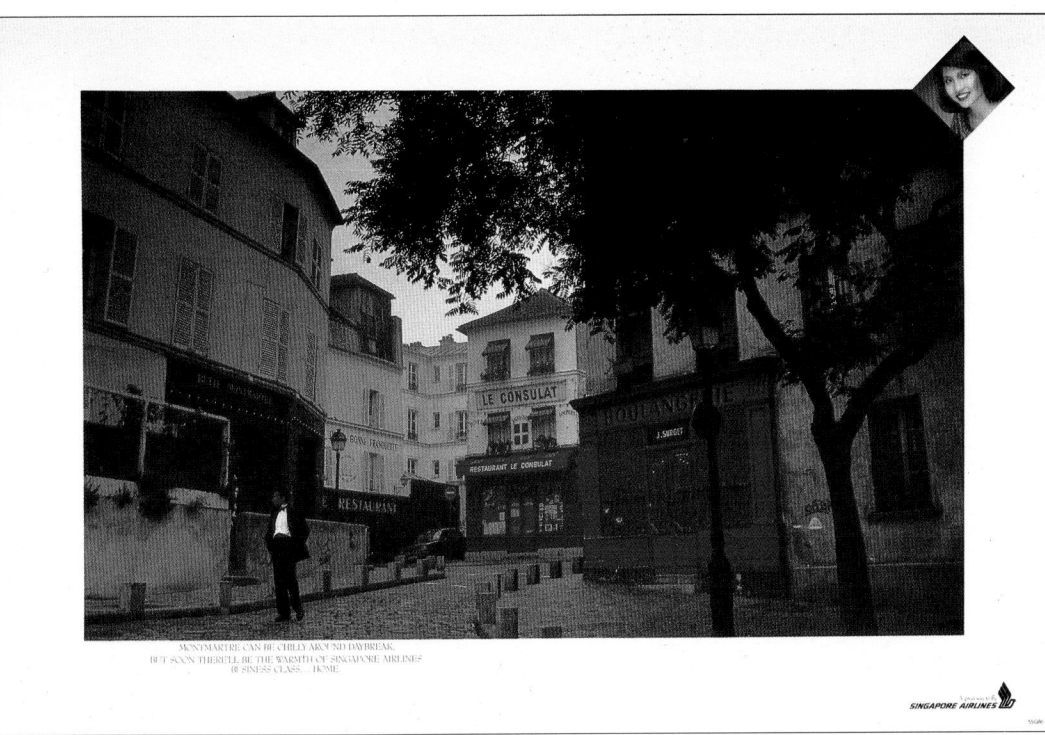

1874
SILVER AWARD

ART DIRECTOR
Neil French
PHOTOGRAPHER
Robert Dowling, London
WRITER
Neil French
CLIENT
Singapore Airlines
AGENCY
Batey Ads.

1874

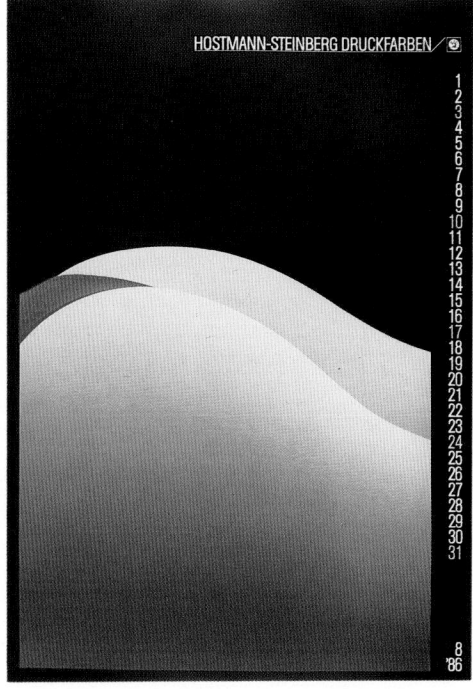

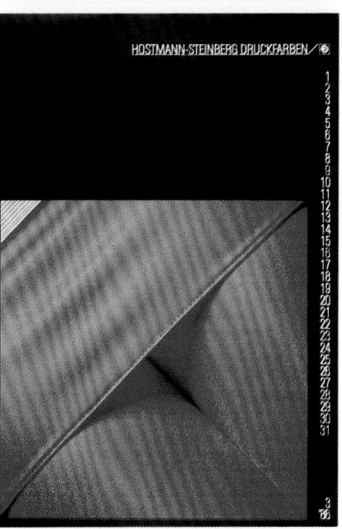

1875
GOLD AWARD

DESIGNER
Noth & Hauer
PHOTOGRAPHER
Hartwig Klappert, Berlin
CLIENT
Hostmann Steinberg Druckfarben

1875

1876
GOLD AWARD

ART DIRECTOR
Paul Arden
PHOTOGRAPHER
Extracts from 'La Bete Humaine'
directed by Jean Renoir
WRITER
Jeff Stark
CLIENT
British Rail Red Star
EDITOR
Mike Kaufman
DIRECTOR
Jeff Stark, Paul Arden
AGENCY
Saatchi & Saatchi Compton Ltd,
London
PRODUCER
Arnold Pearce

1876

FIELD
30-second
WOMAN: What's up Jacques?
MAN: It seems Red Star are now delivering parcels to 5 countries in
Europe.
WOMAN: To the door?
MAN: Yup—Right to the door, lady.
WOMAN: Wee?
MAN: No, big parcels too.
WOMAN: Why do I find this so strangely fascinating?
MAN: It's the way I tell them.
VO: Red Star. To the door. Now in 6 languages.

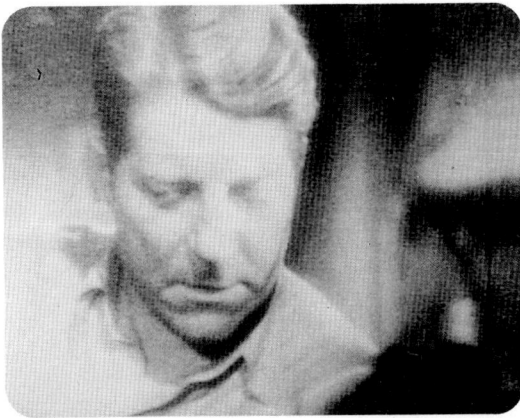

1877
DISTINCTIVE MERIT

ART DIRECTOR
Peter Gibb
WRITER
James Lowther
CLIENT
Allied National Brands
DIRECTOR
John Marles
AGENCY
Saatchi & Saatchi Compton Ltd,
London
PRODUCER
Louise Kidman

1878
SILVER AWARD

ART DIRECTOR
Paul Arden
PHOTOGRAPHER
Extracts from 'La Bete Humaine'
directed by Jean Renoir
WRITER
Jeff Stark
CLIENT
British Rail Red Star
EDITOR
Mike Kaufman
DIRECTOR
Jeff Stark, Arnold Pearce
AGENCY
Saatchi & Saatchi Compton Ltd,
London
PRODUCER
Arnold Pearce

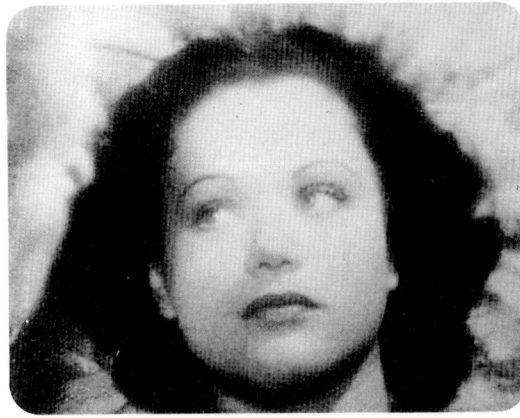

1877

SHARKS
30-second
1ST MAN: Gee . . . now look what you done!
2ND MAN: Hold on . . . I'll get 'em.
. . . aren't any sharks in here are there?
1ST MAN: No.
. . . (AFTER PAUSE) . . . The crocodiles ate all the sharks.
MVO: Australian's wouldn't give a Castlemaine XXXX for anything else.

1878

BED
30-second
MAN: What's the matter luv?
HER: I hear Red Star now deliver parcels to 6 countries in Europe.
MAN: To the door?
SHE: Too right mate.
HE: I love it when you talk parcels.
SHE: I've sent for a leaflet.
SUPER: Red Star to the door.
Freefone Red Star for details.
VO: Red Star. To the door. Now in 6 languages.

1879
ART DIRECTOR
Paul Arden
ILLUSTRATOR/ARTIST
Mick Brownfield
WRITER
Jeff Stark
CLIENT
InterCity British Rail
AGENCY
Saatchi & Saatchi Compton Ltd., London
PUBLICATION
National Press

1880
ART DIRECTOR
Paul Arden
PHOTOGRAPHER
Michael Joseph
WRITER
Jeff Stark
CLIENT
InterCity British Rail
AGENCY
Saatchi & Saatchi Compton Ltd, London
PUBLICATION
National Presss

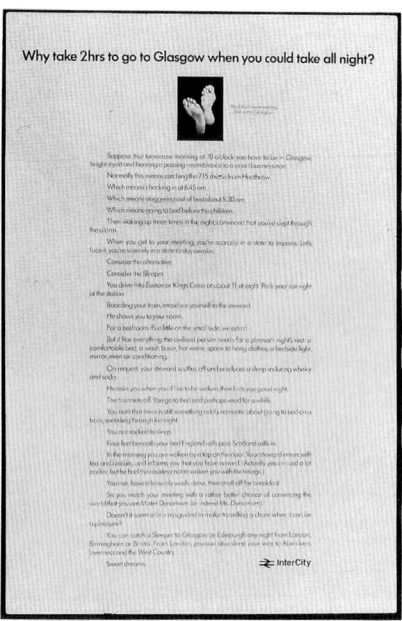

1879

1880

1881
ART DIRECTOR
Yvonne Sumter
PHOTOGRAPHER
Arthur Massey
WRITER
David Hatty
CLIENT
Taylor Ferguson
AGENCY
Saatchi & Saatchi Compton, Melbourne
PUBLICATION
Business Review Weekly
CREATIVE DIRECTOR
Boris Damast

1881

1882
ART DIRECTOR
Charles Johnston
DESIGNER
Charles Johnston
WRITER
Anthony O'Sullivan
CLIENT
Fiat Auto (Ireland) Ltd
AGENCY
Hunter Advertising Ltd., Dublin

1883
ART DIRECTOR
Ernst Bächtold, Beat Keller
PHOTOGRAPHER
Several
WRITER
Rudy Felber, Fabian Zwygart
CLIENT
Swissair
AGENCY
GGK, Zürich

1882

1883

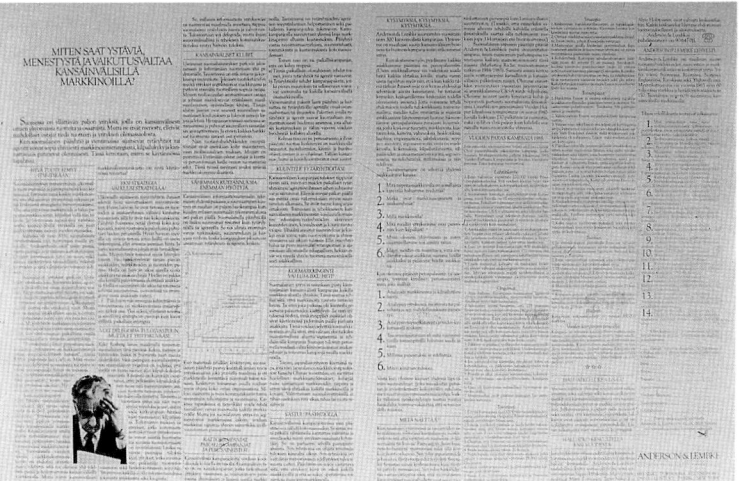

1884

1885

1884
ART DIRECTOR
Veli-Matti Hilli
DESIGNER
Reijo Virolainen
PHOTOGRAPHER
Tommi Heinonen, Ismo Hölttö
ILLUSTRATOR/ARTIST
Reijo Virolainen
WRITER
Alpo Holopainen
CLIENT
Anderson & Lembke Oy image campaign
DIRECTOR
Seppo Hilakari
AGENCY
Anderson & Lembke Oy, Helsinki
PUBLICATION
Kauppalehti (Trade newspaper)

1885
ART DIRECTOR
Tsuguya Inoue
DESIGNER
Kenji Yamaguchi
PHOTOGRAPHER
Curtis Knapp
WRITER
Tokiharu Kiuchi
CLIENT
Gillette Japan Incorporated
DIRECTOR
Barry Hill, Mitsuhiko Sasao
PRODUCER
Susumu Yoshinaga
AGENCY
McCann-Erickson Hakuhodo, Tokyo

ALL 16 YEAR OLDS HAVE A TALENT.

ALL THEY NEED IS TRAINING.

THE NEW 2 YEAR YTS. TRAINING FOR SKILLS.

1886

1886
ART DIRECTOR
Matt Ryan
PHOTOGRAPHER
John Londei, James Cotier
WRITER
Peers Carter
CLIENT
C.O.I.
AGENCY
Saatchi & Saattchi Compton Ltd., London
PUBLICATION
National Press

爸爸的光采下巴

PHILIPS

1887

1887
ART DIRECTOR
Marvin Lin
PHOTOGRAPHER
Lee-Yuan-ben
WRITER
David Sun
AGENCY
Ogilvy + Mather Taiwan Ltd., Taiwan

1888
ART DIRECTOR
Daisuke Nakatsuka, Kohei Terasaka
PHOTOGRAPHER
Unknown
WRITER
Daisuke Nakatsuka, Hiroshi Kuboyama
CLIENT
Kirin Beer Co. (Ltd.)
CREATIVE DIRECTOR
Daisuke Nakatsuka, Tokyo

1889
ART DIRECTOR
Mike Rossi
WRITER
Mike Freedman
CLIENT
Plus
AGENCY
Venture Freedman & Rossi/BBDO, Sandton,
South Africa

1890
ART DIRECTOR
Daisuke Nakatsuka, Kohei Terasaka
PHOTOGRAPHER
Hiroshi Kubota
WRITER
Daisuke Nakatsuka, Hiroshi Kuboyama
CLIENT
Kirin Beer Co. (Ltd.)
CREATIVE DIRECTOR
Daisuke Nakatsuka, Tokyo

1891
ART DIRECTOR
Digby Atkinson
PHOTOGRAPHER
James Cotier
WRITER
Tim Mellors, Chris Waite
CLIENT
British Airways
AGENCY
Saatchi & Saatchi Compton Ltd., London
PUBLICATION
Daily Telegraph

1892
ART DIRECTOR
Kjell Bryngell
PHOTOGRAPHER
Morten Krogvold
WRITER
Kaj Hafr
CLIENT
Ulf Berg
AGENCY
Ted Bates Advance, Oslo

1893
ART DIRECTOR
Marc Law
PHOTOGRAPHER
Don Ashby
WRITER
Andrew Olds
CLIENT
Tourism Commission of NSW
AGENCY
USP Needham, North Sydney

1888

1890

1892

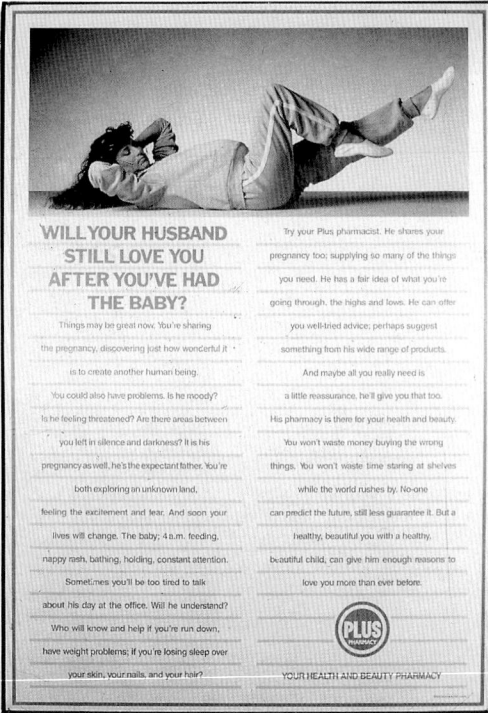

1889

1891

1893

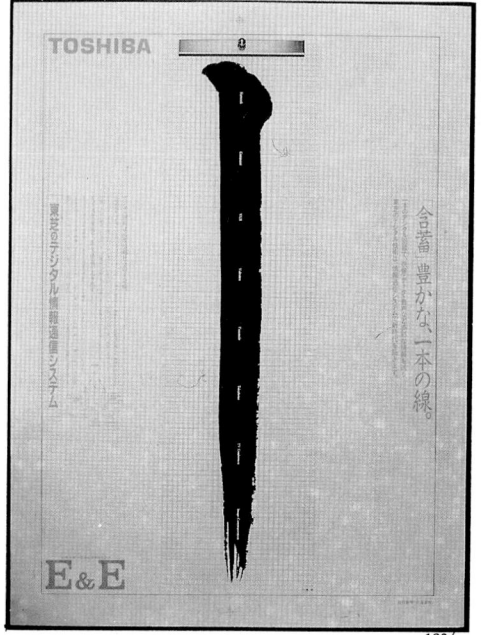

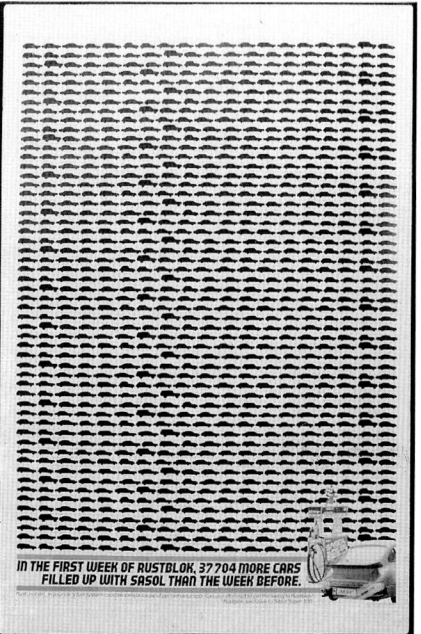

1894

1895

1896

1897

1894

ART DIRECTOR
Atsuo Fujita
DESIGNER
Noriyuki Ogai
ILLUSTRATOR/ARTIST
Chikuo Nakamura (calligrapher)
WRITER
Takayoshi Okajima
CLIENT
Toshiba Ltd.
AGENCY
Hakuhodo Incorporated, Tokyo

1895

ART DIRECTOR
Jules Joubert
PHOTOGRAPHER
Nick Nolton
ILLUSTRATOR/ARTIST
Jules Joubert
WRITER
Kevin Kleynhans
CLIENT
Sasol
DIRECTOR
Carl Preller
AGENCY
McCann National, Johannesburg

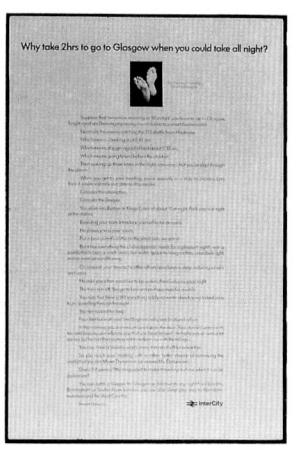

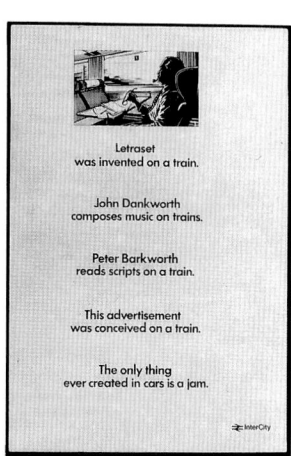

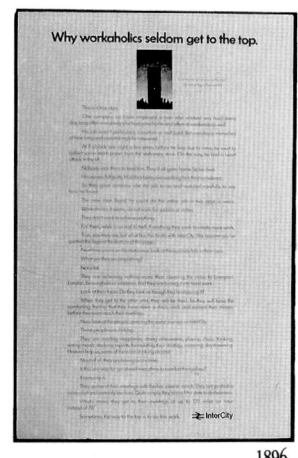

1896

ART DIRECTOR
Paul Arden
PHOTOGRAPHER
Michael Joseph
ILLUSTRATOR/ARTIST
Mick Brownfield
WRITER
Jeff Stark
CLIENT
InterCity British Rail
AGENCY
Saatchi & Saatchi Compton Ltd, London

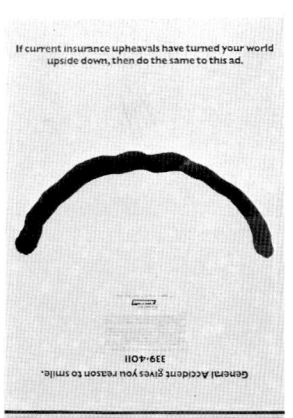

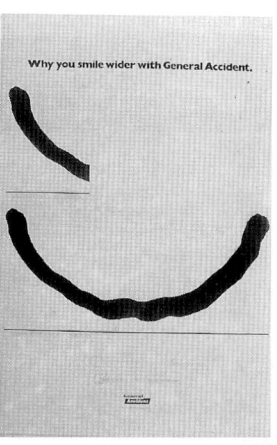

1897

ART DIRECTOR
John Eboral
ILLUSTRATOR/ARTIST
John Eboral
WRITER
Wynellen Crane
CLIENT
General Accident
DIRECTOR
Carl Preller
AGENCY
McCann National, Johannesburg

1898
ART DIRECTOR
Muneaki Andoh
DESIGNER
Muneaki Andoh
ILLUSTRATOR/ARTIST
Kazutoshi Yagami, Muneaki Andoh
WRITER
Hiroyoshi Yamada, Yasuhisa Kisaki
CLIENT
Kirin Beer Co., Ltd.
DIRECTOR
Muneaki Andoh
AGENCY
Dentsu Incorporated, Nagoya Branch, Nagoya
City, Japan

1898

1899
ART DIRECTOR
David May, Digby Atkinson, Chris Gregory
DESIGNER
David May, Chris Gregory
PHOTOGRAPHER
Peter Hall, Jack Bankhead
WRITER
Christopher Waite
CLIENT
The Independent
AGENCY
Saatchi & Saatchi Compton Ltd., London
TYPE
Roger Kennedy, Jeff Merrells

1899

1900
ART DIRECTOR
Makoto Saito, Tokyo
DESIGNER
Soko Hosonome
PHOTOGRAPHER
Tsutomu Wakatsuki
CLIENT
Kashiyama Co., Ltd.
DIRECTOR
Masayasu Okabe

1900

1901
ART DIRECTOR
Iwao Miyanaga
PHOTOGRAPHER
Kenji Ishikawa
WRITER
Daisuke Nakatsuka, Hiroshi Kuboyama
CLIENT
Hayashibara Co. (Ltd.)
CREATIVE DIRECTOR
Daisuke Nakatsuka, Tokyo

 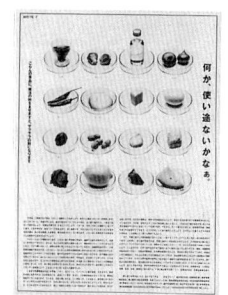 

1901

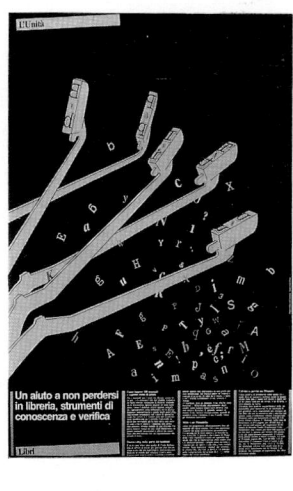

1902
ART DIRECTOR
Lauro Giovanetti, Modena, Italy
CLIENT
L'Unità

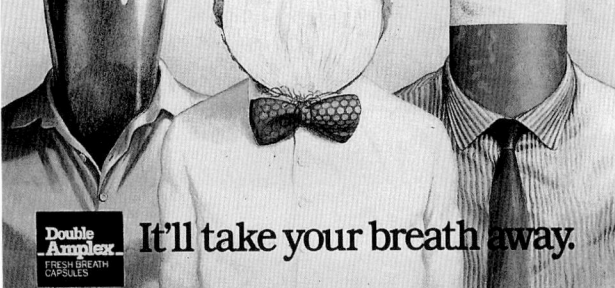

1903

1903
ART DIRECTOR
Yvonne Sumter
ILLUSTRATOR/ARTIST
Geoff Cook
WRITER
David Hatty
CLIENT
Beecham (Australia)
AGENCY
Saatchi & Saatchi Compton, Melbourne
PUBLICATION
Bulletin With Newsweek
CREATIVE DIRECTOR
Boris Damast

1904

1904
ART DIRECTOR
Sylvia Schildge
PHOTOGRAPHER
Martin Fraudreau
WRITER
Gregoire Delacourt
CLIENT
Charles Jourdan
AGENCY
FCB, Neuilly Cedex, France
ART BUYER
Christine Pugeaux

1905

1905
ART DIRECTOR
Titti Fabiani
PHOTOGRAPHER
Orio Raffo
CLIENT
Cassina
AGENCY
B Communications, Milano

1906
ART DIRECTOR
Koji Mizutani, Tokyo
DESIGNER
Hirokazu Kurebayashi, Osamu Kitazima
PHOTOGRAPHER
Kastuo Hanzawa

1907
ART DIRECTOR
Sylvia Schildge
PHOTOGRAPHER
Martin Fraudreau
WRITER
Gregoire Delacourt
CLIENT
Charles Jourdan
AGENCY
FCB, Neuilly Cedex, France
ART BUYER
Christine Pugeaux

1908
ART DIRECTOR
Pentti Pilve
DESIGNER
Pentti Pilve
PHOTOGRAPHER
Markku Alatalo
WRITER
Pentti Pilve
CLIENT
Oy Nokia Ab Paper
AGENCY
Creator Oy, Helsinki

1909
ART DIRECTOR
Eric Holden
PHOTOGRAPHER
Michel DuBois
WRITER
Gregoire Delacourt
CLIENT
Sopad
AGENCY
FCB, Neuilly Cedex, France
ART BUYER
Christine Pugeaux

1910
ART DIRECTOR
Gerard v.d. Hart
PHOTOGRAPHER
Will v.d. Vlugt
WRITER
Ron Walvisch
AGENCY
Noordervliet & Winninghoff/Leo Burnett,
Amsterdam

1906

1907

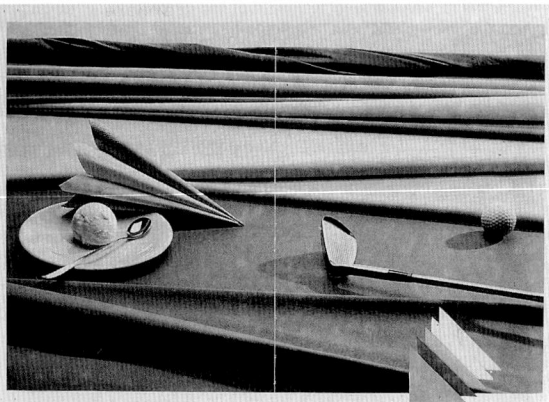

1908

1909

1910

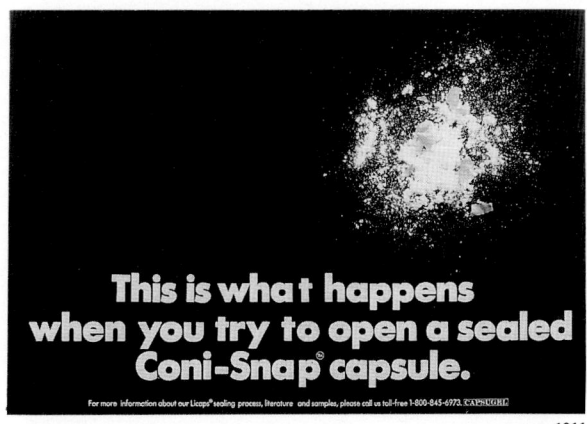

This is what happens
when you try to open a sealed
Coni-Snap® capsule.

1911

1911
ART DIRECTOR
Pierre Mendell
DESIGNER
Pierre Mendell
PHOTOGRAPHER
Klaus Oberer
WRITER
Reinhard Siemes
CLIENT
Capsugel
AGENCY
Mendell & Oberer, Munich

Sony introduceert Micro Black Trinitron. Dat geeft
ineens een heel ander beeld van de concurrentie.

1912

1912
ART DIRECTOR
Pieter van Velsen
PHOTOGRAPHER
Chris Lewis
WRITER
Pieter van der Wijk
CLIENT
Brandsteder Electronics
AGENCY
GGK, Amsterdam

Contre les désodorisants un peu forts, il y a Brise Confort.

Brise Confort.
Formule sans retombées.

1913

1913
ART DIRECTOR
Benoit Chavane, Sylvia Schildge
PHOTOGRAPHER
Peter Winfield
WRITER
Gregoire Delacourt
CLIENT
Johnson
AGENCY
FCB, Neuilly Cedex, France
ART BUYER
Christine Pugeaux

Why have a car that moves like the wind
if your tyres handle like meatballs?

QUICK 1

1914

1914
ART DIRECTOR
Mark Linhart
PHOTOGRAPHER
Ezio Sanelli
WRITER
Boris Damast
CLIENT
Dunlop Olympic Tyres
AGENCY
Saatchi & Saatchi Compton, Melbourne
PUBLICATION
Street Machine
CREATIVE DIRECTOR
Boris Damast

1915

ART DIRECTOR
Pieter van Velsen
PHOTOGRAPHER
Chris Lewis
WRITER
Peter van der Wijk
CLIENT
Brandsteder Electronics
AGENCY
GGK Amsterdam

1915

1916

ART DIRECTOR
Horacio Bertolotti
DESIGNER
Horacio Bertolotti
PHOTOGRAPHER
Lucio Villalba
WRITER
Carlos Mouzo
CLIENT
Leo Burnet Spain
AGENCY
Leo Burnett Spain, Madrid
PRODUCER
Rodrigo Roco
CREATIVE DIRECTOR
Carlos Mouzo

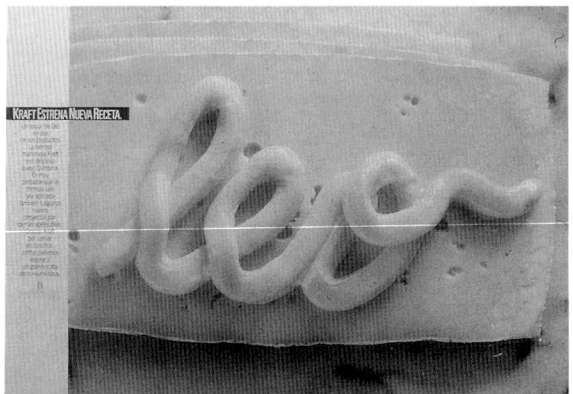

1916

1917

ART DIRECTOR
August Maurer
DESIGNER
August Maurer
ILLUSTRATOR/ARTIST
August Maurer
WRITER
Ruth Grunt
CLIENT
Dyestuffs Division
AGENCY
Werbung CIBA-Geigy , Basle, Switzerland
PRODUCER
Frobenius AG, Basle

1917

1918

ART DIRECTOR
Gerard v.d. Hart
PHOTOGRAPHER
Will v.d. Vlugt
WRITER
Ron Walvisch
AGENCY
Noordervliet & Winninghoff/Leo Burnett,
Amsterdam

1918

1919

1920

1921

1922

1919
ART DIRECTOR
Henny van Varik
PHOTOGRAPHER
Michael Steenmeyer
WRITER
Ron Meijer
CLIENT
RVS Verzekeringen (Insurances)
AGENCY
GGK Amsterdam

1920
ART DIRECTOR
Henny van Varik
PHOTOGRAPHER
Boudewijn Smit
WRITER
Ron Meijer
CLIENT
RVS Verzekeringen (Insurances)
AGENCY
GGK Amsterdam

1921
ART DIRECTOR
Sylvia Schildge
PHOTOGRAPHER
Martin Fraudreau
WRITER
Gregoire Delacourt
CLIENT
Charles Jourdan
AGENCY
FCB, Neuilly Cedex, France
ART BUYER
Christine Pugeaux

1922
ART DIRECTOR
Titti Fabiani
PHOTOGRAPHER
Orio Raffo
CLIENT
Cassina
AGENCY
B Communications, Milano

1923

ART DIRECTOR
John Pace
ILLUSTRATOR/ARTIST
Doug Powell
WRITER
Jonathan Shubitz
CLIENT
Sea Harvest
AGENCY
O&M RS-T&M, Cape Town, South Africa
PUBLICATION
Woman's Value

1923

1924

ART DIRECTOR
Sylvia Schildge
PHOTOGRAPHER
Martin Fraudreau
WRITER
Gregoire Delacourt
CLIENT
Charles Jourdan
AGENCY
FCB, Neuilly Cedex, France
ART BUYER
Christine Pugeaux

1924

1925

ART DIRECTOR
Brian Searle-Tripp
PHOTOGRAPHER
Jorge Rubia
ILLUSTRATOR/ARTIST
Tony Butler
WRITER
Roger Makin
CLIENT
Volkswagen of South Africa
AGENCY
O&M RS-T&M, Capetown, South Africa
PUBLICATION
The Star
TYPOGRAPHER
Di Gersowsky

1925

1926

ART DIRECTOR
Horacio Bertolotti
DESIGNER
Horacio Bertolotti
PHOTOGRAPHER
Lucio Villalba
WRITER
Carlos Mouzo
CLIENT
Leo Burnett Spain
AGENCY
Leo Burnett Spain, Madrid
PRODUCER
Rodrigo Roco
CREATIVE DIRECTOR
Carlos Mouzo

1926

1927

1927
ART DIRECTOR
Kaoru Kasai, Tokyo
DESIGNER
Hiroyuki Takahashi
PHOTOGRAPHER
Yoshihiko Ueda
WRITER
Takao Onoda
CLIENT
Suntory Ltd.

1928

1928
ART DIRECTOR
H. Daniel, H. Burkert
PHOTOGRAPHER
L. Sieff, Chr. v. Alvensleben
WRITER
G. Anlauf, S. Hessing
CLIENT
Kodak AG
AGENCY
Young & Rubicam Gmbh, Frankfurt

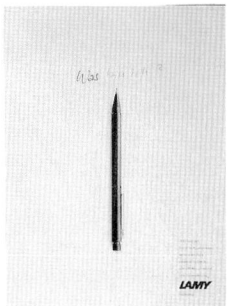

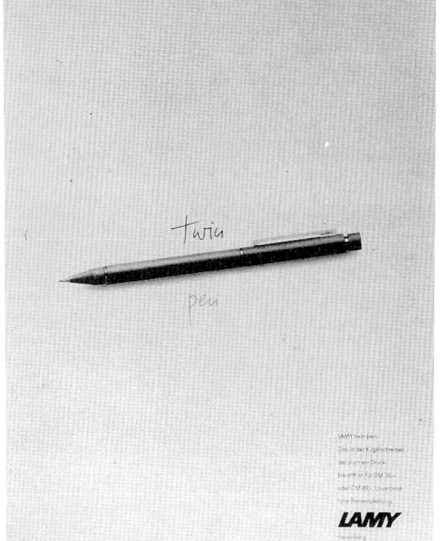

1929
ART DIRECTOR
Waldemar Meister
PHOTOGRAPHER
Rolf Herkner
WRITER
Hans Gerd Klein
AGENCY
Leonhardt & Kern, Stuttgart

1929

1930

1930
ART DIRECTOR
Hermann Gottschalk, Klaus Heckhoff
PHOTOGRAPHER
Christian Délu
WRITER
Monica Fammler
CLIENT
SOPEXA, Mr. François Pommereau
DIRECTOR
Klaus Heckhoff
AGENCY
IdeenService, Meerbusch, West Germany
PRODUCER
Vera Hufnagel
PUBLICATION
Stern

1931
ART DIRECTOR
Roger Pearce
PHOTOGRAPHER
Mike Parsons, Christine Hanscombe
WRITER
Adrian Holmes
CLIENT
Campbell's Soups
AGENCY
Saatchi & Saatchi Compton Ltd., London
PUBLICATION
Sunday Times Magazine

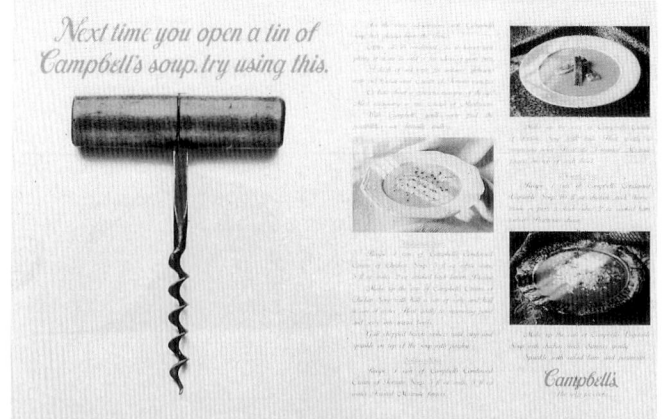
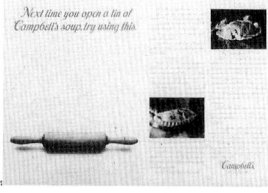
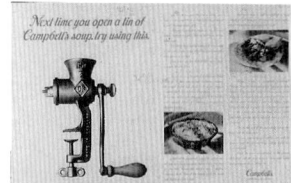

1931

1932
ART DIRECTOR
Fritz Tschirren
PHOTOGRAPHER
Jean-Pierre Maurer
WRITER
Cesare Casiraghi
CLIENT
S.I.S.A.L. S.p.A.
AGENCY
STZ S.r.l., Milano

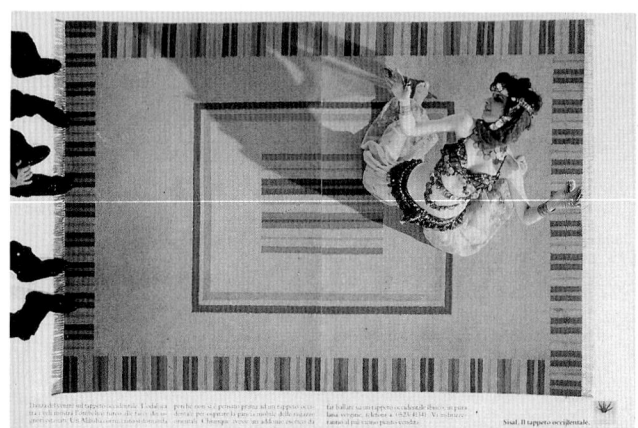

1932

1933
ART DIRECTOR
Ernst Bächtold, Beat Keller
PHOTOGRAPHER
various
WRITER
Rudy Felber, Fabian Zwygart
CLIENT
Swissair
DIRECTOR
Hermann Strittmatter
AGENCY
GGK Zürich
PRODUCER
GGK Zürich

1934
ART DIRECTOR
Hans Goedicke
PHOTOGRAPHER
stock photography
WRITER
Rob Floor
CLIENT
CPC Benelux B.V.
AGENCY
Snabilie, Goedicke, Floor, Amsterdam
PUBLICATION
Autokampioen

1934

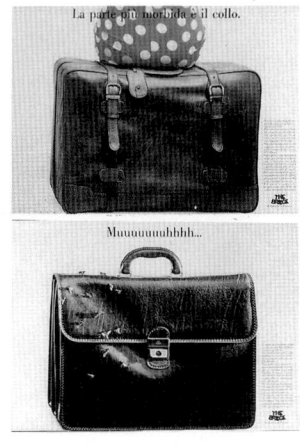

1935

1936

1935
ART DIRECTOR
Fritz Tschirren
PHOTOGRAPHER
Jean-Pierre Maurer
WRITER
Cesare Casiraghi
CLIENT
Il Ponte Pelletteria S.p.A./ The Bridge
AGENCY
STZ S.r.l., Milano

1936
ART DIRECTOR
Urs Schwerzmann
PHOTOGRAPHER
Dietmar Henneka, Stuttgart
CLIENT
Michael Cromer
ADVERTISING MANAGER
Michaela Schmidt

1937
ART DIRECTOR
Laszlo Körössy
PHOTOGRAPHER
Tom Gläser, Ben Oyne, Iver Hansen
ILLUSTRATOR/ARTIST
Dorothee Walter, Michaela Mittelbach
WRITER
Josef Hickl
CLIENT
Fordwerke AG, Köln
AGENCY
Young & Rubicam GmbH, Frankfurt

1938
ART DIRECTOR
Matt Ryan
PHOTOGRAPHER
James Cotier
WRITER
Peers Carter
CLIENT
British Airways
AGENCY
Saatchi & Saatchi Compton Ltd, London

1937

1938

1939

ART DIRECTOR
Pieter van Velsen
PHOTOGRAPHER
stock ABC Press
WRITER
Céline van Gent
CLIENT
NRC Handelsblad
AGENCY
GGK Amsterdam

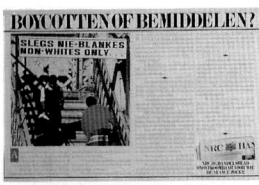
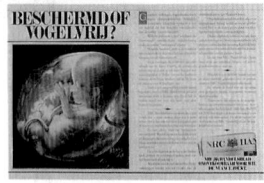

1939

1940

ART DIRECTOR
Rafeeq Ellias
PHOTOGRAPHER
Rafeeq Ellias
CLIENT
JASRA Graphics Pvt. Ltd.
AGENCY
NUCLEUS Advtg & Mktg, Bombay

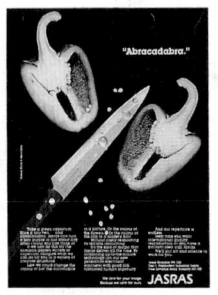

1940

1941

ART DIRECTOR
Fritz Tschirren
PHOTOGRAPHER
Jean-Pierre Maurer
WRITER
Cesare Casiraghi
CLIENT
B&B Italia S.p.A.
AGENCY
STZ S.r.l.,, Milano

1941

1942

ART DIRECTOR
Jean-François Dufay
PHOTOGRAPHER
phototheque, O. Cuvelette (packshot)
CLIENT
Fralib
AGENCY
Lintas-Paris

1942

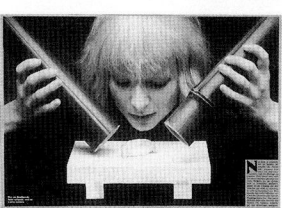

1943

1943

ART DIRECTOR
Hans-Georg Pospischil
DESIGNER
Bernadette Gotthardt
PHOTOGRAPHER
Detlef Odenhausen
PUBLISHER
Dr. Bruno Dechamps
PUBLICATION
Frankfurter Allgemeine Magazin, Frankfurt

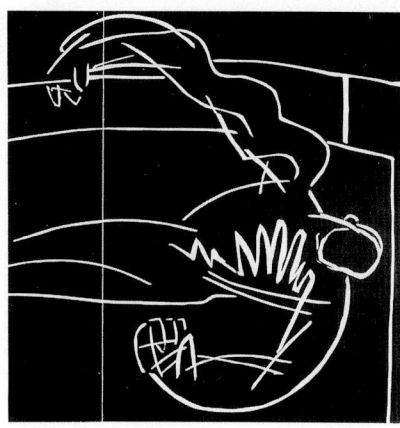

1944

1944

ART DIRECTOR
Hans-Georg Pospischil
DESIGNER
Bernadette Gotthardt
ILLUSTRATOR/ARTIST
Heinz Edelmann
PUBLISHER
Dr. Bruno Dechamps
PUBLICATION
Frankfurter Allgemeine Magazin, Frankfurt

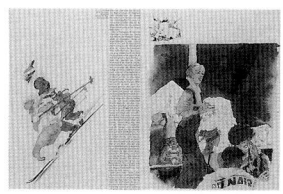

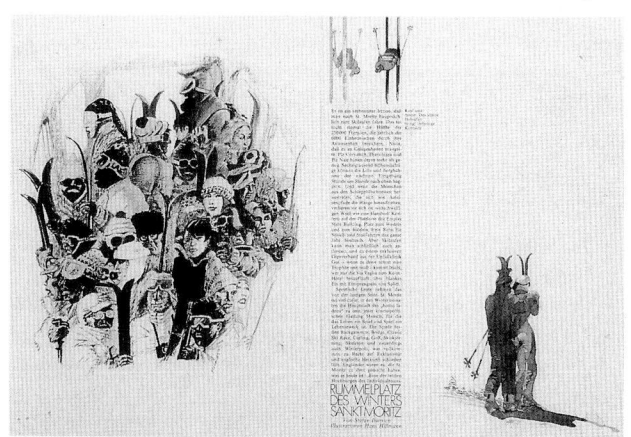

1945

1945

ART DIRECTOR
Hans-Georg Pospischil
DESIGNER
Bernadette Gotthardt
ILLUSTRATOR/ARTIST
Hans Hillmann
PUBLISHER
Dr. Bruno Dechamps
PUBLICATION
Frankfurter Allgemeine Magazin, Frankfurt

1946

1946

ART DIRECTOR
Wolfgang Behnken
DESIGNER
Wolf Dammann
PHOTOGRAPHER
Tom Jacobi
PUBLICATION
Stern, Hamburg

1947

ART DIRECTOR
Hans-Georg Pospischil
DESIGNER
Bernadette Gotthardt
PHOTOGRAPHER
Abe Frajndlich
PUBLISHER
Dr. Bruno Dechamps
PUBLICATION
Frankfurter Allgemeine Magazin, Frankfurt

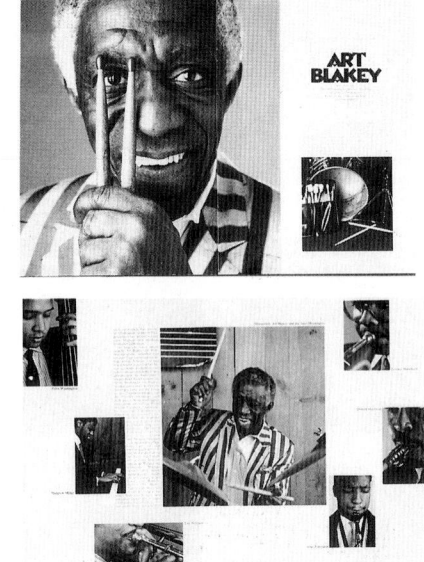

1947

1948

ART DIRECTOR
Hans-Georg Pospischil
DESIGNER
Bernadette Gotthardt
ILLUSTRATOR/ARTIST
Heinz Edelmann
PUBLISHER
Dr. Bruno Dechamps
PUBLICATION
Frankfurter Allgemeine Magazin, Frankfurt

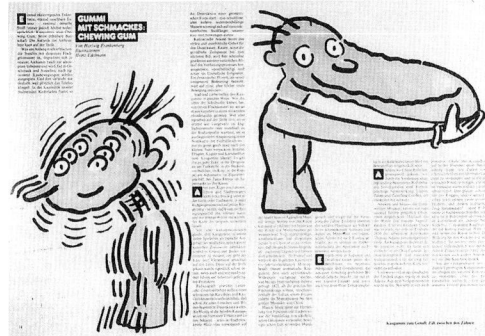
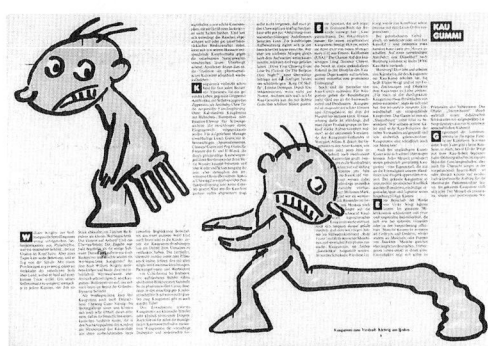

1948

1949

ART DIRECTOR
Wolfgang Behnken, Thomas Höpker
DESIGNER
Norbert Kleiner
PHOTOGRAPHER
Albert Watson
PUBLICATION
Stern, Hamburg

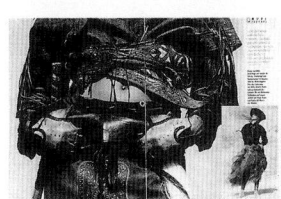

1949

1950

ART DIRECTOR
Paul Wagner
PHOTOGRAPHER
Giacobetti, Paris
EDITOR
Vogue
PUBLISHER
Condé Nast

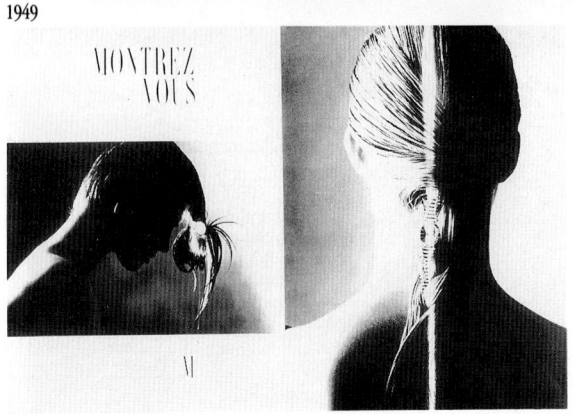
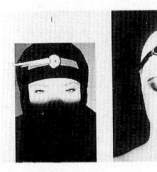
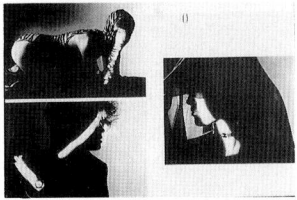

1950

XING-PING

1951

ART DIRECTOR
Hans-Georg Pospischil
DESIGNER
Bernadette Gotthardt
PHOTOGRAPHER
Hermann Dornhege
PUBLISHER
Dr. Bruno Dechmps
PUBLICATION
Frankfurter Allgemeine Magazin, Frankfurt

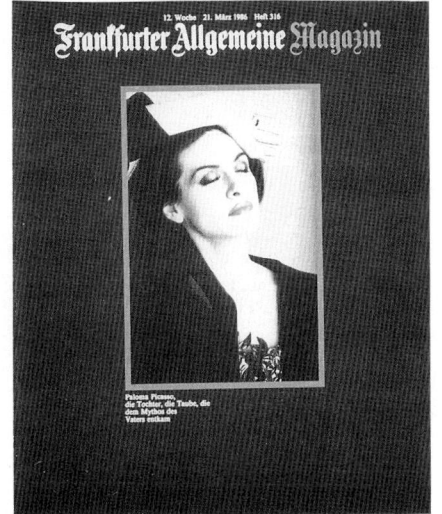

1951

1952

ART DIRECTOR
Hans-Georg Pospischil
DESIGNER
Bernadette Gotthardt
PHOTOGRAPHER
Serge Cohen
PUBLICATION
Frankfurter Allgemeine Magazin, Frankfurt

WEITER SO, DEUTSCHLAND?

1952

1953

ART DIRECTOR
Wolfgang Behnken
DESIGNER
Otto Reinecke
PHOTOGRAPHER
Manfred Michel
PUBLICATION
Stern, Hamburg

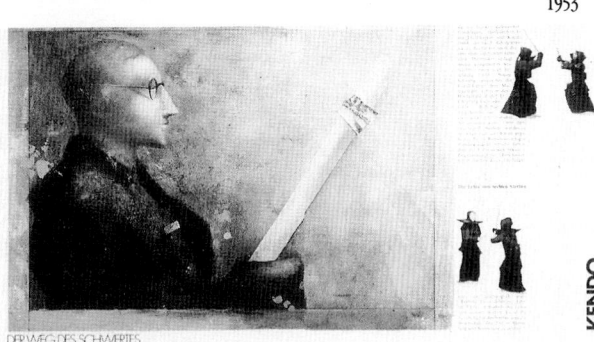

DER WEG DES SCHWERTES

1953

1954

ART DIRECTOR
Hans-Georg Pospischil
DESIGNER
Bernadette Gotthardt
ILLUSTRATOR/ARTIST
Paoloa Piglia
PUBLISHER
Dr. Bruno Dechamps
PUBLICATION
Frankfurter Allgemeine Magazin, Frankfurt

1954

1955
ART DIRECTOR
Thomas Höpker
DESIGNER
Norbert Kleiner
PHOTOGRAPHER
Harry Gruyeart
PUBLICATION
Stern, Hamburg

1955

1956
ART DIRECTOR
Oswaldo Miranda, Curitiba, Brazil
PUBLICATION
Grafica Magazine

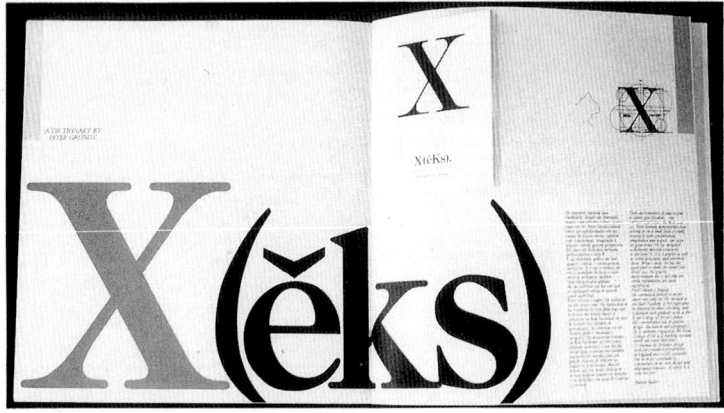

1956

1957
ART DIRECTOR
Urshila Kerkar, Dhun Cordo
DESIGNER
Urshila Kerkar, Dhun Cordo
AGENCY
Graphitecture, Bombay

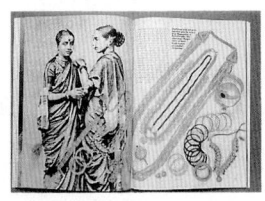

1957

1958
ART DIRECTOR
Wolfgang Behnken
DESIGNER
Diemar Schulze
PHOTOGRAPHER
Bernd Hoff
PUBLICATION
Stern, Hamburg

1958

1959

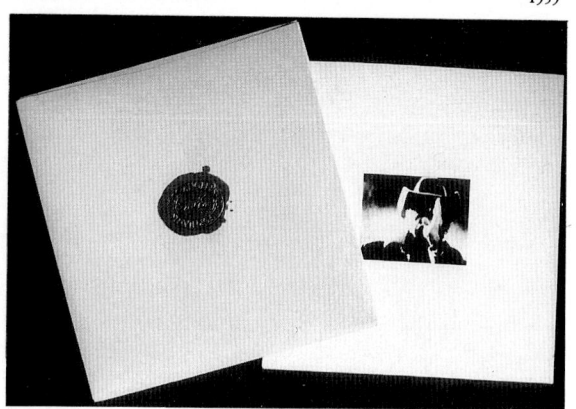

1960

ART DIRECTOR
Klaus-Jochen Nengelken, Köln
DESIGNER
Klaus-Jochen Nengelken, Köln
CLIENT
ZANDERS Feinpapiere AG, Bergisch
Gladbach, West Germany
EDITOR
ZANDERS Feinpapiere AG
DIRECTOR
Wolfgang Heuwinkel, ZANDERS
PRODUCER
Anton Meyer, ZANDERS
ADVERTISING MANAGER
Dietmar Fehse, ZANDERS

1960

ART DIRECTOR
Oswaldo Miranda, Curitiba, Brazil
CLIENT
Saul Bass

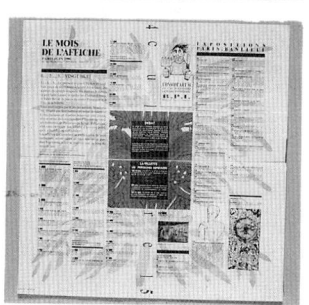

1961

ART DIRECTOR
Bulnes & Robaglia, Laure Predine,
Charenton Le Pont, France
ILLUSTRATOR/ARTIST
Laure Predine and Bulnes & Robaglia
CLIENT
S.N.G.
PRINTER
Ceppi

1962

ART DIRECTOR
Uwe Loesch, Düsseldorf
DESIGNER
Uwe Loesch
PHOTOGRAPHER
Siegbert Kercher
WRITER
Friedwald Schüttler, ZANDERS
CLIENT
ZANDERS Feinpapiere AG, Bergisch
Gladbach, West Germany
EDITOR
ZANDERS Feinpapiere AG
DIRECTOR
Wolfgang Heuwinkel, ZANDERS
PRODUCER
Richard Peters, ZANDERS
ADVERTISING MANAGER
F. Schüttler, ZANDERS

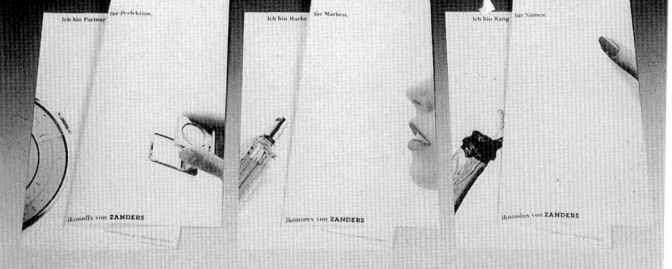

1962

1963
ART DIRECTOR
Oswaldo Miranda, Curitiba, Brazil
CLIENT
Gráfica

1963

1964
ART DIRECTOR
Gerd F. Setzke, Hamburg

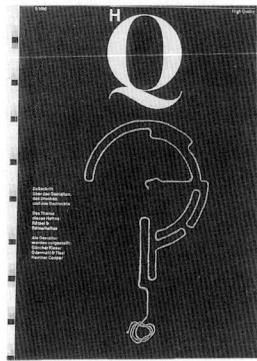

1964

1965
ART DIRECTOR
Rolf Müller, München
DESIGNER
Barbara Miedaner, Roman Lorenz
CLIENT
Heidelberger Druckmaschinen AG
EDITOR
Rolf Müller, Günter Braus
PRODUCER
Paul Simon

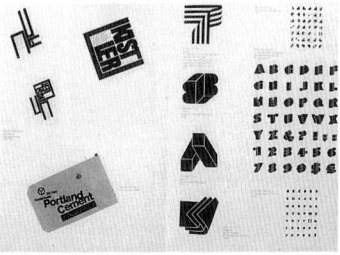

1966
ART DIRECTOR
Harald Schlüter, Essen
DESIGNER
Harald Schlüter
CLIENT
ZANDERS Feinpapiere AG, Bergisch
Gladbach, West Germany
EDITOR
ZANDERS Feinpapiere AG
DIRECTOR
Wolfgang Heuwinkel, ZANDERS
PRODUCER
Anton Meyer, ZANDERS
ADVERTISING MANAGER
Dietmar Fehse, ZANDERS

1966

1967

ART DIRECTOR
Mr. Lasse Nevalainen
WRITER
Mr. Kalevi Koivunen
CLIENT
Enso-Gutzeit Oy, Fine Papers
AGENCY
Anderson & Lembke OY, Helsinki

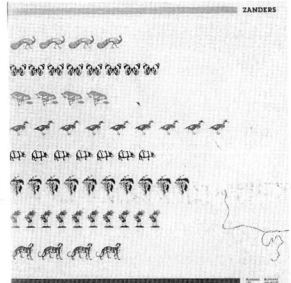

1967

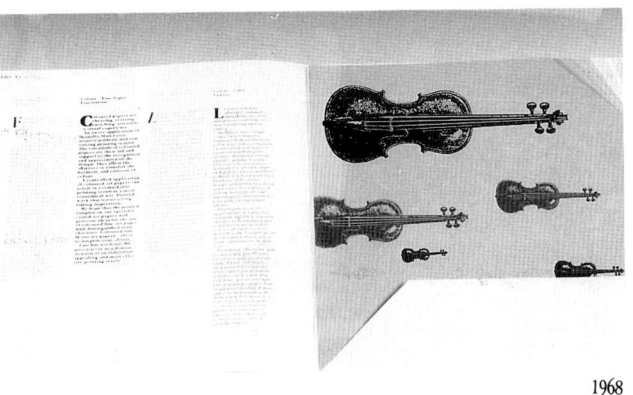

1968

ART DIRECTOR
Burkhard Neumann, Düsseldorf
DESIGNER
Burkhard Neumann
WRITER
Friedwald Schüttler, ZANDERS
CLIENT
ZANDERS Feinpapiere AG, Bergisch
Gladbach, West Germany
EDITOR
ZANDERS Feinpapiere AG
DIRECTOR
Wolfgang Heuwinkel, ZANDERS
PRODUCER
Richard Peters, ZANDERS
ADVERTISING MANAGER
F. Schüttler, ZANDERS

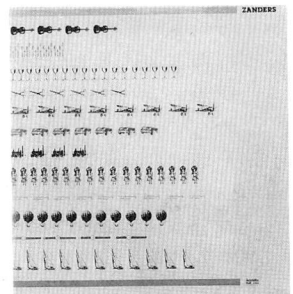

1968

1969

ART DIRECTOR
Otl Aicher
EDITOR
ERCO Leuchten GmbH, Lüdenscheid, West
Germany
PRINTER
Druckhaus Maack

1969

1970

1970

ART DIRECTOR
Gernot Lauffer
DESIGNER
Herms Fritz (cover)
PHOTOGRAPHER
Helmut Utri
EDITOR
Heinrich von Kalnein
PUBLICATION
Sterz, Graz, Austria

1971

ART DIRECTOR
Jürgen Weber
WRITER
Joh.-Friedr. Eddelbüttel
CLIENT
Herman Miller Deutschland
AGENCY
Dommnich & Eddelbüttel, Stuttgart

1971

1972

ART DIRECTOR
Hiroshi Takahara, Tokyo
DESIGNER
Hiroshi Takahara
PHOTOGRAPHER
Javier Vallhonrat
CLIENT
Nicole Co. Ltd.
PUBLISHER
Mitsuhiro Matsuda

1972

1973

ART DIRECTOR
Hayim Shtayer, Haifa
DESIGNER
Hayim Shtayer
PHOTOGRAPHER
Archives
CLIENT
Beth Hatefutsoth, The Jewish Diaspora
Museum
EDITOR
Yossi Avner
PRODUCER
Hayim Shtayer

1973

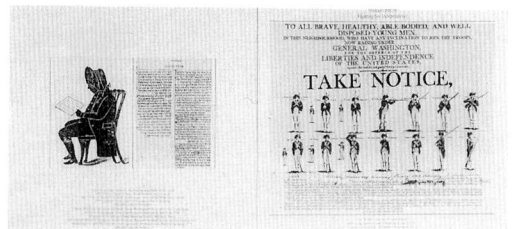

1974

ART DIRECTOR
Otl Aicher
EDITOR
ERCO Leuchten GmbH, Lüdenscheid, West
Germany
PRINTER
Druckhaus Maack

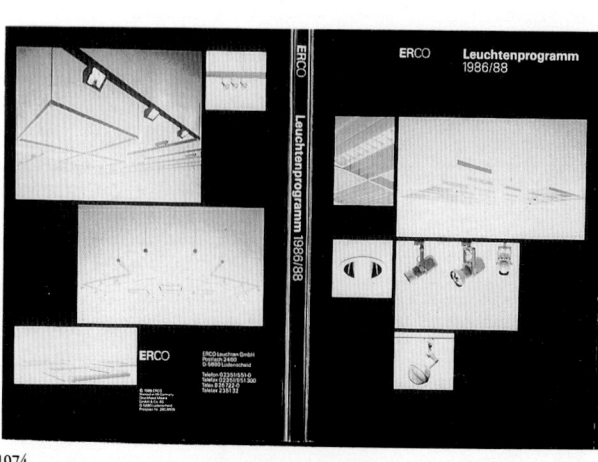

1974

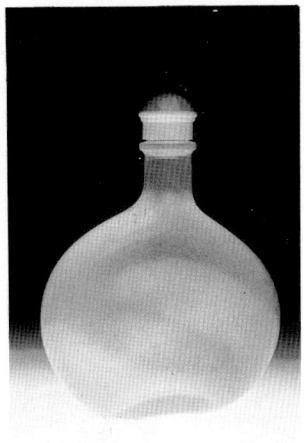

1975

1975
ART DIRECTOR
Annegret Beier, Paris
DESIGNER
Annegret Beier
ILLUSTRATOR/ARTIST
Annegret Beier
CLIENT
Shiseido Co., Japan

1976

1976
ART DIRECTOR
Salvatore Adduci
DESIGNER
Salvatore Adduci
PHOTOGRAPHER
Pedro Pons
CLIENT
Nabisco España
AGENCY
Tandem/DDB/Campmany/Guasch, Barcelona

1977

1977
ART DIRECTOR
Rowland Heming
DESIGNER
Rowland Heming
ILLUSTRATOR/ARTIST
Richard Birks
CLIENT
Andrew Doyle, Delacre
DESIGN FIRM
Pineapple Design, Brussels

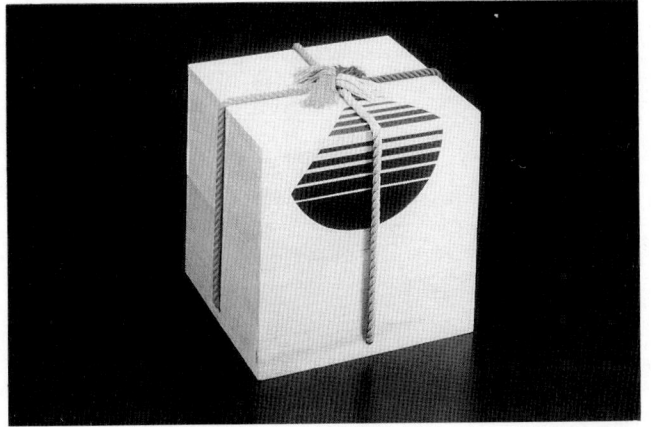

1978

1978
ART DIRECTOR
Kenji Maezawa, Tokyo
DESIGNER
Kenji Maezawa

1979

ART DIRECTOR
Clive Gay
DESIGNER
Clive Gay, Dirk Voorneveld, Yvonne Brummer
ILLUSTRATOR/ARTIST
Dirk Voorneveld
CLIENT
Dewhurst Fresh Foods Limited
AGENCY
Pentagraph, Excom, South Africa

1979

1980

ART DIRECTOR
Kenji Iwasaki
DESIGNER
Shu Kataoka, Tokyo
ILLUSTRATOR/ARTIST
Shu Kataoka
CLIENT
Sagano Matsukaze Co.

1980

1981

ART DIRECTOR
Mario Eskenazi
DESIGNER
Mario Eskenazi, Pablo Martin
CLIENT
Levi Strauss & Co. España
AGENCY
McCann Erickson (Barcelona)
DESIGN FIRM
Mario Eskenazi & Asociados, Barcelona

1981

1982

1982

ART DIRECTOR
Yoshitomo Ohama
DESIGNER
Kazunori Umezawa
CLIENT
Avon Products Co., Ltd. Japan, Tokyo

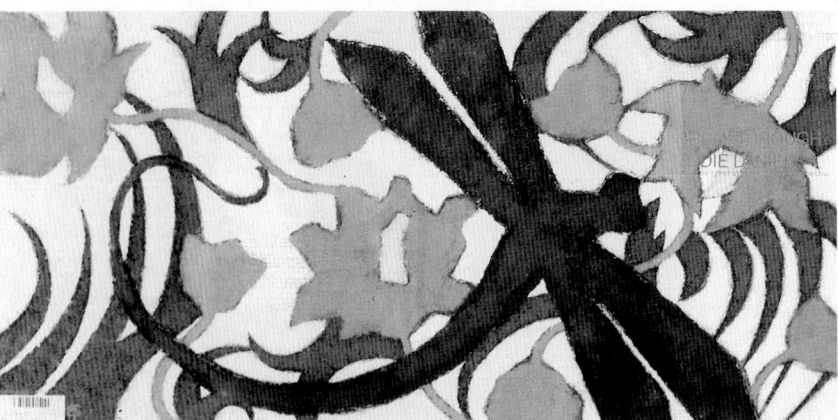

1983

ART DIRECTOR
Kaoru Kasai, Tokyo
DESIGNER
Kaoru Kasai
ILLUSTRATOR/ARTIST
Keiko Hirano
CLIENT
Victor Musical Industries, Inc.

1983

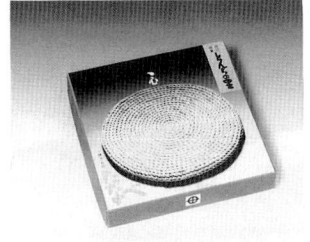

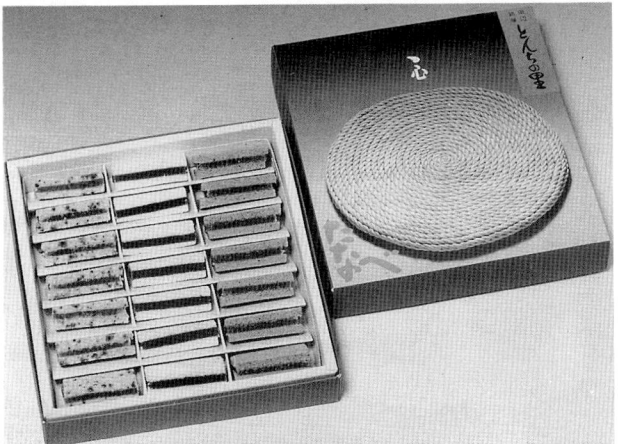

1984

ART DIRECTOR
Shozo Itoi, Kyoto City
DESIGNER
Shozo Itoi
PHOTOGRAPHER
Kenji Hiramatu
CLIENT
Tanabe Chiyo Wagashi Sinkokai

1984

1985

ART DIRECTOR
Yuji Baba, Tokyo
DESIGNER
Yuji Baba
CLIENT
Seibu Department Store

1985

1986

ART DIRECTOR
Roni & Aryeh Hecht
DESIGNER
Roni & Aryeh Hecht
PHOTOGRAPHER
Avi Ganor
CLIENT
Yarden Food Export Ltd.
AGENCY
Hecht Ltd., Tel Aviv

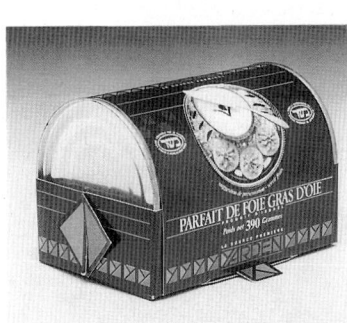

1986

1987

ART DIRECTOR
Tokihiko Kimata
DESIGNER
Yosei Kawaji
WRITER
Natsue Terunuma
CLIENT
Yamagata-Ken Shuzo Kumiai
DIRECTOR
Masaaki Hozumi
AGENCY
Hakuhodo, Inc., Tokyo

1987

1988
ART DIRECTOR
Toru Ando, Tokyo
DESIGNER
Yukio Kashizaki

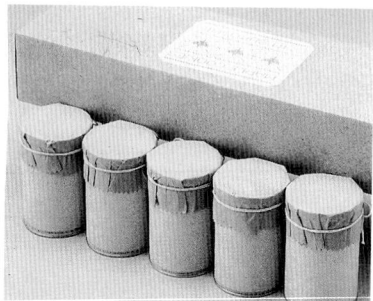

1988

1989
ART DIRECTOR
Annegret Beier
DESIGNER
Annegret Beier
ILLUSTRATOR/ARTIST
Dominique Auboire
CLIENT
Parfums Cacharel, Paris

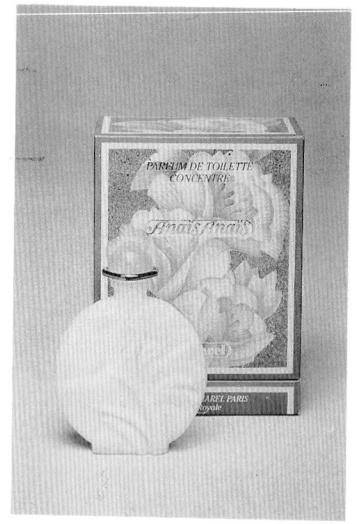
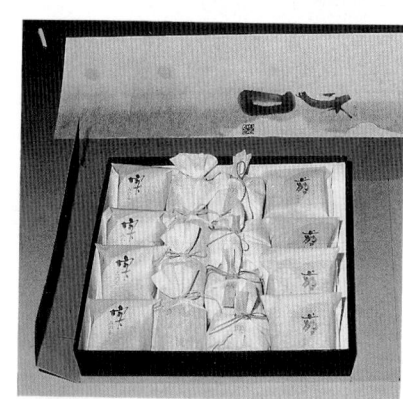

1989

1990
ART DIRECTOR
Kazuki Maeda, Osaka
DESIGNER
Seiichi Maeda
ILLUSTRATOR/ARTIST
Seiichi Maeda
WRITER
Mari Kurihara

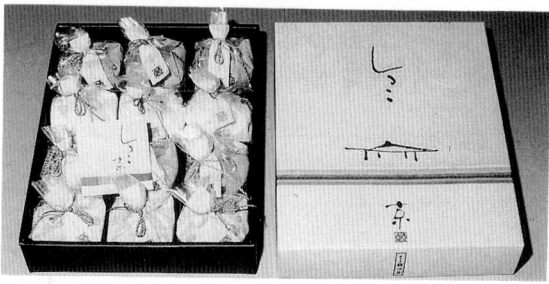

1990

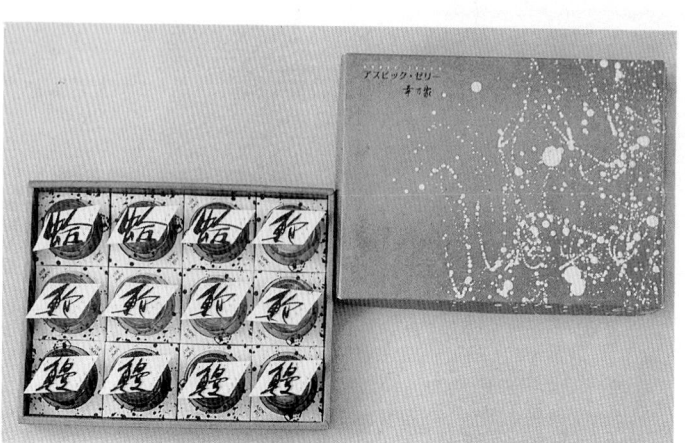

1991
ART DIRECTOR
Toru Ando, Tokyo
DESIGNER
Masako Kiyota

1991

1992

ART DIRECTOR
Toru Ando, Tokyo
DESIGNER
Masanori Kobayashi
ILLUSTRATOR/ARTIST
Sara Midda

1992

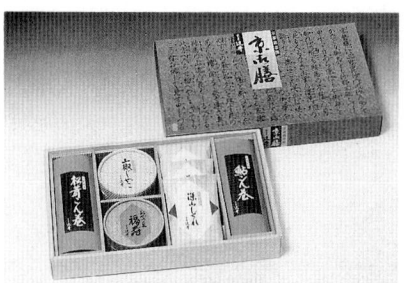

1993

ART DIRECTOR
Shozo Itoi, Kyoto City
DESIGNER
Shozo Itoi
CLIENT
Kurama Tujii Co., Ltd.

1993

1994

1994

ART DIRECTOR
Shozo Itoi, Kyoto City
DESIGNER
Shozo Itoi
ILLUSTRATOR/ARTIST
Kyozo Ashida
CLIENT
Kimura Co., Ltd.

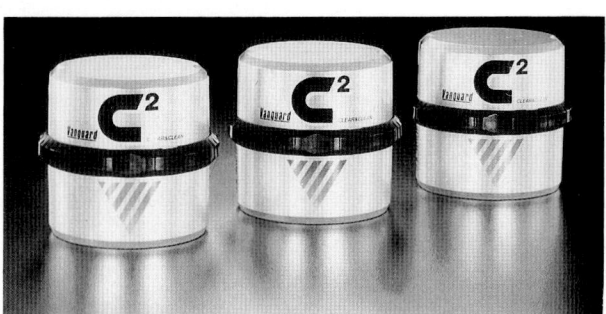

1995

1995

ART DIRECTOR
Yoshiharu Obata
DESIGNER
Toyoharu Obata, Kozo Oda, Haruo Tanaka
CLIENT
Penguin Wax Co., Osaka
AGENCY
Hakuhodo Advertising, Tokyo

1996
ART DIRECTOR
Takenobu Igarashi, Tokyo
DESIGNER
Takenobu Igarashi, Debi Shimamoto
CLIENT
The Museum of Modern Art, New York, NY

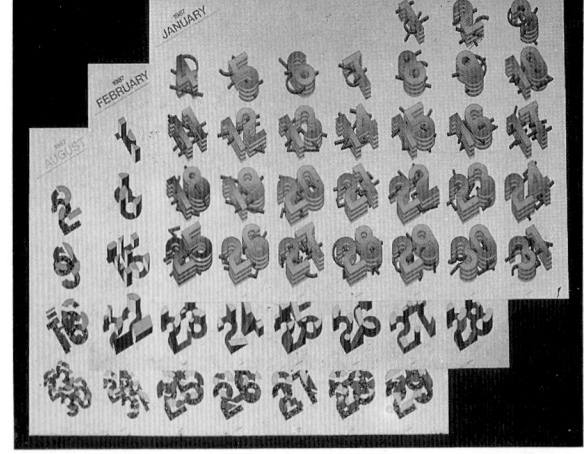

1996

1997
ART DIRECTOR
Robert Dowling
DESIGNER
Trickett & Webb
PHOTOGRAPHER
Robert Dowling
CLIENT
Robert Dowling Productions, London

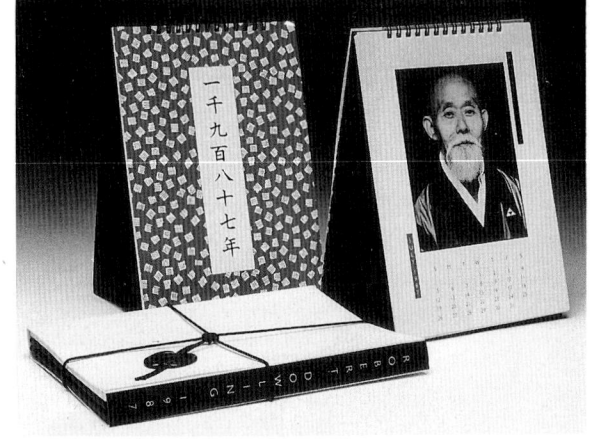

1997

1998
ART DIRECTOR
Bettina Brieger-Geffen, Tel Aviv
DESIGNER
Bettina Brieger-Geffen, David Geffen
WRITER
David Geffen
CLIENT
Bettina Brieger-Geffen, David Geffen
PRODUCER
PRO-1 Interntional Production

1998

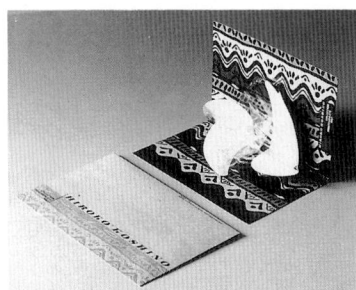

1999
ART DIRECTOR
Keizo Matsui, Osaka
DESIGNER
Keizo Matsui
CLIENT
Hiroko Koshino International Corporation

1999

2000

ART DIRECTOR
Muneaki Andoh
DESIGNER
Muneaki Andoh
ILLUSTRATOR/ARTIST
Yoshio Hayakawa
WRITER
Yukari Hasegawa
CLIENT
Central Finance
DIRECTOR
Muneaki Andoh
AGENCY
Dentsu Incorporated, Nagoya Branch, Nagoya
City

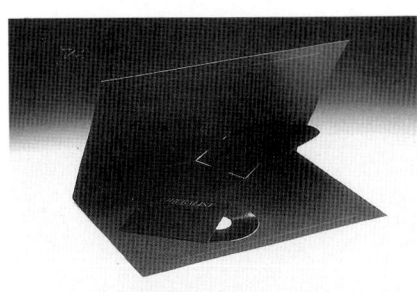

2000

2001

ART DIRECTOR
Keizo Matsui, Osaka
DESIGNER
Keizo Matsui
CLIENT
World Co., Ltd.

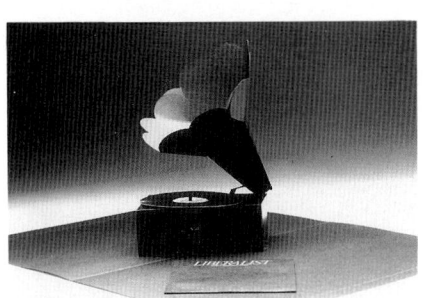

2001

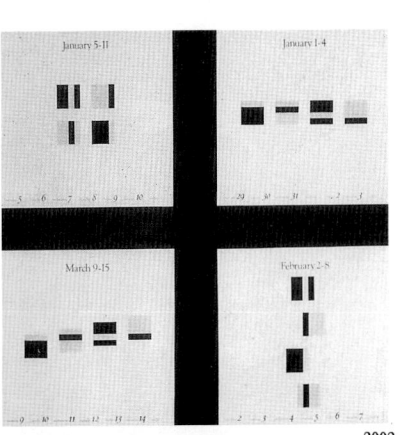

2002

ART DIRECTOR
Masakazu Sawa, Tokyo
DESIGNER
Masakazu Sawa
ILLUSTRATOR/ARTIST
Masakazu Sawa
CLIENT
Loire Co., Ltd.

2002

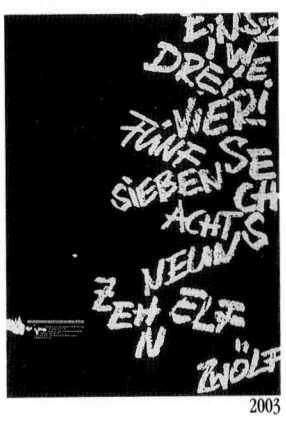

2003

ART DIRECTOR
Jan-Peter Rieken
CLIENT
Typostudio Kophal
AGENCY
Horstmann & Werbung, Hamburg
PRODUCER
Hans M.P. Will

2003

2004
ART DIRECTOR
Hans Kirschbaum
DESIGNER
Walter Kreutzberg
ILLUSTRATOR/ARTIST
Prof. Heinz Mack
WRITER
Prof. Heinz Mack
CLIENT
Kirschbaum Laserscan GmbH
EDITOR
Kirschbaum Laserscan GmbH
AGENCY
Kirschbaum Laserscan GmbH, Düsseldorf
PRODUCER
Horst Krebs

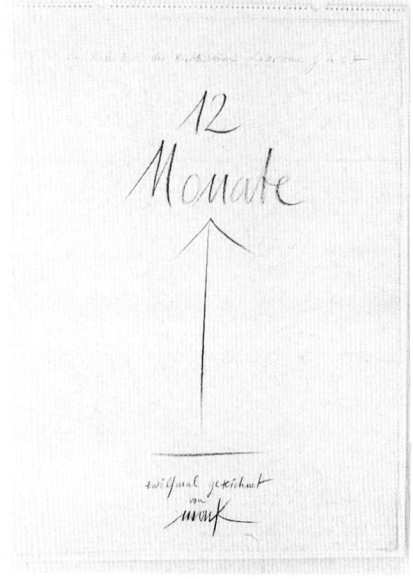
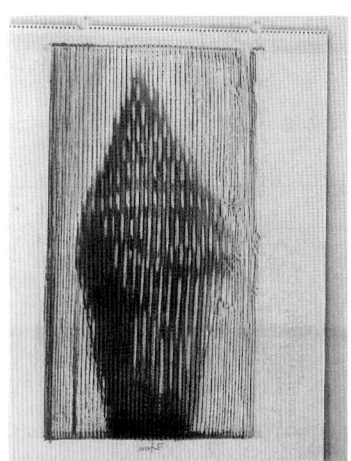

2004

2005
ART DIRECTOR
M. Domberger
DESIGNER
Conny Winter
PHOTOGRAPHER
Conny Winter
CLIENT
Co-Produktion Bertsch/Domberger/C. Winter
PUBLISHER
Domberger, Filderstadt, West Germany

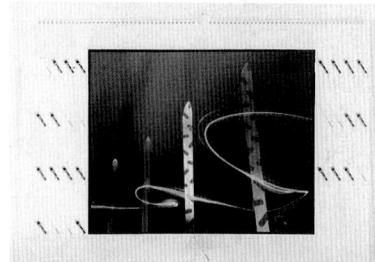
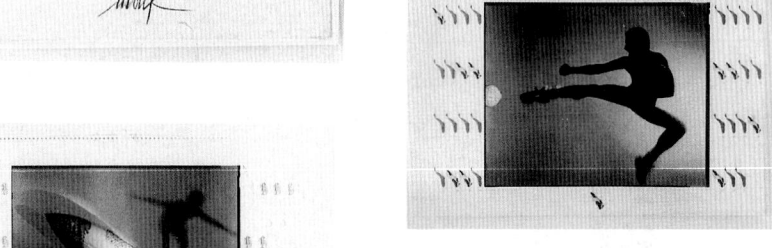

2005

2006
ART DIRECTOR
Giacobetti
DESIGNER
Esther Cavalie
PHOTOGRAPHER
Giacobetti, Paris
CLIENT
Legovic

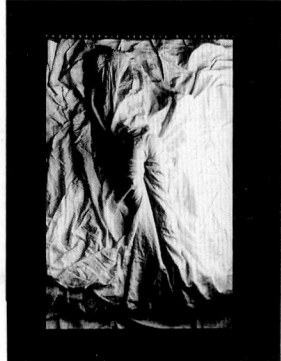

2006

2007
ART DIRECTOR
Gerhard Schwekender
CLIENT
Hirt + Carter, Roggebaai, South Africa

2007

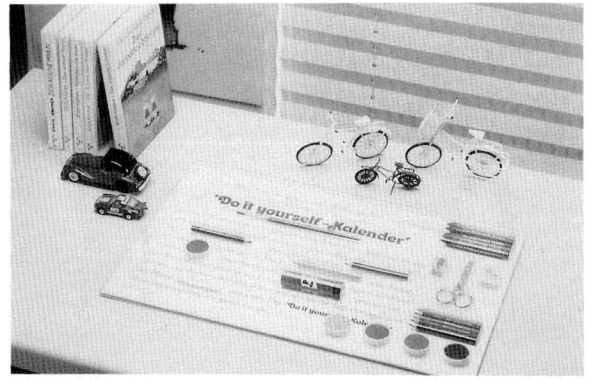

2008

2008
DESIGNER
Michael Domberger
EDITOR
Domberger
PUBLISHER
Domberger, Filderstadt, West Germany
PRODUCER
Fa. Domberger KG

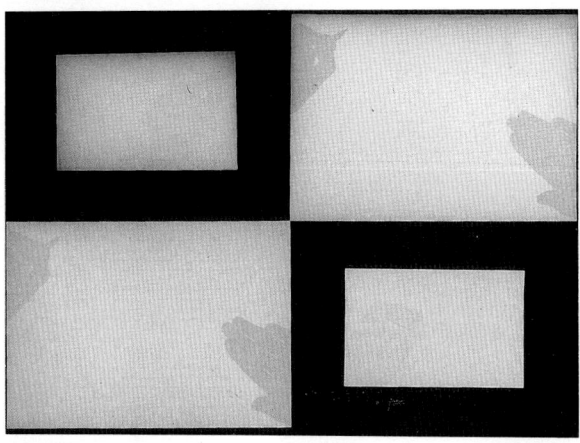

2009
ART DIRECTOR
Kyoji Nakatani, Tokyo
DESIGNER
Kyoji Akatani
PHOTOGRAPHER
Tamotu Kawaguchi
ILLUSTRATOR/ARTIST
Kyoji Nakatani
CLIENT
Seibu Department Stores
PRODUCER
Akio Okumura

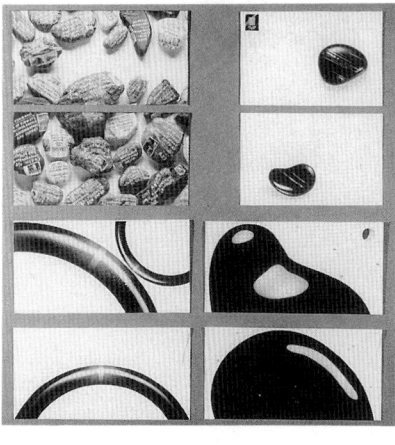

2010
ART DIRECTOR
Haroldo Valente
DESIGNER
Oswaldo Mendes
ILLUSTRATOR/ARTIST
Haroldo Valente
CLIENT
Museu Paraense Emílio Goeldi
AGENCY
Mendes Publicidade Ltda, Belém, Brazil
PRODUCER
Márcia Martins

2009

2011
ART DIRECTOR
Erkki Ruuhinen
DESIGNER
Keijo Halttunen
ILLUSTRATOR/ARTIST
Erkki Ruuhinen
CLIENT
Stripe Castle Ltd
AGENCY
Erkki Ruuhinen Design, Helsinki

2010

2011

2012
ART DIRECTOR
Ernst Bächtold
DESIGNER
Ernst Bächtold
WRITER
Rudy Felber
CLIENT
IWC, Schaffhausen
DIRECTOR
Hermann Strittmatter
AGENCY
GGK Zürich

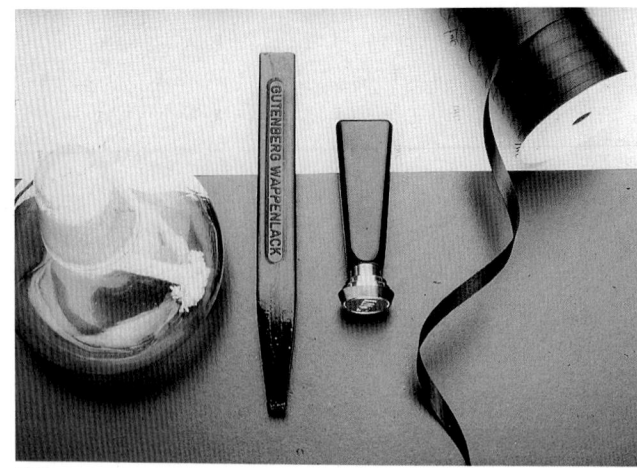

2012

2013
ART DIRECTOR
Roland Mehler
DESIGNER
Roland Mehler
CLIENT
Steigenberger Hotels AG
AGENCY
Knut Hartmann Design, Frankfurt
PRODUCER
Druckerei Koch, Frankfurt

2014
ART DIRECTOR
Roland Mehler
DESIGNER
Roland Mehler
ILLUSTRATOR/ARTIST
Christiane Pralle
CLIENT
Steigenberger Hotels AG
AGENCY
Knut Hartmann Design, Frankfurt
PRODUCER
Hauserpresse, Frankfurt

2013   2014

2015
ART DIRECTOR
Tore Claesson
DESIGNER
Mikko Timonen
CLIENT
Bowl
AGENCY
Claesson & Company, Göteborg, Sweden

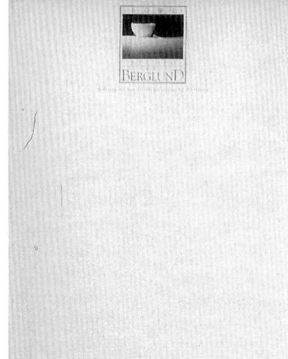

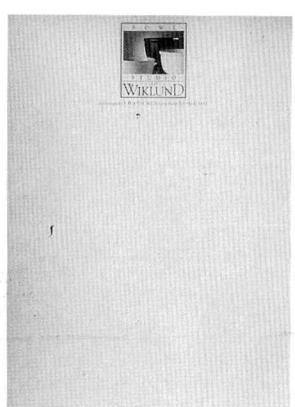

2015

2016
ART DIRECTOR
Oswaldo Miranda, Curitiba, Brazil
AGENCY
Modulo 3 Studio

2017
ART DIRECTOR
Clive Gay
DESIGNER
Clive Gay, Kees Schilperoort
ILLUSTRATOR/ARTIST
Dirk Voorneveld
CLIENT
Triax, Triatic International
AGENCY
Pentagraph (Pty) Ltd, Excom, South Africa

2016

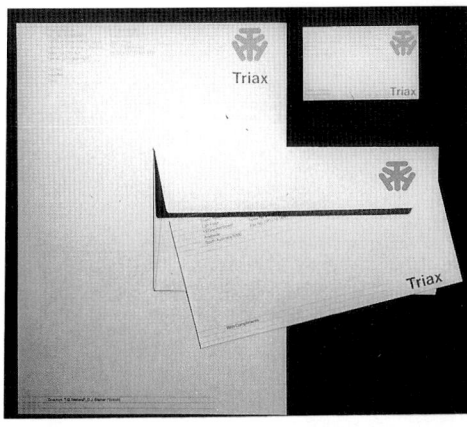

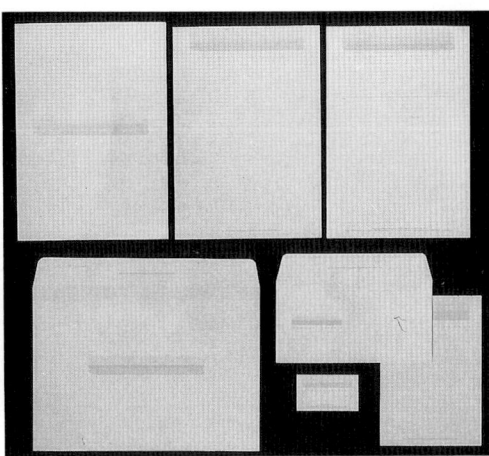

2017

2018
ART DIRECTOR
Erkki Ruuhinen
DESIGNER
Kristiina Varttinen
ILLUSTRATOR/ARTIST
Erkki Ruuhinen
CLIENT
Leena Kaijanranta Ltd
AGENCY
Erkki Ruuhinen Design, Helsinki

2018

2019
ART DIRECTOR
Takenobu Igarashi, Tokyo
DESIGNER
Takenobu Igarashi, Yukimi Sasago
PHOTOGRAPHER
Kenji Taguchi
CLIENT
Meiji Milk Products Co. Ltd.
AGENCY
Dentsu Incorporated

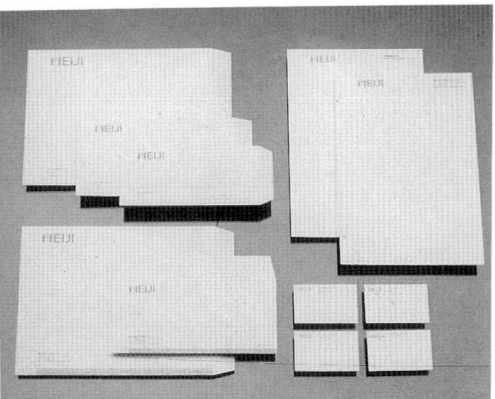

2020
ART DIRECTOR
Bruno Monguzzi
DESIGNER
Bruno Monguzzi
CLIENT
Al Castello Film Productions
DIRECTOR
Heinz Bütler
AGENCY
Bruno Monguzzi, Meride, Switzerland

2020

2019

2021
ART DIRECTOR
Masahisa Nakamura
DESIGNER
Yoichi Kawasaki and others
PHOTOGRAPHER
Masayuki Owa
ILLUSTRATOR/ARTIST
Tatsuhide Matsuoka
WRITER
Noboru Kimura, Naomichi Pete Kobayashi
CLIENT
Suntory Ltd.
EDITOR
Eizo Fukunishi
DIRECTOR
Noboru Kimura, Naomichi Pete Kobayashi
PUBLISHER
TBS Britanica Ltd.
AGENCY
Dentsu Inc., Tokyo
PRODUCER
Kozo Nakajima
PUBLICATION
The Suntory Cocktail Book

2021

2022
DESIGNER
Bruno Pfäffli
ILLUSTRATOR/ARTIST
Granger, Paris
PUBLISHER
Glenat

2023
ART DIRECTOR
Hiroshi Sato, Tokyo
DESIGNER
Toshio Nomura, Kazuhisa Iwakata, Michiko Hirama
PHOTOGRAPHER
Staff photographers at Kodansha
EDITOR
Pec Co., Ltd.
DIRECTOR
Minoru Fujita
PUBLISHER
Kodansha Co., Ltd.
PUBLICATION
Kodansha Co., Ltd.

2022

2023

2024
ART DIRECTOR
Prof. Kurt Weidemann
DESIGNER
Prof. Kurt Weidemann
PHOTOGRAPHER
Dieter Blum
WRITER
P. Bizer, E. Eckardt, Dr. Follath, S. Offinbach, E. Vindmoelles
CLIENT
ECON
EDITOR
ECON
PUBLISHER
ECON, Düsseldorf/Vien

2024

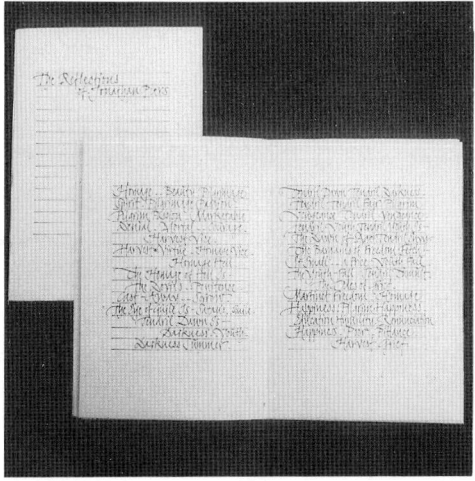

2025

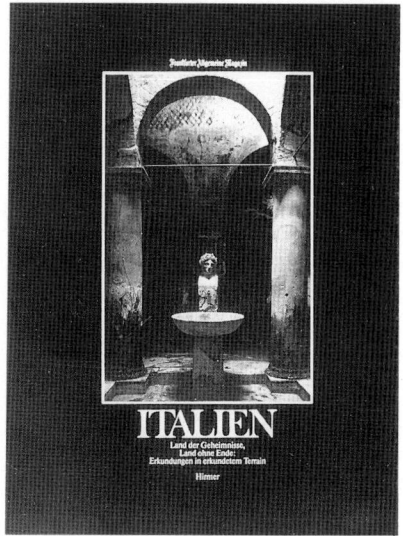

2026

2025
ART DIRECTOR
Gunnlaugur SE Briem, London
CALLIGRAPHER
Werner Schneider

2026
ART DIRECTOR
Hans-Georg Pospischil
DESIGNER
Bernadette Gotthardt
PUBLISHER
Hirmer Verlag, Frankfurter Allgemeine
Zeitung, Frankfurt

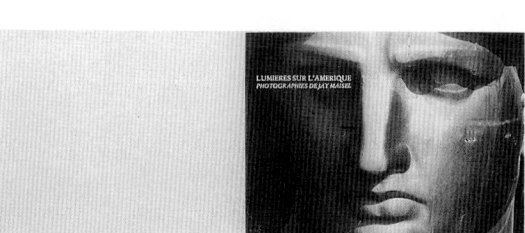

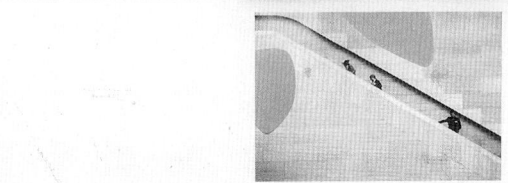

2027

2027
ART DIRECTOR
Derek Birdsall
DESIGNER
Derek Birdsall
PHOTOGRAPHER
Jay Maisel
WRITER
Gordon Bowman
CLIENT
United Technologies Corporation
PUBLISHER
United Technologies Corporation
PRODUCER
Omnific Studios, London

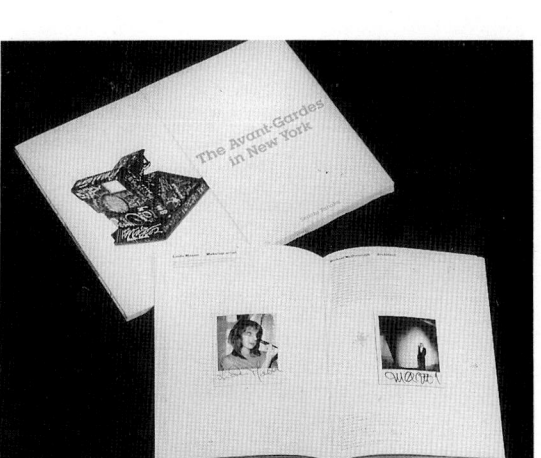

2029

2029
ART DIRECTOR
Tadanori Itakura, Osaka
DESIGNER
Tadanori Itakura
PHOTOGRAPHER
Seiichi Tanaka
CLIENT
Tanaka Studio Inc.
EDITOR
Tadanori Itakura
PUBLISHER
Tanaka Studio Inc.

2030
ART DIRECTOR
Derek Birdsall
DESIGNER
Derek Birdsall
PHOTOGRAPHER
Harri Peccinotti
WRITER
Claudio Nobis
CLIENT
Otis Elevators
PUBLISHER
Otis Elevators
PRODUCER
Omnific Studios, London

2031
ART DIRECTOR
Vladimír Nározník
DESIGNER
Zdenek Ziegler
ILLUSTRATOR/ARTIST
Jiří Šalamoun, Prague
WRITER
Laurence Sterne
CLIENT
Odeon, Prague
EDITOR
Eva Řečinská, Václav Jamek
DIRECTOR
Dr. J. Čermák
PUBLISHER
Odeon
PRODUCER
Odeon, Publishing House
PUBLICATION
Tristram Shandy

2032
ART DIRECTOR
Alfred Lutz, Schwäbisch Gmünd, West
Germany
DESIGNER
Alfred Lutz
EDITOR
Steibeis Stiftung Für Wirtschaftsförderung,
Stuttgart
PRODUCER
SCS Schwartz Computersatz GmbH & Co.,
Stuttgart & Stadler Verlagsgesellschaft,
Konstanz

2033
ART DIRECTOR
Rolf Gillhausen, Hamburg
DESIGNER
Franz Epping
PHOTOGRAPHER
Erwin Fieger, Rainer Martini, Hans
Rauchensteiner
WRITER
Sport-Informations-Dienst
PUBLISHER
proSport Verlag, München
PRODUCER
Busche-Verlag, Dortmund
PUBLICATION
proSport Verlag, München

2034
ART DIRECTOR
Vladimír Nárožník
DESIGNER
Jiří Šalamoun
ILLUSTRATOR/ARTIST
Jiří Šalamoun
WRITER
Richard Brautigan
CLIENT
Odeón, Prague
DIRECTOR
Dr. J. Čermák
PRODUCER
Odeon, Publishing House
PUBLICATION
In Watermelon Sugar

2030

2031

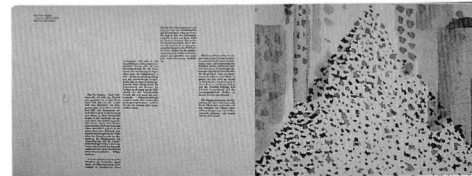

2032

2033

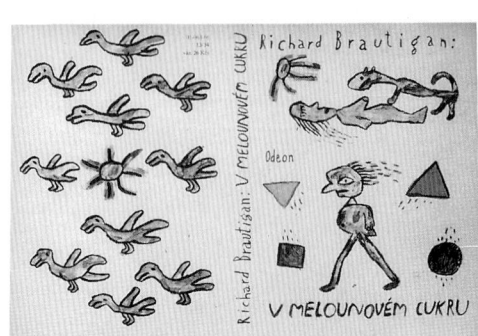

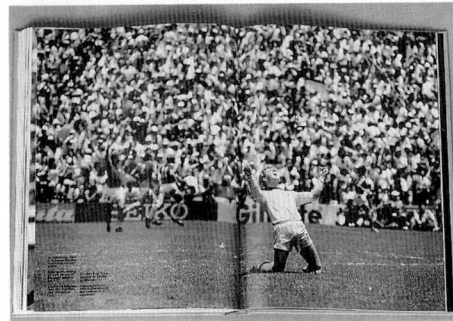

2034

2035
ILLUSTRATOR/ARTIST
Stefan Ignar, Warszawa
EDITOR
Ludowa Spotdzielnia Wydawnicza

2036
ART DIRECTOR
Bruno Monguzzi
DESIGNER
Bruno Monguzzi
PHOTOGRAPHER
Serge Libis, Nini Mulas
WRITER
Bruno Monguzzi
CLIENT
Editrice Abitare Segesta
EDITOR
Renato Minetto
DIRECTOR
Franca Santi
PUBLISHER
Editrice Abitare Segesta
AGENCY
Bruno Monguzzi, Meride, Switzerland
PUBLICATION
Abitare

2035

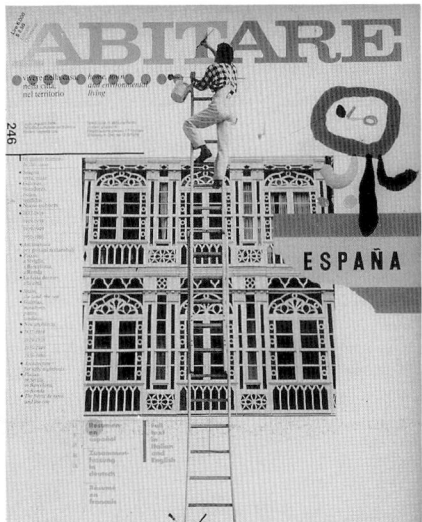

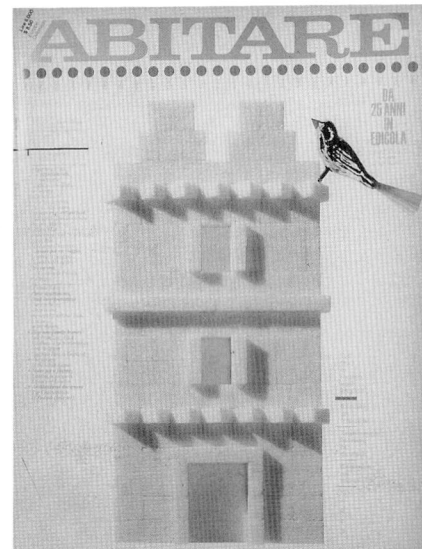

2037
ART DIRECTOR
Bruno Monguzzi
DESIGNER
Bruno Monguzzi
PHOTOGRAPHER
Thomas Libisewski
WRITER
Bruno Monguzzi
CLIENT
Editrice Abitare Segesta
EDITOR
Renato Minetto
DIRECTOR
Franca Santi
PUBLISHER
Editrice Abitare Segesta
AGENCY
Bruno Monguzzi, Meride, Switzerland
PUBLICATION
Abitare

2038
ART DIRECTOR
Mario Eskenazi
DESIGNER
Mario Eskenazi — Teresa Company
WRITER
A. Garau
CLIENT
Editorial Paidós Ibérica
AGENCY
Mario Eskenazi & Asociados, Barcelona

2036

2037

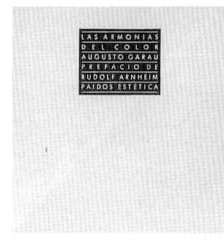

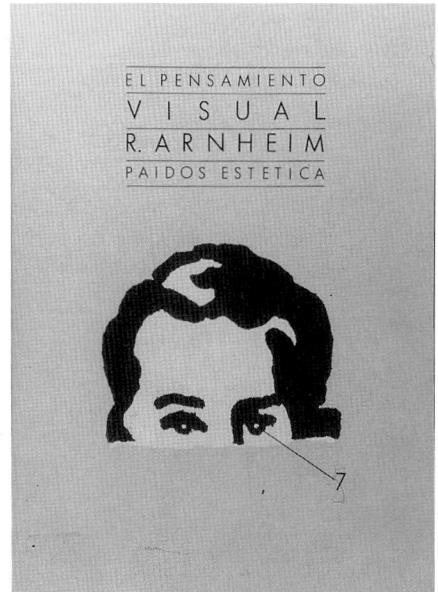

2039
ART DIRECTOR
Mario Eskenazi
DESIGNER
Mario Eskenazi
ILLUSTRATOR/ARTIST
Mario Eskenazi
WRITER
A. Barre, A. Flocon
CLIENT
Editorial Paidós Ibérica
EDITOR
Editorial Paidós
AGENCY
M. Eskenazi & Asociados, Barcelona

2040
ART DIRECTOR
Mario Eskenazi
DESIGNER
Mario Eskenazi
ILLUSTRATOR/ARTIST
Mario Eskenazi
WRITER
R. Arnheim
CLIENT
Editorial Paidós Ibérica
AGENCY
M. Eskenazi & Asociados, Barcelona

2038

2039

2040

2041
ART DIRECTOR
Henes Maier, Frankfurt
DESIGNER
Henes Maier
ILLUSTRATOR/ARTIST
Henes Maier
CLIENT
Buechergilde Gutenberg
PUBLISHER
Buechergilde Gutenberg

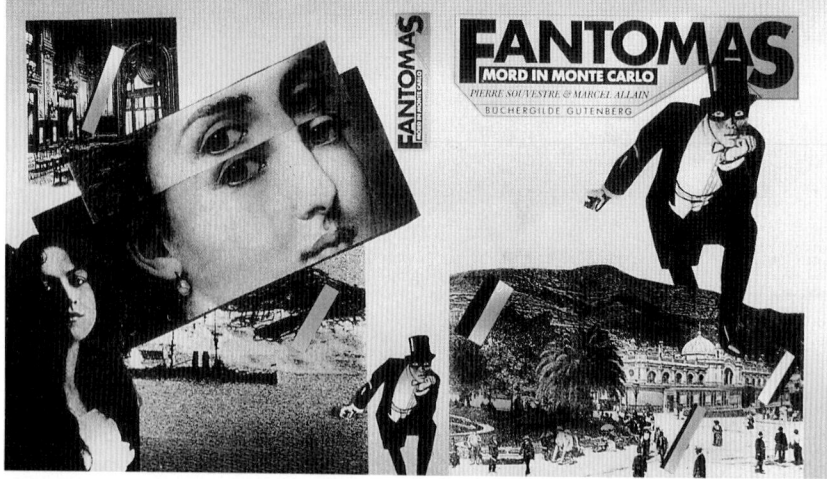

2041

2042
ART DIRECTOR
Katsu Asano, Tokyo
DESIGNER
Kinue Yonezawa
PHOTOGRAPHER
Katsu Asano, Hideo Fujii
CLIENT
Lunetta Bada

2042

2043
DESIGNER
Gabriele Burde, Berlin
PHOTOGRAPHER
Mechthild Wilhelmi
PUBLISHER
Berliner Festspiele GmbH

2043

2044
ART DIRECTOR
Takashi Akiyama, Tokyo
DESIGNER
Takashi Akiyama
ILLUSTRATOR/ARTIST
Takashi Akiyama

2044

2045

ART DIRECTOR
Makoto Saito, Tokyo
DESIGNER
Soko Hosonome
PHOTOGRAPHER
Tsutomu Wakatsuki
CLIENT
Junco, Ltd.

2046

ART DIRECTOR
Makoto Saito, Tokyo
DESIGNER
Soko Hosonome
PHOTOGRAPHER
Tsutomu Wakatsuki
CLIENT
Junco, Ltd

2045

2046

2047

ART DIRECTOR
Stephan Bundi
DESIGNER
Stephan Bundi
ILLUSTRATOR/ARTIST
Stephan Bundi
CLIENT
SCI.ARC
EDITOR
SCI.ARC
DIRECTOR
Daniel Herren
AGENCY
Atelier Bundi, Bern, Switzerland
PRODUCER
SCI.ARC

2047

2048

ART DIRECTOR
Michael McAuley
DESIGNER
Charles Johnston
PHOTOGRAPHER
Neil McDougald
WRITER
Anthony O'Sullivan
CLIENT
Cantrell & Cochrane Ltd.
AGENCY
Hunter Advertising Ltd., Dublin

2048

2049
ART DIRECTOR
Pierre Mendell
DESIGNER
Pierre Mendell
PHOTOGRAPHER
Hans Döring
CLIENT
Kiel
AGENCY
Mendell & Oberer, München

2050
ART DIRECTOR
Jukka Veistola
DESIGNER
Jukka Veistola
PHOTOGRAPHER
Timo Viljakainen
WRITER
Jukka Rautapää
CLIENT
Maxi-mediat Oy
AGENCY
Veistola Oy, Helsinki

2051
ART DIRECTOR
J.M. Haurdeé
DESIGNER
T.A. Lewandowski, Paris
ILLUSTRATOR/ARTIST
T.A. Lewandowski
CLIENT
Théatre des Arts Cergy Pontoise
EDITOR
CAC de Cergy Pontoise

2052
ART DIRECTOR
H. R. Feltus, Düsseldorf
DESIGNER
H. R. Feltus
PHOTOGRAPHER
H. R. Feltus
ILLUSTRATOR/ARTIST
Rolf Isken
WRITER
Rolf Isken
CLIENT
Ste. Trotinette
PUBLISHER
Ste. Trotinette

2049

2050

2051

2052

2053

2054

2053
ART DIRECTOR
Michio Kubo
DESIGNER
Katsumi Tonomura
PHOTOGRAPHER
Shosuke Tanaka
WRITER
Kazuo Nishikawa, Masaaki Kato
CLIENT
Holbein Works, Ltd.
AGENCY
Hakuhodo Incorporated, Tokyo

2055

2054
ART DIRECTOR
Masuteru Aoba, Tokyo
DESIGNER
Masuteru Aoba
PHOTOGRAPHER
Masuteru Aoba
CLIENT
G7 Gallery

2056

2055
ART DIRECTOR
Koji Mizutani, Tokyo
DESIGNER
Hirokazu Kurebayashi
PHOTOGRAPHER
Kastuo Hanzawa

2056
ART DIRECTOR
Koji Mizutani, Tokyo
DESIGNER
Hirokazu Kurebayashi
PHOTOGRAPHER
Kastuo Hanzawa

2057
ART DIRECTOR
Kaoru Kasai, Tokyo
DESIGNER
Hiroyuki Takahashi
PHOTOGRAPHER
Jyumonji Bishin
ILLUSTRATOR/ARTIST
Chiaki Hirota
CLIENT
SONY Corp.

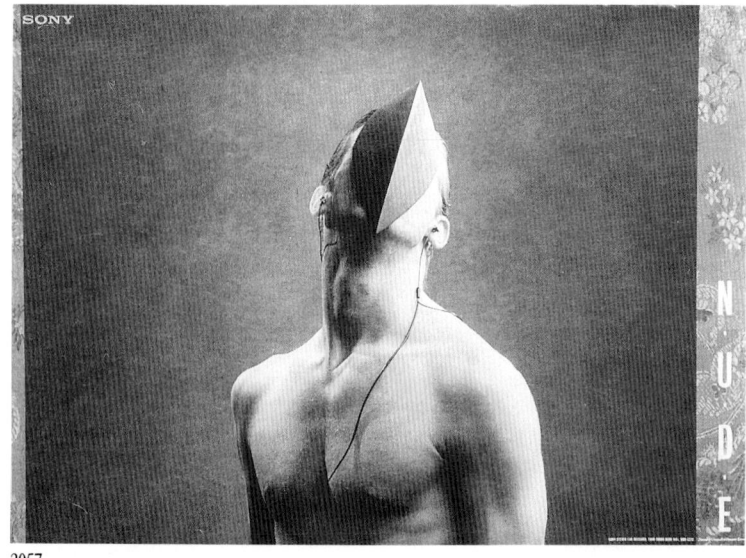

2057

2058
ART DIRECTOR
Renate Herter, Berlin
DESIGNER
Renate Herter
ILLUSTRATOR/ARTIST
Renate Herter
WRITER
Renate Herter
EDITOR
Renate Herter

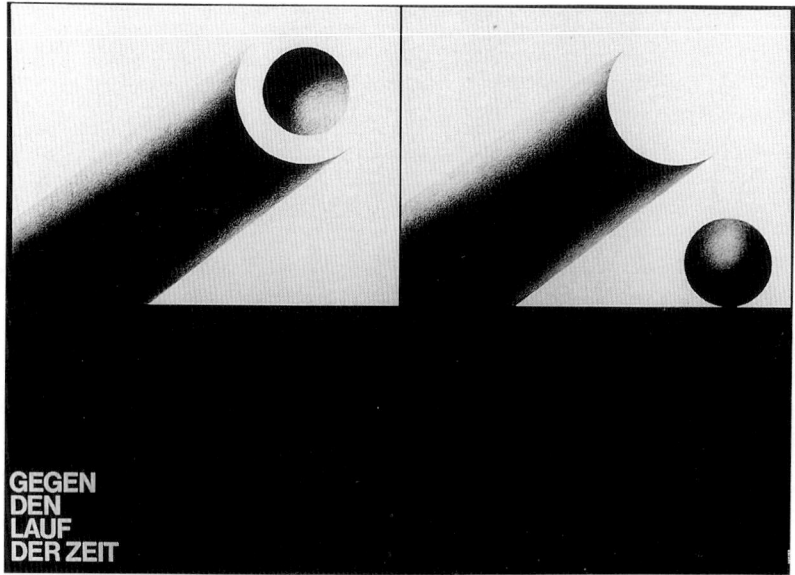

2058

2059
ART DIRECTOR
Michel Bouvet, Paris
DESIGNER
Michel Bouvet
PHOTOGRAPHER
Rachel Levy
CLIENT
Maison des Arts de Créteil

2060
DESIGNER
Gabriele Burde, Berlin
PHOTOGRAPHER
Mechtild Wilhelmi
PUBLISHER
Berliner Festspiele GmH

2059

2060

2061

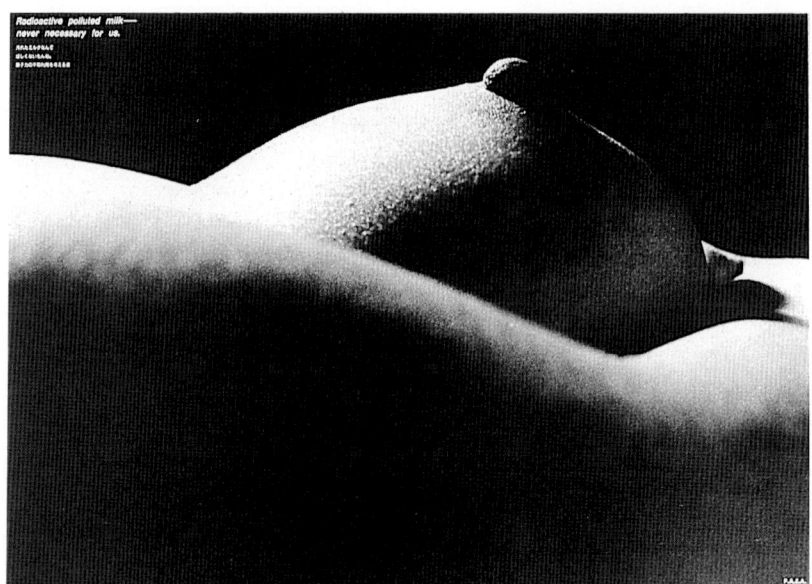

2062

2063

2064

2061
ART DIRECTOR
Yasuyuki Uno, Tokyo
DESIGNER
Yasuyuki Uno
PHOTOGRAPHER
Yasuyuki Uno, Tsuneo Nakamura
CLIENT
Japan Graphic Designers Association

2062
ART DIRECTOR
Asai Yoshiteru, Nagoya
DESIGNER
Suzuki Tomoyuk
PHOTOGRAPHER
Asai Yoshiteru
WRITER
Itoh Hiroyasu
CLIENT
Peaceful Use of Atomic Energy
PUBLISHER
Agni Studio

2063
ART DIRECTOR
Karel Misek, Prague
CLIENT
Divadlo S.K. Neumanna Theatre, Prague

2064
ART DIRECTOR
Michel Bouvet, Paris
DESIGNER
Michel Bouvet
PHOTOGRAPHER
Francis Laharrague
ILLUSTRATOR/ARTIST
Michel Bouvet
CLIENT
Théâtre Populaire de Lorraine

2065
ILLUSTRATOR/ARTIST
Finn Nygaard, Hadsten, Denmark

2066
ART DIRECTOR
Byung Kwon OH, Seoul
DESIGNER
Byung Kwon OH
CLIENT
Gallery YEDANG

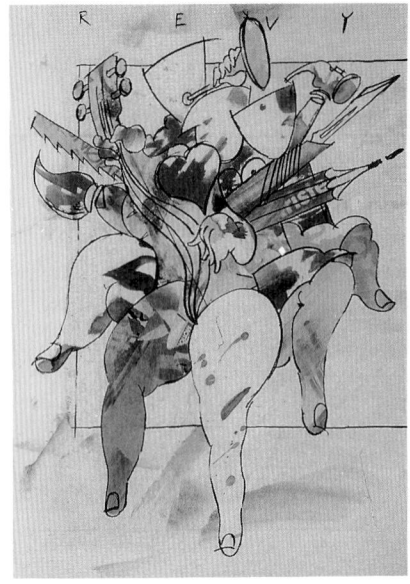

2065

2066

2067
ART DIRECTOR
Takanori Aiba
DESIGNER
Hiroyuki Hayashi ToshihiroOnimaru
ILLUSTRATOR/ARTIST
Seitaro Kuroda
WRITER
Muneharu Okada, Tetsuo Yamazaki
CLIENT
Nichinoken
AGENCY
Grafix International Inc., Tokyo

2067

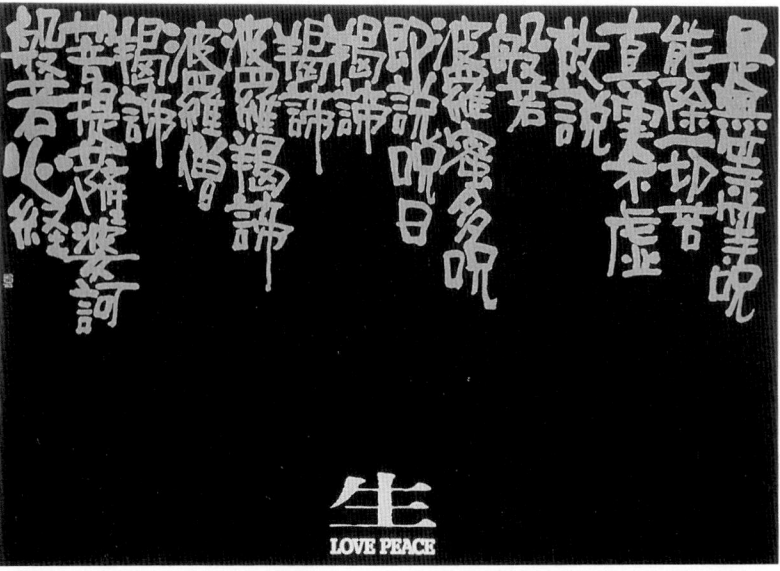

2068
ART DIRECTOR
Shu Kataoka, Tokyo

2068

2069

2070

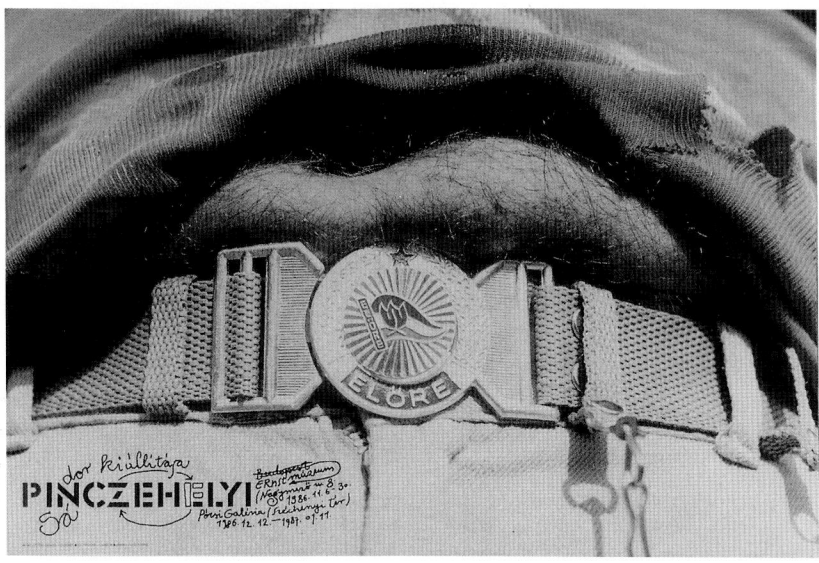

2071

2072

2069
ART DIRECTOR
Michel Bouvet, Paris
DESIGNER
Michel Bouvet
PHOTOGRAPHER
Fabrice Boissière
CLIENT
Maison des Arts de Créteil

2070
ART DIRECTOR
Mr. Lasse Nevalainen
PHOTOGRAPHER
Mr. Kaj Ewart
CLIENT
Enso-Gutzeit Oy, Fine Papers
AGENCY
Anderson & Lembke OY, Helsinki

2071
ART DIRECTOR
Peter Pocs

2072
ART DIRECTOR
Peter Pocs

2073
ART DIRECTOR
Pierre Mendell
DESIGNER
Pierre Mendell
ILLUSTRATOR/ARTIST
Heinz Hiltbrunner
CLIENT
Design Funktion
AGENCY
Mendell & Oberer, München

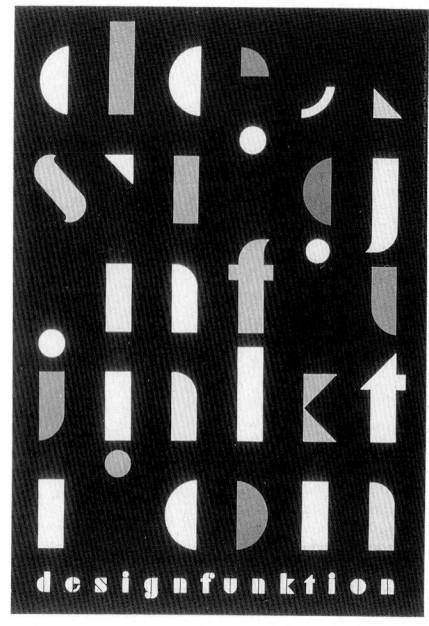

2074
ART DIRECTOR
Michel Bouvet, Paris
DESIGNER
Michel Bouvet
ILLUSTRATOR/ARTIST
Michel Bouvet
CLIENT
City of Paris

2073

2074

2075
ART DIRECTOR
Masaru Sakaguchi, Tokyo
DESIGNER
Masaru Sakaguchi
PHOTOGRAPHER
Toru Kinoshita
WRITER
Keizo Aoki
CLIENT
Itokin Co., Ltd.

2075

2076
ART DIRECTOR
Takanori Aiba
DESIGNER
Hiroyuki Hyashi
PHOTOGRAPHER
Eiichiro Sakata
WRITER
Muneharu Okada
CLIENT
Nihon Kodo
AGENCY
Grafix International, Inc., Tokyo

2076

2077

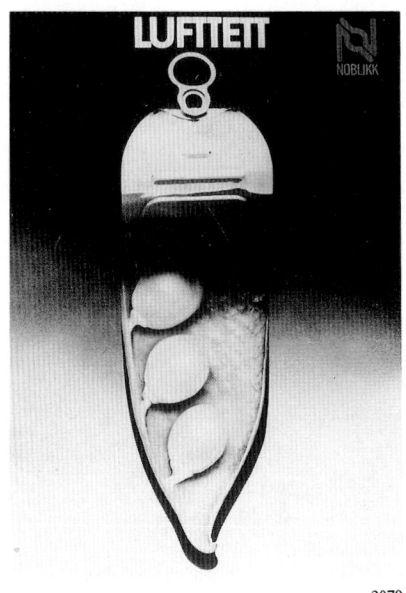

2079

2080

2077
ART DIRECTOR
Karel Misek, Prague
CLIENT
Divadlo S.K. Neumanna, Theatre, Prague

2078
ART DIRECTOR
Pierre Keller
DESIGNER
Jean Tinguely
ILLUSTRATOR/ARTIST
Jean Tinguely
CLIENT
Montreux Tourist Office
EDITOR
Montreux International Jazz Festival
PUBLISHER
Montreux International Jazz Festival,
Switzerland
PUBLICATION
Montreaux International Jazz Festival

2079
ART DIRECTOR
Trygve Foss
PHOTOGRAPHER
Jon Halvorsen, Sven Lorentzen
CLIENT
Noblikk-Sannem A/S
AGENCY
FOSS R & M A/S, Oslo

2080
ART DIRECTOR
Pentti Pilve
DESIGNER
Pentti Pilve
ILLUSTRATOR/ARTIST
Pentti Pilve
CLIENT
A-Lehdet Oy
AGENCY
Creator Oy, Helsinki

2081
ART DIRECTOR
Leszek Drzewinski
DESIGNER
Trio Drzewinski
ILLUSTRATOR/ARTIST
Trio Drzewinski
WRITER
Leszek Drzewinski
CLIENT
Friedens Haus—Berlin
EDITOR
Friedens Haus—Berlin
AGENCY
Trio Drzewinski
PRODUCER
Friedens Haus—Berlin

2082
ART DIRECTOR
Gunter Rambow
DESIGNER
Gunter Rambow
PHOTOGRAPHER
G. Rambow, M. van de Sand
ILLUSTRATOR/ARTIST
Gunter Rambow
CLIENT
Kultaranst der Stadt Kassel
DIRECTOR
Dr. Berndt Nordhoff

2083
ART DIRECTOR
Gunter Rambow, Frankfurt
DESIGNER
Gunter Rambow
PHOTOGRAPHER
G. Rambow, M. van de Sand
CLIENT
S. Fischer Verlag
DIRECTOR
Monika Schoeller
PUBLISHER
Monika Schoeller

2084
ART DIRECTOR
Tadanori Itakura, Osaka
DESIGNER
Tadanori Itakura
PHOTOGRAPHER
Seiichi Tanaka
CLIENT
Tanaka Studio Inc.

2081

2082

2083

2084

2085

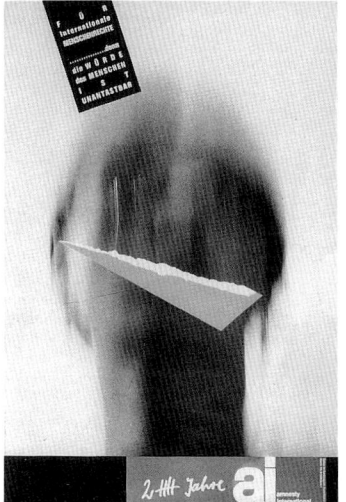

2086

2087

2088

2085
ART DIRECTOR
Kaoru Kasai, Tokyo
DESIGNER
Tetsuo Nishikawa
PHOTOGRAPHER
Yasushi Haiuda
WRITER
Shunichi Iwasaiki
CLIENT
Suntory Co. Ltd

2086
ART DIRECTOR
H.F. Neumann, G.M. Haase
DESIGNER
H.F. Neumann, G.M. Haase
PHOTOGRAPHER
H. F. Neumann
WRITER
Gerda Maria Haase
CLIENT
Amnesty International—Bonn
PUBLISHER
Amnesty International—Bonn
AGENCY
Neumann Kommunikations Design,
Wuppertal, West Germany

2087
ART DIRECTOR
Béla Csoma
DESIGNER
György Kemény
ILLUSTRATOR/ARTIST
György Kemény, Budapest
CLIENT
Mokép (Hungarian Film-Trade)
EDITOR
Mokép (Hungarian Film-Trade)
DIRECTOR
Jozsef Gombár
PUBLISHER
Mokép (Hungarian Film-Trade)

2088
ART DIRECTOR
Kazutami Nishimoto, Tokyo
DESIGNER
Kazutami Nishimoto
PHOTOGRAPHER
Toshiaki Takeuchi
ILLUSTRATOR/ARTIST
Kazutami Nishimoto
CLIENT
Canyon Records

2089
ART DIRECTOR
H.R. Feltus, Düsseldorf
DESIGNER
H.R. Feltus
PHOTOGRAPHER
H.R. Feltus
ILLUSTRATOR/ARTIST
Rolf Isken
WRITER
Rolf Isken
CLIENT
Ste. Trotinette
PUBLISHER
Ste. Trotinette

2089

2090

2090
ART DIRECTOR
Masakazu Tanabe, Nagoya
DESIGNER
Masakazu Tanabe
ILLUSTRATOR/ARTIST
Hiroshi Yoshii
CLIENT
Media Co. Ltd

2091

2091
ART DIRECTOR
Koji Mizutani, Tokyo
DESIGNER
Hirokazu Kurebayashi, Osamu Kitazima
PHOTOGRAPHER
Hiroshi Yoda
CLIENT
PARCO

2092
ART DIRECTOR
Takahisa Kamijyo, Tokyo
DESIGNER
Takahisa Kamijyo
ILLUSTRATOR/ARTIST
Takahisa Kamijyo
CLIENT
Sunshine City Corp.
DIRECTOR
Takahisa Kamijyo

2092

2093
ART DIRECTOR
Agnes Faragó
DESIGNER
Gábor Gyárfás, Budapest
EDITOR
Mokep
DIRECTOR
Cinema Béla
AGENCY
Magyar Hirdető

2094
ART DIRECTOR
O.ASS. Gerhard Frömel
DESIGNER
Ruth Sprenger, Mauthausen, Austria

2093

2094

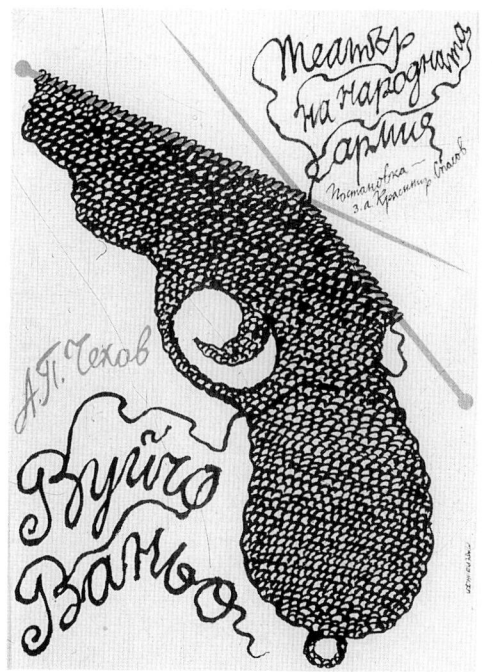

2095
ILLUSTRATOR/ARTIST
Assen Stareischinsky, Sofia, Bulgaria

2096
ILLUSTRATOR/ARTIST
Assen Stareischinsky, Sofia, Bulgaria

2095

2096

2097
ART DIRECTOR
Koichi Sato, Tokyo
DESIGNER
Koichi Sato
ILLUSTRATOR/ARTIST
Koichi Sato
WRITER
Katsuhiko Sasaki
CLIENT
Ohara School of Ikebana
DIRECTOR
Kuni Kizawa

2097

2098

2098
ILLUSTRATOR/ARTIST
Assen Stareischinsky, Sofia, Bulgaria

2099

2099
ART DIRECTOR
Nicolae Corneliu, Bucharest

2100

2100
ART DIRECTOR
Tsuguya Inoue, Tokyo
DESIGNER
Tsuguya Inoue
PHOTOGRAPHER
Cornell Capa
WRITER
Shigesato Itoi
CLIENT
Bungei Shunju Ltd.
COORDINATOR
Kiyoshi Nishikawa

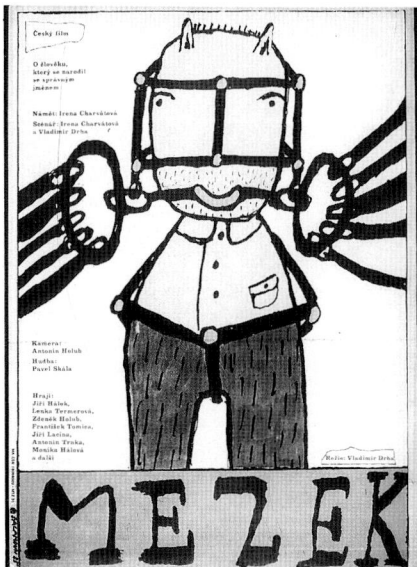

2101

2102

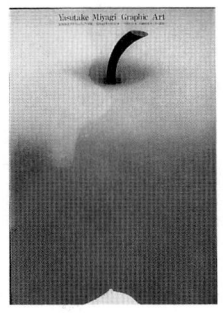

2103

2104

2101
DESIGNER
Jiří Šalamoun
ILLUSTRATOR/ARTIST
Jiří Šalamoun, Prague
CLIENT
Úpf-Film Distributions, Prague
EDITOR
Hana Kalousová
PUBLISHER
ÚPF-Film Distributions, Prague

2102
ART DIRECTOR
Gábor Deák
DESIGNER
Gábor Gyárfás, Budapest
EDITOR
Theater Radnóti
DIRECTOR
András Bálint
PRODUCER
Miklós Slinetár
PUBLICATION
Editrg

2103
ART DIRECTOR
Yasutake Miyagi
DESIGNER
Yasutake Miyagi
ILLUSTRATOR/ARTIST
Yasutake Miyagi
CLIENT
Miyagi Design Studio, Okinawa

2104
ART DIRECTOR
Bruno Monguzzi
DESIGNER
Bruno Monguzzi
PHOTOGRAPHER
Lartigue
WRITER
Bruno Monguzzi
CLIENT
Musée d'Orsay, Paris
DIRECTOR
Jean Jenger
AGENCY
Bruno Monguzzi, Meride, Switzerland
PRODUCER
Léone Nora

2105
ART DIRECTOR
Bruno Monguzzi
DESIGNER
Bruno Monguzzi
PHOTOGRAPHER
Bruno Monguzzi
CLIENT
Al Castello Film Production
DIRECTOR
Heinz Bütler
AGENCY
Bruno Monguzzi , Meride, Switzerland

2106

DESIGNER
Heinz Handschick, Berlin
PUBLISHER
Progress Film-Verleih

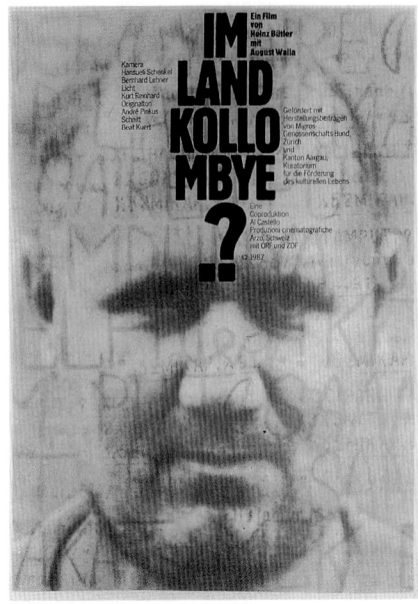

2105

2106

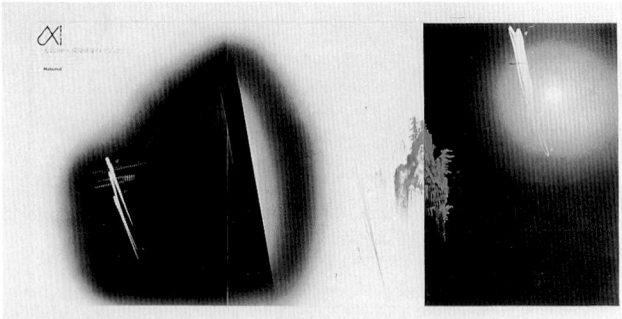

2107

2107
ART DIRECTOR
Koichi Sato, Tokyo; Tsutomu Takada, Osaka
DESIGNER
Tatsushi Hariya
PHOTOGRAPHER
Nobuo Asayama
ILLUSTRATOR/ARTIST
Koichi Sato
WRITER
Koichi Arai
CLIENT
Matsushita Electric Co., Ltd.
DIRECTOR
Hisato Sasaki
AGENCY
Daiko Advertising Inc.
PRODUCER
Yuzo Tsukamoto.

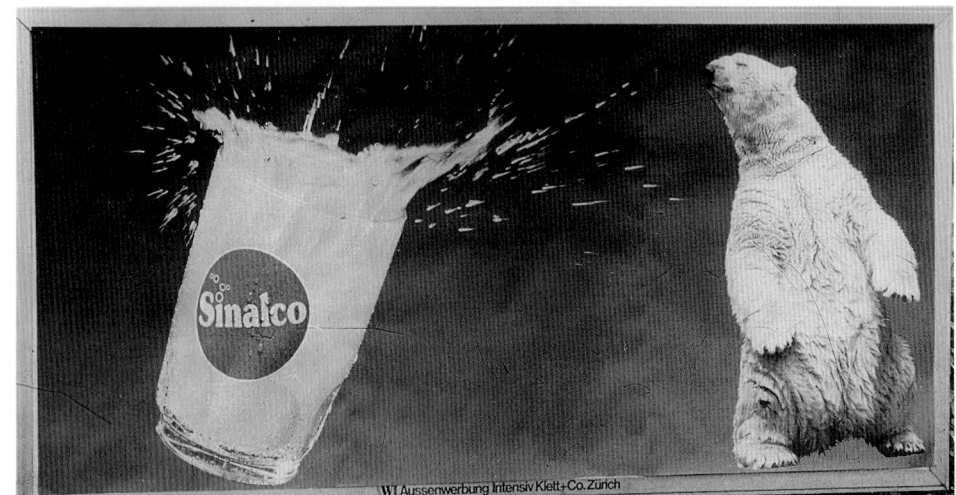

2108

2108
ART DIRECTOR
Ruedi Külling
DESIGNER
Ruedi Külling
PHOTOGRAPHER
Archives
CLIENT
Sibra Management, Fribourg
AGENCY
Advico , Zurich

2109

2111

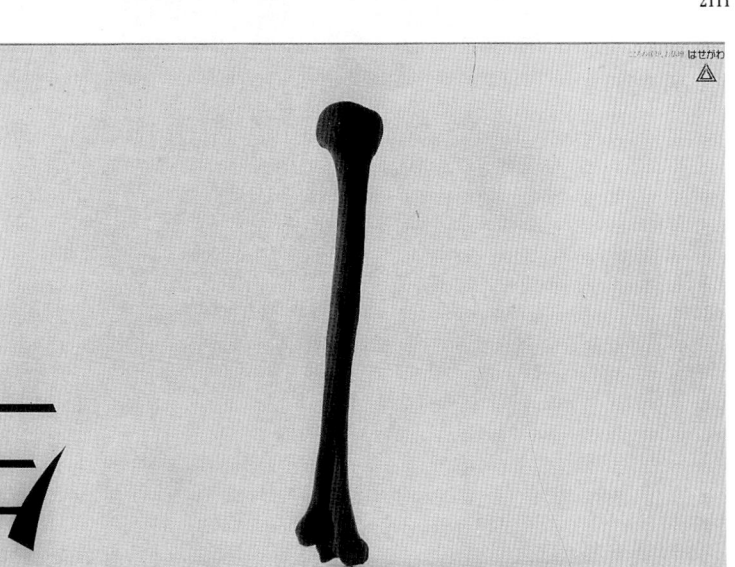

2112

2109
ART DIRECTOR
Koichi Sato, Tokyo
DESIGNER
Koichi Sato
ILLUSTRATOR/ARTIST
Koichi Sato
CLIENT
Uny Co., Ltd.

2110

2110
ART DIRECTOR
Florin Ionescu, Bucharest
DESIGNER
Florin Ionescu
ILLUSTRATOR/ARTIST
Florin Ionescu
CLIENT
Romaniafilm
EDITOR
Romaniafilm

2111
ART DIRECTOR
Tsuguya Inoue, Tokyo
DESIGNER
Tsuguya Inoue
PHOTOGRAPHER
Yoshihiko Ueda
CLIENT
Melrose Co., Ltd.
PRODUCER
Hiroshi Ito

2112
ART DIRECTOR
Makoto Saito, Tokyo
DESIGNER
Minoru Kanda
PHOTOGRAPHER
Kazumi Kurigami
ILLUSTRATOR/ARTIST
Makoto Saito
WRITER
Masayasu Okabe
CLIENT
Hasegawa Co., Ltd.
DIRECTOR
Yoshifumi Nakashima

2113
ART DIRECTOR
Futó Ilona
DESIGNER
Gábor Gyárfás, Budapest
DIRECTOR
Futó Ilona
PUBLISHER
Magyar Hirdetö

2113

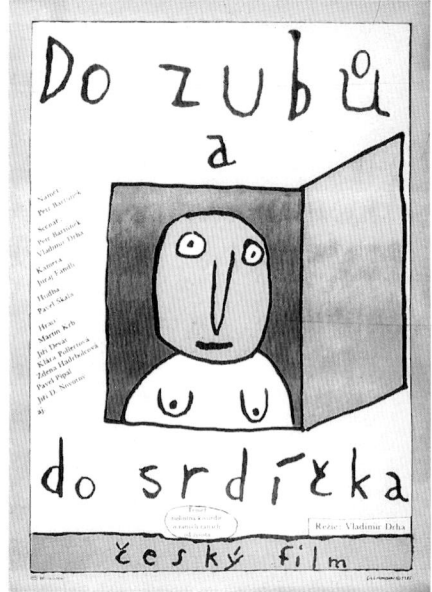

2114

2114
DESIGNER
Jiří Šalamoun
ILLUSTRATOR/ARTIST
Jiří Šalamoun, Prague
CLIENT
Úpf—Film Distributions Prague
DIRECTOR
Hana Kalousová

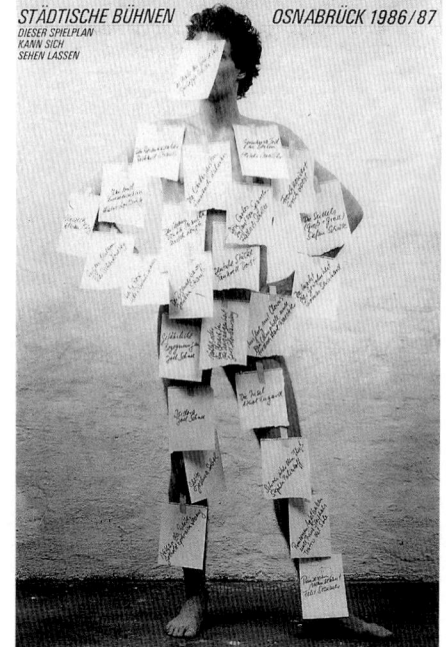

2115
ART DIRECTOR
Dr. E.C. August
DESIGNER
Holger Matthies, Hamburg
PHOTOGRAPHER
Holger Matthies
CLIENT
Städt. Bühnen Osnabruck

2115

2116
DESIGNER
Jiří Šalamoun
ILLUSTRATOR/ARTIST
Jiří Šalamoun, Prague
CLIENT
The Castle Gallery of Kladno, ČSSR

2116

2117

2117
ART DIRECTOR
Masami Shimizu, Tokyo
DESIGNER
Masami Shimizu
PHOTOGRAPHER
Eiichiro Sakata
WRITER
Shigesato Itoi
CLIENT
Ryuko Tsushin Co. Ltd

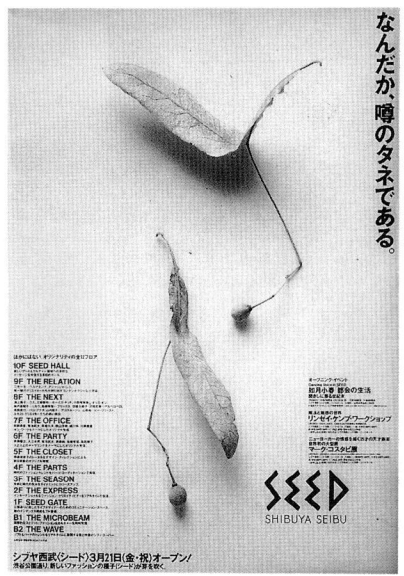

2118

2118
ART DIRECTOR
Tsuguya Inoue
DESIGNER
Tsuguya Inoue
PHOTOGRAPHER
Kazumi Kurigami
WRITER
Shinzo Higurashi
CLIENT
The Seibu Dept. Stores Co., Ltd.

2119

2119
ART DIRECTOR
Jaroslav Fatka
DESIGNER
Jiří Šalamoun
ILLUSTRATOR/ARTIST
Jiří Šalamoun, Prague
WRITER
Vladimír Skrepl
CLIENT
Gallery of the Capitol of Prague
DIRECTOR
Jaroslav Fatka
PUBLISHER
G.H.M.P.
AGENCY
Cultural House of Prague
PRODUCER
Capitol Gallery of Prague

2120
ART DIRECTOR
Susumu Miyazaki
DESIGNER
Takuya Ohnuki
PHOTOGRAPHER
Shintaro Shiratori
ILLUSTRATOR/ARTIST
Amimoto of Choshi Harbor, Haruo Takino
WRITER
Naoya Okada
CLIENT
TOSHIMAEN Inc.
AGENCY
Hakuhodo Incorporated , Tokyo

2120

2121
ART DIRECTOR
Takaharu Matsumoto, Tokyo
DESIGNER
Takaharu Matsumoto
ILLUSTRATOR/ARTIST
Janusz Stanny
CLIENT
Green Peace Publisher Co. Ltd

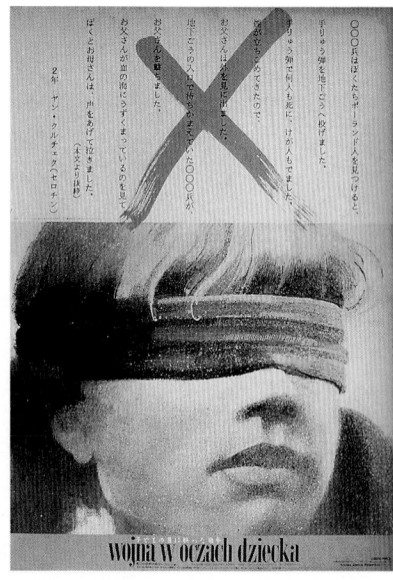

2121

2122
ART DIRECTOR
Tsuguya Inoue, Tokyo
DESIGNER
Tsuguya Inoue
PHOTOGRAPHER
Kazumi Kurigami
WRITER
Shinzo Higurashi
CLIENT
The Seibu Dept. Stores Co., Ltd.

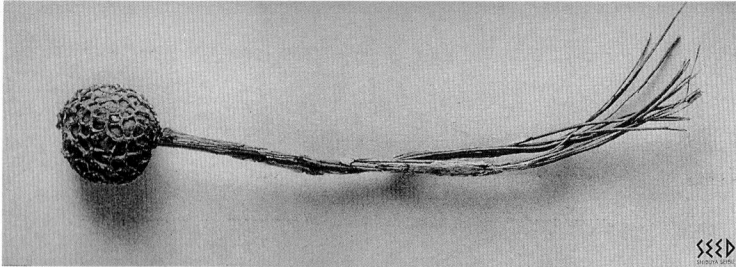
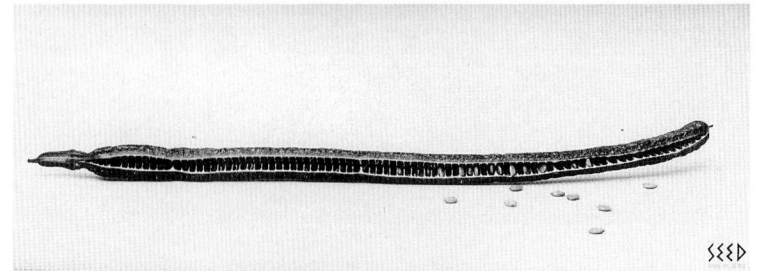

2122

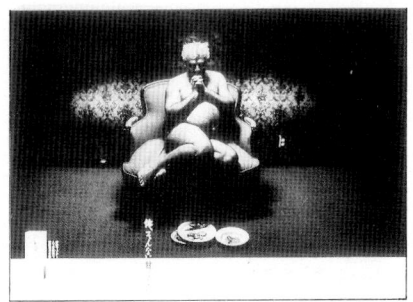

2123

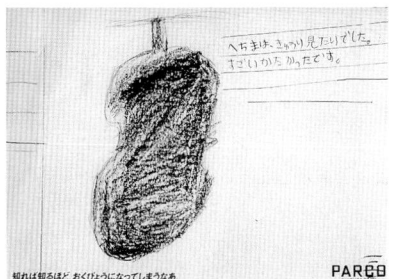

2124

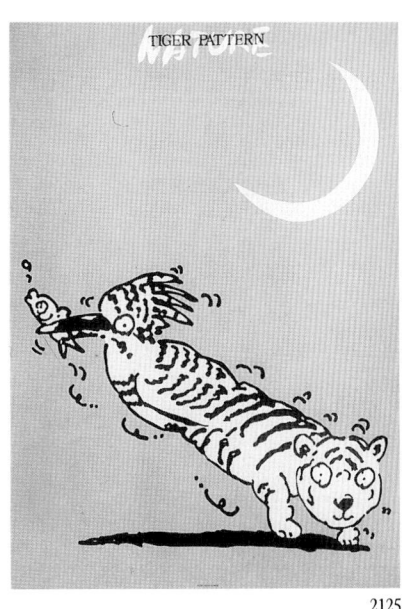

2125

2123
ART DIRECTOR
Iwao Miyanaga
PHOTOGRAPHER
Bishin Jumonji
WRITER
Daisuke Nakatsuka
CLIENT
Hayashibara Biochemical Laboratories Inc.
CREATIVE DIRECTOR
Daisuke Nakatsuka, Tokyo

2124
ART DIRECTOR
Tsuguya Inoue
DESIGNER
Tsuguya Inoue
PHOTOGRAPHER
Eiichiro Sakata
WRITER
Takashi Nakahata
CLIENT
Parco Co., Ltd.

2125
ART DIRECTOR
Takashi Akiyama, Tokyo
DESIGNER
Takashi Akiyama
ILLUSTRATOR/ARTIST
Takashi Akiyama

2126
ART DIRECTOR
Masato Watanabe, Kanagawa, Japan
DESIGNER
Masato Watanabe
PHOTOGRAPHER
Hiroo Watanabe
WRITER
Tomoko Inoue

 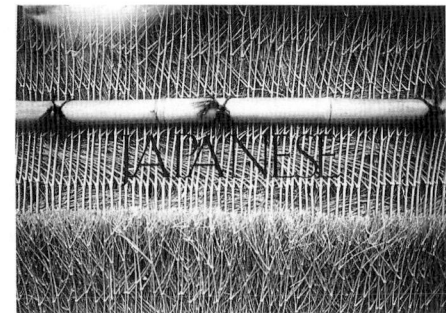

2126

 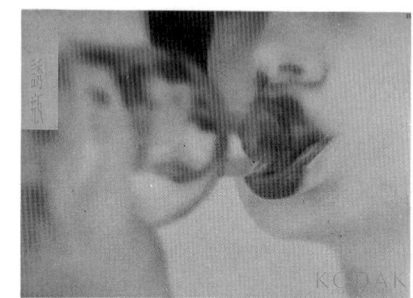

2127

2127
ART DIRECTOR
Junichiro Morita
DESIGNER
Junichiro Morita
PHOTOGRAPHER
Hiroshi Yoda, Sachiko Kuru
WRITER
Eisaku Sekihashi
CLIENT
Kodak Nagase KK
AGENCY
J. Walter Thompson Company Japan , Tokyo

 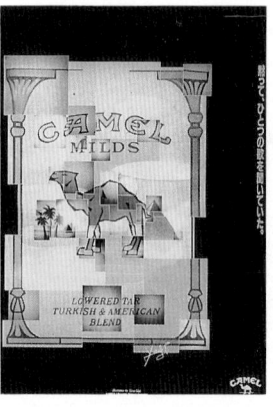 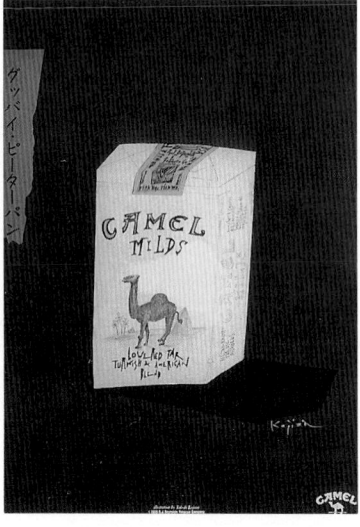

2128

2128
ART DIRECTOR
Michio Nakahara
DESIGNER
Michio Nakahara
ILLUSTRATOR/ARTIST
Takeshi Kojima, Yasuo Yagi, Ten Tomizwa
WRITER
Naoyuki Ito
CLIENT
R.J. Renolds Tobacco Company
AGENCY
McCann-Erickson Hakuhodo, Tokyo

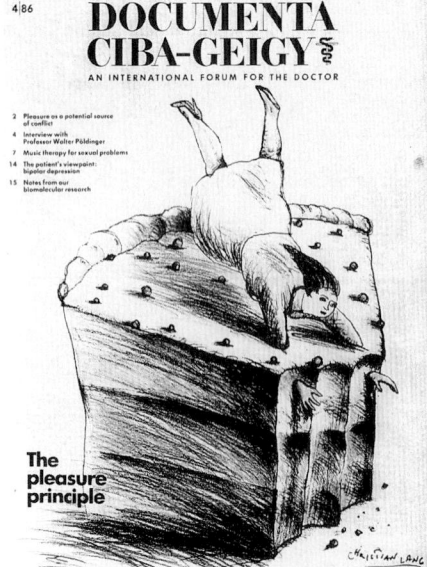  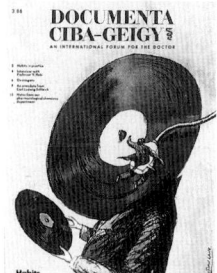

2129
ART DIRECTOR
Christian Lang
DESIGNER
Christian Lang
ILLUSTRATOR/ARTIST
Christian Lang
WRITER
Werner Kayser
CLIENT
CIBA-GEIGY Pharma
AGENCY
Werbung CIBA-GEIGY, Basle, Switzerland

2129

2130

ART DIRECTOR
Hans-Georg Pospischil
DESIGNER
Bernadette Gotthardt
ILLUSTRATOR/ARTIST
Hans Hillmann
PUBLISHER
Dr. Bruno Dechamps
PUBLICATION
Frankfurter Allgemeine Magazin, Frankfurt

2131

ART DIRECTOR
Hans Georg Pospischil
ILLUSTRATOR/ARTIST
Hans Hillmann, Frankfurt
WRITER
Klaus Harpprecht
CLIENT
Frankfurter Allgemeine
EDITOR
Bruno Dechamps
DIRECTOR
Thomas Schröder

2130

2131

2132

ART DIRECTOR
Oswaldo Miranda, Curitiba, Brazil
ILLUSTRATOR/ARTIST
Rubem Grilo

2132

2133

2133

ART DIRECTOR
Oswaldo Miranda, Curitiba, Brasil
ILLUSTRATOR/ARTIST
Chichohi

2134

ART DIRECTOR
Giulio C. Italiani
DESIGNER
Franco Italiani
ILLUSTRATOR/ARTIST
Sergio Tappa, Zurich
WRITER
Edgar Allan Poe
EDITOR
Gruppo Editoriale Leader
PRODUCER
Giulio C. Italiani

2134

2135

ART DIRECTOR
Christof Gassner
DESIGNER
Isolde Monson-Baumgart, Frankfurt
ILLUSTRATOR/ARTIST
Isolde Monson-Baumgart
CLIENT
ÖKO-TEST Verlag GmbH
PUBLISHER
ÖKO-TEST Magazine

2135

2136

2136
DESIGNER
David Lancashire
ILLUSTRATOR/ARTIST
Fay Plamka, East. St. Kilda, Australia
AGENCY
David Lancashire Design

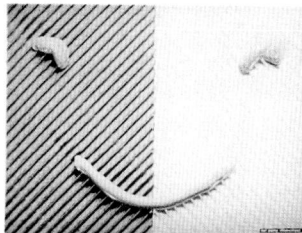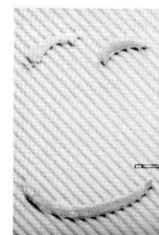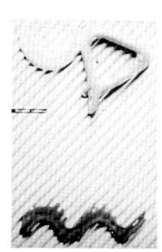

2137

2137
ART DIRECTOR
Ryoji Fujisaki, Tokyo
DESIGNER
Ryoji Fujisaki
PHOTOGRAPHER
Tamotsu Kawaguchi
ILLUSTRATOR/ARTIST
Ryoji Fujisaki
CLIENT
Seibu Tsukashin Department Store
PRODUCER
Akio Okumura

2138

2138
ART DIRECTOR
Sebastian Sancho
ILLUSTRATOR/ARTIST
Hermenegildo Sábat, Buenos Aires
EDITOR
Miguel Brascó
PUBLICATION
Pautas y Contraseñas

2139
ART DIRECTOR
Sigi Mayer
DESIGNER
Sigi Mayer
PHOTOGRAPHER
Horst Stasny, Pasching/Linz, Austria
CLIENT
Laska Repro
PUBLISHER
Modern Times, Linz, Austria
AGENCY
Die Agentur, Linz, Austria

2139

2140
DESIGNER
Wolfgang Hohndorf
PHOTOGRAPHER
Wolfgang Hohndorf, Düsseldorf
CLIENT
Select Magazin
PUBLISHER
Select Magazin

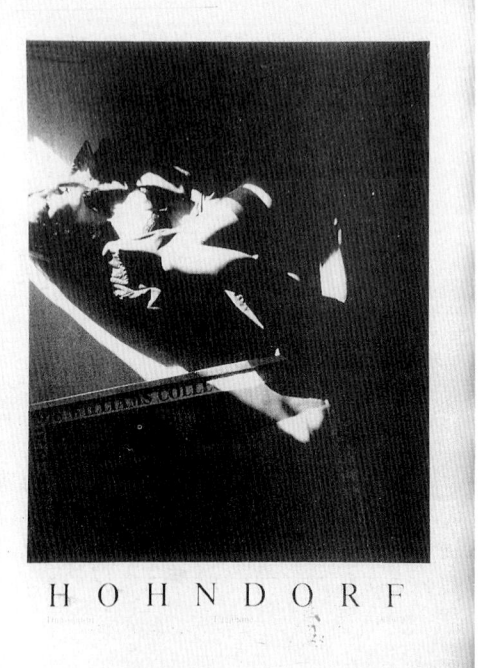

HOHNDORF

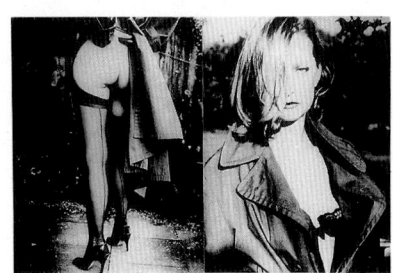

2140

2141

2141

ART DIRECTOR
David Colby, Willi Moser
PHOTOGRAPHER
Wolfgang Hohndorf
CLIENT
The Manipulator, Düsseldorf
PUBLISHER
The Manipulator, Düsseldorf

2142

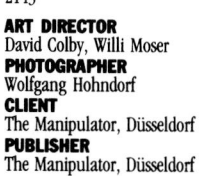

2143

2142

2143

ART DIRECTOR
David Colby, Willi Moser
PHOTOGRAPHER
Wolfgang Hohndorf
CLIENT
The Manipulator, Düsseldorf
PUBLISHER
The Manipulator, Düsseldorf

ART DIRECTOR
David Colby, Willi Moser
PHOTOGRAPHER
Wolfgang Hohndorf
CLIENT
The Manipulator, Düsseldorf
PUBLISHER
The Manipulator, Düsseldorf

2144

2144

ART DIRECTOR
David Colby, Willi Moser
PHOTOGRAPHER
Wolfgang Hohndorf
CLIENT
The Manipulator, Düsseldorf
PUBLISHER
The Manipulator, Düsseldorf

2146

ART DIRECTOR
Morton Kirschner
WRITER
Henk Roozendaal
CLIENT
IBM Nederland
DIRECTOR
Gidi van Liempd
AGENCY
GGK Amsterdam
PRODUCER
Carl Tewes

2147

ART DIRECTOR
Hector Tortallano, Ric Wylie, Sue Solie
WRITER
Sue Reed
CLIENT
Eastman Kodak International
AGENCY
J. Walter Thompson, Sao Paulo and New York
CREATIVE DIRECTOR
Sue Reed

2146

CANAL
15-second
If you want to know more about automation, talk with IBM.
Because IBM is more than computers and word processing.
IBM is ideas.
Ideas that help people to do their work faster and more accurately.
Ideas that help people get more pleasure in their work.
A: Do you know why they're still working next door?
B: No idea!

2147

AZUL
30-second
VO: New Kodacolor VR-G film. See a new color.
SINGERS: Blue, blue . . . Kodak just changed blue.
VO: With new Kodacolor VR-G film, blue has never been as blue.
SINGERS: Blue, blue, blue . . .
Kodak just changed blue.
Kodak is color.

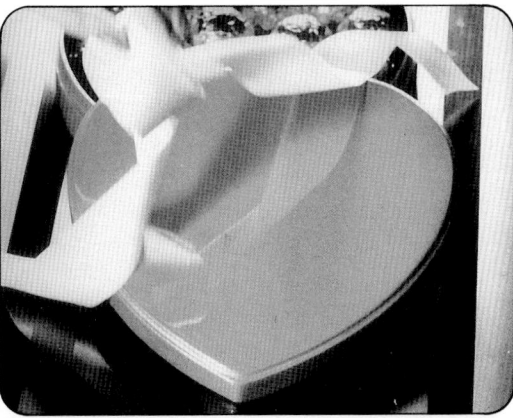

2148
ART DIRECTOR
Hector Tortallano, Ric Wylie, Sue
Solie
WRITER
Sue Reed
CLIENT
Eastman Kodak International
AGENCY
J. Walter Thompson, Sao Paulo and
New York
CREATIVE DIRECTOR
Sue Reed

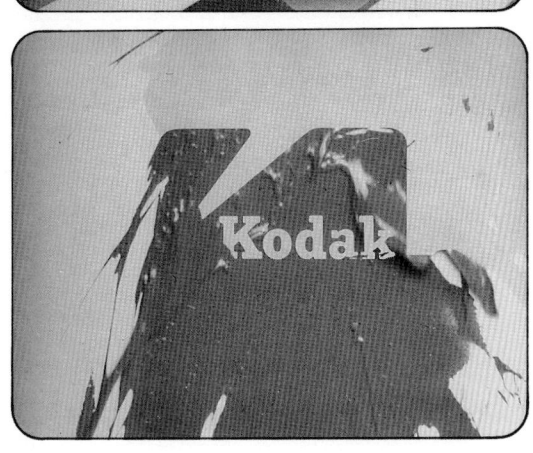

2149
ART DIRECTOR
Hector Tortallano, Ric Wyle, Sue
Solie
WRITER
Sue Reed
CLIENT
Eastman Kodak International
AGENCY
J. Walter Thompson, Sao Paulo and
New York
CREATIVE DIRECTOR
Sue Reed

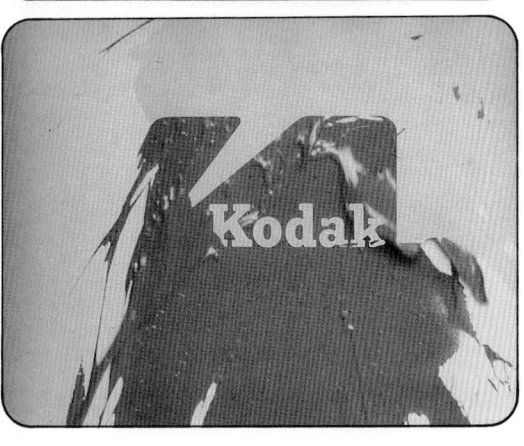

2148

AMARILLO
30-second
VO:New Kodacolor VR-G film. See a new color.
SINGERS: Yellow, yellow, yellow. Kodak just changed yellow.
VO: With new Kodacolor VR-G film, yellow has never been as yellow.
SINGERS: Yellow, yellow, yellow . . . Kodak just changed yellow. Kodak is color.

2149

ROJO
30-second
VO: New Kodacolor VR-G film. See a new color.
SINGERS: Red, red, red . . .
VO: Red has never been as red.
SINGERS: Kodak just changed red.
VO: With new Kodacolor VR-G film.
SINGERS: Red, red, red . . .
Kodak just changed red.
Kodak is color.

2150

ART DIRECTOR
Digby Atkinson
WRITER
Tim Mellors
CLIENT
The Independent
EDITOR
Dave Garland
DIRECTOR
Graham Rose
AGENCY
Saatchi & Saatchi Compton, Ltd,
London
PRODUCER
Arnold Pearce

2151

WRITER
Jürgen Braun
CLIENT
Ford Werke AG
EDITOR
Derik Williams
DIRECTOR
Ben Oyne
AGENCY
Young & Rubicam, Frankfurt
PRODUCER
Dieter Losch

2150

OPINIONS
30-second
MAN (POMPOUS): In our opinion (RAP), in our opinion (RAP), in our
opinion (RAP), in our opinion (RAP) in our opinion . . .
WOMAN (STRIDENT): BUT in our opinion (RAP), in our opinion (RAP),
in our opinion (RAP), in our opinion (RAP), in our opinion (RAP) . . .
2ND MAN: AND in our opinion (RAP).
MVO: On October 7th the first new quality daily newspaper in 131 years
will be on the newsstands.
Financially independent, intellectually independent, editorially independent
and politically independent.
From October 7th.
The Independent.
It is. Are you?

2151

GIRL FRIENDS
45-second
The Ford Fiesta Diesel only consumes 3,8 1 per 100 kms, that means with
one tank full of gas you can drive from Frankfurt to Cologne.And back to
Frankfurt, and to Cologne again. Back to Frankfurt. Return to Cologne
and back again to . . . Frankfurt. Of course this only works, when you go
at a constant speed of 90 kms/hour.

2152
ART DIRECTOR
Ian Blake
WRITER
Eugene Hardy
CLIENT
Beechams SA.
AGENCY
Grey Phillips, Bunton, Mundel &
Blake, Sandown, South Africa

2153
ART DIRECTOR
Zelda Malan
WRITER
Tim Mellors
CLIENT
French Connection
EDITOR
Peter Beston
DIRECTOR
Willie Patterson
AGENCY
Saatchi & Saatchi Compton Ltd.,
London
PRODUCER
Arnold Pearce

2152

BUTTERFLY
30-second
MUSICAL MOOD AMBIENCE THROUGHOUT
SFX: AT APPROPRIATE MOMENTS, SPLASHES, DEEP BREATHS IN SHARP
EXHALATIONS
MVO: In your mind you've set yourself a goal. But to achieve it takes hard
work, and every scrap of energy you can dredge up. You push yourself
until your muscles feel like lead, until your chest burns and your heart
pounds with exhaustion.
When you've earned a rest . . .
. . . there's nothing more refreshing . . .
than Lucozade.
Locozade is rich in glucose
. . . to replace lost energy.
Giving you the strength to carry on . . .
SFX: UUUUUGH!
. . . until you've reached your goal.

2153

REVOLVING DOOR
30-second
SFX: FRENCH CONNECTION MUSIC.
VO: French Connection. Clothes you can't wait to get into.

2154
ART DIRECTOR
Norman Lam
WRITER
Eugene Hardy
CLIENT
Robertsons
AGENCY
Grey Phillips Bunton Mundel &
Blake, Sandown, South Africa

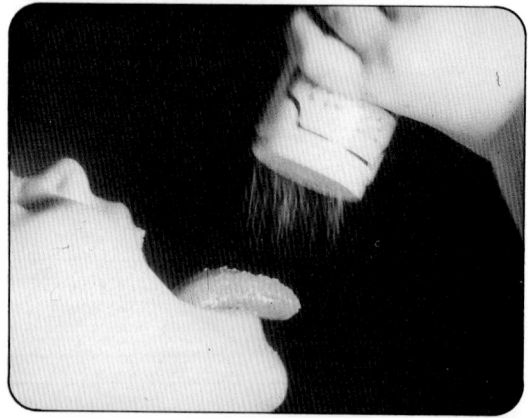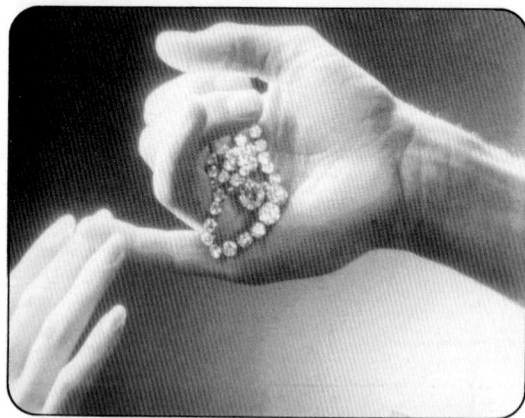

2155
ART DIRECTOR
Reiko Koike
PHOTOGRAPHER
Masamitsu Yokusuka
WRITER
Naoki Watanabe
CLIENT
De Beers Consolidated Mine
EDITOR
Soichi Kimura
DIRECTOR
Soichi Kimura
PRODUCER
Seiichi Takahashi
AGENCY
J. Walter Thompson Company
Japan, Tokyo

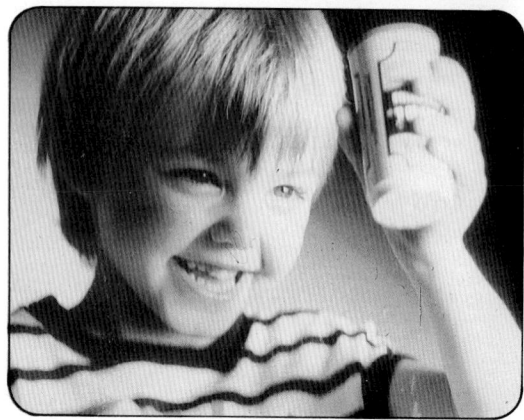

2154

AROMAT BLACK
30-second
JINGLE: Food fills my tummy
But what makes it yummy . . .
Is shake Aromat shake!
Arorice!
Aromealie!
Shake up the taste with a shake of Aromat.
Food's ok
but it's a real hooray
With shake Aromat shake.
Aroeggs!
Arochips!
Shake up the taste with a shake of Aromat.

2155

HANDS
30-second
MUSIC
VO: More profound than words: Diamonds

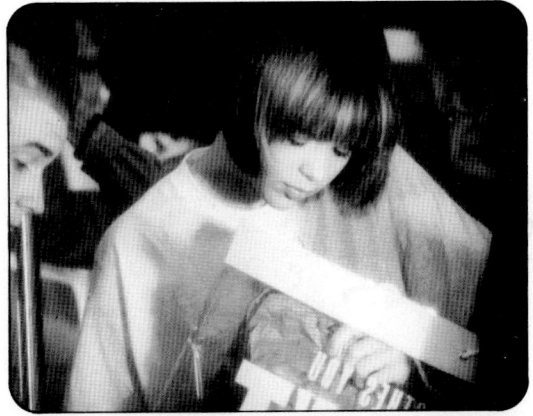

2156
ART DIRECTOR
Zelda Malan
WRITER
Tim Mellors
CLIENT
French Connection
EDITOR
Simon Laurie
DIRECTOR
Willie Patterson
AGENCY
Saatchi & Saatchi Compton Ltd.,
London
PRODUCER
Arnold Pearce

2157
ART DIRECTOR
Toni Guasch
CLIENT
Sanyo España; S.A. /VCR
AGENCY
Tandem DDB Campmany Guasch,
S.A., Barcelona
PRODUCER
Gemma Soler
PRODUCTION COMPANY
Albiñana Films
CREATIVE DIRECTOR
Toni Guasch

2156

TUBE
30-second
SFX: MUSIC & NATURAL SOUNDS OF TUBE.
VO: French Connection. Clothes you can't wait to get into.

2157

MEXICO
30-second
Do you know who invented the first video-cassette of ½ inch?
And the first home videocassette recorder with four heads.
Do you know which Company has been awarded by the Japanese
Government for its video technology?
And which brand has made video equipment affordable?
And do you know which brand has created a special model for the Soccer
World Cup of Mexico?
Sanyo, the first technology in video.

2158

ART DIRECTOR
Ian Blake, Howard Smiedt
WRITER
Eugene Hardy
CLIENT
S. Wainstein
AGENCY
Grey, Phillips, Bunton, Mundel &
Blake, Sandown, South Africa

2159

ART DIRECTOR
Toni Guasch
CLIENT
Sanyo España
AGENCY
Tandem DDB Campmany Guasch,
S.A., Barcelona
PRODUCER
Gemma Soler
PRODUCTION COMPANY
Albiñana Films
CREATIVE DIRECTOR
Toni Guasch

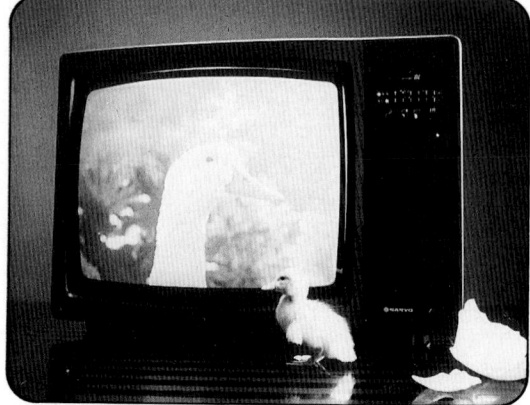

2158

TASTIC—CHINESE
30-second
MVO: Chinese Tastic Fan See Foo.
MR. F: (IN CHINESE) Talks about the beauty of Chinese cooking.
MVO: See Foo . . . tell us a little about the Tastic . . . How it's
guaranteed to cook up perfectly fluffy and white?
MR. F: (IN CHINESE TALKS ABOUT HOW FRESH THE VEGETABLES ARE
AND THAT THE FINISHED DISH IS GOING TO BE WONDERFUL—AND
DON'T WORRY ABOUT THE RICE)
MVO: Oh really?
MVO: He says don't worry about the Tastic . . . let's concentrate on the
cooking.
MVO: See Foo . . . surely there's something to say about Tastic?
MR. F: OK Lemembr if you want to be fantastic, must be Tastic. Tank
you.

2159

DUCK
30-second
Present company excepted, we introduce you to the new TV sets:
Sanyo Metallic.
With remote control at reach.
Electronic memory with 16 programs.
Hi-Fi sound with two loudspeakers.
Present company excepted,
new color TV sets Sanyo.

2160
ART DIRECTOR
Peter Gibb
PHOTOGRAPHER
Peter Lavery
WRITER
Richard Myers
CLIENT
Allied National Brands
DIRECTOR
John Marles
AGENCY
Saatchi & Saatchi Compton Ltd.,
London
PRODUCER
Louise Kidman

2161
ART DIRECTOR
Mike Chu
WRITER
Delia Oakins, Betty Choi
CLIENT
Crocodile Garments Ltd.
EDITOR
Nelson Ng/PPS
DIRECTOR
Louis Ng
AGENCY
Synergie/Hong Kong
PRODUCER
Mike Chu, Hydi Chan

2160

WIFE
40-second
MAN: I've been wonderin' Arlene, would you marry again if I died?
WOMAN: Probably.
MAN: Would you still live here?
WOMAN: Yeah I reckon.
MAN: Would you sleep . . . in the same bed?
WOMAN: Why not?
MAN: Well, would you let him drink me stock of Castlemaine XXXX then?
WOMAN: Course I would.
He doesn't drink anything else.
MVO: Australian's wouldn't give a Castlemaine XXXX for anything else.

2161

LONG HOT CITY SUMMER
30-second
MVO: A lazy summer with Crocodile hot . . . so hot . . . too hot . . . The long, hot, city summer . . . A Crocodile summer with hot spells to make you take it off, show off . . .
You can feel when summer hits Cos summer sits . . . waiting for you to indulge in it.
Summer with Crocodile. It's hot . . . It's here . . .

2162
ART DIRECTOR
Hans Goedicke
WRITER
Rob Floor
CLIENT
CPC Benelux B.V.
AGENCY
Snabilie, Goedicke, Floor,
Amsterdam
PRODUCER
Pim Bentinck, Movieventures

2163
ART DIRECTOR
Gerard v.d. Hart
WRITER
Ron Walvisch
DIRECTOR
Frans Weisz
AGENCY
Noordervliet & Winninghoff/Leo
Burnett, Amsterdam
PRODUCER
Frits Harkema

 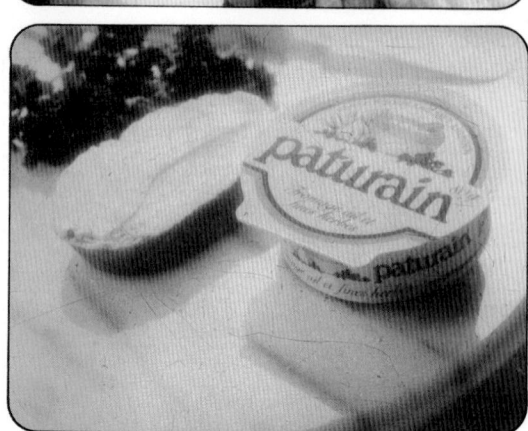

2162

DEXTRO ENERGY
30-second
From time to time we all feel our concentration lapse.
Or we have a bit of an off day.
The reason's often very simple: not enough dextrose.
You see, not enough dextrose means not enough fuel.
But your troubles are over with Dextro Energy: the tasty energy source.
Dextro Energy gives you that little bit extra in no time.

2163

PATURAIN
30-second
Ou est le Paturain?
Ou est le Paturain?
Ou est le Paturain?
Ou est le Paturain?
Ou est le Paturain?
Ou est le Paturain?
VO: Yes, whenever the French enjoy themselves, you'll find Paturain on
the table.
Because no other cheese is so creamy and easy to spread as Paturain,
made with the very finest herbs.
In fact the French aren't quite themselves without Paturain.
Ou es le Paturain?
Ah! S'il vous plait le Paturain.

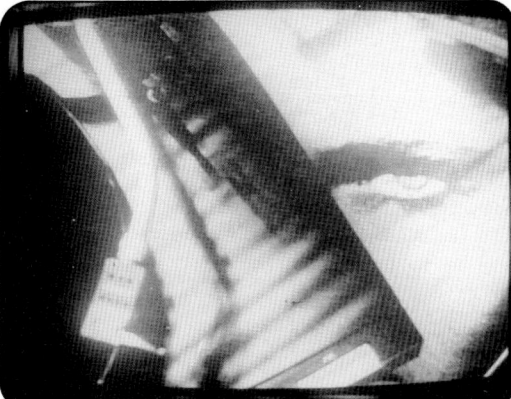

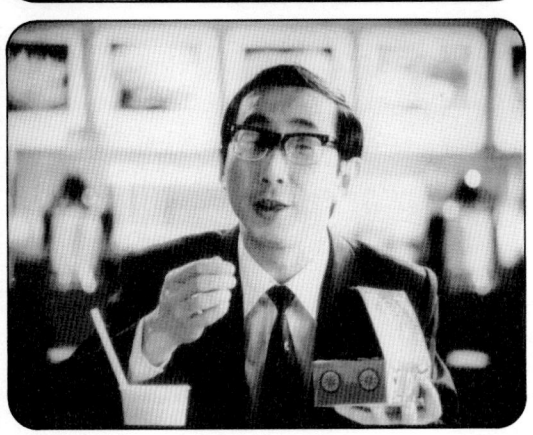

2164
ART DIRECTOR
Norbert Herold
WRITER
Dirk Gutzeit
CLIENT
McDonald's System of Germany
EDITOR
Karl-Heinz Danguillier
AGENCY
Heye, Needham & Partner, Munich
PRODUCER
Dirk Gutzeit, Stephanie Klein
PRODUCTION COMPANY
PPM, Munich

2165
ART DIRECTOR
Mike Rossi
WRITER
Mike Freedman
CLIENT
Edgars
AGENCY
Venture Freedman & Rossi/BBDO,
Sandton, South Africa

2164

CHICKEN MCNUGGETS SHANGHAI
30-second
CHINESE MAN: (SPEAKS GERMAN WITH STRONG CHINESE ACCENT)
Hello!
Right now, McDonald's has something really terrific.
Chicken McNuggets Shanghai.
With 4 delicious sauces . . .
soy,
hot and spicy Kung Fu,
curry,
and sweet and sour.
With Chopsticks!
SONG: I've got a taste for McDonalds'
and Chicken McNuggets Shanghai!
CHINESE MAN: They're also good without chopsticks!

2165

SHAKING HEADS
30-second
SHAKING HEADS LYRICS: When I wear
When I wear my shaking heads
I getta lot
getta lot of shaking heads
I don't care
I don't care what you say
Shake your head
Shake your head
Go and shake your head, Shaking heads
CHORUS: Oooh oooh oooh
When I wear
When I wear my shaking heads
I getta lot
getta lot of shaking heads
I don't care
I don't care what people say
Shake your head
Shake your head
Go and shake your head, Shaking heads
CHORUS: Oooh oooh oooh

2166

ART DIRECTOR
Brian Searle-Tripp
WRITER
Jonathan Shubitz
CLIENT
Volkswagen of South Africa
EDITOR
Roger Harrison
DIRECTOR
David Cornell
AGENCY
Peter Gird, O&M RS-T&M, Cape
Town, South Africa
PRODUCER
David Feldman

 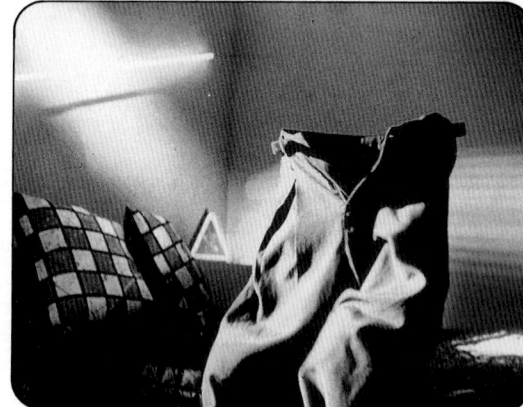

2167

ART DIRECTOR
Heinz Mennecken
DESIGNER
Steve Hendrickson
PHOTOGRAPHER
Robert Liiv
WRITER
Mario Baier
CLIENT
Grundig AG
EDITOR
Mark Scott, Larry Plastrik
DIRECTOR
Richard Greenberg
AGENCY
Heye, Needham & Partner, Munich
PRODUCER
Janet Fox
PRODUCTION COMPANY
R/Greenberg Assoc.

2166

SAREL AND SAREL
30-second
NATURAL SFX.
SAREL: I'm lucky enough to be able to drive only the cars that I like.
And I like this car.
It's extremely driveable.
With all that under-the-skin engineering you expect from a German
machine.
It sticks to the road like boerewors to a braai grid. Watch this.
There aren't too many cars you can do that in.

2167

GLAD RAGS
60-second
SCRIPT: GRUNDIG HIFI!

2168
ART DIRECTOR
Barry Bromley
WRITER
Barry Bromley
CLIENT
Nissan New Zealand
DIRECTOR
Peter Avery
AGENCY
D'Arcy Masius Benton & Bowles,
Auckland
PRODUCER
Tom Baragwanath
ACCOUNT DIRECTOR
Andrew Mazey

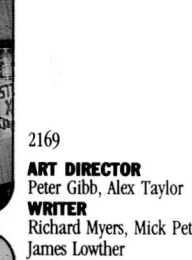

2169
ART DIRECTOR
Peter Gibb, Alex Taylor
WRITER
Richard Myers, Mick Petherick,
James Lowther
CLIENT
Allied National Brands
DIRECTOR
John Marles
AGENCY
Saatchi & Saatchi Compton Ltd,
London
PRODUCER
Louise Kidman

2168

PATROL
60-second
When Alec Metcalfe ordered his new Nissan, he had his reasons.
But there is one reason he may just have overlooked and that is that the
same Japanese technology that built his Patrol is why Nissan is Japan's
number one in Europe, and that is going to make Alec a very happy man.
VOICE OVER: Nissan—The Drive of Europe Through The Technology of
Japan.

2169

SHERRY
30-second
SFX: MOSSIES BUZZING.
STOREKEEPER: So there's going to be a few of you out shearing this time
then.
SFX: SUSPENSION CREAKING.
STOREKEEPER: Something for the ladies.
TRUCK OWNER: Oh yeah. Two bottles of sweet sherry . . .
TRUCK OWNER: Looks like we've over done it with the sherry.
STOREKEEPER: Yeah.
MVO: Australian's wouldn't give a Castlemaine XXXX for anything else.

2170

ART DIRECTOR
Ian Blake
WRITER
Eugene Hardy
CLIENT
Beechams South Africa
AGENCY
Grey Phillips, Bunton, Mundel &
Blake, Sandown, South Africa

2171

ART DIRECTOR
Hector Tortallano, Ric Wylie, Sue
Solie
WRITER
Sue Reed
CLIENT
Eastman Kodak International
AGENCY
J. Walter Thompson, Sao Paulo and
New York
CREATIVE DIRECTOR
Sue Reed

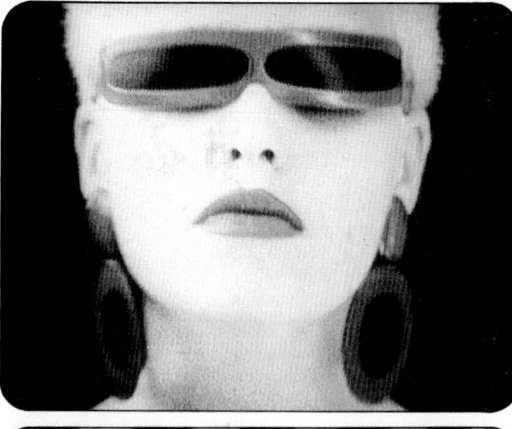

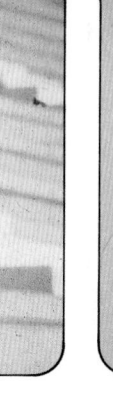

2170

BLACK SPRINTER
30-second
MUSICAL MOOD AMBIENCE THROUGHOUT.
SFX: AT APPROPRIATE MOMENTS, BREATHING, GASPS AND PANTS ARE
MIXED INTO VO.
MVO: In your mind you've got goals which you have set for yourself. But
to achieve them you need to use a lot of energy. Yet the energy gets used
up, and you exert yourself to a point of your muscles quivering through
exhaustion, you can feel your chest burn and your throat dry as a bone.
When you've finally needed to rest . . .
. . . there is nothing more refreshing
. . . than Locozade
Lucozade is rich with glucose.
. . . so that you can replace the energy which has been used up.
So as to give you the strength to carry on . . .
SFX: UUUUGH
. . . until you've reached your goal.

2171

ROJO
30-second
VO: New Kodacolor VR-G film. See a new color.
SINGERS: Red, red, red . . .
VO: Red has never been as red.
SINGERS: Kodak just changed red.
VO: With new Kodacolor VR-G film.
SINGERS: Red, red, red . . .
Kodak just changed red.
Kodak is color.

2172
ART DIRECTOR
Ron Collins
ANIMATOR
Richard Williams, London
WRITER
Andrew Rutherford
CLIENT
News U.K.
EDITOR
Nick Fletcher
DIRECTOR
Richard Williams
AGENCY
Wight Collins Rutherford Scott
PRODUCER
Karen Egan
MUSIC
Ken Emrys-Roberts

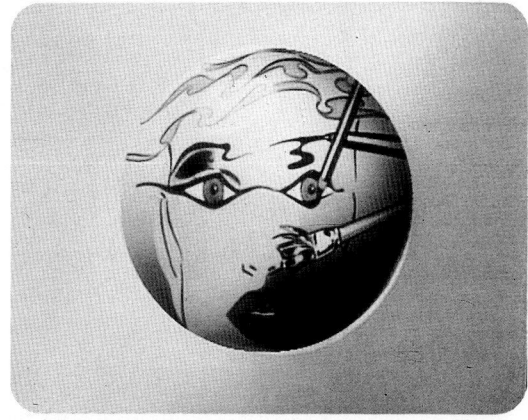

2173
ART DIRECTOR
Barry O'Riordan, Thames
Television, Middlesex, England
PHOTOGRAPHER
Mike Cumpper
PRODUCER
Kate Marlow
ROSTRUM CAMERA
Vic Cummings

2172

TODAY WITHOUT BIAS

No script.

2173

SPLASH

No script.

YEAR END REVIEW THE ART DIRECTORS CLUB

Norman Rockwell's self-portrait, "Artist Faced
With Blank Canvas," appeared on the cover of
the October 8, 1938, Saturday Evening Post.
Although not a trademark or logo, it is a
definitive and timeless symbol of frustrated
creativity.

ED BRODSKY
President, The Art Directors Club

These past two years have been extremely active ones for the Art Directors Club.

We of course, have moved into our new 8,000 square-foot headquarters located at 250 Park Avenue South at the corner of 20th Street. We are at the center of what's been called "The New Madison Avenue." The Club's new space is magnificent! If you haven't seen it yet, I urge you to visit us soon. You are going to be very impressed.

All of the Club's activities have been and are still going strong. During the last two years, our Portfolio Review Committee has seen over six-hundred art students. Our Wednesday Lunch Programs have featured a superstar line-up of speakers and the Tuesday Jazz Concerts are still shaking the rafters! As of this writing, our new gallery has already had fourteen major exhibitions. In the last year alone, our Visual Communicators Education Fund has given $11,000 to twenty-five talented art students. We've also given $1,000 to the Herb Lubalin Study Center at the Cooper Union. In addition, we've successfully launched our First Annual International Exhibition this year.

During the past year, 128 people have joined the Art Directors Club. That's more than twice the amount of the previous year. Think about that. It means that every other business day last year, one of you has become a member of the Art Directors Club. We now have over nine-hundred members worldwide!

The Art Directors Club has been very fortunate. We've had lots of terrific help. From Diane Moore, our Executive Director, her sensational staff, the wonderfully enthusiastic Committee Chairpeople and a very active club membership. I've also been very fortunate. When you elected me your President, you also elected into office what I think is the best and hardest working Board of Directors the Club has ever had.

Thank you for allowing me the privilege of serving as your President these past two years. It has been an experience and honor I will treasure for the rest of my life.

ART DIRECTORS CLUB BOARD OF DIRECTORS

Officers
Ed Brodsky, President
Kurt Haiman, First Vice President
Jack Tauss, Second Vice President
Gladys Barton, Secretary
Richard Wilde, Treasurer
Jack Odette, Assistant Secretary/Treasurer

Executive Committee
Robert Best
Steven Heller
B. Martin Pedersen
Len Sirowitz
Shinichiro Tora
Jessica Weber

ADVISORY BOARD

Gordon Aymar
Frank Baker
Robert H. Blattner
William P. Brockmeier
William H. Buckley
John Peter
Stuart Campbell
David Davidian
Louis Dorfsman
Walter Grotz

John Jamison
Walter Kaprielian
Andrew Kner
George Lois
Garret Orr
Eileen Hedy Schultz
Paul Smith
Robert S. Smith
William Taubin

COMMITTEES AND CHAIRPEOPLE

Agency Relations	Kurt Haiman
Awards Judging	Bill McCaffery
International Judging	Karl H. Steinbrenner
Awards Presentation	Roy Grace
Gallery	Richard Wilde
Hall of Fame Selection	Amil Gargano
Hall of Fame Patrons	Sam Scali
Hall of Fame Management	William Buckley
	Jack Tauss
Membership	Sal Lazzarotti
Newsletter	Ruth Lubell
Portfolio Review	Richard MacFarlane
	Sal Lazzarotti
Luncheon	Dorothy Wachtenheim
	Dick Smith
Traveling Show	Minoru Morita
Members Events	Amy Goldman
	Gladys Barton
Constitution	Jack Jamison
Finance	Jack Odette

The Art Directors Club 66th Annual Awards

Chairman, 66th Annual Awards
William McCaffery

Judges of The 66th Annual Exhibition

Section Chairmen
Advertising, Sal Bue and Meg Crane
Editorial, Alan Peckolick
Promotion, Jessica Weber
Books, Dorothy Wachtenheim
Posters, Martin Solomon
Illustration, Sara Giovanitti
Photography, Onofrio Paccione
Television, Jack Tauss

Advertising
Ralph Casado
Angelo Castelli
Bob Crozier
David Davidian
John F. Dignam
Jim Gager
Ruth Lubell
Jean Marcellino
Sheila McCaffery
Joanne Pateman
Neil Raphan
Robin Sweet
Theo Welti

Editorial
John M. Baxter
John Berg
Donald Burgess
Bryan Canniff
Donald H. Duffy
Ken Kendrick
Tom Phon
Wendy Reingold
Ina Saltz
Melcon Tashian
Elizabeth Woodson

Promotion
Ed Brodsky
Adrienne Brooks
Bob Bruce
Cissy Bruce
Tom Carnase
Younghee Choi
Hoi Ling Chu
Joann Coates
Kathryn Davidian
Bob Defrin
Jerry Demoney
Diane DePasque
Dave Epstein
Amy Fread
S. Neil Fujita
Irving Grunbaum
Dorothy Hayes
Bill Jensen
Minoru Morita
Martin Saint-Martin
Michael Yurick

Books
Lynne Dreese Breslin
Leonard Fury
Abril Lamarque
Sue Llewellyn
Peter Thorpe

Posters
Peter Adler
Gladys Barton
Jane Haber
Larry Lurin
Andrew Newman
Mike Quon
Pamela White

Illustration
Tina Adamek
Ethel Cutler
Roselee Moskowitz
Jacques Parker
Jurek Wajdowicz

Photography
Peter Brandt
Kiyoshi Kanai
Walter Kaprielian
Karl E. Steinbrenner

Television
Bruce Arendash
Phyllis Cayton
Jerry Cotts
Rosalyn Dunham
Greg Flanagan
Tom Forman
Louise Kozminski
Paul LePelletier
Michael Litman
George Maravegias
Lyle Metzdorf
Richard Murnak
Ralph Parenio
Robert Pliskin
Charles Rosner
Karl H. Steinbrenner
Ira Sturtevant

Karl Eric Steinbrenner

1

1

Barbara Steinbrenner, Bill McCaffery, Sheila McCaffery, Jack Tauss, and Pam White

Karl Eric Steinbrenner

3

Karl Eric Steinbrenner

2

2

Jack Tauss and Dorothy Wachtenheim enjoy the festivities

3

The 66th Annual Exhibition and First International Exhibition open at the ADC Gallery June 1, 1987.

5

4

4, 5

66th Annual National Judging

VISUAL COMMUNICATORS EDUCATION FUND

V.C.E.F. PRESIDENT, JESSICA WEBER
presents a scholarship at a reception honoring recipients at the Art Directors Club

VISUAL COMMUNICATORS EDUCATION FUND
Board of Directors 1986–1987

PRESIDENT
Jessica Weber

FIRST VICE PRESIDENT
Walter Kaprielian

SECOND VICE PRESIDENT
Tony Cappiello

SECRETARY
Jerry Demoney

TREASURER
William Brockmeier

EXECUTIVE COMMITTEE
Robert Blattner
Arline Campbell
Daniel Marshall

The Visual Communicators Education Fund, Inc., is a non-profit organization within the Art Directors Club having one simple mission: to provide tuition scholarships to talented design students attending metropolitan area art schools. Our endowment fund is modest. Yet, on May 12, 1987, at ceremonies held at the Club, the VCEF gave tuition awards totaling $11,000 to twenty-five wonderfully talented students. The students who received Art Directors Club Awards of Excellence were:

1987 Visual Communicators Educational Fund, Inc. Scholarship Winners
　　School of Visual Arts: Anthony Ranieri, Heidi North, Mary Ann Salvato, Kathy De Vecchio
　　Pratt Institute: Michael Yoder, Mark Morrissey
　　Pratt Manhattan Center: Arabella Vande Wiele, Jon Muench, Leslie Bock
　　Fashion Institute of Technology: Dawn Vitale, Jean Batthany, Diana King, John Sica
　　Cooper Union School of Art: Michael Van Patten, Jacqueline Kachman
　　New York City Technical College: John Liy, Lashe Birgmon, Darren McMillan, Martha Restrepo, Jaclyn Levine, Jane Gibson, Noemi Ayuso
　　Parsons School of Design
　　Book-of-the-Month Club Award: Elizabeth Rosen
　　Richard Taubin Award: Alexandra Ginns
　　VCEF Award: Victor Rivera

The endowment fund's chief guardian angel has been the *Lila Acheson Wallace/High Winds Fund;* which, through the help of Bob Blattner, has supported the VCEF with substantial tuition gifts. In 1985, Mr. & Mrs. Bill Taubin established the *Richard Taubin Award* in memory of their son. For the third consecutive year, the *Book-of-the-Month Club* has given a tuition scholarship which I helped attain for the fund. Through the efforts of Bob Best, *New York Magazine* has again made a generous contribution to this year's fund.

In the fall of 1986, the *Image Bank* hosted a cocktail party/reception at the restaurant *America.* The proceeds of the evening benefitted the VCEF. We are deeply indebted to Stanley Kanney, President of the *Image Bank* for sponsoring the event.

In 1986, we also instituted a new way to further fund the scholarships. Entry fees from the Club's Annual Exhibition included a one-dollar contribution to the VCEF. The VCEF is actively seeking your support. Other than the income received from sponsoring the Hall of Fame Dinner each autumn, we depend solely on individual and corporate contributions to help the endowment fund. Thank you.

Richard Marx

2

Abbe Lubell

1

LUNCHEON COMMITTEE

**DOROTHY WACHTENHEIM,
DICK SMITH**
Chairpersons,
Luncheon Committee

1

Christo! comes for lunch

2

Dorothy Wachtenheim & Dick Smith
Chairpersons, Luncheon Committee

The Luncheon Committee has enjoyed presenting entertaining and informative Wednesday programs to our members. We've succeeded in providing lively matinee performances ranging from celebrity photographer Harry Benson to Macy's Thanksgiving Day Parade producer Jean McFadden. Also stopping by were award winning illustrators Braldt Bralds and Eugene Mihaesco, Will Vinton Productions with the California Raisins and ADC Hall of Famer Massimo Vignelli. Artist Christo made a surprise visit after the Maysles brothers screened their film, *Island.*

It's been a joy working with fellow committee members: Ethel Cutler, Diane DePasque, Abril Lamarque, Ruth Lubell, Joe Montibello and Robin Sweet. We would also like to thank Club staffers: Diane Moore, Debra Bock-Woo, Glenn Kubota, Cookie Busweiler, Lisa Cohen and Roxann Gantt for their support in making our Wednesdays together a great success.

1

2

MEMBERS EVENTS COMMITTEE

**AMY GOLDMAN &
GLADYS BARTON**
Co-Chairpersons,
Members Events Committee

This year's Members Events Committee (formerly the New Breed Committee), began something new and exciting. Each and every Friday from 5:30–8:30 pm, the Art Directors Club is transformed into Club P.M. Three happy hours for members and their guests to stop by for a drink and unwind after a busy week. For entertainment, we've brought in bands, films, slideshows and music videos.

Getting Club P.M. off the ground would have been impossible without the support and enthusiasm of the Club's membership. Special thanks go to the entire committee: Diane DePasque, Gary DiLuca, Bobbi Rosenthal, Herb Rosenthal, Karl Eric Steinbrenner, Dorothy Wachtenheim and Michael Yurick; who plan, book and create the promotional pieces. The Club's staff is to be commended as well for their extra help in making Club P.M. run smoothly and successfully.

1 & 2
Club PM "Happy Hour"

3
Walter Kaprielian in one of a continuing lecture series of "An Evening With One of the Best" at the Club

3

GALLERY

Chairman, Gallery

1

Silas Rhodes and Marshall Arisman
congratulating artist Peter Scanlan
(center) at The School of Visual Arts
Show.

1

2

The Bohem Press Illustration
Show attracted
a large International crowd.

Moving into the new premises at 250 Park Avenue
South gives the Art Directors Club a truly magnificent, multi-leveled gallery space. The main floor
has thirty foot high ceilings, while the lower floor can
accommodate an exhibition upwards of 1,000 pieces.
The Club also has plans to build a multi-media
screening & conference room equipped with the latest
audio-visual equipment.

The Art Directors Club Gallery has become a showcase exhibition facility for both advertising and
graphic design communities. This year alone, the
Club has held fourteen exhibitions; each unique and
visually stimulating:

Antique Advertising Poster Exhibit
ADC 65th Annual Show
Lindenmeyr Paper Company Exhibit
London Design & Art Direction Show
Japan Peace Poster Exhibit
Los Angeles Art Directors Club Show
Bohem Press Illustrators Exhibit
MacMillan Publishing Illustrators Show
Out-of-Town Agency Exhibit
The Type Shop's Children's Show
School of Visual Arts Student's Exhibit
Japan Advertising Photographer's Show
Association of Graphic Artists Exhibit
Art Directors Club 66th National & First Interna-
tional Show

2

3

Six agencies from across the
country gathered their collective
talents for the "Out-of-Towners"
Show at the Art Directors Club
Gallery.

3

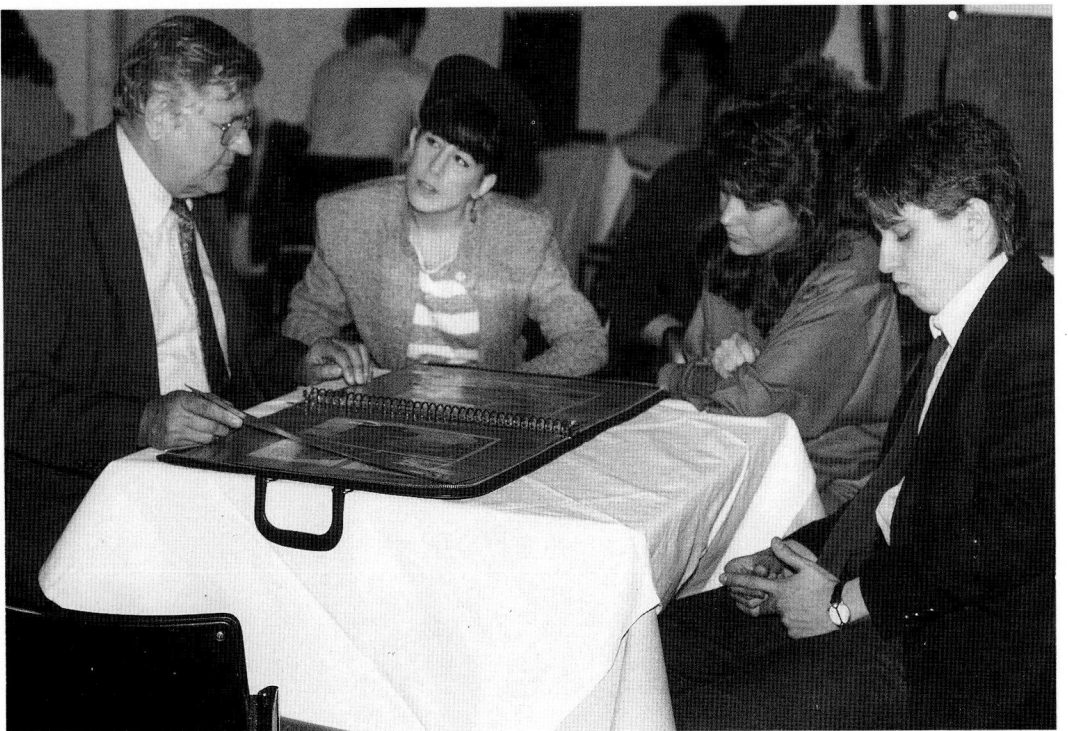

PORTFOLIO REVIEW COMMITTEE

SAL LAZZAROTTI
RICHARD MACFARLANE
Joint-Chairmen,
Portfolio Review Committee

1

LENDING A HELPING HAND ARE ART DIRECTORS:

1
Richard MacFarlane

Every Spring, the Art Directors Club Portfolio Review Committee gives its valuable time and expertise to graduating college and university students. It's a way of preparing them for what lies just ahead in the real advertising and design world. Over lunch, we give students constructive criticism and encourage them to pursue their careers.

This past year, the Portfolio Review Committee has seen over three hundred students from ten major colleges and universities: The Cooper Union, Fashion Institute of Technology, Kutztown State University, Long Island University/C.W. Post College, Moore College, New York Technical College, Pratt Institute, University of Delaware, University of Massachusetts and Youngstown University.

The Committee certainly enjoyed meeting these enthusiastic and talented students. We wish them well . . .

2

2
David Stahlberg

3

3
Denise Breslin

4

4
Eva Costabel

5
Herb Rosenthal

TRAVELING EXHIBITION COMMITTEE

ADC TRAVELING SHOW COMMITTEE
L. Mr. Minoru Morita, Chairman
R. Mr. Shinichiro Tora, Liaison

With the continued support from Japan's *Idea Magazine,* the Club's 65th Annual Exhibition toured Tokyo, Osaka and Nagoya from December, 1986 to March, 1987. The show was well received by throngs of enthusiastic Japanese art directors and designers. Special thanks to ADC members: Takeo Yao, Masutera Aoba and Shigeo Okamoto for their help in setting-up the show.

Back in the United States, selected pieces from the 65th Annual Exhibition were displayed in Nashville, Tennessee, St. Louis, Missouri and Salt Lake City, Utah.

In April of 1988, work from the 66th Annual and First Annual International Exhibition will be shown in China! This will be the first design exhibition of this kind ever presented in the People's Republic. Through the efforts of Club member Shinichiro Tora and officials from the *Chinese Exhibition Agency,* the show will be displayed at Beijing's National Arts Museum. It is sponsored jointly by the New York and Tokyo Art Directors Clubs. Plans are also underway to promote a tour for Club members to attend the Beijing opening.

In addition to its customary yearly showing in Japan, 400 selected pieces from the 66th Exhibition will travel to Europe by special arrangements made through Club member Olaf Leu.

MEMBERSHIP COMMITTEE

SAL LAZZAROTTI
Chairman, Membership Committee

The number of new members accepted and subsequently joining the Club in 1986 swelled to an all-time high of 128.

Sixty-six became regular members while the remaining sixty-two members were initiated through the various other membership categories we offer. Joining our ranks in increasing numbers are young art directors as well as some well-known, established "old timers."

To what do we attribute this steady growth of our club's membership? Some say it's our new, spacious headquarters. Others claim it's our exciting and informative Wednesday luncheons. Still, others think it's a great place to meet clients and friends. Those of us on the Membership Committee agree with all of the above. However, we believe that one underlying reason for our success as a Club can be summed-up in one word: HONOR. It is indeed an honor for people in our business to be chosen for membership in *the* most prestigious and respected art directors organization in the country—and yes, maybe the world!

NEWSLETTER

RUTH LUBELL
Chairperson, Newsletter

This year's Newsletter was produced by art director/ editor, Ruth Lubell, Club-staffer, Roxann Gantt and a group of voluntary, sometimes conscripted member contributors.

As editor, major responsibilities include gathering news, gossip, fact, fiction, reviews, photos and any other material of interest to our readers. Additional member input is always welcome. Please participate by sending us anything worthwhile and or newsworthy. If it's timely, pertinent or decorative, we'll make every effort to include it.

My thanks to Ralph Casado, Eileen Hedy Schultz, Dave Stahlberg, Shinichiro Tora and all committee chairpeople who took the time to chronicle their group's activities.

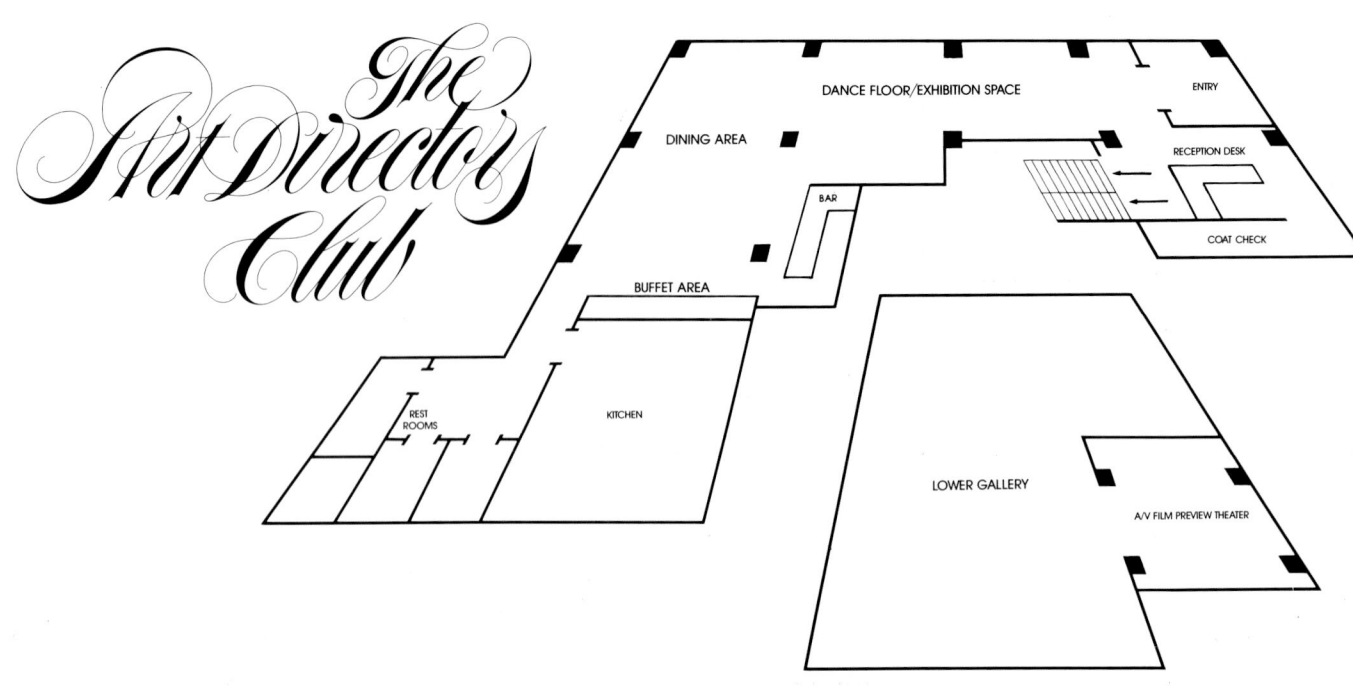

The Art Directors Club

DANCE FLOOR/EXHIBITION SPACE

ENTRY

DINING AREA

RECEPTION DESK

BAR

COAT CHECK

BUFFET AREA

REST ROOMS

KITCHEN

LOWER GALLERY

A/V FILM PREVIEW THEATER

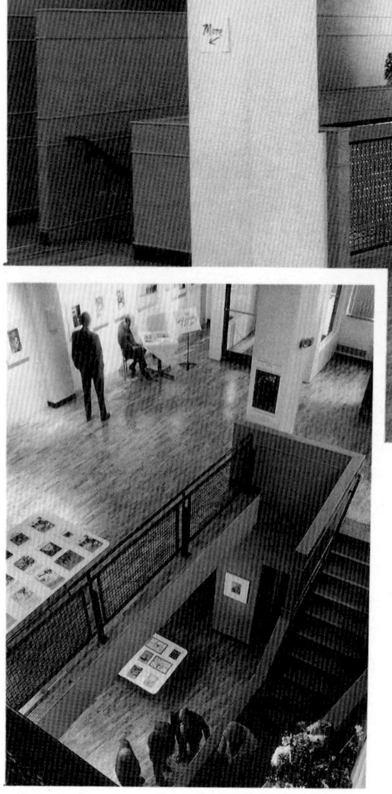

Concept: Promotion Solutions, Inc.

Photography: James R. Morse

Situated near the corner of Park Avenue South and 20th Street, just west of Gramercy Park, is the new quarters of the New York Art Directors Club, a professional organization established in 1921.

The facility was totally redesigned to accommodate two continuous levels of uncluttered exhibition and meeting space. Located in the heart of one of the city's most stimulating neighborhoods, the Art Directors Club is a vital part of advertisiing and its auxiliary creative services.

The Art Directors Club, Inc.
250 Park Avenue South
New York, NY 10003
Telephone: 212-674-0500

ADC MEMBERSHIP LIST

Kazuhiko Adachi
Donald Adamec
Gaylord Adams
George C. Adams
Patricia Addiss
Jane Adler
Peter Adler
Charles Adorney
David Alcorn
Warren Aldoretta
Charles E. Allen
Lorraine Allen
Carlo Ammirati
Gennaro Andreozzi
Ted Andreseakes
Harry Anesta
Al Anthony
Robert Anthony
Arnold Arlow
Herman Aronson
Rochelle L. Arthur
Tadashi Asano
Marvin Asch
John Athorn
Seymour Augenbraun
Gordon C. Aymar
Joel Azerrad

Jeff Babitz
Alberto Baccari
Robert O. Bach
Jeffrey S. Bacon
Ronald Bacsa
Priscilla Baer
Frank Baker
Leslie Baker
Ron Ballister
David Bamford
Letitia Barroll
Don Barron
Robert Barthelmes
Gladys Barton
Matthew Basile
Mary K. Baumann
John M. Baxter
Allen Beaver
Peter Belliveau
Marcia Ben-Eli
Ephram E. Benguiat
Edward J. Bennett
Howard Benson
Laurence Key Benson
John Berg
Sy Berkley
Pamme J. Berman
Park Berry
Barbara Bert
Peter J. Bertolami
Frank Bertulis
Robert Best
Roger Black
Peter J. Blank
Robert Blattner
Robert Blend
Bruce Bloch
David S. Block
Robert Blue
Arnold Blumberg
Robert Bode
Ronne Bonder
George Warren Booth
John Milne Boothroyd
Jeroen Bours
Harold A. Bowman

Carolyn Bowyer
Doug Boyd
Douglas C. Boyd
Jean L. Brady
Simeon Braguin
Joan Brandt
Fred Brauer
Al Braverman
Barry Braverman
Carolyn W. Bray
Denise Breslin
Lynn Dreese Breslin
William P. Brockmeier
Ed Brodsky
Ruth Brody
Adrienne G. Brooks
Joe Brooks
Ilene Renee Brown
Cissy Bruce
Robert Bruce
Bruno E. Brugnatelli
Bernard Brussel-Smith
Lee Buchar
William H. Buckley
Aaron Burns
Herman F. Burns
Laurie Burns
Cipe Pineles Burtin

William Cadge
Albert J. Calzetta
Arline Campbell
Jack D. Campbell
Stuart Campbell
Bryan G. Canniff
Michael R. Capobianco
Tony Cappiello
Thomas Carnase
John C.W. Carroll
David E. Carter
Ralph Casado
Angelo Castelli
C. Edward Cerullo
Jean Chambers
Anthony Chaplinsky Jr.
Vivian Chen
John Cherry
Roberta Chiarella
Young Hee Choi
Shui-Fong Chong
Alan Christie
Hoi Ling Chu
Stanley Church
Seymour Chwast
Bob Ciano
Thomas Clemente
Mahlon Cline
Mattlyn Cline-Natoli
Victor Closi
Joann C. Coates
Joel Cohen
Charles Coiner
Michael Coll
Catherine Connors
Daniel Cooper-Bey
Dinah Coops
Lee Corey
Eva Costabel
Sheldon Cotler
Ron Couture
Robert Cox
Thomas Craddock
James Craig
Meg Crane

Brian A. Cranner
Constance Craven
Elaine Crawford
Adam Cricchio
Robert Crozier
Louis F. Cruz
Jerry Cummins
Charles Cutler
Ethel R. Cutler
Gregory F. Cutshaw

Royal Dadmun
Derek Dalton
Wendy Seabrook Damico
David Davidian
Kathryn Davidian
David Davis
Herman Davis
Joseph Davis
Philip Davis
Jan De Chabert
Robert Defrin
Michael Delia
Vincent del Mese
Joseph del Sorbo
Donald C. Demaio
Erick DeMartino
Jerry Demoney
Diane DePasque
David Deutsch
Frank M. DeVino
Francis DeVito
Peter J. DeWeerdt
Charles Dickinson
Arthur Hill Diedrick
Carolyn Diehl
Edward P. Diehl
John F. Dignam
Gary DiLuca
Joyce DiMauro
Al Di Orio
Lou Donato
Chel S. Dong
Louis Dorfsman
Marc Dorian
Andra Douglas
Kay Elizabeth Douglas
Nick Driver
Rina Drucker
Faye Ellen Druiz
Ann Dubiel
Donald H. Duffy
William R. Duffy
Laura K. Duggan
Rosalyn C. Dunham
Rudolph Dusek
Michael Dweck

Stephen T. Eames
Bernard Eckstein
Peter Edgar
Don Egensteiner
Jack Ehn
Antonie Eichenberg
Zeneth Eidel
Stanley Eisenman
Robert Eisner
Jane Eldershaw
Wallace W. Elton
Malcolm End
David Epstein
Henry Epstein
Lee Epstein
Lois A. Erlacher

Suren Ermoyan
Dorothy Evans

Carolyn Fanelli
Abe Farrell
Gene Federico
Judy Fendelman
Michael Fenga
Roger Ferriter
Michael Fidanzato
William F. Finn
Blanche Fiorenza
Gon Firpo
Carl Fischer
Wayne Fitzpatrick
John Flanagan
Morton Fleischer
Donald P. Flock
Peggy Ford-Fyffe
Jan Foster
John Fraioli
Stephen O. Frankfurt
Richard G. Franklin
Gennaro Franzese
Amy Fread
Cheryl Freed
Frederick B. Freyer
Oren S. Frost
Paul Fuentes
S. Neil Fujita
Takeshi Fukunaga
Leonard W. Fury

Harvey Gabor
Raymond M. Gaeta
Robert Gage
Danielle Gallo
Gene Garlanda
David Gatti
Joseph T. Gauss
Alberto Gavasci
Howard Geissler
Charles Gennarelli
Gloria Gentile
Joseph Gering
Michael Germakian
Linda Gersh
Victor Gialleonardo
Edward Gibbs
Carol Bonnie Gildar
Donald Gill
Peter C. Gilleran
Frank C. Ginsberg
Sara Giovanitti
Akin Girav
Jon M. Giunta
George Guisti
Milton Glaser
Eric Gluckman
Marc Gobe
Barbara Gold
Bennett Gold
Bill Gold
Irwin Goldberg
Roz Goldfarb
Amy E. Goldman
Eli W. Goldowsky
Jo Ann Goldsmith
Cyd Kilbey Gorman
Jean Govoni
Roy Grace
Richard Grider
Jack Griffin
Walter Grotz

Susan Grube
Irving Grunbaum
Maurice Grunfeld
Nelson Gruppo
Delores Gudzin
Rollins S. Guild
Jean-Manuel Guyader

John B. Haag
Thomas W. Haas
Jane Haber
Julie Habner
Henry Hachmann
Robert Hack
Kurt Haiman
Graham Halky
Everett Halvorsen
Edward Hamilton
Frances M. Hamilton
Jerome A. Handman
Carlene Harris
Paul Hartelius, Jr.
George Hartman
Lillian June Hartung
Alan Hartwell
Carolyn Hawks
Dorothy E. Hayes
Mark Hecker
Saul Heff
Amy Heit
Shelley L. Heller
Steven Heller
Garnet E. Henderson
Randall Hensley
Robert S. Herald
Louis F. Hernandez
Susan Herr
Chris Hill
Peter M. Hirsch
Jitsuo Hoashi
Ronald Hodes
Marilyn Hoffner
Leslie Hopkins
William Hopkins
W. David Houser
Jonathan Houston
Joe Hovanec
Elizabeth Howard
Paul Howard
Janet Huet
Roy Alan Hughes
Thomas Hughes
Virginia M. Hull
Wayne Hulse
Jud Hurd
Gary Husk
Melanie Jennings Husk
Morton Hyatt

Tom J. Ide
Ana J. Inoa
Henry Isdith
Edouard Israel

Joseph Jackson
Robert T. Jackson
Harry Jacobs
Holly Jaffee
Lee Ann Jaffee
Jack Jamison
John C. Jay
Bill Jensen
Patricia Jerina
Barbara John

Shaun Johnston
Susan Johnston
Homer Lynn Jolly
Anne M. Jones
Bob Jones
Kristina M. Jorgensen
Roger Joslyn
Len Jossel
Barbara L. Junker

Nita J. Kalish
Kiyoshi Kanai
Cheryl Kaplan
Walter Kaprielian
Judy Katz
Rachel Katzen
M. Richard Kaufman
Milton Kaye
Ken Kendrick
Alice Kenny
Nancy Kent
Myron W. Kenzer
Michele Kestin
Ellen Sue Keir

Leslie Kirschenbaum
Gerald Klein
Judith Klein
Mark Kleinfeld
Hilda Stanger Klyde
Andrew Kner
Henry Knoepfler
Ray Komai
Robert F. Kopelman
Nick Koudis
Oscar Krauss
Helmut Krone
Thaddeus B. Kubis
Bill Kuchler
Anna Kurz

James E. Laird
Howard LaMarca
Abril Lamarque
Joseph O. Landi
Michael Lanotte
John Larkin
Kenneth T. Lassiter
Ann Latrobe
Pearl Lau
Kenneth H. Lavey
Marie-Christine Lawrence
Sal Lazzarotti
Jeffery Leder
Daniel Lee
Edwin Lee
John Lenaas
Robert C. Leung
Richard Levensen
Robert Leydenfrost
Alexander Lieberman
Victor Liebert
Beverly Littlewood
Susan Llewellyn
Leo Lobell
Henry R. Loomis
Michael Losardo
Rocco Lotito
George Gilbert Lott
Robert Louey
Jackson Lovell
Alfred Lowry
Ruth Lubell
John Lucci

Richard Luden
John H. Luke
Thomas R. Lunde
Larry Lurin
Robert W. Lyon, Jr.
Michael J. Lyons

Charles MacDonald
Richard MacFarlane
David H. MacInnes
Frank Macri
Sam Magdoff
Louis Magnani
Carol A. Maisto
Anthony Mancino
Jean Marcellino
John Margeotes
John S. Marmaras
David R. Margolis
Andrea Marquez
Hector W. Marrero
Al Marshall
Daniel Marshall
William R. Martin
Caren J. Martineau
Michael Mastros
Theodore Matyas
Andrea Freund Mauro
Marce Mayhew
Victor John Mazurkiewicz
William McCaffery
Constance McCaffrey
Gerald McConnell
John McCuen
Mandi McIntyre
Scott A. Mednick
William Meehan
Nancy A. Meher
Mario G. Messina
Lyle Metzdorf
Jackie Merri Meyer
Emil T. Micha
Eugene Milbauer
Jean Miller
Lawrence Miller
John Milligan
Isaac Millman
William Minko
Michael Miranda
Leonard J. Mizerek
Cheryl Mohrman
Joseph E. Montebello
Burton A. Morgan
Jeffrey Moriber
Minoru Morita
William R. Morrison
Thomas Morton
Roger Paul Mosconi
Louie Moses
Roselee Moskowitz
Geoffrey Moss
Tobias Moss
Dale Moyer
Marty Muller
Virginia Murphy-Hamill
Ralph J. Mutter

Daniel Nelson
John Newcomb
Andrew M. Newman
Stuart Nezin
Deborah Nichols
Mary Ann Nichols
Raymond Nichols

Marcus Nispel
Joseph Nissen
Evelyn C. Noether
David November
C. Alexander Nuckols

Frank O'Blak
Bernard O'Connor
Edward O'Connor
John O'Neil
Hugh O'Neill
Jack W. Odette
Noriyuki Okazaki
John Okladek
Susan Alexis Orlie
Garrett P. Orr
Larry Ottino
Nina Ovryn
Bernard S. Owett

Onofrio Paccione
Zlata Paces
Maxine Paetro
Robert Paganucci
Roxanne Panero
Nicholas Peter Pappas
Jacques Parker
Paul E. Parker, Jr.
Joanne Pateman
Charles W. Pates
Arthur Paul
Dianne Pavacic
Leonard Pearl
Robert Pearlman
Barbara Pearson
Alan Peckolick
B. Martin Pedersen
Carol Peligian
Paul Pento
Vincent Pepi
David S. Perry
Harold A. Perry
Roberta Perry
Victoria I. Peslak
John Peter
Christos Peterson
Robert L. Peterson
Robert Petrocelli
Theodore D. Pettus
Allan Philiba
Gerald M. Philips
Alma M. Phipps
Joseph Piatti
George Pierson
Michael Pilla
Ernest Pioppo
Peter Pioppo
Robert Pliskin
Raymond Podeszwa
Richard Portner
Louis Portuesi
Anthony Pozsonyi
Benjamin Pride
Bob Procida
Jay Purvis

Charles W. Queener
Elissa Querze
Anny Queyroy
Mario Quilles
Kathleen Quinn
Mike Quon

Judith C. Radice

Paul Rand
Neil Raphan
Robert C. Reed
Samuel Reed
Shelden Reed
Patrick Reeves
Wendy Talve Reingold
Herbert O. Reinke
Edwin C. Ricotta
Arthur Ritter
Valerie Ritter
Michelle M. Roberge
Judy Roberts
Ray Robertson
Bennett Robinson
Harry Rocker
Harlow Rockwell
Andy Romano
Corey Rosenberg
Lee Rosenberg
Barbara Rosenthal
Ed Rosenthal
Herbert M. Rosenthal
Charles Rosner
Andrew Ross
James Francis Ross
Richard Ross
Richard J. Ross
Warren Rossell
Arnold Roston
Leah Roth
Thomas Roth
Wayne Roth
Iska Rothovius
Mort Rubinstein
Randee Rubin
Thomas P. Ruis
Robert Miles Runyan
Henry N. Russell
Albert Russo
Don Ruther
Thomas Ruzicka

Stewart Sacklow
Carmine Saint Andrea
Martin Saint-Martin
Robert Saks
Tracey D. Salaway
Richard M. Salcer
Ludvic Saleh
Robert Salpeter
Ina Saltz
William Samenko
George Samerjan
Jim Sant'Andrea
John Sargeant
Betty B. Saronson
Audrey Satterwhite
Vincent Sauchelli
Hans Sauer
Sam Scali
Peter Scannell
Ernie Scarfone
Beth Schack
Peter Schaefer
Paula Scher
Samuel Scherr
Glen Scheuer
Mark Schimmell
Klaus F. Schmidt
Michael A. Schnact
Joyce Schnaufer
William H. Schneider
Annette Schonhaut
Beverly Faye Schrager
Sharon Schuermann
Carol Schulter
Eileen Hedy Schultz
Nancy K. Schulz
Victor Scocozza
Ruth Scott
William C. Seabrook III
David M. Seager
Leslie Segal
Sheldon Seidler
Amy Seissler

John L. Sellers
Kaede Seville
Ellen Shapiro
Alexander Shear
William Sheldon
Mindee H. Shenkman
Orit Shiffman
Jerry Siano
Arthur Silver
Joyce Silverman
Louis Silverstein
Milt Simpson
Len Sirowitz
Jack Skolnik
Paul Slutsky
Richard Jay Smith
Robert S. Smith
Edward Sobel
Martin Solomon
Harold Sosnow
Michelle R. Spellman
Victor E. Spindler
Leonard A. St. Louis
David Stahlberg
Mindy Phelps Stanton
Karsten Stapelfeldt
Alexander Stauf
Irena Steckiv
Barrie Stein
Douglas Steinbauer
Karl Eric Steinbrenner
Karl H. Steinbrenner
Vera Steiner
Charles M. Stern
Gerald Stewart
Linda Stillman
Stephen Stinehour
Ray Stollerman
Bernard Stone
Otto Storch
Celia Frances Stothard
William Strosahl
Ira F. Sturtevant
Len Sugarman
Brenda Suler
Ken Sweeny
Robin Sweet

Barbara Taff
Robert Talarczyk
Lita Talarico
Nina Tallarico
Norman Tannen
JoAnn Tansman
Melissa K. Tardiff
Melcon Tashian
Bill Taubin
Jack George Tauss
Mark Tekushan
Ciro Tesoro
Giovanna Testani
Richard Thomas
Bradbury Thompson
Marion Thunberg
Robin Ticho
Harold Toledo
Shinichiro Tora
Edward L. Towles
Victor Trasoff
Charles Trovato
Susan B. Trowbridge
Joseph P. Tully
Karen Tureck
Anne Twomey

Catherine Ullman
Clare Ultimo
Frank Urrutia

Gerard Vaglio
Michael Valli
Haydee N. Verdia
Elizabeth Thayer Verney
Karl Vessec
Frank A. Vitale
Thuy Vuong

Dorothy Wachtenheim
Ernest Waivada
Jurek Wajdowicz
Joseph O. Wallace
Paul Waner
Jill Wasserman
Rose Wasserman
Laurence S. Waxberg
Jessica Weber
Art Weithas
Theo Welti
Ron Wetzel
Ken White
Pamela J. White
Ronald Wickham
Gail Wiggin
Richard Wilde
Rodney Craig Williams
Jack Williamson
Anna Willis
David Wiseltier
Rupert Witalis
David Wojdyla
Henry Wolf
Sam Woo
Elizabeth G. Woodson
Robert S. Woolman
Orest Woronewych
Michael Wright
William K. Wurtzel

Ira Yoffe
Zen Yonkovig
Michael Yurick

Susan Broman Zambelli
Bruce Zahor
Carmile S. Zaino
Gary Zamchick
Paul H. Zasada
Richard Zoehrer
Alan Zwiebel

ADC INTERNATIONAL MEMBERS LIST

ARGENTINA
Daniel Verdino

AUSTRALIA
Leighton D. Gage
Ron Kambourian

AUSTRIA
M. J. Demmer
Franz Merlicek

BERMUDA
Paul Smith

BRAZIL
Oswaldo Miranda
Adeir Rampazzo

CANADA
John D. Brooke
Claude Demoulin
Israel Fraiman
Brian C. Hannigan
Ran Hee Kim
Pierre Pepin

DENMARK
Peter Von Schilling

ENGLAND
Jean Govoni
Barbara John
Roland Schenk

HOLLAND
Pieter Brattinga

INDIA
Brendan C. Pereira

ISRAEL
Asher Kalderon
Dan Reisinger

ITALY
Titti Fabiani

JAPAN
Masuteru Aoba
Katsumi Asaba
Yuji Baba
Satoru Fujii
Terunobu Fukushima
Tadanori Hakura
Mitsutoshi Hosaka
Michio Iwaki
Toshio Iwata
Takahisa Kamijyo
Shiu Kataoka
Ryohei Jojima
Yoshikatsu Kosakai
Kazuki Maeda
Keizo Matsumi
Takao Matsumoto
Shin Matsunaga
Hideo Mukai
Keisuke Nagatomo
Yasuharu Nakahara
Makoto Nakamura
Toshiuki Ohashi
Takeshi Ohtaka
Shigeo Okamoto
Motoaki Okuizumi
Akio Okumura
Shigeshi Omori
Tomouiki Ono
Susumu Sakane
Takayuki Shirasu
Kataoka Shiu
Seiji Sugii
Yasuo Suzuki
Itakura Tadanori
Teruaki Takao
Masakazu Tanabe
Ikko Tanaka
Soji George Tanaka
Yusaku Tomoeda
Norio Uejo
Peter Wong
A. Hidehito Yamamato
Yoji Yamamoto
Takeo Yao

MEXICO
Felix Beltran
Diana Garcia De Tolone
Luis Efren Ramirez Flores

NORWAY
Kjell Wollner

PHILIPPINES
Emily A. Abrera

SINGAPORE
Chiet-Husen Eng

SRI LANKA
Kosala Rohana Wickramanayake

SWITZERLAND
Bilal Dallenbach
Fernand Hofer
Moritz S. Jaggi
Hans Looser

WEST GERMANY
Uwe Horstmann
Olaf Leu
Hans-Georg Pospischil

ADC AFFILIATE MEMBERS LIST

AVON PRODUCTS, INC.
Ronald Longsdorf
Timothy Musios
Perry Zompa

CARDINAL TYPE SERVICE, INC.
Mark Darlow
John Froehlich
Allan R. Wahler

CONSTANCE KOVAR & COMPANY
Constance Kovar
Anthony Taibi

NEW YORK CITY TECHNICAL COLLEGE
George Halpern
Seymour Pearlstein

PARSONS SCHOOL OF DESIGN
David Levy
Al Greenberg

PETER ROGERS ASSOCIATES
Leonard Favara
Peter Rogers

TISDELL/CAPESCHA
Daniel Capescha
Clifford Tisdell

TOPPAN PRINTING COMPANY, LTD.
Takeo Hayano
Ryuichi Minakawa
Teru Tanabe

UNION CAMP CORPORATION
Stuart Phelps
Robert Todd

WARNER AMEX SATELLITE ENTERTAINMENT COMPANY
Juli Davidson
Leslie Leventman
Jim Warren

INDEX

ART DIRECTORS

CLIENTS

CREATIVE DIRECTORS

DESIGN FIRMS

DESIGNERS

DIRECTORS

INDEX

New York, 49, 241, 444, 477, 478, 480, 1215, 1233
New York Daily News, 362, 452, 1285
New York Times, 31, 32, 38, 45, 101, 113, 123, 195, 293, 294, 295, 296, 297, 298, 299, 300, 301, 310, 353, 354, 395, 434, 435, 1214, 1229
Newsday, 414, 415, 446, 1201, 1205, 1206, 1265
Newsweek, 399, 445
Northeast, 443

Oceans, 332
Omni, 440, 1216, 1228, 1241, 1242, 1245, 1255, 1256, 1282, 1324, 1327, 1346, 1352, 1353, 1355
1,001 Home Ideas, 338
Orange County Register, 304

Pacific, 474
Packaging, 453
Pautas y Contraseñas, 2138
PC Week, 276
Penthouse International, 39, 341, 342, 1231, 1240, 1243, 1244, 1247, 1250, 1284, 1323, 1349, 1356
Penthouse Letters, 373, 1266, 1310
People, 216, 228, 230, 243, 248
Phi Delta Kappan, 1263
Philip Morris, 455
Physician, 1275
Playboy, 1260
Polaroid Corporation Annual Report, 497
Popular Mechanics, 315, 316, 317, 318, 319, 334, 1283
Postgraduate Medicine, 1271, 1276, 1279, 1280
Progressive Architecture, 46, 461, 463, 464, 1345
proSport Verlag, 2033
Providence Journal, 153
Psychology, 82

Quality, 320, 375, 398
Quarterly, 465
Quincy Patriot Ledger, 156

Reader's Digest, 216, 1847
Real Estate Today, 459, 460
Redbook, 216
Review, 343, 344, 1296
Road & Track, 1249, 1253
Road & Track Presents Exotic Cars, 345
Road & Track Sports & GT Cars 1987, 370
Rolling Stone, 26, 243
Run, 1251, 1257

St. Paul Pioneer Press, 8, 208
San Diego, 251
San Diego Union Tribune, 159, 206
San Jose Mercury News, 285, 1202
Scholastic, 277
Security Management, 1270
Select, 2140
Shreveport Times, 187
Solutions, 457
Spick, 1864
Spirit of Audi, 365, 385, 472
Sports Afield, 369
Sportsmedicine, 1275
Spy, 349
Star, 25, 1925
Stereo Review, 236
Stern, 1852, 1930, 1946, 1949, 1953, 1954, 1958
Sterz, 1970
Street Machine, 1914
Success, 351, 352, 400
Sunday Times Magazine, 1931
Suntory Cocktail Book, 2021

Tatler, 1848
Temple Review, 1213
Think, 454, 1230, 1254
Time, 28, 219, 441, 1354

Topic, 312, 387, 426, 427, 439
Toronto Blue Jays Scorebook, 326
Toronto Life, 1321
Toronto Star, 305
Town & Country, 322, 358, 397, 422, 423
Trees and Turf, 275
Tristam Shandy, 2031

U & lc (Upper and Lowercase), 34
USA Today, 12, 14, 202
U.S. News & World Report, 1322

Variety, 117
Video Review, 24
Vogue, 1157, 1160, 1950

W, 321, 323, 1305
Wall Street Journal, 196
Warfield's, 449, 450, 451, 487
Washington Post, 286, 290, 1264
Weeds, 276
Whisper of the Muse, 959
Wisconsin Trails, 394
Woman's Value, 1923
Women's Day, 216
World, 100
World Tennis, 40, 221, 346, 357, 1235

Yacht, 442

Zoom, 1350

PUBLISHERS

Abbeville Press, 81, 83
Harry N. Abrams, Inc., 79, 84, 962, 965, 966, 1004
Agni Studio, 2062
Wick Allison, 33, 42, 367, 368, 382, 383
American Institute of Graphic Arts, Texas Chapter, 1293
Amnesty International, 2086
Apple Computer, Inc., 803, 1192
Arbor House, 1005, 1007, 1015, 1017
Art Center College of Design, 584
Atlantic Monthly Press, 1022

L. Scott Bailey, 363
Gordon Baird, 327, 329, 330, 331, 333
Dan Barron, 1332
Richard A. Bartkus, 355, 378, 1249, 1253
Gene Bay, 1232
Berliner Festspiele GmbH, 2043, 2060
Best Western International, 465
Peter Betuel, 1277
William F. Bondlow, 110, 118, 1348, 1351
Boston Business Magazine, 1331
Boston Globe, 291, 292, 313, 372, 410, 411, 412, 413, 416, 417, 418, 419, 420, 421, 436, 437
Boston Symphony Orchestra, 1162
Tom Braun, 369
Buechergilde Gutenberg, 2041
Charles S. Bullock, 351, 352, 400

Howard Cadel, 41, 456, 469, 470
Barbara Cady, 390
Cahners Publishing Co., 453
CBS Magazines, 345, 355, 363, 370, 378
Champion Products, 1333
Charlie Cipolla, 326
Comac Communications Inc., 1325
Condé Nast Publications Inc., 110, 118, 281, 388, 389, 895, 1348, 1351
H. H. Coninx, 1864
Controlled Media Communications, 326
Cooper Union, 1126
Crown Publishers, Inc., 957

Daily Record/Warfield's, 449, 450, 451, 487
Daniels Printing, 1191
D'Aubrey & Associates, 336
Bruno Dechamps, 1851, 1853, 1855, 1943, 1944, 1945, 1947, 1948, 1951, 1954, 2130, 2131
Yuri Dojc Inc., 120
Domberger Filderstadt, 2008
Doubleday & Company, 1011

East-West Round Table, 488
Eaton Court Publications, 455
ECON, 2024
Editrice Abitaire Segesta, 2037
Errolgraphics, Inc., 1091

Fairchild Publications, 321, 323, 325, 402, 403
Howard Fish, 438
Fjord Press, 1013
Foremost Publishers, Inc., 1358

J. Paul Getty Museum, 959
Glenat, 2022
Bob Guccione, 39, 341, 342, 373, 440, 1216, 1228, 1231, 1240, 1241, 1242, 1243, 1244, 1245, 1247, 1250, 1255, 1256, 1266, 1282, 1284, 1310, 1323, 1324, 1327, 1346, 1349, 1352, 1363, 1355, 1356
Gulfshore Publishing Co., 1272

Harp Press, 1150
Harper & Row, Publishers, Inc., 82, 972, 974, 980, 982, 983, 984, 997, 999, 1000, 1001, 1002, 1003, 1009

Hartford Courant, 443, 1090
Hearst Business Communications, 1326
Hearst Corporation, 35, 322, 358, 397, 404, 405, 406, 407, 408, 422, 423, 479
Herrndorf, Peter, 1321
Hirmer Verlag, Frankfurter Allgemeine Zeitung, 2026
Hunter Publishing, 604, 608

IBM, 454, 1230, 1254
Institute of Industrial Launderers, 47, 48, 466, 467, 468
Insurance Information Institute, 1258
International Typeface Corporation, 34
Richard D. Irwin, Inc., 967

Jim Jenkins, 1236
G. Douglas Johnston, 634
Junior Scholastic, 471

William M. Kelly, 320, 375, 398
Kipling Washington Editors, 324, 1259
Bob G. Kliesch, 484
Knapp Communications, 1319
Alfred A. Knopf, 977, 979, 1010, 1021, 1212, 1246
Kodansha Co., Ltd., 2023
Anthony Korner, 433
Arthur Kornhaber, 401
Edward Kosner, 444, 477, 480, 1215, 1233

Labelcraft Lithographics, 1102
Joel Laroche, 1350
Steve Levinson, 338
SB Lewis & Co., 638
Owen J. Lipstein, 337, 340, 347, 371, 1238, 1320
Los Angeles Times, 306, 311, 1204
C. S. Lovelace, 360, 361, 377, 482, 1328
James Ludin, 1102

Madison Square Press, 1008
Magyar Hirdetö, 2113
Manipulator, 2142, 2143, 2144
Mitsuhiro Matsuda, 1972
Randolph McAusland, 481
McGraw-Hill Publishing, 1271, 1275, 1276, 1279, 1280
MD Publications, Inc., 364
Nancy Mead, 394
Media Five Limited, 542
Modern Times, 2139
Mokép (Hungarian Film-Trade), 2087
Montreux International Jazz Festival, 2078
Murdoch Magazines, 49, 444, 478, 480, 1215, 1233
Terry Murphy, 447
Museum of American Folk Art, 462
Museum of Broadcasting, 1072
Mysterious Press, 993

National Association of Realtors, 459, 460
National Audubon Society, 448
National Geographic Society, 1225, 1252
NBC Affiliate Advertising & Promotion Services, 598
New American Library (Onyx Books), 1006
New York Times, 31, 32, 38, 45, 101, 113, 293, 294, 295, 296, 297, 298, 299, 300, 301, 353, 354, 395, 434, 435, 685, 1214, 1229
Newsday, 414, 415, 446, 1201, 1206
Normal Inc., 44
Tiina Nunnally, 1013

Odeon, 2031
ÖKO-TEST Magazine, 2135
Otis Elevators, 2030
Oxford University Press, 989

WRITERS